**Glencoe Science**

W9-AAO-281

# Indiana Science

Grade 7

## Features of *Indiana Science*

- Each chapter and section is correlated to the Indiana Science Standards.
- Standards checks are located throughout the book at point-of-use.
- Two pages of assessment in every chapter are correlated to the Indiana Science Standards.
- The **Daily Intervention Guide** at the beginning of the book helps link the program to Indiana Science Standards.

## Additional Resources

- **Interactive Chalkboard** CD-ROM Microsoft® PowerPoint® provides presentations you can customize for each lesson.
- **TeacherWorks™** CD-ROM is a complete lesson planner and resource center that helps you customize lesson plans and reproduce classroom resources.
- **StudentWorks Plus™** CD-ROM provides an all-in-one interactive Student Edition and student resources—a backpack solution in Spanish and English.
- **Exam*View*® Pro Testmaker** CD-ROM is a customizable testmaker with built-in Indiana Science Standards correlations available in Spanish and English.
- **Mastering the Grade 7 Indiana Science Standards** provides Standards-based questions in ISTEP+ Test format.
- **Reading Essentials, An Interactive Student Textbook** presents each chapter at a lower reading level, to help struggling readers master the content.
- **MindJogger Videoquizzes** (VHS and DVD) provide a game-show style interactive quiz for each chapter.
- **Video Labs, Virtual Labs,** the **Science Lab Manual,** the **Probeware Lab Manual,** and the **Science Inquiry Lab Manual** provide additional opportunities to learn and practice laboratory techniques.

**Log on to in7.msscience.com**

# SAFETY SYMBOLS

| SAFETY SYMBOLS | HAZARD | EXAMPLES | PRECAUTION | REMEDY |
|---|---|---|---|---|
| DISPOSAL | Special disposal procedures need to be followed. | certain chemicals, living organisms | Do not dispose of these materials in the sink or trash can. | Dispose of wastes as directed by your teacher. |
| BIOLOGICAL | Organisms or other biological materials that might be harmful to humans | bacteria, fungi, blood, unpreserved tissues, plant materials | Avoid skin contact with these materials. Wear mask or gloves. | Notify your teacher if you suspect contact with material. Wash hands thoroughly. |
| EXTREME TEMPERATURE | Objects that can burn skin by being too cold or too hot | boiling liquids, hot plates, dry ice, liquid nitrogen | Use proper protection when handling. | Go to your teacher for first aid. |
| SHARP OBJECT | Use of tools or glassware that can easily puncture or slice skin | razor blades, pins, scalpels, pointed tools, dissecting probes, broken glass | Practice common-sense behavior and follow guidelines for use of the tool. | Go to your teacher for first aid. |
| FUME | Possible danger to respiratory tract from fumes | ammonia, acetone, nail polish remover, heated sulfur, moth balls | Make sure there is good ventilation. Never smell fumes directly. Wear a mask. | Leave foul area and notify your teacher immediately. |
| ELECTRICAL | Possible danger from electrical shock or burn | improper grounding, liquid spills, short circuits, exposed wires | Double-check setup with teacher. Check condition of wires and apparatus. | Do not attempt to fix electrical problems. Notify your teacher immediately. |
| IRRITANT | Substances that can irritate the skin or mucous membranes of the respiratory tract | pollen, moth balls, steel wool, fiberglass, potassium permanganate | Wear dust mask and gloves. Practice extra care when handling these materials. | Go to your teacher for first aid. |
| CHEMICAL | Chemicals can react with and destroy tissue and other materials | bleaches such as hydrogen peroxide; acids such as sulfuric acid, hydrochloric acid; bases such as ammonia, sodium hydroxide | Wear goggles, gloves, and an apron. | Immediately flush the affected area with water and notify your teacher. |
| TOXIC | Substance may be poisonous if touched, inhaled, or swallowed. | mercury, many metal compounds, iodine, poinsettia plant parts | Follow your teacher's instructions. | Always wash hands thoroughly after use. Go to your teacher for first aid. |
| FLAMMABLE | Flammable chemicals may be ignited by open flame, spark, or exposed heat. | alcohol, kerosene, potassium permanganate | Avoid open flames and heat when using flammable chemicals. | Notify your teacher immediately. Use fire safety equipment if applicable. |
| OPEN FLAME | Open flame in use, may cause fire. | hair, clothing, paper, synthetic materials | Tie back hair and loose clothing. Follow teacher's instruction on lighting and extinguishing flames. | Notify your teacher immediately. Use fire safety equipment if applicable. |

 **Eye Safety** Proper eye protection should be worn at all times by anyone performing or observing science activities.

 **Clothing Protection** This symbol appears when substances could stain or burn clothing.

 **Animal Safety** This symbol appears when safety of animals and students must be ensured.

 **Handwashing** After the lab, wash hands with soap and water before removing goggles.

Glencoe Science

# Indiana
# Science

## Grade 7

Lake County

 **Glencoe**

New York, New York    Columbus, Ohio    Chicago, Illinois    Peoria, Illinois    Woodland Hills, California

ISBN: 0-07-861781-2 *(Indiana Student Edition)*    *0-07-861782-0 (Indiana Teacher Wraparound Edition)*

# Contents

Lafayette wolf preserve

# Indiana Teacher Advisory Board

The Indiana Teacher Advisory Board gave the editorial staff and design team feedback on the content and design of the Student Edition. They provided valuable input in the development of the 2005 edition of *Glencoe Indiana Science.*

# The Glencoe Formula

for successfully mastering Indiana's Academic Standards for Science, Grade 7.

## Learning + Practicing = *Success!*

**Learning**

### Academic Standards

- Each chapter opener lists the Academic Standards you'll learn in that chapter.

### Standards

- Each section opener lists the portion of the Standard you'll learn in that section.

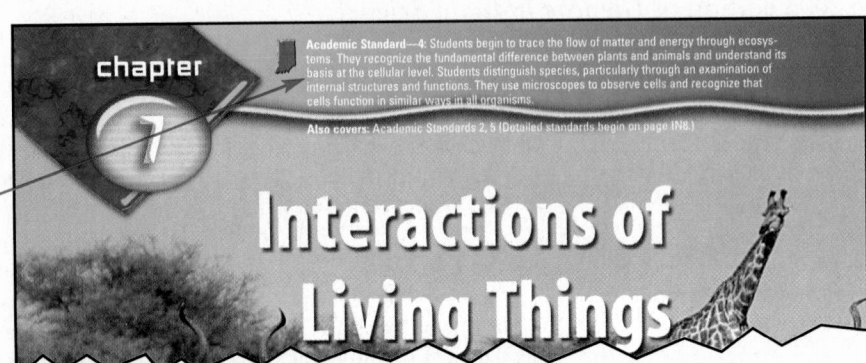

**chapter 7**

Academic Standard—4: Students begin to trace the flow of matter and energy through ecosystems. They recognize the fundamental difference between plants and animals and understand its basis at the cellular level. Students distinguish species, particularly through an examination of internal structures and functions. They use microscopes to observe cells and recognize that cells function in similar ways in all organisms.

Also covers: Academic Standards 2, 5 (Detailed standards begin on page IN8.)

## Interactions of Living Things

**section 3**

Standards—7.4.2: Describe that all organisms, including the human species, are part of and depend on two main interconnected global food webs, the ocean food web and the land food web. 7.4.8: Describe how organisms that eat plants break down the plant structures to produce the materials and energy that they need to survive, and in turn, how they are consumed by other organisms.

Also covers: 7.4.6, 7.5.3 (Detailed standards begin on page IN8.)

## Matter and Energy

**as you read**

*What* You'll Learn

■ Explain the difference between a food chain and food w

### Energy Flow Through Ecosystems

Life on Earth is not simply a collection of independent organisms. Even organisms that seem to spend most of their time alone interact with other members of their species. They also interact with members of other species.

Indiana State Capitol Building

# Practicing

## Standard Check
- focuses on and assesses the Standard covered on that page

## Indiana Academic Standard Check

**7.4.2:** Describe that all organisms . . . are part of and depend on two main interconnected global food webs, the ocean food web and the land food web.

✔ Where might humans fit in an ocean food web?

## Indiana Standards Review
Two pages created specifically for Indiana covering Indiana's Academic Standards for Science.

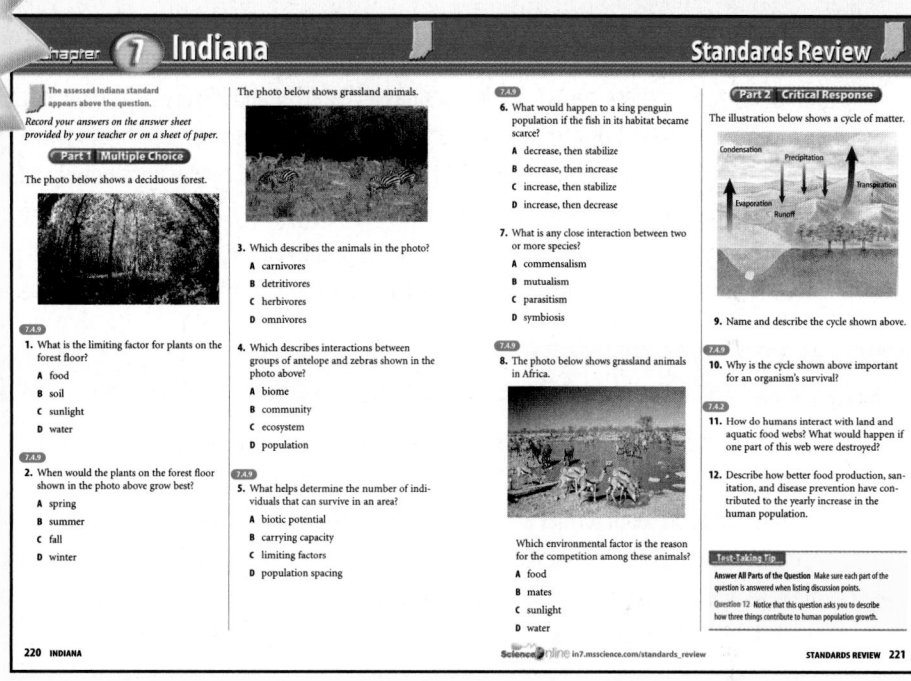

Chapter 7 Indiana — Standards Review

The assessed Indiana standard appears above the question.

*Record your answers on the answer sheet provided by your teacher or on a sheet of paper.*

**Part 1 | Multiple Choice**

The photo below shows a deciduous forest.

7.4.9
1. What is the limiting factor for plants on the forest floor?
   A food
   B soil
   C sunlight
   D water

7.4.9
2. When would the plants on the forest floor shown in the photo above grow best?
   A spring
   B summer
   C fall
   D winter

The photo below shows grassland animals.

3. Which describes the animals in the photo?
   A carnivores
   B detritivores
   C herbivores
   D omnivores

4. Which describes interactions between groups of antelope and zebras shown in the photo above?
   A biome
   B community
   C ecosystem
   D population

7.4.9
5. What helps determine the number of individuals that can survive in an area?
   A biotic potential
   B carrying capacity
   C limiting factors
   D population spacing

7.4.9
6. What would happen to a king penguin population if the fish in its habitat became scarce?
   A decrease, then stabilize
   B decrease, then increase
   C increase, then stabilize
   D increase, then decrease

7. What is any close interaction between two or more species?
   A commensalism
   B mutualism
   C parasitism
   D symbiosis

7.4.9
8. The photo below shows grassland animals in Africa.

Which environmental factor is the reason for the competition among these animals?
   A food
   B mates
   C sunlight
   D water

**Part 2 | Critical Response**

The illustration below shows a cycle of matter.

Condensation   Precipitation   Transpiration   Evaporation   Runoff

9. Name and describe the cycle shown above.

7.4.9
10. Why is the cycle shown above important for an organism's survival?

7.4.2
11. How do humans interact with land and aquatic food webs? What would happen if one part of this web were destroyed?

12. Describe how better food production, sanitation, and disease prevention have contributed to the yearly increase in the human population.

**Test-Taking Tip** Answer All Parts of the Question Make sure each part of the question is answered when listing discussion points.

Question 12 Notice that this question asks you to describe how three things contribute to human population growth.

220 INDIANA

Science Online in7.msscience.com/standards_review

STANDARDS REVIEW 221

## Test-Taking Tips

✔ Go to bed early the night before the test. You will think more clearly after a good night's rest.

✔ Read each problem carefully, underline key words, and think about ways to solve the problem before answering the question.

✔ Relax. It's natural to be nervous when taking a test. Just do your best.

✔ Try to answer each question in order. If you are unsure of an answer, mark your best guess and then mark the question in your test booklet. This will be a reminder to come back to the question at the end of the test.

✔ Think positively. Some problems may seem hard to you, but you may be able to figure out what to do if you read each question carefully.

✔ If no figure is provided, draw one. If one is furnished, mark it up to help you solve the problem.

✔ When you have finished each problem, reread it to make sure your answer is complete and reasonable.

✔ Make sure that the number of the question on the answer sheet matches the number of the question on which you are working in your test booklet.

# Indiana's Academic Standards Overview

*Beginning with Grade 6, Indiana's Academic Standards for science contain seven Standards, with the addition of Historical Perspectives. Each Standard is described below. On the pages that follow, age-appropriate concepts are listed underneath each Standard. These ideas build a foundation for understanding the intent of each Standard.*

## Standard 1  THE NATURE OF SCIENCE AND TECHNOLOGY

It is the union of science and technology that forms the scientific endeavor and that makes it so successful. Although each of these human enterprises has a character and history of its own, each is dependent on and reinforces the other. This first Standard draws portraits of science and technology that emphasize their roles in the scientific endeavor and reveal some of the similarities and connections between them. In order for students to truly understand the nature of science and technology, they must model the process of scientific investigation through inquiries, fieldwork, lab work, etc. Through these experiences, students will practice designing investigations and experiments, making observations, and formulating theories based on evidence.

## Standard 2  SCIENTIFIC THINKING

There are certain thinking skills associated with science, mathematics, and technology that young people need to develop during their school years. These are mostly, but not exclusively, mathematical and logical skills that are essential tools for both formal and informal learning and for a lifetime of participation in society as a whole. Good communication is also essential in order to both receive and disseminate information and to understand others' ideas as well as have one's own ideas understood. Writing, in the form of journals, essays, lab reports, procedural summaries, etc., should be an integral component of students' experiences in science.

## Standard 3  THE PHYSICAL SETTING

One of the grand success stories of science is the unification of the physical universe. It turns out that all natural objects, events, and processes are connected to each other. This Standard contains recommendations for basic knowledge about the overall structure of the universe and the physical principles on which it seems to run, with emphasis on Earth and the solar system. This Standard focuses on two principle subjects: the structure of the universe and the major processes that have shaped planet Earth, and the concepts with which science describes the physical world in general—organized under the headings of *Matter and Energy* and *Forces of Nature*. In Grade 7, students continue to learn about the relationships between physical objects, events, and processes in the universe.

## Standard 4  THE LIVING ENVIRONMENT

People have long been curious about living things—how many different species there are, what they are like, how they relate to each other, and how they behave. Living organisms are made of the same components as all other matter, involve the same kinds of transformations of energy, and move using the same basic kinds of forces. Thus, all of the physical principles discussed in Standard 3—The Physical Setting, apply to life as well as to stars, raindrops, and television sets. This Standard offers recommendations on basic knowledge about how living things function and how they interact with one another and their environment. In Grade 7, students trace the flow of matter and energy through ecosystems.

## Standard 5  THE MATHEMATICAL WORLD

Mathematics is essentially a process of thinking that involves building and applying abstract, logically connected networks of ideas. These ideas often arise from the need to solve problems in science, technology, and everyday life—problems ranging from how to model certain aspects of a complex scientific problem to how to balance a checkbook.

## Standard 6  HISTORICAL PERSPECTIVES

Examples of historical events provide a context for understanding how the scientific enterprise operates. By studying these events, one understands that new ideas are limited by the context in which they are conceived, are often rejected by the scientific establishment, sometimes spring from unexpected findings, and grow or transform slowly through the contributions of many different investigators. The historical events listed in Grade 7 are certainly not the only events that could be used to illustrate this Standard, but they provide an array of examples. Through these examples, students will gain insight into germ theory.

## Standard 7  COMMON THEMES

Some important themes pervade science, mathematics, and technology and appear over and over again, whether we are looking at ancient civilization, the human body, or a comet. These ideas transcend disciplinary boundaries and prove fruitful in explanation, in theory, in observation, and in design. A focus on *Constancy and Change* within this Standard provides students opportunities to engage in long-term and on-going laboratory and fieldwork, and thus understand the role of change over time in studying The Physical Setting and The Living Environment.

# Indiana's Academic Standards Expanded and Correlated to *Glencoe Indiana Science, Grade 7*

This correlation "expands," or breaks down, each standard into its components. The chapter and section that address each component are listed. Some standards do not require expanding.

| Academic Standards | Chapter-Section |
|---|---|
| **Standard 1 THE NATURE OF SCIENCE AND TECHNOLOGY** | |
| *Students further their scientific understanding of the natural world through investigations, experiences, and readings. They design solutions to practical problems by using a variety of scientific methodologies.* | |
| **7.1.1** Recognize and explain that when similar investigations give different results, the scientific challenge is to judge whether the differences are trivial or significant, which often takes further studies to decide. | 1-1, 19-1, Science Skill Handbook |
| **7.1.2** Explain that what people expect to observe often affects what they actually do observe and provide an example of a solution to this problem. | |
| **expanded standard** — what people expect to observe affects what is observed | 1-3, Science Skill Handbook |
| provide a solution to the problem of bias. | Science Skill Handbook |
| **7.1.3** Explain why it is important in science to keep honest, clear, and accurate records. | 1-1, 1-4, Science Skill Handbook |
| **7.1.4** Describe that different explanations can be given for the same evidence, and it is not always possible to tell which one is correct without further inquiry. | |
| **expanded standard** — different explanations can be given for the same evidence | 1-1, 1-3, 19-1, 21-3, Science Skill Handbook |
| it is not always possible to tell which explanation is correct | 1-1, 1-3, 19-1, 21-3, Science Skill Handbook |
| **7.1.5** Identify some important contributions to the advancement of science, mathematics, and technology that have been made by different kinds of people, in different cultures, at different times. | 1-3, 2-2, 2-3, 4-3, 6-4, 9-1, 9-2, 9-3, 12-1, 12-2, 14-3, 15-2, 16-1, 16-3, 16-4, 17-3, 18-1, 21-2, 22-3 |
| **7.1.6** Provide examples of people who overcame bias and/or limited opportunities in education and employment to excel in the fields of science. | 2-3, 5-4, 17-3 |
| **7.1.7** Explain how engineers, architects, and others who engage in design and technology use scientific knowledge to solve practical problems. | 2-2, 2-3, 7-1, Unit 6 Project |
| **7.1.8** Explain that technologies often have drawbacks as well as benefits. Consider a technology, such as the use of pesticides, which help some organisms but may hurt others, either deliberately or inadvertently. | 1-1, 4-3, 8-1, 8-2, 13-3, 15-2, Unit 3 Project |
| **7.1.9** Explain how societies influence what types of technology are developed and used in fields such as agriculture, manufacturing, sanitation, medicine, warfare, transportation, information processing, and communication. | 5-4, 6-1 |

| | Academic Standards | Chapter-Section |
|---|---|---|
| **7.1.10** | Identify ways that technology has strongly influenced the course of history and continues to do so. | |
| expanded standard | technology has influenced the course of history | 4-3, 13-2 |
| | technology continues to influence the course of history | 4-3 |
| **7.1.11** | Illustrate how numbers can be represented using sequences of only two symbols, such as 1 and 0 or on and off, and how that affects the storage of information in our society. | |
| expanded standard | illustrate how numbers can be represented using sequences | 15-2 |
| | illustrate how numbers represented using sequences affects the storage of information | 15-2 |

## Standard 2   SCIENTIFIC THINKING

*Students use instruments and tools to measure, calculate, and organize data. They frame arguments in quantitative terms when possible. They question claims and understand that findings may be interpreted in more than one acceptable way.*

| | | |
|---|---|---|
| **7.2.1** | Find what percentage one number is of another and figure any percentage of any number. | Applied and reinforced in the Math Skill Handbook and Applying Math Features |
| **7.2.2** | Use formulas to calculate the circumferences and areas of rectangles, triangles, and circles, and the volumes of rectangular solids. | Applied and reinforced in the Math Skill Handbook and Applying Math Features |
| **7.2.3** | Decide what degree of precision is adequate, based on the degree of precision of the original data, and round off the result of calculator operations to significant figures that reasonably reflect those of the inputs. | Applied and reinforced in the Math Skill Handbook and Applying Math Features |
| **7.2.4** | Express numbers like 100, 1,000, and 1,000,000 as powers of 10. | Applied and reinforced in the Math Skill Handbook and Applying Math Features |
| **7.2.5** | Estimate probabilities of outcomes in familiar situations, on the basis of history or the number of possible outcomes. | Applied and reinforced in the Math Skill Handbook and Applying Math Features |
| **7.2.6** | Read analog and digital meters on instruments used to make direct measurements of length, volume, weight, elapsed time, rates, or temperatures, and choose appropriate units. | 11-1, 12-3, 13-3, 21-3 |
| **7.2.7** | Incorporate circle charts, bar and line graphs, diagrams, scatterplots, and symbols into writing, such as lab or research reports, to serve as evidence for claims and/or conclusions. | |
| expanded standard | incorporate circle charts into writing | 1-4 |
| | incorporate bar and line graphs into writing | 1-4, 8-2, 11-1, 11-2, 13-2, 13-3, 21-3 |
| | incorporate diagrams into writing | 1-4, 4-1, 4-3, 5-4, 7-1, 11-3, 15-2, 19-2 |
| | incorporate scatterplots into writing | 1-4, Unit 2 Project |
| | incorporate symbols into writing | 1-4, 4-3, 5-4 |
| **7.2.8** | Question claims based on vague attributes, such as "Leading doctors say...," or on statements made by celebrities or others outside the area of their particular expertise. | 1-1 |

| Academic Standards | Chapter-Section |
|---|---|

## Standard 3   THE PHYSICAL SETTING

*Students collect and organize data to identify relationships between physical objects, events, and processes. They use logical reasoning to question their own ideas as new information challenges their conceptions of the natural world.*

| | | |
|---|---|---|
| 7.3.1 | Recognize and describe that the sun is a medium-sized star located near the edge of a disk-shaped galaxy of stars and that the universe contains many billions of galaxies and each galaxy contains many billions of stars. | 16-4 |
| 7.3.2 | Recognize and describe that the sun is many thousands of times closer to Earth than any other star, allowing light from the sun to reach Earth in a few minutes. Note that this may be compared to time spans of longer than a year for all other stars. | 14-3, 16-2 |
| 7.3.3 | Describe how climates sometimes have changed abruptly in the past as a result of changes in Earth's crust, such as volcanic eruptions or impacts of huge rocks from space. | 21-3 |
| 7.3.4 | Explain how heat flow and movement of material within Earth causes earthquakes and volcanic eruptions and creates mountains and ocean basins. | |
| expanded standard | heat flow and movement of material within Earth causes earthquakes and volcanic eruptions | 19-1, 19-2, 20-3 |
| | heat flow and movement of material within Earth creates mountains and ocean basins | 19-1, 19-2 |
| 7.3.5 | Recognize and explain that heat energy carried by ocean currents has a strong influence on climate around the world. | 21-1, 21-3 |
| 7.3.6 | Describe how gas and dust from large volcanoes can change the atmosphere. | 21-3 |
| 7.3.7 | Give examples of some changes in Earth's surface that are abrupt, such as earthquakes and volcanic eruptions, and some changes that happen very slowly, such as uplift and wearing down of mountains and the action of glaciers. | |
| expanded standard | some changes in Earth's surface are abrupt | 19-1, 19-2, 20-1, 20-2, 20-3 |
| | some changes in Earth's surface happen slowly | 19-1, 19-2 |
| 7.3.8 | Describe how sediments of sand and smaller particles, sometimes containing the remains of organisms, are gradually buried and are cemented together by dissolved minerals to form solid rock again. | 18-4, 22-1 |
| 7.3.9 | Explain that sedimentary rock, when buried deep enough, may be reformed by pressure and heat, perhaps melting and recrystallizing into different kinds of rock. Describe that these reformed rock layers may be forced up again to become land surface and even mountains, and subsequently erode. | |
| expanded standard | sedimentary rock may be reformed by pressure and heat | 18-3, 18-4 |
| | reformed rock layers may be forced up again and subsequently erode | 18-4 |
| 7.3.10 | Explain how the thousands of layers of sedimentary rock can confirm the long history of the changing surface of Earth and the changing life forms whose remains are found in successive layers, although the youngest layers are not always found on top, because of folding, breaking, and uplift of layers. | |
| expanded standard | thousands of layers of sedimentary rock can confirm the long history of the changing surface of Earth and the changing life forms | 22-1, 22-2 |
| | the youngest layers are not always found on top | 22-2 |
| 7.3.11 | Explain that the sun loses energy by emitting light. Note that only a tiny fraction of that light reaches Earth. Understand that the sun's energy arrives as light with a wide range of wavelengths, consisting of visible light, infrared, and ultraviolet radiation. | 14-3, 16-2, 16-3 |
| 7.3.12 | Investigate how the temperature and acidity of a solution influences reaction rates, such as those resulting in food spoilage. | 10-2, 10-3 |
| 7.3.13 | Explain that many substances dissolve in water. Understand that the presence of these substances often affects the rates of reactions that are occurring in the water as compared to the same reactions occurring in the water in the absence of the substance. | 3-1, 3-2, 10-1, 10-2 |
| 7.3.14 | Explain that energy in the form of heat is almost always one of the products of an energy transformation, such as in the examples of exploding stars, biological growth, the operation of machines, and the motion of people. | 3-3, 13-1, 13-2 |

| Academic Standards | | Chapter-Section |
|---|---|---|
| **7.3.15** | Describe how electrical energy can be produced from a variety of energy sources and can be transformed into almost any other form of energy, such as light or heat. | |
| expanded standard | electrical energy can be produced from a variety of energy sources | 13-2, 13-3 |
| | electrical energy can be transformed into almost any other form of energy | 13-2, 13-3 |
| **7.3.16** | Recognize and explain that different ways of obtaining, transforming, and distributing energy have different environmental consequences. | |
| expanded standard | different ways of obtaining energy have different environmental consequences | 8-1, 8-2, 8-3, 13-3 |
| | different ways of transforming energy have different environmental consequences | 8-1, 8-2, 8-3, 13-3 |
| | different way of distributing energy have different environmental consequences | 13-3 |
| **7.3.17** | Investigate that an unbalanced force, acting on an object, changes its speed or path of motion or both, and know that if the force always acts toward the same center as the object moves, the object's path may curve into an orbit around the center. | |
| expanded standard | an unbalanced force, acting on an object, changes its speed or path or both | 12-1, 12-2, 12-3 |
| | if the force always acts toward the same center as the object moves, the object's path may curve | 12-2 |
| **7.3.18** | Describe that light waves, sound waves, and other waves move at different speeds in different materials. | |
| expanded standard | light waves move at different speeds in different materials | 14-1, 14-3 |
| | sound waves move at different speeds in different materials | 14-1, 14-2 |
| | other waves move at different speeds in different materials | 14-1, 19-1, 20-1, 20-3 |
| **7.3.19** | Explain that human eyes respond to a narrow range of wavelengths of the electromagnetic spectrum. | 14-3 |
| **7.3.20** | Describe that something can be "seen" when light waves emitted or reflected by it enter the eye just as something can be "heard" when sound waves from it enter the ear. | |
| expanded standard | something can be "seen" when light waves emitted or reflected enter the eye | 14-3 |
| | something can be "heard" when sound waves enter the ear | 14-2 |

## Standard 4  THE LIVING ENVIRONMENT

*Students begin to trace the flow of matter and energy through ecosystems. They recognize the fundamental difference between plants and animals and understand its basis at the cellular level. Students distinguish species, particularly through an examination of internal structures and functions. They use microscopes to observe cells and recognize that cells function in similar ways in all organisms.*

| | | |
|---|---|---|
| **7.4.1** | Explain that similarities among organisms are found in external and internal anatomical features, including specific characteristics at the cellular level, such as the number of chromosomes. Understand that these similarities are used to classify organisms since they may be used to infer the degree of relatedness among organisms. | |
| expanded standard | similarities among organisms are found in external anatomical features | 1-2, 1-4, 4-2 |
| | similarities among organisms are found in internal anatomical features | 1-2, 4-2 |
| | similarities are used to classify organisms | 1-4, 4-2 |
| **7.4.2** | Describe that all organisms, including the human species, are part of and depend on two main interconnected global food webs, the ocean food web and the land food web. | 5-2, 7-3 |
| **7.4.3** | Explain how, in sexual reproduction, a single specialized cell from a female merges with a specialized cell from a male and this fertilized egg carries genetic information from each parent and multiplies to form the complete organism. | |
| expanded standard | a single specialized female cell merges with a single specialized male cell | 4-2 |
| | a fertilized egg carries genetic information | 4-2 |
| | a fertilized egg multiplies to complete the organism | 4-2 |

| Academic Standards | | Chapter-Section |
|---|---|---|
| **7.4.4** | Explain that cells continually divide to make more cells for growth and repair and that various organs and tissues function to serve the needs of cells for food, air, and waste removal. | |
| expanded standard | cells continually divide for growth and repair | 1-2, 2-2, 2-3, 4-1, 4-3, 6-1 |
| | various organs and tissues function to serve the needs of cells for food | 2-1, 3-3, 5-1, 5-2, 6-1, 6-2, 6-4 |
| | various organs and tissues function to serve the needs of cells for air | 2-1, 3-3, 5-3, 6-1, 6-2, 6-4 |
| | various organs and tissues function to serve the needs of cell for waste removal | 2-1, 3-3, 5-4, 6-1, 6-2, 6-4 |
| **7.4.5** | Explain that the basic functions of organisms, such as extracting energy from food and getting rid of wastes, are carried out within the cell and understand that the way which cells function is similar in all organisms. | |
| expanded standard | basic functions of organisms are carried out within the cell | 1-2, 1-4, 2-1, 2-2, 2-3, 3-2, 3-3 |
| | cells function in similar ways in all organisms | 1-2, 1-4, 2-1, 2-2, 2-3, 3-2, 3-3 |
| **7.4.6** | Explain how food provides the fuel and the building material for all organisms. | |
| expanded standard | food provides the fuel for all organisms | 1-2, 5-1, 5-2, 7-3 |
| | food provides the building materials for all organisms | 1-2, 5-2, 5-4, 7-3 |
| **7.4.7** | Describe how plants use the energy from light to make sugars from carbon dioxide and water to produce food that can be used immediately or stored for later use. | 2-1, 2-3, 3-3 |
| **7.4.8** | Describe how organisms that eat plants break down the plant structures to produce the materials and energy that they need to survive, and in turn, how they are consumed by other organisms. | |
| expanded standard | organisms break down plant structures to produce materials and energy needed to survive | 1-2, 3-3, 5-1, 5-2, 7-2, 7-3 |
| | organisms are consumed by other organisms | 1-2, 3-3, 5-2, 7-2, 7-3 |
| **7.4.9** | Understand and explain that as any population of organisms grows, it is held in check by one or more environmental factors. These factors could result in depletion of food or nesting sites and/or increase loss to increased numbers of predators or parasites. Give examples of some consequences of this. | |
| expanded standard | a population of organisms is held in check by depletion of food or nesting sites and give examples | 1-2, 7-1, 7-2 |
| | a population of organisms is held in check by an increased number of predators or parasites and give examples | 7-1, 7-2 |
| **7.4.10** | Describe how technologies having to do with food production, sanitation, and disease prevention have dramatically changed how people live and work and have resulted in changes in factors that affect the growth of human population. | |
| expanded standard | food production and sanitation technologies have dramatically changed how people live and work | 6-3, 6-4 |
| | disease prevention technologies have dramatically changed how people live and work | 6-3 |
| **7.4.11** | Explain that the amount of food energy (calories) a person requires varies with body weight, age, sex, activity level, and natural body efficiency. Understand that regular exercise is important to maintain a healthy heart/lung system, good muscle tone, and strong bone structure. | |
| expanded standard | the amount of calories required by a person varies with body weight, age, sex, activity level, and natural body efficiency | 5-2 |
| | regular exercise is important to maintain a healthy heart/lung system, good muscle tone, and strong bone structure | 6-2 |
| **7.4.12** | Explain that viruses, bacteria, fungi, and parasites may infect the human body and interfere with normal body functions. Recognize that a person can catch a cold many times because there are many varieties of cold viruses that cause similar symptoms. | |
| expanded standard | viruses may infect the human body and interfere with normal body functions | 2-3, 5-3, 6-4 |
| | bacteria may infect the human body and interfere with normal body functions | 2-3, 5-3, 6-4 |
| | fungi may infect the human body and interfere with normal body functions | 5-3, 6-4 |
| | parasites may infect the human body and interfere with normal body functions | 5-3, 6-4 |
| | many varieties of cold viruses cause similar symptoms | 2-3, 6-4 |

| Academic Standards | | Chapter-Section |
|---|---|---|
| 7.4.13 | Explain that white blood cells engulf invaders or produce antibodies that attack invaders or mark the invaders for killing by other white blood cells. Know that the antibodies produced will remain and can fight off subsequent invaders of the same kind. | |
| expanded standard | white blood cells engulf invaders or produce antibodies that attack invaders or mark invaders for killing by other white blood cells | 6-1, 6-3 |
| | antibodies produced will remain and fight off subsequent invaders | 6-1, 6-3 |
| 7.4.14 | Explain that the environment may contain dangerous levels of substances that are harmful to human beings. Understand, therefore, that the good health of individuals requires monitoring the soil, air, and water as well as taking steps to keep them safe. | |
| expanded standard | the environment may contain dangerous levels of harmful substances | 6-4, 8-2, 8-3 |
| | good health requires monitoring the soil as well as steps to keep them safe | 8-2, 8-3 |
| | good health requires monitoring the air as well as steps to keep them safe | 8-2, 8-3 |
| | good health require monitoring the water as well as steps to keep them safe | 8-2, 8-3 |

## Standard 5    THE MATHEMATICAL WORLD

*Students apply mathematics in scientific contexts. They use mathematical ideas, such as relations between operations, symbols, statistical relationships, and the use of logical reasoning, in the representation and synthesis of data.*

| | | |
|---|---|---|
| 7.5.1 | Demonstrate how a number line can be extended on the other side of zero to represent negative numbers and give examples of instances where this is useful. | 21-1 |
| 7.5.2 | Illustrate how lines can be parallel, perpendicular, or oblique. | 14-1 |
| 7.5.3 | Demonstrate how the scale chosen for a graph or drawing determines its interpretation. | 1-4, 4-2, 6-4, 7-2, 7-3, Math Skill Handbook |
| 7.5.4 | Describe that the larger the sample, the more accurately it represents the whole. Understand, however, that any sample can be poorly chosen and this will make it unrepresentative of the whole. | Unit 2 Project, Science Skill Handbook |

## Standard 6    HISTORICAL PERSPECTIVE

*Students gain understanding of how the scientific enterprise operates through examples of historical events. Through the study of these events, they understand that new ideas are limited by the context in which they are conceived, are often rejected by the scientific establishment, sometimes spring from unexpected findings, and grow or transform slowly through the contributions of many different investigators.*

| | | |
|---|---|---|
| 7.6.1 | Understand and explain that throughout history, people have created explanations for disease. Note that some held that disease had spiritual causes, but that the most persistent biological theory over the centuries was that illness resulted from an imbalance in the body fluids. Realize that the introduction of germ theory by Louis Pasteur and others in the nineteenth century led to the modern understanding of how many diseases are caused by microorganisms, such as bacteria, viruses, yeasts, and parasites. | |
| expanded standard | throughout history people have created explanations for disease | 2-3, 6-4 |
| | the introduction of germ theory by Pasteur led to the modern understanding of how diseases are caused by microorganisms | 2-3, 6-4 |

| Academic Standards | | Chapter-Section |
|---|---|---|
| 7.6.2 | Understand and explain that Louis Pasteur wanted to find out what caused milk and wine to spoil. Note that he demonstrated that spoilage and fermentation occur when microorganisms enter from the air, multiply rapidly, and produce waste products, with some desirable results, such as carbon dioxide in bread dough, and some undesirable, such as acetic acid in wine. Understand that after showing that spoilage could be avoided by keeping germs out or by destroying them with heat, Pasteur investigated animal diseases and showed that microorganisms were involved in many of them. Also note that other investigators later showed that specific kinds of germs caused specific diseases. | |
| expanded standard | Pasteur demonstrated that spoilage and fermentation occur from microorganisms with some desirable results and some undesirable results | 3-3, 6-4 |
| | after showing spoilage can be avoided by keeping germs out or by destroying them with heat, Pasteur showed that microorganisms are involved in many animal diseases | 6-4 |
| | other investigators showed that specific germs cause specific diseases | 2-3, 6-4 |
| 7.6.3 | Understand and explain that Louis Pasteur found that infection by disease organisms (germs) caused the body to build up an immunity against subsequent infection by the same organisms. Realize that Pasteur then demonstrated more widely what Edward Jenner had shown for smallpox without understanding the underlying mechanism: that it was possible to produce vaccines that would induce the body to build immunity to a disease without actually causing the disease itself. | |
| expanded standard | Pasteur found that infection by disease organisms caused the body to build up an immunity | 6-4 |
| | Edward Jenner had shown smallpox immunity without understanding the underlying mechanism | 2-3 |
| | Pasteur demonstrated that it was possible to produce vaccines that induce the body to build immunity without causing the disease | 6-4 |
| 7.6.4 | Understand and describe that changes in health practices have resulted from the acceptance of the germ theory of disease. Realize that before germ theory, illness was treated by appeals to supernatural powers or by trying to adjust body fluids through induced vomiting or bleeding. Note that the modern approach emphasizes sanitation, the safe handling of food and water, the pasteurization of milk, quarantine, and aseptic surgical techniques to keep germs out of the body; vaccinations to strengthen the body's immune system against subsequent infection by the same kind of microorganisms; and antibiotics and other chemicals and processes to destroy microorganisms. | |
| expanded standard | the modern approach to illness emphasizes sanitation, safe handling of food and water, pasteurization of milk, quarantine, aseptic surgical techniques to destroy microorganisms | 2-3, 6-3, 6-4 |
| | the modern approach to illness emphasizes vaccinations to destroy microorganisms | 2-3, 6-3, 6-4 |
| | the modern approach to illness emphasizes antibiotics, chemicals, and processes to destroy microorganisms | 2-3, 6-3, 6-4 |

## Standard 7  COMMON THEMES

*Students analyze the relationships within systems. They investigate how different models can represent the same data, rates of change, cyclic changes, and changes that counterbalance one another.*

| | | |
|---|---|---|
| 7.7.1 | Explain that the output from one part of a system, which can include material, energy, or information, can become the input to other parts and this feedback can serve to control what goes on in the system as a whole. | 3-3 |
| 7.7.2 | Use different models to represent the same thing, noting that the kind of model and its complexity should depend on its purpose. | 4-3, 5-4, 6-3, 9-1 |
| 7.7.3 | Describe how physical and biological systems tend to change until they reach equilibrium and remain that way unless their surroundings change. | |
| expanded standard | physical systems tend to change until they reach equilibrium and remain that way unless their surroundings change | 3-2, 19-3 |
| | biological systems tend to change until they reach equilibrium and remain that way unless their surroundings change | 3-2 |
| 7.7.4 | Use symbolic equations to show how the quantity of something changes over time or in response to changes in other quantities. | |
| expanded standard | use symbolic equations to show how the quantity of something changes over time | 3-1, 11-1, 11-2 |
| | use symbolic equations to show how the quantity of something changes in response to other quantities | 3-1, 11-1, 11-2, 11-3, 12-1, 14-1 |

# Grade 7
# Daily Intervention Guide
## *Glencoe Indiana Science*
### correlated to
## Indiana's Academic Standards

Standards are defined on pp. IN8 – IN14.

| Indiana's Standards | Student & Teacher Edition Activities | Reproducible Resources | Technology Resources |
|---|---|---|---|
| **Unit 1 ● The Basis of Life** | | | |
| **Chapter 1 ● Exploring and Classifying Life** | | | |
| **Section 1 ● What is science?** | | | |
| 7.1.1, 7.1.3, 7.1.4, 7.1.8, 7.2.8 | **Science Online,** p. 8<br>**MiniLAB:** Analyzing Data, p. 9<br>**Applying Science:** Does temperature affect the rate of bacterial reproduction?, p. 11 | **Chapter *Fast File* Resources**<br>Transparency Activity, p. 44<br>MiniLAB, p. 3<br>Enrichment, p. 29<br>Reinforcement, p. 25<br>Lab Activity, pp. 9–10<br>Directed Reading, p. 18<br>**Reading Essentials,** Section 1 | Section Focus Transparencies<br><br>Virtual Labs CD-ROM<br><br>Interactive Chalkboard CD-ROM |
| **Section 2 ● Living Things** | | | |
| 7.4.1, 7.4.4, 7.4.5, 7.4.6, 7.4.8, 7.4.9 | **Science Online,** p. 15<br>**Integrate Social Studies,** p. 17 | **Chapter *Fast File* Resources**<br>Transparency Activity, p. 45<br>Enrichment, p. 30<br>Reinforcement, p. 26<br>Directed Reading, p. 18<br>**Reading Essentials,** Section 2 | Video Lab<br><br>ExamView® Pro Testmaker CD-ROM |
| **Section 3 ● Where does life come from?** | | | |
| 7.1.2, 7.1.4, 7.1.5 | **Visualizing the Origins of Life,** p. 20<br>**Integrate Earth Science,** p. 21 | **Chapter *Fast File* Resources**<br>Transparency Activity, p. 46<br>Enrichment, p. 31<br>Reinforcement, p. 27<br>Directed Reading, p. 19<br>**Reading Essentials,** Section 3 | IN Test Prep and Practice ExamView® Pro<br><br>StudentWorks+™ Audio |

| Indiana Objectives | Student & Teacher Edition Activities | Reproducible Resources | Technology Resources |
|---|---|---|---|
| **Section 4 ● How are living things classified?** | | | |
| 7.1.3, 7.2.7, 7.4.1, 7.4.5, 7.5.3 | **Science Online,** p. 23<br>**MiniLAB:** Communicating Ideas, p. 25<br>**Lab:** Classifying Seeds, p. 27<br>**Lab:** Using Scientific Methods, p. 28<br>**Science and Society:** Monkey Business, p. 30 | **Chapter *Fast File* Resources**<br>Transparency Activity, p. 47<br>MiniLAB, p. 4<br>Enrichment, p. 32<br>Reinforcement, p. 28<br>Directed Reading, pp. 19, 20<br>Transparency Activity, pp. 49–50<br>Lab Activity, pp. 11–13<br>Lab Worksheet, pp. 5–6, 7–8<br>**Reading Essentials,** Section 4 | StudentWorks+™ Audio<br><br><br>TeacherWorks™ |
| **End of Chapter Assessment** | | | |
| | **Chapter Review,** pp. 32–33<br>**Indiana Standards Review,** pp. 34–35 | **Mastering the Grade 7 Indiana Science Standards** | in7.msscience.com |
| **Chapter 2 ● Cells** | | | |
| **Section 1 ● Cell Structure** | | | |
| 7.4.4, 7.4.5, 7.4.7 | **MiniLAB:** Modeling Cytoplasm, p. 40<br>**Integrate Environment,** p. 44<br>**Applying Math:** Cell Ratio, p. 44<br>**Lab:** Comparing Cells, p. 46 | **Chapter *Fast File* Resources**<br>Transparency Activity, p. 44<br>MiniLAB, p. 3<br>Enrichment, p. 30<br>Reinforcement, p. 27<br>Directed Reading, p. 20<br>Transparency Activity, pp. 47–48<br>Lab Worksheet, pp. 5–6<br>**Reading Essentials,** Section 1 | Section Focus Transparencies<br><br>Virtual Labs CD-ROM<br><br>Interactive Chalkboard CD-ROM |
| **Section 2 ● Viewing Cells** | | | |
| 7.1.5, 7.1.7, 7.4.4, 7.4.5 | **Visualizing Microscopes,** p. 48<br>**MiniLAB:** Observing Magnified Objects, p. 50<br>**Integrate Career,** p. 50 | **Chapter *Fast File* Resources**<br>Transparency Activity, p. 45<br>MiniLAB, p. 4<br>Enrichment, p. 31<br>Reinforcement, p. 28<br>Directed Reading, p. 20<br>Lab Activity, pp. 9–12, 13–16<br>**Reading Essentials,** Section 2 | Video Lab<br><br>ExamView® Pro Testmaker CD-ROM |
| **Section 3 ● Viruses** | | | |
| 7.1.5, 7.1.6, 7.1.7, 7.4.7, 7.4.12, 7.6.3, 7.6.4 | **Science Online,** p. 53<br>**Science Online,** p. 54<br>**Lab:** Comparing Light Microscopes, p. 56<br>**Science and History:** Cobb Against Cancer, p. 58 | **Chapter *Fast File* Resources**<br>Transparency Activity, p. 46<br>Enrichment, p. 32<br>Reinforcement, p. 29<br>Directed Reading, pp. 21, 22<br>Lab Worksheet, pp. 7–8<br>**Reading Essentials,** Section 3 | IN Test Prep and Practice ExamView® Pro<br><br>StudentWorks+™ Audio |

| Indiana Objectives | Student & Teacher Edition Activities | Reproducible Resources | Technology Resources |
|---|---|---|---|
| **End of Chapter Assessment** | | | |
| | Chapter Review, pp. 60–61 Indiana Standards Review, pp. 62–63 | Mastering the Grade 7 Indiana Science Standards | TeacherWorks™ in7.msscience.com |
| **Chapter 3 ● Cell Processes** | | | |
| **Section 1 ● Chemistry of Life** | | | |
| 7.3.13, 7.7.4 | Science Online, p. 70 MiniLAB: Observing How Enzymes Work, p. 71 Applying Math: Calculating the Importance of Water, p. 72 | Chapter *Fast File* Resources Transparency Activity, p. 42 MiniLAB, p. 3 Enrichment, p. 28 Reinforcement, p. 25 Directed Reading, p. 18 Transparency Activity, pp. 45–46 Reading Essentials, Section 1 | Section Focus Transparencies Virtual Labs CD-ROM Interactive Chalkboard CD-ROM |
| **Section 2 ● Moving Cellular Materials** | | | |
| 7.3.13, 7.4.5, 7.7.3 | MiniLAB: Observing Diffusion, p. 75 Integrate Health, p. 77 Visualizing Cell Membrane Transport, p. 79 Lab: Observing Osmosis, p. 80 | Chapter *Fast File* Resources Transparency Activity, p. 43 MiniLAB, p. 4 Enrichment, p. 29 Reinforcement, p. 26 Directed Reading, p. 18 Lab Activity, pp. 9–10 Lab Worksheet, pp. 5–6 Reading Essentials, Section 2 | Video Lab ExamView® Pro Testmaker CD-ROM |
| **Section 3 ● Energy for Life** | | | |
| 7.3.14, 7.4.4, 7.4.5, 7.4.7, 7.4.8, 7.6.2, 7.7.1 | Integrate Career, p. 83 Science Online, p. 84 Lab: Photosynthesis and Respiration, p. 86 Science and Language Arts: from "Tulip," p. 88 | Chapter *Fast File* Resources Transparency Activity, p. 44 Enrichment, p. 30 Reinforcement, p. 27 Directed Reading, pp. 19, 20 Lab Activity, pp. 11–14 Lab Worksheet, pp. 7–8 Reading Essentials, Section 3 | IN Test Prep and Practice ExamView® Pro StudentWorks+™ Audio TeacherWorks™ |
| **End of Chapter Assessment** | | | |
| | Chapter Review, pp. 90–91 Indiana Standards Review, pp. 92–93 | Mastering the Grade 7 Indiana Science Standards | in7.msscience.com |

# Daily Intervention Guide

| Indiana Objectives | Student & Teacher Edition Activities | Reproducible Resources | Technology Resources |
|---|---|---|---|
| **Chapter 4** ● **Cell Reproduction** | | | |
| **Section 1** ● **Cell Division and Mitosis** | | | |
| 7.2.7, 7.4.4 | **Integrate Career,** p. 97<br>**MiniLAB:** Modeling Mitosis, p. 101<br>**Lab:** Mitosis in Plant Cells, p. 103 | **Chapter *Fast File* Resources**<br>Transparency Activity, p. 42<br>MiniLAB, p. 3<br>Enrichment, p. 28<br>Reinforcement, p. 25<br>Transparency Activity, pp. 45–46<br>Lab Worksheet, pp. 5–6<br>Directed Reading, p. 18<br>Lab Activity, pp. 9–10<br>**Reading Essentials,** Section 1 | Section Focus Transparencies<br><br>Virtual Labs CD-ROM<br><br>Interactive Chalkboard CD-ROM |
| **Section 2** ● **Sexual Reproduction and Meiosis** | | | |
| 7.4.1, 7.4.3, 7.5.3 | **Integrate Chemistry,** p. 105<br>**Applying Science:** How can chromosome numbers be predicted?, p. 107<br>**Visualizing Polyploidy in Plants,** p. 108 | **Chapter *Fast File* Resources**<br>Transparency Activity, p. 43<br>Enrichment, p. 29<br>Reinforcement, p. 26<br>Directed Reading, p. 18<br>**Reading Essentials,** Section 2 | Video Lab<br><br>ExamView® Pro Testmaker CD-ROM |
| **Section 3** ● **DNA** | | | |
| 7.1.5, 7.1.8, 7.1.10, 7.2.7, 7.4.3, 7.4.4, 7.7.2 | **MiniLAB:** Modeling DNA Replication, p. 111<br>**Science Online,** p. 113<br>**Science Online,** p. 115<br>**Lab:** Mutations, p. 116<br>**Oops! Accidents in Science:** A Tangled Tale, p. 118 | **Chapter *Fast File* Resources**<br>Transparency Activity, p. 44<br>MiniLAB, p. 4<br>Enrichment, p. 30<br>Reinforcement, p. 27<br>Directed Reading, pp. 19, 20<br>Lab Worksheet, pp. 7–8<br>Lab Activity, pp. 11–13<br>**Reading Essentials,** Section 3 | IN Test Prep and Practice ExamView® Pro<br><br>StudentWorks+™ Audio<br><br>TeacherWorks™ |
| **End of Chapter Assessment** | | | |
| | **Chapter Review,** pp. 120–121<br>**Indiana Standards Review,** pp. 122–123 | **Mastering the Grade 7 Indiana Science Standards** | in7.msscience.com |
| **Unit 2** ● **The Interdependence of Life** | | | |
| **Chapter 5** ● **Digestion, Respiration, and Excretion** | | | |
| **Section 1** ● **The Digestive System** | | | |
| 7.4.4, 7.4.6, 7.4.8 | **Integrate Health,** p. 132 | **Chapter *Fast File* Resources**<br>Transparency Activity, p. 46<br>Enrichment, p. 31<br>Reinforcement, p. 27<br>Directed Reading, p. 20<br>Lab Activity, pp. 9–12<br>**Reading Essentials,** Section 1 | Section Focus Transparencies<br><br>Virtual Labs CD-ROM |

| Indiana Objectives | Student & Teacher Edition Activities | Reproducible Resources | Technology Resources |
|---|---|---|---|
| **Section 2 ● Nutrition** | | | |
| 7.4.2, 7.4.4, 7.4.6, 7.4.8, 7.4.11 | **Science Online,** p. 134<br>**MiniLAB:** Comparing the Fat Content of Foods, p. 135<br>**Integrate Social Studies,** p. 136<br>**Lab:** Identifying Vitamin C Content, p. 139 | **Chapter *Fast File* Resources**<br>Transparency Activity, p. 47<br>MiniLAB, p. 3<br>Enrichment, p. 32<br>Reinforcement, p. 28<br>Directed Reading, p. 20<br>Lab Worksheet, pp. 5–6<br>**Reading Essentials, Section 2** | Interactive Chalkboard CD-ROM<br><br>Video Lab |
| **Section 3 ● The Respiratory System** | | | |
| 7.4.4, 7.4.12 | **MiniLAB:** Comparing Surface Area, p. 143<br>**Visualizing Abdominal Thrusts,** p. 144<br>**Science Online,** p. 145 | **Chapter *Fast File* Resources**<br>Transparency Activity, p. 48<br>MiniLAB, p. 4<br>Enrichment, p. 33<br>Reinforcement, p. 29<br>Directed Reading, p. 21<br>Lab Activity, pp. 13–16<br>**Reading Essentials,** Section 3 | ExamView® Pro Testmaker CD-ROM<br><br>IN Test Prep and Practice ExamView® Pro |
| **Section 4 ● The Excretory System** | | | |
| 7.1.6, 7.1.9, 7.2.7, 7.4.4, 7.4.6, 7.7.2 | **Applying Science:** How does your body gain or lose water? p. 150<br>**Lab:** Particle Size and Absorption, pp. 152–153<br>**Science and History:** Overcoming the Odds, p. 154 | **Chapter *Fast File* Resources**<br>Transparency Activity, p. 49<br>Enrichment, p. 34<br>Reinforcement, p. 30<br>Directed Reading, pp. 21, 22<br>Lab Worksheet, pp. 7–8<br>Transparency Activity, pp. 50–51<br>**Reading Essentials,** Section 4 | StudentWorks+™ Audio<br><br>TeacherWorks™ |
| **End of Chapter Assessment** | | | |
| | **Chapter Review,** pp. 156–157<br>**Indiana Standards Review,** pp. 158–159 | **Mastering the Grade 7 Indiana Science Standards** | in7.msscience.com |
| **Chapter 6 ● Circulation and Immunity** | | | |
| **Section 1 ● Blood** | | | |
| 7.1.9, 7.4.4, 7.4.13 | **Science Online,** p. 163<br>**MiniLAB:** Modeling Scab Formation, p. 164<br>**Integrate History,** p. 165 | **Chapter *Fast File* Resources**<br>Transparency Activity, p. 46<br>MiniLAB Worksheet, p. 3<br>Enrichment, p. 31<br>Reinforcement, p. 27<br>Directed Reading, p. 20<br>Transparency Activity, p. 45<br>**Reading Essentials,** Section 1 | Section Focus Transparencies<br><br>Virtual Labs CD-ROM |

# Daily Intervention Guide

| Indiana Objectives | Student & Teacher Edition Activities | Reproducible Resources | Technology Resources |
|---|---|---|---|
| **Section 2 ● Circulation** | | | |
| 7.4.4, 7.4.11 | **Science Online,** p. 172 | **Chapter *Fast File* Resources**<br>Transparency Activity, p. 47<br>Enrichment, p. 32<br>Reinforcement, p. 28<br>Directed Reading, p. 20<br>Transparency Activity, pp. 50–51<br>**Reading Essentials,** Section 2 | Interactive Chalkboard CD-ROM<br><br><br>Video Lab |
| **Section 3 ● Immunity** | | | |
| 7.4.10, 7.4.13, 7.6.4, 7.7.2 | **Integrate Social Studies,** p. 174<br>**MiniLAB,** p. 175 | **Chapter *Fast File* Resources**<br>Transparency Activity, p. 48<br>MiniLAB, p. 4<br>Enrichment, p. 33<br>Reinforcement, p. 29<br>Directed Reading, p. 21<br>**Reading Essentials,** Section 3 | Exam*View*® Pro Testmaker CD-ROM<br><br><br>IN Test Prep and Practice Exam*View*® Pro |
| **Section 4 ● Diseases** | | | |
| 7.1.5, 7.4.4, 7.4.10, 7.4.12, 7.4.14, 7.5.3, 7.6.1, 7.6.2, 7.6.3, 7.6.4 | **Science Online,** p. 178<br>**Visualizing Koch's Rules,** p. 179<br>**Applying Science:** Has the annual percentage of deaths from major diseases changed? p. 180<br>**Lab:** Microorganisms and Disease, p. 185<br>**Lab:** Blood Type Reactions, p. 186<br>**Science and History:** Have a Heart, p. 188 | **Chapter *Fast File* Resources**<br>Transparency Activity, p. 49<br>Enrichment, p. 34<br>Reinforcement, p. 30<br>Directed Reading, p. 21<br>Lab Worksheets, pp. 5–8<br>Lab Activities, pp. 9–16<br>**Reading Essentials,** Section 4 | StudentWorks+™ Audio<br><br><br>TeacherWorks™ |
| **End of Chapter Assessment** | | | |
| | **Chapter Review,** pp. 190–191<br>**Indiana Standards Review,** pp. 192–193 | **Mastering the Grade 7 Indiana Science Standards** | in7.msscience.com |
| **Chapter 7 ● Interactions of Living Things** | | | |
| **Section 1 ● The Environment** | | | |
| 7.1.7, 7.2.7, 7.4.9 | **Integrate Career,** p. 198<br>**Science Online,** p. 200<br>**Lab:** Delicately Balanced Ecosystems, p. 202 | **Chapter *Fast File* Resources**<br>Transparency Activity, p. 44<br>Enrichment, p. 30<br>Reinforcement, p. 27<br>Directed Reading, p. 20<br>Lab Worksheets, pp. 5–6<br>Lab Activity, pp. 9–12<br>**Reading Essentials,** Section 1 | Section Focus Transparencies<br><br><br>Virtual Labs CD-ROM |

| Indiana Objectives | Student & Teacher Edition Activities | Reproducible Resources | Technology Resources |
|---|---|---|---|
| **Section 2 ● Interactions Among Living Organisms** | | | |
| 7.4.8, 7.5.3 | **Science Online,** p. 204<br>**MiniLAB: Observing Symbiosis,** p. 206 | **Chapter *Fast File* Resources**<br>Transparency Activity, p. 45<br>MiniLAB, p. 3<br>Enrichment, p. 31<br>Reinforcement, p. 28<br>Directed Reading, p. 20<br>Lab Activity, pp. 13–15<br>**Reading Essentials,** Section 2 | Interactive Chalkboard CD-ROM<br><br><br>Video Lab |
| **Section 3 ● Matter and Energy** | | | Exam*View*® Pro Testmaker CD-ROM |
| 7.4.2, 7.4.6, 7.4.8, 7.5.3 | **Visualizing a Food Chain,** p. 209<br>**Applying Science:** How do changes in Antarctic food webs affect populations?, p. 210<br>**Integrate Chemistry,** p. 211<br>**MiniLAB:** Modeling the Water Cycle, p. 212<br>**Lab:** Identifying a Limiting Factor, p. 214<br>**Science and Language Arts:** The Solace of Open Spaces, p. 216 | **Chapter *Fast File* Resources**<br>Transparency Activity, p. 46<br>MiniLAB, p. 4<br>Enrichment, p. 32<br>Reinforcement, p. 29<br>Directed Reading, p. 21, 22<br>Lab Worksheets, pp. 7–8<br>Transparency Activity, pp. 47–48<br>**Reading Essentials,** Section 3 | IN Test Prep and Practice ExamView® Pro<br><br><br>StudentWorks+™ Audio<br><br><br>TeacherWorks™ |
| **End of Chapter Assessment** | | | |
| | **Chapter Review,** pp. 218–219<br>**Indiana Standards Review,** pp. 220–221 | **Mastering the Grade 7 Indiana Science Standards** | in7.msscience.com |
| **Chapter 8 ● Conserving Resources** | | | |
| **Section 1 ● Resources** | | | |
| 7.1.8, 7.3.16 | **MiniLAB:** Observing Mineral Mining Effects, p. 226<br>**Integrate Social Studies,** p. 227<br>**Visualizing Solar Energy,** p. 231 | **Chapter *Fast File* Resources**<br>Transparency Activity, p. 44<br>MiniLAB, p. 3<br>Enrichment, p. 30<br>Reinforcement, p. 27<br>Directed Reading, p. 20<br>**Reading Essentials,** Section 1 | Section Focus Transparencies<br><br><br>Virtual Labs CD-ROM |
| **Section 2 ● Pollution** | | | |
| 7.1.8, 7.2.7, 7.3.16, 7.4.14 | **MiniLAB:** Measuring Acid Rain, p. 233<br>**Science Online,** p. 234<br>**Integrate Health,** p. 236<br>**Lab:** The Greenhouse Effect, p. 241 | **Chapter *Fast File* Resources**<br>Transparency Activity, p. 45<br>MiniLAB, p. 4<br>Enrichment, p. 31<br>Reinforcement, p. 28<br>Directed Reading, p. 21<br>Lab Worksheet, pp. 5–6<br>Lab Activity, pp. 9–12<br>Transparency Activity, pp. 47–48<br>**Reading Essentials,** Section 2 | Interactive Chalkboard CD-ROM<br><br><br>Video Lab |

| Indiana Objectives | Student & Teacher Edition Activities | Reproducible Resources | Technology Resources |
|---|---|---|---|
| **Section 3 ● The Three Rs of Conservation** | | | |
| 7.3.16, 7.4.14 | **Science Online,** p. 244 <br> **Applying Science:** What items are you recycling at home?, p. 244 <br> **Lab:** Solar Cooking, p. 246 <br> **Science and Language Arts:** Beauty Plagiarized, p. 248 | **Chapter *Fast File* Resources** <br> Transparency Activity, p. 46 <br> Enrichment, p. 32 <br> Reinforcement, p. 29 <br> Directed Reading, pp. 21, 22 <br> Lab Worksheet, pp. 7–8 <br> Lab Activity, pp. 13–16 <br> **Reading Essentials,** Section 3 | ExamView® Pro Testmaker CD-ROM <br><br> IN Test Prep and Practice ExamView® Pro <br><br> StudentWorks+™ Audio <br><br> TeacherWorks™ <br><br> in7.msscience.com |
| **End of Chapter Assessment** | | | |
| | **Chapter Review,** pp. 250–251 <br> **Indiana Standards Review,** pp. 252–253 | **Mastering the Grade 7 Indiana Science Standards** | |
| **Unit 3 ● The Nature of Matter** | | | |
| **Chapter 9 ● Atoms, Elements, and the Periodic Table** | | | |
| **Section 1 ● Structure of Matter** | | | |
| 7.1.5, 7.7.2 | **Integrate History,** p. 259 <br> **MiniLAB:** Investigating the Unseen, p. 260 <br> **Science Online,** p. 262 <br> **Integrate Career,** p. 264 | **Chapter *Fast File* Resources** <br> Transparency Activity, p. 40 <br> MiniLAB, p. 3 <br> Enrichment, p. 26 <br> Reinforcement, p. 23 <br> Directed Reading, p. 16 <br> Transparency Activity, pp. 43–44 <br> **Reading Essentials,** Section 1 | Section Focus Transparencies <br><br> Virtual Labs CD-ROM <br><br> Interactive Chalkboard CD-ROM |
| **Section 2 ● The Simplest Matter** | | | |
| 7.1.5 | **Science Online,** p. 267 <br> **Visualizing the Periodic Table,** p. 268 <br> **Lab:** Elements and the Periodic Table, p. 272 | **Chapter *Fast File* Resources** <br> Transparency Activity, p. 41 <br> Enrichment, p. 27 <br> Reinforcement, p. 24 <br> Directed Reading, p. 17 <br> Lab Worksheet, pp. 5–6 <br> **Reading Essentials,** Section 2 | Video Lab <br><br> ExamView® Pro Testmaker CD-ROM |
| **Section 3 ● Compounds and Mixtures** | | | |
| 7.1.5 | **MiniLAB:** Comparing Compounds, p. 274 <br> **Applying Science:** What's the best way to desalt ocean water?, p. 275 <br> **Science Online,** p. 276 <br> **Integrate Earth Science,** p. 277 <br> **Lab:** Mystery Mixture, p. 278 <br> **Science and History:** Ancient Views of Matter, p. 280 | **Chapter *Fast File* Resources** <br> Transparency Activity, p. 42 <br> MiniLAB, p. 4 <br> Enrichment, p. 28 <br> Reinforcement, p. 25 <br> Directed Reading, pp. 17, 18 <br> Lab Worksheet, pp. 7–8 <br> Lab Activity, pp. 9–10, 11–12 <br> **Reading Essentials,** Section 3 | IN Test Prep and Practice ExamView® Pro <br><br> StudentWorks+™ Audio <br><br> TeacherWorks™ |
| **End of Chapter Assessment** | | | |
| | **Chapter Review,** pp. 282–283 <br> **Indiana Standards Review,** pp. 284–285 | **Mastering the Grade 7 Indiana Science Standards** | in7.msscience.com |

| Indiana Objectives | Student & Teacher Edition Activities | Reproducible Resources | Technology Resources |
|---|---|---|---|
| **Chapter 10 ● Substances, Mixtures, and Solubility** | | | |
| **Section 1 ● What is a solution?** | | | |
| 7.3.13 | **Science Online,** p. 289 | **Chapter *Fast File* Resources**<br>Transparency Activity, p. 44<br>Lab Activity, pp. 9–12<br>Enrichment, p. 30<br>Reinforcement, p. 27<br>Directed Reading, p. 20<br>**Reading Essentials,** Section 1 | Section Focus Transparencies<br><br>Virtual Labs CD-ROM |
| **Section 2 ● Solubility** | | | Interactive Chalkboard CD-ROM |
| 7.3.12, 7.3.13 | **Integrate Environment,** p. 295<br>**MiniLAB:** Observing Chemical Processes, p. 298<br>**Integrate Career,** p. 299<br>**Applying Science:** How can you compare concentrations?, p. 299<br>**Lab:** Observing Gas Solubility, p. 301 | **Chapter *Fast File* Resources**<br>Transparency Activity, p. 45<br>MiniLAB, p. 3<br>Lab Activity, pp. 13–16<br>Enrichment, p. 31<br>Reinforcement, p. 28<br>Directed Reading, p. 20<br>Lab Worksheet, pp. 5–6<br>**Reading Essentials,** Section 2 | Video Lab<br><br>Exam*View*® Pro Testmaker CD-ROM |
| **Section 3 ● Acidic and Basic Solutions** | | | |
| 7.3.12 | **MiniLAB:** Observing a Nail in a Carbonated Drink, p. 303<br>**Visualizing Acid Precipitation,** p. 304<br>**Science Online,** p. 305<br>**Integrate Life Science,** p. 306<br>**Science Online,** p. 308<br>**Lab:** Testing pH Using Natural Indicators, p. 310<br>**Science Stats:** Salty Solutions, p. 312 | **Chapter *Fast File* Resources**<br>Transparency Activity, p. 46<br>MiniLAB, p. 4<br>Enrichment, p. 32<br>Reinforcement, p. 29<br>Transparency Activity, pp. 47–48<br>Directed Reading, pp. 21, 22<br>Lab Worksheet, pp. 7–8<br>**Reading Essentials,** Section 3 | IN Test Prep and Practice Exam*View*® Pro<br><br>StudentWorks+™ Audio |
| **End of Chapter Assessment** | | | TeacherWorks™ |
| | **Chapter Review,** pp. 314–315<br>**Indiana Standards Review,** pp. 316–317 | **Mastering the Grade 7 Indiana Science Standards** | in7.msscience.com |
| **Unit 4 ● Motion, Forces, and Energy** | | | |
| **Chapter 11 ● Motion and Momentum** | | | |
| **Section 1 ● What is motion?** | | | |
| 7.2.6, 7.2.7, 7.7.4 | **Integrate Life Science,** p. 324<br>**Applying Math:** Speed of a Swimmer, p. 324<br>**MiniLAB:** Measuring Average Speed, p. 325<br>**Science Online,** p. 326 | **Chapter *Fast File* Resources**<br>Transparency Activity, p. 44<br>MiniLAB: p. 3<br>Enrichment, p. 30<br>Reinforcement, p. 27<br>Directed Reading, p. 20<br>Lab Activity, pp. 9–11<br>Transparency Activity, pp. 47–48<br>**Reading Essentials,** Section 1 | Section Focus Transparencies<br><br>Virtual Labs CD-ROM |

| Indiana Objectives | Student & Teacher Edition Activities | Reproducible Resources | Technology Resources |
|---|---|---|---|
| **Section 2 ● Acceleration** | | | |
| 7.2.7, 7.7.4 | **Applying Math:** Acceleration of a Bus, p. 330<br>**MiniLAB:** Modeling Acceleration, p. 331 | **Chapter *Fast File* Resources**<br>Transparency Activity, p. 45<br>MiniLAB, p. 4<br>Enrichment, p. 31<br>Reinforcement, p. 28<br>Directed Reading, p. 20<br>Transparency Activity, pp. 47–48<br>**Reading Essentials,** Section 2 | Interactive Chalkboard CD-ROM<br><br>Video Lab<br><br>ExamView® Pro Testmaker CD-ROM |
| **Section 3 ● Momentum** | | | |
| 7.2.7, 7.7.4 | **Integrate Social Studies,** p. 334<br>**Applying Math:** Momentum of a Bicycle, p. 334<br>**Science Online,** p. 336<br>**Visualizing Conservation of Momentum,** p. 337<br>**Lab:** Collisions, p. 339<br>**Lab:** Care Safety Testing, pp. 340–341<br>**Oops! Accidents in Science:** What Goes Around Comes Around, p. 342 | **Chapter *Fast File* Resources**<br>Transparency Activity, p. 46<br>Enrichment, p. 32<br>Reinforcement, p. 29<br>Directed Reading, p. 21, 22<br>Lab Worksheets, pp. 5–6, 7–8<br>**Reading Essentials,** Section 3 | IN Test Prep and Practice ExamView® Pro<br><br>StudentWorks+™ Audio<br><br>TeacherWorks™ |
| **End of Chapter Assessment** | | | |
| | **Chapter Review,** pp. 344–345<br>**Indiana Standards Review,** pp. 346–347 | **Mastering the Grade 7 Indiana Science Standards** | in7.msscience.com |
| **Chapter 12 ● Force and Newton's Laws** | | | |
| **Section 1 ● Newton's First Law** | | | |
| 7.1.5, 7.3.17, 7.7.4 | **Integrate Life Science,** p. 351<br>**Science Online,** p. 353<br>**MiniLAB:** Observing Friction, p. 354 | **Chapter *Fast File* Resources**<br>Transparency Activity, p. 44<br>MiniLAB, p. 3<br>Lab Activity, pp. 9–12<br>Enrichment, p. 30<br>Reinforcement, p. 27<br>Directed Reading, p. 20<br>Transparency Activity, pp. 47–48<br>**Reading Essentials,** Section 1 | Section Focus Transparencies<br><br>Virtual Labs CD-ROM<br><br>Interactive Chalkboard CD-ROM |
| **Section 2 ● Newton's Second Law** | | | |
| 7.1.5, 7.3.17 | **Integrate History,** p. 357<br>**Applying Math:** Acceleration of a Car, p. 359 | **Chapter *Fast File* Resources**<br>Transparency Activity, p. 45<br>Lab Activity, pp. 13–16<br>Enrichment, p. 31<br>Reinforcement, p. 28<br>Directed Reading, p. 21<br>Transparency Activity, p. 47–48<br>**Reading Essentials,** Section 2 | Video Lab<br><br>ExamView® Pro Testmaker CD-ROM |

| Indiana Objectives | Student & Teacher Edition Activities | Reproducible Resources | Technology Resources |
|---|---|---|---|
| **Section 3** ● **Newton's Third Law** | | | |
| 7.2.6, 7.3.17 | **Science Online,** p. 364<br>**Visualizing Newton's Laws in Sports,** p. 365<br>**MiniLAB:** Measuring Force Pairs, p. 367<br>**Lab:** Balloon Races, p. 369<br>**Lab:** Modeling Motion in Two Directions, pp. 370–371<br>**Science and Society:** Air Bag Safety, p. 372 | **Chapter *Fast File* Resources**<br>Transparency Activity, p. 46<br>MiniLAB, p. 4<br>Enrichment, p. 32<br>Reinforcement, p. 29<br>Directed Reading, pp. 20, 22<br>Lab Worksheets, pp. 5–6, 7–8<br>Transparency Activity, pp. 47–48<br>**Reading Essentials,** Section 3 | IN Test Prep and Practice ExamView® Pro<br><br>StudentWorks+™ Audio<br><br>TeacherWorks™ |
| **End of Chapter Assessment** | | | |
| | **Chapter Review,** pp. 374–375<br>**Indiana Standards Review,** pp. 376–377 | **Mastering the Grade 7 Indiana Science Standards** | in7.msscience.com |
| **Chapter 13** ● **Energy and Energy Resources** | | | |
| **Section 1** ● **What is energy?** | | | |
| 7.3.14 | | **Chapter *Fast File* Resources**<br>Transparency Activity, p. 42<br>Enrichment, p. 28<br>Reinforcement, p. 25<br>Directed Reading, p. 18<br>**Reading Essentials,** Section 1 | Section Focus Transparencies<br><br>Virtual Labs CD-ROM |
| **Section 2** ● **Energy Transformations** | | | |
| 7.1.10, 7.2.7, 7.3.14, 7.3.15 | **Science Online,** p. 386<br>**MiniLAB:** Analyzing Energy Transformations, p. 387<br>**Visualizing Energy Transformations,** p. 388<br>**Integrate History,** p. 389<br>**Lab:** Hearing with Your Jaw, p. 392 | **Chapter *Fast File* Resources**<br>Transparency Activity, p. 43<br>MiniLAB, p. 3<br>Enrichment, p. 29<br>Reinforcement, p. 26<br>Directed Reading, p. 19<br>Lab Activity, pp. 9–10<br>Lab Worksheet, pp. 5–6<br>**Reading Essentials,** Section 2 | Interactive Chalkboard CD-ROM<br><br>Video Lab<br><br>ExamView® Pro Testmaker CD-ROM |
| **Section 3** ● **Sources of Energy** | | | |
| 7.1.8, 7.2.6, 7.2.7, 7.3.15, 7.3.16 | **Integrate Earth Science,** p. 394<br>**Science Online,** p. 396<br>**Applying Science:** Is energy consumption outpacing production?, p. 396<br>**MiniLAB:** Building a Solar Collector, p. 397<br>**Lab:** Energy to Power Your Life, p. 402<br>**Science Stats:** Energy to Burn, p. 404 | **Chapter *Fast File* Resources**<br>Transparency Activity, p. 44<br>MiniLAB, p. 4<br>Enrichment, p. 30<br>Reinforcement, p. 27<br>Directed Reading, pp. 19, 20<br>Lab Activity, pp. 11–13<br>Lab Worksheet, pp. 7–8<br>Transparency Activity, pp. 45–46<br>**Reading Essentials,** Section 3 | IN Test Prep and Practice ExamView® Pro<br><br>StudentWorks+™ Audio |

| Indiana Objectives | Student & Teacher Edition Activities | Reproducible Resources | Technology Resources |
|---|---|---|---|
| **End of Chapter Assessment** | | | TeacherWorks™ |
| | **Chapter Review,** pp. 406–407 **Indiana Standards Review,** pp. 408–409 | **Mastering the Grade 7 Indiana Science Standards** | in7.msscience.com |
| **Chapter 14 ● Waves, Sound, and Light** | | | |
| **Section 1 ● Waves** | | | |
| 7.3.18, 7.7.4 | **Applying Math:** Speed of Sound, p. 416 **MiniLAB:** Refraction of Light, p. 417 | **Chapter *Fast File* Resources** Transparency Activity, p. 44 MiniLAB, p. 3 Enrichment, p. 30 Reinforcement, p. 27 Directed Reading, p. 20 **Reading Essentials,** Section 1 | Section Focus Transparencies |
| **Section 2 ● Sound Waves** | | | Virtual Labs CD-ROM |
| 7.3.18, 7.3.20 | **Integrate Health,** p. 421 **Lab:** Sound Waves in Matter, p. 424 | **Chapter *Fast File* Resources** Transparency Activity, p. 45 Enrichment, p. 31 Reinforcement, p. 28 Directed Reading, p. 20 Lab Worksheet, pp. 5–6 Lab Activity, pp. 9–12 **Reading Essentials,** Section 2 | Interactive Chalkboard CD-ROM  Video Lab  Exam*View*® Pro Testmaker CD-ROM |
| **Section 3 ● Light** | | | |
| 7.1.5, 7.3.2, 7.3.11, 7.3.18, 7.3.19, 7.3.20 | **Science Online,** p. 426 **MiniLAB:** Separating Wavelengths, p. 428 **Visualizing Common Vision Problems,** p. 430 **Lab:** Bending Light, p. 432 **Oops! Accidents in Science:** Jansky's Merry-Go-Round, p. 434 | **Chapter *Fast File* Resources** Transparency Activity, p. 46 MiniLAB, p. 4 Enrichment, p. 32 Reinforcement, p. 29 Directed Reading, p. 21 Lab Worksheet, pp. 7–8 Lab Activity, pp. 13–16 **Reading Essentials,** Section 3 | IN Test Prep and Practice Exam*View*® Pro  StudentWorks+™ Audio  TeacherWorks™ |
| **End of Chapter Assessment** | | | |
| | **Chapter Review,** pp. 436–437 **Indiana Standards Review,** pp. 438–439 | **Mastering the Grade 7 Indiana Science Standards** | in7.msscience.com |
| **Chapter 15 ● Electronics and Computers** | | | |
| **Section 1 ● Electronics** | | | |
| This section builds a foundation for Standard 7.1.11. | **Science Online,** p. 445 **Lab:** Investigating Diodes, p. 448 | **Chapter *Fast File* Resources** Transparency Activity, p. 42 Lab Activity, pp. 9–11 Enrichment, p. 29 Reinforcement, p. 27 Directed Reading, p. 20 Lab Worksheet, pp. 5–6 **Reading Essentials,** Section 1 | Section Focus Transparencies  Virtual Labs CD-ROM  Interactive Chalkboard CD-ROM |

| Indiana Objectives | Student & Teacher Edition Activities | Reproducible Resources | Technology Resources |
|---|---|---|---|
| **Section 2** • **Computers** | | | |
| **7.1.5, 7.1.7, 7.1.8, 7.1.9, 7.1.11, 7.2.7** | **MiniLAB:** Using Binary Numbers, p. 450<br>**Applying Science:** How much information can be stored?, p. 451<br>**Science Online,** p. 452<br>**MiniLAB:** Observing Memory, p. 453<br>**Integrate Career:** p. 454<br>**Integrate Environment:** p. 456<br>**Science Online,** p. 456<br>**Visualizing a Hard Disk,** p. 457<br>**Science Online,** p. 458<br>**Lab:** Does your computer have a virus?, pp. 460–461<br>**Science and Society:** E-Lectrifying E-books, p. 462 | **Chapter *Fast File* Resources**<br>Transparency Activity, p. 43<br>MiniLAB, p. 4<br>Transparency Activity, pp. 45–46<br>Lab Activity, pp. 13–16<br>Enrichment, p. 30<br>Reinforcement, p. 28<br>Directed Reading, pp. 21, 22<br>Lab Worksheet, pp. 7–8<br>**Reading Essentials,** Section 2 | Video Lab<br><br>Exam*View*® Pro Testmaker CD-ROM<br><br>IN Test Prep and Practice Exam*View*® Pro<br><br>StudentWorks+™ Audio<br><br>TeacherWorks™ |
| **End of Chapter Assessment** | | | |
| | **Chapter Review,** pp. 464–465<br>**Indiana Standards Review,** pp. 466–467 | **Mastering the Grade 7 Indiana Science Standards** | in7.msscience.com |
| **Unit 5** • **Galaxies, Stars, and Earth** | | | |
| **Chapter 16** • **Stars and Galaxies** | | | |
| **Section 1** • **Stars** | | | |
| **7.1.5** | **MiniLAB:** Observing Star Patterns, p. 473<br>**Applying Science:** Are distance and brightness related?, p. 474 | **Chapter *Fast File* Resources**<br>Transparency Activity, p. 48<br>MiniLAB, p. 3<br>Enrichment, p. 31<br>Reinforcement, p. 27<br>Directed Reading, p. 20<br>Lab Activity, pp. 9–12, 13–15<br>Transparency Activity, pp. 53–54<br>**Reading Essentials,** Section 1 | Section Focus Transparencies<br><br>Virtual Labs CD-ROM<br><br>Interactive Chalkboard CD-ROM |
| **Section 2** • **The Sun** | | | |
| **7.3.2, 7.3.11** | **Science Online,** p. 479<br>**Lab:** Sunspots, p. 481 | **Chapter *Fast File* Resources**<br>Transparency Activity, p. 49<br>Lab Worksheets, pp. 5–6<br>Enrichment, p. 32<br>Reinforcement, p. 28<br>Directed Reading, p. 20<br>**Reading Essentials,** Section 2 | Video Lab<br><br>Exam*View*® Pro Testmaker CD-ROM |
| **Section 3** • **Evolution of Stars** | | | |
| **7.1.5, 7.3.11** | **Science Online,** p. 484<br>**Integrate Chemistry,** p. 485<br>**Integrate History,** p. 486 | **Chapter *Fast File* Resources**<br>Transparency Activity, p. 50<br>Enrichment, p. 33<br>Reinforcement, p. 29<br>Directed Reading, p. 21<br>**Reading Essentials,** Section 3 | IN Test Prep and Practice Exam*View*® Pro |

| Indiana Objectives | Student & Teacher Edition Activities | Reproducible Resources | Technology Resources |
|---|---|---|---|
| **Section 4 • Galaxies and the Universe** | | | |
| 7.1.5, 7.3.1 | **MiniLAB:** Measuring Distance in Space, p. 490<br>**Visualizing the Big Bang Theory,** p. 492<br>**Lab:** Measuring Parallax, p. 494<br>**Science Stats:** Stars and Galaxies, p. 496 | **Chapter *Fast File* Resources**<br>Transparency Activity, p. 51<br>Lab Worksheets, pp. 7–8<br>MiniLAB, p. 4<br>Enrichment, p. 34<br>Reinforcement, p. 30<br>Directed Reading, pp. 21, 22<br>**Reading Essentials,** Section 4 | StudentWorks+™ Audio<br><br>TeacherWorks™ |
| **End of Chapter Assessment** | | | |
| | **Chapter Review,** pp. 498–499<br>**Indiana Standards Review,** pp. 500–501 | **Mastering the Grade 7 Indiana Science Standards** | in7.msscience.com |
| **Chapter 17 • Minerals** | | | |
| **Section 1 • Minerals** | | | |
| 7.5.3 | **MiniLAB:** Inferring Salt's Crystal System, p. 505<br>**Visualizing Crystal Systems,** p. 506<br>**Integrate Physics,** p. 507<br>**Lab:** Crystal Formation, p. 509 | **Chapter *Fast File* Resources**<br>Transparency Activity, p. 40<br>MiniLAB, p. 3<br>Enrichment, p. 26<br>Reinforcement, p. 23<br>Directed Reading, p. 16<br>Lab Worksheets, pp. 5–6<br>Lab Activity, pp. 9–10<br>**Reading Essentials,** Section 1 | Section Focus Transparencies<br><br>Virtual Labs CD-ROM<br><br>Interactive Chalkboard CD-ROM |
| **Section 2 • Mineral Identification** | | | |
| This section builds a foundation for Standards 7.3.8 and 7.3.9. | **Applying Science:** How can you identify minerals?, p. 512<br>**MiniLAB:** Observing Mineral Properties, p. 514 | **Chapter *Fast File* Resources**<br>Transparency Activity, p. 41<br>MiniLAB, p. 4<br>Enrichment, p. 27<br>Reinforcement, p. 24<br>Directed Reading, p. 17<br>Transparency Activity, pp. 43–44<br>**Reading Essentials,** Section 2 | Video Lab<br><br>ExamView® Pro Testmaker CD-ROM<br><br>IN Test Prep and Practice ExamView® Pro |
| **Section 3 • Uses of Minerals** | | | |
| 7.1.5, 7.1.6 | **Science Online,** p. 518<br>**Integrate Social Studies,** p. 519<br>**Lab:** Mineral Identification, p. 522<br>**Science and History:** Dr. Dorothy Crowfoot Hodgkin, p. 524 | **Chapter *Fast File* Resources**<br>Transparency Activity, p. 42<br>Enrichment, p. 28<br>Reinforcement, p. 25<br>Directed Reading, p. 17, 18<br>Lab Worksheets, pp. 7–8<br>Lab Activity, p. 11–12<br>**Reading Essentials,** Section 3 | StudentWorks+™ Audio<br><br>TeacherWorks™ |
| **End of Chapter Assessment** | | | |
| | **Chapter Review,** pp. 526–527<br>**Indiana Standards Review,** pp. 528–529 | **Mastering the Grade 7 Indiana Science Standards** | in7.msscience.com |

| Indiana Objectives | Student & Teacher Edition Activities | Reproducible Resources | Technology Resources |
|---|---|---|---|
| **Chapter 18  •  Rocks** | | | |
| **Section 1  •  The Rock Cycle** | | | |
| 7.1.5 | **MiniLAB:** Modeling Rock, p. 533<br>**Visualizing the Rock Cycle,** p. 534 | **Chapter *Fast File* Resources**<br>Transparency Activity, p. 42<br>MiniLAB, p. 3<br>Enrichment, p. 27<br>Reinforcement, p. 23<br>Directed Reading, p. 16<br>Lab Activity, pp. 9–10<br>Transparency Activity, pp. 47–48<br>**Reading Essentials,** Section 1 | Section Focus Transparencies<br><br>Virtual Labs CD-ROM |
| **Section 2  •  Igneous Rocks** | | | |
| This section builds a foundation for Standards 7.3.8 and 7.3.9. | **Science Online,** p. 538<br>**Integrate Chemistry,** p. 539<br>**Lab:** Igneous Rock Clues, p. 540 | **Chapter *Fast File* Resources**<br>Transparency Activity, p. 43<br>Lab Worksheets, pp. 5–6<br>Enrichment, p. 28<br>Reinforcement, p. 24<br>Directed Reading, p. 16<br>**Reading Essentials,** Section 2 | Interactive Chalkboard CD-ROM<br><br>Video Lab |
| **Section 3  •  Metamorphic Rocks** | | | |
| 7.3.9 | **Science Online,** p. 542 | **Chapter *Fast File* Resources**<br>Transparency Activity, p. 44<br>Enrichment, p. 29<br>Reinforcement, p. 25<br>Directed Reading, p. 17<br>Lab Activity, pp. 11–12<br>**Reading Essentials,** Section 3 | Exam*View*® Pro Testmaker CD-ROM<br><br>IN Test Prep and Practice Exam*View*® Pro |
| **Section 4  •  Sedimentary Rocks** | | | |
| 7.3.8, 7.3.9 | **MiniLAB:** Classifying Sediments, p. 546<br>**Integrate Career,** p. 548<br>**Applying Math:** Coal Formation, p. 550<br>**Lab:** Sedimentary Rocks, pp. 552–553<br>**Science and Society:** Australia's Controversial Rock Star, p. 554 | **Chapter Fast File Resources**<br>Transparency Activity, p. 45<br>MiniLAB, p. 4<br>Enrichment, p. 30<br>Reinforcement, p. 26<br>Directed Reading, pp. 17, 18<br>Lab Worksheets, pp. 7–8<br>**Reading Essentials,** Section 4 | StudentWorks+™ Audio<br><br>TeacherWorks™ |
| **End of Chapter Assessment** | | | |
| | **Chapter Review,** pp. 556–557<br>**Indiana Standards Review,** pp. 558–559 | **Mastering the Grade 7 Indiana Science Standards** | in7.msscience.com |

| Indiana Objectives | Student & Teacher Edition Activities | Reproducible Resources | Technology Resources |
|---|---|---|---|
| **Unit 6 ● Processes that Shape Earth** | | | |
| **Chapter 19 ● Forces Shaping Earth** | | | |
| **Section 1 ● Earth's Moving Plates** | | | |
| 7.1.1, 7.1.4, 7.3.4, 7.3.7, 7.3.18 | **Integrate Chemistry,** p. 566<br>**Science Online,** p. 569<br>**Visualizing Rift Valleys,** p. 570<br>**MiniLAB:** Modeling Tension and Compression, p. 571<br>**Lab:** Earth's Moving Plates, p. 574 | **Chapter** *Fast File* **Resources**<br>Transparency Activity, p. 44<br>MiniLAB, p. 3<br>Enrichment, p. 31<br>Reinforcement, p. 29<br>Directed Reading, p. 22<br>Lab Worksheet, pp. 5–6<br>Lab Activity, pp. 9–13<br>Transparency Activity, pp. 47–48<br>**Reading Essentials,** Section 1 | Section Focus Transparencies<br><br>Virtual Labs CD-ROM<br><br>Interactive Chalkboard CD-ROM<br><br>Video Lab |
| **Section 2 ● Uplift of Earth's Crust** | | | |
| 7.2.7, 7.3.4, 7.3.7 | **MiniLAB:** Modeling Mountains, p. 577<br>**Science Online,** p. 578<br>**Integrate Language Arts,** p. 580<br>**Applying Science:** How can glaciers cause land to rise?, p. 580<br>**Lab:** Isostasy, p. 582<br>**Science Stats:** Mountains, p. 584 | **Chapter** *Fast File* **Resources**<br>Transparency Activity, p. 45<br>MiniLAB, p. 4<br>Enrichment, p. 32<br>Reinforcement, p. 30<br>Directed Reading, pp. 23, 24<br>Lab Worksheet, pp. 7–8<br>Lab Activity, pp. 15–18<br>**Reading Essentials,** Section 2 | ExamView® Pro Testmaker CD-ROM<br><br>IN Test Prep and Practice ExamView® Pro<br><br>StudentWorks+™ Audio<br><br>TeacherWorks™<br><br>in7.msscience.com |
| **End of Chapter Assessment** | | | |
| | **Chapter Review,** pp. 586–587<br>**Indiana Standards Review,** pp. 588–589 | **Mastering the Grade 7 Indiana Science Standards** | |
| **Chapter 20 ● Earthquakes and Volcanoes** | | | |
| **Section 1 ● Earthquakes** | | | |
| 7.3.7, 7.3.18 | **MiniLAB:** Observing Deformation, p. 593<br>**Science Online,** p. 597<br>**Visualizing Tsunamis,** p. 598 | **Chapter** *Fast File* **Resources**<br>Transparency Activity, p. 42<br>MiniLAB, p. 3<br>Enrichment, p. 28<br>Reinforcement, p. 25<br>Directed Reading, p. 18<br>Transparency Activity, pp. 45–46<br>Lab Activity, pp. 9–10<br>**Reading Essentials,** Section 1 | Section Focus Transparencies<br><br>Virtual Labs CD-ROM |
| **Section 2 ● Volcanoes** | | | |
| 7.3.7 | **MiniLAB:** Modeling an Eruption, p. 602<br>**Science Online,** p. 603<br>**Lab:** Disruptive Eruptions, p. 607 | **Chapter** *Fast File* **Resources**<br>Transparency Activity, p. 43<br>MiniLAB, p. 4<br>Enrichment, p. 29<br>Reinforcement, p. 26<br>Directed Reading, p. 19<br>Lab Worksheets, pp. 5–6<br>Lab Activity, pp. 11–14<br>**Reading Essentials,** Section 2 | Interactive Chalkboard CD-ROM<br><br>Video Lab |

| Indiana Objectives | Student & Teacher Edition Activities | Reproducible Resources | Technology Resources |
|---|---|---|---|
| **Section 3 ● Earthquakes, Volcanoes, and Plate Tectonics** | | | |
| 7.3.4, 7.3.7, 7.3.18 | **Integrate Chemistry,** p. 610<br>**Integrate Language Arts,** p. 611<br>**Applying Math:** P-wave Travel Time, p. 612<br>**Lab:** Seismic Waves, pp. 614–615<br>**Science and History:** Quake, p. 616 | **Chapter *Fast File* Resources**<br>Transparency Activity, p. 44<br>Enrichment, p. 30<br>Reinforcement, p. 27<br>Directed Reading, pp. 19–20<br>Lab Worksheet, pp. 7–8<br>**Reading Essentials,** Section 3 | ExamView® Pro Testmaker CD-ROM<br><br>IN Test Prep and Practice ExamView® Pro<br><br>StudentWorks+™ Audio<br><br>TeacherWorks™<br><br>in7.msscience.com |
| **End of Chapter Assessment** | | | |
| | **Chapter Review,** pp. 618–619<br>**Indiana Standards Review,** pp. 620–621 | **Mastering the Grade 7 Indiana Science Standards** | |
| **Chapter 21 ● Climate** | | | |
| **Section 1 ● What is climate?** | | | |
| 7.3.5, 7.5.1 | **MiniLAB:** Observing Solar Radiation, p. 625<br>**Integrate Physics,** p. 626<br>**Applying Science:** How do cities influence temperature?, p. 626 | **Chapter *Fast File* Resources**<br>Transparency Activity, p. 44<br>MiniLAB, p. 3<br>Enrichment, p. 30<br>Reinforcement, p. 27<br>Directed Reading, p. 20<br>Lab Activity, pp. 9–11<br>**Reading Essentials,** Section 1 | Section Focus Transparencies<br><br>Virtual Labs CD-ROM<br><br>Interactive Chalkboard CD-ROM<br><br>Video Lab<br><br>ExamView® Pro Testmaker CD-ROM<br><br>IN Test Prep and Practice ExamView® Pro<br><br>StudentWorks+™ Audio |
| **Section 2 ● Climate Types** | | | |
| 7.1.5 | | **Chapter *Fast File* Resources**<br>Transparency Activity, p. 45<br>Enrichment, p. 31<br>Reinforcement, p. 28<br>Directed Reading, p. 20<br>Transparency Activity, pp. 47–48<br>**Reading Essentials,** Section 2 | |
| **Section 3 ● Climatic Changes** | | | |
| 7.1.4, 7.2.6, 7.2.7, 7.3.3, 7.3.5, 7.3.6 | **MiniLAB:** Modeling El Niño, p. 633<br>**Visualizing El Niño and La Niña,** p. 634<br>**Science Online,** p. 639<br>**Integrate Career,** p. 641<br>**Science Online,** p. 641<br>**Lab:** The Greenhouse Effect, p. 643<br>**Lab:** Microclimates, p. 644<br>**Science and History:** The Year There Was No Summer, p. 646 | **Chapter *Fast File* Resources**<br>Transparency Activity, p. 46<br>MiniLAB, p. 4<br>Enrichment, p. 32<br>Reinforcement, p. 29<br>Lab Worksheets, pp. 5–6, 7–8<br>Directed Reading, pp. 21, 22<br>**Reading Essentials,** Section 3 | |

| Indiana Objectives | Student & Teacher Edition Activities | Reproducible Resources | Technology Resources |
|---|---|---|---|
| **End of Chapter Assessment** | | | |
| | **Chapter Review,** pp. 648–649 **Indiana Standards Review,** pp. 650–651 | **Mastering the Grade 7 Indiana Science Standards** | TeacherWorks™<br><br>in7.msscience.com |
| **Chapter 22 ● Clues to Earth's Past** | | | |
| **Section 1 ● Fossils** | | | |
| 7.3.8, 7.3.10 | **MiniLAB:** Predicting Fossil Preservation, p. 655 **Integrate Social Studies,** p. 657 **Integrate Life Science,** p. 660 | **Chapter *Fast File* Resources** Transparency Activity, p. 44 MiniLAB, p. 3 Enrichment, p. 30 Reinforcement, p. 27 Directed Reading, p. 20 Transparency Activity, pp. 47–48 Lab Activities, pp. 9–12 **Reading Essentials,** Section 1 | Section Focus Transparencies<br><br>Virtual Labs CD-ROM<br><br>Interactive Chalkboard CD-ROM |
| **Section 2 ● Relative Ages of Rocks** | | | |
| 7.3.10 | **Science Online,** p. 663 **Visualizing Unconformities,** p. 665 **Science Online,** p. 666 **Lab:** Relative Ages, p. 668 | **Chapter *Fast File* Resources** Transparency Activity, p. 45 Enrichment, p. 31 Reinforcement, p. 28 Directed Reading, p. 21 Lab Worksheets, pp. 5–6 Lab Activity, pp. 13–15 **Reading Essentials,** Section 2 | Video Lab<br><br>ExamView® Pro Testmaker CD-ROM |
| **Section 3 ● Absolute Ages of Rocks** | | | |
| 7.1.5 | **MiniLAB:** Modeling Carbon-14 Dating, p. 670 **Science Online,** p. 672 **Applying Science:** What did the Iceman die?, p. 672 **Lab:** Trace Fossils, p. 674 **Oops! Accidents in Science:** The World's Oldest Fish Story, p. 676 | **Chapter *Fast File* Resources** Transparency Activity, p. 46 MiniLAB, p. 4 Enrichment, p. 32 Reinforcement, p. 29 Directed Reading, pp. 21, 22 Lab Worksheets, pp. 7–8 **Reading Essentials,** Section 3 | IN Test Prep and Practice ExamView® Pro<br><br>StudentWorks+™ Audio<br><br>TeacherWorks™ |
| **End of Chapter Assessment** | | | |
| | **Chapter Review,** pp. 678–679 **Indiana Standards Review,** pp. 680–681 | **Mastering the Grade 7 Indiana Science Standards** | in7.msscience.com |

Glencoe Science

# Indiana Science

## Grade 7

NATIONAL GEOGRAPHIC

*in7.msscience.com*

Mc Graw Hill **Glencoe**

New York, New York   Columbus, Ohio   Chicago, Illinois   Peoria, Illinois   Woodland Hills, California

## Grade 7

Turkey Run State Park, located in western central Indiana, boasts sandstone features 300 to 600 million years old. The wheel bearings and the drive-train in these bikes cause friction resulting in a loss of efficiency, while the friction caused by the brakes helps stop the bike safely. The coronary artery supplies the heart muscle with oxygen-rich blood.

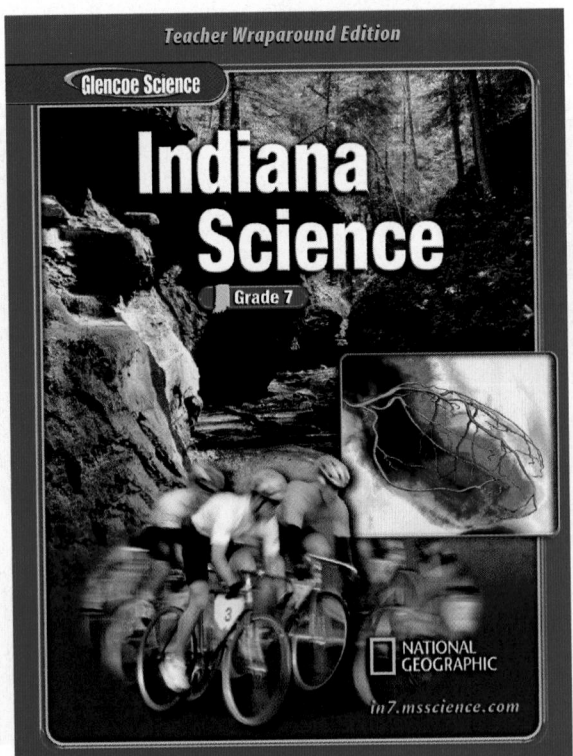

Teacher Wraparound Edition

Glencoe Science

# Indiana Science
### Grade 7

NATIONAL GEOGRAPHIC

in7.msscience.com

# Glencoe

The McGraw-Hill Companies

Send all inquiries to:
Glencoe/McGraw-Hill
8787 Orion Place
Columbus, OH 43240-4027

ISBN 0-07-861781-2 (Student Edition)
ISBN 0-07-861782-0 (Teacher Wraparound Edition)

Printed in the United States of America.

1 2 3 4 5 6 7 8 9 10  058/111  09 08 07 06 05 04

## Authors

**NATIONAL GEOGRAPHIC**
Education Division
Washington, D.C.

**Lucy Daniel, PhD**
Teacher/Consultant
Rutherford County Schools
Rutherfordton, NC

**Ralph M. Feather Jr., PhD**
Assistant Professor
Geoscience Department
Indiana University of Pennsylvania
Indiana, PA

**Edward Ortleb**
Science Consultant
St. Louis, MO

**Peter Rillero, PhD**
Professor of Science Education
Arizona State University West
Phoenix, AZ

**Susan Leach Snyder**
Retired Earth Science Teacher, Consultant
Jones Middle School
Upper Arlington, OH

**Dinah Zike**
Educational Consultant
Dinah-Might Activities, Inc.
San Antonio, TX

## Series Consultants

### CONTENT

**Alton J. Banks, PhD**
Director of the Faculty Center
for Teaching and Learning
North Carolina State University
Raleigh, NC

**Jack Cooper**
Ennis High School
Ennis, TX

**Sandra K. Enger, PhD**
Associate Director,
Associate Professor
UAH Institute for Science Education
Huntsville, AL

**David G. Haase, PhD**
North Carolina State University
Raleigh, NC

**Michael A. Hoggarth, PhD**
Department of Life and
Earth Sciences
Otterbein College
Westerville, OH

**Jerome A. Jackson, PhD**
Whitaker Eminent Scholar in Science
Program Director
Center for Science, Mathematics,
and Technology Education
Florida Gulf Coast University
Fort Meyers, FL

**William C. Keel, PhD**
Department of Physics
and Astronomy
University of Alabama
Tuscaloosa, AL

**Linda McGaw**
Science Program Coordinator
Advanced Placement Strategies, Inc.
Dallas, TX

**Madelaine Meek**
Physics Consultant Editor
Lebanon, OH

**Robert Nierste**
Science Department Head
Hendrick Middle School, Plano ISD
Plano, TX

**Connie Rizzo, MD, PhD**
Department of Science/Math
Marymount Manhattan College
New York, NY

**Dominic Salinas, PhD**
Middle School Science Supervisor
Caddo Parish Schools
Shreveport, LA

**Cheryl Wistrom, PhD**
St. Joseph's College
Rensselaer, IN

**Carl Zorn, PhD**
Staff Scientist
Jefferson Laboratory
Newport News, VA

## Teacher Advisory Board

The Teacher Advisory Board gave the editorial staff and design team feedback on the content and design of the Student Edition. They provided valuable input in the development of the 2005 editions of *Glencoe Science.*

**John Gonzales**
Challenger Middle School
Tucson, AZ

**Rachel Shively**
Aptakisic Jr. High School
Buffalo Grove, IL

**Roger Pratt**
Manistique High School
Manistique, MI

**Kirtina Hile**
Northmor Jr. High/High School
Galion, OH

**Marie Renner**
Diley Middle School
Pickerington, OH

**Nelson Farrier**
Hamlin Middle School
Springfield, OR

**Jeff Remington**
Palmyra Middle School
Palmyra, PA

**Erin Peters**
Williamsburg Middle School
Arlington, VA

**Rubidel Peoples**
Meacham Middle School
Fort Worth, TX

**Kristi Ramsey**
Navasota Jr. High School
Navasota, TX

## Student Advisory Board

The Student Advisory Board gave the editorial staff and design team feedback on the design of the Student Edition. We thank these students for their hard work and creative suggestions in making the 2005 editions of *Glencoe Science* student friendly.

**Jack Andrews**
Reynoldsburg Jr. High School
Reynoldsburg, OH

**Peter Arnold**
Hastings Middle School
Upper Arlington, OH

**Emily Barbe**
Perry Middle School
Worthington, OH

**Kirsty Bateman**
Hilliard Heritage Middle School
Hilliard, OH

**Andre Brown**
Spanish Emersion Academy
Columbus, OH

**Chris Dundon**
Heritage Middle School
Westerville, OH

**Ryan Manafee**
Monroe Middle School
Columbus, OH

**Addison Owen**
Davis Middle School
Dublin, OH

**Teriana Patrick**
Eastmoor Middle School
Columbus, OH

**Ashley Ruz**
Karrar Middle School
Dublin, OH

Aaron Haupt

The Glencoe middle school science Student Advisory Board taking a timeout at COSI, a science museum in Columbus, Ohio.

# Teacher Handbook

## Table of Contents

# Dynamic Instruction

The consistent instructional strategies in each chapter strengthen students' learning—from the beginning of each chapter where students see "Chapter Preview," to the end where they have a chance to test the knowledge they have acquired and prepare for the next lesson.

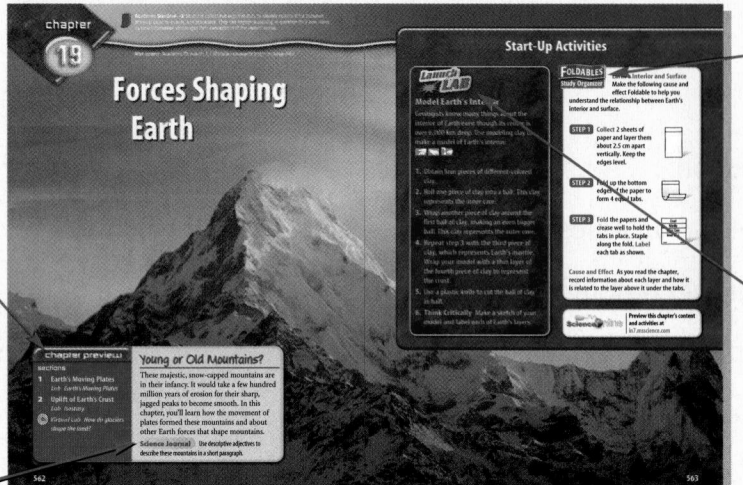

**Dinah Zike's Foldables™** let students create interactive study guides.

**Launch Lab** gives students an opportunity to explore new ideas at the beginning of the chapter.

**Chapter Preview** at the beginning of each chapter introduces the main concepts.

**Science Journal** promotes writing and critical-thinking skills.

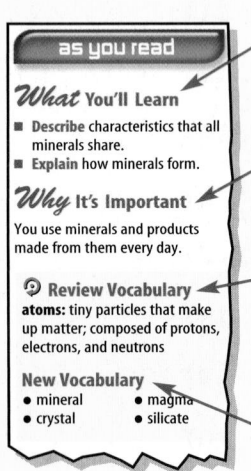

**What You'll Learn** at the beginning of each section introduces the main concepts.

**Why It's Important** provides an answer to "Why do we have to learn this?"

**Review Vocabulary** reviews a term that helps students better understand section content.

**New Vocabulary** highlights new terms students will learn in the section.

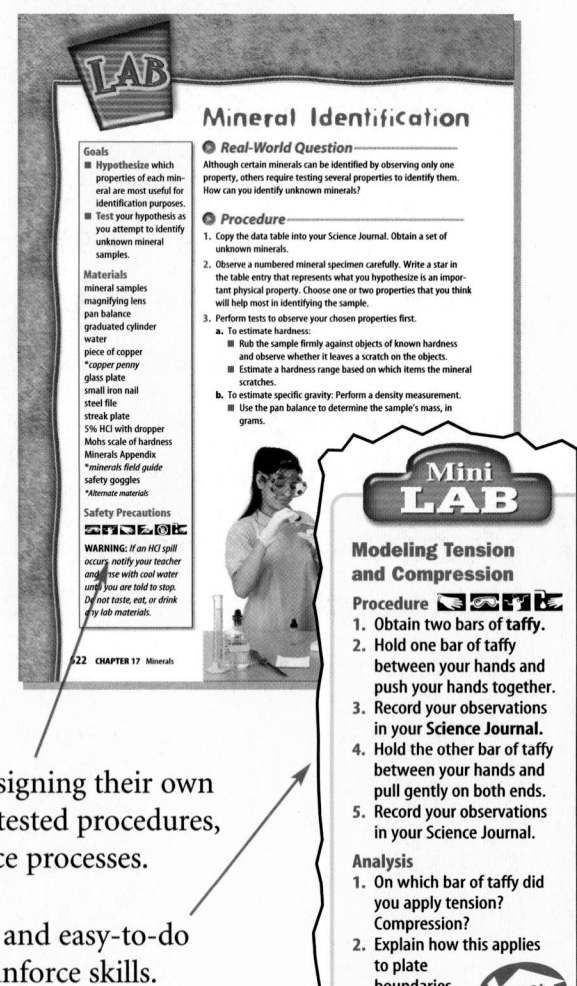

**Labs** Whether students are designing their own experiments or following well-tested procedures, they'll learn and practice science processes.

**MiniLABs** offer students quick and easy-to-do ways to clarify concepts and reinforce skills.

# Multi-Level Review and Assessment

Each chapter provides five pages of review and testing to help you evaluate students' knowledge and ability to apply science concepts.

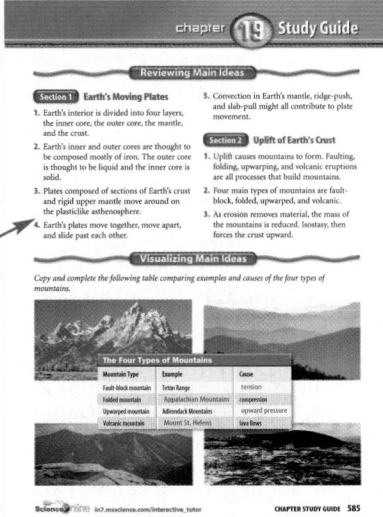

## Section Review
- Summary pinpoints important concepts in the section.
- Skill-based questions promote critical thinking skills.

## Study Guide
- Main idea summary of each section
- Concept mapping activity to help students visualize the main ideas

## Chapter Review
- Using Vocabulary
- Checking Concepts
- Thinking Critically
- Performance Activities
- Applying Math

## Indiana Standards Review
- Multiple Choice
- Critical Response Questions

# Time-Saving Teacher Resources

Glencoe Science provides an extensive array of support materials and resources designed to help you create and customize your science course quickly and easily.

## FAST FILE Chapter Resources

For each chapter, Chapter Resources contain key reproducible masters along with additional teaching strategies, teacher support, and answer keys.

### Reproducible Student Resources include:

- Worksheets for all MiniLABs and Labs
- *Directed Reading for Content Mastery* (in English and Spanish), *Reinforcement* and *Enrichment* worksheets for each chapter
- *Section Focus, Teaching,* and *Assessment Transparencies* masters
- Chapter Review and Chapter Test masters

### Teacher Support and Planning includes:

- Additional student preparation materials for each chapter
- Spanish Resources provide translations of all objectives, vocabulary, and main ideas
- Answer keys and teaching strategies

## Teacher Wraparound Edition

The *Teacher Wraparound Edition* is your key to the teaching resources available. In addition to teaching strategies and suggestions, the *Teacher Wraparound Edition* provides a guide for all print and software materials available for each lesson.

## Transparencies

- Section Focus Transparency
- Assessment Transparency
- Teaching Transparency
- Transparency masters and worksheets

## ExamView® Pro Testmaker CD-ROM

- Create, edit, and customize tests
- Create multiple versions of tests
- Translate tests from English to Spanish and vice versa
- Build tests aligned with state standards

## Video Labs

- Step-by-step lab procedures for selected *Student Edition* labs
- Lab safety skills
- Teacher support
- Troubleshooting advice

# Technology Support

## TeacherWorks™

This CD-ROM is your all-in-one teacher resource center. Personalize a lesson plan, access resources from the *Teacher Wraparound Edition,* connect to the Internet, or make a to-do list. These are only a few of the many features that can assist you in the planning and organizing of your lessons.

### Includes:

- A calendar feature
- Access to all program blackline masters
- Standards correlations and more

## StudentWorks™

This CD-ROM is a valuable resource for students to access content online and use online resources to continue learning chapter concepts.

### Includes:

- Complete *Student Edition* on CD-ROM
- Links to online activities and resources
- Access to all student worksheets

**PowerPoint® Presentations**

**This CD-ROM** brings Microsoft® PowerPoint® presentations right to your door. With the large number of graphics provided, students can use a visual approach to learning chapter content.

### Includes:

- A pre-made presentation for every chapter
- Image bank and interactive graphics
- Animations and audio clips
- All new section and chapter questions
- Standardized test practice
- Transparencies
- Pre-lab questions for all labs
- Foldables™ directions
- Links to in7.msscience.com

## Virtual Labs CD-ROM Program

The Virtual Labs CD-ROM contains a collection of labs that allow students to complete labs that are too expensive, take too long to complete, or might be too dangerous in a classroom laboratory.

in7.msscience.com

### For students:

- Prescreened Internet sites (Web links) that correlate to text chapters
- Interactive activities that review chapter concepts
- Internet Labs where students can share data with each other
- Access to *Student Edition* online
- Interactive self-check quizzes for each chapter section as well as the entire chapter

### For teachers:

- *WebQuest* activities
- Teacher Forum for teachers to share activities and ideas

 **Learning Network**
**mhln.com**

**mhln.com** is an online teaching and learning space for teachers, students, and parents.

- For students, **mhln.com** provides an interactive online textbook. This means a lighter student backpack.
- For teachers, **mhln.com** provides a customizable online learning space for posting assignments, web-based instruction, student resources, and a class calendar.
- For parents, **mhln.com** provides tools to help their child succeed in school. Parents have instant access to their child's progress and daily assignments.

# Help Your Students with Reading and Writing

Glencoe Science increases science literacy, improves reading comprehension, and deepens students' understanding of ideas and concepts. The reading strategies are active, constructive, and engaging.

## In the *Student Edition*

**Reading Checks** stimulate quick recall and keep students focused on the main idea.

**Caption Questions** offer a visual approach to learning. Students are asked to recall what they have read by interpreting the visual.

> **Figure 18** Three allotropes of carbon are depicted here.
> **Identify** *the geometric shapes that make up each allotrope.*

**Science Journals** provide opportunities to write responses to questions that require critical thinking, to conduct research and write about it, or to practice creative writing skills.

**Skill Words** such as *compare and contrast, describe, explain,* and *state* are included in the Self Check at the end of each section, in the goals of each Lab, and in the chapter reviews.

## Technology Support

**Vocabulary PuzzleMaker** allows you to create crossword puzzles, jumble puzzles, or word searches in minutes to review chapter vocabulary. The puzzles can be printed or played on the computer screen.

**Guided Reading Audio Program** (available on MP3-formatted CD-ROMs) provides a comprehensive overview in Spanish and English for auditory learners, students with reading difficulties, and English-language learners (ELL).

## In the *Teacher Edition*

**Project CRISS**™ (Creating Independence through Student-Owned Strategies) strategies are highlighted in the Unit Openers where an activity is supplied that relates to unit content. For more information about Project CRISS™, visit www.projectcriss.com.

**Use Science Words** features encourage students to look up biology terms. Use these as a pre-reading activity, or have students keep a vocabulary journal.

> **Use Science Words**
> **Word Usage** The distinction between distance and displacement can be confusing. Have students use each of these words correctly in a sentence. Possible response: When I go to school and then back home, my displacement is zero, even though the distance from home to school is 2 km.

**Additional Science Journal** writing activities promote writing and critical thinking skills and extend the *Student Edition* journaling activity.

**Active Reading Strategies** utilize a variety of learning styles, and encourage cooperative learning and intrapersonal reflection on chapter content.

## Additional Teacher Resources

**Reading Essentials** provides summaries of each section of the textbook, focusing on the most important scientific concepts.

**Reading and Writing in the Science Classroom** provides teachers with effective strategies for building students' skills in reading and writing about science.

*Reading and Writing*

## Making Concept Maps and Charts

**Bubble Map** Students brainstorm and organize words in clusters to describe concepts.

**Flow Chart** Students logically analyze and draw a sequence of events.

**Cause-and-Effect Chart** Students visually represent the causes and effects of an event or process.

**Supporting-Idea Chart** Students make a concept map to analyze relationships between a whole and its parts.

**Network-Tree Concept Map** Students show a hierarchy and use branching procedures.

**Events-Chain Concept Map** Students order steps or stages in a linear procedure.

**Cycle Concept Map** Students show how a series of events interact.

**Spider Concept Map** Students use for brainstorming and grouping nonrelated terms to a central idea.

## Using the Science Journal

**Double-Reference Journal** Students read and record ideas.

**Metacognition** Students analyze what and how they have learned.

**Learning Journal** Students create notes and reflect on the content.

**Problem-Solution Journal** Students analyze problems and suggest workable solutions.

**Speculation About Effects/Prediction Journal** Students examine events and speculate about their possible long-term effects.

**Synthesis Journal** Students reflect on a project, a paper, or a performance task and plan how to apply what they have learned to their own lives.

**Reflective Journal** Students identify what they learned in an activity and record responses.

**Quickwrites** Students use spontaneous writing to discover what they already know.

## Collaborative Learning Strategies

**Pair of Pairs** Partners respond to a question and compare their response to other pairs and to the class.

**Write-Draw-Discuss** Students write about and draw a picture of a concept, then share it with the class.

### Active Reading

**Learning Reading** Have students divide a sheet of paper in half. Have them record research notes, lecture notes, and vocabulary terms related to the laws of motion in the left column. Tell them to use the right column to respond, interpret, question, and analyze left-column entries. L2 **Intrapersonal**

**Four-Corner Discussion** The class works in four groups to debate a complex issue.

**Jigsaw** Students work in groups to become experts on a portion of text and share what they've learned with the class.

**Buddy Interviews** Students interview one another to find out what strategies they use to learn the text.

**Reciprocal Teaching** Students take turns reading a section of text, retelling it in their own words, then asking questions about it.

**News Summary** Students are given several minutes to summarize, retell, or analyze an activity for a "TV" audience.

**ReQuest** The teacher reads aloud an article or story. Student pairs then construct discussion questions and review the content.

Reading and Writing

# Foldables™

Foldables™ are easy-to-make, three-dimensional, interactive graphic organizers that students create out of simple sheets of paper. These unique hands-on tools for studying and reviewing were created exclusively for Glencoe by education specialist Dinah Zike.

## Research Behind Foldables™

According to research (Bransford, 1979; Corno, 1994), study strategies help students understand, organize, remember and apply new information presented in science textbooks. Some study strategies include concept mapping, highlighting, outlining, note taking, summarizing, and underlining (Peverly, Brobst, Graham & Shaw, 2003). Glencoe Science offers Dinah Zike's Foldables™ Study Organizers as an organizational tool and study guide for students.

## Build Prereading Skills

- Encourages students to prepare for what they will be learning
- Gives students an opportunity to recall what they already know about a subject

## Encourage Active Reading and Writing

- Practices basic reading and writing skills
- Develops skills in finding and reporting main ideas
- Organizes information
- Reviews key vocabulary terms

## Summarize Content for Review

- Creates a comprehensive, interactive snapshot of the chapter
- Provides preparation support for chapter, unit, and end-of-course exams, as well as standardized tests

**FOLDABLES™ Study Organizer**

**Minerals** Make the following Foldable to help you better understand minerals.

**STEP 1** Fold a vertical sheet of notebook paper from side to side.

**STEP 2** Cut along every third line of only the top layer to form tabs.

**STEP 3** Label each tab with a question.

**Ask Questions** Before you read the chapter, write questions you have about minerals on the front of the tabs. As you read the chapter, add more questions and write answers under the appropriate tabs.

## Dinah Zike's *Teaching Science with Foldables*™

- Comprehensive presentations of Foldables™ instructions
- More ideas on how to incorporate Foldables™ into your lessons
- Easy-to-read folding instruction pages in color

# Course Planning Guide

Glencoe Science programs provide a complete selection of core concepts that can be presented in a way that meets the needs of all your students. As the teacher, you are in the best position to design a science course that sets the pace at which the content is covered and determines what material should be given the most emphasis. To assist you in planning the course, the following Course Planning Guide is provided.

The chart shown below offers general suggestions for pacing your students through the book. Pacing for both standard class periods and block schedule class periods is given. The total number of days in each level of pacing is the typical 178-day school year and 89.5-day semester.

| Chapter | Single-Class (178 days) | Block (89.5 days) |
|---|---|---|
| 1 | 8 | 4 |
| 2 | 7 | 3.5 |
| 3 | 7 | 3.5 |
| 4 | 7 | 3.5 |
| 5 | 10 | 5 |
| 6 | 9 | 5 |
| 7 | 7 | 3.5 |
| 8 | 7 | 3.5 |
| 9 | 8 | 4 |
| 10 | 9 | 4.5 |
| 11 | 9 | 4.5 |
| 12 | 9 | 4.5 |
| 13 | 10 | 5 |
| 14 | 10 | 5 |
| 15 | 8 | 4 |
| 16 | 9 | 4.5 |
| 17 | 6 | 3 |
| 18 | 9 | 4.5 |
| 19 | 8 | 4 |
| 20 | 8 | 4 |
| 21 | 6 | 3 |
| 22 | 7 | 3.5 |

# Assessment

Glencoe Science offers the Glencoe Assessment Advantage, a system designed to give you all the tools you need to prepare your students for success in any testing situation.

## In the *Student Edition*

**Section Review** and **Applying Math** questions appear in every chapter.

**Chapter Review** questions help you evaluate students' knowledge and ability to apply science concepts.

**Standardized Test Practice** questions at the end of each chapter provide students with additional opportunities to practice their test-taking skills.

## In the *Teacher Wraparound Edition*

Assessments located throughout the *Teacher Wraparound Edition* provide methods for assessing students' comprehension with Performance, Process, and Content exercises.

## Teacher Classroom Resources

**Performance Assessment in the Science Classroom**
- Guidelines for assessing the performance of a task
- Reproducible activities for evaluating students
- Sample rubrics and checklists

***Fast File* Chapter Resources** provides six pages of assessment for every chapter including *Testing Concepts*, *Applying Concepts*, and *Writing Skills*.

## Technology Support

**MindJogger Videoquizzes** are interactive video quizzes set in game show format. Each is designed for the full range of student learning styles.

**Exam*View*® Pro Testmaker CD-ROM** for Windows® and Macintosh® provides an easy way to create, edit, and customize your tests. Select your own test items by objective from two different levels of difficulty, or write and edit your own. Translate tests from English to Spanish and vice versa.

## Rubrics

The following rubric is a sample scoring device for critical response questions.

**Critical Response**

| Points | Description |
|--------|-------------|
| 4 | The student demonstrates a thorough understanding of the science of the task. The response may contain minor flaws that do not detract from the demonstration of a thorough understanding. |
| 3 | The student demonstrates an understanding of the science of the task. The response is essentially correct and demonstrates an essential but less than thorough understanding of the science. |
| 2 | The student demonstrates only a partial understanding of the science of the task. Although the student may have used the correct approach to a solution or may have provided a correct solution, the work lacks an essential understanding of the underlying science concepts. |
| 1 | The student demonstrates a very limited understanding of the science of the task. The response is incomplete and exhibits many flaws. |
| 0 | The student provides a completely incorrect solution or no response at all. |

Assessment

# Educational Partnerships

### NATIONAL GEOGRAPHIC

Some topics in the chapter either require or benefit from a larger, more detailed visual explanation. The National Geographic Society has created *Visualizing* features that call out an important concept from the chapter and illustrate it in a way that will inform, excite, and motivate your students.

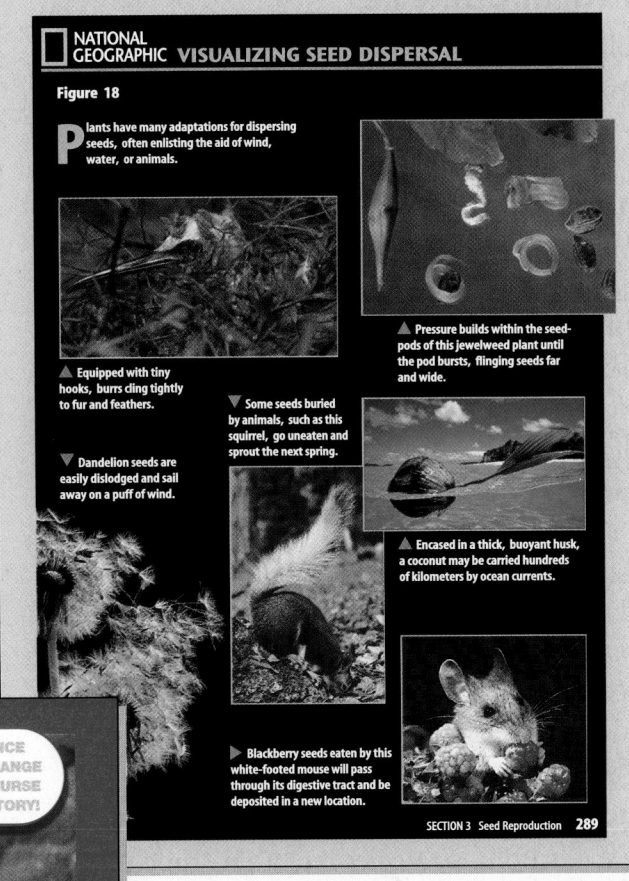

NATIONAL GEOGRAPHIC **VISUALIZING SEED DISPERSAL**

**Figure 18**

Plants have many adaptations for dispersing seeds, often enlisting the aid of wind, water, or animals.

▲ Equipped with tiny hooks, burrs cling tightly to fur and feathers.

▲ Pressure builds within the seed-pods of this jewelweed plant until the pod bursts, flinging seeds far and wide.

▼ Dandelion seeds are easily dislodged and sail away on a puff of wind.

▼ Some seeds buried by animals, such as this squirrel, go uneaten and sprout the next spring.

▲ Encased in a thick, buoyant husk, a coconut may be carried hundreds of kilometers by ocean currents.

▶ Blackberry seeds eaten by this white-footed mouse will pass through its digestive tract and be deposited in a new location.

SECTION 3  Seed Reproduction  **289**

**TIME** SCIENCE AND HISTORY

SCIENCE CAN CHANGE THE COURSE OF HISTORY!

Overcoming the Odds

Guts and determination helped one pioneering doctor to save the lives of thousands

### Fixing the Problem

Kountz discovered the root of the problem—why and how a patient's body rejected the transplanted kidney. He discovered that the patient's cells attacked and destroyed the small blood vessels of the transplanted kidney. So the new kidney would die from lack of blood-supplied oxygen. From this, doctors knew when to give patients the right kinds of drugs, so that their bodies could overcome the rejection process.

Overcoming the odds is a challenge that many people face. Dr. Samuel Lee Kountz, Jr. had the odds stacked against him. Thanks to his determination he beat them.

Dr. Kountz was interested in kidney transplants, a process that was still brand new in the 1950s. For many patients, a kidney transplant added months or a year to one's life. But then a patient's body would reject the kidney, and the patient would die. Dr. Kountz was determined to see that kidney transplants saved lives and kept patients healthy for years.

A donated organ is on its way to save a life.

In 1959, Kountz performed the first successful kidney transplant. He went on to develop a procedure to keep body organs healthy for up to 60 hours after being taken from a donor. He also set up a system of organ donor cards through the National Kidney Foundation. And in his career, Dr. Kountz transplanted more than 1,000 kidneys himself—and paved the way for thousands more.

**Research** What kinds of medical breakthroughs has the last century brought? Locate an article that explains either a recent advance in medicine or the work that doctors and medical researchers are doing. Share your findings with your class.

Science Online

## TIME

TIME magazine brings science topics and history together to further explain the chapter's main ideas and show how science relates to real life.

# Differentiated Instruction

## Teaching Strategies

Following each suggested assessment and activity, ability levels are supplied to accommodate all students.

- **LS** Multiple Learning Styles logos are used throughout the text to indicate strategies that address different learning styles.
- **L1** Level 1 activities should be appropriate for students with learning difficulties.
- **L2** Level 2 activities should be within the ability range of all students.
- **L3** Level 3 activities are designed for above-average students.
- **ELL** English-Language Learners activities should be within the ability range of English-Language Learners or students who speak English as a second language (ESL).
- **COOP LEARN** Cooperative Learning activities are designed for small group work.
- **PBL** Problem-Based Learning activities apply real-world situations to learning.
- **P** Portfolio strategies represent student products that can be placed into a best-work portfolio.

## Identifying Misconceptions

These short, diagnostic, and perscriptive lessons target common science misconceptions.

## Multiple Learning Styles

Look for these italicized designations under various activities to help you target your lessons to each student's preferred learning style.

- **Kinesthetic** learners learn through touch, movement, and manipulating objects.
- **Visual-Spatial** learners think in terms of images, illustrations, and models.
- **Interpersonal** learners understand and work well with other people.
- **Intrapersonal** learners can analyze their own strengths and weaknesses and may prefer to work on their own.
- **Linguistic** learners write clearly and easily understand the written word.
- **Logical-Mathematical** learners understand numbers easily and have highly-developed reasoning skills.

## Daily Interventions

Found at the end of each chapter section, this feature is designed to intercept students who are struggling and prescribe a system to help them get back on track. *Reteach* provides reinforcement of the section's concepts through visual activities.

**Necessary Metals** Students may think it strange that metals are needed by the body. Explain that the metals calcium, potassium, and sodium, for example, help transmit electrical signals within the nervous system.

---

**DAILY INTERVENTION**

**Check for Understanding**
**Kinesthetic** Have a student light a match and allow it to burn. Also, place an ice cube in a glass container and allow it to melt. Have students explain what type of changes took place with each item and describe the final properties of each.

## Differentiated Instruction

These activities present various teaching strategies designed to help you meet the special needs of students with learning disabilities, physical challenges, visual impairment, and hearing impairment. Challenge activities provide opportunities for students who excel to engage in activities and research projects that extend the chapter's concepts. English-language learners in the classroom will also find exercises that bridge the gap between language barriers and the chapter content.

### Differentiated Instruction

**English-Language Learners** Have students make flashcards with the name of a gland on one side and the hormone it produces on the other. Student pairs can quiz each other using the flashcards.

## Cultural Diversity

These readings provide insights into the unique ways in which people of different ethnicities and cultural heritage have approached science. The intent of these features is to build awareness and appreciation for the global community in which we live.

### Cultural Diversity

**Tsunami!** Tsunamis occur in many areas around the world and have been reported since ancient times. One of the earliest record tsunamis struck Syria around 2,000 B.C. Thera, one of the Cyclades Islands in the Mediterranean, may be the remnant of a volcano that erupted—causing tsunamis that ended the Minoan civilization on Crete. Tsunami is a Japanese word for "harbor wave." Many have struck the Japanese shore. Because Japan is an island nation, the threat of tsunamis is a national safety concer. Today, by using expected tsunami characteristics, the Japan Meteorological Agency can forecast tsunami heights for the Japanese coastline. This provides residents with the knowledge necessary to move a safe distance away from the shore.

## Inquiry-Based Science

The call for more inquiry-based science by the *National Science Education Standards* has been met by Glencoe Science.

Glencoe Science recognizes the importance of conducting inquiry-based science activities in the classroom. The process of doing inquiry models actual science practice, encouraging problem-solving strategies and developing critical thinking skills. Inquiry gets students actively involved in the learning process by allowing them to determine materials, procedures, or the topics and questions they want to investigate.

Inquiry can range from a very structured activity for those students who need more guidance to a more open-ended approach where students lead the investigations. Glencoe Science recognizes that the inquiry activities suggested will not look the same in every classroom. We encourage teachers to modify the suggested activities in a manner that best supports your students.

Glencoe also provides teachers with Alternative Inquiry Labs, teaching strategies or suggestions for making existing labs more inquiry-based.

### Alternative Inquiry Lab

**Extend the Experience** To make this Lab an Inquiry Lab, have students examine the magnetic field around the motor, using a compass or iron fillings. Test the armature and rotor before final assembly, as it will be difficult to fit the compass inside the motor. Encourage students to make various adaptations to the motor. Ask them to figure out how to make the motor spin the other way, spin faster, and spin slower. How could the motor be turned into a generator? How could they make the motor consume less power? Finally, students might research how these issues are handled by industry or other questions they find interesting.

# Research-Based Learning Strategies

Glencoe Science incorporates the most current and applicable educational research on science learning and follows recommendations from the American Association for the Advancement of Science and the National Science Teachers Association. The following research-based strategies can be found throughout the text.

## Learning Strategies

The following research-based strategies can be found throughout the text:

- **Using Prior Knowledge** Glencoe Science encourages students to use their prior knowledge to learn information because this adds relevance to the material. Students are referred back to other parts of the text or to their own real-life experiences.

- **Practicing Important Tasks** By offering students an opportunity to practice important tasks using a variety of labs and activities in the *Student Edition, Teacher Wraparound Edition,* ancillaries and technology, Glencoe Science makes learning fun and relevant for students.

- **Using Visuals to Communicate, Organize, and Reinforce Learning** High-quality art and photos throughout the text communicate concepts more efficiently and reinforce learning, while allowing students to organize information.

- **Motivating Students to Achieve** Active strategies and real-world experiences motivate students to achieve. Throughout Glencoe's programs, students are encouraged to apply their knowledge in ways that will motivate them to learn.

- **Developing Decoding and Reading Comprehension Strategies** Throughout the text, students are supplied with caption questions, reading checks, and other strategies to aid in comprehension.

- **Using Study Strategies** Through the use of highlighting, outlining, note-taking, summarizing, and other such strategies, students can monitor their own progress and organize information more effectively, thereby increasing their scientific literacy. These strategies are found throughout the text and ancillaries.

The use of these strategies within Glencoe Science will help teachers to achieve the goals set forth by the *National Science Education Standards.*

## White Paper

The Glencoe Science White Paper outlines the educational strategies on which this program was based. This document provides specific examples from the *Student Edition, Teacher Wraparound Edition,* ancillary program, and technology resources, highlighting extensive use of educationally sound strategies that help students learn science.

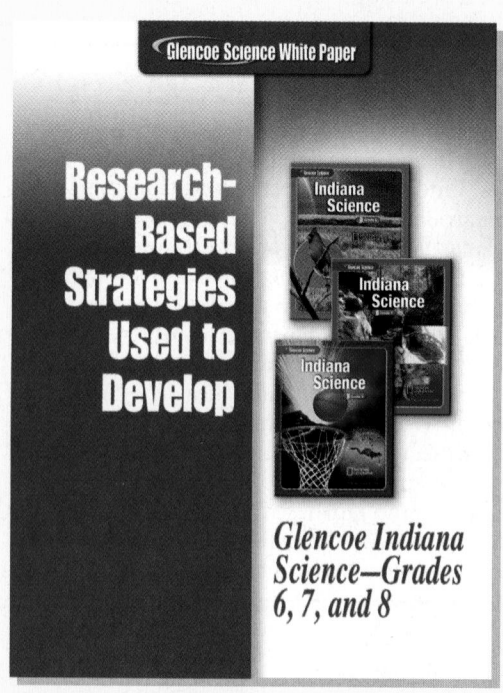

# Field Research and Testing

Feedback from students, teachers, curriculum supervisors, department chairpersons, parents, learning specialists, and science content experts was invaluable in the development of this program. The following pre-publication and post-publication research was conducted.

## Prior to Publication

- Detailed classroom teacher and curriculum supervisor **surveys** were conducted by independently contracted researchers.
- A **nationwide panel** of science teachers, curriculum supervisors, and department chairpersons provided countless hours of feedback and assistance throughout program development.
- A wide range of **educator and content reviewers** provided in-depth reviews of and suggestions for manuscripts and pre-publication versions of the program.
- **Face-to-face interviews** with science teachers provided insight into teachers' day-to-day challenges.

## After Publication

- Field tests were conducted in which students and teachers used a pre-publication manuscript in the classroom.
- Follow-up interviews, observations, and surveys of Glencoe Science users provide ongoing opportunities for program development and verification of program success.

### Field-Test Results

- Field-test research indicates that test scores increased among students using Glencoe Science programs.
- Nine out of ten students earned higher scores after using Glencoe programs.
- Scores improved among both male and female students.
- Scores improved among both minority and non-minority students.
- Overall, the gap between the average pre-test score and a perfect score closed by 33 percent. Stated differently, on average, **scores increased 77 percent after students used the Glencoe program.**

KS Studios

# National Education Standards

Correlation of *Indiana Science Grade 7* to the National Science Education Standards.

| Content Standard | Chapter and Section |
|---|---|
| **(UCP) Unifying Concepts and Processes** | |
| 1. Systems, order, and organization | 1-1, 1-2, 1-3, 1-4, 2-1, 2-2, 2-3, 3-1, 3-2, 3-3, 4-1, 4-2, 4-3, 5-1, 5-2, 5-3, 5-4, 6-1, 6-2, 6-3, 6-4, 7-1, 7-2, 7-3, 9-1, 9-2, 9-3, 10-1, 10-2, 10-3, 12-1, 12-2, 12-3, 13-1, 13-2, 13-3, 14-1, 14-2, 14-3, 15-1, 15-2, 15-3, 16-1, 16-2, 16-3, 17-1, 17-2, 17-3, 17-4, 18-1, 18-2, 19-1, 19-2, 19-3, 20-1, 20-2, 20-3, 21-1, 21-2, 21-3 |
| 2. Evidence, models, and explanation | 1-1, 1-2, 1-3, 1-4, 2-1, 2-2, 2-3, 3-1, 3-2, 3-3, 4-1, 4-2, 4-3, 5-1, 5-2, 5-3, 5-4, 6-1, 6-2, 6-3, 6-4, 7-1, 7-2, 7-3, 8-1, 8-2, 8-3, 9-1, 9-2, 9-3, 10-1, 10-2, 10-3, 11-1, 11-2, 11-3, 12-1, 12-2, 12-3, 13-1, 13-2, 13-3, 14-1, 14-2, 14-3, 15-1, 15-2, 15-3, 16-1, 16-2, 16-3, 17-1, 17-2, 17-3, 17-4, 18-1, 18-2, 19-1, 19-2, 19-3, 20-1, 20-2, 20-3, 21-1, 21-2, 21-3 |
| 3. Change, constancy, and measurement | 1-1, 1-2, 1-3, 1-4, 2-1, 2-2, 3-1, 3-2, 3-3, 4-1, 4-3, 5-1, 5-2, 5-3, 5-4, 6-1, 6-2, 6-3, 6-4, 7-1, 7-2, 7-3, 8-1, 8-2, 8-3, 9-1, 9-2, 9-3, 10-1, 10-2, 10-3, 11-1, 11-2, 11-3, 12-1, 12-2, 12-3, 13-1, 13-2, 13-3, 14-1, 14-2, 14-3, 15-1, 15-2, 15-3, 16-1, 16-2, 16-3, 17-1, 17-2, 17-3, 17-4, 18-1, 18-2, 19-1, 19-2, 19-3, 20-1, 20-2, 20-3, 21-1, 21-2, 21-3 |
| 4. Evolution and equilibrium | 4-3, 15-3 |
| 5. Form and function | 1-1, 1-2, 1-3, 1-4, 2-1, 2-2, 2-3, 3-1, 3-2, 3-3, 4-3, 5-1, 5-2, 5-3, 5-4, 6-1, 6-2, 6-3, 6-4, 7-1, 7-2, 7-3, 9-1, 9-2, 9-3, 10-1, 10-2, 10-3, 11-1, 11-2, 11-3, 12-1, 12-2, 12-3, 13-1, 13-2, 13-3, 14-1, 14-2, 14-3, 15-1, 15-2, 15-3, 16-1, 16-2, 16-3, 17-1, 17-2, 17-3, 17-4, 18-1, 18-2, 19-1, 19-2, 19-3, 20-1, 20-2, 20-3, 21-1, 21-2, 21-3 |
| **(A) Science as Inquiry** | |
| 1. Abilities necessary to do scientific inquiry | 1-1, 1-2, 1-3, 1-4, 2-1, 2-2, 2-3, 3-1, 3-2, 3-3, 4-1, 4-2, 4-3, 5-1, 5-2, 5-3, 5-4, 6-1, 6-2, 6-3, 6-4, 7-1, 7-2, 7-3, 8-1, 8-2, 8-3, 9-1, 9-2, 9-3, 10-1, 10-2, 10-3, 11-1, 11-2, 11-3, 12-1, 12-2, 12-3, 13-1, 13-2, 13-3, 14-1, 14-2, 14-3, 15-1, 15-2, 15-3, 16-1, 16-2, 16-3, 17-1, 17-2, 17-3, 17-4, 18-1, 18-2, 19-1, 19-2, 19-3, 20-1, 20-2, 20-3, 21-1, 21-2, 21-3 |
| 2. Understandings about scientific inquiry | 1-1, 1-2, 1-3, 1-4, 2-1, 2-2, 2-3, 3-1, 3-2, 4-1, 4-3, 5-1, 5-2, 5-3, 5-4, 6-1, 6-2, 6-3, 6-4, 7-1, 7-2, 7-3, 8-1, 8-2, 8-3, 9-1, 9-2, 9-3, 10-1, 10-2, 10-3, 11-1, 11-2, 11-3, 12-1, 12-2, 13-1, 13-2, 13-3, 14-1, 14-2, 14-3, 15-1, 15-2, 15-3, 16-1, 16-2, 16-3, 17-1, 17-2, 17-3, 17-4, 18-1, 18-2, 19-1, 19-2, 19-3, 20-1, 20-2, 20-3, 21-1, 21-2, 21-3 |
| **(B) Physical Science** | |
| 1. Properties and changes of properties in matter | 3-1, 9-1, 9-2, 9-3, 10-1, 10-2, 10-3, 11-1, 11-2, 11-3, 12-1, 12-2, 12-3, 13-1, 13-2, 14-1, 14-2, 21-3 |
| 2. Motions and forces | 10-2, 11-1, 11-2, 11-3, 12-2, 12-3, 13-1, 13-2, 14-3, 16-2, 19-1, 19-2, 19-3, 20-3 |
| 3. Transfer of energy | 7-3, 10-2, 12-2, 12-3, 13-1, 13-2, 13-3, 14-1, 14-2, 14-3, 19-1, 19-2, 19-3, 20-3 |
| **(C) Life Science** | |
| 1. Structure and function in living systems | 1-2, 1-3, 2-1, 2-2, 2-3, 3-1, 3-2, 3-3, 4-1, 4-2, 4-3, 5-1, 5-2, 5-3, 5-4, 6-1, 6-2, 6-3, 6-4, 7-1, 7-2, 7-3, 15-3 |
| 2. Reproduction and heredity | 1-2, 2-3, 4-1, 4-2, 4-3, 5-3, 15-3, 18-1, 18-2 |
| 3. Regulation and behavior | 1-2, 2-1, 3-2, 4-1, 4-2, 4-3, 5-1, 5-2, 5-3, 5-4, 6-1, 6-2, 6-3, 6-4, 15-3, 18-1, 18-2 |
| 4. Populations and ecosystems | 6-3, 6-4, 7-1, 7-2, 7-3 |
| 5. Diversity and adaptations of organisms | 1-4, 2-3, 4-2 |
| **(D) Earth and Space Science** | |
| 1. Structure of the Earth system | 16-1, 16-2, 17-1, 17-2, 17-3, 17-4, 18-1, 18-2, 19-1, 19-2, 19-3, 20-1, 20-2, 20-3 |
| 2. Earth's history | 16-1, 16-3, 17-1, 17-2, 17-3, 17-4, 18-1, 18-2, 19-2, 19-3, 20-3 |
| 3. Earth in the solar system | 15-2 |
| **(E) Science and Technology** | |
| 1. Abilities of technological design | 1-3, 6-3, 11-3, 12-3 |
| 2. Understandings about science and technology | 1-1, 1-3, 2-2, 2-3, 4-3, 6-4, 8-1, 8-2, 9-1, 9-2, 9-3, 12-1, 12-2, 13-3, 14-3, 15-2, 16-1, 16-3, 16-4, 17-3, 18-1, 21-2, 22-3 |

| Content Standard | Chapter and Section |
|---|---|
| **(F) Science in Personal and Social Perspectives** | |
| 1. Personal health | 5-2, 5-3, 6-1, 6-3 |
| 2. Populations, resources, and environments | 2-3, 13-3 |
| 3. Natural hazards | 8-1, 8-2, 8-3, 19-1, 20-3 |
| 4. Risks and benefits | 13-3 |
| 5. Science and technology in society | 12-3, 21-1, 21-3 |
| **(G) History and Nature of Science** | |
| 1. Science as a human endeavor | 9-1, 9-3, 16-3 |
| 2. Nature of science | 1-1, 3-3, 9-1, 9-3, 12-1, 13-1, 16-2, 16-3 |
| 3. History of science | 1-3, 1-4, 2-2, 2-3, 3-3, 5-4, 9-1, 9-2, 9-3, 12-1, 13-1, 15-3, 16-2, 16-3, 19-3, 21-3 |

## How Glencoe Science Aligns with the National Science Education Standards

The correlations at the left show the close alignment between Glencoe Science and the grade-appropriate standards. Glencoe Science allows students to discover concepts within each of the content standards and gives students opportunities to make connections among the science disciplines. Hands-on activities and inquiry-based lessons reinforce the science processes emphasized in the standards.

## How Glencoe Science Aligns with the NCTM Standards for Grades 6–8

Glencoe Science provides students with practice and applications of the mathematical concepts in the NCTM Standards. These opportunities, concentrated in the Applying Math activities, serve to reinforce mathematical skills in real-life situations.

### Correlation of *Indiana Science Grade 7* to NCTM Standards

| Math Standard | Page |
|---|---|
| 1. Number and Operations | 33, 44, 72, 91, 121, 157, 191, 219, 251, 283, 315, 324, 330, 334, 345, 359, 375, 396, 407, 416, 437, 446, 471, 499, 522, 529, 559, 584, 651 |
| 2. Algebra | 33, 44, 91, 191, 251, 283, 324, 330, 334, 345, 359, 375, 396, 407, 416, 437, 522, 529, 559, 584, 591, 651 |
| 3. Geometry | 471 |
| 4. Measurement | 33, 44, 61, 315, 446, 621 |
| 5. Data Analysis and Probability | 33, 91, 191, 219, 251, 315, 345, 396, 446, 499, 559, 591, 651 |
| 6. Problem Solving | 44, 91, 121, 396, 446, 499, 651 |
| 7. Reasoning and Proof | 29, 187, 341, 371 |
| 8. Communication | 396, 446 |
| 9. Connections | 33, 44, 61, 72, 91, 121, 157, 191, 219, 251, 315, 324, 330, 334, 345, 359, 375, 396, 407, 416, 437, 446, 471, 522, 529, 559, 584, 591, 621 |
| 10. Representation | 396, 446, 591, 651 |

National Education Standards

# Learning in the Laboratory

## In the *Student Edition*

Working in the lab is perhaps the most exciting part of science. Labs and MiniLABs give your students the hands-on opportunity to create, investigate, and explore science. Students will learn new material, while having fun.

**Traditional Labs** provide guided inquiry as students hypothesize, plan investigations, and collect and analyze data.

**Design Your Own Labs** challenge students to design their own experiments that will provide answers to lab problems.

**Model and Invent Labs** allow students to create a model or invent a product that can demonstrate scientific concepts.

**Use the Internet Labs** help students share and retrieve data from others around the country and world, by posting data they have collected on in7.msscience.com. These activities show students the possible range of data, importance of collecting large amounts of data, and data analysis.

**MiniLABs** and **Applying Science** activities are a quick way for students to practice specific process skills as they learn science concepts. Many of them can be classroom demonstrations or homework assignments.

## In the *Teacher Wraparound Edition*

**Quick Demos** allow students to visualize biology concepts.

**Inquiry Labs** in each chapter can be used to support inquiry-based science or as alternatives to traditional labs.

## Technology Support

**Virtual Labs CD-ROM** includes a collection of interactive activities involving major chapter themes that allow students to understand science concepts in a virtual setting. These labs provide a way to conduct experiments without classroom time, cost, and safety constraints.

**Video Labs** show students step-by-step lab procedures while emphasizing important lab safety skills. The lab videos also include teacher support, troubleshooting advice, and expected outcomes.

## Additional Resources

**Laboratory Activities** offer a variety of traditional laboratory experiences that reinforce the biology principles in the text. The *Teacher Wraparound Edition* provides full support.

**Probeware Labs** present activities for students to explore scientific concepts using a probeware data collection system. These hand-held systems provide a fast and simple way to collect, view, and analyze data in the classroom or during a field investigation. Integrating technology in the classroom is made simple with step-by-step instructions for setting up and using probeware.

**Science Inquiry Lab Manual** gives students the opportunity to become increasingly independent in stating hypotheses, designing and performing experiments, and collecting and analyzing data.

Learning in the Laboratory

# Safety in the Laboratory

All activities are designed to minimize dangers in the laboratory. Careful laboratory planning and management by both the instructor and the student are essential to a safe laboratory experience. **Local, state, and federal laboratory safety laws and regulations must be strictly followed.** The information provided here is one of the many resources to which you can refer for information about laboratory safety.

## Classroom and Laboratory Preparation

1. Label and store chemicals properly and securely. See p. 20T.
2. Store equipment properly and securely and other thing.
   a. Clean and dry all equipment before storing.
   b. Protect electronic equipment and microscopes from dust, humidity, and extreme temperatures.
   c. Number, catalog, and organize equipment.
3. Ensure adequate work space for each student.
4. Ensure adequate classroom and storeroom ventilation.
5. Explain and post safety and evacuation guidelines along with expectations of conduct.
6. Ensure that all safety equipment is functioning properly and is clearly visible.
7. Provide hot plates as a heat source whenever possible. If gas burners are used, know where the central gas supply shutoff valve is located.
8. Ensure that each workstation has a GFCI-protected electrical source.
9. Provide safety goggles consistent with ANSI Standard Z87.1 for each student, including students who wear corrective lenses.

## First Day of Class (with students)

1. Distribute and discuss safety rules, safety symbols, and first aid guidelines. Have students to review safety symbols and guidelines.
2. Review safe use of equipment and chemicals.
3. Review use and location of safety equipment.
4. Discuss safe disposal of materials and laboratory cleanup policy.
5. Discuss proper laboratory attitude and conduct.
6. Document students' understanding of the preceding points. Have students sign a safety contract and return it.

## Before Each MiniLAB or Lab

1. Perform each investigation yourself before assigning it.
2. Arrange the lab in such a way that equipment and supplies are clearly labeled and easily accessible.
3. Have available only equipment and supplies needed to complete the assigned investigation.
4. Review the procedure with students, emphasizing any caution statements or safety symbols that appear.
5. Be sure all students know the proper procedures to follow if an accident should occur.
6. Provide containers for disposing of chemicals, waste products, and biological specimens. Disposal methods should meet local guidelines.

## During the MiniLAB or Lab

1. Make sure the lab is clean and free of clutter.
2. Insist that students wear goggles and aprons.
3. Never allow a student to work alone in the lab.
4. Never allow students to use a cutting device with more than one edge.
5. Students should not point the open end of a heated test tube toward anyone.
6. Remove broken glassware or frayed cords from use. Also clean up any spills immediately. Dilute solutions with water before removing.
7. Be sure all glassware that is to be heated is of a heat-treated type that will not shatter.
8. Remind students that hot glassware looks cool.
9. Prohibit eating and drinking in the lab.

## After the MiniLAB or Lab

1. Be sure that the lab is clean.
2. Be certain that students have returned all equipment and disposed of broken glassware and chemicals properly.
3. Be sure that all hot plates and electrical connections are off.
4. Insist that each student wash his or her hands when lab work is completed.

# Chemical Storage and Disposal

## General Guidelines

Be sure to store all chemicals properly. The following are guidelines commonly used. Your school, city, county, or state may have additional requirements for handling chemicals. It is the responsibility of each teacher to become informed of the rules or guidelines in effect in his or her area.

1. Separate chemicals by reaction type. Strong acids should be stored together. Likewise, strong bases should be stored together and should be separated from acids. Oxidants should be stored away from easily oxidized materials, and so on.

2. Be sure all chemicals are stored in labeled containers indicating contents, concentration, source, date purchased (or prepared), any precautions for handling and storage, and expiration date.

3. Dispose of any outdated or waste chemicals properly according to accepted disposal procedures.

4. Do not store chemicals above eye level.

5. Wood shelving is preferable to metal. All shelving should be firmly attached to the wall and should have anti-roll edges.

6. Store only those chemicals that you plan to use.

7. Hazardous chemicals require special storage containers and conditions. Be sure to know which chemicals those are and the accepted practices for your area. Some substances must be stored outside the building.

8. When working with chemicals or preparing solutions, observe the same general safety precautions that you would expect from students. These include wearing an apron and goggles. Wear gloves and use the fume hood when necessary. Students will want to do as you do whether they admit it or not.

9. If you are a new teacher in a particular laboratory, it is your responsibility to survey the chemicals stored there to be sure they are stored properly. If not, they should be disposed of. Consult the rules and laws in your area concerning which chemicals can be kept in your classroom. For disposal, consult up-to-date disposal information from state and federal governments.

## Disposal of Chemicals

Local, state, and federal laws regulate the proper disposal of chemicals. These laws should be consulted before chemical disposal is attempted. Although many substances encountered in the science classroom can be flushed down the drain with plenty of water, it is not safe to assume that this is always true. Teachers who use chemicals should consult the following book from the National Research Council:

*Prudent Practices in the Laboratory.* Washington, DC: National Academy Press, 1995. This book is useful and was revised in 1995. Current laws in your area would, of course, supersede the information in this book.

## DISCLAIMER

Glencoe Publishing Company makes no claims to the completeness of this discussion of laboratory safety and chemical storage. The material presented is not all-inclusive, nor does it address all of the hazards associated with handling, storing, and disposing of chemicals, or with laboratory management.

Clement Mok/PictureQuest

# Preparation of Solutions

It is important to use safe laboratory techniques when handling all chemicals. Always check the MSDS (Material Safety Data Sheet) for each chemical before using it in the classroom. Many substances might appear harmless, but might be toxic, corrosive, or very reactive. Chemicals should never be ingested. Use proper techniques to smell any chemical, wear safety goggles and an apron in the laboratory, and observe the following precautions.

1. **Dilution of Acids and Bases** When diluting acids with water, always add the acids to the water. Never add water to acids. When sulfuric acid and sodium hydroxide are added to water, a large amount of thermal energy is released. Use extra care when handling these substances.

2. **Poisonous and Corrosive Liquids or Vapors** Use a fume hood if possible. Examples include hydrochloric acid, acetic acid, nitric acid, and ammonium hydroxide.

3. **Poisonous and Corrosive to Eyes, Lungs, and Skin** Examples include acids, bases, silver nitrate, iodine, and potassium permanganate.

**Bromthymol blue:** Add 0.5 g bromthymol blue powder to 500 mL distilled water to make a BTB stock solution. Dilute 40 mL BTB stock solution to 2 L with distilled water. Solution should be bright blue. If not, add one drop of NaOH at a time, swirling to mix. Check color.

**Hydrochloric acid (HCL) solution:** To make a 5% solution, add 13.6 mL concentrated HCl to 73 mL water while stirring. To make a $0.1M$ solution, add 1 mL concentrated hydrochloric acid to 100 mL water while stirring.

**Iodine solution/Iodine stain:** Dilute 1 part Lugol's solution with 15 parts water.

**Lugol's solution:** Dissolve 10 g potassium iodide in 100 mL distilled water. Then add and dissolve 5 g iodine. Store in dark bottle. Keeps indefinitely.

**Phenolphthalein indicator:** From a drug store, buy a package of any laxative that contains phenolphthalein. To make 1% solution, mash 4 tablets and pour the powder into 10 mL of rubbing alcohol. Let mixture soak for 15 minutes. Pour liquid into and store in a dropper bottle.

**Potassium permanganate:** For a $0.01M$ solution of potassium permanganate, dissolve 0.15 g $KMnO_4$ in 100 mL water.

**Red cabbage concentrate:** Put 5 leaves of red cabbage in a pot. Add 1 L of water, bring to a boil, and simmer until water turns a deep purple. Pour liquid through a strainer or piece of cheesecloth into a storage bottle. Keep refrigerated.

**Salt solution:** For a 3.5% salt (NaCl) solution that simulates the concentration of ocean water, dissolve 35 g of salt (NaCl) in 965 mL of water. For a 1% solution (weak), dissolve 1 g of salt (NaCl) in 99 mL of water. For a 6% solution, dissolve 6 g of salt (NaCl) in 94 mL of water.

**Silver nitrate solution:** To make a 10% solution, put 5 g of silver nitrate in 50 mL of distilled water.

**Sugar solution:** Add 1 tablespoon of sugar to 1 cup of warm water in a deep jar or flask. Stir to dissolve.

**Sodium hydroxide (dilute):** To make a 1% solution, dissolve 1 g NaOH in 99 mL of water.

# Equipment and Materials List

These easy-to-use tables of equipment and consumable materials can help you prepare for your science classes for the year. Refer to the Chapter Organizer in front of each chapter for a list of equipment and materials used for each laboratory activity in the chapter.

| Consumables | | | |
| --- | --- | --- | --- |
| **Material** | **Launch Lab (Chapter)** | **MiniLAB (Chapter-Section)** | **Lab (Chapter-Section)** |
| alcohol, rubbing | | 9-3 | 6-1 |
| alum powder | | | 10-2 |
| aluminum foil | | 6-1 | 7-3, 8-3, 19-1 |
| ammonia, household | | | 10-3 |
| apple | | | 6-1 |
| baking soda | | | 9-3, 20-2 |
| baking soda (solution) | | | 10-3 |
| balloon(s) | 16 | 10-2 | 12-3 |
| bean seeds | 4 | | 7-3 |
| black plastic | | 13-3 | |
| borax soap (solution) | | | 10-3 |
| bottles, clear, 1-L, plastic, soft-drink | | | 8-2 |
| bouillon cube | 10 | | |
| bowl, paper | 22 | | |
| boxes, cardboard | | | 8-3 |
| bromothymol blue solution | | | 3-3 |
| carbonated beverage bottle | | 10-2 | |
| carbonated soft drink (colorless) | | | 10-3 |
| cardboard | 20 | | 14-3, 17-1, 22-3 |
| cardboard tube | | 5-3 | |
| carrot sticks | 3 | | |
| cheese | | 5-2 | |
| clay | 14, 19 | 13-2, 19-2 | 14-3, 22-3 |
| clear-plastic wrap | | 13-3 | 7-1 |
| coat hangers, wire | | | 8-3 |
| construction paper | | 17-1 | 17-1, 22-3 |
| cookie, chocolate-chip | | 8-1 | |
| corn syrup | | | 3-2, 14-2 |
| cornstarch | | | 5-2, 9-3 |
| cotton ball | | | 6-1 |
| cups, insulated foam | | | 11-3 |
| cups, small paper | | | 6-4 |
| dirt or sand | | 18-1 | |
| egg, unshelled | | | 3-2 |
| eraser, flat | | 12-1 | |
| food coloring | | 3-2 | 6-4, 19-1 |
| fruit cubes | | 5-2 | |
| garden fertilizer | | | 7-1 |
| gauze | | 6-1 | |
| gelatin, prepared | | 2-1, 3-1, 20-2 | |
| grocery bag, brown | | 5-2 | |
| hydrochloric acid solution, 5% | | | 17-3, 18-4 |
| hydrochloric acid, 0.1$M$ (solution) | | | 10-3 |
| index cards, large, 3 × 5 | | 15-2 | 9-2 |
| iodine solution | | | 9-3 |
| iodine, 2% tincture | | | 5-2 |
| jelly beans | | 22-3 | |
| label(s) | | | 1-4, 6-1, 7-3 |
| lemon juice | | | 6-4 |
| liquid bandage solution | | 6-1 | |
| meat | | 5-2 | |
| meat trays, insulated foam | | | 11-3 |
| milk, low-fat | | | 6-4 |

# Equipment and Materials List

| Material | Launch Lab (Chapter) | MiniLAB (Chapter-Section) | Lab (Chapter-Section) |
|---|---|---|---|
| moss | 8 | | |
| newspaper | | 2-2 | 6-1 |
| orange juice, canned | | | 5-2 |
| orange juice, dairy carton | | | 5-2 |
| orange juice, freshly squeezed | | | 5-2 |
| orange juice, from frozen concentrate | | | 5-2 |
| paper cup, small | | 18-1 | |
| paper towel(s) | 4, 9 | | 6-1, 18-4 |
| pencil, grease | | | 10-3 |
| pH indicator paper | | 8-2 | |
| pin | | 20-2 | |
| pineapple, fresh | | 3-1 | |
| pipe cleaners | | | 22-3 |
| plaster of paris | 22 | | 22-3 |
| plastic bag(s), self-sealing | 4 | 20-2 | 6-1 |
| plastic sheets, clear | | | 8-3 |
| plastic wrap | | 7-2 | 8-2 |
| plate, paper | | 8-1 | |
| poster board | | | 8-3 |
| potato chips | | 5-2 | |
| powdered sugar | | | 9-3 |
| pretzels | | 5-2 | |
| rainwater | | 8-2 | |
| red cabbage, concentrated | | | 10-3 |
| rubber band | 20 | 7-2 | 7-1, 8-2, 19-1 |
| salad oil | | 9-3 | |
| salt | 3, 17 | 17-1 | |
| salt solution, strong | | | 1-4 |
| salt solution, weak | | | 1-4 |
| sand, moist | 8 | | |
| sandpaper | | | 6-1 |
| sediment samples | | 18-4 | |
| seeds, packaged | | | 1-4 |
| shells, small | 22 | | |
| shoe box | | 9-1 | |
| slide of an onion root tip | | | 4-1 |
| soap | | 12-1 | 6-1 |
| soap (solution) | | | 10-3 |
| soil | 8 | | 7-3, 8-2 |
| straws, drinking | | | 12-3 |
| straws, narrow and wide | | | 11-3 |
| string | 16 | | 8-3, 10-2, 12-3, 17-1 |
| sugar cubes | | | 5-4 |
| sugar, granulated | | 9-3 | 5-4, 17-1 |
| taffy | | 19-1, 20-1 | |
| tap water, aged | | | 3-3 |
| tape, masking | | 11-1, 11-2 | 5-2, 8-2, 12-3, 16-4 |
| toothpick(s) | | 8-1 | 22-3 |
| vegetable oil | | | 14-2 |
| vegetables | | 5-2 | |
| vinegar | | | 9-3, 10-3, 20-2 |
| water, carbonated | | | 3-3 |
| water, distilled | | 8-2 | 1-4, 2-3, 3-2, 10-3 |
| water, pond | | | 7-1 |
| weighing paper | | | 5-2, 5-4, 7-1 |
| wooden stick, flat | | | 17-1 |
| yarn or string | | | 20-3 |

# Equipment and Materials List

## Nonconsumables

| Material | Launch Lab (Chapter) | MiniLAB (Chapter-Section) | Lab (Chapter-Section) |
|---|---|---|---|
| baking pan, 9" × 13" | | 21-3 | |
| balance | | 1-1 | 3-2, 10-2, 17-3 |
| ball | | 19-2 | |
| basalt | | | 18-2 |
| baseball | 11 | | |
| basin, plastic or aluminum-foil baking pan | 8 | | |
| beaker(s) | 8, 10 | | 5-4, 9-3, 10-2, 14-2, 14-3, 17-1, 19-1 |
| blocks, wooden | 20 | | 19-2 |
| bottles, labeled | | | 10-3 |
| bowl | 9 | 5-3 | |
| bulletin board, large | | | 9-2 |
| CD case, clear-plastic | | | 14-3 |
| calcite | 17 | 17-2 | |
| can, large | | | 21-3 |
| clipboard | | | 16-2 |
| coiled spring toy | | | 20-3 |
| compound light microscope | | | 2-3 |
| computer probe | | 13-3 | |
| container | | 2-1, 10-2 | 1-4, 3-2 |
| cookware, black | | | 8-3 |
| copper or copper penny | | | 17-3 |
| coverslip(s) | | | 2-1, 2-3 |
| cup, plastic | 9 | 7-3 | 19-1 |
| D-cell battery and holder | | | 15-1 |
| dissecting probe | | 18-4 | |
| dropper | | 6-1 | 2-1, 2-3, 5-2, 6-4, 10-3, 18-4 |
| dropper bottle(s) | | | 5-2, 10-3, 9-3 |
| eggs, plastic | | | 11-3 |
| electrical motor, small | | | 13-2 |
| encyclopedia | | | 9-2 |
| file, steel | | | 17-3 |
| film canisters, plastic | | | 20-2 |
| flashlight | | 2-1, 14-1, 14-3, 21-1 | 14-3 |
| forceps | | 18-4 | 2-1 |
| gabbro | | | 18-2 |
| glass plate | | 2-2 | 17-3 |
| glasses | | 9-3 | |
| glass-marking pencil | | | 5-2 |
| gloves | | | 6-1 |
| golf ball | | 13-2 | 12-3 |
| graduated cylinder | | | 5-2, 6-4, 17-3, 20-2 |
| granite | 16 | | 18-2 |
| gypsum | | 17-2 | |
| halite | | 17-2 | |
| headphone jack | | | 13-2 |
| hot plate | | | 9-3, 10-2, 17-1 |
| jar lid | | | 21-3 |
| jar | 22 | | 7-1, 21-3 |
| key | | 12-1 | |
| knife, plastic | | 19-2 | |
| lamp (100-W lightbulb) | | | 8-2 |
| laser pointer | | 14-3 | |
| lid, plastic | | | 12-3 |
| lightbulb and holder | | | 15-1 |
| light-emitting diode | | | 15-1 |
| magazine picture of a piece of furniture | | 1-4 | |
| magnifying lens | 2, 17, 18 | 7-2, 17-1, 18-4 | 1-4, 17-1, 17-3, 18-2, 18-4 |
| map | 6 | | |
| marbles | 12, 13 | 5-3, 13-2 | 11-3 |

# Equipment and Materials List

| Material | Launch Lab (Chapter) | MiniLAB (Chapter-Section) | Lab (Chapter-Section) |
|---|---|---|---|
| Merck Index | | | 9-2 |
| mica | 17 | | |
| mica, muscovite | | 17-2 | |
| microscope | | | 2-1, 4-1 |
| microscope slide(s) | | | 2-1, 2-3 |
| mineral samples | | | 17-3 |
| mirror | | 14-1 | 14-3 |
| Mohs scale of hardness | | | 17-3 |
| mortar and pestle | 10 | | 5-4 |
| nail, small iron | | | 17-3 |
| obsidian | | | 18-2 |
| pan, shallow | | | 17-1 |
| penny | | 6-3 | |
| petri dishes, plastic | | | 2-3 |
| pie pan, small | | | 9-3 |
| pins, straight | | | 11-3 |
| planting containers, small | | | 7-3 |
| plastic, rigid | | | 22-3 |
| pot, large | | 13-3 | |
| prism | | 14-3 | 14-3 |
| psychometer | | | 21-3 |
| pumice | | | 18-2 |
| quartz crystals | 17 | | |
| radio or CD player | | | 13-2 |
| refracting telescope | | | 16-2 |
| rhyolite | | | 18-2 |
| rock samples | 18 | | |
| rock samples, sedimentary | | | 18-4 |
| sandstone | 17 | | |
| schist | 17 | | |
| scoops, small | | | 9-3 |
| sponge, dry | | 1-1 | |
| spoon | | | 3-2, 7-1, 17-1, 20-2 |
| spray bottle | 8 | | |
| spring scale (in Newtons) | | 12-3 | 12-3 |
| stereomicroscope | | | 2-3 |
| stirring rod | | | 3-3, 5-4, 10-2 |
| stopwatch | 5, 15 | 11-1 | 5-4, 8-2, 8-3, 12-3 |
| storage box, clear-plastic | | | 19-2 |
| streak plate | | | 17-3 |
| tennis ball(s) | 11 | | |
| test tubes | | | 3-3, 5-2, 9-3, 10-3 |
| test-tube holder | | | 9-3 |
| test-tube rack | | | 3-3, 5-2 |
| thermal mitt | | | 10-2, 17-1 |
| thermometer | | 13-3 | 5-4, 8-2, 8-3, 10-2, 21-3 |
| thumbtacks or pins | | | 9-2 |
| tripod, small | | | 16-2 |
| triple-beam balance | | | 5-2, 5-4, 7-1 |
| trowel | | | 7-3 |
| vesicular basalt | | | 18-2 |
| wind sock | | | 21-3 |
| wire | | | 15-1, 22-3 |
| wooden stirrer | | | 5-2 |
| world atlas, globe, or map | 21 | 21-1 | |
| **Biological** | | | |
| brine shrimp eggs | | | 1-4 |
| *Elodea* | | | 2-1, 3-3 |
| human cheek cells | | | 2-1 |

# Suppliers

## Equipment Suppliers

**American Science & Surplus**
P.O. Box 1030
Skokie, IL 60076
(847) 647-0011
www.sciplus.com

**Bio-Rad Laboratories**
2000 Alfred Nobel Dr.
Life Science Group
Hercules, CA 94547
(800) 424-6723
www.bio-rad.com

**Carolina Biological Supply Co.**
2700 York Road
Burlington, NC 27215
(800) 334-5551
www.carolina.com

**Edmund Scientific Company**
60 Pearce Ave.
Tonawanda, NY 14150
(800) 728-6999
scientificsonline.com

**Fisher Science Education**
Educational Materials Division
4500 Turnberry Dr.
Hanover Park, IL 60133
(800) 955-1177
www.fisheredu.com

**Nasco Science**
901 Janesville Avenue
P.O. Box 901
Fort Atkinson, WI 53538-0901
(800) 558-9595
www.enasco.com

**Nebraska Scientific**
3823 Leavenworth St.
Omaha, NE 68105-1180
(800) 228-7117
nebraskascientific.com

**PASCO Scientific**
10101 Foothills Blvd.
P.O. Box 619011
Roseville, CA 95747
(800) 772-8700
www.pasco.com

**Sargent-Welch/VWR Scientific Products**
P.O. Box 5229
Buffalo Grove, IL 60089-5229
(800) SAR-GENT 727-4368
www.SargentWelch.com

**Science Kit and Boreal Laboratories**
777 East Park Dr.
P.O. Box 5003
Tonawanda, NY 14150
(800) 828-7777
www.sciencekit.com

**Ward's Natural Science Est.**
5100 W. Henrietta Road
P.O. Box 92912
Rochester, NY 14692-9012
(800) 962-2660
www.wardsci.com

## Audiovisual Distributors

**Bullfrog Films**
P.O. Box 149
Oley, PA 19547
(800) 543-FROG
www.bullfrogfilms.com

**Coronet/MTI Film & Video**
2349 Chaffee Dr.
St. Louis, MO 63146
(800) 221-1274

**Discovery Channel School**
1 Discovery Place
Silver Springs, MD 20910
(240) 662-2000
www.discoveryschool.com

**Films for the Humanities and Sciences**
P.O. Box 2053
Princeton, NJ 08543
(800) 257-5126

**Flinn Scientific**
P.O. Box 219
770 N. Raddant Rd.
Batavia, IL 60510
(800) 452-1261
www.flinnsci.com

**Frey Scientific, Div. of Beckley Cardy**
100 Paragon Parkway
Mansfield, OH 44903
(800) 225-FREY
www.freyscientific.com

**Media Design Associates**
1731 15th St.
Suite 220
Boulder, CO 80302
(866) 546-9151
www.indra.com

**National Geographic Society Educational Services**
1145 17th Street, N.W.
Washington, DC 20036
(800) 368-2728
www.nationalgeographic.com

**Scholastic, Inc.**
555 Broadway
New York, NY 10012-3999
(800) 325-6149
www.scholastic.com

**Videodiscovery Inc.**
920 N. 34th St.
Suite 300
Seattle, WA 98103
(800) 548-3472
www.videodiscovery.com

## Software Distributors

**Boreal Laboratories, Ltd.**
399 Vansickle Rd.
St. Catharines, Ontario,
L2S 3T4
Canada
(800) 387-9393
boreal.com

**Educational Activities, Inc.**
1937 Grand Ave.
P.O. Box 87
Baldwin, NY 11510
(800) 645-3739
www.edact.com

**IBM Education**
www.solutions.ibm.com/k12

**J. Weston Walch, Publisher**
321 Valley St.
P.O. Box 658
Portland, ME 04104-0658
(800) 341-6094
www.walch.com

**Scholastic, Inc.**
555 Broadway
New York, NY 10012-3999
(800) 325-6149
www.scholastic.com

**Sunburst Technology**
1550 Executive Drive
Elgin, IL 60123
(800) 321-7511
www.SUNBURST.com

# Contents
# In Brief

# HOW TO...

## Use Your Science Book

## Before You Read

- **Chapter Opener** Science is occurring all around you, and the opening photo of each chapter will preview the science you will be learning about. The **Chapter Preview** will give you an idea of what you will be learning about, and you can try the **Launch Lab** to help get your brain headed in the right direction. The **Foldables** exercise is a fun way to keep you organized.

- **Section Opener** Chapters are divided into two to four sections. The **As You Read** in the margin of the first page of each section will let you know what is most important in the section. It is divided into four parts. **What You'll Learn** will tell you the major topics you will be covering. **Why It's Important** will remind you why you are studying this in the first place! The **Review Vocabulary** word is a word you already know, either from your science studies or your prior knowledge. The **New Vocabulary** words are words that you need to learn to understand this section. These words will be in **boldfaced** print and highlighted in the section. Make a note to yourself to recognize these words as you are reading the section.

Glencoe Science

Indiana Science

Grade 7

NATIONAL GEOGRAPHIC

# As You Read

- **Headings** Each section has a title in large red letters, and is further divided into blue titles and small red titles at the beginnings of some paragraphs. To help you study, make an outline of the headings and subheadings.

- **Margins** In the margins of your text, you will find many helpful resources. The **Science Online** exercises and **Integrate** activities help you explore the topics you are studying. **MiniLabs** reinforce the science concepts you have learned.

- **Building Skills** You also will find an **Applying Math** or **Applying Science** activity in each chapter. This gives you extra practice using your new knowledge, and helps prepare you for standardized tests.

- **Student Resources** At the end of the book you will find **Student Resources** to help you throughout your studies. These include **Science, Technology,** and **Math Skill Handbooks,** an **English/Spanish Glossary,** and an **Index.** Also, use your **Foldables** as a resource. It will help you organize information, and review before a test.

- **In Class** Remember, you can always ask your teacher to explain anything you don't understand.

**FOLDABLES** Study Organizer

**Science Vocabulary** Make the following Foldable to help you understand the vocabulary terms in this chapter.

**STEP 1** Fold a vertical sheet of notebook paper from side to side.

**STEP 2** Cut along every third line of only the top layer to form tabs.

**STEP 3** Label each tab with a vocabulary word from the chapter.

**Build Vocabulary** As you read the chapter, list the vocabulary words on the tabs. As you learn the definitions, write them under the tab for each vocabulary word.

Look For...
**FOLDABLES**™
At the beginning of every section.

# In Lab

Working in the laboratory is one of the best ways to understand the concepts you are studying. Your book will be your guide through your laboratory experiences, and help you begin to think like a scientist. In it, you not only will find the steps necessary to follow the investigations, but you also will find helpful tips to make the most of your time.

- Each lab provides you with a **Real-World Question** to remind you that science is something you use every day, not just in class. This may lead to many more questions about how things happen in your world.

- Remember, experiments do not always produce the result you expect. Scientists have made many discoveries based on investigations with unexpected results. You can try the experiment again to make sure your results were accurate, or perhaps form a new hypothesis to test.

- Keeping a **Science Journal** is how scientists keep accurate records of observations and data. In your journal, you also can write any questions that may arise during your investigation. This is a great method of reminding yourself to find the answers later.

Look For...
- Launch Labs start every chapter.
- MiniLabs in the margin of each chapter.
- Two Full-Period Labs in every chapter.
- EXTRA Try at Home Labs at the end of your book.
- the Web site with laboratory demonstrations.

## Before a Test

Admit it! You don't like to take tests! However, there *are* ways to review that make them less painful. Your book will help you be more successful taking tests if you use the resources provided to you.

- Review all of the **New Vocabulary** words and be sure you understand their definitions.

- Review the notes you've taken on your **Foldables,** in class, and in lab. Write down any question that you still need answered.

- Review the **Summaries** and **Self Check questions** at the end of each section.

- Study the concepts presented in the chapter by reading the **Study Guide** and answering the questions in the **Chapter Review.**

### Look For...

- **Reading Checks** and **caption questions** throughout the text.
- the **Summaries** and **Self Check questions** at the end of each section.
- the **Study Guide** and **Review** at the end of each chapter.
- the **Standards Review** after each chapter.

# Let's Get Started

To help you find the information you need quickly, use the Scavenger Hunt below to learn where things are located in Chapter 1.

1 What is the title of this chapter?

2 What will you learn in Section 1?

3 Sometimes you may ask, "Why am I learning this?" State a reason why the concepts from Section 2 are important.

4 What is the main topic presented in Section 2?

5 How many reading checks are in Section 1?

6 What is the Web address where you can find extra information?

7 What is the main heading above the sixth paragraph in Section 2?

8 There is an integration with another subject mentioned in one of the margins of the chapter. What subject is it?

9 List the new vocabulary words presented in Section 2.

10 List the safety symbols presented in the first Lab.

11 Where would you find a Self Check to be sure you understand the section?

12 Suppose you're doing the Self Check and you have a question about concept mapping. Where could you find help?

13 On what pages are the Chapter Study Guide and Chapter Review?

14 Look in the Table of Contents to find out on which page Section 2 of the chapter begins.

15 You complete the Chapter Review to study for your chapter test. Where could you find another quiz for more practice?

# unit 1 The Basis of Life—2

In each chapter, look for these opportunities for review and assessment:
- **Reading Checks**
- **Caption Questions**
- **Section Review**
- **Chapter Study Guide**
- **Chapter Review**
- **Standards Review**
- **Online practice at in7.msscience.com**

# Contents

# The Nature of Matter—254

In each chapter, look for these opportunities for review and assessment:
- Reading Checks
- Caption Questions
- Section Review
- Chapter Study Guide
- Chapter Review
- Standards Review
- Online practice at in7.msscience.com

# Motion, Forces, and Energy—318

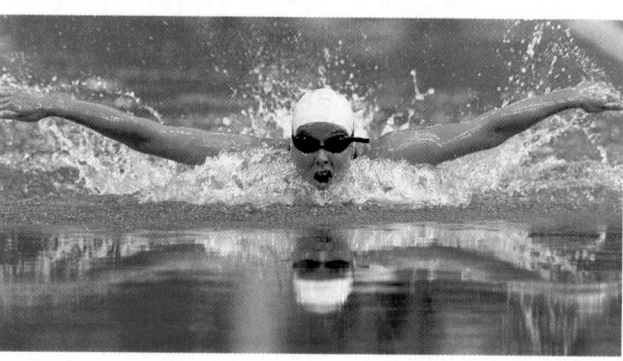

# Contents

In each chapter, look for these opportunities for review and assessment:

- Reading Checks
- Caption Questions
- Section Review
- Chapter Study Guide
- Chapter Review
- Standards Review
- Online practice at in7.msscience.com

# Galaxies, Stars, and Earth—468

# Contents

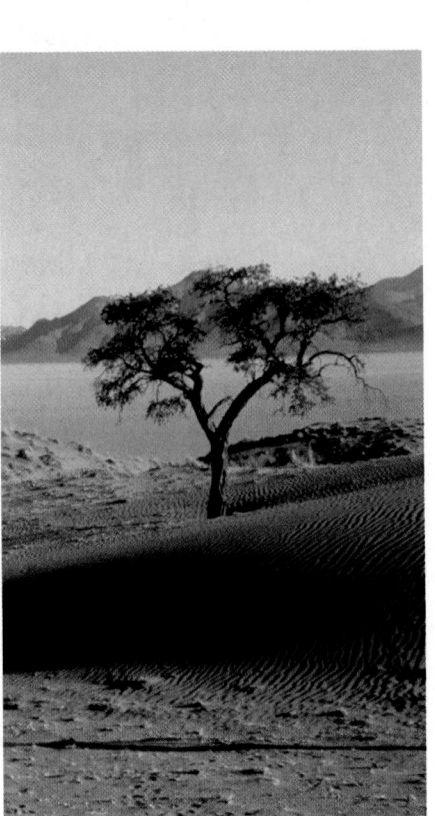

# Student Resources—682

In each chapter, look for these opportunities for review and assessment:
- Reading Checks
- Caption Questions
- Section Review
- Chapter Study Guide
- Chapter Review
- Standards Review
- Online practice at in7.msscience.com

## Cross-Curricular Readings

# Cross-Curricular Readings

**LABS**

available as a video lab

**Mini LAB**

Content Details

Mini LAB Try at Home

Content Details

available as a video lab

## One-Page Labs

Content Details

LABS

Content Details

### Applying Math

### Applying Science

**INTEGRATE**

**Astronomy:** 21
**Career:** 50, 83, 97, 198, 264, 299, 454, 548, 641
**Chemistry:** 105, 110, 211, 212, 233, 298, 446, 485, 519, 539, 566, 603, 610
**Earth Science:** 21, 277, 394, 414
**Environment:** 44, 291, 295, 456
**Health:** 77, 132, 145, 236, 421
**History:** 165, 259, 357, 389, 486
**Language Arts:** 580, 611
**Life Science:** 88, 216, 248, 276, 306, 324, 351, 364, 387, 629, 660
**Physics:** 42, 73, 170, 484, 507, 535, 564, 626, 669
**Social Studies:** 17, 136, 174, 227, 334, 519, 657

**Science Online**

8, 15, 23, 53, 54, 70, 84, 113, 115, 134, 145, 163, 172, 178, 200, 204, 234, 244, 262, 267, 276, 289, 305, 308, 326, 336, 364, 386, 396, 426, 445, 452, 456, 458, 479, 484, 518, 538, 542, 569, 578, 597, 603, 639, 641, 663, 666, 672

**Standards Review**

34–35, 62–63, 92–93, 122–123, 158–159, 192–193, 220–221, 252–253, 284–285, 316–317, 346–347, 376–377, 408–409, 438–439, 466–467, 500–501, 528–529, 558–559, 588–589, 620–621, 650–651, 680–681

## Unit Contents

WebQuest *New Research on Cells* is an investigation of current cell research and an exploration into the roles that different cells play in our bodies. After answering a set of questions designed to guide student learning, students will write a paragraph summarizing one of the topics, using a style suited for posting on a Web site.

# How Are Cargo Ships & Cancer Cells Connected?

2

**PROJECT CRISS**℠

## Study Skills

**Discussion** The Think-Pair-Share strategy ensures active participation of all students. Given the parts of the cell, have students brainstorm ideas about the appearance and function of each cell part on their own. Then have pairs discuss their notes and ideas before returning to share with the whole class.

**NATIONAL GEOGRAPHIC**

**B**elow, a present-day cargo ship glides through a harbor in New Jersey. In 1943, during World War II, another cargo ship floated in an Italian harbor. The ship carried a certain type of chemical. When a bomb struck the ship, the chemical accidentally was released. Later, when doctors examined the sailors who were exposed to the chemical, they noticed that the sailors had low numbers of white blood cells. The chemical had interfered with the genetic material in certain cells, preventing the cells from reproducing. Since cancer cells (like the ones at lower left) are cells that reproduce without control, scientists wondered whether this chemical could be used to fight cancer. A compound related to the chemical became the first drug developed to fight cancer. Since then, many other cancer-fighting drugs have been developed.

## unit projects

**Careers** Have students brainstorm a list of questions they might ask a pharmacist, nurse, pathologist, veterinarian, medical researcher, or other health-care professional. Questions might focus on bacteria or virus reproduction, adaptation of cells to their environment, or drug immunity or resistance. Students might explore homeopathic remedies, historical medicines and treatments, Native American treatments, or medicines and procedures of the future. Acquired information can be displayed in a Venn diagram.

**Technology** Have students imagine that a cell is placed in a dish of nutrient-enriched agar. Twenty minutes later, the virtual cell would have divided to form two cells. Assuming that the cells continue to divide every 20 minutes, how many cells would be in the dish an hour after the first division? Two hours after the first division? Using a computer graphing program, have students illustrate the pattern of cell reproduction with the correct number of cells at 20-minute intervals.

**Model** Have students design a small flip book of approximately 40 pages to demonstrate mitosis. Original illustrations clearly should show the four phases of cell division. Students may produce a second book on meiosis that allows for the comparison of the two processes.

**Additional Resources** For more information, resources, and assessment rubrics, visit in7.msscience.com/unit_project.

---

## unit projects

The assessed Indiana objective appears in blue.

To find project ideas and resources, visit nc7.msscience.com/unit_project.

Projects include:
- **Career** Brainstorm a list of questions for a health professional about cell reproduction, or bacteria and virus resistance to drugs. 7.4.12
- **Technology** Design a chart and graph that presents information on cell reproduction rate during specific time intervals. 7.4.4
- **Model** Construct a thumb flip book that models mitosis. Complete a second book for meiosis to analyze and compare the two processes. 7.4.4

**WebQuest** *New Research on Cells* provides an opportunity to explore current research on cells, and how different cells work in the human body. 7.4.5

---

**NATIONAL GEOGRAPHIC**    **How Are Cargo Ships & Cancer Cells Connected?**

Agar, a gelatinlike product, is made primarily from red seaweeds. It is used in cosmetics, medicines, dentistry, and as a clarifying agent in brewing and wine making. It also is used as a thickening agent in ice cream, pastries, desserts, and salad dressings.

It was in 1883 that Frau Hess developed this medium for culturing cells. Unlike gelatin, agar can be liquefied by only a few microorganisms and is not a food source, thus it allows better control of the nutrient content of the medium.

| Section/Objectives | Standards | | Labs/Features |
|---|---|---|---|
| **Chapter Opener** | **National** | **State/Local** | **Launch Lab:** Classify Organisms, p. 5 **Foldables**, p. 5 |
| | See pp. 16T–17T for a Key to Standards. | Detailed Standards begin on page IN8. | |
| **Section 1 What is science?** ⏱ 2 sessions 📦 1 block 1. **Apply** scientific methods to problem solving. 2. **Demonstrate** how to measure using scientific units. | National Content Standards: UCP.1–UCP.3, UCP.5, A.1, A.2, G.2 | Indiana Standards: 7.1.1, 7.1.3, 7.14, 7.1.8 | **Science Online,** p. 8 **MiniLAB:** Analyzing Data, p. 9 **Applying Science:** Does temperature affect the rate of bacterial reproduction?, p. 11 |
| **Section 2 Living Things** ⏱ 2 sessions 📦 1 block 3. **Distinguish** between living and nonliving things. 4. **Identify** what living things need to survive. | National Content Standards: UCP.1–UCP.3, UCP.5, A.1, A.2, C.1–C.3 | Indiana Standards: 7.4.1, 7.4.4–7.4.6, 7.4.8, 7.4.9 | **Science Online,** p. 15 **Integrate Social Studies,** p. 17 |
| **Section 3 Where does life come from?** ⏱ 1 session 📦 0.5-block 5. **Describe** experiments about spontaneous generation. 6. **Explain** how scientific methods led to the idea of biogenesis. | National Content Standards: UCP.1–UCP.3, UCP.5, A.1, A.2, C.1, G.3 | Indiana Standards: 7.1.2, 7.1.4, 7.1.5 | **Visualizing the Origins of Life,** p. 20 **Integrate Earth Science,** p. 21 |
| **Section 4 How are living things classified?** ⏱ 3 sessions 📦 1.5 block 7. **Describe** how early scientists classified living things. 8. **Explain** how similarities are used to classify organisms. 9. **Explain** the system of binomial nomenclature. 10. **Demonstrate** how to use a dichotomous key. | National Content Standards: UCP.1–UCP.3, UCP.5, A.1, A.2, C.5, G.3 | Indiana Standards: 7.1.3, 7.2.7, 7.4.1, 7.4.5, 7.5.3 | **Science Online,** p. 23 **MiniLAB:** Communicating Ideas, p. 25 **Lab:** Classifying Seeds, p. 27 **Lab:** Using Scientific Methods, p. 28 **Science and Society:** Monkey Business, p. 30 |

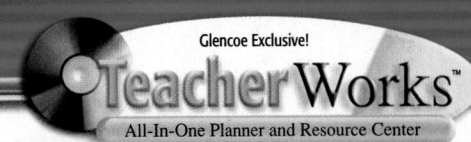

| Lab Materials | Reproducible Resources | Section Assessment | Technology |
|---|---|---|---|
| **Launch Lab:** insect collection | **Chapter** *FAST FILE* **Resources**<br>Foldables Worksheet, p. 15<br>Directed Reading Overview, p. 17<br>Note-taking Worksheets, pp. 33–35 | **ASSESSMENT** GLENCOE'S ADVANTAGE | **Teacher Works** includes:<br>• Interactive Teacher Edition<br>• Lesson Planner with calendar<br>• Access to all program blacklines<br>• Correlations to standards<br>• Web links |
| **MiniLAB:** pan balance, dry sponge, water, Science Journal | **Chapter** *FAST FILE* **Resources**<br>Transparency Activity, p. 44<br>MiniLAB, p. 3<br>Enrichment, p. 29<br>Reinforcement, p. 25<br>Lab Activity, pp. 9–10<br>Directed Reading, p. 18 | **Portfolio**<br>Science Journal, p. 7<br>**Performance**<br>MiniLAB, p. 9<br>Applying Science, p. 11<br>Applying Skills, p. 13<br>**Content**<br>Section Review, p. 13 | Section Focus Transparency<br>Guided Reading Audio Program<br>Interactive Chalkboard CD-ROM<br>Video Lab |
| | **Chapter** *FAST FILE* **Resources**<br>Transparency Activity, p. 45<br>Enrichment, p. 30<br>Reinforcement, p. 26<br>Directed Reading, p. 18 | **Portfolio**<br>Curriculum Connection, p. 16<br>**Performance**<br>Applying Skills, p. 18<br>**Content**<br>Section Review, p. 18 | Section Focus Transparency<br>Guided Reading Audio Program<br>Interactive Chalkboard CD-ROM |
| *Need materials?* Contact Science Kit at 1-800-828-7777 or www.sciencekit.com on the Internet. | **Chapter** *FAST FILE* **Resources**<br>Transparency Activity, p. 46<br>Enrichment, p. 31<br>Reinforcement, p. 27<br>Directed Reading, p. 19 | **Portfolio**<br>Reteach, p. 21<br>**Performance**<br>Applying Skills, p. 21<br>**Content**<br>Section Review, p. 21 | Section Focus Transparency<br>Guided Reading Audio Program<br>Interactive Chalkboard CD-ROM |
| **MiniLAB:** magazine picture of a piece of furniture<br>**Lab:** packets of seeds (10 different kinds), metric ruler, magnifying lens<br>**Lab:** 3 500-mL, wide-mouthed containers; brine shrimp eggs; small, plastic spoon; distilled water; weak salt solution; strong salt solution; 3 labels; magnifying lens | **Chapter** *FAST FILE* **Resources**<br>Transparency Activity, p. 47<br>MiniLAB, p. 4<br>Enrichment, p. 32<br>Reinforcement, p. 28<br>Directed Reading, pp. 19, 20<br>Transparency Activity, pp. 49–50<br>Lab Activity, pp. 11–13<br>Lab Worksheets, pp. 5–6, 7–8 | **Portfolio**<br>Assessment, p. 26<br>**Performance**<br>MiniLAB, p. 25<br>Applying Skills, p. 26<br>**Content**<br>Section Review, p. 26 | Section Focus Transparency<br>Teaching Transparency<br>Virtual Labs CD-ROM<br>Guided Reading Audio Program<br>Interactive Chalkboard CD-ROM |

**ASSESSMENT** GLENCOE'S ADVANTAGE

## End of Chapter Assessment

| Blackline Masters | Technology | Professional Series |
|---|---|---|
| **Chapter** *FAST FILE* **Resources**<br>Chapter Review, pp. 37–38<br>Chapter Tests, pp. 39–42<br>**Mastering the Grade 7 Indiana Science Standards** | MindJogger Videoquiz<br>IN Test Prep and Practice Exam*View*®<br>Exam*View*® Pro Testmaker<br>TeacherWorks CD-ROM<br>Interactive Chalkboard CD-ROM | **Performance Assessment in the Science Classroom (PASC)** |

# Exploring and Classifying Life

## Transparencies

### Section Focus

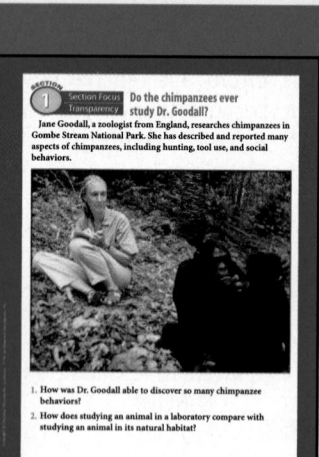

**Section Focus Transparency 1** Do the chimpanzees ever study Dr. Goodall?

Jane Goodall, a zoologist from England, researches chimpanzees in Gombe Stream National Park. She has described and reported many aspects of chimpanzees, including hunting, tool use, and social behaviors.

1. How was Dr. Goodall able to discover so many chimpanzee behaviors?
2. How does studying an animal in a laboratory compare with studying an animal in its natural habitat?

L2

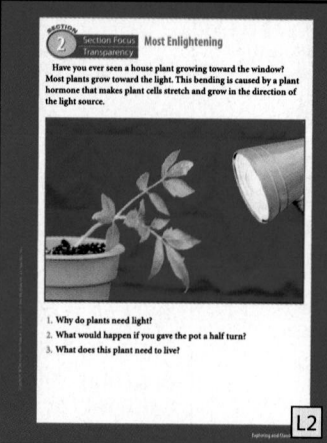

**Section Focus Transparency 2** Most Enlightening

Have you ever seen a house plant growing toward the window? Most plants grow toward the light. This bending is caused by a plant hormone that makes plant cells stretch and grow in the direction of the light source.

1. Why do plants need light?
2. What would happen if you gave the pot a half turn?
3. What does this plant need to live?

L2

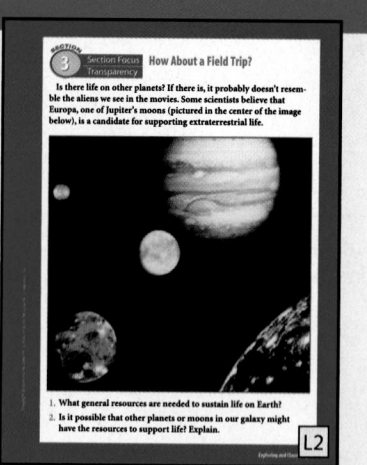

**Section Focus Transparency 3** How About a Field Trip?

Is there life on other planets? If there is, it probably doesn't resemble the aliens we see in the movies. Some scientists believe that Europa, one of Jupiter's moons (pictured in the center of the image below), is a candidate for supporting extraterrestrial life.

1. What general resources are needed to sustain life on Earth?
2. Is it possible that other planets or moons in our galaxy might have the resources to support life? Explain.

L2

This is a representation of key blackline masters available in the Teacher Classroom Resources. See Resource Manager boxes within the chapter for additional information.

### Assessment

**Assessment Transparency** Exploring and Classifying Life

Directions: *Carefully review the table and answer the following questions.*

**Fruit and Vegetable Seed Germination Rate**

| Type of seed | Number of seeds | Amount of water added (mL) | Number of seeds germinating | | |
|---|---|---|---|---|---|
| | | | Day 3 | Day 5 | Day 7 |
| Orange | 10 | 50 | 0 | 0 | 1 |
| Lemon | 10 | 50 | 0 | 1 | 1 |
| Cucumber | 10 | 50 | 6 | 7 | 7 |
| Onion | 10 | 50 | 7 | 9 | 10 |

1. Which hypothesis was probably being tested?
   A Less than 25 percent of vegetable seeds will germinate.
   B Seeds prefer to grow in soil versus sand.
   C Vegetable seeds germinate faster than fruit seeds.
   D A period of one week is required before seeds will germinate.
2. Which of the following would improve an experiment to compare the rate of seed germination?
   F using more types of seeds
   G measuring the length of the plants
   H adding 100mL of water to each seed
   J conducting the experiment for a shorter time
3. Which factor would have the LEAST effect on the results?
   A the amount of light to which the seeds were exposed
   B the amount of soil used for the seeds
   C the color of the pots used
   D the depth the seeds were planted in the soil

L2

### Teaching

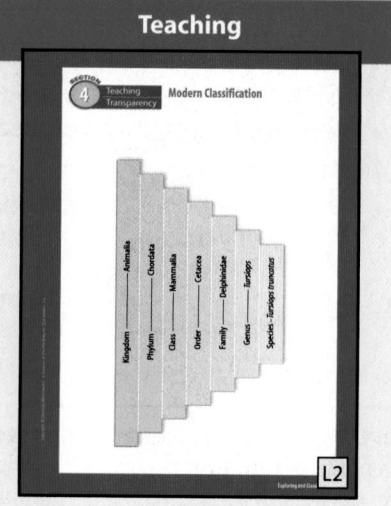

**Teaching Transparency** Modern Classification

L2

## Key to Teaching Strategies

The following designations will help you decide which activities are appropriate for your students.

**L1** Level 1 activities should be appropriate for students with learning difficulties.

**L2** Level 2 activities should be within the ability range of all students.

**L3** Level 3 activities are designed for above-average students.

**ELL** ELL activities should be within the ability range of English-Language Learners.

**COOP LEARN** Cooperative Learning activities are designed for small group work.

**LS** Multiple Learning Styles logos, as described on page 12T, are used throughout to indicate strategies that address different learning styles.

**P** These strategies represent student products that can be placed into a best-work portfolio.

**PBL** Problem-Based Learning activities apply real-world situations to learning.

## Hands-on Activities

### Student Text Lab Worksheet

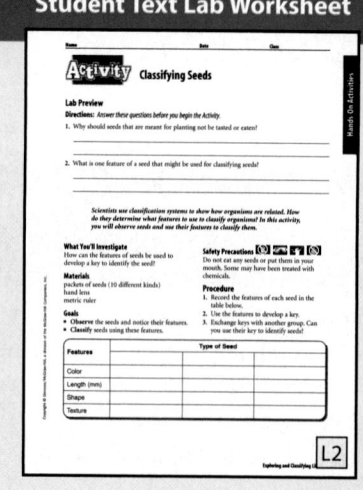

**Activity** Classifying Seeds

L2

### Laboratory Activities

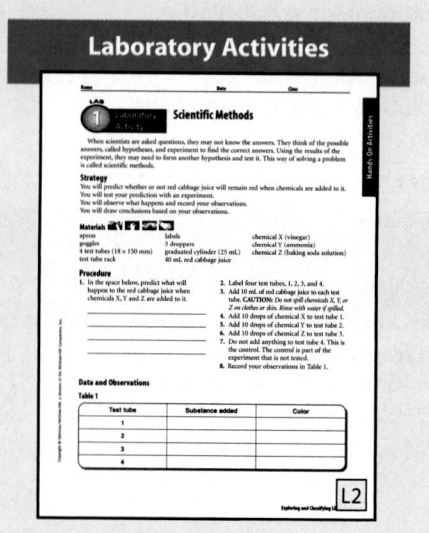

**Lab 1** Scientific Methods

L2

## Meeting Different Ability Levels

### Content Outline

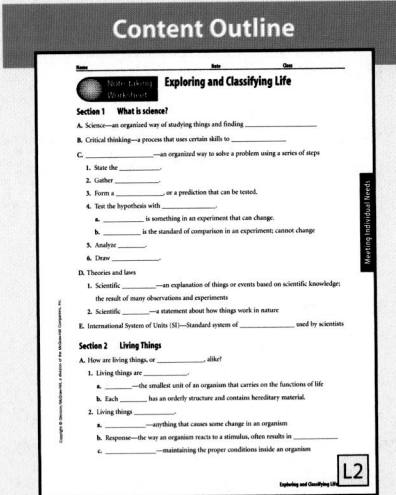

**Note-Taking Worksheet**

**Exploring and Classifying Life**

**Section 1    What is science?**

A. Science—an organized way of studying things and finding _____

B. Critical thinking—a process that uses certain skills to _____

C. _____—an organized way to solve a problem using a series of steps

1. State the _____
2. Gather _____
3. Form a _____, or a prediction that can be tested.
4. Test the hypothesis with _____
   a. _____ is something in an experiment that can change.
   b. _____ is the standard of comparison in an experiment; cannot change
5. Analyze _____
6. Draw _____

D. Theories and laws

1. Scientific _____—an explanation of things or events based on scientific knowledge; the result of many observations and experiments
2. Scientific _____ a statement about how things work in nature

E. International System of Units (SI)—Standard system of _____ used by scientists

**Section 2    Living Things**

A. How are living things, or _____, alike?

1. Living things are _____
   a. _____—the smallest unit of an organism that carries on the functions of life
   b. Each _____ has an orderly structure and contains hereditary material.
2. Living things _____
   a. _____—anything that causes some change in an organism
   b. Response—the way an organism reacts to a stimulus, often results in _____
   c. _____—maintaining the proper conditions inside an organism

*Exploring and Classifying Life*

**L2**

### Reinforcement

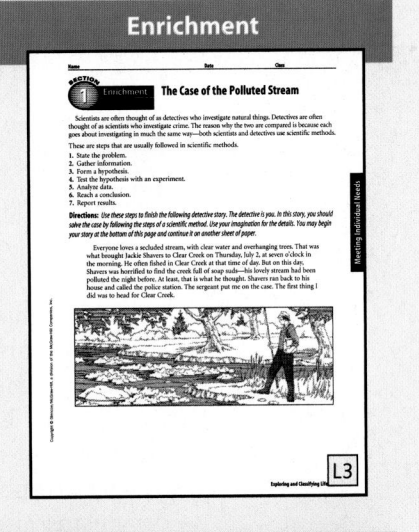

**SECTION 1  Reinforcement**

**What is science?**

**Directions:** *List the steps that are usually followed in scientific methods in the order in which they should be performed.*

1. _____
2. _____
3. _____
4. _____
5. _____
6. _____
7. _____
8. What does SI stand for?

**Directions:** *Match the SI unit with what it measures by writing the correct letter in the space provided.*

_____  9. meter         a. length
_____ 10. liter         b. mass
_____ 11. kilogram      c. volume

**Directions:** *Answer the following questions on the lines provided.*

12. Suppose a scientist wants to test a new drug to fight the flu. The scientist injects the drug into three people with the flu. The scientist injects a harmless solution into three other people with the flu. In this experiment, what is the variable group and what is the control group?

13. Why is it necessary to follow safety rules in the science laboratory?

14. What is the difference between a theory and a scientific law?

*Exploring and Classifying Life*

**L2**

### Enrichment

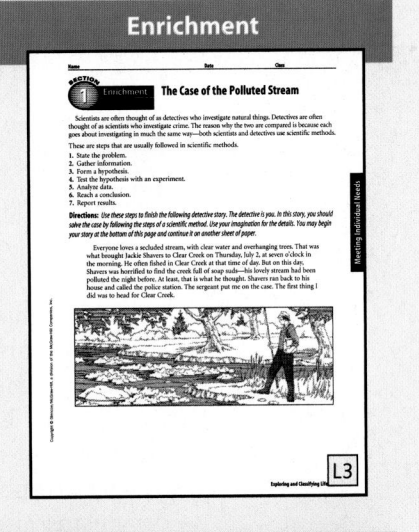

**SECTION 1  Enrichment**

**The Case of the Polluted Stream**

Scientists are often thought of as detectives who investigate natural things. Detectives are often thought of as scientists who investigate crime. The reason why the two are compared is because each goes about investigating in much the same way—both scientists and detectives use scientific methods.

These are steps that are usually followed in scientific methods.

1. State the problem.
2. Gather information.
3. Form a hypothesis.
4. Test the hypothesis with an experiment.
5. Analyze data.
6. Reach a conclusion.
7. Report results.

**Directions:** *Use these steps to finish the following detective story. The detective is you. In this story, you should solve the case by following the steps of a scientific method. Use your imagination for the details. You may begin your story at the bottom of this page and continue it on another sheet of paper.*

Everyone loves a secluded stream, with clear water and overhanging trees. That was what brought Jackie Shavers to Clear Creek on Thursday, July 2, at seven o'clock in the morning. He often fished in Clear Creek at that time of day. But on this day, Shavers was horrified to find the creek full of soap suds—his lovely stream had been polluted the night before. At least, that is what he thought. Shavers ran back to his house and called the police station. The sergeant put me on the case. The first thing I did was to head for Clear Creek.

*Exploring and Classifying Life*

**L3**

### Directed Reading (English/Spanish)

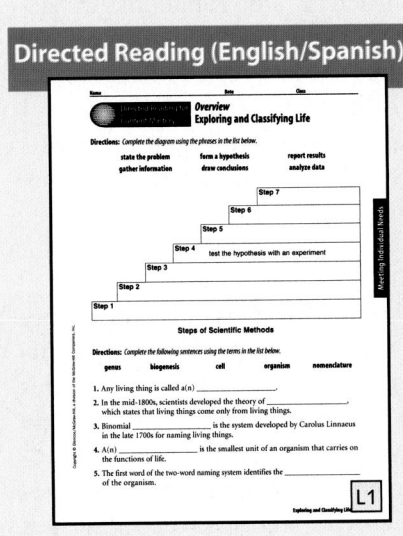

**Directed Reading for Content Mastery**

**Overview**

**Exploring and Classifying Life**

**Directions:** *Complete the diagram using the phrases in the list below.*

state the problem    form a hypothesis    report results
gather information    draw conclusions     analyze data

Step 7
Step 6
Step 5
Step 4   test the hypothesis with an experiment
Step 3
Step 2
Step 1

**Steps of Scientific Methods**

**Directions:** *Complete the following sentences using the terms in the list below.*

genus    biogenesis    cell    organism    nomenclature

1. Any living thing is called a(n) _____
2. In the mid-1800s, scientists developed the theory of _____, which states that living things come only from living things.
3. Binomial _____ is the system developed by Carolus Linnaeus in the late 1700s for naming living things.
4. A(n) _____ is the smallest unit of an organism that carries on the functions of life.
5. The first word of the two-word naming system identifies the _____ of the organism.

*Exploring and Classifying Life*

**L1**

### Study Guide

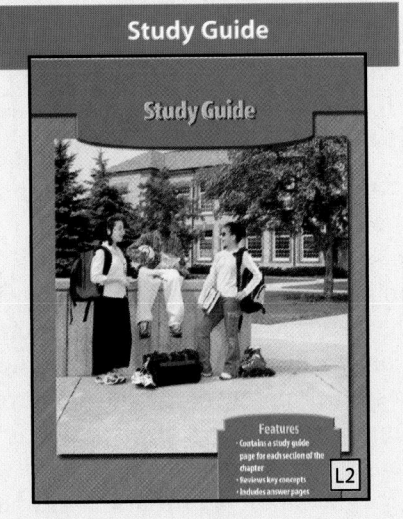

**Study Guide**

**Features**
• Contains a study guide page for each section of the chapter
• Reviews key concepts
• Includes answer pages

**L2**

### Reading Essentials

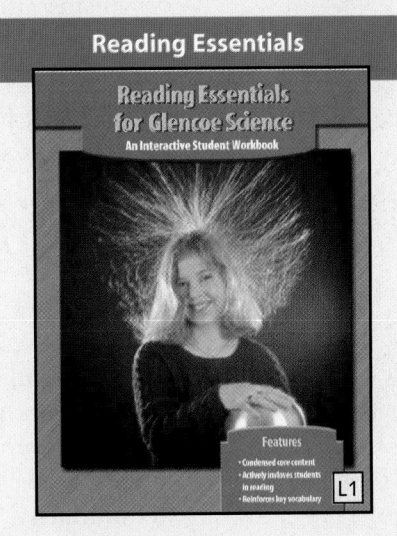

**Reading Essentials for Glencoe Science**

**An Interactive Student Workbook**

**Features**
• Condensed core content
• Actively involves students in reading
• Reinforces key vocabulary

**L1**

## Assessment

### Test Practice Workbook

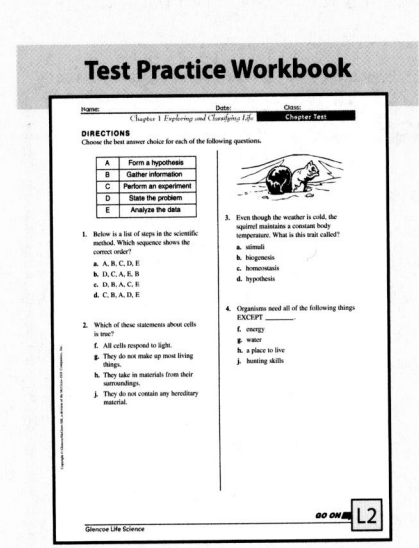

Name:                Date:        Class:
*Chapter 1 Exploring and Classifying Life*    **Chapter Test**

**DIRECTIONS**
Choose the best answer choice for each of the following questions.

| A | Form a hypothesis |
|---|---|
| B | Gather information |
| C | Perform an experiment |
| D | State the problem |
| E | Analyze the data |

1. Below is a list of steps in the scientific method. Which sequence shows the correct order?
   a. A, B, C, D, E
   b. D, C, A, E, B
   c. D, B, A, C, E
   d. C, B, A, D, E

2. Which of these statements about cells is true?
   f. All cells respond to light.
   g. They do not make up most living things.
   h. They take in materials from their surroundings.
   j. They do not contain any hereditary material.

3. Even though the weather is cold, the squirrel maintains a constant body temperature. What is this trait called?
   a. stimuli
   b. biogenesis
   c. homeostasis
   d. hypothesis

4. Organisms need all of the following things EXCEPT _____
   f. energy
   g. water
   h. a place to live
   j. hunting skills

Glencoe Life Science                    **GO ON**  **L2**

### Chapter Review

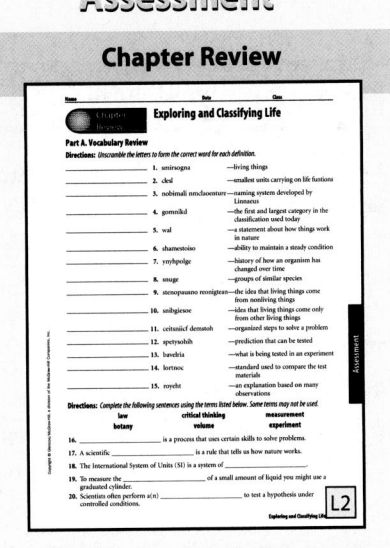

**Chapter Review**

**Exploring and Classifying Life**

**Part A. Vocabulary Review**

**Directions:** *Unscramble the letters to form the correct word for each definition.*

_____  1. smirosgnu    —living things
_____  2. cleol        —smallest units carrying on life fuctions
_____  3. nobimall nrmclaoomture—naming system developed by Linnaeus
_____  4. gommklid     —the first and largest category in the classification used today
_____  5. wal          —a statement about how things work in nature
_____  6. shamestoiso  —ability to maintain a steady condition
_____  7. rynhpolge    —history of how an organism has changed over time
_____  8. snuge        —groups of similar species
_____  9. stenopauano resnigtean—the idea that living things come only from other living things
_____ 10. snibgeosie   —idea that living things come only from nonliving things
_____ 11. ceitsincf dematoh—organized steps to solve a problem
_____ 12. spetrsuhiih  —prediction that can be tested
_____ 13. bavelria     —what is being tested in an experiment
_____ 14. lortnoc      —standard used to compare the test materials
_____ 15. royetht      —an explanation based on many observations

**Directions:** *Complete the following sentences using the terms listed below. Some terms may not be used.*

law    critical thinking    measurement
botany    volume    experiment

16. _____ is a process that uses certain skills to solve problems.
17. A scientific _____ is a rule that tells you how nature works.
18. The International System of Units (SI) is a system of _____
19. To measure the _____ of a small amount of liquid you might use a graduated cylinder.
20. Scientists often perform a(n) _____ to test a hypothesis under controlled conditions.

*Exploring and Classifying Life*

**L2**

### Chapter Tests

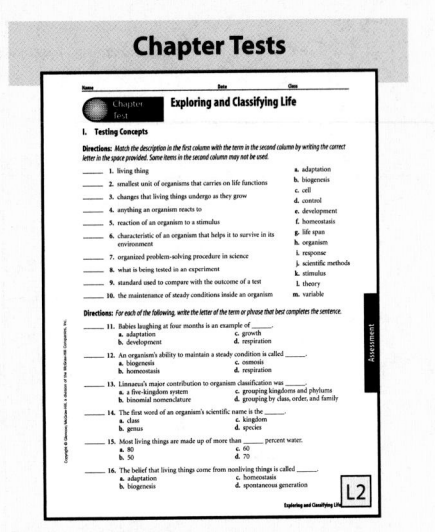

**Chapter Test**

**Exploring and Classifying Life**

**I.   Testing Concepts**

**Directions:** *Match the description in the first column with the term in the second column by writing the correct letter in the space provided. Some terms in the second column may not be used.*

_____  1. living thing                                         a. adaptation
_____  2. smallest unit of organisms that carries on life functions   b. biogenesis
_____  3. changes that living things undergo as they grow       c. cell
_____  4. anything an organism reacts to                        d. control
_____  5. reaction of an organism to a stimulus                 e. development
_____  6. characteristic of an organism that helps it to survive in its environment   f. homeostasis
_____  7. organized problem-solving procedure in science        g. life span
_____  8. what is being tested in an experiment                 h. organism
_____  9. standard used to compare with the outcome of a test   i. response
_____ 10. the maintenance of steady conditions inside an organism   j. scientific methods
                                                                k. stimulus
                                                                l. theory
                                                                m. variable

**Directions:** *For each of the following, write the letter of the term or phrase that best completes the sentence.*

11. Babies laughing at four months is an example of _____
    a. adaptation    c. growth
    b. development   d. respiration

12. An organism's ability to maintain a steady condition is called _____
    a. biogenesis    c. osmosis
    b. homeostasis   d. respiration

13. Linnaeus's major contribution to organism classification was _____
    a. a five-kingdom system    c. grouping kingdoms and phylums
    b. binomial nomenclature    d. grouping by class, order, and family

14. The first word of an organism's scientific name is the _____
    a. class    c. kingdom
    b. genus    d. species

15. Most living things are made up of more than _____ percent water.
    a. 40    c. 60
    b. 50    d. 70

16. The belief that living things come from nonliving things is called _____
    a. adaptation    c. homeostasis
    b. biogenesis    d. spontaneous generation

*Exploring and Classifying Life*

**L2**

# Science Content Background

**section 2** **Living Things**

**Living Versus Nonliving**

Living organisms consist of highly organized systems that interact and are dependent upon one another. Living systems require a constant source of energy. All living organisms have metabolic processes by which the energy in carbohydrates is released for use. All living organisms respond to their environment in adaptive ways, including physiological responses as well as behaviors. Living organisms also have a means of reproduction, growth, and development.

**section 4** **How are living things classified?**

**Modern Classification**

This textbook uses a combination of phenetics and cladistics to classify organisms. Phenetics is based on particular features. Cladistics uses shared, derived characteristics to classify organisms. By comparing DNA nucleotide sequences between species and by measuring the amount of bonding between DNA from different species, taxonomists infer the degree of similarity between organisms. Scientists hypothesize that organisms with similar proteins are closely related. A comparison of the amino acid sequences between species' proteins provides objective, quantitative data for taxonomists because the structure of proteins is genetically determined.

**Domains**

Most taxonomists currently divide the six-kingdom system into groups called domains. The three domains are Eubacteria, Archaea, and Eukarya. The domains Eubacteria and Archaea contain Kingdom Eubacteria and Kingdom Archaebacteria, respectively.

Kingdom Eubacteria and Kingdom Archaebacteria differ. Eubacteria have muramic acid in their cell walls, but archaebacteria do not. The RNA sequences of the two groups also differ.

Domain Eukarya contains four kingdoms—Kingdom Protista, Kingdom Fungi, Kingdom Plantae, and Kingdom Animalia.

**Scientific Names**

A system of classification avoids ambiguity among species, reflects the phylogeny (evolutionary history) of organisms, and provides clues about the organism's habits and possible features shared with similar organisms. The second word of a scientific name is called the specific epithet, usually an adjective that describes the organism, indicates the organism's place of origin, or is a Latinized surname to honor someone. Subspecies have two specific epithets.

## chapter content resources

**Internet Resources**

For additional content background, visit **in7.msscience.com** to:

- access your book online
- find references to related articles in popular science magazines
- access Web links with related content background
- access current events with science journal topics

**Print Resources**

*The Science of Life: Projects and Principles for Beginning Biologists,* by Frank G. Bottone, Chicago Review Press, 2001

*The Origins of Life,* by Roy A. Gallant, Marshall Cavendish, 2000

*Carl Linnaeus: Father of Classification,* by Margaret Jean Anderson, Enslow Publishers, 1997

*National Audubon Society First Field Guide: Reptiles,* by John L. Behler, Scholastic Inc., 1999

## IDENTIFYING ▷ Misconceptions

### Find Out What Students Think

**Students may think that . . .**

**All things that move are alive.**

Students generally define "living" according to the characteristics of large animals. Hence they associate "living" with movement. Students often do not consider plants and fungi to be alive because they do not appear to move, but may classify rivers or clouds as living because they do move. Students may add other mammalian characteristics to their definitions of life such as eating, breathing, or the presence of a heartbeat.

Clouding the concept further is the confusion between "nonliving" and "dead." Students may classify both a dead animal and a rock as "nonliving" objects, even though they classify animals in general as alive.

**Discussion**

Place a rock, a houseplant, and a living animal (such as a caged hamster or a volunteer student) in view of the class. Ask students if they think any of the three items are alive. As students respond, ask them why they think the item is or is not alive. From this, generate a list of characteristics that students believe belong to all living organisms. Students will probably recognize that the animal is alive. Some will understand that the plant is alive, but have difficulty explaining why. Most will know that the rock is not alive.

### Promote Understanding

**Activity**

Have the students read **Section 2** in this chapter, then review the list they generated in the discussion suggestion above. Ask the students if they want to change anything on the list.

Next, place a candle in full view of the class and light it. Ask students if they think the flame is alive. Then do the following:

- Blow gently on the flame to show that it responds.

- Light another candle or a match from the flame to show that the flame can reproduce.

- Point out that the wax of the candle is being consumed, showing that the flame uses energy.

Remind students that many nonliving things have some characteristics of living things.

- Ask the class what characteristics the candle flame lacks. Students should recognize that the flame is not highly organized, it is not made up of organic molecules, and it contains no cells. L2

### Assess

After completing the chapter, see *Identifying Misconceptions* in the Study Guide at the end of the chapter.

## Chapter Vocabulary

**Science Journal** Students' answers will vary. Characteristics might include method of movement, shape of body, and what they eat.

**PowerPoint® Presentations**

This CD-ROM is an editable Microsoft® PowerPoint® presentation that includes:
- a pre-made presentation for every chapter
- interactive graphics
- animations
- audio clips
- image bank
- all new section and chapter questions
- Standardized Test Practice
- transparencies
- pre-lab questions for all labs
- Foldables directions
- links to in7.msscience.com

**Academic Standard—4:** Students begin to trace the flow of matter and energy through ecosystems. They recognize the fundamental difference between plants and animals and understand its basis at the cellular level. Students distinguish species, particularly through an examination of internal structures and functions. They use microscopes to observe cells and recognize that cells function in similar ways in all organisms.

**Also covers:** Academic Standards 1, 2, 5 (Detailed standards begin on page IN8.)

# Exploring and Classifying Life

## chapter preview

**sections**

**1** What is science?

**2** Living Things

**3** Where does life come from?

**4** How are living things classified?
  *Lab* Classifying Seeds
  *Lab* Using Scientific Methods
  *Virtual Lab* How are living things classified into groups?

4

## Life Under the Sea

This picture contains many living things—including living coral. These living things have both common characteristics and differences. Scientists classify life according to similarities.

**Science Journal** List three characteristics that you would use to classify underwater life.

## Theme Connection

**Systems and Interactions** Scientists have devised systems for classifying organisms. These systems use an organism's traits, which have changed over time often as a result of natural selection as organisms interact with the environment.

### About the Photo

**Diversity of Life** The diver is surrounded by a wide variety of living organisms. Some are easily recognizable as living, while others may look more like nonliving rocks. While all the organisms, including the diver, share characteristics that classify them as living, those that are more closely classified share the most characteristics.

# Start-Up Activities

## Classify Organisms

Life scientists discover, describe, and name hundreds of organisms every year. How do they decide if a certain plant belongs to the iris or orchid family of flowering plants, or if an insect is more like a grasshopper or a beetle?

1. Observe the organisms on the opposite page or in an insect collection in your class.
2. Decide which feature could be used to separate the organisms into two groups, then sort the organisms into the two groups.
3. Continue to make new groups using different features until each organism is in a category by itself.
4. **Think Critically** How do you think scientists classify living things? List your ideas in your Science Journal.

 Preview this chapter's content and activities at in7.msscience.com

**Vocabulary** Make the following Foldable to help you understand the vocabulary terms in this chapter.

**STEP 1** Fold a vertical sheet of notebook paper from side to side.

**STEP 2** Cut along every third line of only the top layer to form tabs.

**STEP 3** Label each tab.

**Build Vocabulary** As you read the chapter, write the vocabulary words on the tabs. As you learn the definitions, write them under the tab for each vocabulary word.

**Bellringer**

**Section Focus Transparencies** also are available on the Interactive Chalkboard CD-ROM.

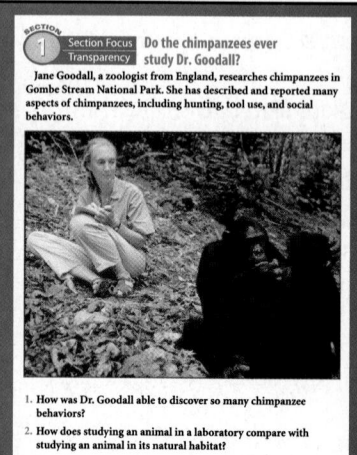

SECTION 1 Section Focus Transparency

**Do the chimpanzees ever study Dr. Goodall?**

Jane Goodall, a zoologist from England, researches chimpanzees in Gombe Stream National Park. She has described and reported many aspects of chimpanzees, including hunting, tool use, and social behaviors.

1. How was Dr. Goodall able to discover so many chimpanzee behaviors?
2. How does studying an animal in a laboratory compare with studying an animal in its natural habitat?

Exploring and Classifying Life

## Tie to Prior Knowledge

**Daily Decisions** Students use problem-solving skills daily. Discuss how they solve everyday problems, such as deciding what outfit to wear or how to manage homework with extra-curricular activities. Relate solving everyday problems to scientific methods.

## Text Question Answer

bacteria

**Standards—7.1.1:** Recognize and explain that when similar investigations give different results, the scientific challenge is to judge whether the differences are trivial or significant, which often takes further studies to decide. **7.1.3:** Explain why it is important in science to keep honest, clear, and accurate records.

**Also covers:** 7.1.4, 7.1.8 (Detailed standards begin on page IN8.)

# section 1

# What is science?

## as you read

### *What* You'll Learn

- **Apply** scientific methods to problem solving.
- **Demonstrate** how to measure using scientific units.

### *Why* It's Important

Learning to use scientific methods will help you solve ordinary problems in your life.

### ⊙ Review Vocabulary

**experiment:** using controlled conditions to test a prediction

### New Vocabulary

- ● scientific methods
- ● hypothesis
- ● control
- ● variable
- ● theory
- ● law

## The Work of Science

Movies and popcorn seem to go together. So before you and your friends watch a movie, sometimes you pop some corn in a microwave oven. When the popping stops, you take out the bag and open it carefully. You smell the mouthwatering, freshly popped corn and avoid hot steam that escapes from the bag. What makes the popcorn pop? How do microwaves work and make things hot? By the way, what are microwaves anyway?

Asking questions like these is one way scientists find out about anything in the world and the universe. Science is often described as an organized way of studying things and finding answers to questions.

**Types of Science** Many types of science exist. Each is given a name to describe what is being studied. For example, energy and matter have a relationship. That's a topic for physics. A physicist could answer most questions about microwaves.

On the other hand, a life scientist might study any of the millions of different animals, plants, and other living things on Earth. Look at the objects in **Figure 1.** What do they look like to you? A life scientist could tell you that some of the objects are living plants and some are just rocks. Life scientists who study plants are botanists, and those who study animals are zoologists. What do you suppose a bacteriologist studies?

**Figure 1** Examine the picture carefully. Some of these objects are actually *Lithops* plants. They commonly are called stone plants and are native to deserts in South Africa.

**6 CHAPTER 1**

## Section 1 Resource Manager

**Chapter *FAST FILE* Resources**
Transparency Activity, p. 44
Directed Reading for Content Mastery, pp. 17, 18
Note-taking Worksheets, pp. 33–35
MiniLAB, p. 3

Reinforcement, p. 25
Enrichment, p. 29
Lab Activity, pp. 9–10
**Life Science Critical Thinking/Problem Solving,** p. 4
**Mathematics Skill Activities,** p. 33
**Reading and Writing Skill Activities,** pp. 17, 33

## Critical Thinking

Whether or not you become a trained scientist, you are going to solve problems all your life. You probably solve many problems every day when you sort out ideas about what will or won't work. Suppose your CD player stops playing music. To figure out what happened, you have to think about it. That's called critical thinking, and it's the way you use skills to solve problems.

If you know that the CD player does not run on batteries and must be plugged in to work, that's the first thing you check to solve the problem. You check and the player is plugged in so you eliminate that possible solution. You separate important information from unimportant information—that's a skill. Could there be something wrong with the first outlet? You plug the player into a different outlet, and your CD starts playing. You now know that it's the first outlet that doesn't work. Identifying the problem is another skill you have.

## Solving Problems

Scientists use the same types of skills that you do to solve problems and answer questions. Although scientists don't always find the answers to their questions, they always use critical thinking in their search. Besides critical thinking, solving a problem requires organization. In science, this organization often takes the form of a series of procedures called **scientific methods. Figure 2** shows one way that scientific methods might be used to solve a problem.

**State the Problem** Suppose a veterinary technician wanted to find out whether different types of cat litter cause irritation to cats' skin. What would she do first? The technician begins by observing something she cannot explain. A pet owner brings his four cats to the clinic to be boarded while he travels. He leaves his cell phone number so he can be contacted if any problems arise. When they first arrive, the four cats seem healthy. The next day however, the technician notices that two of the cats are scratching and chewing at their skin. By the third day, these same two cats have bare patches of skin with red sores. The technician decides that something in the cats' surroundings or their food might be irritating their skin.

**Figure 2** The series of procedures shown below is one way to use scientific methods to solve a problem.

SECTION 1 What is science? **7**

### 2 | Teach

**Activity**

**Life Scientists** Divide the class into small groups. Ask: What do you think life scientists do? Where might they work? Allow time for groups to discuss the questions and record their responses. Have each group use their results to write a Help Wanted advertisement seeking a life scientist. Ask groups to present their advertisements to the class.
[L2] COOP LEARN [IS] **Interpersonal**

### IDENTIFYING Misconceptions

**Science for Everybody** Science is often thought of as a discipline out of reach of most people. Many believe that only well-educated or specially trained people can practice science. Explain that science is a process of understanding and that anyone can use the methods of science in daily life.

## Visual Learning

**Figure 2** Are all the steps shown here always followed in the exact same sequence? No; if a hypothesis is not supported, the scientist starts over by forming a new hypothesis. Sometimes, only a few of the steps are used.

## Science Journal

**Critical-Thinking Log** Ask students to keep in their journals a log of instances in which they used critical thinking to solve problems. Logs should note the date, problem, and solution. At the end of one week, have students share their logs with classmates. Guide students in recognizing that critical thinking is a life skill. [L2] [IS] **Interpersonal** [P]

**Testing a Hypothesis**

**Materials** 2-L clear container, pond water

**Estimated Time** 20 minutes

**Procedure** Fill the container with pond water and place it in a well-lighted area. Have students write a hypothesis about how the water will appear in ten days. Collect the hypotheses and in ten days, have students check their hypotheses against the conditions in the jar.

## Fun Fact

Scientists use computer models to study how cloud cover affects Earth's climate.

## Caption Answer

**Figure 3** Accept any reasonable answers. Possible answers include: an observatory, space station, rain forest, or underwater.

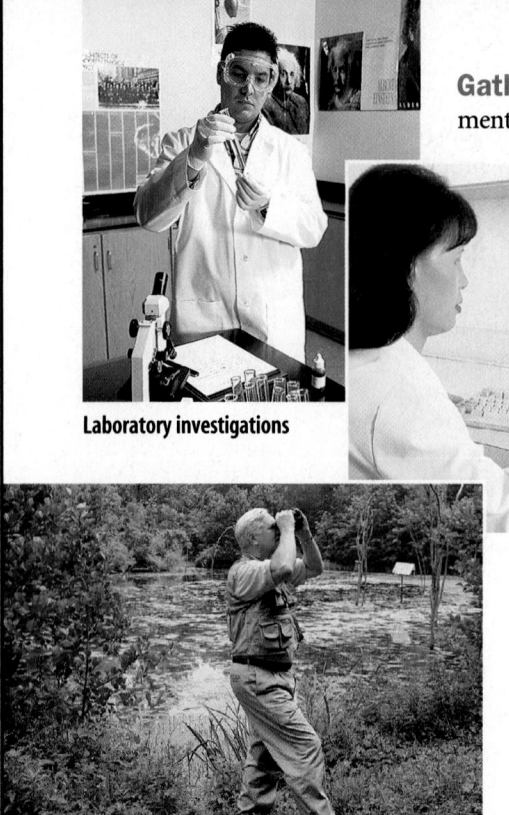

**Laboratory investigations**

**Computer models**

**Fieldwork**

**Figure 3** Observations can be made in many different settings. **List** *three other places where scientific observations can be made.*

**Science Online**

**Topic: Truth in Advertising**
Visit in7.msscience.com for Web links to information about celebrity endorsements.

**Activity** Find and print an advertisement with a celebrity endorsement. What qualification does this person have for endorsing the product? Have a discussion about the validity of celebrity endorsements.

**Gather Information** Laboratory observations and experiments are ways to collect information. Some data also are gathered from fieldwork. Fieldwork includes observations or experiments that are done outside of the laboratory. For example, the best way to find out how a bird builds a nest is to go outside and watch it. **Figure 3** shows some ways data can be gathered.

The technician gathers information about the problem by watching the cats closely for the next two days. She knows that cats sometimes change their behavior when they are in a new place. She wants to see if the behavior of the cats with the skin sores seems different from that of the other two cats. Other than the scratching and chewing at their skin, all four cats' behavior seems to be the same.

The technician calls the owner and tells him about the problem. She asks him what brand of cat food he feeds his cats. Because his brand is the same one used at the clinic, she decides that food is not the cause of the skin irritation. She decides that the cats probably are reacting to something in their surroundings. There are many things in the clinic that the cats might react to. How does she decide what it is?

During her observations she notices that the cats seem to scratch and chew themselves most after using their litter boxes. The cat litter used by the clinic contains a deodorant. The technician calls the owner and finds out that the cat litter he buys does not contain a deodorant.

**Form a Hypothesis** Based on this information, the next thing the veterinary technician does is form a hypothesis. A **hypothesis** is a prediction that can be tested. After discussing her observations with the clinic veterinarian, she hypothesizes that something in the cat litter is irritating the cats' skin.

**Test the Hypothesis with an Experiment** The technician gets the owner's permission to test her hypothesis by performing an experiment. In an experiment, the hypothesis is tested using controlled conditions. The technician reads the labels on two brands of cat litter and finds that the ingredients of each are the same except that one contains a deodorant.

**8 CHAPTER 1** Exploring and Classifying Life

## LAB DEMONSTRATION

**Purpose** to compare observations and inferences

**Materials** one red apple

**Alternate Materials** one purple grape for each student pair

**Preparation** Wash the fruit.

**Procedure** Have students record visual observations of the fruit and then classify the following statements as observations or inferences. 1. The apple's covering is red. 2. The apple is edible. 3. There are seeds inside the apple.

**Expected Outcome** 1 is an observation; 2 and 3 are inferences.

## Assessment

How are observations and inferences different? Observations are information gathered through the senses. Inferences result from past observations.
`L2`

**Controls** The technician separates the cats with sores from the other two cats. She puts each of the cats with sores in a cage by itself. One cat is called the experimental cat. This cat is given a litter box containing the cat litter without deodorant. The other cat is given a litter box that contains cat litter with deodorant. The cat with deodorant cat litter is the control.

A **control** is the standard to which the outcome of a test is compared. At the end of the experiment, the control cat will be compared with the experimental cat. Whether or not the cat litter contains deodorant is the variable. A **variable** is something in an experiment that can change. An experiment should have only one variable. Other than the difference in the cat litter, the technician treats both cats the same.

 **Reading Check** *How many variables should an experiment have?*

**Analyze Data** The veterinary technician observes both cats for one week. During this time, she collects data on how often and when the cats scratch or chew, as shown in **Figure 4**. These data are recorded in a journal. The data show that the control cat scratches and chews more often than the experimental cat does. The sores on the skin of the experimental cat begin to heal, but those on the control cat do not.

**Draw Conclusions** The technician then draws the conclusion—a logical answer to a question based on data and observation—that the deodorant in the cat litter probably irritated the skin of the two cats. To accept or reject the hypothesis is the next step. In this case, the technician accepts the hypothesis. If she had rejected it, new experiments would have been necessary.

Although the technician decides to accept her hypothesis, she realizes that to be surer of her results she should continue her experiment. She should switch the experimental cat with the control cat to see what the results are a second time. If she did this, the healed cat might develop new sores. She makes an ethical decision and chooses not to continue the experiment. Ethical decisions, like this one, are important in deciding what science should be done.

### Mini LAB

**Analyzing Data**

**Procedure**
1. Obtain a **pan balance**. Follow your teacher's instructions for using it.
2. Record all data in your **Science Journal**.
3. Measure and record the mass of a **dry sponge**.
4. Soak this sponge in **water**. Measure and record its mass.
5. Calculate how much water your sponge absorbed.
6. Combine the class data and calculate the average amount of water absorbed.

**Analysis**
What other information about the sponges might be important when analyzing the data from the entire class?

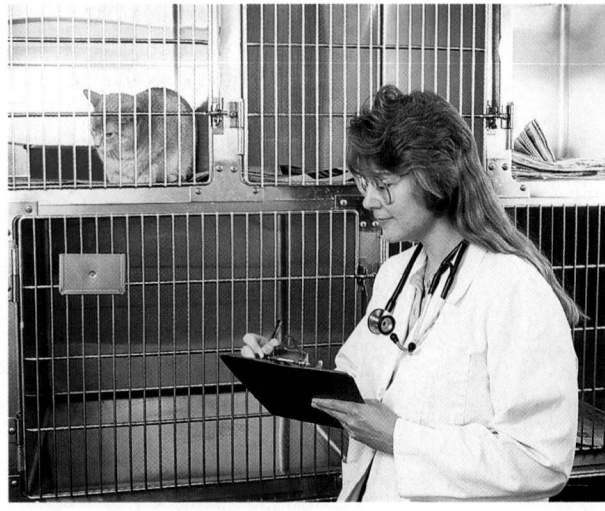

**Figure 4** Collecting and analyzing data is part of scientific methods.

## Reading Check

**Answer** scientific knowledge resulting from observations and experiments

**Figure 5** If data collected from several experiments over a period of time all support the hypothesis, it finally can be called a theory.

**Report Results** When using scientific methods, it is important to share information. The veterinary technician calls the cats' owner and tells him the results of her experiment. She tells him she has stopped using the deodorant cat litter.

The technician also writes a story for the clinic's newsletter that describes her experiment and shares her conclusions. She reports the limits of her experiment and explains that her results are not final. In science it is important to explain how an experiment can be made better if it is done again.

## Developing Theories

After scientists report the results of experiments supporting their hypotheses, the results can be used to propose a scientific theory. When you watch a magician do a trick you might decide you have an idea or "theory" about how the trick works. Is your idea just a hunch or a scientific theory? A scientific **theory** is an explanation of things or events based on scientific knowledge that is the result of many observations and experiments. It is not a guess or someone's opinion. Many scientists repeat the experiment. If the results always support the hypothesis, the hypothesis can be called a theory, as shown in **Figure 5.**

## Reading Check  *What is a theory based on?*

A theory usually explains many hypotheses. For example, an important theory in life sciences is the cell theory. Scientists made observations of cells and experimented for more than 100 years before enough information was collected to propose a theory. Hypotheses about cells in plants and animals are combined in the cell theory.

A valid theory raises many new questions. Data or information from new experiments might change conclusions and theories can change. Later in this chapter you will read about the theory of spontaneous generation and how this theory changed as scientists used experiments to study new hypotheses.

**Laws** A scientific **law** is a statement about how things work in nature that seems to be true all the time. Although laws can be modified as more information becomes known, they are less likely to change than theories. Laws tell you what will happen under certain conditions but do not necessarily explain why it happened. For example, in life science you might learn about laws of heredity. These laws explain how genes are inherited but do not explain how genes work. Due to the great variety of living things, laws that describe them are few. It is unlikely that a law about how all cells work will ever be developed.

## Active Reading

**Learning Journal** In this strategy, students analyze their own learning processes. Have students fold a paper in half. On the left, have them record what they have learned about a topic. On the right, have them record the page number of the text and any illustrations that helped them learn it. Have students write a Learning Journal about scientific methods.  L2

## Cultural Diversity

**Development of Cell Theory** One theory in life science that has been widely accepted by scientists is the cell theory. The cell theory originated through the work of English scientist Robert Hooke in 1665. Almost two hundred years later, the works of three German scientists—Matthias Schleiden, Theodor Schwann, and Rudolph Virchow—were incorporated to form the modern cell theory.

**Scientific Methods Help Answer Questions** You can use scientific methods to answer all sorts of questions. Your questions may be as simple as "Where did I leave my house key?" or as complex as "Will global warming cause the polar ice caps to melt?" You probably have had to find the answer to the first question. Someday you might try to find the answer to the second question. Using these scientific methods does not guarantee that you will get an answer. Often scientific methods just lead to more questions and more experiments. That's what science is about—continuing to look for the best answers to your questions.

## Applying Science

### Does temperature affect the rate of bacterial reproduction?

**S**ome bacteria make you sick. Other bacteria, however, are used to produce foods like cheese and yogurt. Understanding how quickly bacteria reproduce can help you avoid harmful bacteria and use helpful bacteria. It's important to know things that affect how quickly bacteria reproduce. How do you think temperature will affect the rate of bacterial reproduction? A student makes the hypothesis that bacteria will reproduce more quickly as the temperature increases.

#### Identifying the Problem

The table below lists the reproduction-doubling rates at specific temperatures for one type of bacteria. A rate of 2.0 means that the number of bacteria doubled two times that hour (e.g., 100 to 200 to 400).

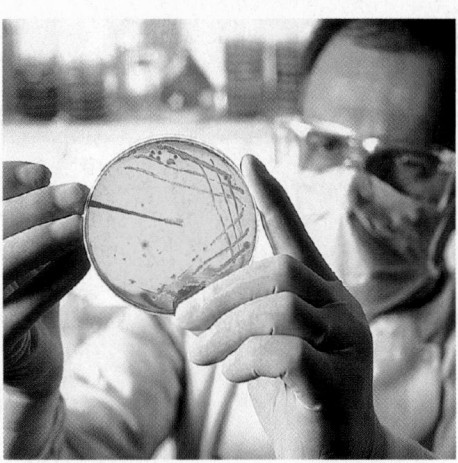

Look at the table. What conclusions can you draw from the data?

#### Solving the Problem

1. Do the data in the table support the student's hypothesis?
2. How would you write a hypothesis about the relationship between bacterial reproduction and temperature?
3. Make a list of other factors that might have influenced the results in the table.
4. Are you satisfied with these data? List other things that you wish you knew.
5. Describe an experiment that would help you test these other ideas.

| Bacterial Reproductive Rates | |
|---|---|
| Temperature (°C) | Doubling Rate per Hour |
| 20.5 | 2.0 |
| 30.5 | 3.0 |
| 36.0 | 2.5 |
| 39.2 | 1.2 |

**Measuring Coins**

**Materials** nickel, dime, other coins, calipers, triple-beam balance

**Estimated Time** 20 minutes

**Procedure** Show students a nickel and a dime. Tell them the nickel has a mass of about 5 g and the dime is 1 mm thick. Using a triple-beam balance and calipers, have students determine the mass and thickness of other coins they have. L2

## IDENTIFYING Misconceptions

**Gravity and Weight** Students may not understand that the weight of an object can vary, depending on the force of gravity. Explain that an object on the moon weighs less than an object on Earth because the pull of gravity is weaker on the moon than on Earth. However, the amount of matter (mass) that makes up the object does not change with location.

### ✔ Reading Check

**Answer** to be able to repeat an experiment; to have valid results

## Discussion

**Safety Symbols** What is the purpose of safety symbols? Each safety symbol alerts experimenters to a potential danger associated with a particular situation. L2

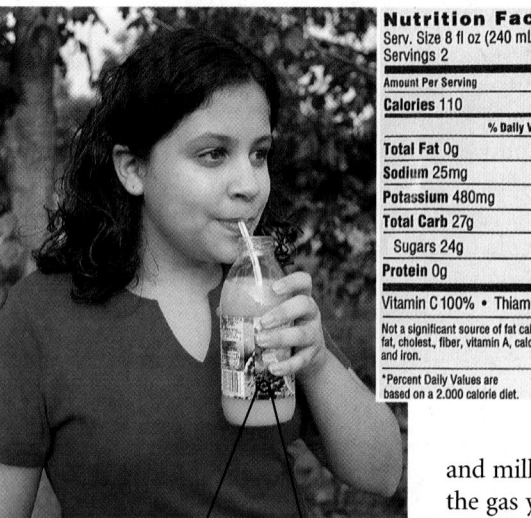

**Figure 6** Your food often is measured in metric units. Nutritional information on the label is listed in grams or milligrams.

The label of this juice bottle shows you that it contains 473 mL of juice.

## Measuring with Scientific Units

An important part of most scientific investigations is making accurate measurements. Think about things you use every day that are measured. Ingredients in your hamburger, hot dog, potato chips, or soft drink are measured in units such as grams and milliliters, as shown in **Figure 6.** The water you drink, the gas you use, and the electricity needed for a CD player are measured, too.

### ✔ Reading Check
*Why is it important to make accurate measurements?*

In your classroom or laboratory this year, you will use the same standard system of measurement scientists use to communicate and understand each other's research and results. This system is called the International System of Units, or SI. For example, you may need to calculate the distance a bird flies in kilometers. Perhaps you will be asked to measure the amount of air your lungs can hold in liters or the mass of an automobile in kilograms. Some of the SI units are shown in **Table 1.**

### Table 1  Common SI Measurements

| Measurement | Unit | Symbol | Equal to |
|---|---|---|---|
| Length | 1 millimeter | mm | 0.001 (1/1,000) m |
|  | 1 centimeter | cm | 0.01 (1/100) m |
|  | 1 meter | m | 100 cm |
|  | 1 kilometer | km | 1,000 m |
| Volume | 1 milliliter | mL | 0.001 (1/1,000) L |
|  | 1 liter | L | 1,000 mL |
| Mass | 1 gram | g | 1,000 mg |
|  | 1 kilogram | kg | 1,000 g |
|  | 1 tonne | t | 1,000 kg = 1 metric ton |

## Teacher FYI

**SI in the U.S.** The U.S. is the only industrialized country that has not officially adopted SI. To compete in world markets, many products made in the U.S. are labeled in SI and customary units. Students can hunt for five items from their homes marked with both types of measures.

## Cultural Diversity

**Ancient Measurements** The ancient Chinese system of weights and measures included an acoustical dimension. The quantity of content in a vessel was defined by both weight and by the pitch produced when the vessel was struck. Have students research and report on other measurement instruments and systems. Students might investigate the cubit and thermoscope or the history of the metric system. L3

## Safety First

Doing science is usually much more interesting than just reading about it. Some of the scientific equipment that you will use in your classroom or laboratory is the same as what scientists use. Laboratory safety is important. In many states, a student can participate in a laboratory class only when wearing proper eye protection. Don't forget to wash your hands after handling materials. Following safety rules, as shown in **Figure 7,** will protect you and others from injury during your lab experiences. Symbols used throughout your text will alert you to situations that require special attention. Some of these symbols are shown below. A description of each symbol is in the Safety Symbols chart at the front of this book.

**Caption Answer**
**Figure 7** something might accidentally enter the eye and cause permanent damage resulting in a loss of vision

**Figure 7** Proper eye protection should be worn whenever you see this safety symbol.
**Predict** *what might happen if you do not wear eye protection in the lab.*

### section 1 review

#### Summary

**The Work of Science**
- Science is an organized way of studying things and finding answers to questions.

**Solving Problems and Developing Theories**
- Scientific methods are procedures used to solve problems and answer questions.
- A theory is an explanation based on many scientific observations.

**Measuring with Scientific Units**
- Scientists use the SI system for measurements.

**Safety First**
- Follow safety rules in the lab.

#### Self Check

1. **Describe** scientific methods.
2. **Infer** why it is important to test only one variable at a time during an experiment.
3. **Identify** the SI unit you would use to measure the width of your classroom.
4. **Compare and contrast** a theory with a hypothesis.
5. **Think Critically** Can the veterinary technician in this section be sure that deodorant caused the cats' skin problems? How could she improve her experiment?

##### Applying Skills

6. **Write a paper** that explains what the veterinary technician discovered from her experiment.

**Science Online** in7.msscience.com/self_check_quiz

SECTION 1 What is science? **13**

#### DAILY INTERVENTION

**Check for Understanding**
**Intrapersonal** Have students make a set of flash cards they can use to review important terms from this section. [L1]

**Reteach**
**Scientific Methods** Divide the class into groups. Give each student in a group a slip of paper labeled with a step of a scientific method. After all the papers have been distributed, have students arrange themselves in a line that shows the order in which the steps are often carried out. Have groups compare their results and discuss why each group may not necessarily have the steps in the same order. [L2]

#### ✓ Assessment

**Portfolio** Safety is just as important at home as it is in the laboratory. For each safety symbol in the chart at the front of the book, have students write one safety rule to follow at home in the kitchen, bathroom, or outdoors. Use **Performance Assessment in the Science Classroom,** p. 157. [L1]

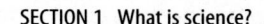

### section 1 review

1. State the problem, gather information, form a hypothesis, experiment to test the hypothesis, analyze data, and draw conclusions.
2. so the scientist can understand which condition caused the results
3. meters
4. theory—an explanation based on many observations; hypothesis—
   a testable prediction
5. Possible answer: Both cats may not be allergic to the same thing. She could repeat the experiment, this time giving the other cat non-deodorized litter. If the skin problem clears up, she has likely identified the problem.
6. The paper should include observations that led to stating the problem, how she gathered the information to form the hypothesis, how she experimented to test the hypothesis, analyzed the data, drew conclusions, and reported the results.

Standards—**7.4.5:** Explain that the basic functions of organisms . . . are carried out within the cell and understand that the way which cells function is similar in all organisms. **7.4.6:** Explain how food provides the fuel and the building material for all organisms. **7.4.8:** Describe how organisms that eat plants break down the plant structures to produce the materials and energy that they need to survive . . .

Also covers: 7.4.1, 7.4.4, 7.4.9 (Detailed standards begin on page IN8.)

**section**

**2**

# Living Things

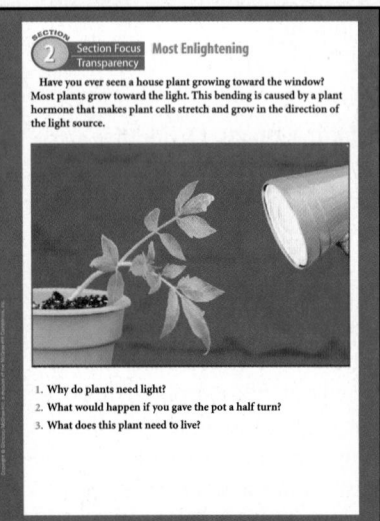
**as you read**

### *What* You'll Learn
■ **Distinguish** between living and nonliving things.
■ **Identify** what living things need to survive.

### *Why* It's Important
All living things, including you, have many of the same traits.

### Review Vocabulary
**raw materials:** substances needed by organisms to make other necessary substances

### New Vocabulary
● organism
● cell
● homeostasis

## What are living things like?

What does it mean to be alive? If you walked down your street after a thunderstorm, you'd probably see earthworms on the sidewalk, birds flying, clouds moving across the sky, and puddles of water. You'd see living and nonliving things that are alike in some ways. For example, birds and clouds move. Earthworms and water feel wet when they are touched. Yet, clouds and water are nonliving things, and birds and earthworms are living things. Any living thing is called an **organism.**

Organisms vary in size from the microscopic bacteria in mud puddles to gigantic oak trees and are found just about everywhere. They have different behaviors and food needs. In spite of these differences, all organisms have similar traits. These traits determine what it means to be alive.

**Living Things Are Organized** If you were to look at almost any part of an organism, like a plant leaf or your skin, under a microscope, you would see that it is made up of small units called cells. A **cell** is the smallest unit of an organism that carries on the functions of life. Some organisms are composed of just one cell while others are composed of many cells. Cells take in materials from their surroundings and use them in complex ways. Each cell has an orderly structure and contains hereditary material. The hereditary material contains instructions for cellular organization and function. **Figure 8** shows some organisms that are made of many cells. All the things that these organisms can do are possible because of what their cells can do.

**Muscle cells**

Color-enhanced LM Magnification: 106×

**Nerve cells**

**Figure 8** Your body is organized into many different types of cells. Two types are shown here.

Color-enhanced SEM Magnification: 2500×

**Living Things Respond** Living things interact with their surroundings. Watch your cat when you use your electric can opener. Does your cat come running to find out what's happening even when you're not opening a can of cat food? The cat in **Figure 9** ran in response to a stimulus—the sound of the can opener. Anything that causes some change in an organism is a stimulus (plural, *stimuli*). The reaction to a stimulus is a response. Often that response results in movement, such as when the cat runs toward the sound of the can opener. To carry on its daily activity and to survive, an organism must respond to stimuli.

Living things also respond to stimuli that occur inside them. For example, water or food levels in organisms' cells can increase or decrease. The organisms then make internal changes to keep the right amounts of water and food in their cells. Their temperature also must be within a certain range. An organism's ability to keep the proper conditions inside no matter what is going on outside the organism is called **homeostasis.** Homeostasis is a trait of all living things.

 **Reading Check** *What are some internal stimuli living things respond to?*

**Living Things Use Energy** Staying organized and carrying on activities like homeostasis require energy. The energy used by most organisms comes either directly or indirectly from the Sun. Plants and some other organisms use the Sun's energy and the raw materials carbon dioxide and water to make food. You and most other organisms can't use the energy of sunlight directly. Instead, you take in and use food as a source of energy. You get food by eating plants or other organisms that ate plants. Most organisms, including plants, also must take in oxygen in order to release the energy of foods.

Some bacteria live at the bottom of the oceans and in other areas where sunlight cannot reach. They can't use the Sun's energy to produce food. Instead, the bacteria use energy stored in some chemical compounds and the raw material carbon dioxide to make food. Unlike most other organisms, many of these bacteria do not need oxygen to release the energy that is found in their food.

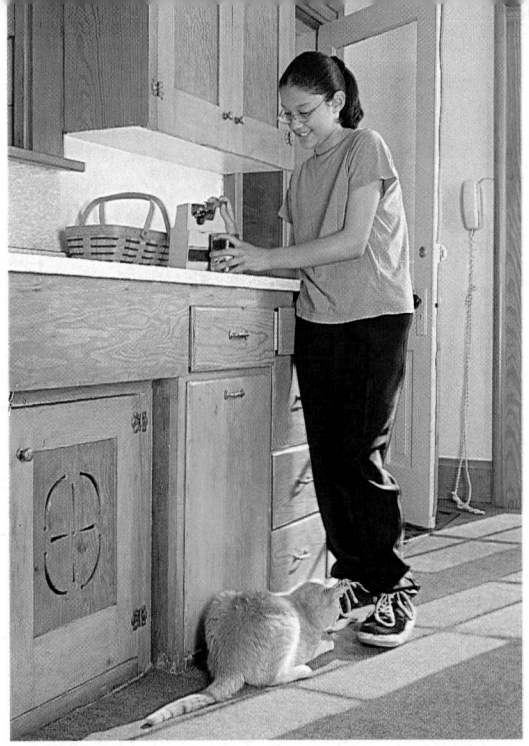

**Figure 9** Some cats respond to a food stimulus even when they are not hungry.
**Infer** why a cat comes running when it hears a can opener.

**Science Online**

**Topic: Homeostasis**
Visit in7.msscience.com for Web links to information about homeostasis.

**Activity** Describe the external stimuli and the corresponding internal changes for three different situations.

SECTION 2  Living Things  **15**

## 2 Teach

**Quick Demo**
**Plant Responses**
**Materials** mimosa plant
**Estimated Time** 5 minutes
**Procedure** Responses in plants are usually less obvious than in animals. However, if you touch a mimosa plant, all the small leaflets on the branch fold upward. Use a mimosa plant to demonstrate this rapid response.

**Caption Answer**
**Figure 9** The cat is responding to the stimulus of the sound of the can opener which means food to the cat.

 **Reading Check**

**Answer** water and food levels, temperature

**Use an Analogy**
**Car Necessities** Compare the homeostasis that must be maintained by the body to the conditions necessary for a car to function. For example, a car must have fuel, oil, and other fluids in proper balance in order to run. In the same way, organisms must have fuel and other materials in order to remain alive. L2

## Differentiated Instruction

**Learning Disabled** Have students choose and draw a scene on poster board or mural paper. Have them label the objects in the drawing as living or nonliving. L1 **Visual-Spatial**

## Fun Fact

Some bacteria can use petroleum as a food source. These bacteria have been used to help clean up oil spills.

**Seed Development** How does an acorn grow and develop? An acorn sprouts and produces roots, stems, and leaves that continue to grow for years. As it grows, it takes in substances from the air and soil and changes those substances into living cells. It continues to add new cells and tissues to replace those that wear out. L2

## Misconceptions

**Nonliving Movement** Students may think that all things that move are alive. Refer to page F at the beginning of this chapter for teaching strategies that address this misconception.

## Teacher FYI

**Energy Uses** Nonliving things use energy just as living things do. Windmills, solar calculators, solar panels, and thunderclouds all use energy from their environments and change it into different forms. However, living things take in energy from their environments and use it for specialized purposes such as growth, development, and reproduction.

---

**Indiana Academic Standard Check**

**7.4.5:** Explain that the basic functions of organisms . . . are carried out within the cell . . .

✓ How does a one-celled organism grow?

✓ Its cell size increases.

**Figure 10** Complete development of an organism can take a few days or several years. The pictures below show the development of a dog, a human, a pea plant, and a butterfly.

---

**Living Things Grow and Develop** When a puppy is born, it might be small enough to hold in one hand. After the same dog is fully grown, you might not be able to hold it at all. How does this happen? The puppy grows by taking in raw materials, like milk from its female parent, and making more cells. Growth of many-celled organisms, such as the puppy, is mostly due to an increase in the number of cells. In one-celled organisms, growth is due to an increase in the size of the cell.

Organisms change as they grow. Puppies can't see or walk when they are born. In eight or nine days, their eyes open, and their legs become strong enough to hold them up. All of the changes that take place during the life of an organism are called development. **Figure 10** shows how four different organisms changed as they grew.

The length of time an organism is expected to live is its life span. Dogs can live for 20 years and a cat for 25 years. Some organisms have a short life span. Mayflies live only one day, but a land tortoise can live for more than 180 years. Some bristlecone pine trees have been alive for more than 4,600 years. Your life span is about 80 years.

---

## Science Journal

**Characteristics of Living Things** Have students choose an animal that they have observed. In their Science Journals, have them write an essay explaining how their observations show that the animal is a living organism. L1 IS **Linguistic**

## Curriculum Connection

**Math** Have students obtain data that illustrates how they have changed as they have grown older. Ask them to research their heights at three different ages. (If this information is not available at home, have students obtain the data from their school records.) Then have students work in pairs to measure their current heights. Ask students to present their results as bar graphs. L2 IS **Logical-Mathematical** P

**Figure 11** Living things reproduce themselves in many different ways. A *Paramecium* reproduces by dividing into two. Beetles, like most insects, reproduce by laying eggs. Every spore released by the puffballs can grow into a new fungus.

Beetle

*Paramecium* dividing
Color-enhanced LM
Magnification: 400×

Puffballs

**Living Things Reproduce** Cats, dogs, alligators, fish, birds, bees, and trees eventually reproduce. They make more of their own kind. Some bacteria reproduce every 20 minutes while it might take a pine tree two years to produce seeds. **Figure 11** shows some ways organisms reproduce.

Without reproduction, living things would not exist to replace those individuals that die. An individual cat can live its entire life without reproducing. However, if cats never reproduced, all cats soon would disappear.

**✓ Reading Check** *Why is reproduction important?*

## What do living things need?

What do you need to live? Do you have any needs that are different from those of other living things? To survive, all living things need a place to live and raw materials. The raw materials that they require and the exact place where they live can vary.

**A Place to Live** The environment limits where organisms can live. Not many kinds of organisms can live in extremely hot or extremely cold environments. Most cannot live at the bottom of the ocean or on the tops of mountains. All organisms also need living space in their surroundings. For example, thousands of penguins build their nests on an island. When the island becomes too crowded, the penguins fight for space and some may not find space to build nests. An organism's surroundings must provide for all of its needs.

**INTEGRATE Social Studies**

**Social Development** Human infants quickly develop their first year of life. Research to find out how infants interact socially at different stages of development. Make a chart that shows changes from birth to one year old.

## Visual Learning

**Figure 11** How do these organisms reproduce? Beetles lay eggs, a fungus releases spores, and a paramecium undergoes cell division to become two organisms. L2

**Activity**

**Illustrate Living Things** Label five sheets of paper with one of the subheads in this section. Divide the class into five groups. Give each group a sheet of paper. Ask group members to cut pictures from magazines that illustrate the subhead, to paste the pictures on the paper, and write a caption for each picture. When all groups have finished their tasks, combine the pages into a booklet titled "How Living Things Are Alike." L1 COOP LEARN

**✓ Reading Check**

**Answer** Organisms must reproduce to replace members of their species that die, or the species will become extinct.

**INTEGRATE Social Studies**

**Social Development** 1 month: movements are clumsy, throaty sounds can be made; 3 months: can sit up with assistance and laugh; 6 months: birth weight doubles, can roll over, sit alone and babble; 9 months: can crawl and repeat syllables; 1 year: birth weight triples, can walk and speak first words

## Teacher FYI

**Survival** All the characteristics of living things are needed for survival of the individual, except for reproduction. Reproduction is needed for survival of the species.

## Differentiated Instruction

**English-Language Learners** Have students name the characteristics and needs of living things that can be observed in a classroom aquarium or terrarium. Have them make a poster that shows two of the organisms and their characteristics. L1

## Caption Answer

**Figure 12** Plants take in water through their roots.

### DAILY INTERVENTION

#### Check for Understanding

**Linguistic** Have students use information in the chapter to compare and contrast characteristics of life of plants and animals. They should then write a paragraph concerning their findings. L2

#### Reteach

**Cards of Life** Write the characteristics of living things on 3" × 5" cards. Have students draw a card and give an example of the characteristic. L1

### ✔ Assessment

**Process** Have students heat water in a beaker and dissolve as much sugar in the beaker as they can. Tie a string around a stirring rod. Place the rod across the top of the beaker so the string is immersed in the cooled water. Leave the string in the beaker until sugar crystals begin to grow. Ask students why these crystals are not alive. They have none of the other characteristics of living things. Use **Performance Assessment in the Science Classroom,** p. 89. L1

**Figure 12** You and a corn plant each take in and give off about 2 L of water in a day. Most of the water you take in is from water you drink or from foods you eat. **Infer** *where plants get water to transport materials.*

**Raw Materials** Water is important for all living things. Plants and animals take in and give off large amounts of water each day, as shown in **Figure 12.** Organisms use homeostasis to balance the amounts of water lost with the amounts taken in. Most organisms are composed of more than 50 percent water. You are made of 60 to 70 percent water. Organisms use water for many things. For example, blood, which is about 90 percent water, transports digested food and wastes in animals. Plants have a watery sap that transports materials between roots and leaves.

Living things are made up of substances such as proteins, fats, and sugars. Animals take in most of these substances from the foods they eat. Plants and some bacteria make them using raw materials from their surroundings. These important substances are used over and over again. When organisms die, substances in their bodies are broken down and released into the soil or air. The substances can then be used again by other living organisms. Some of the substances in your body might once have been part of a butterfly or an apple tree.

At the beginning of this section, you learned that things such as clouds, sidewalks, and puddles of water are not living things. Now do you understand why? Clouds, sidewalks, and water do not reproduce, use energy, or have other traits of living things.

---

## section 2 review

### Summary

**What are living things like?**

- A cell is the smallest unit of an organism that carries on the functions of life.
- Anything that causes some change in an organism is a stimulus.
- Organisms use energy to stay organized and perform activities like homeostasis.
- All of the changes that take place during an organism's life are called development.

**What do living things need?**

- Living things need a place to live, water, and food.

### Self Check

1. **Identify** the source of energy for most organisms.
2. **List** five traits that most organisms have.
3. **Infer** why you would expect to see cells if you looked at a section of a mushroom cap under a microscope.
4. **Determine** what most organisms need to survive.
5. **Think Critically** Why is homeostasis important to organisms?

#### Applying Skills

6. **Use a Database** Use references to find the life span of ten animals. Use your computer to make a database. Then, graph the life spans from shortest to longest.

 **Science Online** in7.msscience.com/self_check_quiz

---

## section 2 review

1. the Sun
2. Living things are organized, respond, take in and use energy, grow and develop, and reproduce.
3. All living things are made of cells.
4. Organisms need raw materials and a place to live.
5. Without homeostasis—the maintaining of proper conditions inside an organism regardless of external conditions—the organism would die.
6. Life spans will vary in different references. Sample data (in years): humans: 76; horses: 30; cows: 24; dogs: 15; cats: 12; turtles: 125; elephants: 60; penguins: 23; shrews: 1; snakes: 11; spiders: 3

# section

# 3

# Where does life come from?

## Life Comes from Life

You've probably seen a fish tank, like the one in **Figure 13,** that is full of algae. How did the algae get there? Before the seventeenth century, some people thought that insects and fish came from mud, that earthworms fell from the sky when it rained, and that mice came from grain. These were logical conclusions at that time, based on repeated personal experiences. The idea that living things come from nonliving things is known as **spontaneous generation.** This idea became a theory that was accepted for several hundred years. When scientists began to use controlled experiments to test this theory, the theory changed.

**✔ Reading Check** *Why did the theory of spontaneous generation change?*

**Spontaneous Generation and Biogenesis** From the late seventeenth century through the middle of the eighteenth century, experiments were done to test the theory of spontaneous generation. Although these experiments showed that spontaneous generation did not occur in most cases, they did not disprove it entirely.

It was not until the mid-1800s that the work of Louis Pasteur, a French chemist, provided enough evidence to disprove the theory of spontaneous generation. It was replaced with **biogenesis** (bi oh JE nuh suss), which is the theory that living things come only from other living things.

### as you read

**What You'll Learn**
■ **Describe** experiments about spontaneous generation.
■ **Explain** how scientific methods led to the idea of biogenesis.

**Why It's Important**
You can use scientific methods to try to find out about events that happened long ago or just last week. You can even use them to predict how something will behave in the future.

**⊙ Review Vocabulary**
**contaminate:** to make impure by coming into contact with an unwanted substance

**New Vocabulary**
● spontaneous generation
● biogenesis

**Figure 13** The sides of this tank were clean and the water was clear when the aquarium was set up. Algal cells, which were not visible on plants and fish, reproduced in the tank. So many algal cells are present now that the water is cloudy.

SECTION 3   Where does life come from?   **19**

---

### Section 3 Resource Manager

**Chapter *FAST FILE* Resources**
Transparency Activity, p. 46
Directed Reading for Content Mastery, p. 19
Enrichment, p. 31
Reinforcement, p. 27

**Earth Science Critical Thinking/Problem Solving,** pp. 1, 12, 14

---

## Visualizing the Origins of Life

Have students examine the pictures and read the captions. Then ask the following questions.

**What are the similarities of Spallanzani's and Redi's work?** Students should note that both Spallanzani and Redi did experiments that questioned the idea of spontaneous generation.

**What must have been present in the neck of the S-necked flasks used by Pasteur in his experiments?** The necks of the S-neck flasks must have contained microorganisms, which contaminated the broth when the flask was tilted.

## Activity

**Matching Game** Students should work in small groups to create and play a matching game based on the scientists in the this feature and their work. In the game, points should be awarded for correctly matching a scientist with his work. Have students explain the rules of their game to the class.

### Fun Fact

A seventeenth-century recipe for mice called for sweaty underwear and wheat to be placed in an open container for 21 days.

## Visual Learning

**Figure 14** Have students create a poster showing the progression of scientific thought on life origins, as evidenced by the experiments in this feature.

---

**NATIONAL GEOGRAPHIC   VISUALIZING THE ORIGINS OF LIFE**

### Figure 14

For centuries scientists have theorized about the origins of life. As shown on this timeline, some examined spontaneous generation—the idea that nonliving material can produce life. More recently, scientists have proposed theories about the origins of life on Earth by testing hypotheses about conditions on early Earth.

**1668** Francesco Redi put decaying meat in some jars, then covered half of them. When fly maggots appeared only on the uncovered meat (see below, left), Redi concluded that they had hatched from fly eggs and had not come from the meat.

John Needham heated broth in sealed flasks. When **1745** the broth became cloudy with microorganisms, he mistakenly concluded that they developed spontaneously from the broth.

Lazzaro Spallanzani boiled **1768** broth in sealed flasks for a longer time than Needham did. Only the ones he opened became cloudy with contamination.

Not contaminated     Contaminated

Not contaminated

Contaminated

**1859** Louis Pasteur disproved spontaneous generation by boiling broth in S-necked flasks that were open to the air. The broth became cloudy (see above, bottom right) only when a flask was tilted and the broth was exposed to dust in the S-neck.

Gases of Earth's early atmosphere

Electric current

Oceanlike mixture forms

Cools

Materials in present-day cells

**1924** Alexander Oparin hypothesized that energy from the Sun, lightning, and Earth's heat triggered chemical reactions early in Earth's history. The newly-formed molecules washed into Earth's ancient oceans and became a part of what is often called the primordial soup.

Stanley Miller and Harold Urey sent electric currents **1953** through a mixture of gases like those thought to be in Earth's early atmosphere. When the gases cooled, they condensed to form an oceanlike liquid that contained materials such as amino acids, found in present-day cells.

**20   CHAPTER 1** Exploring and Classifying Life

---

## Differentiated Instruction

**Challenge** Have students research world events that occurred in the years the experiments shown in this feature took place. Students can construct an expanded time line showing these events, and share their findings with the class. L3

**Hearing Impaired** Have students pantomime the work of one of the scientists who studied life's origins. Other students must guess which scientist is being represented.

# Life's Origins

If living things can come only from other living things, how did life on Earth begin? Some scientists hypothesize that about 5 billion years ago, Earth's solar system was a whirling mass of gas and dust. They hypothesize that the Sun and planets were formed from this mass. It is estimated that Earth is about 4.6 billion years old. Rocks found in Australia that are more than 3.5 billion years old contain fossils of once-living organisms. Where did these living organisms come from?

**Oparin's Hypothesis** In 1924, a Russian scientist named Alexander I. Oparin suggested that Earth's early atmosphere had no oxygen but was made up of the gases ammonia, hydrogen, methane, and water vapor. Oparin hypothesized that these gases could have combined to form the more complex compounds found in living things.

Using gases and conditions that Oparin described, American scientists Stanley L. Miller and Harold Urey set up an experiment to test Oparin's hypothesis in 1953. Although the Miller-Urey experiment showed that chemicals found in living things could be produced, it did not prove that life began in this way.

For many centuries, scientists have tried to find the origins of life, as shown in **Figure 14.** Although questions about spontaneous generation have been answered, some scientists still are investigating ideas about life's origins.

**Oceans** Scientists hypothesize that Earth's oceans originally formed when water vapor was released into the atmosphere from many volcanic eruptions. Once it cooled, rain fell and filled Earth's lowland areas. Identify five lowland areas on Earth that are now filled with water. Record your answer in your Science Journal.

**Oceans** Students may list five of Earth's oceans and seas.

**Career** Explore the jobs of ocean-ographers and what they might study.

## 3 Assess

### DAILY INTERVENTION

**Check for Understanding**

**Interpersonal** Have groups of students write true and false statements concerning spontaneous generation and biogenesis and share them with each other. L2

**Reteach**

**Making Charts** Have students make a three-column chart to summarize the experiments described in this section. Columns should be headed *Experimenter, Summary of Experiment,* and *Conclusions.* L2 P

---

## section 3 review

### Summary

**Life Comes from Life**
- Spontaneous generation is the idea that living things come from nonliving things.
- The work of Louis Pasteur in 1859 disproved the theory of spontaneous generation.
- Biogenesis is the theory that living things come only from other living things.

**Life's Origins**
- Alexander I. Oparin hypothesized about the origin of life.
- The Miller-Urey experiment did not prove that Oparin's hypothesis was correct.

### Self Check

1. **Compare and contrast** spontaneous generation with biogenesis.
2. **Describe** three controlled experiments that helped disprove the theory of spontaneous generation and led to the theory of biogenesis.
3. **Summarize** the results of the Miller-Urey experiment.
4. **Think Critically** How do you think life on Earth began?

**Applying Skills**

5. **Draw Conclusions** Where could the organisms have come from in the 1768 broth experiment described in **Figure 14?**

 in7.msscience.com/self_check_quiz

SECTION 3 Where does life come from? **21**

---

## section 3 review

1. spontaneous generation: living things come from nonliving matter; biogenesis: living things come only from other living things of the same kind

2. Students should describe the experiments performed by Redi, Pasteur, and Spallanzani.

3. Miller and Urey passed electricity through gasses as suggested by Oparin's hypothesis and produced chemicals found in living things.

4. Students' answers will vary. Accept all reasonable responses.

5. The organisms could have come from the air.

## ✔ Assessment

**Performance** Have students review the results of Redi's experiment and write their interpretation. Jars left open to the air attracted flies, and maggots appeared on the meat. Flies could not get to the meat in the covered jars. Use **Performance Assessment in the Science Classroom,** p. 99.

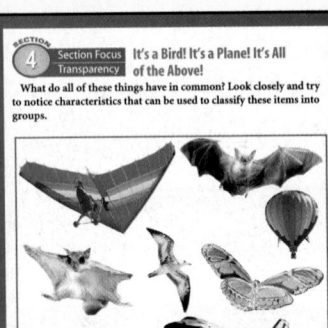
**Standards—7.4.1:** Explain that similarities among organisms are found in external ... features ... Understand that these similarities are used to classify organisms since they may be used to infer the degree of relatedness among organisms. **7.4.5:** Explain that the basic functions of organisms ... are carried out within the cell and understand that the way which cells function is similar in all organisms.

**Also covers:** 7.1.3, 7.2.7, 7.5.3 (Detailed standards begin on page IN8.)

# section 4

# How are living things classified?

## Classification

If you go to a library to find a book about the life of Louis Pasteur, where do you look? Do you look for it among the mystery or sports books? You expect to find a book about Pasteur's life with other biography books. Libraries group similar types of books together. When you place similar items together, you classify them. Organisms also are classified into groups.

**History of Classification** When did people begin to group similar organisms together? Early classifications included grouping plants that were used in medicines. Animals were often classified by human traits such as courageous—for lions—or wise—for owls.

More than 2,000 years ago, a Greek named Aristotle observed living things. He decided that any organism could be classified as either a plant or an animal. Then he broke these two groups into smaller groups. For example, animal categories included hair or no hair, four legs or fewer legs, and blood or no blood. **Figure 15** shows some of the organisms Aristotle would have grouped together. For hundreds of years after Aristotle, no one way of classifying was accepted by everyone.

**Figure 15** Using Aristotle's classification system, all animals without hair would be grouped together.
**List** *other animals without hair that Aristotle would have put in this group.*

**22 CHAPTER 1** Exploring and Classifying Life

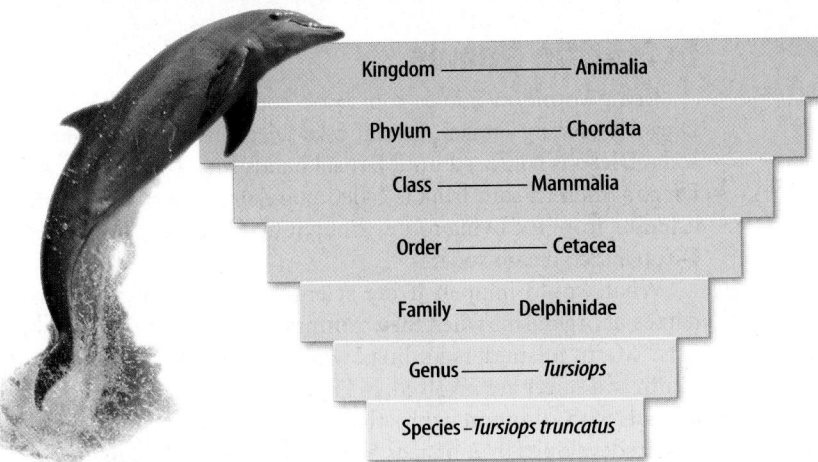

Kingdom ——————— Animalia

Phylum —————— Chordata

Class —————— Mammalia

Order —————— Cetacea

Family ———— Delphinidae

Genus ———— *Tursiops*

Species – *Tursiops truncatus*

**Figure 16** The classification of the bottlenosed dolphin shows that it is in the order Cetacea. This order includes whales and porpoises.

**Linnaeus** In the late eighteenth century, Carolus Linnaeus, a Swedish naturalist, developed a new system of grouping organisms. His classification system was based on looking for organisms with similar structures. For example, plants that had similar flower structure were grouped together. Linnaeus's system eventually was accepted and used by most other scientists.

**Modern Classification** Like Linnaeus, modern scientists use similarities in structure to classify organisms. They also use similiarities in both external and internal features. Specific characteristics at the cellular level, such as the number of chromosomes, can be used to infer the degree of relatedness among organisms. In addition, scientists study fossils, hereditary information, and early stages of development. They use all of this information to determine an organism's phylogeny. **Phylogeny** (fi LAH juh nee) is the evolutionary history of an organism, or how it has changed over time. Today, it is the basis for the classification of many organisms.

✔ **Reading Check** *What information would a scientist use to determine an organism's phylogeny?*

**Six Kingdoms** A classification system commonly used today groups organisms into six kingdoms. A **kingdom** is the first and largest category. Organisms are placed into kingdoms based on various characteristics. Kingdoms can be divided into smaller groups. The smallest classification category is a species. Organisms that belong to the same species can mate and produce fertile offspring. To understand how an organism is classified, look at the classification of the bottle-nosed dolphin in **Figure 16**. Some scientists propose that before organisms are grouped into kingdoms, they should be placed in larger groups called domains. One proposed system groups all organisms into three domains.

**Indiana Academic Standard Check**

**7.4.1:** Explain that similarities among organisms are found in external . . . features . . . Understand that these similarities are used to classify organisms . . .

✔ What plant feature did Linnaeus use for his classification system?

✔ flower structure

**Topic: Domains**
Visit in7.msscience.com for Web links to information about domains.

**Activity** List all the domains and give examples of organisms that are grouped in each domain.

SECTION 4 How are living things classified? **23**

SECTION 4 How are living things classified? **23**

---

## Inquiry Lab

**Classifying with Bones**

**Question** While excavating for a new building, the skeleton of a large animal is found. How could scientists determine the classification of this animal?

**Possible Materials** photos of skeletons of mammoth, elephant, dinosaurs, and other large animals; real or model skeletons of smaller animals; books concerning fossils and animal structure

**Estimated Time** 1 class session

**Teaching Strategies**

• Students can look at photos of animal skeletons and determine how to use them to gain information about classification.

• Students can compare photos of mammoth and elephant skeletons and note similarities.

• Students can hypothesize what animals would have similar skeletons and then use pictures or bones of the animals to collect data; they can research to find out what scientists think.

• A trip to a museum may be planned to look at skeletons of larger animals. L2

**For additional inquiry activities, see** *Science Inquiry Labs.*

✔ **Reading Check**

**Answer** similar structures, fossils, hereditary information, and early stages of development

---

## Fun Fact

Amber is the hardened resin of some trees. Some amber contains fossils of insects that became trapped in the resin.

## Differentiated Instruction

**English-Language Learners** Have students listen to a variety of songs and determine how the songs might be classified into different categories. L2

# Scientific Names

Using common names can cause confusion. Suppose that Diego is visiting Jamaal. Jamaal asks Diego if he would like a soda. Diego is confused until Jamaal hands him a soft drink. At Diego's house, a soft drink is called pop. Jamaal's grandmother, listening from the living room, thought that Jamaal was offering Diego an ice-cream soda.

What would happen if life scientists used only common names of organisms when they communicated with other scientists? Many misunderstandings would occur, and sometimes health and safety are involved. In **Figure 17,** you see examples of animals with common names that can be misleading. A naming system developed by Linnaeus helped solve this problem. It gave each species a unique, two-word scientific name.

**Figure 17** Common names can be misleading.

**Binomial Nomenclature** The two-word naming system that Linnaeus used to name the various species is called **binomial nomenclature** (bi NOH mee ul • NOH mun klay chur). It is the system used by modern scientists to name organisms. The first word of the two-word name identifies the genus of the organism. A **genus** is a group of similar species. The second word of the name might tell you something about the organism—what it looks like, where it is found, or who discovered it.

In this system, the tree species commonly known as red maple has been given the name *Acer rubrum.* The maple genus is *Acer.* The word *rubrum* is Latin for red, which is the color of a red maple's leaves in the fall. The scientific name of another maple is *Acer saccharum.* The Latin word for sugar is *saccharum.* In the spring, the sap of this tree is sweet.

Sea lions are more closely related to seals than to lions. **Identify** *another misleading common name.*

Jellyfish are neither fish nor jelly.

**Figure 18** These two lizards have the same common name, iguana, but are two different species.

## Uses of Scientific Names

Two-word scientific names are used for four reasons. First, they help avoid mistakes. Both of the lizards shown in **Figure 18** have the name *iguana*. Using binomial nomenclature, the green iguana is named *Iguana iguana*. Someone who studied this *iguana*, shown in the left photo, would not be confused by information he or she read about *Dispsosaurus dorsalis*, the desert iguana, shown in the right photo. Second, organisms with similar evolutionary histories are classified together. Because of this, you know that organisms in the same genus are related. Third, scientific names give descriptive information about the species, like the maples mentioned earlier. Fourth, scientific names allow information about organisms to be organized easily and efficiently. Such information may be found in a book or a pamphlet that lists related organisms and gives their scientific names.

**Reading Check** *What are four functions of scientific names?*

## Tools for Identifying Organisms

Tools used to identify organisms include field guides and dichotomous (di KAH tuh mus) keys. Using these tools is one way you and scientists solve problems scientifically.

Many different field guides are available. You will find some field guides at the back of this book. Most have descriptions and illustrations of organisms and information about where each organism lives. You can identify species from around the world using the appropriate field guide.

### Mini LAB

**Communicating Ideas**

**Procedure**
1. Find a **magazine picture of a piece of furniture** that can be used as a place to sit and to lie down.
2. Show the picture to ten people and ask them to tell you what word they use for this piece of furniture.
3. Keep a record of the answers in your **Science Journal.**

**Analysis**
1. In your Science Journal, infer how using common names can be confusing.
2. How do scientific names make communication among scientists easier?

*Try at Home*

**Dichotomous Keys** A dichotomous key is a detailed list of identifying characteristics that includes scientific names. Dichotomous keys are arranged in steps with two descriptive statements at each step. If you learn how to use a dichotomous key, you can identify and name a species.

Did you know many types of mice exist? You can use **Table 2** to find out what type of mouse is pictured to the left. Start by choosing between the first pair of descriptions. The mouse has hair on its tail, so you go to 2. The ears of the mouse are small, so you go on to 3. The tail of the mouse is less that 25 mm. What is the name of this mouse according to the key?

| Table 2  Key to Some Mice of North America | |
|---|---|
| 1. Tail hair | **a.** no hair on tail; scales show plainly; house mouse, *Mus musculus* <br> **b.** hair on tail, go to 2 |
| 2. Ear size | **a.** ears small and nearly hidden in fur, go to 3 <br> **b.** ears large and not hidden in fur, go to 4 |
| 3. Tail length | **a.** less than 25 mm; woodland vole, *Microtus pinetorum* <br> **b.** more than 25 mm; prairie vole, *Microtus ochrogaster* |
| 4. Tail coloration | **a.** sharply bicolor, white beneath and dark above; deer mouse, *Peromyscus maniculatus* <br> **b.** darker above than below but not sharply bicolor; white-footed mouse, *Peromyscus leucopus* |

## section 4 review

### Summary

**Classification**

- Organisms are classified into groups based on their similarities.
- Scientists today classify organisms into six kingdoms.
- Species is the smallest classification category.

**Scientific Names**

- Binomial nomenclature is the two-word naming system that gives organisms their scientific names.

**Tools for Identifying Organisms**

- Field guides and dichotomous keys are used to identify organisms.

### Self Check

1. **State** Aristotle's and Linnaeus' contributions to classifying living things.
2. **Identify** a specific characteristic used to classify organisms.
3. **Describe** what each of the two words identifies in binomial nomenclature.
4. **Think Critically** Would you expect a field guide to have common names as well as scientific names? Why or why not?

**Applying Skills**

5. **Classify** Create a dichotomous key that identifies types of cars.

**26 CHAPTER 1** Exploring and Classifying Life

 Science Online  in7.msscience.com/self_check_quiz

## section 4 review

# Classifying Seeds

Scientists use classification systems to show how organisms are related. How do they determine which features to use to classify organisms? In this lab, you will observe seeds and use their features to classify them.

## Real-World Question

How can the features of seeds be used to develop a key to identify the seed?

### Goals

■ **Observe** the seeds and notice their features.
■ **Classify** seeds using these features.

### Materials

packets of seeds (10 different kinds)
magnifying lens
metric ruler

### Safety Precautions

**WARNING:** *Some seeds may have been treated with chemicals. Do not put them in your mouth.*

## Procedure

1. Copy the following data table in your Science Journal and record the features of each seed. Your table will have a column for each different type of seed you observe.

### Seed Data

| Feature | Type of Seed | | |
| --- | --- | --- | --- |
| | corn | kidney bean | wheat |
| Color | yellow | dark brown | light brown |
| Length (mm) | 10 | 17 | 5 |
| Shape | triangle | oval | oval |
| Texture | smooth | smooth | smooth |

2. Use the features to develop a key.
3. Exchange keys with another group. Can you use their key to identify seeds?

## Conclude and Apply

1. **Determine** how different seeds can be classified.
2. **Explain** how you would classify a seed you had not seen before using your data table.
3. **Explain** why it is an advantage for scientists to use a standardized system to classify organisms. What observations did you make to support your answer?

### Communicating Your Data

**Compare** your conclusions with those of other students in your class. **For more help, refer to the** Science Skill Handbook.

**LAB 27**

### Communicating Your Data

Comparisons may or may not result in agreement. If one group can use another group's key, the second group was successful.

### ✔ Assessment

**Performance** Give students photocopies of ten different leaves. Have them devise and describe a classification system for the leaves. Use **Performance Assessment in the Science Classroom,** p. 121.

## Real-World Question

**Purpose** Students observe seed features and then classify the seeds. L2 IS **Kinesthetic**

**Process Skills** observe and infer, classify, form operational definitions, communicate, make and use tables, compare and contrast

**Time Required** 45 minutes

## Procedure

**Alternate Materials** Any objects may be used, but biological specimens should be used if possible.

**Safety Precautions** Use only edible seeds, not seeds that have been treated for planting.

**Teaching Strategy** Prepare packets of ten different kinds of easily classified seeds, such as black-eyed peas, squash, beans (lima, kidney, pinto, black), green peas, popcorn, seed corn, and sunflower.

## Conclude and Apply

1. color, shape, size, texture, how they are attached to the plant
2. You would use the data table to categorize identifying characteristics of seeds.
3. Different classification systems could result in confusion. Answers should be based on the observation that students classified the same seeds in different ways.

**Design Your Own**

# Using Scientific Methods

## Real-World Question

### Real-World Question

**Purpose** Design and carry out an experiment using scientific methods to infer why brine shrimp live in salty waters. L2
COOP LEARN **IS** Interpersonal

**Process Skills** observe and infer, compare and contrast, recognize cause and effect, interpret data, hypothesize, communicate, make and use tables, make and use graphs, design an experiment, separate and control variables, measure in SI

**Time Required** 50 minutes on Day 1, 5 minutes a day for 3 days, 30 minutes to summarize

**Materials** Purchase brine shrimp eggs from a pet store or a biological supply house. Do not place too many brine shrimp eggs in each container. Brine shrimp are orange-colored and swim with a jerking motion. To maintain the brine shrimp, add a pinch of yeast to the container two or three times a week.

**Safety Precautions** Students should use care when working with live animals.

### Form a Hypothesis

**Possible Hypothesis** Brine shrimp will best grow in a strong salt solution since they naturally live in salty lakes.

### Test Your Hypothesis

**Possible Procedures** The same amount of brine shrimp eggs can be added to the three solutions and observed.

### Goals
- **Design** and carry out an experiment using scientific methods to infer why brine shrimp live in the ocean.
- **Observe** the jars for one week and notice whether the brine shrimp eggs hatch.

### Possible Materials
500-mL, widemouthed containers (3)
brine shrimp eggs
small, plastic spoon
distilled water (500 mL)
weak salt solution (500 mL)
strong salt solution (500 mL)
labels (3)
magnifying lens

### Safety Precautions
[safety icons]

**WARNING:** *Protect eyes and clothing. Be careful when working with live organisms.*

### Real-World Question

Brine shrimp are relatives of lobsters, crabs, crayfish, and the shrimp eaten by humans. They are often raised as a live food source in aquariums. In nature, they live in the oceans where fish feed on them. They can hatch from eggs that have been stored in a dry condition for many years. How can you use scientific methods to determine whether salt affects the hatching and growth of brine shrimp?

**Brine shrimp**

### Form a Hypothesis

Based on your observations, form a hypothesis to explain how salt affects the hatching and growth of brine shrimp.

### Test Your Hypothesis

**Make a Plan**

1. As a group, agree upon the hypothesis and decide how you will test it. Identify what results will confirm the hypothesis.

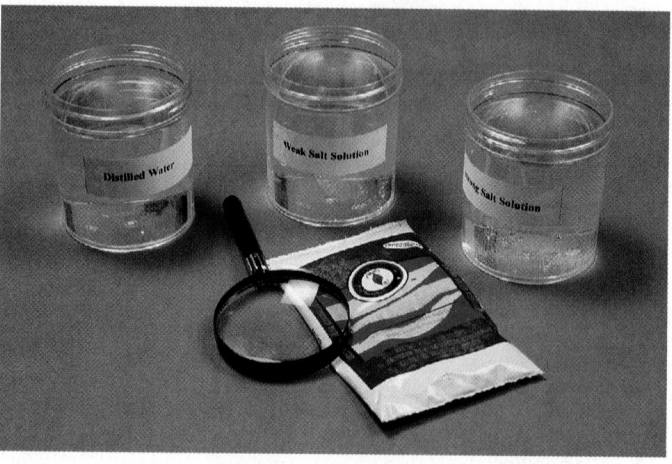

**28 CHAPTER 1** Exploring and Classifying Life

## Alternative Inquiry Lab

**Environmental Change** Have students investigate how other environmental conditions, like temperature and light, might affect the development and growth of brine shrimp. Allow students to prepare variable salt solutions. Since brine shrimp are an important food for birds, have students hypothesize how changing salinity levels might affect both shrimp and bird populations. L2

2. **List** steps that you need to test your hypothesis. Be specific. Describe exactly what you will do at each step.

3. **List** your materials.

4. **Prepare** a data table in your Science Journal to record your data.

5. Read over your entire experiment to make sure that all planned steps are in logical order.

6. **Identify** any constants, variables, and controls of the experiment.

### Follow Your Plan

1. Make sure your teacher approves your plan before you start.

2. Carry out the experiment as planned by your group.

3. While doing the experiment, record any observations and complete the data table in your Science Journal.

4. Use a bar graph to plot your results.

### ◉ Analyze Your Data

1. **Describe** the contents of each jar after one week.

2. **Identify** your control in this experiment.

3. **Identify** your variable in this experiment.

### ◉ Conclude and Apply

1. **Explain** whether or not the results support your hypothesis.

2. **Predict** the effect that increasing the amount of salt in the water would have on the brine shrimp eggs.

3. **Compare** your results with those of other groups.

### *Communicating* Your Data

Prepare a set of instructions on how to hatch brine shrimp to use to feed fish. Include diagrams and a step-by-step procedure.

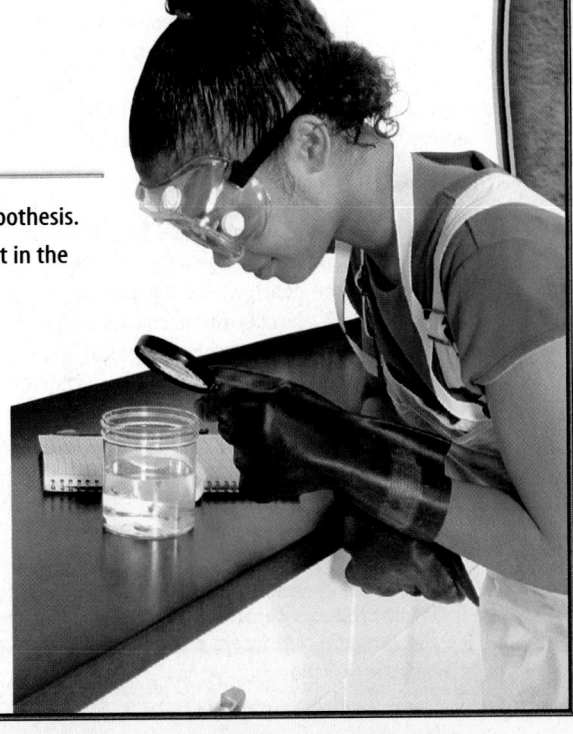

### *Communicating* Your Data

Instructions should include information on the amount of salt to add to the water, light conditions, and so on. Students can use word-processing software programs to write their instructions.

### ✔ Assessment

**Performance** Have students design an experiment to determine how ocean currents affect brine shrimp. Use **Performance Assessment in the Science Classroom,** p. 95.

### Teaching Strategies

Prepare the solutions as follows:

• Dechlorinated water: Allow tap water to stand for 48 hours.

• Weak salt solution: Add 20 mL non-iodized salt to 4 L dechlorinated water. Stir until dissolved.

• Strong salt solution: Add 75 mL non-iodized salt to 4 L dechlorinated water. Stir until dissolved.

**Expected Outcome** Results likely will reflect that the brine shrimp grew best in the strong salt solution.

### ◉ Analyze Your Data

#### Answers to Questions

1. There were no shrimp in the distilled water or weak salt solution. There were many shrimp in the strong salt solution.

2. The dechlorinated water without salt was the control.

3. The amount of salt in the water was the variable.

**Error Analysis** Have students compare their results and their hypotheses and explain any differences.

### ◉ Conclude and Apply

1. Answers will be determined by students' hypotheses.

2. Answers will vary. Some may predict that more brine shrimp will hatch.

3. Results will vary.

## Content Background

The rain forests of the world are home to fifty percent of all species of plants and animals. Some insect species evolve and become extinct without ever having been seen alive by humans. Most rain forest species live in the forest canopy between 18 to 46 meters (60–150 ft) above the ground. While observing wildlife in the canopy is extremely difficult, the need for extensive study is pressing as logging and slash and burn agriculture destroys more forest habitat.

One method being attempted to halt uncontrolled agriculture is the development of programs that preserve wild areas by attracting tourists, or ecotourism. Building an economy based on service industries can relieve pressure to clear more land for farming. One version of ecotourism is the canopy tour ranging from climbing harnesses to walkways and aerial tramways. A benefit of these tours is that canopy research can be conducted from these structures.

## Discussion

**Invisible Species** What features of the rain forest cause a large number species to remain unknown? Possible answer: The difficulty of travel and the remoteness of some areas make observation points difficult to get to. The fact that most of the species live in the canopy further complicates surveys. L2

## Investigate the Issue

**Numbers of Species** Direct students to research the estimated number of plant and animal species worldwide and chart their distribution on a map using colored pins. How many species are in the rain forests? How will deforestation affect these species? L2

---

# TIME › SCIENCE AND Society

SCIENCE ISSUES THAT AFFECT YOU!

Manicore marmoset

Acari marmoset

# M**o**nkey BUSINESS

In 2000, a scientist from Brazil's Amazon National Research Institute came across two squirrel-sized monkeys in a remote and isolated corner of the rain forest, about 2,575 km from Rio de Janeiro.

It turns out that the monkeys had never been seen before, or even known to exist.

## Acari marmoset

The new species were spotted by a scientist who named them after two nearby rivers the Manicore and the Acari, where the animals were discovered. Both animals are marmosets, which is a type of monkey found only in Central and South America. Marmosets have claws instead of nails, live in trees, and use their extraordinarily long tail like an extra arm or leg. Small and light,

both marmosets measure about 23 cm in length with a 38 cm tail, and weigh no more than 0.4 kg.

The Manicore marmoset has a silvery-white upper body, a light-gray cap on its head, a yellow-orange underbody, and a black tail.

The Acari marmoset's upper body is snowy white, its gray back sports a stripe running to the knee, and its black tail flashes a bright-orange tip.

## Amazin' Amazon

The Amazon Basin is a treasure trove of unique species. The Amazon River is Earth's largest body of freshwater, with 1,100 smaller tributaries. And more than half of the world's plant and animal species live in its rain forest ecosystems.

**Research and Report** Working in small groups, find out more about the Amazon rain forest. Which plants and animals live there? What products come from the rain forest? How does what happens in the Amazon rain forest affect you? Prepare a multimedia presentation.

**Science Online**

For more information, visit in7.msscience.com/time

---

**Research and Report** As an extension, have students discuss the pros and cons of ecotourism in light of their research of current rain forest uses and conditions.

## Resources for Teachers and Students

*Rain Forests of the World: Water, Fire, Earth, Air,* by Art Wolfe and Sir Ghillean Prance, New York: Crown Publishers, 1998

*Amazonia: the Land, the Wildlife, the River, the People,* by Afonso Capelas, Firefly Books, 2003

## Reviewing Main Ideas

### Section 1 What is science?

1. Scientists use problem-solving methods to investigate observations about living and nonliving things.

2. Scientists use SI measurements to gather measurable data.

3. Safe laboratory practices help you learn more about science.

### Section 2 Living Things

1. Organisms are made of cells, use energy, reproduce, respond, grow, and develop.

2. Organisms need energy, water, food, and a place to live.

### Section 3 Where does life come from?

1. Controlled experiments finally disproved the theory of spontaneous generation.

2. Pasteur's experiment proved biogenesis.

### Section 4 How are living things classified?

1. Classification is the grouping of ideas, information, or objects based on their similar characteristics.

2. Scientists today use phylogeny to group organisms into six kingdoms.

3. All organisms are given a two-word scientific name using binomial nomenclature.

## Visualizing Main Ideas

*Copy and complete this events-chain concept map that shows the order in which you might use a scientific method. Use these terms:* analyze data, perform an experiment, *and* form a hypothesis.

State the problem

↓

Form a hypothesis

↓

Perform an experiment

↓

Analyze data

↓

Report results

 Science Online in7.msscience.com/interactive_tutor

CHAPTER STUDY GUIDE 31

### Reviewing Main Ideas

Summary statements can be used by students to review the major concepts of the chapter.

### Visualizing Main Ideas

See student page.

**Visit** in7.msscience.com
/self_check_quiz
/interactive_tutor
/vocabulary_puzzlemaker
/chapter_review
/standards_review

### Assessment Transparency

For additional assessment questions, use the *Assessment Transparency* located in the transparency book.

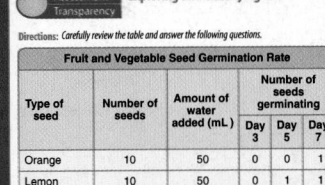

#### Assessment

Assessment Transparency — Exploring and Classifying Life

Directions: *Carefully review the table and answer the following questions.*

**Fruit and Vegetable Seed Germination Rate**

| Type of seed | Number of seeds | Amount of water added (mL) | Number of seeds germinating Day 3 | Day 5 | Day 7 |
|---|---|---|---|---|---|
| Orange | 10 | 50 | 0 | 0 | 1 |
| Lemon | 10 | 50 | 0 | 1 | 1 |
| Cucumber | 10 | 50 | 6 | 7 | 7 |
| Onion | 10 | 50 | 7 | 9 | 10 |

1. Which hypothesis was probably being tested?
A Less than 25 percent of vegetable seeds will germinate.
B Seeds prefer to grow in soil versus sand.
C Vegetable seeds germinate faster than fruit seeds.
D A period of one week is required before seeds will germinate.

2. Which of the following would improve an experiment to compare the rate of seed germination?
F using more types of seeds
G measuring the length of the plants
H adding 100mL of water to each seed
J conducting the experiment for a shorter time

3. Which factor would have the LEAST effect on the results?
A the amount of light to which the seeds were exposed
B the amount of soil used for the seeds
C the color of the pots used
D the depth the seeds were planted in the soil

## Identifying Misconceptions

**Assess**

**Activity** Have students record whether items in several pictures are living or nonliving and their reason. Have students share ideas and generate a list of characteristics that they think describe living things. Compare this list to the list in **Section 2** and ask the class if they would like to make any changes in their list.

**Expected Outcome** Most students should be forming a more sophisticated definition that includes characteristics from the text. L2

## Using Vocabulary

1. variable—condition tested; control—standard used to compare with outcome of the test

2. theory—explanation of things or events based on many observations; law—a statement about how things work in nature

3. The theory of spontaneous generation (living things come from non-living things) was replaced with the theory of biogenesis (living things come only from other living things).

4. Phylogeny is the evolutionary history of an organism; binomial nomenclature is a naming system based on phylogeny.

5. A cell is the smallest unit of an organism that carries out the functions of life. All organisms are made of cells.

6. Phylogeny is the basis for placing organisms into kingdoms.

7. Forming a hypothesis is an important part of solving a problem with scientific methods.

8. Homeostasis—keeping proper internal conditions no matter what external conditions are—is a trait of all organisms.

9. A genus is a subgroup of a kingdom.

10. If the results of repeated experiments always support the same hypothesis, the hypothesis may be called a theory.

## Checking Concepts

| 11. D | 16. D |
|-------|-------|
| 12. D | 17. A |
| 13. A | 18. B |
| 14. D | 19. D |
| 15. C | 20. B |

## Using Vocabulary

| | |
|---|---|
| binomial nomenclature p. 24 | law p. 10 |
| | organism p. 14 |
| biogenesis p. 19 | phylogeny p. 23 |
| cell p. 14 | scientific methods p. 7 |
| control p. 9 | spontaneous |
| genus p. 24 | generation p. 19 |
| homeostasis p. 15 | theory p. 10 |
| hypothesis p. 8 | variable p. 9 |
| kingdom p. 23 | |

*Explain the differences in the vocabulary words in each pair below. Then explain how they are related.*

1. control—variable

2. law—theory

3. biogenesis—spontaneous generation

4. binomial nomenclature—phylogeny

5. organism—cell

6. kingdom—phylogeny

7. hypothesis—scientific methods

8. organism—homeostasis

9. kingdom—genus

10. theory—hypothesis

## Checking Concepts

*Choose the word or phrase that best answers the question.*

11. What category of organisms can mate and produce fertile offspring?
    A) family        C) genus
    B) class         D) species

12. What is the closest relative of *Canis lupus*?
    A) *Quercus alba*    C) *Felis tigris*
    B) *Equus zebra*     D) *Canis familiaris*

13. What is the source of energy for plants?
    A) the Sun           C) water
    B) carbon dioxide    D) oxygen

14. What makes up more than 50 percent of all living things?
    A) oxygen            C) minerals
    B) carbon dioxide    D) water

15. Who finally disproved the theory of spontaneous generation?
    A) Oparin            C) Pasteur
    B) Aristotle         D) Miller

16. What gas do some scientists think was missing from Earth's early atmosphere?
    A) ammonia           C) methane
    B) hydrogen          D) oxygen

17. What is the length of time called that an organism is expected to live?
    A) life span         C) homeostasis
    B) stimulus          D) theory

18. What is the part of an experiment that can be changed called?
    A) conclusion        C) control
    B) variable          D) data

19. What does the first word in a two-word name of an organism identify?
    A) kingdom           C) phylum
    B) species           D) genus

**Use the photo below to answer question 20.**

20. What SI unit is used to measure the volume of soda shown above?
    A) meter             C) gram
    B) liter             D) degree

 Science Online in7.msscience.com/vocabulary_puzzlemaker

**Use the ExamView® Pro Testmaker CD-ROM to:**

- create multiple versions of tests
- create modified tests with one mouse click for inclusion students
- edit existing questions and add your own questions
- build tests aligned with state standards using built-in State Curriculum Tags
- change English tests to Spanish with one mouse click and vice versa

## Thinking Critically

**21. Predict** what *Lathyrus odoratus*, the scientific name for a sweet pea plant, tells you about one of its characteristics.

**Use the photo below to answer question 22.**

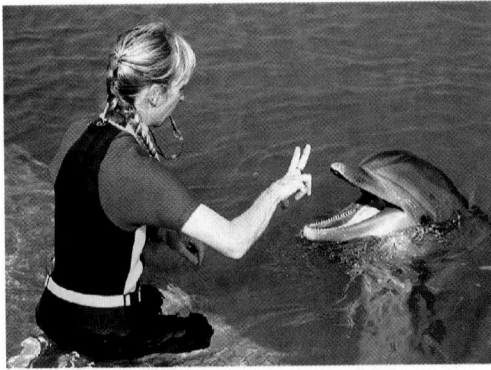

**22. Determine** what problem-solving techniques this scientist would use to find how dolphins learn.

**Use the graph below to answer question 23.**

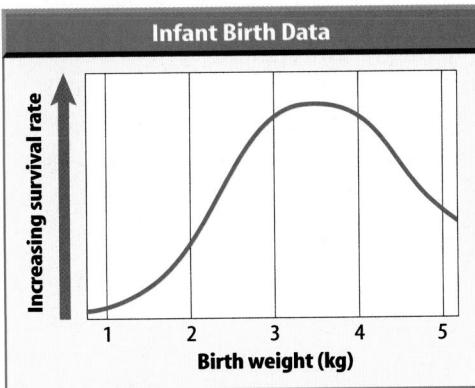

**Infant Birth Data**

Increasing survival rate

Birth weight (kg)

**23. Interpret Data** Do the data in the graph above support the hypothesis that babies with a birth weight of 2.5 kg have the best chance of survival? Explain.

**24. List** advantages of using SI units.

**25. Form a Hypothesis** A lima bean plant is placed under green light, another is placed under red light, and a third under blue light. Their growth is measured for four weeks to determine which light is best for plant growth. What are the variables in this experiment? State a hypothesis for this experiment.

## Performance Activities

**26. Bulletin Board** Interview people in your community whose jobs require a knowledge of life science. Make a Life Science Careers bulletin board. Summarize each person's job and what he or she had to study to prepare for that job.

## Applying Math

**27. Body Temperature** Normal human body temperature is 98.6°F. What is this temperature in degrees Celsius? Use the following expression, 5/9(°F−32), to find degrees Celsius.

**Use the graph below to answer question 28.**

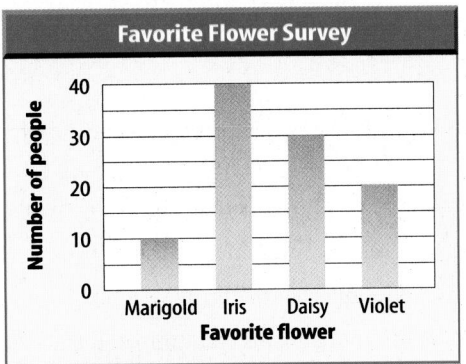

**Favorite Flower Survey**

Number of people

Marigold   Iris   Daisy   Violet
**Favorite flower**

**28. Favorite Flower** The graph above shows how many people selected a certain type of flower as their favorite. According to the graph, what percentage of the people picked daisy as their favorite?

 **Science**online  in7.msscience.com/chapter_review

## Thinking Critically

**21.** The name *odoratus* tells you that the sweet pea probably has an odor.

**22.** critical thinking including scientific methods of observation, forming hypotheses, performing experiments, and analyzing data

**23.** No. The graph indicates that a birth weight of 3.5 kg is best for survival.

**24.** Scientists can compare and repeat experiments; they have a common tool for measurement.

**25.** The colors of light used are variables. A possible hypothesis is that plants will grow better under some colors of light than under other colors.

## Performance Activities

**26.** Careers could include farmers, produce clerks, florists, veterinary technicians, health care workers, and teachers. Use **Performance Assessment in the Science Classroom**, p. 131.

## Applying Math

**Indiana Math Standards**
7.5.1, 7.6.1

**27.** 5/9(98.6−32) = 37°C

**28.** 30 people out of the 100 surveyed chose the daisy or 30/100 = 0.3 = 30%

**Answer Sheet** A practice answer sheet can be found at in7.msscience.com/answer_sheet.

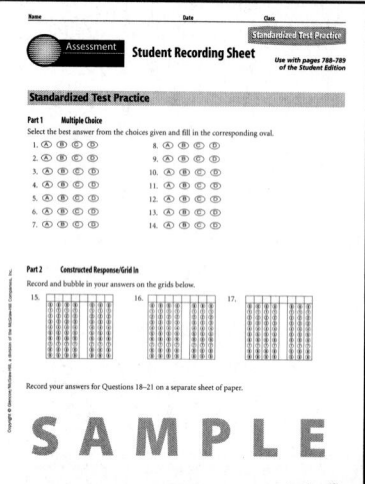

SAMPLE

**Part 1 | Multiple Choice**

1. D
2. D
3. B
4. A
5. C
6. D

The assessed Indiana standard appears above the question.

*Record your answers on the answer sheet provided by your teacher or on a sheet of paper.*

**Part 1 | Multiple Choice**

**7.1.3**

1. Which unit might a biologist use when measuring the length of a mouse's tail?

   **A** gram

   **B** kilometer

   **C** milliliter

   **D** millimeter

2. The illustration below shows an experiment performed to support the theory of biogenesis.

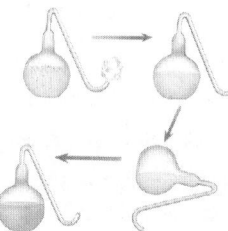

   Why did the boiled broth become cloudy after the flask was tilted?

   **A** The broth was contaminated by decay.

   **B** A disease was added to the broth.

   **C** Flies infected the broth.

   **D** Microorganisms contaminated the broth.

The photos below show two life stages of one dog species.

**7.4.4**

3. Which is responsible for most of the observable changes shown above?

   **A** an increase in the energy of cells

   **B** an increase in the number of cells

   **C** an increase in the size of cells

   **D** an increase in the water in cells

**7.4.4**

4. What characteristic of life do the photos above illustrate?

   **A** growth and development

   **B** use of energy

   **C** reproduction

   **D** response to stimulus

**7.4.5**  **7.4.6**

5. What gas must most organisms take in to release the energy in food?

   **A** carbon dioxide

   **B** hydrogen

   **C** oxygen

   **D** water vapor

**6.** The illustrations below show an experiment to study the response of plants to the stimulus of light.

Day 1

1   2   3

Day 4

1   2   3

Which hypothesis is likely being tested by this experiment?

**A** Plants do not grow in the dark.

**B** Plants do not grow in boxes.

**C** Plants grow away from light.

**D** Plants grow toward light.

**Test-Taking Tip**

**Practice Skills** Remember that test-taking skills can improve with practice. If possible, take at least one practice test and familiarize yourself with the test format and instructions.

Science Online in7.msscience.com/standards_review

---

**Part 2   Critical Response**

7.1.4   7.1.5

**7.** Some scientists think that lightning might have caused chemicals in Earth's early atmosphere to combine and begin the origin of life. Explain how the experiment of Miller and Urey supports this hypothesis but does not prove this hypothesis.

7.4.1

**8.** What information would you need to write a field guide used to identify garden plants? What other information would you need if the guide included a dichotomous key?

The photo below shows beetles on a plant.

7.4.5

**9.** Describe the difference between the source of energy for the beetle and for the plant. In what similar ways would each of these organisms use energy?

7.4.6   7.4.8

**10.** How are the needs of these two organisms in the photo above alike? Explain why the plant is raw material for the beetle. When the beetle dies, how could it become raw material for the plant?

---

## Rubrics

The following rubric is a sample scoring device for critical response questions.

**Critical Response**

| Points | Description |
|--------|-------------|
| 4 | The student demonstrates a thorough understanding of the science of the task. The response may contain minor flaws that do not detract from the demonstration of a thorough understanding. |
| 3 | The student demonstrates an understanding of the science of the task. The response is essentially correct and demonstrates an essential but less than thorough understanding of the science. |
| 2 | The student demonstrates only a partial understanding of the science of the task. Although the student may have used the correct approach to a solution or may have provided a correct solution, the work lacks an essential understanding of the underlying science concepts. |
| 1 | The student demonstrates a very limited understanding of the science of the task. The response is incomplete and exhibits many flaws. |
| 0 | The student provides a completely incorrect solution or no response at all. |

**STANDARDS REVIEW   35**

---

**Part 2   Critical Response**

**7.** Miller and Urey used an electric current and a mixture of gases and produced chemicals found in present day cells. However, the experiment did not produce living things.

**8.** You would need to collect information describing each plant, pictures of each plant, and information about where each grows. A dichotomous key, would include scientific names of each plant and detailed identifying characteristics.

**9.** Plants use the Sun's energy. Since the beetles eat plants for energy, they indirectly use the Sun. Both use energy for organization and homeostasis.

**10.** Both need an environment with proper condition including water and oxygen. Plants also need carbon dioxide and soil minerals. The beetles need plants for food. Dead beetles will be broken down in the soil into substances that plants use as raw materials.

| Section/Objectives | Standards | | Labs/Features |
|---|---|---|---|
| | National | State/Local | |
| **Chapter Opener** | See pp. 16T–17T for a Key to Standards. | Detailed Standards begin on page IN8. | **Launch Lab:** Magnifying Cells, p. 37 **Foldables**, p. 37 A data-collection lab using Probeware technology can be found in the **Probeware Lab Manual**, pp. 1–4 |
| **Section 1 Cell Structure** ⏱ 2 sessions 📦 1 block 1. **Identify** names and functions of each part of a cell. 2. **Explain** how important a nucleus is in a cell. 3. **Compare** tissues, organs, and organ systems. | National Content Standards: UCP.1–UCP.3, UCP.5, A.1, A.2, C.1, C.3 | Indiana Standards: 7.4.4, 7.4.5, 7.4.7 | **MiniLAB:** Modeling Cytoplasm, p. 40 **Integrate Environment**, p. 44 **Applying Math:** Cell Ratio, p. 44 **Lab:** Comparing Cells, p. 46 |
| **Section 2 Viewing Cells** ⏱ 2 sessions 📦 1 block 4. **Compare** the differences between the compound light microscope and the electron microscope. 5. **Summarize** the discoveries that led to the development of the cell theory. | National Content Standards: UCP.1–UCP.3, UCP.5, A.1, A.2, C.1, G.3 | Indiana Standards: 7.1.5, 7.1.7, 7.4.4, 7.4.5 | **Visualizing Microscopes**, p. 48 **MiniLAB:** Observing Magnified Objects, p. 50 **Integrate Career**, p. 50 |
| **Section 3 Viruses** ⏱ 3 sessions 📦 1.5 blocks 6. **Explain** how a virus makes copies of itself. 7. **Identify** the benefits of vaccines. 8. **Investigate** some uses of viruses. | National Content Standards: UCP.1, UCP.2, UCP.5, A.1, A.2, C.1, C.2, C.5, F.2, G.3 | Indiana Standards: 7.1.5–7.1.7, 7.4.7, 7.4.12, 7.6.3, 7.6.4 | **Science Online**, p. 53 **Science Online**, p. 54 **Lab:** Comparing Light Microscopes, p. 56 **Science and History:** Cobb Against Cancer, p. 58 |

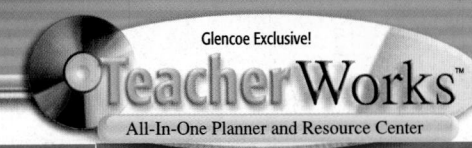
| Lab Materials | Reproducible Resources | Section Assessment | Technology |
|---|---|---|---|
| **Launch Lab:** hand lens, metric ruler | **Chapter** *FAST FILE* **Resources** <br> Foldables Worksheet, p. 17 <br> Directed Reading Overview, p. 19 <br> Note-taking Worksheets, pp. 33–35 | **GLENCOE'S** **ASSESSMENT** **ADVANTAGE** | **TeacherWorks** includes: <br> • Interactive Teacher Edition <br> • Lesson Planner with calendar <br> • Access to all program blacklines <br> • Correlations to standards <br> • Web links |
| **MiniLAB:** water, clear container, unflavored gelatin, flashlight, stirring rod <br> **Lab:** microscope, microscope slide, coverslip, forceps, tap water, dropper, *Elodea* plant, prepared slide of human cheek cells | **Chapter** *FAST FILE* **Resources** <br> Transparency Activity, p. 44 <br> MiniLAB, p. 3 <br> Enrichment, p. 30 <br> Reinforcement, p. 27 <br> Directed Reading, p. 20 <br> Transparency Activity, pp. 47–48 <br> Lab Worksheet, pp. 5–6 <br> **Mathematics Skill Activities,** p. 5 | Portfolio <br> Visual Learning, p. 41 <br> Performance <br> MiniLAB, p. 40 <br> Applying Math, p. 44 <br> Applying Skills, p. 45 <br> Content <br> Section Review, p. 45 | Section Focus Transparency <br> Virtual Labs CD-ROM <br> Guided Reading Audio Program <br> Interactive Chalkboard CD-ROM <br> Video Lab |
| **MiniLAB:** newspaper, clear empty glass, clear empty glass bowl, water, magnifying lens <br> *Need materials?* Contact Science Kit at 1-800-828-7777 or www.sciencekit.com on the Internet. | **Chapter** *FAST FILE* **Resources** <br> Transparency Activity, p. 45 <br> MiniLAB, p. 4 <br> Enrichment, p. 31 <br> Reinforcement, p. 28 <br> Directed Reading, p. 20 <br> Lab Activity, pp. 9–12, 13–16 | Portfolio <br> Assessment, p. 51 <br> Performance <br> MiniLAB, p. 50 <br> Applying Math, p. 51 <br> Content <br> Section Review, p. 51 | Section Focus Transparency <br> Guided Reading Audio Program <br> Interactive Chalkboard CD-ROM |
| **Lab:** compound light microscope, stereomicroscope, 8 classroom items to view, microscope slides and coverslips, plastic petri dishes, distilled water, dropper | **Chapter** *FAST FILE* **Resources** <br> Transparency Activity, p. 46 <br> Enrichment, p. 32 <br> Reinforcement, p. 29 <br> Directed Reading, pp. 21, 22 <br> Lab Worksheet, pp. 7–8 <br> **Lab Management and Safety,** p. 58 <br> **Reading and Writing Skill Activities,** p. 31 | Performance <br> Applying Skills, p. 55 <br> Content <br> Section Review, p. 55 | Section Focus Transparency <br> Guided Reading Audio Program <br> Interactive Chalkboard CD-ROM <br> Probeware Lab |

## End of Chapter Assessment

**GLENCOE'S** **ASSESSMENT** **ADVANTAGE**

| Blackline Masters | Technology | Professional Series |
|---|---|---|
| **Chapter** *FAST FILE* **Resources** <br> Chapter Review, pp. 37–38 <br> Chapter Tests, pp. 39–42 <br> **Mastering the Grade 7 Indiana Science Standards** | MindJogger Videoquiz <br> IN Test Prep and Practice Exam*View*® <br> Exam*View*® Pro Testmaker <br> TeacherWorks CD-ROM <br> Interactive Chalkboard CD-ROM | **Performance Assessment in the Science Classroom (PASC)** |

# Transparencies

## Section Focus

**SECTION 1 Section Focus Transparency — A Factory Analogy**

If this factory were a cell, it would run 24 hours a day and 7 days a week. Just like a factory, cells use raw materials to produce what's needed. Like a factory, they have a control center, a source of power, and a way to move products and waste.

Control center
Factory wall
Electric generator
Storage barrel

1. What part of the drawing directs the activities in the factory?
2. Identify the part of the drawing that provides energy to the factory.
3. What function do the storage barrels have?

L2

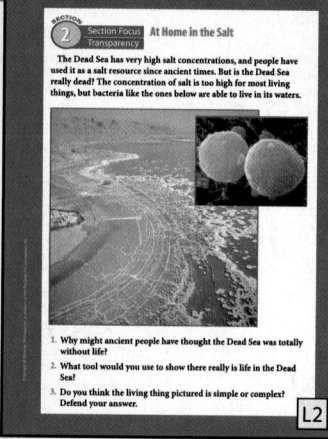

**SECTION 2 Section Focus Transparency — At Home in the Salt**

The Dead Sea has very high salt concentrations, and people have used it as a salt resource since ancient times. But is the Dead Sea really dead? The concentration of salt is too high for most living things, but bacteria like the ones below are able to live in its waters.

1. Why might ancient people have thought the Dead Sea was totally without life?
2. What tool would you use to show there really is life in the Dead Sea?
3. Do you think the living thing pictured is simple or complex? Defend your answer.

L2

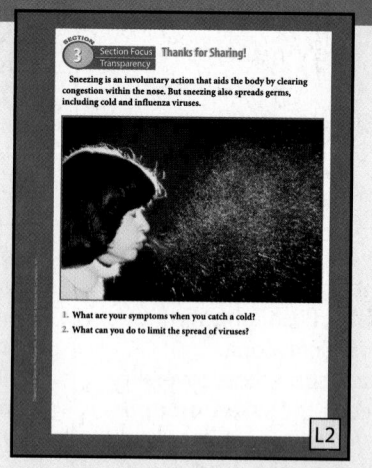

**SECTION 3 Section Focus Transparency — Thanks for Sharing!**

Sneezing is an involuntary action that aids the body by clearing congestion within the nose. But sneezing also spreads germs, including cold and influenza viruses.

1. What are your symptoms when you catch a cold?
2. What can you do to limit the spread of viruses?

L2

---

This is a representation of key blackline masters available in the Teacher Classroom Resources. See Resource Manager boxes within the chapter for additional information.

## Key to Teaching Strategies

The following designations will help you decide which activities are appropriate for your students.

**L1** Level 1 activities should be appropriate for students with learning difficulties.

**L2** Level 2 activities should be within the ability range of all students.

**L3** Level 3 activities are designed for above-average students.

**ELL** ELL activities should be within the ability range of English-Language Learners.

**COOP LEARN** Cooperative Learning activities are designed for small group work.

**LS** Multiple Learning Styles logos, as described on page 12T, are used throughout to indicate strategies that address different learning styles.

**P** These strategies represent student products that can be placed into a best-work portfolio.

**PBL** Problem-Based Learning activities apply real-world situations to learning.

## Assessment

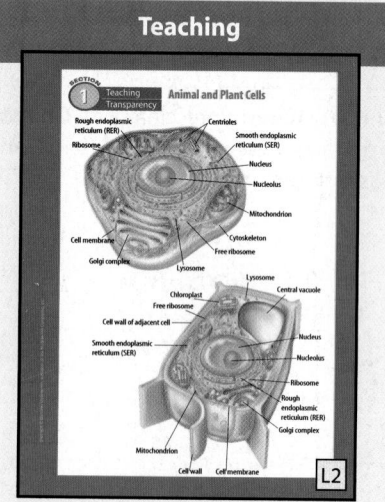

**Assessment Transparency — Cells**

*Directions: Carefully review the diagram and answer the following questions.*

Virus
Cell
Nucleus
Cytoplasm
Vacuole
Interferon
Chromosome
Cell

1. The chromosomes are located in the ___.
   A cytoplasm
   B vacuoles
   C nucleus
   D nucleolus
2. The scientist performing this experiment wants to study interferon because it may work as a powerful medicine. If the scientist wanted to learn how powerful interferon is, the experiment could be repeated ___.
   F at a higher temperature       H with less interferon
   G at a lower altitude            J with more labels
3. The cell on the far right of the picture will probably soon ___.
   A grow                           C move
   B divide                         D die

L2

## Teaching

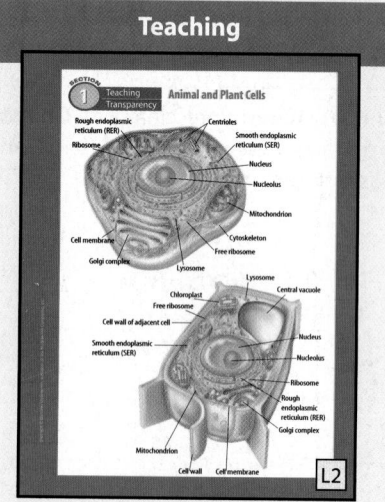

**SECTION 1 Teaching Transparency — Animal and Plant Cells**

Rough endoplasmic reticulum (RER)
Ribosome
Centrioles
Smooth endoplasmic reticulum (SER)
Nucleus
Nucleolus
Mitochondrion
Cell membrane
Cytoskeleton
Golgi complex
Free ribosome
Lysosome
Lysosome
Central vacuole
Chloroplast
Free ribosome
Cell wall of adjacent cell
Smooth endoplasmic reticulum (SER)
Nucleus
Nucleolus
Ribosome
Rough endoplasmic reticulum (RER)
Golgi complex
Mitochondrion
Cell wall   Cell membrane

L2

---

# Hands-on Activities

## Student Text Lab Worksheet

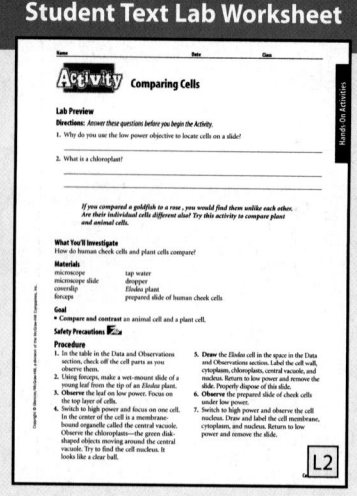

**Activity — Comparing Cells**

**Lab Preview**

*Directions: Answer these questions before you begin the Activity.*

1. Why do you use the low power objective to locate cells on a slide?

2. What is a chloroplast?

*If you compared a goldfish to a rose, you would find them unlike each other. Are their individual cells different also? Try this activity to compare plant and animal cells.*

**What You'll Investigate**
How do human cheek cells and plant cells compare?

**Materials**
microscope            tap water
microscope slide      dropper
coverslip             Elodea plant
forceps               prepared slide of human cheek cells

**Goal**
• Compare and contrast an animal cell and a plant cell.

**Safety Precautions**

**Procedure**
1. In the table in the Data and Observations section, check off the cell parts as you observe them.
2. Using forceps, make a wet-mount slide of a young leaf from the tip of an *Elodea* plant.
3. **Observe** the leaf on low power. Focus on the top layer of cells.
4. Switch to high power and focus on one cell. In the center of the cell is a membrane-bound organelle called the central vacuole. Observe the chloroplasts—the green disk-shaped objects moving around the central vacuole. Try to find the cell nucleus. It looks like a clear ball.
5. **Draw** the *Elodea* cell in the space in the Data and Observations section. Label the cell wall, cytoplasm, chloroplasts, central vacuole, and nucleus. Properly dispose of this slide.
6. **Observe** the prepared slide of check cells under low power.
7. Switch to high power and observe the cell nucleus. Draw and label the cell membrane, cytoplasm, and nucleus. Return to low power and remove the slide.

L2

## Laboratory Activities

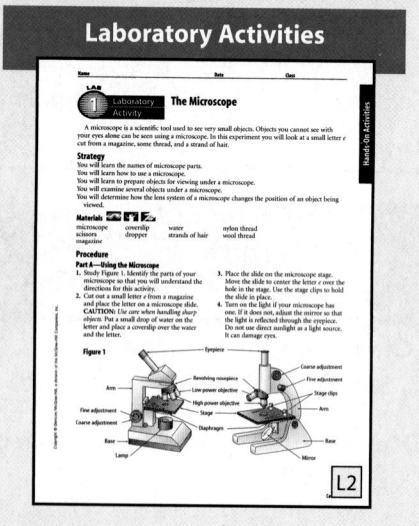

**LAB 1 Laboratory Activity — The Microscope**

A microscope is a scientific tool used to see very small objects. Objects you cannot see with your eyes alone can be seen using a microscope. In this experiment you will look at a small letter *e* cut from a magazine, some thread, and a strand of hair.

**Strategy**
You will learn the names of microscope parts.
You will learn how to use a microscope.
You will learn to prepare objects for viewing under a microscope.
You will examine several objects under a microscope.
You will determine how the lens system of a microscope changes the position of an object being viewed.

**Materials**
microscope    coverslip    water           nylon thread
scissors      dropper      strands of hair  wool thread
magazine

**Procedure**
**Part A—Using the Microscope**
1. Study Figure 1. Identify the parts of your microscope so that you will understand the directions for this activity.
2. Cut out a small letter *e* from a magazine and place the letter on a microscope slide. **CAUTION:** *Use care when handling sharp objects.* Put a small drop of water on the letter and place a coverslip over the water and the letter.
3. Place the slide on the microscope stage. Move the slide to center the letter *e* over the hole in the stage. Use the stage clips to hold the slide in place.
4. Turn on the light if your microscope has one. If it does not, adjust the mirror so that the light is reflected through the eyepiece. Do not use direct sunlight as a light source. It can damage eyes.

**Figure 1**

Eyepiece
Revolving nosepiece
Coarse adjustment
Arm
Fine adjustment
Low power objective
High power objective
Stage clips
Arm
Fine adjustment
Coarse adjustment
Stage
Diaphragm
Base
Lamp
Mirror

L2

# Meeting Different Ability Levels

## Content Outline

## Reinforcement

## Enrichment

## Directed Reading (English/Spanish)

## Study Guide

## Reading Essentials

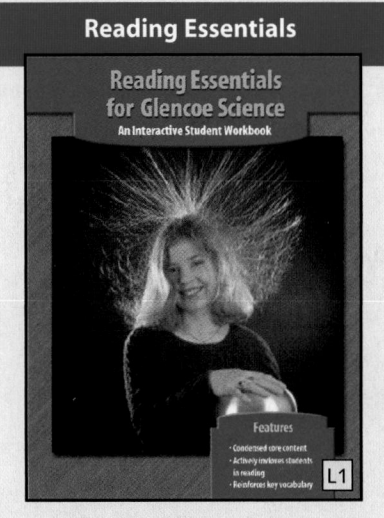

# Assessment

## Test Practice Workbook

## Chapter Review

## Chapter Tests

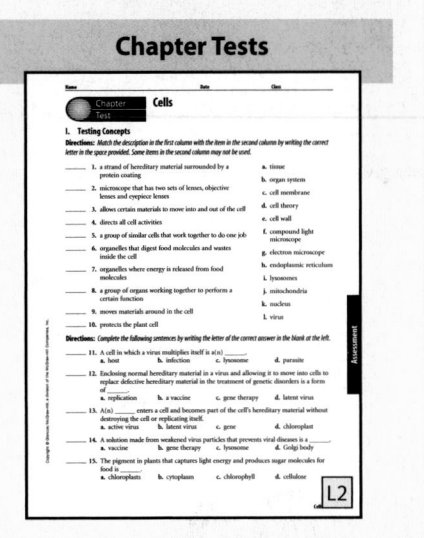

# Science Content Background

## section 1
### Cell Structure
### Common Cell Traits

The two kinds of cells are prokaryotes and eukaryotes. Each type is surrounded by a cell membrane and contains cytoplasm, DNA, and ribosomes. Prokaryotes have a relatively uniform cytoplasm that is not divided into separate compartments by interior membranes. The ribosomes of prokaryotes are different from those of eukaryotes. Prokaryotic DNA is a single molecule and is found floating freely in the cell's cytoplasm. The nucleus is the organelle that contains the eukaryotic cell's many molecules of DNA. All prokaryotic cells are one-celled organisms. Eukaryotic cells make up all multicellular organisms and some one-celled organisms.

*Dwight R. Kuhn/DRK Photo*

## Cell Wall

Although structurally they resemble plant cell walls, the walls of fungi cells are chemically quite different. Some contain cellulose, but most fungal cell walls are made up of chitin, a polysaccharide that also is found in the exoskeletons of insects. Just like cellulose in plants, the chitin is laid down in bundles of fibers that make the fungal cell walls tough and able to support the fungal body.

Bacterial cell walls are different from those found in either plants or fungi. Bacterial cell walls are composed in large part of a compound called peptidoglycan. Various other substances coat and bind to the cell wall. Other bacteria have an outer membrane that surrounds the peptidoglycan cell wall.

## Cell Organization

The cytoskeleton, found only in eukaryotic cells, anchors cell organelles. This "scaffolding" cannot be seen with a normal light microscope but stands out clearly when special fluorescent dyes are used on the cell. Three different kinds of protein fibers—microfilaments, microtubules, and intermediate fibers—make up the cytoskeleton.

---

**Teacher to Teacher**
Steve Federman, 6th Grade Teacher
Loveland Middle School
Loveland, Ohio

"I reinforce the concepts of cell structures and functions by having students create a cell from a light colored flavored gelatin mixed with unflavored gelatin (6-oz. package will make 5 cells). Pour into a small cup or petri dish. Students then use items such as cake sprinkles for ribosomes, hot tamale candies for mitochondria, a gumball for the nucleus, and so on."

*Steve Federman*

---

## section 2 Viewing Cells

### Magnifying Cells

Microscopes enlarge the image of an object and show its details. The change of an object's apparent size is magnification. The power to show details is resolution. The resolution power of light microscopes is limited by the wavelengths of visible light. Unless the wavelength of light can pass between two objects, the objects are seen as one unit, not two. The electron microscope allows for greater resolution because it uses a beam of electrons to generate an image of the specimen. Because they move in waves that have extremely short wavelengths, electron waves can easily pass through microscopic spaces that visible light cannot enter.

### Development of the Cell Theory

The cell theory is sometimes called the cell doctrine. Those scientists who use the term *cell doctrine* want to make it clear that extensive data support the cell theory and that it is universally accepted by biologists.

*Telegraph Colour Library/FPG International*

### Internet Resources

For additional content background, visit **in7.msscience.com** to:

- access your book online
- find references to related articles in popular science magazines
- access Web links with related content background
- access current events with science journal topics

### Print Resources

*Cells (The Kidhaven Science Library),* by Jeanne Duprau, Kidhaven, 2001

*Science Experiments with a Microscope,* by Shar Levine and Leslie Johnstone, Sterling Publications, 2002

*Influenza and Other Viruses (Perspectives on Disease and Illness),* by Judy Monroe, Lifematters Press, 2001

## section 3 Viruses

### Living or Not?

To a biologist, living organisms are cellular and are able to grow and reproduce independently. The smallest organisms that satisfy these criteria are bacteria. Viruses do not meet most criteria for being a living organism.

Viruses are segments of DNA or RNA wrapped in a protein coat. A membranous envelope surrounds many animal viruses. The lipids of the envelope are taken from the host cell, but the proteins are coded by the virus's genetic material. Viruses cannot reproduce on their own but multiply only within host cells using the cellular machinery of the host cell. The host cells often are destroyed when viruses multiply. For the host organism, infection by a virus may have a minor effect like a cold or may be devastating like AIDS. Several types of cancer, including some skin and cervical cancers, are now known to be caused by viruses. Viruses continue to have a major impact on the living world.

## Chapter Vocabulary

cell membrane, p. 38
cytoplasm, p. 38
cell wall, p. 39
organelle, p. 40
nucleus, p. 40
chloroplast, p. 42
mitochondrion, p. 42
ribosome, p. 42
endoplasmic reticulum, p. 43
Golgi body, p. 43
tissue, p. 45
organ, p. 45
cell theory, p. 51
virus, p. 52
host cell, p. 52

**Science Journal** Student responses will vary, but may include how they became a scientist, how can cancer be treated, and when will there be a cure for cancer.

**INTERACTIVE CHALKBOARD** with Image Bank

**PowerPoint® Presentations**

This CD-ROM is an editable Microsoft® PowerPoint® presentation that includes:
- a pre-made presentation for every chapter
- interactive graphics
- animations
- audio clips
- image bank
- all new section and chapter questions
- Standardized Test Practice
- transparencies
- pre-lab questions for all labs
- Foldables directions
- links to in7.msscience.com

# Cells

### chapter preview

**sections**

1 **Cell Structure**
  *Lab  Comparing Cells*

2 **Viewing Cells**

3 **Viruses**
  *Lab  Comparing Light Microscopes*

  *Virtual Lab  How do animal and plant cells work?*

### Too Small To Be Seen

The world around you is filled with organisms that you could overlook, or even be unable to see. Some of these organisms are one-celled and some are many-celled. You can study these organisms and the cells of other organisms by using microscopes.

**Science Journal** Write three questions that you would ask a scientist researching cancer cells.

36

## Theme Connection

**Scale and Structure** All organisms are made up of cells, which are the basic unit organisms. Cells are made up of many types of smaller structures, or organelles. This idea wasn't conceived of until the invention of the microscope.

### About the Photo

**Brain Cells** These are brain cells from the cortex of a mammalian brain. Astrocytes are star-shaped cells that might play a role in the storage of information. A technique called immunofluorescence was used to stain the cells shown here. Fluorescent dyes are attached to antibodies that recognize specific molecules in the cells. Under ultraviolet light, the dye fluoresces. Each cell's cytoplasm appears green, and each astrocyte's nucleus and other neighboring cells appear blue.

# Start-Up Activities

## Magnifying Cells

If you look around your classroom, you can see many things of all sizes. Using a magnifying lens, you can see more details. You might examine a speck of dust and discover that it is a living or dead insect. In the following lab, use a magnifying lens to search for the smallest thing you can find in the classroom.

1. Obtain a magnifying lens from your teacher. Note its power (the number followed by ×, shown somewhere on the lens frame or handle).

2. Using the magnifying lens, look around the room for the smallest object that you can find.

3. Measure the size of the image as you see it with the magnifying lens. To estimate the real size of the object, divide that number by the power. For example, if it looks 2 cm long and the power is 10×, the real length is about 0.2 cm.

4. **Think Critically** Write a paragraph that describes what you observed. Did the details become clearer? Explain.

 **Cells** Make the following Foldable to help you illustrate the main parts of cells.

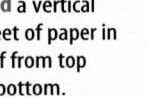 **STEP 1** Fold a vertical sheet of paper in half from top to bottom.

 **STEP 2** Fold in half from side to side with the fold at the top.

 **STEP 3** Unfold the paper once. Cut only the fold of the top flap to make two tabs.

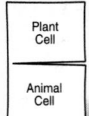 **STEP 4** Turn the paper vertically and write on the front tabs as shown.

**Illustrate and Label** As you read the chapter, draw and identify the parts of plant and animal cells under the appropriate tab.

 Preview this chapter's content and activities at in7.msscience.com

37

**Purpose** Students will use a magnifying lens to study very small objects. Students will calculate the actual size of the object from a measured size seen through the magnifying lens. L2

**Preparation** Obtain magnifying lenses and make sure the power is clearly visible on each one.

**Materials** magnifying lenses, rulers

**Teaching Strategy** Have some very small objects, such as grains of sand, salt, sugar, etc., available for students to study with their magnifying lenses.

## Think Critically

Details of small objects will become larger and clearer when seen through a magnifying lens.

## Assessment

**Oral** Have students describe aloud additional features of small objects, such as sand, salt, sugar, dust particles, etc., that they can observe through a magnifying lens. Use **Performance Assessment in the Science Classroom,** p. 89. L2

 **Dinah Zike Study Fold**

Student preparation materials for this Foldable are available in the Chapter *FAST FILE* Resources.

**Probeware Labs**
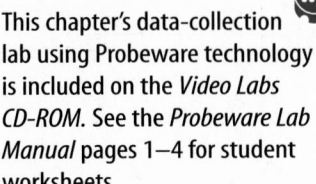

This chapter's data-collection lab using Probeware technology is included on the *Video Labs CD-ROM*. See the *Probeware Lab Manual* pages 1–4 for student worksheets.

**38 CHAPTER 2** Cells

## 1 Motivate

### Bellringer

**INTERACTIVE CHALKBOARD**
PowerPoint® Presentations

**Section Focus Transparencies**
also are available on the
Interactive Chalkboard CD-ROM.

L2 ELL

**Section 1 Section Focus Transparency** — A Factory Analogy

If this factory were a cell, it would run 24 hours a day and 7 days a week. Just like a factory, cells use raw materials to produce what's needed. Like a factory, they have a control center, a source of power, and a way to move products and waste.

Control center
Factory wall
Electric generator
Storage barrel

1. What part of the drawing directs the activities in the factory?
2. Identify the part of the drawing that provides energy to the factory.
3. What function do the storage barrels have?

### Tie to Prior Knowledge

**Body Systems** Ask students what body systems they need to live. Write their responses on the board or overhead projector. Use this list to help students understand that the functions of life are carried out in the cell.

L2

---

**section**
**1**

Standards—7.4.4: …various organs and tissues function to serve the needs of cells for food, air, and waste removal. **7.4.5:** Explain that the basic functions of organisms, such as extracting energy from food and getting rid of wastes, are carried out within the cell and understand that the way which cells function is similar in all organisms.

Also covers: 7.2.2, 7.4.7 (Detailed standards begin on page IN8.)

# Cell Structure

## as you read

### *What* You'll Learn

- **Identify** names and functions of each part of a cell.
- **Explain** how important a nucleus is in a cell.
- **Compare** tissues, organs, and organ systems.

### *Why* It's Important

If you know how organelles function, it's easier to understand how cells survive.

### Review Vocabulary

**photosynthesis:** process by which most plants, some protists, and many types of bacteria make their own food

### New Vocabulary

- cell membrane
- cytoplasm
- cell wall
- organelle
- nucleus
- chloroplast
- mitochondrion
- ribosome
- endoplasmic reticulum
- Golgi body
- tissue
- organ

## Common Cell Traits

Living cells are dynamic and have several things in common. A cell is the smallest unit that is capable of performing life functions. All cells have an outer covering called a **cell membrane.** Inside every cell is a gelatinlike material called **cytoplasm** (SI tuh pla zum). In the cytoplasm of every cell is hereditary material that controls the life of the cell.

**Comparing Cells** Cells come in many sizes. A nerve cell in your leg could be a meter long. A human egg cell is no bigger than the dot on this *i*. A human red blood cell is about one-tenth the size of a human egg cell. A bacterium is even smaller—8,000 of the smallest bacteria can fit inside one of your red blood cells.

A cell's shape might tell you something about its function. The nerve cell in **Figure 1** has many fine extensions that send and receive impulses to and from other cells. Though a nerve cell cannot change shape, muscle cells and some blood cells can. In plant stems, some cells are long and hollow and have openings at their ends. These cells carry food and water throughout the plant.

Bacterium

Nerve cell

**Figure 1** The shape of the cell can tell you something about its function. These cells are drawn 700 times their actual size.

Red blood cell

Muscle cell

**38 CHAPTER 2** Cells

---

## Section 1 Resource Manager

**Chapter *FAST FILE* Resources**
Transparency Activity, pp. 44, 47–48
Directed Reading for Content Mastery, pp. 19, 20
Note-taking Worksheets, pp. 33–35
MiniLAB, p. 3
Enrichment, p. 30

Lab Worksheet, pp. 5–6
Reinforcement, p. 27
**Life Science Critical Thinking/Problem Solving**, p. 1
**Mathematics Skill Activities**, p. 5

Prokaryotic cell

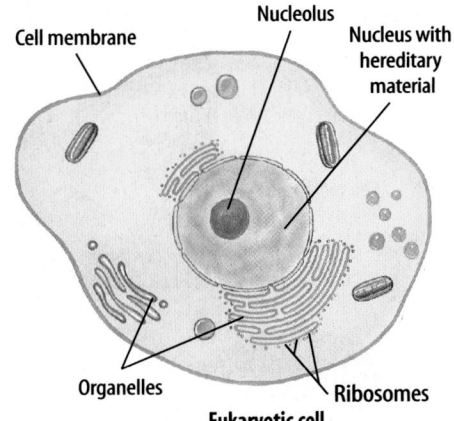

Eukaryotic cell

**Cell Types** Scientists have found that cells can be separated into two groups. One group has no membrane-bound structures inside the cell and the other group does, as shown in **Figure 2.** Cells without membrane-bound structures are called prokaryotic (proh KAYR ee yah tihk) cells. Cells with membrane-bound structures are called eukaryotic (yew KAYR ee yah tihk) cells.

**Reading Check** *Into what two groups can cells be separated?*

## Cell Organization

Each cell in your body has a specific function. You might compare a cell to a busy delicatessen that is open 24 hours every day. Raw materials for the sandwiches are brought in often. Some food is eaten in the store, and some customers take their food with them. Sometimes food is prepared ahead of time for quick sale. Wastes are put into trash bags for removal or recycling. Similarly, your cells are taking in nutrients, secreting and storing chemicals, and breaking down substances 24 hours every day.

**Cell Wall** Just like a deli that is located inside the walls of a building, some cells are enclosed in a cell wall. The cells of plants, algae, fungi, and most bacteria are enclosed in a cell wall. **Cell walls** are tough, rigid outer coverings that protect the cell and give it shape.

A plant cell wall, as shown in **Figure 3,** mostly is made up of a carbohydrate called cellulose. The long, threadlike fibers of cellulose form a thick mesh that allows water and dissolved materials to pass through it. Cell walls also can contain pectin, which is used in jam and jelly, and lignin, which is a compound that makes cell walls rigid. Plant cells responsible for support have a lot of lignin in their walls.

**Figure 2** Examine these drawings of cells. Prokaryotic cells are only found in one-celled organisms, such as bacteria. Protists, fungi, plants, and animals are made of eukaryotic cells.
**Describe** *differences you see between them.*

**Figure 3** The protective cell wall of a plant cell is outside the cell membrane.

Color-enhanced TEM Magnification: 9000×

Cell wall

## Curriculum Connection

**Health** Cellulose, found in all plant cell walls, is not digestible by humans. However, it provides fiber, which is important because it helps in the elimination of wastes. Have students make a list of foods that contain fiber. Lists should include fruits, grains, and leafy vegetables. L2

## 2 Teach

**Quick Demo**

**Different Cell**

**Materials** microprojector, prepared slides of plant, animal, and bacterial cells

**Estimated Time** 10 minutes

**Procedure** Show the prepared slides to students using the microprojector. Have students identify the characteristics of each cell shown. L2 ℕ **Visual-Spatial**

**Caption Answer**

**Figure 2** Answers may include the prokaryotic cell has no membrane-bound structures inside; the eukaryotic cell does have membrane-bound structures.

**Reading Check**

**Answer** prokaryotic and eukaryotic

**Use an Analogy**

**Cell Wall** To show how a plant cell wall provides strength, inflate a balloon and place it inside a small cardboard box. The balloon represents the cell membrane and the box represents the cell wall.

**Discussion**

**Similarities** How are prokaryotic and eukaryotic cells similar? Both have cell membranes, cytoplasm, and DNA as their genetic material.

## Discussion

**Damaged Cells** What would happen if the nucleus of a cell were damaged? The cell would no longer function correctly because the nucleus controls all the cell's activities.

**Purpose** Students model cytoplasm. [L2] **ELL** **IS** **Kinesthetic**

**Materials** 250-mL beaker, unflavored gelatin (one package per student group), water, flashlight, stirring rod

**Teaching Strategy** Be certain students stir the gelatin well before shining the light on the beaker.

**Analysis**

1. particles suspended in the gelatin, which represent organelles suspended in the cytoplasm
2. A model is a representation of an abstract object that is used to help visualize and better understand it.

## Assessment

**Oral** Have students infer how the chemical composition of cytoplasm compares to that of gelatin. Both are water-based suspensions. Cytoplasm is 80% water. Use **Performance Assessment in the Science Classroom,** p. 89.

---

**Figure 4** A cell membrane is made up of a double layer of fatlike molecules.

Cell membranes

Color-enhanced TEM Magnification: 125000×

**Figure 5** Cytoskeleton, a network of fibers in the cytoplasm, gives cells structure and helps them maintain shape.

Stained LM Magnification: 700×

**Modeling Cytoplasm**

**Procedure**

1. Add 100 mL of **water** to a **clear container.**
2. Add **unflavored gelatin** and stir.
3. Shine a **flashlight** through the solution.

**Analysis**

1. Describe what you see.
2. How does a model help you understand what cytoplasm might be like?

---

**Cell Membrane** The protective layer around all cells is the cell membrane, as shown in **Figure 4.** If cells have cell walls, the cell membrane is inside of it. The cell membrane regulates interactions between the cell and the environment. Water is able to move freely into and out of the cell through the cell membrane. Food particles and some molecules enter and waste products leave through the cell membrane.

**Cytoplasm** Cells are filled with a gelatinlike substance called cytoplasm that constantly flows inside the cell membrane. Many important chemical reactions occur within the cytoplasm.

Throughout the cytoplasm is a framework called the cytoskeleton, which helps the cell maintain or change its shape. Cytoskeletons enable some cells to move. An amoeba, for example, moves by stretching and contracting its cytoskeleton. The cytoskeleton is made up of thin, hollow tubes of protein and thin, solid protein fibers, as shown in **Figure 5.** Proteins are organic molecules made up of amino acids.

✔ **Reading Check** *What is the function of the cytoskeleton?*

Most of a cell's life processes occur in the cytoplasm. Within the cytoplasm of eukaryotic cells are structures called **organelles.** Some organelles process energy and others manufacture substances needed by the cell or other cells. Certain organelles move materials, while others act as storage sites. Most organelles are surrounded by membranes. The nucleus is usually the largest organelle in a cell.

**Nucleus** The nucleus is like the deli manager who directs the store's daily operations and passes on information to employees. The **nucleus,** shown in **Figure 6,** directs all cell activities and is separated from the cytoplasm by a membrane. Materials enter and leave the nucleus through openings in the membrane. The nucleus contains the instructions for everything the cell does. These instructions are found on long, threadlike, hereditary material made of DNA. DNA is the chemical that contains the code for the cell's structure and activities. During cell division, the hereditary material coils tightly around proteins to form structures called chromosomes. A structure called a nucleolus also is found in the nucleus.

---

## Teacher FYI

**Electron Microscopes** Before electron microscopes, scientists could only theorize about many cell structures and their makeups. Even the best compound microscope cannot reveal what can be seen with electron microscopes.

## Curriculum Connection

**Health** Students may think that any cholesterol in the body presents a health risk. Cholesterol is an important component of the cell membrane. It creates a health risk only when it is present in high levels in the blood, where it builds up in arteries and obstructs blood flow. Ask students to investigate cholesterol to differentiate between blood cholesterol and dietary cholesterol. [L3]

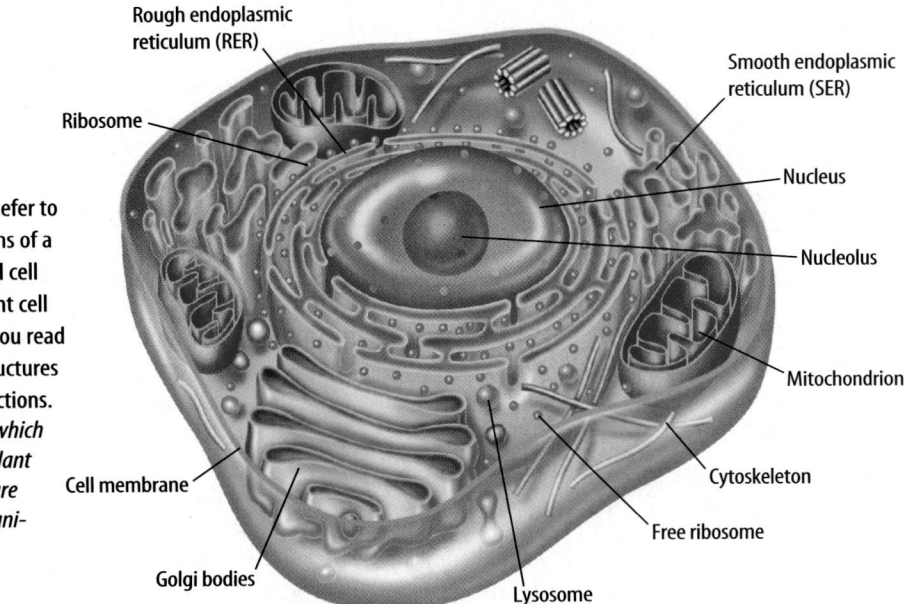

**Figure 6** Refer to these diagrams of a typical animal cell (top) and plant cell (bottom) as you read about cell structures and their functions. **Determine** *which structures a plant cell has that are not found in animal cells.*

Rough endoplasmic reticulum (RER)

Ribosome

Smooth endoplasmic reticulum (SER)

Nucleus

Nucleolus

Mitochondrion

Cell membrane

Cytoskeleton

Free ribosome

Golgi bodies

Lysosome

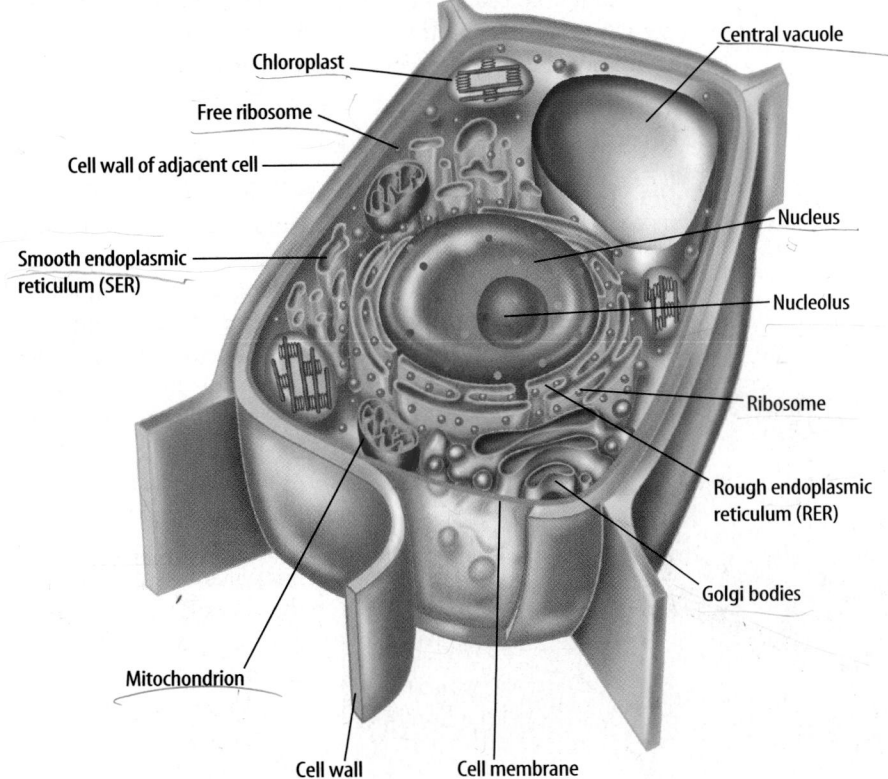

Chloroplast

Free ribosome

Cell wall of adjacent cell

Smooth endoplasmic reticulum (SER)

Central vacuole

Nucleus

Nucleolus

Ribosome

Rough endoplasmic reticulum (RER)

Golgi bodies

Mitochondrion

Cell wall

Cell membrane

## Use an Analogy

**Organelle Functions** Point out that just as each part of a car engine performs a different function to enable the car to run, each organelle performs a different function in the cell.

## Use Science Words

**Word Origin** Greek and Latin words are used in naming cell parts. Have students make a list of cell parts and use a dictionary to find the origins of the words and their meanings. L2 IS **Linguistic**

## IDENTIFYING
## Misconceptions

**Water in Cells** Students may think that cells are solid. Explain that almost 80 percent of a cell is water. The water is enclosed in a membrane that allows certain materials to enter and leave.

## Caption Answer

**Figure 6** cell wall, central vacuole, chloroplast

## Virtual Labs

**Cells** *How do animal and plant cells work?*

# Visual Learning

**Figure 6** Have students create a network tree concept map comparing and contrasting plant and animal cells. Diagrams should make clear which organelles appear in both cells and which are specific to only one type of cell. L2 IS **Visual-Spatial** P

# Differentiated Instruction

**Challenge** Have students do research on the cylindrical organelles in animal cells that are called centrioles. Have students discuss the function of these organelles. How many centrioles are contained within a cell? What is their function in mitosis and meiosis? Students can draw what they learn and share their findings. L3

**Figure 7** Chloroplasts use light energy to make sugar from carbon dioxide and water.

Color-enhanced TEM Magnification: 37000×

### Indiana Academic Standard Check

7.4.5: Explain how the basic functions of organisms . . . are carried out within the cell . . . .

✔ Why are ribosomes important to prokaryotic and eukaryotic cells?

✔ Because they are where proteins are made, which are needed for nearly every cell activity.

**Figure 8** Mitochondria release energy that is needed by the cell from food.

 **INTEGRATE Physics**

**Energy-Processing Organelles** Cells require a continuous supply of energy to process food, make new substances, eliminate wastes, and communicate with each other. In plant cells, food is made in green organelles in the cytoplasm called **chloroplasts** (KLOR uh plasts), as shown in **Figure 7.** Chloroplasts contain the green pigment chlorophyll, which gives many leaves and stems their green color. Chlorophyll captures light energy that is used to make a sugar called glucose. Glucose molecules store the captured light energy as chemical energy. Many cells, including animal cells, do not have chloroplasts for making food. They must get food from their environment.

The energy in food is stored until it is released by the mitochondria. **Mitochondria** (mi tuh KAHN dree uh) (singular, *mitochondrion*), such as the one shown in **Figure 8,** are organelles where energy is released from breaking down food into carbon dioxide and water. Just as the gas or electric company supplies fuel for the deli, a mitochondrion releases energy for use by the cell. Some types of cells, such as muscle cells, are more active than other cells. These cells have large numbers of mitochondria. Why would active cells have more or larger mitochondria?

**Manufacturing Organelles** One substance that takes part in nearly every cell activity is protein. Proteins are part of cell membranes. Other proteins are needed for chemical reactions that take place in the cytoplasm. Cells make their own proteins on small structures called **ribosomes.** Even though ribosomes are considered organelles, they are not membrane bound. Some ribosomes float freely in the cytoplasm; others are attached to the endoplasmic reticulum. Ribosomes are made in the nucleolus and move out into the cytoplasm. Ribosomes receive directions from the hereditary material in the nucleus on how, when, and in what order to make specific proteins.

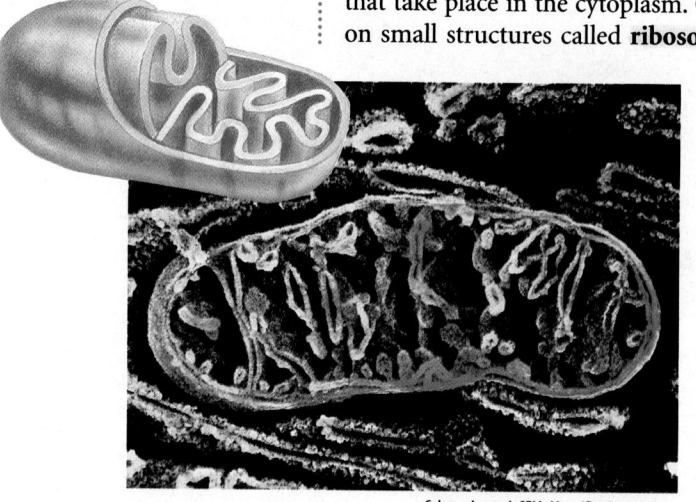

Color-enhanced SEM Magnification: 48000×

**42 CHAPTER 2** Cells

**Figure 9** Endoplasmic reticulum (ER) is a complex series of membranes in the cytoplasm of the cell.
**Infer** *what smooth ER would look like.*

Color-enhanced TEM Magnification: 65000×

## Processing, Transporting, and Storing Organelles

The **endoplasmic reticulum** (en duh PLAZ mihk • rih TIHK yuh lum) or ER, as shown in **Figure 9,** extends from the nucleus to the cell membrane. It is a series of folded membranes in which materials can be processed and moved around inside of the cell. The ER takes up a lot of space in some cells.

The endoplasmic reticulum may be "rough" or "smooth." ER that has no attached ribosomes is called smooth endoplasmic reticulum. This type of ER processes other cellular substances such as lipids that store energy. Ribosomes are attached to areas on the rough ER. There they carry out their job of making proteins that are moved out of the cell or used within the cell.

✓ **Reading Check** *What is the difference between rough ER and smooth ER?*

After proteins are made in a cell, they are transferred to another type of cell organelle called the Golgi (GAWL jee) bodies. The **Golgi bodies,** as shown ion **Figure 10,** are stacked, flattened membranes. The Golgi bodies sort proteins and other cellular substances and package them into membrane-bound structures called vesicles. The vesicles deliver cellular substances to areas inside the cell. They also carry cellular substances to the cell membrane where they are released to the outside of the cell.

Just as a deli has refrigerators for temporary storage of some of its foods and ingredients, cells have membrane-bound spaces called vacuoles for the temporary storage of materials. A vacuole can store water, waste products, food, and other cellular materials. In plant cells, the vacuole may make up most of the cell's volume.

**Figure 10** The Golgi body packages materials and moves them to the outside of the cell.
**Explain** *why materials are removed from the cell.*

Color-enhanced TEM
Magnification: 28000×

## Reading Check

### Applying Math

**Indiana Math Standards**
7.5.1, 7.5.4

### Answers to Practice Problems

1. $A = 2\,cm \times 2\,cm \times 6 = 24\,cm^2$
   $V = 2\,cm \times 2\,cm \times 2\,cm$
   $= 8\,cm^3$
   $R = 24\,cm^2/8\,cm^3 = 3\,cm^2/cm^3$
   As the size of the cube decreases, the ratio increases.

2. $A = 2(4\,cm \times 4\,cm) + 4(4\,cm \times 8\,cm) = 160\,cm^2$
   $V = 4\,cm \times 4\,cm \times 8\,cm$
   $= 128\,cm^3$
   $R = 160\,cm^2/128\,cm^3$
   $= 1.25\,cm^2/cm^3$
   The ratio decreases.

**Recycling** Just like a cell, you can recycle materials. Paper, plastics, aluminum, and glass are materials that can be recycled into usable items. Make a promotional poster to encourage others to recycle.

**Recycling Organelles** Active cells break down and recycle substances. Organelles called lysosomes (LI suh sohmz) contain digestive chemicals that help break down food molecules, cell wastes, and worn-out cell parts. In a healthy cell, chemicals are released into vacuoles only when needed. The lysosome's membrane prevents the digestive chemicals inside from leaking into the cytoplasm and destroying the cell. When a cell dies, a lysosome's membrane disintegrates. This releases digestive chemicals that allow the quick breakdown of the cell's contents.

## Reading Check

*What is the function of the lysosome's membrane?*

### Applying Math    Calculate a Ratio

**CELL RATIO** Assume that a cell is like a cube with six equal sides. Find the ratio of surface area to volume for a cube that is 4 cm high.

4 cm
4 cm   4 cm

**Solution**

**1** *This is what you know:*    A cube has 6 equal sides of 4 cm × 4 cm.

**2** *This is what you need to find out:*    What is the ratio (R) of surface area to volume for the cube?

**3** *These are the equations you use:*
- surface area ($A$) = width × length × 6
- volume ($V$) = length × width × height
- $R = A/V$

**4** *This is the procedure you need to use:*
- Substitute in known values and solve the equations
  $A = 4\,cm \times 4\,cm \times 6 = 96\,cm^2$
  $V = 4\,cm \times 4\,cm \times 4\,cm = 64\,cm^3$
  $R = 96\,cm^2/64\,cm^3 = 1.5\,cm^2/cm^3$

**5** *Check your answer:*    Multiply the ratio by the volume. Did you calculate the surface area?

### Practice Problems

1. Calculate the ratio of surface area to volume for a cube that is 2 cm high. What happens to this ratio as the size of the cube decreases?

2. If a 4-cm cube doubled just one of its dimensions, what would happen to the ratio of surface area to volume?

 For more practice, visit in7.msscience.com/math_practice

## Active Reading

# From Cell to Organism

Many one-celled organisms perform all their life functions by themselves. Cells in a many-celled organism, however, do not work alone. Each cell carries on its own life functions while depending in some way on other cells in the organism.

In **Figure 11,** you can see cardiac muscle cells grouped together to form a tissue. A **tissue** is a group of similar cells that work together to do one job. Each cell in a tissue does its part to keep the tissue alive.

Tissues are organized into organs. An **organ** is a structure made up of two or more different types of tissues that work together. Your heart is an organ made up of cardiac muscle tissue, nerve tissue, and blood tissues. The cardiac muscle tissue contracts, making the heart pump. The nerve tissue brings messages that tell the heart how fast to beat. The blood tissue is carried from the heart to other organs of the body.

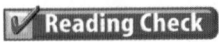 **Reading Check** *What types of tissues make up your heart?*

A group of organs working together to perform a certain function is an organ system. Your heart, arteries, veins, and capillaries make up your cardiovascular system. In a many-celled organism, several systems work together in order to perform life functions efficiently. Your nervous, circulatory, respiratory, muscular, and other systems work together to keep you alive.

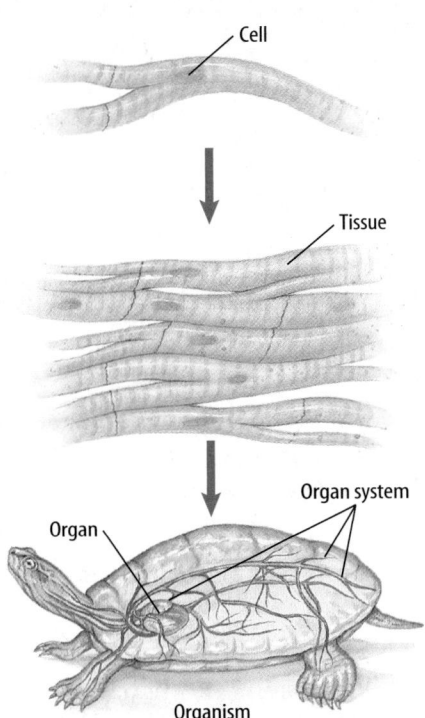

Cell

Tissue

Organ system

Organ

Organism

**Figure 11** In a many-celled organism, cells are organized into tissues, tissues into organs, organs into systems, and systems into an organism.

---

## section 1 review

### Summary

**Common Cell Traits**
- All cells have an outer covering called a cell membrane.
- Cells can be classified as prokaryotic or eukaryotic.

**Cell Organization**
- Each cell in your body has a specific function.
- Most of a cell's life processes occur in the cytoplasm.

**From Cell to Organism**
- In a many-celled organism, several systems work together to perform life functions.

### Self Check

1. **Explain** why the nucleus is important in the life of a cell.
2. **Determine** why digestive enzymes in a cell are enclosed in a membrane-bound organelle.
3. **Discuss** how cells, tissues, organs, and organ systems are related.
4. **Think Critically** How is the cell of a one-celled organism different from the cells in many-celled organisms?

#### Applying Skills

5. **Interpret Scientific Illustrations** Examine **Figure 6.** Make a list of differences and similarities between the animal cell and the plant cell.

## section 1 review

1. It directs the activities of the cell and stores hereditary information.
2. It prevents the digestive chemicals inside from destroying the cell.
3. Organ systems are made of organs, which are made of tissues. Tissues are made of cells.
4. one-celled—performs all life functions; multicellular—cells depend on each other
5. Plant cells have chloroplasts and cell walls which animal cells do not have. Unlike plant cells, animal cells have centrioles.

# Comparing Cells

## Real-World Question

**Purpose** Students identify and compare the parts of a plant and animal cell. L2 ELL IS **Visual-Spatial**

**Process Skills** observe, identify, infer, diagram, compare and contrast, classify

**Time Required** 45 minutes

## Procedure

**Alternate Materials** If *Elodea* is unavailable, the thin, newest leaves of a coleus plant or similar houseplant.

**Safety Precautions** Caution students to use extreme care when working with a microscope and microscope slides.

### Teaching Strategies

• Have students work in pairs. One student obtains and sets up the microscope while the other prepares the wet mount and obtains the cheek-cell slide. Both observe the slides and record data.

• Have students clean slides and coverslips after use.

**Troubleshooting** To see movement of cytoplasm, use only leaves from the tips of *Elodea*. Help students focus so they will see cell layers. Students may not be able to see the nucleus. Many students may mistake the chloroplast for the cells.

## Conclude and Apply

1. The *Elodea* cell is rectangular; the cheek cell is oval.

2. Only plant cells have a cell wall and chloroplasts.

---

If you compared a goldfish to a rose, you would find them unlike each other. Are their individual cells different also?

## Real-World Question

How do human cheek cells and plant cells compare?

### Goals

■ **Compare and contrast** an animal cell and a plant cell.

### Materials

microscope     dropper
microscope slide     *Elodea* plant
coverslip     prepared slide of human
forceps        cheek cells
tap water

### Safety Precautions

## Procedure

1. Copy the data table in your Science Journal. Check off the cell parts as you observe them.

| Cell Observations | | |
|---|:---:|:---:|
| **Cell Part** | **Cheek** | ***Elodea*** |
| Cytoplasm | ✔ | ✔ |
| Nucleus | ✔ | ✔ |
| Chloroplasts | | ✔ |
| Cell wall | | ✔ |
| Cell membrane | ✔ | ✔ |

2. Using forceps, make a wet-mount slide of a young leaf from the tip of an *Elodea* plant.

---

3. **Observe** the leaf on low power. Focus on the top layer of cells.

4. Switch to high power and focus on one cell. In the center of the cell is a membrane-bound organelle called the central vacuole. Observe the chloroplasts—the green, disk-shaped objects moving around the central vacuole. Try to find the cell nucleus. It looks like a clear ball.

5. **Draw** the *Elodea* cell. Label the cell wall, cytoplasm, chloroplasts, central vacuole, and nucleus. Return to low power and remove the slide. Properly dispose of the slide.

6. **Observe** the prepared slide of cheek cells under low power.

7. Switch to high power and observe the cell nucleus. Draw and label the cell membrane, cytoplasm, and nucleus. Return to low power and remove the slide.

## Conclude and Apply

1. **Compare and contrast** the shapes of the cheek cell and the *Elodea* cell.

2. **Draw conclusions** about the differences between plant and animal cells.

### Communicating Your Data

Draw the two kinds of cells on one sheet of paper. Use a green pencil to label the organelles found only in plants, a red pencil to label the organelles found only in animals, and a blue pencil to label the organelles found in both. **For more help, refer to the** Science Skill Handbook.

---

### ✔ Assessment

**Performance** To further assess students' abilities to compare plant and animal cells, have them examine cells from lettuce leaves and other types of animal cells on prepared slides. Use **Performance Assessment in the Science Classroom,** p. 97. L2

### Communicating Your Data

Chloroplasts and cell walls should be labeled in green on the plant cell. No organelles are labeled red. Cytoplasm, nuclei, and cell membranes should be labeled in blue on plant and animal cells. L2

# section 2
## Viewing Cells

## Magnifying Cells

The number of living things in your environment that you can't see is much greater than the number that you can see. Many of the things that you cannot see are only one cell in size. To see most cells, you need to use a microscope.

Trying to see separate cells in a leaf, like the ones in **Figure 12,** is like trying to see individual photos in a photo mosaic picture that is on the wall across the room. As you walk toward the wall, it becomes easier to see the individual photos. When you get right up to the wall, you can see details of each small photo. A microscope has one or more lenses that enlarge the image of an object as though you are walking closer to it. Seen through these lenses, the leaf appears much closer to you, and you can see the individual cells that carry on life processes.

**Early Microscopes** In the late 1500s, the first microscope was made by a Dutch maker of reading glasses. He put two magnifying glasses together in a tube and got an image that was larger than the image that was made by either lens alone.

In the mid 1600s, Antonie van Leeuwenhoek, a Dutch fabric merchant, made a simple microscope with a tiny glass bead for a lens, as shown in **Figure 13.** With it, he reported seeing things in pond water that no one had ever imagined. His microscope could magnify up to 270 times. Another way to say this is that his microscope could make the image of an object 270 times larger than its actual size. Today you would say his lens had a power of 270×. Early compound microscopes were crude by today's standards. The lenses would make an image larger, but it wasn't always sharp or clear.

Magnification: 250×

### as you read

**What You'll Learn**
- **Compare** the differences between the compound light microscope and the electron microscope.
- **Summarize** the discoveries that led to the development of the cell theory.

**Why It's Important**
Humans are like other living things because they are made of cells.

**Review Vocabulary**
**magnify:** to increase the size of something

**New Vocabulary**
- cell theory

**Figure 12** Individual cells become visible when a plant leaf is viewed using a microscope with enough magnifying power.

## 1 Motivate

INTERACTIVE CHALKBOARD
PowerPoint® Presentations

**Bellringer**

**Section Focus Transparencies** also are available on the Interactive Chalkboard CD-ROM.
L2  ELL

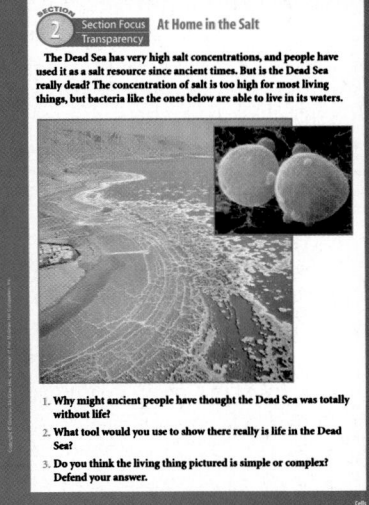

SECTION 2  Section Focus Transparency  At Home in the Salt

The Dead Sea has very high salt concentrations, and people have used it as a salt resource since ancient times. But is the Dead Sea really dead? The concentration of salt is too high for most living things, but bacteria like the ones below are able to live in its waters.

1. Why might ancient people have thought the Dead Sea was totally without life?
2. What tool would you use to show there really is life in the Dead Sea?
3. Do you think the living thing pictured is simple or complex? Defend your answer.

**Tie to Prior Knowledge**

**Magnification** Students may have used magnifying glasses and binoculars. Explain that a microscope magnifies in the same way.

---

### Section 2 Resource Manager

**Chapter FAST FILE Resources**
    Transparency Activity, p. 45
    Directed Reading for Content Mastery, p. 20
    Enrichment, p. 31
    Lab Activity, pp. 9–12, 13–16
    MiniLAB, p. 4

Reinforcement, p. 28

## Visualizing Microscopes

Have students examine the pictures and read the captions. Then ask the following questions.

What are the similarities and differences between a fluorescence microscope and a phase-contrast microscope? Possible answers: Both microscopes magnify up to 1500×. With the fluorescence microscope, the specimen must be stained and can be viewed through the scope directly. With the phase-contrast microscope, the specimen is not stained and can only be viewed on a monitor or in a photograph. Phase-contrast microscopes are good for viewing living things.

Compare and contrast the features of a TEM and an SEM. Possible answers: Both microscopes use electrons to help produce the magnified image. Also, with both microscopes the specimen can only be viewed on a monitor or in a photograph. In a TEM the electrons go through the specimen and the magnification is up to 1,000,000×. With an SEM, the electrons sweep over the surface of the specimen and a three-dimensional image is produced. The magnification of an SEM is only up to 200,000×.

### Activity

**Microscope Types** Have students identify the type of microscope(s) they use in science class. Then have students view different slides under the microscope (e.g. onion slices, hair, sliver from a grass blade, color-comics section of the newspaper). Have students draw what they observe. If possible, use several types of microscopes and a magnifying glass and have students compare how the same slide looks under each one. Ask students to list the similarities and differences between them, and hypothesize what accounts for these differences. L2

# NATIONAL GEOGRAPHIC VISUALIZING MICROSCOPES

## Figure 13

Microscopes give us a glimpse into a previously invisible world. Improvements have vastly increased their range of visibility, allowing researchers to study life at the molecular level. A selection of these powerful tools—and their magnification power—is shown here.

**Up to 250×**
**LEEUWENHOEK MICROSCOPE** Held by a modern researcher, this historic microscope allowed Leeuwenhoek to see clear images of tiny freshwater organisms that he called "beasties."

**Up to 2,000× BRIGHTFIELD / DARKFIELD MICROSCOPE** The light microscope is often called the brightfield microscope because the image is viewed against a bright background. A brightfield microscope is the tool most often used in laboratories to study cells. Placing a thin metal disc beneath the stage, between the light source and the objective lenses, converts a brightfield microscope to a darkfield microscope. The image seen using a darkfield microscope is bright against a dark background. This makes details more visible than with a brightfield microscope. Below are images of a *Paramecium* as seen using both processes.

Darkfield

Brightfield

**Up to 1,500× FLUORESCENCE MICROSCOPE** This type of microscope requires that the specimen be treated with special fluorescent stains. When viewed through this microscope, certain cell structures or types of substances glow, as seen in the image of a *Paramecium* above.

## Science Journal

**Magnification** Have students make a time line showing discoveries made with the light microscope, beginning with Robert Hooke (1665) identifying and drawing cells. L2

## Teacher FYI

**Artifacts** Any phenomenon that occurs as a result of the fixing or staining procedure used to prepare a specimen to be viewed on a slide is called an artifact. An artifact is not a feature of the living organism. Sometimes an artifact can be a simple air bubble; other times the procedure can change the shape of a particular feature.

▶ **Up to 1,000,000×** TRANSMISSION ELECTRON MICROSCOPE A TEM aims a beam of electrons through a specimen. Denser portions of the specimen allow fewer electrons to pass through and appear darker in the image. Organisms, such as the *Paramecium* at right, can only be seen when the image is photographed or shown on a monitor. A TEM can magnify hundreds of thousands of times.

◀ **Up to 1,500×** PHASE-CONTRAST MICROSCOPE A phase-contrast microscope emphasizes slight differences in a specimen's capacity to bend light waves, thereby enhancing light and dark regions without the use of stains. This type of microscope is especially good for viewing living cells, like the *Paramecium* above left. The images from a phase-contrast microscope can only be seen when the specimen is photographed or shown on a monitor.

▶ **Up to 200,000×** SCANNING ELECTRON MICROSCOPE An SEM sweeps a beam of electrons over a specimen's surface, causing other electrons to be emitted from the specimen. SEMs produce realistic, three-dimensional images, which can only be viewed as photographs or on a monitor, as in the image of the *Paramecium* at right. Here a researcher compares an SEM picture to a computer monitor showing an enhanced image.

SECTION 2 Viewing Cells **49**

## Visualizing Microscopes

### Content Background

Microscopes are used by many different types of scientists, including biologists, microbiologists, botanists, geologists, and epidemiologists. In 1665, Robert Hooke was the first person to see cells through a microscope of his creation. The idea of cell theory—that all living things are made of cells—was borne from his discovery. Although Hooke could see the individual cells clearly, he did not stain any of his specimens; therefore, he would not have been able to see other single-celled organisms such as bacteria. It was Antoni van Leeuwenhoek who first examined living organisms through a simple microscope in the late seventeenth century. He found organisms in the rain-water he collected, as well as in the scrapings he took from the surface of his teeth.

## Differentiated Instruction

**English-Language Learners** Have students work in pairs to create an advertisement for a microscope. Students should discuss all of the parts of a microscope in their advertisement. The advertisement should also include all of the parts of a cell that can be visualized using the microscope. L2

## Visual Learning

**Figure 13** Have students make a chart comparing and contrasting the different types of microscopes in this figure. They should include information on lenses and the uses of each. L2
**LS** Visual-Spatial

## Mini LAB

**Purpose** Students discover objects that can be used to magnify. L2 ELL IS **Kinesthetic**

**Materials** clear drinking glass, clear glass bowl, water, magnifying lens, newspaper pages

**Teaching Strategy** Try this lab with the glasses students will use. Determine beforehand the amount of water that will be needed.

**Analysis**
Each of the objects magnifies the newsprint.

### Assessment

**Performance** Cover newsprint with clear plastic wrap. Place a drop of water on the plastic wrap. Have students explain what they see and why. The words appear magnified because the water drop acts like a convex lens. Use **Performance Assessment in the Science Classroom**, p. 89.

Try at Home

INTEGRATE Career

**Cell Biologist** The field of cell biology is very diverse. Many techniques require the use of different microscopes. As students research the drugs that cell biologists are studying, also have them identify techniques that require microscopes, and the types of microscopes that cell biologists use.

---

## Mini LAB

**Observing Magnified Objects**

**Procedure**
1. Look at a **newspaper** through the curved side and through the flat bottom of an **empty, clear glass.**
2. Look at the newspaper through a **clear glass bowl filled with water** and then with a **magnifying lens.**

**Analysis**
In your Science Journal, compare how well you can see the newspaper through each of the objects.

Try at Home

INTEGRATE Career

**Cell Biologist** Microscopes are important tools for cell biologists as they research diseases. In your Science Journal, make a list of diseases for which you think cell biologists are trying to find effective drugs.

---

**Modern Microscopes** Scientists use a variety of microscopes to study organisms, cells, and cell parts that are too small to be seen with the human eye. Depending on how many lenses a microscope contains, it is called simple or compound. A simple microscope is similar to a magnifying lens. It has only one lens. A microscope's lens makes an enlarged image of an object and directs light toward your eye. The change in apparent size produced by a microscope is called magnification. Microscopes vary in powers of magnification. Some microscopes can make images of individual atoms.

The microscope you probably will use to study life science is a compound light microscope, similar to the one in the Reference Handbook at the back of this book. The compound light microscope has two sets of lenses—eyepiece lenses and objective lenses. The eyepiece lenses are mounted in one or two tubelike structures. Images of objects viewed through two eyepieces, or stereomicroscopes, are three-dimensional. Images of objects viewed through one eyepiece are not. Compound light microscopes usually have two to four movable objective lenses.

**Magnification** The powers of the eyepiece and objective lenses determine the total magnifications of a microscope. If the eyepiece lens has a power of $10\times$ and the objective lens has a power of $43\times$, then the total magnification is $430\times$ ($10\times$ times $43\times$). Some compound microscopes, like those in **Figure 13**, have more powerful lenses that can magnify an object up to 2,000 times its original size.

**Electron Microscopes** Things that are too small to be seen with other microscopes can be viewed with an electron microscope. Instead of using lenses to direct beams of light, an electron microscope uses a magnetic field in a vacuum to direct beams of electrons. Some electron microscopes can magnify images up to one million times. Electron microscope images must be photographed or electronically produced.

Several kinds of electron microscopes have been invented, as shown in **Figure 13**. Scanning electron microscopes (SEM) produce a realistic, three-dimensional image. Only the surface of the specimen can be observed using an SEM. Transmission electron microscopes (TEM) produce a two-dimensional image of a thinly-sliced specimen. Details of cell parts can be examined using a TEM. Scanning tunneling microscopes (STM) are able to show the arrangement of atoms on the surface of a molecule. A metal probe is placed near the surface of the specimen and electrons flow from the tip. The hills and valleys of the specimen's surface are mapped.

---

## Curriculum Connection

**Art** Discuss the use of art in science before the camera was invented. Photocopy a picture of Hooke's drawing of cells for each student. Ask them to compare it with the photographs of cells throughout the chapter and write in their Science Journals their opinions of the advantages and disadvantages of using artwork and photography. L2 IS **Linguistic and Visual-Spatial**

## Differentiated Instruction

**Challenge** Have students research the Italian scientist who discover the Golgi body. Their research should include how this discovery was made possible and why this organelle was not seriously studied until the 1950s. Students can use references to find electron micrographs of the Golgi body to learn about it in greater depth. Students can write a biographical report on Camillo Golgi and the Golgi body. L3

## Cell Theory

During the seventeenth century, scientists used their new invention, the microscope, to explore the newly discovered microscopic world. They examined drops of blood, scrapings from their own teeth, and other small things. Cells weren't discovered until the microscope was improved. In 1665, Robert Hooke cut a thin slice of cork and looked at it under his microscope. To Hooke, the cork seemed to be made up of empty little boxes, which he named cells.

In the 1830s, Matthias Schleiden used a microscope to study plants and concluded that all plants are made of cells. Theodor Schwann, after observing different animal cells, concluded that all animals are made up of cells. Eventually, they combined their ideas and became convinced that all living things are made of cells.

Several years later, Rudolf Virchow hypothesized that cells divide to form new cells. Virchow proposed that every cell came from a cell that already existed. His observations and conclusions and those of others are summarized in the **cell theory**, as described in **Table 1.**

**Reading Check**  *Who first concluded that all animals are made of cells?*

| Table 1  The Cell Theory | |
| --- | --- |
| **All organisms are made up of one or more cells.** | An organism can be one cell or many cells like most plants and animals. |
| **The cell is the basic unit of organization in organisms.** | Even in complex organisms, the cell is the basic unit of structure and function. |
| **All cells come from cells.** | Most cells can divide to form two new, identical cells. |

**Indiana Academic Standard Check**

7.4.5: Explain . . . and understand that the way in which cells function is similar in all organisms.

✔ Which scientists concluded that the cell was the basic unit of structure in all organisms?

✔ Schleiden and Schwann

## section 2 review

### Summary

**Magnifying Cells**

- The powers of the eyepiece and objective lenses determine the total magnification of a microscope.
- An electron microscope uses a magnetic field in a vacuum to direct beams of electrons.

**Development of the Cell Theory**

- In 1665, Robert Hooke looked at a piece of cork under his microscope and called what he saw cells.
- The conclusions of Rudolf Virchow and those of others are summarized in the cell theory.

### Self Check

1. **Determine** why the invention of the microscope was important in the study of cells.
2. **State** the cell theory.
3. **Compare** a simple and a compound light microscope.
4. **Explain** Virchow's contribution to the cell theory.
5. **Think Critically**  Why would it be better to look at living cells than at dead cells?

### Applying Math

6. **Solve One-Step Equations**  Calculate the magnifications of a microscope that has an 8× eyepiece and 10× and 40× objectives.

## section 2 review

1. Microscopes made cells visible, which established them as a scientific fact. This led to the understanding that all living things are made of cells.
2. All organisms are made of one or more cells. The cell is the basic unit of organization in organisms. All cells come from other cells.
3. A simple light microscope has one lens. A compound light microscope has two or more lenses.
4. Virchow proposed that every cell came from a cell that already existed.
5. Possible answer: some cell parts disintegrate when the cell dies.
6. The low-power magnification is $80\times = (8 \times 10)$ and the high-power magnification is $320\times = (8 \times 40)$.

**Standards—7.4.12:** Explain that viruses . . . may infect the human body . . . Recognize that a person can catch a cold many times . . . . **7.6.3:** . . . Edward Jenner had shown for smallpox . . . that it was possible to produce vaccines that would induce the body to build immunity to a disease without actually causing the disease itself.

**Also covers:** 7.1.5, 7.1.6, 7.1.7, 7.4.7, 7.6.4 (Detailed standards begin on page IN8.)

## section 3

# Viruses

### as you read

**What You'll Learn**

- **Explain** how a virus makes copies of itself.
- **Identify** the benefits of vaccines.
- **Investigate** some uses of viruses.

**Why It's Important**

Viruses infect nearly all organisms, usually affecting them negatively yet sometimes affecting them positively.

**Review Vocabulary**

**disease:** a condition that results from the disruption in function of one or more of an organism's normal processes

**New Vocabulary**

- virus
- host cell

## What are viruses?

Cold sores, measles, chicken pox, colds, the flu, and AIDS are diseases caused by nonliving particles called viruses. A **virus** is a strand of hereditary material surrounded by a protein coating. Viruses don't have a nucleus or other organelles. They also lack a cell membrane. Viruses, as shown in **Figure 14,** have a variety of shapes. Because they are too small to be seen with a light microscope, they were discovered only after the electron microscope was invented. Before that time, scientists only hypothesized about viruses.

## How do viruses multiply?

All viruses can do is make copies of themselves. However, they can't do that without the help of a living cell called a **host cell.** Crystalized forms of some viruses can be stored for years. Then, if they enter an organism, they can multiply quickly.

Once a virus is inside of a host cell, the virus can act in two ways. It can either be active or it can become latent, which is an inactive stage.

**Figure 14** Viruses come in a variety of shapes.

Color-enhanced TEM Magnification: 160000×

Filoviruses do not have uniform shapes. Some of these *Ebola* viruses have a loop at one end.

The potato leafroll virus, *Polervirus,* damages potato crops worldwide.

Color-enhanced SEM Magnification: 140000×

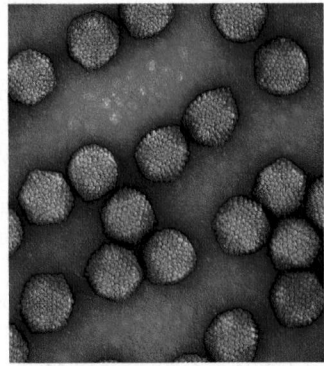

This is one of many adenoviruses that can cause a cold. Each time you have a cold, you've contacted a different adenovirus.

**52 CHAPTER 2** Cells

**Figure 15** An active virus multiplies and destroys the host cell.

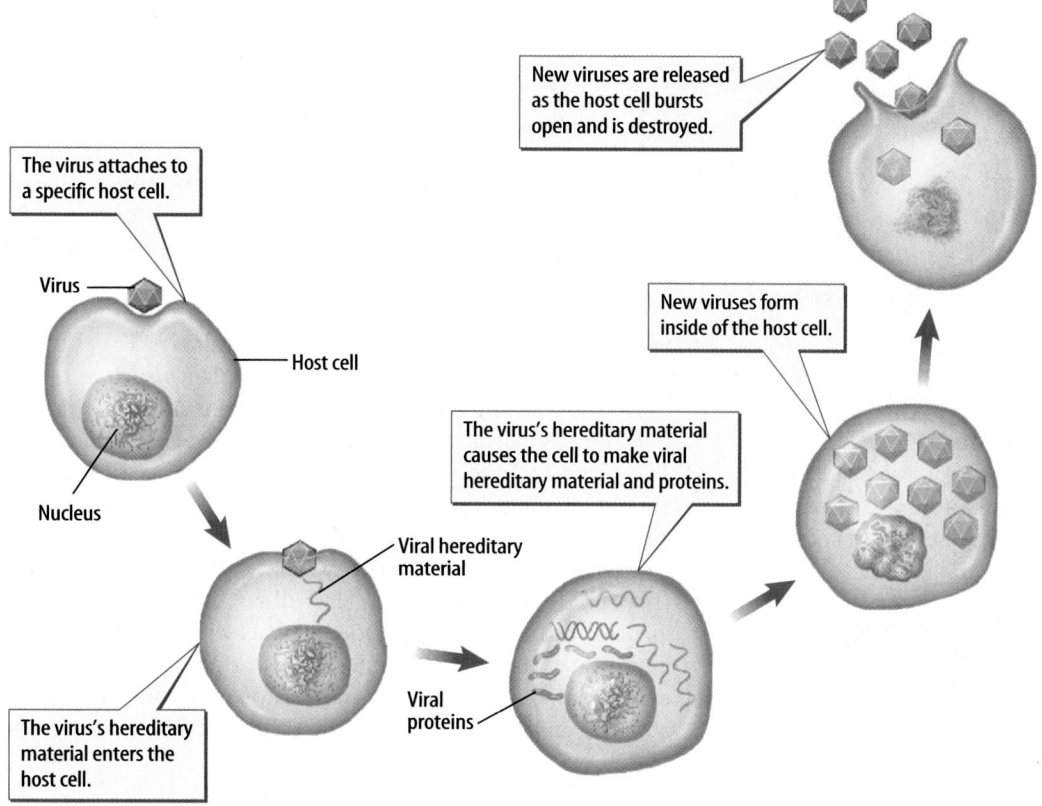

New viruses are released as the host cell bursts open and is destroyed.

The virus attaches to a specific host cell.

Virus

Host cell

Nucleus

The virus's hereditary material enters the host cell.

Viral hereditary material

Viral proteins

The virus's hereditary material causes the cell to make viral hereditary material and proteins.

New viruses form inside of the host cell.

**Active Viruses** When a virus enters a cell and is active, it causes the host cell to make new viruses. This process destroys the host cell. Follow the steps in **Figure 15** to see one way that an active virus functions inside a cell.

**Latent Viruses** Some viruses can be latent. That means that after the virus enters a cell, its hereditary material can become part of the cell's hereditary material. It does not immediately make new viruses or destroy the cell. As the host cell reproduces, the viral DNA is copied. A virus can be latent for many years. Then, at any time, certain conditions, either inside or outside your body, can activate the virus.

If you have had a cold sore on your lip, a latent virus in your body has become active. The cold sore is a sign that the virus is active and destroying cells in your lip. When the cold sore disappears, the virus has become latent again. The virus is still in your body's cells, but it is hiding and doing no apparent harm.

**Science Online**

**Topic: Virus Reactivation**
Visit in7.msscience.com for Web links to information about viruses.

**Activity** In your Science Journal, list five stimuli that might activate a latent virus.

**54 CHAPTER 2** Cells

## Use Science Words

**Word Usage** Have students use the word *vaccine* in a sentence describing its characteristics. **LS Linguistic**

### Fun Fact

Scientist have found small spore-like cells in mammal tissues that are involved in tissue repair. They have been used to repair breaks in the spinal cords of rats.

### ✓ Reading Check

**Answer** a preparation of weakened virus particles that helps prevent disease

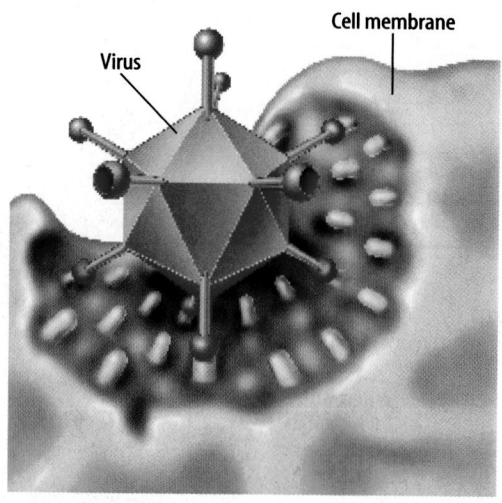

Cell membrane

Virus

**Figure 16** Viruses and the attachment sites of the host cell must match exactly. That's why most viruses infect only one kind of host cell.

---

**Indiana Academic Standard Check**

7.6.3: ... Edward Jenner, ... without understanding the underlying mechanism, ... produced a vaccine.

✓ What was the source of Jenner's vaccine?

✓ sores of people with cowpox

---

**Science Online**

**Topic: Filoviruses**

Visit in7.msscience.com for Web links to information about the virus family *Filoviridae*.

**Activity** Make a table that displays the virus name, location, and year of the initial outbreaks associated with the *Filoviridae* family.

---

## How do viruses affect organisms?

Viruses attack animals, plants, fungi, protists, and all prokaryotes. Some viruses can infect only specific kinds of cells. For instance, many viruses, such as the potato leafroll virus, are limited to one host species or to one type of tissue within that species. A few viruses affect a broad range of hosts. An example of this is the rabies virus. Rabies can infect humans and many other animal hosts.

A virus cannot move by itself, but it can reach a host's body in several ways. For example, it can be carried onto a plant's surface by the wind or it can be inhaled by an animal. In a viral infection, the virus first attaches to the surface of the host cell. The virus and the place where it attaches must fit together exactly, as shown in **Figure 16.** Because of this, most viruses attack only one kind of host cell.

Viruses that infect bacteria are called bacteriophages (bak TIHR ee uh fay jihz). They differ from other kinds of viruses in the way that they enter bacteria and release their hereditary material. Bacteriophages attach to a bacterium and inject their hereditary material. The entire cycle takes about 20 min, and each virus-infected cell releases an average of 100 viruses.

## Fighting Viruses

Vaccines are used to prevent disease. A vaccine is made from weakened virus particles that can't cause disease anymore. Vaccines have been made to prevent many diseases, including measles, mumps, smallpox, chicken pox, polio, and rabies.

### ✓ Reading Check *What is a vaccine?*

**The First Vaccine** Edward Jenner is credited with developing the first vaccine in 1796. He developed a vaccine for smallpox, a disease that was still feared in the early twentieth century. Jenner noticed that people who got a disease called cowpox didn't get smallpox. He prepared a vaccine from the sores of people who had cowpox. When injected into healthy people, the cowpox vaccine protected them from smallpox. Jenner didn't know he was fighting a virus. At that time, no one understood what caused disease or how the body fought disease.

**54 CHAPTER 2** Cells

---

## Curriculum Connection

**Math** A common unit of measure for viruses is the nanometer (nm), which is 1,000 times smaller than a micrometer (μm) and 1 million times smaller than a millimeter. A typical virus is 20 nm in size. What part of a millimeter is that? 0.000 02 mm A virus of 0.3 micrometers is how many nanometers? 300 nm **LS Logical-Mathematical**

## Differentiated Instruction

**Challenge** Have students do research on the use of viruses in genetic engineering. Students should research how genetic engineering works and what specific genetic disorders have been or could be treated using genetically engineered viruses. Students can write a newspaper article that describes their findings. **L3**

**Treating Viral Diseases** Antibiotics treat bacterial infections but are not effective against viral diseases. One way your body can stop viral infections is by making interferons. Interferons are proteins that are produced rapidly by virus-infected cells and move to noninfected cells in the host. They cause the noninfected cells to produce protective substances.

Antiviral drugs can be given to infected patients to help fight a virus. A few drugs show some effectiveness against viruses but some have limited use because of their adverse side effects.

**Preventing Viral Diseases** Public health measures for preventing viral diseases include vaccinating people, improving sanitary conditions, quarantining patients, and controlling animals that spread disease. For example, annual rabies vaccinations of pets and farm animals protect them and humans from infection. To control the spread of rabies in wild animals such as coyotes and wolves, wildlife workers place bait containing an oral rabies vaccine, as shown in **Figure 17,** where wild animals will find it.

## Research with Viruses

You might think viruses are always harmful. However, through research, scientists are discovering helpful uses for some viruses. One use, called gene therapy, substitutes normal hereditary material for a cell's defective hereditary material. The normal material is enclosed in viruses that "infect" targeted cells. The new hereditary material enters the cells and replaces the defective hereditary material. Using gene therapy, scientists hope to help people with genetic disorders and find a cure for cancer.

**Figure 17** This oral rabies bait is being prepared for an aerial drop by the Texas Department of Health as part of their Oral Rabies Vaccination Program. This five-year program has prevented the expansion of rabies into Texas.

### Summary

**What are viruses?**

- A virus is a strand of hereditary material surrounded by a protein coating.

**How do viruses multiply?**

- An active virus immediately destroys the host cell but a latent virus does not.

**Fighting Viruses and Research with Viruses**

- Antiviral drugs can be given to infected patients to help fight a virus.
- Scientists are discovering helpful uses for some viruses.

### Self Check

1. **Describe** how viruses multiply.
2. **Explain** how vaccines are beneficial.
3. **Determine** how some viruses might be helpful.
4. **Discuss** how viral diseases might be prevented.
5. **Think Critically** Explain why a doctor might not give you any medication if you have a viral disease.

**Applying Skills**

6. **Concept Map** Make an events-chain concept map to show what happens when a latent virus becomes active.

 Science Online in7.msscience.com/self_check_quiz

## section 3 review

1. An active virus enters a cell and causes the host cell to make new viruses. When a latent virus enters a cell, its DNA is copied as the host cell reproduces. Under certain conditions, the body can activate the virus.
2. Vaccines, when properly adminis-

tered, help prevent many viral infections.
3. They may be used to transfer normal DNA into a cell.
4. vaccinating people, improving sanitary conditions, quarantining patients, and controlling animals that spread disease

5. No medications cure a viral disease.
6. Maps should show the following: latent virus enters cell; virus becomes part of cell's DNA; cell divides; virus reproduces as part of cell division; virus becomes active; virus forms new virus particles; cell is destroyed.

## Teacher FYI

**Virus Invasion** Even though bacteriophages typically inject their DNA into the host cell, not all viruses invade a host cell in this way. Many animal viruses enter the host cell through endocytosis, the binding of the virus to the cell membrane. Once inside the host cell, the virus sheds its protein coat and either undergoes replication or becomes part of the host's DNA.

### Use Science Words

**Word Meaning** Have students look up the terms *lysis*, *virion*, and *virology*. Have them write a paragraph about the relevance of each to the study of viruses. [L2] IS **Linguistic**

### 3 Assess

### DAILY INTERVENTION

### Check for Understanding

**Visual-Kinesthetic** Have students make a puzzle that shows the steps of viral infection and replication. Students can exchange puzzles to test each other's knowledge of the information. [L2]

### Reteach

**Viruses** Have students write a paragraph that describes the differences between active and latent viruses. [L1] IS **Linguistic**

### ✓ Assessment

**Oral** How does a virus invade a cell? The virus's hereditary material enters the cell, which becomes infected and eventually replicates the virus.

## ⦿ Real-World Question

**Purpose** Students will design an experiment to compare uses of stereomicroscopes and compound light microscopes.

L2 COOP LEARN
**Logical-Mathematical**

**Process Skills** observe, identify, recognize and use spatial relationships, classify, communicate

**Time Required** 15 minutes to plan and 45 minutes to do the experiment

**Safety Precautions** Caution students to use care when working with microscope slides and coverslips.

## ⦿ Form a Hypothesis

**Possible Hypothesis** Students may hypothesize that large items can be viewed with the stereomicroscope and small objects can be viewed with the compound light microscope.

## ⦿ Test Your Hypothesis

**Possible Procedures** Separate items into two groups: those that can be viewed with the stereomicroscope, and those that can be viewed with the light microscope.

### Teaching Strategies
• Demonstrate how to make a wet-mount.
• If microscopes have mirrors, explain how to use them.

# LAB
## Design Your Own

# Comparing Light Microscopes

## ⦿ Real-World Question

You're a technician in a police forensic laboratory. You use a stereomicroscope and a compound light microscope in the laboratory. A detective just returned from a crime scene with bags of evidence. You must examine each piece of evidence under a microscope. How do you decide which microscope is the best tool to use? Will all of the evidence that you've collected be viewable through both microscopes?

**Goals**
- **Learn** how to correctly use a stereo-microscope and a compound light microscope.
- **Compare** the uses of the stereomicroscope and compound light microscope.

**Possible Materials**
compound light microscope
stereomicroscope
items from the classroom—include some living or once-living items (8)
microscope slides and coverslips
plastic petri dishes
distilled water
dropper

**Safety Precautions**
🚫 ☣ ✋ 🔥 🤚

## ⦿ Form a Hypothesis

Compare the items to be examined under the microscopes. Form a hypothesis to predict which microscope will be used for each item and explain why.

## Alternative Inquiry Lab

**Comparing Light Microscopes** To make this Lab an Inquiry Lab, tell students that they are forensics technicians. They are leading a crime scene investigation, and they need to determine the best way to examine the evidence. Have them determine what sorts of evidence would be collected at a crime scene. They also should evaluate which type of microscope would be used with each piece of evidence to help with their examination. Which microscope works best to view a piece of clothing? For examining blood samples, hair, or clothing fibers, which microscope(s) could be used? This can be expanded to include predicting what microscopes, other than a compound light microscope or stereomicroscope, could be used by forensics technicians.

## ▶ Test Your Hypothesis

**Make a Plan**

1. As a group, decide how you will test your hypothesis.

2. **Describe** how you will carry out this experiment using a series of specific steps. Make sure the steps are in a logical order. Remember that you must place an item in the bottom of a plastic petri dish to examine it under the stereomicroscope and you must make a wet mount of any item to be examined under the compound light microscope. For more help, see the Reference Handbook.

3. If you need a data table or an observation table, design one in your Science Journal.

**Follow Your Plan**

1. Make sure your teacher approves the objects you'll examine, your plan, and your data table before you start.

2. Carry out the experiment.

3. While doing the experiment, record your observations and complete the data table.

## ▶ Analyze Your Data

1. **Compare** the items you examined with those of your classmates.

2. **Classify** the eight items you observed based on this experiment.

## ▶ Conclude and Apply

1. **Infer** which microscope a scientist might use to examine a blood sample, fibers, and live snails.

2. **List** five careers that require people to use a stereomicroscope. List five careers that require people to use a compound light microscope. Enter the lists in your Science Journal.

3. **Infer** how the images would differ if you examined an item under a compound light microscope and a stereomicroscope.

4. **Determine** which microscope is better for looking at large, or possibly live, items.

### ℂommunicating Your Data

In your Science Journal, **write** a short description of an imaginary crime scene and the evidence found there. Sort the evidence into two lists—items to be examined under a stereomicroscope and items to be examined under a compound light microscope. **For more help, refer to the** Science Skill Handbook.

### ℂommunicating Your Data

Items small enough to fit under a coverslip should be examined with a compound light microscope; larger items should be examined with a stereomicroscope.

### ✔ Assessment

**Performance** To further assess students' understanding of the differences in microscopes, provide other items and have students demonstrate how to use the appropriate microscope to view each item. Use **Performance Assessment in the Science Classroom,** p. 97. L2

---

**Troubleshooting** Place slides and coverslips for each group in a plastic petri dish to prevent breakage.

**Expected Outcome** The stereomicroscope is used for items that are too large to fit under a coverslip on a slide. The compound light microscope reveals greater detail. Students should note that the image produced by the compound light microscope is upside down and reversed left to right.

## ▶ Analyze Your Data

**Answers to Questions**

1. Answers will vary.
2. Large items should be classified together, and items small enough to fit on a slide should be grouped together.

**Error Analysis** Have students compare their results and their hypotheses and explain why differences occurred.

## ▶ Conclude and Apply

1. A scientist might use a stereomicroscope to examine live snails and a compound light microscope to examine blood and fibers.
2. Answers will vary, but may include lab technicians, forensic scientists, and cell biologists for the compound light microscope and surgeons, botanists, entomologists, geologists, and gemologists for the stereomicroscope.
3. The image under the compound light microscope will be magnified more, show greater detail, be upside down, and reversed left to right.
4. stereomicroscope

## Content Background

Jewel Plummer Cobb hoped to discover if there was a particular drug or combination of drugs which would be effective in destroying specific types of cancer. She would also need to determine whether these drugs would also destroy healthy tissues. Cobb exposed cells from both cancerous and non-cancerous tissues to chemotherapy drugs.

Her results demonstrated that some drugs could stop the uncontrolled growth of certain types of cancer cells. Although normal cells were also harmed, they never showed the dramatic destruction produced in some cancer cells.

## Discussion

**Experimental Results** Using Cobb's research as an example, discuss the value of experiments even if the results do not meet the researcher's specific goals. Possible answer: Science is a continuing process of discovery. Cobb's work is a necessary first step to new approaches to treatment like Levy's.

## Historical Significance

The structure and function of DNA were not discovered until 1953. Cobb's research began shortly thereafter, long before the role of genes in the development of cancer was understood. Research like Cobb's leads to questions about how certain drugs can stop the unchecked growth of tumors. In combination with an increasing understanding of how genes work, these results allow scientists to refine the methods of administering treatments and to target the development of drugs specifically aimed at preventing the replication of DNA, a process that all cells require.

# TIME SCIENCE AND HISTORY
### SCIENCE CAN CHANGE THE COURSE OF HISTORY!

# Cobb Against Cancer

This colored scanning electron micrograph (SEM) shows two breast cancer cells in the final stage of cell division.

**J**ewel Plummer Cobb is a cell biologist who did important background research on the use of drugs against cancer in the 1950s. She removed cells from cancerous tumors and cultured them in the lab. Then, in a controlled study, she tried a series of different drugs against batches of the same cells. Her goal was to find the right drug to cure each patient's particular cancer. Cobb never met that goal, but her research laid the groundwork for modern chemotherapy—the use of chemicals to treat cancer.

Jewel Cobb also influenced science in another way. She was a role model, especially in her role as dean or president of several universities. Cobb promoted equal opportunity for students of all backgrounds, especially in the sciences.

## Light Up a Cure

*Vancouver, British Columbia 2000.* While Cobb herself was only able to infer what was going on inside a cell from its reactions to various drugs, her work has helped others go further. Building on Cobb's work, Professor Julia Levy and her research team at the University of British Columbia actually go inside cells, and even organelles, to work against cancer. One technique they are pioneering is the use of light to guide cancer drugs to the right cells. First, the patient is given a chemotherapy drug that reacts to light. Then, a fiber optic tube is inserted into the tumor. Finally, laser light is passed through the tube, which activates the light-sensitive drug—but only in the tumor itself. This will hopefully provide a technique to keep healthy cells healthy while killing sick cells.

**Write** Report on Cobb's experiments on cancer cells. What were her dependent and independent variables? What would she have used as a control? What sources of error did she have to guard against? Answer the same questions about Levy's work.

**Science Online**
For more information, visit in7.msscience.com/time

**Write** Levy and Cobb were both targeting cancer cells and working to avoid harming normal cells. In both studies, the control group would be normal human cells that were exposed to the chemotherapeutic drugs. The independent variables were the specific drugs administered to the cells. The dependent variables were the response of the cells to the treatment.

## Resources for Teachers and Students

*Advancing Current Treatments for Cancer,* by Samuel Hellman and Everett E. Vokes, Scientific American, September 2000

*How Cancer Arises,* by Robert A. Weinberg, Scientific American, September 2001

## Reviewing Main Ideas

### Section 1 — Cell Structure

1. Prokaryotic and eukaryotic are the two cell types.

2. The DNA in the nucleus controls cell functions.

3. Organelles such as mitochondria and chloroplasts process energy.

4. Most many-celled organisms are organized into tissues, organs, and organ systems.

### Section 2 — Viewing Cells

1. A simple microscope has just one lens. A compound light microscope has an eyepiece and objective lenses.

2. To calculate the magnification of a microscope, multiply the power of the eyepiece by the power of the objective lens.

3. According to the cell theory, the cell is the basic unit of life. Organisms are made of one or more cells, and all cells come from other cells.

### Section 3 — Viruses

1. A virus is a structure containing hereditary material surrounded by a protein coating.

2. A virus can make copies of itself only when it is inside a living host cell.

## Visualizing Main Ideas

*Copy and complete the following concept map of the basic units of life.*

Science Online  in7.msscience.com/interactive_tutor

**CHAPTER STUDY GUIDE** 59

## Reviewing Main Ideas

Summary statements can be used by students to review the major concepts of the chapter.

## Visualizing Main Ideas

See student page.

**Science Online**

**Visit** in7.msscience.com
/self_check_quiz
/interactive_tutor
/vocabulary_puzzlemaker
/chapter_review
/standards_review

## Assessment Transparency

For additional assessment questions, use the *Assessment Transparency* located in the transparency book.

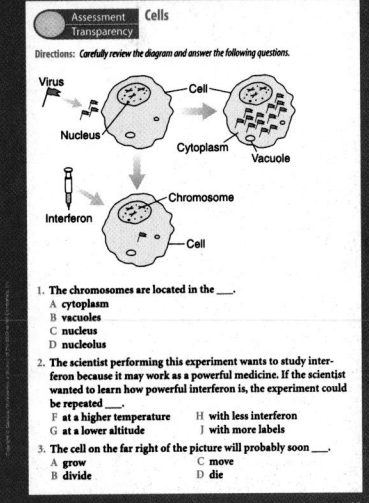

chapter 2 **Review**

## Using Vocabulary

1. tissue
2. chloroplast, ER, Golgi body, mitochondrion, nucleus, organelle, ribosome, or virus
3. chloroplast, ER, Golgi body, nucleus, or ribosome
4. cell membrane or cytoplasm
5. mitochondrion
6. cell theory
7. cytoplasm, nucleus, or virus
8. cell membrane or cell wall
9. host cell
10. organ or tissue

## Checking Concepts

| | |
|---|---|
| 11. B | 15. C |
| 12. D | 16. C |
| 13. B | 17. A |
| 14. A | 18. A |

## Thinking Critically

19. Once a virus infects a cell, it uses the cell to produce more viruses. No drugs will kill viruses.

20. Answers may vary, but a stereomicroscope would enable you to view a large specimen as well as to look closely at the mold.

21. The plant cell would die or become dependent on other cells to provide its food.

## Using Vocabulary

| | |
|---|---|
| cell membrane  p. 38 | host cell  p. 52 |
| cell theory  p. 51 | mitochondrion  p. 42 |
| cell wall  p. 39 | nucleus  p. 40 |
| chloroplast  p. 42 | organ  p. 45 |
| cytoplasm  p. 38 | organelle  p. 40 |
| endoplasmic | ribosome  p. 42 |
| reticulum  p. 43 | tissue  p. 45 |
| Golgi body  p. 43 | virus  p. 52 |

*Using the vocabulary words, give an example of each of the following.*

1. found in every organ
2. smaller than one cell
3. a plant-cell organelle
4. part of every cell
5. powerhouse of a cell
6. used by biologists
7. contains hereditary material
8. a structure that surrounds the cell
9. can be damaged by a virus
10. made up of cells

## Checking Concepts

*Choose the word or phrase that best answers the question.*

11. What structure allows only certain things to pass in and out of the cell?
    A) cytoplasm          C) ribosomes
    B) cell membrane      D) Golgi body

12. What is the organelle to the right?
    A) nucleus
    B) cytoplasm
    C) Golgi body
    D) endoplasmic reticulum

**Use the illustration below to answer question 13.**

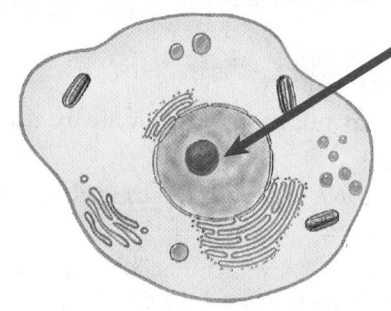

13. In the figure above, what is the function of the structure that the arrow is pointing to?
    A) recycles old cell parts
    B) controls cell activities
    C) protection
    D) releases energy

14. Which scientist gave the name *cells* to structures he viewed?
    A) Hooke          C) Schleiden
    B) Schwann        D) Virchow

15. Which of the following is a viral disease?
    A) tuberculosis   C) smallpox
    B) anthrax        D) tetanus

16. Which microscope can magnify up to a million times?
    A) compound light microscope
    B) stereomicroscope
    C) transmission electron microscope
    D) atomic force microscope

17. Which of the following is part of a bacterial cell?
    A) a cell wall    C) mitochondria
    B) lysosomes      D) a nucleus

18. Which of the following do groups of different tissues form?
    A) organ          C) organ system
    B) organelle      D) organism

Science Online in7.msscience.com/vocabulary_puzzlemaker

**Use the Exam*View*® Pro Testmaker CD-ROM to:**
• create multiple versions of tests
• create modified tests with one mouse click for inclusion students
• edit existing questions and add your own questions
• build tests aligned with state standards using built-in State Curriculum Tags
• change English tests to Spanish with one mouse click and vice versa

## Thinking Critically

19. **Infer** why it is difficult to treat a viral disease.

20. **Explain** which type of microscope would be best to view a piece of moldy bread.

21. **Predict** what would happen to a plant cell that suddenly lost its chloroplasts.

22. **Predict** what would happen if the animal cell shown to the right didn't have ribosomes.

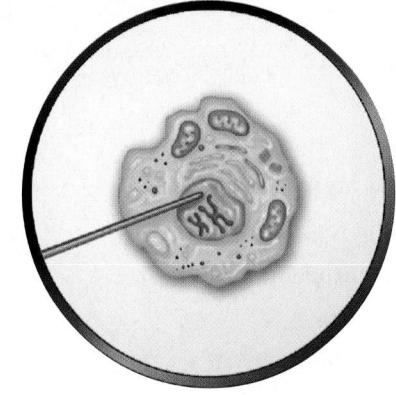

23. **Determine** how you would decide whether an unknown cell was an animal cell, a plant cell, or a bacterial cell.

24. **Concept Map** Make an events-chain concept map of the following from simple to complex: *small intestine, circular muscle cell, human,* and *digestive system.*

25. **Interpret Scientific Illustrations** Use the illustrations in **Figure 1** to describe how the shape of a cell is related to its function.

**Use the table below to answer question 26.**

### Cell Structures

| Structure | Prokaryotic Cell | Eukaryotic Cell |
|---|---|---|
| Cell membrane | Yes | Yes |
| Cytoplasm | Yes | Yes |
| Nucleus | No | Yes |
| Endoplasmic reticulum | No | Yes |
| Golgi bodies | No | Yes |

26. **Compare and Contrast** Copy and complete the table above.

 **Science** nline in7.msscience.com/chapter_review

27. **Make a Model** Make and illustrate a time line about the development of the cell theory. Begin with the development of the microscope and end with Virchow. Include the contributions of Leeuwenhoek, Hooke, Schleiden, and Schwann.

## Performance Activities

28. **Model** Use materials that resemble cell parts or represent their functions to make a model of a plant cell or an animal cell. Include a cell-parts key.

29. **Poster** Make a poster about the history of vaccinations. Contact your local Health Department for current information.

## Applying Math

**Use the illustration below to answer question 30.**

30. **Cell Width** If the pointer shown above with the cell is 10 micrometers ($\mu$m) in length, then about how wide is this cell?

   A) 20 $\mu$m          C) 5 $\mu$m
   B) 10 $\mu$m          D) 0.1 $\mu$m

31. **Magnification** Calculate the magnification of a microscope with a 20× eyepiece and a 40× objective.

## Thinking Critically

22. No proteins could be made, and the animal cell would die.

23. If there is a cell wall and chloroplasts, it is a plant cell. A cell with no chloroplasts or cell wall is an animal cell. If no membrane-bound organelles are present, it is a bacterial cell.

24. circular muscle cell, small intestine, digestive system, human

25. Answers will vary but should relate each shape to a function of the cell, such as the elongated shape of the nerve cell and its function in transmitting impulses.

26. See student page.

27. The time line should have equal divisions of time and cover from the late 1500s to the late 1800s. Include these dates: late 1500s, microscope invented; late 1600s, Leeuwenhoek improves microscope; 1665, Hooke uses the word *cell;* 1830s, Schleiden discovers plants are made of cells; mid 1800s, Schwann discovers animals are made of cells; mid 1800s, Virchow concludes that all cells come from cells.

## Performance Activities

28. Model should include cell parts and a key to identify them. Use **PASC,** p. 123.

29. Posters should correctly show the history of vaccinations. Use **PASC,** p. 145.

## Applying Math

### Indiana Math Standards
7.5.1
30. B
31. the magnification would be 800×

## ☑ Assessment      Resources

**📁 Reproducible Masters**

**Chapter** *Fast File* **Resources**
   Chapter Review, pp. 37–38
   Chapter Tests, pp. 39–42
   Assessment Transparency Activity, p. 49
**Glencoe Science Web site**
   Chapter Review Test
   IN Standards Review

**Glencoe Technology**
   🔋 Assessment Transparency
   💿 Exam*View*® Pro Testmaker
   📼 MindJogger Videoquiz
   💿 Interactive Chalkboard

**Answer Sheet** A practice answer sheet can be found at in7.msscience.com/answer_sheet.

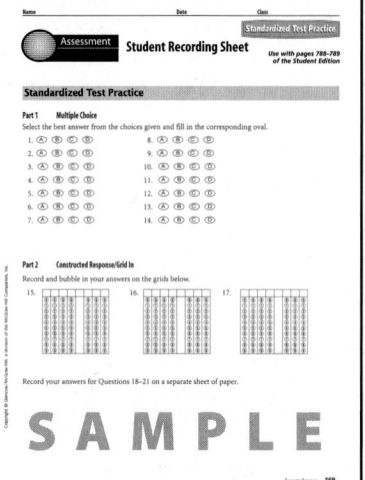

Part 1 | Multiple Choice

| 1. B | 6. C |
| 2. B | 7. D |
| 3. A | 8. B |
| 4. D | 9. B |
| 5. B | |

Part 2 | Critical Response

10. A virus is attaching to a host cell at the cell surface. If the virus and the cell match, the virus will infect the cell, will be replicated, and eventually kill the cell. If the virus and the cell do not match, there will be no infection.

11. Hooke coined the term "cells" by observing cork cells. Schleiden observed plant cells and stated that all plants were made up of cells. Schwann observed animal cells and stated that animals were made up of cells.

12. Many important chemical reactions take place in the cytoplasm. The cytoplasm contains the framework cytoskeleton, which supports the organelles and maintains shape of the cell. Eukaryotic cells have organelles in the cytoplasm.

 The assessed Indiana standard appears above the question.

*Record your answers on the answer sheet provided by your teacher or on a sheet of paper.*

Part 1 | Multiple Choice

1. Why is a virus **NOT** considered a living cell?

   A It does not have a cell wall.

   B It has defective hereditary material.

   C It has few organelles.

   D It cannot reproduce by itself.

The images below show the same organelle.

**7.4.1**

2. What organelle is shown?

   A chloroplast

   B mitochondrion

   C nucleus

   D ribosome

**7.4.5**

3. What is the primary function of the organelle shown above?

   A capturing light energy

   B directing cell processes

   C releasing energy stored in food

   D making proteins

**7.4.5**

4. Which organelle receives the directions from the DNA in the nucleus about which proteins to make?

   A cytoplasm

   B endoplasmic reticulum

   C Golgi body

   D ribosome

**7.4.1**

5. Which do a bacterial cell, a plant cell, and a nerve cell have in common?

   A cell wall and nucleus

   B cytoplasm and cell membrane

   C endoplasmic reticulum

   D flagella and chloroplasts

**7.4.12**

6. The illustration below shows a process that can occur in the human body.

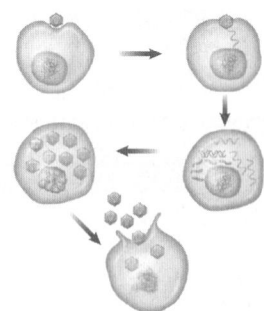

What does the illustration represent?

   A cell reproduction

   B bacterial reproduction

   C active virus multiplication

   D vaccination

13. Jenner noticed that individuals with cowpox did not get smallpox. He used material from the cowpox sores to make a vaccine against smallpox.

**7.4.5**

**7.** Which is a **NOT** a function of an organelle?

A  cell heredity

B  cell protection

C  energy release

D  oxygen release

**7.4.5**

**8.** Where do most life processes occur in a cell?

A  cell wall

B  cytoplasm

C  nucleus

D  organ

**7.4.1**

**9.** The photo below shows Japanese beetles eating a plant.

Which statement is **TRUE** for both organisms?

A  Carbon dioxide and water release energy that its cells use.

B  DNA contains the code for its cells' structures.

C  Organelles in its cells can transform light energy into chemical energy.

D  Reproducing requires a host organism.

---

**Part 2  Critical Response**

The illustration below is an interaction that can occur in the human body.

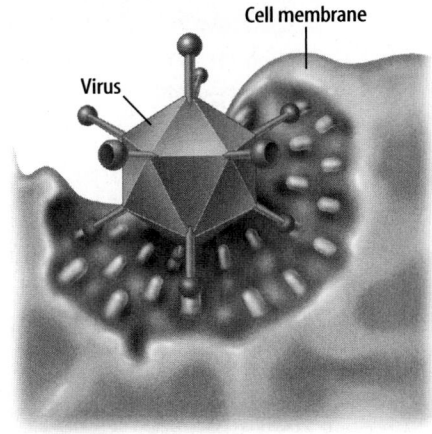

Cell membrane

Virus

**7.4.12**

**10.** What interaction is taking place in the illustration above? What are two possible outcomes of this interaction?

**11.** Explain how Hooke, Schleiden, and Schwann contributed to the cell theory.

**7.4.5**

**12.** Discuss the importance of the structure and function of cytoplasm to a cell.

**7.6.3**

**13.** Describe the development of the first vaccine by Edward Jenner.

**Test-Taking Tip**

**Read Carefully**  Read each question carefully for full understanding.

---

## Rubrics

The following rubric is a sample scoring device for critical response questions.

### Critical Response

| Points | Description |
| --- | --- |
| 4 | The student demonstrates a thorough understanding of the science of the task. The response may contain minor flaws that do not detract from the demonstration of a thorough understanding. |
| 3 | The student demonstrates an understanding of the science of the task. The response is essentially correct and demonstrates an essential but less than thorough understanding of the science. |
| 2 | The student demonstrates only a partial understanding of the science of the task. Although the student may have used the correct approach to a solution or may have provided a correct solution, the work lacks an essential understanding of the underlying science concepts. |
| 1 | The student demonstrates a very limited understanding of the science of the task. The response is incomplete and exhibits many flaws. |
| 0 | The student provides a completely incorrect solution or no response at all. |

| Section/Objectives | Standards | | Labs/Features |
|---|---|---|---|
| **Chapter Opener** | **National** | **State/Local** | **Launch Lab:** Why does water enter and leave plant cells?, p. 65 **Foldables,** p. 65 |
| | See pp. 16T–17T for a Key to Standards. | Detailed Standards begin on page IN8. | |
| **Section 1 Chemistry of Life** ⏱ 2 sessions 📦 1 block 1. **List** the differences among atoms, elements, molecules, and compounds. 2. **Explain** the relationship between chemistry and life science. 3. **Discuss** how organic compounds are different from inorganic compounds. | National Content Standards: UCP.1, UCP.2, UCP.3, UCP.5, A.1, A.2, B.1, C.1 | Indiana Standards: 7.3.13, 7.7.4 | **Science Online,** p. 70 **MiniLAB:** Observing How Enzymes Work, p. 71 **Applying Math:** Calculate the Importance of Water, p. 72 |
| **Section 2 Moving Cellular Materials** ⏱ 2 sessions 📦 1 block 4. **Describe** the function of a selectively permeable membrane. 5. **Explain** how the processes of diffusion and osmosis move molecules in living cells. 6. **Explain** how passive transport and active transport differ | National Content Standards: UCP.1, UCP.2, UCP.3, UCP.5, A.1, A.2, C.1, C.3 | Indiana Standards: 7.3.13, 7.4.5, 7.7.3 | **MiniLAB:** Observing Diffusion, p. 75 **Integrate Health,** p. 77 **Visualizing Cell Membrane Transport,** p. 79 **Lab:** Observing Osmosis, p. 80 |
| **Section 3 Energy for Life** ⏱ 3 sessions 📦 1.5 blocks 7. **List** the differences between producers and consumers. 8. **Explain** how the processes of photosynthesis and respiration store and release energy. 9. **Describe** how cells get energy from glucose through fermentation. | National Content Standards: UCP.1, UCP.2, UCP.3, UCP.5, A.1, C.1, G.1, G.2, G.3 | Indiana Standards: 7.3.14, 7.4.4, 7.4.5, 7.4.7, 7.4.8, 7.6.2, 7.7.1 | **Integrate Career,** p. 83 **Science Online,** p. 84 **Lab:** Photosynthesis and Respiration, p. 86 **Science and Language Arts:** from "Tulip," p. 88 |

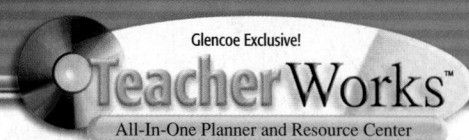

| Lab Materials | Reproducible Resources | Section Assessment | Technology |
|---|---|---|---|
| **Launch Lab:** bowl (2), label, water (500 mL), salt (15 g), carrot sticks (6), watch or clock, beaker (250mL), stirrer | **Chapter *FAST FILE* Resources**<br>Foldables Worksheet, p. 15<br>Directed Reading Overview, p. 17<br>Note-taking Worksheets, pp. 31–33 | **GLENCOE'S ASSESSMENT ADVANTAGE** | **TeacherWorks** includes:<br>• Interactive Teacher Edition<br>• Lesson Planner with calendar<br>• Access to all program blacklines<br>• Correlations to standards<br>• Web links |
| **MiniLAB:** 2 small cups of prepared gelatin, fresh pineapple pieces<br><br>*Need materials?* Contact Science Kit at 1-800-828-7777 or www.sciencekit.com on the Internet. | **Chapter *FAST FILE* Resources**<br>Transparency Activity, p. 42<br>MiniLAB, p. 3<br>Enrichment, p. 28<br>Reinforcement, p. 25<br>Directed Reading, p. 18<br>Transparency Activity, pp. 45–46<br>**Cultural Diversity,** p. 65 | **Portfolio**<br>Science Journal, p. 70<br>**Performance**<br>MiniLAB, p. 71<br>Applying Math, p. 72<br>Applying Skills, p. 73<br>**Content**<br>Section Review, p. 73 | Section Focus Transparency<br>Teaching Transparency<br>Guided Reading Audio Program<br>Interactive Chalkboard CD-ROM |
| **MiniLAB:** clean glasses (2 of equal size), labels, very warm water, cold water, food coloring, dropper, clock, marker or wax pencil<br>**Lab:** unshelled egg, balance, spoon, distilled water (250 mL), light corn syrup (250 mL), 500-mL container | **Chapter *FAST FILE* Resources**<br>Transparency Activity, p. 43<br>MiniLAB, p. 4<br>Enrichment, p. 29<br>Reinforcement, p. 26<br>Directed Reading, p. 18<br>Lab Activity, pp. 9–10<br>Lab Worksheet, pp. 5–6<br>**Home and Community Involvement,** p. 47 | **Portfolio**<br>Visual Learning, p. 79<br>**Performance**<br>MiniLAB, p. 75<br>Applying Skills, p. 78<br>**Content**<br>Section Review, p. 78 | Section Focus Transparency<br>Virtual Labs CD-ROM<br>Guided Reading Audio Program<br>Interactive Chalkboard CD-ROM<br>Video Lab |
| **Lab:** 16-mm test tubes (3), 150-mm test tubes with stoppers (4), test-tube rack, stirring rod, scissors, carbonated water (5 mL), bromthymol blue solution in dropper bottle, aged tap water (20 mL), sprig of *Elodea* | **Chapter *FAST FILE* Resources**<br>Transparency Activity, p. 44<br>Enrichment, p. 30<br>Reinforcement, p. 27<br>Directed Reading, pp. 19, 20<br>Lab Activity, pp. 11–14<br>Lab Worksheet, pp. 7–8<br>**Lab Management and Safety,** p. 63 | **Portfolio**<br>Visual Learning, p. 85<br>**Performance**<br>Applying Math, p. 85<br>**Content**<br>Section Review, p. 85 | Section Focus Transparency<br>Guided Reading Audio Program<br>Interactive Chalkboard CD-ROM |

## End of Chapter Assessment

**GLENCOE'S ASSESSMENT ADVANTAGE**

| Blackline Masters | Technology | Professional Series |
|---|---|---|
| **Chapter *FAST FILE* Resources**<br>Chapter Review, pp. 35–36<br>Chapter Tests, pp. 37–40<br>**Mastering the Grade 7 Indiana Science Standards** | MindJogger Videoquiz<br>IN Test Prep and Practice Exam*View*®<br>Exam*View*® Pro Testmaker<br>TeacherWorks CD-ROM<br>Interactive Chalkboard CD-ROM | **Performance Assessment in the Science Classroom (PASC)** |

## Transparencies

### Section Focus

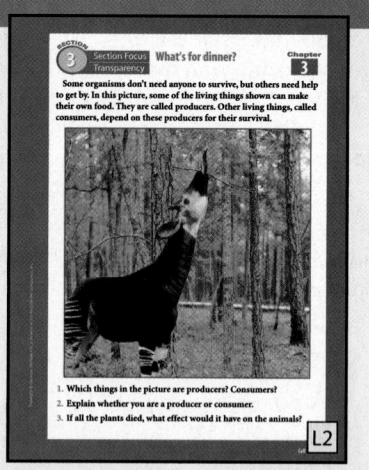

This is a representation of key blackline masters available in the Teacher Classroom Resources. See Resource Manager boxes within the chapter for additional information.

### Assessment

### Teaching

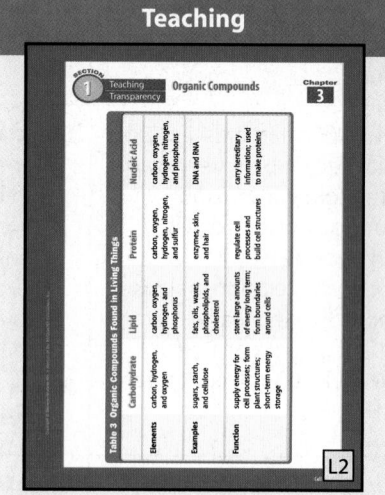

## Key to Teaching Strategies

The following designations will help you decide which activities are appropriate for your students.

**L1** Level 1 activities should be appropriate for students with learning difficulties.

**L2** Level 2 activities should be within the ability range of all students.

**L3** Level 3 activities are designed for above-average students.

**ELL** ELL activities should be within the ability range of English-Language Learners.

**COOP LEARN** Cooperative Learning activities are designed for small group work.

**LS** Multiple Learning Styles logos, as described on page 12T, are used throughout to indicate strategies that address different learning styles.

**P** These strategies represent student products that can be placed into a best-work portfolio.

**PBL** Problem-Based Learning activities apply real-world situations to learning.

## Hands-on Activities

### Student Text Lab Worksheet

### Laboratory Activities

# Resource Manager

## Meeting Different Ability Levels

### Content Outline

### Reinforcement

### Enrichment

### Directed Reading (English/Spanish)

### Study Guide

### Reading Essentials
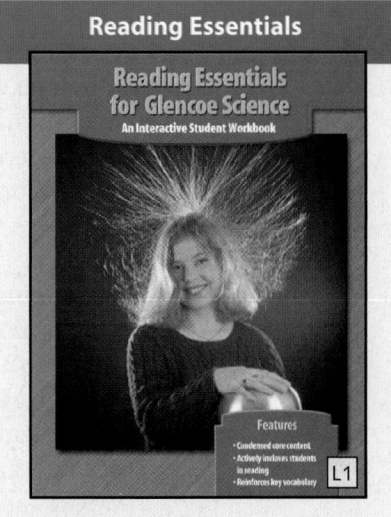

## Assessment

### Test Practice Workbook

### Chapter Review

### Chapter Tests

# Science Content Background

 **Chemistry of Life**
**The Nature of Matter**

Democritus, an ancient Greek philosopher, proposed that atoms were small, solid spheres. Until recently, it was thought that negatively-charged electrons orbited the positively-charged nucleus in specific paths. Quantum mechanics provide us with the current model of a positively-charged nucleus surrounded by a region in which the electrons move. The location of the electrons depends on each electron's energy level.

## Compounds and Mixtures

Compounds are formed when two or more elements combine by a chemical reaction. Molecular components form when atoms share electrons. Ionic compounds form when negative and positive ions join. Organic compounds all contain carbon atoms and most are produced within living organisms. However, organic compounds such as plastics and synthetic fibers are made from organic substances such as petroleum. Inorganic compounds usually are made from elements other than carbon. Water is the most important inorganic compound.

Most things in nature are mixtures of elements. Components of homogeneous mixtures, such as solutions, cannot be distinguished from one another. The components of a heterogeneous mixture are generally visibly identifiable.

 **Moving Cellular Materials**
**Maintaining Balance**

The cell membrane regulates what enters and leaves a cell. The path taken through a membrane depends on the substance's size, shape, and electrical charge. A cell must maintain its internal concentrations of substances such as water, glucose, and other nutrients and eliminate waste products.

## Transport

Passive transport—transport without the input of energy—depends on temperature. One form of passive transport, called diffusion, occurs when molecules move from an area where their concentration is greater into an area where they are less concentrated. Osmosis is the diffusion of water into or out of a cell. Active transport, transport with energy input, requires transport proteins.

**Energy for Life**
**Photosynthesis, Respiration, and Fermentation**

During photosynthesis, plants and other producers convert light energy to chemical energy and make carbohydrates (food). During respiration, the food is broken down and the released energy can be used by the producer, other producers, and consumers. When there is a shortage of oxygen, fermentation is a process some cells can use to release energy from glucose.

## chapter content resources

**Internet Resources**
For additional content background, visit
**in7.msscience.com** to:
- access your book online
- find references to related articles in popular science magazines
- access Web links with related content background
- access current events with science journal topics

**Print Resources**
*Cells and Systems (Life Processes),* by Holly Wallace and Anita Ganeri, Heinemann Library, 2001
*Atoms and Molecules,* by Phil Roxbee Cox, E D C Publications, 1993
*Illustrated Dictionary of Science,* by Corinne Stockley, Usborne Books, 2000

**Misconceptions**

## Find Out What Students Think

### Students may think that . . .

**Plants do not use oxygen and do not release carbon dioxide.**

Students may not understand the complementary nature of photosynthesis and respiration, especially with respect to exchange of gases.

### Demonstration

Ask students to give the relationship among producers, consumers, oxygen, and carbon dioxide. Summarize students' responses on the board. If students do not respond that plants also give off carbon dioxide, let that understanding come from the activities below.

## Promote Understanding

### Activity 1
**WARNING:** *Remind students not to suck on the straw.*

Prepare a 0.1% solution of bromthymol blue.

- Have students blow through a straw into the bromthymol blue solution. The solution should turn yellow as the carbon dioxide dissolves forming carbonic acid.

- Have students add drops of dilute ammonium hydroxide so that the solution again turns blue. Explain that the bromthymol blue is an indicator that turns yellow in an acidic solution and blue in a neutral or alkaline solution.

- Ask students what gas is given off in the process of respiration. (carbon dioxide) Explain that the carbon dioxide blown into the solution dissolves and makes the solution slightly acidic. Point out that adding the ammonium hydroxide made the solution slightly basic. L2

### Activity 2
Acidify a large test tube of bromthymol blue by adding carbonated water to the solution. Add a sprig of *Elodea* to the tube.

- Put the test tube in sunlight or under a bright light. The solution should begin to turn blue in 30 to 45 minutes. Have students record results.

- Also, have students put a sprig of *Elodea* in a test tube of bromthymol blue solution that is slightly alkaline and blue. Place the tube in a dark area. Within 24 hours the solution should change to a pale yellow as the plant respires and releases carbon dioxide. Again have students record their results. L2

### Discussion

- Ask why the bromthymol blue solution turned blue in the light. Ask students what evidence supports their answer. Explicitly reinforce the fact the carbon dioxide was absorbed by the plant and used in the process of photosynthesis.

- Ask students whether they think carbon dioxide was given off by the *Elodea* kept in the dark. Light-independent photosynthesis and respiration occur in the dark, so less carbon dioxide is used and released. Stress that their results indicate that plants give off carbon dioxide during respiration. Point out that all living things must carry out some form of respiration.

### Assess

After completing the chapter, see *Identifying Misconceptions* in the Study Guide at the end of the chapter.

## Chapter Vocabulary

mixture, p. 69
organic compound, p. 70
enzyme, p. 71
inorganic compound, p. 71
passive transport, p. 74
diffusion, p. 75
equilibrium, p. 75
osmosis, p. 76
active transport, p. 77
endocytosis, p. 78
exocytosis, p. 78
metabolism, p. 81
photosynthesis, p. 82
respiration, p. 83
fermentation, p. 84

**Science Journal** Student responses will vary, but may include "from the Sun" and "from the ground."

### PowerPoint® Presentations

This CD-ROM is an editable Microsoft® PowerPoint® presentation that includes:

- a pre-made presentation for every chapter
- interactive graphics
- animations
- audio clips
- image bank
- all new section and chapter questions
- Standardized Test Practice
- transparencies
- pre-lab questions for all labs
- Foldables directions
- links to in7.msscience.com

**Academic Standard—4:** Students begin to trace the flow of matter and energy through ecosystems. They recognize the fundamental difference between plants and animals and understand its basis at the cellular level . . . They use microscopes to observe cells and recognize that cells function in similar ways in all organisms.

**Also covers:** Academic Standards 2, 3, 6, 7 (Detailed standards begin on page IN8.)

# Cell Processes

### chapter preview

**sections**

1 **Chemistry of Life**

2 **Moving Cellular Material**
   *Lab Observing Osmosis*

3 **Energy for Life**
   *Lab Photosynthesis and Respiration*

 *Virtual Lab Under what conditions do cells gain or lose water?*

### The Science of Gardening

Growing a garden is hard work for both you and the plants. Like you, plants need water and food for energy. How plants get food and water is different from you. Understanding how living things get the energy they need to survive will make a garden seem like much more than just plants and dirt.

**Science Journal** Describe two ways in which you think plants get food for energy.

64

## Theme Connection

**Stability and Change** Living things function as a result of chemical reactions in cells. The equilibrium maintained by cells results from their selectively permeable membranes. This is critical to the life of cells and the organism as a whole.

### About the Photo

**A Growing Garden** Growing a bountiful garden requires sunlight, soil, and lots of water. Each plant in a garden, however, has individual requirements. The amount of sunlight, nutrients required, and amount of water needed have to be considered for all the types of plants.

# Start-Up Activities

## Why does water enter and leave plant cells?

If you forget to water a plant, it will wilt. After you water the plant, it probably will straighten up and look healthier. In the following lab, find out how water causes a plant to wilt and straighten.

1. Label a small bowl *Salt Water*. Pour 250 mL of water into the bowl. Then add 15 g of salt to the water and stir.

2. Pour 250 mL of water into another small bowl.

3. Place two carrot sticks into each bowl. Also, place two carrot sticks on the lab table.

4. After 30 min, remove the carrot sticks from the bowls and keep them next to the bowl they came from. Examine all six carrot sticks, then describe them in your Science Journal.

5. **Think Critically** Write a paragraph in your Science Journal that describes what would happen if you moved the carrot sticks from the plain water to the lab table, the ones from the salt water into the plain water, and the ones from the lab table into the salt water for 30 min. Now move the carrot sticks as described and write the results in your Science Journal.

 **How Living Things Survive**
Make the following vocabulary Foldable to help you understand the chemistry of living things and how energy is obtained for life.

**STEP 1** Fold a vertical sheet of notebook paper from side to side.

**STEP 2** Cut along every third line of only the top layer to form tabs.

**Build Vocabulary** As you read this chapter, list the vocabulary words about cell processes on the tabs. As you learn the definitions, write them under the tab for each vocabulary word. Write a sentence about one of the cell processes using the vocabulary word on the tab.

 Preview this chapter's content and activities at in7.msscience.com

# 1 Motivate

## Bellringer

**Section Focus Transparencies** also are available on the Interactive Chalkboard CD-ROM.

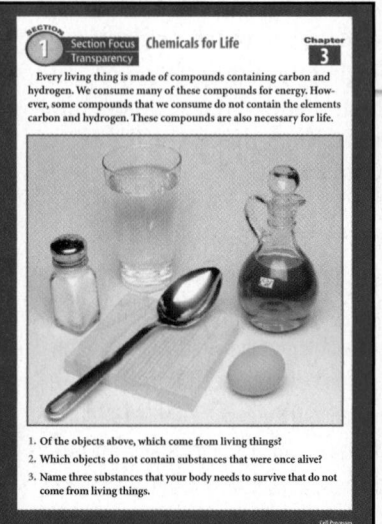

## Tie to Prior Knowledge

**Food Labels** Bring in labels from foods and cleaning products. Have students use the periodic table at the back of the book to determine what elements are in the compounds contained in these products. L2

---

## section 1

Also covers: 7.2.1, 7.7.4 (Detailed standards begin on page IN8.)

# Chemistry of Life

### as you read

#### *What* You'll Learn

- **List** the differences among atoms, elements, molecules, and compounds.
- **Explain** the relationship between chemistry and life science.
- **Discuss** how organic compounds are different from inorganic compounds.

#### *Why* It's Important

You grow because of chemical reactions in your body.

#### Review Vocabulary
**cell:** the smallest unit of a living thing that can perform the functions of life

#### New Vocabulary
- mixture
- organic compound
- enzyme
- inorganic compound

## The Nature of Matter

Think about everything that surrounds you—chairs, books, clothing, other students, and air. What are all these things made up of? You're right if you answer "matter and energy." Matter is anything that has mass and takes up space. Energy is anything that brings about change. Everything in your environment, including you, is made of matter. Energy can hold matter together or break it apart. For example, the food you eat is matter that is held together by chemical energy. When food is cooked, energy in the form of heat can break some of the bonds holding the matter in food together.

**Atoms** Whether it is solid, liquid, or gas, matter is made of atoms. **Figure 1** shows a model of an oxygen atom. At the center of an atom is a nucleus that contains protons and neutrons. Although they have nearly equal masses, a proton has a positive charge and a neutron has no charge. Outside the nucleus are electrons, each of which has a negative charge. It takes about 1,837 electrons to equal the mass of one proton. Electrons are important because they are the part of the atom that is involved in chemical reactions. Look at **Figure 1** again and you will see that an atom is mostly empty space. Energy holds the parts of an atom together.

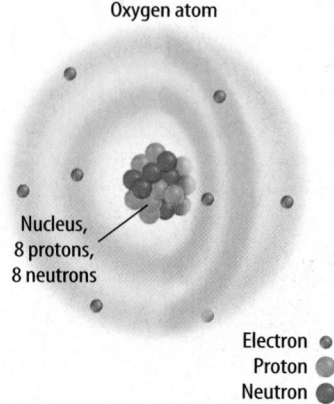

**Figure 1** An oxygen atom model shows the placement of electrons, protons, and neutrons.

Oxygen atom

Nucleus, 8 protons, 8 neutrons

Electron
Proton
Neutron

---

## Section 1 Resource Manager

### Chapter *FAST FILE* Resources
Transparency Activity, p. 42

Directed Reading for Content Mastery, pp. 17, 18

Note-taking Worksheets, pp. 31–33

Enrichment, p. 28

MiniLAB, p. 3

Reinforcement, p. 25

## Table 1  Elements in the Human Body

| Symbol | Element | Percent |
|--------|---------|---------|
| O | Oxygen | 65.0 |
| C | Carbon | 18.5 |
| H | Hydrogen | 9.5 |
| N | Nitrogen | 3.2 |
| Ca | Calcium | 1.5 |
| P | Phosphorus | 1.0 |
| K | Potassium | 0.4 |
| S | Sulfur | 0.3 |
| Na | Sodium | 0.2 |
| Cl | Chlorine | 0.2 |
| Mg | Magnesium | 0.1 |
| | Other elements | 0.1 |

Oxygen 65.0%

Carbon 18.5%

Hydrogen 9.5%

Nitrogen 3.2%

Calcium 1.5%

Phosphorus 1.0%

Other elements 1.3%

**Elements**  When something is made up of only one kind of atom, it is called an element. An element can't be broken down into a simpler form by chemical reactions. The element oxygen is made up of only oxygen atoms, and hydrogen is made up of only hydrogen atoms. Scientists have given each element its own one- or two-letter symbol.

All elements are arranged in a chart known as the periodic table of elements. You can find this table at the back of this book. The table provides information about each element including its mass, how many protons it has, and its symbol.

Everything is made up of elements. Most things, including all living things, are made up of a combination of elements. Few things exist as pure elements. **Table 1** lists elements that are in the human body. What two elements make up most of your body?

Six of the elements listed in the table are important because they make up about 99 percent of living matter. The symbols for these elements are S, P, O, N, C, and H. Use **Table 1** to find the names of these elements.

**Reading Check**  *What types of things are made up of elements?*

## Differentiated Instruction

**Visually Impaired**  To help visually impaired students understand the structure of an atom, make a model of an atom. Outline the nucleus and energy levels by gluing yarn to cardboard. Use marshmallows for protons, gumdrops for neutrons, and red hots for electrons. Have students feel the model to compare the sizes of the different parts.  L1  **Kinesthetic**

## Teacher FYI

**Element Names**  Elements are often given names by their discoverers. An element's name may reflect a property of the element. For example, chlorine, a greenish gas, comes from the Greek word *chloros*, which means "green." Some elements, such as ytterbium—discovered in Ytterby, Sweden—are named for the place where they were discovered. Other elements are named to honor someone. Einsteinium is named in honor of Albert Einstein, fermium for Enrico Fermi, and curium for Marie and Pierre Curie.

## Activity

**Elements Song**  Play Tom Lehrer's *Elements Song*, which lists the elements. Have students listen to see how many elements they recognize.  L2

## Fun Fact

The symbols of many elements are derived from the first one or two letters of the Greek, Latin, or English name of the elements. Scientists worldwide use these symbols.

## Text Question Answer

oxygen and carbon

**Reading Check**

**Answer**  Everything is made up of elements or a combination of elements.

**Figure 2** The words *atoms, molecules,* and *compounds* are used to describe substances.
**Explain** *how these terms are related to each other.*

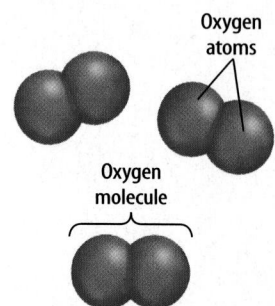

A Some elements, like oxygen, occur as molecules. These molecules contain atoms of the same element bonded together.

B Compounds also are composed of molecules. Molecules of compounds contain atoms of two or more different elements bonded together, as shown by these water molecules.

## Compounds and Molecules

Suppose you make a pitcher of lemonade using a powdered mix and water. The water and the lemonade mix, which is mostly sugar, contain the elements oxygen and hydrogen. Yet, in one, they are part of a nearly tasteless liquid—water. In the other they are part of a sweet solid—sugar. How can the same elements be part of two materials that are so different? Water and sugar are compounds. Compounds are made up of two or more elements in exact proportions. For example, pure water, whether one milliliter of it or one million liters, is always made up of hydrogen atoms bonded to oxygen atoms in a ratio of two hydrogen atoms to one oxygen atom. Compounds have properties different from the elements they are made of. There are two types of compounds—molecular compounds and ionic compounds.

**Molecular Compounds** The smallest part of a molecular compound is a molecule. A molecule is a group of atoms held together by the energy of chemical bonds, as shown in **Figure 2.** When chemical reactions occur, chemical bonds break, atoms are rearranged, and new bonds form. The molecules produced are different from those that began the chemical reaction.

Molecular compounds form when different atoms share their outermost electrons. For example, two atoms of hydrogen each can share one electron on one atom of oxygen to form one molecule of water, as shown in **Figure 2B.** Water does not have the same properties as oxygen and hydrogen. Under normal conditions on Earth, oxygen and hydrogen are gases. Yet, water can be a liquid, a solid, or a gas. When hydrogen and oxygen combine, changes occur and a new substance forms.

**Ions** Atoms also combine because they've become positively or negatively charged. Atoms are usually neutral—they have no overall electric charge. When an atom loses an electron, it has more protons than electrons, so it becomes positively charged. When an atom gains an electron, it has more electrons than protons, so it becomes negatively charged. Electrically charged atoms—positive or negative—are called ions.

**68** **CHAPTER 3** Cell Processes

## Differentiated Instruction

**Hearing Impaired** Provide discussion questions to hearing-impaired students before discussion. Assign another student to record the answers to the questions when they are discussed. Remind hearing students to face hearing-impaired students during the discussion if possible. L2

IS **Auditory-Musical**

## Curriculum Connection

**History** Have students research alchemy. During the Middle Ages, alchemists searched for a way to turn common metals into gold. Though unsuccessful, they were precursors to modern chemists. Much of alchemy was based on Aristotle's idea that matter tries to reach perfection. Alchemists concluded that there must be a way to turn other metals into gold, since it was the "perfect" metal.

L3 IS **Linguistic**

**Ionic Compounds** Ions of opposite charges attract one another to form electrically neutral compounds called ionic compounds. Table salt is made of sodium (Na) and chlorine (Cl) ions, as shown in **Figure 3B.** When they combine, a chlorine atom gains an electron from a sodium atom. The chlorine atom becomes a negatively charged ion, and the sodium atom becomes a positively charged ion. These oppositely charged ions then are attracted to each other and form the ionic compound sodium chloride, NaCl.

Ions are important in many life processes that take place in your body and in other organisms. For example, messages are sent along your nerves as potassium and sodium ions move in and out of nerve cells. Calcium ions are important in causing your muscles to contract. Ions also are involved in the transport of oxygen by your blood. The movement of some substances into and out of a cell would not be possible without ions.

LM Magnification: 8×

**A** Magnified crystals of salt look like this.

Na⁺ Cl⁻

**B** A salt crystal is held together by the attractions between sodium ions and chlorine ions.

**Figure 3** Table salt crystals are held together by ionic bonds.

## Mixtures

Some substances, such as a combination of sugar and salt, can't change each other or combine chemically. A **mixture** is a combination of substances in which individual substances retain their own properties. Mixtures can be solids, liquids, gases, or any combination of them.

> ☑ **Reading Check** *Why is a combination of sugar and salt said to be a mixture?*

Most chemical reactions in living organisms take place in mixtures called solutions. You've probably noticed the taste of salt when you perspire. Sweat is a solution of salt and water. In a solution, two or more substances are mixed evenly. A cell's cytoplasm is a solution of dissolved molecules and ions.

Living things also contain mixtures called suspensions. A suspension is formed when a liquid or a gas has another substance evenly spread throughout it. Unlike solutions, the substances in a suspension eventually sink to the bottom. If blood, shown in **Figure 4,** is left undisturbed, the red blood cells and white blood cells will sink gradually to the bottom. However, the pumping action of your heart constantly moves your blood and the blood cells remain suspended.

**Figure 4** When a test tube of whole blood is left standing, the blood cells sink in the watery plasma.

SECTION 1 Chemistry of Life **69**

**70** CHAPTER 3 Cell Processes

**Table 2 Organic Compounds Found in Living Things**

|  | Carbohydrates | Lipids | Proteins | Nucleic Acids |
|---|---|---|---|---|
| Elements | carbon, hydrogen, and oxygen | carbon, oxygen, hydrogen, and phosphorus | carbon, oxygen, hydrogen, nitrogen, and sulfur | carbon, oxygen, hydrogen, nitrogen, and phosphorus |
| Examples | sugars, starch, and cellulose | fats, oils, waxes, phospholipids, and cholesterol | enzymes, skin, and hair | DNA and RNA |
| Function | supply energy for cell processes; form plant structures; short-term energy storage | store large amounts of energy long term; form boundaries around cells | regulate cell processes and build cell structures | carry hereditary information; used to make proteins |

## Organic Compounds

You and all living things are made up of compounds that are classified as organic or inorganic. Rocks and other nonliving things contain inorganic compounds, but most do not contain large amounts of organic compounds. **Organic compounds** always contain carbon and hydrogen and usually are associated with living things. One exception would be nonliving things that are products of living things. For example, coal contains organic compounds because it was formed from dead and decaying plants. Organic molecules can contain hundreds or even thousands of atoms that can be arranged in many ways. **Table 2** compares the four groups of organic compounds that make up all living things—carbohydrates, lipids, proteins, and nucleic acids.

**Carbohydrates** Carbohydrates are organic molecules that supply energy for cell processes. Sugars and starches are carbohydrates that cells use for energy. Some carbohydrates also are important parts of cell structures. For example, a carbohydrate called cellulose is an important part of plant cells.

**Lipids** Another type of organic compound found in living things is a lipid. Lipids do not mix with water. Lipids such as fats and oils store and release even larger amounts of energy than carbohydrates do. One type of lipid, the phospholipid, is a major part of cell membranes.

**Reading Check** *What are three types of lipids?*

---

## IDENTIFYING Misconceptions

**Lipids** Student awareness of the emphasis on maintaining a "low-fat" diet may lead them to believe that all lipids are harmful. Explain that fats and other lipids have many useful functions in living organisms, such as energy storage, and are a vital component of cell membranes.

### Activity

**Organic Compounds** Display a Food Guide Pyramid and discuss the types of organic compounds represented by foods in each group. Ask students to use this information to create a bulletin board display of foods rich in carbohydrates, lipids, and proteins. Have students illustrate the display with pictures of the foods. L2

## Fun Fact

A paste made of meat tenderizer and water is often used to treat bee and jellyfish stings. An enzyme in the meat tenderizer helps to break down the proteins in the venom, making the area less painful.

**Reading Check**

**Answer** fats, oils, and phospholipids

## Science Journal

**CFCs** Have students research and summarize in their Science Journals the organic compounds known as chlorofluorocarbons (CFCs). Summaries should include a description of the composition of these compounds, their use as refrigerants, and a description of how the use of these substances has impacted the environment. L3 P

**Proteins** Organic compounds called proteins have many important functions in living organisms. They are made up of smaller molecules called amino acids. Proteins are the building blocks of many structures in organisms. Your muscles contain large amounts of protein. Proteins are scattered throughout cell membranes. Certain proteins called **enzymes** regulate nearly all chemical reactions in cells.

**Nucleic Acids** Large organic molecules that store important coded information in cells are called nucleic acids. One nucleic acid, deoxyribonucleic acid, or DNA—genetic material—is found in all cells at some point in their life. It carries information that directs each cell's activities. Another nucleic acid, ribonucleic acid, or RNA, is needed to make enzymes and other proteins.

## Inorganic Compounds

Most **inorganic compounds** are made from elements other than carbon. Generally, inorganic molecules contain fewer atoms than organic molecules. Inorganic compounds are the source for many elements needed by living things. For example, plants take up inorganic compounds from the soil. These inorganic compounds can contain the elements nitrogen, phosphorus, and sulfur. Many foods that you eat contain inorganic compounds. **Table 3** shows some of the inorganic compounds that are important to you. One of the most important inorganic compounds for living things is water.

| Table 3 Some Inorganic Compounds Important in Humans | |
|---|---|
| **Compound** | **Use in Body** |
| Water | makes up most of the blood; most chemical reactions occur in water |
| Calcium phosphate | gives strength to bones |
| Hydrochloric acid | breaks down foods in the stomach |
| Sodium bicarbonate | helps the digestion of food to occur |
| Salts containing sodium, chlorine, and potassium | important in sending messages along nerves |

## Mini LAB

**Observing How Enzymes Work**

**Procedure**

1. Get two small cups of **prepared gelatin** from your teacher. Do not eat or drink anything in lab.
2. On the gelatin in one of the cups, place a piece of **fresh pineapple**.
3. Let both cups stand undisturbed overnight.
4. Observe what happens to the gelatin.

**Analysis**

1. What effect did the piece of fresh pineapple have on the gelatin?
2. What does fresh pineapple contain that caused it to have the effect on the gelatin you observed?
3. Why do the preparation directions on a box of gelatin dessert tell you not to mix it with fresh pineapple?

## Mini LAB

**Purpose** to observe the effects of enzymes on gelatin [L1] [IS]
**Visual-Spatial**

**Materials** two small cups of prepared gelatin, one slice of fresh pineapple

**Teaching Strategies**

• To prepare gelatin, add only half the amount of water indicated on the gelatin package.
• After students add pineapple to one cup, allow both cups of gelatin to sit overnight.

**Analysis**

1. The gelatin under the fresh pineapple turned to a liquid.
2. an enzyme
3. The gelatin would not solidify if in contact with fresh pineapple.

**Assessment**

**Performance** Have students design an experiment to show conclusively that fresh pineapple contains enzymes that keep gelatin from becoming solid. They can repeat the experiment using canned pineapple. Use **Performance Assessment in the Science Classroom,** p. 95.

## Teacher FYI

**Water** Life on Earth could not have evolved without water. Wherever life is found, water is found. Life is found in water at all temperatures. Bacteria can live under snow and in the near-boiling water of hot springs.

## Curriculum Connection

**Health** Provide students with copies of the periodic table. Ask them to research which elements are important for good health. They can find this information on food labels, in reference books, and on the Internet. Ask students to shade each element they discover on the table and to share their results with the class. [L2] [IS] **Interpersonal**

**Importance of Water** Some scientists hypothesize that life began in the water of Earth's ancient oceans. Chemical reactions might have occurred that produced organic molecules. Similar chemical reactions can take place in cells in your body.

Living things are composed of more than 50 percent water and depend on water to survive. You can live for weeks without food but only for a few days without water. **Figure 5** shows where water is found in your body. Although seeds and spores of plants, fungi, and bacteria can exist without water, they must have water if they are to grow and reproduce. All the chemical reactions in living things take place in water solutions, and most organisms use water to transport materials through their bodies. For example, many animals have blood that is mostly water and moves materials. Plants use water to move minerals and sugars between the roots and leaves.

### Applying Math      Solve an Equation

**CALCULATE THE IMPORTANCE OF WATER** All life on Earth depends on water for survival. Water is the most vital part of humans and other animals. It is required for all of the chemical processes that keep us alive. At least 60 percent of an adult human body consists of water. If an adult man weighs 90 kg, how many kilograms of water does his body contain?

**Solution**

1 *This is what you know:*
- adult human body $= 60\%$ water
- man $= 90$ kg

2 *This is what you need to find:*
How many kilograms of water does the adult man have?

3 *This is the procedure you need to use:*
- Set up the ratio: $60/100 = x/90$.
- Solve the equation for $x$: $(60 \times 90)/100$.
- The adult man has 54 kg of water.

4 *Check your answer:*
Divide your answer by 90, then multiply by 100. You should get 60%.

#### Practice Problems

1. A human body at birth consists of 78 percent water. This gradually decreases to 60 percent in an adult. Assume a baby weighed 3.2 kg at birth and grew into an adult weighing 95 kg. Calculate the approximate number of kilograms of water the human gained.

2. Assume an adult woman weighs 65 kg and an adult man weighs 90 kg. Calculate how much more water, in kilograms, the man has compared to the woman.

 Science Online   For more practice, visit in7.msscience.com/math_practice

## Curriculum Connection

**Art** Have students cut out pictures from magazines that illustrate water use by organisms, in industry, and in the environment. Then, have each student make a water collage using the pictures they chose. Display collages in the classroom. L1 **LS** **Visual-Spatial**

**Characteristics of Water** The atoms of a water molecule are arranged in such a way that the molecule has areas with different charges. Water molecules are like magnets. The negative part of a water molecule is attracted to the positive part of another water molecule just like the north pole of a magnet is attracted to the south pole of another magnet. This attraction, or force, between water molecules is why a film forms on the surface of water. The film is strong enough to support small insects because the forces between water molecules are stronger than the force of gravity on the insect.

When heat is added to any substance, its molecules begin to move faster. Because water molecules are so strongly attracted to each other, the temperature of water changes slowly. The large percentage of water in living things acts like an insulator. The water in a cell helps keep its temperature constant, which allows life-sustaining chemical reactions to take place.

You've seen ice floating on water. When water freezes, ice crystals form. In the crystals, each water molecule is spaced at a certain distance from all the others. Because this distance is greater in frozen water than in liquid water, ice floats on water. Bodies of water freeze from the top down. The floating ice provides insulation from extremely cold temperatures and allows living things to survive in the cold water under the ice.

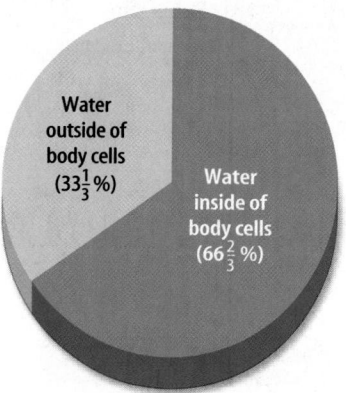

Water outside of body cells $(33\frac{1}{3}\%)$

Water inside of body cells $(66\frac{2}{3}\%)$

**Figure 5** About two-thirds of your body's water is located within your body's cells. Water helps maintain the cells' shapes and sizes. One-third of your body's water is outside of your body's cells.

---

## section 1 review

### Summary

**The Nature of Matter**
- Atoms are made up of protons, neutrons, and electrons.
- Elements are made up of only one kind of atom.
- Compounds are made up of two or more elements.

**Mixtures**
- Solutions are made of two or more substances and are mixed evenly, whereas substances in suspension eventually will sink to the bottom.

**Organic Compounds**
- All living things contain organic compounds.

**Inorganic Compounds**
- Water is one of the most important inorganic compounds for living things.

### Self Check

1. **Compare and contrast** atoms and molecules.
2. **Describe** the differences between an organic and an inorganic compound. Given an example of each type of compound.
3. **List** the four types of organic compounds found in all living things.
4. **Infer** why life as we know it depends on water.
5. **Think Critically** If you mix salt, sand, and sugar with water in a small jar, will the resulting mixture be a suspension, a solution, or both?

#### Applying Skills

6. **Interpret** Carefully observe **Figure 1** and determine how many protons, neutrons, and electrons an atom of oxygen has.

Science Online in7.msscience.com/self_check_quiz

---

### DAILY INTERVENTION

**Check for Understanding**
**Visual-Spatial** Display different liquids, such as a glass of fruit juice, a jar of paint, a bottle of oil, and a glass of water. Discuss the uniqueness of water, in that it is mostly found in liquid form on Earth, that it expands when it freezes, and that it is the most common solvent in the world.

### Reteach

**Organic Compounds** Display carbon compounds such as starch, soap, vinegar, and alcohol. Ask students to explain why these are considered to be organic compounds. They all contain carbon and hydrogen. L2
IS **Logical-Mathematical**

### ✔ Assessment

**Portfolio** Have students write an essay to explain why water is important to them. Ask them to think about their family's use of water each day and what would happen if they were asked to cut their water usage. Use **Performance Assessment in the Science Classroom,** p. 157. L1

---

## section 1 review

1. Possible answer: similarities—both are made of smaller units. Atoms consist of protons, neutrons, and electrons and molecules consist of two or more atoms; differences— molecules are larger than atoms. Molecules can be formed or broken down in a chemical reaction but atoms cannot.
2. Organic compounds, such as lipids, contain carbon; most inorganic compounds, such as water, do not.
3. lipids, carbohydrates, proteins, and nucleic acids
4. Most life processes can occur only in water solutions.
5. Salt and sugar dissolve in water forming a solution; if shaken, sand will spread throughout the solution and form a suspension.
6. 8 protons, 8 neutrons, and 8 electrons

Standards—7.4.5: Explain that the basic functions of organisms, such as extracting energy from food and getting rid of wastes, are carried out within the cell and understand that the way which cells function is similar in all organisms. 7.7.3: Describe how physical and biological systems tend to change until they reach equilibrium and remain that way unless their surroundings change.

Also covers: 7.3.13 (Detailed standards begin on page IN8.)

## section 2

# Moving Cellular Materials

### as you read

#### *What* You'll Learn
- **Describe** the function of a selectively permeable membrane.
- **Explain** how the processes of diffusion and osmosis move molecules in living cells.
- **Explain** how passive transport and active transport differ.

#### *Why* It's Important
Cell membranes control the substances that enter and leave the cells in your body.

#### Review Vocabulary
**cytoplasm:** constantly moving gel-like mixture inside the cell membrane that contains hereditary material and is the location of most of a cell's life process

#### New Vocabulary
- passive transport
- diffusion
- equilibrium
- osmosis
- active transport
- endocytosis
- exocytosis

**Figure 6** A cell membrane, like a screen, will let some things through more easily than others. Air gets through a screen, but insects are kept out.

## Passive Transport

"Close that window. Do you want to let in all the bugs and leaves?" How do you prevent unwanted things from coming through the window? As seen in **Figure 6,** a window screen provides the protection needed to keep unwanted things outside. It also allows some things to pass into or out of the room like air, unpleasant odors, or smoke.

Cells take in food, oxygen, and other substances from their environments. They also release waste materials into their environments. A cell has a membrane around it that works for a cell like a window screen does for a room. A cell's membrane is selectively permeable (PUR mee uh bul). It allows some things to enter or leave the cell while keeping other things outside or inside the cell. The window screen also is selectively permeable based on the size of its openings.

Things can move through a cell membrane in several ways. Which way things move depends on the size of the molecules or particles, the path taken through the membrane, and whether or not energy is used. The movement of substances through the cell membrane without the input of energy is called **passive transport.** Three types of passive transport can occur. The type depends on what is moving through the cell membrane.

### Section 2 Resource Manager

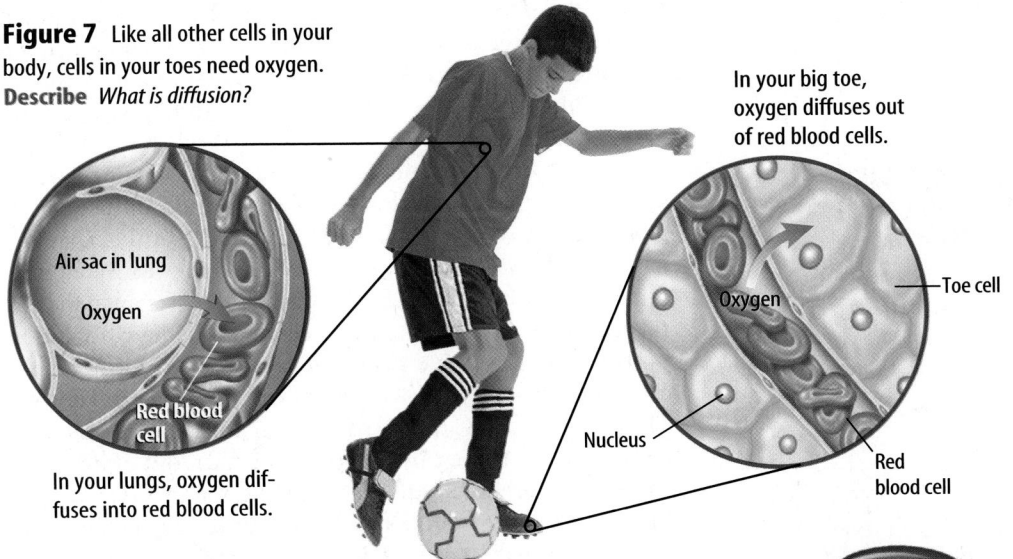

**Figure 7** Like all other cells in your body, cells in your toes need oxygen.
**Describe** *What is diffusion?*

Air sac in lung

Oxygen

Red blood cell

In your lungs, oxygen diffuses into red blood cells.

In your big toe, oxygen diffuses out of red blood cells.

Oxygen

Toe cell

Nucleus

Red blood cell

**Diffusion** Molecules in solids, liquids, and gases move constantly and randomly. You might smell perfume when you sit near or as you walk past someone who is wearing it. This is because perfume molecules randomly move throughout the air. This random movement of molecules from an area where there is relatively more of them into an area where there is relatively fewer of them is called **diffusion.** Diffusion is one type of cellular passive transport. Molecules of a substance will continue to move from one area into another until the relative number of these molecules is equal in the two areas. When this occurs, **equilibrium** is reached and diffusion stops. After equilibrium occurs, it is maintained because molecules continue to move.

☑ **Reading Check** *What is equilibrium?*

Every cell in your body uses oxygen. When you breathe, how does oxygen get from your lungs to cells in your big toe? Oxygen is carried throughout your body in your blood by the red blood cells. When your blood is pumped from your heart to your lungs, your red blood cells do not contain much oxygen. However, your lungs have more oxygen molecules than your red blood cells do, so the oxygen molecules diffuse into your red blood cells from your lungs, as shown in **Figure 7.** When the blood reaches your big toe, there are more oxygen molecules in your red blood cells than in your big toe cells. The oxygen diffuses from your red blood cells and into your big toe cells, as shown also in **Figure 7.**

## Mini LAB

### Observing Diffusion
**Procedure**

1. Use two clean glasses of equal size. Label one *Hot,* then fill it until half full with **very warm water.** Label the other *Cold,* then fill it until half full with **cold water. WARNING:** *Do not use boiling hot water.*
2. Add one drop of **food coloring** to each glass. Carefully release the drop just at the water's surface to avoid splashing the water.
3. Observe the water in the glasses. Record your observations immediately and again after 15 min.

**Analysis**
1. Describe what happens when food coloring is added to each glass.
2. How does temperature affect the rate of diffusion?

**Try at Home**

SECTION 2 Moving Cellular Materials **75**

SECTION 2 Moving Cellular Materials **75**

## 2 Teach

### Caption Answer
**Figure 7** the random movement of molecules from where there is more of them to where there is fewer of them

## Mini LAB

**Purpose** to investigate the effect of temperature on diffusion rate
L1 **ELL** COOP LEARN IS **Logical-Mathematical**

**Materials** two clean glasses, very warm water, cold water, food coloring, dropper, marker or wax pencil, clock, labels

**Teaching Strategies**
• Have students record how long it takes the food coloring to diffuse evenly throughout each beaker.
• Caution students not to move the water-filled beakers.

**Analysis**
1. The food coloring spreads throughout the water; it spreads faster in the hot water.
2. Heat increases the rate of diffusion.

### Assessment

**Performance** To further assess understanding of the effect of temperature on diffusion, have students repeat the activity using ice water instead of hot water. Use **Performance Assessment in the Science Classroom,** p. 105. L1

**Try at Home**

☑ **Reading Check**

**Answer** when the relative number of molecules of a substance is equal in the two areas

## Teacher FYI

**Membranes** A permeable membrane allows all molecules to pass through. An impermeable membrane doesn't allow any to pass. Only some molecules can pass through a semi-permeable membrane—usually only small molecules that can pass through quickly.

**Materials** sand, salt, marbles, water, kitchen strainer

**Estimated Time** five minutes

**Procedure** Pour different substances through the kitchen strainer. Select some substances that will pass through the strainer and some that will not.

## Inquiry Lab

**Observing the Effect of Salt on Plants**

**Purpose** to design an experiment to grow plants treated with salt

**Possible Materials** container, soil, fast-growing plants or seeds such as grass or radishes, table salt or road salt

**Estimated Time** one month

**Teaching Strategies**

• Students can vary the amount of salt, and whether it is added to the soil or to leaves.

• Students can predict what the effect of the salt will be by testing rate of growth, plant height, plant color, and leaf number. L2

**For additional inquiry activities, see Science Inquiry Labs.**

**Caption Answer**

**Figure 8** diffusion of water through a cell membrane

### ✔ Reading Check

**Answer** Because there are fewer water molecules around the carrot cells than inside the carrot cells, water leaves the carrot and moves into the salt solution.

---

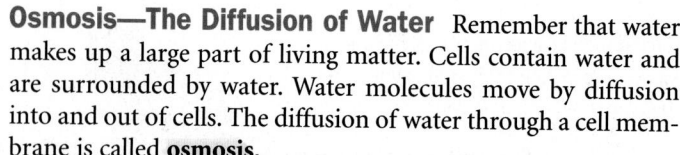

**Indiana Academic Standard Check**

**7.7.3:** Describe how . . . biological systems tend to change until they reach equilibrium and remain that way unless their surrounds change.

✔ How do molecules undergo diffusion?

✔ Molecules randomly move from an area where there are relatively more of them, into an area where there are relatively fewer of them.

**Figure 8** Cells respond to differences between the amount of water inside and outside the cell. **Define** What is osmosis?

---

**Osmosis—The Diffusion of Water** Remember that water makes up a large part of living matter. Cells contain water and are surrounded by water. Water molecules move by diffusion into and out of cells. The diffusion of water through a cell membrane is called **osmosis.**

If cells weren't surrounded by water that contains few dissolved substances, water inside of cells would diffuse out of them. This is why water left the carrot cells in this chapter's Launch Lab. Because there were relatively fewer water molecules in the salt solution around the carrot cells than in the carrot cells, water moved out of the cells and into the salt solution.

Losing water from a plant cell causes its cell membrane to come away from its cell wall, as shown on the left in **Figure 8.** This reduces pressure against its cell wall, and a plant cell becomes limp. If the carrot sticks were taken out of salt water and put in pure water, the water around the cells would move into them and they would fill with water. Their cell membranes would press against their cell walls, as shown on the right in **Figure 8,** pressure would increase, and the cells would become firm. That is why the carrot sticks would be crisp again.

### ✔ Reading Check *Why do carrots in salt water become limp?*

Osmosis also takes place in animal cells. If animal cells were placed in pure water, they too would swell up. However, animal cells are different from plant cells. Just like an overfilled water balloon, animal cells will burst if too much water enters the cell.

The carrot stick becomes limp when more water leaves each of its cells than enters them.

Equilibrium occurs when water leaves and enters the cells at the same rate.

---

## 🔬 LAB DEMONSTRATION

**Purpose** to observe diffusion

**Materials** self-sealing plastic sandwich bag, cooked rice, tincture of iodine, 8-oz clear plastic cups, tablespoon

**Preparation** Half-fill the plastic cups with water and add 6 drops of tincture of iodine. Cook rice before class.

**Procedure** Seal a sandwich bag containing 2 tbsp of rice, and place it into the water that contains iodine. Observe after 10 min.

**Expected Outcome** Iodine molecules will move through the plastic bag, turning the rice blue-black. Iodine turns blue-black in the presence of starch.

**Assessment**

**What did you observe?** The rice inside the plastic bag turned blue-black. **Explain what occurred.** Iodine molecules diffused from an area where there was a large number of iodine molecules (outside the bag) to an area where there were few iodine molecules (inside the bag).

**Facilitated Diffusion** Cells take in many substances. Some substances pass easily through the cell membrane by diffusion. Other substances, such as glucose molecules, are so large that they can enter the cell only with the help of molecules in the cell membrane called transport proteins. This process, a type of passive transport, is known as facilitated diffusion. Have you ever used the drive through at a fast-food restaurant to get your meal? The transport proteins in the cell membrane are like the drive-through window at the restaurant. The window lets you get food out of the restaurant and put money into the restaurant. Similarly, transport proteins are used to move substances into and out of the cell.

## Active Transport

Imagine that a football game is over and you leave the stadium. As soon as you get outside of the stadium, you remember that you left your jacket on your seat. Now you have to move against the crowd coming out of the stadium to get back in to get your jacket. Which required more energy—leaving the stadium with the crowd or going back to get your jacket? Something similar to this happens in cells.

Sometimes, a substance is needed inside a cell even though the amount of that substance inside the cell is already greater than the amount outside the cell. For example, root cells require minerals from the soil. The roots of the plant in **Figure 9** already might contain more of those mineral molecules than the surrounding soil does. The tendency is for mineral molecules to move out of the root by diffusion or facilitated diffusion. But they need to move back across the cell membrane and into the cell just like you had to move back into the stadium. When an input of energy is required to move materials through a cell membrane, **active transport** takes place.

Active transport involves transport proteins, just as facilitated diffusion does. In active transport, a transport protein binds with the needed particle and cellular energy is used to move it through the cell membrane. When the particle is released, the transport protein can move another needed particle through the membrane.

Higher mineral levels    Lower mineral levels

Minerals

Active transport

Soil particles    Root hair

**Figure 9** Some root cells have extensions called root hairs that may be 5 mm to 8 mm long. Minerals are taken in by active transport through the cell membranes of root hairs.

INTEGRATE Health

**Transport Proteins** Your health depends on transport proteins. Sometimes transport proteins are missing or do not function correctly. What would happen if proteins that transport cholesterol across membranes were missing? Cholesterol is an important lipid used by your cells. Write your ideas in your Science Journal.

**Salt and Thirst** Why do salty foods make you thirsty? The salt present in the food causes water to leave your cells; the lost water needs to be replaced by the body.

### Caption Answer

**Figure 8** The diffusion of water through a cell membrane.

### Use an Analogy

**Active and Passive Transport** Have students compare active and passive transport with the energy they must exert to get a bicycle to the top of a hill and then ride it back down. Students must exert energy to get the bicycle up the hill. In the same way, the cell uses energy to move substances from areas of low concentration to areas of high concentration. Students do not need to exert energy to ride the bicycle down the hill. In passive transport, cells do not have to use energy to move substances from areas of high concentration to areas of low concentration. L2 IS **Logical-Mathematical**

### Text Question Answer

going back for the jacket

INTEGRATE Health

**Transport Proteins** Cholesterol would not be transported to different areas of the body. Without cholesterol, the body could not synthesize bile acids, steroid hormones, or Vitamin D.

**Research** Have students research the "good" types and "bad" types of cholesterol. Why does the body need cholesterol? They should include why the body needs "good" cholesterol and why certain types of cholesterol are bad for people's health. Students can design a health pamphlet on the ways to lower health risks associated with high cholesterol. L2

## Cultural Diversity

**Preserving Foods** A practical use of osmosis is the drying and salting of food. Have students report on the processes and uses of dried and salted foods in Native American and other cultures. For example, the French developed a vegetable dehydrator in 1795. Both processes remove water from cells in order to preserve the food. In drying, water evaporates. In salting, a salt solution is used to remove water from cells. L2

## Teacher FYI

**Membranes** Cell membranes contain spaces through which some substances (water molecules, mineral ions, sugar molecules) can pass easily. The spaces are too small for large molecules to pass through. Some ions cannot pass through membranes due to their charge. These move into a cell via channels or active transport.

# Endocytosis and Exocytosis

Some molecules and particles are too large to move by diffusion or to use the cell membrane's transport proteins. Large protein molecules and bacteria, for example, can enter a cell when they are surrounded by the cell membrane. The cell membrane folds in on itself, enclosing the item in a sphere called a vesicle. Vesicles are transport and storage structures in a cell's cytoplasm. The sphere pinches off, and the resulting vesicle enters the cytoplasm. A similar thing happens when you poke your finger into a partially inflated balloon. Your finger is surrounded by the balloon in much the same way that the protein molecule is surrounded by the cell membrane. This cell process that takes in a substance by surrounding it with the cell membrane is called **endocytosis** (en duh si TOH sus). Some one-celled organisms, as shown in **Figure 10,** take in food this way.

The contents of a vesicle can be released by a cell using the process called **exocytosis** (ek soh si TOH sus). Exocytosis occurs in the opposite way that endocytosis does. A vesicle's membrane fuses with a cell's membrane, and the vesicle's contents are released. Cells in your stomach use this process to release chemicals that help digest food. The ways that materials can enter or leave a cell are summarized in **Figure 11.**

Color-enhanced TEM Magnification: 1,400×

**Figure 10** One-celled organisms like this egg-shaped one can take in other one-celled organisms using endocytosis.

## section 2 review

### Summary

**Passive Transport**
- Cells take in substances and release waste through their cell membranes.
- Facilitated diffusion and osmosis are types of passive transport.

**Active Transport**
- Transport proteins are involved in active transport.
- Transport proteins can be reused many times.

**Endocytosis and Exocytosis**
- Vesicles are formed when a cell takes in a substance by endocytosis.
- Contents of a vesicle are released to the outside of a cell by exocytosis.

### Self Check

1. **Describe** how cell membranes are selectively permeable.
2. **Compare and contrast** the processes of osmosis and diffusion.
3. **Infer** why endocytosis and exocytosis are important processes to cells.
4. **Think Critically** Why are fresh fruits and vegetables sprinkled with water at produce markets?

#### Applying Skills

5. **Communicate** Seawater is saltier than tap water. Explain why drinking large amounts of seawater would be dangerous for humans.

 Science Online in7.msscience.com/self_check_quiz

## section 2 review

1. They allow some molecules to pass through, but not others.
2. In both, molecules move from areas with many molecules to areas with few molecules. Osmosis is the diffusion of water across a cell membrane; diffusion can apply to any form of matter.
3. Molecules and particles that are too large to move by diffusion or by the cell's transport proteins can move into and out of cells using endocytosis and exocytosis.
4. Water will diffuse into the fruits and vegetables and keep them crisp.
5. The high levels of salt in seawater would cause water to move out of the cells, resulting in dehydration.

**Figure 11**

**A** flexible yet strong layer, the cell membrane is built of two layers of lipids (gold) pierced by protein "passageways" (purple). Molecules can enter or exit the cell by slipping between the lipids or through the protein passageways. Substances that cannot enter or exit the cell in these ways may be surrounded by the membrane and drawn into or expelled from the cell.

**Diffusion and Osmosis**

**Facilitated Diffusion**

Outside cell

**Active Transport**

Cell membrane

Inside cell

**DIFFUSION AND OSMOSIS** Small molecules such as oxygen, carbon dioxide, and water can move between the lipids into or out of the cell.

**FACILITATED DIFFUSION** Larger molecules such as glucose also diffuse through the membrane ——but only with the help of transport proteins.

**ACTIVE TRANSPORT** Cellular energy is used to move some molecules through protein passageways. The protein binds to the molecule on one side of the membrane and then releases the molecule on the other side.

Nucleolus    Nucleus

**ENDOCYTOSIS AND EXOCYTOSIS** In endocytosis, part of the cell membrane wraps around a particle and engulfs it in a vesicle. During exocytosis, a vesicle filled with molecules bound for export moves to the cell membrane, fuses with it, and the contents are released to the outside.

Endocytosis

Exocytosis

SECTION 2 Moving Cellular Materials **79**

## Visualizing Cell Membrane Transport

Have students examine the pictures and read the captions. Then ask students the following questions.

Why do some substances move through the cell membrane through exocytosis and endocytosis instead of one of the other transport methods? These substances, which include proteins and nucleic acids, are too large to use the other methods. For example, cholesterol enters by endocytosis; neurotransmitters exit by exocytosis.

Which transport method(s) is like floating downstream? Which is like paddling upstream? Why? In diffusion (osmosis and facilitated diffusion), a substance moves from an area of higher concentration to an area of lower concentration. This does not require energy because it goes with the flow, like floating downstream. In active transport, the substance must go against the concentration gradient which, like paddling upstream, requires energy.

### Activity

**Cell Membrane Transport** Have students make a model of a cell that illustrates one type of cell membrane transport. L2
**IS** Kinesthetic

## Visual Learning

**Figure 11** Transport of a molecule across a cell membrane can occur in several ways, such as diffusion and osmosis, facilitated diffusion, active transport, and endocytosis and exocytosis. Have students make an outline of the transport of a molecule across a membrane by using this figure. L2 P

# Differentiated Instruction

**English-Language Learners** Pair students and on flashcards have them write key terms and definitions that deal with the movement of cellular materials. Students should include diffusion, osmosis, facilitated diffusion, active transport, exocytosis and endocytosis on their cards. L2

**Challenge** Have students investigate transport proteins and the substances each transports. Students can make a card game to teach other students what they learned. L3

## Real-World Question

**Purpose** to observe and measure the amount of water diffusing through an egg membrane
**L2** **IS** **Logical-Mathematical**

**Process Skills** observe and infer, measure, communicate, recognize cause and effect, form operational definitions

**Time Required** 50 minutes to set up, 5 minutes each day to observe, 15 minutes to summarize

## Procedure

**Alternate Materials** Food containers with lids may be used to hold the unshelled egg.

**Teaching Strategy** Cover raw eggs with vinegar. Leave undisturbed for two or three days until the shells dissolve.

**Troubleshooting**

• Remind students to handle unshelled eggs carefully.
• Thick syrup works better than thin syrup.
• Make sure students replace lids on containers.

## Conclude and Apply

1. water— increased in size; corn syrup—decreased in size
2. about 30 mL of water entered; about 40 mL of water left
3. The eggshell is not permeable to water and syrup.
4. cell membrane

# Observing Osmosis

It is difficult to observe osmosis in cells because most cells are so small. However, a few cells can be seen without the aid of a microscope. Try this lab to observe osmosis.

## Real-World Question

How does osmosis occur in an egg cell?

**Materials**

unshelled egg*    distilled water (250 mL)
balance    light corn syrup (250 mL)
spoon    500-mL container

*an egg whose shell has been dissolved by vinegar

**Goals**

■ **Observe** osmosis in an egg cell.
■ **Determine** what affects osmosis.

**Safety Precautions**

**WARNING:** *Eggs may contain bacteria. Avoid touching your face.*

## Procedure

1. Copy the table below into your Science Journal and use it to record your data.

**Egg Mass Data**

| | Beginning Egg Mass | Egg Mass After Two Days |
|---|---|---|
| Distilled water | Answers will vary. | |
| Corn syrup | | |

2. Obtain an unshelled egg from your teacher. Handle the egg gently. Use a balance to find the egg's mass and record it in the table.

3. Place the egg in the container and add enough distilled water to cover it.

4. **Observe** the egg after 30 min, one day, and two days. After each observation, record the egg's appearance in your Science Journal.

5. After day two, remove the egg with a spoon and allow it to drain. Find the egg's mass and record it in the table.

6. Empty the container, then put the egg back in. Now add enough corn syrup to cover it. Repeat steps 4 and 5.

## Conclude and Apply

1. **Explain** the difference between what happened to the egg in water and in corn syrup.
2. **Calculate** the mass of water that moved into and out of the egg.
3. **Hypothesize** why you used an unshelled egg for this investigation.
4. **Infer** what part of the egg controlled water's movement into and out of the egg.

### Communicating Your Data

**Compare** your conclusions with those of other students in your class. **For more help, refer to the** Science Skill Handbook.

---

### ✓ Assessment

**Performance** Have students place ten dried beans in water overnight. Direct them to explain their observations. Use **Performance Assessment in the Science Classroom,** p. 97 **L3**

### Communicating Your Data

Students should discuss why their conclusions did or did not agree with those of other students.

**Standards—7.4.5:** Explain that the basic functions of organisms, such as extracting energy from food and getting rid of wastes, are carried out within the cell . . . . **7.4.7:** Describe how plants use the energy from light to make sugars from carbon dioxide and water to produce food that can be used immediately or stored for later use.

**Also covers:** 7.3.12, 7.3.14, 7.4.4, 7.4.8, 7.6.2, 7.7.1 (Detailed standards begin on page IN8.)

# Energy for Life

## Trapping and Using Energy

Think of all the energy that players use in a basketball game. Where does the energy come from? The simplest answer is "from the food they eat." The chemical energy stored in food molecules is changed inside of cells into forms needed to perform all the activities necessary for life. In every cell, these changes involve chemical reactions. All of the activities of an organism involve chemical reactions in some way. The total of all chemical reactions in an organism is called **metabolism.**

The chemical reactions of metabolism need enzymes. What do enzymes do? Suppose you are hungry and decide to open a can of spaghetti. You use a can opener to open the can. Without a can opener, the spaghetti is unusable. The can of spaghetti changes because of the can opener, but the can opener does not change. The can opener can be used again later to open more cans of spaghetti. Enzymes in cells work something like can openers. The enzyme, like the can opener, causes a change, but the enzyme is not changed and can be used again, as shown in **Figure 12.** Unlike the can opener, which can only cause things to come apart, enzymes also can cause molecules to join. Without the right enzyme, a chemical reaction in a cell cannot take place. Each chemical reaction in a cell requires a specific enzyme.

### as you read

**_What_ You'll Learn**

- **List** the differences between producers and consumers.
- **Explain** how the processes of photosynthesis and respiration store and release energy.
- **Describe** how cells get energy from glucose through fermentation.

**_Why_ It's Important**

Because of photosynthesis and respiration, you use the Sun's energy.

**Review Vocabulary**
**mitochondrion:** cell organelle that breaks down lipids and carbohydrates and releases energy

**New Vocabulary**
- metabolism
- photosynthesis
- respiration
- fermentation

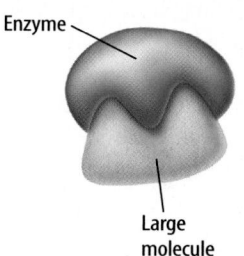

Enzyme

Large molecule

The enzyme attaches to the large molecule it will help change.

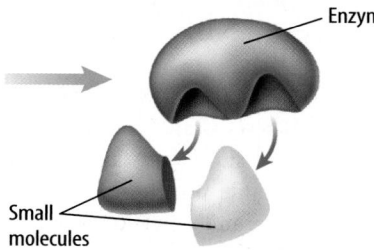

Enzyme

Small molecules

The enzyme causes the larger molecule to break down into two smaller molecules. Like a can opener, the enzyme is not changed and can be used again.

**Figure 12** Enzymes are needed for most chemical reactions that take place in cells.
**Determine** _What is the sum of all chemical reactions in an organism called?_

SECTION 3 Energy for Life **81**

---

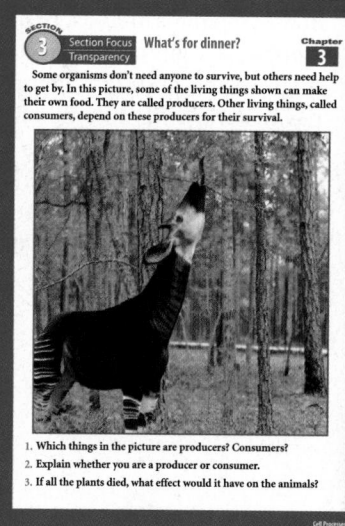
---

### Section 3 Resource Manager

**Chapter _Fast File_ Resources**
Transparency Activity, p. 44
Directed Reading for Content Mastery, pp. 19, 20
Lab Activity, pp. 11–14
Enrichment, p. 30

Reinforcement, p. 27
Lab Worksheet, pp. 7–8
**Life Science Critical Thinking/Problem Solving,** p. 15
**Lab Management and Safety,** p. 63

## Activity

**Bubbles** Pick a leaf from a plant that has been exposed to sunlight for a few hours. Submerge it in water. Observe the surface of the leaf. What forms on the leaf? Why? Bubbles; the leaf is giving off oxygen. L2

## Use an Analogy

**Construction and Photosynthesis** Compare the construction of a house to photosynthesis. Building a house is a physical process that requires the putting together of raw materials. Photosynthesis is a chemical process of putting raw materials together. They both require raw materials and result in a usable product. **IS** **Logical-Mathematical**

## Caption Answer

**Figure 13** carbon dioxide, water, light energy, and chlorophyll

## IDENTIFYING
## Misconceptions

**Plant Food** Some students may think that plants obtain food from the soil. Plants take in a variety of minerals and other substances from the soil, but these are not used as food. They are dissolved in water and absorbed through the plant's roots. Once absorbed, they are transported to structures in the plant where they are needed. The food of plants—glucose—is produced by plants in the chloroplasts of their cells from carbon dioxide and water and using light energy.

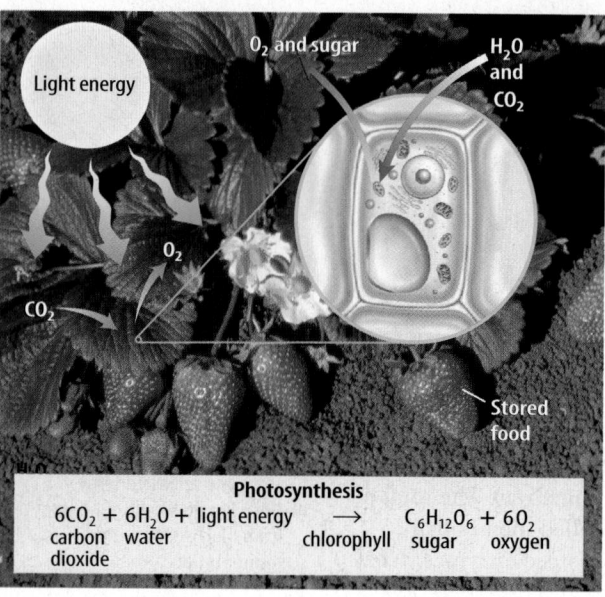

**Figure 13** Plants use photosynthesis to make food.
**Determine** *According to the chemical equation, what raw materials would the plant pictured need for photosynthesis?*

**Photosynthesis**

$$6CO_2 + 6H_2O + \text{light energy} \longrightarrow[\text{chlorophyll}] C_6H_{12}O_6 + 6O_2$$

carbon dioxide   water                    sugar   oxygen

**Indiana Academic Standard Check**

**7.4.7:** Describe how plants use the energy from light to make sugars from carbon dioxide and water to produce food that can be used immediately or stored for later use.

✔ Where in plant cells does photosynthesis occur?

✔ chloroplasts

**Photosynthesis** Living things are divided into two groups—producers and consumers—based on how they obtain their food. Organisms that make their own food, such as plants, are called producers. Organisms that cannot make their own food are called consumers.

If you have ever walked barefoot across a sidewalk on a sunny summer day, you probably moved quickly because the sidewalk was hot. Sunlight energy was converted into thermal energy and heated the sidewalk. Plants and many other producers can convert light energy into another kind of energy—chemical energy. The process they use is called photosynthesis. During **photosynthesis,** producers use light energy to make sugars, which can be used as food.

**Producing Carbohydrates** Producers that use photosynthesis are usually green because they contain a green pigment called chlorophyll (KLOR uh fihl). Chlorophyll and other pigments are used in photosynthesis to capture light energy. In plant cells, these pigments are found in chloroplasts.

The captured light energy is used to drive chemical reactions during which the raw materials, carbon dioxide and water, are used to produce sugar and oxygen. For plants, the raw materials come from air and soil. Some of the captured light energy is stored in the chemical bonds that hold the sugar molecules together. **Figure 13** shows what happens during photosynthesis in a plant. Enzymes also are needed before these reactions can occur.

**Storing Carbohydrates** Plants make more sugar during photosynthesis than they need for survival. Excess sugar is changed and stored as starches or used to make other carbohydrates. Plants use these carbohydrates as food for growth, maintenance, and reproduction.

Why is photosynthesis important to consumers? Do you eat apples? Apple trees use photosynthesis to produce apples. Do you like cheese? Some cheese comes from milk, which is produced by cows that eat plants. Consumers take in food by eating producers or other consumers. No matter what you eat, photosynthesis was involved directly or indirectly in its production.

## Differentiated Instruction

**Challenge** There are certain plants, such as the Indian pipe (*Monotropa uniflora*) and dodder (*Cuscuta*), that lack chlorophyll. Have students research these plants and write a report about how they obtain food to present to the class. L3

## Science Journal

**Energy and Photosynthesis** In their Science Journals, have students list all the foods they eat in one day. Have them to divide the list into two groups: (1) foods formed directly by photosynthesis, (2) foods not formed directly by photosynthesis. Use the lists to help students see that all food energy comes from photosynthesis, whether directly or indirectly. L2

**Respiration** Imagine that you get up late for school. You dress quickly, then run three blocks to school. When you get to school, you feel hot and are breathing fast. Why? Your muscle cells use a lot of energy when you run. To get this energy, muscle cells break down food. Some of the energy from the food is used when you move and some of it becomes thermal energy, which is why you feel warm or hot. Most cells also need oxygen to break down food. You were breathing fast because your body was working to get oxygen to your muscles. Your muscle cells were using the oxygen for the process of respiration. During **respiration,** chemical reactions occur that break down food molecules into simpler substances and release their stored energy. Just as in photosynthesis, enzymes are needed for the chemical reactions of respiration.

**Reading Check** *What must happen to food molecules for respiration to take place?*

**Breaking Down Carbohydrates** The type of food molecules most easily broken down by cells is carbohydrates. Respiration of carbohydrates begins in the cytoplasm of the cell. The carbohydrates are broken down into glucose molecules. Each glucose molecule is broken down further into two simpler molecules. As the glucose molecules are broken down, energy is released.

The two simpler molecules are broken down again. This breakdown occurs in the mitochondria of the cells of plants, animals, fungi, and many other organisms. This process uses oxygen, releases much more energy, and produces carbon dioxide and water as wastes. When you exhale, you breathe out carbon dioxide and some of the water.

Respiration occurs in the cells of all living things. **Figure 14** shows how respiration occurs in one consumer. As you are reading this section of the chapter, millions of cells in your body are breaking down glucose, releasing energy, and producing carbon dioxide and water.

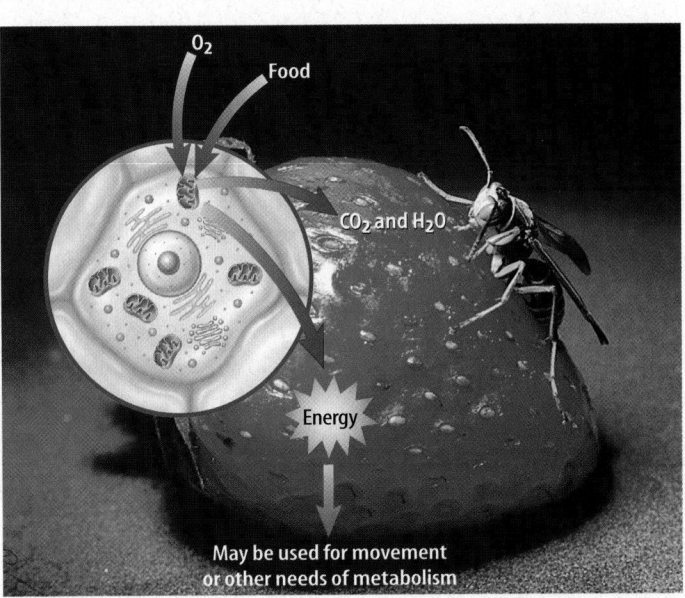

**Figure 14** Producers and consumers carry on respiration that releases energy from foods.

**Microbiologist** Dr. Harold Amos is a microbiologist who has studied cell processes in bacteria and mammals. He has a medical degree and a doctorate in bacteriology and immunology. He has also received many awards for his scientific work and his contributions to the careers of other scientists. Research microbiology careers, and write what you find in your Science Journal.

**Microbiologist** Scientists in the field of microbiology study organisms of microscopic or submicroscopic size. A bachelor's degree is required to work in this field. Students interested in a career in microbiology should study sciences, math, and Latin.

**Use Science Words**

**Word Origin** Have students study the parts of the word *photosynthesis.* It comes from the Greek *photo, syn-,* and *thesis.* Have them find the meaning of these words and word parts and describe how the word is defined. photo: "light;" syn-: "together;" thesis: "to place;" Photosynthesis uses light to place compounds together. L2

**Reading Check**

**Answer** They must be broken down into simpler substances and their stored energy released.

**IDENTIFYING Misconceptions**

**Plant Gases** Students often think that plants do not use oxygen, only that they produce oxygen and use carbon dioxide during photosynthesis. See page F at the beginning of this chapter for teaching strategies that address this misconception.

**Active Reading**

**Buddy Interviews** This strategy helps students understand and clarify the reading. Have students interview one another to find out what helps them to understand what they are reading, how they find answers, and how they assimilate new vocabulary terms. Have students use Buddy Interviews to help them master photosynthesis and respiration. L2

**Teacher FYI**

**Athletes' Oxygen** The body of an average person running a 100-yard dash in 12 seconds would require 6 L (1.6 gal.) of air. The person's lungs could supply only about 1.2 L of air. As a result, oxygen debt would occur, and the muscles would produce lactic acid. Most athletes take in at least 10 percent more oxygen than the average person; trained marathon runners take in up to 45 percent more oxygen. They have more efficient respiratory and circulatory systems and can exert greater effort without incurring oxygen debt.

## Discussion

**Yeast** Why do bakers use yeast for breadmaking? Yeast carry out processes that release energy in the absence of oxygen and produce carbon dioxide, which causes bread to rise.

## Quick Demo

**Fermentation**

**Materials** sugar, water, jar, yeast

**Estimated Time** five minutes to prepare, several hours before class; 10 minutes to observe

**Procedure** Prepare a sugar solution by mixing 1 tablespoon of sugar with 1 cup of warm water. Add some yeast to the solution a few hours before class and cover it. Have students note the odor of alcohol and the bubbles of carbon dioxide. Point out that these products result from alcoholic fermentation.

**Science Online**

**Topic: Beneficial Microorganisms**
Visit in7.msscience.com for Web links to information about how microorganisms are used to produce many useful products.

**Activity** Find three other ways that microorganisms are beneficial.

---

**Indiana Academic Standard Check**

**7.4.5:** Explain that the basic functions of organisms, such as extracting energy from food . . . .

✔ Where does fermentation occur in a cell?

✔ cytoplasm

---

**Figure 15** Organisms that use fermentation produce several different wastes.

**Fermentation** Remember imagining you were late and had to run to school? During your run, your muscle cells might not have received enough oxygen, even though you were breathing rapidly. When cells do not have enough oxygen for respiration, they use a process called **fermentation** to release some of the energy stored in glucose molecules.

Like respiration, fermentation begins in the cytoplasm. Again, as the glucose molecules are broken down, energy is released. But the simple molecules from the breakdown of glucose do not move into the mitochondria. Instead, more chemical reactions occur in the cytoplasm. These reactions release some energy and produce wastes. Depending on the type of cell, the wastes may be lactic acid, alcohol, and carbon dioxide, as shown in **Figure 15.** Your muscle cells can use fermentation to change the simple molecules into lactic acid while releasing energy. The presence of lactic acid is why your muscle cells might feel stiff and sore after you run to school.

 **Reading Check** *Where in a cell does fermentation take place?*

Some microscopic organisms, such as bacteria, carry out fermentation and make lactic acid. Some of these organisms are used to produce yogurt and some cheeses. These organisms break down a sugar in milk to release energy. The lactic acid produced causes the milk to become more solid and gives these foods some of their flavor.

Have you ever used yeast to make bread? Yeasts are one-celled living organisms. Yeast cells use fermentation to break down sugar in bread dough. They produce alcohol and carbon dioxide as wastes. The carbon dioxide waste is a gas that makes bread dough rise before it is baked. The alcohol is lost as the bread bakes.

Color-enhanced SEM Magnification: 18,000×

Yeast cells produce carbon dioxide and alcohol as wastes when they use fermentation.

Stained LM Magnification: 500×

Your muscle cells produce lactic acid as a waste when they use fermentation.

## Cultural Diversity

**Fermenting Food** Lactic acid fermentation by bacteria is responsible for a number of foods from different cultures. Have students research these foods and report their findings to the class in oral reports. Possible topics: Hawaiian *poi*, Japanese soy sauce, Korean *kimchi*, German sauerkraut, yogurt. L3

CO$_2$, H$_2$O

Photosynthesis (producers)

Respiration (all living things)

Sugars, O$_2$

**Figure 16** The chemical reactions of photosynthesis and respiration could not take place without each other.

**Related Processes** How are photosynthesis, respiration, and fermentation related? Some producers use photosynthesis to make food. All living things use respiration or fermentation to release energy stored in food. If you think carefully about what happens during photosynthesis and respiration, you will see that what is produced in one is used in the other, as shown in **Figure 16.** These two processes are almost the opposite of each other. Photosynthesis produces sugars and oxygen, and respiration uses these products. The carbon dioxide and water produced during respiration are used during photosynthesis. Most life would not be possible without these important chemical reactions.

---

### section ③ review

#### Summary

**Trapping and Using Energy**

- Metabolism is the total of all chemical reactions in an organism.
- During photosynthesis, light energy is used to make sugars.
- Chlorophyll and other pigments capture light energy.
- Consumers take in energy by eating producers and other consumers.
- Living cells break down glucose and release energy. This is called respiration.
- Fermentation changes simple molecules and releases energy.
- Without photosynthesis and respiration, most life would not be possible.

#### Self Check

1. **Explain** the difference between producers and consumers and give three examples of each.
2. **Infer** how the energy used by many living things on Earth can be traced back to sunlight.
3. **Compare and contrast** respiration and fermentation.
4. **Think Critically** How can some indoor plants help to improve the quality of air in a room?

#### Applying Math

5. **Solve** Refer to the chemical equation for photosynthesis. Calculate then compare the number of carbon, hydrogen, and oxygen atoms before and after photosynthesis.

### section ③ review

1. Producers make food. Consumers get energy by eating producers, food made by producers, or other consumers. Examples will vary.
2. Energy used by living things is released from food molecules during cellular respiration. Photosynthetic producers convert light energy—usually from the
Sun—into the chemical energy in the sugar molecules that they produce. Consumers get this energy by eating producers or other consumers that eat producers.
3. The amount of energy released by fermentation is less than that released by respiration.
4. Plants remove carbon dioxide from the air, use it in photosynthesis, and produce oxygen.
5. The number of atoms is the same before and after photosynthesis; C = 6, H = 12, O = 18.

## Visual Learning

**Figure 16** The arrows in the figure illustrate the interdependence of photosynthesis and respiration. Producers take in carbon dioxide and water, undergo photosynthesis, and produce oxygen and sugars. Other living organisms take in oxygen and sugars, undergo respiration, and give off carbon dioxide and water. Have students create an events chain concept map to illustrate what is occurring in the pictures in this figure. L2 P

### 3 Assess

#### DAILY INTERVENTION

### Checking for Understanding

**Logical-Mathematical** Using a three-column chart, have students brainstorm with the class about different organisms and whether they use photosynthesis, respiration, or fermentation. Discuss how these processes are related and under what circumstances an organism would use them. L2

### Reteach

**Using Energy** Have students identify organisms that photosynthesize and those that respire. Only organisms with chlorophyll photosynthesize; all organisms respire. L1

### ☑ Assessment

**Content** Have students make a table to compare and contrast photosynthesis and respiration. Use **Performance Assessment in the Science Classroom,** p. 109. L2

## Real-World Question

**Purpose** Students observe photosynthesis and respiration in plants and infer whether the processes occur in light or darkness. `L2` **ELL** COOP LEARN **IS** Visual-Spatial

**Process Skills** measure, observe, infer, communicate, compare and contrast, recognize cause and effect, separate and control variables, interpret data

**Time Required** 50 minutes (leave overnight if using artificial light)

**Safety Precautions** Students should use care when working with chemicals.

## Procedure

**Tie to Prior Knowledge** Most students are aware that plants use light energy to make food and that photosynthesis will occur in the tube placed near the light.

**Troubleshooting** *Elodea* should be kept in the dark for two days before the activity. Use sharp scissors to make a clean diagonal cut at the bottom of each stem.

### Goals
- **Observe** green water plants in the light and dark.
- **Determine** whether plants carry on photosynthesis and respiration.

### Materials
16-mm test tubes (3)
150-mm test tubes with stoppers (4)
*small, clear-glass baby food jars with lids (4)
test-tube rack
stirring rod
scissors
carbonated water (5 mL)
bromthymol blue solution in dropper bottle
aged tap water (20 mL)
*distilled water (20 mL)
sprigs of *Elodea* (2)
*other water plants
*Alternate materials

### Safety Precautions

**WARNING:** *Wear splash-proof safety goggles to protect eyes from hazardous chemicals.*

# Photosynthesis and Respiration

LM Magnification: 225×

## Real-World Question

Every living cell carries on many chemical processes. Two important chemical processes are respiration and photosynthesis. All cells, including the ones in your body, carry on respiration. However, some plant cells can carry on both processes. In this experiment you will investigate when these processes occur in plant cells. How could you find out when plants were using these processes? Are the products of photosynthesis and respiration the same? When do plants carry on photosynthesis and respiration?

## Procedure

1. In your Science Journal, copy and complete the test-tube data table as you perform this lab.

### Test-Tube Data

| Test Tube | Color at Start | Color After 30 Minutes |
|---|---|---|
| 1 | yellow | blue |
| 2 | yellow | yellow |
| 3 | blue | yellow |
| 4 | blue | blue |

## Alternative Inquiry Lab

**Photosynthesis and Respiration** To make this Lab an Inquiry Lab, have students relate the problem to nature. Explain to students that plants undergo some form of respiration. What happens to plants that survive during periods without light? Students can observe photosynthesis and respiration in plants. To determine if they both occur in plants, have students design an experiment to measure the outputs of photosynthesis and respiration. They can use *Elodea* or other water plants and the materials described above to set up the experiment. Unsafe or impractical questions should be eliminated.

2. Label each test tube using the numbers *1, 2, 3,* and *4.* Pour 5 mL of aged tap water into each test tube.

3. Add 10 drops of carbonated water to test tubes *1* and *2.*

4. Add 10 drops of bromthymol blue to all of the test tubes. Bromthymol blue turns green to yellow in the presence of an acid.

5. Cut two 10-cm sprigs of *Elodea.* Place one sprig in test tube *1* and one sprig in test tube *3.* Stopper all test tubes.

6. Place test tubes *1* and *2* in bright light. Place tubes *3* and *4* in the dark. Observe the test tubes for 30 min or until the color changes. Record the color of each of the four test tubes.

### ◉ Analyze Your Data

1. **Identify** what is indicated by the color of the water in all four test tubes at the start of the activity.

2. **Infer** what process occurred in the test tube or tubes that changed color after 30 min.

### ◉ Conclude and Apply

1. **Describe** the purpose of test tubes *2* and *4* in this experiment.

2. **Explain** whether or not the results of this experiment show that photosynthesis and respiration occur in plants.

#### 𝒞ommunicating Your Data

Choose one of the following activities to **communicate** your data. Prepare an oral presentation that explains how the experiment showed the differences between products of photosynthesis and respiration. Draw a cartoon strip to **explain** what you did in this experiment. Use each panel to show a different step. **For more help, refer to the** Science Skill Handbook.

### ◉ Analyze Your Data

**Expected Outcome** Most results will reflect that plants used carbon dioxide in the light and gave off carbon dioxide in the dark.

**Answers to Questions**

1. Test tubes 1 and 2 contain carbon dioxide. Tubes 3 and 4 do not.
2. They underwent photosynthesis or respiration.

**Error Analysis** Have students compare their results and explain why any differences occurred. [L2]

### ◉ Conclude and Apply

1. Tubes 2 and 4 were controls.
2. Yes, the experimental results showed that both processes happen in plant cells. In test tube 1, the green plant used carbon dioxide for photosynthesis. In test tube 3, the green plant gave off carbon dioxide as a result of respiration.

#### ☑ Assessment

**Oral** How are fermentation and respiration similar? Both processes release energy through the breakdown of other substances. Use **Performance Assessment in the Science Classroom,** p. 99. [L2]

**LAB 87**

## Differentiated Instruction

**Visually Impaired** Pair students who are visually impaired with those who can describe to them the colors in the test tubes and other observations, both before and after the experiment. [L2]

#### 𝒞ommunicating Your Data

Students should use data from the experiment for the presentation or cartoon.

## Understanding Literature

**Personification** When she states that the tulip inspires love.

## Respond to the Reading

1. Possible answers: The tulip bulb is buried deep in the ground; the tulip is a hardy plant.

2. the yellow color at the base of each petal

3. **Linking Science and Writing** As they observe the plant, students should record the change in the plant's growth.

 **Plant Dormancy**

Plant stems play a part in the transport of materials from roots to leaves. Stems vary greatly in size and shape from one plant species to another. Some grow entirely underground and other stems can store water and nutrients. Plants often store food in their stems during their growth period. When a plant's growth stops, this stored food enables them to survive dormancy. Dormancy occurs during a cold winter or a long dry period. The dormant plant uses the stored food to begin growing when conditions again become favorable.

# from "Tulip"
### by Penny Harter

I watched its first green push
through bare dirt, where the builders
had dropped boards, shingles,
plaster—
killing everything.
    I could not recall what grew there,
what returned each spring,
but the leaves looked tulip,
and one morning it arrived,
a scarlet slash against the aluminum siding.
    Mornings, on the way to my car,
I bow to the still bell
of its closed petals; evenings,
it greets me, light ringing
at the end of my driveway.
    Sometimes I kneel
to stare into the yellow throat . . . .
It opens and closes my days.
It has made me weak with love . . . .

## Understanding Literature

**Personification** Using human traits or emotions to describe an idea, animal, or inanimate object is called personification. When the poet writes that the tulip has a "yellow throat," she uses personification. Where else does the poet use personification?

## Respond to the Reading

1. Why do you suppose the tulip survived the builders' abuse?

2. What is the yellow throat that the narrator is staring into?

3. **Linking Science and Writing** Keep a gardener's journal of a plant for a month, describing weekly the plant's condition, size, health, color, and other physical qualities.

 Because most chemical reactions in plants take place in water, plants must have water in order to grow. The water carries nutrients and minerals from the soil into the plant. The process of active transport allows needed nutrients to enter the roots. The cell membranes of root cells contain proteins that bind with the needed nutrients. Cellular energy is used to move these nutrients through the cell membrane.

**88** CHAPTER 3 Cell Processes

## Resources for Teachers and Students

*Tulipa: A Photographer's Botonical,* by Christopher Baker (Photographer), Willem Lemmers, Emma Sweeny, and Michael Pollan, Artisan, 1999

*Photosynthesis,* by Krishna Rao and David O. Hall, Cambridge University Press, 1999

*Plant Identification Terminology: An Illustrated Glossary,* by James G. Harris and Melinda Woolf Harris, Spring Lake Publishers, 2001

American Society for Microbiology, Office of Education, 1325 Massachusetts Avenue, NW, Washington, DC 20005–4171

## Reviewing Main Ideas

### Section 1 Chemistry of Life

1. Matter is anything that has mass and takes up space.

2. Energy in matter is in the chemical bonds that hold matter together.

3. All organic compounds contain the elements hydrogen and carbon. The organic compounds in living things are carbohydrates, lipids, proteins, and nucleic acids.

4. Organic and inorganic compounds are important to living things.

### Section 2 Moving Cellular Materials

1. The selectively permeable cell membrane controls which molecules can pass into and out of the cell.

2. In diffusion, molecules move from areas where there are relatively more of them to areas where there are relatively fewer of them.

3. Osmosis is the diffusion of water through a cell membrane.

4. Cells use energy to move molecules by active transport but do not use energy for passive transport.

5. Cells move large particles through cell membranes by endocytosis and exocytosis.

### Section 3 Energy for Life

1. Photosynthesis is the process by which some producers change light energy into chemical energy.

2. Respiration that uses oxygen releases the energy in food molecules and produces waste carbon dioxide and water.

3. Some one-celled organisms and cells that lack oxygen use fermentation to release small amounts of energy from glucose. Wastes such as alcohol, carbon dioxide, and lactic acid are produced.

## Visualizing Main Ideas

*Copy and complete the following table on energy processes.*

| Energy Processes | Photosynthesis | Respiration | Fermentation |
|---|---|---|---|
| Energy source | light | food (glucose) | food (glucose) |
| In plant and animal cells, occurs in | chloroplast | mitochondria | cytoplasm |
| Reactants are | water, carbon dioxide | glucose, oxygen | glucose, oxygen |
| Products are | glucose, oxygen | water, carbon dioxide | lactic acid, alcohol, carbon dioxide |

 in7.msscience.com/interactive_tutor

**CHAPTER STUDY GUIDE 89**

## Reviewing Main Ideas

Summary statements can be used by students to review the major concepts of the chapter.

## Visualizing Main Ideas

See student page.

**Visit** in7.msscience.com
/self_check_quiz
/interactive_tutor
/vocabulary_puzzlemaker
/chapter_review
/standards_review

### Assessment Transparency

For additional assessment questions, use the *Assessment Transparency* located in the transparency book.

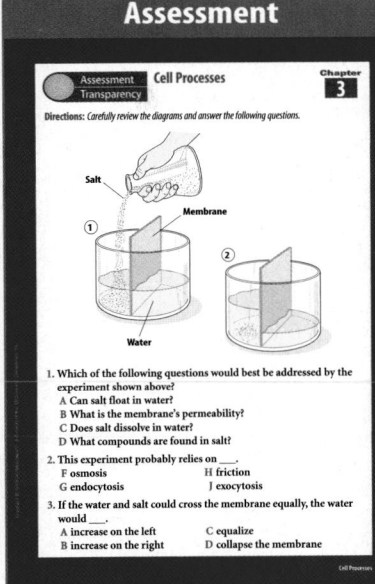

## Identifying Misconceptions

**Assess**

**Discussion** Do animals ever give off oxygen as a product of their metabolic activities? No Explain Oxygen is given off as a product of photosynthesis, thus only organisms that can carry out photosynthesis produce this gas. Animals are not photosynthetic organisms. What products do plants release during their metabolic processes? both oxygen and carbon dioxide

Specifically reinforce the idea that plants carry out both photosynthesis and respiration.

**Expected Outcome** At this point students should understand and be able to explain the complementary processes of photosynthesis and respiration in plants and animals.

## Using Vocabulary

1. osmosis
2. enzymes
3. by endocytosis
4. inorganic compound
5. photosynthesis
6. organic compounds
7. respiration
8. metabolism

## Checking Concepts

| | |
|---|---|
| 9. C | 13. D |
| 10. B | 14. C |
| 11. A | 15. A |
| 12. B | 16. C |

## Using Vocabulary

| | |
|---|---|
| active transport p. 77 | metabolism p. 81 |
| diffusion p. 75 | mixture p. 69 |
| endocytosis p. 78 | organic compound p. 70 |
| enzyme p. 71 | osmosis p. 76 |
| equilibrium p. 75 | passive transport p. 74 |
| exocytosis p. 78 | photosynthesis p. 82 |
| fermentation p. 84 | respiration p. 83 |
| inorganic | |
| compound p. 71 | |

*Use what you know about the vocabulary words to answer the following questions.*

1. What is the diffusion of water called?

2. What type of protein regulates nearly all chemical reactions in cells?

3. How do large food particles enter an amoeba?

4. What type of compound is water?

5. What process is used by some producers to convert light energy into chemical energy?

6. What type of compounds always contain carbon and hydrogen?

7. What process uses oxygen to break down glucose?

8. What is the total of all chemical reactions in an organism called?

## Checking Concepts

*Choose the word or phrase that best answers the question.*

9. What is it called when cells use energy to move molecules?
   **A)** diffusion       **C)** active transport
   **B)** osmosis         **D)** passive transport

**Use the photo below to answer question 10.**

10. What cell process is occurring in the photo?
    **A)** osmosis        **C)** exocytosis
    **B)** endocytosis    **D)** diffusion

11. What occurs when the number of molecules of a substance is equal in two areas?
    **A)** equilibrium    **C)** fermentation
    **B)** metabolism     **D)** cellular respiration

12. Which of the following substances is an example of a carbohydrate?
    **A)** enzymes        **C)** waxes
    **B)** sugars         **D)** proteins

13. What is RNA an example of?
    **A)** carbon dioxide **C)** lipid
    **B)** water          **D)** nucleic acid

14. What organic molecule stores the greatest amount of energy?
    **A)** carbohydrate   **C)** lipid
    **B)** water          **D)** nucleic acid

15. Which of these formulas is an example of an organic compound?
    **A)** $C_6H_{12}O_6$   **C)** $H_2O$
    **B)** $NO_2$           **D)** $O_2$

16. What are organisms that cannot make their own food called?
    **A)** biodegradables **C)** consumers
    **B)** producers      **D)** enzymes

 Science online in7.msscience.com/vocabulary_puzzlemaker

**Use the ExamView® Pro Testmaker CD-ROM to:**

- create multiple versions of tests
- create modified tests with one mouse click for inclusion students
- edit existing questions and add your own questions
- build tests aligned with state standards using built-in State Curriculum Tags
- change English tests to Spanish with one mouse click and vice versa

## Thinking Critically

**17. Concept Map** Copy and complete the events-chain concept map to sequence the following parts of matter from smallest to largest: *atom, electron,* and *compound.*

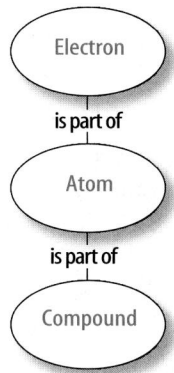

Electron

is part of

Atom

is part of

Compound

**Use the table below to answer question 18.**

### Photosynthesis in Water Plants

| Beaker Number | Distance from Light (cm) | Bubbles per Minute |
|---|---|---|
| 1 | 10 | 45 |
| 2 | 30 | 30 |
| 3 | 50 | 19 |
| 4 | 70 | 6 |
| 5 | 100 | 1 |

**18. Interpret Data** Water plants were placed at different distances from a light source. Bubbles coming from the plants were counted to measure the rate of photosynthesis. What can you say about how the distance from the light affected the rate?

**19. Infer** why, in snowy places, salt is used to melt ice on the roads. Explain what could happen to many roadside plants as a result.

 Science⌂nline in7.msscience.com/chapter_review

**20. Draw a conclusion** about why sugar dissolves faster in hot tea than in iced tea.

**21. Predict** what would happen to the consumers in a lake if all the producers died.

**22. Explain** how meat tenderizers affect meat.

**23. Form a hypothesis** about what will happen to wilted celery when placed in a glass of plain water.

## Performance Activities

**24. Puzzle** Make a crossword puzzle with words describing ways substances are transported across cell membranes. Use the following words in your puzzle: *diffusion, osmosis, facilitated diffusion, active transport, endocytosis,* and *exocytosis.* Make sure your clues give good descriptions of each transport method.

## Applying Math

**25. Light and Photosynthesis** Using the data from question 18, make a line graph that shows the relationship between the rate of photosynthesis and the distance from light.

**26. Importance of Water** Assume the brain is 70% water. If the average adult human brain weighs 1.4 kg, how many kilograms of water does it contain?

**Use the equation below to answer question 27.**

**Photosynthesis**
$$6CO_2 + 6H_2O + \text{light energy} \xrightarrow{\text{chlorophyll}} C_6H_{12}O_6 + 6O_2$$
carbon dioxide   water   chlorophyll   sugar   oxygen

**27. Photosynthesis** Refer to the chemical equation above. If 18 $CO_2$ molecules and 18 $H_2O$ molecules are used with light energy to make sugar, how many sugar molecules will be produced? How many oxygen molecules will be produced?

**CHAPTER REVIEW** 91

## Thinking Critically

**17.** See student page.

**18.** The closer a plant is to light, the faster its rate of photosynthesis.

**19.** Plants die as water molecules move out of the cells into the salty soil.

**20.** The molecules in hot water move faster than those in cold. These faster-moving molecules bump into the sugar molecules more often and more vigorously, dissolving the sugar faster.

**21.** Consumers would also die; they depend on producers for food.

**22.** The enzymes increase the rate at which protein bonds are broken; this makes the meat more tender.

**23.** Wilted celery will become crisp as water molecules move by osmosis into its cells to reach equilibrium.

## Performance Activities

**24.** Definitions in the chapter for these terms can be used. Use **PASC,** p. 91.

## Applying Math

### Indiana Math Standards
7.2.1, 7.6.1

**25.**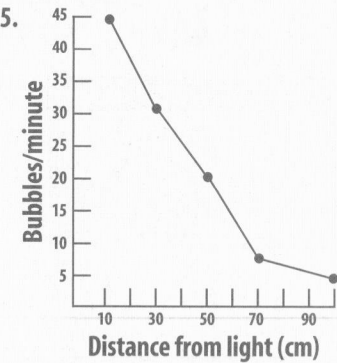

**26.** 0.98 kg

**27.** 3 sugar molecules and 18 oxygen molecules will be produced.

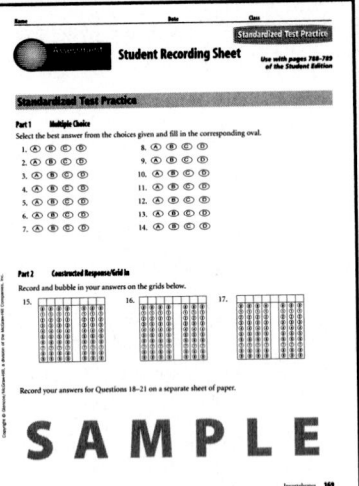

**Answer Sheet** A practice
answer sheet can be found
at in7.msscience.com/answer_sheet.

S A M P L E

**Part 1 | Multiple Choice**

1. C
2. B
3. B
4. C
5. B
6. D
7. D
8. D

**Part 2 | Critical Response**

9. Endocytosis is a cell process that
takes in a substance by surrounding
it with the cell membrane.
Exocytosis removes the contents of a
vesicle from the cell. The vesicle's
membrane fuses with the cell membrane, and the vesicle's contents are
released. Cells in the stomach
release chemicals by exocytosis.

---

The assessed Indiana standard
appears above the question.

*Record your answers on the answer sheet*
*provided by your teacher or on a sheet of paper.*

**Part 1 | Multiple Choice**

1. Which describes a substance that is made
up of only one kind of atom and cannot be
broken down by chemical reactions?

   A carbohydrate

   B electron

   C element

   D molecule

2. The illustration below shows the crystal
structure of salt, NaCl.

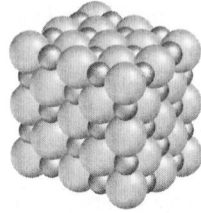

What type of substance is salt?

   A element

   B ionic compound

   C mixture

   D molecular compound

**Test-Taking Tip**

**Diagrams** Study a diagram carefully, being sure to read all
labels and captions.

---

**7.7.3**

3. A cell that contains 40% water is placed in
a solution that is 20% water. Which percent
represents equilibrium for the water and
the cell?

   A 20%

   B 30%

   C 40%

   D 60%

4. Which is the sum of all the chemical reactions in an organism?

   A endocytosis

   B fermentation

   C metabolism

   D respiration

5. The table below shows the flexibility of cell
substances.

| Cell Substances | | |
| --- | --- | --- |
| Organic Compound | Flexibility | Found In |
| Keratin | Not very flexible | Hair and skin of mammals |
| Collagen | Not very flexible | Skin, bones, and tendons of mammals |
| Chitin | Very rigid | Tough outer shell of insects and crabs |
| Cellulose | Very flexible | Plant cell walls |

Which organic compound is least flexible?

   A cellulose

   B chitin

   C collagen

   D keratin

---

10. In this diagram, an enzyme is regulating a chemical reaction. The
enzyme allows a larger molecule to
break down into smaller molecules.
This is significant because enzymes
are needed for all chemical reactions that take place in a cell.

11. Carbon dioxide and water are converted to sugar and oxygen in the
presence of chlorophyll. Light

energy drives this reaction.
Photosynthesis transforms light
energy into chemical energy,
which is the source of energy for
most living things. The oxygen produced replenished that in Earth's
atmosphere.

12. Plant cells need oxygen for respiration. Without respiration, the
chemical energy stored in sugar

would not be available for use in a
plant.

13. In plant cells, photosynthesis produces oxygen. This oxygen is
released into the air, inhaled by
humans, and diffuses into the
bloodstream in the lungs. Then it is
carried to cells where it defuses
into them and is used in the mitochondria for respiration.

**7.4.5**

**6.** Which process has the carbon dioxide that you exhale as an end product?

   **A** DNA synthesis

   **B** osmosis

   **C** photosynthesis

   **D** respiration

**7.4.5**

**7.** Which process releases the most energy for an athlete's muscles?

   **A** fermentation

   **B** osmosis

   **C** photosynthesis

   **D** respiration

**8.** The table below shows how some substances in the body are classified.

| Compound | Organic or Inorganic | Type of Substance |
|---|---|---|
| Fat | Organic | |
| Skin | Organic | |
| DNA | Organic | |
| Sugar | Organic | |
| Water | Inorganic | Molecular compound |
| Potassium | Inorganic | Element |

Which correctly completes the table for *Fat, Skin, DNA,* and *Sugar,* in that order?

   **A** carbohydrate, lipid, nucleic acid, protein

   **B** carbohydrate, nucleic acid, protein, lipid

   **C** lipid, nucleic acid, carbohydrate, protein

   **D** lipid, protein, nucleic acid, carbohydrate

**Part 2   Critical Response**

**7.4.4**

**9.** Compare and contrast endocytosis and exocytosis. List an example of how the body uses each process.

**7.4.5**

**10.** The illustration below shows a process that takes place in all organisms.

What process is taking place? What is the significance of this process for a cell?

**7.4.5**

**11.** Describe the chemical reaction for photosynthesis. What is the importance of the products of photosynthesis?

**7.4.5**

**12.** Why would plants need oxygen?

**7.4.5**

**13.** How do oxygen molecules get from plant cells to cells in your skin?

## Rubrics

The following rubric is a sample scoring device for critical response questions.

### Critical Response

| Points | Description |
|---|---|
| 4 | The student demonstrates a thorough understanding of the science of the task. The response may contain minor flaws that do not detract from the demonstration of a thorough understanding. |
| 3 | The student demonstrates an understanding of the science of the task. The response is essentially correct and demonstrates an essential but less than thorough understanding of the science. |
| 2 | The student demonstrates only a partial understanding of the science of the task. Although the student may have used the correct approach to a solution or may have provided a correct solution, the work lacks an essential understanding of the underlying science concepts. |
| 1 | The student demonstrates a very limited understanding of the science of the task. The response is incomplete and exhibits many flaws. |
| 0 | The student provides a completely incorrect solution or no response at all. |

| Section/Objectives | Standards | | Labs/Features |
|---|---|---|---|
| **Chapter Opener** | **National** | **State/Local** | **Launch Lab:** Infer About Seed Growth, p. 95 **Foldables,** p. 95 |
| | See pp. 16T–17T for a Key to Standards. | Detailed Standards begin on page IN8. | A data-collection lab using Probeware technology can be found in **Probeware Labs,** pp. 1–4 |
| **Section 1 Cell Division and Mitosis** 2 sessions 1 block 1. **Explain** why mitosis is important. 2. **Examine** the steps of mitosis. 3. **Compare** mitosis in plant and animal cells. 4. **List** two examples of asexual reproduction. | National Content Standards: UCP.1, UCP.2, UCP.3, A.1, A.2, C.1, C.2, C.3 | Indiana Standards: 7.2.7, 7.4.4 | **Integrate Career,** p. 97 **MiniLAB:** Modeling Mitosis, p. 101 **Lab:** Mitosis in Plant Cells, p. 103 |
| **Section 2 Sexual Reproduction and Meiosis** 2 sessions 1 block 5. **Describe** the stages of meiosis and how sex cells are produced. 6. **Explain** why meiosis is needed for sexual reproduction. 7. **Name** the cells that are involved in fertilization. 8. **Explain** how fertilization occurs in sexual reproduction. | National Content Standards: UCP.1, UCP.2, A.1, C.1, C.2, C.3, C.5 | Indiana Standards: 7.4.1, 7.4.3, 7.5.3 | **Integrate Chemistry,** p. 105 **Applying Science:** How can chromosome numbers be predicted? p. 107 **Visualizing Polyploidy in Plants,** p. 108 |
| **Section 3 DNA** 3 sessions 1.5 blocks 9. **Identify** the parts of a DNA molecule and its structure. 10. **Explain** how DNA copies itself. 11. **Describe** the structure and function of each kind of RNA. | National Content Standards: UCP.1–UCP.5, A.1, A.2, C.1, C.2, C.3 | Indiana Standards: 7.1.5, 7.1.8, 7.1.10, 7.2.7, 7.4.3, 7.4.4, 7.7.2 | **MiniLAB:** Modeling DNA Replication, p. 111 **Science Online,** p. 113 **Science Online,** p. 115 **Lab:** Mutations, p. 116 **Oops! Accidents in Science:** A Tangled Tale, p. 118 |

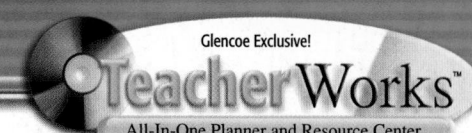

| Lab Materials | Reproducible Resources | Section Assessment | Technology |
|---|---|---|---|
| **Launch Lab:** soaked bean seeds, water, paper towels, self-sealing plastic bags, magnifying lens | **Chapter FAST FILE Resources** Foldables Worksheet, p. 15 Directed Reading Overview, p. 17 Note-taking Worksheets, pp. 31–33 | GLENCOE'S ASSESSMENT ADVANTAGE | Teacher**Works** includes: • Interactive Teacher Edition • Lesson Planner with calendar • Access to all program blacklines • Correlations to standards • Web links ▭ Video Lab |
| **MiniLAB:** colored paper, poster board, markers, toothpicks, yarn, thread, glue, scissors **Lab:** prepared slide of onion root tip, microscope | **Chapter FAST FILE Resources** Transparency Activity, p. 42 MiniLAB, p. 3 Enrichment, p. 28 Reinforcement, p. 25 Transparency Activity, pp. 45–46 Lab Worksheet, pp. 5–6 Directed Reading, p. 18 Lab Activity, pp. 9–10 | Portfolio Visual Learning, p. 97 Performance MiniLAB, p. 101 Applying Math, p. 102 Content Challenge, p. 99 Section Review, p. 102 | Section Focus Transparency Teaching Transparency Guided Reading Audio Program Interactive Chalkboard CD-ROM |
| *Need materials?* Contact Science Kit at 1-800-828-7777 or www.sciencekit.com on the Internet. | **Chapter FAST FILE Resources** Transparency Activity, p. 43 Enrichment, p. 29 Reinforcement, p. 26 Directed Reading, p. 18 **Life Science Critical Thinking/ Problem Solving,** p. 19 **Mathematics Skill Activities,** p. 3 **Performance Assessment in the Science Classroom,** p. 57 | Portfolio Make a Model, p. 107 Performance Applying Science, p. 107 Applying Skills, p. 109 Content Challenge, p. 106 Section Review, p. 109 | Section Focus Transparency Guided Reading Audio Program Interactive Chalkboard CD-ROM |
| **MiniLAB:** pencil, paper **Lab:** Web sites and other resources on mutations | **Chapter FAST FILE Resources** Transparency Activity, p. 44 MiniLAB, p. 4 Enrichment, p. 30 Reinforcement, p. 27 Directed Reading, pp. 19, 20 Lab Worksheet, pp. 7–8 Lab Activity, pp. 11–13 **Home and Community Involvement,** p. 36 | Portfolio Curriculum Connection, p. 113 Performance MiniLAB, p. 111 Applying Skills, p. 115 Content Challenge, p. 114 Section Review, p. 115 | Section Focus Transparency Virtual Labs CD-ROM Guided Reading Audio Program Interactive Chalkboard CD-ROM ▭ Probeware Lab |

## End of Chapter Assessment

| Blackline Masters | Technology | Professional Series |
|---|---|---|
| **Chapter FAST FILE Resources** Chapter Review, pp. 35–36 Chapter Tests, pp. 37–40 Mastering the Grade 7 Indiana Science Standards | ▭ MindJogger Videoquiz IN Test Prep and Practice ExamView® ExamView® Pro Testmaker TeacherWorks CD-ROM Interactive Chalkboard CD-ROM | **Performance Assessment in the Science Classroom (PASC)** |

# Transparencies

## Section Focus

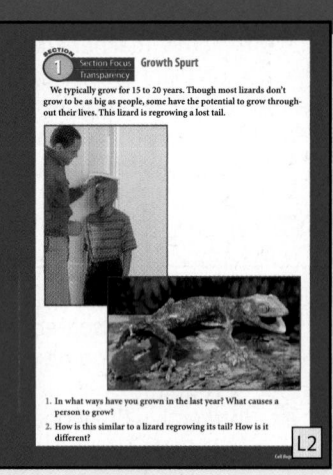

SECTION 1 Section Focus Transparency — **Growth Spurt**

We typically grow for 15 to 20 years. Though most lizards don't grow to be as big as people, some have the potential to grow throughout their lives. This lizard is regrowing a lost tail.

1. In what ways have you grown in the last year? What causes a person to grow?
2. How is this similar to a lizard regrowing its tail? How is it different?

L2

SECTION 2 Section Focus Transparency — **I Think He Has Your Eyes**

The Santa Gertrudis bull flourishes in the arid plains of Texas. The King Ranch developed the Santa Gertrudis by cross-breeding Brahman cattle with Shorthorns. As you can see, the Santa Gertrudis inherited characteristics from both of its parents.

Brahman  Shorthorn  Santa Gertrudis

1. Why might ranchers have wanted to cross-breed Brahmans and Shorthorns?
2. Which of the Santa Gertrudis' traits can you identify in the Brahman and the Shorthorn?

L2

SECTION 3 Section Focus Transparency — **Curly Cat**

This unusual cat is a Devon Rex. It appeared in Devonshire, England in 1960 when a genetic change occurred among British barn cats. The Devon Rex has a small head and a curly coat.

1. Based on the picture and the description above, what do you think a genetic change is?
2. How can cat breeders attempt to continue the characteristics of the Devon Rex?

L2

This is a representation of key blackline masters available in the Teacher Classroom Resources. See Resource Manager boxes within the chapter for additional information.

## Key to Teaching Strategies

The following designations will help you decide which activities are appropriate for your students.

**L1** Level 1 activities should be appropriate for students with learning difficulties.

**L2** Level 2 activities should be within the ability range of all students.

**L3** Level 3 activities are designed for above-average students.

**ELL** ELL activities should be within the ability range of English-Language Learners.

**COOP LEARN** Cooperative Learning activities are designed for small group work.

**LS** Multiple Learning Styles logos, as described on page 12T, are used throughout to indicate strategies that address different learning styles.

**P** These strategies represent student products that can be placed into a best-work portfolio.

**PBL** Problem-Based Learning activities apply real-world situations to learning.

## Assessment

Assessment Transparency — **Cell Reproduction**

Directions: Carefully review the diagram and answer the following questions.

**Interphase**

Chromosomes — Nucleolus — Centrioles (two parts) — Nuclear membrane — Chromatin — Nucleus — Cell membrane

1. A cell produced by the fruit fly cell pictured above will most likely be ___.
   A identical to the fruit fly cell
   B a combination of its two parent fruit fly cells
   C unable to reproduce
   D a genetic mutation
2. In which part of the cell are the chromosomes located?
   F Cell membrane
   G Cytoplasm
   H Nucleus
   J Mitochondrion
3. The fruit fly cell above contains eight chromosomes. How many chromosomes will cells produced by the above cell probably have?
   A sixteen     B eight     C four     D sixty-four

L2

## Teaching

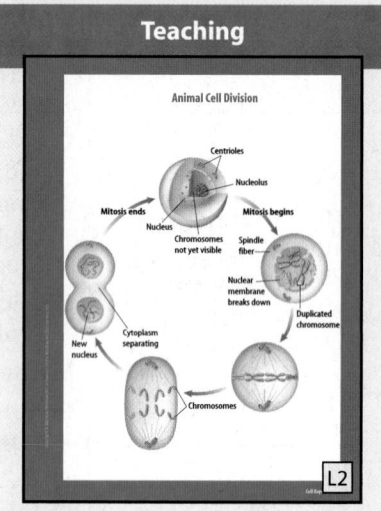

Teaching Transparency — **Animal Cell Division**

Centrioles — Nucleolus — Mitosis begins — Spindle fiber — Nuclear membrane breaks down — Duplicated chromosome — Chromosomes — New nucleus — Cytoplasm separating — Chromosomes not yet visible — Nucleus — Mitosis ends

L2

# Hands-on Activities

## Student Text Lab Worksheet

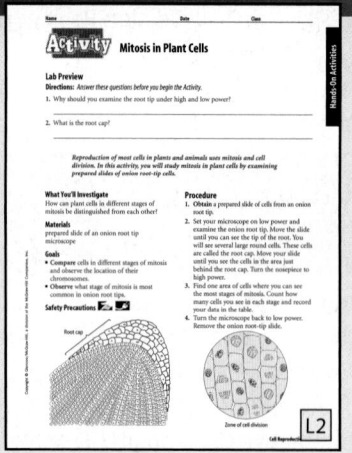

**Activity** Mitosis in Plant Cells

**Lab Preview**

Directions: Answer these questions before you begin the Activity.

1. Why should you examine the root tip under high and low power?

2. What is the root cap?

Reproduction of most cells in plants and animals uses mitosis and cell division. In this activity, you will study mitosis in plant cells by examining prepared plates of onion root-tip cells.

**What You'll Investigate**
How can plant cells in different stages of mitosis be distinguished from each other?

**Materials**
prepared plate of an onion root tip
microscope

**Goals**
• Compare cells in different stages of mitosis and observe the location of their chromosomes.
• Observe what stage of mitosis is most common in the root tip.

**Safety Precautions**

**Procedure**
1. Obtain a prepared slide of cells from an onion root tip.
2. Set your microscope on low power and examine the onion root tip. Move the slide until you can see the tip of the root. You will see several large round cells. These cells are called the root cap. Move your slide until you see the cells in the area just behind the root cap. Turn the nosepiece to high power.
3. Find one area of cells where you can see the most stages of mitosis. Count how many cells you see in each stage and record your data in the table.
4. Turn the microscope back to low power. Remove the onion root-tip slide.

Root cap — Zone of cell division

L2

## Laboratory Activities

LAB 1 Laboratory Activity — **Modeling Cell Division in Early Development**

Every person starts out as a single cell. Cell division is responsible for the development of a baby from the single cell. As the single cell begins developing, cell division results in exponential growth in the number of cells present. Exponential growth is growth that occurs at an ever-increasing rate. On a graph, exponential growth is represented by a J-shaped curve.

**Strategy**
You will model how cell division results in exponential growth in the number of cells in a developing human.
You will determine why exponential growth cannot continue indefinitely during human development.
You will infer why uncontrolled cell divisions, which occurs in cancer, can be so harmful to human health.

**Materials**
uncooked rice
paper cups (11)
graph paper

**Procedure**
1. Obtain a container of uncooked rice from your teacher. Each grain of rice represents one human cell.
2. Place one grain of rice in a paper cup. This grain of rice represents the single cell that results when sperm and egg unite.
3. Label paper cups 1 through 10, and place them in a row next to the cup containing the original cell. During the first 10 cell divisions, the cells in the developing human all have the same cell cycle length.
4. Place two grains of rice into cup 1 to represent the number of cells present after the original cell undergoes the first round of mitosis. Record the number 2 in the table in the Data and Observations section.
5. Place grains of rice into cup 2 to represent the number of cells that will be present after the second round of mitosis. Record the number of cells in your data table.
6. Repeat step 5 for cups 3 through 10.
7. Using your data and graph paper, make a line graph that shows the growth in the number of cells. Label the x-axis Number of cell divisions and the y-axis Number of cells.

L2

# Meeting Different Ability Levels

## Content Outline

L2

## Reinforcement

L2

## Enrichment

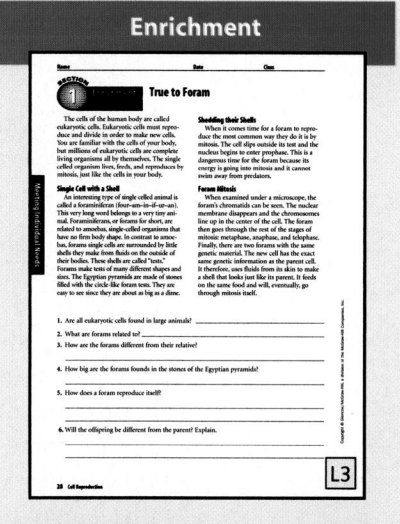

L3

## Directed Reading (English/Spanish)

L1

## Study Guide

L2

## Reading Essentials

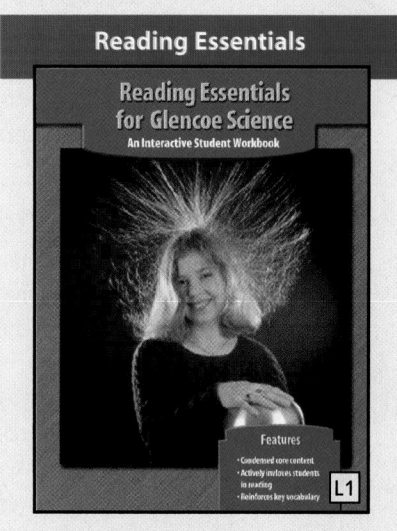

L1

# Assessment

## Test Practice Workbook

L2

## Chapter Review

L2

## Chapter Tests

L2

# Science Content Background

### section 1 — Cell Division and Mitosis
### Results of Mitosis

Every species has a characteristic number of chromosomes in each cell. A cat has 38 chromosomes, whereas a potato and a chimpanzee each have 48 chromosomes. In all sexually reproducing organisms, chromosomes occur in homologous pairs. Except for some sex chromosomes, homologous chromosomes are of equal length and have the same genes at the same relative locations. The alleles may or may not be identical. For example, the gene for hair color would be at the same location on homologous chromosomes but may code for brunette on one chromosome and blonde on the other.

---

**Teacher to Teacher**

Patricia M. Horton, Mentor Teacher
Summit Intermediate School
Etiwanda, California

"To demonstrate osmosis, I put liquid starch in a plastic sandwich bag and close it with a twist tie. I then place the plastic bag into a beaker filled with a mixture of water and iodine. As the iodine moves through the plastic bag membrane, the starch begins to turn purple."

*Patricia M. Horton*

---

*Reuters New Media Inc./Corbis*

Animals and some plants have one pair of sex chromosomes. In most animals, including humans, the sex chromosomes of the female are truly homologous, whereas the male sex chromosomes are of unequal lengths and have many different genes. This is reversed in birds and butterflies, with males having the truly homologous sex chromosomes.

### Asexual Reproduction

Eukaryotes, which include many protists, some fungi, and plants, reproduce asexually by mitosis. Prokaryotes, like bacteria, reproduce by fission. Depending on the organism, one or several new organisms can be created that are genetically identical to, or clones of, the original organism. Most animals do not use asexual reproduction. Recently scientists have been able to stimulate cells from adult animals to divide by mitosis and reproduce new animals that are clones of the organism from which the cells were taken.

### section 2 — Sexual Reproduction and Meiosis
### Sexual Reproduction

Sex cells, or gametes, are the result of meiosis. Because of a process that happens at metaphase I called independent assortment, the possible combination of chromosomes for each sex cell varies every time sex cells form. When duplicated homologous chromosomes line up at a cell's center during metaphase I, there are no rules about how a particular pair is aligned relative to any other pair. The only requirement is that the alignment results in one half of each duplicated chromosome moving in one direction and the other half moving in the opposite direction during anaphase I. The offspring formed by fertilization has its own unique combination of genetic material. This produces variation between parents and offspring and may give offspring a better chance of surviving in a changing environment.

## Meiosis and Sex Cells

This process is often called reduction division since the number of chromosomes in the cells produced is half that of the original cell. Meiosis provides for great diversity within a species because of the many ways the chromosomes can align during metaphase I. There are more than 8 million possible gametes that can be produced from the 23 pairs of human chromosomes.

In animals, meiosis results in haploid egg and sperm cells. In plants, meiosis results in haploid spores that later produce egg and sperm cells.

## section 3 DNA

### What is DNA?

The information in DNA that determines what an organism will be is contained in a code dictated by the order of subunits called nucleotides. A nucleotide consists of the sugar deoxyribose, a phosphate molecule, and one of the four possible nitrogen bases. A DNA molecule is two chains of nucleotides. These two chains are antiparallel and run in opposite directions. One chain ends with a phosphate, and the other chain ends with deoxyribose. Just as the order of letters on this page determines what words you are reading, the order of nucleotides determines the message on the DNA. Because DNA is copied from one generation to the next, any change, or mutation, in a gene is also preserved. If the change occurs in cells that become gametes, it is passed on to future generations in a process called heredity.

### A DNA Model

The process of DNA replication is directed by the enzyme called DNA polymerase. It moves along the separated DNA molecule and inserts the correct, complementary nucleotides onto the exposed nitrogen bases. This happens at many locations along the length of the DNA molecule simultaneously. Otherwise the time it would take to match up the millions of nitrogen bases would be astronomical.

### Mutations

A change in a cell's genetic message is called a mutation. Some mutations affect the message itself, altering the sequence of DNA nucleotides. Other classes of mutations involve sequences of DNA that can move from place to place and are often called jumping genes. When a particular gene is mutated, its function is often destroyed.

*Michael Simpson/FPG International*

## chapter content resources

**Internet Resources**
For additional content background, visit
in7.msscience.com to:
- access your book online
- find references to related articles in popular science magazines
- access Web links with related content background
- access current events with science journal topics

**Print Resources**
*James Watson & Francis Crick: Discovery of the Double Helix and Beyond (Makers of Modern Science),* by David E. Newton and David B. Newton, Facts on File, Inc., 1992
*DNA (Science Concepts),* by Alvin Silverstein, Virginia B. Silverstein, Laura Silverstein Nunn, Twenty-First Century Books (E), 2002
*My Name Is Gene,* Second Edition, N.L. Eskeland, N.C. Bailey, Science2Discover, 2002

**Academic Standard—4:** Students . . . recognize the fundamental difference between plants and animals and understand its basis at the cellular level. Students distinguish species, particularly through an examination of internal structures and functions. They use microscopes to observe cells and recognize that cells function in similar ways in all organisms.

**Also covers:** Academic Standards 1, 2, 3, 5, 7 (Detailed standards begin on page IN8.)

# Cell Reproduction

## Chapter Vocabulary

**Science Journal** Student responses will vary, but may include that cells split into two and that they reproduce so that an organism can grow.

**INTERACTIVE CHALKBOARD**
**with Image Bank**

**PowerPoint® Presentations**

This CD-ROM is an editable Microsoft® PowerPoint® presentation that includes:

- a pre-made presentation for every chapter
- interactive graphics
- animations
- audio clips
- image bank
- all new section and chapter questions
- Standardized Test Practice
- transparencies
- pre-lab questions for all labs
- Foldables directions
- links to in7.msscience.com

### chapter preview

**sections**

**1** Cell Division and Mitosis
  *Lab Mitosis in Plant Cells*

**2** Sexual Reproduction and Meiosis

**3** DNA
  *Lab Mutations*

*Virtual Lab What is the role of DNA and RNA in protein synthesis?*

94

### Why a turtle, not a chicken?

A sweet potato plant can be grown from just one potato, but turtles and most other animals need to have two parents. A cut on your finger heals. How do these things happen? In this chapter, you will find answers to these questions as you learn about cell reproduction.

**Science Journal** Write three things that you know about how and why cells reproduce.

## Theme Connection

**Stability and Change** DNA controls all cell activities by directing the production of proteins in living organisms. Changes in DNA can result in evolutionary changes that are inherited.

### About the Photo

**Hatchlings** Turtles reproduce on land. Female turtles lay eggs, usually at night, and then bury them to protect them from predators, to keep the eggs moist, and to help maintain the proper temperature for development. Eggs usually hatch in 60–140 days. Hatchling turtles use an "egg tooth" to break their way out of the egg. Hatchlings usually emerge in early evening.

# Start-Up Activities

## Infer About Seed Growth

Most flower and vegetable seeds sprout and grow into entire plants in just a few weeks. Although all of the cells in a seed have information and instructions to produce a new plant, only some of the cells in the seed use the information. Where are these cells in seeds? Do the following lab to find out.

1. Carefully split open two bean seeds that have soaked in water overnight.
2. Observe both halves and record your observations.
3. Wrap all four halves in a moist paper towel. Then put them into a self-sealing, plastic bag and seal the bag.
4. Make observations every day for a few days.
5. **Think Critically** Write a paragraph that describes what you observe. Hypothesize which cells in seeds use information about how plants grow.

**Science Online** Preview this chapter's content and activities at in7.msscience.com

**FOLDABLES** **How and Why Cells Divide**
**Study Organizer** Make the following Foldable to help you organize information from the chapter about cell reproduction.

**STEP 1** Draw a mark at the midpoint of a vertical sheet of paper along the side edge.

**STEP 2** Turn the paper horizontally and fold the outside edges in to touch at the midpoint mark.

**STEP 3** Use a pencil to draw a cell on the front of your Foldable as shown.

**Analyze** As you read the chapter, write under the flaps how cells divide. In the middle section, list why cells divide.

---

**Purpose** Use the Launch Lab to introduce students to growth; as they read the chapter, they will understand that growth is the result of mitosis. L2 LS
**Kinesthetic**

**Preparation** Soak pinto beans or other large seeds for 24 hours.

**Materials** 2 soaked seeds, paper towels, self-sealing plastic bag, magnifying lens, water

**Teaching Strategy** After soaking, the seeds should split easily. If students have difficulty, forceps can be used to separate the seeds.

## Think Critically

Students should observe and record the growth of a new plant from one-half of each seed. They should predict that the cells of the seed embryo are able to use the information needed to grow into a plant.

## Assessment

**Performance** Have students repeat the experiment using corn seeds and observe the new plant that grows from each seed. Use **Performance Assessment in the Science Classroom**, p. 89. L2

**FOLDABLES** **Dinah Zike**
**Study Organizer** **Study Fold**

Student preparation materials for this Foldable are available in the Chapter *FAST FILE* Resources.

**Probeware Labs**

This chapter's data-collection lab using Probeware technology is included on the *Video Labs CD-ROM*. See the *Probeware Lab Manual* pages 1–4 for student worksheets.

95

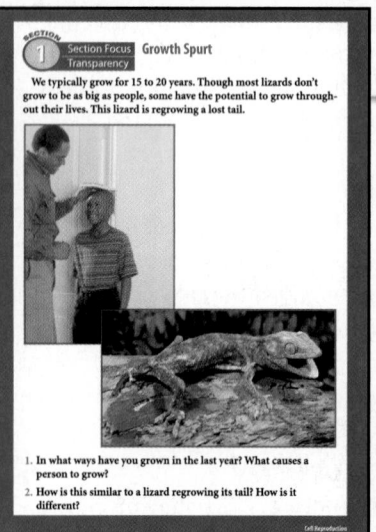
## section 1

**Also covers:** 7.2.7 (Detailed standards begin on page IN8.)

# Cell Division and Mitosis

### as you read

*What* **You'll Learn**

- **Explain** why mitosis is important.
- **Examine** the steps of mitosis.
- **Compare** mitosis in plant and animal cells.
- **List** two examples of asexual reproduction.

*Why* **It's Important**

Your growth, like that of many organisms, depends on cell division.

 **Review Vocabulary**
**nucleus:** organelle that controls all the activities of a cell and contains hereditary material made of proteins and DNA

**New Vocabulary**
- mitosis
- chromosome
- asexual reproduction

## Why is cell division important?

What do you, an octopus, and an oak tree have in common? You share many characteristics, but an important one is that you are all made of cells—trillions of cells. Where did all of those cells come from? As amazing as it might seem, many organisms start as just one cell. That cell divides and becomes two, two become four, four become eight, and so on. Many-celled organisms, including you, grow because cell division increases the total number of cells in an organism. Even after growth stops, cell division is still important. Every day, billions of red blood cells in your body wear out and are replaced. During the few seconds it takes you to read this sentence, your bone marrow produced about six million red blood cells. Cell division is important to one-celled organisms, too—it's how they reproduce themselves, as shown in **Figure 1.** Cell division isn't as simple as just cutting the cell in half, so how do cells divide?

## The Cell Cycle

A living organism has a life cycle. A life cycle begins with the organism's formation, is followed by growth and development, and finally ends in death. Right now, you are in a stage of your life cycle called adolescence, which is a period of active growth and development. Individual cells also have life cycles.

**Figure 1** All organisms use cell division. Many-celled organisms, such as this octopus, grow by increasing the numbers of their cells.

Like this dividing amoeba, a one-celled organism reaches a certain size and then reproduces.

**96 CHAPTER 4** Cell Reproduction

---

**Figure 2** Interphase is the longest part of the cell cycle.
**Identify** *When do chromosomes duplicate?*

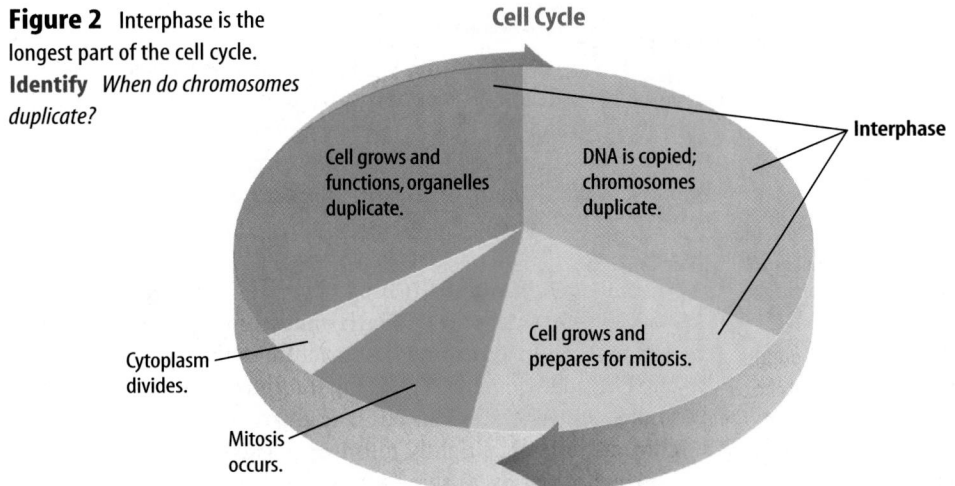

**Cell Cycle**

Cell grows and functions, organelles duplicate.

DNA is copied; chromosomes duplicate.

Interphase

Cell grows and prepares for mitosis.

Cytoplasm divides.

Mitosis occurs.

**Length of Cycle** The cell cycle, as shown in **Figure 2,** is a series of events that takes place from one cell division to the next. The time it takes to complete a cell cycle is not the same in all cells. For example, the cycle for cells in some bean plants takes about 19 h to complete. Cells in animal embryos divide rapidly and can complete their cycles in less than 20 min. In some human cells, the cell cycle takes about 16 h. Cells in humans that are needed for repair, growth, or replacement, like skin and bone cells, constantly repeat the cycle.

**Interphase** Most of the life of any eukaryotic cell—a cell with a nucleus—is spent in a period of growth and development called interphase. Cells in your body that no longer divide, such as nerve and muscle cells, are always in interphase. An actively dividing cell, such as a skin cell, copies its hereditary material and prepares for cell division during interphase.

Why is it important for a cell to copy its hereditary information before dividing? Imagine that you have a part in a play and the director has one complete copy of the script. If the director gave only one page to each person in the play, no one would have the entire script. Instead the director makes a complete, separate copy of the script for each member of the cast so that each one can learn his or her part. Before a cell divides, a copy of the hereditary material must be made so that each of the two new cells will get a complete copy. Just as the actors in the play need the entire script, each cell needs a complete set of hereditary material to carry out life functions.

After interphase, cell division begins. The nucleus divides, and then the cytoplasm separates to form two new cells.

**Oncologist** The cell cycle is well controlled in most cells, but cancer cells have uncontrolled cell division. Doctors who diagnose, study, and treat cancer are called oncologists. To be an oncologist, you must complete medical school, then have training in oncology. Research the subspecialities of oncology. List and describe them in your Science Journal.

**Indiana Academic Standard Check**

**7.4.4:** Explain that cells continually divide to make more cells for growth and repair . . .

✔ When might cell division occur for repair?

✔ Possible answers: to heal a cut or broken bone, or after surgery

SECTION 1  Cell Division and Mitosis **97**

**2 | Teach**

**Caption Answer**
**Figure 2** during interphase

## Visual Learning

**Figure 2** Have students make an events chain concept map that outlines the steps of the cell cycle as illustrated in **Figure 2.**
L2  IS  **Visual-Spatial**  P

**INTEGRATE Career**

**Oncologist** There are many oncology specialties, including medical oncology, pediatric oncology, radiation oncology, and surgical oncology. After completion of medical school and training in a specialty, physicians must pass a certifying exam.

**Research** Have students research ways that help prevent cancerous cells from forming. Some preventive measures include using sunscreen, not smoking, and eating certain foods. Can cancer be prevented completely? Are there vaccinations against cancer? Students can write a health pamphlet that encourages a healthy lifestyle to minimize cancer risks.  L2

## Science Journal

**Life of a Cell** Have students write creative stories about the life cycle of a cell from its beginning to its end. Have them use section vocabulary words as they describe what happens in the cell. L2  IS
**Linguistic**

## IDENTIFYING Misconceptions

**Nondividing Cells** Students may assume that all cells divide. However, some cells do not divide at all. Red blood cells circulating in the blood vessels do not have a nucleus and do not divide; they live for 90 days before they are replaced by new cells.

## Use an Analogy

**Telephone Cord** Compare chromosome thickening to a coiled telephone cord. When stretched out, the cord is long and thin, like chromosomes during interphase. When the cord returns to its usual position, it shortens and thickens, like chromosomes preparing to divide. L1 IS **Visual-Spatial**

### Reading Check

**Answer** A duplicated chromosome is made up of two chromatids.

## Fun Fact

Most cells are not actively engaged in mitosis. Skin cells spend 15–20 days in interphase. After infancy, nerve cells stay in interphase.

## Caption Answer

**Figure 4** interphase

**Figure 3** DNA is copied during interphase. An unduplicated chromosome has one strand of DNA. A duplicated chromosome has two identical DNA strands, called chromatids, that are held together at a region called the centromere.

**Figure 4** The cell plate shown in this plant cell appears when the cytoplasm is being divided. **Identify** what phase of mitosis will be next.

Cell plate

98

## Mitosis

**Mitosis** (mi TOH sus) is the process in which the nucleus divides to form two identical nuclei. Each new nucleus also is identical to the original nucleus. Mitosis is described as a series of phases, or steps. The steps of mitosis in order are named prophase, metaphase, anaphase, and telophase.

**Steps of Mitosis** When any nucleus divides, the chromosomes (KROH muh sohmz) play the important part. A **chromosome** is a structure in the nucleus that contains hereditary material. During interphase, each chromosome duplicates. When the nucleus is ready to divide, each duplicated chromosome coils tightly into two thickened, identical strands called chromatids, as shown in **Figure 3.**

### Reading Check *How are chromosomes and chromatids related?*

During prophase, the pairs of chromatids are fully visible when viewed under a microscope. The nucleolus and the nuclear membrane disintegrate. Two small structures called centrioles (SEN tree olz) move to opposite ends of the cell. Between the centrioles, threadlike spindle fibers begin to stretch across the cell. Plant cells also form spindle fibers during mitosis but do not have centrioles.

In metaphase, the pairs of chromatids line up across the center of the cell. The centromere of each pair usually becomes attached to two spindle fibers—one from each side of the cell.

In anaphase, each centromere divides and the spindle fibers shorten. Each pair of chromatids separates, and chromatids begin to move to opposite ends of the cell. The separated chromatids are now called chromosomes. In the final step, telophase, spindle fibers start to disappear, the chromosomes start to uncoil, and a new nucleus forms.

**Division of the Cytoplasm** For most cells, after the nucleus has divided, the cytoplasm separates and two new cells are formed. In animal cells, the cell membrane pinches in the middle, like a balloon with a string tightened around it, and the cytoplasm divides. In plant cells, the appearance of a cell plate, as shown in **Figure 4,** tells you that the cytoplasm is being divided. New cell walls form along the cell plate, and new cell membranes develop inside the cell walls. Following division of the cytoplasm, most new cells begin the period of growth, or interphase, again. Review cell division for an animal cell using the illustrations in **Figure 5.**

## Differentiated Instruction

**Visually Impaired** Have selected students make three-dimensional models of mitosis on poster board. Display the posters in the classroom for visually impaired students to feel. L2 IS **Visual-Spatial**

## Cultural Diversity

**Historic Contributions** In 1887, Edouard-Joseph-Marie van Beneden, a Belgian scientist, discovered that each species has a fixed number of chromosomes. He also observed the formation of a haploid cell. In 1956, J. Hin Tjio and Albert Levan showed that each human cell has 46 chromosomes.

**Figure 5** Cell division for an animal cell is shown here. Each micrograph shown in this figure is magnified 600 times.

Centrioles

Nucleus

Nucleolus

Spindle fibers

**Prophase**
The chromatid pairs are now visible and the spindle is beginning to form.

Duplicated chromosome (2 chromatids)

**Interphase**
During interphase, the cell's chromosomes duplicate. The nucleolus is clearly visible in the nucleus.

**Metaphase**
Chromatid pairs are lined up in the center of the cell.

The two new cells enter interphase and cell division usually begins again.

**Mitosis begins**

**Anaphase**
The chromosomes have separeted.

**Mitosis ends**

**Telophase**
In the final step, the cytoplasm is beginning to separate.

Chromosomes

Cytoplasm separating

New nucleus

## Quick Demo

**Mitosis**

**Materials** microprojector, fertilized frog eggs

**Estimated Time** 10 minutes

**Procedure** Demonstrate mitotic cell divisions in the growth of fertilized frog eggs. The increasing numbers of cells can be seen readily during the early stages of tadpole development.

## Teacher FYI

**Interphase Duplication** The fact that chromosomes are duplicated in the nucleus during interphase has been hypothesized for more than a hundred years, but evidence for the hypothesis did not appear until 1981.

## Use Science Words

**Word Meaning** Explain that the word *mitosis* derives from the Greek word for "thread." Have students explain the derivation. During mitosis, the replicated chromosomes—threadlike structures—separate. Then point out that *phase* is another word for "stage." Have students use a dictionary to find the meanings of the prefixes *inter-* (between), *pro-* (before), *meta-* (after), *ana-* (up), and *telo-* (end). L2

# Differentiated Instruction

**Challenge** Have students make a paper-and-string model of mitosis. The stages of mitosis can be connected using string, and colored string can be used to represent duplicated chromosomes. Students should include labels and descriptions of what occurs at each stage. The models can then be displayed in the classroom. L3

# Curriculum Connection

**Math** It takes 15 minutes for certain embryo cells to divide. Have students calculate how many cells would be produced from one embryo cell after four hours. 240 minutes divided by 15 minutes = 16 cell divisions; $2^{16} = 65,536$ cells L2 IS **Logical-Mathematical**

Chromosomes of a human cell

## Discussion

**Spinal Cord Damage** Have students use their knowledge of the cell cycle to infer why even slight injuries to the brain and spinal cord can be serious and permanent. Because nerve cells do not undergo mitosis, damaged cells are not replaced, although some repair does occur. L2

## Discussion

**Nonliving Growth** Many nonliving things such as icicles, stalagmites, crystals, and sand dunes appear to grow. Ask students to give examples of other nonliving things that appear to grow. Possible answers: highway systems, buildings, developments, shopping malls Have students distinguish between the processes involved in the growth of living things and the growth of nonliving things. In nonliving things, growth is caused by the surrounding environment. In living things, growth is caused by processes within the organism. L1

## Caption Answer

**Figure 6** the sex of the organism

## Activity

**Cancer** Have students research and report on cancer. The report should include how cancer relates to mitosis and some of the technology used to diagnose and treat cancer. Display written reports.

Chromosomes of a fruit fly cell

**Figure 6** Pairs of chromosomes are found in the nucleus of most cells. All chromosomes shown here are in their duplicated form. Most human cells have 23 pairs of chromosomes including one pair of chromosomes that help determine sex such as the XY pair above. Most fruit fly cells have four pairs of chromosomes.

**Infer** *What do you think the XX pair in fruit flies helps determine?*

**Results of Mitosis** You should remember two important things about mitosis. First, it is the division of a nucleus. Second, it produces two new nuclei that are identical to each other and the original nucleus. Each new nucleus has the same number and type of chromosomes. Every cell in your body, except sex cells, has a nucleus with 46 chromosomes—23 pairs. This is because you began as one cell with 46 chromosomes in its nucleus. Skin cells, produced to replace or repair your skin, have the same 46 chromosomes as the original single cell you developed from. Each cell in a fruit fly has eight chromosomes, so each new cell produced by mitosis has a copy of those eight chromosomes. **Figure 6** shows the chromosomes found in most human cells and those found in most fruit fly cells.

Each of the trillions of cells in your body, except sex cells, has a copy of the same hereditary material. Even though all actors in a play have copies of the same script, they do not learn the same lines. Likewise, all of your cells use different parts of the same hereditary material to become different types of cells.

Cell division allows growth and replaces worn out or damaged cells. You are much larger and have more cells than a baby mainly because of cell division. If you cut yourself, the wound heals because cell division replaces damaged cells. Another way some organisms use cell division is to produce new organisms.

**100    CHAPTER 4** Cell Reproduction

---

 **LAB DEMONSTRATION**

**Purpose** to observe asexual reproduction in a sweet potato

**Materials** sweet potato with leaf buds, water, widemouthed glass jar, 4 toothpicks

**Preparation** Obtain a sweet potato that has purple leaf buds growing at its scarred end.

**Procedure** Fill a jar almost full of water, and place sweet potato with buds or scarred end up so at least half of the potato is in water. Toothpicks can hold the potato in place. Keep the water level constant and observe for three weeks.

**Expected Outcome** Students should observe the formation of roots and leaf growth.

**Assessment**

Ask students what part of the sweet potato produced leaves and roots. Leaves developed from the buds; roots grew from the bottom half of the sweet potato. Is this an example of sexual or asexual reproduction? Explain. Asexual; a new organism is produced from one parent. L2

## Asexual Reproduction

Reproduction is the process by which an organism produces others of its same kind. Among living organisms, there are two types of reproduction—sexual and asexual. Sexual reproduction usually requires two organisms. In **asexual reproduction,** a new organism (sometimes more than one) is produced from one organism. The new organism will have hereditary material identical to the hereditary material of the parent organism.

**Reading Check** *How many organisms are needed for asexual reproduction?*

**Cellular Asexual Reproduction** Organisms with eukaryotic cells asexually reproduce by cell division. A sweet potato growing in a jar of water is an example of asexual reproduction. All the stems, leaves, and roots that grow from the sweet potato have been produced by cell division and have the same hereditary material. New strawberry plants can be reproduced asexually from horizontal stems called runners. **Figure 7** shows asexual reproduction in a potato and a strawberry plant.

Recall that mitosis is the division of a nucleus. However, bacteria do not have a nucleus so they can't use mitosis. Instead, bacteria reproduce asexually by fission. During fission, an organism whose cells do not contain a nucleus copies its genetic material and then divides into two identical organisms.

**Figure 7** Many plants can reproduce asexually.

A new potato plant can grow from each sprout on this potato.

**Infer** *how the genetic material in the small strawberry plant above compares to the genetic material in the large strawberry plant.*

### Mini LAB

**Modeling Mitosis**

**Procedure**
1. Make models of cell division using **materials supplied by your teacher.**
2. Use four chromosomes in your model.
3. When finished, arrange the models in the order in which mitosis occurs.

**Analysis**
1. In which steps is the nucleus visible?
2. How many cells does a dividing cell form?

**Figure 8** Some organisms use cell division for budding and regeneration.

 Hydra, a freshwater animal, can reproduce asexually by budding. The bud is a small exact copy of the adult.

Bud

 This sea star is regenerating four new arms.

**Budding and Regeneration** Look at **Figure 8A.** A new organism is growing from the body of the parent organism. This organism, called a hydra, is reproducing by budding. Budding is a type of asexual reproduction made possible because of cell division. When the bud on the adult becomes large enough, it breaks away to live on its own.

Could you grow a new finger? Some organisms can regrow damaged or lost body parts, as shown in **Figure 8B.** Regeneration is the process that uses cell division to regrow body parts. Sponges, planaria, sea stars, and some other organisms can use regeneration for asexual reproduction. If these organisms break into pieces, a whole new organism will grow from each piece. Because sea stars eat oysters, oyster farmers dislike them. What would happen if an oyster farmer collected sea stars, cut them into pieces, and threw them back into the ocean?

## section 1 review

### Summary

**The Cell Cycle**
● The cell cycle is a series of events from one cell division to the next.
● Most of a eukaryotic cell's life is interphase.

**Mitosis**
● Mitosis is a series of four phases or steps.
● Each new nucleus formed by mitosis has the same number and type of chromosomes.

**Asexual Reproduction**
● In asexual reproduction, a new organism is produced from one organism.
● Cellular, budding, and regeneration are forms of asexual reproduction.

### Self Check

1. **Define** mitosis. How does it differ in plants and animals?
2. **Identify** two examples of asexual reproduction in many-celled organisms.
3. **Describe** what happens to chromosomes before mitosis.
4. **Compare and contrast** the two new cells formed after mitosis and cell division.
5. **Think Critically** Why is it important for the nuclear membrane to disintegrate during mitosis?

**Applying Math**

6. **Solve One-Step Equations** If a cell undergoes cell division every 5 min, how many cells will there be after 1 h?

Science Online in7.msscience.com/self_check_quiz

## section 1 review

1. a process in which a cell nucleus divides into two nuclei, each of which has the same genetic information; in animal cells, the cytoplasm divides as the cell membrane pinches in the middle of the cell; in plant cells, the appearance of the cell plate indicates that the cytoplasm is being divided.

2. Possible answers: budding and regeneration

3. The chromosomes duplicate.

4. They both have the same genetic information.

5. Otherwise, the chromosomes would not be able to move to opposite ends of the cell.

6. 60 minutes divided by 5 minutes = 12 cell divisions; $2^{12}$ = 4,096 cells

# Mit💠sis in Plant Cells

Reproduction of most cells in plants and animals uses mitosis and cell division. In this lab, you will study mitosis in plant cells by examining prepared slides of onion root-tip cells.

## ▶ Real-World Question

How can plant cells in different stages of mitosis be distinguished from each other?

### Goals

- **Compare** cells in different stages of mitosis and observe the location of their chromosomes.
- **Observe** what stage of mitosis is most common in onion root tips.

### Materials

prepared slide of an onion root tip
microscope

### Safety Precautions

## ▶ Procedure

1. Copy the data table in your Science Journal.

### Number of Root-Tip Cells Observed

| Stage of Mitosis | Number of Cells Observed | Percent of Cells Observed |
|---|---|---|
| Prophase | 78 | 65 |
| Metaphase | 23 | 19 |
| Anaphase | 12 | 10 |
| Telophase | 7 | 6 |
| Total | 120 | 100 |

2. **Obtain** a prepared slide of cells from an onion root tip.

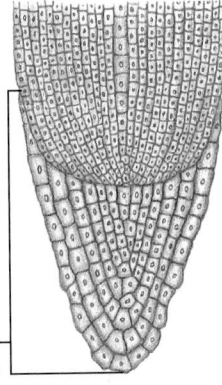

Zone of cell division     Root cap

3. Set your microscope on low power and examine the slide. The large, round cells at the root tip are called the root cap. Move the slide until you see the cells just behind the root cap. Turn to the high-power objective.

4. Find an area where you can see the most stages of mitosis. Count and record how many cells you see in each stage.

5. Return the nosepiece to low power. Remove the onion root-tip slide.

## ▶ Conclude and Apply

1. **Compare** the cells in the region behind the root cap to those in the root cap.

2. **Calculate** the percent of cells found in each stage of mitosis. Infer which stage of mitosis takes the longest period of time.

### 𝒞ommunicating
#### Your Data

Write and illustrate a story as if you were a cell undergoing mitosis. Share your story with your class. **For more help, refer to the Science Skill Handbook.**

## ▶ Real-World Question

**Purpose** Students observe the stages of mitosis. L2 ELL IS **Visual-Spatial**

**Process Skills** observe, infer, compare and contrast

**Time Required** 40 minutes

## ▶ Procedure

**Teaching Strategy** Review the stages of mitosis before beginning the activity.

**Troubleshooting** Students may have difficulty locating all the phases. You may want to place an onion root tip slide on the microprojector and point out the phases.

## ▶ Conclude and Apply

1. The cells behind the root cap are smaller than those in the root cap. Mitosis occurs at a faster rate in cells behind the root cap.

2. See student page; prophase takes the longest.

### ✔ Assessment

**Performance** To further assess students' understanding of mitosis, give each one a sheet of paper listing a stage and have them describe what comes before and after that stage. Use **Performance Assessment in the Science Classroom**, p. 163. L2

### 𝒞ommunicating
#### Your Data

The story and drawings should include the stages in mitosis.

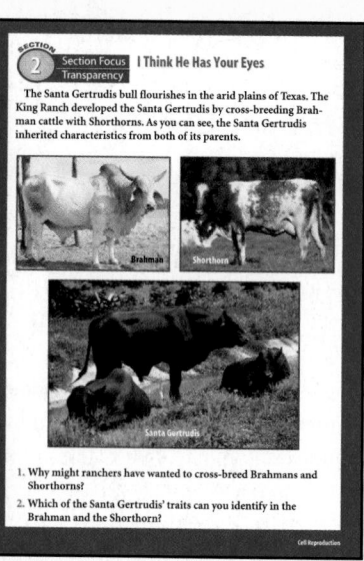
## section 2

# Sexual Reproduction and Meiosis

Also covers: 7.4.1, 7.5.3 (Detailed standards begin on page IN8.)

### as you read

**What You'll Learn**

- **Describe** the stages of meiosis and how sex cells are produced.
- **Explain** why meiosis is needed for sexual reproduction.
- **Name** the cells that are involved in fertilization.
- **Explain** how fertilization occurs in sexual reproduction.

**Why It's Important**

Meiosis and sexual reproduction are the reasons why no one else is exactly like you.

**Review Vocabulary**

**organism:** any living thing; uses energy, is made of cells, reproduces, responds, grows, and develops

**New Vocabulary**

- sexual reproduction
- sperm
- egg
- fertilization
- zygote
- diploid
- haploid
- meiosis

## Sexual Reproduction

Sexual reproduction is another way that a new organism can be produced. During **sexual reproduction,** two sex cells, sometimes called an egg and a sperm, come together. Sex cells, like those in **Figure 9,** are formed from cells in reproductive organs. **Sperm** are formed in the male reproductive organs. **Eggs** are formed in the female reproductive organs. The joining of an egg and a sperm is called **fertilization,** and the cell that forms is called a **zygote** (ZI goht). Generally, the egg and the sperm come from two different organisms of the same species. Following fertilization, cell division begins. A new organism with a unique identity develops.

**Diploid Cells** Your body forms two types of cells—body cells and sex cells. Body cells far outnumber sex cells. Your brain, skin, bones, and other tissues and organs are formed from body cells. A typical human body cell has 46 chromosomes. Each chromosome has a mate that is similar to it in size and shape and has similar DNA. Human body cells have 23 pairs of chromosomes. When cells have pairs of similar chromosomes, they are said to be **diploid** (DIH ployd).

**Figure 9** A human egg and a human sperm at fertilization.

**Haploid Cells** Because sex cells do not have pairs of chromosomes, they are said to be **haploid** (HA ployd). They have only half the number of chromosomes as body cells. *Haploid* means "single form." Human sex cells have only 23 chromosomes—one from each of the 23 pairs of similar chromosomes. Compare the chromosomes found in a sex cell, as shown in **Figure 9,** to the full set of human chromosomes seen in **Figure 6.**

✓ **Reading Check** *How many chromosomes are usually in each human sperm?*

## Meiosis and Sex Cells

A process called **meiosis** (mi OH sus) produces haploid sex cells. What would happen in sexual reproduction if two diploid cells combined? The offspring would have twice as many chromosomes as its parent. Although plants with twice the number of chromosomes as the parent plants are often produced, most animals do not survive with a double number of chromosomes. Meiosis ensures that the offspring will have the same diploid number as its parent, as shown in **Figure 10.** After two haploid sex cells combine, a diploid zygote is produced that develops into a new diploid organism.

During meiosis, two divisions of the nucleus occur. These divisions are called meiosis I and meiosis II. The steps of each division have names like those in mitosis and are numbered for the division in which they occur.

**Indiana Academic Standard Check**

**7.4.3:** Explain how . . . information . . . multiplies to form the complete organism.

✓ How do the genetics of an organism compare to those of the zygote from which it developed?

✓ the same

**Male lion**

**Female lion**

**Figure 10** When sex cells join, a zygote forms. The zygote divides by cell division and develops into a new organism. **Compare** *the number of chromosomes present in the different cells.*

Meiosis → **Sperm** (Haploid number = 24)

**Fertilization**

Mitosis →

**Zygote** (Diploid number = 48)

**Development**

**Cub**

Meiosis → **Egg** (Haploid number = 24)

### ✔ Reading Check

**Answer** The duplicated chromosomes of each similar pair are pulled to opposite ends of the cell.

## Use Science Words

**Word Meaning** Have students use a dictionary to find out what *triploid* and *tetraploid* mean. Have them write an explanation of how this condition occurs. *Triploid*— each cell in the organism contains three sets of chromosomes; plant endosperm is triploid and normal. *Tetraploid* organisms have four sets of chromosomes in each cell; these conditions arise from total nondisjunction during mitosis or meiosis. L2 IS **Linguistic**

## Discussion

**Controlled Traits** In areas throughout the world, people have similar genetically controlled traits including skin color, height, and face shape. Cultures of people were unable to travel long distances for thousands of years and, therefore, reproduced mainly among themselves. As a result, genetic instructions for such traits remained within given cultures.

**Meiosis I**

Pair of duplicated chromosomes — Spindle fibers — Duplicated chromosomes

Nuclear membrane — Centrioles

Prophase I — Metaphase I — Anaphase I — Telophase I

**Figure 11** Meiosis has two divisions of the nucleus—meiosis I and meiosis II.
**Determine** *how many sex cells are finally formed after both divisions are completed.*

**Meiosis I** Before meiosis begins, each chromosome is duplicated, just as in mitosis. When the cell is ready for meiosis, each duplicated chromosome is visible under the microscope as two chromatids. As shown in **Figure 11,** the events of prophase I are similar to those of prophase in mitosis. In meiosis, each duplicated chromosome comes near its similar duplicated mate. In mitosis they do not come near each other.

In metaphase I, the pairs of duplicated chromosomes line up in the center of the cell. The centromere of each chromatid pair becomes attached to one spindle fiber, so the chromatids do not separate in anaphase I. The two pairs of chromatids of each similar pair move away from each other to opposite ends of the cell. Each duplicated chromosome still has two chromatids. Then, in telophase I, the cytoplasm divides, and two new cells form. Each new cell has one duplicated chromosome from each similar pair.

### ✔ Reading Check
What happens to duplicated chromosomes during anaphase I?

**Meiosis II** The two cells formed during meiosis I now begin meiosis II. The chromatids of each duplicated chromosome will be separated during this division. In prophase II, the duplicated chromosomes and spindle fibers reappear in each new cell. Then in metaphase II, the duplicated chromosomes move to the center of the cell. Unlike what occurs in metaphase I, each centromere now attaches to two spindle fibers instead of one. The centromere divides during anaphase II, and the chromatids separate and move to opposite ends of the cell. Each chromatid now is an individual chromosome. As telophase II begins, the spindle fibers disappear, and a nuclear membrane forms around the chromosomes at each end of the cell. When meiosis II is finished, the cytoplasm divides.

**106** CHAPTER 4 Cell Reproduction

## Differentiated Instruction

**Challenge** To encourage students to understand all of the stages of meiosis, have them create an eight-stage puzzle that demonstrates each phase of meiosis. Pieces of the puzzle can include cells, chromosomes, and centrioles. Students can work in pairs to test their ability to use the puzzle pieces to represent any stage of meiosis or the entire eight-stage process. L3

**Learning Disabled** Students who are dyslexic may have trouble distinguishing between the first and second parts of meiosis. Instead of Roman numbers, as in prophase I and prophase II, use Arabic numbers for easier identification (prophase 1 and prophase 2). L2

## Meiosis II

Prophase II    Metaphase II    Anaphase II    Telophase II

Unduplicated chromosomes

**Summary of Meiosis** Two cells form during meiosis I. In meiosis II, both of these cells form two cells. The two divisions of the nucleus result in four sex cells. Each has one-half the number of chromosomes in its nucleus that was in the original nucleus. From a human cell with 46 paired chromosomes, meiosis produces four sex cells each with 23 unpaired chromosomes.

## Applying Science

### How can chromosome numbers be predicted?

Offspring get half of their chromosomes from one parent and half from the other. What happens if each parent has a different diploid number of chromosomes?

**Identifying the Problem**

A zebra and a donkey can mate to produce a zonkey. Zebras have a diploid number of 46. Donkeys have a diploid number of 62.

**Solving the Problem**

1. How many chromosomes would the zonkey receive from each parent?
2. What is the chromosome number of the zonkey?
3. What would happen when meiosis occurs in the zonkey's reproductive organs?
4. Predict why zonkeys are usually sterile.

Donkey
62 chromosomes

Zonkey

Zebra
46 chromosomes

SECTION 2 Sexual Reproduction and Meiosis  **107**

---

---

## Active Reading

**Flow Chart** A flow chart helps students logically sequence events. Students will write major stages of the sequence in large ovals and write substages in smaller ovals under the larger ovals. Have students design a flow chart for a concept in this section. Sample flow chart: L2

## Visualizing Polyploidy in Plants

Have students examine the pictures and read the captions. Then ask the following questions.

**What kinds of mistakes in meiosis or mitosis could result in a polyploid plant?** A mistake that caused chromosome sets not to separate, allowing more than one full set to be present in a cell after division to form sex cells.

**What is the main advantage of bananas being triploid?** Triploid plants have very small seeds, so people can eat bananas without removing seeds.

**Why wouldn't you find triploid peanuts in the grocery store?** The part of a peanut plant you eat is a seed, but triploid plants have little or no seeds.

### Activity

**Plant Chromosomes** Have students use pipe cleaners to model the chromosomes of one of the plants featured here. For example, a banana with 3 sets of 11 chromosomes, a strawberry with 8 sets of 7 chromosomes, or a peanut with 4 sets of 10 chromosomes. [L2]

---

**NATIONAL GEOGRAPHIC** **VISUALIZING POLYPLOIDY IN PLANTS**

**Figure 12**

**Y**ou received a haploid (n) set of chromosomes from each of your parents, making you a diploid (2n) organism. In nature, however, many plants are polyploid—they have three (3n), four (4n), or more sets of chromosomes. We depend on some of these plants for food.

▲ **TRIPLOID** Bright yellow bananas typically come from triploid (3n) banana plants. Plants with an odd number of chromosome sets usually cannot reproduce sexually and have very small seeds or none at all.

▲ **TETRAPLOID** Polyploidy occurs naturally in many plants—including peanuts and daylilies—due to mistakes in mitosis or meiosis.

▼ **HEXAPLOID** Modern cultivated strains of oats have six sets of chromosomes, making them hexaploid (6n) plants.

▲ **OCTAPLOID** Polyploid plants often are bigger than nonpolyploid plants and may have especially large leaves, flowers, or fruits. Strawberries are an example of octaploid (8n) plants.

**108**

## Visual Learning

**Figure 13** Have students follow the unseparated chromosome pair through each stage of meiosis. How did this error affect the sex cells? Some had too many chromosomes; others not enough. [L2]

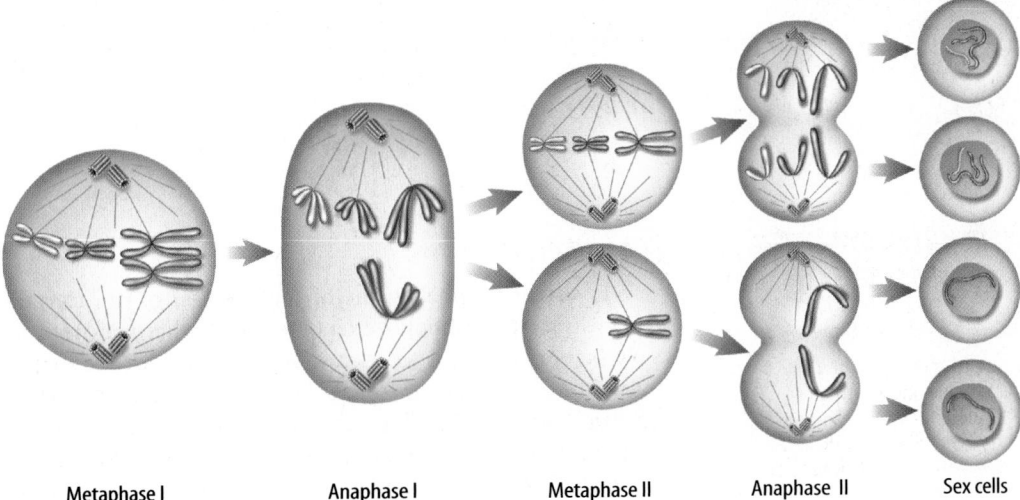

| Metaphase I | Anaphase I | Metaphase II | Anaphase II | Sex cells |

**Mistakes in Meiosis** Meiosis occurs many times in reproductive organs. Although mistakes in plants, as shown in **Figure 12,** are common, mistakes are less common in animals. These mistakes can produce sex cells with too many or too few chromosomes, as shown in **Figure 13.** Sometimes, zygotes produced from these sex cells die. If the zygote lives, every cell in the organism that grows from that zygote usually will have the wrong number of chromosomes. Organisms with the wrong number of chromosomes may not grow normally.

**Figure 13** This diploid cell has four chromosomes. During anaphase I, one pair of duplicated chromosomes did not separate. **Infer** *how many chromosomes each sex cell usually has.*

## section 2 review

### Summary

**Sexual Reproduction**

- During sexual reproduction, two sex cells come together.
- Cell division begins after fertilization.
- A typical human body cell has 46 chromosomes, and a human sex cell has 23 chromosomes.

**Meiosis and Sex Cells**

- Each chromosome is duplicated before meiosis, then two divisions of the nucleus occur.
- During meiosis I, duplicated chromosomes are separated into new cells.
- Chromatids separate during meiosis II.
- Meiosis I and meiosis II result in four sex cells.

### Self Check

1. **Describe** a zygote and how it is formed.
2. **Explain** where sex cells form.
3. **Compare** what happens to chromosomes during anaphase I and anaphase II.
4. **Think Critically** Plants grown from runners and leaf cuttings have the same traits as the parent plant. Plants grown from seeds can vary from the parent plants in many ways. Why can this happen?

#### Applying Skills

5. **Make and use a table** to compare mitosis and meiosis in humans. Vertical headings should include: *What Type of Cell (Body or Sex), Beginning Cell (Haploid or Diploid), Number of Cells Produced, End-Product Cell (Haploid or Diploid),* and *Number of Chromosomes in New Cells.*

## section 2 review

1. A zygote is the cell that forms when a sperm fertilizes an egg.
2. Sperm cells form in male reproductive organs; egg cells form in female reproductive organs.
3. Anaphase I—duplicated chromosome pairs separate and move to opposite ends of the cell; anaphase II—chromatids separate and move to opposite ends of the cell.
4. Plants produced by asexual reproduction are the result of mitosis. Plants grown from seeds vary from their parents, because seeds are produced by sexual reproduction.
5. See table.

## 3 Assess

### DAILY INTERVENTION

#### Check for Understanding

**Visual-Spatial** Have students use colored pipe cleaners as chromosomes to demonstrate the process of meiosis. Pipe cleaners of the same color can be paired as duplicated chromosomes. Students should repeat the process with varying numbers of chromosomes. Students should also demonstrate the result when a pair of duplicated chromosomes does not separate properly. L2

#### Reteach

**Meiosis** Show the phases of meiosis out of sequence. Have students identify each phase and place the phases in order. L2
ELL LS **Visual-Spatial**

### ✔ Assessment

**Content** Write these chromosome numbers on the board: *horse—66; cat—38; potato—48.* How many chromosomes would be in a cell of each organism produced by mitosis and meiosis? horse—66, 33; cat—38, 19; potato—48, 24 Use **PASC,** p. 101.

| Feature | Mitosis | Meiosis |
|---|---|---|
| Type of cell | Body cell | Sex cell |
| Beginning cell | Diploid | Diploid |
| Number of cells produced | Two | Four |
| End product | Diploid | Haploid |
| Number of chromosomes | Same as original cell | Half the original cell |

## section

**3**

Also covers: 7.1.5, 7.1.8, 7.1.10, 7.2.7, 7.7.2 (Detailed standards begin on page IN8.)

# DNA

### Bellringer

**Section Focus Transparencies** also are available on the Interactive Chalkboard CD-ROM.

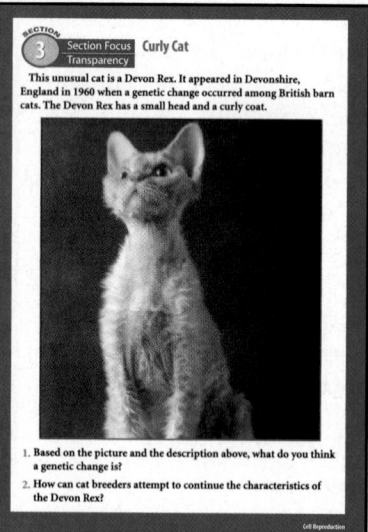

### Tie to Prior Knowledge

**Template Games** Students should be familiar with template systems, such as keys and locks and peg-and-hole games. Ask for other examples. Use this knowledge to explain that DNA in the nucleus serves as a template for RNA.

### Virtual Labs

**Protein Synthesis** *What is the role of DNA and RNA in protein synthesis?*

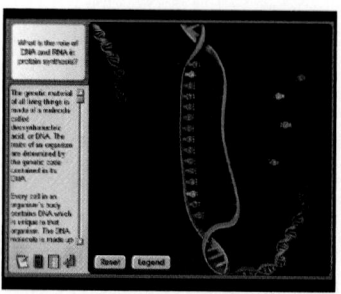

---

### as you read

***What*** **You'll Learn**

- **Identify** the parts of a DNA molecule and its structure.
- **Explain** how DNA copies itself.
- **Describe** the structure and function of each kind of RNA.

***Why*** **It's Important**

DNA helps determine nearly everything your body is and does.

**Review Vocabulary**
**heredity:** the passing of traits from parents to offspring

**New Vocabulary**
- DNA
- gene
- RNA
- mutation

**Figure 14** DNA is part of the chromosomes found in a cell's nucleus.

---

## What is DNA?

Why was the alphabet one of the first things you learned when you started school? Letters are a code that you need to know before you learn to read. A cell also uses a code that is stored in its hereditary material. The code is a chemical called deoxyribonucleic (dee AHK sih ri boh noo klay ihk) acid, or **DNA**. It contains information for an organism's growth and function. **Figure 14** shows how DNA is stored in cells that have a nucleus. When a cell divides, the DNA code is copied and passed to the new cells. In this way, new cells receive the same coded information that was in the original cell. Every cell that has ever been formed in your body or in any other organism contains DNA.

**Discovering DNA** Since the mid-1800s, scientists have known that the nuclei of cells contain large molecules called nucleic acids. By 1950, chemists had learned what the nucleic acid DNA was made of, but they didn't understand how the parts of DNA were arranged.

Duplicated chromosome

Nucleus

Each chromosome is composed of a long strand of DNA wrapped around proteins, like thread wrapped around a spool.

DNA

Proteins

**110** **CHAPTER 4** Cell Reproduction

---

## Section 3 Resource Manager

**Chapter *FAST FILE* Resources**

Transparency Activity, p. 44

Directed Reading for Content Mastery, pp. 19, 20

MiniLAB, p. 4

Enrichment, p. 30

Reinforcement, p. 27

Lab Activity, pp. 11–13

Lab Worksheet, pp. 7–8

**Home and Community Involvement**, p. 36

**Cultural Diversity**, p. 19

**Lab Management and Safety**, p. 58

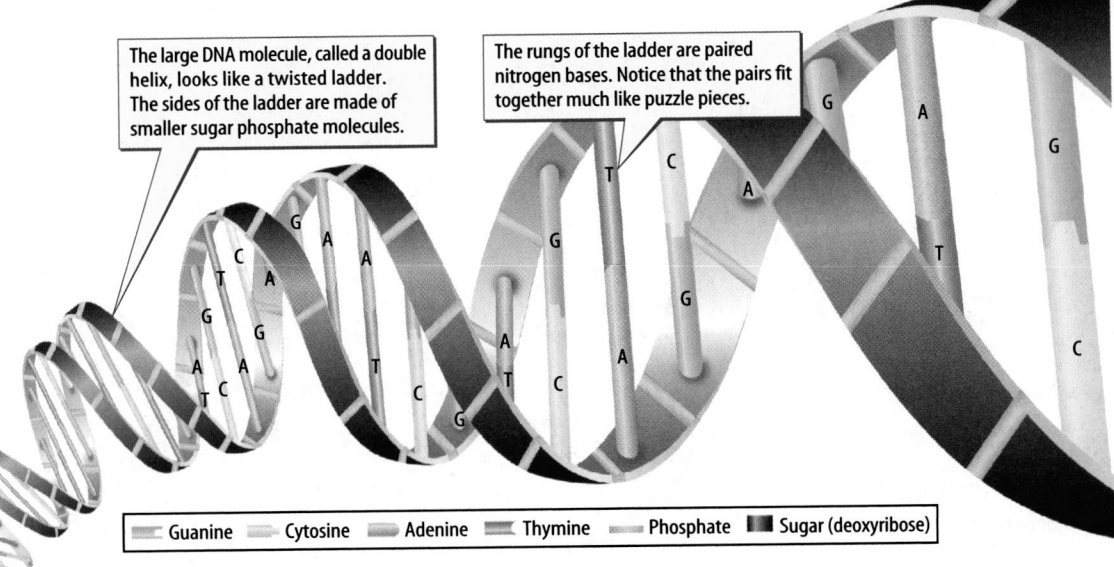

The large DNA molecule, called a double helix, looks like a twisted ladder. The sides of the ladder are made of smaller sugar phosphate molecules.

The rungs of the ladder are paired nitrogen bases. Notice that the pairs fit together much like puzzle pieces.

▬▬ Guanine   ▬▬ Cytosine   ▬▬ Adenine   ▬▬ Thymine   ▬▬ Phosphate   ■ Sugar (deoxyribose)

**DNA's Structure** In 1952, scientist Rosalind Franklin discovered that DNA is two chains of molecules in a spiral form. By using an X-ray technique, Dr. Franklin showed that the large spiral was probably made up of two spirals. As it turned out, the structure of DNA is similar to a twisted ladder. In 1953, using the work of Franklin and others, scientists James Watson and Francis Crick made a model of a DNA molecule.

**A DNA Model** What does DNA look like? According to the Watson and Crick DNA model, each side of the ladder is made up of sugar-phosphate molecules. Each molecule consists of the sugar called deoxyribose (dee AHK sih ri bohs) and a phosphate group. The rungs of the ladder are made up of other molecules called nitrogen bases. Four kinds of nitrogen bases are found in DNA—adenine (A duh neen), guanine (GWAH neen), cytosine (SI tuh seen), and thymine (THI meen). The bases are represented by the letters A, G, C, and T. The amount of cytosine in cells always equals the amount of guanine, and the amount of adenine always equals the amount of thymine. This led to the hypothesis that these bases occur as pairs in DNA. **Figure 14** shows that adenine always pairs with thymine, and guanine always pairs with cytosine. Like interlocking pieces of a puzzle, each base bonds only with its correct partner.

✔ **Reading Check** *What are the nitrogen base pairs in a DNA molecule?*

## Mini LAB

### Modeling DNA Replication

**Procedure**
1. Suppose you have a segment of DNA that is six nitrogen base pairs in length. On **paper,** using the letters A, T, C, and G, write a combination of six pairs, remembering that A and T are always a pair and C and G are always a pair.
2. Duplicate your segment of DNA. On paper, diagram how this happens and show the new DNA segments.

**Analysis**
Compare the order of bases of the original DNA to the new DNA molecules.

Try at Home

SECTION 3 DNA **111**

## Mini LAB

**Purpose** Students will model DNA replication. L2 **IS** **Visual-Spatial**

**Materials** pencil and paper

**Teaching Strategy** Make sure students understand that they are to make up a sample strand of DNA, then make the complementary strand, then split the two strands and make those complementary strands, so they can see that the new strands are identical to the original.

**Analysis**

Answers will vary with the bases chosen, but bases should be in the same order as the original DNA.

**Assessment**

**Performance** Draw and label one strand of DNA. Have students draw the complementary strand. Use **Performance Assessment in the Science Classroom,** p. 127. L2

Try at Home

✔ **Reading Check**

**Answer** Adenine pairs with thymine, and guanine with cytosine.

## Differentiated Instruction

**English-Language Learners** Use unifix cubes to demonstrate the various bases. Have students make their own models of base pairs, using a different color for each base. L2 **ELL** **IS** **Kinesthetic**

**Step 1**
Enzyme separates DNA sides

**Step 2**
New bases pair with bases on original DNA.

**Step 3**
Two new identical DNA molecules are produced.

Original DNA molecule

**Figure 15** DNA unzips when it is about to be copied. A protein called an enzyme helps unzip the DNA.

**Figure 16** This diagram shows just a few of the genes that have been identified on human chromosome 7. The bold print is the name that has been given to each gene.

**Chromosome 7**

- **Diabetes**
- **Williams-Beuren syndrome**
  *Physical- and mental-development disorder*
- **Cystic fibrosis**
- **Pendred syndrome**
  *A form of deafness*
- **Obesity**

**112    CHAPTER 4** Cell Reproduction

**Copying DNA** When chromosomes are duplicated before mitosis or meiosis, the amount of DNA in the nucleus is doubled. The Watson and Crick model shows how this takes place. The two sides of DNA unwind and separate. Each side then becomes a pattern on which a new side forms, as shown in **Figure 15.** The new DNA has bases that are identical to those of the original DNA and are in the same order.

## Genes

Most of your characteristics, such as the color of your hair, your height, and even how things taste to you, depend on the kinds of proteins your cells make. DNA in your cells stores the instructions for making these proteins.

Proteins build cells and tissues or work as enzymes. The instructions for making a specific protein are found in a **gene** which is a section of DNA on a chromosome. As shown in **Figure 16,** each chromosome contains hundreds of genes. Proteins are made of chains of hundreds or thousands of amino acids. The gene determines the order of amino acids in a protein. Changing the order of the amino acids makes a different protein. What might occur if an important protein couldn't be made or if the wrong protein was made in your cells?

**Making Proteins** Genes are found in the nucleus, but proteins are made on ribosomes in cytoplasm. The codes for making proteins are carried from the nucleus to the ribosomes by another type of nucleic acid called ribonucleic acid, or **RNA.**

**Ribonucleic Acid** RNA is made in the nucleus on a DNA pattern. However, RNA is different from DNA. If DNA is like a ladder, RNA is like a ladder that has all its rungs sawed in half. Compare the DNA molecule in **Figure 14** to the RNA molecule in **Figure 17**. RNA has the bases A, G, and C like DNA but has the base uracil (U) instead of thymine (T). The sugar-phosphate molecules in RNA contain the sugar ribose, not deoxyribose.

The three main kinds of RNA made from DNA in a cell's nucleus are messenger RNA (mRNA), ribosomal RNA (rRNA), and transfer RNA (tRNA). Protein production begins when mRNA moves into the cytoplasm. There, ribosomes attach to it. Ribosomes are made of rRNA. Transfer RNA molecules in the cytoplasm bring amino acids to these ribosomes. Inside the ribosomes, three nitrogen bases on the mRNA temporarily match with three nitrogen bases on the tRNA. The same thing happens for the mRNA and another tRNA molecule, as shown in **Figure 17.** The amino acids that are attached to the two tRNA molecules bond. This is the beginning of a protein.

The code carried on the mRNA directs the order in which the amino acids bond. After a tRNA molecule has lost its amino acid, it can move about the cytoplasm and pick up another amino acid just like the first one. The ribosome moves along the mRNA. New tRNA molecules with amino acids match up and add amino acids to the protein molecule.

**Science Online**

**Topic: The Human Genome Project**

Visit in7.msscience.com for Web links to information about the Human Genome Project.

**Activity** Find out when chromosomes 5, 16, 29, 21, and 22 were completely sequenced. Write about what scientists learned about each of these chromosomes.

**Figure 17** Cells need DNA, RNA, and amino acids to make proteins.

DNA in the nucleus is used to make RNA. RNA carries the code for a protein from the nucleus to the ribosome.

At the ribosome, the RNA's message is translated into a specific protein.

SECTION 3 DNA **113**

**Make a Model**

**Protein Synthesis** Have students draw a cell on a poster board and make a model demonstrating protein synthesis using materials such as craft sticks, beads, yarn, and so on. L2 IS **Visual-Spatial**

**Activity**

**Corresponding Sequence** On the board or an overhead transparency, write the sequence for one strand of DNA. Have students copy the sequence and write the corresponding sequence for mRNA and tRNA. L2 IS **Visual-Spatial**

**Quick Demo**

**DNA Replication**

**Materials** pipe cleaners in multiple colors

**Estimated Time** 5 minutes

**Procedure** Demonstrate the replication of DNA. Begin with two pipe cleaners of different colors, wrapped around one another as in a double helix. Unwind the strands and separate them. Wrap a new pipe cleaner around each strand, using the opposite color to demonstrate the complimentary strands.

## Visual Learning

**Figure 17** Have students make an events-chain concept map to outline the stages of protein synthesis. L2 IS **Visual-Spatial**

## Curriculum Connection

**History** Have students study the history of DNA research. Then using poster board, students should draw and label a timeline showing the events of DNA research since DNA was first removed from a cell nucleus in 1869. L3 IS **Visual-Spatial and Kinesthetic** P

Cells in the iris of the eye produce proteins needed for eye color.

Muscle cells produce proteins that help make muscles move.

Cells in the stomach produce proteins necessary to digest food.

**Figure 18** Each cell in the body produces only the proteins that are necessary to do its job.

**Controlling Genes** You might think that because most cells in an organism have exactly the same chromosomes and the same genes, they would make the same proteins, but they don't. In many-celled organisms like you, each cell uses only some of the thousands of genes that it has to make proteins. Just as each actor uses only the lines from the script for his or her role, each cell uses only the genes that direct the making of proteins that it needs. For example, muscle proteins are made in muscle cells, as represented in **Figure 18,** but not in nerve cells.

Cells must be able to control genes by turning some genes off and turning other genes on. They do this in many different ways. Sometimes the DNA is twisted so tightly that no RNA can be made. Other times, chemicals bind to the DNA so that it cannot be used. If the incorrect proteins are produced, the organism cannot function properly.

## Mutations

Sometimes mistakes happen when DNA is being copied. Imagine that the copy of the script the director gave you was missing three pages. You use your copy to learn your lines. When you begin rehearsing for the play, everyone is ready for one of the scenes except for you. What happened? You check your copy of the script against the original and find that three of the pages are missing. Because your script is different from the others, you cannot perform your part correctly.

If DNA is not copied exactly, the proteins made from the instructions might not be made correctly. These mistakes, called **mutations,** are any permanent change in the DNA sequence of a gene or chromosome of a cell. Some mutations include cells that receive an entire extra chromosome or are missing a chromosome. Outside factors such as X rays, sunlight, and some chemicals have been known to cause mutations.

### ✔ Reading Check  *When are mutations likely to occur?*

**114   CHAPTER 4** Cell Reproduction

**Figure 19** Because of a defect on chromosome 2, the mutant fruit fly has short wings and cannot fly.

**Predict** *Could this defect be transferred to the mutant's offspring? Explain.*

**Results of a Mutation** Genes control the traits you inherit. Without correctly coded proteins, an organism can't grow, repair, or maintain itself. A change in a gene or chromosome can change the traits of an organism, as illustrated in **Figure 19.**

If the mutation occurs in a body cell, it might or might not be life threatening to the organism. However, if a mutation occurs in a sex cell, then all the cells that are formed from that sex cell will have that mutation. Mutations add variety to a species when the organism reproduces. Many mutations are harmful to organisms, often causing their death. Some mutations do not appear to have any effect on the organism, and some can even be beneficial. For example, a mutation to a plant might cause it to produce a chemical that certain insects avoid. If these insects normally eat the plant, the mutation will help the plant survive.

**Science Online**

**Topic: Fruit Fly Genes**
Visit in7.msscience.com for Web links to information about what genes are present on the chromosomes of a fruit fly.

**Activity** Draw a picture of one of the chromosomes of a fruit fly and label some of its genes.

---

## section 3 review

### Summary

**What is DNA?**
- Each side of the DNA ladder is made up of sugar-phosphate molecules, and the rungs of the ladder are made up of nitrogenous bases.
- When DNA is copied, the new DNA has bases that are identical to those of the original DNA.

**Genes**
- The instructions for making a specific protein are found in genes in the cell nucleus. Proteins are made on ribosomes in the cytoplasm.
- There are three main kinds of RNA—mRNA, rRNA, and tRNA.

**Mutations**
- If DNA is not copied exactly, the resulting mutations may cause proteins to be made incorrectly.

### Self Check

1. **Describe** how DNA makes a copy of itself.
2. **Explain** how the codes for proteins are carried from the nucleus to the ribosomes.
3. **Apply** A strand of DNA has the bases AGTAAC. Using letters, show a matching DNA strand.
4. **Determine** how tRNA is used when cells build proteins.
5. **Think Critically** You begin as one cell. Compare the DNA in your brain cells to the DNA in your heart cells.

#### Applying Skills

6. **Concept Map** Using a Venn diagram, compare and contrast DNA and RNA.
7. **Use a word processor** to make an outline of the events that led up to the discovery of DNA. Use library resources to find this information.

**Science Online** in7.msscience.com/self_check_quiz

## 3 Assess

### DAILY INTERVENTION

#### Check for Understanding

**Visual-Spatial** Have students make puzzle pieces that represent the key elements in protein synthesis—three types of RNA, ribosome, amino acids, chemical bond, and protein. Working in pairs, the students can put the puzzle together to demonstrate the process of protein synthesis and students can test each other's ability to identify what each puzzle piece represents. L2

#### Reteach

**DNA and Protein** Have students make a drawing of DNA replication and protein synthesis. L2 IS **Visual-Spatial**

### ✓ Assessment

**Oral** What are the three kinds of RNA and their functions? Messenger RNA, transfer RNA, and ribosomal RNA; mRNA is copied from DNA and moves from the nucleus to a ribosome; tRNA carries amino acids to ribosomes; rRNA makes up ribosomes. Use **Performance Assessment in the Science Classroom,** p. 89. L2

---

## section 3 review

1. The two sides unwind and separate; a complementary strand is formed for each, and the resulting double-stranded DNA has one original strand and one new strand.
2. The codes are carried by mRNA from the nucleus to the ribosome.
3. TCATTG

4. The tRNA in the cytoplasm brings amino acids to the ribosomes. There, three nitrogen bases on the mRNA template match with three bases on the tRNA. The amino acids bond, and protein synthesis begins.
5. The DNA is identical.

6. Answers should be similar to the table for question 23 in the Chapter Review.
7. Students should be sure to include the contributions of Miescher, Griffith, Avery, Hershey, Chase, Chargraff, Wilkins, Franklin, Crick, and Watson.

## Real-World Question

**Purpose**

**Internet** Students use Internet sites that can be accessed through in7.msscience.com/internet_lab. They will observe genetic traits and mutations in animals. L2

**Process Skills** collect data, observe, research, communicate, make and use tables, form a hypothesis, compare, describe, record

**Time Required** about three days

## Make a Plan

**Preparation**

**Internet** To run through the steps that the students will follow, visit in7.msscience.com/internet_lab.

**Non-Internet** Have students use books to select an animal and one of its traits to investigate.

# LAB Use the Internet

# Mutations

**Fantail pigeon**

## Real-World Question

Mutations can result in dominant or recessive genes. A recessive characteristic can appear only if an organism has two recessive genes for that characteristic. However, a dominant characteristic can appear if an organism has one or two dominant genes for that characteristic. Why do some mutations result in more common traits while others do not? Form a hypothesis about how a mutation can become a common trait.

## Make a Plan

1. **Observe** common traits in various animals, such as household pets or animals you might see in a zoo.

2. **Learn** what genes carry these traits in each animal.

3. **Research** the traits to discover which ones are results of mutations. Are all mutations dominant? Are any of these mutations beneficial?

**Goals**

■ **Observe** traits of various animals.

■ **Research** how mutations become traits.

■ Gather data about mutations.

■ Make a frequency table of your findings and communicate them to other students.

**Data Source**

Visit in7.msscience.com/internet_lab for more information on common genetic traits in different animals, recessive and dominant genes, and data from other students.

**White tiger**

## Alternative Inquiry Lab

**Real-World Connection** To observe genetic traits and mutations in animals, give students a more personal investment into the Real-World Question by telling them that they are animal professionals at the zoo trying to maintain variety in the animals that are kept there. They can explore the Web sites of zoos on the Internet. To track what they learn, students can make a table of the different species that are found at the zoos that they investigate. What species are found at only a few zoos? For species that are found at many zoos, what unique traits do species have at the different zoos? Encourage students to research what zoos do to keep variety in the species of animals. Also, have them collect information on species that are becoming extinct.

## Follow Your Plan

1. Make sure your teacher approves your plan before you start.
2. Visit the link shown below to access different Web sites for information about mutations and genetics.
3. **Decide** if a mutation is beneficial, harmful, or neither. Record your data in your Science Journal.

## Analyze Your Data

1. **Record** in your Science Journal a list of traits that are results of mutations.
2. **Describe** an animal, such as a pet or an animal you've seen in the zoo. Point out which traits are known to be the result of a mutation.
3. **Make** a chart that compares recessive mutations to dominant mutations. Which are more common?
4. **Share** your data with other students by posting it at the link shown below.

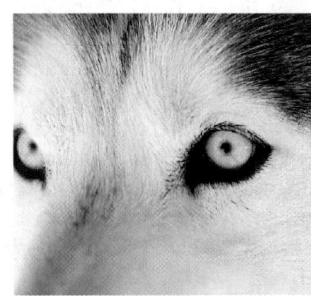

**Siberian Husky's eyes**

## Conclude and Apply

1. **Compare** your findings to those of your classmates and other data at the link shown below. What were some of the traits your classmates found that you did not? Which were the most common?
2. Look at your chart of mutations. Are all mutations beneficial? When might a mutation be harmful to an organism?
3. **Predict** how your data would be affected if you had performed this lab when one of these common mutations first appeared. Do you think you would see more or less animals with this trait?
4. Mutations occur every day but we only see a few of them. Infer how many mutations over millions of years can lead to a new species.

### Communicating Your Data

Find this lab using the link below. **Post** your data in the table provided. Combine your data with that of other students and make a chart that shows all of the data.

**Science Online**

in7.msscience.com/internet_lab

**LAB 117**

---

### Communicating Your Data

Have students use the Internet resources to collect pictures of the animal they are investigating. Have them find pictures that show the mutation.

## Follow Your Plan

**Teaching Strategy** Have students use animal population data to see how often that mutation is found. L2

## Analyze Your Data

1. Answers will vary. Color can result from a mutation.
2. Answers will depend upon animals chosen.
3. Answers will vary, but dominant genes are not necessarily more common.
4. Students may need help posting data.

## Conclude and Apply

1. Answers will vary. Remind students that the most common traits may be the result of mutations.
2. Answers will vary. Have students think about the mutation they are investigating and how helpful or harmful it is to the animal.
3. If you had investigated the mutation when it first appeared, you may have seen fewer animals with the trait. With the passage of time, you can determine if the mutation is beneficial.
4. Organisms with mutations may be better suited to a particular environment. These traits would be passed on to their offspring. Many mutations may lead to a new species.

### ✓ Assessment

**Oral** Students describe mutations they researched and discuss how helpful they are to animals. Show pictures of animals with the mutation. Use **Performance Assessment in the Science Classroom,** p. 143. L2

## Content Background

Cytogenetics is the branch of science that studies heredity both through genetics and studies of the cell. In 1956, modern human cytogenetics began, thanks to the discovery of the number of human chromosomes present in each cell of the body. As early as 1905, scientists had determined that chromosomes are found in pairs, and in 1915 Thomas Hunt Morgan discovered that genes were found on chromosomes. It was not until 1952 that Dr. Hsu's work occurred, and 1953 when Watson and Crick used Rosalind Franklin's work to determine the structure of DNA. Studies of human chromosomes and genes have progressed at an astounding rate since that time. Scientists have determined the particular chromosome that carries the gene for many human diseases and other traits.

## Discussion

**Explain** What type of mistake could the lab technician in Dr. Hsu's lab have made while mixing the solution to cause mysterious behavior of the chromosomes? Possible answer: The technician either added too little of the solute to a set amount of water, or too much water to a set amount of solute, causing the solution to have a higher water content than the cells.

## Activity

**Genetics** Have students work in teams to research the major discoveries in the field of genetics. Have each team display their results on a time line made on a long piece of paper. Students should be encouraged to include discoveries from early research until present times and to include the names of the scientists who made the discoveries. L2

# A Tangled Tale
### How did a scientist get chromosomes to separate?

Thanks to chromosomes, each of us is unique!

**V**iewed under the microscope, chromosomes in cells sometimes look a lot like spaghetti. That's why scientists had such a hard time figuring out how many chromosomes are in each human cell. Imagine, then, how Dr. Tao-Chiuh Hsu (dow shew•SEW) must have felt when he looked into a microscope and saw "beautifully scattered chromosomes." The problem was, Hsu didn't know what he had done to separate the chromosomes into countable strands.

"I tried to study those slides and set up some more cultures to repeat the miracle," Hsu explained. "But nothing happened."

These chromosomes are magnified 500 times.

For three months Hsu tried changing every variable he could think of to make the chromosomes separate again. In April 1952, his efforts were finally rewarded. Hsu quickly realized that the chromosomes separated because of osmosis.

Osmosis is the movement of water molecules through cell membranes. This movement occurs in predictable ways. The water molecules move from areas with higher concentrations of water to areas with lower concentrations of water. In Hsu's case, the solution he used to prepare the cells had a higher concentration of water then the cell did. So water moved from the solution into the cell and the cell swelled until it finally exploded. The chromosomes suddenly were visible as separate strands.

What made the cells swell the first time? Apparently a technician had mixed the solution incorrectly. "Since nearly four months had elapsed, there was no way to trace who actually had prepared that particular [solution]," Hsu noted. "Therefore, this heroine must remain anonymous."

**Research** What developments led scientists to conclude that the human cell has 46 chromosomes? Visit the link shown to the right to get started.

Science Online
For more information, visit
in7.msscience.com/oops

**Research** As students research the history of research on human chromosomes, have them consider the rate at which discoveries occurred then and now. Point out that the Human Genome Project has increased the knowledge of genetics at an amazing rate. L2

## Resources for Teachers and Students

*DNA and Genetic Engineering (Cells & Life)*, by Robert Snedden, Heinemann Library, 2003

*The Big Idea*, by Paul Strathern. New York: Doubleday, 1999

## Reviewing Main Ideas

### Section 1 — Cell Division and Mitosis

1. The life cycle of a cell has two parts—growth and development, and cell division.

2. In mitosis, the nucleus divides to form two identical nuclei. Mitosis occurs in four continuous steps, or phases—prophase, metaphase, anaphase, and telophase.

3. Cell division in animal cells and plant cells is similar, but plant cells do not have centrioles and animal cells do not form cell walls.

4. Organisms use cell division to grow, to replace cells, and for asexual reproduction. Asexual reproduction produces organisms with DNA identical to the parent's DNA. Fission, budding, and regeneration can be used for asexual reproduction.

### Section 2 — Sexual Reproduction and Meiosis

1. Sexual reproduction results when an egg and sperm join. This event is called fertilization, and the cell that forms is called the zygote.

2. Meiosis occurs in the reproductive organs, producing four haploid sex cells.

3. During meiosis, two divisions of the nucleus occur.

4. Meiosis ensures that offspring produced by fertilization have the same number of chromosomes as their parents.

### Section 3 — DNA

1. DNA is a large molecule made up of two twisted strands of sugar-phosphate molecules and nitrogen bases.

2. All cells contain DNA. The section of DNA on a chromosome that directs the making of a specific protein is a gene.

3. DNA can copy itself and is the pattern from which RNA is made. Messenger RNA, ribosomal RNA, and transfer RNA are used to make proteins.

4. Permanent changes in DNA are called mutations.

## Visualizing Main Ideas

*Think of four ways that organisms can use mitosis. Copy and complete the spider diagram below.*

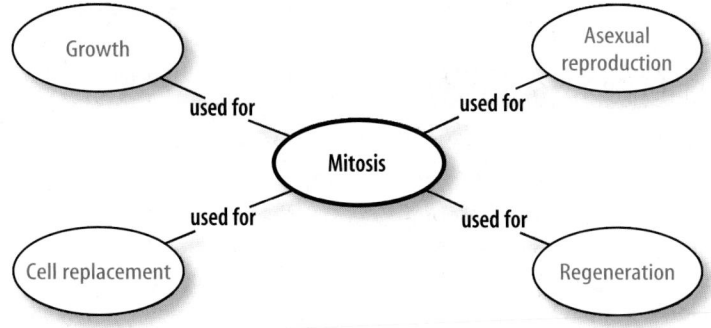

Science Online in7.msscience.com/interactive_tutor

**CHAPTER STUDY GUIDE** 119

## Reviewing Main Ideas

Summary statements can be used by students to review the major concepts of the chapter.

## Visualizing Main Ideas

See student page.

**Visit** in7.msscience.com
/self_check_quiz
/interactive_tutor
/vocabulary_puzzlemaker
/chapter_review
/standards_review

### Assessment Transparency

For additional assessment questions, use the *Assessment Transparency* located in the transparency book.

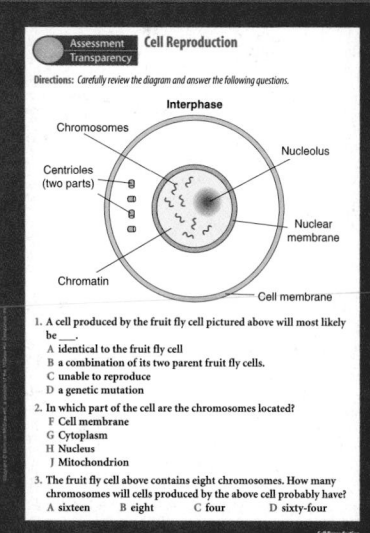

## Using Vocabulary

1. Egg, sperm
2. Mitosis
3. DNA or RNA
4. gene
5. haploid
6. asexual reproduction
7. chromosome
8. Meiosis
9. Fertilization, meiosis, or sexual reproduction
10. mutation

## Checking Concepts

11. D
12. D
13. B
14. C
15. A
16. A
17. D
18. C
19. B

## Using Vocabulary

asexual reproduction p.101
chromosome p.98
diploid p.104
DNA p.110
egg p.104
fertilization p.104
gene p.112
haploid p.105
meiosis p.105
mitosis p.98
mutation p.114
RNA p.112
sexual reproduction p.104
sperm p.104
zygote p.104

*Fill in the blanks with the correct vocabulary word or words.*

1. _____ and _____ cells are sex cells.
2. _____ produces two identical cells.
3. An example of a nucleic acid is _____.
4. A(n) _____ is the code for a protein.
5. A(n) _____ sperm is formed during meiosis.
6. Budding is a type of _____.
7. A(n) _____ is a structure in the nucleus that contains hereditary material.
8. _____ produces four sex cells.
9. As a result of _____, a new organism develops that has its own unique identity.
10. An error made during the copying of DNA is called a(n) _____.

## Checking Concepts

*Choose the word or phrase that best answers the question.*

11. Which of the following is a double spiral molecule with pairs of nitrogen bases?
A) RNA  C) protein
B) amino acid  D) DNA

12. What is in RNA but not in DNA?
A) thymine  C) adenine
B) thyroid  D) uracil

13. If a diploid tomato cell has 24 chromosomes, how many chromosomes will the tomato's sex cells have?
A) 6  C) 24
B) 12  D) 48

14. During a cell's life cycle, when do chromosomes duplicate?
A) anaphase  C) interphase
B) metaphase  D) telophase

15. When do chromatids separate during mitosis?
A) anaphase  C) metaphase
B) prophase  D) telophase

16. How is the hydra shown in the picture reproducing?
A) asexually, by budding
B) sexually, by budding
C) asexually, by fission
D) sexually, by fission

17. What is any permanent change in a gene or a chromosome called?
A) fission  C) replication
B) reproduction  D) mutation

18. What does meiosis produce?
A) cells with the diploid chromosome number
B) cells with identical chromosomes
C) sex cells
D) a zygote

19. What type of nucleic acid carries the codes for making proteins from the nucleus to the ribosome?
A) DNA  C) protein
B) RNA  D) genes

 Science Online in7.msscience.com/vocabulary_puzzlemaker

**Use the ExamView® Pro Testmaker CD-ROM to:**
- create multiple versions of tests
- create modified tests with one mouse click for inclusion students
- edit existing questions and add your own questions
- build tests aligned with state standards using built-in State Curriculum Tags
- change English tests to Spanish with one mouse click and vice versa

## Thinking Critically

**20.** **List** the base sequence of a strand of RNA made using the DNA pattern ATCCGTC. Look at **Figure 14** for a hint.

**21.** **Predict** whether a mutation in a human skin cell can be passed on to the person's offspring. Explain.

**22.** **Explain** how a zygote could end up with an extra chromosome.

**23.** **Classify** Copy and complete this table about DNA and RNA.

### DNA and RNA

| | DNA | RNA |
|---|---|---|
| Number of strands | 2 | 1 |
| Type of sugar | deoxyribose | ribose |
| Letter names of bases | G, A, C, T | G, A, C, U |
| Where found | nucleus | nucleus & cytoplasm |

**24.** **Concept Map** Make an events-chain concept map of what occurs from interphase in the parent cell to the formation of the zygote. Tell whether the chromosome's number at each stage is haploid or diploid.

**25.** **Concept Map** Copy and complete the events-chain concept map of DNA synthesis.

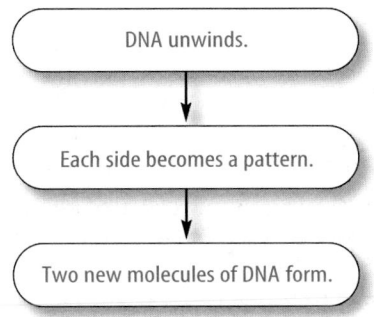

DNA unwinds.

↓

Each side becomes a pattern.

↓

Two new molecules of DNA form.

 in7.msscience.com/chapter_review

**26.** **Compare and Contrast** Meiosis is two divisions of a reproductive cell's nucleus. It occurs in a continuous series of steps. Compare and contrast the steps of meiosis I to the steps of meiosis II.

**27.** **Describe** what occurs in mitosis that gives the new cells identical DNA.

**28.** **Form a hypothesis** about the effect of an incorrect mitotic division on the new cells produced.

**29.** **Determine** how many chromosomes are in the original cell compared to those in the new cells formed by cell division. Explain.

## Performance Activities

**30.** **Flash Cards** Make a set of 11 flash cards with drawings of a cell that show the different stages of meiosis. Shuffle your cards and then put them in the correct order. Give them to another student in the class to try.

## Applying Math

**31.** **Cell Cycle** Assume an average human cell has a cell cycle of 20 hours. Calculate how many cells there would be after 80 hours.

**Use the diagram below to answer question 32.**

**32.** **Amino Acids** Sets of three nitrogen bases code for an amino acid. How many amino acids will make up the protein molecule that is coded for by the mRNA molecule above?

---

## Thinking Critically

**20.** UAGGCAG

**21.** No; in order for a mutation to be passed to offspring, the mutation must take place in a sex cell.

**22.** This could happen if nondisjunction (failure of like chromosomes or chromatids to separate) occurs during anaphase I or II.

**23.** See student page.

**24.** The order of events given for meiosis should reflect **Figure 11** and formation of the zygote, **Figure 10**. The cell at the beginning of meiosis is diploid. The four cells at the end of meiosis are all haploid.

**25.** See student page.

**26.** Student answers should reflect the information in Section 2 and **Figure 11**.

**27.** the copying of chromosomes in interphase; the separation of the copies at anaphase; the separation of two new cells at telophase

**28.** Incorrect division can result in an incorrect number of chromosomes, often leading to abnormal offspring.

**29.** The number of chromosomes in the new cell are the same as in the original cell; DNA is copied before mitosis so new cells retained the correct number of chromosomes.

## Performance Activities

**30.** Cards should be sequenced as shown in **Figure 11**. If interphase is included, it should come before prophase I. **Use Performance Assessment in the Science Classroom**, p. 163.

## Applying Math

### Indiana Math Standards

7.2.1

**31.** 80 hours divided by 20 hours = 4 cycles; $2^4$ = 16 cells

**32.** 7

---

chapter 4 Indiana

**Answer Sheet** A practice answer sheet can be found at in7.msscience.com/answer_sheet.

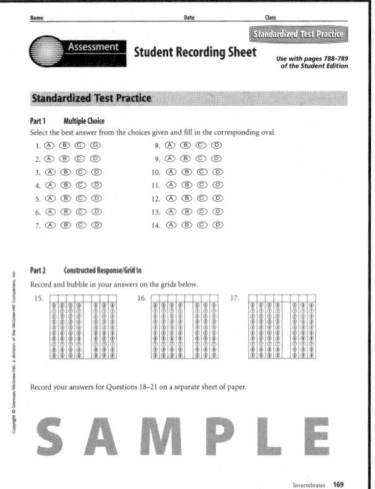

**SAMPLE**

### Part 1 | Multiple Choice

| | | |
|---|---|---|
| **1.** D | **4.** B | **7.** B |
| **2.** A | **5.** B | |
| **3.** C | **6.** A | |

### Part 2 | Critical Response

**8.** It is a plant cell undergoing cell division. A cell plate that will develop into the cell walls for the two new cells is forming between the cells.

**9.** Sex cells transfer genetic information to offspring from each parent. The sperm carries half the genetic information of the male parent and the egg carries half of the genetic information of the female parent.

---

The assessed Indiana standard appears above the question.

*Record your answers on the answer sheet provided by your teacher or on a sheet of paper.*

### Part 1 | Multiple Choice

The photo below shows a potato undergoing reproduction.

**7.4.1**

**1.** How does the genetic material of the new organism compare to the genetic material of the parent organism?

   **A** different genes

   **B** double the amount

   **C** half the amount

   **D** the same genes

**7.4.4**

**2.** What is the form of reproduction shown above?

   **A** asexual

   **B** meiosis

   **C** regeneration

   **D** sexual

---

The illustration below shows a model of genetic material.

**3.** What does the illustration represent?

   **A** cell cycle

   **B** cell division

   **C** DNA duplication

   **D** RNA synthesis

**4.** When does the process shown above occur?

   **A** anaphase

   **B** interphase

   **C** metaphase

   **D** prophase

**Test-Taking Tip**

**Prepare** Avoid rushing on test day. Prepare your clothes and test supplies the night before. Wake up early and arrive at school on time on test day.

**122 INDIANA**

---

**10.** DNA and RNA are nucleic acids. A DNA molecule is a double helix with a dextrose-phosphate backbone and nitrogen bases adenine, cytosine, guanine, and thymine. DNA controls all activities of cells. A RNA molecule is a single strand with a ribose-phosphate backbone and nitrogen bases adenine, cytosine, guanine, and uracil. RNA transfers genetic information from the nucleus to ribosomes for protein synthesis.

**11.** Messenger RNA is made from DNA in the nucleus and moves to ribosomes in the cytoplasm. Transfer RNA (t RNA) in the cytoplasm brings amino acids to the ribosome. A code on the tRNA pairs with a code on the mRNA, the chain of amino acids begins, and a protein forms.

**7.4.1**

**5.** If an organism's sex cell has eight chromosomes, how many chromosomes are in the body cells of that organism?

**A** 8 chromosomes

**B** 16 chromosomes

**C** 32 chromosomes

**D** 64 chromosomes

The table below is about cell division.

| Phase of Cell Division | Action |
|---|---|
| 1 | Chromosomes duplicate |
| 2 | Chromatid pairs are visible |
| Metaphase | |
| 3 | Chromosomes separate |
| 4 | Cytoplasm separates |

**6.** What term correctly replaces phase 3?

**A** anaphase

**B** interphase

**C** prophase

**D** telephase

**7.** Which completes the action for metaphase in the table above?

**A** cell organelles migrate

**B** chromatid pairs line up

**C** mitosis begins again

**D** spindles form

## Part 2 Critical Response

The photo below shows a cell undergoing cell division.

**8.** Is this cell an animal or a plant cell? Provide evidence to support your conclusion.

**7.4.3**

**9.** Describe the transfer of genetic information in sexual reproduction.

**10.** Compare and contrast DNA and RNA.

**11.** The diagram below shows protein synthesis.

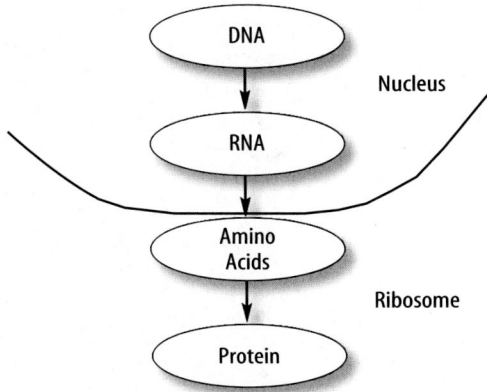

Give a detailed explanation of this diagram.

## Rubrics

The following rubric is a sample scoring device for critical response questions.

### Critical Response

| Points | Description |
|---|---|
| 4 | The student demonstrates a thorough understanding of the science of the task. The response may contain minor flaws that do not detract from the demonstration of a thorough understanding. |
| 3 | The student demonstrates an understanding of the science of the task. The response is essentially correct and demonstrates an essential but less than thorough understanding of the science. |
| 2 | The student demonstrates only a partial understanding of the science of the task. Although the student may have used the correct approach to a solution or may have provided a correct solution, the work lacks an essential understanding of the underlying science concepts. |
| 1 | The student demonstrates a very limited understanding of the science of the task. The response is incomplete and exhibits many flaws. |
| 0 | The student provides a completely incorrect solution or no response at all. |

## Unit Contents

**WebQuest** *History of Disease Prevention* investigates five different diseases and science through history. Students will choose one disease to study further, and then create a time line of discoveries that help prevent the spread of disease.

# How are Chickens & Rice Connected?

124

**PROJECT CRISS**ˢᴹ

## Study Skills

**Cooperative Team Research** Cooperative team assignments are a reliable means of involving every student. Break into cooperative teams and assign each member of the team a human body system. Each should research the system, its function, and any diseases associated with that system. Team members come back together to share information and draft a group report.

# NATIONAL GEOGRAPHIC

Back in the 1800s, a mysterious disease called beriberi affected people in certain parts of Asia. One day, a doctor in Indonesia noticed some chickens staggering around, a symptom often seen in people with beriberi. It turned out that the chickens had been eating white rice—the same kind of rice that was being eaten by human beriberi sufferers. White rice has had the outer layers, including the bran, removed. When the sick chickens were fed rice that still had its bran, they quickly recovered. It turned out that the same treatment worked for people with beriberi! Research eventually showed that rice bran contains a vitamin, $B_1$, which is essential for good health. Today, white rice usually is "vitamin-enriched" to replace $B_1$ and other nutrients lost in processing.

## unit projects

The assessed Indiana objective appears in blue.

To find project ideas and resources, visit in7.msscience.com/unit_project.

Projects include:
- **History** Contribute to a class "remedy journal" with interesting, out-dated medical treatments, and how techniques have improved. **7.6.1**
- **Technology** Investigate rare and interesting medical conditions, including their history, characteristics, and treatments. Present a colorful poster with photos and information for class display. **7.6.4**
- **Model** Gather data on hand span versus height for 20 people. Design a scatter plot to analyze trends and draw conclusions about growth, age, and gender relationships. **7.2.7**

**WebQuest** In *Investigating Disease and Prevention,* explore a variety of diseases and science through history, study one disease more in-depth, and then create a time line of new information. **7.6.1, 7.6.4**

## unit projects

**History** Have students investigate unusual, old-fashioned, or native-culture medicines and treatments practiced throughout history. After writing a one-page summary about their historical medicine or treatment, the ailment associated with it, and any connection to modern medicine, have the class compile an alphabetical "medical remedy" journal to share.

**Technology** Have students explore an assigned disease or syndrome. Research should include a paragraph on each of the following topics: discovered by whom and when, symptoms, diagnosis, therapy, medications, inherited or how contracted and where, and a photo, chart, or other visual. Information may be displayed in a poster or brochure and presented to the class.

**Model** Ask each student to measure the hand span and height of 20 different people. Subjects should vary in age and sex. Have students graph their data on a scatter plot. Design a class scatter plot of all student data. Ask students to analyze and draw conclusions about the relationship between hand span and height as a person grows older, changes height, and female versus male data. Students should express why a scatter plot is an effective way to interpret trends in large amounts of data.

**Additional Resources** For more information, resources, and assessment rubrics, visit in7.msscience.com/unit_project.

## NATIONAL GEOGRAPHIC  How Are Chickens & Rice Connected?

Deficiencies of vitamin $B_1$ affect many human systems. This vitamin allows cells to use many other nutrients. When $B_1$ is deficient, blood vessels expand in an attempt to deliver more blood and more nutrients to cells. This, in turn, leads to increased work for the heart. Each body system must perform its functions in order for the other systems to do so.

All vertebrates share a common body plan and similar organ systems. Observations of animals in nature and in the laboratory provide valuable clues for an understanding of human health and biology.

| Section/Objectives | Standards | | Labs/Features |
|---|---|---|---|
| **Chapter Opener** | **National** | **State/Local** | **Launch Lab:** Breathing Rate, p. 127<br>**Foldables,** p. 127 |
| | See pp. 16T–17T for a Key to Standards. | Detailed Standards begin on page IN8. | |
| **Section 1 The Digestive System**<br>🕐 2 sessions   📦 1 block<br><br>1. **Distinguish** the differences between mechanical digestion and chemical digestion.<br>2. **Identify** the organs of the digestive system and what takes place in each.<br>3. **Explain** how homeostasis is maintained in digestion. | National Content Standards:<br>UCP.1–UCP.3, UCP.5, A.1, A.2, C.1, C.3 | Indiana Standards:<br>7.4.4, 7.4.6, 7.4.8 | **Integrate Health,** p. 132 |
| **Section 2 Nutrition**<br>🕐 1 session   📦 .5 block<br><br>4. **Distinguish** among the six classes of nutrients.<br>5. **Identify** the importance of each type of nutrient.<br>6. **Explain** the relationship between diet and health. | National Content Standards:<br>UCP.1–UCP.3, UCP.5, A.1, A.2, C.1, C.3, F.1 | Indiana Standards:<br>7.4.2, 7.4.4, 7.4.6, 7.4.8, 7.4.11 | **Science Online,** p. 134<br>**MiniLAB:** Comparing the Fat Content of Foods, p. 135<br>**Integrate Social Studies,** p. 136<br>**Lab:** Identifying Vitamin C Content, p. 139 |
| **Section 3 The Respiratory System**<br>🕐 1.5 sessions   📦 .5 block<br><br>7. **Describe** the functions of the respiratory system.<br>8. **Explain** how oxygen and carbon dioxide are exchanged in the lungs and in tissues.<br>9. **Identify** the pathway of air in and out of the lungs.<br>10. **Explain** the effects of smoking on the respiratory system. | National Content Standards:<br>UCP.1–UCP.3, UCP.5, A.1, A.2, C.1–C.3, F.1 | Indiana Standards:<br>7.4.4, 7.4.12 | **MiniLAB,** p. 143<br>**Visualizing Abdominal Thrusts,** p. 144<br>**Science Online,** p. 145 |
| **Section 4 The Excretory System**<br>🕐 2.5 sessions   📦 1 block<br><br>11. **Distinguish** between the excretory and urinary systems.<br>12. **Describe** how the kidneys work.<br>13. **Explain** what happens when urinary organs don't work. | National Content Standards:<br>UCP.1–UCP.3, UCP.5, A.1, A.2, C.1, C.3, G.3 | Indiana Standards:<br>7.1.6, 7.1.9, 7.2.7, 7.4.4, 7.4.6, 7.7.2 | **Applying Science,** p. 150<br>**Lab:** Particle Size and Absorption, pp. 152–153<br>**Science and History:** Overcoming the Odds, p. 154 |

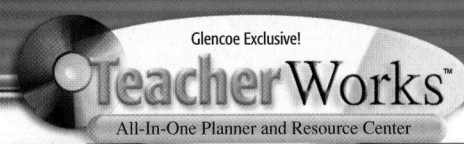
| Lab Materials | Reproducible Resources | Section Assessment | Technology |
|---|---|---|---|
| **Launch Lab:** watch or clock with second hand, calculator | **Chapter FAST FILE Resources** Foldables Worksheet, p. 17 Directed Reading Overview, p. 19 Note-taking Worksheets, pp. 35–37 | ASSESSMENT ADVANTAGE | TeacherWorks includes: • Interactive Teacher Edition • Lesson Planner with calendar • Access to all program blacklines • Correlations to standards • Web links |
| *Need materials?* Contact Science Kit at 1-800-828-7777 or www.sciencekit.com on the Internet. | **Chapter FAST FILE Resources** Transparency Activity, p. 46 Enrichment, p. 31 Reinforcement, p. 27 Directed Reading, p. 20 Lab Activity, pp. 9–12 | **Performance** Assessment, p. 132 Applying Skills, p. 132 **Content** Section Review, p. 132 | Section Focus Transparency Teaching Transparency Guided Reading Audio Program Interactive Chalkboard CD-ROM |
| **MiniLAB:** 3 each: potato chips, pretzels, peanuts, cubes of fruit, cheese, vegetables, and meat; brown paper bag **Lab:** test tubes, tape, wooden stirrers, graduated cylinder, dropper bottles of orange juice, iodine, dropper, cornstarch, balance, weighing paper, water, wax pencil | **Chapter FAST FILE Resources** Transparency Activity, p. 47 MiniLAB, p. 3 Enrichment, p. 32 Reinforcement, p. 28 Directed Reading, p. 20 Lab Worksheet, pp. 5–6 | **Performance** MiniLAB, p. 135 Assessment, p. 138 Applying Skills, p. 138 **Content** Section Review, p. 138 | Section Focus Transparency Guided Reading Audio Program Interactive Chalkboard CD-ROM Video Lab |
| **MiniLAB:** bathroom-tissue cardboard tube, marbles, bowl, calculator | **Chapter FAST FILE Resources** Transparency Activity, p. 48 MiniLAB, p. 4 Enrichment, p. 33 Reinforcement, p. 29 Directed Reading, p. 21 Lab Activity, pp. 13–16 | **Performance** MiniLAB, p. 143 Assessment, p. 146 Applying Skills, p. 146 **Content** Section Review, p. 146 | Section Focus Transparency Virtual Labs CD-ROM Guided Reading Audio Program Interactive Chalkboard CD-ROM |
| **Lab:** beakers or jars (3), thermometers (3), sugar granules, mortar and pestle, triple-beam balance, stirring rod, sugar cubes, weighing paper, warm water, stopwatch | **Chapter FAST FILE Resources** Transparency Activity, p. 49 Enrichment, p. 34 Reinforcement, p. 30 Directed Reading, pp. 21, 22 Lab Worksheet, pp. 7–8 Transparency Activity, pp. 50–51 | **Performance** Applying Science, p. 150 Assessment, p. 151 Applying Math, p. 151 **Content** Section Review, p. 151 | Section Focus Transparency Guided Reading Audio Program Interactive Chalkboard CD-ROM |

## End of Chapter Assessment

GLENCOE'S ASSESSMENT ADVANTAGE

| Blackline Masters | Technology | Professional Series |
|---|---|---|
| **Chapter FAST FILE Resources** Chapter Review, pp. 39–40 Chapter Tests, pp. 41–44 **Mastering the Grade 7 Indiana Science Standards** | MindJogger Videoquiz IN Test Prep and Practice ExamView® ExamView® Pro Testmaker TeacherWorks CD-ROM Interactive Chalkboard CD-ROM | **Performance Assessment in the Science Classroom (PASC)** |

# Transparencies

## Section Focus

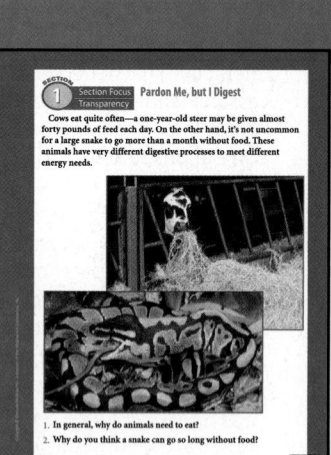

**SECTION 1** Section Focus Transparency — **Pardon Me, but I Digest**

Cows eat quite often—a one-year-old steer may be given almost forty pounds of feed each day. On the other hand, it's not uncommon for a large snake to go more than a month without food. These animals have very different digestive processes to meet different energy needs.

1. In general, why do animals need to eat?
2. Why do you think a snake can go so long without food?

L2

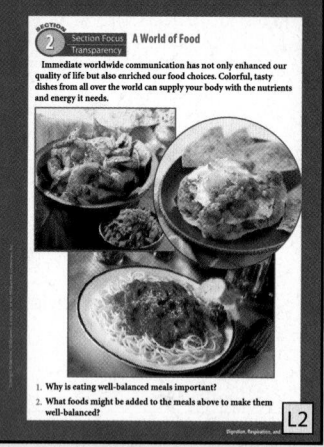

**SECTION 2** Section Focus Transparency — **A World of Food**

Immediate worldwide communication has not only enhanced our quality of life but also enriched our food choices. Colorful, tasty dishes from all over the world can supply your body with the nutrients and energy it needs.

1. Why is eating well-balanced meals important?
2. What foods might be added to the meals above to make them well-balanced?

L2

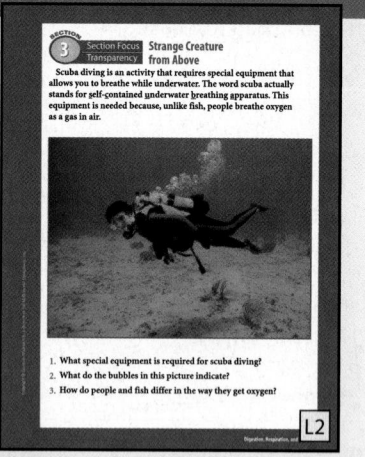

**SECTION 3** Section Focus Transparency — **Strange Creature from Above**

Scuba diving is an activity that requires special equipment that allows you to breathe while underwater. The word scuba actually stands for self-contained underwater breathing apparatus. This equipment is needed because, unlike fish, people breathe oxygen as a gas in air.

1. What special equipment is required for scuba diving?
2. What do the bubbles in this picture indicate?
3. How do people and fish differ in the way they get oxygen?

L2

This is a representation of key blackline masters available in the Teacher Classroom Resources. See Resource Manager boxes within the chapter for additional information.

## Key to Teaching Strategies

The following designations will help you decide which activities are appropriate for your students.

L1 Level 1 activities should be appropriate for students with learning difficulties.

L2 Level 2 activities should be within the ability range of all students.

L3 Level 3 activities are designed for above-average students.

ELL ELL activities should be within the ability range of English-Language Learners.

COOP LEARN Cooperative Learning activities are designed for small group work.

LS Multiple Learning Styles logos, as described on page 12T, are used throughout to indicate strategies that address different learning styles.

P These strategies represent student products that can be placed into a best-work portfolio.

PBL Problem-Based Learning activities apply real-world situations to learning.

## Assessment

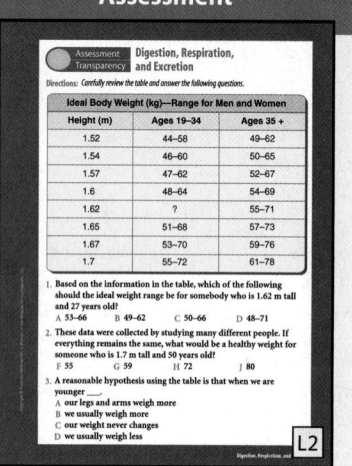

Assessment Transparency — **Digestion, Respiration, and Excretion**

Directions: *Carefully review the table and answer the following questions.*

| Ideal Body Weight (kg)—Range for Men and Women | | |
|---|---|---|
| Height (m) | Ages 19–34 | Ages 35 + |
| 1.52 | 44–58 | 49–62 |
| 1.54 | 46–60 | 50–65 |
| 1.57 | 47–62 | 52–67 |
| 1.6 | 48–64 | 54–69 |
| 1.62 | ? | 55–71 |
| 1.65 | 51–68 | 57–73 |
| 1.67 | 53–70 | 59–76 |
| 1.7 | 55–72 | 61–78 |

1. Based on the information in the table, which of the following should the ideal weight range be for somebody who is 1.62 m tall and 27 years old?
   A 53–66  B 49–62  C 50–66  D 48–71
2. These data were collected by studying many different people. If everything remains the same, what would be a healthy weight for someone who is 1.7 m tall and 50 years old?
   F 55  G 59  H 72  J 80
3. A reasonable hypothesis using the table is that when we are younger ____.
   A our legs and arms weigh more
   B we usually weigh more
   C our weight never changes
   D we usually weigh less

L2

## Teaching

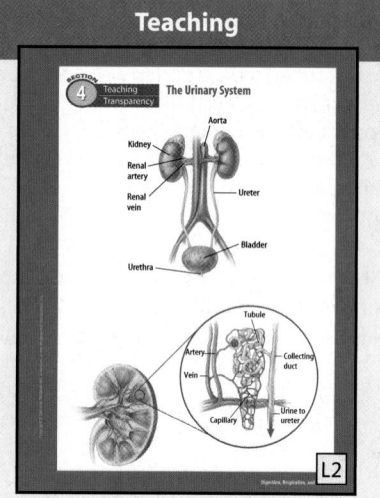

**SECTION 4** Teaching Transparency — **The Urinary System**

L2

# Hands-on Activities

## Student Text Lab Worksheet

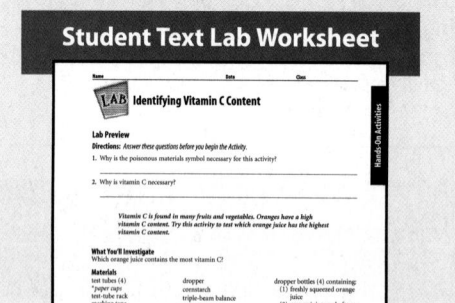

**LAB** Identifying Vitamin C Content

**Lab Preview**
Directions: *Answer these questions before you begin the Activity.*
1. Why is the poisonous materials symbol necessary for this activity?

2. Why is vitamin C necessary?

*Vitamin C is found in many fruits and vegetables. Oranges have a high vitamin C content. Try this activity to test which orange juice has the highest vitamin C content.*

**What You'll Investigate**
Which orange juice contains the most vitamin C?

**Materials**
test tubes (4)          dropper          dropper bottles (4) containing:
*paper cups            cornstarch          (1) freshly squeezed orange
test-tube rack          triple-beam balance          juice
masking tape          weighing paper          (2) orange juice made from
wooden skewers (15)          water (50mL)          frozen concentrate
graduated cylinder          glass-marking pencil          (3) canned orange juice
*graduated container          *Alternate materials          (4) dairy carton orange juice
2% tincture of iodine

**Goals**
• **Observe** the vitamin C content of different orange juices.

**Safety Precautions**
Wear your goggles and apron. Do not taste any of the juices. Iodine is poisonous and can stain skin and clothing. It is an irritant and can cause damage if it comes in contact with your eyes. Notify your teacher if a spill occurs.

**Procedure**
1. Label four test tubes 1 through 4 and place them in the test-tube rack.
2. **Measure** and pour 5 mL of juice from bottle 1 into test tube 1, 5 mL from bottle 2 into test tube 2, 5 mL from bottle 3 into

test tube 3, and 5 mL from bottle 4 into test tube 4.
3. **Measure** 0.3 g of cornstarch, then put it in a container. Slowly mix in 50 mL of water until the cornstarch completely dissolves.
4. Add 5 mL of the cornstarch solution to each of the four test tubes. Stir well.
5. Add iodine to test tube 1, one drop at a time. Stir after each drop. In the table on the next page, record the number of drops it takes for the juice to change to a purple color. The more vitamin C that is present, the more drops it takes to change color.
6. Repeat step 5 with test tubes 2, 3, and 4.
7. Empty and clean the test tubes. Repeat steps 2 through 6 two more times. Record your results.

L2

## Laboratory Activities

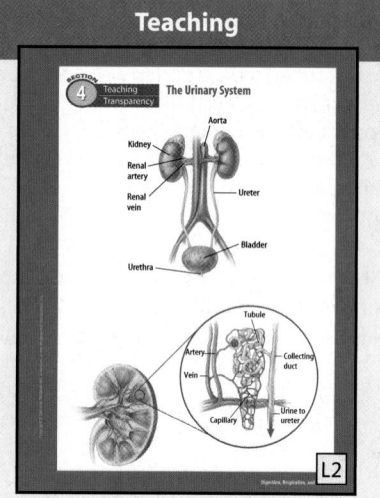

**LAB 1** Laboratory Activity — **Testing for Carbohydrates**

Carbohydrates provide energy for the body. Your body needs more carbohydrates than fats and proteins each day. Foods that contain starch and foods that contain sugar are sources of carbohydrates.

**Strategy**
You will test foods for starch by using iodine solution.
You will test foods for sugar by using sugar test tablets.
You will use your test results to determine which foods are sources of carbohydrates.

**Materials**
12 test tubes (18 × 150-mm)          egg white (hard-boiled)          honey
test-tube rack          potato (cooked)          milk
water          iodine in dropper bottle          molasses
starch          labels          forceps
bread          glucose          sugar test tablets
rice (cooked)          syrup

**Procedure**
CAUTION: *Do not taste, eat, or drink any materials used in the lab.*
CAUTION: *Inform your teacher if you come in contact with any chemicals.*
1. Label six test tubes 1 through 6. Place them in a test-tube rack.
2. Fill the test tubes to about 1 cm with the following:
   1—Water      4—Rice
   2—Starch      5—Egg White
   3—Bread      6—Potato
3. Add 5 drops of iodine to test tubes 1–6. CAUTION: *Iodine is poisonous. Do not inhale iodine fumes. Do not allow iodine to get on your hands. Wash immediately if iodine comes in contact with your skin. Inform your teacher.* Examine the color. A blue-black color means that starch is present. Record the colors in Table 1. (See Data and Observations.)

4. Label the remaining test tubes 7 through 12. Place them in a test-tube rack.
5. Fill these test tubes to a depth of about 1 cm with the following:
   7—Water      10—Honey
   8—Glucose      11—Milk
   9—Syrup      12—Molasses
6. Use forceps to add one sugar test tablet each to test tubes 7–12. CAUTION: *Sugar tablets are poisonous. DO NOT touch the tablet with your fingers. Wash hands immediately if sugar test tablets or solution containing them come in contact with your skin. The test tubes will get hot as the tablets dissolve. Do not remove the test tubes from the test rack, DO NOT TOUCH.* Observe the color of each of the five tubes. Green, yellow, or orange color means that sugar is present. Record the colors in Table 2.

L2

## Meeting Different Ability Levels

### Content Outline

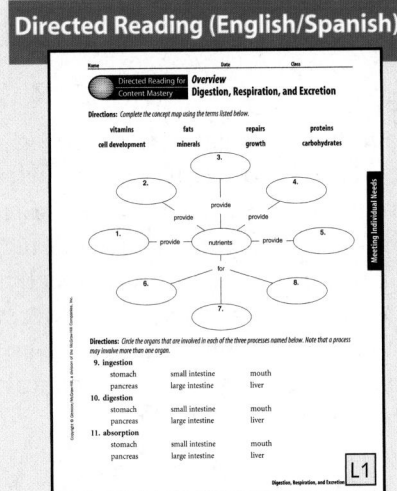

L2

### Reinforcement

L2

### Enrichment

L3

### Directed Reading (English/Spanish)

L1

### Study Guide

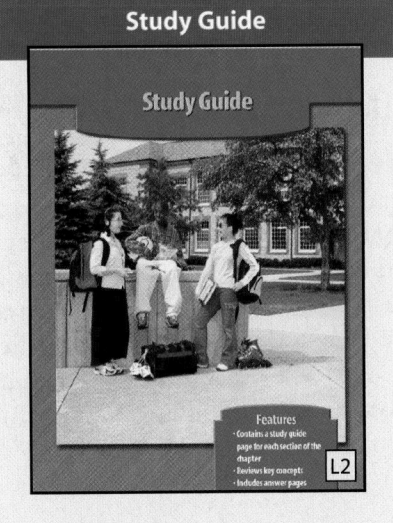

**Study Guide**

Features
· Contains a study guide page for each section of the chapter
· Reviews key concepts
· Includes answer pages

L2

### Reading Essentials

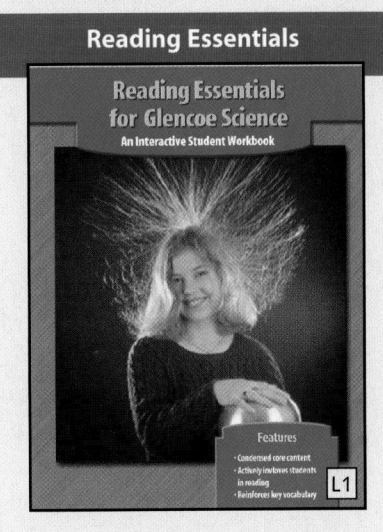

**Reading Essentials for Glencoe Science**
An Interactive Student Workbook

Features
· Condensed core content
· Actively involves students in reading
· Reinforces key vocabulary

L1

## Assessment

### Test Practice Workbook

L2

### Chapter Review

L2

### Chapter Tests

L2

# Science Content Background

## The Digestive System
### Digestion

The process of transforming foods into usable nutrients is called digestion. This extracellular process takes place in the digestive system, specifically in the stomach and small intestine. Enzymes that serve as catalysts for chemical reactions often require precise environmental conditions, including the proper temperature, pH, and substrate, to be active. For example, the enzyme pepsin, which is found in the stomach, is only active in a medium having a pH of 1.5 to 2.2 and only helps digest proteins.

## Nutrition
### Calorie Needs

The rate at which the body consumes energy when at rest is termed the basal metabolic rate. The basal metabolic rate and the physical activity metabolic rate are two of the factors that help determine the number of Calories a person's body requires each day. Other factors include age, body mass, size, sex, endocrine gland activity, and external temperature.

## Carbohydrates

Carbohydrates and proteins supply about four Calories per gram, and fats supply about nine Calories per gram. Excess sugar is stored in the liver and muscles in the form of glycogen. When energy is required, a series of activities involving the brain, nerves, and adrenal glands brings about the conversion of glycogen to glucose. The amino acids of protein can be converted into carbohydrates, and then these can be utilized for energy production. Excess fat stored in the body can oxidize and supply energy. This reaction produces a great deal of heat as a waste product.

## Vitamins

The role of vitamins as nutrients was not recognized until the early 1900s. During the early years of research, each new vitamin that was identified was given a letter designation. This method proved to be inadequate to correctly classify the substances. Vitamins then were called by their chemical names. Niacin is an example of a vitamin that goes by its chemical name rather than a letter designation.

---

## chapter content resources

**Internet Resources**

For additional content background, visit **in7.msscience.com** to:

- access your book online
- find references to related articles in popular science magazines
- access Web links with related content background
- access current events with science journal topics

**Print Resources**

*Contemporary Nutrition,* by Gordon M. Wardlaw, McGraw-Hill, 2000

*The Digestive System,* by Carol Ballard, Heinemann Library, 2002

*Lungs: Learning How We Breathe,* by Chris Hayhurst, The Rosen Publishing Group Incorporated, 2002

*The Excretory System,* by Alvin Silverstein, Robert Silverstein and Virginia B. Silverstein, Millbrook Press, 1997

## section 3 The Respiratory System
### Functions of the Respiratory System

In order to function, cells need nutrients, which must be oxidized in order to release energy. The process of obtaining energy from nutrients is called cellular respiration. In respiration, the most commonly used carbohydrate is glucose. The oxidation of glucose produces water and carbon dioxide, and releases energy.

$$C_6H_{12}O_6 + 6O_2 \rightarrow 6H_2O + 6\ CO_2 + energy$$

Obtaining oxygen and removing carbon dioxide are the major functions of the respiratory system. These processes occur in two successive phases of functioning—breathing and transporting gases. In order to effectively exchange the gases involved in respiration, a large surface area is required. There are 300 million to 400 million alveoli in each lung. The air sacs of both lungs have a total surface area of about 93 $m^2$, nearly 50 times the total surface area of the skin.

### Diseases and Disorders of the Respiratory System

Many diseases and disorders affect the health of the human respiratory system and interfere with its effectiveness. Allergies affect so many people that pollen counts of the atmosphere are reported in the media. The worst allergens include the pollen of wind-pollinated trees, grasses, and ragweed, and air pollutants.

Pneumonia is the term used to describe any condition that results in alveoli filling up with fluid. It can be caused by a number of different factors, including chemicals, bacteria, viruses, or fungi. Blood infections, chronic alcoholism, inhalation of fluids into the lungs, or even prolonged bed rest can predispose a person to infection of the lungs by microorganisms. Chronic smoking has the potential to promote emphysema and lung cancer.

### Teacher to Teacher
Jeff Remington
Palmyra Middle School
Palmyra, PA

"To sensitize students to breathing problems such as asthma or emphysema, I have them exercise for a minute then count the number of breaths they take per minute. After they recover, they repeat the same procedure using a straw to breathe through. They have to breathe shallow and fast when using the straw, much like a person with a breathing disorder might have."

*Jeff Remington*

## section 4 The Excretory System
### The Urinary System

The metabolic processes of the body produce waste products. The respiratory system rids the body of carbon dioxide and other waste gases. The digestive system eliminates solid wastes. The urinary system removes a variety of dissolved salts and nitrogenous wastes from the blood and lymph systems.

The major organs of the respiratory system are a pair of bean-shaped structures called kidneys, each of which is approximately 10 cm long and 5 cm wide. They weigh about 170 g each. The functioning unit of the kidney is the nephron. All of the blood in the body flows through the kidneys about once every five minutes.

### Urinary Diseases and Disorders

Urinary tract infections are common, second only to respiratory infections. Normally urine is sterile. An infection occurs when microbes, usually bacteria from the digestive tract, adhere to the opening of the urethra and begin to multiply. Most urinary tract infections can be traced to one type of colon bacteria, *Escherichia coli* (*E. coli*). Often the bacteria move from the urethra to the bladder causing a bladder infection. Such infections are usually treated with specific antibacterial drugs.

## Chapter Vocabulary

nutrient, p. 128
enzyme, p. 128
peristalsis, p. 130
chyme, p. 131
villi, p. 131
amino acid, p. 133
carbohydrate, p. 134
vitamin, p. 135
mineral, p. 136
larynx, p. 142
trachea, p. 142
bronchi, p. 142
alveoli, p. 142
nephron, p. 149
ureter, p. 149
bladder, p. 149

**Science Journal** Student responses will vary but may include drinking fluids, eating, resting, and taking a shower.

**INTERACTIVE CHALKBOARD with Image Bank**

**PowerPoint® Presentations**

This CD-ROM is an editable Microsoft® PowerPoint® presentation that includes:
- a pre-made presentation for every chapter
- interactive graphics
- animations
- audio clips
- image bank
- all new section and chapter questions
- Standardized Test Practice
- transparencies
- pre-lab questions for all labs
- Foldables directions
- links to in7.msscience.com

**Academic Standard—4:** Students begin to trace the flow of matter and energy through ecosystems. They recognize the fundamental difference between plants and animals and understand its basis at the cellular level. Students distinguish species, particularly through an examination of internal structures and functions. They use microscopes to observe cells and recognize that cells function in similar ways in all organisms.

**Also covers:** Academic Standards 1, 2, 5, 7 (Detailed standards begin on page IN8.)

# Digestion, Respiration, and Excretion

## chapter preview

### sections

**1** The Digestive System

**2** Nutrition
  *Lab* Identifying Vitamin C Content

**3** The Respiratory System

**4** The Excretory System
  *Lab* Particle Size and Absorption

⊙ *Virtual Lab* How do the parts of the respiratory system work together?

### Playing soccer is hard work.

If you're like most people, when you play an active game like soccer you probably breathe hard and perspire. You need a constant supply of oxygen and energy to keep your body cells functioning. Your body is adapted to meet that need.

**Science Journal** Write a paragraph describing what you do to help your body recover after an active game.

## Theme Connection

**Energy** A major theme in this chapter is energy. Nutrients contain chemical energy. During digestion, complex food molecules are broken down into simpler forms that body cells can use for metabolism. Human cells require oxygen in order to utilize nutrients and provide energy for cellular activities. Chemical energy is transformed into thermal and mechanical energy.

### About the Photo

**Using Energy** To play active games, the human body requires energy. Deep breaths during physical activity provide the body's cells with oxygen. Perspiring cools the body and helps get rid of wastes. The respiratory and excretory systems work together to help the body maintain homeostasis.

# Start-Up Activities

## Breathing Rate

Your body can store food and water, but it cannot store much oxygen. Breathing brings oxygen into your body. In the following lab, find out about one factor that can change your breathing rate.

1. Put your hand on the side of your rib cage. Using a watch or clock with a second hand, count the number of breaths you take for 15 s. Multiply this number by four to calculate your normal breathing rate for one minute.

2. Repeat step 1 two more times, then calculate your average breathing rate.

3. Do a physical activity described by your teacher for one minute and repeat step 1 to determine your breathing rate now.

4. Time how long it takes for your breathing rate to return to normal.

5. **Think Critically** In your Science Journal, write a paragraph explaining how breathing rate appears to be related to physical activity.

**Respiration** Make the following Foldable to help identify what you already know, what you want to know, and what you learn about respiration.

**STEP 1** Fold a vertical sheet of paper from side to side. Make the front edge about 1.25 cm shorter than the back edge.

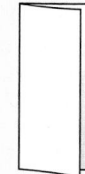

**STEP 2** Turn lengthwise and **fold** into thirds.

**STEP 3** Unfold and cut only the top layer along both folds to make three tabs. Label each tab.

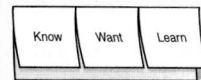

Know | Want | Learn

**Identify Questions** Before you read the chapter, write *I breathe* under the left tab, and write *Why do I breathe?* under the center tab. As you read the chapter, write the answer you learn under the right tab.

Preview this chapter's content and activities at in7.msscience.com

**Purpose** Students are introduced to the respiratory system. Students will discover how the respiratory system responds to physical activity. L2 ELL
LS **Kinesthetic**

**Preparation** Ask your school nurse if there are any students in your class who should not jog or engage in activities that stress the heart and respiratory system.

**Materials** watch or a clock with second hand, calculator

### Teaching Strategies
• Any students not able to participate in the physical part of this activity can be designated as timekeepers or recorders.
• Review the reason for multiplying by four to obtain the pulse rate for one minute.

## Think Critically
Breathing rates increase after physical activity.

## Assessment
**Performance** Have students design another activity that will result in an increase in breathing rate, do the activity, and gather the data. Use **Performance Assessment in the Science Classroom,** p. 105.

 **Dinah Zike Study Fold**

Student preparation materials for this Foldable are available in the **Chapter FAST FILE Resources.**

127

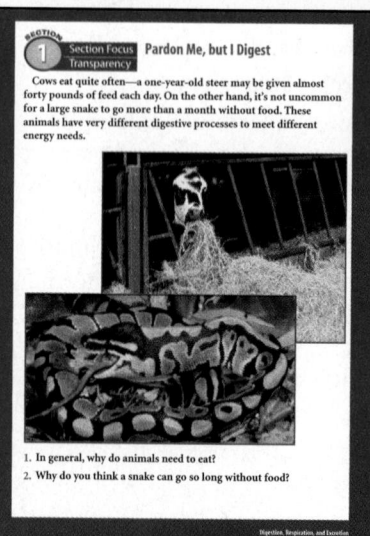
**Standards—7.4.4:** ... various organs and tissues function to serve the needs of cells for food ...
**7.4.6:** Explain how food provides the fuel ... for all organisms. **7.4.8:** Describe how organisms that eat plants break down the plant structures to produce the materials and energy that they need to survive ...

## section 1

# The Digestive System

### as you read

*What* You'll Learn

- **Distinguish** the differences between mechanical digestion and chemical digestion.
- **Identify** the organs of the digestive system and what takes place in each.
- **Explain** how homeostasis is maintained in digestion.

*Why* It's Important

The processes of the digestive system make the food you eat available to your cells.

**Review Vocabulary**
**bacteria:** one-celled organisms without membrane-bound organelles

**New Vocabulary**
- nutrient
- enzyme
- peristalsis
- chyme
- villi

## Functions of the Digestive System

Food is processed in your body in four stages—ingestion, digestion, absorption, and elimination. Whether it is a piece of fruit or an entire meal, all the food you eat is treated to the same processes in your body. As soon as food enters your mouth, or is ingested, digestion begins. Digestion breaks down food so that nutrients (NEW tree unts) can be absorbed and moved into the blood. **Nutrients** are substances in food that provide energy and materials for cell development, growth, and repair. From the blood, these nutrients are transported across the cell membrane to be used by the cell. Unused substances pass out of your body as wastes.

Digestion is mechanical and chemical. Mechanical digestion takes place when food is chewed, mixed, and churned. Chemical digestion occurs when chemical reactions break down food.

## Enzymes

Chemical digestion is possible only because of enzymes (EN zimez). An **enzyme** is a type of protein that speeds up the rate of a chemical reaction in your body. One way enzymes speed up reactions is by reducing the amount of energy necessary for a chemical reaction to begin. If enzymes weren't there to help, the rate of chemical reactions would be too slow. Some reactions might not even happen at all. As shown in **Figure 1**, enzymes work without being changed or used up.

**Figure 1** Enzymes speed up the rate of certain body reactions.
**Explain** *what happens to the enzyme after it separates from the new molecule.*

**128 CHAPTER 5** Digestion, Respiration, and Excretion

---

### Section 1 Resource Manager

**Chapter FAST FILE Resources**
Transparency Activity, p. 46
Enrichment, p. 31
Reinforcement, p. 27
Directed Reading, p. 20
Lab Activity, pp. 9–12

**Cultural Diversity,** pp. 15–16
**Performance Assessment in the Science Classroom,** pp. 66–67
**Reading and Writing Skill Activities,** pp. 37–38

**Enzymes in Digestion** Many enzymes help you digest carbohydrates, proteins, and fats. These enzymes are produced in the salivary glands, stomach, small intestine, and pancreas.

**Reading Check** *What is the role of enzymes in the chemical digestion of food?*

**Other Enzyme Actions** Enzyme-aided reactions are not limited to the digestive process. Enzymes also help speed up chemical reactions responsible for building your body. They are involved in the energy-releasing activities of your muscle and nerve cells. Enzymes also aid in the blood-clotting process. Without enzymes, the chemical reactions in your body would happen too slowly for you to exist.

## Organs of the Digestive System

Your digestive system has two parts—the digestive tract and the accessory organs. The major organs of your digestive tract—mouth, esophagus (ih SAH fuh gus), stomach, small intestine, large intestine, rectum, and anus—are shown in **Figure 2.** Food passes through all of these organs. The tongue, teeth, salivary glands, liver, gallbladder, and pancreas, also shown in **Figure 2,** are the accessory organs. Although food doesn't pass through them, they are important in mechanical and chemical digestion. Your liver, gallbladder, and pancreas produce or store enzymes and other chemicals that help break down food as it passes through the digestive tract.

Salivary glands — Tongue
Esophagus
Liver
Stomach
Pancreas
Gallbladder
Small intestine
Large intestine
Rectum
Anus

**Figure 2** The human digestive system can be described as a tube divided into several specialized sections. If stretched out, an adult's digestive system is 6 m to 9 m long.

**Reading Check**

**Answer** to speed up the rate of chemical digestion

### Quick Demo

**Enzymes**

**Materials** two cubes of beef, meat tenderizer, sugar, oven, plastic fork, cooking pan

**Estimated Time** 20 minutes

**Procedure** Sprinkle some meat tenderizer on a small cube of beef. (Meat tenderizers often contain the enzyme papain, which is made from papaya juice.) On another cube of beef, sprinkle some sugar. Heat both pieces in an oven at 250°F until brown. When cooled, have students examine both pieces and probe with a plastic fork to compare tenderness.

## Visual Learning

**Figure 2** Tell students that the small intestine is 4 m to 7 m in length. Use the diagram to reinforce how an organ of this length can be contained within the body.

### Discussion

**Characteristics of Enzymes** What characteristics of enzymes enable them to affect chemical reactions within the body? Enzymes remain unchanged by their activity; they are effective in small amounts; they speed up chemical change; and they are specific in the chemicals that they effect.

**IS Linguistic**

## Differentiated Instruction

**Visually Impaired and Learning Disabled** Cut from a foam-core board pairs of shapes that fit together as shown in **Figure 1.** Mix up several pairs and have students find the enzyme for the molecule by matching the shapes. Compare the matching of shapes to a key fitting in a lock or pieces of a puzzle fitting together. L1 **IS Kinesthetic**

## Curriculum Connection

**Language Arts** In one of Robert Frost's poems, he describes a rotting woodpile as the "smokeless burning of decay." Have students compare this to the oxidation of foods that is part of the digestive system. L3 **IS Linguistic**

## IDENTIFYING
# Misconceptions

**Peristalsis** Students may think that peristalsis cannot occur in the "weightless" environment of a spacecraft. Because peristalsis is an action controlled by muscles, the lack of gravity does not affect swallowing and the movement of food through the digestive system.

## Teacher FYI

**Animal Digestive Systems** The digestive systems of various animals reflect their lifestyles and diets. Birds have a specialized stomach chamber, the gizzard, that contains small stones. These stones aid in grinding food—a process that is needed in the absence of teeth. Mammals that subsist on grasses have stomach storage pouches or more than one stomach in which their food is ground more thoroughly for subsequent bacterial action.

**Figure 3** About 1.5 L of saliva are produced each day by salivary glands in your mouth. **Describe** *what happens in your mouth when you think about a food you like.*

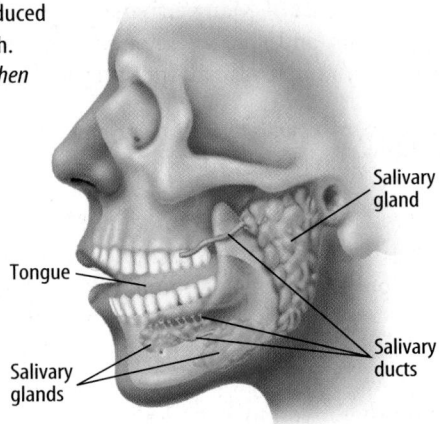

**The Mouth** Mechanical and chemical digestion begin in your mouth. Mechanical digestion happens when you chew your food with your teeth and mix it with your tongue. Chemical digestion begins with the addition of a watery substance called saliva (suh LI vuh), which contains water, mucus, and an enzyme that aids in the breakdown of starch into sugar. Saliva is produced by three sets of glands near your mouth, shown in **Figure 3.** Food mixed with saliva becomes a soft mass and is moved to the back of your mouth by your tongue. It is swallowed and passes into your esophagus. Now ingestion is complete, but the process of digestion continues.

**The Esophagus** Food moving into the esophagus passes over a flap of tissue called the epiglottis (eh puh GLAH tus). This structure automatically covers the opening to the windpipe to prevent food from entering it, otherwise you would choke. Your esophagus is a muscular tube about 25 cm long. No digestion takes place in the esophagus. Smooth muscles in the wall of the esophagus move food downward with a squeezing action. These waves of muscle contractions, called **peristalsis** (per uh STAHL sus), move food through the entire digestive tract. Secretions from the mucous glands in the wall of the esophagus keep food moist.

**The Stomach** The stomach is a muscular bag. When empty, it is somewhat sausage shaped with folds on the inside. As food enters from the esophagus, the stomach expands and the folds smooth out. Mechanical and chemical digestion take place here. Mechanically, food is mixed in the stomach by peristalsis. Chemically, food is mixed with enzymes and strong digestive solutions, such as hydrochloric acid solution, to help break it down.

## Active Reading

**Metacognition Journal** In this strategy, each student analyzes his or her own thought processes. Have students divide the paper in half. On the left, have them record what they have learned about a topic. On the right, have them record the reason they learned it. Have students write a Metacognition Journal about the digestive system.

Specialized cells in the stomach's walls release about two liters of hydrochloric acid solution each day. This solution works with the enzyme pepsin to digest protein and destroys bacteria that are present in food. The stomach also produces mucus, which makes food more slippery and protects the stomach from the strong, digestive solutions. Food is changed in the stomach into a thin, watery liquid called **chyme** (KIME). Slowly, chyme moves out of your stomach and into your small intestine.

**✔ Reading Check** *Why isn't your stomach digested by the acidic digestive solution?*

**The Small Intestine** Your small intestine, shown in **Figure 4,** is small in diameter, but it measures 4 m to 7 m in length. As chyme leaves your stomach, it enters the first part of your small intestine, called the duodenum (doo AH duh num). Most digestion takes place in your duodenum. Here, bile—a greenish fluid from the liver—is added. The acidic solution from the stomach makes large fat particles float to the top of the chyme. Bile breaks up the large fat particles, similar to the way detergent breaks up grease.

Chemical digestion of carbohydrates, proteins, and fats occurs when a digestive solution from the pancreas is mixed in. This solution contains bicarbonate ions and enzymes. The bicarbonate ions help neutralize the stomach acid that is mixed with chyme. Your pancreas also makes insulin, a hormone that allows glucose to pass from the bloodstream into your cells.

Absorption of broken down food takes place in the small intestine. The wall of the small intestine, shown in **Figure 4,** has many ridges and folds. These folds are covered with fingerlike projections called **villi** (VIH li). Villi increase the surface area of the small intestine, which allows more places for nutrients to be absorbed. Nutrients move into blood vessels within the villi. From here, blood transports the nutrients to all cells of your body. Peristalsis continues to force the remaining undigested and unabsorbed materials slowly into the large intestine.

**Indiana Academic Standard Check**

7.4.4: Explain . . . that various organs and tissues function to serve the needs of cells for food . . .

✔ Which organ absorbs broken food before it is transported by blood to cells?

✔ small intestine

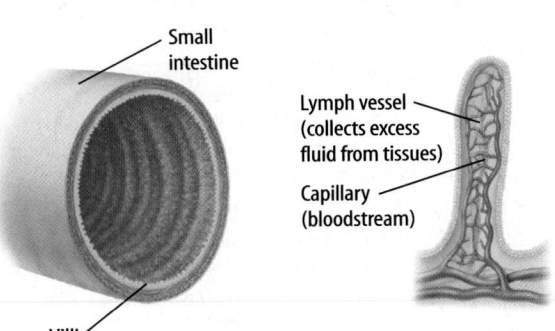

Small intestine

Lymph vessel (collects excess fluid from tissues)

Capillary (bloodstream)

Villi

**Figure 4** Hundreds of thousands of densely packed villi give the impression of a velvet cloth surface. If the surface area of your villi could be stretched out, it would cover an area the size of a tennis court.
**Infer** *what would happen to a person's weight if the number of villi were drastically reduced. Why?*

# Differentiated Instruction

**Challenge** Have students demonstrate the chemical process involved in neutralizing an acid. First have them use litmus paper to test a vinegar solution (5 mL in 100 mL water) and a baking soda solution (5 mL in 100 mL water). After the two solutions are combined, have students again test to show that the combined solution is no longer acidic or basic. Note: The reaction will produce bubbles of carbon dioxide gas. L3

**Large Intestine Bacteria** The bacteria might die, ending the breakdown of materials and the production of certain vitamins.

**Research** Have students research types of bacteria that live in extreme environments. Some live without oxygen or in very salty or very hot habitats. Students can design a comic strip about the environment of one type of these bacteria.

## 3 Assess

DAILY INTERVENTION

### Check for Understanding

**Linguistic** Have students prepare a two-column chart that lists these parts of the digestive system in the first column: mouth, stomach, small intestine, and large intestine, and the function of each in the second column. L1

### Reteach

**Enzyme Models** Have each student construct a three-dimensional model of an enzyme and demonstrate how it works. L3

### ✓ Assessment

**Oral** Have students suggest what might happen to digestion and nutrition in people who have lost their teeth. Use **Performance Assessment in the Science Classroom**, p. 93.

**Large Intestine Bacteria** The species of bacteria that live in your large intestine are adapted to their habitat. What do you think would happen to the bacteria if their environment were to change? How would this affect your large intestine? Discuss your ideas with a classmate and write your answers in your Science Journal.

**The Large Intestine** When the chyme enters the large intestine, it is still a thin, watery mixture. The large intestine absorbs water from the undigested mass, which helps maintain homeostasis (hoh mee oh STAY sus). Peristalsis usually slows down in the large intestine. After the excess water is absorbed, the remaining undigested materials become more solid. Muscles in the rectum, which is the last section of the large intestine, and the anus control the release of semisolid wastes from the body in the form of feces (FEE seez).

## Bacteria Are Important

Many types of bacteria live in your body. Some bacteria live in many of the organs of your digestive tract including your mouth and large intestine. Some of these bacteria live in a relationship that is beneficial to the bacteria and to your body. The bacteria in your large intestine feed on undigested material like cellulose and make vitamins you need—vitamin K and two B vitamins. Vitamin K is needed for blood clotting. The two B vitamins, niacin and thiamine, are important for your nervous system and for other body functions. Bacterial action also converts bile pigments into new compounds. The breakdown of intestinal materials by bacteria produces gas.

### section 1 review

#### Summary

**Functions of the Digestive System**
● Food is processed in four stages—ingestion, digestion, absorption, and elimination.

**Enzymes**
● Enzymes make chemical digestion possible.
● Enzymes are used in other chemical reactions, including blood clotting.

**Organs of the Digestive System**
● In the digestive system, food passes through the mouth, esophagus, stomach, small intestine, large intestine, rectum, and anus.
● Accessory digestive organs help in mechanical and chemical digestion.

**Bacteria Are Important**
● Some bacteria that live in the organs of the digestive tract are helpful to your body.

#### Self Check

1. **Compare and contrast** mechanical digestion and chemical digestion.
2. **Describe** the function of each organ through which food passes as it moves through the digestive tract.
3. **Explain** how activities in the large intestine help maintain homeostasis.
4. **Describe** how the accessory organs aid digestion.
5. **Think Critically** Crackers contain starch. Explain why a cracker begins to taste sweet after it is in your mouth for five minutes without being chewed.

##### Applying Skills

6. **Recognize Cause and Effect** What would happen to some of the nutrients in chyme if the pancreas did not secrete its solution into the small intestine?
7. **Communicate** Write a paragraph in your Science Journal explaining what would happen to the mechanical and chemical digestion in a person missing a large portion of his or her stomach.

Science Online in7.msscience.com/self_check_quiz

### section 1 review

1. Both break down food for use by the body. Mechanical digestion involves cutting, grinding, tearing, and crushing by teeth and moving of food by the tongue and peristalsis. Chemical digestion involves the chemical breakdown of food into usable materials.

2. mouth: ingestion, mechanical and chemical digestion; esophagus: moves food into stomach; stomach: mechanical and chemical digestion; small intestine: chemical digestion, absorption; large intestine: absorption; rectum and anus: excretion

3. water is removed from wastes and returned to the body

4. The liver produces digestive juices and bile to break up fat particles. The pancreas also produces digestive juices.

5. Complex carbohydrates in the cracker are broken down into simple sugars by saliva.

6. Food would be acidic in the remainder of the digestive tract, possibly causing ulcers.

7. Journal entries should reflect that both churning action and the digestion of proteins are probably reduced because the stomach is not as large as it was.

# section 2

Also covers: 7.4.2, 7.4.4, 7.4.11 (Detailed standards begin on page IN8.)

# Nutrition

**1 Motivate**

## Why do you eat?

You might choose a food because of its taste, because it's readily available, or quickly prepared. However, as much as you don't want to admit it, the nutritional value of and Calories in foods are more important. A Calorie is a measurement of the amount of energy available in food. The amount of food energy a person requires varies with body weight, age, sex, activity level, and natural body efficiency. A chocolate donut might be tasty, quick to eat, and provide plenty of Calories, but it has only some of the nutrients that your body needs.

## Classes of Nutrients

Six kinds of nutrients are available in food—proteins, carbohydrates, fats, vitamins, minerals, and water. Proteins, carbohydrates, vitamins, and fats all contain carbon and are called organic nutrients. Inorganic nutrients, such as water and minerals, do not contain carbon. Foods containing carbohydrates, fats, and proteins need to be digested or broken down before your body can use them. Water, vitamins, and minerals don't require digestion and are absorbed directly into your bloodstream.

**Proteins** Your body uses proteins for replacement and repair of body cells and for growth. Proteins are large molecules that contain carbon, hydrogen, oxygen, nitrogen, and sometimes sulfur. A molecule of protein is made up of a large number of smaller units, or building blocks, called **amino acids.** You can see some sources of proteins in **Figure 5.**

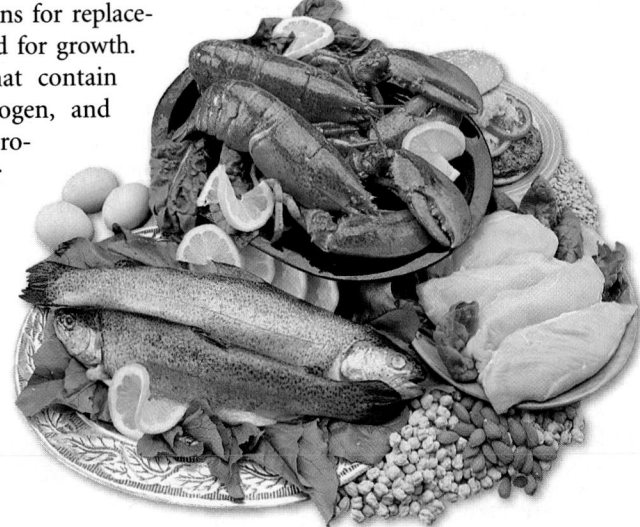

**Figure 5** Meats, poultry, eggs, fish, peas, beans, and nuts are all rich in protein.

### as you read

*What* You'll Learn
- **Distinguish** among the six classes of nutrients.
- **Identify** the importance of each type of nutrient.
- **Explain** the relationship between diet and health.

*Why* It's Important
You can make healthful food choices if you know what nutrients your body uses daily.

🔎 **Review Vocabulary**
**molecule:** the smallest particle of a substance that retains the properties of the substance and is composed of one or more atoms

**New Vocabulary**
- amino acid
- carbohydrate
- vitamin
- mineral

**1 Motivate**

**Bellringer**

**Section Focus Transparencies** also are available on the Interactive Chalkboard CD-ROM.

L2 ELL

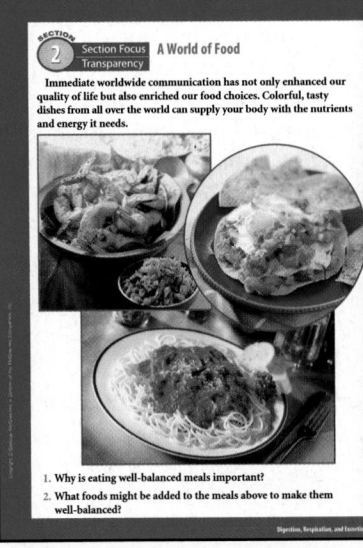

### Tie to Prior Knowledge

**Balanced Diet** Have students discuss what they know about eating a "balanced" diet.

SECTION 2 Nutrition **133**

## Section 2 Resource Manager

**Chapter *FAST FILE* Resources**
- Transparency Activity, p. 47
- MiniLAB, p. 3
- Enrichment, p. 32
- Reinforcement, p. 28
- Directed Reading, p. 20
- Lab Worksheet, pp. 5–6

**Life Science Critical Thinking/Problem Solving,** p. 15
**Laboratory Management and Safety,** p. 69
**Mathematics Skill Activities,** pp. 47–48

## Quick Demo

**Energy in Fat**

**Materials** Brazil nut, pecan, and whole peanut, safety goggles, apron, matches, needle, cork, metal pan, stopwatch or clock with second hand

**Estimated Time** 10 minutes

**Procedure** Observe safety precautions for sharp objects, flames, eye safety, and clothing protection. Insert the sharp end of a needle into one of the nuts. Push the eye of the needle into a cork. Stand the entire apparatus in a metal pan. Ignite the nut and have students observe the length of time the nut burns. Repeat with the other types of nuts, and have students compare the burning times.

## Discussion

**Why You Eat** Are you what you eat? The food you eat supplies materials for the production of new cells, which become part of your body. It also supplies energy, which allows you to do the things you like to do.

## Activity

**Discovering Unique Protein and Carbohydrate Sources** Have students research unique sources of proteins and carbohydrates used in different countries. Make labels with the food names and place them in the proper geographic locations on a world map. Examples include amaranth in South America and Africa and taro root in the Pacific Islands. [L1] [IS] **Visual-Spatial**

## Caption Answer

**Figure 6** Carbohydrates are the main source of energy for your body.

**Science Online**

**Topic: Fiber**

Visit in7.msscience.com for Web links to recent news or magazine articles about the importance of fiber in your diet.

**Activity** In your Science Journal, classify your favorite foods into two groups—*Good source of fiber* and *Little or no fiber*.

---

**Indiana Academic Standard Check**

**7.4.8:** Describe how organisms that eat plants break down plant structures to produce the materials and energy that they need to survive . . .

✔ What complex carbohydrate is in plant cell walls and what is its function in human diets?

✔ cellulose; provides dietary fiber

**Figure 6** These foods contain carbohydrates that provide energy for all the things that you do. **Describe** *the role of carbohydrates in your body.*

**Protein Building Blocks** Your body needs only 20 amino acids in various combinations to make the thousands of proteins used in your cells. Most of these amino acids can be made in your body's cells, but eight of them cannot. These eight are called essential amino acids. They have to be supplied by the foods you eat. Complete proteins provide all of the essential amino acids. Eggs, milk, cheese, and meat contain complete proteins. Incomplete proteins are missing one or more of the essential amino acids. If you are a vegetarian, you can get all of the essential amino acids by eating a wide variety of protein-rich vegetables, fruits, and grains.

**Carbohydrates** Study the nutrition label on several boxes of cereal. You'll notice that the number of grams of carbohydrates found in a typical serving of cereal is higher than the amounts of the other nutrients. **Carbohydrates** (kar boh HI drayts) usually are the main sources of energy for your body.

Three types of carbohydrates are sugar, starch, and fiber, shown in **Figure 6.** Sugars are called simple carbohydrates. You're probably most familiar with table sugar. However, fruits, honey, and milk also contain forms of sugar. Your cells break down glucose, a simple sugar.

The other two types of carbohydrates—starch and fiber—are called complex carbohydrates. Starch is found in potatoes and foods made from grains such as pasta. Starches are made up of many simple sugars. Fiber, such as cellulose, is found in the cell walls of plant cells. Foods like whole-grain breads and cereals, beans, peas, and other vegetables and fruits are good sources of fiber. Because different types of fiber are found in foods, you should eat a variety of fiber-rich plant foods. You cannot digest fiber, but it is needed to keep your digestive system running smoothly.

**Fats** The term *fat* has developed a negative meaning for some people. However, fats, also called lipids, are necessary because they provide energy and help your body absorb vitamins. Fat tissue cushions your internal organs. A major part of every cell membrane is made up of a type of fat.

---

# Differentiated Instruction

**Learning Disabled** Ask students to list the simple and complex carbohydrates they ate during the last 24 hours. Ask each student to analyze the length of the two lists and write answers to these questions: Do I eat more simple or complex carbohydrates? How could I improve my diet? Eat fewer simple carbohydrates. [L1] [IS] **Linguistic**

# Curriculum Connection

**History** The extraction of sugar from sugarcane is an ancient practice. Sugarcane grass was first discovered either in the South Pacific or in India. It most likely spread to Europe via Chinese and Arab traders. Have students research how and when sugarcane was brought to the Americas.

Nucleus

Fat deposit

Cytoplasm

**Figure 7** Fat is stored in certain cells in your body. Fat deposits push the cytoplasm and nucleus to the edge of the cell.

A gram of fat can release more than twice as much energy as a gram of carbohydrate can. Because fat is a good storage unit for energy, excess energy from the foods you eat is converted to fat and stored for later use, as shown in **Figure 7.**

☑ **Reading Check** *Why is fat a good storage unit for energy?*

Fats are classified as unsaturated or saturated based on their chemical structure. Unsaturated fats are usually liquid at room temperature. Vegetable oils as well as fats found in seeds are unsaturated fats. Saturated fats are found in meats, animal products, and some plants and are usually solid at room temperature. Saturated fats have been associated with high levels of blood cholesterol. Your body makes cholesterol in your liver. Cholesterol is part of the cell membrane in all of your cells. However, a diet high in cholesterol may result in deposits forming on the inside walls of blood vessels. These deposits can block the blood supply to organs and increase blood pressure. This can lead to heart disease and strokes.

**Vitamins** Your bone cells need vitamin D to use calcium, and your blood needs vitamin K in order to clot. **Vitamins** are organic nutrients needed in small quantities for growth, regulating body functions, and preventing some diseases.

Vitamins are classified into two groups. Some vitamins dissolve easily in water and are called water-soluble vitamins. They are not stored by your body so you have to take them daily. Other vitamins dissolve only in fat and are called fat-soluble vitamins. These vitamins are stored by your body. Although you eat or drink most vitamins, some are made by your body. Vitamin D is made when your skin is exposed to sunlight. Recall that vitamin K and two of the B vitamins are made in your large intestine with the help of bacteria that live there.

### Mini LAB

**Comparing the Fat Content of Foods**

**Procedure** 🤚 🔪 ⓧ 🔬

1. Collect three pieces of each of the following foods: **potato chips; pretzels; peanuts;** and **small cubes of fruits, cheese, vegetables,** and **meat.**
2. Place the food items on a piece of **brown grocery bag.** Label the paper with the name of each food. Do not taste the foods.
3. Allow foods to sit for 30 min.
4. Remove the items, properly dispose of them, and observe the paper.

**Analysis**

1. Which items left a translucent (greasy) mark? Which left a wet mark?
2. How are the foods that left a greasy mark on the paper alike?
3. Use this test to determine which other foods contain fats. A greasy mark means the food contains fat. A wet mark means the food contains a lot of water.

SECTION 2 Nutrition **135**

**Reading Check**

**Answer** gram of fat can release twice as much energy as a gram of carbohydrate

### Mini LAB

**Purpose** Students test for fats in foods. L1 ELL IS **Kinesthetic**

**Materials** 3 potato chips, pretzels, and peanuts; small cubes of fruits, cheeses, vegetables, and meat; brown craft paper or brown paper bag

**Teaching Strategy** Point out the difference between a water mark and a greasy mark.

**Safety Precaution** Use only cooked meat.

**Analysis**

1. Potato chips, peanuts, cheeses, and meat will leave a translucent mark. Pretzels may leave a greasy mark if they are fresh. Fruits and vegetables will leave a wet mark.
2. They have some fat content.
3. Other foods that contain fat include butter, oils, and many crackers and chips.

### Assessment

**Process** Have students test an unknown food item for fat. Use **Performance Assessment in the Science Classroom,** p. 97.

---

# Differentiated Instruction

**Challenge** Have students research and report on a particular vitamin deficiency. Their reports should include information about how the vitamin was discovered, the symptoms of a deficiency, and foods that are high in the vitamin. Have students work together to present their findings on a "Vitamins for Good Health" bulletin board. L3 COOP LEARN IS **Linguistic**

# Science Journal

**Taking Your Vitamins** Have students write a paragraph about why it might be a disadvantage to substitute vitamin pills for a proper diet. Their entries should indicate an understanding that other nutrients besides vitamins are needed for maintaining health. A well-balanced diet supplies the range of needed vitamins. L2 IS **Logical-Mathematical**

**Table 1 Minerals**

| Mineral | Health Effect | Food Sources |
|---------|---------------|--------------|
| Calcium | strong bones and teeth, blood clotting, muscle and nerve activity | dairy products, eggs, green leafy vegetables, soy |
| Phosphorus | strong bones and teeth, muscle contraction, stores energy | cheese, meat, cereal |
| Potassium | balance of water in cells, nerve impulse conduction, muscle contraction | bananas, potatoes, nuts, meat, oranges |
| Sodium | fluid balance in tissues, nerve impulse conduction | meat, milk, cheese, salt, beets, carrots, nearly all foods |
| Iron | oxygen is transported in hemoglobin by red blood cells | red meat, raisins, beans, spinach, eggs |
| Iodine (trace) | thyroid activity, metabolic stimulation | seafood, iodized salt |

INTEGRATE
Social Studies

**Salt Mines** The mineral halite is processed to make table salt. In the United States, most salt comes from underground mines. Research to find the location of these mines, then label them on a map.

**Indiana Academic Standard Check**

7.4.6: Explain how food provides the fuel and the building material for all organisms.

✔ What mineral comes from seafood and is needed for thyroid activity?

✔ iodine

**Minerals** Inorganic nutrients—nutrients that lack carbon and regulate many chemical reactions in your body—are called **minerals.** Of about 14 minerals that your body uses, calcium and phosphorus are used in the largest amounts for a variety of body functions. One of these functions is the formation and maintenance of bone. Some minerals, called trace minerals, are required only in small amounts. Copper and iodine usually are listed as trace minerals. Minerals are not used by the body as a source of energy. However, they do serve many different functions. Several minerals, their health effects, and some food sources for them are listed in **Table 1.**

### ✔ Reading Check  *Why is copper considered a trace mineral?*

**Water** Next to oxygen, water is the most important factor for survival. Different organisms need different amounts of water to survive. You could live for a few weeks without food but for only a few days without water because your cells need water to carry out their work. Most of the nutrients you have studied in this chapter can't be used by your body unless they are carried in a solution. This means that they have to be dissolved in water. In cells, chemical reactions take place in solutions.

**136  CHAPTER 5** Digestion, Respiration, and Excretion

The human body is about 60 percent water by mass. About two-thirds of your body water is located in your body cells. Water also is found around cells and in body fluids such as blood. **Table 2** shows how your body loses water every day. To replace water lost each day, you need to drink about 2 L of liquids. However, drinking liquids isn't the only way to supply cells with water. Most foods have more water than you realize. An apple is about 80 percent water, and many meats are 90 percent water.

**Why do you get thirsty?** Your body is made up of systems that operate together. When your body needs to replace lost water, messages are sent to your brain that result in a feeling of thirst. Drinking water satisfies your thirst and usually restores the body's homeostasis. When homeostasis is restored, the signal to the brain stops and you no longer feel thirsty.

## Food Groups

Because no naturally occurring food has every nutrient, you need to eat a variety of foods. Nutritionists have developed a simple system, called the food pyramid, shown in **Figure 8,** to help people select foods that supply all the nutrients needed for energy and growth. The recommended daily amount for each food group will supply your body with the nutrients it needs for good health.

| Table 2  Water Loss | |
|---|---|
| Method of Loss | Amount (mL/day) |
| Exhaled air | 350 |
| Feces | 150 |
| Skin (mostly as sweat) | 500 |
| Urine | 1,500 |

**Figure 8** The pyramid shape reminds you that you should consume more servings from the bread and cereal group than from other groups.
**Analyze** *Where should the least number of servings come from?*

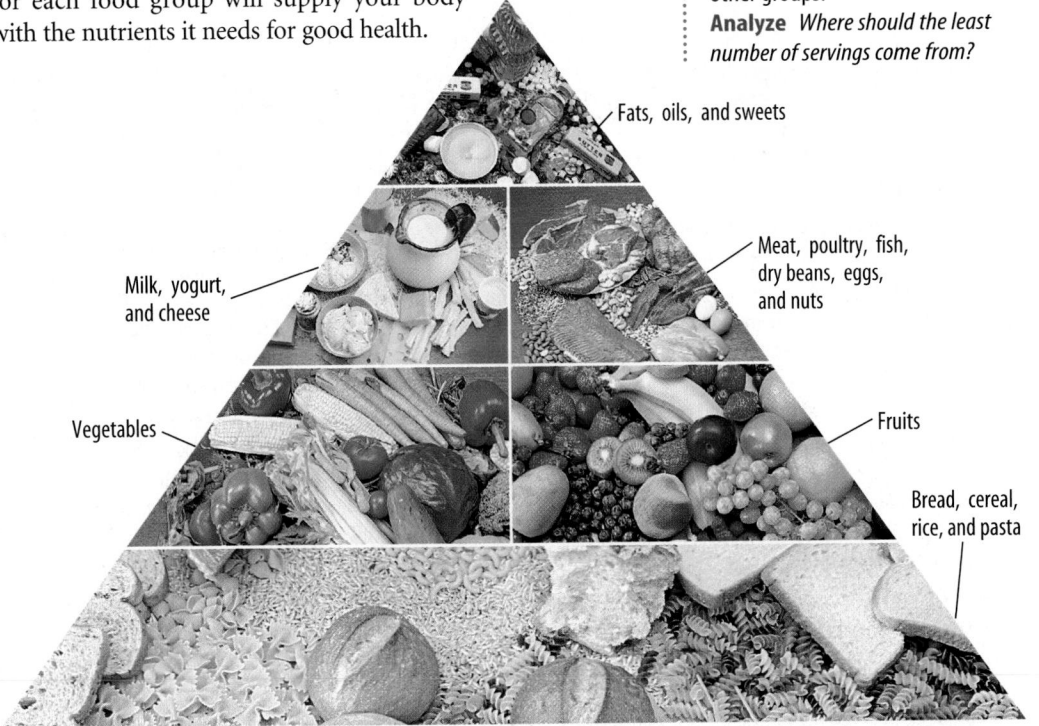

Fats, oils, and sweets

Milk, yogurt, and cheese

Meat, poultry, fish, dry beans, eggs, and nuts

Vegetables

Fruits

Bread, cereal, rice, and pasta

SECTION 2 Nutrition **137**

**Use an Analogy**

**Perspiration and Transpiration** Perspiration of water from the body is like the transpiration of water from plants. In both animals and plants, excessive water loss can have profoundly negative effects on the health of the organism.

**Make a Model**

**Food Pyramid** Have students work together to make a three-dimensional display of the food pyramid using empty food packages to represent food groups. **L2 ELL** COOP LEARN **LS Kinesthetic**

**Caption Answer**

**Figure 8** from fats, oils, sweets group at the top of the pyramid

## LAB DEMONSTRATION

**Purpose** to measure the water content of food
**Materials** pan balance, 250-mL beaker, sliced celery, tray
**Preparation** Use the pan balance to find the mass of the beaker.
**Procedure** Fill the beaker with celery and find its mass. Spread the celery on the tray to dry for 2 or 3 days, then mass the celery again.
**Expected Outcome** Students should find that dried celery has much less mass than fresh celery. Have them calculate the percentage of celery that is water.

**Assessment**

Why was the beaker massed when empty? so its mass could be subtracted from the mass of the beaker and celery Infer how much water might be in other fresh vegetables. Answers will vary. Leafy vegetables have more water than hard vegetables such as broccoli.

SECTION 2 Nutrition **137**

## DAILY INTERVENTION

### Check for Understanding

**Visual-Spatial** Have students make flash cards with names of fruits and vegetables. On the reverse side, have them identify the major vitamin content of each food. Students can test each other using the flash cards. L1

### Reteach

**Food Labels** Have students read the labels of canned and packaged foods. Discuss the major sources of various nutrients in the foods they eat each day. L2
IS **Logical-Mathematical**

## ✔ Assessment

**Performance** Assess students' abilities to make and use tables by having them use Table 2 to determine how much water (in liters) is lost through the skin. Use **Performance Assessment in the Science Classroom,** p. 109.

---

**Figure 9** The information on a food label can help you decide what to eat.

**Nutrition Facts**
Serving Size 1 Meal

**Amount Per Serving**

| | |
|---|---|
| **Calories** 330 | Calories from Fat 60 |

| | % Daily Value* |
|---|---|
| **Total Fat** 7g | **10%** |
| Saturated Fat 3.5g | **17%** |
| Polyunsaturated Fat 1g | |
| Monounsaturated Fat 2.5g | |
| **Cholesterol** 35mg | **12%** |
| **Sodium** 460mg | **19%** |
| **Total Carbohydrate** 52g | **18%** |
| Dietary Fiber 6g | **24%** |
| Sugars 17g | |
| **Protein** 15g | |

| | | | |
|---|---|---|---|
| Vitamin A 15% | • | Vitamin C 70% | |
| Calcium 4% | • | Iron 10% | |

* Percent Daily Values are based on a 2,000 calorie diet. Your daily values may be higher or lower depending on your calorie needs.

| | | Calories | 2,000 | 2,500 |
|---|---|---|---|---|
| Total Fat | Less than | | 65g | 80g |
| Sat Fat | Less than | | 20g | 25g |
| Cholesterol | Less than | | 300mg | 300mg |
| Sodium | Less than | | 2,400mg | 2,400mg |
| Total Carbohydrate | | | 300g | 375g |
| Dietary Fiber | | | 25g | 30g |

**Daily Servings** Each day you should eat six to eleven servings from the bread and cereal group, three to five servings from the vegetable group, two to four servings from the fruit group, two to three servings from the milk group, and two to three servings from the meat and beans group. Only small amounts of fats, oils, and sweets should be consumed.

The size of a serving is different for different foods. For example, a slice of bread or one ounce of ready-to-eat cereal is a bread and cereal group serving. One cup of raw leafy vegetables or one-half cup of cooked or chopped raw vegetables make a serving from the vegetable group. One medium apple, banana, or orange, one-half cup of canned fruit, or three-quarter cup of fruit juice is a fruit serving. A serving from the milk group can be one cup of milk or yogurt. Two ounces of cooked lean meat, one-half cup of cooked dry beans, one egg, or two tablespoons of peanut butter counts as a serving from the meat and beans group.

**Food Labels** The nutritional facts found on all packaged foods make it easier to make healthful food choices. These labels, as shown in **Figure 9,** can help you plan meals that supply the daily recommended amounts of nutrients and meet special dietary requirements (for example, a low-fat diet).

## section 2 review

### Summary

**Why do you eat?**

- Nutrients in food provide energy and materials for cell development, growth, and repair.

**Classes of Nutrients**

- Six kinds of nutrients are found in food—proteins, carbohydrates, fats, vitamins, minerals, and water.

- Proteins are used for growth and repair, carbohydrates provide energy, and fats store energy and cushion organs.

- Vitamins and minerals regulate body functions.

- Next to oxygen, water is the most important factor for your survival.

**Food Groups**

- The food pyramid and nutritional labels can help you choose foods that supply all the nutrients you need for energy and growth.

### Self Check

1. **List** one example of a food source for each of the six classes of nutrients.
2. **Explain** how your body uses each class of nutrients.
3. **Discuss** how food choices can positively and negatively affect your health.
4. **Explain** the importance of water in the body.
5. **Think Critically** What foods from each food group would provide a balanced breakfast? Explain.

### Applying Skills

6. **Interpret Data** Nutritional information can be found on the labels of most foods. Interpret the labels found on three different types of food products.
7. **Use a Spreadsheet** Make a spreadsheet of the minerals listed in **Table 1.** Use reference books to gather information about minerals and add these to the table: *sulfur, magnesium, copper, manganese, cobalt,* and *zinc.*

Science Online in7.msscience.com/self_check_quiz

---

## section 2 review

1. Possible answers: carbohydrates: bread; proteins: fish; fats: butter; vitamins: fruit; minerals: vegetables; water: juice
2. Possible answers: carbohydrates: source of energy; proteins: growth of cells; fats: source of energy; vitamins: growth; minerals: nerve activity; water: enables chemical reactions to occur
3. An unbalanced diet can be detrimental to your health. For example, an inadequate intake of certain vitamins and minerals can hinder your body's energy supply and functions.

A diet low in cholesterol can reduce the risk of heart disease.
4. dissolves and carries nutrients, removes wastes, enables chemical reactions to occur
5. Accept all correct responses.
6. Answers will vary.

7. sulfur—all protein-rich foods; magnesium—green vegetables, meats, nuts; copper—liver, legumes, shellfish, whole grains; manganese—legumes, whole grains, nuts, dark green vegetables; cobalt—leafy vegetables, shellfish, liver, milk; zinc—seafood, meat, dairy products

# Identifying Vitamin C Content

Vitamin C is found in many fruits and vegetables. Oranges have a high vitamin C content. Try this lab to test the vitamin C content in different orange juices.

## Real-World Question

Which orange juice contains the most vitamin C?

### Goals

■ **Observe** the vitamin C content of different orange juices.

### Materials

| | |
|---|---|
| test tube (4) | 2% tincture of iodine |
| *paper cups | dropper |
| test-tube rack | cornstarch |
| masking tape | triple-beam balance |
| wooden stirrer (13) | weighing paper |
| graduated cylinder | water (50 mL) |
| *graduated container | glass-marking pencil |

dropper bottles (4) containing orange juice that is:
    (1) freshly squeezed    (3) canned
    (2) from frozen concentrate  (4) in a carton

\* Alternate materials

### Safety Precautions

**WARNING:** *Do not taste any of the juices. Iodine is poisonous and can stain skin and clothing. It is an irritant and can cause damage if it comes in contact with your eyes. Notify your teacher if a spill occurs.*

## Procedure

1. Make a data table like the example shown to record your observations.

2. Label four test tubes 1 through 4 and place them in the test-tube rack.

**Drops of Iodine Needed to Change Color**

| Juice | Trial 1 | Trial 2 | Trial 3 | Average |
|---|---|---|---|---|
| 1 Fresh juice | 8 | 7 | 8 | 8 |
| 2 Frozen juice | 7 | 8 | 8 | 8 |
| 3 Canned juice | 6 | 6 | 6 | 6 |
| 4 Carton juice | 14 | 12 | 10 | 12 |

3. Measure and pour 5 mL of juice from bottle 1 into test tube 1, 5 mL from bottle 2 into test tube 2, 5 mL from bottle 3 into test tube 3, and 5 mL from bottle 4 into test tube 4.

4. Measure 0.3 g of cornstarch, then put it in a container. Slowly mix in 50 mL of water until the cornstarch completely dissolves.

5. Add 5 mL of the cornstarch solution to each of the four test tubes. Stir well.

6. Add iodine to test tube 1, one drop at a time. Stir after each drop. Record the number of drops it takes for the juice to change to a purple color. The more vitamin C that is present, the more drops it takes to change color.

7. Repeat step 6 with test tubes 2, 3, and 4.

8. Empty and clean the test tubes. Repeat steps 3 through 7 two more times, then average your results.

9. Dispose of all materials as directed by your teacher. Wash your hands thoroughly.

## Conclude and Apply

1. **Compare and contrast** the amount of vitamin C in the orange juices tested.

2. **Infer** why the amount of vitamin C varies in the orange juices.

**LAB 139**

---

---

# section 3

# The Respiratory System

### Tie to Prior Knowledge

**Oxygen** Students are aware that they need oxygen to live. Ask students how they get oxygen into their bodies. Most will say breathing. Point out that oxygen taken in by the respiratory system is transported to the body's cells by the circulatory system.

**Answer** chemical reaction in which glucose and oxygen combine and produce $CO_2$ and $H_2O$ with the release of energy

---

## as you read

### *What* You'll Learn

- **Describe** the functions of the respiratory system.
- **Explain** how oxygen and carbon dioxide are exchanged in the lungs and in tissues.
- **Identify** the pathway of air in and out of the lungs.
- **Explain** the effects of smoking on the respiratory system.

### *Why* It's Important

Your body's cells depend on your respiratory system to supply oxygen and remove carbon dioxide.

### Review Vocabulary

**diaphragm:** muscle beneath the lungs that contracts and relaxes to move gases in and out of the body

### New Vocabulary

- larynx
- trachea
- bronchi
- alveoli

---

## Functions of the Respiratory System

Can you imagine an astronaut walking on the Moon without a space suit or a diver exploring the ocean without scuba gear? Of course not. They couldn't survive in either location under those conditions because humans need to breathe air.

People often confuse the terms *breathing* and *respiration*. Breathing is the movement of the chest that brings air into the lungs and removes waste gases. The air entering the lungs contains oxygen. It passes from the lungs into the circulatory system because there is less oxygen in blood when it enters the lungs than in cells of the lungs.

Blood carries oxygen and glucose from digested food to individual cells. The oxygen delivered to the cells is used to release energy from glucose. This chemical reaction, shown in the equation in **Figure 10,** is called cellular respiration. Without oxygen, this reaction would not take place. Carbon dioxide and water molecules are waste products of cellular respiration. They are carried back to the lungs in the blood. Exhaling, or breathing out, eliminates waste carbon dioxide and some water molecules.

**✓ Reading Check** *What is cellular respiration?*

Respiration

Oxygen supplied to body

Oxygen carried to body cells

Carbon dioxide removed from cells to lungs

Carbon dioxide waste expelled

Circulation

Breathing (Inhale)

Breathing (Exhale)

**Figure 10** Several processes are involved in how the body obtains, transports, and uses oxygen.

---

## Section 3 Resource Manager

**Chapter *FAST FILE* Resources**

Transparency Activity, p. 48

MiniLAB, p. 4

Enrichment, p. 33

Reinforcement, p. 29

Directed Reading, p. 21

Lab Activity, pp. 13–16

**Earth Science Critical Thinking/Problem Solving,** p. 3

**Physical Science Critical Thinking/Problem Solving,** p. 9

**Making a low-pitched sound**
- Thyroid cartilage
- Vocal cords relaxed
- Muscles
- Cartilages pull vocal cords open and shut.

**Making a high-pitched sound**
- Vocal cords contracted
- Muscles

Cilia

- Nasal cavity
- Mouth cavity
- Pharynx
- Larynx
- Trachea
- Lung

About 300 million alveoli are in each lung. The exchange of oxygen and carbon dioxide with the environment takes place between the alveoli and the surrounding capillaries.

- Bronchi
- Capillaries

Sound made by your vocal cords gets louder with increased air pressure. Pitch gets higher as muscles pull your vocal cords tighter, thus causing the glottis to close.

- Alveoli
- Hollow center of alveolus containing air

**Figure 11** Air can enter the body through the nostrils and the mouth.
**Explain** *an advantage of having air enter through the nostrils.*

## Organs of the Respiratory System

The respiratory system, shown in **Figure 11,** is made up of structures and organs that help move oxygen into the body and waste gases out of the body. Air enters your body through two openings in your nose called nostrils or through the mouth. Fine hairs inside the nostrils trap particles from the air. Air then passes through the nasal cavity, where it gets moistened and warmed by the body's heat. Glands that produce sticky mucus line the nasal cavity. The mucus traps particles that were not trapped by nasal hairs. This process helps filter and clean the air you breathe. Tiny, hairlike structures, called cilia (SIH lee uh), sweep mucus and trapped material to the back of the throat where it can be swallowed.

**Pharynx** Warmed, moist air then enters the pharynx (FER ingks), which is a tubelike passageway for food, liquids, and air. At the lower end of the pharynx is the epiglottis. When you swallow, your epiglottis folds down, which allows food or liquids to enter your esophagus instead of your airway. What do you think has happened if you begin to choke?

SECTION 3 The Respiratory System **141**

**Text Question Answer**
The food or drink gets in your airway.

**Caption Answer**
**Figure 11** It can be cleaned, warmed, and moistened before moving to the pharynx.

**Quick Demo**
**Examining Lungs**
**Materials** pig lungs (from meat-packing house or biological supply company)
**Estimated Time** 10 minutes
**Procedure** Have students examine the lungs and note their weight. Lead a discussion on why lungs aren't heavy. Lungs are composed of alveoli, which are hollow.

**Activity**
**Observing the Presence of Carbon Dioxide** Have students blow through a straw into a test tube one-fourth full of limewater. Note the change from a clear liquid to a cloudy liquid. This indicates the presence of carbon dioxide. L1 IS **Kinesthetic**

**Make a Model**
**Vocal Cords** Blow up a balloon and stretch the opening into a narrow slit. Explain to students that the balloon represents a lung and its neck is the trachea. Stretch the slit to make it longer and release a bit to make it shorter, noting the changes in pitch. Correlate the higher-pitched sounds and tighter stretch with the shorter vocal cords of females and the lower-pitched sounds and looser stretch with the longer vocal cords of males.

## Differentiated Instruction

**Challenge** An opera singer's ability to be heard over an orchestra in a large auditorium for an extended period of time is a result of breath control. Breath control enables singers to sustain a long musical phrase and change volume for dramatic effect. Invite students who have studied voice or a wind instrument to perform for the class and demonstrate their breathing techniques. L3 ELL IS **Auditory-Musical**

## Curriculum Connection

**Health** The pharynx serves as the passageway of food into the esophagus and air into the trachea. The epiglottis is a small flap of tissue that normally closes over the tracheal opening when food is swallowed. Sometimes food or liquid gets past the epiglottis and goes into the trachea, triggering the choking reflex. Ask students to discuss ways to prevent choking. L2 IS **Logical-Mathematical**

Alveolus

$CO_2$

$O_2$

Red blood cell

Capillary

**Figure 12** The thin capillary walls allow gases to be exchanged easily between the alveoli and the capillaries.
**Name** *the two gases that are exchanged by the capillaries and alveoli.*

**Larynx and Trachea** Next, the air moves into your larynx (LER ingks). The **larynx** is the airway to which two pairs of horizontal folds of tissue, called vocal cords, are attached, as shown in **Figure 11** on the previous page. Forcing air between the cords causes them to vibrate and produce sounds. When you speak, muscles tighten or loosen your vocal cords, resulting in different sounds. Your brain coordinates the movement of the muscles in your throat, tongue, cheeks, and lips when you talk, sing, or just make noise. Your teeth also are involved in forming letter sounds and words.

From the larynx, air moves into the **trachea** (TRAY kee uh). Strong, C-shaped rings of cartilage prevent the trachea from collapsing. It is lined with mucous membranes and cilia, also shown in **Figure 11** on the previous page. The mucous membranes trap dust, bacteria, and pollen. The cilia move the mucus upward, where it is either swallowed or expelled from the nose or mouth. Why must the trachea stay open all the time?

**Bronchi and the Lungs** Air is carried into your lungs by two short tubes called **bronchi** (BRAHN ki) (singular, *bronchus*) at the lower end of the trachea. Within the lungs, the bronchi branch into smaller and smaller tubes. The smallest tubes are called bronchioles (BRAHN kee ohlz). At the end of each bronchiole are clusters of tiny, thin-walled sacs called **alveoli** (al VEE uh li) (singular, *alveolus*). Air passes into the bronchi, then into the bronchioles, and finally into the alveoli. Lungs are masses of alveoli, like the one shown in **Figure 12,** arranged in grapelike clusters. The capillaries surround the alveoli like a net.

The exchange of oxygen and carbon dioxide takes place between the alveoli and capillaries. The walls of the alveoli and capillaries are only one cell thick, as shown in **Figure 12.** Oxygen moves through the cell membranes of alveoli and through cell membranes of the capillaries into the blood. In blood, oxygen is picked up by hemoglobin (HEE muh gloh bun), a molecule in red blood cells, and carried to all body cells. At the same time, carbon dioxide and other cellular wastes leave the body cells and move into capillaries. Then they are carried by the blood to the lungs. In the lungs, waste gases move through cell membranes from capillaries into alveoli. Then waste gases leave the body when you exhale.

## Cultural Diversity

## Why do you breathe?

Signals from your brain tell the muscles in your chest and abdomen to contract and relax. You don't have to think about breathing to breathe, just like your heart beats without you telling it to beat. Your brain can change your breathing rate depending on the amount of carbon dioxide present in your blood. If a lot of carbon dioxide is present, your breathing rate increases. It decreases if less carbon dioxide is in your blood. You do have some control over your breathing—you can hold your breath if you want to. Eventually, your brain will respond to the buildup of carbon dioxide in your blood and signal your chest and abdomen muscles to work automatically. You will breathe whether you want to or not.

**Inhaling and Exhaling** Breathing is partly the result of changes in volume and resulting air pressure. Under normal conditions, a gas moves from an area of higher pressure to an area of lower pressure. When you squeeze an empty, soft-plastic bottle, air is pushed out. This happens because air pressure outside the top of the bottle is less than the pressure you create inside the bottle when you changed its volume. As you release your grip on the bottle, the air pressure inside the bottle becomes less than it is outside the bottle because the bottle's volume changed. Air rushes back in, and the bottle returns to its original shape.

Your lungs work in a way similar to the squeezed bottle. Your diaphragm (DI uh fram) contracts and relaxes, changing the volume of the chest, which helps move gases into and out of your lungs. **Figure 13** illustrates breathing.

> **✓ Reading Check** *How does your diaphragm help you breathe?*

When a person's airway is blocked, a rescuer can use abdominal thrusts, as shown in **Figure 14,** to save the life of the choking victim.

**Inhale**

**Exhale**

---

**Figure 13** Your lungs inhale and exhale about 500 mL of air with an average breath. This can increase to 2,000 mL of air per breath when you do strenuous activity.

---

---

## Visual Learning

**Figure 13** The position of the diaphragm during the process of inhaling and expanding is shown. Compare this process with the squeezing of the plastic bottle discussed in the text.

## Teacher FYI

**Reflex Action** Hiccups are caused by spasmodic contractions of the diaphragm. The result is a sudden inhaling of air. Choking could result if a reflex action did not automatically cause the epiglottis to close over the trachea and prevent any food from entering.

## Visualizing Abdominal Thrusts

Have students examine the picture and read the captions. Then ask the following questions.

Why should abdominal thrusts only be performed in emergencies, and never performed on other people for practice or for fun? Abdominal thrusts could cause injury if performed on a person who is not choking.

Why is it important that the rescuer's fist be located below the ribs of the choking victim? The fist must be below the diaphragm in order for an upward force to be applied to the diaphragm. A fist located on the rib cage or breastbone could cause injury to the victim.

### Activity

**Creating a Mnemonic** Have students work in small grips to develop a mnemonic, or memory device, that will allow them to quickly and accurately remember the steps of proper abdominal thrusts to save a choking victim.

---

NATIONAL GEOGRAPHIC **VISUALIZING ABDOMINAL THRUSTS**

### Figure 14

When food or other objects become lodged in the trachea, airflow between the lungs and the mouth and nasal cavity is blocked. Death can occur in minutes. However, prompt action by someone can save the life of a choking victim. The rescuer uses abdominal thrusts to force the victim's diaphragm up. This decreases the volume of the chest cavity and forces air up in the trachea. The result is a rush of air that dislodges and expels the food or other object. The victim can breathe again. This technique is shown at right and should only be performed in emergency situations.

Food is lodged in the victim's trachea.

The rescuer places her fist against the victim's stomach.

The rescuer's second hand adds force to the fist.

An upward thrust dislodges the food from victim's trachea.

**A** The rescuer stands behind the choking victim and wraps her arms around the victim's upper abdomen. She places a fist (thumb side in) against the victim's stomach. The fist should be below the ribs and above the navel.

**B** With a violent, sharp movement, the rescuer thrusts her fist up into the area below the ribs. This action should be repeated as many times as necessary.

**144** CHAPTER 5 Digestion, Respiration, and Excretion

---

## Differentiated Instruction

**Visually Impaired** Have students use the non-emergency number to contact the local rescue squad. Have the students obtain statistics on the number of choking incidents that occur each year in your area, and share the information with the class. L2

## Curriculum Connection

**Health** Arrange a visit to a Red Cross center or have a health specialist come to school and demonstrate how to use abdominal thrusts and cardiopulmonary resuscitation (CPR) to revive a person who is not breathing. Ask students to find out where CPR training is available in their area. L2

## Diseases and Disorders of the Respiratory System

**INTEGRATE Health**  If you were asked to make a list of some things that can harm your respiratory system, you probably would put smoking at the top. As you can see in **Table 3,** many serious diseases are related to smoking. The chemical substances in tobacco—nicotine and tars—are poisons and can destroy cells. The high temperatures, smoke, and carbon monoxide produced when tobacco burns also can injure a smoker's cells. Even if you are a nonsmoker, inhaling smoke from tobacco products—called secondhand smoke—is unhealthy and has the potential to harm your respiratory system. Smoking, polluted air, coal dust, and asbestos (as BES tus) have been related to respiratory problems such as asthma (AZ muh), bronchitis (brahn KI tus), emphysema (em fuh SEE muh), and cancer.

**Respiratory Infections**  Bacteria, viruses, and other microorganisms can cause infections that affect any of the organs of the respiratory system. The common cold usually affects the upper part of the respiratory system—from the nose to the pharynx. The cold virus also can cause irritation and swelling in the larynx, trachea, and bronchi. The cilia that line the trachea and bronchi can be damaged. However, cilia usually heal rapidly.

**Chronic Bronchitis**  When bronchial tubes are irritated and swell and too much mucus is produced, a disease called bronchitis develops. Many cases of bronchitis clear up within a few weeks, but the disease sometimes lasts for a long time. When this happens, it is called chronic (KRAH nihk) bronchitis.

**Emphysema**  A disease in which the alveoli in the lungs enlarge is called emphysema. When cells in the alveoli are reddened and swollen, an enzyme is released that causes the walls of the alveoli to break down. As a result, alveoli can't push air out of the lungs, so less oxygen moves into the bloodstream from the alveoli. When blood becomes low in oxygen and high in carbon dioxide, shortness of breath occurs.

**Table 3  Smokers' Risk of Death from Disease**

| Disease | Smokers' Risk Compared to Nonsmokers' Risk |
|---|---|
| Lung cancer | 23 times higher for males; 11 times higher for females |
| Chronic bronchitis and emphysema | 5 times higher |
| Heart disease | 2 times higher |

**Topic: Secondhand Smoke**
Visit in7.msscience.com for Web links to information about the health aspects of secondhand smoke.

**Activity**  Write a paragraph in your Science Journal summarizing the possible effects of secondhand smoke on your health.

**Indiana Academic Standard Check**

7.4.12: Explain that viruses . . . may infect the human body and interfere with normal body functions.

✔ What part of the respiratory system does a cold virus usually affect?

✔ the upper part from the nose to the pharynx

---

## Inquiry Lab

**Comparing Cilia Function**

**Purpose**  To compare cilia function in the presence and absence of tar, have students design and construct simple models of cilia.

**Possible Materials**  fine-tooth comb, water, black pepper, molasses, newspaper

**Estimated Time**  30 minutes

**Teaching Strategies**

• Students can make a simple model of cilia by using a fine-toothed comb. The comb's teeth can represent cilia. Vibration of the comb's teeth can model cilia movement.

• Students can make a simple model of dust and tar by using pepper to represent dust, and molasses to represent tar. (They may try applying water to the comb and then applying pepper to model dust without tar; molasses instead of water can be used to model dust with tar.)

• Students can predict and then observe how well the cilia function with and without tar.

• Allow students to explore other questions that arise.

**For additional inquiry activities, see**
**Science Inquiry Labs.**

### Use an Analogy

**Emphysema**  The alveoli of persons with emphysema are like balloons that have been blown up too many times and with too much air. In both cases the walls have been stretched, become thin, and can rupture.

---

## Teacher FYI

**Tobacco Smoke**  Inhaling tobacco smoke or other chemical irritants stimulates an increase in goblet cells and the enlargement of mucous cells in the lining of the bronchial tubes. This is the cause of the increased mucus in the bronchi of bronchitis sufferers.

**Check for Understanding**

**Visual-Spatial** Use a lung demonstration apparatus to illustrate how the downward movement of the diaphragm causes reduced pressure within the chest cavity.

**Reteach**

**Inhalation** Have students write a paragraph describing why air moves into the lungs when the ribs move upward and the diaphragm moves downward. This action reduces air pressure within the chest cavity, and the higher external air pressure causes air to rush into the lungs.

### ✓ Assessment

**Process** Have students use a chart of the respiratory system to describe the passage of air into and out of the lungs. Use **Performance Assessment in the Science Classroom, p. 143.**

### Virtual Labs

**The Respiratory System**
*How do the parts of the respiratory system work together?*

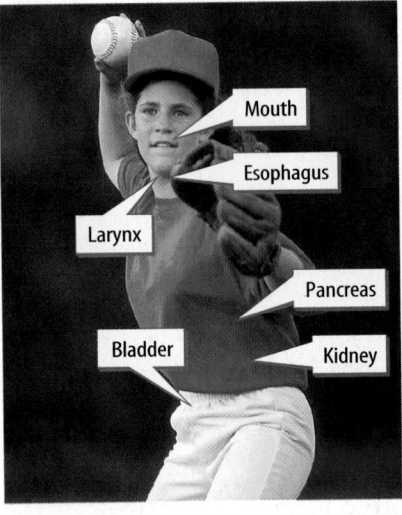

**Lung Cancer** The third leading cause of death in men and women in the United States is lung cancer. Inhaling the tar in cigarette smoke is the greatest contributing factor to lung cancer. In the body, tar and other ingredients found in smoke act as carcinogens (kar SIH nuh junz). Carcinogens are substances that can cause an uncontrolled growth of cells. In the lungs, this is called lung cancer. Lung cancer is not easy to detect in its early stages. Smoking also has been linked to the development of cancers of the mouth, esophagus, larynx, pancreas, kidney, and bladder. See **Figure 15.**

**Figure 15** More than 85 percent of all lung cancer is related to smoking. Smoking also can play a part in the development of cancer in other body organs indicated above.

**Asthma** Shortness of breath, wheezing, or coughing can occur in a lung disorder called asthma. When a person has an asthma attack, the bronchial tubes contract quickly. Inhaling medicine that relaxes the bronchial tubes is the usual treatment for an asthma attack. Asthma can be an allergic reaction. An allergic reaction occurs when the body overreacts to a foreign substance. An asthma attack can result from breathing certain substances such as cigarette smoke or certain plant pollen, eating certain foods, or stress in a person's life.

### section 3 review

#### Summary

**Functions of the Respiratory System**
- Breathing moves the chest to bring air into and remove wastes from the lungs.
- Cellular respiration uses oxygen to release energy from glucose.

**Organs of the Respiratory System**
- Air flows from your nostrils or mouth through the pharynx, larynx, trachea, bronchi, and into the alveoli of your lungs.
- Alveoli and capillaries exchange oxygen and carbon dioxide.

**Why do you breathe?**
- Your brain sends signals to your chest and abdominal muscles to contract and relax, which controls breathing rate.

**Diseases of the Respiratory System**
- Problems of the respiratory system include chronic bronchitis, emphysema, and lung cancer.

#### Self Check

1. **State** the main function of the respiratory system.
2. **Describe** the exchange of oxygen, carbon dioxide, and other waste gases in the lungs and body tissues.
3. **Explain** how air moves into and out of the lungs.
4. **Describe** the effects of smoking on the respiratory and circulatory systems.
5. **Think Critically** How is the work of the digestive and circulatory systems related to the respiratory system?

##### Applying Skills

6. **Research Information** Nicotine in tobacco is a poison. Using library references, find out how nicotine affects the body.
7. **Communicate** Use references to find out about lung disease common among coal miners, stonecutters, and sandblasters. Find out what safety measures are required now for these trades. In your Science Journal, write a paragraph about these safety measures.

**146**

Science Online in7.msscience.com/self_check_quiz

### section 3 review

1. supply oxygen and remove carbon dioxide
2. Oxygen, carbon dioxide, and waste gases are exchanged by diffusion into and out of the blood.
3. movement of the diaphragm and rib cage; differences in pressure
4. Smoking damages the lungs, making breathing labored and causing the heart to work harder.
5. digestive system—provides food for cell respiration; circulatory system—transports oxygen for food break down and carries respiration waste products to the lungs for expulsion
6. Nicotine causes blood vessels to constrict, resulting in increased blood pressure. It also causes nausea, headaches, and gastric upset.
7. Student answers will vary.

Standards—**7.1.6:** Provide examples of people who overcame bias and/or limited opportunities in education and employment to excel in the fields of science. **7.4.4:** … various organs and tissues function to serve the needs of cells for … waste removal.

Also covers: 7.1.9, 7.2.7, 7.2.8, 7.4.6, 7.7.2 (Detailed standards begin on page IN8.)

# The Excretory System

## Functions of the Excretory System

It's your turn to take out the trash. You carry the bag outside and put it in the trash can. The next day, you bring out another bag of trash, but the trash can is full. When trash isn't collected, it piles up. Just as trash needs to be removed from your home to keep it livable, your body must eliminate wastes to remain healthy. Undigested material is eliminated by your large intestine. Waste gases are eliminated through the combined efforts of your circulatory and respiratory systems. Some salts are eliminated when you sweat. These systems function together as parts of your excretory system. If wastes aren't eliminated, toxic substances build up and damage organs. If not corrected, serious illness or death occurs.

## The Urinary System

**Figure 16** shows how the urinary system functions as a part of the excretory system. The urinary system rids the blood of wastes produced by the cells. It controls blood volume by removing excess water produced by body cells during cellular respiration. The urinary system also balances the amounts of certain salts and water that must be present for all cellular activities.

### as you read

**What You'll Learn**
- **Distinguish** between the excretory and urinary systems.
- **Describe** how the kidneys work.
- **Explain** what happens when urinary organs don't work.

**Why It's Important**
The urinary system helps clean your blood of cellular wastes.

**Review Vocabulary**
**capillary:** blood vessel that connects arteries and veins

**New Vocabulary**
- nephron
- ureter
- bladder

**Figure 16** The urinary, digestive, and respiratory systems, and the skin, make up the excretory system.

**Bellringer**

**Section Focus Transparencies** also are available on the Interactive Chalkboard CD-ROM.
L2 ELL

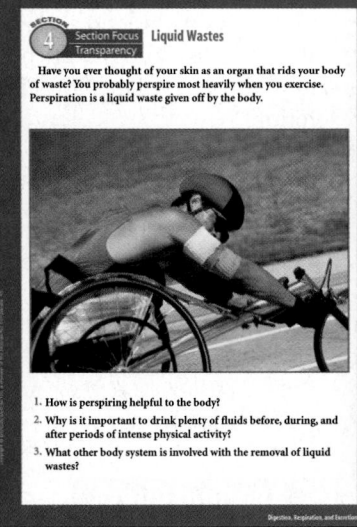

**Tie to Prior Knowledge**

**Filters** Remind students of how the filter on a coffeemaker works. Only liquid is allowed to flow through. Explain that, in a similar way, the urinary system acts as a filter.

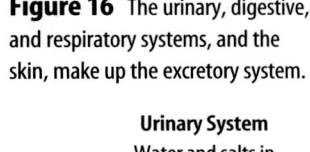

| Digestive System | Respiratory System | Skin | Urinary System |
|---|---|---|---|
| Food and liquid in | Oxygen in | | Water and salts in |
| Water and undigested food out | Carbon dioxide and water out | Salt and some organic substances out | Excess water, metabolic wastes, and salts out |

Excretion

---

### Section 4 Resource Manager

**Chapter FAST FILE Resources**
Transparency Activity, p. 49
Enrichment, p. 34
Reinforcement, p. 30
Directed Reading, pp. 21, 22
Lab Worksheet, pp. 7–8

Transparency Activity, pp. 50–51
**Home and Community Involvement,** p. 39

**Diffusion**

**Materials** cellophane bag, container, sugar, food coloring, water

**Estimated Time** 20 minutes

**Procedure** Make up a sugar solution. Add several drops of food coloring to the solution. Place the solution in a cellophane bag. Place the bag in a container of water. To demonstrate diffusion in the opposite direction, place a cellophane bag of colored pure water into a container of sugar solution.

### Activity

**Composition of Urine** Have students do research and construct a circle graph to illustrate the composition of urine. water = 95%, urea = 2%, sodium chloride = 1%, other substances = 2% L3

[IS] **Visual-Spatial**

### ✓ Reading Check

**Answer** by increasing and decreasing the amount of wastewater excreted

### Teacher FYI

**Cells and Salt** Every body cell requires a certain concentration of salt water to function properly. Cell membranes are selectively permeable and regulate the amount of water and salt that go into and out of the cell.

### Caption Answer

**Figure 17** If there is too much water in the blood, a specific hormone signals the kidneys to return less water to the blood and excrete more urine.

---

**Regulating Fluid Levels** To stay in good health, the fluid levels within the body must be balanced and normal blood pressure must be maintained. An area in the brain, the hypothalamus (hi poh THA luh mus), constantly monitors the amount of water in the blood. When the brain detects too much water in the blood, the hypothalamus releases a lesser amount of a specific hormone. This signals the kidneys to return less water to the blood and increase the amount of urine that is excreted.

### ✓ Reading Check
*How does the urinary system control the volume of water in the blood?*

**Organs of the Urinary System** Excretory organs is another name for the organs of the urinary system. The main organs of the urinary system are two bean-shaped kidneys. Kidneys are located on the back wall of the abdomen at about waist level. The kidneys filter blood that contains wastes collected from cells. In approximately 5 min, all of the blood in your body passes through the kidneys. The red-brown color of the kidneys is due to their enormous blood supply. In **Figure 17,** you can see that blood enters the kidneys through a large artery and leaves through a large vein.

**Figure 17** The urinary system removes wastes from the blood. The urinary system includes the kidneys, the bladder, and the connecting tubes.
**Explain** *how the kidneys help the body balance its fluid levels.*

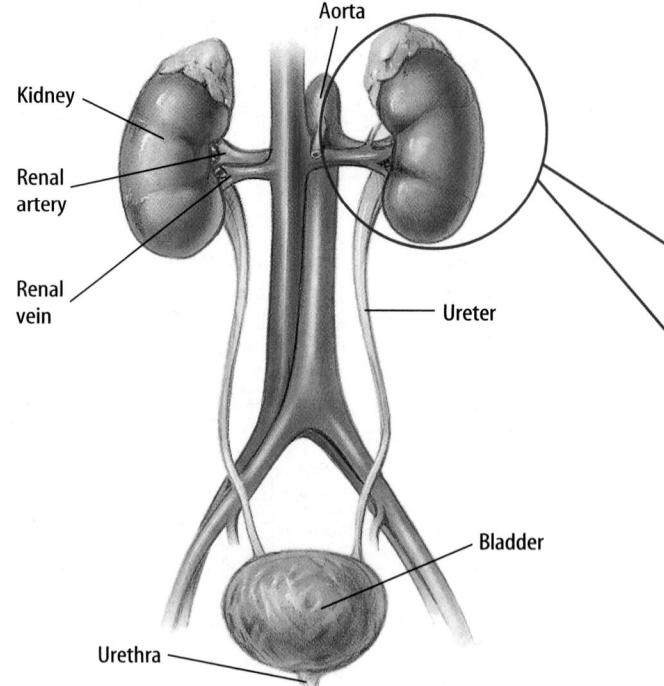

Aorta
Kidney
Renal artery
Renal vein
Ureter
Bladder
Urethra

---

## Visual Learning

**Figure 17** Have students use their finger or pencil to trace the pathway of fluids through the urinary system and out of the body.

## Curriculum Connection

**Math** Calculate the ratio of body weight to amount of urine excreted. If an 11-kg child excretes 600 mL, what would you expect a 45-kg adult to excrete? 2,453 mL The amount is actually only about 1500 mL. The amount excreted by children is greater in proportion to their weight.
L2 [IS] **Logical-Mathematical**

**Filtration in the Kidney** A two-stage filtration system is an accurate description of a kidney, shown in **Figure 18.** It is made up of about 1 million tiny filtering units called **nephrons** (NE frahnz), also shown in **Figure 18.** Each nephron has a cuplike structure and a tubelike structure called a duct. Blood moves from a renal artery to capillaries in the cuplike structure. The first filtration occurs when water, sugar, salt, and wastes from the blood pass into the cuplike structure. Left behind in the blood are the red blood cells and proteins. Next, liquid in the cuplike structure is squeezed into a narrow tubule.

Capillaries that surround the tubule perform the second filtration. Most of the water, sugar, and salt are reabsorbed and returned to the blood. These collection capillaries merge to form small veins, which merge to form a renal vein in each kidney. Purified blood is returned to the main circulatory system. The liquid left behind flows into collecting tubules in each kidney. This wastewater, or urine, contains excess water, salts, and other wastes that are not reabsorbed by the body. An average-sized person produces about 1 L of urine per day.

**Urine Collection and Release** The urine in each collecting tubule drains into a funnel-shaped area of each kidney that leads to the **ureter** (YOO ruh tur). Ureters are tubes that lead from each kidney to the bladder. The **bladder** is an elastic, muscular organ that holds urine until it leaves the body. The elastic walls of the bladder can stretch to hold up to 0.5 L of urine. When empty, the bladder looks wrinkled and the cells lining the bladder are thick. When full, the bladder looks like an inflated balloon and the cells lining the bladder are stretched and thin. A tube called the urethra (yoo REE thruh) carries urine from the bladder to the outside of the body.

**Indiana Academic Standard Check**

7.4.4: Explain . . . that various organs and tissues function to serve the needs of cells for . . . waste removal.

✔ Which structures in a kidney filter wastes from the blood?

✔ nephrons

**Figure 18** A single nephron is a complex structure.
**Describe** *the main function of a nephron.*

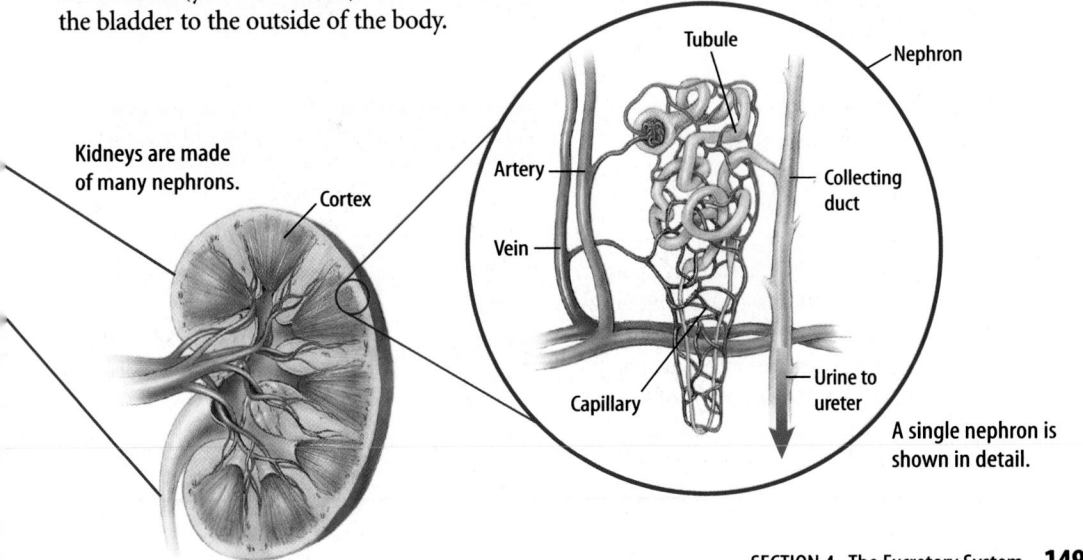

Kidneys are made of many nephrons.

Cortex

Tubule

Nephron

Artery

Vein

Collecting duct

Capillary

Urine to ureter

A single nephron is shown in detail.

# Differentiated Instruction

**Challenge** Small stones made up of precipitated minerals such as uric acid or calcium sometimes may form in the kidneys. These kidney stones may move into the ureter and can cause severe pain. Drinking large quantities of water help prevent the formation of the stones. Have students investigate what foods may contribute to the formation of kidney stones. L3

**150** CHAPTER 5 Digestion, Respiration, and Excretion

## Activity

**Amount of Liquid Processed by Kidneys** Adult kidneys weigh only about 170 g each. The kidneys of an average adult process about 1,600 L of liquid per day, most of which is recycled. Have students calculate how many liters an adult's kidneys process in a year, in a decade, and in 75 years. 584,000 L; 5,840,000 L; 43,800,000 L L2

IS **Logical-Mathematical**

---

### Applying Science

**Answers**

1. ingested liquids; urine
2. More water would be lost than taken in; the skin.

---

## Urinary Diseases and Disorders

What happens when someone's kidneys don't work properly or stop working? Waste products that are not removed build up and act as poisons in body cells. Without excretion, an imbalance of salts occurs. The body responds by trying to restore this balance. If the balance isn't restored, the kidneys and other organs can be damaged. Kidney failure occurs when the kidneys don't work as they should. This is always a serious problem because the kidneys' job is so important to the rest of the body.

---

### Applying Science

**How does your body gain and lose water?**

Your body depends on water. Without water, your cells could not carry out their activities and body systems could not function. Water is so important to your body that your brain and other body systems are involved in balancing water gain and water loss.

**Identifying the Problem**

**Table A** shows the major sources by which your body gains water. Oxidation of nutrients occurs when energy is released from nutrients by your body's cells. Water is a waste product of these reactions. **Table B** lists the major sources by which your body loses water. The data show you how daily gain and loss of water are related.

| Table A Major Sources by Which Body Water Is Gained | | |
|---|---|---|
| Source | Amount (mL) | Percent |
| Oxidation of nutrients | 250 | 10 |
| Foods | 750 | 30 |
| Liquids | 1,500 | 60 |
| Total | 2,500 | 100 |

**Solving the Problem**

1. What is the greatest source of water gained by your body? What is the greatest source of water lost by your body?
2. How would the percentages of water gained and lost change in a person who was working in extremely warm temperatures? In this case, what organ of the body would be the greatest contributor to water loss?

| Table B Major Sources by Which Body Water Is Lost | | |
|---|---|---|
| Source | Amount (mL) | Percent |
| Urine | 1,500 | 60 |
| Skin | 500 | 20 |
| Lungs | 350 | 14 |
| Feces | 150 | 6 |
| Total | 2,500 | 100 |

**150** CHAPTER 5 Digestion, Respiration, and Excretion

---

## Differentiated Instruction

**Learning Disabled and English-Language Learners**
Ask students to compare a kidney to a recycling center. Have them consider substances that can and cannot be recycled. Have them make a list or draw pictures to show what they have discovered. Kidney—water, salt, and sugar can be recycled, waste cannot; recycling center—paper, glass, and plastic can be recycled, some synthetic materials cannot. L1 IS **Linguistic**

Because the ureters and urethra are narrow tubes, they can be blocked easily in some disorders. A blockage can cause serious problems because urine cannot flow out of the body properly. If the blockage is not corrected, the kidneys can be damaged.

 **Reading Check** *Why is a blocked ureter or urethra a serious problem?*

**Dialysis** A person who has only one kidney still can live normally. The remaining kidney increases in size and works harder to make up for the loss of the other kidney. However, if both kidneys fail, the person will need to have his or her blood filtered by an artificial kidney machine in a process called dialysis (di AH luh sus), as shown in **Figure 19.**

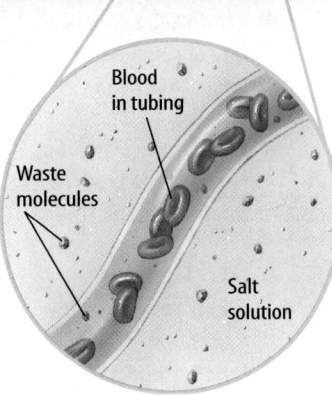

**Figure 19** A dialysis machine can replace or help with some of the activities of the kidneys in a person with kidney failure. Like the kidney, the dialysis machine removes wastes from the blood.

Blood in tubing

Waste molecules

Salt solution

line in7.msscience.com/self_check_quiz

## section 4 review

### Summary

**Functions of the Excretory System**

- The excretory system removes wastes from your body.
- The digestive, respiratory, and urinary systems and skin make up your excretory system.

**The Urinary System**

- The kidneys, which filter wastes from the blood, are the major organs of the urinary system.
- Urine moves from the kidneys through the ureters, into the bladder, then leaves the body through the urethra.

**Urinary Diseases and Disorders**

- Kidney failure can lead to a buildup of waste products in the body.
- An artificial kidney can be used to filter the blood in a process called dialysis.

### Self Check

1. **List** the functions of a person's urinary system.
2. **Explain** how the kidneys remove wastes and keep fluids and salts in balance.
3. **Describe** what happens when the urinary system does not function properly.
4. **Compare** the excretory system and urinary system.
5. **Think Critically** Explain why reabsorption of certain materials in the kidneys is important to your health.

**Applying Math**

6. **Make and Use Graphs** Make a circle graph of major sources by which body water is gained. Use the data in **Table A** of the Applying Science activity.
7. **Concept Map** Using a network-tree concept map, compare the excretory functions of the kidneys and the lungs.

## 3 Assess

### DAILY INTERVENTION

#### Check for Understanding

**Visual-Spatial** Have students prepare a basic diagram of the sequence involved in the processing of liquid wastes in the body. L2

#### Reteach

**Two-stage Filtration** Have students look again at **Figure 18.** Have them explain the two stages of filtration in the kidney and point out where each stage takes place.

### Assessment

**Portfolio** Provide students with diagrams of the circulatory, respiratory, and excretory systems. Have them construct concept maps from these diagrams. Use **Performance Assessment in the Science Classroom,** p. 161.

## section 4 review

1. rids the body of wastes, controls blood volume, balances salts and water
2. Kidneys filter the blood to remove wastes, sugar, water, and salt. Necessary amounts of water, sugar, and salt are returned to the blood.
3. Waste products not removed cause the destruction of cells. Fluids not removed from body tissue cause swellings in the extremities and buildup of fluids around the heart. Salts are in imbalance in body fluids, which can lead to organ damage.
4. excretory system—includes all systems that rid the body of wastes; urinary system—consists of organs that produce urine as waste
5. Many of the substances are needed by the body to maintain homeostasis.
6. Graphs should include the correct information.
7. Wastes in blood are carried to the lungs, which remove water and carbon dioxide, and to the kidney, which removes water and excess salts and other wastes.

## Real-World Question

**Purpose** Students will observe the relationship between particle size and rate of dissolving. L2 ELL

**Process Skills** observe and infer, communicate, recognize cause and effect, separate and control variables, interpret data, compare and contrast

**Time Required** 50 minutes

**Safety Precautions** Remind students not to taste, eat, or drink any materials used in the lab.

## Procedure

**Teaching Strategy** Demonstrate the way to use the mortar and pestle to grind the sugar cube into powder.

**Troubleshooting** Be sure the water temperature and amount of water is the same in each beaker.

---

### Goals

- **Compare and contrast** the dissolving rates of different sized particles.
- **Predict** the dissolving rate of sugar particles larger than sugar cubes.
- **Predict** the dissolving rate of sugar particles smaller than particles of ground sugar.
- **Infer**, using the lab results, why the body must break down and dissolve food particles.

### Materials

beakers or jars (3)
thermometers (3)
sugar granules
mortar and pestle
triple-beam balance
stirring rod
sugar cubes
weighing paper
warm water
stopwatch

### Safety Precautions

**WARNING:** *Never taste, eat, or drink any materials used in the lab.*

---

# Particle Size and Absorption

## Real-World Question

Before food reaches the small intestine, it is digested mechanically in the mouth and the stomach. The food mass is reduced to small particles. You can chew an apple into small pieces, but you would feed applesauce to a small child who didn't have teeth. What is the advantage of reducing the size of the food material? Does reducing the size of food particles aid the process of digestion?

## Procedure

1. Copy the data table below into your Science Journal.

### Dissolving Times of Sugar Particles

| Size of Sugar Particles | Mass | Time Until Dissolved |
|---|---|---|
| Sugar cube | | |
| Sugar granules | | |
| Ground sugar particles | | |

2. Place a sugar cube into your mortar and grind up the cube with the pestle until the sugar becomes powder.

3. Using the triple-beam balance and weighing paper, measure the mass of the powdered sugar from your mortar. Using separate sheets of weighing paper, measure the mass of a sugar cube and the mass of a sample of the granular sugar. The masses of the powdered sugar, sugar cube, and granular sugar should be approximately equal to each other. Record the three masses in your data table.

4. Place warm water into the three beakers. Use the thermometers to be certain the water in each beaker is the same temperature.

**152** **CHAPTER 5** Digestion, Respiration, and Excretion

---

### Alternative Inquiry Lab

**Extend the Experience** Students may investigate the rate of dissolving of another substance such as hard candy. They can use them whole, crushed, and broken into pieces. Rate of dissolving of the different substances can be compared. Have students brainstorm questions that arise from this extension.

5. Place the sugar cube in a beaker, the powdered sugar in a second beaker, and the granular sugar in a third beaker. Place all the sugar samples in the beakers at the same time and start the stopwatch when you put the sugar samples in the beaker.

6. Stir each sample equally.

7. Measure the time it takes each sugar sample to dissolve and record the times in your data table.

### ⊙ Analyze Your Data

1. **Identify** the experiment's constants and variables.

2. **Compare** the rates at which the sugar samples dissolved. What type of sugar dissolved most rapidly? Which was the slowest to dissolve?

### ⊙ Conclude and Apply

1. **Predict** how long it would take sugar particles larger than the sugar cubes to dissolve. Predict how long it would take sugar particles smaller than the powdered sugar to dissolve.

2. **Infer** and explain the reason why small particles dissolve more rapidly than large particles.

3. **Infer** why you should thoroughly chew your food.

4. **Explain** how reducing the size of food particles aids the process of digestion.

### Communicating Your Data

Write a news column for a health magazine explaining to health-conscious people what they can do to digest their food better.

**LAB 153**

### ⊙ Analyze Your Data

**Expected Outcome** Students will observe differences in the rate of dissolving. Sugar cube will take the longest, powdered sugar the least amount of time.

**Answers to Questions**

1. The size of the beakers, mass of the sugar samples, temperature of water in the beakers, and the amount of time each sample is stirred are the constants. The three particle sizes of the sugar are the variables.

2. The sugar cube should dissolve the slowest. The ground sugar particles should dissolve in the least amount of time.

**Error Analysis** Have students compare their results and attempt to explain any significant differences.

### ⊙ Conclude and Apply

1. Answers will vary, but larger sugar cubes would require more time to dissolve than the three samples used in the experiment, and smaller ground granules would require less time.

2. Small particles have much more surface area exposed to a dissolving agent than large particles.

3. Smaller particles of food will digest more easily than larger food particles. Chewing food thoroughly speeds up the digestion process.

4. To be used by the body, foods must be broken down into nutrients. Once digested, the blood carries these nutrients to all the cells of the body.

### ✔ Assessment

**Process** Have students investigate and compare the rate of dissolving among table salt, kosher salt, and rock salt. Use **Performance Assessment in the Science Classroom,** p. 97.

### Communicating Your Data

Articles should emphasize the idea that smaller particles of food will digest more easily than larger food particles. Chewing food thoroughly speeds up the digestion process. To be used by the body, foods must be broken down into nutrients. Once digested, the blood carries these nutrients to all the cells of the body.

## Content Background

It is important to know the function of the kidney and to relay this information to students. The kidney washes the blood as a filtering system, ridding it of toxins and balancing the body's water levels by producing urine to get rid of this waste.

Before making discoveries with regard to kidney transplants, Samuel Kountz had to overcome many odds. He was born in extreme poverty in an all-black town in Arkansas in 1930. His grandmother, born a slave, encouraged and inspired him when he tried to get into college. He became the first African-American to be accepted to the University of Arkansas Medical School.

## Discussion

**Rejected Kidneys** What did Kountz discover as the reason for kidneys being rejected after transplant surgeries? Possible answer: The patient's cells attacked and destroyed the small blood vessels of the transplanted kidney, thus, the kidney would die from lack of blood-supplied oxygen.

## Historical Significance

**Transplant Surgeries** The significance of Kountz's work for people who suffer from kidney disease is obvious. Point out to students that Kountz's work also had a significant impact on other transplant surgeries. Because other transplant procedures were associated with similar rejection problems, similar immunosuppressive drug treatments have been developed for heart, liver, and lung transplants.

---

## TIME SCIENCE AND HISTORY

SCIENCE CAN CHANGE THE COURSE OF HISTORY!

# Overcoming the Odds

O vercoming the odds—especially when the odds seem stacked against you—is a challenge that many people face. Dr. Samuel Lee Kountz, Jr. (right) had the odds stacked against him. Thanks to his determination, however, he beat them.

Samuel Kountz decided at age eight to become a doctor. He faced his first challenge when he failed the entrance exam to his local Arkansas college. That didn't stop him, though. He asked the college president to give him another chance, and the president did. Kountz got into school and earned As and Bs. He went on to get a graduate degree in biochemistry and was admitted to the University of Arkansas's

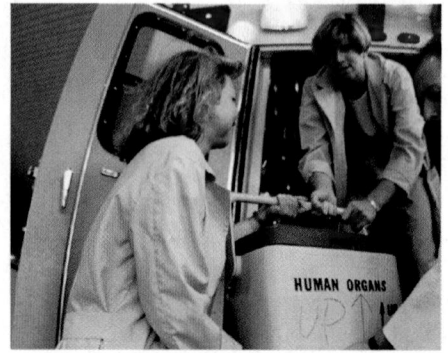

HUMAN ORGANS
UP 1

medical school. Kountz was especially interested in a process that was still brand new in the 1950s—the kidney transplant. At that time, a kidney transplant added months or a year to the lives of many patients. But then, a patient's body would reject the kidney, and the patient would die. Dr. Kountz was determined to see that kidney transplants saved lives and kept patients healthy for years.

### Fixing the Problem

Kountz discovered the root of the problem—why and how a patient's body rejected the transplanted kidney. He and others at Stanford University developed a way for doctors to watch the flow of the kidney's blood supply following surgery. As a result, doctors can give patients the right kinds of drugs at the right time, so that their bodies can overcome the rejection process.

In 1959, Kountz performed the first successful kidney transplant. He went on to develop a procedure to keep body organs healthy for up to 60 hours after being taken from a donor. He also set up a system of organ donor cards through the National Kidney Foundation. And in his career, Dr. Kountz transplanted more than 1,000 kidneys himself—and paved the way for thousands more.

**Research** What kinds of medical breakthroughs has the last century brought? Locate an article that explains either a recent advance in medicine or the work that doctors and medical researchers are doing. Share your findings with your class.

Science online

For more information, visit in7.msscience.com/time

---

**Research** First ask students to focus on one part of medicine or one specialization in medicine that interests them. If a student is interested in the brain, suggest a search for an article about neurological advancements in medicine. Suggest avenues that are available for your students to successfully fulfill research in whatever interest they present for this project.

### Resources for Teachers and Students

"The Black Surgeon in the Twentieth Century: A Tribute to Samuel L. Kountz" by Claude Organ. *Journal of the National Medical Association*, (September, 1978)

*Understanding Kidney Transplantation* by Edith T. Oberley and Neal R. Glass. Thomas: Springfield, Ill. 1987

## Reviewing Main Ideas

### Section 1 The Digestive System

1. Mechanical digestion breaks down food through chewing and churning. Enzymes and other chemicals aid chemical digestion.

2. Food passes through the mouth, esophagus, stomach, small intestine, large intestine, and rectum and then out the anus.

3. The large intestine absorbs water, which helps the body maintain homeostasis.

### Section 2 Nutrition

1. Proteins, carbohydrates, fats, vitamins, minerals, and water are the six nutrients found in foods.

2. Health is affected by the combination of foods that make up a diet.

### Section 3 The Respiratory System

1. The respiratory system brings oxygen into the body and removes carbon dioxide.

2. Breathing is the movement of the chest that allows air to move into the lungs and waste gases to leave the lungs.

3. The chemical reaction in cells that needs oxygen to release energy and produces carbon dioxide and water as wastes is called cellular respiration.

4. Smoking causes many respiratory problems, including chronic bronchitis, emphysema, and lung cancer.

### Section 4 The Excretory System

1. The urinary system is part of the excretory system. The skin, lungs, liver, and large intestine are also excretory organs.

2. The kidneys are the major organs of the urinary system and have a two-stage filtration system that removes wastes.

3. When kidneys fail to work, an artificial kidney can be used to filter the blood in a process called dialysis.

## Visualizing Main Ideas

*Copy and complete the following table on the respiratory and excretory systems.*

| Human Body Systems | | |
|---|---|---|
| | **Respiratory System** | **Excretory System** |
| **Major Organs** | lungs | kidneys, lungs, large intestine, skin, liver |
| **Wastes Eliminated** | carbon dioxide, water vapor | water, salts, toxins |
| **Disorders** | chronic bronchitis, emphysema, lung cancer, asthma | buildup of wastes, infections |

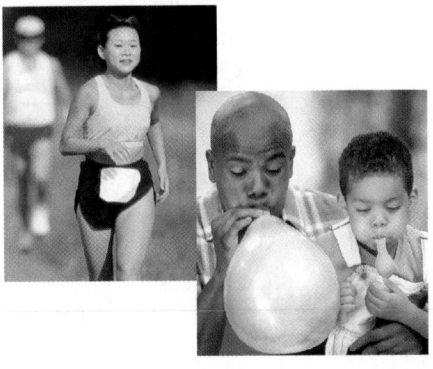

Science Online in7.msscience.com/interactive_tutor

### Reviewing Main Ideas

Summary statements can be used by students to review the major concepts of the chapter.

### Visualizing Main Ideas

See student page.

**Science Online**

**Visit** in7.msscience.com
/self_check_quiz
/interactive_tutor
/vocabulary_puzzlemaker
/chapter_review
/standards_review

### Assessment Transparency

For additional assessment questions, use the *Assessment Transparency* located in the transparency book.

**Assessment**

Assessment Transparency — Digestion, Respiration, and Excretion

Directions: *Carefully review the table and answer the following questions.*

| Ideal Body Weight (kg)—Range for Men and Women | | |
|---|---|---|
| **Height (m)** | **Ages 19–34** | **Ages 35 +** |
| 1.52 | 44–58 | 49–62 |
| 1.54 | 46–60 | 50–65 |
| 1.57 | 47–62 | 52–67 |
| 1.6 | 48–64 | 54–69 |
| 1.62 | ? | 55–71 |
| 1.65 | 51–68 | 57–73 |
| 1.67 | 53–70 | 59–76 |
| 1.7 | 55–72 | 61–78 |

1. Based on the information in the table, which of the following should the ideal weight range be for somebody who is 1.62 m tall and 27 years old?
   A 53–66   B 49–62   C 50–66   D 48–71

2. These data were collected by studying many different people. If everything remains the same, what would be a healthy weight for someone who is 1.7 m tall and 50 years old?
   F 55   G 59   H 72   J 80

3. A reasonable hypothesis using the table is that when we are younger ____.
   A our legs and arms weigh more
   B we usually weigh more
   C our weight never changes
   D we usually weigh less

Digestion, Respiration, and Excretion

## Using Vocabulary

1. Peristalsis
2. amino acids
3. chyme
4. Minerals
5. Nephrons
6. Alveoli
7. bladder

## Checking Concepts

| | |
|---|---|
| 8. A | 13. B |
| 9. D | 14. A |
| 10. D | 15. D |
| 11. C | 16. B |
| 12. A | 17. C |

## Thinking Critically

18. mouth: ingestion, mechanical and chemical digestion; esophagus: ingestion; stomach: mechanical and chemical digestion; small intestine: digestion and absorption; large intestine: absorption and elimination

19. Sugar—simple carbohydrate, dissolves in water, tastes sweet; starch and fiber—complex carbohydrates, do not dissolve in water; fiber absorbs water, starch does not.

## Using Vocabulary

| | |
|---|---|
| alveoli p. 142 | mineral p. 136 |
| amino acid p. 133 | nephron p. 149 |
| bladder p. 149 | nutrient p. 128 |
| bronchi p. 142 | peristalsis p. 130 |
| carbohydrate p. 134 | trachea p. 142 |
| chyme p. 131 | ureter p. 149 |
| enzyme p. 128 | villi p. 131 |
| larynx p. 142 | vitamin p. 135 |

*Fill in the blanks with the correct vocabulary word or words.*

1. _____ is the muscular contractions of the esophagus.

2. The building blocks of proteins are _____.

3. The liquid product of digestion is called _____.

4. _____ are inorganic nutrients.

5. _____ are the filtering units of the kidney.

6. _____ are thin-walled sacs in the lungs.

7. The _____ is an elastic muscular organ that holds urine.

## Checking Concepts

*Choose the word or phrase that best answers the question.*

8. Where in humans does most chemical digestion occur?
   A) duodenum      C) liver
   B) stomach       D) large intestine

9. In which organ is water absorbed?
   A) liver         C) small intestine
   B) esophagus     D) large intestine

10. Which of these organs is an accessory organ?
    A) mouth        C) small intestine
    B) stomach      D) liver

11. What beneficial substances are produced by bacteria in the large intestine?
    A) fats         C) vitamins
    B) minerals     D) proteins

12. Which food group contains yogurt and cheese?
    A) dairy        C) meat
    B) grain        D) fruit

13. When you inhale, which of the following contracts and moves down?
    A) bronchioles  C) nephrons
    B) diaphragm    D) kidneys

14. Exchange of gases occurs between capillaries and which of the following structures?
    A) alveoli      C) bronchioles
    B) bronchi      D) trachea

15. Which of the following conditions does smoking worsen?
    A) arthritis    C) excretion
    B) respiration  D) emphysema

16. Urine is held temporarily in which of the following structures?

17. Which of the following substances is not reabsorbed by blood after it passes through the kidneys?
    A) salt         C) wastes
    B) sugar        D) water

 **Science** online in7.msscience.com/vocabulary_puzzlemaker

**Use the Exam*View*® Pro Testmaker CD-ROM to:**
• create multiple versions of tests
• create modified tests with one mouse click for inclusion students
• edit existing questions and add your own questions
• build tests aligned with state standards using built-in State Curriculum Tags
• change English tests to Spanish with one mouse click and vice versa

## Thinking Critically

**18.** **Make and use a table** to sequence the order of organs in the digestive system through which food passes. Indicate whether ingestion, digestion, absorption, or elimination takes place in each.

**19.** **Compare and contrast** the three types of carbohydrates—sugar, starch, and fiber.

**20.** **Classify** the parts of your favorite sandwich into three of the nutrient categories—carbohydrates, proteins, and fats.

**21.** **Recognize cause and effect** by discussing how lack of oxygen is related to lack of energy.

**22.** **Form a hypothesis** about the number of breaths a person might take per minute in each of these situations: asleep, exercising, and on top of Mount Everest. Give a reason for each hypothesis.

**23.** **Concept Map** Make an events-chain concept map showing how urine forms in the kidneys. Begin with, "In the nephron …"

**Use the table below to answer question 24.**

| Materials Filtered by the Kidneys | | |
|---|---|---|
| Substance Filtered in Urine | Amount Moving Through Kidney | Amount Excreted |
| Water | 125 L | 1 L |
| Salt | 350 g | 10 g |
| Urea | 1 g | 1 g |
| Glucose | 50 g | 0 g |

**24.** **Interpret Data** Study the data above. How much of each substance is reabsorbed into the blood in the kidneys? What substance is excreted completely in the urine?

**25.** **Describe** how bile aids the diegestive process.

**26.** **Explain** how the bacteria that live in your large intestine help your body.

 Science Online in7.msscience.com/chapter_review

## Performance Activities

**27.** **Questionnaire and Interview** Prepare a questionnaire that can be used to interview a health specialist who works with lung cancer patients. Include questions on reasons for choosing the career, new methods of treatment, and the most encouraging or discouraging part of the job.

## Applying Math

**28.** **Kidney Blood Flow** In approximately 5 min, all 5 L of blood in the body pass through the kidneys. Calculate the average rate of flow through the kidneys in liters per minute.

**Use the graph below to answer question 29.**

### Total Lung Capacity

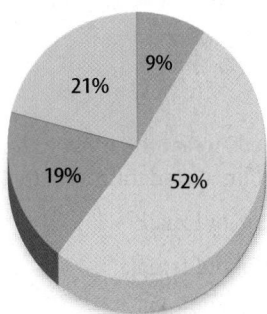

9%
21%
19%
52%

**Total Lung Capacity = 5800 mL**

■ Volume of air normally inhaled or exhaled

■ Volume of additional air that can be inhaled forcefully

■ Volume of additional air that can be exhaled forcefully

■ Volume of air left in lungs after forcefully exhaling

**29.** **Total Lung Capacity** What volume of air (mL) is left in the lungs after forcefully exhaling?

## Thinking Critically

**20.** Answers will vary: bread is a carbohydrate; meat and cheese are proteins and fats; margarine is fat; peanut butter is protein and fat; jelly is carbohydrate.

**21.** Cells need oxygen to break down food and release energy.

**22.** Possible answers: Sleeping—breathing rate is low because less respiration is occurring; exercising—breathing rate would increase to get oxygen to the muscles; on Mount Everest—breathing rate would increase because less oxygen is present.

**23.** In the nephron, wastes, water, salt, and sugar are removed from blood; water, sugar, and salt are reabsorbed; urine is produced and removed from the kidneys through the ureter.

**24.** Water: 124 L; salt: 340 g; glucose: 50 g; all urea is excreted.

**25.** Bile breaks up the large fat particles.

**26.** Bacteria that live in the large intestine make vitamin K and two B vitamins, niacin and thiamine. Bacteria also convert bile pigments into new compounds.

## Performance Activities

**27.** Students should prepare questionnaires and conduct interviews. Use **Performance Assessment in the Science Classroom**, p. 91.

## Applying Math

### Indiana Math Standards

7.5.4, 7.6.1

**28.** 5 L/5 min = 1 L/min

**29.** 1,200 mL

---

## ✓ Assessment   Resources

📁 **Reproducible Masters**
**Chapter *Fast File* Resources**
  Chapter Review, pp. 39–40
  Chapter Tests, pp. 41–44
  Assessment Transparency Activity, p. 52
**Glencoe Science Web site**
  Chapter Review Test
  IN Standards Review

**Glencoe Technology**
  🖌 Assessment Transparency
  ⊕ Exam*View*® Pro Testmaker
  ▭ MindJogger Videoquiz
  ⬤ Interactive Chalkboard

**Answer Sheet** A practice answer sheet can be found at in7.msscience.com/answer_sheet.

SAMPLE

## Part 1 | Multiple Choice

1. C
2. A
3. B
4. D
5. A
6. A
7. A

 The assessed Indiana standard appears above the question.

*Record your answers on the answer sheet provided by your teacher or on a sheet of paper.*

### Part 1 | Multiple Choice

The table below shows the recommended energy intake.

| Recommended Energy Intake | | | | |
|---|---|---|---|---|
| Gender | Age | Calories Per Day | | |
| | | Light Activity | Moderate Activity | Heavy Activity |
| Male | 19–24 | 2,700 | 3,000 | 3,600 |
| Male | 25–50 | 3,000 | 3,200 | 4,000 |
| Female | 19–24 | 2,000 | 2,100 | 2,600 |
| Female | 25–50 | 2,200 | 2,300 | 2,800 |

Data from the National Academy of Sciences

**7.4.11**

1. Who needs to eat the most Calories per day to maintain a moderate activity level?

   A  20-year-old male

   B  20-year-old female

   C  30-year-old male

   D  30-year-old female

**7.4.11**

2. Using the table above, determine how many more Calories a 35-year-old female needs to eat if she increases her activity level from moderate to high?

   A  500 Calories

   B  600 Calories

   C  700 Calories

   D  800 Calories

**7.4.8**

3. Foods derived from grains usually contain large amounts of what type of nutrient?

   A  carbohydrate

   B  fat

   C  mineral

   D  protein

The illustration below shows a body system.

**7.4.4**

4. What is the organ labeled A?

   A  alveolus

   B  bladder

   C  gallbladder

   D  kidney

**7.4.4**

5. To which body system does the above organ labeled A belong?

   A  circulatory

   B  digestive

   C  respiratory

   D  urinary

### Part 2 | Critical Response

8. Cilia remove mucus, bacteria, and dirt particles from the respiratory system. If the cilia are damaged, these materials cannot be removed, so they build up in the airways and the airways cannot work properly.

9. The antibiotics may kill some or many of the bacteria normally found in the large intestine. Vitamin K, niacin, and thiamine may not be produced. Bacterial breakdown of bile pigments may be reduced. Breakdown of other intestinal materials may be affected.

10. In the digestive system, mucus moistens food and has protective functions in the stomach. In the respiratory system, mucus protects the airways by trapping particles.

**6.** Which disease is related to smoking?

**A** bronchitis

**B** diabetes

**C** influenza

**D** measles

**7.** For one week, research scientists collected and accurately measured the amount of body water lost and gained per day for four different patients. The table below lists results from their investigation.

| Body Water Gained (+) and Lost (−) | | | | |
|---|---|---|---|---|
| Patient | Day 1 (L) | Day 2 (L) | Day 3 (L) | Day 4 (L) |
| 1 | +0.15 | +0.15 | −0.35 | +0.12 |
| 2 | −0.01 | 0.00 | −0.20 | −0.01 |
| 3 | 0.00 | +0.20 | −0.28 | +0.01 |
| 4 | −0.50 | −0.50 | −0.55 | −0.32 |

Which patient had the greatest total gain in body water over the four-day period?

**A** 1

**B** 2

**C** 3

**D** 4

---

**Test-Taking Tip**

**Answer All Questions** Never skip a question. If you are unsure of an answer, mark your best guess on another sheet of paper and mark the question in your test booklet to remind you to come back to it at the end of the test.

---

## Part 2 Critical Response

**7.4.4**

**8.** Explain the role of cilia in the respiratory system. In chronic bronchitis, cilia are damaged. What effects does this damage have on the respiratory system?

**7.4.12**

**9.** If a person is taking antibiotics to fight off a bacterial infection, what might happen to the normal bacteria living in the large intestine? How would this affect the body?

**10.** Compare and contrast the roles of mucus in the digestive and respiratory systems.

**7.4.6**

**11.** The illustration below shows the food pyramid.

Explain why the greatest number of servings should come from the food group shown at the base of the food pyramid.

**12.** A person had a urine test that showed protein in the urine. Is protein normally present in the urine? How do you know? What might the results of this urine test mean?

## Rubrics

The following rubric is a sample scoring device for critical response questions.

### Critical Response

| Points | Description |
|---|---|
| 4 | The student demonstrates a thorough understanding of the science of the task. The response may contain minor flaws that do not detract from the demonstration of a thorough understanding. |
| 3 | The student demonstrates an understanding of the science of the task. The response is essentially correct and demonstrates an essential but less than thorough understanding of the science. |
| 2 | The student demonstrates only a partial understanding of the science of the task. Although the student may have used the correct approach to a solution or may have provided a correct solution, the work lacks an essential understanding of the underlying science concepts. |
| 1 | The student demonstrates a very limited understanding of the science of the task. The response is incomplete and exhibits many flaws. |
| 0 | The student provides a completely incorrect solution or no response at all. |

---

**11.** The greatest number of servings should come from the bread and cereal group because these foods are carbohydrates. Carbohydrates are the main sources of energy for the body.

**12.** First line: skin, and respiratory, digestive, and circulatory systems. Respiratory system traps disease organisms with mucus and cilia. Circulatory system has white blood cells that destroy invaders. Second line: specific immunity against invaders that make it past first line. Antibodies that destroy the disease-causing organisms are made.

| Section/Objectives | Standards | | Labs/Features |
|---|---|---|---|
| **Chapter Opener** | **National** | **State/Local** | **Launch Lab:** Transportation by Road and Vessel, p. 161 **Foldables,** p. 161 |
| | See pp. 16T–17T for a Key to Standards. | Detailed standards begin on page IN8. | A data-collection lab using Probeware technology can be found in the **Probeware Lab Manual,** pp. 5–8 |
| **Section 1 Blood** ⏱ 2 sessions 📦 1 block  1. **Identify** the parts and functions of blood. 2. **Explain** why blood types are checked before a transfusion. 3. **Give** examples of diseases of blood. | National Content Standards: UCP.1–UCP.3, UCP.5, A.1, A.2, C.1, C.3, F.1 | Indiana Standards: 7.1.9, 7.4.4, 7.4.13 | **Science Online,** p. 163 **MiniLAB:** Modeling Scab Formation, p. 164 **Integrate History,** p. 165 |
| **Section 2 Circulation** ⏱ 3 sessions 📦 1.5 blocks  4. **Compare and contrast** arteries, veins, and capillaries. 5. **Explain** how blood moves through the heart. 6. **Identify** the functions of the pulmonary and systemic circulation systems. 7. **Describe** functions of the lymphatic system. | National Content Standards: UCP.1–UCP.3, UCP.5, A.1, A.2, C.1, C.3 | Indiana Standards: 7.4.4, 7.4.11 | **Science Online,** p. 172 |
| **Section 3 Immunity** ⏱ 2 sessions 📦 1 block  8. **Explain** the difference between an antigen and an antibody. 9. **Compare and contrast** active and passive immunity. | National Content Standards: UCP.1–UCP.3, UCP.5, A.1, A.2, C.1, C.3, C.4, F.1 | Indiana Standards: 7.4.10, 7.4.13, 7.6.4, 7.7.2 | **Integrate Social Studies,** p. 174 **MiniLAB:** Determining Reproduction Rates, p. 175 |
| **Section 4 Diseases** ⏱ 2.5 sessions 📦 1.5 blocks  10. **Describe** the work of Pasteur, Koch, and Lister in the discovery and prevention of disease. 11. **Identify** diseases caused by viruses and bacteria. 12. **Explain** how HIV affects the immune system. 13. **Define** noninfectious diseases and list their causes. 14. **Explain** what happens during an allergic reaction. | National Content Standards: UCP.1–UCP.3, UCP.5, A.1, A.2, C.1, C.3, C.4, F.1 | Indiana Standards: 7.1.5, 7.4.4, 7.4.10, 7.4.12, 7.4.14, 7.5.3, 7.6.1–7.6.4 | **Science Online,** p. 178 **Visualizing Koch's Rules,** p. 179 **Applying Science,** p. 180 **Lab:** Microorganisms and Disease, p. 185 **Lab:** Blood Type Reactions, p. 186 **Science and History:** Have a Heart, p. 188 |

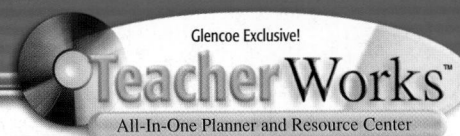

| Lab Materials | Reproducible Resources | Section Assessment | Technology |
|---|---|---|---|
| **Launch Lab:** maps of your city, county, or state, Science Journal | **Chapter FAST FILE Resources**<br>Foldables Worksheet, p. 17<br>Directed Reading Overview, p. 19<br>Note-taking Worksheets, pp. 35–37 | | **TeacherWorks includes:**<br>• Interactive Teacher Edition<br>• Lesson Planner with calendar<br>• Access to all program blacklines<br>• Correlations to standards<br>• Web links |
| **MiniLAB:** 5-cm by 5-cm square of gauze, aluminum foil, liquid bandage solution, dropper, water | **Chapter FAST FILE Resources**<br>Transparency Activity, p. 46<br>MiniLAB Worksheet, p. 3<br>Enrichment, p. 31<br>Reinforcement, p. 27<br>Directed Reading, p. 20<br>Transparency Activity, p. 45 | **Portfolio**<br>Differentiated Instruction, p. 165<br>**Performance**<br>MiniLAB, p. 164<br>Applying Skills, p. 166<br>**Content**<br>Section Review, p. 166 | Section Focus Transparency<br>Teaching Transparency<br>Guided Reading Audio Program<br>Interactive Chalkboard CD-ROM |
| *Need materials?* Contact Science Kit at 1-800-828-7777 or www.sciencekit.com on the Internet. | **Chapter FAST FILE Resources**<br>Transparency Activity, p. 47<br>Enrichment, p. 32<br>Reinforcement, p. 28<br>Directed Reading, p. 20<br>Transparency Activity, pp. 50–51 | **Portfolio**<br>Assessment, p. 172<br>**Performance**<br>Applying Skills, p. 172<br>**Content**<br>Section Review, p. 172 | Section Focus Transparency<br>Guided Reading Audio Program<br>Interactive Chalkboard CD-ROM |
| **MiniLAB:** pennies, paper, pencil, calculator | **Chapter FAST FILE Resources**<br>Transparency Activity, p. 48<br>MiniLAB Worksheet, p. 4<br>Enrichment, p. 33<br>Reinforcement, p. 29<br>Directed Reading, p. 21 | **Portfolio**<br>Differentiated Instruction, p. 175<br>**Performance**<br>MiniLAB, p. 175<br>Applying Skills, p. 176<br>**Content**<br>Section Review, p. 176 | Section Focus Transparency<br>Guided Reading Audio Program<br>Interactive Chalkboard CD-ROM |
| **Lab:** fresh apples, rotting apple, rubbing alcohol, self-sealing plastic bags, labels, paper towels, sandpaper, cotton ball, soapy water, newspaper<br>**Lab:** simulated blood, lemon juice, water, droppers, paper cups, pen, graduated cylinder | **Chapter FAST FILE Resources**<br>Transparency Activity, p. 49<br>Enrichment, p. 34<br>Reinforcement, p. 30<br>Directed Reading, p. 21<br>Lab Worksheets, pp. 5–8<br>Lab Activities, pp. 9–16 | **Portfolio**<br>Differentiated Instruction, p. 179<br>**Performance**<br>Applying Science, p. 180<br>Applying Math, p. 184<br>**Content**<br>Section Review, p. 184 | Section Focus Transparency<br>Virtual Labs CD-ROM<br>Guided Reading Audio Program<br>Interactive Chalkboard CD-ROM<br>Probeware Lab<br>Video Lab |

## End of Chapter Assessment

| Blackline Masters | Technology | Professional Series |
|---|---|---|
| **Chapter FAST FILE Resources**<br>Chapter Review, pp. 39–40<br>Chapter Tests, pp. 41–44<br>**Mastering the Grade 7 Indiana Science Standards** | MindJogger Videoquiz<br>IN Test Prep and Practice ExamView®<br>ExamView® Pro Testmaker<br>TeacherWorks CD-ROM<br>Interactive Chalkboard CD-ROM | **Performance Assessment in the Science Classroom (PASC)** |

## Transparencies

### Section Focus

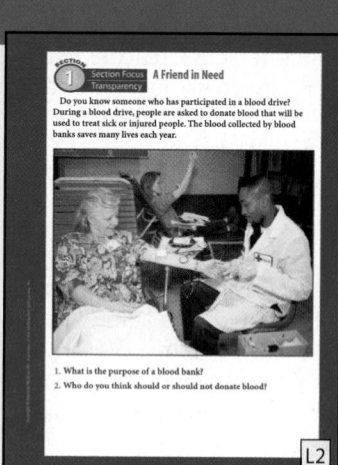

**Section Focus Transparency — A Friend in Need**

Do you know someone who has participated in a blood drive? During a blood drive, people are asked to donate blood that will be used to treat sick or injured people. The blood collected by blood banks saves many lives each year.

1. What is the purpose of a blood bank?
2. Who do you think should or should not donate blood?

L2

**Section Focus Transparency — How to Relax in Traffic**

Venice is a city in Italy that includes over one hundred islands. Because there's so much water, Venetians use canals instead of streets for transportation. There is a main canal, called the Grand Canal, and many smaller canals branching off the main canal.

1. If you compared the canals in Venice to blood vessels, what would the water represent?
2. What might the gondolas represent?

L2

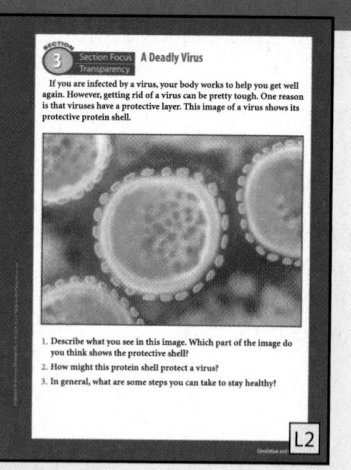

**Section Focus Transparency — A Deadly Virus**

If you are infected by a virus, your body works to help you get well again. However, getting rid of a virus can be pretty tough. One reason is that viruses have a protective layer. This image of a virus shows its protective protein shell.

1. Describe what you see in this image. Which part of the image do you think shows the protective shell?
2. How might this protein shell protect a virus?
3. In general, what are some steps you can take to stay healthy?

L2

This is a representation of key blackline masters available in the Teacher Classroom Resources. See Resource Manager boxes within the chapter for additional information.

## Key to Teaching Strategies

The following designations will help you decide which activities are appropriate for your students.

**L1** Level 1 activities should be appropriate for students with learning difficulties.

**L2** Level 2 activities should be within the ability range of all students.

**L3** Level 3 activities are designed for above-average students.

**ELL** ELL activities should be within the ability range of English-Language Learners.

**COOP LEARN** Cooperative Learning activities are designed for small group work.

**LS** Multiple Learning Styles logos, as described on page 12T, are used throughout to indicate strategies that address different learning styles.

**P** These strategies represent student products that can be placed into a best-work portfolio.

**PBL** Problem-Based Learning activities apply real-world situations to learning.

### Assessment

**Assessment Transparency — Circulation and Immunity**

*Directions: Carefully review the table and answer the following questions.*

**Estimated HIV/AIDS in Western Europe, 1999**

| Country | Adult Population Living with HIV/AIDS | Transmission | |
| --- | --- | --- | --- |
| | | IV Drug Use | Contaminated Blood |
| France | 0.43% | 24% | 5% |
| Germany | 0.10% | 15% | 5% |
| Greece | 0.16% | 5% | 9% |
| Portugal | 0.74% | 49% | 3% |
| Spain | 0.58% | 66% | 2% |

1. According to the table, which country has the highest percentage of people with HIV/AIDS?
   A France    C Portugal
   B Germany   D Spain
2. According to the table, which country has the highest percentage of infection by blood transfusions?
   F France
   G Germany
   H Greece
   J Portugal
3. According to the table, which country has the highest percentage of people infected by drug use?
   A France
   B Germany
   C Spain
   D Greece

L2

### Teaching

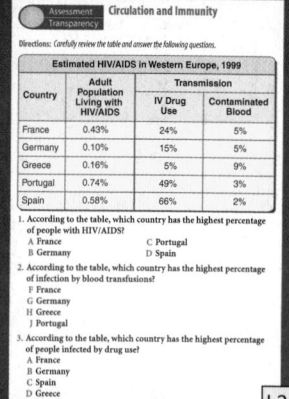

**Teaching Transparency — Pulmonary Circulation**

L2

## Hands-on Activities

### Student Text Lab Worksheet

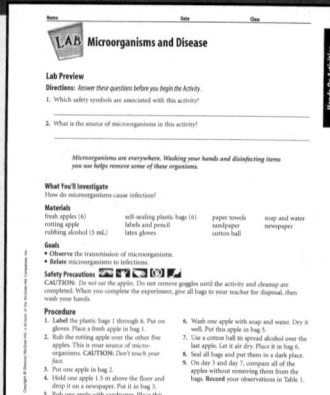

**LAB — Microorganisms and Disease**

**Lab Preview**
**Directions:** *Answer these questions before you begin the Activity.*
1. Which safety symbols are associated with this activity?

2. What is the source of microorganisms in this activity?

*Microorganisms are everywhere. Washing your hands and disinfecting items you use help remove some of these organisms.*

**What You'll Investigate**
How do microorganisms cause infection?

**Materials**
fresh apples (6)
rotting apple
rubbing alcohol (5 mL)
self-sealing plastic bags (6)
labels and pencil
latex gloves
paper towels
sandpaper
cotton ball
soap and water
newspaper

**Goals**
• Observe the transmission of microorganisms.
• Relate microorganisms to infections.

**Safety Precautions**
CAUTION: *Do not eat the apples. Do not remove goggles until the activity and cleanup are completed. When you complete the experiment, give all bags to your teacher for disposal, then wash your hands.*

**Procedure**
1. Label the plastic bags 1 through 6. Put on gloves. Place a fresh apple in bag 1.
2. Rub the rotting apple over the other five apples. This is your source of microorganisms. CAUTION: Don't touch your face.
3. Put one apple in bag 2.
4. Hold one apple 1.5 m above the floor and drop it on a newspaper. Put it in bag 3.
5. Rub one apple with sandpaper. Place this apple in bag 4.
6. Wash one apple with soap and water. Dry it well. Put this apple in bag 5.
7. Use a cotton ball to spread alcohol over the last apple. Let it air dry. Place it in bag 6.
8. Seal all bags and put them in a dark place.
9. On days 3 and 7, compare all of the apples without removing them from the bags. Record your observations in Table 1.

L2

### Laboratory Activities

**Laboratory Activity — Immunity Simulation**

To defend itself against disease, the human body is able to chemically "recognize" proteins and chemicals that are foreign to its system. Any protein or chemical that the body recognizes as not one of its own is called an antigen. When an antigen enters the body, a healthy immune system responds by producing a protein called an antibody. The antibody binds with the antigen, making the antigen useless. Large white blood cells then digest the antigen. In this way, the body develops an immunity to that antigen.

**Strategy**
You will simulate antigens in the blood.
You will simulate antibodies in the blood.
You will infer from the results of the simulation how antibody immunity works in the human body.

**Materials**
10 labels and pencils
5 beakers, glass
cylinder, graduated
milk
food coloring, red
5 stirring rods, glass
water
lemon juice
vinegar
5 test tubes, glass
test-tube rack
mortar and pestle
antacid, tablets
antacid, liquid
CAUTION: *Use care when handling sharp objects. Do not taste, eat, or drink any materials used in the lab.*

**Figure 1**

**Procedure**
**Part A—Antibodies Attack Antigens**
1. Using the labels, mark the glass beakers A–E, as in Figure 1.
2. Using the graduated cylinder, add 25 mL of milk to each of the glass beakers.
3. Set beaker A aside.
4. Place one drop of red food coloring into beakers B, C, D, and E. Stir the contents of each beaker with a glass stirring rod. Set beaker B aside.
5. Using the graduated cylinder, add 10 mL of tap water to beaker C. Stir the contents with a glass stirring rod and set beaker C aside.
6. Clean the graduated cylinder and add 10 mL of lemon juice to beaker D. Stir the contents with a glass stirring rod and set beaker D aside.
7. Clean the graduated cylinder and add 10 mL of vinegar to beaker E. Stir the contents with a glass stirring rod and set beaker E aside.
8. Wait 5 min. Then, observe each beaker and write your observations in Table 1.

L2

## Meeting Different Ability Levels

### Content Outline

L2

### Reinforcement

L2

### Enrichment

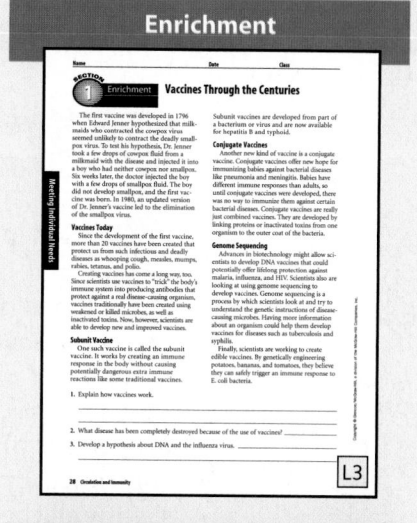

L3

### Directed Reading (English/Spanish)

L1

### Study Guide

L2

### Reading Essentials

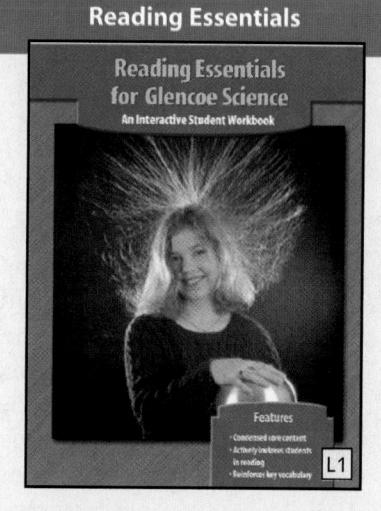

L1

## Assessment

### Test Practice Workbook

L2

### Chapter Review

L2

### Chapter Tests

L2

# Science Content Background

## section 1

### Blood

### A Liquid Tissue

The liquid component of blood, plasma, is a complex solution of organic and inorganic substances dissolved in water. Blood is about 90 percent water and eight percent proteins. The remaining two percent is made up of dissolved substances such as electrolytes, gases, and nutrients. Blood characteristics such as pH and sugar content are precisely controlled by the body. The pH of blood is slightly alkaline, and serious problems can occur if the pH changes only slightly.

## section 2

### Circulation

### The Heart

The heart is a muscular organ that lies in the thoracic cavity between the lungs. It is enclosed by a protective sac of fibrous tissue, the pericardium.

The initiation of the heartbeat originates within the heart muscle. The sinoatrial node is a modified piece of cardiac muscle tissue located near the superior vena cava. An impulse for this node spreads to the atria of the heart, causing them to contract. Another node (atrioventricular) receives the signal and then transmits it to the ventricles, causing them to contract.

### Blood Vessels

A cross section of arteries and veins shows that the walls have three layers. The inner lining of the vessels is covered with two types of tissue; one of these is a network of elastic connective tissue. The middle layer is smooth muscle and elastic tissue. The outer layer is collagenous connective tissue. The middle layer in veins is less developed than it is in arteries, and therefore collapses more easily. Capillaries have walls only one cell thick. This allows materials to diffuse through them.

### Blood Pressure

The pressure in the blood vessels is the result of a greater amount of blood being pumped into the arteries than can be absorbed by the arterioles and capillaries. Blood pressure is measured in millimeters of mercury with a sphygmomanometer.

### The Lymphatic System

Lymph is blood plasma that has diffused and filtered from the blood capillaries into the spaces between cells. Like blood plasma, lymph consists mainly of water, some dissolved substances, and white blood cells called lymphocytes.

Lymph passes through lymph capillaries, larger lymph vessels, lymph nodes, and lymph glands before entering a vein. Lymph is not under great pressure; therefore, external forces are needed to cause it to flow. Gravity and muscle contractions play a role in the movement of lymph.

## chapter content resources

**Internet Resources**
For additional content background, visit **in7.msscience.com** to:
- access your book online
- find references to related articles in popular science magazines
- access Web links with related content background
- access current events with science journal topics

**Print Resources**
*The Circulatory System,* by Regina Avraham, Chelsea House Publishers, 2000
*101 Questions about Blood and Circulation with Answers Straight from the Heart,* by Faith Hickman Brynie, Millbrook Press, 2001
*How the Immune System Works,* by Lauren Sompayrac, Blackwell Publishers, 2002

## Immunity

### Active Immunity

A natural active immunity is developed after a person contracts and recovers from diseases such as measles or mumps. Defensive proteins, called antibodies, produced in the body counteract the invading microorganism's proteins called antigens. The interaction between antigens and antibodies stimulates the release of histamine and complement compounds.

Artificial active immunity is an induced immunity. A person is given an injection or an oral dose of a noninfectious disease antigen. Noninfectious antigens can come from three sources: 1) microorganism secretions that have been detoxified, 2) dead microorganisms, and 3) living microorganisms. The body forms antibodies against the antigen providing immunity. Booster shots may be required to keep artificial immunity active.

### Passive Immunity

Passive artificial immunity is acquired when antibodies produced in another animal are injected into the body. The serum containing the antibodies is often obtained from horses that were inoculated with disease antigens and then produced antibodies within their own body systems.

Passive natural immunity is that which an infant receives from the mother via the placenta.

### Teacher to Teacher
Jeff Remington
Palmyra Middle School
Palmyra, PA

"Obtain a non-toxic 100% synthetic organic colorant (orange or blue) whose plastic particles are five microns or smaller to simulate germs. Sprinkle a small amount of the powder on the hands of a few students and on classroom surfaces. After your students shake hands or touch the surfaces, use an ultra-violet lamp (black light) to demonstrate the transfer of 'germs' to one another."

*Jeff Remington*

Because this protection only lasts for a few months, the child must be given inoculations to establish his or her own immunity to diseases.

## Diseases

### Germ Theory

In early history, the causes of diseases were associated with the anger of the gods, evil vapors, or imbalances in body fluids. By the early and mid 1800s, researchers, such as French chemist Louis Pasteur, developed a germ theory that indicated microorganisms might be responsible for disease. It is now known that pathogenic organisms such as viruses, bacteria, yeasts, protozoans, and hookworms cause disease by secreting toxins, by destroying red blood cells, or by ingesting tissues.

### Infectious Diseases

Infectious or communicable diseases can be transmitted from one organism to another by food, through the air, by insects, by parasites, or by sexual contact or exchange of body fluids. Bacteria and viruses cause sexually transmitted diseases. Some organisms are able to gain entrance to the body through the thin membranes of the eyes, nose, and mouth. Good hygiene habits of washing with soap and water remove many potentially troublesome organisms from the surface of the skin.

### Noninfectious Diseases

Some diseases and disorders are noninfectious. Although they are not contracted from other people or from objects, these conditions are usually unavoidable. Some noncommunicable diseases and disorders are the result of inheriting certain genes. Included in such genetic disorders are cystic fibrosis, hemophilia, Huntington's chorea, muscular dystrophy, sickle-cell anemia, and Tay-Sachs disease. Toxins, or chemicals, introduced into the body through breathing, touching, drinking, or eating, can cause noninfectious diseases such as allergies, emphysema, and cancer.

## Chapter Vocabulary

plasma, p. 162
hemoglobin, p. 163
platelet, p. 163
capillary, p. 169
artery, p. 169
vein, p. 169
lymph, p. 172
antigen, p. 174
antibody, p. 174
active immunity, p. 175
passive immunity, p. 175
pasteurization, p. 177
infectious disease, p. 178
noninfectious disease, p.182
allergen, p. 182

**Science Journal** Student responses will vary. Students may include questions about blood transfusions, heart diseases, or illnesses that they have heard about in the news.

## INTERACTIVE CHALKBOARD
### with Image Bank

**PowerPoint® Presentations**

This CD-ROM is an editable Microsoft® PowerPoint® presentation that includes:
- a pre-made presentation for every chapter
- interactive graphics
- animations
- audio clips
- image bank
- all new section and chapter questions
- Standardized Test Practice
- transparencies
- pre-lab questions for all labs
- Foldables directions
- links to in7.msscience.com

**Academic Standards—4:** Students . . . recognize that cells function in similar ways in all organisms. **6:** Students gain understanding of how the scientific enterprise operates through examples of historical events . . . new ideas . . . grow or transform slowly through the contributions of many different investigators.
**Also covers:** Academic Standards 1, 5, 7 (Detailed standards begin on page IN8.)

# Circulation and Immunity

## chapter preview

### sections

1  **Blood**

2  **Circulation**

3  **Immunity**

4  **Diseases**
   *Lab* **Microorganisms and Disease**
   *Lab* **Blood Type Reactions**
   *Virtual Lab* **How does the body protect itself against foreign substances?**

160

### The Flow of Traffic

This highway interchange is simple compared to how blood travels within your body. In this chapter, you will discover how complex your circulatory system is—from parts of your blood to how it travels through your body and fights disease.

**Science Journal** Write three questions that you have about blood, circulation, or how diseases are spread.

## Theme Connection

**Systems and Interactions** One major theme of science is interactions among systems. This chapter focuses on interactions within the body. Blood pressure remains relatively constant so that enough blood reaches all organs and tissues in the body. Natural defenses in the body aid in preventing disease.

### About the Photo

**Flow of Traffic** The complexity of a highway interchange can be related to the complexity of blood flow through the body. Tracing the path of blood flow through the complex pulmonary circulation system can be compared to the route a vehicle takes through the simpler highway interchange. The road analogy can be continued as students learn how substances are moved through the body via blood vessels.

# Start-Up Activities

## Transportation by Road and Vessel

Your circulatory system is like a road system. Just as roads are used to transport goods to homes and factories, your blood vessels transport substances throughout your body. You'll find out how similar roads and blood vessels are in this lab.

1. Observe a map of your city, county, or state.
2. Identify roads that are interstates, as well as state and county roads, using the map key.
3. Plan a route to a destination that your teacher describes. Then plan a different return trip.
4. Draw a diagram in your Science Journal showing your routes to and from the destination.
5. **Think Critically** If the destination represents your heart, what do the routes represent? In your Science Journal, draw a comparison between a blocked road on your map and a clogged artery in your body.

**Circulation** Make the following Foldable to help you organize information and diagram ideas about circulation.

**STEP 1** Fold a sheet of paper in half lengthwise. Make the back edge about 5 cm longer than the front edge.

**STEP 2** Turn the paper so the fold is on the bottom. Then fold it into thirds.

**STEP 3** Unfold and cut only the top layer along both folds to make three tabs.

**STEP 4** Label the Foldable as shown.

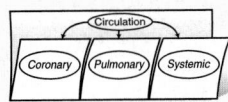

**Read and Write** As you read the chapter, write information about each circulatory system under the appropriate tab.

Preview this chapter's content and activities at in7.msscience.com

---

**Purpose** Students model how the circulatory system transports substances throughout the body.
**L2** **IS** **Visual-Spatial**

**Preparation** Obtain enough maps so that each group can plan a route to and from a different destination.

**Materials** maps of your city, county, or state; Science Journal

**Teaching Strategy** Help students interpret the map key. Point out that colors as well as symbols can be used to denote different types of roads.

## Think Critically

Possible answer: The routes represent the blood vessels that transport materials to and from the heart. If a road is blocked, cars cannot travel on it; if an artery is clogged, blood cannot flow through it.

## Assessment

**Oral** Again refer students to their map's legend. Have them infer why there are different types of roads and how they might be analogous to the circulatory system. Different types of roads carry different amounts of traffic at different speeds. They are analogous to different sizes of blood vessels in the body. Use **Performance Assessment in the Science Classroom,** p. 89.

 **Dinah Zike Study Fold**

Student preparation materials for this Foldable are available in the Chapter *FAST FILE* Resources.

### Probeware Labs

This chapter's data-collection lab using Probeware technology is included on the *Video Labs CD-ROM.* See the *Probeware Lab Manual* pages 5–8 for student worksheets.

Standards—**7.4.4**: Explain . . . that various organs and tissues function to serve the needs of cells for food, air, and waste removal. **7.4.13**: Explain that white blood cells engulf invaders or produce antibodies that attack invaders or mark the invaders for killing by other white blood cells. Know that the antibodies produced will remain and can fight off subsequent invaders of the same kind.

Also covers: 7.1.9 (Detailed standards begin on page IN8.)

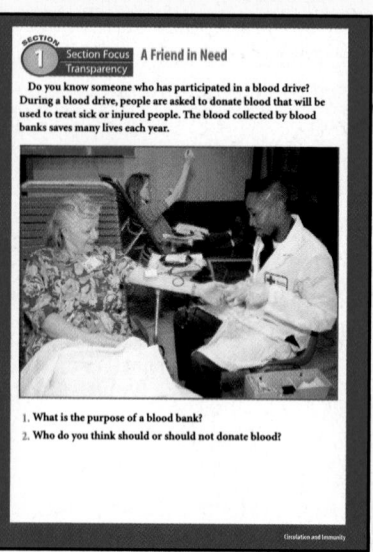
# Section 1

# Blood

## as you read

### *What* You'll Learn
- **Identify** the parts and functions of blood.
- **Explain** why blood types are checked before a transfusion.
- **Give** examples of diseases of blood.

### *Why* It's Important
Blood plays a part in every major activity of your body.

### Review Vocabulary
**diffusion:** a type of passive transport within cells in which molecules move from areas where there are more of them to areas where there are fewer of them

### New Vocabulary
- plasma
- platelet
- hemoglobin

## Functions of Blood

You take a last, deep, calming breath before plunging into a dark, vessel-like tube. Water is everywhere. You take a hard right turn, then left as you streak through a narrow tunnel of twists and turns. The water transports you down the slide much like the way blood carries substances to all parts of your body. Blood has four important functions.

1. Blood carries oxygen from your lungs to all your body cells. Carbon dioxide diffuses from your body cells into your blood. Your blood carries carbon dioxide to your lungs to be exhaled.

2. Blood carries waste products from your cells to your kidneys to be removed.

3. Blood transports nutrients and other substances to your body cells.

4. Cells and molecules in blood fight infections and help heal wounds.

Anything that disrupts or changes these functions affects all the tissues of your body. Can you understand why blood is sometimes called the tissue of life?

## Parts of Blood

A close look at blood tells you that blood is not just a red-colored liquid. Blood is a tissue made of plasma (PLAZ muh), red and white blood cells, and platelets (PLAYT luts), shown in **Figure 1.** Blood makes up about eight percent of your body's total mass. If you weigh 45 kg, you have about 3.6 kg of blood moving through your body.

**Plasma** The liquid part of blood, which is made mostly of water, is called **plasma.** It makes up more than half the volume of blood. Nutrients, minerals, and oxygen are dissolved in plasma so that they can be carried to body cells. Wastes from body cells also are carried in plasma.

| 55% | Plasma |
| 45% | White blood cells / Red blood cells |

**Figure 1** The blood in this graduated cylinder has separated into its parts. Each part plays a key role in body functions.

**162 CHAPTER 6** Circulation and Immunity

**Blood Cells** Disk-shaped red blood cells, shown in **Figure 2,** are different from other cells in your body because they have no nuclei. They contain **hemoglobin** (HEE muh gloh bun), which is a molecule that carries oxygen and carbon dioxide. Hemoglobin carries oxygen from your lungs to your body cells. Then it carries some of the carbon dioxide from your body cells back to your lungs. The rest of the carbon dioxide is carried in the cytoplasm of red blood cells and in plasma.

Red blood cells have a life span of about 120 days. They are made at a rate of 2 million to 3 million per second in the center of long bones, like the femur in your thigh. Red blood cells wear out and are destroyed at about the same rate.

A cubic millimeter of blood, about the size of a grain of rice, has about 5 million red blood cells. In contrast, a cubic millimeter of blood has about 5,000 to 10,000 white blood cells. White blood cells fight bacteria, viruses, and other invaders of your body. Your body reacts to invaders by increasing the number of white blood cells. These cells leave the blood through capillary walls and go into the tissues that have been invaded. Here, they destroy bacteria and viruses and absorb dead cells. The life span of white blood cells varies from a few days to many months.

Circulating with the red and white blood cells are platelets. **Platelets** are irregularly shaped cell fragments that help clot blood. A cubic millimeter of blood can contain as many as 400,000 platelets. Platelets have a life span of five to nine days.

**Science Online**

**Topic: Human White Blood Cells**

Visit in7.msscience.com for Web links to information about the types of human white blood cells and their functions.

**Activity** Make a table showing the functions of the various types of white blood cells.

**Indiana Academic Standard Check**

**7.4.13:** Explain that white blood cells engulf invaders or produce antibodies....

✓ How do white blood cells enter body tissues to attack pathogens?

✓ They move through capillary walls.

**Figure 2** Blood cells have different roles.

Color-enhanced SEM
Magnification: 1000×

Red blood cells supply your body with oxygen. Platelets help stop bleeding and release chemicals that help form filaments of fibrin.

Several types, sizes, and shapes of white blood cells exist. These cells destroy bacteria, viruses, and foreign substances.

*Platelets*
*Red blood cells*
*Nuclei*
*White blood cells*

SECTION 1 Blood **163**

## 2 Teach

### Make a Model
**Parts of Blood** Have students make models of red and white blood cells from modeling clay. Encourage students to make the models to scale to reinforce concepts about the relative sizes, shapes, and colors of the cells.
L2 IS **Kinesthetic**

### Use an Analogy
**White Blood Cell Movement** Have students view a film clip of amoeba activity to draw an analogy to white blood cell movement and ingestion.

### Discussion
**Platelet Function** How do blood platelets function in maintaining homeostasis when the skin is cut? Platelets form clots to help prevent further blood loss.

### Quick Demo
**Blood Cells**
**Materials** microscope, prepared microscope slide of human blood
**Estimated Time** five minutes
**Procedure** Have students look at a slide of red blood cells, white blood cells, and platelets to get an idea of the sizes of each of these components of blood.

## Differentiated Instruction

**English-Language Learners** Explain that words can be understood by analyzing the different parts of words to discover their meanings. Have students find out what *CPR* stands for, analyze the parts of the words to determine their meanings, and then describe this technique in their Science Journals.

*CPR* stands for "cardiopulmonary resuscitation." *Cardio* = "heart"; *pulmonary* = "lungs"; *resuscitation* = "to revive." CPR is an emergency procedure that includes clearing air passages, mouth-to-mouth resuscitation, and heart massage.
L2

## Mini LAB

**Purpose** Students use a model to discover how a scab forms. **L2** **ELL** **IS** **Visual-Spatial**

**Materials** 5-cm × 5-cm square of gauze, aluminum foil, liquid bandage solution, dropper, water

**Teaching Strategy** Explain that the gauze represents the fibers formed in the clotting process.

**Analysis**

1. The water soaks into the untreated gauze but not into the treated area.
2. The treated area is like a scab because it forms a covering that prevents leakage of liquids and protects the area underneath it.

### Assessment

**Process** Have students use cotton cloth and white glue to make another model of scab formation and repeat the water drop test. Use **Performance Assessment in the Science Classroom,** p. 123.

### Discussion

**Hemophilia** Why would relatively minor cuts and bruises be hazardous to a person with hemophilia? Even minor cuts and bruises would cause major bleeding problems that could result in death.

**Answer** platelets, clotting factors, fibrin

---

**Figure 3** When the skin is damaged, a sticky blood clot seals the leaking blood vessel. Eventually, a scab forms to protect the wound from further damage and allow it to heal.

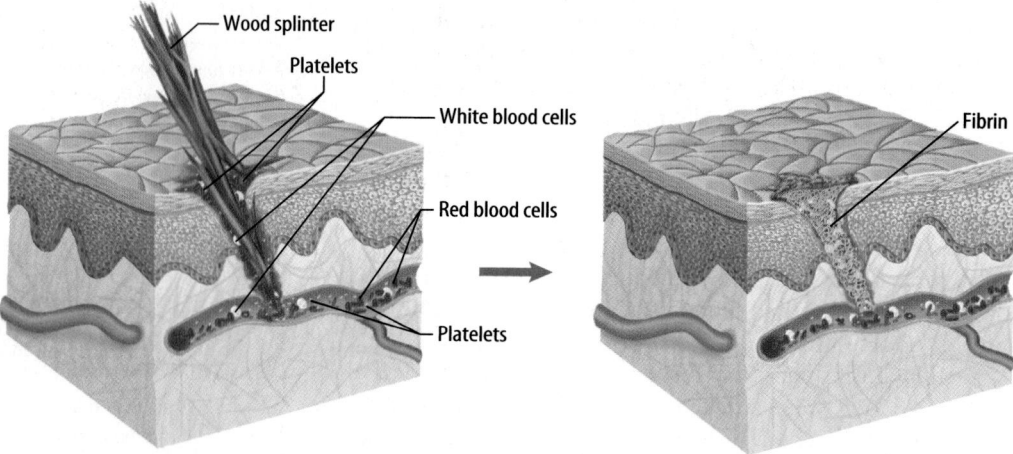

## Mini LAB

**Modeling Scab Formation**

**Procedure**

1. Place a 5-cm × 5-cm square of **gauze** on a piece of **aluminum foil.**
2. Place several drops of a **liquid bandage solution** onto the gauze and let it dry. Keep the liquid bandage away from eyes and mouth.
3. Use a **dropper** to place one drop of **water** onto the area of the liquid bandage. Place another drop of water in another area of the gauze.

**Analysis**

1. Compare the drops of water in both areas.
2. Describe how the treated area of the gauze is like a scab.

## Blood Clotting

You're running with your dog in a park, when suddenly you trip and fall down. Your knee starts to bleed, but the bleeding stops quickly. Already the wounded area has begun to heal. Bleeding stops because platelets and clotting factors in your blood make a blood clot that plugs the wounded blood vessels.

A blood clot also acts somewhat like a bandage. When you cut yourself, platelets stick to the wound and release chemicals. Then substances, called clotting factors, carry out a series of chemical reactions. These reactions cause threadlike fibers called fibrin (FI brun) to form a sticky net, as shown in **Figure 3.** This net traps escaping blood cells and plasma and forms a clot. The clot helps stop more blood from escaping. After the clot is in place and becomes hard, skin cells begin the repair process under the scab. Eventually, the scab is lifted off. Bacteria that get into the wound during the healing process usually are destroyed by white blood cells.

**✓ Reading Check** *What blood components help form blood clots?*

Most people will not bleed to death from a minor wound, such as a cut or scrape. However, some people have a genetic condition called hemophilia (hee muh FIH lee uh). Their plasma lacks one of the clotting factors that begins the clotting process. A minor injury can be a life-threatening problem for a person with hemophilia.

**164** **CHAPTER 6** Circulation and Immunity

---

## Science Journal

**Blood Clotting** Have students find out about the role of vitamin K, prothrombin, calcium ions, thrombin, fibrinogen, and fibrin in the mechanism of blood clotting. Suggest they use this information to draw in their Science Journals a labeled diagram showing the sequence of events and the components involved in this process. **L3** **IS** **Linguistic**

> **Vitamin K** is used in the liver to produce **prothrombin.**
>
> ↓
>
> In the presence of clotting factors, **calcium ions,** and platelets, prothrombin is converted to **thrombin.**
>
> ↓
>
> Thrombin acts as a catalyst to change **fibrinogen** to **fibrin.**
>
> ↓
>
> **Fibrin** produces long threads that stick to the damaged surface of the blood vessel and form the webbing of the clot, trapping blood cells and platelets, which strengthen the clot.

## Blood Types

Blood clots stop blood loss quickly in a minor wound, but with a serious wound a person might lose a lot of blood. A blood transfusion might be necessary. During a blood transfusion, a person receives donated blood or parts of blood. The medical provider must be sure that the right type of blood is given. If the wrong type is given, the red blood cells will clump together. Then, clots form in the blood vessels and the person could die.

**The ABO Identification System** People can inherit one of four types of blood: A, B, AB, or O. Types A, B, and AB have chemical identification tags called antigens (AN tih junz) on their red blood cells. Type O red blood cells have no antigens.

Each blood type also has specific antibodies in its plasma. Antibodies are proteins that destroy or neutralize substances that do not belong in or are not part of your body. Because of these antibodies, certain blood types cannot be mixed. This limits blood transfusion possibilities, as shown in **Table 1.** If type A blood is mixed with type B blood, the antibodies in type A blood determine that type B blood does not belong there. The antibodies in type A blood cause the type B red blood cells to clump. In the same way, type B blood antibodies cause type A blood to clump. Type AB blood has no antibodies, so people with this blood type can receive blood from A, B, AB, and O types. Type O blood has both A and B antibodies.

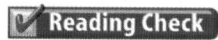 **Reading Check** *Why are people with type O blood called universal donors?*

**The Rh Factor** Another inherited chemical identification tag in blood is the Rh factor. If the Rh factor is on red blood cells, the person has Rh-positive (Rh+) blood. If it is not present, the person has Rh-negative (Rh−) blood. If an Rh− person receives a blood transfusion from an Rh+ person, he or she will produce antibodies against the Rh factor. These antibodies can cause Rh+ cells to clump. Clots then form in the blood vessels and the person could die. In the same way, an Rh− mother can make antibodies against her Rh+ baby during pregnancy. If the antibodies pass into the baby's blood, they can destroy the baby's red blood cells. To prevent deadly results, blood groups and Rh factor are checked before transfusions and during pregnancies.

**INTEGRATE History**

**Blood Transfusions** In 1665, the first successful blood transfusion was performed between two dogs. The first successful human-to-human blood transfusion was performed in 1818. However, many failures followed. The different blood types and the problems that result when they are mixed were unknown at that time. Research the discovery of the four types of blood and write a summary in your Science Journal.

| Table 1 Blood Transfusion Possibilities | | |
|------|-------------|-------------|
| **Type** | **Can Receive** | **Can Donate To** |
| A | O, A | A, AB |
| B | O, B | B, AB |
| AB | all | AB |
| O | O | all |

SECTION 1 Blood **165**

**INTEGRATE History**

**Blood Transfusions** The three main human blood groups—A, B, and C (later changed to O) were discovered in 1901 by Austrian physician Karl Landsteiner. One year later, his colleagues, Alfred von Decastello and Adriano Sturli, identified a fourth blood group—AB. In 1912, Roger Lee determined that O blood type is the universal donor and AB blood type is the universal recipient.

**Career** Investigate the duties of a Blood Bank Technology Specialist.

**Reading Check**

**Answer** able to give blood to people with all other blood types

**Activity**

**Blood Transfusions** Explain to students that even if the donor's and recipient's blood types are the same, a blood transfusion can be unsafe. Have students research reasons for this. A number of other blood factors can cause harmful reactions. Also, repeated transfusions of even the same blood type may eventually cause agglutination. This is because there are other antigens on red blood cells besides the A and B antigens. L3

## Teacher FYI

**Determining Blood Type** To determine the blood type of an individual, suspensions of the person's red blood cells are mixed separately with different serums. Each serum has a known, particular antibody. When a serum causes agglutination of blood cells, it indicates that the cells contain the antigen with which that specific antibody agglutinates. This reaction identifies the blood type of the individual.

## Visual Learning

**Table 1** After students have studied the information in this table, have them explain why people with blood type AB are sometimes called universal recipients. These people can receive all blood types.

## Differentiated Instruction

**Challenge** Students can research how blood transfusion experiments started in the early 1800s. Have them design a poster to report their findings. The first successful blood transfusion was performed in the seventeenth century by a French physician, Jean Baptiste Denis. He used lamb's blood. L3 P

**Figure 4** Persons with sickle-cell disease have misshapened red blood cells. The sickle-shaped cells clog the capillaries of a person with this disease. Oxygen cannot reach tissues served by the capillaries, and wastes cannot be removed. **Explain** *how this damages the affected tissues.*

## Diseases of Blood

Because blood circulates to all parts of your body and performs so many important functions, any disease of the blood is a cause for concern. One common disease of the blood is anemia (uh NEE mee uh). In this disease of red blood cells, body tissues can't get enough oxygen and are unable to carry on their usual activities. Anemia has many causes. Sometimes, anemia is caused by the loss of large amounts of blood. A diet lacking iron or certain vitamins also might cause anemia. Still other types of anemia are inherited problems related to the structure of the red blood cells. Cells from one such type of anemia, sickle-cell disease, are shown in **Figure 4.**

Leukemia (lew KEE mee uh) is a disease in which one or more types of white blood cells are made in excessive numbers. These cells are immature and do not fight infections well. These immature cells fill the bone marrow and crowd out the normal, mature cells. Then not enough red blood cells, normal white blood cells, and platelets can be made. Some types of leukemia affect children. Other kinds are more common in adults. Medicines, blood transfusions, and bone marrow transplants are used to treat this disease. If the treatments are not successful, the person will eventually die from related complications.

### section 1 review

#### Summary

**Functions and Parts of Blood**

- Blood carries oxygen, carbon dioxide, wastes, and nutrients.
- Blood contains cells that help fight infections and heal wounds.
- Blood is a tissue made of plasma, red and white blood cells, and platelets.

**Blood Clotting and Blood Types**

- Platelets and clotting factors form blood clots to stop bleeding from a wound.
- Blood type—A, B, AB, or O—must be identified before a person receives a transfusion.

**Diseases of Blood**

- Anemia affects red blood cells, while leukemia affects white blood cells.

#### Self Check

1. **List** the four functions of blood in the body.
2. **Compare and contrast** red blood cells, white blood cells, and platelets.
3. **Describe** how anemia and leukemia affect the blood.
4. **Explain** why blood type and Rh factor are checked before a transfusion.
5. **Think Critically** Think about the main job of your red blood cells. If red blood cells couldn't deliver oxygen to your cells, what would be the condition of your body tissues?

##### Applying Skills

6. **Interpret Data** Look at the data in **Table 1** about blood group interactions. To which group(s) can people with blood type AB donate blood?

 Science Online in7.msscience.com/self_check_quiz

### section 1 review

1. carries oxygen to cells and removes carbon dioxide; carries wastes to kidneys; transports nutrients from the digestive system to cells; has materials to fight infections and heal wounds

2. red: transport oxygen and carbon dioxide; white: fight infections;

   platelets: help in blood clotting

3. Anemia is a disease in which there are too few red blood cells. Leukemia is a disease in which large numbers of white blood cells are made.

4. to prevent blood cells from clumping

5. Wastes would build up and become toxic.

6. only to another person with type AB blood

Standards—**7.4.4:** … various organs and tissues function to serve the needs of cells for food, air, and waste removal. **7.4.11:** … Understand that regular exercise is important to maintain a healthy heart/lung system, good muscle tone, and strong bone structure.

# section 2
# Circulation

## The Body's Delivery System

It's time to get ready for school, but your younger sister is taking a long time in the shower. "Don't use up all the water," you shout. Water is carried throughout your house in pipes that are part of the plumbing system. The plumbing system supplies water for your needs and carries away wastes. Just as you expect water to flow when you turn on the faucet, your body needs a continuous supply of oxygen and nutrients and a way to remove wastes. In a similar way, materials are moved throughout your body by your cardiovascular (kar dee oh VAS kyuh lur) system. It includes your heart, kilometers of blood vessels, and blood. Blood vessels carry the blood to every part of your body, as shown in **Figure 5.** Recall that blood moves oxygen and nutrients to cells and carries carbon dioxide and other wastes away from the cells.

## The Heart

Your heart is an organ made of cardiac muscle tissue. It is located behind your breastbone, called the sternum, and between your lungs. Your heart has four compartments called chambers. The two upper chambers are called the right and left atriums (AY tree umz). The two lower chambers are called the right and left ventricles (VEN trih kulz). A one-way valve separates each atrium from the ventricle below it. The blood flows from an atrium to a ventricle, then from a ventricle into a blood vessel. A wall between the two atriums or the two ventricles keeps blood rich in oxygen separate from blood low in oxygen.

**Figure 5** The blood is pumped by the heart to all the cells of the body and then back to the heart through a network of blood vessels.

### as you read

#### *What* You'll Learn

- **Compare and contrast** arteries, veins, and capillaries.
- **Explain** how blood moves through the heart.
- **Identify** the functions of the pulmonary and systemic circulation systems.
- **Describe** functions of the lymphatic system.

#### *Why* It's Important

Your body's cells depend on blood vessels to deliver nutrients and remove wastes. The lymphatic system helps protect you from infections and disease.

#### Review Vocabulary
**tissue:** group of similar cells that work together to do one job

#### New Vocabulary
- capillary
- artery
- vein
- lymph

## 1 Motivate

**Bellringer**

**Section Focus Transparencies** also are available on the Interactive Chalkboard CD-ROM.

L2 ELL

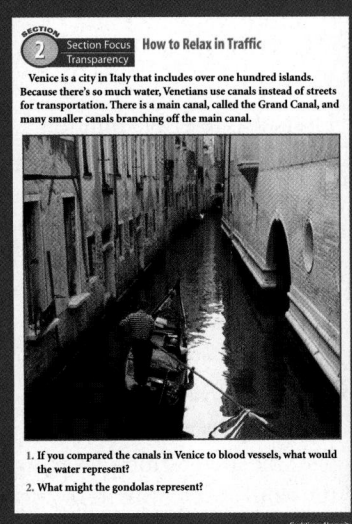

**Tie to Prior Knowledge**

**Transportation Systems** Have students list the parts of a transportation system. They may suggest roads, trucks, other vehicles, and intersections. Explain that parts similar to these exist in their bodies to carry materials from place to place.

### Section 2 Resource Manager

**Chapter *FAST FILE* Resources**
Transparency Activity, p. 47
Directed Reading for Content Mastery, p. 20
Enrichment, p. 32
Reinforcement, p. 28

**Home and Community Involvement,** p. 45

## Visual Learning

**Figure 6** Direct students to trace the flow of blood through the heart. Then have them explain why this definition of veins is correct or incorrect: "Pulmonary veins are vessels that carry more carbon dioxide than oxygen." The statement is incorrect. In pulmonary circulation the veins carry more oxygen than carbon dioxide. **IS Visual-Spatial**

## Quick Demo

**The Heart**

**Estimated Time** five minutes

**Procedure** To reinforce the actual position and size of the heart, make a closed fist with your right hand and hold it on your chest above your breastbone. Then ask each student to do the same.

## Use Science Words

**Word Meaning** Have students compare the architectural meaning of the word *atrium* with its biological meaning. In architectural use, the word *atrium* refers to an entrance hall or open court. In biological terms, the atrium is the entrance chamber that receives blood from the body.

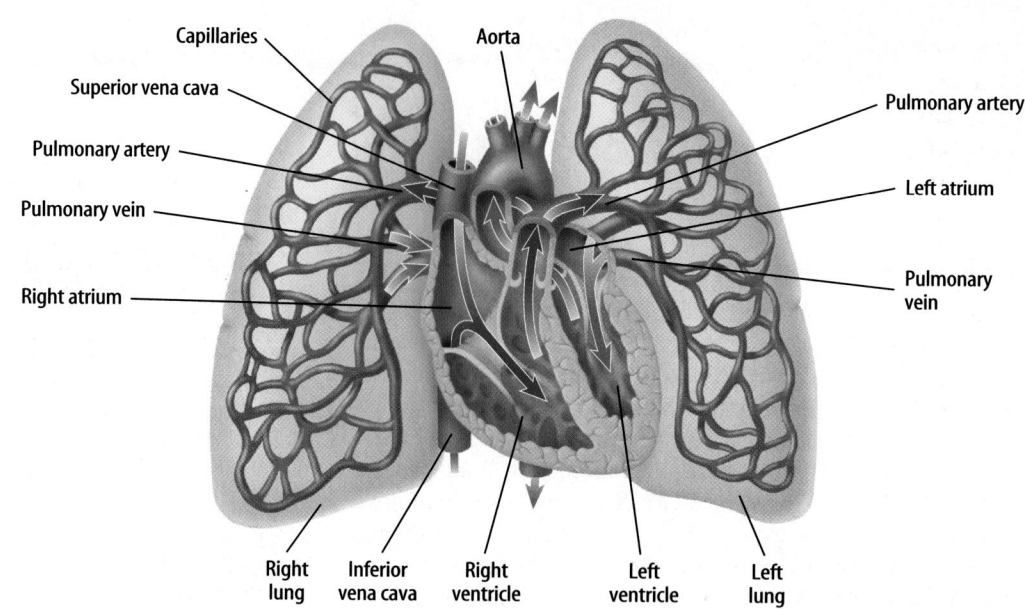

**Figure 6** Pulmonary circulation moves blood between the heart and lungs.

---

### Indiana Academic Standard Check

**7.4.4:** ... various organs and tissues function to serve the needs of cells . . . .

✔ How are pulmonary arteries and veins different from systemic arteries and veins?

✔ Pulmonary arteries carry oxygen-poor blood, while systemic arteries carry oxygen-rich blood. Pulmonary veins carry oxygen-rich blood, while systemic veins carry oxygen-poor blood.

## Types of Circulation

Scientists have divided the circulatory system into three sections—coronary (KOR uh ner ee) circulation, pulmonary (PUL muh ner ee) circulation, and systemic circulation. The beating of your heart controls blood flow through each section.

**Coronary Circulation** Your heart has its own blood vessels that supply it with nutrients and oxygen and remove wastes. Coronary circulation is the flow of blood to and from the tissues of the heart. When the coronary circulation is blocked, oxygen and nutrients cannot reach all the cells of the heart. This can result in a heart attack.

**Pulmonary Circulation** The flow of blood through the heart to the lungs and back to the heart is called pulmonary circulation. Use **Figure 6** to trace the path blood takes through this part of the circulatory system. The blood returning from the body through the right side of the heart and to the lungs contains cellular wastes. The wastes include molecules of carbon dioxide and other substances. In the lungs, gaseous wastes diffuse out of the blood, and oxygen diffuses into the blood. Then the blood returns to the left side of the heart. In the final step of pulmonary circulation, the oxygen-rich blood is pumped from the left ventricle into the aorta (ay OR tuh), the largest artery in your body. From there, the oxygen-rich blood flows to all parts of your body.

**168 CHAPTER 6** Circulation and Immunity

---

### Active Reading

**Double Bubble Map** This strategy uses two bubble maps to compare concepts. Each cluster has qualities that are unique to that idea. In the middle, connecting ideas are similar to both cluster ideas. This technique helps students list common qualities before writing or discussing a topic. Have students design a Double Bubble Map about the circulatory system.

**Sample map:**

- from heart to body and back to heart
- oxygen provided to cells
- wastes removed from cells
- Pulmonary circulation
- Pumped by heart
- Systemic circulation
- from heart to lungs and back to heart
- wastes removed in lungs
- oxygen added

**Systemic Circulation** Oxygen-rich blood moves to all of your organs and body tissues, except the heart and lungs, and oxygen-poor blood returns to the heart by a process called systemic circulation. Systemic circulation is the largest of the three sections of your circulatory system. Oxygen-rich blood flows from your heart in the arteries of this system. Then nutrients and oxygen are delivered by blood to your body cells and exchanged for carbon dioxide and wastes. Finally, the blood returns to your heart in the veins of the systemic circulation system.

## Blood Vessels

In the middle 1600s, scientists discovered that blood moves by the pumping of the heart and flows in one direction from arteries to veins. But they couldn't explain how blood gets from arteries to veins. Using a new invention of that time, the microscope, scientists discovered **capillaries** (KA puh ler eez), the blood vessels that connect arteries and veins.

**Arteries** As blood is pumped out of the heart, it travels through arteries, capillaries, and then veins, shown in **Figure 7.** **Arteries** are blood vessels that carry blood away from the heart. Arteries have thick, elastic walls made of connective tissue and smooth muscle tissue.

**Veins** The blood vessels that carry blood back to the heart are called **veins.** Veins have one-way valves that keep blood moving toward the heart. If blood flows backward, the pressure of the blood against the valves causes them to close. Blood flow in veins also is helped by your skeletal muscles. When skeletal muscles contract, this action squeezes veins and helps blood move toward the heart.

**✓ Reading Check** *What are the similarities and differences between arteries and veins?*

**Capillaries** The walls of capillaries are only one cell thick. Nutrients and oxygen diffuse into body cells from capillaries. Waste materials and carbon dioxide diffuse from body cells into the capillaries.

**Figure 7** The structures of arteries, veins, and capillaries are different. Valves in veins prevent blood from flowing backward. Capillaries are much smaller. Capillary walls are only one cell thick.

**Activity**

**Capillary Walls** Have students prepare a brief report on how the one-cell-thick capillary walls are held together and why a covering would not be practical. A cementing material holds the cells together. A covering would not easily allow materials to pass in and out of the walls. L2 IS **Logical-Mathematical**

## Fun Fact

All tissues in the body are nourished by materials from the circulatory system. Every cell is within 0.10 to 0.15 mm of a capillary. Some arteries have such thick walls that they have their own system of capillaries.

### ✓ Reading Check

**Answer** Both have walls consisting of three layers of tissue. Arteries move blood away from the heart; veins move blood to the heart. Veins have valves that keep blood from flowing backward.

### Use Science Words

**Word Origins** The body's largest artery is the aorta. The name has its origin in the Greek word *aorte*, meaning "to raise or lift." Discuss why this is an appropriate word for this vessel. The aorta rises from the top of the heart.

## Differentiated Instruction

**Visually Impaired** Provide visually impaired students with a three-dimensional model of the heart and lungs. Have students trace with their fingers both pulmonary and coronary circulation. As they trace the flow of blood, have a sighted peer identify major vessels and chambers of the heart. L1 IS **Kinesthetic**

## Teacher **FYI**

**Blood Pressure** The force produced by the blood against the walls of blood vessels, because of the pumping action of the heart, is called blood pressure. Blood pressure tends to force fluids into capillaries at their artery end (where blood pressure is higher); osmosis tends to force water out of capillaries at their venous end (where blood pressure is lower).

## IDENTIFYING Misconceptions

**Cholesterol** The main component of fatty deposits, *atheroma*, in arteries is cholesterol, a steroid lipid. Some students will assume that any cholesterol is unhealthy. In fact, the liver produces cholesterol. It is a component of nerve cells, and it is involved in the synthesis of certain hormones. Normal levels of cholesterol are essential for good health.

## Fun Fact

Not all persons with atherosclerosis suffer discomfort. Sometimes even those with a severe condition do not have any symptoms.

# Blood Pressure

**INTEGRATE Physics**

If you fill a balloon with water and then push on it, the pressure moves through the water in all directions, as shown in **Figure 8.** Your circulatory system is like the water balloon. When your heart pumps blood through the circulatory system, the pressure of the push moves through the blood. The force of the blood on the walls of the blood vessels is called blood pressure. This pressure is highest in arteries and lowest in veins. When you take your pulse, you can feel the waves of pressure. This rise and fall of pressure occurs with each heartbeat.

**Controlling Blood Pressure** Special nerve cells in the walls of some arteries sense changes in blood pressure. When pressure is higher or lower than normal, messages are sent to your brain. Then the brain sends messages that speed up or slow the heart rate. This helps keep blood pressure constant within your arteries so that enough blood reaches all organs and tissues in your body and delivers needed nutrients to every cell.

## Cardiovascular Disease

Any disease that affects the cardiovascular system—the heart, blood vessels, and blood—can seriously affect the health of your entire body. Heart disease is the leading cause of death in humans.

**Atherosclerosis** One leading cause of heart disease is called atherosclerosis (ah thur oh skluh ROH sus). In this condition, fatty deposits build up on arterial walls. Atherosclerosis can occur in any artery in the body, but fatty deposits in coronary arteries are especially serious. If a coronary artery is blocked, a heart attack can occur. Open-heart surgery then may be needed to correct the problem.

**Figure 8** When pressure is exerted on a fluid in a closed container, the pressure is transmitted through the liquid in all directions. Your circulatory system is like a closed container. Blood pressure is measured using a blood pressure cuff and a stethoscope.

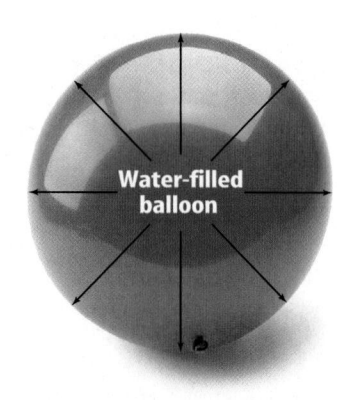

Water-filled balloon

---

### LAB DEMONSTRATION

**Purpose** to compare the flow of liquid through an open tube and a partially blocked tube

**Materials** two 10-cm pieces of plastic tubing, dropper, mineral oil, modeling clay, tweezers

**Preparation** Be sure there is enough clay to impede but not stop the flow of oil.

**Procedure** Insert a dropper full of oil into the tubing. Squeeze the oil through the tubing. Observe the amount of oil that comes out. Compare this to the amount of oil that comes out of a clay-clogged tube.

**Expected Outcome** Students will observe less oil escape from the clogged tube.

**Assessment**

How does this demonstrate what happens in clogged arteries? The clay represents deposits that may collect on the walls of arteries. Blood flow in these tubes is slower, and blocked tubes can carry less blood than unblocked tubes.

**Hypertension** Another condition of the cardiovascular system is called hypertension (hi pur TEN chun), or high blood pressure. When blood pressure is higher than normal most of the time, the heart must work harder to keep blood flowing. One cause of hypertension is atherosclerosis. A clogged artery can increase pressure within the vessel, causing the walls to become stiff and hard. The artery walls no longer contract and dilate easily because they have lost their elasticity.

### Preventing Cardiovascular Disease

Having a healthy lifestyle is important for the health of your cardiovascular system. The choices you make now to maintain good health may reduce your risk of future serious illness. Regular checkups, a healthful diet, and exercise are all part of a heart-healthy lifestyle.

Another way to prevent cardiovascular disease is to not smoke. Smoking causes blood vessels to contract and makes the heart beat faster and harder. Smoking also increases carbon monoxide levels in the blood. Not smoking helps prevent heart disease and a number of respiratory system problems.

## Functions of the Lymphatic System

You turn on the water faucet and fill a glass with water. The excess water runs down the drain. In a similar way, your body's tissue fluid is removed by the lymphatic (lihm FA tihk) system, shown in **Figure 9.** The nutrient, water, and oxygen molecules in blood diffuse through capillary walls to nearby cells. Water and other substances become part of the tissue fluid that is found between cells. This fluid is collected and returned to the blood by the lymphatic system.

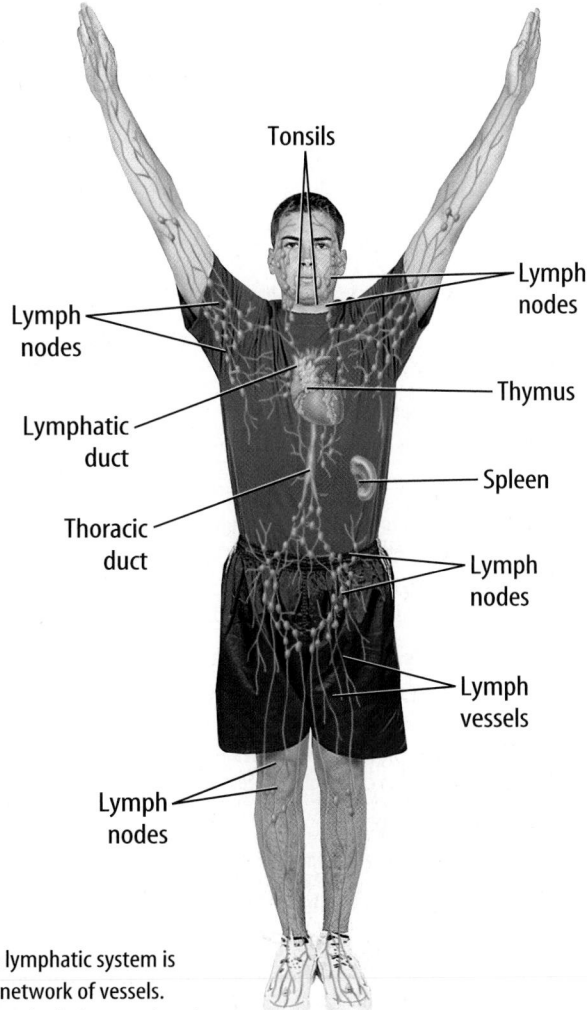

**Figure 9** The lymphatic system is connected by a network of vessels.
**Explain** *how muscles help move lymph.*

Tonsils

Lymph nodes

Thymus

Spleen

Lymph nodes

Lymph vessels

Lymph nodes

Lymph nodes

Lymphatic duct

Thoracic duct

### Discussion

**Low-Cholesterol Foods** Why might a food label that proclaims the item has little or no cholesterol be a poor choice for a healthful diet? Foods rated low in cholesterol may be very high in fat and have a negative effect on the cardiovascular system.

### Activity

**Healthful Diet** Have students keep a log of all the foods they eat for a few days. Then have them identify foods they have eaten that are high in fat or cholesterol or both. Have them think of low-fat substitutes for those foods. L2

## Fun Fact

The fluid in the ears is known as endolymph, but it is not true lymph fluid.

### Caption Answer

**Figure 9** As skeletal muscles contract, they force lymph to move within the lymph vessels.

## Differentiated Instruction

**Challenge** Have students find statistics on atherosclerosis. This can include percentages in categories such as age, race, gender, countries, or other characteristics that may be associated with the condition. Have them present their findings in a graph or table. L3 **Logical-Mathematical**

**Science Online**

**Topic: Hodgkin's Disease**
Visit in7.msscience.com for Web links to information about Hodgkin's Disease.

**Activity** Create a brochure about Hodgkin's Disease, including what it is, its symptoms, risk factors, and treatment.

**Lymph** After tissue fluid diffuses into the lymphatic capillaries, it is called **lymph** (LIHMF). In addition to water and dissolved substances, lymph contains lymphocytes (LIHM fuh sites), a type of white blood cell. Lymphocytes help your body defend itself against disease-causing organisms. If the lymphatic system is not working properly, severe swelling occurs because the tissue fluid cannot get back to the blood.

### ✓ Reading Check *What is lymph?*

Your lymphatic system carries lymph through a network of lymph capillaries and larger lymph vessels. Then, the lymph passes through lymph nodes, which are bean-shaped organs found throughout the body. Lymph nodes filter out microorganisms and foreign materials that have been taken up by lymphocytes. After it is filtered, lymph enters the bloodstream through large veins near the neck. No heartlike structure pumps the lymph through the lymphatic system. The movement of lymph depends on the contraction of smooth muscles in lymph vessels and skeletal muscles. Lymphatic vessels, like veins, have valves that keep lymph from flowing backward.

## section 2 review

### Summary

**The Body's Delivery System**
- Blood vessels carry blood to the body.

**The Heart and Types of Circulation**
- Your heart controls blood flow through the circulatory system.
- In the lungs, carbon dioxide leaves the blood and oxygen diffuses into the blood.

**Blood Vessels and Blood Pressure**
- The three types of blood vessels are arteries, veins, and capillaries.
- The force of the blood on the walls of the blood vessels is called blood pressure.

**Cardiovascular Disease**
- Heart disease is a leading cause of death.

**Functions of the Lymphatic System**
- Lymph is tissue fluid from cells that has entered the lymph vessels.
- Lymphocytes help fight disease.

### Self Check

1. **Compare and contrast** veins, arteries, and capillaries.
2. **Identify** the vessels in the pulmonary and systemic circulation systems that carry oxygen-rich blood.
3. **Describe** the functions of the lymphatic system.
4. **Explain** how blood moves through the heart.
5. **Explain** why blood type and Rh factor are checked before a transfusion.
6. **Think Critically** What waste product builds up in blood and cells when the heart is unable to pump blood efficiently?

#### Applying Skills

7. **Use a Database** Research diseases of the circulatory system. Make a database showing what part of the circulatory system is affected by each disease. Categories should include the organs and vessels of the circulatory system.
8. **Concept Map** Make an events-chain concept map to show pulmonary circulation beginning at the right atrium and ending at the aorta.

 **Science**nline in7.msscience.com/self_check_quiz

## section 2 review

1. Arteries have thick walls. Veins have valves. Capillary walls are only one cell thick.
2. pulmonary system—veins; systemic system—arteries
3. collects tissue fluid and returns it to blood; contains lymphocytes that defend body against disease-causing organisms; lymph nodes: filter out microorganisms and foreign particles
4. right atrium, right ventricle, lungs, left atrium, left ventricle
5. to prevent blood cells from clumping
6. carbon dioxide
7. Sample entries: atherosclerosis—arteries; myocardial infarction—heart; leukemia—white blood cells
8. Map should show: right atrium, right ventricle, pulmonary artery, lungs, pulmonary vein, left atrium, left ventricle, aorta.

**Standards—7.4.10:** Describe how technologies having to do with . . . disease prevention have . . . resulted in changes in factors that affect the growth of human population. **7.4.13:** . . . Know that the antibodies produced will remain and can fight off subsequent invaders of the same kind. **7.6.4:** Understand and describe that changes in health practices have resulted from the acceptance of the germ theory of disease. . . .

**Also covers:** 7.7.2 (Detailed standards begin on page IN8.)

# Immunity

## Lines of Defense

Your body has many ways to defend itself. Its first-line defenses work against harmful substances and all types of disease-causing organisms, called pathogens (PA thuh junz). Your second-line defenses are specific and work against specific pathogens. This complex group of defenses is called your immune system. Tonsils are one of the organs in the immune system that protect your body.

> **Reading Check** *What types of defenses does your body have?*

**First-Line Defenses** Your skin and respiratory, digestive, and circulatory systems are first-line defenses against pathogens, like those in **Figure 10.** The skin is a barrier that prevents many pathogens from entering your body. However, pathogens can get into your body easily through a cut or through your mouth and the membranes in your nose and eyes. The conditions on the skin can affect pathogens. Perspiration contains substances that can slow the growth of some pathogens. At times, secretions from the skin's oil glands and perspiration are acidic. Some pathogens cannot grow in this acidic environment.

**Internal First-Line Defenses** Your respiratory system traps pathogens with hairlike structures, called cilia (SIH lee uh), and mucus. Mucus contains an enzyme that weakens the cell walls of some pathogens. When you cough or sneeze, you get rid of some of these trapped pathogens.

Your digestive system has several defenses against pathogens—saliva, enzymes, hydrochloric acid solution, and mucus. Saliva in your mouth contains substances that kill bacteria. Also, enzymes (EN zimez) in your stomach, pancreas, and liver help destroy pathogens. Hydrochloric acid solution in your stomach helps digest your food. It also kills some bacteria and stops the activity of some viruses that enter your body on the food that you eat. The mucus found on the walls of your digestive tract contains a chemical that coats bacteria and prevents them from binding to the inner lining of your digestive organs.

### as you read

*What* **You'll Learn**
- **Explain** the difference between an antigen and an antibody.
- **Compare and contrast** active and passive immunity.

*Why* **It's Important**
Your body's defenses fight the pathogens that you are exposed to every day.

**Review Vocabulary**
**enzyme:** a type of protein that speeds up the rate of a chemical reaction in your body

**New Vocabulary**
- antigen
- antibody
- active immunity
- passive immunity

Stained LM Magnification: 1000×

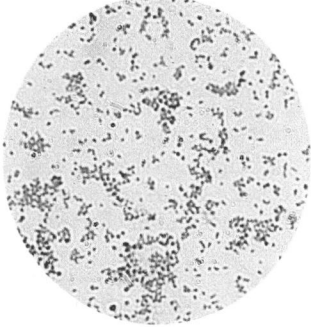

**Figure 10** Most pathogens, such as the staphylococci bacteria shown below, cannot get through unbroken skin.

---

### Section 3 Resource Manager

**Chapter *FAST FILE* Resources**
Transparency Activity, p. 48
Directed Reading for Content Mastery, p. 21
MiniLAB, p. 4
Enrichment, p. 33
Reinforcement, p. 29

**Cultural Diversity,** pp. 23–24
**Performance Assessment,** pp. 59–60

---

**Bellringer**

**Section Focus Transparencies** also are available on the Interactive Chalkboard CD-ROM.
L2 ELL

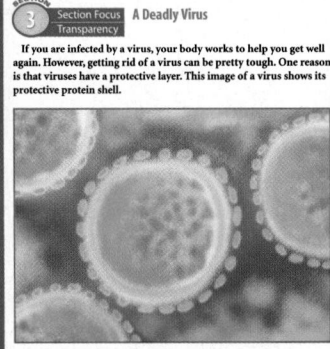

**Tie to Prior Knowledge**

**Immunizations** Have students recall the shots they received before entering school. Ask them to describe any immunizations they have been given in recent years.

## **2** **Teach**

> **Reading Check**

**Answer** first-line (general) and second-line (specific) defenses

### Activity

**Lines of Defense** Have students test the acidity of their sweat after physical activity using pH indicator paper. Sweat may range from pH 3.0 to slightly alkaline. L2 IS **Kinesthetic**

## Discussion

**Fever** Why should a fever not be ignored? Fevers are an indication of infection, a sign that the body is fighting a pathogen. Temperatures over 104°F are potentially dangerous and medical help should be sought immediately.

**INTEGRATE Social Studies**

**Disease Immunity** Jenner realized that dairy workers were resistant to catching smallpox if they had acquired cowpox, a similar, but milder disease. To test his theory, he infected a young boy with cowpox, then later with smallpox. The boy became ill, then made a full recovery.

## Visual Learning

**Figure 11** All antibodies are y-shaped and specific to one type of antigen. The ends of arms fit binding sites on an antigen and the base of the antibody determines how it affects the antigen. Recognition of an antigen by an antibody is similar to a lock and key.

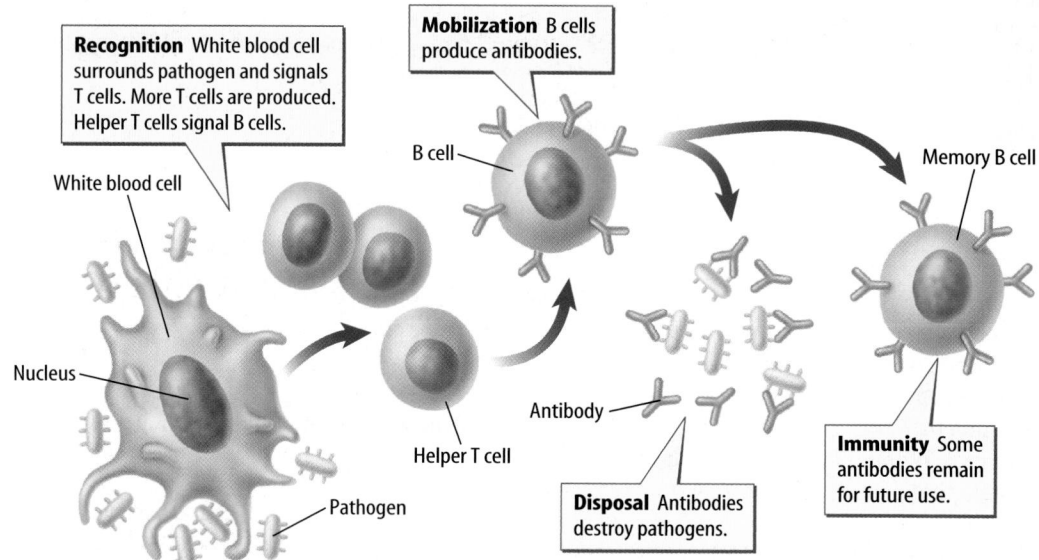

**Recognition** White blood cell surrounds pathogen and signals T cells. More T cells are produced. Helper T cells signal B cells.

White blood cell

Nucleus

Helper T cell

Pathogen

**Mobilization** B cells produce antibodies.

B cell

Antibody

**Disposal** Antibodies destroy pathogens.

Memory B cell

**Immunity** Some antibodies remain for future use.

**Figure 11** The response of your immune system to disease-causing organisms can be divided into four steps—recognition, mobilization, disposal, and immunity. **Describe** the function of B cells.

**INTEGRATE Social Studies**

**Disease Immunity** Edward Jenner discovered a vaccine that prevented smallpox. However, Louis Pasteur demonstrated that germs cause diseases and that vaccines, which contained small amounts of disease organisms, could cause the body to build immunity to that disease without causing it. Research and write a summary in your Science Journal about Jenner's discovery of the smallpox vaccine.

**174 CHAPTER 6** Circulation and Immunity

**White Blood Cells** Your circulatory system contains white blood cells that surround and digest foreign organisms and chemicals. These white blood cells constantly patrol your body, sweeping up and digesting bacteria that invade.

**Inflammation** When tissue is damaged or infected by pathogens, it can become inflamed—becomes red, feels warm, swells, and hurts. Chemicals released by damaged cells expand capillary walls, allowing more blood to flow into the area. Other chemicals released by damaged tissue attract certain white blood cells that surround and take in pathogenic bacteria. If pathogens get past these first-line defenses, your body uses another line of defense called specific immunity.

**Specific Immunity** When your body fights disease, it is battling complex molecules called **antigens** that don't belong there. Antigens can be separate molecules or they can be found on the surface of a pathogen.

When your immune system recognizes foreign molecules, as in **Figure 11,** special lymphocytes called T cells respond. One type of T cells, called killer T cells, releases enzymes that help destroy invading foreign matter. Another type of T cells, called helper T cells, turns on the immune system. They stimulate other lymphocytes, known as B cells, to form antibodies. An **antibody** is a protein made in response to a specific antigen. The antibody attaches to the antigen and makes it useless.

## Fun Fact

The saliva of cats and dogs contains various substances that can kill bacteria. The licking of wounds aids in the healing process.

## Differentiated Instruction

**Learning Disabled** Have students use the write-draw-discuss strategy about the immune system's lines of defense. Have students write about their idea, clarify it, then make an illustration or drawing. Ask students to share responses with the class and display several examples. L2

**Memory B Cells** Another type of lymphocyte, called memory B cells, also has antibodies for the specific pathogen. Memory B cells remain in the blood, ready to defend against an invasion by that same pathogen at another time.

**Active Immunity** Antibodies help your body build defenses in two ways—actively and passively. In **active immunity** your body makes its own antibodies in response to an antigen. **Passive immunity** results when antibodies that have been produced in another animal are introduced into your body.

When a pathogen invades your body, the pathogen quickly multiplies and you get sick. Your body immediately starts to make antibodies to attack the pathogen. After enough antibodies form, you usually get better. Some antibodies stay on duty in your blood, and more are produced rapidly if the pathogen enters your body again. Because of this defense system, you usually don't get certain diseases, such as chicken pox, more than once.

 **Reading Check** *How does active immunity differ from passive immunity?*

**Vaccination** Another way to develop active immunity to a disease is to be inoculated with a vaccine, as shown in **Figure 12.** The process of giving a vaccine by injection or by mouth is called vaccination. A vaccine is a form of the antigen that gives you active immunity against a disease.

A vaccine can prevent a disease, but it is not a cure. As you grow older, you will be exposed to many more types of pathogens and will build a separate immunity to each one.

**Figure 12** Many vaccines are injected into the arm.

---

## Mini LAB

**Determining Reproduction Rates**

**Procedure**

1. Place **one penny** on a table. Imagine that the penny is a bacterium that can divide every 10 min.
2. Place **two pennies** below to form a triangle with the first penny. These indicate the two new bacteria present after a bacterium divides.
3. Repeat three more divisions, placing two pennies under each penny in the row above.
4. Calculate how many bacteria you would have after 5 h of reproduction. Graph your data.

**Analysis**

1. How many bacteria are present after 5 h?
2. Why is it important to take antibiotics promptly if you have an infection?

 Try at Home

---

### Indiana Academic Standard Check

**7.4.10:** Describe how technologies having to do with . . . disease prevention have dramatically changed how people live and work.

✓ What kind of immunity is acquired from a vaccination?

✓ active immunity

---

---

 **Reading Check**

active immunity: body makes its own antibodies in response to an antigen; passive immunity: antibodies produced in another animal and introduced into the body

## Mini LAB

**Purpose** to model bacterial reproduction

**Materials** pennies, paper, pencil, calculator

**Teaching Strategies**
• Make sure students understand that bacteria reproduce exponentially, allowing their populations to grow very quickly.
• Students should label the *y*-axis of the graph *Bacteria* (thousands) and the *x*-axis *Time* (hours).

**Analysis**

1. At the five-hour point, there will be 1,073,741,824 bacteria.
2. Taking antibiotics promptly will inhibit the reproduction of bacteria. It is also important to take all of the antibiotics prescribed. Failing to do so will leave a few bacteria that can reinfect the body.

### Assessment

**Performance** To further assess students' understanding of bacterial infections, have them research a variety of bacteria that cause common infections. Possible topics: *staphylococci, Mycobacterium tuberculosis, Treponema pallidum* Use **Performance Assessment in the Science Classroom,** p. 97.

 Try at Home

---

## Differentiated Instruction

**Challenge** Have students research the discovery of chemicals that are used to destroy or neutralize viruses. Have them write two or three paragraphs on what they have found. L3 ELL LS **Linguistic**
P

## Curriculum Connection

**History** In 1796, Edward Jenner pioneered the use of vaccines by inoculating a young boy with cowpox material to keep him from contracting the deadly disease smallpox. Editorial cartoons in the newspaper ridiculed the treatment and showed illustrations of people growing cow parts on their bodies as a result of being vaccinated. Have students find out more about Jenner's work. L2

## Quick Demo

**Vaccine Specificity**

**Materials** five beads of one color, one bead of a different color

**Estimated Time** five minutes

**Procedure** Take four beads of one color. Explain that these represent antibodies that developed in response to the measles vaccine. The fifth bead represents the virus. Explain that the antibodies protect the person from that virus. Take the single bead of the second color and explain that this represents the flu virus. Point out that no antibodies are present to this disease (no same-colored beads in body) and that a separate immunity must be built up to this disease.

## 3  Assess

### DAILY INTERVENTION

#### Check for Understanding

**Visual-Spatial** Use an anatomy chart or model to illustrate the various body systems involved in defense against microbes. L2 IS

#### Reteach

**Specific Immunity** Have students work together in groups of four. Each group should draw representations of the four steps of the immune system response to disease-causing organisms. Check that each group's representations include all four steps: recognition, mobilization, disposal, and immunity. L2

### ☑ Assessment

**Portfolio** To assess students' understanding of active and passive immunity, have them draw a concept map comparing and contrasting the two. Use **Performance Assessment in the Science Classroom**, p. 161.

---

**Table 2  Cases of Disease Before and After Vaccine Availability in the U.S.**

| Disease | Average Number of Cases per Year Before Vaccine Available | Cases in 1998 After Vaccine Available |
|---|---|---|
| Measles | 503,282 | 89 |
| Diphtheria | 175,885 | 1 |
| Tetanus | 1,314 | 34 |
| Mumps | 152,209 | 606 |
| Rubella | 47,745 | 345 |
| Pertussis (whooping cough) | 147,271 | 6,279 |

Data from the National Immunization Program, CDC

**Passive Immunity** Passive immunity does not last as long as active immunity does. For example, you were born with all the antibodies that your mother had in her blood. However, these antibodies stayed with you for only a few months. Because newborn babies lose their passive immunity in a few months, they need to be vaccinated to develop their own immunity. Vaccines have helped reduce cases of many childhood diseases, as shown in **Table 2**.

### section 3 review

#### Summary

**Lines of Defense**

- The purpose of the immune system is to fight disease.
- Your skin and your respiratory, digestive, and circulatory systems are first-line defenses against pathogens.
- Your body's second line of defense is called specific immunity.
- In active immunity, your body makes its own antibodies in response to an antigen.
- Vaccinations can give you active immunity against a disease.
- Passive immunity results when antibodies that have been produced in another animal are introduced into your body.

#### Self Check

1. **Describe** how harmful bacteria can cause infections in your body.
2. **List** the natural defenses that your body has against harmful substances and disease.
3. **Explain** how an active vaccine works to protect the human body.
4. **Think Critically** Several diseases have symptoms similar to those of measles. Why doesn't the measles vaccine protect you from all of these diseases?

#### Applying Skills

5. **Make Models** Create models of the different types of T cells, antigens, and B cells from clay, construction paper, or other art materials. Use them to explain how T cells function in the immune system.

**176  CHAPTER 6** Circulation and Immunity

 Science Online in7.msscience.com/self_check_quiz

---

### section 3 review

1. Harmful bacteria enter your body and rapidly reproduce, causing you to get sick.
2. white blood cells, cilia, mucus, coughing, enzymes in the digestive system, hydrochloric acid solution, active immunity, sneezing, saliva, skin, perspiration, fever
3. It causes the immune system to produce antibodies against a specific antigen.
4. Antibodies formed to fight a specific antigen will protect only against that antigen.
5. Models should show the role of T cells in the response of the immune system to antigens.

**section**

**4**

Also covers: 7.1.5, 7.4.4, 7.4.12, 7.4.14, 7.5.3 (Detailed standards begin on page IN8.)

# Diseases

## Disease in History

Throughout time, the plague, smallpox, and influenza have killed millions of people worldwide. Today, the causes of these diseases are known, and treatments can prevent or cure them. But even today, some diseases cannot be cured, and outbreaks of new diseases, such as severe acute respiratory syndrome (SARS), occur.

**Discovering Disease Organisms** With the invention of the microscope in the latter part of the seventeenth century, bacteria, yeast, and mold spores were seen for the first time. However, scientists did not make a connection between microorganisms and disease transmission until the late 1800s and early 1900s.

The French chemist Louis Pasteur learned that microorganisms cause disease in humans. Many scientists of his time did not believe that microorganisms could harm larger organisms, such as humans. However, Pasteur discovered that microorganisms could spoil wine and milk. He then realized that microorganisms could attack the human body in the same way. Pasteur invented **pasteurization** (pas chuh ruh ZAY shun), which is the process of heating a liquid to a temperature that kills most bacteria.

**Disease Organisms** **Table 3** lists some of the diseases caused by various groups of pathogens. Bacteria and viruses cause many common diseases.

### as you read

#### *What* You'll Learn

- **Describe** the work of Pasteur, Koch, and Lister in the discovery and prevention of disease.
- **Identify** diseases caused by viruses and bacteria.
- **Explain** how HIV affects the immune system.
- **Define** noninfectious diseases and list their causes.
- **Explain** what happens during an allergic reaction.

#### *Why* It's Important

You can help prevent certain illnesses if you know what causes disease and how disease spreads.

#### Review Vocabulary

**virus:** tiny piece of genetic material surrounded by a protein coating that infects and multiplies in host cells

#### New Vocabulary

- pasteurization
- infectious disease
- noninfectious disease
- allergen

| Table 3  Human Diseases and Their Agents ||
| --- | --- |
| **Agent** | **Diseases** |
| Bacteria | Tetanus, tuberculosis, typhoid fever, strep throat, bacterial pneumonia, plague |
| Protists | Malaria, sleeping sickness |
| Fungi | Athlete's foot, ringworm |
| Viruses | Colds, influenza, AIDS, measles, mumps, polio, smallpox, SARS |

---

**INTERACTIVE CHALKBOARD**
PowerPoint® Presentations

### Bellringer

**Section Focus Transparencies** also are available on the Interactive Chalkboard CD-ROM.

L2  ELL

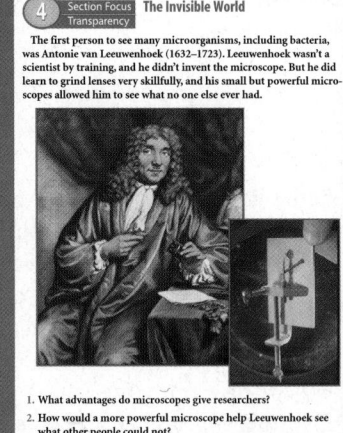

**SECTION 4**  Section Focus Transparency  **The Invisible World**

The first person to see many microorganisms, including bacteria, was Antonie van Leeuwenhoek (1632–1723). Leeuwenhoek wasn't a scientist by training, and he didn't invent the microscope. But he did learn to grind lenses very skillfully, and his small but powerful microscopes allowed him to see what no one else ever had.

1. What advantages do microscopes give researchers?
2. How would a more powerful microscope help Leeuwenhoek see what other people could not?
3. One of Leeuwenhoek's microscopes is shown on the right. Where do you think he placed the sample he wished to magnify?

*Circulation and Immunity*

### Tie to Prior Knowledge

**Noninfectious Diseases** Have students recall that some diseases are not "catching." They are not transmitted by pathogens. Have students list as many of these diseases as they can. Possible answers: cancer, heart disease, leukemia, diabetes

---

### Section 4 Resource Manager

**Chapter *Fast File* Resources**
   Transparency Activity, p. 49
   Directed Reading for Content Mastery, p. 21
   Enrichment, p. 34
   Reinforcement, p. 30
   Lab Worksheets, pp. 5–8
   Lab Activities, pp. 9–16

**Life Science Critical Thinking/Problem Solving,** p. 17

**Earth Science Critical Thinking/Problem Solving,** p. 13

**Physical Science Critical Thinking/Problem Solving,** p. 22

**Reading and Writing Skills Activities,** pp. 31–32

### Quick Demo

**Comparing Bacteria**

**Materials** microscope, slides of various stained bacteria

**Estimated Time** 15 minutes

**Procedure** Have students look at slides of various stained bacteria to get an idea of their sizes and shapes.

### ✔ Reading Check

**Answer** virus invades host cell and multiplies within it; host cell dies when the virus breaks out of it

### Make a Model

**Koch's Rules** Have students prepare a display of Koch's Rules. Use agar or gelatin petri dishes. Place several bright-colored cake decorations (nonpareils) on the surface of the medium. The color will diffuse onto the surface to give the appearance of bacterial colonies. L2 IS **Kinesthetic and Visual-Spatial**

### Use Science Words

**Word Usage** Have students use the word *vector* in a sentence. Possible answer: Certain mosquitoes are vectors of malaria. L2 IS **Linguistic**

---

**Science Online**

**Topic: Disease Theory**
Visit in7.msscience.com for Web links to information about one of the historical theories of disease—the four body humors.

**Activity** Make a picture book describing the humoral theory of disease.

---

**Indiana Academic Standard Check**

**7.6.1:** Realize that the introduction of germ theory . . . led to the modern understanding of how many diseases are caused by microorganisms . . . .

✔ What is the first step of Koch's rules?

✔ The same pathogen must be present in all cases of the disease.

---

**Figure 14** When flies land on food, they can transport pathogens from one location to another.

---

**Pathogens** The conditions in your body, such as temperature and available nutrients, help harmful bacteria that enter your body grow and multiply. Bacteria can slow down the normal growth and metabolic activities of body cells and tissues. Some bacteria even produce toxins that kill cells on contact.

A virus infects and multiplies in host cells. The host cells die when the viruses break out of them. These new viruses infect other cells, leading to the destruction of tissues or the interruption of vital body activities.

### ✔ Reading Check    *What is the relationship between a virus and a host cell?*

Pathogenic protists, such as the organisms that cause malaria, can destroy tissues and blood cells or interfere with normal body functions. In a similar manner, fungus infections can cause athlete's foot, nonhealing wounds, chronic lung disease, or inflammation of the membranes of the brain.

**Koch's Rules** Many diseases caused by pathogens can be treated with medicines. In many cases, these organisms need to be identified before specific treatment can begin. Today, a method developed in the nineteenth century by Robert Koch still is used to identify organisms, as shown in **Figure 13.**

## Infectious Diseases

A disease that is caused by a virus, bacterium, protist, or fungus and is spread from an infected organism or the environment to another organism is called an **infectious disease.** Infectious diseases are spread by direct contact with the infected organism, through water and air, on food, by contact with contaminated objects, and by disease-carrying organisms called biological vectors. Examples of vectors that have been sources of disease are rats, birds, cats, dogs, mosquitoes, fleas, and flies, as shown in **Figure 14.**

**Human Vectors** People also can be carriers of disease. Colds and many other diseases are spread through contact. Each time you turn a doorknob or use a telephone, your skin comes in contact with bacteria and viruses, which is why washing your hands frequently should be part of your daily routine.

Joseph Lister, an English surgeon, recognized the relationship between infections and cleanliness. Lister dramatically reduced the number of deaths among his patients by washing their skin and his hands with carbolic (kar BAH lihk) acid, which is a liquid that kills pathogens.

**178    CHAPTER 6** Circulation and Immunity

---

## Cultural Diversity

**Native American Herbs** Explorers and pioneers in the Americas learned a great deal from Native Americans about the healing power of certain herbs. Have students find out about the use of herbs by Native Americans in the treatment of disease symptoms. Possible topics: ipecac, cinchona, witch hazel, and cascara sagrada. L3 IS **Linguistic**

## Science Journal

**Joseph Lister** Have students research Lister's use of a carbolic spray in the operating room to reduce infection. They should infer how this might affect the surgeon's work and write a brief report. L2 IS **Linguistic**

# NATIONAL GEOGRAPHIC VISUALIZING KOCH'S RULES

**Figure 13**

In the 1880s, German doctor Robert Koch developed a series of methods for identifying which organism was the cause of a particular disease. Koch's Rules are still in use today. Developed mainly for determining the cause of particular diseases in humans and other animals, these rules have been used for identifying diseases in plants as well.

**Anthrax bacteria**

**Ⓐ** In every case of a particular disease, the organism thought to cause the disease—the pathogen—must be present.

**Ⓑ** The suspected pathogen must be separated from all other organisms and grown on agar gel with no other organisms present.

**Ⓒ** When inoculated with the suspected pathogen, a healthy host must come down with the original illness.

**Anthrax bacteria**

**Ⓓ** Finally, when the suspected pathogen is removed from the host and grown on agar gel again, it must be compared with the original organism. Only when they match can that organism be identified as the pathogen that causes the disease.

SECTION 4 Diseases **179**

## Visualizing Koch's Rules

Have students examine the pictures and read the captions. Then ask the following questions.

Why does the suspected pathogen need to be grown on agar with no other organism present? A suspected organism needs to be isolated (grown in a pure culture) to make sure that the suspected pathogen and only the suspected pathogen is inoculated into the healthy host. If not, there would be no way to know which organism caused the disease.

Why is it important to prove that a particular pathogen causes a particular disease? Possible answer: Knowing which pathogen causes a disease can help scientists develop treatments and preventative measures.

### Activity

**Skit** Have students write and perform a skit demonstrating Koch's rules. Possible characters include Robert Koch and a person or animal with a disease. Props: mouse, microscope, and petri dishes. L2 **IS** **Interpersonal**

## Differentiated Instruction

**Challenge** Have students find out more about anthrax, a disease that Koch studied. Possible topics to investigate include which animals are affected, symptoms of the disease, how the disease is detected, and treatment. Have students make posters to explain what they found out. L3
P

## Use an Analogy

**Bacterial Trail** When a fly walks across the table and onto food, you may not be able to see its tracks, but it is analogous to a dog walking across the floor with muddy paws. Both leave a trail of debris that can contain bacteria.

## IDENTIFYING Misconceptions

**STDs** There is a belief that sexually transmitted diseases can be contracted through casual contact, such as touching a person with the disease or handling an object touched by an infected person. STDs are not transmitted through casual contact. There must be direct contact with bodily fluids such as blood, semen, or vaginal secretions.

### ☑ Reading Check

**Answer** to prevent permanent damage to organs

### Applying Science

**Answers**

1. yes; cancer, diabetes, and pneumonia and flu
2. Possible answers: changes in lifestyles, increase in pollution, and better medical disease identification

### Indiana Academic Standard Check

**7.4.12:** Explain that viruses, bacteria . . . may infect the human body and interfere with normal body functions.

☑ Which STDs can be treated with antibodies?

☑ gonorrhea, chlamydia, and syphilis

**Sexually Transmitted Diseases** Infectious diseases that are passed from person to person during sexual contact are called sexually transmitted diseases (STDs). STDs are caused by bacteria or viruses.

Gonorrhea (gah nuh REE uh), chlamydia (kluh MIH dee uh), and syphilis (SIH fuh lus) are STDs caused by bacteria. Antibiotics are used to treat these diseases. If they are untreated, gonorrhea and chlamydia can leave a person sterile because the reproductive organs can be damaged permanently. Untreated syphilis may infect cardiovascular and nervous systems, resulting in damage to body organs that cannot be reversed.

Genital herpes, a lifelong viral disease, causes painful blisters on the sex organs. This type of herpes can be transmitted during sexual contact or from an infected mother to her child during birth. Herpes has no cure, and no vaccine can prevent it. However, the symptoms of herpes can be treated with antiviral medicines.

### ☑ Reading Check  *Why should STDs be treated in the early stages?*

### Applying Science

#### Has the annual percentage of deaths from major diseases changed?

Each year, many people die from diseases. Medical science has found numerous ways to treat and cure disease. Have new medicines, improved surgery techniques, and healthier lifestyles helped decrease the number of deaths from disease? By using your ability to interpret data tables, you can find out.

| Percentage of Deaths Due to Major Diseases | | | | |
|---|---|---|---|---|
| **Disease** | Year | | | |
| | **1950** | **1980** | **1990** | **2000** |
| **Heart** | 37.1 | 38.3 | 33.5 | 29.6 |
| **Cancer** | 14.6 | 20.9 | 23.5 | 23.0 |
| **Stroke** | 10.8 | 8.6 | 6.7 | 7.0 |
| **Diabetes** | 1.7 | 1.8 | 2.2 | 2.9 |
| **Pneumonia and flu** | 3.3 | 2.7 | 3.7 | 2.7 |

#### Identifying the Problem

The table above shows the percentage of total deaths due to six major diseases for a 50-year time period. Study the data for each disease. Can you see any trends in the percentage of deaths?

#### Solving the Problem

1. Has the percentage increased for any disease that is listed?
2. What factors could have contributed to this increase?

**180  CHAPTER 6** Circulation and Immunity

## Curriculum Connection

**Health** The previous indiscriminate use of antibiotics in the treatment of STDs has resulted in the development of drug-resistant strains of bacteria. Modern methods of treatment use more potent forms of antibiotics and combinations of drugs. Ask students to write a paragraph about the problems that drug-resistant bacteria pose for individuals and society. L2 ELL LS **Linguistic**

**180  CHAPTER 6** Circulation and Immunity

# HIV and Your Immune System

Human immunodeficiency virus (HIV) can exist in blood and body fluids. This virus can hide in body cells, sometimes for years. You can become infected with HIV by having sex with an HIV-infected person or by reusing an HIV-contaminated hypodermic needle for an injection. However, a freshly unwrapped sterile needle cannot transmit infection. The risk of getting HIV through blood transfusion is small because all donated blood is tested for the presence of HIV. A pregnant woman with HIV can infect her child when the virus passes through the placenta. The child also may become infected from contacts with blood during the birth process or when nursing after birth.

HIV cannot multiply outside the body, and it does not survive long in the environment. The virus cannot be transmitted by touching an infected person, by handling objects used by the person unless they are contaminated with body fluids, or from contact with a toilet seat.

**AIDS** An HIV infection can lead to Acquired Immune Deficiency Syndrome (AIDS), which is a disease that attacks the body's immune system. HIV, as shown in **Figure 15,** is different from other viruses. It attacks the helper T cells in the immune system. The virus enters the T cell and multiplies. When the infected cell bursts open, it releases more HIV. These infect other T cells. Soon, so many T cells are destroyed that not enough B cells are stimulated to produce antibodies. The body no longer has an effective way to fight invading antigens. The immune system then is unable to fight HIV or any other pathogen.

From 1981 to 2001, more than 816,000 cases of AIDS were documented in the United States. At this time the disease has no known cure. However, several medications help treat AIDS in some patients.

# Fighting Disease

Washing a small wound with soap and water is the first step in preventing an infection. Cleaning the wound with an antiseptic and covering it with a bandage are other steps. Is it necessary to wash your body to help prevent diseases? Yes! In addition to reducing body odor, washing your body removes and destroys some surface microorganisms.

In your mouth, microorganisms are responsible for mouth odor and tooth decay. Using dental floss and routine tooth brushing keep these organisms under control.

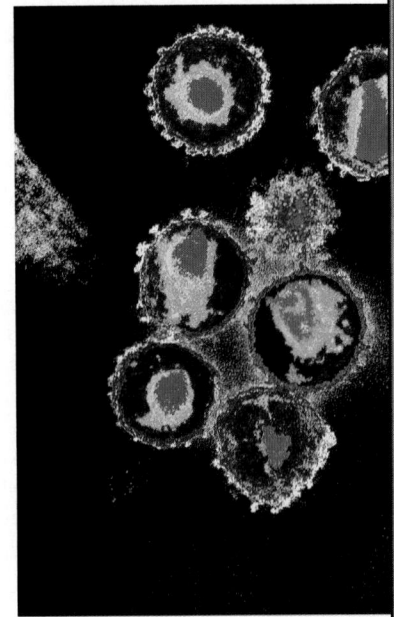

**Figure 15** A person can be infected with HIV and not show any symptoms of the infection for several years.
**Explain** *why this characteristic makes the spread of AIDS more likely.*

## Use an Analogy

**Antihistamines** The neutralizing action of antihistamines to the histamines produced in allergic reactions can be compared to acids neutralizing bases in chemical reactions.

## Visual Learning

**Figure 16** Emphasize the actual size of the dust mite in this illustration (the size of a period at the end of the sentence). Have students explain why it would be hard to get rid of them. Their small size makes it hard to eliminate them by the usual methods of vacuuming and washing.

**Figure 16** Dust mites are smaller than a period at the end of a sentence. They can live in pillows, mattresses, carpets, furniture, and other places.

---

**Indiana Academic Standard Check**

**7.6.4:** . . . the modern approach emphasizes sanitation . . . and aseptic surgical techniques to keep germs out of the body.

✔ How are airborne pathogens controlled in operating rooms?

✔ The air is filtered.

---

**Aseptic Surgical Techniques** Every person involved with a surgery must help fight disease. Thorough washing of hands and wearing sterile gloves, gowns, and masks are standard practices. All surgical tools and operating room equipment must be sterilized. Even the operating room's air is filtered. Also, the patient's skin is cleaned where an incision is to be made, and then covered with sterile cloths.

**Healthy Choices** Exercise and good nutrition help the circulatory and respiratory systems work more effectively. Good health habits, including getting enough rest and eating well-balanced meals, can make you less susceptible to the actions of disease organisms such as those that cause colds and flu. Keeping up with recommended immunizations and having annual health checkups also can help you stay healthy.

## Chronic Disease

Diseases and disorders such as diabetes, allergies, asthma, cancer, and heart disease are **noninfectious diseases.** They are not caused by pathogens and do spread from one person to another. Many are chronic (KRAH nihk). This means that they can last for a long time.

Some infectious diseases can be chronic too. For example, deer ticks carry a bacterium that causes Lyme disease. This bacterium can affect the nervous system, heart, and joints for weeks to years. It can become chronic if not treated. Antibiotics will kill the bacteria, but some damage cannot be reversed.

**Allergies** Many people have allergies. An allergy is an overly strong reaction of the immune system to a foreign substance. Most allergic reactions are minor. However, severe allergic reactions can cause shock and even death if they aren't treated promptly.

Substances that cause an allergic response are called **allergens.** Some chemicals, certain foods, pollen, molds, some antibiotics, and dust are allergens for some people. Dust can contain cat and dog dander and dust mites, shown in **Figure 16.**

When you come in contact with an allergen, your immune system usually forms antibodies. Your body reacts by releasing chemicals called histamines (HIHS tuh meenz) that promote red, swollen tissues. Antihistamines are medications that can be used to treat allergic reactions and asthma, a lung disorder associated with reactions to allergens. Some severe allergies are treated with repeated injections of small doses of the allergen. This allows your body to become less sensitive to the allergen.

**182   CHAPTER 6** Circulation and Immunity

---

## Differentiated Instruction

**Challenge** Have a team of students prepare a joint report and poster on first aid procedures for individuals who are experiencing a severe allergic reaction. Have them present their material to the class. ⬛ L3  **ELL**  COOP LEARN  ⬛ **Interpersonal**

## Teacher FYI

**Anaphylactic Shock** Sometimes the body may experience an intense reaction to an allergen, causing blood vessels to dilate and bronchiole tubes to constrict. This condition is known as anaphylactic shock and can lead to death if not treated. A single bee sting to a hypersensitive person can trigger anaphylactic shock.

**Diabetes** A chronic disease associated with the levels of insulin produced by the pancreas is diabetes. Insulin is a hormone that enables glucose to pass from the bloodstream into your cells. Doctors recognize two types of diabetes—Type 1 and Type 2. Type 1 diabetes is the result of too little or no insulin production. In Type 2 diabetes, your body cannot properly process insulin. Symptoms of diabetes include fatigue, excessive thirst, frequent urination, and tingling sensations in the hands and feet.

If glucose levels in the blood remain high for a long time, other health problems can develop. These problems can include blurred vision, kidney failure, heart attack, stroke, loss of feeling in the feet, and the loss of consciousness (diabetic coma).

## Cancer

Cancer is the name given to a group of closely related diseases that result from uncontrolled cell growth. It is a complicated disease, and no one fully understands how cancers form. Characteristics of cancer cells are shown in **Table 4.** Tumors can occur anywhere in your body. Cancerous cells can leave a tumor, spread throughout the body via blood and lymph vessels, and then invade other tissues.

**Reading Check** *How do cancers spread?*

**Causes** In the latter part of the eighteenth century, a British physician recognized the association of soot to cancer in chimney sweeps. Since that time, scientists have learned more about causes of cancer. Research done in the 1940s and 1950s first related genes to cancer.

Although not all the causes of cancer are known, many causes have been identified. Smoking has been linked to lung cancer—the leading cause of cancer deaths for males in the United States. Exposure to certain chemicals also can increase your chances of developing cancer. These substances, called carcinogens (kar SIH nuh junz), include asbestos, various solvents, heavy metals, alcohol, and home and garden chemicals. Exposure to X rays, nuclear radiation, and ultraviolet radiation of the Sun also increases your risk of cancer.

| Table 4  Characteristics of Cancer Cells |
|---|
| Cell growth is uncontrolled. |
| These cells do not function as part of your body. |
| The cells take up space and interfere with normal body functions. |
| The cells travel throughout the body. |
| The cells produce tumors and abnormal growths anywhere in your body. |

**Indiana Academic Standard Check**

7.4.14: Explain that the environment may contain dangerous levels of substances that are harmful to human beings. . . .

✔ What is a carcinogen?

✔ a substance that can increase your chances of developing cancer

**Teacher FYI**

**Diabetes** An estimated 17 million people in the United States have diabetes, but only two-thirds of them are aware of it. Only about 10 percent of people with diabetes have Type 1; about 90 percent have Type 2.

**Activity**

**Causes of Death** Have students research the top ten causes of death in the United States and identify which are infectious and which are noninfectious. L2 IS **Logical-Mathematical**

**Reading Check**

**Answer** may leave a tumor and move throughout the body via the blood and lymph vessels

**IDENTIFYING Misconceptions**

**Preventing Cancer** People are often heard to say, "Everything causes cancer, so why bother to do anything?" The fact is that there are a number of specific actions a person can take to reduce the risk of cancer. Students should take these seriously.

## Differentiated Instruction

**Hearing Impaired** Have students request pamphlets from health organizations, such as the American Heart Association, the American Cancer Society, the American Diabetes Association, and the Arthritis Foundation, to learn about new treatment methods for some chronic diseases and arrange a bulletin board display for the classroom. L2 IS **Linguistic**

**Table 5  Early Warning Signs of Cancer**

| Changes in bowel or bladder habits |
| --- |
| A sore that does not heal |
| Unusual bleeding or discharge |
| Thickening or lump in the breast or elsewhere |
| Indigestion or difficulty swallowing |
| Obvious change in a wart or mole |
| Nagging cough or hoarseness |

from the National Cancer Institute

**Prevention** Knowing some causes of cancer might help you prevent it. The first step is to know the early warning signs, shown in **Table 5.** Medical attention and treatments such as chemotherapy or surgery in the early stages of some cancers can cure or keep them inactive.

A second step in cancer prevention concerns lifestyle choices. Choosing not to use tobacco and alcohol products can help prevent mouth and lung cancers and the other associated respiratory and circulatory system diseases. Selecting a healthy diet without many foods that are high in fats, salt, and sugar also might reduce your chances of developing cancer. Using sunscreen and limiting the amount of time that you expose your skin to direct sunlight are good preventive measures against skin cancer. Careful handling of harmful home and garden chemicals will help you avoid the dangers connected with these substances.

## section 4 review

### Summary

**Disease in History**
- Pasteur, Koch, and Lister made important discoveries about the causes and how to prevent the spread of diseases.

**Infectious Diseases and HIV**
- Bacteria, fungi, protists, and viruses can cause infectious disease.
- STDs are passed during sexual contact and are caused by bacteria or viruses.
- HIV infection can lead to AIDS, a disease that attacks the immune system.

**Fighting Disease**
- Good health habits can help prevent the spread of disease.

**Chronic Disease and Cancer**
- Allergies, diabetes, and cancer are chronic noninfectious diseases.
- Early detection and lifestyle choices can help treat or prevent some cancers.

### Self Check

1. **Name** an infectious disease caused by each of the following: a virus, a bacterium, a protist, and a fungus.
2. **Compare and contrast** how HIV and other viruses affect the immune system.
3. **Explain** why diabetes is classified as a noninfectious disease.
4. **Recognize** how poor hygiene is related to the spread of disease.
5. **Describe** how your body might respond to an allergen.
6. **Think Critically** In what ways does Koch's procedure demonstrate the use of scientific methods?

**Applying Math**

7. **Make and Use Graphs** Make a bar graph using the following data about the number of deaths from AIDS-related diseases for children younger than 13 years old: 1995, 536; 1996, 420; 1997, 209; 1998, 115; and 1999, 76.

**184 CHAPTER 6** Circulation and Immunity

 **Science** *Online* in7.msscience.com/self_check_quiz

## section 4 review

1. Possible answers: virus—colds; bacterium—tetanus; protist—malaria; fungus—athlete's foot
2. HIV: attacks the helper T cells in the immune system, can hide in the body cells sometimes for years; other viruses: infect and multiply in other types of host cells not helper T cells, do not hide in the body cells for years
3. Diabetes is not caused by a pathogen.
4. Poor cleanliness can allow disease organisms on the body to be transmitted to other people through physical contact or contact with a common object.
5. Your immune system forms antibodies; your body reacts by releasing chemicals called histamines.
6. Possible answer: Koch used strict isolation techniques and retested suspected pathogens.
7. Check bar graph to ensure it matches data given.

# Micro•rganisms and Disease

Microorganisms are everywhere. Washing your hands and disinfecting items you use helps remove some of these organisms.

## ● Real-World Question

How do microorganisms cause infection?

### Goals

■ **Observe** the transmission of microorganisms.
■ **Relate** microorganisms to infections.

### Materials

fresh apples (6)                 paper towels
rotting apple                    sandpaper
rubbing alcohol (5 mL)           cotton ball
self-sealing plastic bags (6)    soap and water
labels and pencil                newspaper
gloves

### Safety Precautions

**WARNING:** *Do not eat the apples. Do not remove goggles until the lab and cleanup are completed. When you complete the experiment, give all bags to your teacher for disposal.*

## ● Procedure

1. **Label** the plastic bags 1 through 6. Put on gloves. Place a fresh apple in bag 1.
2. Rub the rotting apple over the other five apples. This is your source of microorganisms. **WARNING:** *Don't touch your face.*
3. Put one apple in bag 2.
4. Hold one apple 1.5 m above the floor and drop it on a newspaper. Put it in bag 3.
5. Rub one apple with sandpaper. Place this apple in bag 4.

6. Wash one apple with soap and water. Dry it well. Put this apple in bag 5.
7. Use a cotton ball to spread alcohol over the last apple. Let it air-dry. Place it in bag 6.
8. Seal all bags and put them in a dark place.
9. On day 3 and day 7, compare all of the apples without removing them from the bags. Record your observations in a data table.

### Apple Observations

| Condition | Day 3 | Day 7 |
| --- | --- | --- |
| 1. Fresh | no change | no change |
| 2. Untreated | no change | some decay |
| 3. Dropped | brown spots | some decay |
| 4. Rubbed with sandpaper | some brown at soft areas | decay at soft areas |
| 5. Washed with soap and water | no change | little or no change |
| 6. Covered with alcohol | no change | no change |

## ● Conclude and Apply

1. **Infer** How does this experiment relate to infections on your skin?
2. **Explain** why it is important to clean a wound.

### Communicating Your Data

Prepare a poster illustrating the advantages of washing hands to avoid the spread of disease. Get permission to put the poster near a school rest room. **For more help, refer to the** Science Skill Handbook.

**LAB  185**

## ● Real-World Question

**Purpose**  to predict and explain how microbes spread  L2

**Process Skills**  observe and infer, predict, interpret data, compare and contrast, recognize cause and effect, separate and control variables

**Time Required**  30 minutes for initial setup; 15 minutes of observation time on days 3 and 7

**Safety Precautions**  Have students wash their hands after handling microorganisms. Provide for safe disposal of the rotting apples.

## ● Procedure

**Teaching Strategy**  Point out that bruises may be caused by bacteria.

## ● Conclude and Apply

1. Pathogens can cause infections by entering damaged or cut surfaces on an organism's skin.
2. Cleaning a wound removes pathogens and prevents infection.

---

### ✔ Assessment

**Performance**  To further assess students' understanding of microorganisms and disease, repeat the activity using 3% hydrogen peroxide to clean an infected apple. Determine whether it stops bacterial growth. Use **Performance Assessment in the Science Classroom,** p. 97.

### Communicating Your Data

Students may want to include other good health habits that will help them fight disease. Posters dealing with good nutrition might be posted near the school cafeteria.

## BENCH TESTED

### Real-World Question

**Purpose** Students determine how different blood types react when mixed. [L2] [ELL]

[IS] **Visual-Spatial**

**Process Skills** design an experiment, form a hypothesis, observe and infer, communicate, recognize cause and effect, separate and control variables, interpret data

**Time Required** 50 minutes

**Materials** For simulated blood, mix 10 mL of lowfat milk with 10 mL of water and add 2 or 3 drops of red food coloring. The lemon juice and water are used as antigens.

### Form a Hypothesis

**Possible Hypothesis** Most students' hypotheses will reflect that there will be clumping when some blood types are mixed.

### Test Your Hypothesis

**Possible Procedures**

- Mark four paper cups with blood type names A, B, AB, and O.
- Add 5 mL simulated blood to each cup.
- Use the lemon juice as antigen A for blood types B and O. Add 2 to 3 drops of lemon juice to cups B and O. Clumping occurs.
- Use water as antigen A for blood types A and AB. Add 2 to 3 drops to cups A and AB. No clumping occurs.

---

## LAB — Design Your Own

### Goals

- **Design** an experiment that simulates the reactions between different blood types.
- **Identify** which blood types can donate to which other blood types.

### Possible Materials

simulated blood (10 mL low-fat milk and 10 mL water plus red food coloring)
lemon juice as antigen A (for blood types B and O)
water as antigen A (for blood types A and AB)
droppers
small paper cups
marking pen
10-mL graduated cylinder

### Safety Precautions

**WARNING:** *Do not taste, eat, or drink any materials used in the lab.*

---

# Blood Type Reactions

### Real-World Question

Human blood can be classified into four main blood types—A, B, AB, and O. These types are determined by the presence or absence of antigens on the red blood cells. After blood is collected into a transfusion bag, it is tested to determine the blood type. The type is labeled clearly on the bag. Blood is refrigerated to keep it fresh and available for transfusion. What happens when two different blood types are mixed?

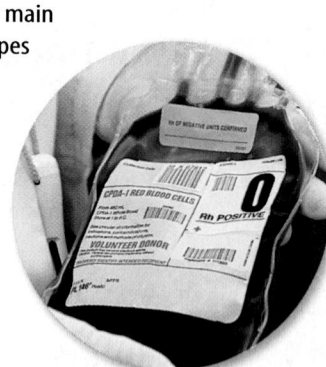

### Form a Hypothesis

Based on your reading and observations, form a hypothesis to explain how different blood types will react to each other.

### Test Your Hypothesis

**Make a Plan**

1. As a group, agree upon a hypothesis and decide how you will test it. Identify the results that will confirm the hypothesis.

2. **List** the steps you must take and the materials you will need to test your hypothesis. Be specific. Describe exactly what you will do in each step.

3. **Prepare** a data table like the one at the right in your Science Journal to record your observations.

| Blood Type Reactions | |
|---|---|
| Blood Type | Clumping (Yes or No) |
| A | no |
| B | yes |
| AB | no |
| O | yes |

---

## Alternative Inquiry Lab

**Blood Thickness** Students can extend the experience by designing an investigation to explore the question "How do antigens affect blood samples of different thicknesses?" Students can substitute the low-fat milk in the experiment with skim milk, whole milk, half-and-half, or cream to simulate how antigens affect blood samples of different thicknesses. Students can use metric rulers to estimate the diameters of the clumps formed in the different dairy products. Students can also design an experiment in which antigens A and B are added to each blood type.

4. Reread the entire experiment to make sure all steps are in logical order.

5. **Identify** constants and variables. Blood type O will be the control.

**Follow Your Plan**

1. Make sure your teacher approves your plan before you start.

2. Carry out the experiment according to the approved plan.

3. While doing the experiment, record your observations and complete the data table in your Science Journal.

## Analyze Your Data

1. **Compare** the reactions of each blood type (A, B, AB, and O) when antigen A was added to the blood.

2. **Observe** where clumping took place.

3. **Compare** your results with those of other groups.

4. What was the control factor in this experiment?

5. What were your variables?

## Conclude and Apply

1. Did the results support your hypothesis? Explain.

2. **Predict** what might happen to a person if other antigens are not matched properly.

3. What would happen in an investigation with antigen B added to each blood type?

### Communicating Your Data

**Write** a brief report on how blood is tested to determine blood type. Describe why this is important to know before receiving a blood transfusion. **For more help, refer to the** Science Skill Handbook.

LAB 187

### ✔ Assessment

**Oral** Have students explain why persons with blood type O can donate to anyone but can only receive from a person with blood type O. Type O has no A or B antigens and has antibodies A and B. Use **Performance Assessment in the Science Classroom,** p. 89.

### Communicating Your Data

Have students use online and library resources to find information on how blood is checked before a transfusion.

## ◉ Procedure

**Teaching Strategy** Instruct students to look for curdling of the milk in the simulated blood as it reacts with the acidic lemon juice. This represents the "clumping" of blood cells.

**Expected Outcome** Clumping will occur when the lemon juice antigen is mixed with blood types B and O. No clumping will occur when the water antigen is mixed with blood types A and AB.

## ◉ Analyze Your Data

**Answers to Questions**

1. Blood types B and O clumped when lemon juice antigen A was added. Blood types A and AB did not clump when water antigen A was added.

2. Clumping took place in cups with B and O blood types.

3. Students' results should be similar to those of other groups.

4. The control in this experiment was the blood solution and the amount of each antigen added to the blood.

5. The variable was the type of antigen solution used.

**Error Analysis** Have students compare their results with their hypotheses and explain any differences that might have occurred.

## ◉ Conclude and Apply

1. Answers will be determined by student hypotheses.

2. Clumping of blood cells could result.

3. Clumping would occur with blood types A and O and not with blood types B and AB.

# TIME

# TIME

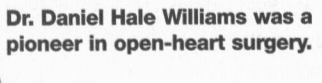

# SCIENCE AND HISTORY

## SCIENCE CAN CHANGE THE COURSE OF HISTORY!

## Content Background

Galen, a Roman physician, taught that there were two types of blood and two separate circulatory systems, venous and arterial. Oxygenated blood supposedly seeped from the right to the left side of the heart to become arterial blood that was then consumed by the body. Galen's theories dominated medieval and early Renaissance medicine.

Renaissance doctors began to question this theory when Arab medical texts became available in the West.

Sixteenth-century European anatomists made direct observations of pulmonary circulation and one-way valves in the heart and veins. This investigation culminated in Harvey's correct description of the circulatory system in 1628.

## Discussion

**Medical Research** What did Harvey do to develop his theory of circulation that is still done in medical research today? Possible answer: He used animals for his early observations and applied his findings to humans.

## Historical Significance

**Scientific Method** Harvey's discovery and theory were based on the observations of his predecessors and measurable phenomenon to construct a result that others could reproduce. He had developed a scientific method. Investigation, as opposed to traditional authority, was a defining aspect of the Renaissance that led to modern scientific practices.

Dr. Daniel Hale Williams was a pioneer in open-heart surgery.

# Have a Heart

## People didn't always know where blood came from or how it moved through the body.

You prick your finger, and when blood starts to flow out of the cut, you put on a bandage. But if you were a scientist living long ago, you might have also asked yourself some questions: How did your blood get to the tip of your finger? And why and how does it flow through (and sometimes out of!) your body?

As early as the 1500s, a Spanish scientist named Miguel Serveto (mee GEL • ser VEH toh) asked that question. His studies led him to the theory that blood circulated throughout the human body, but he didn't know how or why.

About 100 years later, William Harvey, an English doctor, explored Serveto's idea. Harvey studied animals to develop a theory about how the heart and the circulatory system work. Blood was pumped from the heart throughout the body,

Harvey hypothesized. Then it returned to the heart and recirculated. He published his ideas in 1628 in his famous book, *On the Motion of the Heart and Blood in Animals*. His theories were correct, and Harvey's book became the basis for all modern research on heart and blood vessels.

## Medical Pioneer

More than two centuries later, another pioneer, Dr. Daniel Hale Williams, stepped forward and used Harvey's ideas to change the science frontier again. He performed the first open-heart surgery by removing a knife from the heart of a stabbing victim. He stitched the wound in the fluid sac surrounding the heart, and the patient lived for several years afterward.

**Report** Identify a pioneer in science or medicine who has changed our lives for the better. Find out how this person started in the field, and how they came to make an important discovery. Give a presentation to the class.

## Science Online

For more information, visit in7.msscience.com/time

**Report** To help students create some perspective of the results of the last four hundred years of scientific investigation, do the following exercise. Assign student teams. Each team will research an organ of the body and prepare a presentation that compares its functions as they were known before the Renaissance with how they are viewed today.

## Resources for Teachers and Students

*The Greatest Benefit to Mankind: A Medical History of Humanity* by Roy Porter. New York: W. W. Norton, 1998

*Medicine: An Illustrated History* by Albert S. Lyons and R. Joseph Petrucelli, II. New York: Harry N. Abrams, Inc., 1978

## Reviewing Main Ideas

### Section 1 Blood

1. Red blood cells carry oxygen and carbon dioxide, platelets form clots, and white blood cells fight infection.

2. A, B, AB, and O blood types are determined by the presence or absence of antigens on red blood cells.

### Section 2 Circulation

1. Arteries carry blood away from the heart and veins return blood to the heart. Capillaries connect arteries to veins.

2. The circulatory system can be divided into three sections—coronary, pulmonary, and systemic circulation.

3. Lymph structures filter blood, produce white blood cells, and destroy worn out blood cells.

### Section 3 Immunity

1. Your body is protected against most pathogens by the immune system.

2. Active immunity is long lasting, but passive immunity is not.

### Section 4 Diseases

1. Pasteur and Koch discovered that microorganisms cause diseases. Lister learned that cleanliness helps control microorganisms.

2. Bacteria, viruses, fungi, and protists can cause infectious diseases.

3. HIV damages your body's immune system, which can cause AIDS.

4. Causes of noninfectious diseases, such as diabetes and cancer, include genetics, a poor diet, chemicals, and uncontrolled cell growth.

## Visualizing Main Ideas

*Copy and complete this concept map on the functions of the parts of the blood.*

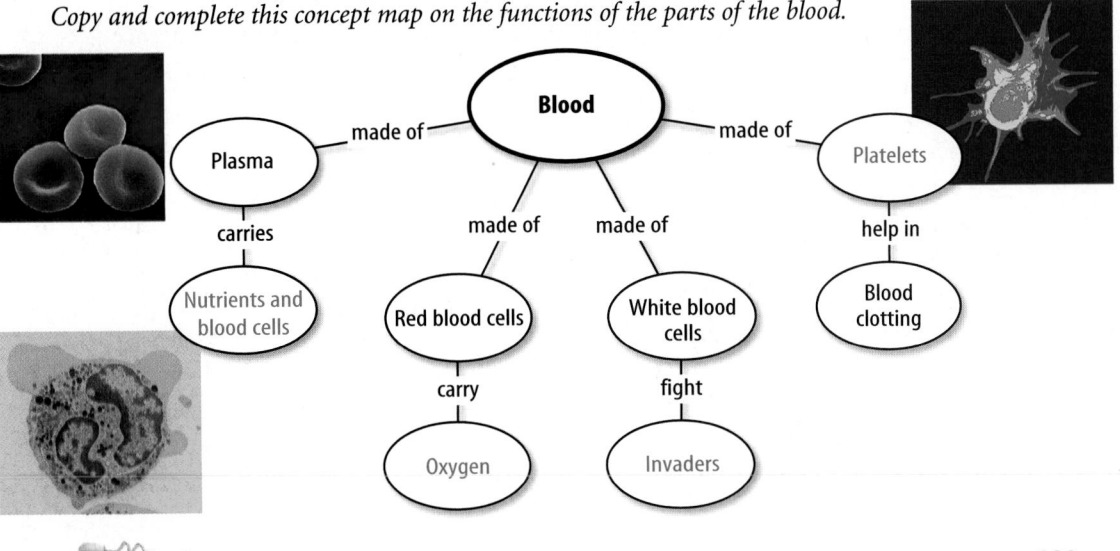

### Reviewing Main Ideas

Summary statements can be used by students to review the major concepts of the chapter.

### Visualizing Main Ideas

See student page.

**Science Online**

**Visit** in7.msscience.com
/self_check_quiz
/interactive_tutor
/vocabulary_puzzlemaker
/chapter_review
/standards_review

### Assessment Transparency

For additional assessment questions, use the *Assessment Transparency* located in the transparency book.

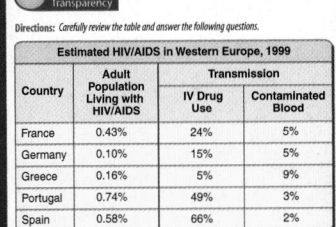

### Using Vocabulary

1. Hemoglobin
2. Platelets
3. Active immunity
4. allergen
5. pasteurization

### Checking Concepts

| | |
|---|---|
| 6. B | 11. C |
| 7. D | 12. D |
| 8. A | 13. B |
| 9. C | 14. D |
| 10. A | 15. A |

### Thinking Critically

16. red blood cells—120 days; white blood cells—a few days to several months; platelets—5 to 9 days

17. Student responses should match **Figure 3.**

18. All transport blood. Arteries carry blood away from the heart. Veins carry blood to the heart. Capillaries connect arteries and veins.

19. Antigens—foreign proteins and chemicals that invade your body; antibodies—formed by your immune system to destroy antigens; antibiotics—medicines that destroy or neutralize pathogens in the body

### Using Vocabulary

| | |
|---|---|
| active immunity p.175 | lymph p.172 |
| allergen p.182 | noninfectious |
| antibody p.174 | disease p.182 |
| antigen p.174 | passive immunity p.175 |
| artery p.169 | pasteurization p.177 |
| capillary p.169 | plasma p.162 |
| hemoglobin p.163 | platelet p.163 |
| infectious disease p.178 | vein p.169 |

*Fill in the blanks with the correct vocabulary word or words.*

1. _____ is the chemical in red blood cells.

2. _____ are cell fragments that help clot blood.

3. _____ occurs when your body makes its own antibodies.

4. A(n) _____ stimulates histamine release.

5. Heating a liquid to kill harmful bacteria is called _____.

### Checking Concepts

*Choose the word or phrase that best answers the question.*

6. Where does the exchange of food, oxygen, and wastes occur?
   - **A)** arteries
   - **B)** capillaries
   - **C)** veins
   - **D)** lymph vessels

7. How can infectious diseases be caused?
   - **A)** heredity
   - **B)** allergies
   - **C)** chemicals
   - **D)** organisms

8. Where is blood under greatest pressure?
   - **A)** arteries
   - **B)** capillaries
   - **C)** veins
   - **D)** lymph vessels

9. Which cells fight off infection?
   - **A)** red blood
   - **B)** bone
   - **C)** white blood
   - **D)** nerve

10. Of the following, which carries oxygen in blood?
    - **A)** red blood cells
    - **B)** platelets
    - **C)** white blood cells
    - **D)** lymph

11. What is required to clot blood?
    - **A)** plasma
    - **B)** oxygen
    - **C)** platelets
    - **D)** carbon dioxide

**Use the table below to answer question 12.**

| Table 1 Blood Types | | |
|---|---|---|
| **Blood Type** | **Antigen** | **Antibody** |
| A | A | Anti-B |
| B | B | Anti-A |
| AB | A, B | None |
| 0 | None | Anti-A, Anti-B |

12. Using the table above, what kind of antigen does type O blood have?
    - **A)** A
    - **B)** B
    - **C)** A and B
    - **D)** no antigen

13. Where does oxygen-rich blood enter first?
    - **A)** right atrium
    - **B)** left atrium
    - **C)** left ventricle
    - **D)** right ventricle

14. What is formed in the blood to fight invading antigens?
    - **A)** hormones
    - **B)** allergens
    - **C)** pathogens
    - **D)** antibodies

15. Which disease is caused by a virus that attacks white blood cells?
    - **A)** AIDS
    - **B)** measles
    - **C)** flu
    - **D)** polio

 Science Online in7.msscience.com/vocabulary_puzzlemaker

**Use the ExamView® Pro Testmaker CD-ROM to:**

- create multiple versions of tests
- create modified tests with one mouse click for inclusion students
- edit existing questions and add your own questions
- build tests aligned with state standards using built-in State Curriculum Tags
- change English tests to Spanish with one mouse click and vice versa

## Thinking Critically

16. **Compare and contrast** the life spans of red blood cells, white blood cells, and platelets.

17. **Sequence** blood clotting from the wound to forming a scab.

18. **Compare and contrast** the functions of arteries, veins, and capillaries.

19. **Analyze** how antibodies, antigens, and antibiotics differ.

20. **Recognize Cause and Effect** Use library references to identify the cause—bacteria, virus, fungus, or protist—of each of these diseases: athlete's foot, AIDS, cold, dysentery, flu, pinkeye, acne, and strep throat.

21. **Classify** Using word processing software, make a table to classify the following diseases as infectious or noninfectious: diabetes, gonorrhea, herpes, strep throat, syphilis, cancer, and flu.

**Use the graph below to answer question 22.**

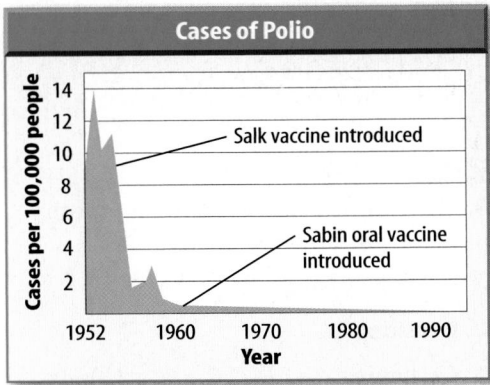

**Cases of Polio**

Salk vaccine introduced

Sabin oral vaccine introduced

22. **Explain** the rate of polio cases between 1952 and 1965. What conclusions can you draw about the effectiveness of the polio vaccine?

 Science Online in7.msscience.com/chapter_review

## Performance Activities

23. **Scientific Drawing** Prepare a drawing of the human heart and label its parts. Use arrows to show the flow of blood through the heart.

24. **Poster** Design and construct a poster to illustrate how a person with the flu could spread the disease to family members, classmates, and others.

25. **Pamphlet** Prepare a pamphlet describing heart transplants. Include an explanation of why the patient is given drugs that suppress the immune system and describe the patient's life after the operation.

## Applying Math

26. **Percentages of Blood Cells** A cubic millimeter of blood has about five million red blood cells, 7,500 white blood cells, and 400,000 platelets. Find the total number of red blood cells, white blood cells, and platelets in 1 mm³ of blood. Calculate what percentage of the total each type is.

**Use the table below to answer question 27.**

| Gender and Heart Rate | |
|---|---|
| **Sex** | **Pulse/Minute** |
| Male 1 | 72 |
| Male 2 | 64 |
| Male 3 | 65 |
| Female 1 | 67 |
| Female 2 | 84 |
| Female 3 | 74 |

27. **Heart Rates** Interpret the data listed in the table above. Find the average heart rate of the three males and the three females and compare the two averages.

## Thinking Critically

20. bacteria: pinkeye, strep throat, acne; virus: AIDS, cold, flu, pinkeye; fungus: athlete's foot; protist: dysentery

21. infectious: gonorrhea, herpes, strep throat, syphilis, flu; noninfectious: diabetes, cancer

22. rate dropped after the vaccine was introduced; the dramatic decline was a result of the vaccine

## Performance Activities

23. Compare student drawings to the illustration of the heart in **Figure 6.** Use **Performance Assessment in the Science Classroom**, p. 127.

24. Poster could show a person sneezing without covering the mouth and nose, coughing over food, and handling objects without washing hands. Use **Performance Assessment in the Science Classroom**, p. 145.

25. Drugs are given to prevent the body from rejecting the transplant (an antigen). Patients must avoid conditions that will bring them into contact with germs while their immune systems are suppressed. Use **Performance Assessment in the Science Classroom**, p. 145.

## Applying Math

**Indiana Math Standards**
7.2.1, 7.2.3, 7.6.1

26. total = 5,407,500 cells; red blood cells = 92.5%; white blood cells = 0.14%; platelets = 7.4%

27. males = 67; females = 75; In general, males' heart rates are lower than females'.

## ✓ **Assessment** **Resources**

📁 **Reproducible Masters**
**Chapter *Fast File* Resources**
  Chapter Review, pp. 39–40
  Chapter Tests, pp. 41–44
  Assessment Transparency Activity, p. 52
**Glencoe Science Web site**
  Chapter Review Test
  IN Standards Review

**Glencoe Technology**
  🔋 Assessment Transparency
  💿 Exam*View*® Pro Testmaker
  📼 MindJogger Videoquiz
  💿 Interactive Chalkboard

**Answer Sheet** A practice answer sheet can be found at in7.msscience.com/answer_sheet.

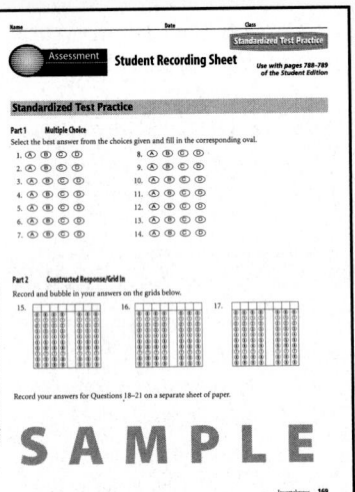

**Part 1  Multiple Choice**

1. B
2. D
3. A
4. D
5. A
6. A
7. C

**Part 2  Critical Response**

8. The blood in the circulatory system brings nutrients, water, and oxygen to the body cells. These substances diffuse through capillary walls into nearby cells. Water and other substances become part of the tissue fluid between cells. The lymphatic system collects and returns this fluid to the blood.

9. In the normal heart, oxygen-poor blood is pumped through the right atrium into the right ventricle and then to the lungs through the pulmonary artery. Then oxygen-rich blood returns from the lungs to the left atrium and into the left ventricle. In this heart, a hole is between the ventricles. This would allow the blood in both ventricles to mix. Because the left ventricle is under

The assessed Indiana standard appears above the question.

*Record your answers on the answer sheet provided by your teacher or on a sheet of paper.*

**Part 1  Multiple Choice**

The graph below shows life expectancy data for some people.

**Life Expectancy by Race and Sex, 1970–1997**

1. Which group had the lowest life expectancy in both 1975 and 1994?

   A  black females

   B  black males

   C  white females

   D  white males

**Test-Taking Tip**

**Answer Bubbles** For each question, double check that you are filling in the correct answer bubble for the question number you are working on.

**7.4.4**

2. Which is a function of blood?

   A  carries saliva to the mouth

   B  excretes salts from the body

   C  removes lymph from around cells

   D  transports substances to body cells

The table below lists recorded body data.

| Results from Exercising | | | |
|---|---|---|---|
| Activity | Pulse Rate (beats/min) | Body Temperature | Degree of Sweating |
| 1 | 80 | 98.6°F | None |
| 2 | 90 | 98.8°F | Minimal |
| 3 | 100 | 98.9°F | Little |
| 4 | 120 | 99.1°F | Moderate |
| 5 | 150 | 99.5°F | Considerable |

**7.4.11**

3. Which activity caused a pulse of less than 100 beats per minute?

   A  2

   B  3

   C  4

   D  5

**7.4.11**

4. Using the data above, what was probably occurring during Activity 2?

   A  brisk walking

   B  resting

   C  running

   D  slow walking

more pressure than the right ventricle, blood will flow through the hole from the left ventricle to the right ventricle.

10. Some ways to prevent cardiovascular disease include having a healthy lifestyle and regular check-ups, eating healthful diet, exercising, and not smoking.

11. Active immunity is longer lasting. In active immunity, the body makes antibodies in response to an antigen. Some antibodies stay on duty in the blood, and more are produced rapidly if the pathogen enters the body again. In passive immunity, antibodies that are produced in another animal are introduced into the human body by vaccination. Some vaccinations require booster shots after a period of time.

12. The scientist can use Koch's Rules. She must identify the bacteria in every case of the disease. She must grow the organism on agar gel. Then she must be sure that no

**7.4.4**

5. This illustration shows part of a human's circulatory system.

A

What might happen if vessel A became blocked?

A Blood could not flow to the lungs.

B Blood could not return to the heart from the body.

C Blood could not flow to the body.

D Blood could not return to the heart from the lungs.

**7.4.12**

6. Which is a noninfectious disease?

A diabetes

B malaria

C SARS

D tetanus

**7.4.12**

7. Which is **NOT** a biological vector?

A bird

B fly

C food

D human

## Part 2 Critical Response

**7.4.4**

8. How do the lymphatic and circulatory systems work together?

**7.4.4**

9. Below is an illustration of the interior of a human heart.

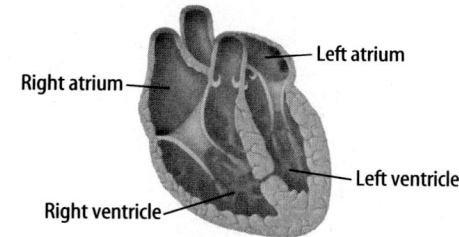

Left atrium
Right atrium
Left ventricle
Right ventricle

The left ventricle pumps blood under higher pressure than the right ventricle does. Compare the circulation in this heart with that of a normal heart.

**7.4.11**

10. What are some ways to prevent cardiovascular disease?

**7.4.13**

11. Which is longer lasting, active immunity or passive immunity? Why?

**7.4.12** **7.6.2**

12. A scientist has isolated a bacterium that she thinks causes a recently discovered disease called red tree. How can she prove it? What steps should she follow?

**7.4.12**

13. Compare and contrast infectious and non-infectious diseases.

## Rubrics

The following rubric is a sample scoring device for critical response questions.

### Critical Response

| Points | Description |
|--------|-------------|
| 4 | The student demonstrates a thorough understanding of the science of the task. The response may contain minor flaws that do not detract from the demonstration of a thorough understanding. |
| 3 | The student demonstrates an understanding of the science of the task. The response is essentially correct and demonstrates an essential but less than thorough understanding of the science. |
| 2 | The student demonstrates only a partial understanding of the science of the task. Although the student may have used the correct approach to a solution or may have provided a correct solution, the work lacks an essential understanding of the underlying science concepts. |
| 1 | The student demonstrates a very limited understanding of the science of the task. The response is incomplete and exhibits many flaws. |
| 0 | The student provides a completely incorrect solution or no response at all. |

Science Online in7.msscience.com/standards_review

other organisms are present. Next, she must inoculate the organism into a healthy host. The healthy host must get the disease. Finally, the organism is removed from the host and grown again on agar gel. The organism that grows on the agar must be identical to the original organism. If they match, then the organism is the pathogen that caused the disease.

13. An infectious disease is caused by a pathogen and is spread from an infected organism or the environment to another organism. Noninfectious diseases result from malfunctions of body cells. Both types of disease can be chronic.

Some infectious and noninfectious diseases can be cured but, in some cases, only symptoms of the disease can be treated.

| Section/Objectives | Standards | | Labs/Features |
|---|---|---|---|
| **Chapter Opener** | **National** | **State/Local** | **Launch Lab:** Space and Interactions, p. 195 **Foldables**, p. 195 |
| | See pp. 16T–17T for a Key to Standards. | Detailed standards begin on page IN8. | A data-collection lab using Probeware technology can be found in the **Probeware Lab Manual**, pp. 17–20 |
| **Section 1  The Environment** ⏱ 2 sessions  📦 1 block 1. **Identify** biotic and abiotic factors in an ecosystem. 2. **Describe** the different levels of biological organizations. 3. **Explain** how ecology and the environment are related. | National Content Standards: UCP.1–UCP.3, UCP.5, A.1, A.2, C.1, C.4 | Indiana Standards: 7.1.7, 7.2.7, 7.4.9 | **Integrate Career**, p. 198 **Science Online**, p. 200 **Lab:** Delicately Balanced Ecosystems, p. 202 |
| **Section 2  Interactions Among Living Organisms** ⏱ 2 sessions  📦 1 block 4. **Identify** the characteristics that describe populations. 5. **Examine** the different types of relationships that occur among populations in a community. 6. **Determine** the habitat and niche of a species in a community. | National Content Standards: UCP.1–UCP.3, UCP.5, A.1, A.2, C.1, C.4 | Indiana Standards: 7.4.8, 7.4.9, 7.5.3 | **Science Online**, p. 204 **MiniLAB:** Observing Symbiosis, p. 206 |
| **Section 3  Matter and Energy** ⏱ 3 sessions  📦 1.5 blocks 7. **Explain** the difference between a food chain and a food web. 8. **Describe** how energy flows through ecosystems. 9. **Examine** how materials such as water, carbon, and nitrogen are used repeatedly. | National Content Standards: UCP.1–UCP.3, UCP.5, A.1, A.2, B.1, B.3, C.1, C.4 | Indiana Standards: 7.4.2, 7.4.6, 7.4.8, 7.5.3 | **Visualizing a Food Chain**, p. 209 **Applying Science:** How do changes in Antarctic food webs affect populations?, p. 210 **Integrate Chemistry**, p. 211 **MiniLAB:** Modeling the Water Cycle, p. 212 **Lab:** Identifying a Limiting Factor, p. 214 **Science and Language Arts:** The Solace of Open Spaces, p. 216 |

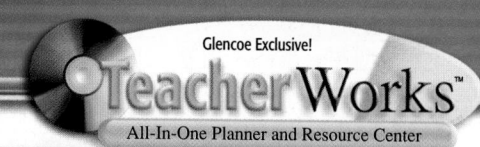

Glencoe Exclusive!
**TeacherWorks™**
All-In-One Planner and Resource Center

| Lab Materials | Reproducible Resources | Section Assessment | Technology |
|---|---|---|---|
| **Launch Lab:** meter stick | **Chapter FAST FILE Resources**<br>Foldables Worksheet, p. 17<br>Directed Reading Overview, p. 19<br>Note-taking Worksheets, pp. 33–35 | GLENCOE'S ASSESSMENT ADVANTAGE | TeacherWorks includes:<br>• Interactive Teacher Edition<br>• Lesson Planner with calendar<br>• Access to all program blacklines<br>• Correlations to standards<br>• Web links |
| **Lab:** large jars of equal size (4), clear-plastic wrap, stalks of *Elodea* (8), garden fertilizer, rubber bands (4), pond water, triple-beam balance, weighing paper, spoon, metric ruler | **Chapter FAST FILE Resources**<br>Transparency Activity, p. 44<br>Enrichment, p. 30<br>Reinforcement, p. 27<br>Directed Reading, p. 20<br>Lab Worksheets, pp. 5–6<br>Lab Activity, pp. 9–12 | **Portfolio**<br>Curriculum Connection, p. 199<br>**Performance**<br>Applying Skills, p. 201<br>**Content**<br>Section Review, p. 201 | Section Focus Transparency<br>Guided Reading Audio Program<br>Interactive Chalkboard CD-ROM |
| **MiniLAB:** legume plant, nonlegume plant, magnifying lens<br><br>*Need materials?*<br>Contact Science Kit at 1-800-828-7777 or www.sciencekit.com on the Internet. | **Chapter FAST FILE Resources**<br>Transparency Activity, p. 45<br>MiniLAB, p. 3<br>Enrichment, p. 31<br>Reinforcement, p. 28<br>Directed Reading, p. 20<br>Lab Activity, pp. 13–15 | **Portfolio**<br>Curriculum Connection, p. 205<br>**Performance**<br>MiniLAB, p. 206<br>Applying Math, p. 207<br>**Content**<br>Section Review, p. 207 | Section Focus Transparency<br>Guided Reading Audio Program<br>Interactive Chalkboard CD-ROM |
| **MiniLAB:** marker, plastic cup, water, plastic wrap, tape, rubber band<br>**Lab:** bean seeds, small planting containers, soil, water, label, trowel, aluminum foil, sunny window, refrigerator or oven | **Chapter FAST FILE Resources**<br>Transparency Activity, p. 46<br>MiniLAB, p. 4<br>Enrichment, p. 32<br>Reinforcement, p. 29<br>Directed Reading, pp. 21, 22<br>Lab Worksheets, pp. 7–8<br>Transparency Activity, pp. 47–48<br>**Lab Management and Safety** p. 39 | **Portfolio**<br>Activity, p. 209<br>Assessment, p. 213<br>**Performance**<br>Applying Science, p. 210<br>MiniLAB, p. 212<br>Applying Skills, p. 213<br>**Content**<br>Section Review, p. 213 | Section Focus Transparency<br>Teaching Transparency<br>Virtual Labs CD-ROM<br>Guided Reading Audio Program<br>Interactive Chalkboard CD-ROM<br>Video Lab |

## End of Chapter Assessment

GLENCOE'S ASSESSMENT ADVANTAGE

| Blackline Masters | Technology | Professional Series |
|---|---|---|
| **Chapter FAST FILE Resources**<br>Chapter Review, pp. 37–38<br>Chapter Tests, pp. 39–42<br>**Mastering the Grade 7 Indiana Science Standards** | MindJogger Videoquiz<br>IN Test Prep and Practice ExamView®<br>ExamView® Pro Testmaker<br>TeacherWorks CD-ROM<br>Interactive Chalkboard CD-ROM | **Performance Assessment in the Science Classroom (PASC)** |

## Transparencies

### Section Focus

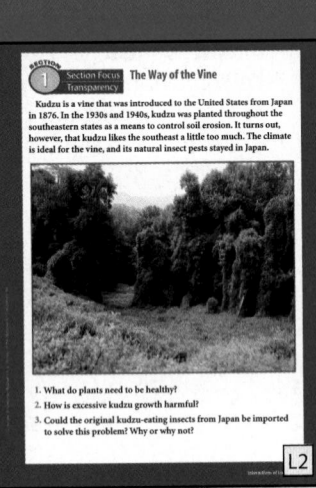

**The Way of the Vine**

Kudzu is a vine that was introduced to the United States from Japan in 1876. In the 1930s and 1940s, kudzu was planted throughout the southeastern states as a means to control soil erosion. It turns out, however, that kudzu likes the southeast a little too much. The climate is ideal for the vine, and its natural insect pests stayed in Japan.

1. What do plants need to be healthy?
2. How is excessive kudzu growth harmful?
3. Could the original kudzu-eating insects from Japan be imported to solve this problem? Why or why not?

L2

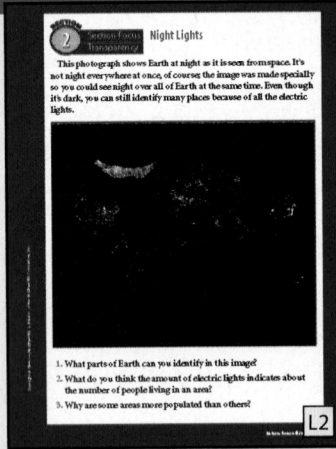

**Night Lights**

This photograph shows Earth at night as it is seen from space. It's not night everywhere at once, of course; the image was made specially so you could see night over all of Earth at the same time. Even though it's dark, you can still identify many places because of all the electric lights.

1. What parts of Earth can you identify in this image?
2. What do you think the amount of electric lights indicates about the number of people living in an area?
3. Why are some areas more populated than others?

L2

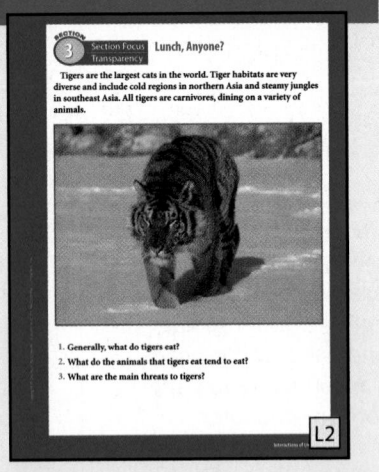

**Lunch, Anyone?**

Tigers are the largest cats in the world. Tiger habitats are very diverse and include cold regions in northern Asia and steamy jungles in southeast Asia. All tigers are carnivores, dining on a variety of animals.

1. Generally, what do tigers eat?
2. What do the animals that tigers eat tend to eat?
3. What are the main threats to tigers?

L2

This is a representation of key blackline masters available in the Teacher Classroom Resources. See Resource Manager boxes within the chapter for additional information.

### Key to Teaching Strategies

The following designations will help you decide which activities are appropriate for your students.

L1 Level 1 activities should be appropriate for students with learning difficulties.

L2 Level 2 activities should be within the ability range of all students.

L3 Level 3 activities are designed for above-average students.

ELL ELL activities should be within the ability range of English Language Learners.

COOP LEARN Cooperative Learning activities are designed for small group work.

LS Multiple Learning Styles logos, as described on page 12T, are used throughout to indicate strategies that address different learning styles.

P These strategies represent student products that can be placed into a best-work portfolio.

PBL Problem-Based Learning activities apply real-world situations to learning.

### Assessment

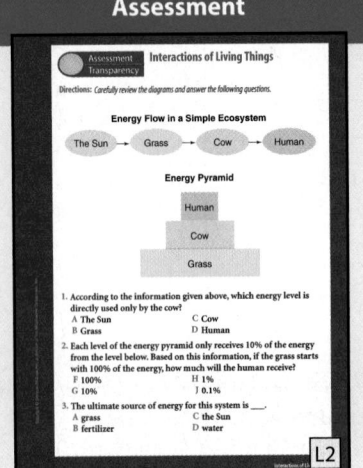

**Interactions of Living Things**

Directions: Carefully review the diagrams and answer the following questions.

**Energy Flow in a Simple Ecosystem**

The Sun → Grass → Cow → Human

**Energy Pyramid**

Human
Cow
Grass

1. According to the information given above, which energy level is directly used only by the cow?
   A The Sun    C Cow
   B Grass      D Human
2. Each level of the energy pyramid only receives 10% of the energy from the level below. Based on this information, if the grass starts with 100% of the energy, how much will the human receive?
   F 100%   H 1%
   G 10%    J 0.1%
3. The ultimate source of energy for this system is ___.
   A grass       C the Sun
   B fertilizer  D water

L2

### Teaching

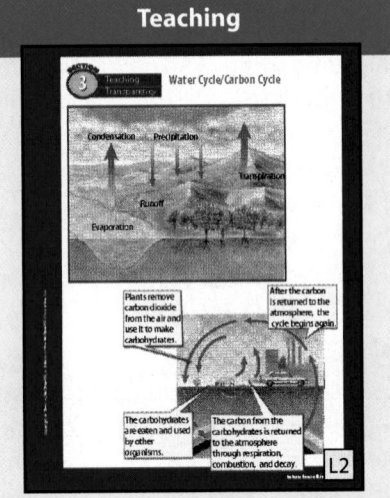

**Water Cycle/Carbon Cycle**

L2

## Hands-on Activities

### Student Text Lab Worksheet

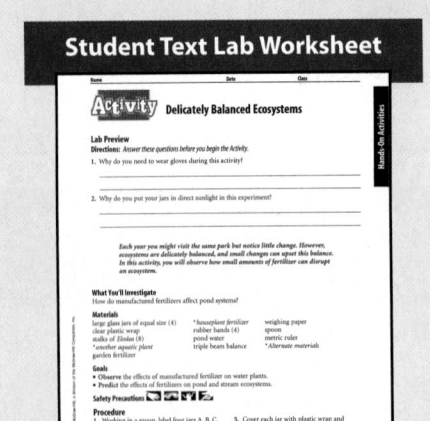

**Activity** Delicately Balanced Ecosystems

**Lab Preview**
Directions: Answer these questions before you begin the Activity.
1. Why do you need to wear gloves during this activity?

2. Why do you put your jar in direct sunlight in this experiment?

Each year you might visit the same park but notice little change. However, ecosystems are delicately balanced, and small changes can upset this balance. In this activity, you will observe how small amounts of fertilizer can disrupt an ecosystem.

**What You'll Investigate**
How do manufactured fertilizers affect pond systems?

**Materials**
large glass jars of equal size (4)       *houseplant fertilizer       weighing paper
clear plastic wrap                        rubber bands (4)             spoon
stalks of Elodea (8)                      pond water                   metric ruler
*another aquatic plant                    triple beam balance          *Alternate materials
garden fertilizer

**Goals**
• Observe the effects of manufactured fertilizer on water plants.
• Predict the effects of fertilizers on pond and stream ecosystems.

**Safety Precautions**

**Procedure**
1. Working in a group, label four jars A, B, C, and D.
2. Measure eight Elodea stalks to be certain that they are all about equal in length.
3. Fill the jars with pond water and place two stalks of Elodea in each jar.
4. Add 3 g of fertilizer to jar B, 10 g to jar C, and 30 g to jar D. Put no fertilizer in jar A.
5. Cover each jar with plastic wrap and secure it with a rubber band. Use your pencil to punch three small holes through the plastic wrap.
6. Place the jars together in direct sunlight.
7. Make daily observations of the jars for three weeks. Record your observations in Table 1.
8. At the end of the three-week period, remove the Elodea stalks. Measure and record the length of each in the table.

L2

### Laboratory Activities

**Laboratory Activity** Your School's Ecosystem

One of the most important reasons that living things interact is to exchange energy. Your school functions in a way that is very similar to an ecosystem. It receives energy and distributes it throughout the school. It is composed of both biotic and abiotic factors. There are interactions occurring constantly throughout the day. In this laboratory you will observe and identify some similarities between your school and a natural ecosystem.

**Strategy**
You will observe the biotic and abiotic factors of your school.
You will describe and classify different kinds of interactions.

**Materials**
pencils      markers      old magazines      paper
poster board glue         scissors

**Procedure**
1. Look around the classroom. Identify all the abiotic factors you can find. For this study, you may consider as abiotic items any items made from once-living products such as wood or cotton. Abiotic factors will include chairs, tables, building materials on walls, and anything else you can think of. Even clothing will be important as you begin to identify connections and interactions between biotic and abiotic factors. Don't forget the temperature and lighting of your classroom. Write these on a piece of paper, but don't put them in your data table yet.
2. Look around your classroom again. Identify all the biotic factors you can find. Biotic factors will include students, living animals in the classroom, snacks in back packs, and anything else you can think of. Even plants will be important as you begin to identify connections and interactions between biotic and abiotic factors. Write these on a piece of paper, but don't put them in your data table yet.
3. Make a second list of abiotic factors, this time outside your classroom. If your teacher permits, you may travel as a class to identify factors around your school. These are the larger views of your school environment and should include such things as the gymnasium or cafeteria.
4. Now, make a second list of biotic factors outside your classroom. If your teacher permits, you may travel as a class to identify factors around your school. These are the larger views of your school environment and should include trees, grass, birds or other animals that live on your campus, food machines, food in the cafeteria, or anything else you can think of.
5. Make a list of populations within your school. There are many populations that are grouped according to what they do. For example, the students in your science classroom and all the students in school. Think about the teachers. Are they divided into subpopulations such as English teachers and science teachers? How about the administration, the people who run the business of the school? Are there any clubs in your school? What about sports teams? List as many as you can think of.
6. Form small groups and share your information. Some people may have noticed things that others did not. Using Table 1, make one large list of all the factors that you, as a group, identified. If you need more room, use a separate sheet of paper.

L2

# Meeting Different Ability Levels

## Content Outline

## Reinforcement

## Enrichment

## Directed Reading (English/Spanish)

## Study Guide

## Reading Essentials

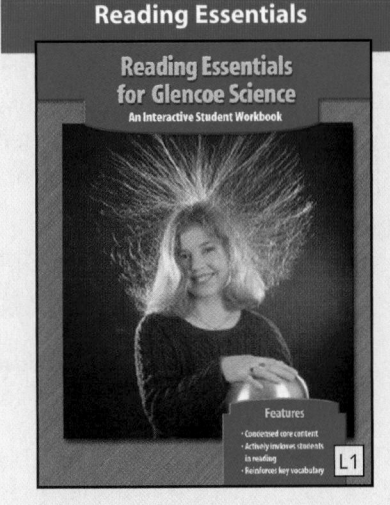

# Assessment

## Test Practice Workbook

## Chapter Review

## Chapter Tests

# Science Content Background

## section 1 The Environment

### Ecology

The interactions of biotic and abiotic factors determine what kinds of organisms live in various environments. Biotic and abiotic factors are not independent of each other. Abiotic factors include air currents, temperature, moisture, light, and soil. The importance of each factor varies from environment to environment and over time.

### Abiotic Factors

Soil, a mixture of humus, decayed organic matter, and particles of weathered rock, sand, silt, and clay, forms as rocks are weathered and eroded. Clay is an important component of soil because it helps hold water in the soil and contains nutrients that plants need for growth. The types of minerals found in clays are largely dependent on the climate. Humus is equally important because it helps separate clay and sand particles, allowing more water and air to enter the soil. It also provides food for soil organisms as well as nutrients for plants.

### Biotic Factors

Ecologists study interactions among organisms at several different levels. They study individual organisms, interactions among organisms of the same species, and interactions among organisms of different species. They also study how abiotic factors affect groups of interacting species.

### Ecological Systems

Hundreds of different systems interact within an ecosystem. An individual organism is a member and interacts with other members of the same species, or population, living in that area. Each population interacts with other populations that live in the same area, forming a community. The size of each population or community is dependent upon the availability of food, shelter, and space.

## section 2 Interactions Among Living Organisms

### Characteristics of Populations

Population size can be difficult to measure. Animal population size can be influenced by the amount of food and space available. Natural populations cannot increase forever. Population density measures how crowded a population is and is expressed as the number of individuals per unit area or volume.

Dispersion is the spatial distribution of individuals within a population. The three patterns of dispersion are recognized: even, clumped, and random. The dispersion pattern sometimes depends on how the population is observed. Waterbirds that live near the shore may appear evenly spaced. However, if the entire island is

---

### chapter content resources

**Internet Resources**
For additional content background, visit in7.msscience.com to:
- access your book online
- find references to related articles in popular science magazines
- access Web links with related content background
- access current events with science journal topics

**Print Resources**
*Discover Nature in Water and Wetlands: Things to Know and Things to Do (Discover Nature Series)* by Elizabeth P. Lawlor, Pat Archer (Illustrator), Stackpole Books, 2000

*Environmental Science: Field Activities and Projects Guide,* HBJ School, 2000

*Woods and Forests (Exploring Ecosystems)* by Patricia Fink, A. Martin, Bob Italiano (Illustrator), Steve Savage (Illustrator), Franklin Watts, Incorporated, 2000

*Environmental Science* by Martin Schachter, Amsco School Publishing, 1999

observed, the birds may appear clumped near the water's edge.

## Carrying Capacity

When a population arrives at the point at which its size is no longer increasing, it has reached the carrying capacity of the environment. The carrying capacity is the greatest number of individuals in a certain population that a given environment can support under a specific set of conditions. The carrying capacity may vary with the time of the year, as conditions change. At carrying capacity the number of organisms born or produced in a given period of time balances the number of organisms that die during that same time. When this happens, the size of the population remains fairly stable.

## section 3 Matter and Energy
### Energy Flow Through Ecosystems

The flow of energy through ecosystems is illustrated by food chains, food webs, ecological pyramids, and energy pyramids.

## Food Chains

Food chains illustrate how energy flows from organism to organism in a community. The main parts of a food chain are the Sun, producers, consumers, and decomposers. The Sun produces energy used by living beings. Producers are green plants, protists, and bacteria that make their own food. A producer is the first step in the food chain. Decomposers are bacteria, fungi, and other organisms that break down dead organisms. They release carbon and nitrogen into the environment.

## Food Webs

The feeding relationships among organisms in a community are called a food web, which illustrates energy flow. A food web is made up of interconnected food chains.

*Steve Kaufman/DRK Photo*

### Teacher to Teacher
Dennis L. Stockdale
Asheville High School
Asheville, NC

"On the left-hand page of their open Science Journals, I have students take 'home notes' and write questions about what they read. In class the following day, they take 'class notes' on the right-hand page of their journals. This arrangement can be used for review of chapter content."

*Dennis L. Stockdale*

## Chapter Vocabulary

ecology, p. 196
abiotic factor, p. 196
biotic factor, p. 196
population, p. 200
community, p. 200
ecosystem, p. 200
biosphere, p. 201
population density, p. 204
limiting factor, p. 205
symbiosis, p. 206
niche, p. 207
habitat, p. 207
food chain, p. 208
food web, p. 210
water cycle, p. 212

**Science Journal** Student responses may include water, sunlight, air, soil, plants, animals, and other organisms

**PowerPoint® Presentations**

This CD-ROM is an editable Microsoft® PowerPoint® presentation that includes:
• a pre-made presentation for every chapter
• interactive graphics
• animations
• audio clips
• image bank
• all new section and chapter questions
• Standardized Test Practice
• transparencies
• pre-lab questions for all labs
• Foldables directions
• links to in7.msscience.com

## Text Question Answer

soil, water, sunlight, and air

---

**Academic Standard—4:** Students begin to trace the flow of matter and energy through ecosystems. They recognize the fundamental difference between plants and animals and understand its basis at the cellular level. Students distinguish species, particularly through an examination of internal structures and functions. They use microscopes to observe cells and recognize that cells function in similar ways in all organisms.

**Also covers:** Academic Standards 2, 5 (Detailed standards begin on page IN8.)

# Interactions of Living Things

## chapter preview

**sections**

**1  The Environment**
   *Lab  Delicately Balanced Ecosystems*

**2  Interactions Among Living Organisms**

**3  Matter and Energy**
   *Lab  Identifying a Limiting Factor*

*Virtual Lab  How is energy transferred through a community of organisms?*

## Interactions at a Waterhole

How many different kinds of animals can you see in the photo? How are the animals interacting with each other? Animals and other organisms in an area not only interact with each other, but with the nonliving factors of the area as well. What non-living factors can you identify?

**Science Journal**  Write a list of things you interact with each day.

194

## Theme Connection

**Systems and Interactions** In learning about relationships among living and nonliving things in populations, communities, and ecosystems, students will discover how all living and nonliving things on Earth are connected.

## About the Photo

**Animal Interactions** On an African savannah, it is common to see a variety of animals taking advantage of a water hole, which is rainwater left from the rainy season. Pictured are ostriches, zebras, giraffes, and kudus. All of these herbivorous animals interact with one another as they drink and bathe at the waterhole.

# Start-Up Activities

## Space and Interactions

Imagine that you are in a crowded elevator. Everyone jostles and bumps each other. The temperature increases and ordinary noises seem louder. Like people in an elevator, plants and animals in an area interact. How does the amount of space available to each organism affect its interaction with other organisms?

1. Use a meterstick to measure the length and width of the classroom.
2. Multiply the length by the width to find the area of the room in square meters.
3. Count the number of individuals in your class. Divide the area of the classroom by the number of individuals. In your Science Journal, record how much space each person has.
4. **Think Critically** Write a prediction in your Science Journal about what might happen if the number of students in your classroom doubled.

 **Preview this chapter's content and activities at** in7.msscience.com

---

**FOLDABLES™**
**Study Organizer**

**Biotic and Abiotic** Make the following Foldable to help you understand the cause and effect relationship of biotic and abiotic things.

**STEP 1** Fold a vertical sheet of paper in half from top to bottom.

**STEP 2** Fold in half from side to side with the fold at the top.

**STEP 3** Unfold the paper once. Cut only the fold of the top flap to make two tabs.

**STEP 4** Turn the paper vertically and label the front tabs as shown.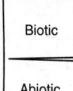

> Biotic
>
> Abiotic

**Illustrate and Label** Before you read the chapter, list examples of biotic and abiotic things around you on the tabs. As you read, write about each.

195

---

**Purpose** Use the Launch Lab to give students firsthand experience in determining population density. L2 ELL COOP LEARN LS

**Logical-Mathematical**

**Preparation** Pair students to work together.

**Materials** meterstick

**Teaching Strategy** One student can measure and the other can record. They can find the answers to the questions together.

### Think Critically

If the student population is 30 and the classroom size is 240 m², then each student would have 8 m². If the number of students in the classroom is doubled, each person would have only 4 m². To calculate population density, divide the number of individuals in a population by the area to get individuals per unit area. In this case, the population density would be:

30 students/240 m² = 0.125 students per m²

### Assessment

**Performance** Provide students with the total number of students and staff in the school and the area of the school building. Have them calculate the population density. Use **Performance Assessment in the Science Classroom,** p. 101.

**FOLDABLES™**
**Study Organizer**
**Dinah Zike**
**Study Fold**

Student preparation materials for this Foldable are available in the **Chapter *FAST FILE* Resources.**

**Probeware Labs**

This chapter's data-collection lab using Probeware technology is included on the *Video Labs CD-ROM*. See the *Probeware Lab Manual* pages 17–20 for student worksheets.

# 1 Motivate

**INTERACTIVE CHALKBOARD**
PowerPoint® Presentations

### Bellringer

**Section Focus Transparencies** also are available on the Interactive Chalkboard CD-ROM.

L2 ELL

SECTION
1 Section Focus Transparency

**The Way of the Vine**

Kudzu is a vine that was introduced to the United States from Japan in 1876. In the 1930s and 1940s, kudzu was planted throughout the southeastern states as a means to control soil erosion. It turns out, however, that kudzu likes the southeast a little too much. The climate is ideal for the vine, and its natural insect pests stayed in Japan.

1. What do plants need to be healthy?
2. How is excessive kudzu growth harmful?
3. Could the original kudzu-eating insects from Japan be imported to solve this problem? Why or why not?

L2

Interactions of Living Things

### Tie to Prior Knowledge

**Organisms** Ask students to name organisms from their own environment. Ask how these organisms interact in their environment.

# 2 Teach

### ✔ Reading Check

**Answer** It was once living.

---

**section**

**1**

Also covers: 7.1.7, 7.2.7 (Detailed standards begin on page IN8.)

# The Environment

as you read

### *What* You'll Learn
- **Identify** biotic and abiotic factors in an ecosystem.
- **Describe** the different levels of biological organization.
- **Explain** how ecology and the environment are related.

### *Why* It's Important
Abiotic and biotic factors interact to make up your ecosystem. The quality of your ecosystem can affect your health. Your actions can affect the health of the ecosystem.

### ⊕ Review Vocabulary
**climate:** the average weather conditions of an area over time

### New Vocabulary
- ecology
- community
- abiotic factor
- ecosystem
- biotic factor
- biosphere
- population

## Ecology

All organisms, from the smallest bacteria to a blue whale, interact with their environment. **Ecology** is the study of the interactions among organisms and their environment. Ecologists, such as the one in **Figure 1,** are scientists who study these relationships. Ecologists organize the environmental factors that influence organisms into two groups—nonliving and living or once-living. **Abiotic** (ay bi AH tihk) **factors** are the nonliving parts of the environment. Living or once-living organisms in the environment are called **biotic** (bi AH tihk) **factors.**

**✔ Reading Check** *Why is a rotting log considered a biotic factor in the environment?*

## Abiotic Factors

In any environment, birds, insects, and other living things, including humans, depend on one another for food and shelter. They also depend on the abiotic factors that surround them, such as water, sunlight, temperature, air, and soil. All of these factors and others are important in determining which organisms are able to live in a particular environment.

**Figure 1** Ecologists study biotic and abiotic factors in an environment and the relationships among them. Many times, ecologists must travel to specific environments to examine the organisms that live there.

---

## Section 1 Resource Manager

**Chapter *FAST FILE* Resources**
Transparency Activity, p. 44
Directed Reading for Content Mastery, pp. 19, 20
Note-taking Worksheets, pp. 33–35
Lab Activity, pp. 9–12
Enrichment, p. 30

Reinforcement, p. 27
Lab Worksheets, pp. 5–6
**Life Science Critical Thinking/Problem Solving,** p. 13
**Performance Assessment in the Science Classroom,** p. 48

**Earth's Water Supply**

The seas and oceans are home to thousands of different species.

This stream is a freshwater environment. It is home to many species of plants and animals.

**Figure 2** Salt water accounts for 97 percent of the water on Earth. It is found in the seas and oceans. Only three percent of Earth's water is freshwater.

**Water** All living organisms need water to survive. The bodies of most organisms are 50 percent to 95 percent water. Water is an important part of the cytoplasm in cells and the fluid that surrounds cells. Respiration, photosynthesis, digestion, and other important life processes can only occur in the presence of water.

More than 95 percent of Earth's surface water is found in the oceans. The saltwater environment in the oceans is home to a vast number of species. Freshwater environments, like the one in **Figure 2,** also support thousands of types of organisms.

**Light and Temperature** The abiotic factors of light and temperature also affect the environment. The availability of sunlight is a major factor in determining where green plants and other photosynthetic organisms live, as shown in **Figure 3.** By the process of photosynthesis, energy from the Sun is changed into chemical energy that is used for life processes. Most green algae live near the water's surface where sunlight can penetrate. In dense forests where little sunlight penetrates through to the forest floor, very few photosynthetic plants grow.

The temperature of a region also determines which plants and animals can live there. Some areas of the world have a fairly consistent temperature year round, but other areas have seasons during which temperatures vary. Water environments throughout the world also have widely varied temperatures. Living organisms are found in the freezing cold Arctic, in the extremely hot water near ocean vents, and at almost every temperature in between.

**Figure 3** Flowers that grow on the forest floor, such as these bluebells, grow during the spring when they receive the most sunlight. **Infer** *why there is little sunlight on the forest floor during the summer.*

## Use Science Words

**Word Origin** Have students look up *ecology* in the dictionary and write its definition, based on its two parts, *oikos*, meaning "house," and *-logy*, meaning "the study of." Ecology is the study of where we live. [L2] **Linguistic**

## Discussion

**Rainfall Variations** What happens to plants when rainfall in an area changes from season to season? During times of little rainfall, plants are smaller and fewer and may die. New plants come back when it rains again.

## Quick Demo

**Aquarium Life**
**Materials** aquarium with live fish and aquatic plants
**Estimated Time** ten minutes
**Procedure** Show students an aquarium with live fish and aquatic plants. What nonliving things influence a fish's life? water quality, temperature, light, the presence of oxygen What living things influence the life of a fish? plants, bacteria, other fish, snails

## Discussion

**Abiotics Climate** Which abiotic factors relate to climate? temperature, wind, soil, light, water

## Caption Answer

**Figure 3** because leaves grow in number and size and shade the forest floor

# Differentiated Instruction

**Challenge** Have students build their own terrarium representing a variety of environments, such as desert, temperate, and rainforest. Students should make a list of all the abiotic and biotic factors, and how these influence the environment. [L3]

# Teacher FYI

**Biotic and Abiotic** Biotic factors affect abiotic factors. The trees in a rain forest hold the topsoil with their roots; fallen leaves return organic matter to the soil; and leaves shade the soil and return water to the atmosphere by evaporation and transpiration. Trees, therefore, influence soil composition, temperature, and humidity.

**Humans and Environment** Have students make a list of the ways humans have changed the environment through pollution. Students may list thermal pollution by heating waters, water pollution by disposing of detergents and fertilizers, air pollution by acid rain and smog, and the ozone hole from release of CFCs. Ask students to list organisms that have been affected by these changes and then discuss changes that have occurred in their neighborhood. L2

**INTEGRATE**
**Career**

**Air Pollution Engineer** *Sick building syndrome* is a term used when a building's occupants experience nonspecific health problems because of environmental conditions in the building. Some common causes are inadequate ventilation, chemical contaminants from indoor and outdoor sources, and biological contaminants.

**Research** Have students research one method an air pollution engineer can currently use to improve indoor air quality. They can present this to the class as an engineer trying to convince a company to implement his or her solution.

**✓ Reading Check**

**Answer** Only species that can tolerate air pollution remain. Some species may die out and others may move out of the area.

**Discussion**

**Fertile Topsoil** Why is topsoil fertile? It contains humus, which is made up of the decayed remains of organisms.

---

**Figure 4** Air pollution can come from many different sources. Air quality in an area affects the health and survival of the species that live there.

**INTEGRATE**
**Career**

**Air Pollution Engineer**
Have you ever wondered who monitors the air you breathe? Air pollution engineers are people who make sure air quality standards are being met. They also design new technologies to reduce air pollution, such as improved machinery, filters, and ventilation systems, to try and solve problems like "sick building syndrome."

**Figure 5** Soil provides a home for many species of animals and other organisms.

**198** CHAPTER 7 Interactions of Living Things

---

**Air** Although you can't see the air that surrounds you, it has an impact on the lives of most species. Air is composed of a mixture of gases including nitrogen, oxygen, and carbon dioxide. Most plants and animals depend on the gases in air for respiration. The atmosphere is the layer of gases and airborne particles that surrounds Earth. Polluted air, like the air in **Figure 4,** can cause the species in an area to change, move, or die off.

Clouds and weather occur in the bottom 8 km to 16 km of the atmosphere. All species are affected by the weather in the area where they live. The ozone layer is 20 km to 50 km above Earth's surface and protects organisms from harmful radiation from the Sun. Air pressure, which is the weight of air pressing down on Earth, changes depending on altitude. Higher altitudes have less air pressure. Few organisms live at extreme air pressures.

**✓ Reading Check** *How does pollution in the atmosphere affect the species in an area?*

**Soil** From one enviroment to another, soil, as shown in **Figure 5,** can vary greatly. Soil type is determined by the amounts of sand, silt, and clay it contains. Various kinds of soil contain different amounts of nutrients, minerals, and moisture. Different plants need different kinds of soil. Because the types of plants in an area help determine which other organisms can survive in that area, soil affects every organism in an environment.

## Biotic Factors

Abiotic factors do not provide everything an organism needs for survival. Organisms depend on other organisms for food, shelter, protection, and reproduction. How organisms interact with one another and with abiotic factors can be described in an organized way.

---

## Differentiated Instruction

**English-Language Learners** Provide photographs from magazines to students who may require reinforcement of the concepts of biotic and abiotic factors. Ask students to identify all the biotic factors in each photograph and explain why they identified these factors as biotic. L1

## Science Journal

**Area Survey** Ask students to observe the natural environment of the area in which they live, and make a table in their Science Journal in which they list the biotic and abiotic factors of their area. Have them summarize the importance of the biotic factors listed in their tables. Then have students summarize the importance of the abiotic factors. L2 ▨ **Linguistic**

**Levels of Organization** The living world is highly organized. Atoms are arranged into molecules, which in turn might be organized into cells. Cells form tissues, tissues form organs, and organs form organ systems. Together, organ systems form organisms. Biotic and abiotic factors also can be arranged into levels of biological organization, as shown in **Figure 6**.

**Figure 6** The living world is organized in levels.

Organism

An organism is one individual from a population.

Population

All of the individuals of one species that live in the same area at the same time make up a population.

Community

The populations of different species that interact in some way are called a community.

Ecosystem

All of the communities in an area and the abiotic factors they interact with make up an ecosystem.

Biome

A biome is a large region with plants and animals well adapted to the soil and climate of the region.

Biosphere

The level of biological organization that is made up of all the ecosystems on Earth is the biosphere.

SECTION 1 The Environment **199**

## Visual Learning

**Figure 6** Have student groups create a concept map showing the differences among organisms, populations, communities, ecosystems, and biomes. Make sure students include abiotic factors and their role. Next, have students identify other populations. Possible answers: oak trees and grasses L2 COOP LEARN
IS **Interpersonal**

## IDENTIFYING Misconceptions

**Changing Biomes** Students may think that the location of a particular biome on Earth is permanent, not realizing that a change in climate would cause the biome to change. To help students understand that biomes and climate change over time, explain that evidence suggests that Earth's average temperature has increased over the past century. Ask them to speculate how a global temperature increase would affect climates and biomes.

## Use Science Words

**Word Meaning** Write *biosphere*, *biotic*, and *abiotic* on the board. Ask students to find the meanings of their parts in the dictionary. *bio:* "life;" *sphere:* "area;" and *-tic:* "relating to" L2 IS **Linguistic**

## Teacher FYI

**Exponential Growth** The exponential model of population growth describes a population that increases rapidly after a few generations. The larger a population gets, the faster it grows. The logistic model of population growth builds on the exponential model but accounts for the influence of limiting factors.

## Curriculum Connection

**Art** Have students create a visual illustrating the levels of organization within the biosphere. Have them include all applicable vocabulary words in their visual. L2 IS **Visual-Spatial and Kinesthetic** P

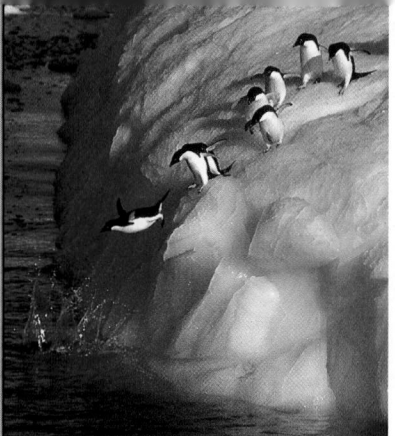

**Figure 7** Members of a penguin population compete for resources. **Infer** *what resources these penguins might be using.*

### Science Online

**Topic: Earth's Biomes**
Visit in7.msscience.com for Web links to information about Earth's different biomes.

**Activity** Select one of Earth's biomes and research what plants, animals, and other organisms live there. Prepare a display that includes pictures and text about your selected biome.

**Populations** All the members of one species that live together make up a **population.** For example, all of the humans living on Earth at the same time make up a population. Part of a population of penguins is shown in **Figure 7.** Members of a population compete for food, water, mates, and space. The resources of the environment and the ways the organisms use these resources determine how large a population can become.

**Communities** Most populations of organisms do not live alone. They live and interact with populations of other types of organisms. Groups of populations that interact with each other in a given area form a **community.** For example, a population of penguins and all of the species that they interact with form a community. Populations of organisms in a community depend on each other for food, shelter, and other needs.

**Ecosystems** In addition to interactions among populations, ecologists also study interactions among populations and their physical surroundings. An **ecosystem** is made up of a biotic community and the abiotic factors that affect it. Examples of ecosystems include coral reefs, forests, and ponds. You will learn more about the interactions that occur in ecosystems later in this chapter.

**Biomes** Scientists divide Earth into different regions called biomes. A biome (BI ohm) is a large region with plant and animal groups that are well adapted to the soil and climate of the region. Many different ecosystems are found in a biome. Examples of biomes include tundra, as shown in **Figure 8,** tropical rain forests, and grasslands.

**Figure 8** Biomes contain many different ecosystems. This mountaintop ecosystem is part of the alpine tundra biome.

The legend on the map reads:

- Ice
- Tundra
- Taiga
- Grassland
- Temperate forests
- Tropical rain forest
- Chaparral
- Savanna
- Desert
- Mountain

**Caption Answer**

**Figure 9** Answers will vary, but might include grassland, savanna, chaparral, temperate forest, etc.

**3 Assess**

**DAILY INTERVENTION**

**Check for Intervention**

**Linguistic** Have students write paragraphs in their Science Journals explaining the relationships among population, community, and ecosystem then share their paragraphs in small groups. Emphasize that populations interact to make a community and that communities and nonliving things make up an ecosystem. L1 LS

**Reteach**

**Rainfall** What happens to vegetation when rainfall amounts gradually decrease over centuries? Plant species either adapt or they die out. New plant species may enter the area. The ecosystem may change from forest to grassland to desert over time.

**Assessment**

**Portfolio** Have students cut out magazine pictures that illustrate soil formation, and make a poster using the pictures. Be sure they include all stages. Use **Performance Assessment in the Science Classroom,** p. 145.

**The Biosphere** Where do all of Earth's organisms live? Living things can be found 11,000 m deep in the ocean, 9,000 m high on mountains, and 4.5 km high in Earth's atmosphere. The part of Earth that supports life is the **biosphere** (BI uh sfihr). It includes the top part of Earth's crust, all the waters that cover Earth's surface, the surrounding atmosphere, and all biomes, including those in **Figure 9.**

**Figure 9** This map shows some of the major biomes of the world. **Determine** *what biome you live in.*

## section 1 review

### Summary

**Abiotic Factors**

- Organisms interact with and depend on factors in their environments.
- More than 95 percent of Earth's surface is water.
- The amount of sunlight determines where green plants can grow.
- Temperature determines which organisms can live in a region.
- Air is needed by most organisms. Polluted air can harm organisms.
- Soil can determine organisms in an area.

**Biotic Factors**

- Organisms depend on other organisms for food, shelter, protection, and reproduction.
- The living world is organized into levels.

### Self Check

1. **Compare and contrast** abiotic factors and biotic factors. Give five examples of each that are in your ecosystem.
2. **Describe** a population and a community.
3. **Define** the term *ecosystem.*
4. **Explain** how the terms *ecology* and *environment* are related.
5. **Think Critically** Explain how biotic factors change in an ecosystem that has flooded.

#### Applying Skills

6. **Record Observations** Each person lives in a population as part of a community. Describe your population and community.
7. **Use a database** to research biomes. Find the name of the biome that best describes where you live.

## section 1 review

1. Biotic factors are living. Abiotic factors are nonliving. Biotic factors: bacteria, protists, fungi, plants, and animals; abiotic factors: soil, temperature, light, water, and wind

2. population—all the organisms of one species living together in the same place at the same time; community—groups of populations

3. all of the communities in an area and the abiotic factors that affect them

4. Ecology is the study of the interactions among organisms and their environment.

5. Organisms that do not live in water would die. Other water organisms might move into the ecosystem.

6. Population: all the human beings in the area where the student lives; community: all other living organisms in the area where he or she lives

7. Answers will vary.

## BENCH TESTED

### ▶ *Real-World Question*

**Purpose** Students will observe the effects of various artificial fertilizers on the organisms comprising a pond ecosystem.

L2  IS  **Kinesthetic**

**Process Skills** observe, predict, compare, infer

**Time Required** 40 minutes; five-minute daily observations for three weeks; 40-minute observation at end

### ▶ *Procedure*

**Teaching Strategies**

• This lab works best in the early fall or late spring.
• Have guidebooks to pond life available for students during their microscope observation period.

**Troubleshooting** Be certain students check the water levels in the jars daily and refill with fresh pond water.

### ▶ *Conclude and Apply*

1. control: Jar A (no fertilizer); variables: amount of fertilizer added to Jars B, C, and D
2. Jars B and C should have shown more *Elodea* growth than Jar A. Jar D likely suffered from eutrophication, causing the *Elodea* to die off.
3. Possible answer: The slow addition of fertilizer may make the *Elodea* grow at a steady rate.
4. The excess nutrients in fertilizers often cause an increase in algal growth, called an "algal bloom." These algae eventually deplete the water's oxygen supply, causing other forms of aquatic life to die.

# LAB

# Delicately Balanced Ec⊕systems

Each year you might visit the same park, but notice little change. However, ecosystems are delicately balanced, and small changes can upset this balance. In this lab, you will observe how small amounts of fertilizer can disrupt an ecosystem.

### ▶ *Real-World Question*

How do manufactured fertilizers affect pond systems?

#### Goals

■ **Observe** the effects of manufactured fertilizer on water plants.
■ **Predict** the effects of fertilizers on pond and stream ecosystems.

#### Materials

large glass jars of      rubber bands (4)
  equal size (4)         pond water
clear plastic wrap       triple-beam balance
stalks of *Elodea* (8)   *electronic scale
*another aquatic plant   weighing paper
garden fertilizer        spoon
*houseplant fertilizer   metric ruler
                         *Alternate materials

#### Safety Precautions

### ▶ *Procedure*

1. Working in a group, label four jars *A, B, C,* and *D.*
2. **Measure** eight *Elodea* stalks to be certain that they are all about equal in length.
3. Fill the jars with equal volumes of pond water and place two stalks of *Elodea* in each jar.
4. Add 5 g of fertilizer to jar B, 10 g to jar C,

and 30 g to jar D. Put no fertilizer in jar A.

5. Cover each jar with plastic wrap and secure it with a rubber band. Use your pencil to punch three small holes through the plastic wrap.
6. Place all jars in a well-lit area.
7. **Observe** the jars daily for three weeks. Record your observations in your Science Journal.
8. **Measure and record** the length of each *Elodea* stalk in your Science Journal.

### ▶ *Conclude and Apply*

1. **List** the control and variables you used in this experiment.
2. **Compare** the growth of *Elodea* in each jar.
3. **Predict** what might happen to jar A if you added 5 g of fertilizer to it each week.
4. **Infer** what effects manufactured fertilizers might have on pond and stream ecosystems.

## *C*ommunicating
### Your Data

Compare your results with the results of other students. Research how fertilizer runoff from farms and lawns has affected aquatic ecosystems in your area.

---

### ✔ Assessment

**Portfolio** Ask students to draw diagrams of the organisms they find in their pond ecosystems. Use **Performance Assessment in the Science Classroom,** p. 127.

## *C*ommunicating
### Your Data

Make a data table on the board to record each group's final Elodea lengths for the different jars. This will be a good way to quickly compare student results.

Standard—7.4.9: Understand and explain that as any population of organisms grows, it is held in check by one or more environmental factors. These factors could result in depletion of food or nesting sites and/or increase loss to increased numbers of predators or parasites. Give examples of some consequences of this.

Also covers: 7.4.8, 7.5.3 (Detailed standards begin on page IN8.)

# Interactions Among Living Organisms

## Characteristics of Populations

You, the person sitting next to you, everyone in your class, and every other organism on Earth is a member of a specific population. Populations can be described by their characteristics such as spacing and density.

**Population Size** The number of individuals in the population is the population's size, as shown in **Figure 10.** Population size can be difficult to measure. If a population is small and made up of organisms that do not move, the size can be determined by counting the individuals. Usually individuals are too widespread or move around too much to be counted. The population size then is estimated. The number of organisms of one species in a small section is counted and this value is used to estimate the population of the larger area.

Suppose you spent several months observing a population of field mice that live in a pasture. You probably would observe changes in the size of the population. Older mice die. Mice are born. Some are eaten by predators, and some mice move away to new nests. The size of a population is always changing. The rate of change in population size varies from population to population. In contrast to a mouse population, the number of pine trees in a mature forest changes slowly, but a forest fire or disease could reduce the pine tree population quickly.

**Figure 10** The size of the human population is increasing each year. By the year 2050, the human population is projected to be more than 9 billion.

### as you read

**What You'll Learn**

- **Identify** the characteristics that describe populations.
- **Examine** the different types of relationships that occur among populations in a community.
- **Determine** the habitat and niche of a species in a community.

**Why It's Important**

You must interact with other organisms to survive.

**Review Vocabulary**
**coexistence:** living together in the same place at the same time

**New Vocabulary**
- population density
- limiting factor
- symbiosis
- niche
- habitat

**World Population: 1950–2050 (projected)**

Human population (billions) vs Year

Source: U.S. Census Bureau, International Data Base 5-10-00.

## Visual Learning

**Figure 11** Test students' abilities to interpret scientific illustrations by having them list two states in each population density color level. See if they can determine what area of the country has the most northern bobwhite birds.

## Make a Model

**Population Spacing** Provide groups of students with a plain sheet of paper, glue or tape, and a self-sealing plastic bag that contains small squares cut from colored construction paper. Tell students that the paper represents a habitat and each square represents an individual member of a population. Have students glue or tape the squares to the paper to illustrate one of the types of population spacing. Display each group's habitat, and have the class identify the type of spacing each represents.  L2    COOP LEARN   LS
**Interpersonal and Kinesthetic**

**Figure 11** Population density can be shown on a map. This map uses different colors to show varying densities of a population of northern bobwhites, a type of bird.

**Science Online**

**Topic: Human Population**
Visit in7.msscience.com for Web links to information about human population and densities.

**Activity** Select at least three different areas of the world and prepare a bar graph to compare population density of each area. Compare the population density of where you live to the three areas of the world you select.

**Figure 12** Some populations, such as creosote bushes in the desert, are evenly spaced throughout an area.

| Average Count per km² | |
|---|---|
| < 1 | 11–30 |
| 1–3 | 31–100 |
| 4–10 | > 100 |

**Population Density** At the beginning of this chapter, when you figured out how much space is available to each student in your classroom, you were measuring another population characteristic. The number of individuals in a population that occupy a definite area is called **population density.** For example, if 100 mice live in an area of one square kilometer, the population density is 100 mice per square kilometer. When more individuals live in a given amount of space, as seen in **Figure 11,** the population is more dense.

**Population Spacing** Another characteristic of populations is spacing, or how the organisms are arranged in a given area. They can be evenly spaced, randomly spaced, or clumped together. If organisms have a fairly consistent distance between them, as shown in **Figure 12,** they are evenly spaced. In random spacing, each organism's location is independent of the locations of other organisms in the population. Random spacing of plants usually results when wind or birds disperse seeds. Clumped spacing occurs when resources such as food or living space are clumped. Clumping results when animals gather in groups or plants grow near each other in groups.

**204  CHAPTER 7** Interactions of Living Things

**Limiting Factors** Populations, such as the antelopes in **Figure 13,** cannot continue to grow larger forever. All ecosystems have a limited amount of food, water, living space, mates, nesting sites, and other resources. A **limiting factor** is any biotic or abiotic factor that limits the number of individuals in a population. A limiting factor also can affect other populations in the community indirectly. For example, a drought might reduce the number of seed-producing plants in a forest clearing. Fewer plants means that food can become a limiting factor for deer that eat the plants and for a songbird population that feeds on the seeds of these plants. Food also could become a limiting factor for animals that feed on the songbirds.

✔ **Reading Check** *What is an example of a limiting factor?*

Competition is the struggle among organisms to obtain the same resources needed to survive and reproduce, as shown in **Figure 14.** As population density increases, so does competition among individuals for the resources in their environment.

**Carrying Capacity** Suppose a population increases in size year after year. At some point, food, nesting space, or other resources become so scarce that some individuals are not able to survive or reproduce. When this happens, the environment has reached its carrying capacity. Carrying capacity is the largest number of individuals of a species that an environment can support and maintain for a long period of time. If a population gets bigger than the carrying capacity of the environment, some individuals are left without adequate resources. They will die or be forced to move elsewhere.

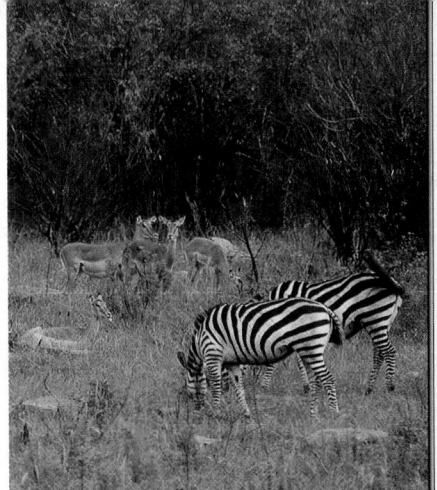

**Figure 13** These antelope and zebra populations live in the grasslands of Africa.
**Infer** *what limiting factors might affect the plant and animal populations shown here.*

> **Indiana Academic Standard Check**
>
> **7.4.9:** Understand and explain that as any population of organisms grows, it is held in check by one or more environmental factors . . . . Give examples of some consequences of this.
>
> ✔ What can happen if the size of a population exceeds the carrying capacity of its environment?
>
> ✔ Individuals die from lack of resources or are forced to move elsewhere.

**Figure 14** During dry summers, the populations of animals at existing watering holes increase because some watering holes have dried up. This creates competition for water, a valuable resource.

**Activity**

**Pill Bug Density** Have groups of students observe 1-L containers of soil, leaf litter, and pill bugs. Each container should have a different number of pill bugs. Ask students to calculate the density of the pill bug population in each container. L2 ⁣IS **Logical-Mathematical**

**Quick Demo**

**Water Capacity**

**Materials** beaker, water, dropper

**Estimated Time** five minutes

**Procedure** Fill a beaker with water. Add water 1 drop at a time until the beaker overflows. Explain that the beaker has exceeded its water-holding capacity. Ecosystems also have a point at which they reach their capacity to support more organisms.

✔ **Reading Check**

**Answer** any biotic or abiotic factor that limits the number of individuals in a population—water, food, living space

**Caption Answer**

**Figure 13** food, water, living space, competition

**Activity**

**Limiting Factors** Have students make lists of limiting factors for human population growth. Factors could include food, living space, pollution, and disease. L2 ⁣IS **Intrapersonal**

---

# Differentiated Instruction

**Learning Disabled** To illustrate limiting factors, have students stand in a circle. Place squares of blue paper, representing water, for each student, and about half the number of green squares, representing food, in the center. Have students walk to the center and try to get one of each piece of paper. Students with both colors have survived. What is the limiting factor in our example? food
L1

# Curriculum Connection

**Art** Have students research populations that live in areas with extreme factors that restrict the kinds of organisms that can live there. Have them create a collage that shows several different populations, such as penguins and cacti. L2 ⁣IS **Visual-Spatial and Kinesthetic** P

**Purpose** Students compare the roots of a legume and a non-legume. L2 IS **Kinesthetic**

**Materials** legume plant (clover, alfalfa), nonlegume plant (geranium, coleus), prepared slide of nitrogen-fixing bacteria, beaker of water, magnifying glass.

**Teaching Strategy** A magnifying lens can be used to observe the nodules on the legume.

**Analysis**

1. The legume has nodules that contain nitrogen-fixing bacteria.
2. Mutualism; the bacteria make nitrogen available to the plant roots and the plant gives the bacteria food.

## Assessment

**Performance** Have students conduct research about symbiotic relationships. They should record the information in their Science Journals. Use **Performance Assessment in the Science Classroom,** p. 175.

## Use Science Words

**Word Meaning** *Symbiosis* comes from a Greek word meaning "living together." Have students find words that begin with *sym-* and discuss their meanings. symbol, symmetry, sympathy, symphony, symposium L2 IS **Linguistic**

**☑ Reading Check**

**Answer** flatworms living in gills of horseshoe crabs, mistletoe growing on trees, yucca plant and yucca moth

**Observing Symbiosis**

**Procedure**

1. Carefully wash and examine the roots of a **legume plant** and a **nonlegume plant.**
2. Use a **magnifying lens** to examine the roots of the legume plant.

**Analysis**

1. What differences do you observe in the roots of the two plants?
2. Bacteria and legume plants help one another thrive. What type of symbiotic relationship is this?

**Figure 15** The partnership between the desert yucca plant and the yucca moth is an example of mutualism.

**Biotic Potential** What would happen if a population's environment had no limiting factors? The size of the population would continue to increase. The maximum rate at which a population increases when plenty of food and water are available, the weather is ideal, and no diseases or enemies exist, is its biotic potential. Most populations never reach their biotic potential, or they do so for only a short period of time. Eventually, the carrying capacity of the environment is reached and the population stops increasing.

## Symbiosis and Other Interactions

In ecosystems, many species of organisms have close relationships that are necessary for their survival. **Symbiosis** (sihm bee OH sus) is any close interaction between two or more different species. Symbiotic relationships can be identified by the type of interaction between organisms. Mutualism is a symbiotic relationship in which two different species of organisms cooperate and both benefit. **Figure 15** shows one example of mutualism.

Commensalism is a form of symbiosis that benefits one organism without affecting the other organism. For example, a species of flatworm benefits by living in the gills of horseshoe crabs, eating scraps of the horseshoe crab's meals. The horseshoe crab is unaffected by the flatworms.

Parasitism is a symbiotic relationship between two species in which one species benefits and the other species is harmed. Some species of mistletoe are parasites because their roots grow into a tree's tissue and take nutrients from the tree.

**☑ Reading Check** *What form of symbiosis exists between a bee and a flower?*

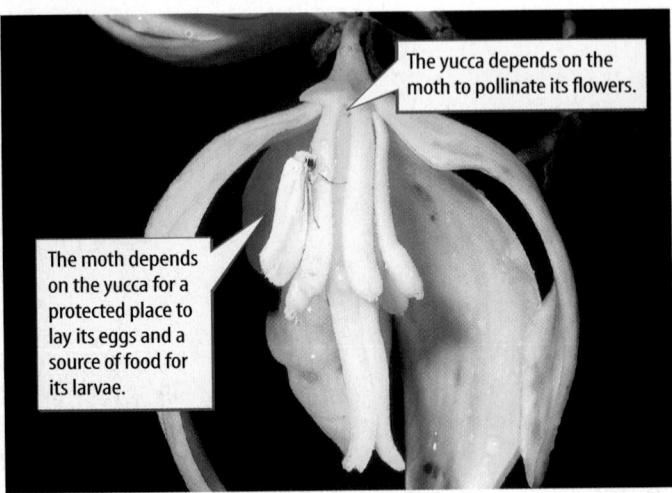

The yucca depends on the moth to pollinate its flowers.

The moth depends on the yucca for a protected place to lay its eggs and a source of food for its larvae.

## Science Journal

**Organism Interaction** Have students explain the relationship between symbiosis and mutualism. Symbiosis includes several kinds of relationships. Mutualism is a type of symbiosis in which both species benefit. Have students find pictures in magazines or references that illustrate symbiosis and mutualism. L2 IS **Linguistic and Visual-Spatial**

## Differentiated Instruction

**Challenge** Have students list as many predator-prey relationships as they can. Write all contributions on the board. Have students determine which prey have more than one predator. L3

**Predation** One way that population size is regulated is by predation (prih DAY shun). Predation is the act of one organism hunting, killing, and feeding on another organism. Owls are predators of mice, as shown in **Figure 16.** Mice are their prey. Predators are biotic factors that limit the size of the prey population. Availability of prey is a biotic factor that can limit the size of the predator population. Because predators are more likely to capture old, ill, or young prey, the strongest individuals in the prey population are the ones that manage to reproduce. This improves the prey population over several generations.

**Habitats and Niches** In a community, every species plays a particular role. For example, some are producers and some are consumers. Each also has a particular place to live. The role, or job, of an organism in the ecosystem is called its **niche** (NICH). What a species eats, how it gets its food, and how it interacts with other organisms are all parts of its niche. The place where an organism lives is called its **habitat.** For example, an earthworm's habitat is soil. An earthworm's niche includes loosening, aerating, and enriching the soil.

**Figure 16** Owls use their keen senses of sight and hearing to hunt for mice in the dark.

## section 2 review

### Summary

**Characteristics of Populations**

- Populations can be described by size, density, and spacing.
- Limiting factors affect population size.
- The number of individuals an environment can support and maintain over time is called the carrying capacity.
- The biotic potential is the rate a population would increase without limiting factors.

**Symbiosis and Other Interactions**

- A close interaction between two or more different species is called symbiosis.
- Mutualism, commensalism, and parasitism are types of symbiotic relationships that can exist between organisms.
- Predators are biotic limiting factors of prey.
- The role an organism plays is called its niche.

### Self Check

1. **Determine** the population of students in your classroom.
2. **Describe** how limiting factors can affect a population.
3. **Explain** the difference between a habitat and a niche.
4. **Describe** and give an example of two symbiotic relationships that occur among populations in a community.
5. **Explain** how sound could be used to relate the size of the cricket population in one field to the cricket population in another field.
6. **Think Critically** A parasite obtains food from its host. Most parasites weaken but do not kill their hosts. Why?

**Applying Math**

7. **Solve One-Step Equations** A 15-m² wooded area has the following: 30 ferns, 150 grass plants, and 6 oak trees. What is the population density per m² of each of the above species?

## section 2 review

1. size, spacing, and density
2. Limiting factors such as food, habitat, drought, and competition can cause a population to become smaller or limit its growth.
3. Where an organism lives is its habitat. The way an organism interacts with its surroundings is its niche.
4. Possible answer: Commensalism—benefits one organism and does not harm the other; parasitism—benefits one organism and the other is harmed; examples will vary.
5. If a parasite kills its host, the parasite is likely to die because its food supply will disappear.
6. The loudest population will probably be the one with the most organisms.
7. 15-m² area = 225 m², ferns = 0.13, grass = 0.67, oak trees = 0.03

### Use an Analogy

**Game Tickets** Use the analogy of two friends and basketball game tickets to discuss types of symbiosis. A friend offers to buy you a ticket if you will give him or her a ride to the game (mutualism). A friend with a free ticket gives it to you (commensalism). A friend sells you a ticket and you later find out he or she charged you much more than the ticket was worth (parasitism).

### Discussion

What advantages does a population that feeds on several kinds of organisms have? Feeding on several kinds of organisms ensures a food supply for the population if one food source becomes unavailable.

## 3 Assess

### DAILY INTERVENTION

### Check for Understanding

**Linguistic** Have students make a list of objects in their classroom and schoolyard. Their list can include living, once-living, and non-living items. Then, have the students classify the relationship that the object has with its environment.

### Reteach

**Symbiosis** Have students make a list of symbiotic relationships with which they are familiar and identify the organisms in each. L1

### ✓ Assessment

**Performance** Have students research data about population growth or decline of a threatened or endangered species. Then ask students to graph the data, with number of individuals on the *y*-axis and year on the *x*-axis. Students should describe the growth curve. Use **PASC**, p. 111.

Standards—**7.4.2:** Describe that all organisms, including the human species, are part of and depend on two main interconnected global food webs, the ocean food web and the land food web. **7.4.8:** Describe how organisms that eat plants break down the plant structures to produce the materials and energy that they need to survive, and in turn, how they are consumed by other organisms.

Also covers: 7.4.6, 7.5.3 (Detailed standards begin on page IN8.)

# section 3

# Matter and Energy

### Bellringer

**INTERACTIVE CHALKBOARD**
PowerPoint® Presentations

**Section Focus Transparencies** also are available on the Interactive Chalkboard CD-ROM.

L2 ELL

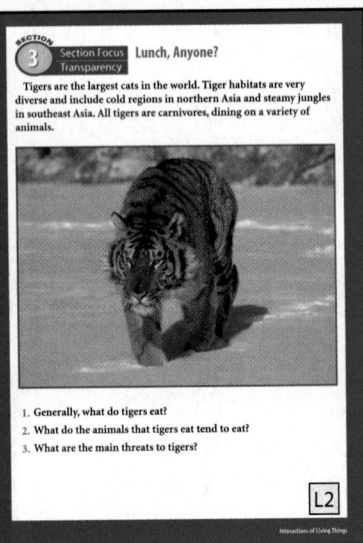

SECTION 3 Section Focus Transparency **Lunch, Anyone?**

Tigers are the largest cats in the world. Tiger habitats are very diverse and include cold regions in northern Asia and steamy jungles in southeast Asia. All tigers are carnivores, dining on a variety of animals.

1. Generally, what do tigers eat?
2. What do the animals that tigers eat tend to eat?
3. What are the main threats to tigers?

L2

Interactions of Living Things

### Tie to Prior Knowledge

**Animal Energy** Remind students that animals get their energy from the food they eat. Have them speculate where plants get their energy from. Plants get their energy from the Sun through the process of photosynthesis.

## 2 Teach

### Activity

Have students use **Figure 17** to construct a decomposition food chain to illustrate interactions of matter and energy in the decay of biomass. Students should label the organisms as biomass and show energy transfers with arrows.

leaves → mushrooms → bacteria

## as you read

### *What* You'll Learn

- **Explain** the difference between a food chain and a food web.
- **Describe** how energy flows through ecosystems.
- **Examine** how materials such as water, carbon, and nitrogen are used repeatedly.

### *Why* It's Important

You are dependent upon the recycling of matter and the transfer of energy for survival.

### ◉ Review Vocabulary

**consumer:** organism that obtains energy by eating other organisms

### New Vocabulary

- food chain
- water cycle
- food web

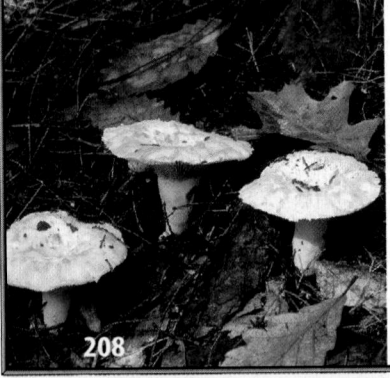

**208**

## Energy Flow Through Ecosystems

Life on Earth is not simply a collection of independent organisms. Even organisms that seem to spend most of their time alone interact with other members of their species. They also interact with members of other species. Most of the interactions among members of different species occur when one organism feeds on another. Food contains nutrients and energy needed for survival. When one organism is food for another organism, some of the energy in the first organism (the food) is transferred to the second organism (the eater).

Producers are organisms that take in and use energy from the Sun or some other source to produce food. Some use the Sun's energy for photosynthesis to produce carbohydrates. For example, plants, algae, and some one-celled, photosynthetic organisms are producers. Consumers are organisms that take in energy when they feed on producers or other consumers. The transfer of energy does not end there. When organisms die, other organisms called decomposers, as shown in **Figure 17,** take in energy as they break down the remains of organisms. This movement of energy through a community can be diagrammed as a food chain or a food web.

**Food Chains** A **food chain,** as shown in **Figure 18,** is a model, a simple way of showing how energy, in the form of food, passes from one organism to another. When drawing a food chain, arrows between organisms indicate the direction of energy transfer. An example of a pond food chain follows.

aquatic plants → insects → bluegill → bass → humans

Food chains usually have only three or four links. This is because the available energy decreases from one link to the next link. At each transfer of energy, a portion of the energy is lost as heat due to the activities of the organisms. In a food chain, the amount of energy left for the last link is only a small portion of the energy in the first link.

**Figure 17** These mushrooms are decomposers. They obtain needed energy for life when they break down organic material.

**Figure 18**

In nature, energy in food passes from one organism to another in a sequence known as a food chain. All living things are linked in food chains, and there are millions of different chains in the world. Each chain is made up of organisms in a community. The photographs here show a food chain in a North American meadow community.

**E** The last link in many food chains is a top carnivore, an animal that feeds on other animals, including other carnivores. This great horned owl is a top carnivore.

**D** The fourth link of this food chain is a garter snake, which feeds on toads.

**A** The first link in any food chain is a producer—in this case, grass. Grass gets its energy from sunlight.

**B** The second link of a food chain is usually an herbivore like this grasshopper. Herbivores are animals that feed only on producers.

**C** The third link of this food chain is a carnivore, an animal that feeds on other animals. This woodhouse toad feeds on grasshoppers.

SECTION 3 Matter and Energy **209**

## NATIONAL GEOGRAPHIC

## Visualizing a Food Chain

### Discussion

**Food Chains** Have students examine the pictures and read the captions. Then ask the following questions.

What makes the first link in a food chain different from all of the other links? In the first step of a food chain the energy comes from the Sun, in all other cases the energy is obtained by eating another organism.

An omnivore can eat plants or animals. Where in a food chain could you find an omnivore? any spot occupied by an herbivore or carnivore in the feature, that is, any spot except the first link

Would the garter snake be classified as a producer, an herbivore, or a carnivore? The garter snake would be classified as a carnivore, an animal that feeds on other animals.

### Activity

**Top Consumer** Have students make a poster that diagrams a food chain with themselves at the top. Have the students consider a food they have eaten recently, and show the food chain that led up to them consuming that particular food. L2 IS **Visual-Spatial** P

### Fun Fact

Mold, bacteria, beetles, centipedes, and worms are all busy recyclers. Without their help, dead plants and animals would just keep piling up. These decomposers break down the residue into rich soil for new plants to grow.

## Differentiated Instruction

**Challenge** Have students consider the effect of a recent local event on local food chains. Some examples might be trees cut down to build a road, or a wetland drained to construct a parking lot. Have the students share their conclusion with the class. L3

## Visual Learning

**Figure 18** Have students practice interpreting scientific illustrations by writing a paragraph in which they summarize the relationships seen in this figure. L2 IS **Linguistic and Visual-Spatial**

## Food Chains

**Purpose** to observe energy flow and relationships that exist in an ecosystem

**Possible Materials** magazine pictures or toys of various organisms, paper, and drawing materials

**Estimated Time** one class period

**Teaching Strategies**

• Assign small student groups.
• Students can develop a food chain with their materials and then, can come together to create a food web.
• Allow students to explore other questions as they arise.

**For additional inquiry activities, see *Science Inquiry Labs*.**

### Applying Science

## Teaching Strategy

Have students write out the food web described, then alter it as necessary to answer the questions.

## Answers

1. The absence of whales made more krill available for the fish and the squid, so their numbers increased. Similarly, large numbers of fish and squid meant that more food was available for seals and penguins.

2. Fish, squid, seal, and penguin populations could decrease because whales are taking some of the food supply.

---

**Indiana Academic Standard Check**

**7.4.2:** Describe that all organisms . . . are part of and depend on two main interconnected global food webs, the ocean food web and the land food web.

✓ Where might humans fit in the ocean food web shown below?

✓ Humans might eat fish or squid.

---

**Food Webs** Food chains are too simple to describe the many interactions among organisms in an ecosystem. A **food web** is a series of overlapping food chains that exist in an ecosystem. A food web provides a more complete model of the way energy moves through an ecosystem. They also are more accurate models because food webs show how many organisms, including humans, are part of more than one food chain in an ecosystem.

Humans are a part of many land and aquatic food webs. Most people eat foods from several different levels of a food chain. Every time you eat a hamburger, an apple, or other food, you have become a link in a food web. Can you picture the steps in the food web that led to the food in your lunch?

### Applying Science

## How do changes in Antarctic food webs affect populations?

The food webs in the icy Antarctic Ocean are based on phytoplankton, which are microscopic algae that float near the water's surface. The algae are eaten by tiny, shrimplike krill, which are consumed by baleen whales, squid, and fish. Toothed whales, seals, and penguins eat the fish and squid. How would changes in any of these populations affect the other populations?

**Identifying the Problem**

Worldwide, the hunting of most baleen whales has been illegal since 1986. It is hoped that the baleen whale population will increase. How will an increase in the whale population affect the food web illustrated below?

**Solving the Problem**

1. Populations of seals, penguins, and krill-eating fish increased in size as populations of baleen whales declined. Explain why this occurred.

2. What might happen if the number of baleen whales increases but the amount of krill does not?

---

 **LAB DEMONSTRATION**

**Purpose** to demonstrate the niches in a mini-ecosystem

**Materials** terrarium with producers and consumers (salamanders, lizards, turtles).

**Preparation** Prepare a terrarium. Place a layer of charcoal under the soil to keep the soil "sweet." Include a pond area by bury-ing a small plastic container in the soil. Use rocks to make a "ladder" for animals to use to enter and leave the pond. Cover the terrarium with a screen.

**Procedure** Have students identify the producers and consumers in the terrarium.

**Expected Outcome** Students observe the interactions in a mini-ecosystem.

## Assessment

Are there decomposers in the terrarium? Explain. Decomposers (bacteria and fungi) are found in the soil.

**Ecological Pyramids** Most of the energy in the biosphere comes from the Sun. Producers take in and transform only a small part of the energy that reaches Earth's surface. When an herbivore eats a plant, some of the energy in the plant passes to the herbivore. However, most of it is given off into the atmosphere as heat. The same thing happens when a carnivore eats an herbivore. An ecological pyramid models the number of organisms at each level of a food chain. The bottom of an ecological pyramid represents the producers of an ecosystem. The rest of the levels represent successive consumers.

**Reading Check** *What is an ecological pyramid?*

**Energy Pyramid** The flow of energy from grass to the hawk in **Figure 19** can be illustrated by an energy pyramid. An energy pyramid compares the energy available at each level of the food chain in an ecosystem. Just as most food chains have three or four links, a pyramid of energy usually has three or four levels. Only about ten percent of the energy at each level of the pyramid is available to the next level. By the time the top level is reached, the amount of energy available is greatly reduced.

**INTEGRATE Chemistry**

**Chemosynthesis** Certain bacteria take in energy through a process called chemosynthesis. In chemosynthesis, the bacteria produce food using the energy in chemical compounds instead of light energy. In your Science Journal, predict where these bacteria are found.

**Figure 19** An energy pyramid illustrates that available energy decreases at each successive feeding step.
**Determine** *why an energy pyramid doesn't have more levels.*

---

## Cultural Diversity

**Food Preferences** Have students research how people in different countries meet their food needs. Suggest that students choose a country and find information about the diets of the people living there. Have them consider whether the people are mainly first-, second-, or third-level consumers. L2

## Differentiated Instruction

**Visually Impaired** Obtain or make a pyramid-shaped model composed of successively smaller blocks placed on top of one another. Allow students to hold the model and identify its shape. Then explain that energy and the number of organisms decrease in an energy pyramid in the same manner as in the model. L2 **IS Kinesthetic**

---

**INTEGRATE Chemistry**

**Chemosynthesis** Chemosynthetic bacteria often live in habitats so extreme that most other organisms cannot exist there. They live in hot springs, thermal pools, salt flats, and around volcanic vents on the bottom of the ocean floor.

**Reading Check**

**Answer** a model that shows the number of organisms at each level of a food chain

**Caption Answer**
**Figure 19** The available energy is greatly reduced with each successive level. By the time the top level is reached, little energy is left.

**Virtual Labs**

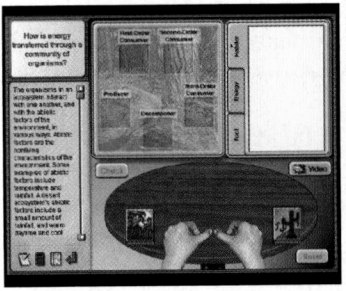
**Energy Transfer** *How is energy transferred through a community of organisms?*

## Mini LAB

**Purpose** to model the water cycle [L2] [ELL] [IS] **Kinesthetic**

**Materials** marker, clear plastic cup, water, plastic wrap, rubber band or tape

**Teaching Strategy** Remind students to observe their model for three days and record their observations.

**Analysis**
1. condensation, evaporation, and precipitation
2. It decreased.

### Assessment

**Performance** Have students diagram the water cycle in their Science Journals. Use **Performance Assessment in the Science Classroom,** p. 163.

Try at Home

---

---

## Mini LAB

### Modeling the Water Cycle

**Procedure**
1. With a **marker,** make a line halfway up on a **plastic cup.** Fill the cup to the mark with water.
2. Cover the top with **plastic wrap** and secure it with a **rubber band or tape.**
3. Put the cup in direct sunlight. Observe the cup for three days. Record your observations.
4. Remove the plastic wrap and observe the cup for seven more days.

**Analysis**
1. What parts of the water cycle did you observe during this activity?
2. How did the water level in the cup change after the plastic wrap was removed?

Try at Home

**Figure 20** A water molecule that falls as rain can follow several paths through the water cycle. **Identify** these paths in this diagram.

212

---

## The Cycles of Matter

The energy available as food is constantly renewed by plants using sunlight. However, think about the matter that makes up the bodies of living organisms. The law of conservation of mass states that matter on Earth is never lost or gained. It is used over and over again. In other words, it is recycled. The carbon atoms in your body might have been on Earth since the planet formed billions of years ago. They have been recycled billions of times. Many important materials that make up your body cycle through the environment. Some of these materials are water, carbon, and nitrogen.

**Water Cycle** Water molecules on Earth constantly rise into the atmosphere, fall to Earth, and soak into the ground or flow into rivers and oceans. The **water cycle** involves the processes of evaporation, condensation, and precipitation.

Heat from the Sun causes water on Earth's surface to evaporate, or change from a liquid to a gas, and rise into the atmosphere as water vapor. As the water vapor rises, it encounters colder and colder air and the molecules of water vapor slow down. Eventually, the water vapor changes back into tiny droplets of water. It condenses, or changes from a gas to a liquid. These water droplets clump together to form clouds. When the droplets become large and heavy enough, they fall back to Earth as rain or other precipitation. This process is illustrated in **Figure 20.**

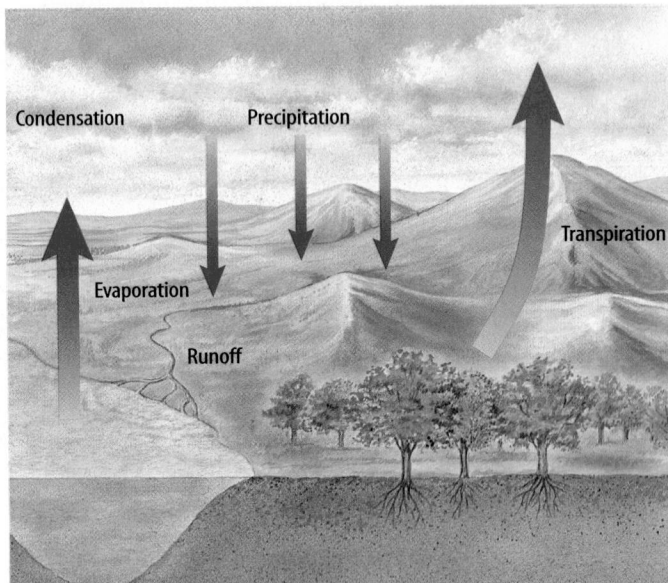

---

---

**Other Cycles in Nature** You and all organisms contain carbon. Earth's atmosphere contains about 0.03 percent carbon in the form of carbon dioxide gas. The movement of carbon through Earth's biosphere is called the carbon cycle, as shown in **Figure 21.**

Nitrogen is an element found in proteins and nucleic acids. The nitrogen cycle begins with the transfer of nitrogen from the atmosphere to producers then to consumers. The nitrogen then moves back to the atmosphere or directly into producers again.

Phosphorus, sulfur, and other elements needed by living organisms also are used and returned to the environment. Just as you recycle aluminum, glass, and paper products, the matter that organisms need to live is recycled continuously in the biosphere.

Plants remove carbon dioxide from the air and use it to make carbohydrates.

After the carbon is returned to the atmosphere, the cycle begins again.

The carbohydrates are eaten and used by other organisms.

The carbon from the carbohydrates is returned to the atmosphere through respiration, combustion, and decay.

**Figure 21** Carbon can follow several different paths through the carbon cycle. Some carbon is stored in Earth's biomass.

## section 3 review

### Summary

**Energy Flow Through Ecosystems**

- A food chain models one pathway of energy through an ecosystem, and a food web is made of many food chains.
- Humans are part of different food webs.
- Ecological pyramids model the number of organisms at each level of a food chain.
- Energy pyramids illustrate the available energy at each level of a food chain.

**The Cycles of Matter**

- Energy is constantly renewed by the Sun, but matter must be recycled.
- The water cycle involves evaporation, condensation, and precipitation.
- Other matter that cycles includes carbon, nitrogen, phosphorus, and sulfur.

### Self Check

1. **Draw and label** a food web that includes you and what you've eaten today.
2. **Compare and contrast** producers, consumers, and decomposers.
3. **Explain** how carbon flows through ecosystems.
4. **Think Critically** Use your knowledge of food chains and the energy pyramid to explain why fewer lions than gazelles live on the African plains.

#### Applying Skills

5. **Classify** Look at the food chain in **Figure 18.** Classify each organism as a producer or a consumer.
6. **Communicate** In your Science Journal, write a short essay about how the water cycle, carbon cycle, and nitrogen cycle are important to living organisms.

### DAILY INTERVENTION

**Check for Understanding**

**Kinesthetic** List producers, consumers, and decomposers in a food web on separate index cards. Give a card to each student. Give each producer a ball of colored yarn to roll to their primary consumers, then each subsequent consumer, until each chain is complete and creates a food web. L2 ELL COOP LEARN LS

### Reteach

**Herbivore or Carnivore?** Do all organisms remain in the same place in the food chain throughout their lives? Explain. No; tadpoles are herbivores, and frogs and toads are carnivores. Many insect larvae are herbivores and then become carnivores as adults.

### ✔ Assessment

**Performance** Place a picture of an underwater pond scene on the overhead projector. Have students identify the producers, consumers, and decomposers. Then, have students diagram a possible food chain or web in their Science Journals. Use **Performance Assessment in the Science Classroom,** p. 163. P

## section 3 review

1. Answer will vary. Check for correct interactions.
2. Producers capture and use energy to produce carbohydrates. Consumers obtain energy when they feed on producers or other consumers. Decomposers obtain energy as they break down the remains of organisms.
3. Plants remove carbon dioxide from the air and produce carbohydrates. Carbohydrates are eaten by other organisms. The carbon from the carbohydrates is returned to the atmosphere through respiration, decomposition, and decay. Then the cycle begins again.
4. Gazelles are lower in the food chain and energy pyramid, lions are higher; therefore there are fewer lions.
5. Check student answers against **Figure 18.**
6. Check student answers.

**BENCH TESTED**

## Real-World Question

**Purpose** Students determine how abiotic factors affect the germination of seeds. L2 ELL

COOP LEARN IS **Interpersonal**

**Process Skills** observe and infer, communicate, make and use tables, compare and contrast, recognize cause and effect, form a hypothesis, design an experiment, use numbers, separate and control variables, interpret data

**Time Required** 50 minutes for setup; 10 minutes every three to four days for data collection for a period of about two weeks

**Materials** Square milk cartons may be used for planters.

**Alternate Materials** Other kinds of seeds, such as pea seeds or flower seeds, may be used.

## Form a Hypothesis

**Possible Hypothesis** Students may hypothesize that seeds will not germinate in the dark, in the refrigerator, or without water.

## Test Your Hypothesis

**Possible Procedures** Plant the same number of seeds in each of two planters and keep all conditions the same, except for the variable. For example, place one planter in a refrigerator and another in a closed cabinet at room temperature. Give each the same amount of water. Observe the results.

---

**LAB**

## Design Your Own

# Identifying a Limiting Factor

**Goals**

- **Observe** the effects of an abiotic factor on the germination and growth of bean seedlings.
- **Design** an experiment that demonstrates whether or not a specific abiotic factor limits the germination of bean seeds.

**Possible Materials**
bean seeds
small planting containers
soil
water
label
trowel
*spoon
aluminum foil
sunny window
*other light source
refrigerator or oven
*Alternate materials

**Safety Precautions**

## Real-World Question

Organisms depend upon many biotic and abiotic factors in their environment to survive. When these factors are limited or are not available, it can affect an organism's survival. How do abiotic factors such as light, water, and temperature affect the germination of seeds?

## Form a Hypothesis

Based on what you have learned about limiting factors, make a hypothesis about how one specific abiotic factor might affect the germination of a bean seed. Be sure to consider factors that you can change easily.

## Test Your Hypothesis

**Make a Plan**

1. As a group, agree upon and write out a hypothesis statement.
2. **Decide** on a way to test your group's hypothesis. Keep available materials in mind as you plan your procedure. List your materials.
3. **Design** a data table in your Science Journal for recording data.
4. Remember to test only one variable at a time and use suitable controls.

214

---

## Alternative Inquiry Lab

**Ask Additional Questions** To extend this Lab into an Inquiry Lab, have students research how gardeners and horticulturists manipulate the growing factors they studied in the lab. Students also might be interested in other factors growers consider, such as light levels, temperature, soil pH, soil type, organic matter, etc. What conditions do certain plants prefer? How does this make plants better suited to certain environments (for example, which plants are best as office plants)? What are optimum growing conditions for greenhouses, flower gardens, vegetable gardens, and/or orchards? How do plant adaptations relate to their climate zone (similar to the factors studied in the lab)?

5. Read over your entire experiment to make sure that all steps are in logical order.

6. **Identify** any constants, variables, and controls in your experiment.

7. Be sure the factor that you will test is measurable.

**Follow Your Plan**

1. Make sure your teacher approves your plan before you start.

2. Carry out your approved plan.

3. While the experiment is going on, record any observations that you make and complete the data table in your Science Journal.

## Analyze Your Data

1. **Compare** the results of this experiment with those of other groups in your class.

2. **Infer** how the abiotic factor you tested affected the germination of bean seeds.

3. **Graph** your results in a bar graph that compares the number of bean seeds that germinated in the experimental container with the number of seeds that germinated in the control container.

## Conclude and Apply

1. **Identify** which factor had the greatest effect on the germination of the seeds.

2. **Determine** whether or not you could change more than one factor in this experiment and still have germination of seeds.

### Communicating Your Data

Write a set of instructions that could be included on a packet of this type of seeds. Describe the best conditions for seed germination.

**LAB 215**

---

**Teaching Strategy**

**Troubleshooting** Caution students not to plant seeds too deeply and not to overwater them.

**Expected Outcome** Most results will reflect that seeds need water and the proper temperature to germinate.

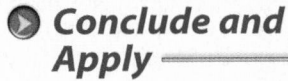

## Analyze Your Data

**Answers to Questions**

1. Results should be consistent among groups using the same variable.

2. Answers will vary.

3. The graph will be determined by the number of seeds used in the experiment.

**Error Analysis** Have students compare their results and their hypotheses and explain why any differences occurred.

## Conclude and Apply

1. Answers will vary.

2. Each different type of abiotic factor is necessary for seeds to germinate.

### ✔ Assessment

**Performance** Have students design an experiment to test the effect of the same variable on another kind of seed. Use **PASC,** p. 95.

---

**Sample Data based on planting 10 seeds**

| Number of Seeds That Germinate | | | | |
|---|---|---|---|---|
| Days | 3 | 6 | 9 | 12 |
| Light | 0 | 3 | 6 | 10 |
| No light | 0 | 0 | 0 | 0 |
| 7.2°C | 0 | 0 | 0 | 0 |
| 21.1°C | 0 | 3 | 6 | 10 |
| No water | 0 | 0 | 0 | 0 |
| 20 mL/day | 0 | 3 | 6 | 10 |

### Communicating Your Data

Instructions should include the results of the data collected.

## Understanding Literature

**Informative Writing** A journalist would offer an objective reporting of the facts regarding the who, what, where, when, why, and how of life on a ranch.

## Respond to the Reading

1. People and animals rely on each other. Both give and take in a relationship based on respect.

2. The author writes that horses are mischievous and dependable, as well as cunning enough to catch us off guard.

3. **Linking Science and Writing** Have students make a chart that compares and contrasts human and animal traits to use in their writing

 **Symbiosis**

*Symbiosis* is a biological term, but it can easily be applied to human relationships as well. Symbiosis usually applies to a dependent relationship that is beneficial to both members. This is called mutualism. Another kind of relationship is commensalism, in which one member benefits and the other is neither helped nor harmed. On the other hand, parasitism is a relationship in which one member depends upon the other and may even injure its host.

# The Solace of Open Spaces
## a novel by Gretel Ehrlich

Animals give us their constant, unjaded[1] faces and we burden them with our bodies and civilized ordeals. We're both humbled by and imperious[2] with them. We're comrades who save each other's lives. The horse we pulled from a boghole this morning bucked someone off later in the day; one stock dog refuses to work sheep, while another brings back a calf we had overlooked. . . . What's stubborn, secretive, dumb, and keen[3] in us bumps up against those same qualities in them. . . .

Living with animals makes us redefine our ideas about intelligence. Horses are as mischievous as they are dependable. Stupid enough to let us use them, they are cunning enough to catch us off guard. . . .

We pay for their loyalty; They can be willful, hard to catch, dangerous to shoe and buck on frosty mornings. In turn, they'll work themselves into a lather cutting cows, not for the praise they'll get but for the simple glory of outdodging a calf or catching up with an errant steer. . . .

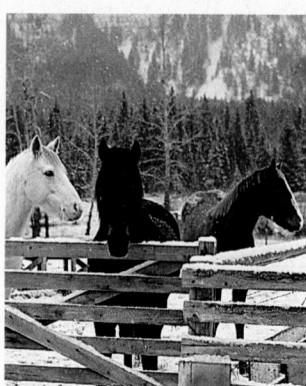

1 *Jaded* means "to be weary with fatigue," so *unjaded* means "not to be weary with fatigue."

2 domineering or overbearing

3 intellectually smart or sharp

## Understanding Literature

**Informative Writing** This passage is informative because it describes the real relationship between people and animals on a ranch in Wyoming. The author speaks from her own point of view, not from the point of view of a disinterested party. How might this story have been different if it had been told from the point of view of a visiting journalist?

## Respond to the Reading

1. Describe the relationship between people and animals in this passage.

2. What words does the author use to indicate that horses are intelligent?

3. **Linking Science and Writing** Write a short passage about an experience you have had with a pet. Put yourself in the passage without overusing the word "I".

 Animals and ranchers are clearly dependent on each other. Ranchers provide nutrition and shelter for animals on the ranch and, in turn, animals provide food, companionship, and perform work for the ranchers. You might consider the relationship between horses and ranchers to be a symbiotic one. Symbiosis (sihm bee OH sus) is any close interaction among two or more different species.

### Resources for Teachers and Students

*All Creatures Great and Small,* by James Herriot, St. Martin's Press, 1972

*Horse: The Complete Guide,* by Mary Gordon Watson, R. Russell Lyons, and Sue Montgomery, Team Media, Ltd., 1999

*Polar Dreams,* by Helen Thayer, Simon & Schuster, Inc., 1992

## Reviewing Main Ideas

### Section 1  The Environment

1. Ecology is the study of interactions among organisms and their environment.

2. The nonliving features of the environment are abiotic factors, and the organisms in the environment are biotic factors.

3. Ecosystems include biotic and abiotic factors.

4. The region of Earth and its atmosphere in which all organisms live is the biosphere.

### Section 2  Interactions Among Living Organisms

1. Characteristics that can describe populations include size, spacing, and density.

2. Any biotic or abiotic factor that limits the number of individuals in a population is a limiting factor.

3. A close relationship between two or more species is a symbiotic relationship.

4. The place where an organism lives is its habitat, and its role in the environment is its niche.

### Section 3  Matter and Energy

1. Food chains and food webs are models that describe the flow of energy.

2. At each level of a food chain, organisms lose energy as heat. Energy on Earth is renewed constantly by sunlight.

3. Matter on Earth is never lost or gained. It is used over and over again, or recycled.

## Visualizing Main Ideas

*Copy and complete the following concept map on the biosphere.*

Science Online  in7.msscience.com/interactive_tutor

**CHAPTER STUDY GUIDE   217**

## Reviewing Main Ideas

Summary statements can be used by students to review the major concepts of the chapter.

## Visualizing Main Ideas

See student page.

Science Online

**Visit** in7.msscience.com
/self_check_quiz
/interactive_tutor
/vocabulary_puzzlemaker
/chapter_review
/standards_review

### Assessment Transparency

For additional assessment questions, use the *Assessment Transparency* located in the transparency book.

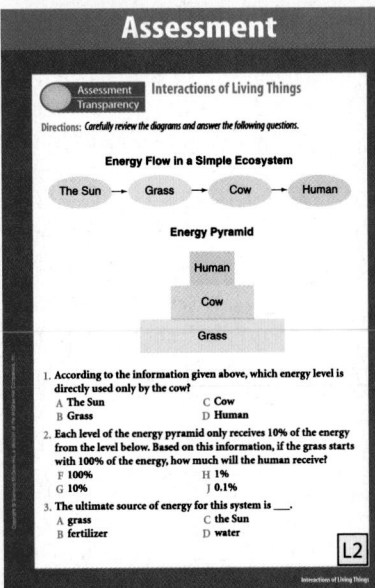

## Using Vocabulary

1. biotic factor
2. food web
3. population density
4. habitat
5. biosphere
6. symbiosis

## Checking Concepts

7. B  12. D
8. A  13. B
9. C  14. B
10. D  15. D
11. C  16. B

## Thinking Critically

17. The amount of energy available to a consumer decreases at each level with the greatest amount available at the bottom level.

18. Producers capture and transfer the Sun's energy into chemical energy. Consumers obtain energy by feeding on producers or other consumers. Decomposers obtain energy from the remains of organisms.

19. The carrying capacity of the environment limits population size. Biotic potential is the largest size the population can reach under the best possible conditions. Carrying capacity usually prevents populations from reaching biotic potential.

20. They break down dead organisms and make the nutrients contained in the organisms' bodies available for plants to use.

## Using Vocabulary

| | |
|---|---|
| abiotic factor p.196 | habitat p.207 |
| biosphere p.201 | limiting factor p.205 |
| biotic factor p.196 | niche p.207 |
| community p.200 | population p.200 |
| ecology p.196 | population density p.204 |
| ecosystem p.200 | symbiosis p.206 |
| food chain p.208 | water cycle p.212 |
| food web p.210 | |

*Fill in the blanks with the correct vocabulary word or words.*

1. A(n) _____ is any living thing in the environment.

2. A series of overlapping food chains makes up a(n) _____.

3. The size of a population that occupies an area of definite size is its _____.

4. Where an organism lives in an ecosystem is its _____.

5. The part of Earth that supports life is the _____.

6. Any close relationship between two or more species is _____.

## Checking Concepts

*Choose the word or phrase that best answers the question.*

7. Which of the following is a model that shows the amount of energy available as it flows through an ecosystem?
   A) niche
   B) energy pyramid
   C) carrying capacity
   D) food chain

8. Which of the following is a biotic factor?
   A) animals    C) sunlight
   B) air         D) soil

9. What is made up of all populations in an area?
   A) niche        C) community
   B) habitat      D) ecosystem

10. What is the term for the total number of individuals in a population occupying a certain area?
    A) clumping     C) spacing
    B) size         D) density

11. What is the tree to the right an example of?
    A) prey
    B) consumer
    C) producer
    D) predator

12. Which level of the food chain has the most energy?
    A) consumer     C) decomposers
    B) herbivores   D) producers

13. What is the symbitotc relationship called in which one organism is helped and the other organism is harmed?
    A) mutualism
    B) parasitism
    C) commensalism
    D) consumer

14. Which of the following is NOT cycled in the biosphere?
    A) nitrogen     C) water
    B) soil         D) carbon

15. What are coral reefs, forests, and ponds examples of?
    A) niches       C) populations
    B) habitats     D) ecosystems

16. What are all of the individuals of one species that live in the same area at the same time called?
    A) community    C) biosphere
    B) population   D) organism

Science ⌇nline in7.msscience.com/vocabulary_puzzlemaker

**Use the ExamView® Pro Testmaker CD-ROM to:**
- create multiple versions of tests
- create modified tests with one mouse click for inclusion students
- edit existing questions and add your own questions
- build tests aligned with state standards using built-in State Curriculum Tags
- change English tests to Spanish with one mouse click and vice versa

## Thinking Critically

**Use the illustration below to answer question 17.**

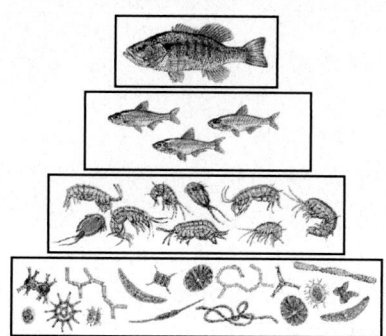

**17.** **Infer** why each level of the energy pyramid shown above is smaller than the one below it.

**18.** **Compare and contrast** the role of producers, consumers, and decomposers in an ecosystem.

**19.** **Explain** what carrying capacity has to do with whether or not a population reaches its biotic potential.

**20.** **Infer** why decomposers are vital to the cycling of matter in an ecosystem.

**21.** **Write** a paragraph that describes your own habitat and niche.

**22.** **Classify** the following as the result of either evaporation or condensation.
  **a.** A puddle disappears after a rainstorm.
  **b.** Rain falls.
  **c.** A lake becomes shallower.
  **d.** Clouds form.

**23.** **Concept Map** Use the following information to draw a food web of organisms living in a goldenrod field. *Aphids eat goldenrod sap, bees eat goldenrod nectar, beetles eat goldenrod pollen and goldenrod leaves, stinkbugs eat beetles, spiders eat aphids, and assassin bugs eat bees.*

**Science**online in7.msscience.com/chapter_review

**24.** **Record Observations** A home aquarium contains water, an air pump, a light, algae, a goldfish, and algae-eating snails. What are the abiotic factors in this environment?

**25.** **Determine** why viruses are considered parasites.

## Performance Activities

**26.** **Poster** Use your own observations or the results of library research to develop a food web for a nearby park, pond, or other ecosystem. Make a poster display illustrating the food web.

**27.** **Oral Presentation** Research the steps in the phosphorous cycle. Find out what role phosphorus plays in the growth of algae in ponds and lakes. Present your findings to the class.

## Applying Math

**Use the table below to answer questions 28 and 29.**

| Arizona Deer Population | |
|---|---|
| Year | Deer Per 400 Hectares |
| 1905 | 5.7 |
| 1915 | 35.7 |
| 1920 | 142.9 |
| 1925 | 85.7 |
| 1935 | 25.7 |

**28.** **Deer Population** Use the data above to graph the population density of a deer population over the years. Plot the number of deer on the *y*-axis and years on the *x*-axis. Predict what might have happened to cause the changes in the size of the population.

**29.** **Population Trend** What might the population of deer be in 1940 if the trend continued?

**21.** Answers will vary. Habitat is the student's home. Niche includes food, ways of getting food and water, relationships with other organisms, and daily activities.

**22.** (a) evaporation, (b) condensation, (c) evaporation, (d) condensation

**23.**

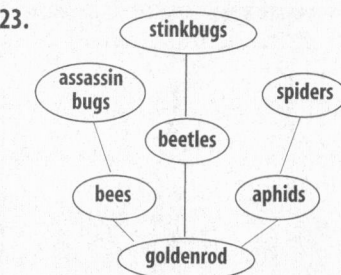

**24.** water, light, and air pump

**25.** The virus benefits, and the host is harmed.

## Performance Activities

**26.** The poster should illustrate the concepts presented in this chapter. Use **PASC**, p. 145.

**27.** Excess phosphorus causes an increase in the growth of algae. When algae die, their decomposition removes much of the oxygen from the pond, affecting all other organisms in the pond. Use **PASC**, p. 143.

## Applying Math

### Indiana Math Standards
7.3.1, 7.6.1

**28.** Possible answer: The deer population became so large that the deer consumed all the available food, and some deer starved. Check student graphs.

**29.** The population would continue to decline, therefore it would be less than 25.7.

---

## ✔ Assessment    Resources

**📁 Reproducible Masters**
**Chapter *Fast File* Resources**
  Chapter Review, pp. 37–38
  Chapter Tests, pp. 39–42
  Assessment Transparency Activity, p. 49
**Glencoe Science Web site**
  Chapter Review Test
  IN Standards Review

**Glencoe Technology**
  🔧 Assessment Transparency
  💿 Exam*View*® Pro Testmaker
  📺 MindJogger Videoquiz
  🔘 Interactive Chalkboard

chapter **7** Indiana

**Answer Sheet** A practice answer sheet can be found at in7.msscience.com/answer_sheet.

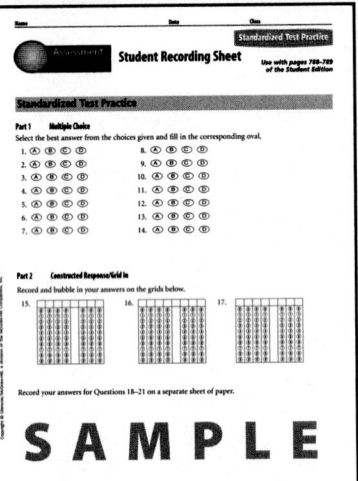

**S A M P L E**

*Record your answers on the answer sheet provided by your teacher or on a sheet of paper.*

**Part 1 Multiple Choice**

The photo below shows a deciduous forest.

**7.4.9**

**1.** What is the limiting factor for plants on the forest floor?

  **A** food

  **B** soil

  **C** sunlight

  **D** water

**7.4.9**

**2.** When would the plants on the forest floor shown in the photo above grow best?

  **A** spring

  **B** summer

  **C** fall

  **D** winter

The photo below shows grassland animals.

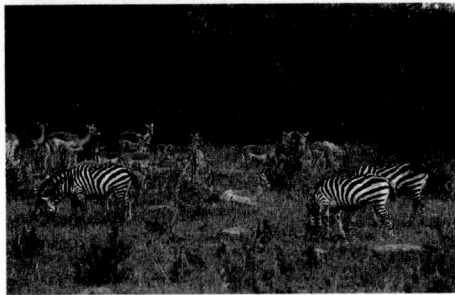

**3.** Which describes the animals in the photo?

  **A** carnivores

  **B** detritivores

  **C** herbivores

  **D** omnivores

**4.** Which describes interactions between groups of antelope and zebras shown in the photo above?

  **A** biome

  **B** community

  **C** ecosystem

  **D** population

**7.4.9**

**5.** What helps determine the number of individuals that can survive in an area?

  **A** biotic potential

  **B** carrying capacity

  **C** limiting factors

  **D** population spacing

**220 INDIANA**

**Part 1 Multiple Choice**

1. C      5. C
2. A      6. A
3. C      7. D
4. B      8. D

**Part 2 Critical Response**

**9.** This is the water cycle, which involves evaporation, condensation and precipitation. Heat from the Sun causes water to change from a liquid to a gas, water vapor. This is evaporation. The water vapor rises and encounters cooler air. As the water vapor cools, its molecules slow down and form a liquid. This is condensation. The tiny drops of water clump together and become clouds. As the drops become bigger, they get heavier and then fall back to Earth as rain or another type of precipitation.

**10.** A food web is a series of overlapping food chains. Humans consume food from both the land (terrestrial) and the water (aquatic) food webs. In the ocean, krill consume phytoplankton and whales and fish consume krill. Humans eat fish in order to obtain energy. On land, herbivores and omnivores eat grass and other plants. Carnivores consume herbivores and omnivores. Humans can eat all three types of consumers to get energy. If any part of this web is destroyed, it eventually could affect humans.

**11.** The amount of food in a given geographical region can be considered a limiting factor for the human population. Humans must consume food in order to survive. They compete with one another and with other organisms for this limited food supply. As humans have gained more knowledge, they can produce more food that has better nutritional value, can have better sanitation, and can better prevent disease. This helps humans approach their biotic potential because limiting factors of food and disease are overcome.

**7.4.9**

**6.** What would happen to a king penguin population if the fish in its habitat became scarce?

  **A** decrease, then stabilize

  **B** decrease, then increase

  **C** increase, then stabilize

  **D** increase, then decrease

**7.** What is any close interaction between two or more species?

  **A** commensalism

  **B** mutualism

  **C** parasitism

  **D** symbiosis

**7.4.9**

**8.** The photo below shows grassland animals in Africa.

Which environmental factor is the reason for the competition among these animals?

  **A** food

  **B** mates

  **C** sunlight

  **D** water

### Part 2   Critical Response

The illustration below shows a cycle of matter.

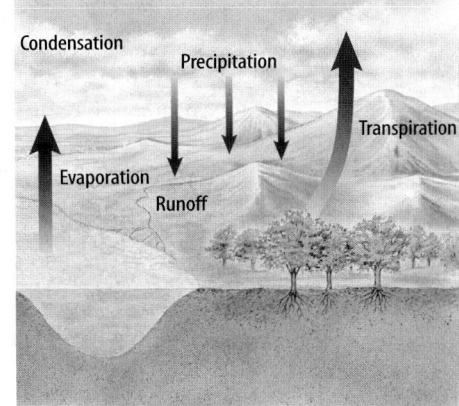

Condensation   Precipitation   Transpiration

Evaporation   Runoff

**9.** Name and describe the cycle shown above.

**7.4.9**

**10.** Why is the cycle shown above important for an organism's survival?

**7.4.2**

**11.** How do humans interact with land and aquatic food webs? What would happen if one part of this web were destroyed?

**12.** Describe how better food production, sanitation, and disease prevention have contributed to the yearly increase in the human population.

### Test-Taking Tip

**Answer All Parts of the Question** Make sure each part of the question is answered when listing discussion points.

**Question 12** Notice that this question asks you to describe how three things contribute to human population growth.

## Rubrics

The following rubric is a sample scoring device for critical response questions.

### Critical Response

| Points | Description |
| --- | --- |
| 4 | The student demonstrates a thorough understanding of the science of the task. The response may contain minor flaws that do not detract from the demonstration of a thorough understanding. |
| 3 | The student demonstrates an understanding of the science of the task. The response is essentially correct and demonstrates an essential but less than thorough understanding of the science. |
| 2 | The student demonstrates only a partial understanding of the science of the task. Although the student may have used the correct approach to a solution or may have provided a correct solution, the work lacks an essential understanding of the underlying science concepts. |
| 1 | The student demonstrates a very limited understanding of the science of the task. The response is incomplete and exhibits many flaws. |
| 0 | The student provides a completely incorrect solution or no response at all. |

 Science Online in7.msscience.com/standards_review

| Section/Objectives | Standards | | Labs/Features |
|---|---|---|---|
| **Chapter Opener** | National | State/Local | **Launch Lab:** What happens when topsoil is left unprotected?, p. 223 **Foldables,** p. 223 |
| | See pp. 16T–17T for a Key to Standards. | Detailed standards begin on page IN8. | |
| **Section 1  Resources** ⏱ 2 sessions 📦 1 block 1. **Compare** renewable and nonrenewable resources. 2. **List** uses of fossil fuels. 3. **Identify** alternatives to fossil fuel use. | National Content Standards: UCP.2, UCP.3, A.1, A.2, F.2 | Indiana Standards: 7.1.8, 7.3.16 | **MiniLAB:** Observing Mineral Mining Effects, p. 226 **Integrate Social Studies,** p. 227 **Visualizing Solar Energy,** p. 231 |
| **Section 2  Pollution** ⏱ 2 sessions 📦 1 block 4. **Describe** types of air pollution. 5. **Identify** causes of water pollution. 6. **Explain** methods that can be used to prevent erosion. | National Content Standards: UCP.2, UCP.3, A.1, A.2, F.2 | Indiana Standards: 7.1.8, 7.2.7, 7.3.16, 7.4.14 | **MiniLAB:** Measuring Acid Rain, p. 233 **Science Online,** p. 234 **Integrate Health,** p. 236 **Lab:** The Greenhouse Effect, p. 241 |
| **Section 3  The Three Rs of Conservation** ⏱ 3 sessions 📦 1.5 blocks 7. **Recognize** ways you can reduce your use of natural resources. 8. **Explain** how you can reuse resources to promote conservation. 9. **Describe** how many materials can be recycled. | National Content Standards: UCP.2, UCP.3, A.1, A.2, F.2 | Indiana Standards: 7.3.16, 7.4.14, 7.5.3, 7.7.2 | **Science Online,** p. 244 **Applying Science:** What items are you recycling at home?, p. 244 **Lab:** Solar Cooking, p. 246 **Science and Language Arts:** Beauty Plagiarized, p. 248 |

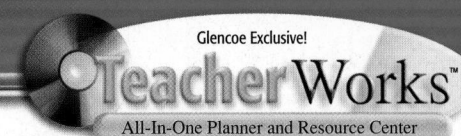

| Lab Materials | Reproducible Resources | Section Assessment | Technology |
|---|---|---|---|
| **Launch Lab:** moist sand, potting soil, plastic basin or aluminum-foil baking pan, moss, water, spray bottle, beaker | **Chapter FAST FILE Resources** Foldables Worksheet, p. 17 Directed Reading Overview, p. 19 Note-taking Worksheets, pp. 33–35 | **GLENCOE'S ASSESSMENT ADVANTAGE** | TeacherWorks includes: • Interactive Teacher Edition • Lesson Planner with calendar • Access to all program blacklines • Correlations to standards • Web links |
| **MiniLAB:** chocolate-chip cookie, paper plate, toothpick *Need materials?* Contact Science Kit at 1-800-828-7777 or www.sciencekit.com on the Internet. | **Chapter FAST FILE Resources** Transparency Activity, p. 44 MiniLAB, p. 3 Enrichment, p. 30 Reinforcement, p. 27 Directed Reading, p. 20 **Cultural Diversity,** p. 41 **Mathematics Skill Activities,** p. 9 | **Portfolio** Activity, p. 231 **Performance** MiniLAB, p. 226 Applying Math, p. 230 **Content** Section Review, p. 230 | Section Focus Transparency Guided Reading Audio Program Interactive Chalkboard CD-ROM |
| **MiniLAB:** cup, rainwater, pH indicator paper, tap water, distilled water **Lab:** 1-L clear plastic soft-drink bottle with top cut off and label removed (2), 2 thermometers, potting soil, masking tape, plastic wrap, rubber band, lamp with 100-W lightbulb, watch or clock with second hand | **Chapter FAST FILE Resources** Transparency Activity, p. 45 MiniLAB, p. 4 Enrichment, p. 31 Reinforcement, p. 28 Directed Reading, p. 21 Lab Worksheet, pp. 5–6 Lab Activity, pp. 9–12 Transparency Activity, pp. 47–48 | **Portfolio** Assessment, p. 240 **Performance** MiniLAB, p. 233 Applying Math, p. 240 **Content** Section Review, p. 240 | Section Focus Transparency Teaching Transparency Virtual Labs CD-ROM Guided Reading Audio Program Interactive Chalkboard CD-ROM Video Lab |
| **Lab:** poster board, cardboard boxes, aluminum foil, string, wire coat hangers, clear plastic sheets, black cookware, thermometer, stopwatch, glue, tape, scissors | **Chapter FAST FILE Resources** Transparency Activity, p. 46 Enrichment, p. 32 Reinforcement, p. 29 Directed Reading, pp. 21, 22 Lab Worksheet, pp. 7–8 Lab Activity, pp. 13–16 **Lab Management and Safety,** p. 37 | **Portfolio** Challenge, p. 244 **Performance** Applying Science, p. 244 Applying Skills, p. 245 **Content** Section Review, p. 245 | Section Focus Transparency Guided Reading Audio Program Interactive Chalkboard CD-ROM |

## End of Chapter Assessment

**GLENCOE'S ASSESSMENT ADVANTAGE**

| Blackline Masters | Technology | Professional Series |
|---|---|---|
| **Chapter FAST FILE Resources** Chapter Review, pp. 37–38 Chapter Tests, pp. 39–42 **Mastering the Grade 7 Indiana Science Standards** | MindJogger Videoquiz IN Test Prep and Practice ExamView® ExamView® Pro Testmaker TeacherWorks CD-ROM Interactive Chalkboard CD-ROM | **Performance Assessment in the Science Classroom (PASC)** |

# chapter 8 Conserving Resources

## Transparencies

### Section Focus

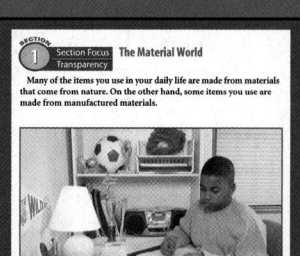

**Section Focus Transparency 1** The Material World

Many of the items you use in your daily life are made from materials that come from nature. On the other hand, some items you use are made from manufactured materials.

1. What kinds of materials can you identify in the scene above?
2. Where do you think the materials you identified come from?
3. Can the materials you named be replaced or will they eventually disappear?

L2

**Section Focus Transparency 2** Ocean-Sized Ice Cubes

One of the concerns with rising worldwide temperatures is the melting of ice at Earth's poles. Ice floating in water, as found in the Arctic Ocean, won't raise sea levels if it melts. But ice-sheets on land, as found in Greenland and Antarctica, do contain enough water to raise sea levels if they melt.

1. What is happening in the picture above?
2. What might cause ice sheets to melt?
3. Do you think human activity could affect the amount of ice that melts in Antarctica? Why or why not?

L2

**Section Focus Transparency 3** The Art of Recycling

Many artists work with paints or other specific materials, but sometimes artists work with whatever happens to be lying around. This goat was made from objects that many people throw away without a second thought.

1. Can you identify the items this goat is made from?
2. What other materials might be reused to make a piece of art?
3. What are some benefits of reusing materials rather than throwing them away?

L2

This is a representation of key blackline masters available in the Teacher Classroom Resources. See Resource Manager boxes within the chapter for additional information.

### Assessment

**Assessment Transparency** Conserving Resources

Directions: Carefully review the table and answer the following questions.

| Alternatives to Fossil Fuels | | |
|---|---|---|
| **Type** | **How it works** | **Environmental impacts** |
| Hydroelectric power | Energy of moving water is converted into electrical energy. | Habitats destroyed by dams |
| Wind power | Energy of moving air is converted into electrical energy. | No significant problem |
| Nuclear power | Energy of nuclear fission heats water, which is used to generate electricity. | Produces hazardous waste and has risk of accidents |
| Solar power | Energy from the Sun is absorbed and converted into heat and electrical energy. | No significant problem |

1. According to the table, a windmill would be an example of ___.
   A hydroelectric power  C nuclear power
   B wind power  D solar power
2. Which of these could be added to the table?
   F Coal power  H Gasoline power
   G Oil power  J Geothermal power
3. According to the table, which fuel is most likely to affect human health?
   A Hydroelectric power  C Nuclear power
   B Wind power  D Solar power

L2

### Teaching

**Teaching Transparency 2** Groundwater

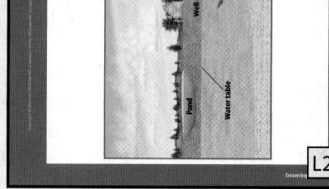

L2

## Key to Teaching Strategies

The following designations will help you decide which activities are appropriate for your students.

L1 Level 1 activities should be appropriate for students with learning difficulties.

L2 Level 2 activities should be within the ability range of all students.

L3 Level 3 activities are designed for above-average students.

**ELL** ELL activities should be within the ability range of English Language Learners.

COOP LEARN Cooperative Learning activities are designed for small group work.

**LS** Multiple Learning Styles logos, as described on page 12T, are used throughout to indicate strategies that address different learning styles.

P These strategies represent student products that can be placed into a best-work portfolio.

PBL Problem-Based Learning activities apply real-world situations to learning.

## Hands-on Activities

### Student Text Lab Worksheet

**Activity** The Greenhouse Effect

**Lab Preview**
Directions: Answer these questions before you begin the Activity.
1. Why is it important to place the lamp exactly 1 cm from each container?

2. What is the greenhouse effect?

You can create models of Earth with and without heat-reflecting greenhouse gases. Then, experiment with the models to observe the greenhouse effect.

**What You'll Investigate**
How does the greenhouse effect influence temperatures on Earth?

**Materials**
1-L, clear, plastic, soft drink bottle with top cut off and label removed (2)
thermometer (2)
*temperature probe
potting soil
masking tape
plastic wrap
rubber band
lamp with 100-W lightbulb
watch or clock with second hand
*Alternate materials

**Goals**
• Observe the greenhouse effect.
• Describe the effect that a heat source has on an environment.

**Safety Precautions**

**Procedure**
1. Put an equal volume of potting soil in the bottom of each container.
2. Use masking tape to attach a thermometer to the inside of each container. Place each thermometer at the same height above the soil. Shield each thermometer bulb by putting a double layer of masking tape over it.

3. Seal the top of one container with plastic wrap held in place with a rubber band.
4. Place the lamp with the exposed 100-W lightbulb between the two containers and exactly 1 cm away from each. Do not turn on the light.
5. Let the setup sit for five min, then record the temperature in each container.
6. Turn on the light. Record the temperature in each container every 2 min for 15 to 20 min.
7. **Record** the data in the Data and Observations table. Graph the results on a separate sheet of paper.

L2

### Laboratory Activities

**Laboratory Activity 1** Water Pollution

Polluting substances are added to the environment in many ways. Detergents, fertilizers, and garbage often wash into streams. These substances can influence the growth of algae in freshwater. Algae add oxygen to water. Problems arise when the algae die and decompose. Decomposition of algae by bacteria uses oxygen resulting in a net oxygen loss from the water. Therefore, other organisms that need oxygen to survive begin to die off.

**Strategy**
You will test the effects of detergent, fertilizer, and garbage on the growth of algae in water. You will observe and record changes that occur in water environments.

**Materials**
apron
labels
4 glass jars (1-L, with lids)
aged tap water
water containing algae
graduated cylinder
detergent
fertilizer (liquid)
plant peelings (potato, apple, orange)

**Procedure**
1. Label the jars, 1, 2, 3, and 4. Half fill each jar with aged tap water. Add water containing algae until each jar is 3/4 full. CAUTION: Always wash your hands after handling microbes.
2. Add 5 mL of detergent to jar 1.
3. Add 5 mL of fertilizer to jar 2.
4. Add some plant peelings to jar 3.
5. Do not add anything to jar 4. It will be the control.
6. Put the lid on each of the jars.
7. Place the jars in the light on a windowsill or underneath a light source.
8. Observe the jars every other day for two weeks. Compare jars 1, 2, and 3, with jar 4. Record your observations in Tables 1–4.

L2

## Meeting Different Ability Levels

### Content Outline

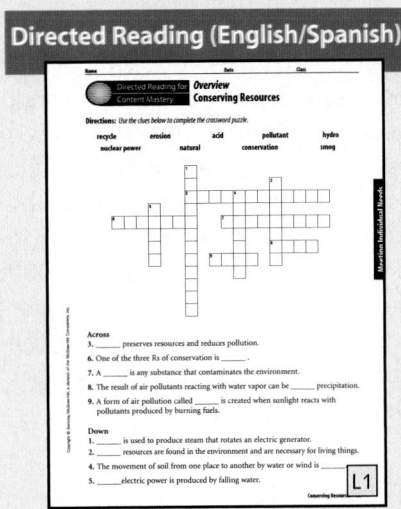

**L2**

### Reinforcement

**L2**

### Enrichment

**L3**

### Directed Reading (English/Spanish)

**L1**

### Study Guide

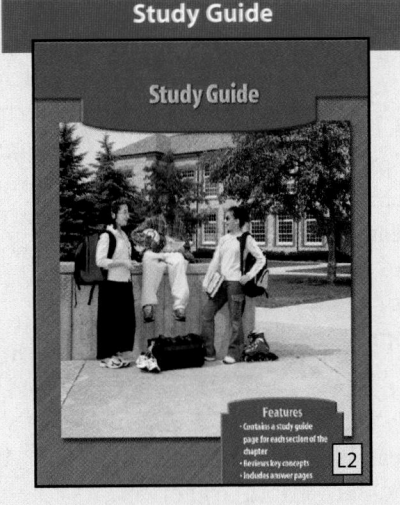

Study Guide

**Features**
- Contains a study guide page for each section of the chapter
- Reviews key concepts
- Includes answer pages

**L2**

### Reading Essentials

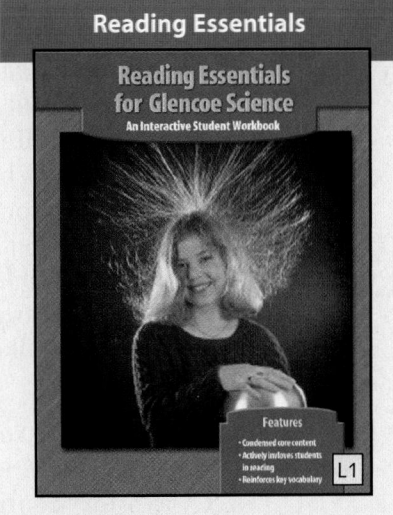

Reading Essentials for Glencoe Science
An Interactive Student Workbook

**Features**
- Condensed core content
- Actively involves students in reading
- Reinforces key vocabulary

**L1**

## Assessment

### Test Practice Workbook

**L2**

### Chapter Review

**L2**

### Chapter Tests

**L2**

# Science Content Background

 **Resources**

### Renewable Resources

Renewable resources include trees in forests; fish in lakes, rivers, and oceans; fertile agricultural soil; and freshwater in lakes and rivers. Nature replaces these resources, and they can be used forever as long as they are not overexploited in the short term. Some resources, like agricultural soil, can be considered renewable or nonrenewable. Soil is constantly replaced but at a very slow rate.

### Nonrenewable Resources

Nonrenewable resources, which include minerals and fossil fuels, are present in limited supplies and are depleted by use. They are not replenished by natural processes within a reasonable amount of time. Fossil fuels, for example, take millions of years to form. Recycling nonrenewable resources can help sustain the supply of certain substances. In the future, most products will contain some recycled material.

### Nuclear Power

In 1942, Enrico Fermi established the first successful controlled nuclear chain reaction. Nuclear fission reactions release a great deal of energy, several million times the energy of a typical chemical reaction. Nuclear reactors use uranium-235 for the production of power. Once started, the reactions are self-sustaining: the neutrons released by each splitting in turn split other atoms, causing a chain reaction. There is no danger of nuclear chain reactions starting in nature since uranium-235 makes up only 0.71% of the naturally occurring uranium. Most of the remainder is uranium-238, which is not fissible.

 **Pollution**

### Acid Precipitation

Acid precipitation is a worldwide problem. Reports of highly acidic precipitation have come from Canada, England, Germany, France, Scandinavia, and the United States. Precipitation is normally slightly acidic, with a pH between 5.6 and 5.7 that is caused by atmospheric carbonic acid. But acid precipitation sometimes has a concentration of acid 1,000 times higher than normal. The average precipitation in much of the northeastern part of the United States and adjoining parts of Ontario has a pH between 4.0 and 4.5.

### Greenhouse Effect

Carbon dioxide is one of the most abundant of the greenhouse gases. It occurs as a natural consequence of respiration. However, carbon dioxide is emitted into the atmosphere as a waste product of energy production. Coal, oil, natural gas, and biomass are burned to provide heat and electricity for industrial processes, home heating, and cooking. These sources are increasing the amount of carbon dioxide in the atmosphere. Some evidence suggests that increased levels of carbon dioxide in the atmosphere may cause Earth's average temperature to increase.

### Ozone Depletion

Ozone, a molecule made up of three oxygen atoms, traps excess ultraviolet radiation and prevents it from reaching Earth. In 1985, it was

---

**Teacher to Teacher**

Steve Federman
Loveland Middle School
Loveland, Ohio

"To emphasize the effect of coal mining on our land, I give each student a soft cookie with raisins or chocolate chips and a toothpick. Their objective is to use a toothpick carefully to mine all the chocolate chips (raisins) out of the cookie while leaving the cookie intact."

*Steve Federman*

---

discovered that a significant thinning of the ozone layer over the Antarctic occurred during the southern hemisphere's spring. Some regions of the ozone layer showed 95 percent depletion. Ozone depletion is also occurring farther north. Measurements in arctic regions suggest a thinning of the ozone layer there. These findings have caused countries to stop producing ozone-destroying chemicals.

## Soil Loss

Erosion is a natural process that has occurred since Earth was formed. Humans have little control over the erosion caused by glaciers, rivers, and oceans. A number of human activities, mainly farming and logging, have increased erosion. Scientists estimate that between 2 and 3 billion metric tons of soil are lost from farmlands in the United States each year.

## Soil Pollution—Solid Wastes

About 90 percent of our solid wastes are disposed of on land, mostly in landfills. Several methods of producing energy from solid waste are used on a small scale and further research is being done in this area. One example is a combustion chamber lined with water lines in which selected wastes are burned and the heat is used to produce steam to power a generator.

*Telegraph Colour Library/FPG International*

## section 3 The Three Rs of Conservation

**Recycle**

In 1999, the overall recycling rate in the U.S. was 28 percent, with the composting of yard waste accounting for 2/5 of this. The overall recycling rate of plastic soft-drink containers was only 34.9 percent, 26.3 percent for glass containers, and 57.2 percent for steel cans. Paper and paper products are the most voluminous waste products, and they make up about 42 percent of the solid waste produced in the United States.

## chapter content resources

**Internet Resources**
For additional content background, visit **in7.msscience.com** to:
- access your book online
- find references to related articles in popular science magazines
- access Web links with related content background
- access current events with science journal topics

**Print Resources**
*Understanding Garbage and Our Environment,* by Andrea Nolan, McGraw-Hill Trade, 1998
*Air Pollution (True Books),* by Rhonda Lucas Donald, Children's Press, 2001
*Global Warming: The Threat of the Earth's Changing Climate,* by Laurence Pringle, SeaStar Books, 2003

**Academic Standard—3:** Students collect and organize data to identify relationships between physical objects, events, and processes. They use logical reasoning to question their own ideas as new information challenges their conceptions of the natural world.

**Also covers:** Academic Standards 1, 2, 4, 5, 7 (Detailed standards begin on page IN8.)

# Conserving Resources

## Chapter Vocabulary

natural resource, p. 224
renewable resource, p. 224
nonrenewable resource, p. 225
petroleum, p. 225
fossil fuel, p. 226
hydroelectric power, p. 227
nuclear energy, p. 228
geothermal energy, p. 229
pollutant, p. 232
acid precipitation, p. 233
greenhouse effect, p. 234
ozone depletion, p. 235
erosion, p. 239
hazardous waste, p. 240
recycling, p. 243

**Science Journal** Woods, food crops, and soil are examples. Wood can provide shelter and home furnishings, food crops are needed for our own consumption and by other animals, and soil is needed by farmers to produce crops and it filters water.

### PowerPoint® Presentations

This CD-ROM is an editable Microsoft® PowerPoint® presentation that includes:
- a pre-made presentation for every chapter
- interactive graphics
- animations
- audio clips
- image bank
- all new section and chapter questions
- Standardized Test Practice
- transparencies
- pre-lab questions for all labs
- Foldables directions
- links to in7.msscience.com

**chapter preview**

sections

**1 Resources**

**2 Pollution**
   *Lab The Greenhouse Effect*

**3 The Three Rs of Conservation**
   *Lab Solar Cooking*

⊙ *Virtual Lab When is water safe to drink?*

### Resources Fuel Our Lives

Resources, such as clean water and air, are commonly taken for granted. We depend on water and air to survive. Fossil fuels are another type of resource, and we depend on them for energy. However, fossil fuels can pollute our air and water.

**Science Journal** List some other resources that we depend on and describe how we use them.

222

## Theme Connection

**Energy** Even though the total amount of energy on Earth remains constant, the sources of usable energy are limited. Energy is often transformed from one form to another, such as fossil fuel energy into electricity and then into light energy.

## About the Photo

**Pollution** Three major sources of pollution are municipal, industrial, and agricultural wastes. It is estimated that 1.5 billion people worldwide lack safe drinking water and at least 5 million people die from waterborne diseases each year.

# Start-Up Activities

## What happens when topsoil is left unprotected?

Plants grow in the top, nutrient-rich layer, called topsoil. Plants help keep topsoil in place by protecting it from wind and rain. Try the following experiment to find out what happens when topsoil is left unprotected.

1. Use a mixture of moist sand and potting soil to create a miniature landscape in a plastic basin or aluminum-foil baking pan. Form hills and valleys in your landscape.

2. Use clumps of moss to cover areas of your landscape. Leave some sloping portions without plant cover.

3. Simulate a rainstorm over your landscape by spraying water on it from a spray bottle or by pouring a slow stream of water on it from a beaker.

4. **Think Critically** In your Science Journal, record your observations and describe what happened to the land that was not protected by plant cover.

Preview this chapter's content and activities at
in7.msscience.com

**Resources** Make the following Foldable to help you organize information and diagram ideas about renewable and nonrenewable resources.

**STEP 1** **Fold** a sheet of paper in half lengthwise. Make the back edge about 5 cm longer than the front edge.

**STEP 2** **Turn** the paper so the fold is on the bottom. Then **fold** in half.

**STEP 3** **Unfold and cut** only the top layer along the fold to make two tabs. **Label** the Foldable as shown.

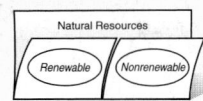

Natural Resources

Renewable   Nonrenewable

**Make a Concept Map** Before you read the chapter, list examples of each type of natural resource you already know on the back of the appropriate tabs. As you read the chapter, add to your lists.

## section
## 1

Also covers: 7.1.8 (Detailed standards begin on page IN8.)

# Resources

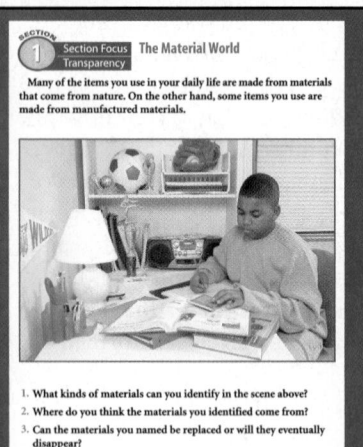
## as you read

### *What* You'll Learn

- **Compare** renewable and nonrenewable resources.
- **List** uses of fossil fuels.
- **Identify** alternatives to fossil fuel use.

### *Why* It's Important

Wise use of natural resources is important for the health of all life on Earth.

### ◉ Review Vocabulary

**geyser:** a spring that emits intermittent jets of heated water and steam

### New Vocabulary

- natural resource
- renewable resource
- nonrenewable resource
- petroleum
- fossil fuel
- hydroelectric power
- nuclear energy
- geothermal energy

**Figure 1** Cotton and wood are renewable resources. Cotton cloth is used for rugs, curtains, and clothing. A new crop of cotton can be grown every year. Wood is used for furniture, building materials, and paper. It will take 20 years for these young trees to grow large enough to harvest.

## Natural Resources

An earthworm burrowing in moist soil eats decaying plant material. A robin catches the worm and flies to a tree. The leaves of the tree use sunlight during photosynthesis. Leaves fall to the ground, decay, and perhaps become an earthworm's meal. What do these living things have in common? They rely on Earth's **natural resources**—the parts of the environment that are useful or necessary for the survival of living organisms.

What kinds of natural resources do you use? Like other organisms, you need food, air, and water. You also use resources that are needed to make everything from clothes to cars. Natural resources supply energy for automobiles and power plants. Although some natural resources are plentiful, others are not.

**Renewable Resources** The Sun, an inexhaustible resource, provides a constant supply of heat and light. Rain fills lakes and streams with water. When plants carry out photosynthesis, they add oxygen to the air. Sunlight, water, air, and the crops shown in **Figure 1** are examples of renewable resources. A **renewable resource** is any natural resource that is recycled or replaced constantly by nature.

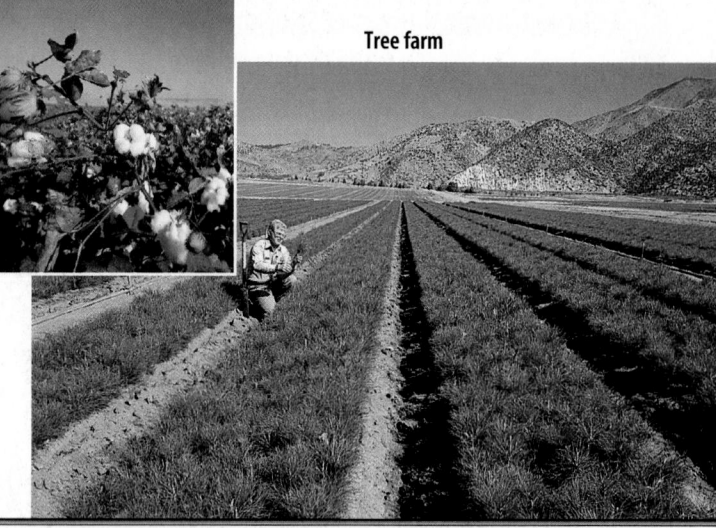

Cotton plants

Tree farm

**224 CHAPTER 8** Conserving Resources

**Supply and Demand** Even though renewable resources are recycled or replaced, they are sometimes in short supply. Rain and melted snow replace the water in streams, lakes, and reservoirs. Sometimes, there may not be enough rain or snowmelt to meet all the needs of people, plants, and animals. In some parts of the world, especially desert regions, water and other resources usually are scarce. Other resources can be used instead, as shown in **Figure 2.**

**Nonrenewable Resources** Natural resources that are used up more quickly than they can be replaced by natural processes are **nonrenewable resources.** Earth's supply of nonrenewable resources is limited. You use nonrenewable resources when you take home groceries in a plastic bag, paint a wall, or travel by car. Plastics, paints, and gasoline are made from an important nonrenewable resource called petroleum, or oil. **Petroleum** is formed mostly from the remains of microscopic marine organisms buried in Earth's crust. It is nonrenewable because it takes hundreds of millions of years for it to form.

✔ **Reading Check** *What are nonrenewable resources?*

Minerals and metals found in Earth's crust are nonrenewable resources. Petroleum is a mineral. So are diamonds and the graphite in pencil lead. The aluminum used to make soft-drink cans is a metal. Iron, copper, tin, gold, silver, tungsten, and uranium also are metals. Many manufactured items, like the car shown in **Figure 3,** are made from nonrenewable resources.

**Figure 2** In parts of Africa, firewood has become scarce. People in this village now use solar energy instead of wood for cooking.

**Figure 3** Iron, a nonrenewable resource, is the main ingredient in steel. Steel is used to make cars, trucks, appliances, buildings, bridges, and even tires.
**Infer** *what other nonrenewable resources are used to build a car.*

SECTION 1 Resources **225**

✔ **Active Reading**

**News Summary** Assign students the job of being television reporters. Allow different students to summarize the information on renewable and nonrenewable resources. Then have students present their summaries to the "television" audience.

**2 Teach**

## Use an Analogy

**Savings Account** Compare nonrenewable resources to a noninterest-bearing savings account to which nothing is added. The depletion of the savings account depends on how fast withdrawals are made and how large they are.
L2

## Activity

**Daily Resource Use** Have pairs work together to make a list of the things they used or relied upon today. Have them categorize the items as food, transportation, clothing, or household items. Finally, have them make check marks by the items they think are renewable. Have groups compare and discuss their answers.
L2 COOP LEARN IS **Interpersonal**

✔ **Reading Check**

**Answer** resources that are used up more quickly than they can be replaced

⚠ **IDENTIFYING Misconceptions**

**Recognize Nonrenewability** Some students may not realize that fossil fuels and other mineral resources are nonrenewable. Point out that much of the coal used today was formed during the Carboniferous Period. Have students research how long ago that was. about 345–280 million years ago

## Caption Answer

**Figure 3** Most of the materials are nonrenewable and include chrome, plastic, and synthetic rubber.

## Mini LAB

### Observing Mineral Mining Effects

**Procedure**
1. Place a **chocolate-chip cookie** on a **paper plate**. Pretend the chips are mineral deposits and the rest of the cookie is Earth's crust.
2. Use a **toothpick** to locate and dig up the mineral deposits. Try to disturb the land as little as possible.
3. When mining is completed, try to restore the land to its original condition.

### Analysis
1. How well were you able to restore the land?
2. Compare the difficulty of digging for mineral deposits found close to the surface with digging for those found deep in Earth's crust.
3. Describe environmental changes that might result from a mining operation.

*Try at Home*

**Figure 4** Coal is a fossil fuel. It often is obtained by strip mining, which removes all the soil above the coal deposit. The soil is replaced, but it takes many years for the ecosystem to recover.

**Identify** *the resource that provided 84 percent of the energy used in the United States in 1999.*

## Fossil Fuels

Coal, oil, and natural gas are nonrenewable resources that supply energy. Most of the energy you use comes from these fossil fuels, as the graph in **Figure 4** shows. **Fossil fuels** are fuels formed in Earth's crust over hundreds of millions of years. Cars, buses, trains, and airplanes are powered by gasoline, diesel fuel, and jet fuel, which are made from oil. Coal is used in many power plants to produce electricity. Natural gas is used in manufacturing, for heating and cooking, and sometimes as a vehicle fuel.

**Fossil Fuel Conservation** Billions of people all over the world use fossil fuels every day. Because fossil fuels are nonrenewable, Earth's supply of them is limited. In the future, they may become more expensive and difficult to obtain. Also, the use of fossil fuels can lead to environmental problems. For example, mining coal can require stripping away thick layers of soil and rock, as shown in **Figure 4,** which destroys ecosystems. Another problem is that fossil fuels must be burned to release the energy stored in them. The burning of fossil fuels produces waste gases that cause air pollution, including smog and acid rain. For these reasons, many people suggest reducing the use of fossil fuels and finding other sources of energy.

You can use simple conservation measures to help reduce fossil fuel use. Switch off the light when you leave a room and turn off the television when you're not watching it. These actions reduce your use of electricity, which often is produced in power plants that burn fossil fuels. Hundreds of millions of automobiles are in use in the United States. Riding in a car pool or taking public transportation uses fewer liters of gasoline than driving alone in a car. Walking or riding a bicycle uses even less fossil fuel. Reducing fossil fuel use has an added benefit—the less you use, the more money you save.

Renewable energy
Nuclear power 8%
8%
Natural gas 23%
Coal 22%
Oil 39%

## Curriculum Connection

**Social Studies** Have students investigate ways petroleum was used in ancient cultures. Egyptians used petroleum to help preserve mummies. The Chinese used petroleum to heat and light their homes and to cook. Tar pits supplied crude oil that was used for fuel, cooking, and lighting in Latin America. At the same time, petroleum was used in Europe for lubricating wagon wheels and to make ointments. L3 IS **Naturalist**

**Figure 5** Most power plants use turbine generators to produce electricity. In fossil fuel plants, burning fuel boils water and produces steam that turns the turbine.

Fast-moving steam, water, or wind rushes across the turbine blades. This flow of energy causes the turbine blades to turn.

The turbine blades are attached to a shaft. When the blades turn, so does the shaft.

Electricity flows from the coil into electrical wires.

Magnet

Generator

Turbine

The turning shaft is connected to an electric generator. A simple generator is a coil of wire that spins inside the field of a magnet. The turbine shaft spins the coil. The spinning coil generates electricity.

## Alternatives to Fossil Fuels

Another approach to reducing fossil fuel use is to develop other sources of energy. Much of the electricity used today comes from power plants that burn fossil fuels. As **Figure 5** shows, electricity is generated when a rotating turbine turns a coil of wires in the magnetic field of an electric generator. Fossil-fuel power plants boil water to produce steam that turns the turbine. Alternative energy sources, including water, wind, and atomic energy can be used instead of fossil fuels to turn turbines. Also, solar cells can produce electricity using only sunlight, with no turbines at all. Some of these alternative energy sources—particularly wind and solar energy—are so plentiful they could be considered inexhaustible resources.

**Water Power** Water is a renewable energy source that can be used to generate electricity. **Hydroelectric power** is electricity that is produced when the energy of falling water is used to turn the turbines of an electric generator. Hydroelectric power does not contribute to air pollution because no fuel is burned. However, it does present environmental concerns. Building a hydroelectric plant usually involves constructing a dam across a river. The dam raises the water level high enough to produce the energy required for electricity generation. Many acres behind the dam are flooded, destroying land habitats and changing part of the river into a lake.

**Energy** Oil and natural gas are used to produce over 60 percent of the energy supply in the United States. Over half of the oil used is imported from other countries. Many scientists suggest that emissions from the burning of fossil fuels are principally responsible for global warming. In your Science Journal, write what you might do to persuade utility companies to increase their use of water, wind, and solar power.

SECTION 1 Resources **227**

SECTION 1 Resources **227**

## Make a Model

**Turbines** Use a pinwheel and a fan to show how wind can be used to turn a turbine. Give some pinwheels to students and ask them to find the spot on the school grounds that would be best for generating electricity using the wind. L1 ELL LS
**Naturalist**

## Discussion

**Windmills** Ask students to compare modern windmills with old-style windmills found in Holland, Spain, or the United States. They both have blades that are turned by the force of the wind. Modern windmills are more streamlined and generate electricity. Older ones were used to grind grain or pump water from underground.

**Wind Power** Wind power is another renewable energy source that can be used for electricity production. Wind turns the blades of a turbine, which powers an electric generator. When winds blow at least 32 km/h, energy is produced. Wind power does not cause air pollution, but electricity can be produced only when the wind is blowing. So far, wind power accounts for only a small percentage of the electricity used worldwide.

**Nuclear Power** Another alternative to fossil fuels makes use of the huge amounts of energy in the nuclei of atoms, as shown in **Figure 6. Nuclear energy** is released when billions of atomic nuclei from uranium, a radioactive element, are split apart in a nuclear fission reaction. This energy is used to produce steam that rotates the turbine blades of an electric generator.

Nuclear power does not contribute to air pollution. However, uranium is a nonrenewable resource, and mining it can disrupt ecosystems. Nuclear power plants also produce radioactive wastes that can seriously harm living organisms. Some of these wastes remain radioactive for thousands of years, and their safe disposal is a problem that has not yet been solved. Accidents also are a danger.

**Figure 6** Nuclear power plants are designed to withstand the high energy produced by nuclear reactions.

1. The containment building is made of concrete lined with steel. The reactor vessel and steam generators are housed inside.

Cooling water pump

Containment building

Steel lining

Steam generators

Control rods

3. Rods made of radiation-absorbing material can be raised and lowered to control the reaction.

Reactor vessel

4. A fast-moving neutron from the nucleus of a uranium atom crashes into another atom.

Uranium atom

Fuel rods

2. The uranium fuel rods are lowered to begin the nuclear reaction.

6. Water circulates through the steel reactor vessel to prevent overheating.

5. The collision splits the atom, releasing more neutrons, which collide with other atoms or are absorbed by control rods. The heat produced by these collisions is used to produce steam.

Radiation

Neutron

**228 CHAPTER 8** Conserving Resources

## Science Journal

**Nuclear Power Plant** Sometimes people think something is a good idea but they don't want it in their own backyards. Have students describe in their journals how they might feel and what they might do if they learned of plans to build a nuclear power plant near their neighborhood.
L2 LS **Intrapersonal**

## Teacher FYI

**Yucca Mountain** The Yucca Mountain nuclear waste disposal site in Nevada has been under consideration since the late 1980s. To date, it is not operational and some people still are not convinced of the site's safety.

**Geothermal Energy** The hot, molten rock that lies deep beneath Earth's surface is also a source of energy. You see the effects of this energy when lava and hot gases escape from an erupting volcano or when hot water spews from a geyser. The heat energy contained in Earth's crust is called **geothermal energy.** Most geothermal power plants use this energy to produce steam to generate electricity.

Geothermal energy for power plants is available only where natural geysers or volcanoes are found. A geothermal power plant in California uses steam produced by geysers. The island nation of Iceland was formed by volcanoes, and geothermal energy is plentiful there. Geothermal power plants supply heat and electricity to about 90 percent of the homes in Iceland. Outdoor swimming areas also are heated with geothermal energy, as shown in **Figure 7.**

✔ **Reading Check** *Where does geothermal energy come from?*

**Solar Energy** The most inexhaustible source of energy for all life on Earth is the Sun. Solar energy is an alternative to fossil fuels. One use of solar energy is in solar-heated buildings. During winter in the northern hemisphere, the parts of a building that face south receive the most sunlight. Large windows placed on the south side of a building help heat it by allowing warm sunshine into the building during the day. Floors and walls of most solar-heated buildings are made of materials that absorb heat during the day. During the night, the stored heat is released slowly, keeping the building warm. **Figure 8** shows how solar energy can be used.

**Figure 7** In Iceland, a geothermal power plant pumps hot water out of the ground to heat buildings and generate electricity. Leftover hot water goes into this lake, making it warm enough for swimming even when the ground is covered with snow.

**Figure 8** The Zion National Park Visitor Center in Utah is a solar-heated building designed to save energy. The roof holds solar panels that are used to generate electricity. High windows can be opened to circulate air and help cool the building on hot days. The overhanging roof shades the windows during summer.

## Check for Understanding

**Logical-Mathematical** Using the board, brainstorm with students about the methods we use to obtain energy. Have them determine whether each source of energy is renewable or not and how the energy is obtained. L2

## Reteach

**Using Resources** Have students list reasons why renewable resources should be used wisely and nonrenewable resources should be conserved. L1

### ✔ Assessment

**Oral** Have students explain which energy alternative to fossil fuels they think has the most promise to decrease fossil fuel use. Have them justify their answers. Use **Performance Assessment in the Science Classroom,** p. 89. L2

Free electrons

Layers of semiconductor atoms

Electric current flows through the calculator and back to the PV cell to form a complete circuit.

Light

**Figure 9** Light energy from the Sun travels in tiny packets of energy called photons. Photons crash into the atoms of PV cells, knocking electrons loose. These electrons create an electric current.

**Solar Cells** Do you know how a solar-powered calculator works? How do spacecraft use sunlight to generate electricity? These devices use photovoltaic (foh toh vohl TAY ihk) cells to turn sunlight into electric current, as shown in **Figure 9.** Photovoltaic (PV) cells are small and easy to use. However, they produce electricity only in sunlight, so batteries are needed to store electricity for use at night or on cloudy days. Also, PV cells presently are too expensive to use for generating large amounts of electricity. Improvements in this technology continue to be made, and prices probably will go down in the future. As **Figure 10** shows, solar buildings and PV cells are just two of the many ways solar energy can be used to replace fossil fuels.

### section 1 review

#### Summary

**Natural Resources**
- All living things depend on natural resources to survive.
- Some resources are renewable, while other resources, such as petroleum, are nonrenewable.

**Fossil Fuels**
- Most of the energy that humans use comes from fossil fuels.
- Fossil fuels must be burned to release the energy stored in them, which causes air pollution.

**Alternatives to Fossil Fuels**
- Alternatives to fossil fuels include water power, wind power, nuclear power, geothermal energy, and solar energy.
- The Sun provides the most inexhaustible supply of energy for all life on Earth.

#### Self Check

1. **Summarize** What are natural resources?
2. **Compare and contrast** renewable and nonrenewable resources. Give five examples of each.
3. **Describe** the advantages and disadvantages of using nuclear power.
4. **Describe** two ways solar energy can be used to reduce fossil fuel use.
5. **Think Critically** Explain why the water that is used to cool the reactor vessel of a nuclear power plant is kept separate from the water that is heated to produce steam for the turbine generators.

##### Applying Math

6. **Solve One-Step Equations** Most cars in the U.S. are driven about 10,000 miles each year. If a car can travel 30 miles on one gallon of gasoline, how many gallons will it use in a year?

Science Online in7.msscience.com/self_check_quiz

### section 1 review

1. the raw materials that organisms use for survival or to enhance life
2. renewable: can be replaced quickly by nature, include water, plants, animals, sunlight, air; nonrenewable: cannot be replaced quickly by nature, include petroleum, diamonds, metals, phosphorous, topsoil.
3. advantage—produces huge amounts of energy, does not contribute to air pollution; disadvantage—nonrenewable, produces radioactive wastes that are difficult to dispose of
4. passively, to heat homes (and water) and thus reduce use of fuels
   for this purpose; directly, to make electricity directly so that fossil fuels don't have to be burned
5. to prevent possible radioactive contamination
6. $10,000/30 = 333.33$ gallons per year

## Figure 10

**S**unlight is a renewable energy source that provides an alternative to fossil fuels. Solar technologies use the Sun's energy in many ways—from heating to electricity generation.

▼ **ELECTRICITY** Photovoltaic (PV) cells turn sunlight into electric current. They are commonly used to power small devices, such as calculators. Panels that combine many PV cells provide enough electricity for a home—or an orbiting satellite, such as the International Space Station, below.

▲ **POWER PLANTS** In California's Mojave Desert, an experimental solar power plant used hundreds of mirrors to focus sunlight on a water-filled tower. The steam produced by this system generates enough electricity to power 2,400 homes.

▼ **COOKING** In hot, sunny weather, a solar oven or panel cooker can be used to cook a pot of rice or heat water. The powerful solar cooker shown below reaches even higher temperatures. It is being used to fry food.

▼ **INDOOR HEATING** South-facing windows and heat-absorbing construction materials turn a room into a solar collector that can help heat an entire building, such as this Connecticut home.

▲ **WATER HEATING** Water is heated as it flows through small pipes in this roof-mounted solar heat collector. The hot water then flows into an insulated tank for storage.

SECTION 1 Resources **231**

## Visualizing Solar Energy

Have students examine the pictures and read the captions. Then ask the following questions.

How are photovoltic cells similar to chloroplasts? How are they different? Possible answer: Both chloroplasts and photovoltic cells capture sunlight and turn it into another form of energy. Chloroplasts convert solar energy to chemical energy, and photovoltic cells convert solar energy into electric energy.

What are some potential disadvantages of using solar energy as the only source of energy for your home? How could you overcome these disadvantages? Possible answer: Solar energy might not be consistent or reliable; a cloudy day could result in no heat or electricity. However, a method of storing solar energy for future use would overcome this problem.

### Activity

**Capture the Sun's Energy** Have students work in pairs to make posters that diagram an innovative way to capture or use the Sun's energy. Encourage creative and different thinking. Have students explain their diagrams to the class. L3 P

## Differentiated Instruction

**Challenge** Have students research the percentage of energy used in the United States that was supplied by solar energy in the past year. Have the students compare this percentage to the percentage in 1950. L3

**232 CHAPTER 8** Conserving Resources

## 1 Motivate

**Bellringer**

**Section Focus Transparencies** also are available on the Interactive Chalkboard CD-ROM.

L2 ELL

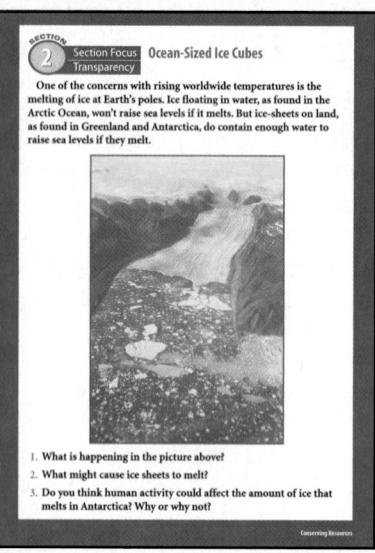

**Section Focus Transparency** Ocean-Sized Ice Cubes

One of the concerns with rising worldwide temperatures is the melting of ice at Earth's poles. Ice floating in water, as found in the Arctic Ocean, won't raise sea levels if it melts. But ice-sheets on land, as found in Greenland and Antarctica, do contain enough water to raise sea levels if they melt.

1. What is happening in the picture above?
2. What might cause ice sheets to melt?
3. Do you think human activity could affect the amount of ice that melts in Antarctica? Why or why not?

### Tie to Prior Knowledge

**Pollution** Most students will be familiar with some forms of pollution. Ask for examples. For each example, have students list what people can do to reduce that form of pollution.

### Caption Answer

**Figure 11** Smog can be reduced by using public transportation, and using vehicles that produce fewer pollutants.

---

**section 2**

Also covers: 7.1.8, 7.2.7, 7.3.16 (Detailed standards begin on page IN8.)

# Pollution

## as you read

**What You'll Learn**
- **Describe** types of air pollution.
- **Identify** causes of water pollution.
- **Explain** methods that can be used to prevent erosion.

**Why It's Important**
By understanding the causes of pollution, you can help solve pollution problems.

**Review Vocabulary**
**atmosphere:** the whole mass of air surrounding Earth

**New Vocabulary**
- pollutant
- acid precipitation
- greenhouse effect
- ozone depletion
- erosion
- hazardous waste

## Keeping the Environment Healthy

More than six billion people live on Earth. This large human population puts a strain on the environment, but each person can make a difference. You can help safeguard the environment by paying attention to how your use of natural resources affects air, land, and water.

## Air Pollution

On a still, sunny day in almost any large city, you might see a dark haze in the air, like that in **Figure 11.** The haze comes from pollutants that form when wood or fuels are burned. A **pollutant** is a substance that contaminates the environment. Air pollutants include soot, smoke, ash, and gases such as carbon dioxide, carbon monoxide, nitrogen oxides, and sulfur oxides. Wherever cars, trucks, airplanes, factories, homes, or power plants are found, air pollution is likely. Air pollution also can be caused by volcanic eruptions, wind-blown dust and sand, forest fires, and the evaporation of paints and other chemicals.

Smog is a form of air pollution created when sunlight reacts with pollutants produced by burning fuels. It can irritate the eyes and make breathing difficult for people with asthma or other lung diseases. Smog can be reduced if people take buses or trains instead of driving or if they use vehicles, such as electric cars, that produce fewer pollutants than gasoline-powered vehicles.

**Figure 11** The term *smog* was used for the first time in the early 1900s to describe the mixture of smoke and fog that often covers large cities in the industrial world. **Infer** *how smog can be reduced in large cities.*

**232 CHAPTER 8** Conserving Resources

---

## Section 2 Resource Manager

**Chapter *FAST FILE* Resources**
Transparency Activity, pp. 45, 47–48
Directed Reading for Content Mastery, p. 21
MiniLAB, p. 4
Enrichment, p. 31
Lab Activity, pp. 9–12

Reinforcement, p. 28
Lab Worksheet, pp. 5–6
**Reading and Writing Skill Activities,** pp. 19, 29
**Performance Assessment in the Science Classroom,** p. 48

---

**Figure 12** Compare these two photographs of the same statue. The photo on the left was taken before acid rain became a problem. The photo on the right shows acid rain damage. The pH scale, shown below, indicates whether a solution is acidic or basic.

## Acid Precipitation

Water vapor condenses on dust particles in the air to form droplets that combine to create clouds. Eventually, the droplets become large enough to fall to the ground as precipitation—mist, rain, snow, sleet, or hail. Air pollutants from the burning of fossil fuels can react with water in the atmosphere to form strong acids. Acidity is measured by a value called pH, as shown in **Figure 12. Acid precipitation** has a pH below 5.6.

**Effects of Acid Rain** Acid precipitation washes nutrients from the soil, which can lead to the death of trees and other plants. Runoff from acid rain that flows into a lake or pond can lower the pH of the water. If algae and microscopic organisms cannot survive in the acidic water, fish and other organisms that depend on them for food also die.

**Preventing Acid Rain** Sulfur from burning coal and nitrogen oxides from vehicle exhaust are the pollutants primarily responsible for acid rain. Using low-sulfur fuels, such as natural gas or low-sulfur coal, can help reduce acid precipitation. However, these fuels are less plentiful and more expensive than high-sulfur coal. Smokestacks that remove sulfur dioxide before it enters the atmosphere also help. Reducing automobile use and keeping car engines properly tuned can reduce acid rain caused by nitrogen oxide pollution. The use of electric cars, or hybrid-fuel cars that can run on electricity as well as gasoline, also could help.

### Mini LAB

**Measuring Acid Rain**

**Procedure**
1. Collect **rainwater** by placing a clean **cup** outdoors. Do not collect rainwater that has been in contact with any object or organism.
2. Dip a piece of **pH indicator paper** into the sample.
3. Compare the color of the paper to the pH chart provided. Record the pH of the rainwater.
4. Use separate pieces of pH paper to test the pH of **tap water** and **distilled water**. Record these results.

**Analysis**
1. Is the rainwater acidic, basic, or neutral?
2. How does the pH of the rainwater compare with the pH of tap water? With the pH of distilled water?

SECTION 2 Pollution **233**

## Curriculum Connection

**Social Studies** Vinegar is a mild acid that has been used for hundreds of years to preserve foods. Pickles and sauerkraut are examples of foods that were developed to take advantage of vinegar's acidic properties, which kill many microorganisms. Have students research other foods that are prepared in pickling solution. Fish, fruits and vegetables, and pig's feet are pickled, to name a few. L2

**Discussion**

**Automobile Usage** Guide students to predict the effects of increased automobile usage on renewable resources such as trees and crops. Have them draw conclusions about the effects of other human activities on Earth's renewable resources.

### Mini LAB

**Purpose** Students collect samples and determine the pH of rainwater. L2 COOP LEARN
**Kinesthetic**

**Materials** cups, pH paper, rain gauge (optional), rainwater, tap water, distilled water

**Teaching Strategies**
• If your school has a rain gauge, this is a convenient place to obtain rainwater. Otherwise, cups can be placed outside to catch rain.
• Have students test the pH of rain on different days throughout the school year to detect variations.

**Analysis**
1. The pH of most rainwater is acidic and averages 5.6. Student results may range from a pH of 4 to 7.
2. Tap water pH varies, but in most of the U.S. it is about 6; distilled water always has a pH of 7.

**Assessment**

**Performance** Set up several liquids of unknown pH. Have students use pH paper to test each and determine whether it is an acid or base. Then have them make a chart showing the pH of each unknown liquid and comparing the liquids with substances of known pH. Use **Performance Assessment in the Science Classroom,** p. 109.

**Greenhouse Effect** Compare the greenhouse effect to getting into a car with the windows rolled up on a summer day. It is much hotter inside the car than outside. L1

**$CO_2$ in the Atmosphere** The greenhouse effect has given Earth a sufficiently warm climate for life to flourish. Venus, however, has such a thick layer of $CO_2$ that its atmosphere is as hot as an oven. Some scientists predict that if people continue to add $CO_2$ to our atmosphere, Earth's atmospheric temperatures will increase. Other scientists think that if we produce more $CO_2$, plants will be able to use it to grow faster.

## Visual Learning

**Figure 13** Ask students what the glass in the greenhouse is analogous to in the atmosphere. carbon dioxide

**Science Online**

**Topic: Global Warming**
Visit in7.msscience.com for Web links to information about global warming.

**Activity** Describe three possible impacts of global warming. Provide one fact that supports global warming and one fact that does not.

**Carbon Dioxide Levels**

**Figure 13** The moment you step inside a greenhouse, you feel the results of the greenhouse effect. Heat trapped by the glass walls warms the air inside. In a similar way, atmospheric greenhouse gases trap heat close to Earth's surface.

# Greenhouse Effect

Sunlight travels through the atmosphere to Earth's surface. Some of this sunlight normally is reflected back into space. The rest is trapped by certain atmospheric gases, as shown in **Figure 13.** This heat-trapping feature of the atmosphere is the **greenhouse effect.** Without it, temperatures on Earth probably would be too cold to support life.

Atmospheric gases that trap heat are called greenhouse gases. One of the most important greenhouse gases is carbon dioxide ($CO_2$). $CO_2$ is a normal part of the atmosphere. It is also a waste product that forms when fossil fuels are burned. Over the past century, more fossil fuels have been burned than ever before, which is increasing the percentage of $CO_2$ in the atmosphere. The atmosphere might be trapping more of the Sun's heat, making Earth warmer. A rise in Earth's average temperature, possibly caused by an increase in greenhouse gases, is known as global warming.

**Global Warming** Temperature data collected from 1895 through 1995 indicate that Earth's average temperature increased about 1°C during that 100-year period. No one is certain whether this rise was caused by human activities or is a natural part of Earth's weather cycle. What kinds of changes might be caused by global warming? Changing rainfall patterns could alter ecosystems and affect the kinds of crops that can be grown in different parts of the world. The number of storms and hurricanes might increase. The polar ice caps might begin to melt, raising sea levels and flooding coastal areas. Warmer weather might allow tropical diseases, such as malaria, to become more widespread. Many people feel that the possibility of global warming is a good reason to reduce fossil fuel use.

Sunlight

Re-emitted energy

Greenhouse gases in atmosphere

Heat trapped near Earth's surface

**234** CHAPTER 8 Conserving Resources

## LAB DEMONSTRATION

**Purpose** to determine relative pH

**Materials** purple cabbage, hot plate, pot, water, strainer, 4 test tubes, stand, goggles, test materials: club soda, vinegar, ammonia, baking soda water

**Preparation** Boil the cabbage, cool, and strain. Retain the liquid.

**Procedure** Explain that purple cabbage juice can be used as a pH indicator. Add 1" juice to each tube. Add a small amount of one test material to each tube. Observe.

**Expected Outcome** Acids turn cabbage juice purple, bases turn it blue. The darker the color, the stronger the acid or base.

**Assessment**

Have students sort the test materials into acids. vinegar, club soda and bases ammonia, baking soda Set up another tube. Add lemon juice until the color changes. Have students identify lemon juice as an acid or base. acid

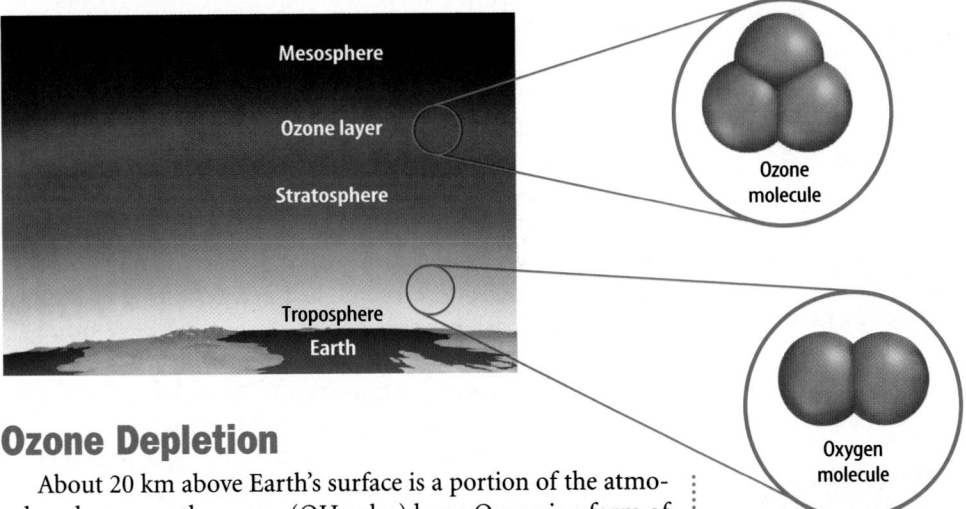

**Figure 14** The atmosphere's ozone layer absorbs large amounts of UV radiation, preventing it from reaching Earth's surface. Ozone molecules are made of three oxygen atoms. They are formed in a chemical reaction between sunlight and oxygen. The oxygen you breathe has two oxygen atoms in each molecule.

**Infer** *what will happen if the ozone layer continues to thin.*

## Ozone Depletion

About 20 km above Earth's surface is a portion of the atmosphere known as the ozone (OH zohn) layer. Ozone is a form of oxygen, as shown in **Figure 14.** The ozone layer absorbs some of the Sun's harmful ultraviolet (UV) radiation. UV radiation can damage living cells.

Every year, the ozone layer temporarily becomes thinner over each polar region during its spring season. The thinning of the ozone layer is called **ozone depletion.** This problem is caused by certain pollutant gases, especially chlorofluorocarbons (klor oh FLOR oh kar bunz) (CFCs). CFCs are used in the cooling systems of refrigerators, freezers, and air conditioners. When CFCs leak into the air, they slowly rise into the atmosphere until they arrive at the ozone layer. CFCs react chemically with ozone, breaking apart the ozone molecules.

**UV Radiation** Because of ozone depletion, the amount of UV radiation that reaches Earth's surface could be increasing. UV radiation could be causing a rise in the number of skin cancer cases in humans. It also might be harming other organisms. The ozone layer is so important to the survival of life on Earth that world governments and industries have agreed to stop making and using CFCs.

Ozone that is high in the upper atmosphere protects life on Earth. Near Earth's surface though, it can be harmful. Ozone is produced when fossil fuels are burned. This ozone stays in the lower atmosphere, where it pollutes the air. Ozone damages the lungs and other sensitive tissues of animals and plants. For example, it can cause the needles of a Ponderosa pine to drop, harming growth.

**Reading Check** *What is the difference between ozone in the upper atmosphere and ozone in the lower atmosphere?*

**Teacher** **FYI**

**CFCs** Although the production of CFC has halted, there is a reserve supply available for air conditioning and refrigeration units. In many cases, HFCs are being used as coolants to replace CFCs, as they do not lead to ozone depletion.

**Quick Demo**

**Chemical Bonds**

**Materials** none

**Estimated Time** one minute

**Procedure** Have two students join hands to represent the normal state of oxygen ($O_2$) and three students join hands to represent ozone ($O_3$). L1

**Reading Check**

**Answer** Ozone in the upper atmosphere is helpful to life; ozone in the lower atmosphere can be harmful to life as it pollutes the air.

**IDENTIFYING**
**Misconceptions**

**Cause and Effect** Students sometimes confuse common environmental problems. For example, they may think that not littering will help with the problem of acid rain. Make sure that for each problem, students understand the related causes and effects and what can be done to reduce the problem.

## Differentiated Instruction

**Challenge** Have students research monthly and annual changes in the ozone layer. Have students present graphs showing their results and discuss what environmental factors might explain the changes in the ozone layer. L3

## Cultural Diversity

**Sun Exposure** Australia leads the world in skin cancer because of the many fair-skinned people, the ozone hole over the country, and changes in culture. In the past, wealthy Australians avoided the Sun. After WWI, Australians embraced a tanned look. As a result, skin cancer rates rapidly increased. It has now become a culturally accepted practice to have children wear hats when they go outside.

**Caption Answer**

**Figure 14** The amount of UV radiation that reaches Earth could increase. This could cause an increase in the number of skin cancer cases in humans and might cause harm to other organisms.

**Indoor Air Pollution** Why might better-insulated buildings make indoor air pollution more of a problem? Less air enters and leaves a building. Why do radon levels tend to be higher in wintertime? People are more likely to keep windows tightly closed. Have students discuss the pros and cons of insulating buildings to this extent.

**Air Quality** Carbon monoxide has an affinity for hemoglobin in red blood cells, so when it attaches, it doesn't let go. This prevents red blood cells from functioning properly. Because of this, appliances designed for outdoor use should only be used outdoors, as they often are not equipped with ventilation devices for indoor use.

## IDENTIFYING Misconceptions

**Natural Pollution** Some students may think that people are responsible for all pollutants. Although many pollutants can be traced to people, radon is a naturally occurring substance. It is formed from the radioactive decay of uranium present in soil.

## Caption Answer

**Figure 15** Soils of the northern and northeastern portions of the U.S. produce more radon gas than in most other areas.

**INTEGRATE Health**

**Air Quality** Carbon monoxide enters the body through the lungs. It attaches to red blood cells, preventing the cells from absorbing oxygen. In your Science Journal, explain why heaters and barbecues designed for outdoor use never should be used indoors.

### Indiana Academic Standard Check

**7.4.14:** Explain that the environment may contain dangerous levels of substances . . . Understand, therefore, . . . steps to keep them safe.

✔ How can radon pollution be controlled in a building?

✔ improve ventilation

**Figure 15** The map shows the potential for radon exposure in different parts of the United States. **Identify** *the area of the country with soils that produce the most radon gas.*

# Indoor Air Pollution

Air pollution can occur indoors. Today's buildings are better insulated to conserve energy. However, better insulation reduces the flow of air into and out of a building, so air pollutants can build up indoors. For example, burning cigarettes release hazardous particles and gases into the air. Even non-smokers can suffer ill effects from secondhand cigarette smoke. As a result, smoking no longer is allowed in many public and private buildings. Paints, carpets, glues and adhesives, printers, and photocopy machines also give off dangerous gases, including formaldehyde. Like cigarette smoke, formaldehyde is a carcinogen, which means it can cause cancer.

**Carbon Monoxide** Carbon monoxide (CO) is a poisonous gas that is produced whenever charcoal, natural gas, kerosene, or other fuels are burned. CO poisoning can cause serious illness or death. Fuel-burning stoves and heaters must be designed to prevent CO from building up indoors. CO is colorless and odorless, so it is difficult to detect. Alarms that provide warning of a dangerous buildup of CO are being used in more and more homes.

**Radon** Radon is a naturally occurring, radioactive gas that is given off by some types of rock and soil, as shown in **Figure 15.** Radon has no color or odor. It can seep into basements and the lower floors of buildings. Radon exposure is the second leading cause of lung cancer in this country. A radon detector sounds an alarm when levels of the gas in indoor air become too high. If radon is present, increasing a building's ventilation can eliminate any damaging effects.

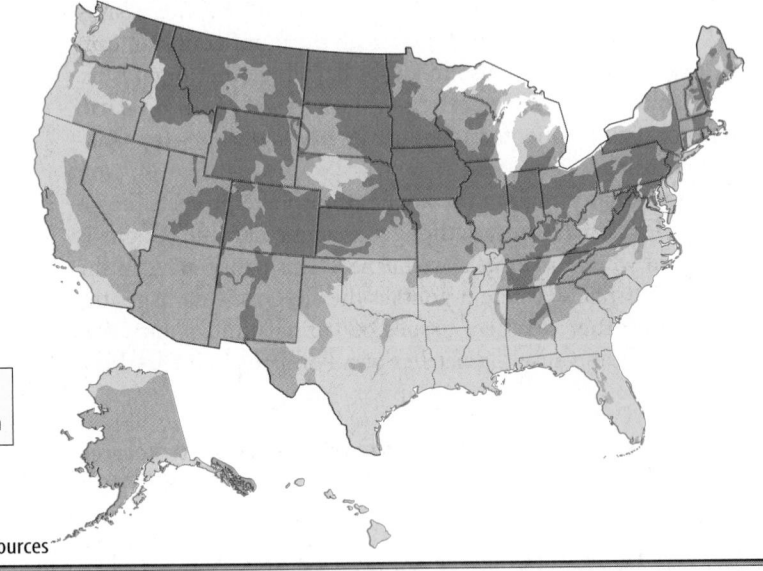

**Geologic radon potential**
Low  Moderate  High

## Teacher FYI

**Complete Combustion** If combustion were complete, only carbon dioxide and water would be produced. Complete combustion is hard to achieve, especially in a barbecue. This is why barbecues should not be used indoors.

## Curriculum Connection

**Health** Have students research sources of indoor air pollution. Suggest different students study the effects of asbestos, formaldehyde, radon, cigarette smoke, and other substances found in homes. Have students combine their findings and present them as an informative bulletin board. L2 COOP LEARN

When rain falls on roads and parking lots, it can wash oil and grease onto the soil and into nearby streams.

Rain can wash agricultural pesticides and fertilizers into lakes, streams, or oceans.

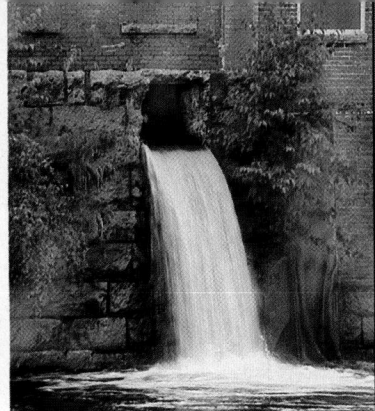

Industrial wastes are sometimes released directly into surface waters.

**Figure 16** Pollution of surface waters can occur in several ways, as shown above.

## Water Pollution

Pollutants enter water, too. Air pollutants can drift into water or be washed out of the sky by rain. Rain can wash land pollutants into waterways, as shown in **Figure 16.** Wastewater from factories and sewage-treatment plants often is released into waterways. In the United States and many other countries, laws require that wastewater be treated to remove pollutants before it is released. But, in many parts of the world, wastewater treatment is not always possible. Pollution also enters water when people dump litter or waste materials into rivers, lakes, and oceans.

**Surface Water** Some water pollutants poison fish and other wildlife, and can be harmful to people who swim in or drink the water. For example, chemical pesticides sprayed on farmland can wash into lakes and streams. These chemicals can harm the insects that fish, turtles, or frogs rely on for food. Shortages of food can lead to deaths among water-dwelling animals. Some pollutants, especially those containing mercury and other metals, can build up in the tissues of fish. Eating contaminated fish and shellfish can transfer these metals to people, birds, and other animals. In some areas, people are advised not to eat fish or shellfish taken from polluted waterways.

Algal blooms are another water pollution problem. Raw sewage and excess fertilizer contain large amounts of nitrogen. If they are washed into a lake or pond, they can cause the rapid growth of algae. When the algae die, they are decomposed by huge numbers of bacteria that use up much of the oxygen in the water. Fish and other organisms can die from a lack of oxygen in the water.

---

**Indiana Academic Standard Check**

**7.4.14:** Explain that the environment may contain dangerous levels of substances that are harmful to human beings. . . .

✔ How can surface water pollutants be harmful?

✔ They can poison wildlife that humans might consume. They also can harm humans that swim in or drink water.

---

---

---

## Cultural Diversity

**Significance of Water** Water is so important for civilization that it has become part of human culture. Water and waterscapes have been described in words, drawings, songs, and other art forms by all cultures on Earth. Water also plays an important part in religion. From Japanese Shintoism to Christianity, water symbolizes cleansing in spiritual ceremonies.

## Visual Learning

**Figure 18** Have students study the illustration. Emphasize that groundwater is an important source of water for many people. Then prepare a beaker with sand or soil on top and gravel on the bottom. Pour a little water on the soil's surface and show students how the water percolates through the layers to the bottom of the beaker. Have students relate this to the movement of groundwater shown in the illustration. L2 IS **Visual-Spatial**

## Oil Cleanup

**Purpose** to explore the process and cleanup of oil spills and discuss waste disposal of materials

**Possible Materials** cooking oil, clear-plastic bin, cotton balls, aquarium net, sand, liquid detergent, string, plastic spoons, paper towels, garbage bag

**Estimated Time** 1 class period

**Teaching Strategies**

• You can have students work in groups and assign each group a bin of water.

• Students can predict and observe what will happen to the oil when it is poured into the water.

• Students can write a procedure using the materials available to clean up the oil spill and then follow their procedure.

• After collecting their data, students can write suggestions for doing the experiment better.

**For additional inquiry activities, see** *Science Inquiry Labs.*

**Figure 18** Water from rainfall slowly filters through sand or soil until it is trapped in underground aquifers. Pollutants picked up by the water as it filters through the soil can contaminate water wells.

**Figure 17** In 1996, the oil tanker *Sea Empress* spilled more than 72 million kg of oil into the sea along the coast of Wales. More than $40 million was spent on the cleanup effort, but thousands of ocean organisms were destroyed, including birds, fish, and shellfish.

**Ocean Water** Rivers and streams eventually flow into oceans, bringing their pollutants along. Also, polluted water can enter the ocean in coastal areas where factories, sewage-treatment plants, or shipping activities are located. Oil spills are a well-known ocean pollution problem. About 4 billion kg of oil are spilled into ocean waters every year. Much of that oil comes from ships that use ocean water to wash out their fuel tanks. Oil also can come from oil tanker wrecks, as shown in **Figure 17.**

**Groundwater** Pollution can affect water that seeps underground, as shown in **Figure 18.** Groundwater is water that collects between particles of soil and rock. It comes from precipitation and runoff that soaks into the soil. This water can flow slowly through permeable layers of rock called aquifers. If this water comes into contact with pollutants as it moves through the soil and into an aquifer, the aquifer could become polluted. Polluted groundwater is difficult—and sometimes impossible—to clean. In some parts of the country, chemicals leaking from underground storage tanks have created groundwater pollution problems.

Pond

Well

Stream

Precipitation

Water table

Aquifer

238

Impermeable rock

## Science Journal

**Well Water** Have students imagine that they depend on a well as their source of water. They find out that pesticides that can injure their health have seeped into the groundwater the well draws from. Have students write in their Science Journals the changes they will make in their use of the well's water. L2 IS **Intrapersonal**

## Differentiated Instruction

**Hearing Impaired** Fill a funnel with soil and place it in a beaker. Add a teaspoon of food coloring to the top of the soil. Slowly pour water through the funnel. At first, water flowing out of the funnel is probably clear, but eventually colored water exits. Explain that soil may act as a filter for a time, but eventually pollutants will work their way through the soil. L1 ELL

Contour plowing reduces the downhill flow of water.

## Soil Loss

Fertile topsoil is important to plant growth. New topsoil takes hundreds or thousands of years to form. The Launch Lab at the beginning of this chapter shows that rain washes away loose topsoil. Wind also blows it away. The movement of soil from one place to another is called **erosion** (ih ROH zhun). Eroded soil that washes into a river or stream can block sunlight and slow photosynthesis. It also can harm fish, clams, and other organisms. Erosion is a natural process, but human activities increase it. When a farmer plows a field or a forest is cut down, soil is left bare. Bare soil is more easily carried away by rain and wind. **Figure 19** shows some methods farmers use to reduce soil erosion.

## Soil Pollution

Soil can become polluted when air pollutants drift to the ground or when water leaves pollutants behind as it flows through the soil. Soil also can be polluted when people toss litter on the ground or dispose of trash in landfills.

**Solid Wastes** What happens to the trash you throw out every week? What do people do with old refrigerators, TVs, and toys? Most of this solid waste is dumped in landfills. Most landfills are designed to seal out air and water. This helps prevent pollutants from seeping into surrounding soil, but it slows normal decay processes. Even food scraps and paper, which usually break down quickly, can last for decades in a landfill. In populated areas, landfills fill up quickly. Reducing the amount of trash people generate can reduce the need for new landfills.

**Figure 19** The farming methods shown here help prevent soil erosion.
**Infer** *why soil erosion is a concern for farmers.*

On steep hillsides, flat areas called terraces reduce downhill flow.

In strip cropping, cover crops are planted between rows to reduce wind erosion.

In no-till farming, soil is never left bare.

SECTION 2 Pollution **239**

**Figure 20** Leftover paints, batteries, pesticides, drain cleaners, and medicines are hazardous wastes that should not be discarded in the trash. They should never be poured down a drain, onto the ground, or into a storm sewer. Most communities have collection facilities where people can dispose of hazardous materials like these.

**Hazardous Wastes** Waste materials that are harmful to human health or poisonous to living organisms are **hazardous wastes.** They include dangerous chemicals, such as pesticides, oil, and petroleum-based solvents used in industry. They also include radioactive wastes from nuclear power plants, from hospitals that use radioactive materials to treat disease, and from nuclear weapons production. Many household items also are considered hazardous, such as those shown in **Figure 20.** If these materials are dumped into landfills, they could seep into the soil, surface water, or groundwater over time. Hazardous wastes usually are handled separately from trash. They are treated in ways that prevent environmental pollution.

**Reading Check** *What are hazardous wastes?*

## section 2 review

### Summary

**Air Pollution and Acid Precipitation**
- Vehicles, volcanoes, forest fires, and even wind-blown dust and sand can cause air pollution.
- Acid rain washes nutrients from the soil, which can harm plants.

**Greenhouse Effect and Ozone Depletion**
- $CO_2$ is a greenhouse gas that helps warm Earth.
- The ozone layer protects life on Earth.

**Indoor Air Pollution, Water Pollution, Soil Loss, and Soil Pollution**
- Pollutants can build up inside of buildings.
- There are many sources of water pollutants.
- Wind and rain can erode bare soil.
- Pollutants in soil decay more slowly than in air.

### Self Check

1. **List** four ways that air pollution affects the environment.
2. **Explain** how an algal bloom can affect other pond organisms.
3. **Describe** possible causes and effects of ozone depletion.
4. **Think Critically** How could hazardous wastes in landfills eventually affect groundwater?

#### Applying Math

5. **Solve a One-Step Equation** A solution of pH 4 is 10 times more acidic than one of pH 5, and it is 10 times more acidic than a solution of pH 6. How many times more acidic is the solution of pH 4 than the one of pH 6?

 Science Online in7.msscience.com/self_check_quiz

## section 2 review

1. smog, acid rain, enhanced greenhouse effect, ozone depletion
2. Algal blooms grow and eventually die. Their decay uses up oxygen, making it difficult for other organisms to survive.
3. CFCs that escape into the air can cause ozone depletion; as ozone is depleted, more UV radiation reached Earth, resulting in more cases of skin cancer.
4. They can leach into the soil and be picked up by groundwater, making the water hazardous for people to drink.
5. A solution with a pH of 4 is 100 times more acidic than a solution with a pH of 6.

# The Greenhouse Effect

You can create models of Earth with and without heat-reflecting green-house gases. Then, experiment with the models to observe the greenhouse effect.

## ◉ Real-World Question

How does the greenhouse effect influence temperatures on Earth?

### Goals
- **Observe** the greenhouse effect.
- **Describe** the effect that a heat source has on an environment.

### Materials
1-L clear-plastic, soft-drink bottles with tops cut off and labels removed (2)
thermometers (2)
*temperature probe
potting soil
masking tape
plastic wrap
rubber band
lamp with 100-W lightbulb
watch or clock with second hand
*Alternate materials

**Safety Precautions** 🥽🧤🔥✋🌡

## ◉ Procedure

1. Copy the data table and use it to record your temperature measurements.
2. Put an equal volume of potting soil in the bottom of each container.
3. Use masking tape to attach a thermometer to the inside of each container. Place each thermometer at the same height above the soil. Shield each thermometer bulb by putting a double layer of masking tape over it.

### Changes in Temperature

| Time (min) | Open Container Temperature (°C) | Closed Container Temperature (°C) |
|---|---|---|
| 0 | | |
| 2 | Answers will vary. | |
| 4 | | |
| 6 | | |

4. Seal the top of one container with plastic wrap held in place with a rubber band.
5. Place the lamp with the exposed 100-W light-bulb between the two containers and exactly 1 cm away from each. Do not turn on the light.
6. Let the setup sit for 5 min, then record the temperature in each container.
7. Turn on the light. Record the temperature in each container every 2 min for 15 min to 20 min. Graph the results.

## ◉ Conclude and Apply

1. **Compare and contrast** temperatures in each container at the end of the experiment.
2. **Infer** What does the lightbulb represent in this experimental model? What does the plastic wrap represent?

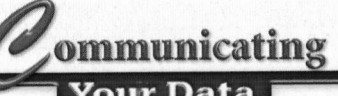

Average the data obtained in the experiments conducted by all the groups in your class. Prepare a line graph of these data. **For more help, refer to the** Science Skill Handbook.

**LAB** 241

## ◉ Real-World Question

**Purpose** Students make models of the atmosphere and determine what happens when light shines on the model. L2
COOP LEARN **IS** **Interpersonal**

**Process Skills** model, observe and infer, interpret data, communicate, compare and contrast, recognize cause and effect, measure in SI, make and use tables, make and use graphs

**Time Required** 50 minutes

## ◉ Procedure

**Safety Precautions** Caution students to use care in working with thermometers and 100-W lightbulbs. Use only alcohol thermometers.

### Teaching Strategies
- Drafts can affect results.
- Make sure the thermometers face outward to make it easier for students to read them.

**Troubleshooting** If the two thermometers did not read the same temperature when the experiment began, adjust readings so both data sets can be plotted on the same graph.

## ◉ Conclude and Apply

1. The temperatures of both containers has increased. The container covered with plastic wrap had a greater increase.
2. The light bulb represents the Sun; the plastic wrap represents carbon dioxide in the atmosphere.

---

### ☑ Assessment

**Oral** Have students summarize the information in their graphs in writing. Make sure summaries are clear and concise. Use **Performance Assessment in the Science Classroom,** p. 113.

### *Communicating* Your Data

Have students write the final temperatures for the two conditions on the board. Students should compare data and see if the results were the same for everyone. Discuss how differences may have occurred.

## section
### 3

Also covers: 7.3.16 (Detailed standards begin on page IN8.)

# The Three Rs of Conservation

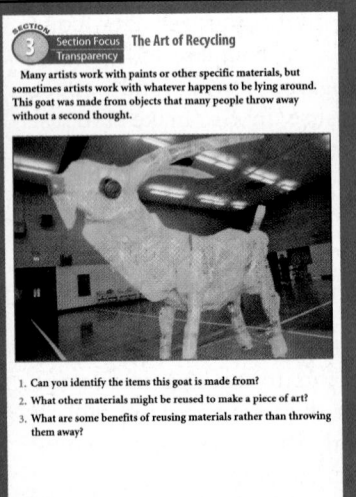
### as you read

#### *What* You'll Learn
- **Recognize** ways you can reduce your use of natural resources.
- **Explain** how you can reuse resources to promote conservation.
- **Describe** how many materials can be recycled.

#### *Why* It's Important
Conservation preserves resources and reduces pollution.

#### Review Vocabulary
**reprocessing:** to subject to a special process or treatment in preparation for reuse

#### New Vocabulary
- recycling

**Figure 21** Worn-out automobile tires can have other useful purposes.

## Conservation

A teacher travels to school in a car pool. In the school cafeteria, students place glass bottles and cans in separate containers from the rest of the garbage. Conservation efforts like these can help prevent shortages of natural resources, slow growth of landfills, reduce pollution levels, and save people money. Every time a new landfill is created, an ecosystem is disturbed. Reducing the need for landfills is a major benefit of conservation. The three Rs of conservation are reduce, reuse, and recycle.

## Reduce

You contribute to conservation whenever you reduce your use of natural resources. You use less fossil fuel when you walk or ride a bicycle instead of taking the bus or riding in a car. If you buy a carton of milk, reduce your use of petroleum by telling the clerk you don't need a plastic bag to carry it in.

You also can avoid buying things you don't need. For example, most of the paper, plastic, and cardboard used to package items for display on store shelves is thrown away as soon as the product is brought home. You can look for products with less packaging or with packaging made from recycled materials. What are some other ways you can reduce your use of natural resources?

## Reuse

Another way to help conserve natural resources is to use items more than once. Reusing an item means using it again without changing it or reprocessing it, as shown in **Figure 21.** Bring reusable canvas bags to the grocery store to carry home your purchases. Donate clothes you've outgrown to charity so that others can reuse them. Take reusable plates and utensils on picnics instead of disposable paper items.

242

### Section 3 Resource Manager

# Recycle

If you can't avoid using an item, and if you can't reuse it, the next best thing is to recycle it. **Recycling** is a form of reuse that requires changing or reprocessing an item or natural resource. If your city or town has a curbside recycling program, you already separate recyclables from the rest of your garbage. Materials that can be recycled include glass, metals, paper, plastics, and yard and kitchen waste.

**✔ Reading Check** *How is recycling different from reusing?*

**Plastics** Plastic is more difficult to recycle than other materials, mainly because several types of plastic are in use. A recycle code marked on every plastic container indicates the type of plastic it is made of. Plastic soft-drink bottles, like the one shown in **Figure 22,** are made of type 1 plastic and are the easiest to recycle. Most plastic bags are made of type 2 or type 4 plastic; they can be reused as well as recycled. Types 6 and 7 can't be recycled at all because they are made of a mixture of different plastics. Each type of plastic must be separated carefully before it is recycled because a single piece of a different type of plastic can ruin an entire batch.

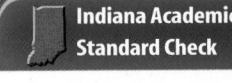
**Indiana Academic Standard Check**

**7.4.14:** Explain that the environment may contain dangerous levels of substances . . . Understand, therefore, . . . steps to keep them safe.

✔ Why are the three Rs of conservation important?

✔ They help prevent shortages of natural resources, slow growth of landfills, reduce pollution levels, and save people money.

**Figure 22** Many soft-drink bottles are made of PETE, which is the most common type of recyclable plastic. It can be melted down and spun into fibers to make carpets, paintbrushes, rope, and clothing. **Identify** *other products made out of recycled materials.*

## Discussion

**Over-Packaging** Bring in a product that is clearly over-packaged. Have students suggest ways to reduce the amount of material used in the packaging of this item.

## Activity

**Brainstorm** Find an item that is commonly thrown out, such as a plastic soft-drink bottle. Have students brainstorm a list of possible ways to reuse the bottle. L2 ELL IS **Interpersonal**

**✔ Reading Check**

**Answer** Reusing does not require reprocessing; recycling does.

## Caption Answer

**Figure 22** Packaging, paper, glass bottles, furniture, auto parts, and construction and landscaping products are some examples of materials made from recycled material.

## Quick Demo

**Recycling**

**Materials** cans, cereal boxes, other products with recycling symbol or made from recycled material

**Estimated Time** one minute

**Procedure** Lay products out on a table and have students note whether the packaging has a recycle symbol or if the package states that it is made of recycled material. Explain that many products can be recycled and made from recycled materials.

# Differentiated Instruction

**Challenge** Have students find as many products as they can that are recycled and what material they are made up of. Then have them research the types of material that are commonly recycled and present a report of their findings. L3

# Visual Learning

**Figure 22** The objects in these photographs are made from the same type 1 plastic (PET). Ask students to bring in materials with this symbol on them. When the objects are collected, discuss why recycling is a good idea. Possible answer: It reduces the amount of nonbiodegradable materials going into landfills. L2

## IDENTIFYING Misconceptions

**Recycled Paper** Many people think that recycled paper is paper that has been used by consumers. Most of it, however, comes from wood or paper scrap in logging or paper manufacturing. Some companies indicate how much recycled paper comes directly from consumers by labeling the percent that is post-consumer content.

## Applying Science

### Answer

Students' lists should include some of each type of item. Possible exceptions would be yard wastes, depending on the season, and newspapers. The percentages will depend on student data. Tin cans are steel cans coated with tin. They should be included.

## Science Online

**Topic: Recycling**

Visit in7.msscience.com for Web links to information about recycling bottles and cans.

**Activity** Write one argument in support of a money deposit for bottles and cans and one argument against it. Provide data to support one of your arguments.

**Metals** The manufacturing industry has been recycling all kinds of metals, especially steel, for decades. At least 25 percent of the steel in cans, appliances, and automobiles is recycled steel. Up to 100 percent of the steel in plates and beams used to build skyscrapers is made from reprocessed steel. About one metric ton of recycled steel saves about 1.1 metric tons of iron ore and 0.5 metric ton of coal. Using recycled steel to make new steel products reduces energy use by 75 percent. Other metals, including iron, copper, aluminum, and lead also can be recycled.

You can conserve metals by recycling food cans, which are mostly steel, and aluminum cans. It takes less energy to make a can from recycled aluminum than from raw materials. Also, remember that recycled cans do not take up space in landfills.

**Glass** When sterilized, glass bottles and jars can be reused. They also can be melted and re-formed into new bottles, especially those made of clear glass. Most glass bottles already contain at least 25 percent recycled glass. Glass can be recycled again and again. It never needs to be thrown away. Recycling about one metric ton of glass saves more than one metric ton of mineral resources and reduces the energy used to make new glass by 25 percent or more.

## Applying Science

### What items are you recycling at home?

Many communities have recycling programs. Recyclable items may be picked up at the curbside, taken to a collection site, or the resident may hire a licensed recycling handler to pick them up. What do you recycle in your home?

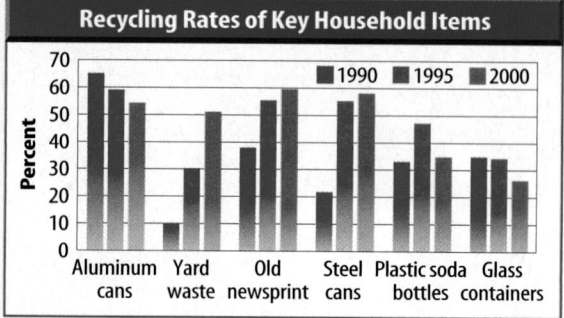

Recycling Rates of Key Household Items

Source: U.S. EPA, 2003

### Identifying the Problem

This bar graph shows the recycling rates in the U. S. of six types of household items for the years 1990, 1995, and 2000. What are you and your classmates' recycling rates?

### Solving the Problem

For one week, list each glass, plastic, and aluminum item you use. Note which items you throw away and which ones you recycle. Calculate the percentage of glass, plastic, and aluminum you recycled. How do your percentages compare with those on the graph?

**244 CHAPTER 8** Conserving Resources

## Teacher FYI

**Compost** Composting is considered recycling because the form of the materials is changed (through decay) so they can be used again.

## Differentiated Instruction

**Challenge** Have students investigate the trash generated by your school's cafeteria. Challenge them to devise a plan to reduce the amount of trash that is thrown away. Have them write a report on their investigation and plan. **L3** **P**

**Paper** Used paper is recycled into paper towels, insulation, newsprint, cardboard, and stationery. Ranchers and dairy farmers sometimes use shredded paper instead of straw for bedding in barns and stables. Used paper can be made into compost. Recycling about one metric ton of paper saves 17 trees, more than 26,000 L of water, close to 1,900 L of oil, and more than 4,000 kW of electric energy. You can do your part by recycling newspapers, notebook and printer paper, cardboard, and junk mail.

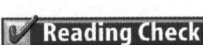 **Reading Check** *What nonrenewable resource(s) do you conserve by recycling paper?*

**Compost** Grass clippings, leaves, and fruit and vegetable scraps that are discarded in a landfill can remain there for decades without breaking down. The same items can be turned into soil-enriching compost in just a few weeks, as shown in **Figure 23**. Many communities distribute compost bins to encourage residents to recycle fruit and vegetable scraps and yard waste.

**Buy Recycled** People have become so good at recycling that recyclable materials are piling up, just waiting to be put to use. You can help by reading labels when you shop and choosing products that contain recycled materials. What other ways of recycling natural resources can you think of?

**Figure 23** Composting is a way of turning plant material you would otherwise throw away into rich garden soil. Dry leaves and weeds, grass clippings, vegetable trimmings, and nonmeat food scraps can be composted.

## section 3 review

### Summary

**Conservation**
- The three Rs of conservation are reduce, reuse, and recycle.

**Reduce**
- You can contribute to conservation by reducing your use of natural resources.

**Reuse**
- Some items can be used more than once, such as reusable canvas bags for groceries.

**Recycle**
- Some items can be recycled, including some plastics, metal, glass, and paper.
- Grass clippings, leaves, and fruit and vegetable scraps can be composted into rich garden soil.

### Self Check

1. **Describe** at least three actions you could take to reduce your use of natural resources.
2. **Describe** how you could reuse three items people usually throw away.
3. **Think Critically** Why is reusing something better than recycling it?

**Applying Skills**

4. **Make and Use Tables** Make a table of data of the number of aluminum cans thrown away in the United States: 2.7 billion in 1970; 11.1 billion in 1974; 21.3 billion in 1978; 22.7 billion in 1982; 35.0 billion in 1986; 33.8 billion in 1990; 38.5 billion in 1994; 45.5 billion in 1998; 50.7 billion in 2001.

 **Science Online** in7.msscience.com/self_check_quiz

## section 3 review

1. Possible answers: turn off lights in vacant rooms, buy materials with less packaging, carpool, buy items made from recycled materials

2. Possible answers: store water in plastic soft-drink bottles, use plastic grocery bags as trash can liners, use margarine tubs to store left-over food.

3. There is less energy used in reusing than in recycling.
4. Check tables for accuracy.

## Model and Invent

### Real-World Question

**Purpose** Students will design and build a solar cooker.

**Process Skills** design and make a model, research, compare

**Time Required** one class period

**Discussion** Discuss with students the problems some people in the world face just trying to cook a meal. Explain to students that in some places where fuel is scarce, people use solar cookers to prepare food. Why do people cook most food? Possible answers: to improve taste, to kill harmful bacteria Why does cooking food require energy? Energy is needed to raise the temperature of the food.

**Alternate Materials** Oven bags are available at most supermarkets. Kitchen timers are available at most hardware stores.

**Safety Precautions** Remind students to use insulated gloves or tongs when handling hot objects.

### Goals
- **Research** designs for solar panel cookers or box cookers.
- **Design** a solar cooker that can be used to cook food.
- **Plan** an experiment to measure the effectiveness of your solar cooker.

### Possible Materials
poster board
cardboard boxes
aluminum foil
string
wire coat hangers
clear plastic sheets
*oven bags
black cookware
thermometer
stopwatch
*timer
glue
tape
scissors
*Alternate materials

### Safety Precautions

**WARNING:** *Be careful when cutting materials. Your solar cooker will get hot. Use insulated gloves or tongs to handle hot objects.*

# Solar Cooking

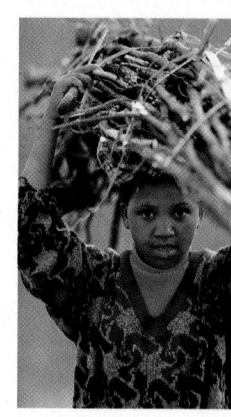

### Real-World Question

The disappearance of forests in some places on Earth has made firewood extremely difficult and expensive to obtain. People living in these regions often have to travel long distances or sell some of their food to get firewood. This can be a serious problem for people who may not have much food to begin with. Is there a way they could cook food without using firewood? How would you design and build a cooking device that uses the Sun's energy?

### Make the Model

1. **Design** a solar cooker. In your Science Journal, explain why you chose this design and draw a picture of it.

2. **Write** a summary explaining how you will measure the effectiveness of your solar cooker. What will you measure? How will you collect and organize your data? How will you present your results?

## Fun Fact

The Sun converts approximately 4 million tons of hydrogen gas into energy every second.

## Differentiated Instruction

**Learning Disabled** Assign these students the task of gathering the materials their group decides they want to use. L1

3. **Compare** your solar cooker design to those of other students.

4. Share your experimental plan with students in your class. Discuss the reasoning behind your plan. Be specific about what you intend to test and how you are going to test it.

5. Make sure your teacher approves your plan before you start working on your model.

6. Using all of the information you have gathered, construct a solar cooker that follows your design.

## ▶ Test the Model

1. **Test** your design to determine how well it works. Try out a classmate's design. How do the two compare?

## ▶ Analyze Your Data

1. Combine the results for your entire class and decide which type of solar cooker was most effective. How could you design a more effective solar cooker, based on what you learned from this activity?

2. **Infer** Do you think your results might have been different if you tested your solar cooker on a different day? Explain. Why might a solar cooker be more useful in some regions of the world than in others?

## ▶ Conclude and Apply

1. **Infer** Based on what you've read and the results obtained by you and your classmates, do you think that your solar cooker could boil water? Explain.

2. **Compare** the amount of time needed to cook food with a solar cooker and with more traditional cooking methods. Assuming plenty of sunlight is available, would you prefer to use a solar cooker or a traditional oven? Explain.

### Communicating Your Data

**Prepare** a demonstration showing how to use a solar cooker. Present your demonstration to another class of students or to a group of friends or relatives. **For more help, refer to the** Science Skill Handbook.

**LAB 247**

---

### ✓ Assessment

**Process** Have students use a foam cup of water with a thermometer in it to test whether their solar ovens can boil water. Be sure that each group uses the same amount of water for the test and that students record the time it takes to boil the water. Based on the results, have students rank the solar cooker designs from best to worst. Use **Performance Assessment in the Science Classroom,** p. 97.

### Communicating Your Data

Students should prepare a poster that shows the construction of their solar cooker and an explanation of how it works.

---

## ▶ Make a Model

### Teaching Strategies

• Comparisons of solar cookers will be difficult if students do not use the same method of testing them.

• You might want to have a cook-off with the two best solar ovens to see which one could cook a small red potato in the shortest time. Be sure both potatoes are the same size.

• Students can move the cookers during the testing to keep them in the sunlight.

## ▶ Test Your Model

**Expected Outcome** Solar cookers should be able to raise the temperature of a cup of water to at least 75°C. A well-designed cooker might reach temperatures approaching 150°C.

## ▶ Analyze Your Data

1. Answers will depend on the designs of the solar cookers that are compared.

2. Results would vary in different weather conditions. Solar cookers function best on clear, sunny days. Solar cookers are more useful in areas that have many clear, sunny days.

## ▶ Conclude and Apply

1. Answers will depend on the success of the design. Some well-designed cookers could boil water.

2. Solar cookers generally take two to three times as long to cook a meal as a traditional oven. However, the energy for a solar cooker is free and the energy for a traditional oven is not.

## Understanding Literature

**Cause and Effect** Answers will vary but might include that bottle caps litter the picnic area and that exhaust fumes from cars make the snow banks dark and gray.

## Respond to the Reading

1. The four verses correspond to the four seasons.
2. Human activity (civilization) has plagiarized beauty.
3. **Linking Science and Writing** Students could review chapter and list conservation methods to include in their poem.

 **Renewing Resources**

Even renewable resources can be rendered nonrenewable. This happens when renewable resources are removed at a rate that prevents their renewal, or if the environment that supports them deteriorates faster than renewal can take place. For example, although forests are considered a renewable resource, if they are not carefully managed they can disappear as a result of excessive logging or clear-cutting. Also, although Earth's supply of air is inexhaustible, the quality of Earth's air can be affected by human activity, and air quality directly affects other renewable resources.

# Beauty Plagiarized
## by Amitabha Mukerjee

I wandered lonely as a cloud –
Except for a motorboat,
Nary a soul in sight.
Beside the lake beneath the trees,
Next to the barbed wire fence,
There was a picnic table
And beer bottle caps from many years.
A boat ramp to the left,
And the chimney from a power station on the
    other side,
A summer haze hung in the air,
And the lazy drone of traffic far away.

Crimson autumn of mists and mellow fruitfulness
Blue plastic covers the swimming pools
The leaves fall so I can see
Dark glass reflections in the building
That came up
where the pine cones crunched underfoot . . .

And then it is snow
White lining on trees and rooftops . . .
And through my windshield wipers
The snow is piled dark and grey . . .
Next to my driveway where I check my mail
Little footprints on fresh snow —
A visiting rabbit.

I knew a bank where the wild thyme blew
Over-canopied with luscious woodbine
It is now a landfill —
Fermentation of civilization
Flowers on TV
Hyacinth rose tulip chrysanthemum
Acres of colour
Wind up wrapped in decorous plastic,
In this landfill where oxlips grew. . .

## Understanding Literature

**Cause and Effect** Recognizing cause-and-effect relationships can help you make sense out of what you read. One event causes another event. The second event is the effect of the first event. In the poem, the author describes the causes and effects of pollution and waste. What effects do pollution and the use of nonrenewable resources have on nature in the poem?

## Respond to the Reading

1. To plagiarize is to copy without giving credit to the source. In this poem, who or what has plagiarized beauty?
2. What do the four verses in the poem correspond to?
3. **Linking Science and Writing** Write a poem that shows how conservation methods could restore the beauty in nature.

 The poet makes a connection between the four seasons of the year and the pollution and waste products created by human activity, or civilization. For example, in the spring, a landfill for dumping garbage replaces a field of wildflowers. Describing four seasons instead of one reinforces the poet's message that the beauty of nature has been stolen, or plagiarized.

## Resources for Teachers and Students

*A Walk in the Woods: Rediscovering America on the Appalachian Trail*, by Bill Bryson, Broadway Books, 1999

*The Best American Science & Nature Writing 2000*, ed. Burkhard Bilger, Houghton Mifflin Co., 2000

*Lost Woods: The Discovered Writing of Rachel Carson*, by Rachel Carson, ed. Linda Lear, Beacon Press, 1999

## Reviewing Main Ideas

### Section 1 Resources

1. Natural resources are the parts of the environment that supply materials needed for the survival of living organisms.

2. Renewable resources are being replaced continually by natural processes.

3. Nonrenewable resources cannot be replaced or are replaced very slowly.

4. Energy sources include fossil fuels, wind, solar energy, geothermal energy, hydroelectric power, and nuclear power.

### Section 2 Pollution

1. Most air pollution is made up of waste products from the burning of fossil fuels.

2. The greenhouse effect is the warming of Earth by a blanket of heat-reflecting gases in the atmosphere.

3. Water can be polluted by acid rain and by the spilling of oil or other wastes into waterways.

4. Solid wastes and hazardous wastes dumped on land or disposed of in landfills can pollute the soil. Erosion can cause the loss of fertile topsoil.

### Section 3 The Three Rs of Conservation

1. You can reduce your use of natural resources in many ways.

2. Reusing items is an excellent way to practice conservation.

3. In recycling, materials are changed in some way so that they can be used again.

4. Materials that can be recycled include paper, metals, glass, plastics, yard waste, and nonmeat kitchen scraps.

## Visualizing Main Ideas

*Copy and complete the following concept map using the terms* smog, acid precipitation, *and* ozone depletion.

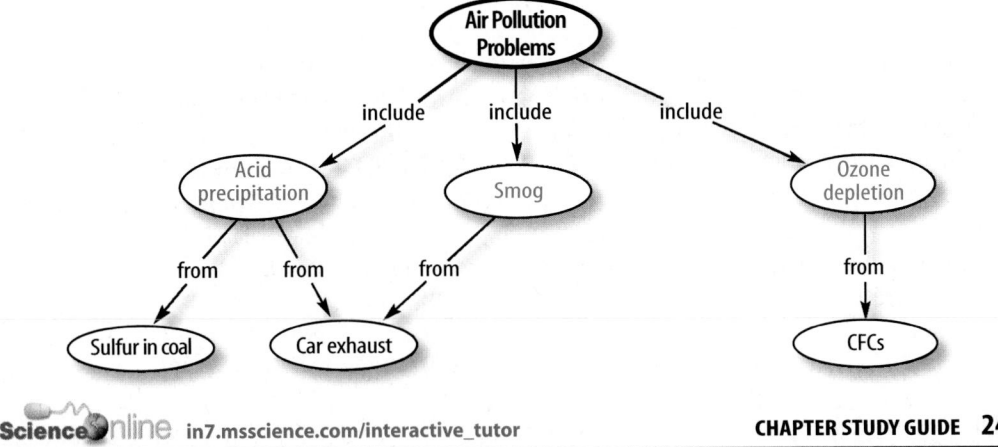

Science Online in7.msscience.com/interactive_tutor

**CHAPTER STUDY GUIDE** 249

## Reviewing Main Ideas

Summary statements can be used by students to review the major concepts of the chapter.

## Visualizing Main Ideas

See student page.

Science Online

**Visit** in7.msscience.com
/self_check_quiz
/interactive_tutor
/vocabulary_puzzlemaker
/chapter_review
/standards_review

## Assessment Transparency

For additional assessment questions, use the *Assessment Transparency* located in the transparency book.

## Using Vocabulary

1. Petroleum is a type of fossil fuel.
2. Erosion produces pollutants and degrades the environment.
3. These are both types of air pollution, but one does not cause the other.
4. The burning of fossil fuels and the release of excess carbon dioxide may enhance the greenhouse effect.
5. The use of nuclear energy generates radioactive materials, which are hazardous wastes.
6. The use of hydroelectric power can decrease the use of fossil fuels.
7. Coal is a fossil fuel. The burning of coal that contains sulfur causes acid precipitation.
8. The pollutant called CFC causes ozone depletion.
9. Recycling is a good way of conserving nonrenewable resources.
10. The use of geothermal energy can decrease the use of fossil fuels.

## Checking Concepts

| 11. B | 14. B | 17. B |
|-------|-------|-------|
| 12. C | 15. C | 18. A |
| 13. C | 16. C | |

## Thinking Critically

19. Most geothermal energy is used to produce steam that rotates turbine blades of an electric generator.
20. Fossil fuels were formed from plants and animals. Wood is from a plant.
21. Desert region; sunshine is more constant there than at the poles.
22. to prevent erosion of topsoil
23. Yes; it is constantly replaced and has many uses.
24. Solar, wind, geothermal, and water energy are renewable resources. Nuclear energy is not a renewable resource, but no severe shortages are expected.
25. Reusing the bag would save energy because it wouldn't need to be changed back into its raw form and then a new bag made.

## Using Vocabulary

| | |
|---|---|
| acid precipitation p. 233 | nonrenewable |
| erosion p. 239 | resource p. 225 |
| fossil fuel p. 226 | nuclear energy p. 228 |
| geothermal energy p. 229 | ozone depletion p. 235 |
| greenhouse effect p. 234 | petroleum p. 225 |
| hazardous waste p. 240 | pollutant p. 232 |
| hydroelectric power p. 227 | recycling p. 243 |
| natural resource p. 224 | renewable resource p. 224 |

*Explain the differences in the vocabulary words given below. Then explain how the words are related. Use complete sentences in your answers.*

1. fossil fuel—petroleum
2. erosion—pollutant
3. ozone depletion—acid precipitation
4. greenhouse effect—fossil fuels
5. hazardous wastes—nuclear energy
6. hydroelectric power—fossil fuels
7. acid precipitation—fossil fuels
8. ozone depletion—pollutant
9. recycle—nonrenewable resources
10. geothermal energy—fossil fuels

## Checking Concepts

*Choose the word or phrase that best answers the question.*

11. An architect wants to design a solar house in the northern hemisphere. For maximum warmth, which side of the house should have the most windows?
    A) north       C) east
    B) south       D) west

12. Of the following, which is considered a renewable resource?
    A) coal        C) sunlight
    B) oil         D) aluminum

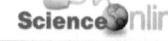 Science Online in7.msscience.com/vocabulary_puzzlemaker

Use the photo below to answer question 13.

13. Which energy resource is shown in the photo?
    A) solar energy
    B) geothermal energy
    C) hydroelectric energy
    D) photovoltaic energy

14. Which of the following is a fossil fuel?
    A) wood        C) nuclear power
    B) oil         D) photovoltaic cell

15. Which of the following contributes to ozone depletion?
    A) carbon dioxide   C) CFCs
    B) radon            D) carbon monoxide

16. What is a substance that contaminates the environment called?
    A) acid rain   C) pollutant
    B) pollution   D) ozone

17. If there were no greenhouse effect in Earth's atmosphere, which of the following statements would be true?
    A) Earth would be much hotter.
    B) Earth would be much colder.
    C) The temperature of Earth would be the same.
    D) The polar ice caps would melt.

18. Which of the following can change solar energy into electricity?
    A) photovoltaic cells
    B) smog
    C) nuclear power plants
    D) geothermal power plants

**Use the Exam*View*® Pro Testmaker CD-ROM to:**
- create multiple versions of tests
- create modified tests with one mouse click for inclusion students
- edit existing questions and add your own questions
- build tests aligned with state standards using built-in State Curriculum Tags
- change English tests to Spanish with one mouse click and vice versa

## Thinking Critically

**19. Explain** how geothermal energy is used to produce electricity.

**20. Infer** why burning wood and burning fossil fuels produce similar pollutants.

**Use the photos below to answer question 21.**

**21. Draw a Conclusion** Which would make a better location for a solar power plant—a polar region (left) or a desert region (right)? Why?

**22. Explain** why it is beneficial to grow a different crop on soil after the major crop has been harvested.

**23. Infer** Is garbage a renewable resource? Why or why not?

**24. Summarize** Solar, nuclear, wind, water, and geothermal energy are alternatives to fossil fuels. Are they all renewable? Why or why not?

**25. Draw Conclusions** Would you save more energy by recycling or reusing a plastic bag?

**26. Recognize Cause and Effect** Forests use large amounts of carbon dioxide during photosynthesis. How might cutting down a large percentage of Earth's forests affect the greenhouse effect?

**27. Form a hypothesis** about why Americans throw away more aluminum cans each year.

**28. Compare and contrast** contour farming, terracing, strip cropping, and no-till farming.

## Performance Activities

**29. Poster** Create a poster to illustrate and describe three things students at your school can do to conserve natural resources.

## Applying Math

**Use the table below to answer questions 30 and 31.**

### Estimated Recycling Rates

| Item | Percent Recycled |
|------|------------------|
| Aluminum cans | 60 |
| Glass beverage bottles | 31 |
| Plastic soft-drink containers | 37 |
| Newsprint | 56 |
| Magazines | 23 |

**30. Recycling Rates** Make a bar graph of the data above.

**31. Bottle Recycling** For every 1,000 glass beverage bottles that are produced, how many are recycled?

**32. Nonrenewable Resources** 45.8 billion (45,800,000,000) cans were thrown away in 2000. If it takes 33.79 cans to equal one pound and the average scrap value is \$0.58/lb, then what was the total dollar value of the discarded cans?

**33. Ozone Depletion** The thin ozone layer called the "ozone hole" over Antarctica reached nearly 27,000,000 $km^2$ in 1998. To conceptualize this, the United States has a geographical area of 9,363,130 $km^2$. How much larger is the "ozone hole" in comparison to the United States?

**34. Increased $CO_2$ Levels** To determine the effects of increased $CO_2$ levels in the atmosphere, scientists increased the $CO_2$ concentration by 70 percent in an enclosed rain forest environment. If the initial $CO_2$ concentration was 430 parts per million, what was it after the increase?

Science online in7.msscience.com/chapter_review

**CHAPTER REVIEW 251**

**26.** Cutting large forests could result in more carbon dioxide in the atmosphere, possibly resulting in an enhanced greenhouse effect and accelerated global warming.

**27.** Answers will vary. Students should support their answers.

**28.** Contour farming and terracing are similar in that they are farming methods for hillsides that reduce soil erosion. Strip cropping compares to no-till farming in that they are both methods of reducing soil erosion by leaving soil covered by vegetation. The first two methods contrast to the last two in that they are used on hillsides, while the last two are used on level ground.

## Performance Activities

**29.** Posters should involve reducing, reusing, or recycling. Use **Performance Assessment in the Science Classroom,** p. 145.

## Applying Math

### Indiana Math Standards
1.02, 4.01

**30.** bars (highest to lowest): aluminum cans, newsprint, plastic soft-drink containers, glass beverage bottles, magazines

**31.** 310 are recycled

**32.** \$786, 149, 748

**33.** 2.88 times larger

**34.** $430 + (430 \times 0.7) = 731$ ppm

---

**Answer Sheet** A practice answer sheet can be found at in7.msscience.com/answer_sheet.

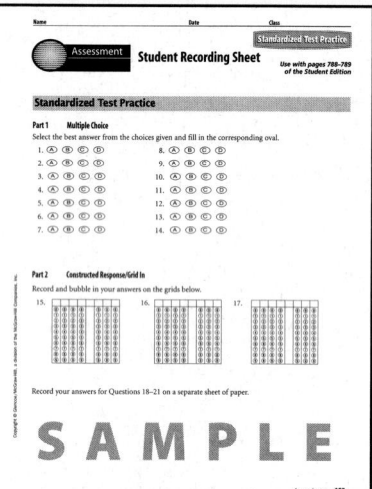

## Part 1 | Multiple Choice

| | | |
|---|---|---|
| **1.** D | **4.** C | **7.** C |
| **2.** A | **5.** D | **8.** A |
| **3.** A | **6.** C | |

## Part 2 | Critical Response

**9.** Excess nutrients, such as raw sewage or fertilizers, entering lakes or ponds

**10.** As a result of global warming, rainfall patterns may change, which could alter ecosystems; other weather patterns may change; polar ice caps might melt, which would raise sea levels. The cause of global warming is unknown. Burning fossil fuels increases the amount of $CO_2$ in the atmosphere, which traps more of the sun's heat, which makes Earth warmer.

**11.** The diagram shows what is happening inside the fuel rods of a nuclear reactor. It is source of energy for the electricity produced by nuclear power.

---

 The assessed Indiana standard appears above the question.

*Record your answers on the answer sheet provided by your teacher or on a sheet of paper.*

### Part 1 | Multiple Choice

**1.** Which natural resource is the source of plastics, paints, and gasoline?

**A** coal

**B** iron ore

**C** natural gas

**D** petroleum

The illustration below shows a turbine generator.

**2.** What does this machine produce?

**A** electricity

**B** microwaves

**C** nuclear power

**D** solar power

**3.** Where does a flow of water cause the blades to turn in the machine shown above?

**A** 1

**B** 2

**C** 3

**D** 4

The photo below shows a method of farming.

**4.** Which method of farming is shown?

**A** contour plowing

**B** no-till farming

**C** strip cropping

**D** terracing

**5.** What is the purpose of the farming method shown above?

**A** to decrease effects of acid rain

**B** to decrease nutrient loss from water erosion

**C** to decrease nutrients returned to the soil

**D** to decrease soil loss from wind erosion

**7.3.16** **7.4.14**

**6.** What type of air pollution results when sunlight reacts with pollutants produced by burning fossil fuels?

**A** acid rain

**B** ozone

**C** smog

**D** UV radiation

**7.** The illustration below shows a type of alternative energy.

What type of alternative energy is being used?

**A** geothermal

**B** hydroelectric

**C** solar

**D** wind

7.1.8   7.3.16

**8.** What is one drawback to using the alternative energy shown above?

**A** available only when the Sun is shining

**B** available only where geysers or volcanoes are found

**C** available only when the wind is blowing

**D** available only where there is falling water

---

**Part 2   Critical Response**

7.1.8

**9.** What is the cause of algal blooms in lakes and ponds? Suggest ways to limit algal blooms.

7.3.16   7.4.14

**10.** What are the possible worldwide effects of global warming? What causes global warming? Why do some people think that using fossil fuels less will decrease global warming?

7.3.16

**11.** The illustration below shows part of the process for an alternative form of energy.

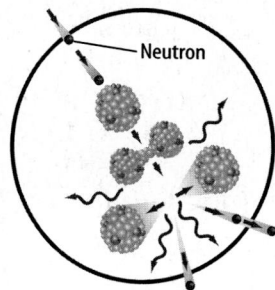

Neutron

What does the illustration represent?

**Test-Taking Tip**

**Qualifying Terms** Look for qualifiers in a question. Such questions are not looking for absolute answers. Qualifiers could be words such as *most likely*, *most common*, or *least common*.

**Question 10** The qualifier in this question is *possible*. This indicates that there is uncertainty about the effects of global warming.

---

## Rubrics

The following rubric is a sample scoring device for critical response questions.

### Critical Response

| Points | Description |
|--------|-------------|
| 4 | The student demonstrates a thorough understanding of the science of the task. The response may contain minor flaws that do not detract from the demonstration of a thorough understanding. |
| 3 | The student demonstrates an understanding of the science of the task. The response is essentially correct and demonstrates an essential but less than thorough understanding of the science. |
| 2 | The student demonstrates only a partial understanding of the science of the task. Although the student may have used the correct approach to a solution or may have provided a correct solution, the work lacks an essential understanding of the underlying science concepts. |
| 1 | The student demonstrates a very limited understanding of the science of the task. The response is incomplete and exhibits many flaws. |
| 0 | The student provides a completely incorrect solution or no response at all. |

---

## Unit Contents

**Web**Quest  *Art of Neon* is a motivating and challenging investigation of the chemistry of noble gases and how they are used in colorful neon signs and glowing sculptures. Using specific internet sites, students will research how the noble gases are inserted into bent tubing and made to glow. As a culminating activity, students will design a "blueprint" of their own neon sign, its components, colors, shape, size, and use.

# How Are Refrigerators & Frying Pans Connected?

I n the late 1930s, scientists were experimenting with a gas that they hoped would work as a new coolant in refrigerators. They filled several metal canisters with the gas and stored the canisters on dry ice. Later, when they opened the canisters, they were surprised to find that the gas had disappeared and that the inside of each canister was coated with a slick, powdery, white solid. The gas had undergone a chemical change. That is, the chemical bonds in its molecules had broken and new bonds had formed, turning one kind of matter into a completely different kind of matter. Strangely, the mysterious white powder proved to be just about the slipperiest substance that anyone had ever encountered. Years later, a creative Frenchman obtained some of the slippery stuff and tried applying it to his fishing tackle to keep the lines from tangling. His wife noticed what he was doing and suggested putting the substance on the inside of a frying pan to keep food from sticking. He did, and nonstick cookware was born!

254

**PROJECT**

**CRISS**℠

*Study Skills*

**Discussion** Creating opportunities for students to initiate their own inquiries and discuss interests is an effective way to ensure full participation in discussions. Have students write down one thing they find interesting or did not fully understand about the changes of states of matter. These "seeds" are used as the basis for class discussion.

## unit projects

**History** Have students explore the development of airships and their relevance to chemistry. Students should become familiar with the design, construction, voyages, and destruction of the Hindenburg. Students might display their research on a informative mobile/model.

**Technology** Have students research an assigned element from the periodic table. Have them present its symbol, atomic number, atomic mass, and name on a 1-inch by 2-inch card. On a second card, have students write the electron configuration, state of matter at room temperature, and synthetic or man-made. The class may display their cards in a wall mural, or class sets may be distributed for a periodic review game.

**Model** Ask students to demonstrate their knowledge of physical and chemical changes in the kitchen. Ask pairs of students to prepare a simple food that focuses on either a physical or chemical change. Students may then present their snack along with an explanation of the characteristics of the change they are demonstrating.

**Additional Resources** For more information, resources, and assessment rubrics, visit in7.msscience.com/unit_project.

## unit projects

The assessed Indiana objective appears in blue.

To find project ideas and resources, visit in7.msscience.com/unit_project.
Projects include:
- **History** Discover the chemistry related to airships. Investigate the design, voyages, and destruction of famous airships. Display your information on a creative mobile. 7.1.5
- **Technology** Design a classroom periodic table wall mural. Use the information as a learning tool and review game.
- **Model** Demonstrate your knowledge of the characteristics of physical and chemical change by preparing a simple snack to share.

**WebQuest** *Art of Neon* is an investigation of the noble gases and how they are inserted into glass tubes to be used in art and signage.

---

**NATIONAL GEOGRAPHIC**    **How Are Refrigerators & Frying Pans Connected?**

It was Roy Plunkett who first discovered phytetrafluoroethylene (PTFE) in 1938. It was used to protect metal equipment from corrosion during World War II. It was 1960 when the first nonstick cookware was released. PTFE is an organic polymer known for its strength, toughness, and slippery surface. It is almost completely indifferent to attack, by all chemicals, and retains its physical properties at high temperatures. These qualities make it ideal for use in gaskets, bearings, cooking utensils, and numerous other products.

| Section/Objectives | Standards | | Labs/Features |
|---|---|---|---|
| **Chapter Opener** | National | State/Local | **Launch Lab:** Observe Matter, p. 257 **Foldables,** p. 257 |
| | See p. 16T–17T for a Key to Standards. | Detailed standards begin on IN8. | |
| **Section 1  Structure of Matter** ⏱ 2 sessions 📦 1 block <br><br> 1. **Describe** the characteristics of matter. <br> 2. **Identify** what makes up matter. <br> 3. **Identify** the parts of an atom. <br> 4. **Compare** the models that are used for atoms. | National Content Standards: UCP.1, UCP.2, UCP.3, UCP.5, A.1, A.2, B.1, G.1, G.2, G.3 | Indiana Standards: 7.1.5, 7.7.2 | **Integrate History,** p. 259 **MiniLAB:** Investigating the Unseen, p. 260 **Science Online,** p. 262 **Integrate Career,** p. 264 |
| **Section 2  The Simplest Matter** ⏱ 2 sessions 📦 1 block <br><br> 5. **Describe** the relationship between elements and the periodic table. <br> 6. **Explain** the meaning of atomic mass and atomic number. <br> 7. **Identify** what makes an isotope. <br> 8. **Contrast** metals, metalloids, and nonmetals. | National Content Standards: UCP.1, UCP.2, UCP.3, UCP.5, A.1, A.2, B.1, G.3 | Indiana Standards: 7.1.5 | **Science Online,** p. 267 **Visualizing the Periodic Table,** p. 268 **Lab:** Elements and the Periodic Table, p. 272 |
| **Section 3  Compounds and Mixtures** ⏱ 4 sessions 📦 2 blocks <br><br> 9. **Identify** the characteristics of a compound. <br> 10. **Compare and contrast** different types of mixtures. | National Content Standards: UCP.1, UCP.2, UCP.3, UCP.5, A.1, A.2, B.1, G.1, G.2, G.3 | Indiana Standards: 7.1.5 | **MiniLAB:** Comparing Compounds, p. 274 **Applying Science:** What's the best way to desalt ocean water?, p. 275 **Science Online,** p. 276 **Integrate Earth Science,** p. 277 **Lab:** Mystery Mixture, p. 278 **Science and History:** Ancient Views of Matter, p. 280 |

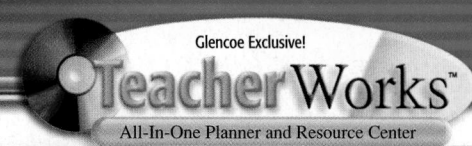

Glencoe Exclusive!
Teacher Works™
All-In-One Planner and Resource Center

| Lab Materials | Reproducible Resources | Section Assessment | Technology |
|---|---|---|---|
| **Launch Lab:** dry paper towel or tissue, tape, plastic cup, bowl, or sink water | **Chapter *FAST FILE* Resources**<br>Foldables Worksheet, p. 13<br>Note-taking Worksheets, pp. 29–31 | GLENCOE'S ASSESSMENT ADVANTAGE | **Teacher Works** includes:<br>• Interactive Teacher Edition<br>• Lesson Planner with calendar<br>• Access to all program blacklines<br>• Correlations to standards<br>• Web links |
| **MiniLAB:** sealed shoe box, one or more items<br><br>*Need materials?* Contact Science Kit at 1-800-828-7777 or www.sciencekit.com on the Internet. | **Chapter *FAST FILE* Resources**<br>Transparency Activity, p. 40<br>MiniLAB, p. 3<br>Enrichment, p. 26<br>Reinforcement, p. 23<br>Directed Reading, p. 16<br>Transparency Activity, pp. 43–44<br>**Reading and Writing Skill Activities,** p. 41<br>**Mathematics Skill Activities,** p. 39 | **Portfolio**<br>Activity, p. 262<br>**Performance**<br>MiniLAB, p. 260<br>Applying Skills, p. 265<br>**Content**<br>Section Review, p. 265 | 🔊 Section Focus Transparency<br>🔊 Teaching Transparency<br>💿 Virtual Labs CD-ROM<br>🎧 Guided Reading Audio Program<br>💿 Interactive Chalkboard CD-ROM |
| **Lab:** colored markers, large index cards, Merck index, encyclopedia, large bulletin board, 8 1/2- × 14-inch paper, thumbtacks | **Chapter *FAST FILE* Resources**<br>Transparency Activity, p. 41<br>Enrichment, p. 27<br>Reinforcement, p. 24<br>Directed Reading, p. 17<br>Activity Worksheet, pp. 5–6<br>**Science Inquiry Labs,** pp. 49–50 | **Portfolio**<br>Science Journal, p. 270<br>Assessment, p. 272<br>**Performance**<br>Applying Math, p. 271<br>**Content**<br>Section Review, p. 271 | 🔊 Section Focus Transparency<br>🎧 Guided Reading Audio Program<br>💿 Interactive Chalkboard CD-ROM |
| **MiniLAB:** sugar, rubbing alcohol, salad oil, spoon, glasses, hot water<br>**Lab:** test tubes and holder, cornstarch, sugar, baking soda, mystery mixture, small scoops, dropper bottles, iodine solution, white vinegar, hot plate, 250-mL beaker, water, small pie pan, matches | **Chapter *FAST FILE* Resources**<br>Transparency Activity, p. 42<br>MiniLAB, p. 4<br>Enrichment, p. 28<br>Reinforcement, p. 25<br>Directed Reading, pp. 17, 18<br>Lab Worksheet, pp. 7–8<br>Lab Activity, pp. 9–10, 11–12<br>**Lab Management and Safety,** p. 44 | **Portfolio**<br>MiniLAB Assessment, p. 274<br>Curriculum Connection, p. 276<br>**Performance**<br>MiniLAB, p. 274<br>Applying Science, p. 275<br>Applying Skills, p. 277<br>**Content**<br>Section Review, p. 277 | 🔊 Section Focus Transparency<br>🎧 Guided Reading Audio Program<br>💿 Interactive Chalkboard CD-ROM<br>📼 Video Lab |

## End of Chapter Assessment

GLENCOE'S ASSESSMENT ADVANTAGE

| Blackline Masters | Technology | Professional Series |
|---|---|---|
| **Chapter *FAST FILE* Resources**<br>Chapter Review, pp. 33–34<br>Chapter Tests, pp. 35–38<br>**Mastering the Grade 7 Indiana Science Standards** | 📼 MindJogger Videoquiz<br>💿 IN Test Prep and Practice Exam*View*®<br>💿 Exam*View*® Pro Testmaker<br>💿 TeacherWorks CD-ROM<br>💿 Interactive Chalkboard CD-ROM | **Performance Assessment in the Science Classroom (PASC)** |

# Transparencies

## Section Focus

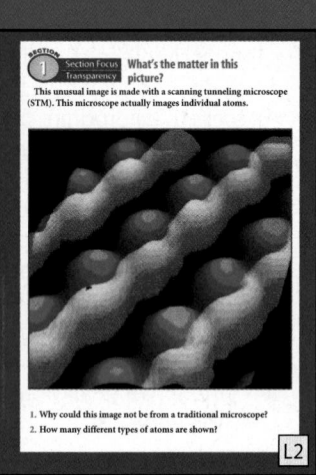

**Section Focus Transparency** What's the matter in this picture?

This unusual image is made with a scanning tunneling microscope (STM). This microscope actually images individual atoms.

1. Why could this image not be from a traditional microscope?
2. How many different types of atoms are shown?

L2

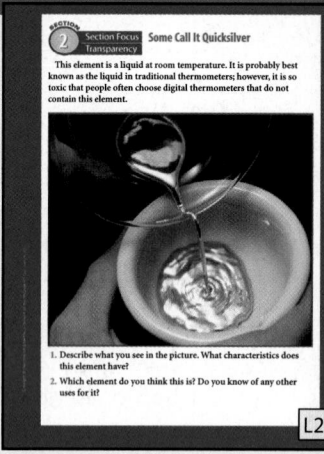

**Section Focus Transparency** Some Call It Quicksilver

This element is a liquid at room temperature. It is probably best known as the liquid in traditional thermometers; however, it is so toxic that people often choose digital thermometers that do not contain this element.

1. Describe what you see in the picture. What characteristics does this element have?
2. Which element do you think this is? Do you know of any other uses for it?

L2

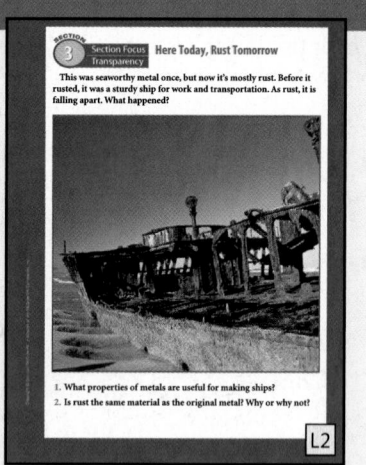

**Section Focus Transparency** Here Today, Rust Tomorrow

This was seaworthy metal once, but now it's mostly rust. Before it rusted, it was a sturdy ship for work and transportation. As rust, it is falling apart. What happened?

1. What properties of metals are useful for making ships?
2. Is rust the same material as the original metal? Why or why not?

L2

This is a representation of key blackline masters available in the Teacher Classroom Resources. See Resource Manager boxes within the chapter for additional information.

## Key to Teaching Strategies

The following designations will help you decide which activities are appropriate for your students.

L1 Level 1 activities should be appropriate for students with learning difficulties.

L2 Level 2 activities should be within the ability range of all students.

L3 Level 3 activities are designed for above-average students.

ELL ELL activities should be within the ability range of English Language Learners.

COOP LEARN Cooperative Learning activities are designed for small group work.

LS Multiple Learning Styles logos, as described on page 12T, are used throughout to indicate strategies that address different learning styles.

P These strategies represent student products that can be placed into a best-work portfolio.

PBL Problem-Based Learning activities apply real-world situations to learning.

## Assessment

**Assessment Transparency** Matter

Directions: Carefully review the table and answer the following questions.

**Characteristics of Some Elements**

| Element | Atomic number | Mass number | Number of protons | Number of electrons | Number of neutrons |
|---|---|---|---|---|---|
| Boron | 5 | 11 | 5 | 5 | 6 |
| Carbon | 6 | 12 | 6 | 6 | 6 |
| Nitrogen | 7 | 14 | 7 | 7 | 7 |
| Oxygen | 8 | 16 | 8 | 8 | 8 |
| Fluorine | 9 | 19 | 9 | 9 | 10 |

1. According to the table, which element has an atomic number of 7?
   A Boron   C Nitrogen
   B Carbon   D Oxygen
2. According to the table, which element has a mass number less than 12?
   F Boron   H Oxygen
   G Carbon   J Fluorine
3. According to the table, an atom with 9 protons in its nucleus is ___.
   A carbon   C oxygen
   B nitrogen   D fluorine

L2

## Teaching

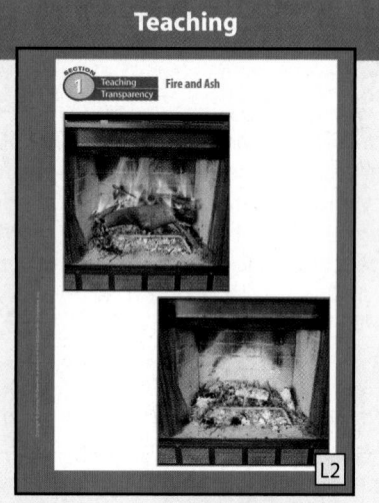

**Teaching Transparency** Fire and Ash

L2

# Hands-on Activities

## Student Text Lab Worksheet

**Activity** Elements and the Periodic Table

**Lab Preview**

**Directions:** Answer these questions before you begin the Activity.

1. What safety practice is indicated by the safety symbol with the hand that is included in this activity?

2. List at least two research sources that might be useful in this activity.

*The periodic table organizes the elements, but what do they look like? What are they used for? In this activity, you'll examine some elements and share your findings with your classmates.*

**What You'll Investigate**
What are some of the characteristics and purposes of the chemical elements?

**Goals**
• **Classify** the chemical elements.
• **Design** your own periodic table that shows the classification of the elements.

**Materials**
colored markers
large index cards
Merck Index
encyclopedia
*other reference materials
large bulletin board
8 ½ × 14-inch paper
thumbtacks
*pushpins
*Alternate materials

**Safety Precautions**
Use care when handling sharp objects.

**Procedure**
1. Select the assigned number of elements from the list provided by your teacher.
2. **Design** an index card for each of your selected elements. On each card, mark the element's atomic number in the upper left-hand corner and write its symbol and name in the upper right-hand corner.
3. **Research** each of the elements and write several sentences on the card about its appearance, its other properties, and its uses.
4. **Classify** each of your elements as a metal, a metalloid, or a nonmetal based upon its properties.
5. **Write** the appropriate classification on each of your cards using the colored marker chosen by your teacher.
6. Work with your classmates to make a large periodic table. Use thumbtacks to attach your cards to a bulletin board in their proper positions on the periodic table.
7. **Draw** your own periodic table. Place the elements' symbols and atomic numbers in the proper locations on your table.

L2

## Laboratory Activities

**Laboratory Activity** Mixtures and Compounds

Matter is anything that has mass and occupies space. Matter exists in different forms. Three classifications of matter are well known to us: elements, mixtures, and compounds. Elements are the basic materials of our world. Elements in a mixture have recognizable boundaries and can be separated by mechanical means. Elements that form a chemical compound can be separated only by a chemical process. The element oxygen(O) combines with the element hydrogen (H) to form water ($H_2O$), which is a compound. Salt water is a mixture of two compounds, water and salt.

**Strategy**
You will separate a mixture into its parts.
You will compare the characteristics of a compound and a mixture.

**Materials**
magnifying glass
sand (coarse)
granite rock
granite (crushed)
water
disposable pie pans (2)
rock salt
heat source

**Procedure**
1. Use the magnifying glass to observe the sand and granite rock. Sketch the granite with the minerals in it, and the shapes of the sand grains under Sketch A.
2. Sort the crushed granite into separate piles according to color.
3. Sketch the general shape of a piece from each pile of the mixed granite, and label each as to color under Sketch B.
4. Mix a spoonful of sand in some water in a pie pan. Sketch what you observed under Sketch C.
5. Examine and sketch the salt crystals under Sketch D. CAUTION: *Do not ingest rock salt. It might contain harmful impurities.*
6. Mix a spoonful of salt in some water in the second pie pan. Record your observations.
7. Heat both pans until the water is evaporated. Sketch what is left in each pan under Sketch E. CAUTION: *Be careful not to get clothes or hair close to the heat source.*

**Data and Observations**

Sketch A

Sketch B

L2

# Meeting Different Ability Levels

## Content Outline

L2

## Reinforcement

L2

## Enrichment

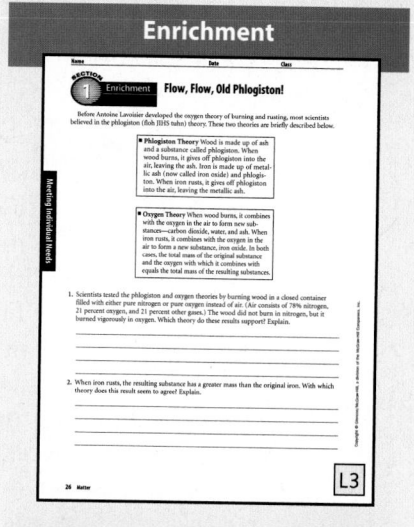

L3

## Directed Reading (English/Spanish)

L1

## Study Guide

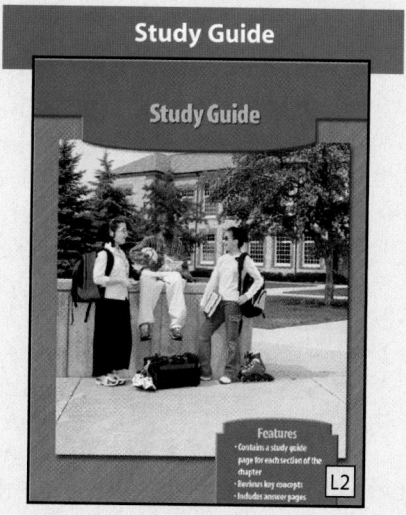

Study Guide

Features
• Contains a study guide page for each section of the chapter
• Reviews key concepts
• Includes answer pages

L2

## Reading Essentials

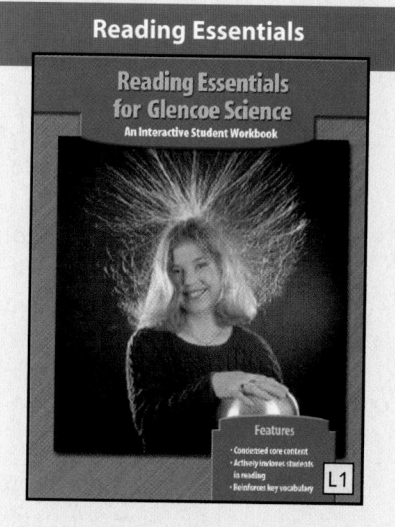

Reading Essentials for Glencoe Science
An Interactive Student Workbook

Features
• Condensed core content
• Actively involves students in reading
• Reinforces key vocabulary

L1

# Assessment

## Test Practice Workbook

L2

## Chapter Review

L2

## Chapter Tests

L2

# Science Content Background

### section 1
## Structure of Matter
### Matter Basics

Solids, liquids, and gases are matter—they take up space and have mass. The amount of space an object occupies is its volume. The mass of an object refers to the amount of matter it contains. On Earth the amount of mass is directly proportional to the weight of the object. Dividing matter into smaller pieces reduces its volume and mass, and because the mass is reduced, so is the weight.

### Ions

Many substances are ionic. That is, they are made up of charged particles called ions rather than neutral atoms. For example, sodium chloride is made up of sodium ions that have 1+ charges and chloride ions that have 1− charges. A sodium ion is formed when a sodium atom loses one of its 11 electrons. A chloride ion is formed when a chlorine atom gains an additional electron to go with the 17 it had as an atom.

### Plasma

Plasma, another fluid state of matter, is a gaslike state of negatively charged electrons and positively charged ions. Most matter in the universe is plasma. Stars are mostly plasma, and the hydrogen ions that occur in interstellar space exist in the plasma state.

### section 2
## The Simplest Matter
### Elements

The arrangement of electrons in the energy levels and sublevels in the atoms of an element determines the properties of that element. Elements whose atoms have identical arrangements of electrons in their highest energy levels have similar properties and make up a family of elements on the periodic table.

### section 3
## Compounds and Mixtures
### Compounds

Electron sharing is called covalent bonding. Covalent bonding between atoms of different elements produces molecular compounds. The molecules of molecular compounds attract each other to varying degrees. In the solid state, these attractions sometimes lead to an orderly arrangement of molecules called a molecular crystal.

When atoms react by losing or gaining electrons, called ionic bonding, ions are formed. The formula for an ionic compound such as sodium chloride (NaCl) is called an empirical formula and gives the simplest ratio of ions in the compound, not the formula for a molecule.

### Mixtures

Solid solutions, made up of uniform mixtures of metals and sometimes nonmetals, are called alloys. Brass and stainless steel are common alloys.

## chapter content resources

**Internet Resources**
For additional content background, visit
**in7.msscience.com** to:
- access your book online
- find references to related articles in popular science magazines
- access Web links with related content background
- access current events with science journal topics

**Print Resources**
*Chemistry*, Steve S. Zumdahl, Susan A. Zumdahl, Houghton Mifflin Company, 2003
*Chemistry*, Raymond Chang, McGraw-Hill College, 2001
*General Chemistry*, Ralph Petrucci, William Harwood, Prentice Hall, 1997

# IDENTIFYING ▷ Misconceptions

## Find Out What Students Think

### Students may think that . . .

**Objects have mass only if you can feel them.**

**If you keep dividing matter, you will eventually get small pieces with no mass.**

Students may have these misconceptions because they are relying on their senses. In this case they are relying on their sense of touch. They may think that if an object does not press down on their hands and feel heavy, it has no mass.

### Demonstration

Hold up a plastic foam cup, and ask students if the cup has mass. Establish that it does. Break a chunk off the cup, and ask how the mass of this part of the cup compares with the mass of the original cup. Establish that it has less mass. Give pieces of the cup to four different students sitting in different parts of the classroom. Ask students to break their pieces and hold up the biggest piece of cup that has no mass. When they hold these up ask other students if they agree that the pieces have no mass.

## Promote Understanding

### Activity

Divide the class into groups. Give a foam cup to each group. Have them discuss whether the cup is matter. Establish that it is because it has mass and takes up space. Explain that on Earth, the mass of a cup is directly proportional to its weight. This means that if a cup has a large mass, it has a large weight, and if it has a small mass, it has a small weight. Perform the following:

- Using a balance that can measure mass to at least 0.1 g, measure the mass of the cup.

- Draw a picture of the cup, and write its mass.

- Use scissors to cut the cup exactly in half.

- Draw a picture of the half cup, calculate its mass (original mass divided by two), and write the new mass by the picture.

- Take one half of the cup and cut it into two equal parts.

- Draw a picture of one of the new pieces, and write its mass next to it.

- Repeat this procedure four more times, each time cutting the piece in half, drawing it, and calculating its mass.

- Make a graph of the data. The *x*-axis should be labeled *Mass (g)*. It should start with zero and have a range that includes the mass of the whole cup. The *y*-axis should be labeled *Fraction of cup*. It should begin with 1/64th of a cup and go up in the following increments: 1/32, 1/16, 1/8, 1/4, 1/2, and 1.

Instruct students to examine their data and discuss whether they will ever get a piece of cup that has absolutely no mass. Make sure students understand that as pieces get smaller and smaller, their masses and their weights get smaller and smaller, but the pieces always have some mass.

## Assess

After completing the chapter, see *Identifying Misconceptions* in the Study Guide at the end of the chapter.

## Chapter Vocabulary

matter, p. 258
atom, p. 259
law of conservation of matter, p. 260
electron, p. 262
nucleus, p. 263
proton, p. 263
neutron, p. 264
element, p. 266
atomic number, p. 269
isotope, p. 269
mass number, p. 269
atomic mass, p. 270
metal, p. 270
nonmetal, p. 271
metalloid, p. 271
substance, p. 273
compound, p. 273
mixture, p. 275

**Science Journal** Student responses will vary but may include questions about flight, balloons, and how matter is involved with flight.

**PowerPoint® Presentations**

This CD-ROM is an editable Microsoft® PowerPoint® presentation that includes:
- a pre-made presentation for every chapter
- interactive graphics
- animations
- audio clips
- image bank
- all new section and chapter questions
- Standardized Test Practice
- transparencies
- pre-lab questions for all labs
- Foldables directions
- links to in7.msscience.com

**Academic Standard—1:** Students further their scientific understanding of the natural world through investigations, experiences, and readings. They design solutions to practical problems by using a variety of scientific methodologies.

**Also covers:** Academic Standard 7 (Detailed standards begin on page IN8.)

# Atoms, Elements, and the Periodic Table

## chapter preview

### sections

**1 Structure of Matter**

**2 The Simplest Matter**
*Lab Elements and the Periodic Table*

**3 Compounds and Mixtures**
*Lab Mystery Mixture*

*Virtual Lab How can a molecular model be built?*

## What a fun ride!

The pilot gives the propane burner a long, loud blast that will heat the air in the balloon, making you soar higher. During your ride, you might start thinking about what is keeping you airborne. In this chapter, as you learn about atoms and elements, you will be able to understand more about matter.

**Science Journal** Make a list of three questions that you think of when you look at the picture.

256

## Theme Connection

**Scale and Structure** Tiny particles called atoms make up elements. Elements are the building blocks of all matter.

| About the Photo |

**Rise and Sink** What keeps a hot air balloon flying? It is the same principle that keeps food frozen in the open chest freezers at the grocery store. The principle is that hot air rises and cold air sinks. While the super-cooled air in a open chest freezer settles down around the food, the hot air in a hot air balloon pushes up, keeping the balloon afloat.

# Start-Up Activities

## Observe Matter

You've just finished playing basketball. You're hot and thirsty. You reach for your bottle of water and take a drink. Releasing your grip, you notice that the bottle is nearly empty. Is the bottle really almost empty? According to the dictionary, *empty* means "containing nothing." When you have finished all the water in the bottle, will it be empty or full?

1. Wad up a dry paper towel or tissue and tape it to the inside of a plastic cup as shown.

2. Fill a bowl or sink with water. Turn the cup upside down and slowly push the cup straight down into the water as far as you can.

3. Slowly raise the cup straight up and out of the water. Remove the paper towel or tissue paper and examine it.

4. **Think Critically** In your Science Journal, describe the lab and its results. Explain what you think happened. Was anything in the cup besides the paper? If so, what was it?

**FOLDABLES™**
**Study Organizer**

**Atoms, Elements, and the Periodic Table** Make the following Foldable to help you identify the main ideas about atoms, elements, compounds, and mixtures.

**STEP 1** Draw a mark at the midpoint of a sheet of paper along the side edge. Then **fold** the top and bottom edges in to touch the midpoint.

**STEP 2** Fold in half from side to side.

**STEP 3** Open and cut along the inside fold lines to form four tabs.

**STEP 4** Label each tab as shown.

**Read and Write** As you read the chapter, list several everyday examples of atoms, elements, compounds, and mixtures on the back of the appropriate tab.

**Science Online** Preview this chapter's content and activities at in7.msscience.com

---

**Launch LAB**

**Purpose** Use the Launch Lab to help students discover that air is matter because it occupies space. **L2** **ELL** **IS** **Kinesthetic**

**Preparation** Obtain water if sinks are not available in your classroom. The sink or bowl used in the lab must be deep enough for the cup to be submerged in water.

**Materials** paper towel or tissue, plastic cup, sink or bowl, water, tape

**Teaching Strategy** In Step 2, remind students to *slowly* push the cup into the water to avoid spills.

## Think Critically

Students should observe that the paper towel was dry when removed from the cup. They should infer that air in the cup took up space and did not allow water to enter.

## Assessment

**Process** Have students work in small groups to make a mini picture book that explains to third graders how air is matter. Use **Performance Assessment in the Science Classroom,** p. 129.

**FOLDABLES™**
**Study Organizer** **Dinah Zike Study Fold**

Student preparation materials for this Foldable are available in the Chapter *FAST FILE* Resources.

## section

Also covers: 7.1.1, 7.7.2 (Detailed standards begin on page IN8.)

# Structure of Matter

## as you read

### *What* You'll Learn

- **Describe** characteristics of matter.
- **Identify** what makes up matter.
- **Identify** the parts of an atom.
- **Compare** the models that are used for atoms.

### *Why* It's Important

Matter makes up almost everything we see—and much of what we can't see.

### ⚙ Review Vocabulary
**density:** the mass of an object divided by its volume

### New Vocabulary
- matter
- atom
- law of conservation of matter
- electron
- nucleus
- proton
- neutron

## What is matter?

Is a glass with some water in it half empty or half full? Actually, neither is correct. The glass is completely full—half full of water and half full of air. What is air? Air is a mixture of several gases, including nitrogen and oxygen, which are kinds of matter. **Matter** is anything that has mass and takes up space. So, even though you can't see it or hold it in your hand, air is matter. What about all the things you can see, taste, smell, and touch? Most are made of matter, too. Look at the things pictured in **Figure 1** and determine which of them are matter.

## What isn't matter?

You can see the words on this page because of the light from the Sun or from a fixture in the room. Does light have mass or take up space? What about the warmth from the Sun or the heat from the heater in your classroom? Light and heat do not take up space, and they have no mass. Therefore, they are not forms of matter. Emotions, thoughts, and ideas are not matter either. Does this information change your mind about the items in **Figure 1?**

 **Reading Check** *Why is air matter, but light is not?*

**Figure 1** A rainbow is formed when light filters through the raindrops, a plant grows from a seed in the ground, and a statue is sculpted from bronze.
**Identify** *which are matter.*

**258 CHAPTER 9** Atoms, Elements, and the Periodic Table

## Figure 2 Early Beliefs About the Composition of Matter

| Many Indian Philosophers (1,000 B.C.) | Kashyapa, an Indian Philosopher (1,000 B.C.) | Many Greek Philosophers (500–300 B.C.) | Democritus (380 B.C.) | Aristotle (330 B.C.) | Chinese Philosophers (300 B.C.) |
|---|---|---|---|---|---|
| • Ether—an invisible substance that filled the heavens<br>• Earth<br>• Water<br>• Air<br>• Fire | • Five elements broken down into smaller units called parmanu<br>• Parmanu of earth elements are heavier than air elements | • Earth<br>• Water<br>• Air<br>• Fire | • Tiny individual particles he called *atomos*<br>• Empty space through which atoms move<br>• Each substance composed of one type of *atomos* | • Empty space could not exist<br>• Earth<br>• Water<br>• Air<br>• Fire | • Metal<br>• Earth<br>• Water<br>• Air<br>• Fire |

## What makes up matter?

Suppose you cut a chunk of wood into smaller and smaller pieces. Do the pieces seem to be made of the same matter as the large chunk you started with? If you could cut a small enough piece, would it still have the same properties as the first chunk? Would you reach a point where the last cut resulted in a piece that no longer resembled the first chunk? Is there a limit to how small a piece can be? For centuries, people have asked questions like these and wondered what matter is made of.

**An Early Idea** Democritus, who lived from about 460 B.C. to 370 B.C., was a Greek philosopher who thought the universe was made of empty space and tiny bits of stuff. He believed that the bits of stuff were so small they could no longer be divided into smaller pieces. He called these tiny pieces atoms. The term *atom* comes from a Greek word that means "cannot be divided." Today an **atom** is defined as a small particle that makes up most types of matter. **Figure 2** shows the difference between Democritus's ideas and those of other early scientists and philosophers. Democritus thought that different types of atoms existed for every type of matter and that the atom's identity explained the characteristics of each type of matter. Democritus's ideas about atoms were a first step toward understanding matter. However, his ideas were not accepted for over 2,000 years. It wasn't until the early 1800s that scientists built upon the concept of atoms to form the current atomic theory of matter.

**INTEGRATE History**

**Atomism** Historians note that Leucippus developed the idea of the atom around 440 B.C. He and his student, Democritus, refined the idea of the atom years later. Their concept of the atom was based on five major points: (1) all matter is made of atoms, (2) there are empty spaces between atoms, (3) atoms are complete solids, (4) atoms do not have internal structure, and (5) atoms are different in size, shape, and weight.

### IDENTIFYING Misconceptions

**Weight/Mass** Students may think that objects have weight only if you can feel them. Refer to the F page at the beginning of the chapter for teaching strategies that address this misconception.

### Activity

**Classifying Matter** Take students outside to make a list of all the things they observe. Return to the classroom and have them classify the items as "Matter" and "Not Matter." What is matter? Possible answers: Matter is anything that has mass and takes up space and includes things that we see, taste, smell, and touch. What isn't matter? Possible answers: Emotions, thoughts, ideas, and light are not matter because they do not have mass and do not take up space. L2

**INTEGRATE History**

**Atomism** Democritus (460–370 B.C.) was born into a noble and wealthy family. The Magi instructed him in astronomy and theology. After the death of his father, Democritus traveled to search for wisdom. It was said that he visited many countries, such as Egypt and Ethiopia. Democritus was known as "The Laughing Philosopher" because he expressed disapproval for human foolishness while laughing. He lived for more than one hundred years.

## Curriculum Connection

**Physics** Ancient astronomers had no understanding of what stars were. This is because they lacked a framework of physics in which to understand how stars worked and what they constituted. The study of modern physics includes a wide variety of fields that are used to understand the origin and evolution of stars, matter, energy and the forces of nature.

**Purpose** Students infer the number and types of objects in a sealed box to model how scientists study atoms. L2 LS
**Logical-Mathematical**

**Materials** sealed shoe box containing various items (eraser, coin, paper clip, ruler)

**Teaching Strategy** Emphasize that students should not open the box.

**Analysis**
1. Answers will vary depending on items in the box.
2. Scientists perform experiments on matter to make models of the atom, but they cannot actually see inside an atom to verify that their models are correct.

## Assessment

**Process** Have students open the box and examine the items contained inside. Ask them to infer why some objects were easier to identify than others. Use **Performance Assessment in the Science Classroom,** p. 89.

---

## Teacher **FYI**

**Creating Matter** According to the law of conservation of matter, matter can neither be created nor destroyed. But experimental data indicate that a high energy X ray can collide with the nucleus of an atom to create an electron and a positron in its place. Also, an electron and positron can collide with and annihilate each other to produce X rays. Although matter is created and destroyed in these instances, the amount of total energy stays the same, but the energy can change its form from electromagnetic radiation to matter.

**Figure 3** When wood burns, matter is not lost. The total mass of the wood and the oxygen it combines with during a fire equals the total mass of the ash, water vapor, carbon dioxide, and other gases produced.
**Infer** *When you burn wood in a fireplace, what is the source of oxygen?*

wood + oxygen = ash + gases + water vapor

### Investigating the Unseen

**Procedure**
1. Your teacher will give you a **sealed shoe box** that contains **one or more items.**
2. Try to find out how many and what kinds of items are inside the box. You cannot look inside the box. The only observations you can make are by handling the box.

**Analysis**
1. How many items do you infer are in the box? Sketch the apparent shapes of the items and identify them if you can.
2. Compare your procedure with how scientists perform experiments and make models to find out more about the atom.

**Lavoisier's Contribution** Lavoisier (la VWAH see ay), a French chemist who lived about 2,000 years after Democritus, also was curious about matter—especially when it changed form. Before Lavoisier, people thought matter could appear and disappear because of the changes they saw as matter burned or rusted. You might have thought that matter can disappear if you've ever watched wood burn in a fireplace or at a bonfire. Lavoisier showed that wood and the oxygen it combines with during burning have the same mass as the ash, water, carbon dioxide, and other gases that are produced, as shown in **Figure 3.** In a similar way, an iron bar, oxygen, and water have the same mass as the rust that forms when they interact. From Lavoisier's work came the **law of conservation of matter,** which states that matter is not created or destroyed—it only changes form.

## Models of the Atom

Models are often used for things that are too small or too large to be observed or that are too difficult to be understood easily. One way to make a model is to make a smaller version of something large. If you wanted to design a new sailboat, would you build a full-sized boat and hope it would float? It would be more efficient, less expensive, and safer to build and test a smaller version first. Then, if it didn't float, you could change your design and build another model. You could keep trying until the model worked.

In the case of atoms, scientists use large models to explain something that is too small to be looked at. These models of the atom were used to explain data or facts that were gathered experimentally. As a result, these models are also theories.

## Visual Learning

**Figure 3** Why could being in a closed space with a fire be hazardous, even if you are in no danger of being burned? As the fuel burns, it consumes oxygen and produces smoke. Thus, being confined with a fire can lead to suffocation, not only from lack of oxygen, but also from smoke inhalation.

**Dalton's Atomic Model** In the early 1800s, an English schoolteacher and chemist named John Dalton studied the experiments of Lavoisier and others. Dalton thought he could design an atomic model that explained the results of those experiments. Dalton's atomic model was a set of ideas—not a physical object. Dalton believed that matter was made of atoms that were too small to be seen by the human eye. He also thought that each type of matter was made of only one kind of atom. For example, gold atoms make up a gold nugget and give a gold ring its shiny appearance. Likewise, iron atoms make up an iron bar and give it unique properties, and so on. Because predictions using Dalton's model were supported by data, the model became known as the atomic theory of matter.

**Sizes of Atoms** Atoms are so small it would take about 1 million of them lined up in a row to equal the thickness of a human hair. For another example of how small atoms are, look at **Figure 4.** Imagine you are holding an orange in your hand. If you wanted to be able to see the individual atoms on the orange's surface, the size of the orange would have to be increased to the size of Earth. Then, imagine the Earth-sized orange covered with billions and billions of marbles. Each marble would represent one of the atoms on the skin of the orange. No matter what kind of model you use to picture it, the result is the same—an atom is an extremely small particle of matter.

**Indiana Academic Standard Check**

**7.1.5:** Identify some important contributions to the advancement of science . . . that have been made by different kinds of people, in different cultures, at different times.

✔ How did Dalton's research build upon the work of Lavoisier?

✔ Lavoisier determined that matter was conserved in a chemical reaction. Dalton proposed a model of the atom to explain these experimental results.

**Discussion**
**Educational Models** Show students several educational models. Examples include plant, solar system, or anatomy models. How can models be helpful? Models can help us understand the structure of things and how they behave. **L1**

## Fun Fact

Our knowledge of Democritus' atomic theory comes from a poem written by the Roman Lucretius, who lived about 300 years after Democritus.

### Virtual Labs

**Atomic Structure** *How can a molecular model be built?*

**Figure 4** If this orange were as large as Earth, each of its atoms would be marble-sized.

## LAB DEMONSTRATION

**Purpose** to demonstrate that matter is neither created nor destroyed

**Materials** fine steel wool, heat-proof mitt, safety goggles, crucible tongs, burner, pan balance

**Preparation** Wear goggles and heat-proof mitt while performing this activity.

**Procedure** Obtain the mass of a piece of steel wool. Hold the steel wool in a burner flame using tongs. After a few fibers burn, ask question 1. After students have responded, obtain the mass of the burned steel wool and then ask question 2.

**Expected Outcome** Mass increases.

**Assessment**

1. Will what's left have a mass greater or less than the original? Most students will likely think the mass has decreased. 2. Why is there a gain in mass? The iron in the steel wool reacted with $O_2$ in the air to form iron oxide, so the mass of the $O_2$ has been added to the original mass.

**Figure 5** In Thomson's experiment, the magnet caused the cathode rays inside the tube to bend. **Describe** *what you think would happen to the cathode rays if the magnet were removed.*

**Science Online**

**Topic: Subatomic Particles**
Visit in7.msscience.com for Web links to information about particles that make up atoms.

**Activity** Can any of the particles be divided further? Display your data in a table.

**Discovering the Electron** One of the many pioneers in the development of today's atomic model was J.J. Thomson, an English scientist. He conducted experiments using a cathode ray tube, which is a glass tube sealed at both ends out of which most of the air has been pumped. Thomson's tube had a metal plate at each end. The plates were connected to a high-voltage electrical source that gave one of the plates—the anode—a positive charge and the other plate—the cathode—a negative charge. During his experiments, Thomson observed rays that traveled from the cathode to the anode. These cathode rays were bent by a magnet, as seen in **Figure 5,** showing that they were made up of particles that had mass and charge. Thomson knew that like charges repel each other and opposite charges attract each other. When he saw that the rays traveled toward a positively charged plate, he concluded that the cathode rays were made up of negatively charged particles. These invisible, negatively charged particles are called **electrons.**

✔ **Reading Check** *Why were the cathode rays in Thomson's cathode ray tube bent by a magnet?*

Try to imagine Thomson's excitement at this discovery. He had shown that atoms are not too tiny to divide after all. Rather, they are made up of even smaller subatomic particles. Other scientists soon built upon Thomson's results and found that the electron had a small mass. In fact, an electron is 1/1,837 the mass of the lightest atom, the hydrogen atom. In 1906, Thomson received the Nobel Prize in Physics for his work on the discovery of the electron.

Matter that has an equal amount of positive and negative charge is said to be neutral—it has no net charge. Because most matter is neutral, Thomson pictured the atom as a ball of positive charge with electrons embedded in it. It was later determined that neutral atoms contained an equal number of positive and negative charges.

## Differentiated Instruction

**Learning Disabled** Have students make up new lyrics to a familiar tune using the vocabulary and definitions from the chapter. The song can focus on one concept, such as the parts of an atom, or cover the entire chapter's content. Some examples for the familiar tune are "Row, Row, Row Your Boat," "Old McDonald," and "Itsy Bitsy Spider." LS **Auditory-Musical**

### ✔ Active Reading

**Reflective Journal** Have students write reflective journals about their experiences in this activity. Have students divide sheets of paper into several columns and record their thoughts under headings such as *What I Did, What I Learned, What Questions I Have, What Surprises I Experienced,* and *Overall Response.* Suggest that volunteers share their reflections with the class.

**Thomson's Model** Thomson's model, shown in **Figure 6,** can be compared to chocolate chips spread throughout a ball of cookie dough. However, the model did not provide all the answers to the questions that puzzled scientists about atoms.

**Rutherford—The Nucleus** Scientists still had questions about how the atom was arranged and about the presence of positively charged particles. In about 1910, a team of scientists led by Ernest Rutherford worked on these questions. In their experiment, they bombarded an extremely thin piece of gold foil with alpha particles. Alpha particles are tiny, high-energy, positively charged particles that he predicted would pass through the foil. Most of the particles passed straight through the foil as if it were not there at all. However, other particles changed direction, and some even bounced back. Rutherford thought the result was so remarkable that he later said, "It was almost as incredible as if you had fired a 15-inch shell at a piece of tissue paper, and it came back and hit you."

**Positive Center** Rutherford concluded that because so many of the alpha particles passed straight through the gold foil, the atoms must be made of mostly empty space. However, because some of the positively charged alpha particles bounced off something, the gold atoms must contain some positively charged object concentrated in the midst of this empty space. Rutherford called the positively charged, central part of the atom the **nucleus** (NEW klee us). He named the positively charged particles in the nucleus **protons**. He also suggested that electrons were scattered in the mostly empty space around the nucleus, as shown in **Figure 7.**

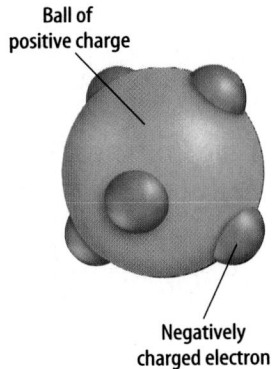

**Figure 6** Thomson's model shows the atom as electrons embedded in a ball of positive charge.
**Explain** *how Thomson knew atoms contained positive and negative charges.*

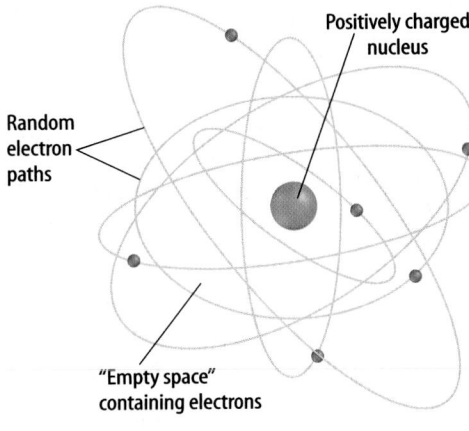

**Figure 7** Rutherford concluded that the atom must be mostly empty space in which electrons travel in random paths around the nucleus. He also thought the nucleus of the atom must be small and positively charged.
**Identify** *where most of the mass of an atom is concentrated.*

---

## Discussion

**Protons and Neutrons** How are protons and neutrons similar and how are they different? Protons and neutrons are both found in atomic nuclei. Both particles are small but massive, and their masses are nearly equal. The proton is positively charged, while the neutron has no charge.

## Inquiry Lab

### Touching Atoms

**Purpose** Students will work with models of atoms to gain a better understanding of their structure and properties.

**Possible Materials** nuts or bolts in two different sizes, long-distance measuring tape, ground stake

**Estimated Time** one or two class sessions

### Teaching Strategies

• Size: Have students calculate where the first electron would be if the nucleus of an atom was the size of the head of a pin (1mm diameter). The average atom is of the order of $10^{-10}$ m, while the average nucleus is of the order of $10^{-15}$ m. It will be about 100 m away.

• Isotopes: Gather a handful of small and large bolts. Tell students it is the element 'bolt' and you want to find its average mass, just like atoms have average masses for all of their real isotopes. Have students weigh a large bolt and a small bolt and record the mass. Then, multiply the mass of the object by the number of objects, add it to the mass of the other size object times the number of objects, and divide by the total number of objects. This is the same method for calculating isotopic mass of elements. You could add a medium-sized bolt to the calculation, too.

• Have students brainstorm other ways to represent this information.

**For additional inquiry activities, see** *Science Inquiry Labs.*

---

### Active Reading

**Buddy Interviews** This strategy helps students to understand and clarify the reading. Having students interview one another to find out what helps them to understand what they are reading, how they find answers, and how they assimilate new vocabulary. Have students use Buddy Interviews to help them master the concept of matter and the atomic theory of matter.

## Visual Learning

**Figures 6 and 7** Have students compare Thomson's model with Rutherford's model. How are they the same? Both are spherical and contain particles. How are they different? Thomson's model is like a solid ball, while Rutherford's is mostly empty space, like a cloud.

**Figure 8** This simplified Bohr model shows a nucleus of protons and neutrons and electron paths based on energy levels.

**Discovering the Neutron** Rutherford had been puzzled by one observation from his experiments with alpha particles. After the collisions, the nuclei seemed to be heavier. Where did this extra mass come from? James Chadwick, a student of Rutherford's, answered this question. The alpha particles themselves were not heavier, but the atoms that had been bombarded had given off new particles. Chadwick experimented with these new particles and found that, unlike electrons, the paths of these particles were not affected by an electric field. To explain his observations, he said that these particles came from the nucleus and had no charge. Chadwick called these uncharged particles **neutrons** (NEW trahn). His proton-neutron model of the atomic nucleus is still accepted today.

## Improving the Atomic Model

Early in the twentieth century, a scientist named Niels Bohr found evidence that electrons in atoms are arranged according to energy levels. The lowest energy level is closest to the nucleus and can hold only two electrons. Higher energy levels are farther from the nucleus and can contain more electrons. To explain these energy levels, some scientists thought that the electrons might orbit an atom's nucleus in paths that are specific distances from the nucleus, as shown in **Figure 8.** This is similar to how the planets orbit the Sun.

**The Modern Atomic Model** As a result of continuing research, scientists now realize that because electrons have characteristics that are similar to waves and particles, their energy levels are not defined, planet-like orbits around the nucleus. Rather, it seems most likely that electrons move in what is called the atom's electron cloud, as shown in **Figure 9.**

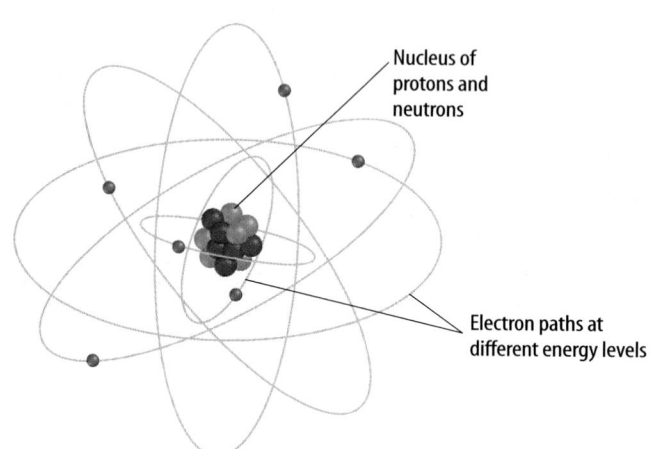

Nucleus of protons and neutrons

Electron paths at different energy levels

**The Electron Cloud** The electron cloud is a spherical cloud of varying density surrounding the nucleus. The varying density shows where an electron is more or less likely to be. Atoms with electrons in higher energy levels have electron clouds of different shapes that also show where those electrons are likely to be. Generally, the electron cloud has a radius 10,000 times that of the nucleus.

**Further Research** By the 1930s, it was recognized that matter was made up of atoms, which were, in turn, made up of protons, neutrons, and electrons. But scientists, called physicists, continued to study the basic parts of this atom. Today, they have succeeded in breaking down protons and neutrons into even smaller particles called quarks. These particles can combine to make other kinds of tiny particles, too. The six types of quarks are *up, down, strange, charmed, top,* and *bottom.* Quarks have fractional electric charges of $+2/3$ or $-1/3$, unlike the $+1$ charge of a proton or the $-1$ charge of an electron. Research will continue as new discoveries are made about the structure of matter.

Nucleus

Electron cloud

**Figure 9** This model of the atom shows the electrons moving around the nucleus in a region called an electron cloud. The dark cloud of color represents the area where the electron is more likely to be found.
**Infer** *What does the intensity of color near the nucleus suggest?*

## section 1 review

### Summary

**What is matter?**
- Matter is anything that has mass and takes up space.
- Matter is composed of atoms.

**Models of the Atom**
- Democritus introduced the idea of an atom. Lavoisier showed matter is neither created nor destroyed, just changed.
- Dalton's ideas led to the atomic theory of matter.
- Thomson discovered the electron.
- Rutherford discovered protons exist in the nucleus.
- Chadwick discovered the neutron.

**Improving the Atomic Model**
- Niels Bohr suggested electrons move in energy levels.
- More recent physicists introduced the idea of the electron cloud and were able to break down protons and neutrons into smaller particles called quarks.

### Self Check

1. **List** five examples of matter and five examples that are not matter. Explain your answers.
2. **Describe** and name the parts of the atom.
3. **Explain** why the word *atom* was an appropriate term for Democritus's idea.
4. **Think Critically** When neutrons were discovered, were these neutrons created in the experiment? How does Lavoisier's work help answer this question?
5. **Explain** the law of conservation of matter using your own examples.
6. **Think Critically** What made Niels Bohr predict that electrons were arranged in energy levels?

#### Applying Skills

7. **Classify** each scientist and his contribution according to the type of discovery each person made. Explain why you grouped certain scientists together.
8. **Evaluate Others' Data and Conclusions** Analyze, review, and critique the strengths and weaknesses of Thomson's "cookie dough" theory using the results of Rutherford's gold foil experiment.

## section 1 review

1. Possible answers: matter: things that have mass and occupy space; not matter: ideas, emotions
2. A nucleus consists of positively charged protons and neutral neutrons; negatively charged electrons move outside the nucleus.
3. *Atom* means cannot be divided.
4. No; According to the law of conservation of matter, matter cannot be created or destroyed.
5. Possible answer: wood burning in a fireplace is an example of the law of conservation of mass. The wood and oxygen from the air have the same mass as the ash, water, and gases

that are produced.
6. The electron cloud model, unlike Bohr's model, does not have the electrons moving around the nucleus in a planet-like orbit.
7. Classification schemes will vary.
8. Thomson: atom is a ball of positive charge with electrons embedded in

it. Rutherford: atom is mostly empty space with electrons scattered around small nucleus. Strength: shows atom is divisible and composed of charged particles. Weakness: does not show atom is mostly space and has "structure".

# section 2

# The Simplest Matter

**Bellringer**

**Section Focus Transparencies** also are available on the Interactive Chalkboard CD-ROM.

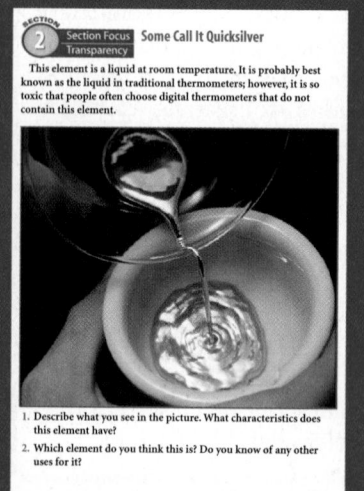

SECTION 2 Section Focus Transparency **Some Call It Quicksilver**

This element is a liquid at room temperature. It is probably best known as the liquid in traditional thermometers; however, it is so toxic that people often choose digital thermometers that do not contain this element.

1. Describe what you see in the picture. What characteristics does this element have?
2. Which element do you think this is? Do you know of any other uses for it?

Matter

## Tie to Prior Knowledge

**Chemical Formulas** Many students are familiar with the chemical formula for water, $H_2O$. Ask whether they know what the symbols *H* and *O* represent. *H* represents the element hydrogen; *O* represents the element oxygen. Have students list the names and symbols of any other elements they know.

## as you read

### *What* You'll Learn

- **Describe** the relationship between elements and the periodic table.
- **Explain** the meaning of atomic mass and atomic number.
- **Identify** what makes an isotope.
- **Contrast** metals, metalloids, and nonmetals.

### *Why* It's Important

Everything on Earth is made of the elements that are listed on the periodic table.

### ⚙ Review Vocabulary

**mass:** a measure of the amount of matter an object has

### New Vocabulary

- element
- atomic number
- isotope
- mass number
- atomic mass
- metal
- nonmetal
- metalloid

## The Elements

Have you watched television today? TV sets are common, yet each one is a complex system. The outer case is made mostly of plastic, and the screen is made of glass. Many of the parts that conduct electricity are metals or combinations of metals. Other parts in the interior of the set contain materials that barely conduct electricity. All of the different materials have one thing in common: they are made up of even simpler materials. In fact, if you had the proper equipment, you could separate the plastics, glass, and metals into these simpler materials.

**One Kind of Atom** Eventually, though, you would separate the materials into groups of atoms. At that point, you would have a collection of elements. An **element** is matter made of only one kind of atom. At least 115 elements are known and about 90 of them occur naturally on Earth. These elements make up gases in the air, minerals in rocks, and liquids such as water. Examples of naturally occurring elements include the oxygen and nitrogen in the air you breathe and the metals gold, silver, aluminum, and iron. The other elements are known as synthetic elements. These elements have been made in nuclear reactions by scientists with machines called particle accelerators, like the one shown in **Figure 10.** Some synthetic elements have important uses in medical testing and are found in smoke detectors and heart pacemaker batteries.

**Figure 10** The Tevatron has a circumference of 6.3 km—a distance that allows particles to accelerate to high speeds. These high-speed collisions can create synthetic elements.

266

---

## Section 2 Resource Manager

**Chapter FAST FILE Resources**
- Transparency Activity, p. 41
- Directed Reading for Content Mastery, p. 27
- Enrichment, p. 27
- Reinforcement, p. 24
- Lab Worksheet, pp. 5–6

**Physical Science Critical Thinking/Problem Solving,** p. 13
**Science Inquiry Labs,** pp. 49–50
**Earth Science Critical Thinking/Problem Solving,** p. 2

Figure 11 When you look for information in the library, a system of organization called the Dewey Decimal Classification System helps you find a book quickly and efficiently.

## The Periodic Table

Suppose you go to a library, like the one shown in **Figure 11,** to look up information for a school assignment. How would you find the information? You could look randomly on shelves as you walk up and down rows of books, but the chances of finding your book would be slim. To avoid such haphazard searching, some libraries use the Dewey Decimal Classification System to categorize and organize their volumes and to help you find books quickly and efficiently.

**Charting the Elements** Chemists have created a chart called the periodic table of the elements to help them organize and display the elements. **Figure 12** shows how scientists changed their model of the periodic table over time.

On the inside back cover of this book, you will find a modern version of the periodic table. Each element is represented by a chemical symbol that contains one to three letters. The symbols are a form of chemical shorthand that chemists use to save time and space—on the periodic table as well as in written formulas. The symbols are an important part of an international system that is understood by scientists everywhere.

The elements are organized on the periodic table by their properties. There are rows and columns that represent relationships between the elements. The rows in the table are called periods. The elements in a row have the same number of energy levels. The columns are called groups. The elements in each group have similar properties related to their structure. They also tend to form similar bonds.

| Dewey Decimal Classification System | |
|---|---|
| 000 | Computers, information and general reference |
| 100 | Philosophy and psychology |
| 200 | Religion |
| 300 | Social sciences |
| 400 | Languages |
| 500 | Science |
| 600 | Technology |
| 700 | Arts and recreation |
| 800 | Literature |
| 900 | History and geography |

**Science Online**

**Topic: New Elements**

Visit in7.msscience.com for Web links to information about new elements.

**Activity** Research physical properties of two synthetic elements.

### Fun Fact

The Fermilab, which is home to the Tevatron particle accelerator, is about 20,000 times longer than Thompson's cathode-ray tube.

## Visualizing the Periodic Table

Have students examine the pictures and read the captions. Then ask the following questions.

Why do you think the periodic table is so useful to scientists? It helps them organize and understand the chemical properties of the elements.

One difference between Mendeleev's table and the one used today is that his table lacks the column containing the elements helium through radon. Why do you think this is? None of the elements in that column had been discovered in Mendeleev's time. This is because they are not common and they don't readily undergo chemical reactions.

### Activity

**Periodic Groups** Divide the class into eighteen groups. Assign each group a different group of elements from the periodic table. Have them research the similarities and differences among the elements in their respective groups and make a poster illustrating the properties of these elements. L2

COOP LEARN **IS** **Interpersonal**

## Fun Fact

Mendeleev left gaps in his periodic table to locate the next element in its proper family and predicted properties of undiscovered elements that would fit these spaces. His predictions were confirmed when three predicted elements, gallium, germanium, and scandium were discovered.

---

## NATIONAL GEOGRAPHIC VISUALIZING THE PERIODIC TABLE

**Figure 12**

The familiar periodic table that adorns many science classrooms is based on a number of earlier efforts to identify and classify the elements. In the 1790s, one of the first lists of elements and their compounds was compiled by French chemist Antoine-Laurent Lavoisier, who is shown in the background picture with his wife and assistant, Marie Anne. Three other tables are shown here.

John Dalton (Britain, 1803) used symbols to represent elements. His table also assigned masses to each element.

An early alchemist put together this table of elements and compounds. Some of the symbols have their origin in astrology.

Dmitri Mendeleev (Russia, 1869) arranged the 63 elements known to exist at that time into groups based on their chemical properties and atomic weights. He left gaps for elements he predicted were yet to be discovered.

268   CHAPTER 9  Atoms, Elements, and the Periodic Table

---

## Teacher FYI

**Mendeleev's Periodic Table** In 1869, Dmitri Mendeleev published a periodic table based on properties and atomic masses of 60 known elements. He made a card for each element. Each card contained the element's symbol, atomic mass, and its characteristic chemical and physical properties. By arranging the cards on a table, in order of increasing atomic mass, and by grouping elements of similar properties together, the resultant "periodic table" showed vertical, horizontal, and diagonal relationships. Mendeleev left gaps in his table for future discovery of some of the then unknown elements.

## Identifying Characteristics

Each element is different and has unique properties. These differences can be described in part by looking at the relationships between the atomic particles in each element. The periodic table contains numbers that describe these relationships.

**Number of Protons and Neutrons** Look up the element chlorine on the periodic table found on the inside back cover of your book. Cl is the symbol for chlorine, as shown in **Figure 13,** but what are the two numbers? The top number is the element's **atomic number.** It tells you the number of protons in the nucleus of each atom of that element. Every atom of chlorine, for example, has 17 protons in its nucleus.

 **Reading Check** *What are the atomic numbers for Cs, Ne, Pb, and U?*

**Isotopes** Although the number of protons changes from element to element, every atom of the same element has the same number of protons. However, the number of neutrons can vary even for one element. For example, some chlorine atoms have 18 neutrons in their nucleus while others have 20. These two types of chlorine atoms are chlorine-35 and chlorine-37. They are called **isotopes** (I suh tohps), which are atoms of the same element that have different numbers of neutrons.

You can tell someone exactly which isotope you are referring to by using its mass number. An atom's **mass number** is the number of protons plus the number of neutrons it contains. The numbers 35 and 37, which were used to refer to chlorine, are mass numbers. Hydrogen has three isotopes with mass numbers of 1, 2, and 3. They are shown in **Figure 14.** Each hydrogen atom always has one proton, but in each isotope the number of neutrons is different.

**Figure 13** The periodic table block for chlorine shows its symbol, atomic number, and atomic mass.
**Determine** *if chlorine atoms are more or less massive than carbon atoms.*

**Figure 14** Three isotopes of hydrogen are known to exist. They have zero, one, and two neutrons in addition to their one proton. Protium, with only the one proton, is the most abundant isotope.

1 Proton
0 Neutrons

1 Proton
1 Neutron

1 Proton
2 Neutrons

Protium

Deuterium

Tritium

---

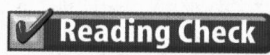
---

**Classifying by Atomic Mass** Mendeleev grouped elements based on their atomic masses. Have students find three pairs of elements on the periodic table at the back of the book that would have been switched in Mendeleev's table based on atomic masses. Cobalt is element 9 and has an atomic mass of 58.933; nickel is element 10 and has an atomic mass of 58.693. Other pairs of elements that would have been switched on Mendeleev's table are iodine and tellurium, and argon and potassium. L2

**IS** **Logical-Mathematical**

## Quick Demo

### Testing for Metals

**Materials** copper wire; 1.5-V mini lightbulb, D-size battery, electrical tape, wire cutter, different metallic and nonmetallic objects or materials to test

**Estimated Time** 15 minutes

**Procedure** Cut a piece of copper wire and tape one end to the positive end of the battery and wrap the other end around the bottom of the lightbulb. Cut another piece of copper wire and tape that end to the negative end of the battery. Cut another piece of copper wire and tape one end to the bottom of the lightbulb. Take one of the objects you are testing and place the wire that is connected to the negative side of the battery to one end of the object and place the wire that is connected to the bottom of the lightbulb to the other end of the object. Repeat the last step until you have tested all the objects. Observe whether the lightbulb lights up or not for each object that is tested. A property of metals is that they conduct electricity. This experiment is based on that property. Make students notice that metallic materials made the lightbulb light up while other nonmetals didn't.

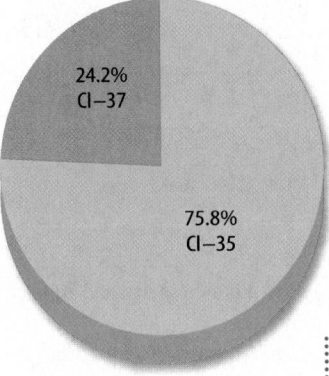

**Circle Graph Showing Abundance of Chlorine Isotopes**

Average atomic mass = 35.45 u

24.2%
Cl–37

75.8%
Cl–35

**Figure 15** If you have 1,000 atoms of chlorine, about 758 will be chlorine-35 and have a mass of 34.97 u each. About 242 will be chlorine-37 and have a mass of 36.97 u each. The total mass of the 1,000 atoms is 35,454 u, so the average mass of one chlorine atom is about 35.45 u.

**Figure 16** The artisan is chasing, or chiseling, the malleable metal into the desired form.

**Atomic Mass** The **atomic mass** is the weighted average mass of the isotopes of an element. The atomic mass is the number found below the element symbol in **Figure 13.** The unit that scientists use for atomic mass is called the atomic mass unit, which is given the symbol u. It is defined as 1/12 the mass of a carbon-12 atom.

The calculation of atomic mass takes into account the different isotopes of the element. Chlorine's atomic mass of 35.45 u could be confusing because there aren't any chlorine atoms that have that exact mass. About 76 percent of chlorine atoms are chlorine-35 and about 24 percent are chlorine-37, as shown in **Figure 15.** The weighted average mass of all chlorine atoms is 35.45 u.

## Classification of Elements

Elements fall into three general categories—metals, metalloids (ME tuh loydz), and nonmetals. The elements in each category have similar properties.

**Metals** generally have a shiny or metallic luster and are good conductors of heat and electricity. All metals, except mercury, are solids at room temperature. Metals are malleable (MAL yuh bul), which means they can be bent and pounded into various shapes. The beautiful form of the shell-shaped basin in **Figure 16** is a result of this characteristic. Metals are also ductile, which means they can be drawn into wires without breaking. If you look at the periodic table, you can see that most of the elements are metals.

## Science Journal

**Medical Uses of Isotopes** Have students research and write essays on isotopes that are used to diagnose and treat diseases. Some isotopes students might research include $^{67}$Cu, $^{111}$In, $^{186}$Re, $^{82}$Sr, $^{68}$Ge, $^{153}$Sm, and $^{103}$Pd. L3 P

## Differentiated Instruction

**Challenge** Have students research the following questions: How were alchemists' ideas about matter different from modern ideas? How is this reflected in their version of the periodic table? How did modern chemistry develop from the methods of alchemy? Ask students to share their findings with the class. L3 **IS** **Linguistic**

**Other Elements** Nonmetals are elements that are usually dull in appearance. Most are poor conductors of heat and electricity. Many are gases at room temperature, and bromine is a liquid. The solid nonmetals are generally brittle, meaning they cannot change shape easily without breaking. The nonmetals are essential to the chemicals of life. More than 97 percent of your body is made up of various nonmetals, as shown in **Figure 17.** You can see that, except for hydrogen, the nonmetals are found on the right side of the periodic table.

**Metalloids** are elements that have characteristics of metals and nonmetals. On the periodic table, metalloids are found between the metals and nonmetals. All metalloids are solids at room temperature. Some metalloids are shiny and many are conductors, but they are not as good at conducting heat and electricity as metals are. Some metalloids, such as silicon, are used to make the electronic circuits in computers, televisions, and other electronic devices.

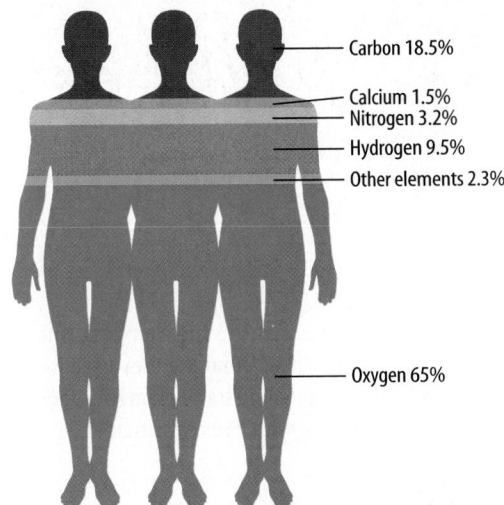

Carbon 18.5%
Calcium 1.5%
Nitrogen 3.2%
Hydrogen 9.5%
Other elements 2.3%
Oxygen 65%

**Figure 17** You are made up of mostly nonmetals.

✔ **Reading Check** *What is a metalloid?*

**3 Assess**

**DAILY INTERVENTION**

**Check for Understanding**
**Linguistic** Have small groups of students classify classroom objects as being made mostly of metals or nonmetals and record their answers on a chart. Then have students write a statement that can be used to determine if their chart is correct.
Possible Answers:

| Metal | Nonmetal |
|---|---|
| File cabinet | Carpet |
| Chair legs | Plastic seat |

Metal items are shiny, solid at room temperature, conduct heat and electricity, and can be pounded into different shapes without breaking. Nonmetals do not have those properties.

**Reteach**
**Periodic Table** Write all the information found on the periodic table for one element on the board. Have students tell what each symbol or number represents. L2 ⓘⓢ **Visual-Spatial**

---

## section 2 review

### Summary

**The Elements**
- An element is matter made of only one type of atom.
- Some elements occur naturally on Earth. Synthetic elements are made in nuclear reactions in particle accelerators.
- Elements are divided into three categories based on certain properties.

**The Periodic Table**
- The periodic table arranges and displays all known elements in an orderly way.
- Each element has a chemical symbol.

**Identifying Characteristics**
- Each element has a unique number of protons, called the atomic mass number.
- Isotopes of an element are important when determining the atomic mass of an element.

### Self Check

1. **Explain** some of the uses of metals based on their properties.
2. **Describe** the difference between atomic number and atomic mass.
3. **Define** the term *isotope*. Explain how two isotopes of an element are different.
4. **Determine** how many isotopes of krypton are known.
5. **Think Critically** Describe how to find the atomic number for the element oxygen. Explain what this information tells you about oxygen.

#### Applying Math

6. **Simple Equation** An atom of niobium has a mass number of 93. How many neutrons are in the nucleus of this atom? An atom of phosphorus has 15 protons and 15 neutrons in the nucleus. What is the mass number of this isotope?

 Science Online in7.msscience.com/self_check_quiz

SECTION 2 The Simplest Matter **271**

---

## section 2 review

1. good conductors of heat and electricity (electrical circuits and cookware), malleable (formed into tools), ductile (drawn into wires)
2. atomic number: the number of protons in the nucleus of each atom of an element; mass number: the sum of an atom's protons and neutrons
3. Isotopes are atoms of the same element that contain different numbers of neutrons.
4. Krypton has six naturally occurring isotopes.
5. Locate oxygen on the periodic table. Oxygen's atomic number (8) is the large number in the element's box and means that every atom of oxygen contains eight protons in its nucleus.
6. $93 - 41 = 52$ n; $15$ p $+ 15$ n $= 30$

✔ **Assessment**

**Oral** Name elements on the periodic table at random. Ask students to tell whether each selected element is a metal, a metalloid, or a nonmetal.

## Real-World Question

**Purpose** Students classify elements and build a periodic table that shows their classifications.

L2  IS  **Visual-Spatial**

**Process Skills** classify, compare and contrast, make and use tables, interpret data, predict

**Time Required** two to three class periods

## Procedure

**Teaching Strategy** Because a large amount of information is available for most elements, advise students to focus their efforts and collect only key information.

## Conclude and Apply

1. The table students make will look like the periodic table, but only certain elements will be present.

2. This element should be shiny in the solid state, have metallic characteristics such as high electrical and thermal conductivities, and be reactive with nonmetals to form compounds.

### ✔ Assessment

**Portfolio** Take a photograph of the class periodic table and have a copy made for each student. Have students include the index cards for their elements and the photograph of the class periodic table in their portfolios. Use **Performance Assessment in the Science Classroom,** pp. 135; 169.  P

# Elements and the Periodic Table

The periodic table organizes the elements, but what do they look like? What are they used for? In this lab, you'll examine some elements and share your findings with your classmates.

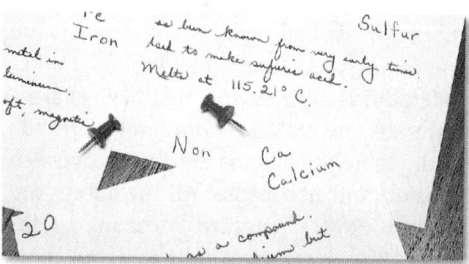

## Real-World Question

What are some of the characteristics and purposes of the chemical elements?

### Goals

■ **Classify** the chemical elements.
■ **Organize** the elements into the groups and periods of the periodic table.

### Materials

colored markers          large bulletin board
large index cards         8½-in × 14-in paper
Merck Index               thumbtacks
encyclopedia              *pushpins
*other reference
  materials               *Alternate materials

### Safety Precaution

**WARNING:** *Use care when handling sharp objects.*

## Procedure

1. Select the assigned number of elements from the list provided by your teacher.

2. **Design** an index card for each of your selected elements. On each card, mark the element's atomic number in the upper left-hand corner and write its symbol and name in the upper right-hand corner.

3. **Research** each of the elements and write several sentences on the card about its appearance, its other properties, and its uses.

4. **Classify** each of your elements as a metal, a metalloid, or a nonmetal based upon its properties.

5. **Write** the appropriate classification on each of your cards using the colored marker chosen by your teacher.

6. Work with your classmates to make a large periodic table. Use thumbtacks to attach your cards to a bulletin board in their proper positions on the periodic table.

7. **Draw** your own periodic table. Place the elements' symbols and atomic numbers in the proper locations on your table.

## Conclude and Apply

1. **Interpret** the class data and classify the elements into the categories metal, metalloid, and nonmetal. Highlight each category in a different color on your periodic table.

2. **Predict** the properties of a yet-undiscovered element located directly under francium on the periodic table.

**272   CHAPTER 9** Atoms, Elements, and the Periodic Table

## Communicating Your Data

Have students use a database program to display their results. The printed database can be shared with a small group or with the class.

## Using Science Words

**Word Meaning** Have students use the dictionary to determine the meaning of the word *element*. Ask them why chemical particles are referred to as elements. In chemistry, the basic chemical particles are called elements because elements are fundamental components of matter.  L2

# Compounds and Mixtures

## Substances

Scientists classify matter in several ways that depend on what it is made of and how it behaves. For example, matter that has the same composition and properties throughout is called a **substance.** Elements, such as a bar of gold or a sheet of aluminum, are substances. When different elements combine, other substances are formed.

**Compounds** What do you call the colorless liquid that flows from the kitchen faucet? You probably call it water, but maybe you've seen it written $H_2O$. The elements hydrogen and oxygen exist as separate, colorless gases. However, these two elements can combine, as shown in **Figure 18,** to form the compound water, which is different from the elements that make it up. A **compound** is a substance whose smallest unit is made up of atoms of more than one element bonded together.

Compounds often have properties that are different from the elements that make them up. Water is distinctly different from the elements that make it up. It is also different from another compound made from the same elements. Have you ever used hydrogen peroxide ($H_2O_2$) to disinfect a cut? This compound is a different combination of hydrogen and oxygen and has different properties from those of water.

Water is a nonirritating liquid that is used for bathing, drinking, cooking, and much more. In contrast, hydrogen peroxide carries warnings on its labels such as *Keep Hydrogen Peroxide Out of the Eyes.* Although it is useful in solutions for cleaning contact lenses, it is not safe for your eyes as it comes from the bottle.

**Figure 18** A space shuttle is powered by the reaction between liquid hydrogen and liquid oxygen. The reaction produces a large amount of energy and the compound water.
**Explain** *why a car that burns hydrogen rather than gasoline would be friendly to the environment.*

### as you read

*What* **You'll Learn**
- **Identify** the characteristics of a compound.
- **Compare and contrast** different types of mixtures.

*Why* **It's Important**
The food you eat, the materials you use, and all matter can be classified by compounds or mixtures.

**Review Vocabulary**
**formula:** shows which elements and how many atoms of each make up a compound

**New Vocabulary**
- substance
- mixture
- compound

**1** **Motivate**

**Bellringer**

**Section Focus Transparencies** also are available on the Interactive Chalkboard CD-ROM.
L2 ELL

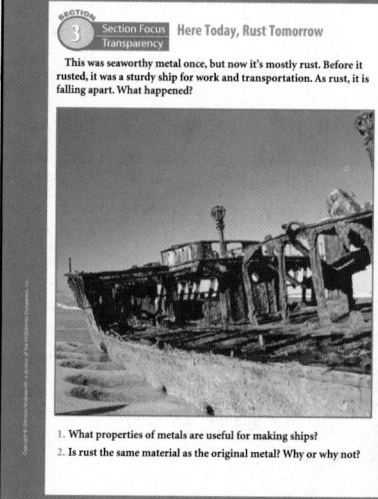

**3** Section Focus Transparency **Here Today, Rust Tomorrow**

This was seaworthy metal once, but now it's mostly rust. Before it rusted, it was a sturdy ship for work and transportation. As rust, it is falling apart. What happened?

1. What properties of metals are useful for making ships?
2. Is rust the same material as the original metal? Why or why not?

### Tie to Prior Knowledge
**Combining Elements** Have students recall chemical formulas for substances such as water or salt. $H_2O$ and NaCl Show a periodic table and point out that these substances represent a combination of elements from the periodic table.

### Caption Answer
**Figure 18** It would release water as a by-product rather than pollution.

---

### Section 3 Resource Manager

**Chapter *FAST FILE* Resources**
Transparency Activity, p. 42
Directed Reading for Content Mastery, pp. 17, 18
MiniLAB, p. 4
Enrichment, p. 28

Lab Worksheet, pp. 7–8
Lab Activity, pp. 9–10, 11–12

### Make a Model

**H₂O₂ and H₂O** While discussing the law of definite proportions, have students make models of the compounds in **Figure 19** using materials such as gumdrops and toothpicks. Have them share their models with the class. L1 ELL IS **Kinesthetic**

### Mini LAB

**Purpose** Students observe and compare the properties of three compounds. L2 ELL IS **Visual-Spatial**

**Materials** sugar, rubbing alcohol, salad oil, glasses (3), hot water

**Teaching Strategy** Warn students to use hot tap water, not boiling water, in Step 3.

### Analysis

1. rubbing alcohol—colorless liquid, strong chemical smell, dissolves in water; salad oil—golden liquid, more viscous than rubbing alcohol, little or no odor, floats on water; sugar—white granular solid, little or no odor, dissolves easily in water

2. The number of atoms of each type of element and their arrangement account for the different properties.

### Assessment

**Content** Have students draw pictures showing how the substances mix with each other in the MiniLAB. Use **Performance Assessment in the Science Classroom,** p. 127. P

Try at Home

### Reading Check

**Answer** $C_3H_8$

---

**Figure 19** The elements hydrogen and oxygen can form two compounds—water and hydrogen peroxide. Note the differences in their structure.

### Mini LAB

**Comparing Compounds**

**Procedure**

1. Collect the following substances—**granular sugar, rubbing alcohol,** and **salad oil.**

2. Observe the color, appearance, and state of each substance. Note the thickness or texture of each substance.

3. Stir a spoonful of each substance into separate **glasses** of **hot tap water** and observe.

**Analysis**

1. Compare the different properties of the substances.

2. The formulas of the three substances are made of only carbon, hydrogen, and oxygen. Infer how they can have different properties.

Try at Home

---

**Compounds Have Formulas** What's the difference between water and hydrogen peroxide? $H_2O$ is the chemical formula for water, and $H_2O_2$ is the formula for hydrogen peroxide. The formula tells you which elements make up a compound as well as how many atoms of each element are present. Look at **Figure 19.** The subscript number written below and to the right of each element's symbol tells you how many atoms of that element exist in one unit of that compound. For example, hydrogen peroxide has two atoms of hydrogen and two atoms of oxygen. Water is made up of two atoms of hydrogen and one atom of oxygen.

Carbon dioxide, $CO_2$, is another common compound. Carbon dioxide is made up of one atom of carbon and two atoms of oxygen. Carbon and oxygen also can form the compound carbon monoxide, CO, which is a gas that is poisonous to all warm-blooded animals. As you can see, no subscript is used when only one atom of an element is present. A given compound always is made of the same elements in the same proportion. For example, water always has two hydrogen atoms for every oxygen atom, no matter what the source of the water is. No matter what quantity of the compound you have, the formula of the compound always remains the same. If you have 12 atoms of hydrogen and six atoms of oxygen, the compound is still written $H_2O$, but you have six molecules of $H_2O$ (6 $H_2O$), not $H_{12}O_6$. The formula of a compound communicates its identity and makeup to any scientist in the world.

### Reading Check

Propane has three carbon and eight hydrogen atoms. What is its chemical formula?

---

## Visual Learning

**Figure 19** Ask students to write the formula for hydrogen peroxide. ($H_2O_2$) Point out how much easier it is to write the chemical formulas than it is to write out all of the words.

## Teacher FYI

**Chemical Formulas** Structural formulas show the bonding relationship (e.g. H-O-O-H); molecular formulas show how many atoms of each element are present (e.g. $H_2O_2$); empirical formulas show kinds of atoms are present, and gives the simplest whole number ratio of atoms in the compound (e.g. HO).

## Mixtures

When two or more substances (elements or compounds) come together but don't combine to make a new substance, a **mixture** results. Unlike compounds, the proportions of the substances in a mixture can be changed without changing the identity of the mixture. For example, if you put some sand into a bucket of water, you have a mixture of sand and water. If you add more sand or more water, it's still a mixture of sand and water. Its identity has not changed. Air is another mixture. Air is a mixture of nitrogen, oxygen, and other gases, which can vary at different times and places. Whatever the proportion of gases, it is still air. Even your blood is a mixture that can be separated, as shown in **Figure 20,** by a machine called a centrifuge.

 **Reading Check** *How do the proportions of a mixture relate to its identity?*

**Figure 20** The layers in this blood sample include plasma, platelets, white blood cells, and red blood cells.

- Plasma
- Platelets and white blood cells
- Red blood cells

---

### Applying Science

#### What's the best way to desalt ocean water?

You can't drink ocean water because it contains salt and other suspended materials. Or can you? In many areas of the world where drinking water is in short supply, methods for getting the salt out of salt water are being used to meet the demand for fresh water. Use your problem-solving skills to find the best method to use in a particular area.

**Methods for Desalting Ocean Water**

| Process | Amount of Water a Unit Can Desalt in a Day ($m^3$) | Special Needs | Number of People Needed to Operate |
|---|---|---|---|
| Distillation | 1,000 to 200,000 | lots of energy to boil the water | many |
| Electrodialysis | 10 to 4,000 | stable source of electricity | 1 to 2 persons |

#### Identifying the Problem

The table above compares desalting methods. In distillation, the ocean water is heated. Pure water boils off and is collected, and the salt is left behind. Electrodialysis uses an electric current to pull salt particles out of water.

#### Solving the Problem

1. What method(s) might you use to desalt the water for a large population where energy is plentiful?
2. What method(s) would you choose to use in a single home?

---

### Discussion

**Compounds** Remind students that a compound is a pure substance whose smallest unit is made up of atoms of more than one element. What compounds do you use in your daily activities? Examples include table salt, water, and sugar.

**Reading Check**

**Answer** They can change without changing the identity of a mixture.

### Applying Science

**Answers**

1. Distillation would be best to use for a large population. Although the unit needs many operators and lots of energy, it produces the largest amount of fresh water.
2. Electrodialysis works in a home or small resort hotel. This method produces smaller amounts of fresh water and does not require many skilled operators. It only needs a stable source of electricity.

## Differentiated Instruction

**Challenge** Have students research the following question and develop answers. If there were a mixture of sand and salt in a beaker, how would you separate the sand from the salt? Ask students to share their findings with the class. The salt can be dissolved using water and later evaporated. L3

---

## Cultural Diversity

**Ocher** Ocher, a naturally occurring iron oxide ($Fe_2O_3$), is formed by the weathering of rocks. Historically, ocher has been used to produce rock paintings and continues to be used for artwork today. It comes in a variety of colors, depending on the percentage of iron oxide present. Hematite ore is one source of ocher that can be ground to produce a bright red color. Ocher also has been found in burial plots of several different cultures. Have students find out the other colors produced by iron oxide ores. Other colors produced include black (magnetite), brown to dark yellow (limonite), and brown (siderite and pyrite).

**Figure 21** Mixtures are part of your everyday life.

**Science Online**

**Topic: Mixtures**
Visit in7.msscience.com for Web links to information about separating mixtures.

**Activity** Describe the difference between mixtures and compounds.

**INTEGRATE Life Science** Your blood is a mixture made up of elements and compounds. It contains white blood cells, red blood cells, water, and a number of dissolved substances. The different parts of blood can be separated and used by doctors in different ways. The proportions of the substances in your blood change daily, but the mixture does not change its identity.

**Separating Mixtures** Sometimes you can use a liquid to separate a mixture of solids. For example, if you add water to a mixture of sugar and sand, only the sugar dissolves in the water. The sand then can be separated from the sugar and water by pouring the mixture through a filter. Heating the remaining solution will separate the water from the sugar.

At other times, separating a mixture of solids of different sizes might be as easy as pouring them through successively smaller sieves or filters. A mixture of marbles, pebbles, and sand could be separated in this way.

**276** CHAPTER 9 Atoms, Elements, and the Periodic Table

**Homogeneous or Heterogeneous** Mixtures, such as the ones shown in **Figure 21,** can be classified as homogeneous or heterogeneous. *Homogeneous* means "the same throughout." You can't see the different parts in this type of mixture. In fact, you might not always know that homogeneous mixtures are mixtures because you can't tell by looking. Which mixtures in **Figure 21** are homogeneous? No matter how closely you look, you can't see the individual parts that make up air or the parts of the mixture called brass in the lamp shown. Homogeneous mixtures can be solids, liquids, or gases.

A heterogeneous mixture has larger parts that are different from each other. You can see the different parts of a heterogeneous mixture, such as sand and water. How many heterogeneous mixtures are in **Figure 21?** A pepperoni and mushroom pizza is a tasty kind of heterogeneous mixture. Other examples of this kind of mixture include tacos, vegetable soup, a toy box full of toys, or a toolbox full of nuts and bolts.

**INTEGRATE Earth Science**

**Rocks and Minerals**
Scientists called geologists study rocks and minerals. A mineral is composed of a pure substance. Rocks are mixtures and can be described as being homogeneous or heterogeneous. Research to learn more about rocks and minerals and note some examples of homogeneous and heterogeneous rocks in your Science Journal.

**INTEGRATE Earth Science**

**Rocks and Minerals** Strictly speaking, the term *rocks* applies to the solid materials that make up Earth's crust. These materials are not homogeneous and have no definite chemical composition. *Minerals,* on the other hand, have more or less definite chemical compositions, crystal structures, and properties.

## 3 Assess

**DAILY INTERVENTION**

### Check for Understanding
**Visual-Spatial** Have students develop a demonstration that differentiates between homogeneous and heterogeneous mixtures. Possible answer: Homogeneous mixtures can include substances such as apple juice or non-carbonated soft drinks. Heterogeneous mixtures can include substances such as a tossed salad, or fruit salad.

### Reteach
**Blood** Ask a medical technologist to make a class presentation explaining the different parts of the mixture known as human blood and describing how these parts can be separated by physical means. ⌊L1⌋

---

### section **3** review

#### Summary

**Substances**
- A substance can be either an element or a compound.
- A compound contains more than one kind of element bonded together.
- A chemical formula shows which elements and how many atoms of each make up a compound.

**Mixtures**
- A mixture contains substances that are not chemically bonded together.
- There are many ways to separate mixtures, based on their physical properties.
- Homogeneous mixtures are those that are the same throughout. These types of mixtures can be solids, liquids, or gases.
- Heterogeneous mixtures have larger parts that are different from each other.

#### Self Check

1. **List** three examples of compounds and three examples of mixtures. Explain your choices.
2. **Determine** Ethanol is an alcohol made up of carbon, hydrogen, and oxygen atoms. How many atoms of each element does ethanol have?
3. **Think Critically** Explain whether your breakfast was a compound, a homogeneous mixture, or a heterogeneous mixture.

##### Applying Skills

4. **Compare and contrast** compounds and mixtures based on what you have learned from this section.
5. **Use a Database** Use a computerized card catalog or database to find information about one element from the periodic table. Include information about the properties and uses of the mixtures and/or compounds in which the element is frequently found.

Science Online  in7.msscience.com/self_check_quiz    SECTION 3 Compounds and Mixtures  **277**

---

### section  review

1. Possible answers: compounds— water, carbon dioxide, table salt; mixtures— air, ocean water, brass; mixtures can be separated by physical means; compounds can't.
2. C:2; H:6; O:1
3. Answers will vary, but most breakfasts, such as orange juice and cold

cereal with milk, will be heterogeneous mixtures.
4. Possible answer: Compounds are pure substances whose properties vary from the original elements that they are made from. Mixtures are made from different parts and can be separated.

5. Sample answer: Carbon is found in the Sun, stars, comets, and atmospheres of most planets. It is present as carbon dioxide in the atmosphere and dissolved in water. It is a component of rocks as carbonates of calcium (limestone), magnesium, and iron.

## ☑ Assessment

**Process** Have students design an experimental procedure that they could use to separate a mixture of white sand and sugar. Use **Performance Assessment in the Science Classroom,** p. 95.

## Real-World Question

**Purpose** Students test for certain compounds and decide which are present in a mystery mixture. L2 ELL IS Logical-Mathematical

**Process Skills** form a hypothesis, communicate, observe and infer, recognize cause and effect, separate and control variables, interpret data

**Time Required** 45 minutes

## Procedure

**Materials** Compounds used are cornstarch, powdered sugar, and baking soda. Combine any two of these compounds to make the mystery mixture. Prepare iodine test solution by adding 7 g of iodine and 5 g of potassium iodide to 5 mL of water, then diluting to 100 mL with denatured alcohol.

### Safety Precautions

• Students must wear goggles and aprons. Remind students that while heating the test tube, the opening of the tube should never be pointed at themselves or others.

• Iodine is poisonous and will stain clothing.

• Remind students that test tubes should not be touched while they are hot.

---

## Goals

■ **Test** for the presence of certain compounds.

■ **Decide** which of these compounds are present in an unknown mixture.

## Materials

test tubes (4)
cornstarch
powdered sugar
baking soda
mystery mixture
small scoops (3)
dropper bottles (2)
iodine solution
white vinegar
hot plate
250-mL beaker
water (125 mL)
test-tube holder
small pie pan

## Safety Precautions

**WARNING:** *Use caution when handling hot objects. Substances could stain or burn clothing. Be sure to point the test tube away from your face and your classmates while heating.*

---

# Mystery Mixture

## Real-World Question

You will encounter many compounds that look alike. For example, a laboratory stockroom is filled with white powders. It is important to know what each is. In a kitchen, cornstarch, baking powder, and powdered sugar are compounds that look alike. To avoid mistaking one for another, you can learn how to identify them. Different compounds can be identified by using chemical tests. For example, some compounds react with certain liquids to produce gases. Other combinations produce distinctive colors. Some compounds have high melting points. Others have low melting points. How can the compounds in an unknown mixture be identified by experimentation?

---

## Alternative Inquiry Lab

**Separating Compounds** To extend this Lab into an Inquiry Lab, have students brainstorm and/or research the difference between mixtures and compounds. Chemical reactions are required to separate compounds. You may have students try reducing copper oxide ore by combining it with carbon powder and heating it in a crucible—they should get pure shiny copper metal as a result (keep the lid on and heat it as hot as possible for at least fifteen minutes). Special instruments (such as magnetic resonance imaging and infrared spectrometers) are available to find out what elements are in compounds, but tell students that these machines involve complex processes. Some students may want to research the MRI and IR processes.

## ▶ Procedure

1. Copy the data table into your Science Journal. Record your results carefully for each of the following steps.
2. Place a small scoopful of cornstarch on the pie pan. Do the same for the sugar and baking soda making separate piles. Add a drop of vinegar to each. Wash and dry the pan after you record your observations.
3. Again, place a small scoopful of cornstarch, sugar, and baking soda on the pie pan. Add a drop of iodine solution to each one. Wash and dry the pan after you record your observations.
4. Again place a small scoopful of each compound in a separate test tube. Hold the test tube with the test-tube holder and with an oven mitt. Gently heat the test tube in a beaker of boiling water on a hot plate.
5. Follow steps 2 through 4 to test your mystery mixture for each compound.

### Identifying Presence of Compounds

| Substance to Be Tested | Fizzes with Vinegar | Turns Blue with Iodine | Melts When Heated |
|---|---|---|---|
| Cornstarch | no | yes | no |
| Sugar | no | no | yes |
| Baking soda | yes | no | no |
| Mystery mix | yes | yes | yes |

## ▶ Analyze Your Data

**Identify** from your data table which compound(s) you have.

## ▶ Conclude and Apply

1. **Describe** how you decided which substances were in your unknown mixture.
2. **Explain** how you would be able to tell if all three compounds were not in your mystery substance.
3. **Draw a Conclusion** What would you conclude if you tested baking powder from your kitchen and found that it fizzed with vinegar, turned blue with iodine, and did not melt when heated?

### Communicating Your Data

Make a different data table to display your results in a new way. **For more help, refer to the Science Skill Handbook.**

---

### Assessment

**Performance** After students have determined the two compounds that were present in the mystery mixture, have them determine other possible two-material combinations and explain how the combinations would react when tested. Use **Performance Assessment in the Science Classroom,** p. 89.

### Communicating Your Data

Students could use illustrations, chemical symbols, or color to revise their data table.

---

## Teaching Strategies

- In Steps 2 and 3, have students use only sufficient amounts of the solids to produce satisfactory test results. Test your scoops to determine how much to use.
- In Step 4, have students use only enough solid to fill the bottom, rounded portion of the test tubes.

## ▶ Analyze Your Data

**Expected Outcome** Cornstarch will react with iodine to make a blue color. Sugar will melt when heated. Baking soda will fizz in the presence of vinegar.

**Error Analysis** If students let their experiments run together or do not clean their equipment, they may get erroneous results. Have students compare their results to the results of other groups. If results differ, discuss errors that could have caused the differences.

## ▶ Conclude and Apply

1. Answers will vary depending on the two compounds used for the mystery mixture. In describing their conclusions, students should include the data they gathered.
2. If all three compounds were absent from the mystery mixture, the mixture would not turn blue in the presence of iodine, it would not melt when heated, and it would not fizz with vinegar.
3. It contained baking soda and cornstarch.

## Content Background

Kashyapa lived during the 6th century B.C., and was the first to use the word *parmanu;* derived from the two Sanskrit words *param*, meaning "beyond", and *anu*, meaning "atom." Among other things, he proposed that two different classes of parmanu could combine to form what he called *dwinuka*, or binary molecules, of new substances.

The Chinese term for the five material agents of matter, as they called the five elements, is *wu hsing*. The Chinese believed that these material agents took part in cyclical patterns of change that resulted in the opposites, yin and yang.

## Discussion

**Atomic Theory** Do you think Kashyapa's ideas were known to Democritus when he developed his theory of the atom? Why or why not? Accept all well-supported answers. Point out to students on a globe the relative locations of Greece and India and remind them of the means of transportation and communication available at the time these two men lived.

## Historical Significance

Both the Chinese and Indian philosophies have roots in ancient history. Encourage students to choose a current scientific theory and use a variety of research tools to trace the idea back to its earliest origins. Make sure students understand that one theory may have origins in ideas that arose independently in different cultures. This activity will help students become aware that our modern theories have had a long history of development.

# Ancient Views of Matter

air

water

metal

**Two cultures observed the world around them differently**

The world's earliest scientists were people who were curious about the world around them and who tried to develop explanations for the things they observed. This type of observation and inquiry flourished in ancient cultures such as those found in India and China. Read on to see how the ancient Indians and Chinese defined matter.

### Indian Ideas

To Indians living about 3,000 years ago, the world was made up of five elements: fire, air, earth, water, and ether, which they thought of as an unseen substance that filled the heavens. Building upon this concept, the early Indian philosopher Kashyapa (kah SHI ah pah) proposed that the five elements could be broken down into smaller units called parmanu (par MAH new). Parmanu were similar to atoms in that they were too small to be seen but still retained the properties of the original element. Kashyapa also believed that each type of parmanu had unique physical and chemical properties.

Parmanu of earth elements, for instance, were heavier than parmanu of air elements. The different properties of the parmanu determined the characteristics of a substance. Kashyapa's ideas about matter are similar to those of the Greek philosopher Democritus, who lived centuries after Kashyapa.

### Chinese Ideas

The ancient Chinese also broke matter down into five elements: fire, wood, metal, earth, and water. Unlike the early Indians, however, the Chinese believed that the elements constantly changed form. For example, wood can be burned and thus changes to fire. Fire eventually dies down and becomes ashes, or earth. Earth gives forth metals from the ground. Dew or water collects on these metals, and the water then nurtures plants that grow into trees, or wood.

This cycle of constant change was explained in the fourth century B.C. by the philosopher Tsou Yen. Yen, who is known as the founder of Chinese scientific thought, wrote that all changes that took place in nature were linked to changes in the five elements.

fire

earth

**Research** Write a brief paragraph that compares and contrasts the ancient Indian and Chinese views of matter. How are they different? Similar? Which is closer to the modern view of matter? Explain.

Science Online

For more information, visit in7.msscience.com/time

## Resources for Teachers and Students

*Chemistry in Action*, by Nina Morgan, Oxford University Press, 1995

*The Periodic Kingdom*, by P.W. Atkins, Basic Books, 1995

**Research** Students will need to research their information by using the school's media center, the library, or visiting the link on the student page.

## Reviewing Main Ideas

### Section 1 Structure of Matter

1. Matter is anything that occupies space and has mass.

2. Matter is made up of atoms.

3. Atoms are made of smaller parts called protons, neutrons, and electrons.

4. Many models of atoms have been created as scientists try to discover and define the atom's internal structure. Today's model has a central nucleus with the protons and neutrons, and an electron cloud surrounding it.

### Section 2 The Simplest Matter

1. Elements are the building blocks of matter.

2. An element's atomic number tells how many protons its atoms contain, and its atomic mass tells the average mass of its atoms.

3. Isotopes are two or more atoms of the same element that have different numbers of neutrons.

### Section 3 Compounds and Mixtures

1. Compounds are substances that are produced when elements combine. Compounds contain specific proportions of the elements that make them up.

2. Mixtures are combinations of compounds and elements that have not formed new substances. Their proportions can change.

## Visualizing Main Ideas

*Copy and complete the following concept map.*

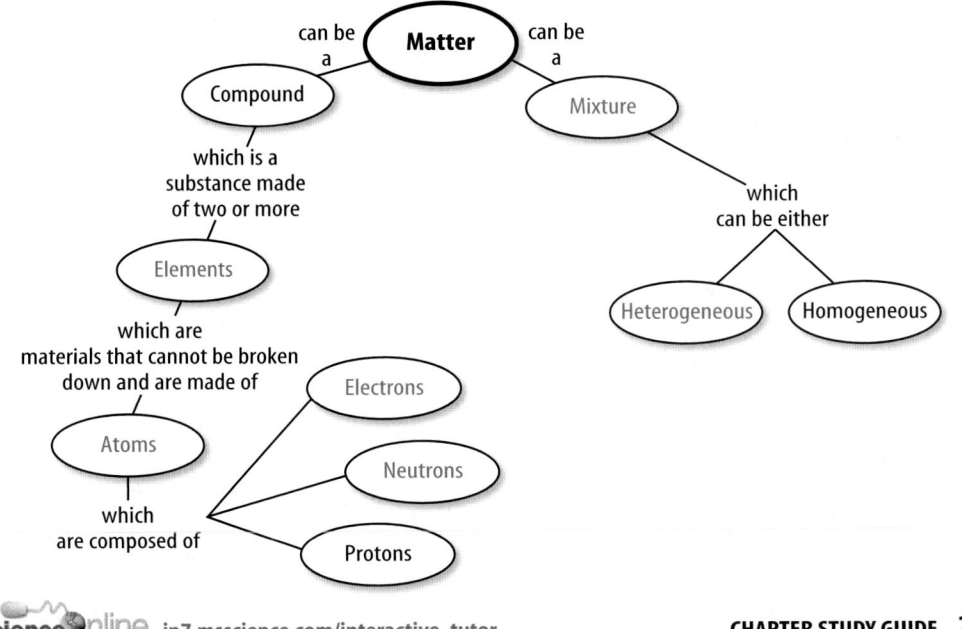

## Reviewing Main Ideas

Summary statements can be used by students to review the major concepts of the chapter.

## Visualizing Main Ideas

See student page.

**Visit in7.msscience.com**
/self_check_quiz
/interactive_tutor
/vocabulary_puzzlemaker
/chapter_review
/standards_review

### Assessment Transparency

For additional assessment questions, use the *Assessment Transparency* located in the transparency book.

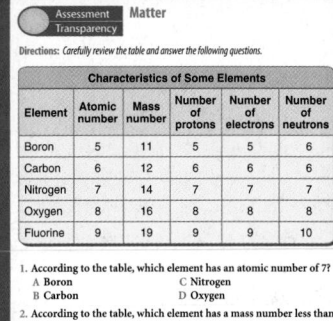

## Identifying Misconceptions

**Assess**

Use the assessment as follow-up to page F at the beginning of the chapter after students have completed the chapter.

**Materials** 50-mL graduated cylinder, beaker, water, droppers, pan balance

**Procedure** Find the mass of the empty graduated cylinder, then pour 50 mL of water into it and find the mass again. Use the dropper to decrease the volume of water by one half and calculate the mass of the water. Repeat this process three more times to obtain volumes of 50 mL, 25 mL, 12.5 mL, 6.25 mL, and 3.125 mL. Will you ever get a drop of water that has no mass?

**Expected Outcome** No matter how small the volume, the water has mass and therefore weight.

## Using Vocabulary

1. proton
2. compound
3. matter
4. neutrons
5. metals

## Checking Concepts

| | |
|---|---|
| 6. D | 11. B |
| 7. C | 12. C |
| 8. B | 13. C |
| 9. C | 14. B |
| 10. D | 15. D |

## Thinking Critically

16. one sulfur atom to two oxygen atoms

17. An atom with seven protons is nitrogen.

18. The element loses its characteristics and a new substance is formed.

19. Cobalt-60 and cobalt-59 are isotopes because they both have 27 protons in their nuclei.

20. Rutherford's gold foil experiment told scientists that the atom contains a small, dense, positively charged structure.

21. Because the nuclei in all atoms are composed of densely packed positive charge (protons), the positive alpha particle would have been deflected by the aluminum foil. Students also may add that the angle of deflection would not be as great because an aluminum nucleus is less dense than a gold nucleus.

## Using Vocabulary

| | |
|---|---|
| atom p.259 | matter p.258 |
| atomic mass p.270 | metal p.270 |
| atomic number p.269 | metalloid p.271 |
| compound p.273 | mixture p.275 |
| electron p.262 | neutron p.264 |
| element p.266 | nonmetal p.271 |
| isotope p.269 | nucleus p.263 |
| law of conservation | proton p.263 |
| of matter p.260 | substance p.273 |
| mass number p.269 | |

*Fill in the blanks with the correct vocabulary word or words.*

1. The _____ is the particle in the nucleus of the atom that carries a positive charge and is counted to identify the atomic number.

2. The new substance formed when elements combine chemically is a(n) _____.

3. Anything that has mass and takes up space is _____.

4. The particles in the atom that account for most of the mass of the atom are protons and _____.

5. Elements that are shiny, malleable, ductile, good conductors of heat and electricity, and make up most of the periodic table are _____.

## Checking Concepts

*Choose the word or phrase that best answers the question.*

6. What is a solution an example of?
   A) element
   B) heterogeneous mixture
   C) compound
   D) homogeneous mixture

7. The nucleus of one atom contains 12 protons and 12 neutrons, while the nucleus of another atom contains 12 protons and 16 neutrons. What are the atoms?
   A) chromium atoms
   B) two different elements
   C) two isotopes of an element
   D) negatively charged

8. What is a compound?
   A) a mixture of chemicals and elements
   B) a combination of two or more elements
   C) anything that has mass and occupies space
   D) the building block of matter

9. What does the atom consist of?
   A) electrons, protons, and alpha particles
   B) neutrons and protons
   C) electrons, protons, and neutrons
   D) elements, protons, and electrons

10. In an atom, where is an electron located?
    A) in the nucleus with the proton
    B) on the periodic table of the elements
    C) with the neutron
    D) in a cloudlike formation surrounding the nucleus

11. How is matter defined?
    A) the negative charge in an atom
    B) anything that has mass and occupies space
    C) the mass of the nucleus
    D) sound, light, and energy

12. What are two atoms that have the same number of protons called?
    A) metals
    B) nonmetals
    C) isotopes
    D) metalloids

13. Which is a heterogeneous mixture?
    A) air          C) a salad
    B) brass          D) apple juice

 Science Online in7.msscience.com/vocabulary_puzzlemaker

**Use the Exam*View*® Pro Testmaker CD-ROM to:**
- create multiple versions of tests
- create modified tests with one mouse click for inclusion students
- edit existing questions and add your own questions
- build tests aligned with state standards using built-in State Curriculum Tags
- change English tests to Spanish with one mouse click and vice versa

Use the illustration below to answer questions 14 and 15.

Krypton
36
Kr
83.80

14. Using the figure above, krypton has
   A) an atomic number of 84.
   B) an atomic number of 36.
   C) an atomic mass of 36.
   D) an atomic mass of 72.

15. From the figure, the element krypton is
   A) a solid.          C) a mixture.
   B) a liquid.         D) a gas.

### Thinking Critically

16. **Analyze Information** A chemical formula is written to indicate the makeup of a compound. What is the ratio of sulfur atoms to oxygen atoms in $SO_2$?

17. **Determine** which element contains seven electrons and seven protons.

18. **Describe** what happens to an element when it becomes part of a compound.

19. **Explain** how cobalt-60 and cobalt-59 can be the same element but have different mass numbers.

20. **Analyze Information** What did Rutherford's gold foil experiment tell scientists about atomic structure?

21. **Predict** Suppose Rutherford had bombarded aluminum foil with alpha particles instead of the gold foil he used in his experiment. What observations do you

predict Rutherford would have made? Explain your prediction.

22. **Draw Conclusions** You are shown a liquid that looks the same throughout. You're told that it contains more than one type of element and that the proportion of each varies throughout the liquid. Is this an element, a compound, or a mixture?

Use the illustrations below to answer question 23.

23. **Interpret Scientific Illustrations** Look at the two carbon atoms above. Explain whether or not the atoms are isotopes.

24. **Explain** how the atomic mass of krypton was determined.

### Performance Activities

25. **Newspaper Article** Research the source, composition, and properties of asbestos. Why was it used in the past? Why is it a health hazard now? What is being done about it? Write a newspaper article to share your findings.

### Applying Math

26. **Atomic Mass** Krypton has six naturally occurring isotopes with atomic masses of 78, 80, 82, 83, 84, and 86. Make a table of the number of protons, electrons, and neutrons in each isotope.

27. **Atomic Ratio** A researcher is analyzing two different compounds, sulfuric acid ($H_2SO_4$) and hydrogen peroxide ($H_2O_2$). What is the ratio of hydrogen to oxygen in hydrogen peroxide? What is the ratio of oxygen to hydrogen in sulfuric acid?

 Science Online in7.msscience.com/chapter_review

**CHAPTER REVIEW** 283

22. The liquid is a mixture. Students also might add that it is homogeneous.

23. The atoms are isotopes because they differ in their number of neutrons. The atom on the left has 6 p and 6 n whereas the one on the right has 6 p and 8 n.

24. The atomic mass of krypton was determined by using the weighted average of the isotopes of krypton.

### Performance Activities

25. Asbestos is a hydrous magnesium silicate—$Mg_3Si_2O_5(OH)_4$. It occurs as fibers, which are spun into yarn or mixed with other materials to form cement board or other fireproof building materials. When asbestos fibers become airborne, they can be inhaled. The sharp fibers penetrate the lungs, and can cause a form of lung cancer. Use **Performance Assessment in the Science Classroom**, p. 141.

### Applying Math

## Indiana Math Standards
7.6.1, 7.7.1
26.

| Isotope/Atomic Mass | P | E | N |
|---|---|---|---|
| $Kr_{78}$ | 36 | 36 | 42 |
| $Kr_{80}$ | 36 | 36 | 44 |
| $Kr_{82}$ | 36 | 36 | 46 |
| $Kr_{83}$ | 36 | 36 | 47 |
| $Kr_{84}$ | 36 | 36 | 48 |
| $Kr_{86}$ | 36 | 36 | 50 |

27. 1:1; 2:1.

### ☑ Assessment  Resources

📁 **Reproducible Masters**
**Chapter *Fast File* Resources**
   Chapter Review, pp. 33–34
   Chapter Tests, pp. 35–38
   Assessment Transparency Activity, p. 45
**Glencoe Science Web site**
   Chapter Review Test
   IN Standards Review

**Glencoe Technology**
   🔧 Assessment Transparency
   💿 Exam*View®* Pro Testmaker
   📼 MindJogger Videoquiz
   💿 Interactive Chalkboard

**Answer Sheet** A practice answer sheet can be found at in7.msscience.com/answer_sheet.

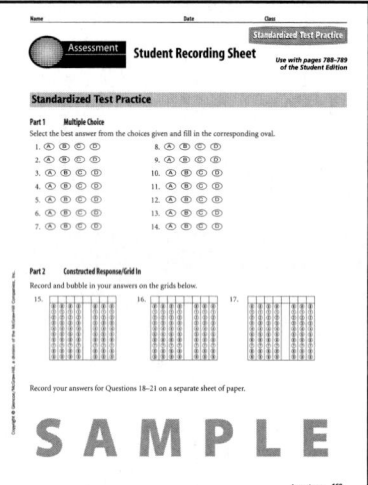

S A M P L E

---

**Part 1** | **Multiple Choice**

| | |
|---|---|
| **1.** B | **5.** D |
| **2.** D | **6.** A |
| **3.** D | **7.** A |
| **4.** D | **8.** C |

**Part 2** | **Critical Response**

**9.** The rows are called periods. Elements in a row have the same number of energy levels. The columns are called groups. Elements in each group have similar properties related to their structure. They also tend to form similar bonds.

**10.** A mixture of sugar and sand can be separated by adding water. The sugar dissolves in the water and the sand can then be filtered out. A mixture of water and sugar can be separated by heating the water so that the water evaporates, leaving the sugar. Mixtures of different-sized solids, such as pebbles and sand, can be separated by filtering out the larger solid.

---

 The assessed Indiana standard appears above the question.

*Record your answers on the answer sheet provided by your teacher or on a sheet of paper.*

**Part 1** | **Multiple Choice**

7.1.5

**1.** Which scientist introduced the idea that matter is made up of tiny, individual bits called atoms?

**A** Chadwick

**B** Democritus

**C** Rutherford

**D** Thomson

**2.** The periodic table block shown below lists properties of the element chlorine.

What does the number 17 represent?

**A** number of electrons

**B** number of isotopes

**C** number of neutrons

**D** number of protons

**Test-Taking Tip**

**Full Understanding** Read each question carefully for full understanding.

---

7.1.5

**3.** Which scientist envisioned the atom as a ball of positive charge with electrons embedded in it?

**A** Crookes

**B** Dalton

**C** Rutherford

**D** Thomson

The illustrations below show three nuclei.

| 1 Proton | 1 Proton | 1 Proton |
|---|---|---|
| 0 Neutrons | 1 Neutron | 2 Neutrons |

**4.** Which correctly identifies the three nuclei?

**A** hydrogen, lithium, sodium

**B** hydrogen, helium, lithium

**C** hydrogen, helium, helium

**D** hydrogen, hydrogen, hydrogen

**5.** What is the mass number for each of the nuclei shown in the illustration above?

**A** 0, 1, 2

**B** 1, 1, 1

**C** 1, 2, 2

**D** 1, 2, 3

---

**11.** Particles labeled *z* were slightly deflected by the gold foil. Particles labeled *x* were strongly deflected by the gold foil. Rutherford thought the positive charge of the atom was spread out throughout the atom and wouldn't be dense enough to deflect alpha particles.

He thought most of the alpha particles would pass straight through the foil.

**12.** Particles that struck the small, dense positive nuclei directly were strongly deflected. Particles that struck the nuclei at an angle were only slightly deflected.

**6.** Which are found close to the right side of the periodic table?

- **A** nonmetals
- **B** metals
- **C** metalloids
- **D** lanthanides

**7.** Which is a characteristic that is typical of a solid, nonmetal element?

- **A** brittle
- **B** good electrical conductor
- **C** good heat conductor
- **D** shiny

**8.** The illustration below shows atoms of two compounds that are combined without making a new compound.

What term describes this combination?

- **A** compound
- **B** element
- **C** mixture
- **D** substance

---

### Part 2 | Critical Response

**9.** What are the rows and columns on the periodic table called? How are elements in the rows similar, and how are elements in the columns similar?

**10.** Describe three possible methods for separating mixtures. Give an example for each method.

The illustration below shows Rutherford's gold foil experiment.

Source of positively charged particles

X

Z

Positively charged particle beam

Gold foil

Detector screen

**11.** What has happened to the positively charged particles labeled Z? What has happened to the positively charged particles labeled X? How is this different from what Rutherford expected?

**12.** How does the structure of the atom explain why particles traveled in both paths Z and X above?

---

## Rubrics

The following rubric is a sample scoring device for critical response questions.

### Critical Response

| Points | Description |
|---|---|
| 4 | The student demonstrates a thorough understanding of the science of the task. The response may contain minor flaws that do not detract from the demonstration of a thorough understanding. |
| 3 | The student demonstrates an understanding of the science of the task. The response is essentially correct and demonstrates an essential but less than thorough understanding of the science. |
| 2 | The student demonstrates only a partial understanding of the science of the task. Although the student may have used the correct approach to a solution or may have provided a correct solution, the work lacks an essential understanding of the underlying science concepts. |
| 1 | The student demonstrates a very limited understanding of the science of the task. The response is incomplete and exhibits many flaws. |
| 0 | The student provides a completely incorrect solution or no response at all. |

| Section/Objectives | Standards | | Labs/Features |
|---|---|---|---|
| | **National** | **State/Local** | |
| **Chapter Opener** | See pp. 16T–17T for a Key to Standards. | Detailed standards begin on page IN8. | **Launch Lab:** Particle Size and Dissolving Rates, p. 287 <br> **Foldables,** p. 287 |
| **Section 1  What is a solution?** <br> ⏱ 2 sessions    📦 1 block <br><br> 1. **Distinguish** between substances and mixtures. <br> 2. **Describe** two different types of mixtures. <br> 3. **Explain** how solutions form. <br> 4. **Describe** different types of solutions. | National Content Standards: UCP.1, UCP.2, UCP.3, UCP.5, A.1, A.2, B.1 | Indiana Standards: 7.3.13 | **Science Online,** p. 289 |
| **Section 2  Solubility** <br> ⏱ 2 sessions    📦 1.5 blocks <br><br> 5. **Explain** why water is a good general solvent. <br> 6. **Describe** how the structure of a compound affects which solvents it dissolves in. <br> 7. **Identify** factors that affect how much of a substance will dissolve in a solvent. <br> 8. **Describe** how temperature affects reaction rate. <br> 9. **Explain** how solute particles affect physical properties of water. | National Content Standards: UCP.1, UCP.2, UCP.3, UCP.5, A.1, A.2, B.1, B.2, B.3 | Indiana Standards: 7.2.2, 7.2.3, 7.3.12, 7.3.13 | **Integrate Environment,** p. 295 <br> **MiniLAB:** Observing Chemical Processes, p. 298 <br> **Integrate Career,** p. 299 <br> **Applying Science:** How can you compare concentrations?, p. 299 <br> **Lab:** Observing Gas Solubility, p. 301 |
| **Section 3  Acidic and Basic Solutions** <br> ⏱ 4 sessions    📦 2 blocks <br><br> 10. **Compare** acids and bases and their properties. <br> 11. **Describe** practical uses of acids and bases. <br> 12. **Explain** how pH is used to describe the strength of an acid or base. <br> 13. **Describe** how acids and bases react when they are brought together. | National Content Standards: UCP.1, UCP.2, UCP.3, UCP.5, A.1, A.2, B.1 | Indiana Standards: 7.2.1, 7.3.12, 7.3.13, 7.3.16, 7.5.3 | **MiniLAB:** Observing a Nail in a Carbonated Drink, p. 303 <br> **Visualizing Acid Precipitation,** p. 304 <br> **Science Online,** p. 305 <br> **Integrate Life Science,** p. 306 <br> **Science Online,** p. 308 <br> **Lab:** Testing pH Using Natural Indicators, p. 310 <br> **Science Stats:** Salty Solutions, p. 312 |

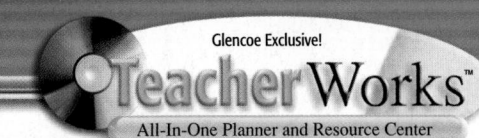
| Lab Materials | Reproducible Resources | Section Assessment | Technology |
|---|---|---|---|
| **Launch Lab:** 2 bouillon cubes, mortar and pestle, 2 large beakers, water, stirring rod, timer | **Chapter *FAST FILE* Resources**<br>Foldables Worksheet, p. 17<br>Directed Reading Overview, p. 19<br>Note-taking Worksheets, pp. 33–35 | **GLENCOE'S ASSESSMENT ADVANTAGE** | TeacherWorks includes:<br>• Interactive Teacher Edition<br>• Lesson Planner with calendar<br>• Access to all program blacklines<br>• Correlations to standards<br>• Web links |
| *Need materials?* Contact Science Kit at 1-800-828-7777 or www.sciencekit.com on the Internet. | **Chapter *FAST FILE* Resources**<br>Transparency Activity, p. 44<br>Lab Activity, pp. 9–12<br>Enrichment, p. 30<br>Reinforcement, p. 27<br>Directed Reading, p. 20<br>**Physical Science Critical Thinking/Problem Solving,** pp. 10, 13 | **Portfolio**<br>Differentiated Instruction, p. 293<br>**Performance**<br>Applying Skills, p. 293<br>**Content**<br>Section Review, p. 293 | Section Focus Transparency<br>Guided Reading Audio Program<br>Interactive Chalkboard CD-ROM |
| **MiniLAB:** 2 small beverage glasses, milk, refrigerator<br>**Lab:** 2 chilled carbonated beverages, tape, 2 balloons, fabric tape measure, container, hot water, clock | **Chapter *FAST FILE* Resources**<br>Transparency Activity, p. 45<br>MiniLAB, p. 3<br>Lab Activity, pp. 13–16<br>Enrichment, p. 31<br>Reinforcement, p. 28<br>Directed Reading, p. 20<br>Lab Worksheet, pp. 5–6<br>**Science Inquiry Labs,** pp. 43–44 | **Portfolio**<br>Assessment, p. 300<br>Assessment, p. 301<br>**Performance**<br>Applying Science, p. 299<br>Applying Skills, p. 300<br>**Content**<br>Section Review, p. 300 | Section Focus Transparency<br>Guided Reading Audio Program<br>Interactive Chalkboard CD-ROM |
| **MiniLAB:** iron nail, carbonated soft drink, cup<br>**Lab:** test tubes and rack; concentrated red cabbage juice; bottles of ammonia, soap solution, baking soda solution, white vinegar, hydrochloric acid solution, borax soap solution, colorless carbonated soft drink, and distilled water; grease pencil; droppers (9) | **Chapter *FAST FILE* Resources**<br>Transparency Activity, p. 46<br>MiniLAB, p. 4<br>Enrichment, p. 32<br>Reinforcement, p. 29<br>Transparency Activity, pp. 47–48<br>Directed Reading, pp. 21, 22<br>Lab Worksheet, pp. 7–8<br>**Home and Community Involvement,** p. 44<br>**Earth Science Critical Thinking/ Problem Solving,** p. 18 | **Portfolio**<br>Differentiated Instruction, p. 304<br>**Performance**<br>MiniLAB, p. 303<br>Applying Math, p. 309<br>**Content**<br>Section Review, p. 309 | Section Focus Transparency<br>Teaching Transparency<br>Virtual Labs CD-ROM<br>Guided Reading Audio Program<br>Interactive Chalkboard CD-ROM<br>Video Lab |

## GLENCOE'S ASSESSMENT ADVANTAGE — End of Chapter Assessment

| Blackline Masters | Technology | Professional Series |
|---|---|---|
| **Chapter *FAST FILE* Resources**<br>Chapter Review, pp. 37–38<br>Chapter Tests, pp. 39–42<br>**Mastering the Grade 7 Indiana Science Standards** | MindJogger Videoquiz<br>IN Test Prep and Practice Exam*View*®<br>Exam*View*® Pro Testmaker<br>TeacherWorks CD-ROM<br>Interactive Chalkboard CD-ROM | **Performance Assessment in the Science Classroom (PASC)** |

## Transparencies

### Section Focus

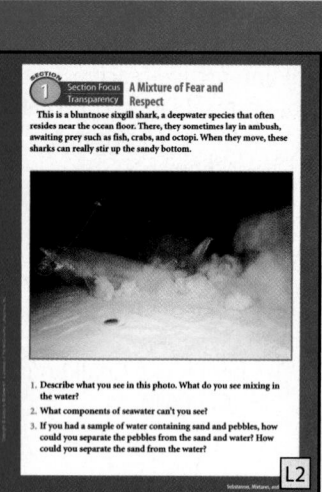

**Section Focus Transparency 1** A Mixture of Fear and Respect

This is a bluntnose sixgill shark, a deepwater species that often resides near the ocean floor. There, they sometimes lay in ambush, awaiting prey such as fish, crabs, and octopi. When they move, these sharks can really stir up the sandy bottom.

1. Describe what you see in this photo. What do you see mixing in the water?
2. What components of seawater can't you see?
3. If you had a sample of water containing sand and pebbles, how could you separate the pebbles from the sand and water? How could you separate the sand from the water?

L2

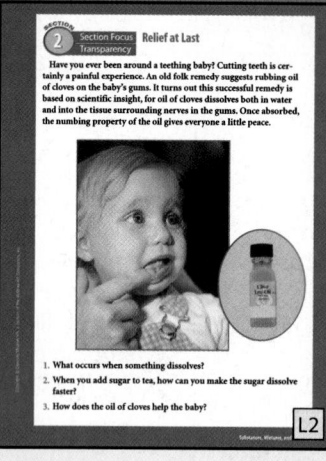

**Section Focus Transparency 2** Relief at Last

Have you ever been around a teething baby? Cutting teeth is certainly a painful experience. An old folk remedy suggests rubbing oil of cloves on the baby's gums. It turns out this successful remedy is based on scientific insight, for oil of cloves dissolves both in water and into the tissue surrounding nerves in the gums. Once absorbed, the numbing property of the oil gives everyone a little peace.

1. What occurs when something dissolves?
2. When you add sugar to tea, how can you make the sugar dissolve faster?
3. How does the oil of cloves help the baby?

L2

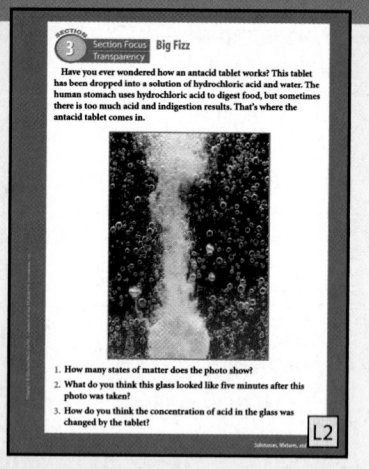

**Section Focus Transparency 3** Big Fizz

Have you ever wondered how an antacid tablet works? This tablet has been dropped into a solution of hydrochloric acid and water. The human stomach uses hydrochloric acid to digest food, but sometimes there is too much acid and indigestion results. That's where the antacid tablet comes in.

1. How many states of matter does the photo show?
2. What do you think this glass looked like five minutes after this photo was taken?
3. How do you think the concentration of acid in the glass was changed by the tablet?

L2

This is a representation of key blackline masters available in the Teacher Classroom Resources. See Resource Manager boxes within the chapter for additional information.

### Assessment

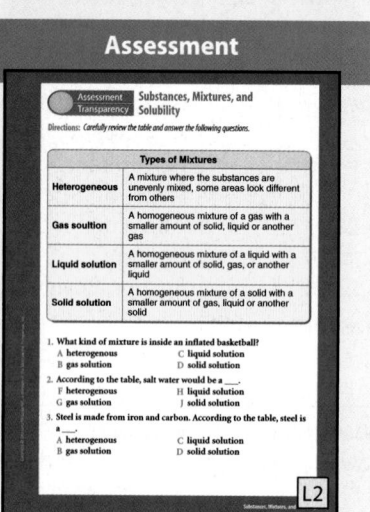

**Assessment Transparency** Substances, Mixtures, and Solubility

*Directions: Carefully review the table and answer the following questions.*

**Types of Mixtures**

| | |
|---|---|
| Heterogeneous | A mixture where the substances are unevenly mixed, some areas look different from others |
| Gas soultion | A homogeneous mixture of a gas with a smaller amount of solid, liquid or another gas |
| Liquid solution | A homogeneous mixture of a liquid with a smaller amount of solid, gas, or another liquid |
| Solid solution | A homogeneous mixture of a solid with a smaller amount of gas, liquid or another solid |

1. What kind of mixture is inside an inflated basketball?
   A heterogeneous  C liquid solution
   B gas solution  D solid solution
2. According to the table, salt water would be a ___.
   F heterogeneous  H liquid solution
   G gas solution  J solid solution
3. Steel is made from iron and carbon. According to the table, steel is a ___.
   A heterogenous  C liquid solution
   B gas solution  D solid solution

L2

### Teaching

**Teaching Transparency** pH Scale

L2

## Key to Teaching Strategies

The following designations will help you decide which activities are appropriate for your students.

**L1** Level 1 activities should be appropriate for students with learning difficulties.

**L2** Level 2 activities should be within the ability range of all students.

**L3** Level 3 activities are designed for above-average students.

**ELL** ELL activities should be within the ability range of English-Language Learners.

**COOP LEARN** Cooperative Learning activities are designed for small group work.

**LS** Multiple Learning Styles logos, as described on page 12T, are used throughout to indicate strategies that address different learning styles.

**P** These strategies represent student products that can be placed into a best-work portfolio.

**PBL** Problem-Based Learning activities apply real-world situations to learning.

## Hands-on Activities

### Student Text Lab Worksheet

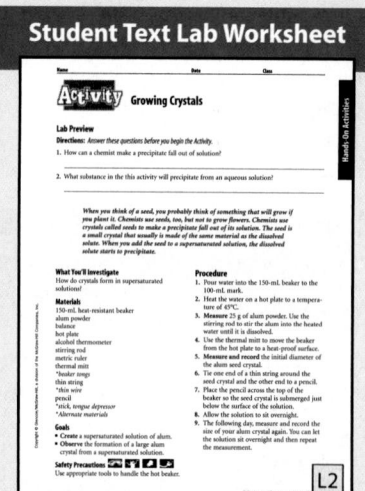

**Activity** Growing Crystals

**Lab Preview**

**Directions:** Answer these questions before you begin the Activity.

1. How can a chemist make a precipitate fall out of solution?

2. What substance in this activity will precipitate from an aqueous solution?

When you think of a seed, you probably think of something that will grow if you plant it. Chemists use seeds, too, but not to grow flowers. Chemists use crystals called seeds to make a precipitate fall out of its solution. The seed is a small crystal that usually is made of the same material as the dissolved solute starts to precipitate.

**What You'll Investigate**
How do crystals form in supersaturated solutions?

**Materials**
150-mL heat-resistant beaker
alum powder
balance
hot plate
alcohol thermometer
stirring rod
metric ruler
thermal mitt
*beaker tongs
thin string
*thin wire
pencil
*stick, tongue depressor
*Alternate materials

**Goals**
- Create a supersaturated solution of alum.
- Observe the formation of a large alum crystal from a supersaturated solution.

**Safety Precautions**
Use appropriate tools to handle the hot beaker.

**Procedure**
1. Pour water into the 150-mL beaker to the 100-mL mark.
2. Heat the water on a hot plate to a temperature of 45°C.
3. Measure 25 g of alum powder. Use the stirring rod to stir the alum into the heated water until it is dissolved.
4. Use the thermal mitt to move the beaker from the hot plate to a heat-proof surface.
5. Measure and record the initial diameter of the alum seed crystal.
6. Tie one end of a thin string around the seed crystal and the other end to a pencil.
7. Place the pencil across the top of the beaker so the seed crystal is submerged just below the surface of the solution.
8. Allow the solution to sit overnight.
9. The following day, measure and record the size of your alum crystal again. You can let the solution sit overnight and then repeat the measurement.

L2

### Laboratory Activities

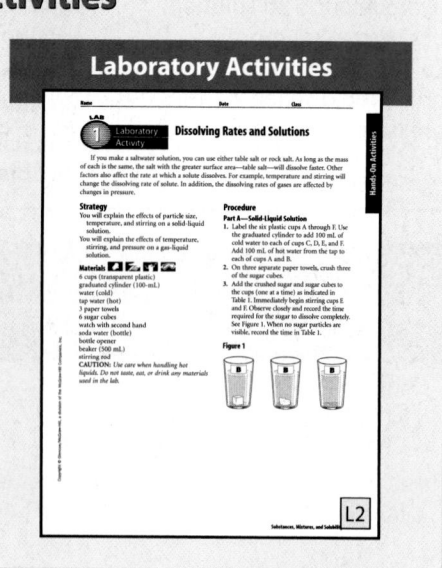

**Laboratory Activity** Dissolving Rates and Solutions

If you make a saltwater solution, you can use either table salt or rock salt. As long as the mass of each is the same, the salt with the greater surface area—table salt—will dissolve faster. Other factors also affect the rate at which a solute dissolves. For example, temperature and stirring will change the dissolving rate of solute. In addition, the dissolving rates of gases are affected by changes in pressure.

**Strategy**
You will explain the effects of particle size, temperature, and stirring on a solid-liquid solution.
You will explain the effects of temperature, stirring, and pressure on a gas-liquid solution.

**Materials**
6 cups (transparent plastic)
graduated cylinder (100-mL)
water (cold)
tap water (hot)
3 paper towels
6 sugar cubes
watch with second hand
soda marker (bottle)
bottle opener
bottle (500 mL)
stirring rod
CAUTION: Use care when handling hot liquids. Do not taste, eat, or drink any materials used in the lab.

**Procedure**
**Part A—Solid-Liquid Solution**
1. Label the six plastic cups A through F. Use the graduated cylinder to add 100 mL of cold water to each of cups C, D, E, and F. Add 100 mL of hot water from the tap to each of cups A and B.
2. On three separate paper towels, crush three of the sugar cubes.
3. Add the crushed sugar and sugar cubes to the cups (one at a time) as indicated in Table 1. Immediately begin stirring cups E and F. Observe closely and record the time required for the sugar to dissolve completely. See Figure 1. When no sugar particles are visible, record the time in Table 1.

**Figure 1**

L2

# Resource Manager

## Meeting Different Ability Levels

### Content Outline

*L2*

### Reinforcement

*L2*

### Enrichment

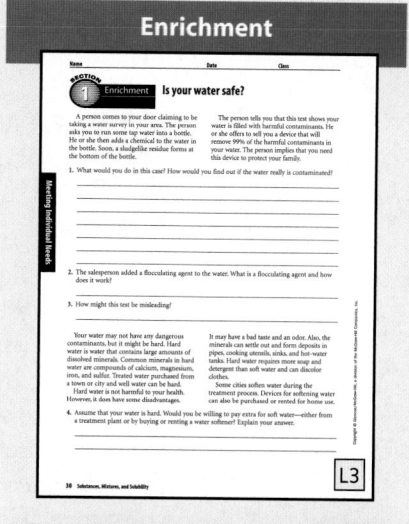

*L3*

### Directed Reading (English/Spanish)

*L1*

### Study Guide

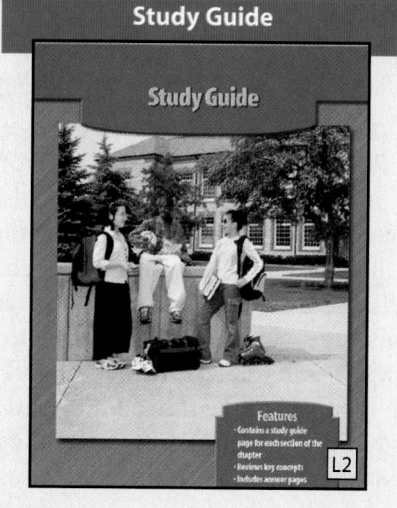

**Study Guide**

Features
- Contains a study guide page for each section of the chapter
- Reviews key concepts
- Includes answer pages

*L2*

### Reading Essentials

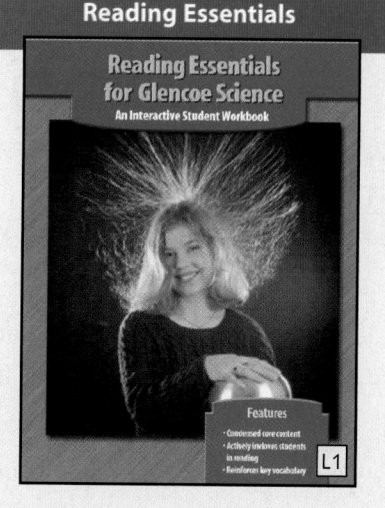

**Reading Essentials for Glencoe Science**
An Interactive Student Workbook

Features
- Condensed core content
- Actively involves students in reading
- Reinforces key vocabulary

*L1*

## Assessment

### Test Practice Workbook

*L2*

### Chapter Review

*L2*

### Chapter Tests

*L2*

# Science Content Background

## section 1

### What is a solution?
### How Solutions Form

Attractive forces between the atoms, ions, or molecules of a substance hold liquid and solid substances together. When a substance is surrounded by a solvent, particles of the substance may be attracted to the solvent by various forces. If the attractive forces of the solvent are strong enough to overcome the internal attractive forces of the solute, the substance will be soluble to some extent. A substance with an extremely low solubility is usually said to be insoluble.

## section 2

### Solubility
### Dissolution

The process of dissolving, called dissolution, involves energy. Energy is absorbed when the structure of the molecular solid is broken down or the ions of an ionic crystal are separated. Energy is released when the particles of solute form new bonds with the solvent. In the cold packs used by athletic trainers, more energy is absorbed in the first part of the dissolution process than released in the second. For that reason, the overall process is endothermic and the liquid becomes colder.

### How much will dissolve?

A solution is saturated when solution equilibrium between the undissolved solute and dissolved solute in a solution is established at a particular temperature. In the state known as solution equilibrium, the solute is dissolving into the solution and forming from the solution at exactly equal rates. If a solution contains less dissolved solute than it can hold at a given temperature, the solution is unsaturated.

## section 3

### Acidic and Basic Solutions
### Strengths of Acids and Bases

When a strong acid dissolves in water, the vast majority of acid molecules dissociate completely into ions. Strong bases react in the same way as strong acids. A weak acid only partially dissociates in water. Students might think this means that each acid molecule only separates partially. Students should understand that "partial dissociation" means that, in a solution of millions of weak acid molecules, only a few molecules completely dissociate, but the vast majority of molecules remain completely undissociated. Weak bases partially dissociate in the same manner as weak acids.

## chapter content resources

**Internet Resources**
For additional content background, visit
**in7.msscience.com** to:
- access your book online
- find references to related articles in popular science magazines
- access Web links with related content background
- access current events with science journal topics

**Print Resources**
*Chemistry; The Molecular Nature of Matter and Change,* by Martin S. Silberberg, McGraw-Hill, 2003
*Crime Lab Chemistry: Grades 4–8,* by Jacqueline Barber, University of California, Berkeley, Lawrence Hall of Science, 1999
*Visualizing Chemistry: Investigations for Teachers,* by Julie B. Ealy, James L. Ealy, and James L. Ealy Jr., American Chemical Society, 1995

## IDENTIFYING Misconceptions

### Find Out What Students Think

**Students may think that . . .**

**When a material dissolves, it goes away.**

**An object that dissolves is melting.**
A solid dissolves when it becomes part of a solution. For example, salt dissolves in water to produce a solution of salt water. After salt has dissolved in water students may think the salt is gone because it cannot be seen. Thus, they may equate dissolving with disappearing. Other students may think dissolving is the same as melting. Language may also play a role in these misconceptions. People say delicious foods "melt in their mouths" and speak of things that "dissolve into thin air."

### Demonstration
As a class, find the mass of 100 mL of water, which should be about 100 g. Start adding and stirring in 5-g portions of table salt. Add a total of 20 g. Show that the salt can no longer be seen. Have students write down what they predict the new mass of the solution to be. Ask them to also write an explanation for what happened to the salt.

### Promote Understanding

**Activity** L2 COOP LEARN
Have students work in groups to repeat the steps of the demonstration. Have each group find the mass of 100 mL of water and dissolve 20 g of table salt in it.

Ask each group to find the mass of its salt solution and compare this mass with the mass they predicted. They will find that the mass of the solution is equal to the mass of the water plus the mass of the salt.

Make sure students understand that even though we can't see the salt, it is still there.

Discuss with students ways you could show the salt is in the water. For example, if the water were boiled away, the salt would be left behind.

Now contrast melting with dissolving. Put an ice cube on your desk and allow students to watch as it melts. Light a candle, show students the liquid wax, and explain that some of the wax has melted.

Discuss the difference between dissolving and melting. Make sure students understand that

- dissolving involves at least two different materials (a solvent and a solute).

- melting happens because solids become warm enough to turn into liquids.

Explain that salt would have to be heated to a temperature of 800°C to melt.

### Assess

After completing the chapter, see *Identifying Misconceptions* in the Study Guide at the end of the chapter.

## Chapter Vocabulary

substance, p. 288
heterogeneous mixture, p. 289
homogeneous mixture, p. 290
solution, p. 290
solute, p. 290
solvent, p. 290
precipitate, p. 290
aqueous, p. 294
solubility, p. 297
saturated, p. 298
concentration, p. 299
acid, p. 302
hydronium ions, p. 302
base, p. 305
pH, p. 306
indicator, p. 308
neutralization, p. 308

**Science Journal** Answers will vary. Look for depth and quality of information.

**with Image Bank**

**PowerPoint® Presentations**

This CD-ROM is an editable Microsoft® PowerPoint® presentation that includes:

- a pre-made presentation for every chapter
- interactive graphics
- animations
- audio clips
- image bank
- all new section and chapter questions
- Standardized Test Practice
- transparencies
- pre-lab questions for all labs
- Foldables directions
- links to in7.msscience.com

**Academic Standard—3:** Students collect and organize data to identify relationships between physical objects, events, and processes. They use logical reasoning to question their own ideas as new information challenges their conceptions of the natural world.

# Substances, Mixtures, and Solubility

## chapter preview

### sections

**1** What is a solution?

**2** Solubility
   *Lab* Observing Gas Solubility

**3** Acidic and Basic Solutions
   *Lab* Testing pH Using Natural Indicators

   *Virtual Lab* What is the pH of common solutions?

## Big-Band Mixtures

It's a parade and the band plays. Just as the mixing of notes produces music, the mixing of substances produces many of the things around you. From the brass in tubas to the lemonade you drink, you live in a world of mixtures. In this chapter, you'll learn why some substances form mixtures and others do not.

**Science Journal** Find and name four items around you that are mixtures.

286

## Theme Connection

**Systems and Interactions** Solutions are systems in which ions, atoms, or molecules of solutes and solvents interact. Acid/base systems exist in solutions that produce hydronium ions or hydroxide ions. Acid/base systems have their own well-defined interactions.

### About the Photo

**Marching Bands** While the tuba is the largest brass instrument in the marching band, a whole band of tubas would not be very exciting. Other instruments are needed to blend with the tubas to create the sounds you hear. The composer of the music took special care that the various instruments' sounds are interfused to produce the perfect mixture.

# Start-Up Activities

## Particle Size and Dissolving Rates

Why do drink mixes come in powder form? What would happen if you dropped a big chunk of drink mix into the water? Would it dissolve quickly? Powdered drink mix dissolves faster in water than chunks do because it is divided into smaller particles, exposing more of the mix to the water. See for yourself how particle size affects the rate at which a substance dissolves.

1. Pour 400 mL of water into each of two 600-mL beakers.

2. Carefully grind a bouillon cube into powder using a mortar and pestle.

3. Place the bouillon powder into one beaker and drop a whole bouillon cube into the second beaker.

4. Stir the water in each beaker for 10 s and observe.

5. **Think Critically** Write a paragraph in your Science Journal comparing the color of the two liquids and the amount of undissolved bouillon at the bottom of each beaker. How does the particle size affect the rate at which a substance dissolves?

**Solutions** Make the following Foldable to help classify solutions based on their common features.

**STEP 1** Fold a vertical sheet of paper from side to side. Make the front edge about 1.25 cm shorter than the back edge.

**STEP 2** Turn lengthwise and fold into thirds.

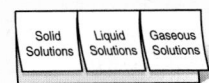

**STEP 3** Unfold and cut only the top layer along both folds to make three tabs.

**STEP 4** Label each tab as shown.

**Find Main Ideas** As you read the chapter, classify solutions based on their states and list them under the appropriate tabs. On your Foldable, circle the solutions that are acids and underline the solutions that are bases.

Science Online **Preview this chapter's content and activities at in7.msscience.com**

287

## SECTION 1

# What is a solution?

### Tie to Prior Knowledge

**Carbonation** Ask students how a carbonated beverage is similar to and different from lemonade. These two drinks are both water solutions. They are different because lemonade has solids and liquids dissolved in the water while soda also includes gases dissolved in the water.

---

### as you read

**What You'll Learn**

- **Distinguish** between substances and mixtures.
- **Describe** two different types of mixtures.
- **Explain** how solutions form.
- **Describe** different types of solutions.

**Why It's Important**

The air you breathe, the water you drink, and even parts of your body are all solutions.

**Review Vocabulary**
**proton:** positively charged particle located in the nucleus of an atom

**New Vocabulary**
- substance
- heterogeneous mixture
- homogeneous mixture
- solution       • solvent
- solute         • precipitate

---

### Substances

Water, salt water, and pulpy orange juice have some obvious differences. These differences can be explained by chemistry. Think about pure water. No matter what you do to it physically—freeze it, boil it, stir it, or strain it—it still is water. On the other hand, if you boil salt water, the water turns to gas and leaves the salt behind. If you strain pulpy orange juice, it loses its pulp. How does chemistry explain these differences? The answer has to do with the chemical compositions of the materials.

**Atoms and Elements** Recall that atoms are the basic building blocks of matter. Each atom has unique chemical and physical properties which are determined by the number of protons it has. For example, all atoms that have eight protons are oxygen atoms. A **substance** is matter that has the same fixed composition and properties. It can't be broken down into simpler parts by ordinary physical processes, such as boiling, grinding, or filtering. Only a chemical process can change a substance into one or more new substances. **Table 1** lists some examples of physical and chemical processes. An element is an example of a pure substance; it cannot be broken down into simpler substances. The number of protons in an element, like oxygen, are fixed—it cannot change unless the element changes.

**Compounds** Water is another example of a substance. It is always water even when you boil it or freeze it. Water, however, is not an element. It is an example of a compound which is made of two or more elements that are chemically combined. Compounds also have fixed compositions. The ratio of the atoms in a compound is always the same. For example, when two hydrogen atoms combine with one oxygen atom, water is formed. All water—whether it's in the form of ice, liquid, or steam—has the same ratio of hydrogen atoms to oxygen atoms.

| Table 1  Examples of Physical and Chemical Processes | |
|---|---|
| **Physical Processes** | **Chemical Processes** |
| Boiling | Burning |
| Changing pressure | Reacting with other chemicals |
| Cooling | Reacting with light |
| Sorting | |

**288 CHAPTER 10** Substances, Mixtures, and Solubility

---

**Separation by magnetism**

**Separation by straining**

**Figure 1** Mixtures can be separated by physical processes.
**Explain** *why the iron-sand mixture and the pulpy lemonade are not pure substances.*

## Mixtures

Imagine drinking a glass of salt water. You would know right away that you weren't drinking pure water. Like salt water, many things are not pure substances. Salt water is a mixture of salt and water. Mixtures are combinations of substances that are not bonded together and can be separated by physical processes. For example, you can boil salt water to separate the salt from the water. If you had a mixture of iron filings and sand, you could separate the iron filings from the sand with a magnet. **Figure 1** shows some mixtures being separated.

Unlike compounds, mixtures do not always contain the same proportions of the substances that they are composed of. Lemonade is a mixture that can be strong tasting or weak tasting, depending on the amounts of water and lemon juice that are added. It also can be sweet or sour, depending on how much sugar is added. But whether it is strong, weak, sweet, or sour, it is still lemonade.

**Heterogeneous Mixtures** It is easy to tell that some things are mixtures just by looking at them. A watermelon is a mixture of fruit and seeds. The seeds are not evenly spaced through the whole melon—one bite you take might not have any seeds in it and another bite might have several seeds. A type of mixture where the substances are not mixed evenly is called a **heterogeneous** (he tuh ruh JEE nee us) **mixture.** The different areas of a heterogeneous mixture have different compositions. The substances in a heterogeneous mixture are usually easy to tell apart, like the seeds from the fruit of a watermelon. Other examples of heterogeneous mixtures include a bowl of cold cereal with milk and the mixture of pens, pencils, and books in your backpack.

**Science Online**

**Topic: Desalination**
Visit in7.msscience.com for Web links to information about how salt is removed from salt water to provide drinking water.

**Activity** Compare and contrast the two most common methods used for desalination.

**IDENTIFYING**
**Misconceptions**

**Substances** The word *substance* is often used to mean "any kind of matter." Make sure students know that in science, *substance* is used only to refer to an element or a compound. Provide students with several common items, such as wood, water, and an iron nail, and have them identify whether each is a substance.

**Caption Answer**

**Figure 1** They can be separated by physical processes.

**Make a Model**

**Marbles and Balls of Clay** To emphasize the difference between compounds and mixtures, have students put marbles of different colors in one container and some soft balls of two different colors of modeling clay in another. Tell them to shake both containers. The clay balls will stick together, simulating the formation of compounds. The marbles will just mix. ⓛ ⓔⓛⓛ ⓘⓢ **Kinesthetic**

SECTION 1 What is a solution? **289**

## Visual Learning

**Figure 1** Ask students whether straining the lemonade will completely separate it into its component parts. Ask them what might have to be done to further separate its parts. Straining lemonade does not separate the dissolved materials. Evaporating the water would separate the dissolved materials from the water.
ⓛ ⓘⓢ **Logical-Mathematical**

**Figure 2** Molecules of sugar and water are evenly mixed in frozen pops.

**Figure 3** Minerals and soap react to form soap scum, which comes out of the water solution and coats the tiles of a shower.

290

**Homogeneous Mixtures** Your shampoo contains many ingredients, but you can't see them when you look at the shampoo. It is the same color and texture throughout. Shampoo is an example of a homogeneous (hoh muh JEE nee us) mixture. A **homogeneous mixture** contains two or more substances that are evenly mixed on a molecular level but still are not bonded together. Another name for a homogeneous mixture is a **solution.** The sugar and water in the frozen pops shown in **Figure 2,** are a solution—the sugar is evenly distributed in the water, and you can't see the sugar.

**Reading Check** *What is another name for a homogeneous mixture?*

## How Solutions Form

How do you make sugar water for a hummingbird feeder? You might add sugar to water and heat the mixture until the sugar disappears. The sugar molecules would spread out until they were evenly spaced throughout the water, forming a solution. This is called dissolving. The substance that dissolves—or seems to disappear—is called the **solute.** The substance that dissolves the solute is called the **solvent.** In the hummingbird feeder solution, the solute is the sugar and the solvent is water. The substance that is present in the greatest quantity is the solvent.

**Forming Solids from Solutions** Under certain conditions, a solute can come back out of its solution and form a solid. This process is called crystallization. Sometimes this occurs when the solution is cooled or when some of the solvent evaporates. Crystallization is the result of a physical change. When some solutions are mixed, a chemical reaction occurs, forming a solid. This solid is called a **precipitate** (prih SIH puh tayt). A precipitate is the result of a chemical change. Precipitates probably have formed in your sink or shower because of chemical reactions. Minerals that are dissolved in tap water react chemically with soap. The product of this reaction leaves the water as a precipitate called soap scum, shown in **Figure 3.**

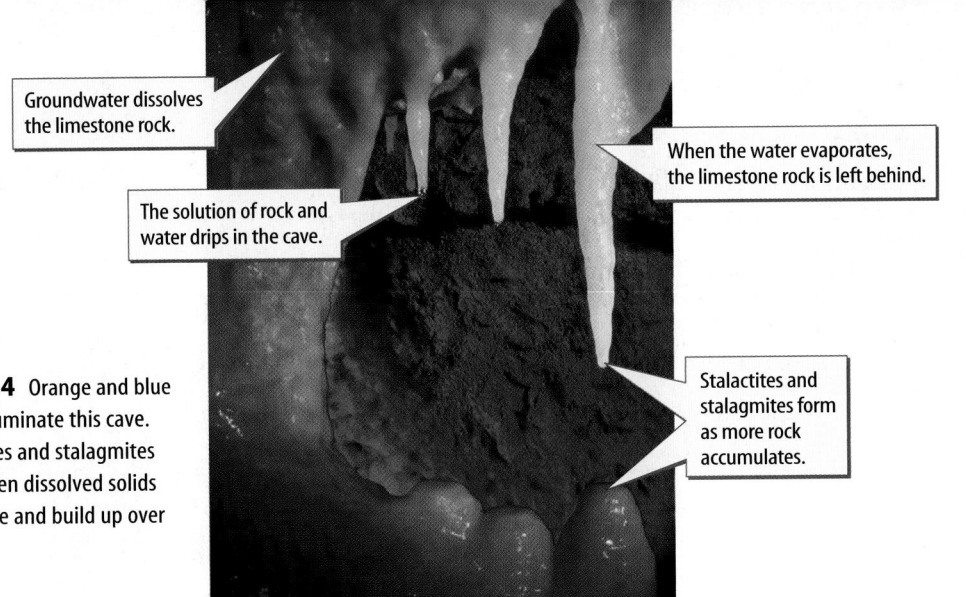

Groundwater dissolves the limestone rock.

When the water evaporates, the limestone rock is left behind.

The solution of rock and water drips in the cave.

Stalactites and stalagmites form as more rock accumulates.

**Figure 4** Orange and blue lights illuminate this cave. Stalactites and stalagmites form when dissolved solids crystallize and build up over time.

**INTEGRATE Environment**

Stalactites and stalagmites in caves are formed from solutions, as shown in **Figure 4.** First, minerals dissolve in water as it flows through rocks at the top of the cave. This solution of water and dissolved minerals drips from the ceiling of the cave. When drops of the solution evaporate from the roof of the cave, the minerals are left behind. They create the hanging rock formations called stalactites. When drops of the solution fall onto the floor of the cave and evaporate, they form stalagmites. Very often, a stalactite develops downward while a stalagmite develops upward until the two meet. One continuous column of minerals is formed. This process will be discussed later.

## Types of Solutions

So far, you've learned about types of solutions in which a solid solute dissolves in a liquid solvent. But solutions can be made up of different combinations of solids, liquids, and gases, as shown in **Table 2.**

| Table 2 Examples of Common Solutions | | | |
|---|---|---|---|
| | **Solvent/ State** | **Solute/ State** | **State of Solution** |
| **Earth's atmosphere** | nitrogen/gas | oxygen/gas carbon dioxide/gas argon/gas | gas |
| **Ocean water** | water/liquid | salt/solid oxygen/gas carbon dioxide/gas | liquid |
| **Carbonated beverage** | water/liquid | carbon dioxide/gas | liquid |
| **Brass** | copper/solid | zinc/solid | solid |

## Caption Answer

**Figure 5** Yes; many carbonated soft drinks contain solid, liquid, and gas solutes.

## Use Science Words

**Word Meaning** The term *miscible* is used when speaking of liquids dissolving in liquids. Have students look up the term and write paragraphs explaining what it means to say that two substances are miscible. Two liquids that are miscible can mix completely with each other in all proportions. Ask students whether it's possible to tell which of two miscible substances is the solvent and which is the solute and explain their answers. The solvent is the liquid present in greater quantity. L2 IS **Linguistic**

### ✓ Reading Check

**Answer** carbon dioxide and components that give it its flavor and color

## Fun Fact

The gases in the gas-gas solution that is air can be separated by fractional distillation. The gases must first undergo several steps to cool until they are liquids. Then fractional distillation can separate them according to their boiling points.

**Figure 5** Acetic acid (a liquid), carbon dioxide (a gas), and drink-mix crystals (a solid) can be dissolved in water (a liquid). **Determine** *whether one liquid solution could contain all three different kinds of solute.*

## Liquid Solutions

You're probably most familiar with liquid solutions like the ones shown in **Figure 5,** in which the solvent is a liquid. The solute can be another liquid, a solid, or even a gas. You've already learned about liquid-solid solutions such as sugar water and salt water. When discussing solutions, the state of the solvent usually determines the state of the solution.

**Liquid-Gas Solutions** Carbonated beverages are liquid-gas solutions—carbon dioxide is the gaseous solute, and water is the liquid solvent. The carbon dioxide gas gives the beverage its fizz and some of its tartness. The beverage also might contain other solutes, such as the compounds that give it its flavor and color.

### ✓ Reading Check *What are the solutes in a carbonated beverage?*

**Liquid-Liquid Solutions** In a liquid-liquid solution, both the solvent and the solute are liquids. Vinegar, which you might use to make salad dressing, is a liquid-liquid solution made of 95 percent water (the solvent) and 5 percent acetic acid (the solute).

## Gaseous Solutions

In gaseous solutions, a smaller amount of one gas is dissolved in a larger amount of another gas. This is called a gas-gas solution because both the solvent and solute are gases. The air you breathe is a gaseous solution. Nitrogen makes up about 78 percent of dry air and is the solvent. The other gases are the solutes.

**292** **CHAPTER 10** Substances, Mixtures, and Solubility

## Science Journal

**Solutions** Ask students to describe in their Science Journals the solutions they encounter on a typical day. Have them classify each solution as a gaseous, liquid, or solid solution. L2 IS **Linguistic**

## Teacher FYI

**Adding to a Solution** Adding a solute raises the boiling point and lowers the freezing point of a liquid solvent. For example, adding antifreeze to the water in an automobile radiator causes the water to freeze at a lower temperature.

**Figure 6** Metal alloys can contain either metal or nonmetal solutes dissolved in a metal solvent.

● Iron atoms
· Carbon atoms

Steel

Steel is a solid solution of the metal iron and the nonmetal carbon.

● Copper atoms
● Zinc atoms

Brass

Brass is a solid solution made of copper and zinc.

**Solid Solutions** In solid solutions, the solvent is a solid. The solute can be a solid, liquid, or gas. The most common solid solutions are solid-solid solutions—ones in which the solvent and the solute are solids. A solid-solid solution made from two or more metals is called an alloy. It's also possible to include elements that are not metals in alloys. For example, steel is an alloy that has carbon dissolved in iron. The carbon makes steel much stronger and yet more flexible than iron. Two alloys are shown in **Figure 6.**

---

## section 1 review

### Summary

**Substances**

- Elements are substances that cannot be broken down into simpler substances.
- A compound is made up of two or more elements bonded together.

**Mixtures and Solutions**

- Mixtures are either heterogeneous or homogeneous.
- Solutions have two parts—solute and solvent.
- Crystallization and precipitation are two ways that solids are formed from solutions.

**Types of Solutions**

- The solutes and solvents can be solids, liquids, or gases.

### Self Check

1. **Compare and contrast** substances and mixtures. Give two examples of each.
2. **Describe** how heterogeneous and homogeneous mixtures differ.
3. **Explain** how a solution forms.
4. **Identify** the common name for a solid-solid solution of metals.
5. **Think Critically** The tops of carbonated-beverage cans usually are made with a different aluminum alloy than the pull tabs are made with. Explain.

#### Applying Skills

6. **Compare and contrast** the following solutions: a helium-neon laser, bronze (a copper-tin alloy), cloudy ice cubes, and ginger ale.

---

## section 1 review

1. A substance is either an element or a compound. Examples may include water or elements, such as oxygen, carbon, or hydrogen. A mixture is two or more substances mixed together. Examples may include salt water, cold cereal and milk, or lemonade.
2. In a homogeneous mixture two or more substances are mixed evenly on a molecular level. In a heterogeneous mixture substances are not mixed evenly on a molecular level.
3. A solution is formed by a solute, a substance that dissolves, combining with a solvent, a substance that dissolves the solute. The substance in greater quantity is the solvent.
4. alloy
5. The alloy for the tab must be stronger so that it will open the can without breaking.
6. Helium-neon is a gas-gas solution; bronze is a solid-solid solution; cloudy ice cubes are a solid-gas solution; and ginger ale is a liquid solvent with gas and solid solutes.

---

# Differentiated Instruction

**Challenge** To make a solid solution, the solids are melted, dissolved, and then cooled back to solid form. Have each student research a particular solid solution, such as brass, steel, or 14-karat gold, and make a poster showing how it is made and how it is used. L3 [LS] **Visual-Spatial** P

## 3 Assess

### DAILY INTERVENTION

**Check for Understanding**

**Auditory-Musical** Working in small groups, have students create either a poem or a song that describes the differences between mixtures and solutions. L1 COOP LEARN [LS]

### Reteach

**Matter** Make a chart on the chalkboard with the word *Matter* at the top. Below it draw two boxes to indicate that matter can be divided into pure substances and mixtures. Draw boxes to show that mixtures can be divided into homogeneous and heterogeneous mixtures. Then, draw boxes to show that pure substances can be divided into elements and compounds. L2 [LS] **Visual-Spatial**

### ✔ Assessment

**Performance** Have students brainstorm a list of solvents used around the house. Water is the most common, but paint thinner, alcohol, spot removers, and nail polish remover also are frequently used. Use **Performance Assessment in the Science Classroom,** p. 89.

# section

# 2 Solubility

### as you read

**What You'll Learn**
- **Explain** why water is a good general solvent.
- **Describe** how the structure of a compound affects which solvents it dissolves in.
- **Identify** factors that affect how much of a substance will dissolve in a solvent.
- **Describe** how temperature affects reaction rate.
- **Explain** how solute particles effect physical properties of water.

**Why It's Important**
How you wash your hands, clothes, and dishes depends on which substances can dissolve in other substances.

**Review Vocabulary**
**polar bond:** a bond resulting from the unequal sharing of electrons

**New Vocabulary**
- aqueous
- saturated
- solubility
- concentration

**Figure 7** Some atoms share electrons to form covalent bonds.

Two atoms of hydrogen share their electrons equally. Such a molecule is nonpolar.

## Water—The Universal Solvent

In many solutions, including fruit juice and vinegar, water is the solvent. A solution in which water is the solvent is called an **aqueous** (A kwee us) solution. Because water can dissolve so many different solutes, chemists often call it the universal solvent. To understand why water is such a great solvent, you must first know a few things about atoms and bonding.

**Molecular Compounds** When certain atoms form compounds, they share electrons. Sharing electrons is called covalent bonding. Compounds that contain covalent bonds are called molecular compounds, or molecules.

If a molecule has an even distribution of electrons, like the one in **Figure 7,** it is called nonpolar. The atoms in some molecules do not have an even distribution of electrons. For example, in a water molecule, two hydrogen atoms share electrons with a single oxygen atom. However, as **Figure 7** shows, the electrons spend more time around the oxygen atom than they spend around the hydrogen atoms. As a result, the oxygen portion of the water molecule has a partial negative charge and the hydrogen portions have a partial positive charge. The overall charge of the water molecule is neutral. Such a molecule is said to be polar, and the bonds between its atoms are called polar covalent bonds.

(Partial negative charge)

The electrons spend more time around the oxygen atom than the hydrogen atoms. Such a molecule is polar.

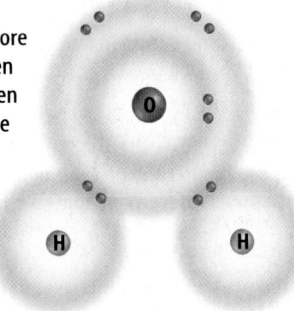

(Partial positive charge)

**294 CHAPTER 10** Substances, Mixtures, and Solubility

## Section 2 Resource Manager

**Ionic Bonds** Some atoms do not share electrons when they join with other atoms to form compounds. Instead, these atoms lose or gain electrons. When they do, the number of protons and electrons within an atom are no longer equal, and the atom becomes positively or negatively charged. Atoms with a charge are called ions. Bonds between ions that are formed by the transfer of electrons are called ionic bonds, and the compound that is formed is called an ionic compound. Table salt is an ionic compound that is made of sodium ions and chloride ions. Each sodium atom loses one electron to a chlorine atom and becomes a positively charged sodium ion. Each chlorine atom gains one electron from a sodium atom, becoming a negatively charged chloride ion.

**Reading Check** *How does an ionic compound differ from a molecular compound?*

**How Water Dissolves Ionic Compounds** Now think about the properties of water and the properties of ionic compounds as you visualize how an ionic compound dissolves in water. Because water molecules are polar, they attract positive and negative ions. The more positive part of a water molecule—where the hydrogen atoms are—is attracted to negatively charged ions. The more negative part of a water molecule—where the oxygen atom is—attracts positive ions. When an ionic compound is mixed with water, the different ions of the compound are pulled apart by the water molecules. **Figure 8** shows how sodium chloride dissolves in water.

**Solutions** Seawater is a solution that contains nearly every element found on Earth. Most elements are present in tiny quantities. Sodium and chloride ions are the most common ions in seawater. Several gases, including oxygen, nitrogen, and carbon dioxide, also are dissolved in seawater.

**Figure 8** Water dissolves table salt because its partial charges are attracted to the charged ions in the salt.

The partially negative oxygen in the water molecule is attracted to a positive sodium ion.

The partially positive hydrogen atoms in another water molecule are attracted to a negative chloride ion.

The sodium and chloride ions are pulled apart from each other, and more water molecules are attracted to them.

---

## Differentiated Instruction

**Challenge** Water alone can't dissolve everything needed to clean oil off your hands. You need to use soap as well. Have students find out how soap works. A soap molecule is hydrophilic (attracted to water) on one end, and hydrophobic (attracted to water-insoluble molecules) on the other end. Its hydrophilic end allows it to dissolve in water, and its hydrophobic end dissolves materials that are insoluble in water and washes them off. L3  IS **Logical-Mathematical**

## Visual Learning

**Figure 8** Review the three illustrations. Point out that an ion is not attracted to one certain water molecule but is attracted to the oppositely charged parts of many water molecules. Many water molecules are attracted to and surround each ion. L2  IS **Visual-Spatial**

---

## 2 Teach

### Quick Demo
**Polar Molecules**

**Materials** balloon, wool cloth or piece of fur, sink with running water

**Estimated Time** 15 min

**Procedure** To make the concept of polar molecules more accessible to students, blow up a balloon and rub it with a wool cloth or a piece of fur to give it a charge. Then hold the balloon next to a thin stream of water. Students will observe that the stream of water bends toward the balloon. The polar water molecules are attracted to the charge on the balloon.

**Reading Check**

**Answer** Ionic compounds are made up of particles that have lost or gained electrons. Molecular compounds are made up of particles that share electrons to form molecules.

**INTEGRATE Environment**

**Solutions** Other elements found in some abundance in seawater include bromine and manganese. Earth's oceans also contain an estimated nine billion metric tons of gold, but obtaining gold from seawater is not cost effective.

### Discussion

**Water Conductivity** Pure water is a poor conductor of electricity. Do you think water with ions dissolved in it conducts electricity? Explain. Water with ions dissolved in it conducts electricity easily because the ions are free to move in the water and can carry electric current. L3  IS **Logical-Mathematical**

## Activity

**Waterproofing** The fact that oil and water don't mix is useful in waterproofing. Have students look up and report on natural and manufactured examples of the oily materials used for waterproofing. Materials include duck feathers, compounds used for waterproofing boots, and oilskin. L2 IS
**Logical-Mathematical**

### ✔ Reading Check

**Answer** Polar solvents dissolve polar solutes and nonpolar solvents dissolve nonpolar solutes.

## Inquiry Lab

### Observing Solubility

**Purpose** Students will gain experience with solubility by trying to dissolve salt and sugar in water or vinegar. L2 ELL

**Possible Materials** water, vinegar, salt, sugar, beakers, weighing scale, hot plate

**Estimated Time** one class session

**Teaching Strategies**

• Challenge students to see who can dissolve the greatest mass of solute in 100 mL of solvent.

• Discuss the contest the day prior to the lab. Which will dissolve in greater mass: salt, sugar, or a mixture? Why do they think so?

• The vinegar can be puzzling. It already has solute in it, so in fact may lower the solubility results (depending on the precision of your weighing scale).

• Have students write their predictions, including the theoretical basis for their guesses, before starting the lab.

• Give the class a basic procedure for weighing and dissolving the solute.

• Ask students to design a lab that increases the solubility of the salt and sugar. heat the solutions

**For additional inquiry activities, see**
*Science Inquiry Labs.*

**Figure 9** Sugar molecules that are dissolved in water spread out until they are spaced evenly in the water.

**Figure 10** Water and oil do not mix because water molecules are polar and oil molecules are nonpolar.

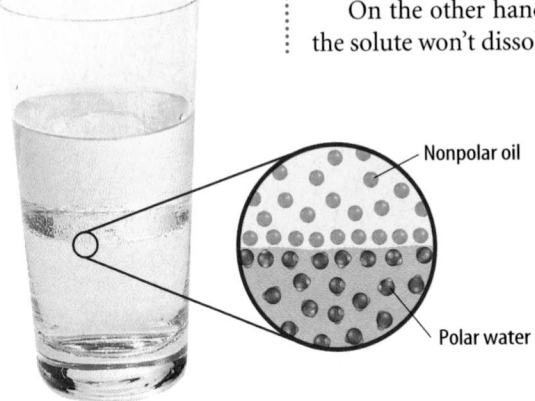

### How Water Dissolves Molecular Compounds

Can water also dissolve molecular compounds that are not made of ions? Water does dissolve molecular compounds, such as sugar, although it doesn't break each sugar molecule apart. Water simply moves between different molecules of sugar, separating them. Like water, a sugar molecule is polar. Polar water molecules are attracted to the positive and negative portions of the polar sugar molecules. When the sugar molecules are separated by the water and spread throughout it, as **Figure 9** shows, they have dissolved.

## What will dissolve?

When you stir a spoonful of sugar into iced tea, all of the sugar dissolves but none of the metal in the spoon does. Why does sugar dissolve in water, but metal does not? A substance that dissolves in another is said to be soluble in that substance. You would say that the sugar is soluble in water but the metal of the spoon is insoluble in water, because it does not dissolve readily.

**Like Dissolves Like** When trying to predict which solvents can dissolve which solutes, chemists use the rule of "like dissolves like." This means that polar solvents dissolve polar solutes and nonpolar solvents dissolve nonpolar solutes. In the case of sugar and water, both are made up of polar molecules, so sugar is soluble in water. In the case of salt and water, the sodium and chloride ion pair is like the water molecule because it has a positive charge at one end and a negative charge at the other end.

### ✔ Reading Check    *What does "like dissolves like" mean?*

On the other hand, if a solvent and a solute are not similar, the solute won't dissolve. For example, oil and water do not mix. Oil molecules are nonpolar, so polar water molecules are not attracted to them. If you pour vegetable oil into a glass of water, the oil and the water separate into layers instead of forming a solution, as shown in **Figure 10.** You've probably noticed the same thing about the oil-and-water mixtures that make up some salad dressings. The oil stays on the top. Oils generally dissolve better in solvents that have nonpolar molecules.

Nonpolar oil

Polar water

## Science Journal

**Alcohol** Molecules such as ethyl alcohol, $C_2H_5OH$, dissolve equally well in the polar solvent water and the nonpolar solvent turpentine. Have students find out why and each write a paragraph summarizing his or her findings. Alcohol dissolves in water because of the polar $-OH$ end of the molecule; it dissolves in nonpolar turpentine because of the nonpolar end of the molecule, $-C_2H_5$. L3 IS **Linguistic**

## Teacher FYI

**Eliminating Water** Water sometimes gets into automobile gas tanks, and can interfere with the combustion process. To get rid of the water, you can add dry gas, which is a methanol solution. The methanol mixes in all proportions with water, and the mixture is combustible. The water is eliminated along with the combustion products.

# How much will dissolve?

Even though sugar is soluble in water, if you tried to dissolve 1 kg of sugar into one small glass of water, not all of the sugar would dissolve. **Solubility** (sahl yuh BIH luh tee) is a measurement that describes how much solute dissolves in a given amount of solvent. The solubility of a material has been described as the amount of the material that can dissolve in 100 g of solvent at a given temperature. Some solutes are highly soluble, meaning that a large amount of solute can be dissolved in 100 g of solvent. For example, 63 g of potassium chromate can be dissolved in 100 g of water at 25°C. On the other hand, some solutes are not very soluble. For example, only 0.00025 g of barium sulfate will dissolve in 100 g of water at 25°C. When a substance has an extremely low solubility, like barium sulfate does in water, it usually is considered insoluble.

✔ **Reading Check** *What is an example of a substance that is considered to be insoluble in water?*

**Solubility in Liquid-Solid Solutions** Did you notice that the temperature was included in the explanation about the amount of solute that dissolves in a quantity of solvent? The solubility of many solutes changes if you change the temperature of the solvent. For example, if you heat water, not only does the sugar dissolve at a faster rate, but more sugar can dissolve in it. However, some solutes, like sodium chloride and calcium carbonate, do not become more soluble when the temperature of water increases. The graph in **Figure 11** shows how the temperature of the solvent affects the solubility of some solutes.

**Figure 11** The solubility of some solutes changes as the temperature of the solvent increases.
**Use a Graph** *According to the graph, is it likely that warm ocean water contains any more sodium chloride than cold ocean water does?*

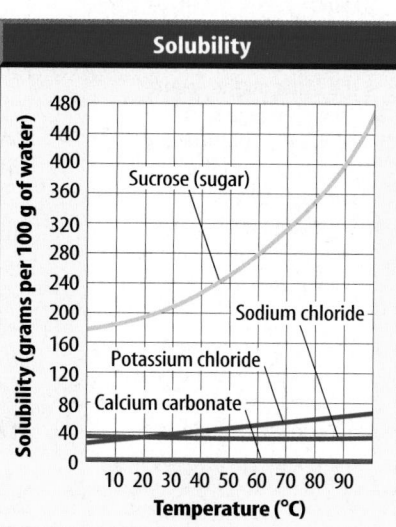

**Solubility in Liquid-Gas Solutions** Unlike liquid-solid solutions, an increase in temperature decreases the solubility of a gas in a liquid-gas solution. You might notice this if you have ever opened a warm carbonated beverage and it bubbled up out of control while a chilled one barely fizzed. Carbon dioxide is less soluble in a warm solution. What keeps the carbon dioxide from bubbling out when it is sitting at room temperature on a supermarket shelf? When a bottle is filled, extra carbon dioxide gas is squeezed into the space above the liquid, increasing the pressure in the bottle. This increased pressure increases the solubility of gas and forces most of it into the solution. When you open the cap, the pressure is released and the solubility of the carbon dioxide decreases.

✔ **Reading Check** *Why does a bottle of carbonated beverage go "flat" after it has been opened for a few days?*

## Science Journal

**Heat and Speed of Dissolution** Remind students that when a material is heated, its molecules move faster. Have them write paragraphs in their Science Journals describing why heating water increases the speed at which sugar dissolves in it.
L2 **IS** **Logical-Mathematical**

## Fun Fact

Hot chocolate mix is a combination of sugars. The instructions say to combine the mix with hot water. More mix is dissolved in hot water since sugars are more soluble in hot water than cold water.

✔ **Reading Check**

**Answer** barium sulfate

**Caption Answer**

**Figure 11** No; the sodium chloride curve is nearly horizontal.

### Quick Demo

**Solubility**

**Materials** 20 g of calcium acetate dehydrate, 20 g of potassium nitrate, 100-mL beaker (2), water, hot plate with magnetic stirring, stirring rod

**Estimated Time** 20 min

**Procedure** Place 20 g of calcium acetate dihydrate in one beaker and 20 g of potassium nitrate in another. Add 50 mL of water to each. Stir with magnetic stirring or a stirring rod and have students observe that all of the calcium acetate dihydrate dissolves but some of the potassium nitrate does not. Heat the beakers on a hot plate, stirring constantly. Then have students observe that more potassium nitrate dissolves, but some of the calcium acetate dihydrate comes out of solution.

### Discussion

**Solute Contact** Why does a solute dissolve faster when it is stirred or when its crystals are broken down into smaller pieces? Stirring brings fresh solvent into contact with the solute, so they can interact faster. When a large piece of solute is broken down into smaller pieces, the surface area with which solvent molecules can come into contact increases. L2 **IS** **Logical-Mathematical**

✔ **Reading Check**

**Answer** Upon opening the carbonated beverage the extra pressure that kept the carbon dioxide in solution is released. After a few days the remaining carbon dioxide comes out of solution and leaves your beverage "flat."

**Purpose** Students observe how temperature affects reaction rate L2 ELL

IS **Visual-Spatial**

**Materials** two small glasses, milk, refrigerator

**Teaching Strategies** If possible, leave the unrefrigerated glass of milk on a window ledge exposed to sunlight.

**Safety Precautions** Warn students not to drink the milk that sat out overnight.

**Analysis**

1. The unrefrigerated milk will smell sour and may have solids in it. The refrigerated milk will not.
2. Refrigeration lowers the temperature of the food and therefore slows the rate of the reaction and spoilage.

## Assessment

**Process** Show students pictures of perishable and nonperishable food items. Have them determine which will spoil faster and why.

**Figure 12** The Dead Sea is a saturated solution. When the water evaporates, minerals are left behind as pillars.

## Mini LAB

### Observing Chemical Processes

**Procedure**

1. Pour **two small glasses of milk.**
2. Place one glass of milk in the **refrigerator.** Leave the other on the counter.
3. Allow the milk to sit overnight. **WARNING:** *Do not drink the milk that sat out overnight.*
4. On the following day, smell both glasses of milk. Record your observations.

**Analysis**

1. Compare and contrast the appearance and odor of both glasses of milk.
2. Explain why refrigeration is needed.

---

**Indiana Academic Standard Check**

**7.3.12:** Investigate how the temperature . . . of a solution influences reaction rates, such as those resulting in food spoilage.

✔ How do the movements of molecules affect food spoilage?

✔ The slower the molecules move, the slower the reaction rate and the rate of spoilage.

---

**Saturated Solutions** If you add calcium carbonate to 100 g of water at 25°C, only 0.0014 g of it will dissolve. Additional calcium carbonate will not dissolve. Such a solution—one that contains all of the solute that it can hold under the given conditions—is called a **saturated** solution. **Figure 12** shows a saturated solution. If a solution is a liquid-solid solution, the extra solute that is added will settle to the bottom of the container. Unsaturated solutions contain less solute than the maximum amount that will dissolve.

When a saturated solution cools, some of the solute usually falls out of the solution. But if a saturated solution is cooled slowly, sometimes the excess solute remains dissolved for a period of time. Such a solution is said to be supersaturated, because it contains more than the maximum amount that will dissolve.

## Rate of Dissolving

Solubility does not tell you how fast a solute will dissolve—it tells you only how much of a solute will dissolve at a given temperature. Some solutes dissolve quickly, but others take a long time to dissolve. A solute dissolves faster when the solution is stirred or shaken or when the temperature of the solution is increased. These methods increase the rate at which the surfaces of the solute come into contact with the solvent. Increasing the area of contact between the solute and the solvent can also increase the rate of dissolving. This can be done by breaking up the solute into smaller pieces, which increases the surface area of the solute that is exposed to the solvent.

Molecules always are moving and colliding. Collisions must take place for chemical reactions to occur. The higher the temperature, the more collisions that occur and the higher the rate of reaction. The opposite also is true. The lower the temperature, the fewer collisions that occur and the lower the rate of reaction. Refrigerators slow reaction rates, preventing food spoilage.

**298 CHAPTER 10** Substances, Mixtures, and Solubility

---

**Active Reading**

**Double-Entry Journal** In this strategy, the student takes notes and adds his or her own reflections while reading the student text. Students are encouraged to explore ideas, make responses, and take risks in giving opinions about the reading. Have students divide sheets of paper in half down the middle. On the left, have them identify a particular passage or quotation of significance in the reading. Students may record anything luminous, enigmatic, stimulating, or disturbing. On the right, students respond, question, elaborate, make personal connections, evaluate, reflect, analyze, or interpret. Have students make a Double-Entry Journal for the discussion of solubility and concentration presented in this section. L2

## Concentration

What makes strong lemonade strong and weak lemonade weak? The difference between the two drinks is the amount of water in each one compared to the amount of lemon. The lemon is present in different concentrations in the solution. The **concentration** of a solution tells you how much solute is present compared to the amount of solvent. You can give a simple description of a solution's concentration by calling it either concentrated or dilute. These terms are used when comparing the concentrations of two solutions with the same type of solute and solvent. A concentrated solution has more solute per given amount of solvent than a dilute solution.

**Measuring Concentration** Can you imagine a doctor ordering a dilute intravenous, or IV, solution for a patient? Because dilute is not an exact measurement, the IV could be made with a variety of amounts of medicine. The doctor would need to specify the exact concentration of the IV solution to make sure that the patient is treated correctly.

**INTEGRATE Career**

**Pharmacist** Doctors rely on pharmacists to formulate IV solutions. Pharmacists begin with a concentrated form of the drug, which is supplied by pharmaceutical companies. This is the solute of the IV solution. The pharmacist adds the correct amount of solvent to a small amount of the solute to achieve the concentration requested by the doctor. There may be more than one solute per IV solution in varying concentrations.

**INTEGRATE Career**

**Pharmacist** Besides making IV solutions, pharmacists are responsible for understanding the use, effects, and chemical composition of drugs including physical, chemical, and biological properties. Pharmacists also advise doctors on the selection, dosage, interactions, and side effects of the drugs.

### Use an Analogy

**Swimming Pools** Suggest that students think of a public swimming pool as being like a solvent and individual swimmers as molecules of solute. A dozen swimmers in the pool would be like a dilute solution. A crowded pool would be like a concentrated solution. L1 ELL IS **Visual-Spatial**

### Applying Science

#### How can you compare concentrations?

A solute is a substance that can be dissolved in another substance called a solvent. Solutions vary in concentration, or strength, depending on the amount of solute and solvent being used. Fruit drinks are examples of such a solution. Stronger fruit drinks appear darker in color and are the result of more drink mix being dissolved in a given amount of water. What would happen if more water were added to the solution?

| Glucose Solutions (g/100 mL) | | |
|---|---|---|
| Solute Glucose (g) | Solvent Water (mL) | Solution Concentration of Glucose (%) |
| 2 | 100 | 2 |
| 4 | 100 | 4 |
| 10 | 100 | 10 |
| 20 | 100 | 20 |

#### Identifying the Problem

The table on the right lists different concentration levels of glucose solutions, a type of carbohydrate your body uses as a source of energy. The glucose is measured in grams, and the water is measured in milliliters.

#### Solving the Problem

A physician writes a prescription for a patient to receive 1,000 mL of a 20 percent solution of glucose. How many grams of glucose must the pharmacist add to 1,000 mL of water to prepare this 20 percent concentration level?

### Applying Science

**Answer**
$$1000 \text{ mL} \times \frac{20 \text{ g}}{100 \text{ mL}} = 200 \text{ g}$$

SECTION 2 Solubility **299**

## Science Journal

**Home Concentrates** Most households contain a variety of solutions, such as frozen juice, or laundry detergent, that are concentrated. Have students list in their Science Journals the concentrated solutions in their homes, and describe why they think these products come in concentrated form. It makes them smaller so they can be shipped easily and cheaply. L2 IS **Logical-Mathematical**

## Differentiated Instruction

**Learning Disabled** Give the students a small box. Have them add five marbles to the box to mimic a dilute solution. Have them add 15 more marbles to exhibit a concentrated solution. L1 ELL IS **Visual-Spatial**

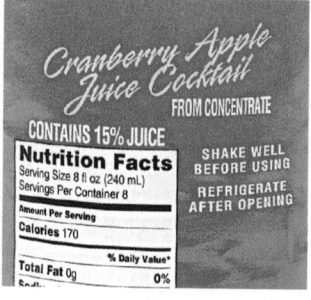

**Figure 13** Concentrations can be stated in percentages.

One way of giving the exact concentration is to state the percentage of the volume of the solution that is made up of solute. Labels on fruit drinks show their concentration like the one in **Figure 13.** When a fruit drink contains 15 percent fruit juice, the remaining 85 percent of the drink is water and other substances such as sweeteners and flavorings. This drink is more concentrated than another brand that contains 10 percent fruit juice, but it's more dilute than pure juice, which is 100 percent juice. Another way to describe the concentration of a solution is to give the percentage of the total mass that is made up of solute.

**Effects of Solute Particles** All solute particles affect the physical properties of the solvent, such as its boiling point and freezing point. The effect that a solute has on the freezing or boiling point of a solvent depends on the number of solute particles.

When a solvent such as water begins to freeze, its molecules arrange themselves in a particular pattern. When a solute, such as sodium chloride, is added, the solute particles interfere with the formation of the solid. To overcome this interference, a lower temperature is needed to freeze the solvent.

When a solvent such as water begins to boil, the solvent molecules are gaining enough energy to move from the liquid state to the gaseous state. When a solute such as sodium chloride is added to the solvent, fewer solvent particles escape the liquid's surface to the gas phase. More energy is needed for the solvent particles to escape from the liquid, and the boiling point of the solution will be higher.

## section 2 review

### Summary

**The Universal Solvent**

- Water is known as the universal solvent.
- A molecule that has an even distribution of electrons is a nonpolar molecule.
- A molecule that has an uneven distribution of electrons is a polar molecule.
- A compound that loses or gains electrons is an ionic compound.

**Dissolving a Substance**

- Chemists use the rule "like dissolves like."

**Concentration**

- Concentration is the quantity of solute present compared to the amount of solvent.

### Self Check

1. **Identify** the property of water that makes it the universal solvent.
2. **Describe** the two methods to increase the rate at which a substance dissolves.
3. **Infer** why it is important to add sodium chloride to water when making homemade ice cream.
4. **Think Critically** Why can the fluids used to dry-clean clothing remove grease even when water cannot?

### Applying Skills

5. **Recognize Cause and Effect** Why is it more important in terms of reaction rate to take groceries straight home from the store when it is 25°C than when it is 2°C?

Science nline in7.msscience.com/self_check_quiz

## section 2 review

1. Water is a polar molecule with a partial negative charge near the oxygen atom and a partial positive charge near the hydrogen atoms. The opposite charges allow water to attract both positive and negative charges on ions or molecules.

2. Possible answers: Change the temperature, increase surface area of solute, stir or shake, increase the pressure if the solute is a gas.

3. It is important to add sodium chloride to water when making homemade ice cream in order to lower the freezing point of the water.

4. The fluids are nonpolar, as are molecules that make up grease.

5. At 25°C the rate at which food spoils is much higher than the rate at 2°C.

# Observing Gas Solubility

On a hot day, a carbonated beverage will cool you off. If you leave the beverage uncovered at room temperature, it quickly loses its fizz. However, if you cap the beverage and place it in the refrigerator, it will still have its fizz hours later. In this lab you will explore why this happens.

## ● Real-World Question

What effect does temperature have on the fizz, or carbon dioxide, in your carbonated beverage?

### Goals

- ■ **Observe** the effect that temperature has on solubility.
- ■ **Compare** the amount of carbon dioxide released at room temperature and in hot tap water.

### Materials

carbonated beverages in plastic bottles, thoroughly chilled (2)
balloons (2)               *ruler
tape                       container
fabric tape measure        hot tap water
*string                    *Alternative materials

### Safety Precautions

WARNING: *DO NOT point the bottles at anyone at any time during the lab.*

## ● Procedure

1. Carefully remove the caps from the thoroughly chilled plastic bottles one at a time. Create as little agitation as possible.
2. Quickly cover the opening of each bottle with an uninflated balloon.

3. Use tape to secure and tightly seal the balloons to the top of the bottles.
4. Gently agitate one bottle from side to side for two minutes. Measure the circumference of the balloon.

WARNING: *Contents under pressure can cause serious accidents. Be sure to wear safety goggles, and DO NOT point the bottles at anyone.*

5. Gently agitate the second bottle in the same manner as in step 4. Then, place the bottle in a container of hot tap water for ten minutes. Measure the circumference of the balloon.

## ● Conclude and Apply

1. **Compare and contrast** the relative amounts of carbon dioxide gas released from the cold and the warm carbonated beverages.
2. **Infer** Why does the warmed carbonated beverage release a different amount of carbon dioxide than the chilled one?

### *C*ommunicating
**Your Data**

Compare the circumferences of your balloons with those of members of your class. **For more help, refer to the** Science Skill Handbook.

---

### ☑ Assessment

**Process** Have students design an experiment that would produce a more qualitative way to measure the amount of carbon dioxide in a carbonated beverage. Use **Performance Assessment in the Science Classroom,** p. 95. **P**

### *C*ommunicating
**Your Data**

Have students make line graphs. Plot the student's name (or team) versus the circumference of the balloons. Make two separate lines. Use blue pen to plot the cold carbonated beverage data. Use red pen to plot the warm carbonated beverage data. Be sure the students plot the cold and warm data on the same *x*-axis point for each team. A computer graphing program may be used.

---

BENCH TESTED

## ● Real-World Question

**Purpose** Students observe how temperature effects solubility. L2 **ELL** COOP LEARN

**Process Skills** observe, measure, record data

**Time Required** 30 min

## ● Procedure

**Alternate Materials** A string of known length can be substituted for a fabric tape measure. Have the students use a ruler to measure the amount of string that wraps around the balloon circumference.

**Safety Precautions** Be sure that all students are wearing safety goggles.

**Teaching Strategy** Consider having students work in pairs. One student can remove the cap from the plastic bottle while the other student covers the opening with a balloon.

**Troubleshooting** The connection between the bottle and the balloon must be secure.

## ● Conclude and Apply

1. The relative amount of carbon dioxide released from the cold carbonated beverage was less than the relative amount of carbon dioxide in the warm carbonated beverage.
2. The warm carbonated beverage releases more carbon dioxide because an increase of temperature decreases the solubility of a gas in a liquid-gas solution.

# section 3

# Acidic and Basic Solutions

**as you read**

## *What* You'll Learn

- **Compare** acids and bases and their properties.
- **Describe** practical uses of acids and bases.
- **Explain** how pH is used to describe the strength of an acid or base.
- **Describe** how acids and bases react when they are brought together.

## *Why* It's Important

Many common products, such as batteries and bleach, work because of acids or bases.

### Review Vocabulary

**physical property:** any characteristic of a material that can be seen or measured without changing the material

### New Vocabulary

- acid
- hydronium ion
- base
- pH
- indicator
- neutralization

## Acids

What makes orange juice, vinegar, dill pickles, and grapefruit tangy? Acids cause the sour taste of these and other foods. **Acids** are substances that release positively charged hydrogen ions, $H^+$, in water. When an acid mixes with water, the acid dissolves, releasing a hydrogen ion. The hydrogen ion then combines with a water molecule to form a hydronium ion, as shown in **Figure 14. Hydronium ions** are positively charged and have the formula $H_3O^+$.

**Properties of Acidic Solutions** Sour taste is one of the properties of acidic solutions. The taste allows you to detect the presence of acids in your food. However, even though you can identify acidic solutions by their sour taste, you should never taste anything in the laboratory, and you should never use taste to test for the presence of acids in an unknown substance. Many acids can cause serious burns to body tissues.

Another property of acidic solutions is that they can conduct electricity. The hydronium ions in an acidic solution can carry the electric charges in a current. This is why some batteries contain an acid. Acidic solutions also are corrosive, which means they can break down certain substances. Many acids can corrode fabric, skin, and paper. The solutions of some acids also react strongly with certain metals. The acid-metal reaction forms metallic compounds and hydrogen gas, leaving holes in the metal in the process.

$$H^+ \quad + \quad H_2O \quad \longrightarrow \quad H_3O^+$$

Hydrogen ion

Water molecule

Hydronium ion

**Figure 14** One hydrogen ion can combine with one water molecule to form one positively charged hydronium ion.
**Identify** *what kinds of substances are sources of hydrogen ions.*

**302** CHAPTER 10 Substances, Mixtures, and Solubility

---

**Figure 15** Each of these products contains an acid or is made with the help of an acid.
**Describe** *how your life would be different if acids were not available to make these products.*

## Uses of Acids

You're probably familiar with many acids. Vinegar, which is used in salad dressing, contains acetic acid. Lemons, limes, and oranges have a sour taste because they contain citric acid. Your body needs ascorbic acid, which is vitamin C. Ants that sting inject formic acid into their victims.

**Figure 15** shows other products that are made with acids. Sulfuric acid is used in the production of fertilizers, steel, paints, and plastics. Acids often are used in batteries because their solutions conduct electricity. For this reason, it sometimes is referred to as battery acid. Hydrochloric acid, which is known commercially as muriatic acid, is used in a process called pickling. Pickling is a process that removes impurities from the surfaces of metals. Hydrochloric acid also can be used to clean mortar from brick walls. Nitric acid is used in the production of fertilizers, dyes, and plastics.

## Acid in the Environment

Carbonic acid plays a key role in the formation of caves and of stalactites and stalagmites. Carbonic acid is formed when carbon dioxide in soil is dissolved in water. When this acidic solution comes in contact with calcium carbonate—or limestone rock—it can dissolve it, eventually carving out a cave in the rock. A similar process occurs when acid rain falls on statues and eats away at the stone, as shown in **Figure 16.** When this acidic solution drips from the ceiling of the cave, water evaporates and carbon dioxide becomes less soluble, forcing it out of solution. The solution becomes less acidic and the limestone becomes less soluble, causing it to come out of solution. These solids form stalactites and stalagmites.

### Mini LAB

**Observing a Nail in a Carbonated Drink**

**Procedure**
1. Observe the initial appearance of an **iron nail.**
2. Pour enough **carbonated soft drink** into a **cup or beaker** to cover the nail.
3. Drop the nail into the soft drink and observe what happens.
4. Leave the nail in the soft drink overnight and observe it again the next day.

**Analysis**
1. Describe what happened when you first dropped the nail into the soft drink and the appearance of the nail the following day.
2. Based upon the fact that the soft drink was carbonated, explain why you think the drink reacted with the nail as you observed.

**2 Teach**

**Caption Answer**
**Figure 15** Answers will vary but might include that many common products would not be available.

### Mini LAB

**Purpose** Students observe the effects of dissolved carbon dioxide on iron. L2 ELL LS
**Visual-Spatial**

**Materials** carbonated soft drink, iron nail, beaker or cup

**Teaching Strategies**
• Suggest that students use a clear beverage rather than a cola to make it easier to observe the nail.

**Analysis**
1. Bubbles formed on the nail, but it stayed shiny. On the following day, the nail appeared dull with signs of corrosion (pitting).
2. Carbon dioxide in soft drinks reacts with water to form carbonic acid, which reacted with the iron.

**Assessment**

**Performance** Ask students to hypothesize what the nail would look like if it were left in the soft drink for a week or more. Suggest they check their predictions. Use **Performance Assessment in the Science Classroom,** p. 93.

## Visual Learning

**Figure 15** Have students examine the items shown in the figure and hypothesize which ones actually contain acids and which ones were made using acids. An example of a product that contains an acid is a battery. Plastics are made using acids. L2 LS **Logical-Mathematical**

## Visualizing Acid Precipitation

Have students examine the pictures and read the captions. Then ask the following questions.

**What are some ways to cut down on the emissions from power plants and cars?** Possible answers: Improve catalytic converters that are currently on cars or have periodic inspections of cars to ensure that the catalytic converters are working properly. Power plants can continue to improve the scrubbers on their emission towers and to periodically inspect scrubbers to ensure that they are working properly.

**What are some ways to repair the damage that has already occurred on statues and forests?** Possible answers: Professionals can repair the damage that has already occurred to statues. Studies can be conducted to see if coatings or coverings can protect them. Soil can be treated and forests can be replanted.

### Activity

**Reducing Emissions** Have students find out if cars and power plants in their area are significantly contributing to the acid rain problem. If so, ask them to determine what measures are being taken to reduce the emissions.
L2  **Linguistic**

---

**NATIONAL GEOGRAPHIC**
## VISUALIZING ACID PRECIPITATION

**Figure 16**

When fossil fuels such as coal and oil are burned, a variety of chemical compounds are produced and released into the air. In the atmosphere, some of these compounds form acids that mix with water vapor and fall back to Earth as acid precipitation—rain, sleet, snow, or fog. The effects of acid precipitation on the environment can be devastating. Winds carry these acids hundreds of miles from their source, damaging forests, corroding statues, and endangering human health.

**B** Sulfur dioxide and nitrogen oxides react with water vapor in the air to form highly acidic solutions of nitric acid ($HNO_3$) and sulfuric acid ($H_2SO_4$). These solutions eventually return to Earth as acid precipitation.

**C** Some acid rain in the United States has a pH as low as 2.3— close to the acidity of stomach acid.

**A** Power plants and cars burn fossil fuels to generate energy for human use. In the process, sulfur dioxide ($SO_2$) and nitrogen oxides are released into the atmosphere.

304

---

## Differentiated Instruction

**Challenge** Challenge students to find out how scrubbers and catalytic converters work. Ask students to make diagrams illustrating their findings. L3  **Visual-Spatial** P

## Teacher FYI

**Binary Acids** Acids that contain only two elements, one of which is hydrogen, are binary acids. An example is HCl. These acids are named by using the prefix *hydro*, the root of the nonhydrogen element, the suffix *-ic*, and the word *acid*. HCl is hydrochloric acid; HI is hydroiodic acid.

## Bases

People often use ammonia solutions to clean windows and floors. These solutions have different properties from those of acidic solutions. Ammonia is called a base. **Bases** are substances that can accept hydrogen ions. When bases dissolve in water, some hydrogen atoms from the water molecules are attracted to the base. A hydrogen atom in the water molecule leaves behind the other hydrogen atom and oxygen atom. This pair of atoms is a negatively charged ion called a hydroxide ion. A hydroxide ion has the formula $OH^-$. Most bases contain a hydroxide ion, which is released when the base dissolves in water. For example, sodium hydroxide is a base with the formula NaOH. When NaOH dissolves in water, a sodium ion and the hydroxide ion separate.

**Properties of Basic Solutions** Most soaps are bases, so if you think about how soap feels, you can figure out some of the properties of basic solutions. Basic solutions feel slippery. Acids in water solution taste sour, but bases taste bitter—as you know if you have ever accidentally gotten soap in your mouth.

Like acids, bases are corrosive. Bases can cause burns and damage tissue. You should never touch or taste a substance to find out whether it is a base. Basic solutions contain ions and can conduct electricity. Basic solutions are not as reactive with metals as acidic solutions are.

**Uses of Bases** Many uses for bases are shown in **Figure 17.** Bases give soaps, ammonia, and many other cleaning products some of their useful properties. The hydroxide ions produced by bases can interact strongly with certain substances, such as dirt and grease.

Chalk and oven cleaner are examples of familiar products that contain bases. Your blood is a basic solution. Calcium hydroxide, often called lime, is used to mark the lines on athletic fields. It also can be used to treat lawns and gardens that have acidic soil. Sodium hydroxide, known as lye, is a strong base that can cause burns and other health problems. Lye is used to make soap, clean ovens, and unclog drains.

**Science Online**

**Topic: Calcium Hydroxide**
Visit in7.msscience.com for Web links to information about the uses for calcium hydroxide.

**Activity** Describe the chemical reaction that converts limestone (calcium carbonate) to calcium hydroxide.

**Figure 17** Many products, including soaps, cleaners, and plaster contain bases or are made with the help of bases.

SECTION 3 Acidic and Basic Solutions **305**

---

## Discussion

**Household Bases** Household cleaners such as ammonia and oven cleaner have health warning labels on their containers. Explain what characteristics of these products make them dangerous. Possible answer: They are corrosive and can cause burns and irritation to the skin, eyes, and lungs. L2 IS **Logical-Mathematical**

## IDENTIFYING Misconceptions

**Alcohol's Formula** The formulas for alcohols might lead students to think that alcohols are bases because they contain an −OH group. This group is nonionic and is known as a hydroxyl group. It is quite different from the hydroxide ion, $OH^-$.

## Activity

**Testing Soap** Have students confirm that soap contains a base by testing a wet bar of soap with red litmus paper. Then have them wash their hands with the soap, observing the slippery feel. L2 ELL IS **Kinesthetic**

## Fun Fact

Although they are named as acids, amino acids have properties of both acids and bases. In the glycine molecule, $NH_2CH_2COOH$, for example, the $NH_2-$ group acts as a base, and the $-COOH$ group acts as an acid.

---

## Curriculum Connection

**Literature** Preserving the best of writing from the past is a problem that has occupied archivists since people recognized that the life of paper is limited. In the nineteenth century, in an effort to preserve the quality of the printing, potassium aluminum sulfate, or alum, was used to absorb moisture and prevent ink from spreading. Have students find out the effect this had on paper and report their findings to the class. Unfortunately, the reaction of alum with water produces the $Al(H_2O)_6^{3+}$ ion, which is acidic. Over time, the acid reacted with the fibers of the paper, causing the paper to disintegrate. Thus, some books from earlier centuries are in better condition than those of the nineteenth century. L2 IS **Linguistic**

**Figure 18** The pH scale classifies a solution as acidic, basic, or neutral.

# What is pH?

You've probably heard of pH-balanced shampoo or deodorant, and you might have seen someone test the pH of the water in a swimming pool. **pH** is a measure of how acidic or basic a solution is. The pH scale ranges from 0 to 14. Acidic solutions have pH values below 7. A solution with a pH of 0 is very acidic. Hydrochloric acid can have a pH of 0. A solution with a pH of 7 is neutral, meaning it is neither acidic nor basic. Pure water is neutral. Basic solutions have pH values above 7. A solution with a pH of 14 is very basic. Sodium hydroxide can have a pH of 14. **Figure 18** shows where various common substances fall on the pH scale.

The pH of a solution is related directly to its concentrations of hydronium ions ($H_3O^+$) and hydroxide ions ($OH^-$). Acidic solutions have more hydronium ions than hydroxide ions. Neutral solutions have equal numbers of the two ions. Basic solutions have more hydroxide ions than hydronium ions.

### Reading Check
*In a neutral solution, how do the numbers of hydronium ions and hydroxide ions compare?*

**pH Scale** The pH scale is not a simple linear scale like mass or volume. For example, if one book has a mass of 2 kg and a second book has a mass of 1 kg, the mass of the first book is twice that of the second. However, a change of 1 pH unit represents a tenfold change in the acidity of the solution. For example, if one solution has a pH of 1 and a second solution has a pH of 2, the first solution is not twice as acidic as the second—it is ten times more acidic. To determine the difference in pH strength, use the following calculation: $10^n$, where $n$ = the difference between pHs. For example: pH3 − pH1 = 2, $10^2$ = 100 times more acidic.

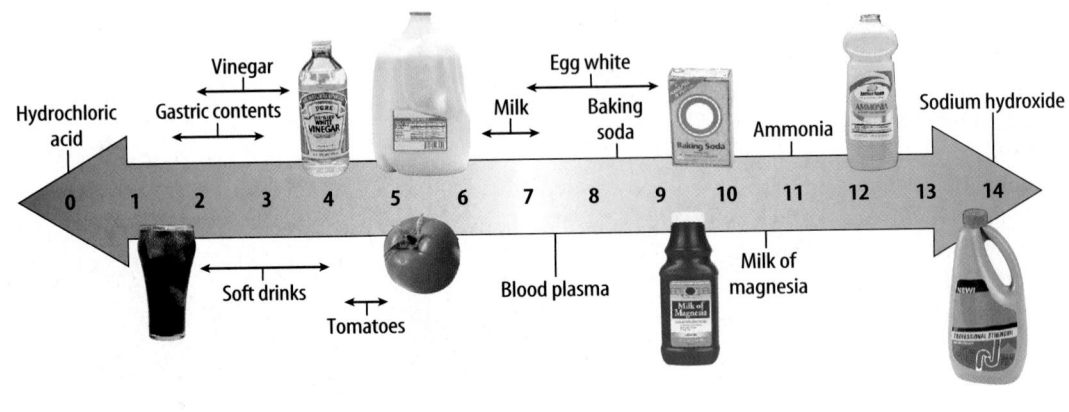

## Cultural Diversity

**Sandbox Trees** Tall sandbox trees are found in the jungles of South and Central America. The sap from these trees is acidic. People throw the sap into lakes and streams that have been dammed. The sap solution stuns the fish, and the people gather the fish for food. Then they remove the dams, and water dilutes the sap so that the remaining fish recover completely.

Hydrochloric Acid    Acetic Acid

Chloride
ion

Acetate ion
Acetic acid

Hydronium
ion

**Figure 19** Hydrochloric acid separates into ions more readily than acetic acid does when it dissolves in water. Therefore, hydrochloric acid exists in water as separated ions. Acetic acid exists in water almost entirely as molecules.

**Strengths of Acids and Bases** You've learned that acids give foods a sour taste but also can cause burns and damage tissue. The difference between food acids and the acids that can burn you is that they have different strengths. The acids in food are fairly weak acids, while the dangerous acids are strong acids. The strength of an acid is related to how easily the acid separates into ions, or how easily a hydrogen ion is released, when the acid dissolves in water. Look at **Figure 19.** In the same concentration, a strong acid—like hydrochloric acid—forms more hydronium ions in solution than a weak acid does—like acetic acid. More hydronium ions means the strong-acid solution has a lower pH than the weak-acid solution. Similarly, the strength of a base is related to how easily the base separates into ions, or how easily a hydroxide ion is released, when the base dissolves in water. The relative strengths of some common acids and bases are shown in **Table 3.**

✔ **Reading Check** *What determines the strength of an acid or a base?*

An acid containing more hydrogen atoms, such as carbonic acid, $H_2CO_3$, is not necessarily stronger than an acid containing fewer hydrogen atoms, such as nitric acid, $HNO_3$. An acid's strength is related to how easily a hydrogen ion separates—not to how many hydrogen atoms it has. For this reason, nitric acid is stronger than carbonic acid.

### Table 3 Strengths of Some Acids and Bases

|  | Acid | Base |
|---|---|---|
| **Strong** | hydrochloric (HCl) sulfuric ($H_2SO_4$) nitric ($HNO_3$) | sodium hydroxide (NaOH) potassium hydroxide (KOH) |
| **Weak** | acetic ($CH_3COOH$) carbonic ($H_2CO_3$) ascorbic ($H_2C_6H_6O_6$) | ammonia ($NH_3$) aluminum hydroxide ($Al(OH)_3$) iron (III) hydroxide ($Fe(OH)_3$) |

**Science Online**

**Topic: Indicators**

Visit in7.msscience.com for Web links to information about the types of pH indicators.

**Activity** Describe how plants can act as indicators in acidic and basic solutions.

**Figure 20** The pH of a solution is more acidic when greater amounts of hydronium ions are present.
**Define** what makes a pH 7 solution neutral.

# Indicators

What is a safe way to find out how acidic or basic a solution is? **Indicators** are compounds that react with acidic and basic solutions and produce certain colors, depending on the solution's pH.

Because they are different colors at different pHs, indicators can help you determine the pH of a solution. Some indicators, such as litmus, are soaked into paper strips. When litmus paper is placed in an acidic solution, it turns red. When placed in a basic solution, litmus paper turns blue. Some indicators can change through a wide range of colors, with each different color appearing at a different pH value.

## Neutralization

Perhaps you've heard someone complain about heartburn or an upset stomach after eating spicy food. To feel better, the person might have taken an antacid. Think about the word *antacid* for a minute. How do antacids work?

Heartburn or stomach discomfort is caused by excess hydrochloric acid in the stomach. Hydrochloric acid helps break down the food you eat, but too much of it can irritate your stomach or digestive tract. An antacid product, often made from the base magnesium hydroxide, $Mg(OH)_2$, neutralizes the excess acid. **Neutralization** (new truh luh ZAY shun) is the reaction of an acid with a base. It is called this because the properties of both the acid and base are diminished, or neutralized. In most cases, the reaction produces a water and a salt. **Figure 20** illustrates the relative amounts of hydronium and hydroxide ions between pH 0 and pH 14.

 **Reading Check** **What are the products of neutralization?**

pH 0       7       14

**308** **CHAPTER 10** Substances, Mixtures, and Solubility

$$H_3O^+ \quad + \quad OH^- \quad \longrightarrow \quad 2H_2O$$

Hydronium ion

Hydroxide ion

Water molecules

**Figure 21** When acidic and basic solutions react, hydronium and hydroxide ions react to form water.
**Determine** *why the pH of the solution changes.*

**How does neutralization occur?** Recall that every water molecule contains two hydrogen atoms and one oxygen atom. As **Figure 21** shows, when one hydronium ion reacts with one hydroxide ion, the product is two water molecules. This reaction occurs during acid-base neutralization. Equal numbers of hydronium ions from the acidic solution and hydroxide ions from the basic solution react to produce water. Pure water has a pH of 7, which means that it's neutral.

✓ **Reading Check** *What happens to acids and bases during neutralization?*

## section ③ review

### Summary

**Acids and Bases**
- Acids are substances that release positively charged hydrogen ions in water.
- Substances that accept hydrogen ions in water are bases.
- Acidic and basic solutions can conduct electricity.

**pH**
- pH measures how acidic or basic a solution is.
- The scale ranges from 0 to 14.

**Neutralization**
- Neutralization is the interaction between an acid and a base to form water and a salt.

### Self Check

1. **Identify** what ions are produced by acids in water and bases in water. Give two properties each of acids and bases.
2. **Name** three acids and three bases and list an industrial or household use of each.
3. **Explain** how the concentration of hydronium ions and hydroxide ions are related to pH.
4. **Think Critically** In what ways might a company that uses a strong acid handle an acid spill on the factory floor?

**Applying Math**

5. **Solve One-Step Equations** How much more acidic is a solution with a pH of 2 than one with a pH of 6? How much more basic is a solution with a pH of 13 than one with a pH of 10?

## section ③ review

1. Hydronium ions are produced by acids and hydroxide ions are produced by bases. Properties of acids include sour taste, corrosive, and conduct electricity. Properties of bases include bitter taste, slippery, corrosive, and conduct electricity.
2. Acids: acetic acid, vinegar; ascorbic acid, vitamin C; hydrochloric acid, pickling; sulfuric acid, fertilizer production; nitric acid, plastics and dyes production. Bases: calcium hydroxide, lawn treatments or lining athletic fields; sodium hydroxide, soap or oven cleaners; ammonia, cleaning products.
3. Solutions with more hydronium ions than hydroxide ions are acidic, pH below 7. Solutions with equal amounts are neutral, pH equal to 7. Solutions with more hydroxide ions than hydronium ions are basic, pH above 7.
4. Answers might include that a base could be used to neutralize it.
5. 10,000 times more acidic; 1,000 times more basic

SECTION 3  Acidic and Basic Solutions  **309**

## ● Real-World Question

**Purpose** Students will measure pH using a red-cabbage-juice indicator. L2 ELL
IS **Kinesthetic**

**Process Skills** observe, make and use tables, compare, classify, predict

**Time Required** 45 min

## ● Procedure

**Materials** Prepare indicator solution by tearing three red cabbage leaves into small pieces and layering them in a 600-mL beaker. Add distilled water until the leaves are just covered. Boil the mixture for 5 minutes. Pour the cooled indicator into dropper bottles and refrigerate until needed.

Prepare 100 mL of 0.1$M$ HCl solution by adding 10 mL 1$M$ HCl to 90 mL distilled water.

**Alternate Materials** Other solutions that could be tested are lemon juice, sodium chloride solution, eyewash, and orange juice.

**Safety Precautions** Caution students not to inhale ammonia fumes, to avoid skin contact with the solutions, and to report any spillage.

### Goals
- ■ **Determine** the relative acidity or basicity of several common solutions.
- ■ **Compare** the strengths of several common acids and bases.

### Materials
small test tubes (9)
test-tube rack
concentrated red cabbage juice in a dropper bottle
labeled bottles containing:
 household ammonia,
 baking soda solution,
 soap solution,
 0.1$M$ hydrochloric acid solution, white vinegar,
 colorless carbonated soft drink, borax soap solution, distilled water
grease pencil
droppers (9)

### Safety Precautions

**WARNING:** *Many acids and bases are poisonous, can damage your eyes, and can burn your skin. Wear goggles and gloves AT ALL TIMES. Tell your teacher immediately if a substance spills. Wash your hands after you finish but before removing your goggles.*

# Testing pH Using Natural Indicators

## ● Real-World Question

You have learned that certain substances, called indicators, change color when the pH of a solution changes. The juice from red cabbage is a natural indicator. How do the pH values of various solutions compare to each other? How can you use red cabbage juice to determine the relative pH of several solutions?

## ● Procedure

1. **Design** a data table to record the names of the solutions to be tested, the colors caused by the added cabbage juice indicator, and the relative strengths of the solutions.

2. Mark each test tube with the identity of the acid or base solution it will contain.

3. Half-fill each test tube with the solution to be tested.
   **WARNING:** *If you spill any liquids on your skin, rinse the area immediately with water. Alert your teacher if any liquid spills in the work area or on your skin.*

| Solutions, Indicators, and Approximate pH Values | | | | | |
|---|---|---|---|---|---|
| Solution | Indicator Color | pH | Solution | Indicator Color | pH |
| Ammonia solution | blue-green | 11–12 | White vinegar | red-purple | 3–4 |
| Baking soda solution | green | 10–11 | Soft drink | red-purple | 3–4 |
| Soap solution | green | 10–11 | Borax soap | purple | 7–8 |
| HCl | red | 0–1 | Distilled water | purple | 6–8 |

4. Add ten drops of the cabbage juice indicator to each of the solutions to be tested. Gently agitate or wiggle each test tube to mix the cabbage juice with the solution.

5. **Observe** and record the color of each solution in your data table.

### Determining pH Values

| Cabbage Juice Color | Relative Strength of Acid or Base |
|---|---|
| | strong acid |
| | medium acid |
| | weak acid |
| | neutral |
| | weak base |
| | medium base |
| | strong base |

## Conclude and Apply

1. **Compare** your observations with the table above. Record in your data table the relative acid or base strength of each solution you tested.

2. **Classify** which solutions were acidic and which were basic.

3. **Identify** which solution was the weakest acid. The strongest base? The closest to neutral?

4. **Predict** what ion might be involved in the cleaning process based upon your data for the ammonia, soap, and borax soap solutions.

5. **List** the solutions by pH value starting with the most acidic and finishing with the most basic.

## Form a Hypothesis

Form a hypothesis that explains why the borax soap solution was less basic than an ammonia solution of approximately the same concentration.

### Communicating Your Data

Use your data to create labels for the solutions you tested. Include the relative strength of each solution and any other safety information you think is important on each label. **For more help, refer to the Science Skill Handbook.**

LAB 311

## Alternative Inquiry Lab

**Indicator Inquiry** Have students research other natural indicators, such as flowers, that change color due to soil acidity. Consult a garden center for specific pH-reliant flowers. Have students try to grow them with soils of different acidities. What methods do gardeners use to alter soil pH? NOTE: leaves changing color in the fall is NOT an acid/base effect.

### Communicating Your Data

Student labels should show which solutions are dangerous to skin and eyes and which solutions might be harmful to metals or other materials they contact.

**Teaching Strategies** Advise students to compare the color of one solution with another and with the color chart. Students should observe the colors by setting the beakers on white paper. This will help them develop sensitivity to small differences in tint.

## Analyze Your Data

**Expected Outcome** See table. Students should be able to classify each solution according to relative strength of acid or base.

## Conclude and Apply

1. See data table.
2. acidic solutions: HCl, vinegar, soft drink; basic solutions: ammonia, baking soda, soap, borax soap solution
3. weakest acid: vinegar or soft drink; strongest base: ammonia solution; closest to neutral: distilled water
4. the hydroxide ion
5. HCl, soft drink, white vinegar, distilled water, borax soap, soap solution, baking soda solution, ammonia solution

## Form a Hypothesis

The ammonia solution produces more hydroxide ions in solution than the borax.

**Error Analysis** Have groups compare results to determine whether they distinguished color in the same way. If data disagree, have students repeat the tests.

### ✓ Assessment

**Content** Ask students to use colored markers or colored pencils to draw and label each solution containing indicator.

# SCIENCE Stats

## Content Background

While salt is necessary for life, too much or too little salt is harmful. If too little salt is present in blood, blood cells swell and become ineffective. If too much salt is present in blood, the cells shrivel up and die.

## Discussion

**How much salt?** Why should your diet limit, but not eliminate, salt? Too much salt can cause health problems, but salt is a part of many body fluids, such as saliva, tears, perspiration, and blood plasma. Correct concentrations of salt are also needed for proper transmission of nerve impulses. L2 IS
**Logical-Mathematical**

## Activity

**Create a Saline Lake** Have students show how the Great Salt Lake formed. Set up a stream table containing a mixture of soil or sand containing a small amount of salt. Have students pour small streams of water over the soil, simulating rain. Have them collect the runoff in a bowl or beaker. Then, have them set the solution in a warm place so that the water can evaporate. Discuss how the salt concentration of the water changes over time. L2 ELL IS **Kinesthetic**

### Applying Math

**Answer** 4,000 km²/32,000 km² × 100% = 12.5%

---

# SCIENCE Stats

## Salty Solutions

### Did you know...

**...Seawater is certainly a salty solution.** Ninety-nine percent of all salt ions in the sea are sodium, chlorine, sulfate, magnesium, calcium, and potassium. The major gases in the sea are nitrogen, oxygen, carbon dioxide, argon, neon, and helium.

**...Tears and saliva have a lot in common.** Both are salty solutions that protect you from harmful bacteria, keep tissues moist, and help spread nutrients. Bland-tasting saliva, however, is 99 percent water. The remaining one percent is a combination of many ions, including sodium and several proteins.

**...The largest salt lake** in the United States is the Great Salt Lake. It covers more than 4,000 km² in Utah and is up to 13.4 m deep. The Great Salt Lake and the Salt Lake Desert were once part of the enormous, prehistoric Lake Bonneville, which was 305 m deep at some points.

**Applying Math** At its largest, Lake Bonneville covered about 32,000 km². What percentage of that area does the Great Salt Lake now cover?

**...Salt can reduce pain.** Gargled salt water is a disinfectant; it fights the bacteria that cause some sore throats.

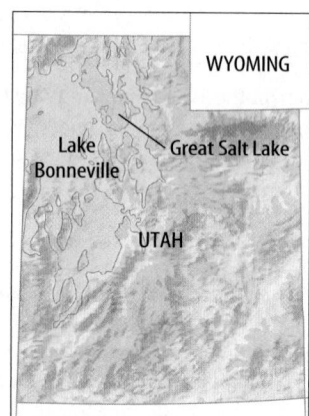

### Graph It

Visit in7.msscience.com/science_stats to research and learn about other elements in seawater. Create a graph that shows the amounts of the ten most common elements in 1 L of seawater.

**312** **CHAPTER 10** Substances, Mixtures, and Solubility

---

## Differentiated Instruction

**English-Language Learners** Each continent has saline lakes. Have students research a saline lake from their native continent. Instruct them to write a summary of their research including the location, the depth, and the area the lake covers. Ask them to present their summaries orally to a classmate. L2 ELL IS **Auditory-Musical**

### Graph It

**Seawater Elements** Be sure student graphs reflect elements, not compounds. Students can use bar or circle graphs to present results. If they use circle graphs, review how to calculate the percentage of each element and how to multiply it by 360° to determine the number of degrees in the circle represented by the element.

## Reviewing Main Ideas

**Section 1** **What is a solution?**

1. Elements and compounds are pure substances, because their compositions are fixed. Mixtures are not pure substances.

2. Heterogeneous mixtures are not mixed evenly. Homogeneous mixtures, also called solutions, are mixed evenly on a molecular level.

3. Solutes and solvents can be gases, liquids, or solids, combined in many different ways.

**Section 2** **Solubility**

1. Because water molecules are polar, they can dissolve many different solutes. Like dissolves like.

2. Temperature and pressure can affect solubility.

3. Solutions can be unsaturated, saturated, or supersaturated, depending on how much solute is dissolved compared to the solubility of the solute in the solvent.

4. The concentration of a solution is the amount of solute in a particular volume of solvent.

**Section 3** **Acidic and Basic Solutions**

1. Acids release H+ ions and produce hydronium ions when they are dissolved in water. Bases accept H+ ions and produce hydroxide ions when dissolved in water.

2. pH expresses the concentrations of hydronium ions and hydroxide ions in aqueous solutions.

3. In a neutralization reaction, an acid reacts with a base to form water and a salt.

## Visualizing Main Ideas

*Copy and complete the concept map on the classification of matter.*

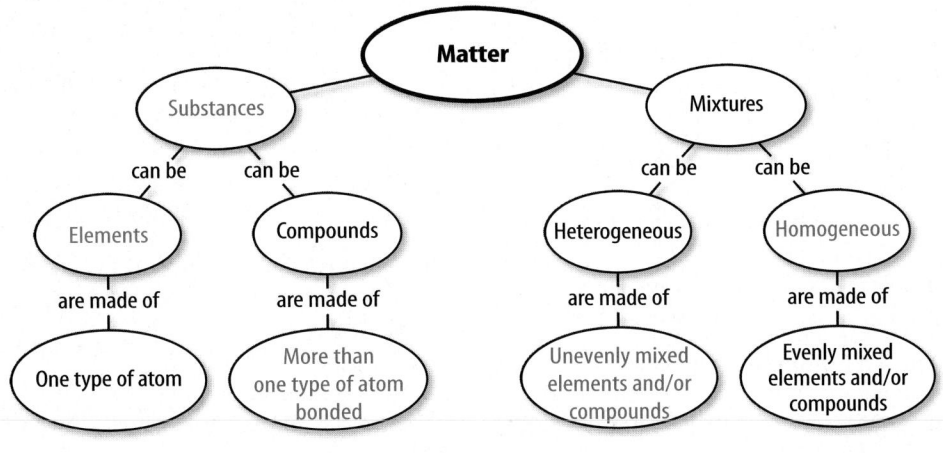

### Reviewing Main Ideas

Summary statements can be used by students to review the major concepts of the chapter.

### Visualizing Main Ideas

See student page.

**Visit** in7.msscience.com
/self_check_quiz
/interactive_tutor
/vocabulary_puzzlemaker
/chapter_review
/standards_review

### Assessment Transparency

For additional assessment questions, use the *Assessment Transparency* located in the transparency book.

**Assessment**

Substances, Mixtures, and Solubility

**Directions:** *Carefully review the table and answer the following questions.*

| Types of Mixtures | |
|---|---|
| Heterogeneous | A mixture where the substances are unevenly mixed, some areas look different from others |
| Gas soultion | A homogeneous mixture of a gas with a smaller amount of solid, liquid or another gas |
| Liquid solution | A homogeneous mixture of a liquid with a smaller amount of solid, gas, or another liquid |
| Solid solution | A homogeneous mixture of a solid with a smaller amount of gas, liquid or another solid |

1. What kind of mixture is inside an inflated basketball?
   A heterogenous     C liquid solution
   B gas solution     D solid solution
2. According to the table, salt water would be a ___.
   F heterogenous     H liquid solution
   G gas solution     J solid solution
3. Steel is made from iron and carbon. According to the table, steel is a ___.
   A heterogenous     C liquid solution
   B gas solution     D solid solution

Substances, Mixtures, and Solubility

## Identifying Misconceptions

**Assess**

After students have done the activity on page F at the beginning of this chapter, have them perform this activity.

**Materials** beaker of water, salt

**Procedure** Give each group a set of materials. Ask them to write observations about the water and salt. Then have them drop the salt into the water and record what they observe. Have them allow the water to evaporate and observe the remaining salt. **L2** COOP LEARN

**Expected Outcome** When the salt is dropped into the water, it seems to disappear. When the water is evaporated, the salt will remain, proving that it was there all the time.

## Using Vocabulary

1. pH
2. concentration
3. solubility
4. solute
5. neutralization
6. substance

## Checking Concepts

| | | | |
|---|---|---|---|
| 7. | D | 12. | A |
| 8. | C | 13. | B |
| 9. | A | 14. | C |
| 10. | B | 15. | C |
| 11. | C | 16. | D |

## Using Vocabulary

| | |
|---|---|
| acid p. 302 | neutralization p. 308 |
| aqueous p. 294 | pH p. 306 |
| base p. 305 | precipitate p. 290 |
| concentration p. 299 | saturated p. 298 |
| heterogeneous | solubility p. 297 |
| mixture p. 289 | solute p. 290 |
| homogeneous | solution p. 290 |
| mixture p. 290 | solvent p. 290 |
| hydronium ion p. 302 | substance p. 288 |
| indicator p. 308 | |

*Fill in the blanks with the correct vocabulary word.*

1. A base has a(n) _____ value above 7.

2. A measure of how much solute is in a solution is its _____.

3. The amount of a solute that can dissolve in 100 g of solvent is its _____.

4. The _____ is the substance that is dissolved to form a solution.

5. The reaction between an acidic and basic solution is called _____.

6. A(n) _____ has a fixed composition.

## Checking Concepts

*Choose the word or phrase that best answers the question.*

7. Which of the following is a solution?
   A) pure water
   B) an oatmeal-raisin cookie
   C) copper
   D) vinegar

8. What type of compounds will not dissolve in water?
   A) polar      C) nonpolar
   B) ionic      D) charged

9. What type of molecule is water?
   A) polar      C) nonpolar
   B) ionic      D) precipitate

10. When chlorine compounds are dissolved in pool water, what is the water?
    A) the alloy
    B) the solvent
    C) the solution
    D) the solute

11. A solid might become less soluble in a liquid when you decrease what?
    A) particle size   C) temperature
    B) pressure        D) container size

12. Which acid is used in the industrial process known as pickling?
    A) hydrochloric    C) sulfuric
    B) carbonic        D) nitric

13. A solution is prepared by adding 100 g of solid sodium hydroxide, NaOH, to 1,000 mL of water. What is the solid NaOH called?
    A) solution        C) solvent
    B) solute          D) mixture

14. Given equal concentrations, which of the following will produce the most hydronium ions in an aqueous solution?
    A) a strong base   C) a strong acid
    B) a weak base     D) a weak acid

15. Bile, an acidic body fluid used in digestion, has a high concentration of hydronium ions. Predict its pH.
    A) 11              C) less than 7
    B) 7               D) greater than 7

16. When you swallow an antacid, what happens to your stomach acid?
    A) It is more acidic.
    B) It is concentrated.
    C) It is diluted.
    D) It is neutralized.

 Science Online in7.msscience.com/vocabulary_puzzlemaker

**Use the ExamView® Pro Testmaker CD-ROM to:**
- create multiple versions of tests
- create modified tests with one mouse click for inclusion students
- edit existing questions and add your own questions
- build tests aligned with state standards using built-in State Curriculum Tags
- change English tests to Spanish with one mouse click and vice versa

## Thinking Critically

**17. Infer** why deposits form in the steam vents of irons in some parts of the country.

**18. Explain** if it is possible to have a dilute solution of a strong acid.

**19. Draw Conclusions** Antifreeze is added to water in a car's radiator to prevent freezing in cold months. It also prevents overheating or boiling. Explain how antifreeze does both.

**Use the illustration below to answer question 20.**

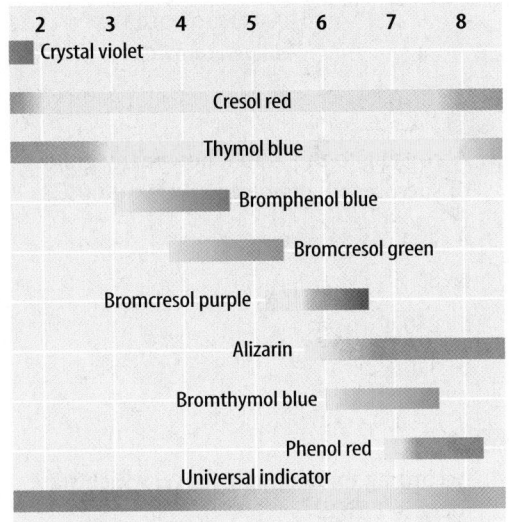

**20. Interpret** Chemists use a variety of indicators. Using the correct indicator is important. The color change must occur at the proper pH or the results could be misleading. Looking at the indicator chart, what indicators could be used to produce a color change at both pH 2 and pH 8?

**21. Explain** Water molecules can break apart to form $H^+$ ions and $OH^-$ ions. Water is known as an amphoteric substance, which is something that can act as an acid or a base. Explain how this can be so.

 Science Online in7.msscience.com/chapter_review

**22. Recognize Cause and Effect** When you slice an apple, the cut surfaces soon turn brown. Brushing fruit with lemon juice slows the browning. Explain why this might occur, in terms of the effect of pH on this reaction.

**23. Compare and contrast** examples of heterogeneous and homogeneous mixtures from your daily life.

**24. Form a Hypotheses** A warm carbonated beverage seems to fizz more than a cold one when it is opened. Explain this based on the solubility of carbon dioxide in water.

## Performance Activities

**25. Poem** Write a poem that explains the difference between a substance and a mixture.

## Applying Math

**Use the graph below to answer question 26.**

**26. Solubility** Using the solubility graph above, estimate the solubilities of potassium chloride and sodium chloride in grams per 100 g of water at 80°C.

**27. Juice Concentration** You made a one-liter (1,000 mL) container of juice. How much concentrate, in mL, did you add to make a concentration of 18 percent?

CHAPTER REVIEW **315**

## Thinking Critically

**17.** Minerals are dissolved in the water. When the water evaporates, the minerals are left behind.

**18.** Yes; if a small amount of a strong acid is dissolved in a large amount of water, the solution will be dilute.

**19.** Antifreeze lowers the freezing point of the water in cold months and raises the boiling point in hot months. This happens because antifreeze acts as a solute particle and changes the physical properties of the solvent, water.

**20.** cresol red, thymol blue, universal indicator

**21.** It meets the definition of a base because it produces hydroxide ions and that of an acid because it produces hydrogen (hydronium) ions.

**22.** Lemon juice is acidic, so it would lower the pH on the surface of the apple.

**23.** Accept all reasonable answers.

**24.** The higher the temperature, the less carbon dioxide can be dissolved in water. Therefore, more carbon dioxide gas escapes from the warm beverage than from the cold one.

## Performance Activities

**25.** Check student poems for accuracy. Use **Performance Assessment in the Science Classroom,** p. 151.

## Applying Math

### Indiana Math Standards
7.2.1, 7.3.1, 7.6.1

**26.** potassium chloride: 60 g/100 g of water; sodium chloride: 35 g/100 g of water

**27.** $x$ mL/1,000 mL $= .18$; $x = 180$ mL

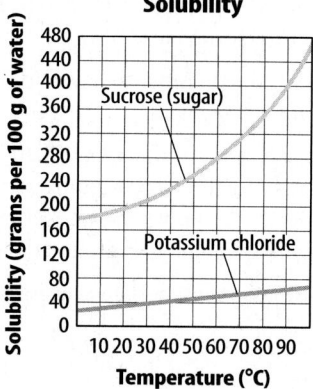

**Answer Sheet** A practice answer sheet can be found at in7.msscience.com/answer_sheet.

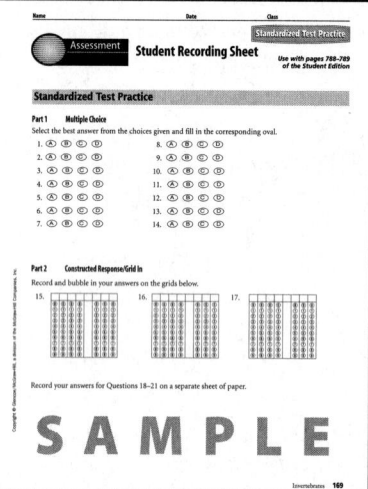

S A M P L E

**Part 1 | Multiple Choice**

1. B
2. D
3. C
4. C
5. B
6. B
7. C

The assessed Indiana standard appears above the question.

*Record your answers on the answer sheet provided by your teacher or on a sheet of paper.*

**Part 1 | Multiple Choice**

1. The graph below displays the compostion of Earth's atmosphere.

**Composition of Earth's Atmosphere**

Nitrogen 78%

Oxygen 21%

Water vapor, carbon dioxide, other gases 1%

Which is the solvent in Earth's atmosphere?

A carbon dioxide

B nitrogen

C oxygen

D water vapor

2. Which term best describes Earth's atmosphere?

A atom

B element

C compound

D solution

The graph below shows the solubilities of two solids.

**Solubility**

Solubility (grams per 100 g of water)

Sucrose (sugar)

Potassium chloride

Temperature (°C)

**7.3.13**

3. According to the graph, how many grams of sucrose will dissolve in water at 60°C?

A 50 g

B 80 g

C 280 g

D 320 g

**7.3.13**

4. According to the graph above, which statement is **TRUE**?

A Potassium chloride is more soluble in water than sucrose.

B As water temperature increases, the solubility of potassium chloride decreases.

C Sucrose is more soluble in water than potassium chloride.

D Temperature does not affect the solubility of either chemical.

**316** INDIANA

**Part 2 | Critical Response**

8. Water is the liquid solvent in a carbonated drink. Carbon dioxide gas is present in addition to other solutes. Over time, $CO_2$ gas escapes into the air, decreasing the amount of solute in the solvent.

9. Each hydrogen atom shares one electron with the oxygen atom. The electrons spend more time around the oxygen atom than the hydrogen atoms. The oxygen end of the water molecule has a partial negative charge, and the hydrogen end has a partial positive charge, resulting in a polar molecule.

10. The positive parts of water molecules attract the negative ions in an ionic compound, while the negative parts of water molecules attract the positive ions in an ionic compound. The ions are pulled away from each other and surrounded by additional polar water molecules, causing them to dissolve.

**5.** Steel is composed of carbon and what other element?

**A** copper

**B** iron

**C** silicon

**D** zinc

**6.** Which is the symbol for a hydronium ion?

**A** $H^+$

**B** $H_3O^+$

**C** $H_3O^-$

**D** $OH^-$

**7.** The photo below shows a mixture of sand and iron filings being separated.

What physical property is used to separate the sand and iron?

**A** density

**B** ductility

**C** magnetism

**D** malleability

**Part 2 | Critical Response**

**8.** Explain why a carbonated beverage can be classified as a liquid-gas solution. Explain how the ratio of liquid solvent to gas solute changes when the container is opened.

**9.** The diagram below shows a water molecule.

(Partial negative charge)

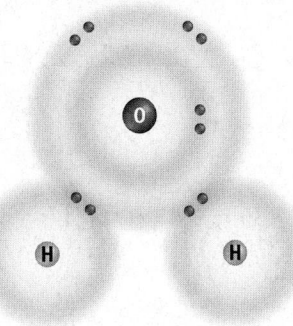

(Partial positive charge)

Use the distribution of electrons to describe this molecule's polarity. What type of bonds does water contain?

7.3.13

**10.** Explain how the polarity of water makes water effective in dissolving ionic compounds.

**Test-Taking Tip**

**Start the Day Right** The morning of the test, eat a healthy breakfast with a balanced amount of protein and carbohydrates.

## Rubrics

The following rubric is a sample scoring device for critical response questions.

### Critical Response

| Points | Description |
|--------|-------------|
| 4 | The student demonstrates a thorough understanding of the science of the task. The response may contain minor flaws that do not detract from the demonstration of a thorough understanding. |
| 3 | The student demonstrates an understanding of the science of the task. The response is essentially correct and demonstrates an essential but less than thorough understanding of the science. |
| 2 | The student demonstrates only a partial understanding of the science of the task. Although the student may have used the correct approach to a solution or may have provided a correct solution, the work lacks an essential understanding of the underlying science concepts. |
| 1 | The student demonstrates a very limited understanding of the science of the task. The response is incomplete and exhibits many flaws. |
| 0 | The student provides a completely incorrect solution or no response at all. |

# unit 4

## Unit Contents

**Web**Quest *Laser Eye Surgery* is a personal journey to investigate the new technology and procedures for corrective vision. Students will make an informed decision as to whether Lasik or PRK procedures are an option for patients with myopia. Students will study the advantages and disadvantages of surgery for this type of procedure and decide if they might be a candidate. A set of questions to guide them in their investigations is provided.

# unit 4 Motion, Forces, and Energy

# How Are Radar & Popcorn Connected?

318

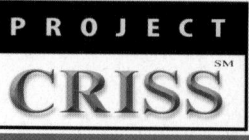

## PROJECT CRISS℠

### Study Skills

**Organize Information** Concept mapping gives students a graphic means of organizing information as they read. Using each type of wave as a main topic, students use the wave's properties and behaviors as arms or branches. The arms can become topics on note cards for use in future study.

# NATIONAL GEOGRAPHIC

Radar systems—such as the one in this modern air traffic control room—use radio waves to detect objects. In the 1940s, the radio waves used for radar were generated by a device called a magnetron. One day, an engineer working on a radar project was standing near a magnetron when he noticed that the candy bar in his pocket had melted. Intrigued, the engineer got some unpopped popcorn and placed it next to the magnetron. Sure enough, the kernels began to pop. The engineer realized that the magnetron's short radio waves, called microwaves, caused the molecules in the food to move more quickly, increasing the food's temperature. Soon, magnetrons were being used in the first microwave ovens. Today, microwave ovens are used to pop popcorn—and heat many other kinds of food—in kitchens all over the world.

## unit ⚡ projects

**The assessed Indiana objective appears in blue.**

To find project ideas and resources, visit nc7.msscience.com/unit_project.

Projects include:

- **History** Research tsunamis, their energy, and other characteristics. Graph and compare height, distance, and lives lost from past waves.
- **Technology** Discover how steel drums are made. Construct your own drum and experiment with sounds and patterns of vibrations.
- **Model** Create an original light show with colored lights and stick puppets expressing your new knowledge of light, mirrors, and lenses. **7.3.19**

**Web Quest** *Laser Eye Surgery* provides an opportunity to be an informed consumer of the advantages and disadvantages of laser eye surgery. **7.3.20**

## unit ⚡ projects

**History** Have students research tsunamis, their energy and characteristics, how they are created, how they travel, and their effects on beach-front communities. Have students graph and compare the lives lost, the height of the waves, and the distance the waves moved inland.

**Technology** Ask students to investigate how steel drums are made. This instrument has a distinct sound that demonstrates different pitch in a simple and effective way. Students may experiment with balloons stretched across an empty can to produce a variety of pitches. Ask students to sprinkle pepper or sand on their drum head and then strike the drum. With the balloon-drum head at different tensions, have students make drawings of the pepper patterns that develop from the range of vibrations and pitch.

**Model** Have students create a light show using three different-colored incandescent light sources and stick puppets. Have students write a short shadow puppet play with a simple plot to demonstrate their knowledge of primary light colors, reflection and absorption, concave and convex mirrors, lenses, prisms, refraction, critical angle, and the uses of these concepts in science and science equipment.

**Additional Resources** For more information, resources, and assessment rubrics, visit in7.msscience.com/unit_project.

## NATIONAL GEOGRAPHIC    How Are Radar & Popcorn Connected?

Popcorn, like all matter, is composed of atoms in constant motion. Heating a substance is one way to increase an object's temperature. Microwaves also can be used to raise an object's temperature by harnessing electromagnetic waves that carry radiant energy.

Popcorn kernels, like most food, contain water. Inside a microwave oven, water molecules absorb the microwave energy, causing the water molecules to move faster until the water turns to steam. The pressure increases until the kernel explodes. The kernel is turned inside out. The end result is the familiar-looking, white puff of popcorn.

| Section/Objectives | Standards | | Labs/Features |
|---|---|---|---|
| **Chapter Opener** | **National** | **State/Local** | **Launch Lab:** Motion After a Collision, p. 321 <br> **Foldables,** p. 321 |
| | See pp. 16T–17T for a Key to Standards. | Detailed standards begin on page IN8. | |
| **Section 1 What is motion?** <br> ⏱ 2 sessions <br> 📦 1 block <br><br> 1. **Define** distance, speed, and velocity. <br> 2. **Graph** motion. | National Content Standards: UCP.2, UCP.3, UCP.5, A.1, A.2, B.1, B.2 | Indiana Standards: 7.2.6, 7.2.7, 7.7.4 | **Integrate Life Science,** p. 324 <br> **Applying Math:** Speed of a Swimmer, p. 324 <br> **MiniLAB:** Measuring Average Speed, p. 325 <br> **Science Online,** p. 326 |
| **Section 2 Acceleration** <br> ⏱ 3 sessions <br> 📦 1.5 blocks <br><br> 3. **Define** acceleration. <br> 4. **Predict** what effect acceleration will have on motion. | National Content Standards: UCP.2, UCP.3, UCP.5, A.1, A.2, B.1, B.2 | Indiana Standards: 7.2.7, 7.7.4 | **Applying Math:** Acceleration of a Bus, p. 330 <br> **MiniLAB:** Modeling Acceleration, p. 331 |
| **Section 3 Momentum** <br> ⏱ 4 sessions <br> 📦 2 blocks <br><br> 5. **Explain** the relationship between mass and inertia. <br> 6. **Define** momentum. <br> 7. **Predict** motion using the law of conservation of momentum. | National Content Standards: UCP.2, UCP.3, UCP.5, A.1, A.2, B.1, B.2 | Indiana Standards: 7.2.7, 7.7.4 | **Integrate Social Studies,** p. 334 <br> **Applying Math:** Momentum of a Bicycle, p. 334 <br> **Science Online,** p. 336 <br> **Visualizing Conservation of Momentum,** p. 337 <br> **Lab:** Collisions, p. 339 <br> **Lab:** Care Safety Testing, pp. 340–341 <br> **Oops! Accidents in Science:** What Goes Around Comes Around, p. 342 |

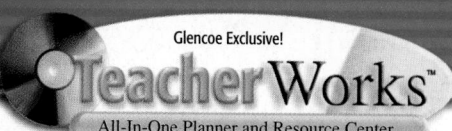
| Lab Materials | Reproducible Resources | Section Assessment | Technology |
|---|---|---|---|
| **Launch Lab:** 2 baseballs, 2 tennis balls | **Chapter _FAST FILE_ Resources**<br>Foldables Worksheet, p. 17<br>Directed Reading Overview, p. 19<br>Note-taking Worksheets, pp. 33–34 | GLENCOE'S **ASSESSMENT** ADVANTAGE | **Teacher**Works includes:<br>• Interactive Teacher Edition<br>• Lesson Planner with calendar<br>• Access to all program blacklines<br>• Correlations to standards<br>• Web links |
| **MiniLAB:** masking tape, meterstick, stopwatch<br><br>*Need materials?* Contact Science Kit at 1-800-828-7777 or www.sciencekit.com on the Internet. | **Chapter _FAST FILE_ Resources**<br>Transparency Activity, p. 44<br>MiniLAB, p. 3<br>Enrichment, p. 30<br>Reinforcement, p. 27<br>Directed Reading, p. 20<br>Lab Activity, pp. 9–11<br>Transparency Activity, pp. 47–48<br>**Physical Science Critical Thinking/Problem Solving,** pp. 2, 21 | **Portfolio**<br>Active Reading, p. 323<br>**Performance**<br>Applying Math, p. 324<br>MiniLAB, p. 325<br>Applying Math, p. 327<br>**Content**<br>Section Review, p. 327 | Section Focus Transparency<br>Teaching Transparency<br>Virtual Labs CD-ROM<br>Guided Reading Audio Program<br>Interactive Chalkboard CD-ROM |
| **MiniLAB:** masking tape, meterstick | **Chapter _FAST FILE_ Resources**<br>Transparency Activity, p. 45<br>MiniLAB, p. 4<br>Enrichment, p. 31<br>Reinforcement, p. 28<br>Directed Reading, p. 20<br>Transparency Activity, pp. 47–48<br>Lab Activity, pp. 13–15 | **Portfolio**<br>Assessment, p. 332<br>**Performance**<br>Applying Math, p. 330<br>MiniLAB, p. 331<br>Applying Math, p. 332<br>**Content**<br>Section Review, p. 332 | Section Focus Transparency<br>Guided Reading Audio Program<br>Interactive Chalkboard CD-ROM |
| **Lab:** 5 small marbles, 2 large marbles, 2 metersticks, tape<br>**Lab:** insulated foam meat trays or fast-food trays, insulated foam cups, straws, straight pins, tape, plastic eggs | **Chapter _FAST FILE_ Resources**<br>Transparency Activity, p. 46<br>Enrichment, p. 32<br>Reinforcement, p. 29<br>Directed Reading, pp. 21, 22<br>Lab Worksheets, pp. 5–6, 7–8<br>**Home and Community Involvement,** p. 48 | **Portfolio**<br>Currculum Connection, p. 334<br>**Performance**<br>Applying Math, p. 334<br>Applying Math, p. 338<br>**Content**<br>Section Review, p. 338 | Section Focus Transparency<br>Guided Reading Audio Program<br>Interactive Chalkboard CD-ROM<br>Video Lab |

## End of Chapter Assessment

GLENCOE'S **ASSESSMENT** ADVANTAGE

| Blackline Masters | Technology | Professional Series |
|---|---|---|
| **Chapter Fast File Resources**<br>Chapter Review, pp. 37–38<br>Chapter Tests, pp. 39–42<br>**Mastering the Grade 7 Indiana Science Standards** | MindJogger Videoquiz<br>IN Test Prep and Practice Exam*View*®<br>Exam*View*® Pro Testmaker<br>TeacherWorks CD-ROM<br>Interactive Chalkboard CD-ROM | **Performance Assessment in the Science Classroom (PASC)** |

# Transparencies

## Section Focus

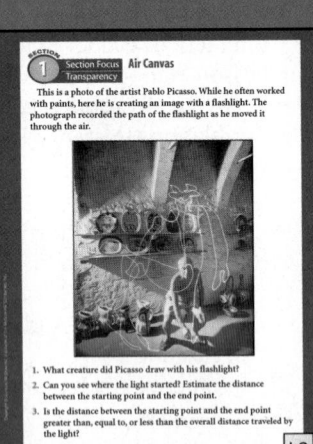

**Section Focus Transparency 1** — Air Canvas

This is a photo of the artist Pablo Picasso. While he often worked with paints, here he is creating an image with a flashlight. The photograph recorded the path of the flashlight as he moved it through the air.

1. What creature did Picasso draw with his flashlight?
2. Can you see where the light started? Estimate the distance between the starting point and the end point.
3. Is the distance between the starting point and the end point greater than, equal to, or less than the overall distance traveled by the light?

L2

**Section Focus Transparency 2** — Nothing but Air!

Very experienced skydivers can work together to make different formations as they free-fall. Called relative work, these formations require the skydivers to carefully control their movements while falling.

1. What happens when a skydiver jumps out of a large plane? How does the jumper's motion change?
2. When the parachute opens, how does the skydiver's motion change?
3. How is a skydiver's speed changing before the parachute opens? After the parachute opens?

L2

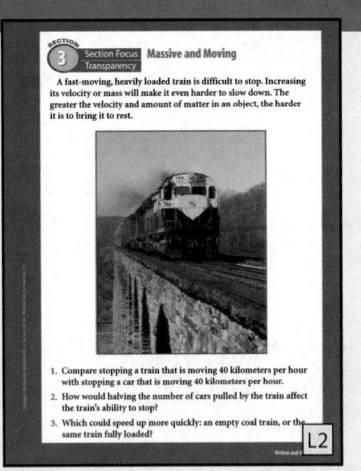

**Section Focus Transparency 3** — Massive and Moving

A fast-moving, heavily loaded train is difficult to stop. Increasing its velocity or mass will make it even harder to slow down. The greater the velocity and amount of matter in an object, the harder it is to bring it to rest.

1. Compare stopping a train that is moving 40 kilometers per hour with stopping a car that is moving 40 kilometers per hour.
2. How would halving the number of cars pulled by the train affect the train's ability to stop?
3. Which could speed up more quickly: an empty coal train, or the same train fully loaded?

L2

This is a representation of key blackline masters available in the Teacher Classroom Resources. See Resource Manager boxes within the chapter for additional information.

## Key to Teaching Strategies

The following designations will help you decide which activities are appropriate for your students.

**L1** Level 1 activities should be appropriate for students with learning difficulties.

**L2** Level 2 activities should be within the ability range of all students.

**L3** Level 3 activities are designed for above-average students.

**ELL** ELL activities should be within the ability range of English Language Learners.

**COOP LEARN** Cooperative Learning activities are designed for small group work.

**LS** Multiple Learning Styles logos, as described on page 12T, are used throughout to indicate strategies that address different learning styles.

**P** These strategies represent student products that can be placed into a best-work portfolio.

**PBL** Problem-Based Learning activities apply real-world situations to learning.

## Assessment

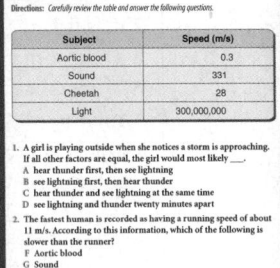

**Assessment Transparency** — Motion and Momentum

Directions: Carefully review the table and answer the following questions.

| Subject | Speed (m/s) |
|---|---|
| Aortic blood | 0.3 |
| Sound | 331 |
| Cheetah | 28 |
| Light | 300,000,000 |

1. A girl is playing outside when she notices a storm is approaching. If all other factors are equal, the girl would most likely ___.
   A hear thunder first, then see lightning
   B see lightning first, then hear thunder
   C hear thunder and see lightning at the same time
   D see lightning and thunder twenty minutes apart
2. The fastest human is recorded as having a running speed of about 11 m/s. According to this information, which of the following is slower than the runner?
   F Aortic blood
   G Sound
   H Cheetah
   J Light
3. Which factor would have the LEAST effect on measuring these speeds?
   A The distance measured
   B The time measured
   C The time of day
   D The speed formula used

L2

## Teaching

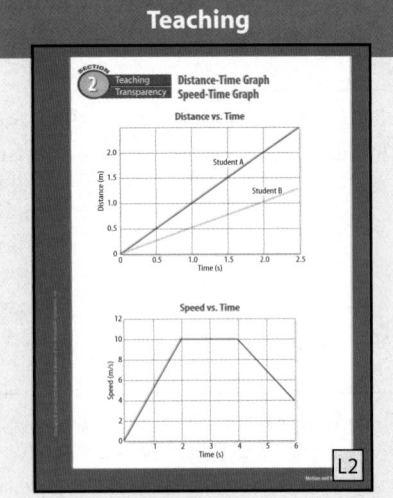

**Teaching Transparency** — Distance-Time Graph Speed-Time Graph

L2

# Hands-on Activities

## Student Text Lab Worksheet

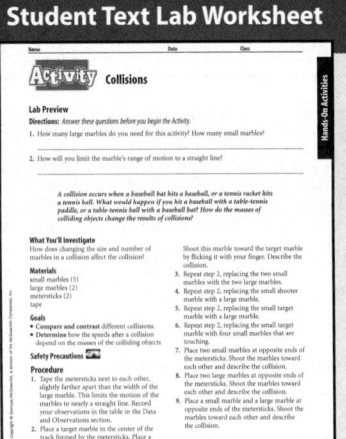

**Activity** — Collisions

**Lab Preview**
Directions: Answer these questions before you begin the Activity.

1. How many large marbles do you need for this activity? How many small marbles?

2. How will you limit the marble's range of motion to a straight line?

*A collision occurs when a baseball bat hits a baseball, or a tennis racket hits a tennis ball. What would happen if you hit a baseball with a table-tennis paddle, or a table-tennis ball with a baseball? How do the masses of colliding objects change the results of collisions?*

**What You'll Investigate**
How does changing the size and number of marbles in a collision affect the collision?

**Materials**
small marbles (5)
large marbles (2)
metersticks (2)
tape

**Goals**
• Compare and contrast different collisions.
• Determine how the speeds after a collision depend on the masses of the colliding objects

**Safety Precautions**

**Procedure**
1. Tape the metersticks next to each other, slightly farther apart than the width of the large marble. This limits the motion of the marbles to nearly a straight line. Record your observations in the table in the Data and Observations section.
2. Place a target marble in the center of the track formed by the metersticks. Place a small marble at one end of the track.

3. Shoot this marble toward the target marble by flicking it with your finger. Describe the collision.
4. Repeat step 2, replacing the two small marbles with two large marbles.
5. Repeat step 2, replacing the small shooter marble with a large marble.
6. Repeat step 2, replacing the small target marble with four small marbles that are touching.
7. Place two small marbles at opposite ends of the metersticks. Shoot the marbles toward each other and describe the collision.
8. Place two large marbles at opposite ends of the metersticks. Shoot the marbles toward each other and describe the collision.
9. Place a small marble and a large marble at opposite ends of the metersticks. Shoot the marbles toward each other and describe the collision.

L2

## Laboratory Activities

**Laboratory Activity 1** — Pushing People Around

When we push something, we unconsciously compensate for how much it weighs. We know that if an object is heavy it will require more force to get it moving and if it is light it will require less force. But how much difference is there? In this experiment, we will see what variables affect acceleration.

**Strategy**
You will see what happens when you use a constant force to pull a skater.
You will examine the relationship between force, acceleration, and mass.

**Materials**
tape
meterstick
roller skates
skating safety equipment (helmet, pads)
spring balance
stopwatch

**Procedure**
1. Mark positions on the floor at intervals of 0 m, 5 m, 10 m, and 15 m with the tape. The floor should be smooth, straight, and level.
2. Have one student stand on the 0-m mark with the skates on. A second student stands behind the mark and holds the skater. The skater holds the spring balance by its hook.
3. The third student holds the other end of the spring balance and exerts a constant pulling force on the skater. When the skater is released, the puller must maintain a constant force throughout the distance.

Measure the time to reach each of the marks. Record this in Table 1 in the Data and Observations section along with the spring balance readings at each mark.
4. Repeat steps 2 and 3 with skaters who have different masses. Keep the force the same. Make sure the skaters hold their skates parallel and do not try to change direction during the trial.
5. Repeat steps 2, 3, and 4 with a different constant force. Use the same three skaters. Record these results in Table 2 in the Data and Observations section.

L2

# Resource Manager

## Meeting Different Ability Levels

### Content Outline

L2

### Reinforcement

L2

### Enrichment

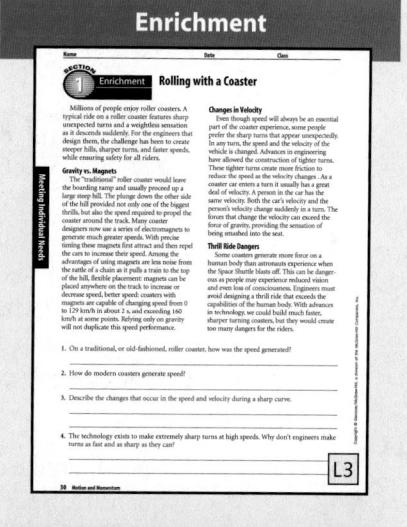

L3

### Directed Reading (English/Spanish)

L1

### Study Guide

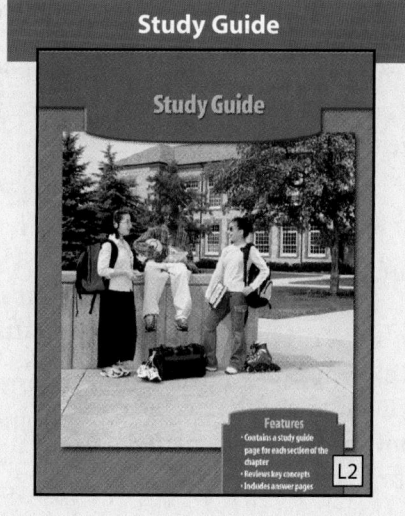

Study Guide

**Features**
• Contains a study guide page for each section of the chapter
• Reviews key concepts
• Includes answer pages

L2

### Reading Essentials

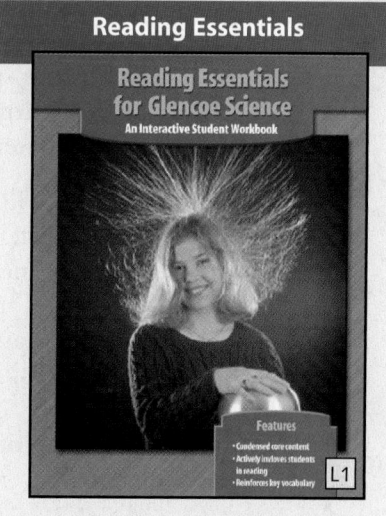

Reading Essentials for Glencoe Science
An Interactive Student Workbook

**Features**
• Condensed core content
• Actively involves students in reading
• Reinforces key vocabulary

L1

## Assessment

### Test Practice Workbook

L2

### Chapter Review

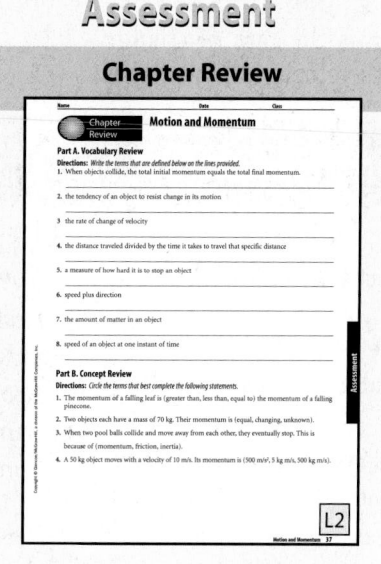

L2

### Chapter Tests

L2

# Science Content Background

section 1

## What is motion?

### Changing Position

Distance is a scalar quantity. This means that it has only a magnitude, such as 6 km. Displacement is a vector quantity; it has both magnitude and direction, such as 8 km south. A car or bike odometer displays distance, not displacement.

### Speed

Speed, unlike displacement and velocity, is a scalar quantity. Speedometers display speed, not velocity, because they do not indicate direction. Speedometers indicate instantaneous speed, which is the speed at a given instant of time. In planning a trip, however, average speed is more useful for determining the time required to travel.

### Graphing Motion

Because distance is how far an object has traveled, a distance-time graph can never have a line that slopes downward in the positive-time direction (has a negative slope). This is because it is impossible to travel a negative distance. However, a displacement-time graph can have a negative slope, which means the object is moving closer to its point of reference.

section 2

## Acceleration

### Acceleration and Motion

Acceleration is the rate of change of an object's velocity. If velocity is expressed as meters/second and time is given in seconds, then acceleration is expressed in units of meters per second per second, m/s/s or (m/s $\times$ 1/s) or m/s$^2$.

If the direction of motion is defined as the positive direction, then when an object's velocity increases, the object experiences positive acceleration. When its velocity decreases, the object experiences negative acceleration. Acceleration also occurs when an object changes direction. For example, as Earth orbits the Sun, it is accelerating. Although Earth travels at a nearly constant speed, its direction is constantly changing.

section 3

## Momentum

### Mass and Inertia

Students may attribute inertia to an object's weight instead of mass, so that a weightless object would have no inertia. However, even in deep space where there is almost no gravitational force on an object, its inertia is unchanged.

### Momentum

Momentum and force are related. The time rate of change of an object's momentum is equal to the force exerted on the object or exerted by the object. In collisions, momentum is conserved only if there are no external forces, such as friction, acting on the colliding objects.

## chapter content resources

**Internet Resources**
For additional content background, visit
**in7.msscience.com** to:
- access your book online
- find references to related articles in popular science magazines
- access Web links with related content background
- access current events with science journal topics

**Print Resources**
*Eyewitness: Force & Motion,* by Peter Lafferty, Dorling Kindersley Publishing, 2000
*Hands-On Physics Activities with Real-Life Applications : Easy-to-Use Labs and Demonstrations for Grades 8–12,* by James Cunningham & Norman Herr, Jossey-Bass, 1994

**IDENTIFYING** ▷ # Misconceptions

## Find Out What Students Think

**Students may think that . . .**

**distance and displacement are the same, and**

**speed and velocity are the same.**
One difficulty with the terms velocity and displacement is that they are both vector quantities, and students are much more familiar with scalar quantities. To confuse matters more, the term velocity is sometimes used in everyday language in a non-scientific way. Finally, the terms displacement and distance sound similar, and this may make it easier to confuse them.

### Demonstration
After initially teaching the difference between distance and displacement, ask students whether the phrase "as the crow flies," when estimating how far something is, is more like distance or more like displacement.

## Promote Understanding

### Activity

- Draw Figures 1 and 2 on the board. Explain that the distance-time graph and the displacement-time graph both show Samantha's walking motion after she left her house.

- Ask students to supply a possible story to describe her motion. Ask them what she might be doing when the lines of the two graphs are horizontal.

- Students should see that the distance-time graph and displacement-time graph for the same motion look very different. In this case, the distance traveled is how far Samantha actually walked. Her displacement shows how far she is from her house.

**Figure 1:
Distance-time graph**

Distance (m/s)

Time (s)

**Figure 2:
Displacement-time graph**

Displacement (m/s North)

Time (s)

- A plausible story for both graphs has Samantha walking at constant speed directly away from her house, then resting a bit, and then walking at constant speed directly back to her house.

### Assess

After completing the chapter, see *Identifying Misconceptions* in the Study Guide at the end of a chapter.

## Chapter Vocabulary

speed, p. 324
average speed, p. 325
instantaneous speed, p. 325
velocity, p. 327
acceleration, p. 328
mass, p. 333
inertia, p. 333
momentum, p. 334
law of conservation of
  momentum, p. 335

**Science Journal**  Student
responses will vary.

### INTERACTIVE CHALKBOARD
**with Image Bank**

**PowerPoint® Presentations**

This CD-ROM is an editable
Microsoft® PowerPoint®
presentation that includes:
- a pre-made presentation for
  every chapter
- interactive graphics
- animations
- audio clips
- image bank
- all new section and chapter
  questions
- Standardized Test Practice
- transparencies
- pre-lab questions for all labs
- Foldables directions
- links to in7.msscience.com

**Academic Standard—7:** Students analyze the relationships within systems. They investigate how different models can represent the same data, rates of change, cyclic changes, and changes that counterbalance one another.

**Also covers:** Academic Standard 2 (Detailed standards begin on page IN8.)

# Motion and Momentum

## chapter preview

### sections

**1**  What is motion?

**2**  Acceleration

**3**  Momentum
  *Lab  Collisions*
  *Lab  Car Safety Testing*
  **Virtual Lab**  *How does horizontal motion affect vertical motion?*

## A Vanishing Act

You hear the crack of the bat and an instant later the ball disappears into a diving infielder's glove. Think of how the motion of the ball changed—it moved toward the batter, changed direction when it collided with the bat, and then stopped when it collided with the infielder's glove.

**Science Journal**  Describe how your motion changed as you moved from your school's entrance to your classroom.

320

## Theme Connection

**Stability and Change**  An object can be in motion or at rest. If in motion, the motion can be constant or accelerated. If accelerated, the acceleration can be constant or changing.

### About the Photo

**Home-Run Hitting**  Many baseball fans love the excitement of seeing long balls hit far into the outfield. The distance the ball travels depends, in part, on the momentum of the bat and ball when they collide. Every year, it seems like hitters send the ball flying further, so some people think the ball must be being changed somehow. However, the mass and size of the baseball has remained the same since 1872.

# Start-Up Activities

## Motion After a Collision

How is it possible for a 70-kg football player to knock down a 110-kg football player? The smaller player usually must be running faster. Mass makes a difference when two objects collide, but the speed of the objects also matters. Explore the behavior of colliding objects during this lab.

1. Space yourself about 2 m away from a partner. Slowly roll a baseball on the floor toward your partner, and have your partner roll a baseball quickly into your ball.

2. Have your partner slowly roll a baseball as you quickly roll a tennis ball into the baseball.

3. Roll two tennis balls toward each other at the same speed.

4. **Think Critically** In your Science Journal, describe how the motion of the balls changed after the collisions, including the effects of speed and type of ball.

Preview this chapter's content and activities at
in7.msscience.com

**Study Organizer**

**Motion and Momentum** Make the following Foldable to help you understand the vocabulary terms in this chapter.

**STEP 1** Fold a vertical sheet of notebook paper from side to side.

**STEP 2** Cut along every third line of only the top layer to form tabs.

**STEP 3** Label each tab.

**Build Vocabulary** As you read the chapter, list the vocabulary words about motion and momentum on the tabs. As you learn the definitions, write them under the tab for each vocabulary word.

321

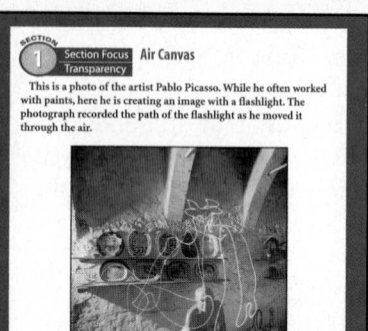
# What is motion?

## Matter and Motion

All matter in the universe is constantly in motion, from the revolution of Earth around the Sun to electrons moving around the nucleus of an atom. Leaves rustle in the wind. Lava flows from a volcano. Bees move from flower to flower as they gather pollen. Blood circulates through your body. These are all examples of matter in motion. How can the motion of these different objects be described?

## Changing Position

To describe an object in motion, you must first recognize that the object is in motion. Something is in motion if it is changing position. It could be a fast-moving airplane, a leaf swirling in the wind, or water trickling from a hose. Even your school, attached to Earth, is moving through space. When an object moves from one location to another, it is changing position. The runners shown in **Figure 1** sprint from the start line to the finish line. Their positions change, so they are in motion.

**Figure 1** When running a race, you are in motion because your position changes.

**Relative Motion** Determining whether something changes position requires a point of reference. An object changes position if it moves relative to a reference point. To visualize this, picture yourself competing in a 100-m dash. You begin just behind the start line. When you pass the finish line, you are 100 m from the start line. If the start line is your reference point, then your position has changed by 100 m relative to the start line, and motion has occurred. Look at **Figure 2.** How can you determine that the dog has been in motion?

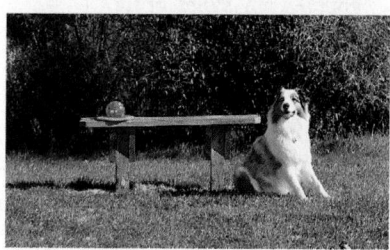

> ✓ **Reading Check** *How do you know if an object has changed position?*

**Distance and Displacement** Suppose you are to meet your friends at the park in five minutes. Can you get there on time by walking, or should you ride your bike? To help you decide, you need to know the distance you will travel to get to the park. This distance is the length of the route you will travel from your house to the park.

Suppose the distance you traveled from your house to the park was 200 m. When you get to the park, how would you describe your location? You could say that your location was 200 m from your house. However, your final position depends on both the distance you travel and the direction. Did you go 200 m east or west? To describe your final position exactly, you also would have to tell the direction from your starting point. To do this, you would specify your displacement. Displacement includes the distance between the starting and ending points and the direction in which you travel. **Figure 3** shows the difference between distance and displacement.

**Figure 2** Motion occurs when something changes position relative to a reference point.
**Explain** *whether the dog's position would depend on the reference point chosen.*

**Figure 3** Distance is how far you have walked. Displacement is the direction and difference in position between your starting and ending points.

Distance: 40 m
Displacement: 40 m east

Distance: 70 m
Displacement: 50 m northeast

Distance: 140 m
Displacement: 0 m

SECTION 1 What is motion? **323**

---

## Cultural Diversity

**Chinese Mapmaking** By the second century A.D., Chang Heng, inventor of the seismometer, was applying uniform grids to maps to make it easier to calculate distances. This was eventually developed to the point where, by the 1300s, some maps eliminated the physical features and simply showed place names and grid lines, as a modern computer might model a map.

## ✓ Active Reading

**Concept Maps** Have students create concept maps using the vocabulary words introduced throughout the chapter. Have students pair up and take turns explaining their concept maps to each other. P

---

## 2 Teach

### ✓ Reading Check
**Answer** It has moved relative to a reference point.

### Caption Answer
**Figure 2** Yes, the description of the dog's position depends on the reference point.

### Activity
**Walking Motion** Have students work in pairs. Ask one student to walk forward while the other stands still. Then have the first student stand still while the other walks forward. Have students describe their motion relative to each other. L2 LS **Kinesthetic**

### Quick Demo
**Distance v. Displacement**
**Material** ball
**Estimated Time** 15 minutes
**Procedure** Toss a ball to a student. Maintaining the same distance from the student, vary the toss. Throw the ball quickly and along a fairly flat path, bounce it, and toss it high in the air. Point out that the ball's displacement remains the same, but its total path (distance) varies. L2 LS **Visual-Spatial**

## Differentiated Instruction

**English-Language Learners** Help these students by assigning each one a partner to provide support in understanding new concepts. Encourage partners to demonstrate or illustrate ideas to add meaning to verbal explanations.

## Speed

To describe motion, you usually want to describe how fast something is moving. The faster something is moving, the less time it takes to travel a certain distance. **Speed** is the distance traveled divided by the time taken to travel the distance. Speed can be calculated from this equation:

**Speed Equation**

$$\text{speed (in meters/second)} = \frac{\text{distance (in meters)}}{\text{time (in seconds)}}$$

$$s = \frac{d}{t}$$

Because speed equals distance divided by time, the unit of speed is the unit of distance divided by the unit of time. In SI units, distance is measured in m and time is measured in s. As a result, the SI unit of speed is the m/s—the SI distance unit divided by the SI time unit.

### Applying Math    Solve a Simple Equation

**SPEED OF A SWIMMER** Calculate the speed of a swimmer who swims 100 m in 56 s.

**Solution**

**1** *This is what you know:*
- distance: $d = 100$ m
- time: $t = 56$ s

**2** *This is what you need to know:*
speed: $s = ?$ m/s

**3** *This is the procedure you need to use:*
Substitute the known values for distance and time into the speed equation and calculate the speed:

$$s = \frac{d}{t} = \frac{100 \text{ m}}{56 \text{ s}} = \frac{100}{56} \frac{\text{m}}{\text{s}} = 1.8 \text{ m/s}$$

**4** *Check your answer:*
Multiply your answer by the time. You should get the distance that was given.

### Practice Problems

1. A runner completes a 400-m race in 43.9 s. In a 100-m race, he finishes in 10.4 s. In which race was his speed faster?

2. A passenger train travels from Boston to New York, a distance of 350 km, in 3.5 h. What is the train's speed?

 For more practice, visit in7.msscience.com/math_practice

## Curriculum Connection

**Music** Ask students to identify the units used to measure speed in music and to demonstrate how speed is used in music. Beats per minute are the units used. A rapid beat or slow beat affects the mood of a piece.

L3 ELL LS **Auditory-Musical**

## Teacher FYI

**Pulse Rate** Before people had accurate timekeeping devices, they used their pulse rate to measure time. Early musicians based the tempo of music on their pulse rate, and Galileo analyzed the movement of a pendulum using his pulse.

**Average Speed** If a sprinter ran the 100-m dash in 10 s, she probably couldn't have run the entire race with a speed of 10 m/s. Consider that when the race started, the sprinter wasn't moving. Then, as she started running, she moved faster and faster, which increased her speed. During the entire race, the sprinter's speed could have been different from instant to instant. However, the sprinter's motion for the entire race can be described by her average speed, which is 10 m/s. **Average speed** is found by dividing the total distance traveled by the time taken.

✔ **Reading Check** *How is average speed calculated?*

An object in motion can change speeds many times as it speeds up or slows down. The speed of an object at one instant of time is the object's **instantaneous speed**. To understand the difference between average and instantaneous speeds, think about walking to the library. If it takes you 0.5 h to walk 2 km to the library, your average speed would be as follows:

$$s = \frac{d}{t}$$
$$= \frac{2 \text{ km}}{0.5 \text{ h}} = 4 \text{ km/h}$$

However, you might not have been moving at the same speed throughout the trip. At a crosswalk, your instantaneous speed might have been 0 km/h. If you raced across the street, your speed might have been 7 km/h. If you were able to walk at a steady rate of 4 km/h during the entire trip, you would have moved at a constant speed. Average speed, instantaneous speed, and constant speed are illustrated in **Figure 4.**

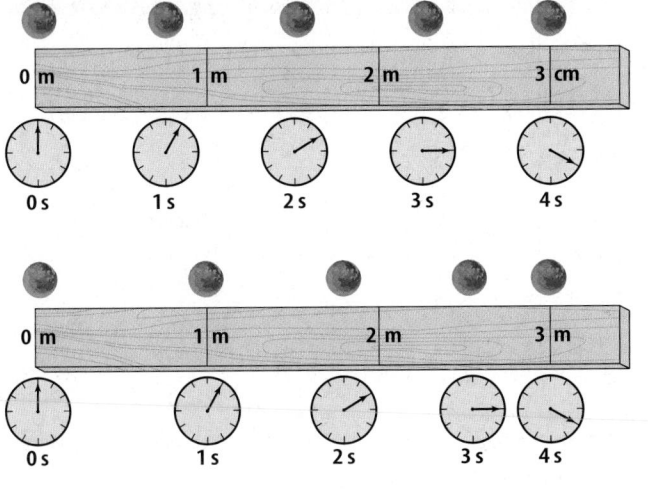

**Figure 4** The average speed of each ball is the same from 0 s to 4 s.

The top ball is moving at a constant speed. In each second, the ball moves the same distance.

The bottom ball has a varying speed. Its instantaneous speed is fast between 0 s and 1 s, slower between 2 s and 3 s, and even slower between 3 s and 4 s.

## Visual Learning

**Figure 4** Point out to students that this drawing illustrates motion over time. Tell them that photographers can take time-lapse photos to show the same thing. If the photographer knows the time between shots, he or she can find the average speed between any two positions.

## Fun Fact

People climbing Mt. Everest by the North Ridge Ascent start at a base camp with an elevation of 5,170 m. Because the summit of Mt. Everest has an elevation of 8,850 m, the ascent has a vertical displacement of only 3,680 m. However, the distance along the ridge from the base camp to the summit is 20 km (20,000 m)!

**Activity**

**Slope** Tell students that to calculate speed from a distance-time graph, they must find the slope of the line. The slope is a measure of the steepness of the graph and is found by dividing the rise, or vertical change, by the run, or horizontal change. In **Figure 5**, the slope of line A between 1 and 2 seconds is (2 m − 1 m) ÷ (2 s − 1 s) = 1 m/s. Have students find the slope of line B for that period of time. (1 m − 0.5 m) ÷ (2 s − 1 s) = 0.5 m/s [L3] **IS** **Logical-Mathematical**

## Caption Answer

**Figure 5** student A

## Inquiry Lab

**Mass, Acceleration, and Inertia**

**Purpose** Students will explore the role of mass in inertia and in acceleration.

**Possible Materials** several toy cars of varying masses, toy car track, rubber bands, stopwatch

**Safety Precaution** Caution students never to direct rubber bands at one another.

**Estimated Time** one class session

**Teaching Strategies**

• Students can use the rubber bands as slingshots to propel the cars and the tracks to keep the cars moving in a straight line.

• Students can predict and then observe how the mass of a car affects how quickly it's accelerated by the rubber bands. They can compare the distances traveled by different cars for the same force or by the same car for different forces.

• Students can also explore how the relative masses of cars (one moving, one initially at rest) affect their velocities after a collision.

**For additional inquiry activities, see** *Science Inquiry Labs.*

**Science Online**

**Topic: Land Speed Record**

Visit in7.msscience.com for Web links to information about how the land speed record has changed over the past century.

**Activity** Make a graph showing the increase in the land speed over time.

## Graphing Motion

You can represent the motion of an object with a distance-time graph. For this type of graph, time is plotted on the horizontal axis and distance is plotted on the vertical axis. **Figure 5** shows the motion of two students who walked across a classroom plotted on a distance-time graph.

**Distance-Time Graphs and Speed** A distance-time graph can be used to compare the speeds of objects. Look at the graph shown in **Figure 5.** According to the graph, after 1 s student A traveled 1 m. Her average speed during the first second is as follows:

$$speed = \frac{distance}{time} = \frac{1\ m}{1\ s} = 1\ m/s$$

Student B, however, traveled only 0.5 m in the first second. His average speed is

$$speed = \frac{distance}{time} = \frac{0.5\ m}{1\ s} = 0.5\ m/s$$

So student A traveled faster than student B. Now compare the steepness of the lines on the graph in **Figure 5.** The line representing the motion of student A is steeper than the line for student B. A steeper line on the distance-time graph represents a greater speed. A horizontal line on the distance-time graph means that no change in position occurs. In that case, the speed, represented by the line on the graph, is zero.

**Figure 5** The motion of two students walking across a classroom is plotted on this distance-time graph.
**Use the graph** *to determine which student had the faster average speed.*

**326** **CHAPTER 11** Motion and Momentum

## Curriculum Connection

**Math** The horizontal axis of a graph represents the independent variable; that is, the variable in which a change causes a change in the other variable. In distance-time graphs the independent variable is time. The vertical axis shows the dependent variable, in this case distance.

## Differentiated Instruction

**Challenge** The motion of groups of objects can be modeled using graph paper. Have students divide a sheet of graph paper into six regions to represent one-second intervals from 0 to 5 s. Have students use the graph paper to illustrate what happens to four objects moving at different speeds and directions at $t$ = 0, 1, 2, 3, 4, and 5 s. Then ask them to predict when and if various pairs of objects meet. [L3] **IS** **Visual-Spatial**

# Velocity

If you are hiking in the woods, it is important to know in which direction you should walk in order to get back to camp. You want to know not only your speed, but also the direction in which you are moving. The **velocity** of an object is the speed of the object and the direction of its motion. This is why a compass and a map, like the one shown in **Figure 6**, are useful to hikers. The map and the compass help the hikers to determine what their velocity must be. Velocity has the same units as speed, but it includes the direction of motion.

The velocity of an object can change if the object's speed changes, its direction of motion changes, or they both change. For example, suppose a car is traveling at a speed of 40 km/h north and then turns left at an intersection and continues on with a speed of 40 km/h. The speed of the car is constant at 40 km/h, but the velocity changes from 40 km/h north to 40 km/h west. Why can you say the velocity of a car changes as it comes to a stop at an intersection?

1.5 m/s west

1.5 m/s south

△ START/FINISH

N

**Figure 6** A map helps determine the direction in which you need to travel. Together with your speed, this gives your velocity.

## section ① review

### Summary

**Changing Position**

- An object is in motion if it changes position relative to a reference point.
- Motion can be described by distance, speed, displacement, and velocity, where displacement and velocity also include direction.

**Speed and Velocity**

- The speed of an object can be calculated by dividing the distance traveled by the time needed to travel the distance.
- For an object traveling at constant speed, its average speed is the same as its instantaneous speed.
- The velocity of an object is the speed of the object and its direction of motion.

**Graphing Motion**

- A line on a distance-time graph becomes steeper as an object's speed increases.

### Self Check

1. **Identify** the two pieces of information you need to know the velocity of an object.

2. **Make and Use Graphs** You walk forward at 1.5 m/s for 8 s. Your friend decides to walk faster and starts out at 2.0 m/s for the first 4 s. Then she slows down and walks forward at 1.0 m/s for the next 4 s. Make a distance-time graph of your motion and your friend's motion. Who walked farther?

3. **Think Critically** A bee flies 25 m north of the hive, then 10 m east, 5 m west, and 10 m south. How far north and east of the hive is it now? Explain how you calculated your answer.

#### Applying Math

4. **Calculate** the average velocity of a dancer who moves 5 m toward the left of the stage over the course of 15 s.

5. **Calculate Travel Time** An airplane flew a distance of 650 km at an average speed of 300 km/h. How much time did the flight take?

## section ① review

1. speed and direction
2. The horizontal axis should be marked from 0 s to 8 s, and the vertical axis should be marked from 0 m to 12 m. The graph of your motion is a diagonal line from (0,0) to (8,12). The graph of your friend's motion is a 2-part line extending from (0,0) to (4,8) and from (4,8) to (8,12). You and your friend walked the same distance, 12 m.

3. 15 m north (25 − 10) and 5 m east (10 − 5)
4. 5 m left ÷ 15 s = 0.33 m/s left
5. 650 km ÷ 300 km/h = 2.17 h

## Discussion

**Distance-Time Graph** Could you use a distance-time graph to show velocity? Why or why not? No, because a distance-time graph would not show the direction of motion.
L2  IS  **Logical-Mathematical**

## Text Question Answer

because its speed changes

## 3 Assess

### DAILY INTERVENTION

### Check for Understanding

**Logical-Mathematical** Have each student make a distance-time graph of the following motion.
0 s to 4 s: walk at 0.8 m/s
4 s to 6 s: stopped
6 s to 10 s: run at 2.3 m/s
What was the average speed over the 10 s? 1.24 m/s  L2

### Reteach

**Distance and Displacement** Have a student start at the door and walk across the classroom in a straight line. Then move a few desks into the path and have the student repeat the test, dodging the desks. What was the distance in each case? The displacement? Was the speed constant or changing? The velocity?  L2
ELL  IS  **Visual-Spatial**

### ✓ Assessment

**Process** Give students a distance-time graph showing the motions of three different people. Ask them to compare the motions. How did each person's speed and position change over time? Use **Performance Assessment in the Science Classroom,** p. 113.

## 1 Motivate

### Bellringer

**Section Focus Transparencies** also are available on the Interactive Chalkboard CD-ROM.

### Tie to Prior Knowledge

**Car Acceleration** Bring to class a car advertising statement like "goes from 0 to 60 in 8.3 s." Ask students to describe acceleration using this example. What would it mean if the car reached a faster speed in 8.3 s? higher acceleration What would it mean if it took 12 s to reach 60 mi/h? lower acceleration What do people mean when they say a car has "no acceleration"? that it won't increase its speed very rapidly

---

## section 2

**Also covers:** 7.2.7, 7.7.4 (Detailed standards begin on page IN8.)

# Acceleration

### as you read

**What You'll Learn**

- **Define** acceleration.
- **Predict** what effect acceleration will have on motion.

**Why It's Important**

Whenever the motion of an object changes, it is accelerating.

**Review Vocabulary**

**kilogram:** SI unit of mass, abbreviated kg; equal to approximately 2.2 lbs

**New Vocabulary**

- acceleration

**Figure 7** The toy car is accelerating to the right. Its speed is increasing.

## Acceleration and Motion

When you watch the first few seconds of a liftoff, a rocket barely seems to move. With each passing second, however, you can see it move faster until it reaches an enormous speed. How could you describe the change in the rocket's motion? When an object changes its motion, it is accelerating. **Acceleration** is the change in velocity divided by the time it takes for the change to occur.

Like velocity, acceleration has a direction. If an object speeds up, the acceleration is in the direction that the object is moving. If an object slows down, the acceleration is opposite to the direction that the object is moving. What if the direction of the acceleration is at an angle to the direction of motion? Then the direction of motion will turn toward the direction of the acceleration.

**Speeding Up** You get on a bicycle and begin to pedal. The bike moves slowly at first, and then accelerates because its speed increases. When an object that is already in motion speeds up, it also is accelerating. Imagine that you are biking along a level path and you start pedaling harder. Your speed increases. When the speed of an object increases, it is accelerating.

Suppose a toy car is speeding up, as shown in **Figure 7.** Each second, the car moves at a greater speed and travels a greater distance than it did in the previous second. When the car stops accelerating, it will move in a straight line at the speed it had when the acceleration stopped.

**328    CHAPTER 11** Motion and Momentum

---

### Section 2 Resource Manager

**Chapter FAST FILE Resources**
Transparency Activity, p. 45
Directed Reading for Content Mastery, p. 20
MiniLAB, p.4

Enrichment, p. 31
Reinforcement, p. 28
Lab Activity, pp. 13–15

0 cm  10 cm  20 cm  30 cm  40 cm  50 cm  60 cm  70 cm

0 s          1 s          2 s    3 s

**Slowing Down** Now suppose you are biking at a speed of 4 m/s and you apply the brakes. This causes you to slow down. It might sound odd, but because your speed is changing, you are accelerating. Acceleration occurs when an object slows down, as well as when it speeds up. The car in **Figure 8** is slowing down. During each time interval, the car travels a smaller distance, so its speed is decreasing.

In both of these examples, speed is changing, so acceleration is occurring. Because speed is decreasing in the second example, the direction of the acceleration is opposite to the direction of motion. Any time an object slows down, its acceleration is in the direction opposite to the direction of its motion.

**Changing Direction** Motion is not always along a straight line. If the acceleration is at an angle to the direction of motion, the object will turn. At the same time, it might speed up, slow down, or not change speed at all.

Again imagine yourself riding a bicycle. When you lean to one side and turn the handlebars, the bike turns. Because the direction of the bike's motion has changed, the bike has accelerated. The acceleration is in the direction that the bicycle turned.

**Figure 9** shows another example of an object that is accelerating. The ball starts moving upward, but its direction of motion changes as its path turns downward. Here the acceleration is downward. The longer the ball accelerates, the more its path turns toward the direction of acceleration.

**Reading Check** What are three ways to accelerate?

**Figure 9** The ball starts out by moving forward and upward, but the acceleration is downward, so the ball's path turns in that direction.

**Figure 8** The car is moving to the right but accelerating to the left. In each time interval, it covers less distance and moves more slowly.
**Determine** how the car's velocity is changing.

SECTION 2 Acceleration **329**

**Squared Seconds** Have students look at the equations on this page. Why is acceleration measured in meters divided by seconds *squared*? Velocity is measured in meters per second. To find acceleration, you divide velocity by time, which has units of seconds. Therefore, the final answer has units of distance divided by time (velocity) divided by time = $m/s^2$.

L2 IS **Logical-Mathematical**

**Answers to Practice Problems**

**1.** $a = (17 \text{ m/s} - 7 \text{ m/s}) \div 120 \text{ s} = 0.083 \text{ m/s}^2$

**2.** $a = (6 \text{ m/s} - 0 \text{ m/s}) \div 2 \text{ s} = 3 \text{ m/s}^2$

## Differentiated Instruction

**Learning Disabled** Provide extra practice problems for students who have difficulty understanding the mathematics discussed on these pages. Make sure students understand the basic principles used both to set up and solve the problems.

## Calculating Acceleration

If an object is moving in a straight line, its acceleration can be calculated using this equation.

**Acceleration Equation**

acceleration (in $m/s^2$) =

$$\frac{(\textbf{final speed (in m/s)} - \textbf{initial speed (in m/s)})}{\textbf{time (in s)}}$$

$$a = \frac{(s_f - s_i)}{t}$$

In this equation, time is the length of time over which the motion changes. In SI units, acceleration has units of meters per second squared ($m/s^2$).

### Applying Math    Solve a Simple Equation

**ACCELERATION OF A BUS** Calculate the acceleration of a bus whose speed changes from 6 m/s to 12 m/s over a period of 3 s.

**Solution**

**1** *This is what you know:*
- initial speed: $s_i = 6$ m/s
- final speed: $s_f = 12$ m/s
- time: $t = 3$ s

**2** *This is what you need to know:*

acceleration: $a = ?$ $m/s^2$

**3** *This is the procedure you need to use:*

Substitute the known values of initial speed, final speed and time in the acceleration equation and calculate the acceleration:

$$a = \frac{(s_f - s_i)}{t} = \frac{(12 \text{ m/s} - 6 \text{ m/s})}{3 \text{ s}} = 6\frac{\text{m}}{\text{s}} \times \frac{1}{3 \text{ s}} = 2 \text{ m/s}^2$$

**4** *Check your answer:*

Multiply the calculated acceleration by the known time. Then add the known initial speed. You should get the final speed that was given.

### Practice Problems

**1.** Find the acceleration of a train whose speed increases from 7 m/s to 17 m/s in 120 s.

**2.** A bicycle accelerates from rest to 6 m/s in 2 s. What is the bicycle's acceleration?

 **For more practice, visit in7.msscience.com/ math_practice**

## Differentiated Instruction

**Challenge** When doing calculations, students may be helped by doing unit analysis. In doing unit analysis, you write the initial problem with units included and cancel appropriately to see what units the answer will have. If the answer does not have the right units, the problem is set up incorrectly. Have students do a unit analysis of the problem of finding the time needed to accel- erate from 3 m/s to 8 m/s at 2 $m/s^2$. The units should cancel leaving the unit of time, seconds. The change in velocity is 5 m/s. Rearrange the equation for acceleration to: time = change in velocity $\div$ acceleration. Substituting units in this equation gives

time = (m/s $-$ m/s) $\div$ m/s$^2$ = m/s $\times$ s$^2$/m = s

$t = (5 \text{ m/s}) \div (2 \text{ m/s}^2) = 2.5 \text{ s}$ L3 IS

**Logical-Mathematical**

**Figure 10** When skidding to a stop, you are slowing down. This means you have a negative acceleration.

**Positive and Negative Acceleration** An object is accelerating when it speeds up, and the acceleration is in the same direction as the motion. An object also is accelerating when it slows down, but the acceleration is in the direction opposite to the motion, such as the bicycle in **Figure 10.** How else is acceleration different when an object is speeding up and slowing down?

Suppose you were riding your bicycle in a straight line and increased your speed from 4 m/s to 6 m/s in 5 s. You could calculate your acceleration from the equation on the previous page.

$$a = \frac{(s_f - s_i)}{t}$$
$$= \frac{(6 \text{ m/s} - 4 \text{ m/s})}{5 \text{ s}} = \frac{+2 \text{ m/s}}{5 \text{ s}}$$
$$= +0.4 \text{ m/s}^2$$

When you speed up, your final speed always will be greater than your initial speed. So subtracting your initial speed from your final speed gives a positive number. As a result, your acceleration is positive when you are speeding up.

Suppose you slow down from a speed of 4 m/s to 2 m/s in 5 s. Now the final speed is less than the initial speed. You could calculate your acceleration as follows:

$$a = \frac{(s_f - s_i)}{t}$$
$$= \frac{(2 \text{ m/s} - 4 \text{ m/s})}{5 \text{ s}} = \frac{-2 \text{ m/s}}{5 \text{ s}}$$
$$= -0.4 \text{ m/s}^2$$

Because your final speed is less than your initial speed, your acceleration is negative when you slow down.

### Modeling Acceleration

**Procedure**
1. Use **masking tape** to lay a course on the floor. Mark a starting point and place marks along a straight path at 10 cm, 40 cm, 90 cm, 160 cm, and 250 cm from the start.
2. Clap a steady beat. On the first beat, the person walking the course should be at the starting point. On the second beat, the walker should be on the first mark, and so on.

**Analysis**
1. Describe what happens to your speed as you move along the course. Infer what would happen if the course were extended farther.
2. Repeat step 2, starting at the other end. Are you still accelerating? Explain.

**Purpose** Students observe constant acceleration. L2 IS **Kinesthetic**

**Materials** meterstick or other measuring device, masking tape

**Teaching Strategy** Explain to students that the actual time interval used doesn't matter, as long as it is constant—it could be 1 s–1 s–1 s, or 3 s–3 s–3 s, or any other regular time interval. Clapping steadily is easier than trying to watch the clock and the course at the same time.

**Safety Precaution** Suggest that students leave space at the fast end of the course to come to a stop.

**Analysis**
1. I speed up. I would go faster and faster with each clap, because I would be covering a greater distance in the same amount of time.
2. Yes, because my speed is changing. In this case, I am slowing down.

### Assessment

**Process** Ask students to repeat the experiment using different steady beats—very slow or very fast. How does this affect the acceleration they experience? The faster the beat, the greater the acceleration, because the time between beats decreases. Use **Performance Assessment in the Science Classroom,** p. 97.

### Activity

**Final Speed** Have students calculate the final speed of a bicyclist who accelerates at 0.3 m/s² for 10 s from an initial speed of 4 m/s.

# Curriculum Connection

**History** An early problem in the study of motion was to measure the acceleration of an object due to gravity. Does the acceleration of an object depend on its mass? Have students do research to find Galileo's contributions to understanding the answers to these problems. He showed that gravity causes all falling objects to have the same constant acceleration. L3 IS **Linguistic**

# Teacher FYI

**Negative Velocity** A negative number multiplied by a positive number results in a negative number. Because time is always positive, a negative acceleration multiplied by a positive time will always give a negative change in velocity.

## 3 Assess

### Check for Understanding

**Logical-Mathematical** Ask students to draw a speed-time graph showing the speed of an object with a constant acceleration of 8 m/s² after starting from rest for 10 s. Have them use points on this graph to calculate the average speed after 8 seconds and the distance traveled in 8 seconds. The average speed is (speed after 8 s − initial speed) ÷ 2 = (64 m/s − 0 m/s) ÷ 2 = 32 m/s. The distance traveled in 8 s is 32 m/s × 8 s = 256 m. L2

### Reteach

**Graphing Acceleration** Draw the following speed-time graph on the board: straight line sloping up, flat line, straight line sloping partway down, another flat line, then a line curving down. Where does the graph show positive acceleration? sloping up Negative acceleration? sloping down No acceleration? flat Constant acceleration? any straight line L2 LS
**Visual-Spatial**

### ✔ Assessment

**Portfolio** Ask students to make speed-time graphs for a possible trip from their homes to school. The graphs should indicate where students speed up, slow down, or move at constant speed and give an idea of the comparative speeds and accelerations. Use **Performance Assessment in the Science Classroom,** p. 111. P

**Speed v. Time**

**Figure 11** A speed-time graph can be used to find acceleration. When the line rises, the object is speeding up. When the line falls, the object is slowing down.
**Infer** *what acceleration a horizontal line represents.*

**Graphing Accelerated Motion** The motion of an object that is accelerating can be shown with a graph. For this type of graph, speed is plotted on the vertical axis and time on the horizontal axis. Take a look at **Figure 11.** On section A of the graph, the speed increases from 0 m/s to 10 m/s during the first 2 s, so the acceleration is +5 m/s². The line in section A slopes upward to the right. An object that is speeding up will have a line on a speed-time graph that slopes upward.

Now look at section C. Between 4 s and 6 s, the object slows down from 10 m/s to 4 m/s. The acceleration is −3 m/s². On the speed-time graph, the line in section C is sloping downward to the right. An object that is slowing down will have a line on a speed-time graph that slopes downward.

On section B, where the line is horizontal, the change in speed is zero. So a horizontal line on the speed-time graph represents an acceleration of zero or constant speed.

## section 2 review

### Summary

**Acceleration and Motion**

- Acceleration is the change in velocity divided by the time it takes to make the change. Acceleration has direction.

- Acceleration occurs whenever an object speeds up, slows down, or changes direction.

**Calculating Acceleration**

- For motion in a straight line, acceleration can be calculated from this equation:

$$a = \frac{s_f - s_i}{t}$$

- If an object is speeding up, its acceleration is positive; if an object is slowing down, its acceleration is negative.

- On a speed-time graph, a line sloping up represents positive acceleration, a line sloping down represents negative acceleration, and a horizontal line represents zero acceleration or constant speed.

### Self Check

1. **Compare and contrast** speed, velocity, and acceleration.

2. **Infer** the motion of a car whose speed-time graph shows a horizontal line, followed by a straight line that slopes downward to the bottom of the graph.

3. **Think Critically** You start to roll backward down a hill on your bike, so you use the brakes to stop your motion. In what direction did you accelerate?

#### Applying Math

4. **Calculate** the acceleration of a runner who accelerates from 0 m/s to 3 m/s in 12 s.

5. **Calculate Speed** An object falls with an acceleration of 9.8 m/s². What is its speed after 2 s?

6. **Make and Use a Graph** A sprinter had the following speeds at different times during a race: 0 m/s at 0 s, 4 m/s at 2 s, 7 m/s at 4 s, 10 m/s at 6 s, 12 m/s at 8 s, and 10 m/s at 10 s. Plot these data on a speed-time graph. During what time intervals is the acceleration positive? Negative? Is the acceleration ever zero?

**332 CHAPTER 11** Motion and Momentum

Science Online in7.msscience.com/self_check_quiz

## section 2 review

1. Speed and velocity both include rate of change in position. Acceleration measures rate of change in velocity. Both velocity and acceleration include direction; speed does not.

2. The car first travels at constant speed (horizontal line) and then slows down (sloping line) and

comes to a stop (bottom of the graph).

3. Against the motion; I accelerated uphill.

4. $a = (3 \text{ m/s} - 0 \text{ m/s}) \div 12 \text{ s} = 0.25 \text{ m/s}^2$

5. $s_f = 0 \text{ m/s} + 9.8 \text{ m/s}^2 \times 2 \text{ s} = 19.6 \text{ m/s}$

6. Check students' graphs; positive from 0 s to 8 s; negative from 8 s to 10 s. The acceleration must become zero for some short time as it changes from positive to negative between 8 and 10 s.

**Standard—7.7.4:** Use symbolic equations to show how the quantity of something changes over time or in response to changes in other quantities.

Also covers: 7.2.7 (Detailed standards begin on page IN8.)

# section 3

# Momentum

## Mass and Inertia

The world you live in is filled with objects in motion. How can you describe these objects? Objects have many properties such as color, size, and composition. One important property of an object is its mass. The **mass** of an object is the amount of matter in the object. In SI units, the unit for mass is the kilogram.

The weight of an object is related to the object's mass. Objects with more mass weigh more than objects with less mass. A bowling ball has more mass than a pillow, so it weighs more than a pillow. However, the size of an object is not the same as the mass of the object. For example, a pillow is larger than a bowling ball, but the bowling ball has more mass.

Objects with different masses are different in an important way. Think about what happens when you try to stop someone who is rushing toward you. A small child is easy to stop. A large adult is hard to stop. The more mass an object has, the harder it is to start it moving, slow it down, speed it up, or turn it. This tendency of an object to resist a change in its motion is called **inertia**. Objects with more mass have more inertia, as shown in **Figure 12.** The more mass an object has, the harder it is to change its motion.

**Reading Check** *What is inertia?*

### as you read

**What You'll Learn**
- **Explain** the relationship between mass and inertia.
- **Define** momentum.
- **Predict** motion using the law of conservation of momentum.

**Why It's Important**

Objects in motion have momentum. The motion of objects after they collide depends on their momentum.

**Review Vocabulary**
**triple-beam balance:** scientific instrument used to measure mass precisely by comparing the mass of a sample to known masses

**New Vocabulary**
- mass
- inertia
- momentum
- law of conservation of momentum

**Figure 12** The more mass an object has, the greater its inertia is. A table-tennis ball responds to a gentle hit that would move a tennis ball only slightly.

SECTION 3 Momentum **333**

---

### Section 3 Resource Manager

**Chapter FAST FILE Resources**
Transparency Activity, p. 46
Directed Reading for Content Mastery, pp. 21, 22
Enrichment, p. 32

Lab Worksheets, pp. 5–6, 7–8
Reinforcement, p. 29
**Cultural Diversity,** p. 63

---

## 1 Motivate

**Bellringer**

**Section Focus Transparencies** also are available on the Interactive Chalkboard CD-ROM.
L2 ELL

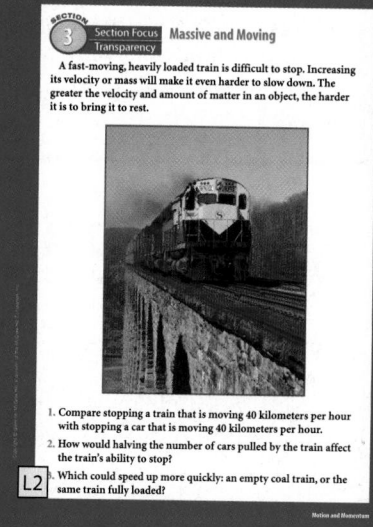

**Tie to Prior Knowledge**

**Dog Walking** Ask students if any of them have dogs they take for walks using a leash. Ask whether it is harder to hold back a charging German shepherd or a charging chihuahua. Tell students that the larger dog has more inertia than the small dog and that they will be studying inertia in this section.

## 2 Teach

**Reading Check**

**Answer** the tendency of an object to resist a change in its motion

**INTEGRATE Social Studies**

**Forensics and Momentum** Student answers will vary. Examples could be tracking a bullet's path, or the path of a person that has fallen from an elevated surface.

### Reading Check

**Answer** An object's momentum increases as its velocity increases and decreases as its velocity decreases.

### Applying Math

**Indiana Math Standards**
**Correlation to Mathematics Objectives**
7.2.1, 7.3.1

## Answers to Practice Problems

1. $p = mv = 10{,}000 \text{ kg} \times 15 \text{ m/s east}$
$= 150{,}000 \text{ kg·m/s east}$

2. $p = mv = 900 \text{ kg} \times 27 \text{ m/s north}$
$= 24{,}300 \text{ kg·m/s north}$

**INTEGRATE Social Studies**

**Forensics and Momentum** Forensic investigations of accidents and crimes often involve determining the momentum of an object. For example, the law of conservation of momentum sometimes is used to reconstruct the motion of vehicles involved in a collision. Research other ways momentum is used in forensic investigations.

# Momentum

You know that the faster a bicycle moves, the harder it is to stop. Just as increasing the mass of an object makes it harder to stop, so does increasing the speed or velocity of the object. The **momentum** of an object is a measure of how hard it is to stop the object, and it depends on the object's mass and velocity. Momentum is usually symbolized by $p$.

**Momentum Equation**
**momentum** (in kg · m/s) = **mass** (in kg) $\times$ **velocity** (in m/s)
$$p = mv$$

Mass is measured in kilograms and velocity has units of meters per second, so momentum has units of kilograms multiplied by meters per second (kg · m/s). Also, because velocity includes a direction, momentum has a direction that is the same as the direction of the velocity.

**Reading Check** *Explain how an object's momentum changes as its velocity changes.*

## Applying Math    Solve a Simple Equation

**MOMENTUM OF A BICYCLE** Calculate the momentum of a 14-kg bicycle traveling north at 2 m/s.

**Solution**

**1** *This is what you know:*
- mass: $m = 14$ kg
- velocity: $v = 2$ m/s north

**2** *This is what you need to find:*
momentum: $p = ?$ kg · m/s

**3** *This is the procedure you need to use:*
Substitute the known values of mass and velocity into the momentum equation and calculate the momentum:
$p = mv = (14 \text{ kg}) (2 \text{ m/s north}) = 28 \text{ kg · m/s north}$

**4** *Check your answer:*
Divide the calculated momentum by the mass of the bicycle. You should get the velocity that was given.

### Practice Problems

1. A 10,000-kg train is traveling east at 15 m/s. Calculate the momentum of the train.

2. What is the momentum of a car with a mass of 900 kg traveling north at 27 m/s?

 **Science Online** For more practice, visit in7.msscience.com/ math_practice

# Curriculum Connection

**Physical Education** Momentum and inertia are part of all sports. Ask each student to choose a sport and prepare a poster illustrating how momentum and inertia are important in that sport. Possibilities include the inertia of a runner racing around an oval track, the momentum of a soccer ball going past a goalie, and the inertia of a wrestler. L2  **Visual-Spatial** P

# Fun Fact

When an object falls toward Earth, its momentum downward is balanced by Earth's momentum upward — but Earth is so massive that its velocity is too tiny to be felt!

## Conservation of Momentum

If you've ever played billiards, you know that when the cue ball hits another ball, the motions of both balls change. The cue ball slows down and may change direction, so its momentum decreases. Meanwhile, the other ball starts moving, so its momentum increases. It seems as if momentum is transferred from the cue ball to the other ball.

In fact, during the collision, the momentum lost by the cue ball was gained by the other ball. This means that the total momentum of the two balls was the same just before and just after the collision. This is true for any collision, as long as no outside forces such as friction act on the objects and change their speeds after the collision. According to the **law of conservation of momentum,** the total momentum of objects that collide is the same before and after the collision. This is true for the collisions of the billiard balls shown in **Figure 13,** as well as for collisions of atoms, cars, football players, or any other matter.

## Using Momentum Conservation

Outside forces, such as gravity and friction, are almost always acting on objects that are colliding. However, sometimes, the effects of these forces are small enough that they can be ignored. Then the law of conservation of momentum enables you to predict how the motions of objects will change after a collision.

There are many ways that collisions can occur. Two examples are shown in **Figure 14.** Sometimes, the objects that collide will bounce off of each other, like the bowling ball and bowling pins. In other collisions, objects will stick to each other after the collision, like the two football players. In both of these types of collisions, the law of conservation of momentum enables the speeds of the objects after the collision to be calculated.

**Figure 13** When the cue ball hits the other billiard balls, it slows down because it transfers some of its momentum to the other billiard balls.
**Predict** *what would happen to the speed of the cue ball if all of its momentum were transferred to the other billiard balls.*

**Figure 14** In these collisions, the total momentum before the collision equals the total momentum after the collision.

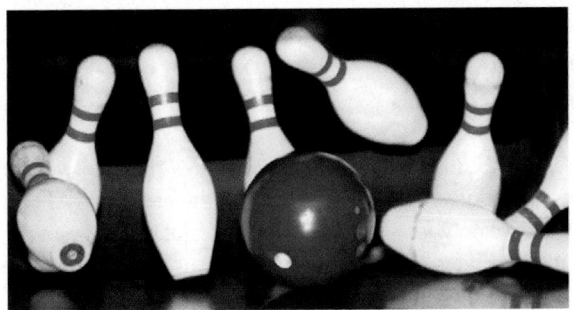

When the bowling ball hits the pins, some of its momentum is transferred to the pins. The ball slows down, and the pins speed up.

When one player tackles the other, they both change speeds, but momentum is conserved.

## Discussion

**Ball Motion** Suppose two balls approach each other at 1 m/s from opposite directions. Their total momentum is zero. After the collision, they both zoom off at 1 m/s in opposite directions. What is their momentum? It is still zero. What do you know about the masses of the two balls? If the total momentum is zero and the two balls have the same speed in opposite directions, the balls must have the same mass. **L2** **IS** **Logical-Mathematical**

## Quick Demo

**Momentum Conservation**

**Materials** ball, rolling cart or roller skates

**Estimated Time** 15 minutes

**Procedure** While sitting on a rolling cart or standing on roller skates, use both hands to throw a ball forcefully forward. Explain that, because you and the ball were initially at rest, the total initial momentum was zero. When you threw the ball, you gave it positive momentum in the forward direction. As a result, you started to roll backward (negative momentum) so that the total momentum would still be zero.

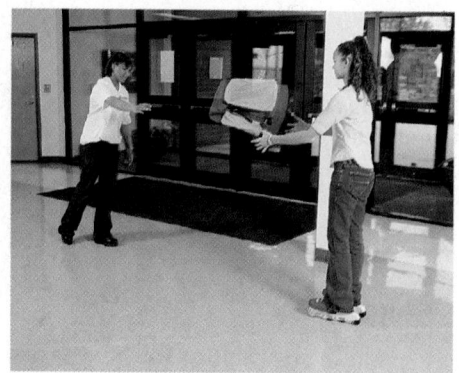

Before the student on skates and the backpack collide, she is not moving.

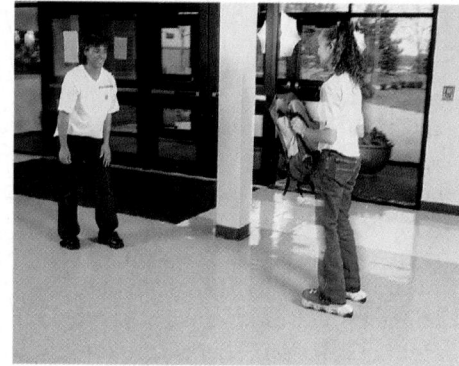

After the collision, the student and the backpack move together at a slower speed than the backpack had before the collision.

**Figure 15** Momentum is conserved in the collision of the backpack and the student.

### Science Online

**Topic: Collisions**

Visit in7.msscience.com for Web links to information about collisions between objects with different masses.

**Activity** Draw diagrams showing the results of collisions between a bowling ball and a tennis ball if they are moving in the same direction and if they are in opposite directions.

**Sticking Together** Imagine being on skates when someone throws a backpack to you, as in **Figure 15**. When you catch the backpack, you and the backpack continue to move in the same direction as the backpack was moving before the collision.

The law of conservation of momentum can be used to find your velocity after you catch the backpack. Suppose a 2-kg backpack is tossed at a speed of 5 m/s. Your mass is 48 kg, and initially you are at rest. Then the total initial momentum is

total momentum = momentum of backpack + your momentum
$$= 2 \text{ kg} \times 5 \text{ m/s} + 48 \text{ kg} \times 0 \text{ m/s}$$
$$= 10 \text{ kg} \cdot \text{m/s}$$

After the collision, the total momentum remains the same, and only one object is moving. Its mass is the sum of your mass and the mass of the backpack. You can use the equation for momentum to find the final velocity.

total momentum = (mass of backpack + your mass) × velocity
$$10 \text{ kg} \cdot \text{m/s} = (2 \text{ kg} + 48 \text{ kg}) \times \text{velocity}$$
$$10 \text{ kg} \cdot \text{m/s} = (50 \text{ kg}) \times \text{velocity}$$
$$0.2 \text{ m/s} = \text{velocity}$$

This is your velocity right after you catch the backpack. As you continue to move on your skates, the force of friction between the ground and the skates slows you down. Because of friction, the momentum of you and the backpack together continually decreases until you come to a stop. **Figure 16** shows the results of some collisions between two objects with various masses and velocities.

---

## LAB DEMONSTRATION

**Purpose** to observe and measure momentum during an inelastic collision

**Materials** 2 toy cars, 2 metersticks, balance, timer

**Preparation** Set up a straight course bounded by two metersticks set end to end.

**Procedure** Measure and record the mass of each toy car. Place one car at the zero mark of the second meterstick. Push the other car so that it starts rolling at the zero mark of the first meterstick and hits the first car. Measure the time it takes the rolling car to reach the standing car, and measure the time and distance the two cars roll after the collision. Calculate the momentum before and after the collision.

### Assessment

Was momentum conserved in this collision? Answers will depend on experimental results. If not, why not? Friction caused the toy cars to slow down, so their total momentum decreased.

**Figure 16**

The law of conservation of momentum can be used to predict the results of collisions between different objects, whether they are subatomic particles smashing into each other at enormous speeds, or the collisions of marbles, as shown on this page. What happens when one marble hits another marble initially at rest? The results of the collisions depend on the masses of the marbles.

**A** Here, a less massive marble strikes a more massive marble that is at rest. After the collision, the smaller marble bounces off in the opposite direction. The larger marble moves in the same direction that the small marble was initially moving.

**B** Here, the large marble strikes the small marble that is at rest. After the collision, both marbles move in the same direction. The less massive marble always moves faster than the more massive one.

**C** If two objects of the same mass moving at the same speed collide head-on, they will rebound and move with the same speed in the opposite direction. The total momentum is zero before and after the collision.

SECTION 3 Momentum **337**

## Visualizing Conservation of Momentum

Have students examine the pictures and read the captions. Then ask the following questions.

If a small car is stopped at a traffic light and is hit from behind by a truck, what will happen? Both vehicles will move forward, with the car moving faster than the truck.

What will happen if two marbles of the same mass, traveling toward each other, collide? The marbles will collide and reverse directions, moving away from each other at the same speed as before the collision.

### Activity

**Marble Tracks** Have small groups of students tape two metersticks to a flat surface. The space between them should be wide enough to allow marbles to travel in the space. Have students form a ramp by placing one end of a grooved ruler on two or three books and the other end at one end of the track. They should place three marbles in the track and roll one marble down the ruler into the track and observe what happens. Ask students to repeat the procedure rolling two and three marbles down the ramp together. Ask them to explain their observations in terms of conservation of momentum. L2 IS **Kinesthetic**

## Differentiated Instruction

**Challenge** Have students research collision tests that are used to rate cars. Ask them to present oral reports on the tests and how the conservation of momentum applies. L3 IS **Linguistic**

### Check for Understanding

**Logical-Mathematical** Ask students to calculate the final velocity of the baseball in the following problem: A tennis ball (57 g) is rolling at a velocity of 5 m/s north. It collides with a baseball (142 g) that is initially at rest. The tennis ball bounces off at a speed of 2 m/s in the opposite direction. (Assume the collision is perfectly elastic.) 2.8 m/s north

### Reteach

**Inertia** Toss a table-tennis ball, tennis ball, and basketball to students. Have the students compare the amounts of force they had to use to stop the three balls and the inertias of the three balls. It took the most force to stop the basketball, which had the most inertia. It took less force to stop the tennis ball, which had less inertia than the basketball. It took very little force to stop the table-tennis ball, which had the least inertia. L2 ELL IS Kinesthetic

### ☑ Assessment

**Process** Ask students to design an experiment to demonstrate qualitatively what happens to velocity in different collisions. Use **Performance Assessment in the Science Classroom,** p. 95.

**Figure 17** When bumper cars collide, they bounce off each other, and momentum is transferred.

**Colliding and Bouncing Off** In some collisions, the objects involved, like the bumper cars in **Figure 17,** bounce off each other. The law of conservation of momentum can be used to determine how these objects move after they collide.

For example, suppose two identical objects moving with the same speed collide head on and bounce off. Before the collision, the momentum of each object is the same, but in opposite directions. So the total momentum before the collision is zero. If momentum is conserved, the total momentum after the collision must be zero also. This means that the two objects must move in opposite directions with the same speed after the collision. Then the total momentum once again is zero.

---

### section **3** review

#### Summary

**Mass, Inertia, and Momentum**

- Mass is the amount of matter in an object.
- Inertia is the tendency of an object to resist a change in motion. Inertia increases as the mass of an object increases.
- The momentum of an object in motion is related to how hard it is to stop the object, and can be calculated from the following equation:
  $$p = mv$$
- Because velocity has a direction, momentum also has a direction.

**The Law of Conservation of Momentum**

- The law of conservation of momentum states that in a collision, the total momentum of the objects that collide is the same before and after the collision.

#### Self Check

1. **Explain** how momentum is transferred when a golfer hits a ball with a golf club.
2. **Determine** if the momentum of an object moving in a circular path at constant speed is constant.
3. **Explain** why the momentum of a billiard ball rolling on a billiard table changes.
4. **Think Critically** Two identical balls move directly toward each other with equal speeds. How will the balls move if they collide and stick together?

##### Applying Math

5. **Calculate Momentum** What is the momentum of a 0.1-kg mass moving with a speed of 5 m/s?
6. **Calculate Speed** A 1-kg ball moving at 3 m/s strikes a 2-kg ball and stops. If the 2-kg ball was initially at rest, find its speed after the collision.

**338 CHAPTER 11** Motion and Momentum

Science Online in7.msscience.com/self_check_quiz

---

### section **3** review

1. Some of the momentum of the moving club is transferred to the ball when the club collides with the ball.

2. No, because momentum depends on velocity and velocity includes direction, which is constantly changing.

3. The momentum of a rolling billiard ball decreases because its velocity decreases as a result of friction with the table.

4. Momentum must be conserved. Before the collision, the momentum is zero because $m_1v_1 = -m_2v_2$, so $m_1v_1 + m_2v_2 = 0$. After the collision, the momentum must also be zero. If the balls stick together, the only way for momentum to be zero is if the balls are at rest ($v = 0$).

5. $p = 0.1$ kg $\times$ 5 m/s $= 0.5$ kg·m/s

6. Before the collision, the momentum is 1 kg $\times$ 3 m/s left + 2 kg $\times$ 0 m/s = 3 kg·m/s left. After the collision, the momentum must also be 3 kg·m/s left, so 1 kg $\times$ $v$ = 3 kg·m/s. $v$ = 3 kg·m/s left $\div$ 2 kg = 1.5 m/s left.

# Collisions

A collision occurs when a baseball bat hits a baseball or a tennis racket hits a tennis ball. What would happen if you hit a baseball with a table-tennis paddle or a table-tennis ball with a baseball bat? How do the masses of colliding objects change the results of collisions?

## ▶ Real-World Question

How does changing the size and number of objects in a collision affect the collision?

### Goals
■ **Compare and contrast** different collisions.
■ **Determine** how the speeds after a collision depend on the masses of the colliding objects.

### Materials
small marbles (5)          metersticks (2)
large marbles (2)          tape

### Safety Precautions 🥽 🧤

## ▶ Procedure

1. Tape the metersticks next to each other, slightly farther apart than the width of the large marbles. This limits the motion of the marbles to nearly a straight line.

2. Place a small target marble in the center of the track formed by the metersticks. Place another small marble at one end of the track. Flick the small marble toward the target marble. Describe the collision.

3. Repeat step 2, replacing the two small marbles with the two large marbles.

4. Repeat step 2, replacing the small shooter marble with a large marble.

5. Repeat step 2, replacing the small target marble with a large marble.

6. Repeat step 2, replacing the small target marble with four small marbles that are touching.

7. Place two small marbles at opposite ends of the metersticks. Shoot the marbles toward each other and describe the collision.

8. Place two large marbles at opposite ends of the metersticks. Shoot the marbles toward each other and describe the collision.

9. Place a small marble and a large marble at opposite ends of the metersticks. Shoot the marbles toward each other and describe the collision.

## ▶ Conclude and Apply

1. **Describe** In which collisions did the shooter marble change direction? How did the mass of the target marble compare with the mass of the shooter marble in these collisions?

2. **Explain** how momentum was conserved in these collisions.

### *C*ommunicating
**Your Data**

Make a chart showing your results. You might want to make before-and-after sketches, with short arrows to show slow movement and long arrows to show fast movement.

---

## ▶ Real-World Question

**Purpose** Students observe the changes in momentum occurring in different collisions. L2 LS **Kinesthetic**

**Process Skills** identify and manipulate variables, observe and infer, interpret data, draw conclusions

**Time Required** 50 minutes

## ▶ Procedure

**Safety Precautions** Make sure no loose marbles remain on the classroom floor when the experiment is done.

**Teaching Strategy** Caution students not to shoot the marbles so hard that they bounce or make the other marbles jump when they hit them.

## ▶ Conclude and Apply

1. The shooter marble changed direction when it hit a target marble with more mass than itself.
2. by being transferred from the shooter marble to the target marble, slowing down or stopping the shooter marble and setting the target marble in motion

---

## ☑ Assessment

**Process** Predict what will happen when a small shooter marble hits a line of five large target marbles. The shooter marble will stop, and the last target marble in line will be set in motion, with a velocity smaller than that of the shooter marble. Use **Performance Assessment in the Science Classroom,** p. 89.

### *C*ommunicating
**Your Data**

Students can work together on a large chart to be displayed as a class poster.

## Real-World Question

**Purpose** Students will construct a car that will protect an egg from a rapid deceleration.

**Time Required** approximately 70 minutes

**Alternate Materials** The list for materials that can be used to create the car is nearly endless. Don't use items that are sharp or breakable.

**Safety Precautions** Because the cars are intended to crash, students should wear safety goggles.

## Form a Hypothesis

**Possible Hypothesis** The egg will be most likely to survive in a car that gradually brings the egg to a stop, thus cushioning it.

## Test Your Hypothesis

**Possible Procedures** The car must roll freely to be fast. The egg must be protected or slowed gradually to a stop by some sort of layers or barriers or restraints.

**Teaching Strategy** Students will often have elaborate and complex ideas that may be too difficult to be practical. Try to steer them clear of such ideas without stifling their creativity

# Design Your Own

# Car Safety Testing

**Goals**
■ **Construct** a fast car.
■ **Design** a safe car that will protect a plastic egg from the effects of inertia when the car crashes.

**Possible Materials**
insulated foam meat trays or fast food trays
insulated foam cups
straws, narrow and wide
straight pins
tape
plastic eggs

**Safety Precautions**

⬚ ⬚ ⬚

**WARNING:** *Protect your eyes from possible flying objects.*

## Real-World Question

Imagine that you are a car designer. How can you create an attractive, fast car that is safe? When a car crashes, the passengers have inertia that can keep them moving. How can you protect the passengers from stops caused by sudden, head-on impacts?

## Form a Hypothesis

Develop a hypothesis about how to design a car to deliver a plastic egg quickly and safely through a race course and a crash at the end.

## Test Your Hypothesis

**Make a Plan**

1. Be sure your group has agreed on the hypothesis statement.

2. **Sketch** the design for your car. List the materials you will need. Remember that to make the car move smoothly, narrow straws will have to fit into the wider straws.

## Differentiated Instruction

**Learning Disabled** Students who have learning challenges are sometimes good at manipulating or building things. Perhaps one student in a group could design an idea and another could physically create it.

## Alternative Inquiry Lab

**Car Materials** To make this Lab an Inquiry Lab, allow students to propose and use alternative materials in the construction of their cars.

3. As a group, make a detailed list of the steps you will take to test your hypothesis.

4. Gather the materials you will need to carry out your experiment.

**Follow Your Plan**

1. Make sure your teacher approves your plan before you start. Include any changes suggested by your teacher in your plans.

2. Carry out the experiment as planned.

3. **Record** any observations that you made while doing your experiment. Include suggestions for improving your design.

### Analyze Your Data

1. **Compare** your car design to the designs of the other groups. What made the fastest car fast? What slowed the slowest car?

2. **Compare** your car's safety features to those of the other cars. What protected the eggs the best? How could you improve the unsuccessful designs?

3. **Predict** What effect would decreasing the speed of your car have on the safety of the egg?

### Conclude and Apply

1. **Summarize** How did the best designs protect the egg?

2. **Apply** If you were designing cars, what could you do to better protect passengers from sudden stops?

**Communicating Your Data**

**Write** a descriptive paragraph about ways a car could be designed to protect its passengers effectively. Include a sketch of your ideas.

**Expected Outcome** Cars that cushioned their eggs will be most successful. Students should try to discover why some were successful and others weren't.

### Analyze Your Data

**Answers to Questions**

1. Reducing friction and air resistance makes the cars go faster.

2. Eggs with layers of protection to gradually slow them to a stop work best. Such protections have the same effects as car seat belts and air bags.

3. Decreasing the speed would give the egg a better chance for survival because the egg would experience a smaller deceleration during a crash.

**Error Analysis** Ask students to name features that allowed eggs to survive.

### Conclude and Apply

1. The best designs protected the egg in the same way seat belts and airbags protect people.

2. Provide devices to restrain people from being thrown as the car stops.

**Assessment**

**Content** Divide the class into groups and ask each group to develop and perform a short skit comparing the cart with the egg to a real car carrying people. Use **Performance Assessment in the Science Classroom,** p. 147.

**Active Reading**

**Synthesis Journal** In this strategy, students reflect on a project, paper, or performance in light of their own experiences and plan to apply it personally. Ask students to write a Synthesis Journal entry for this activity. Have each student divide a sheet of paper into three sections. For this activity, have them record *What I did, What I learned,* and *How I can use it.*

**Communicating Your Data**

To complete their writing, students could also briefly research how the automobile industry tests vehicle safety. Students may also find photos or videos of industry tests to incorporate into their writing.

# Oops! Accidents in SCIENCE

## Content Background

Not all boomerangs return to their throwers. A true boomerang is nothing more than a curved stick that is thrown. The early boomerangs used for hunting by peoples of many ancient cultures (including many tribes in the western United States) were much longer, straighter, and heavier than the more familiar returning types. Returning boomerangs are too light and thin to do much damage to any living thing. Returning boomerangs became popular primarily as playthings for Aborigines in Australia. Some hunters there used them to imitate hawks in flight and so to serve as a decoy to drive other game birds into nets strung from trees. Otherwise, they don't have any real practical uses because they are difficult to throw very accurately. They also probably wouldn't have enough momentum to return to the thrower after hitting something.

## Activity

**Varying Throw Angle** Take students outside and have volunteers throw boomerangs first from a horizontal starting position and then from varying angles. Ask students what is different about the paths of the boomerangs. A boomerang thrown from a horizontal position flies off until it stops spinning and then falls. Boomerangs thrown at different angles curve. Explain to students that when a boomerang is thrown from an angle slightly different from the horizontal, the motions of its wings and its speed through the air cause it to experience a force that makes it circle back to the thrower. L2 LS
**Kinesthetic**

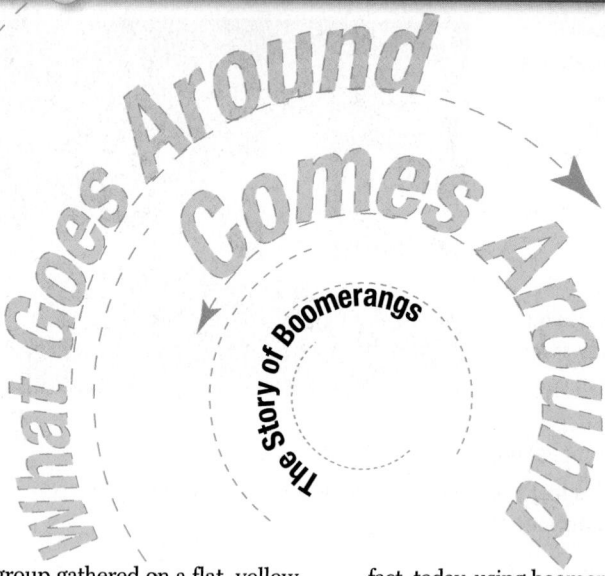

## What Goes Around Comes Around

### The Story of Boomerangs

Imagine a group gathered on a flat, yellow plain on the Australian Outback. One youth steps forward and, with the flick of an arm, sends a long, flat, angled stick soaring and spinning into the sky. The stick's path curves until it returns right back into the thrower's hand. Thrower after thrower steps forward, and the contest goes on all afternoon.

This contest involved throwing boomerangs—elegantly curved sticks. Because of how boomerangs are shaped, they always return to the thrower's hand

This amazing design is over 15,000 years old. Scientists believe that boomerangs developed from simple clubs thrown to stun and kill animals for food. Differently shaped clubs flew in different ways. As the shape of the club was refined, people probably started throwing them for fun too. In fact, today, using boomerangs for fun is still a popular sport, as world-class throwers compete in contests of strength and skill.

Boomerangs come in several forms, but all of them have several things in common. First a boomerang is shaped like an airplane's wing: flat on one side and curved on the other. Second, boomerangs are angled, which makes them spin as they fly. These two features determine the aerodynamics that give the boomerang its unique flight path.

From its beginning as a hunting tool to its use in today's World Boomerang Championships, the boomerang has remained a source of fascination for thousands of years.

**Design** Boomerangs are made from various materials. Research to find instructions for making boomerangs. After you and your friends build some boomerangs, have a competition of your own.

Science Online
For more information, visit in7.msscience.com/oops

**Design** Possible competitions might include the best catch, longest flight time, and greatest curvature in flight. Students might also construct targets to hit or paper barriers to curve through. Caution students that, although boomerangs are very light, they can hit hard when moving fast, so students should be careful when throwing them and wear protective goggles and gloves.

## Resources for Teachers and Students

*Boomerang: Behind an Australian Icon*, by Philip Jones, Ten Speed Press, 1997

*Many Happy Returns*, Quarterly Newsletter of the United States Boomerang Association

## Reviewing Main Ideas

**Section 1** **What is motion?**

1. The position of an object depends on the reference point that is chosen.

2. An object is in motion if the position of the object is changing.

3. The speed of an object equals the distance traveled divided by the time:
$$s = \frac{d}{t}$$

4. The velocity of an object includes the speed and the direction of motion.

5. The motion of an object can be represented on a speed-time graph.

**Section 2** **Acceleration**

1. Acceleration is a measure of how quickly velocity changes. It includes a direction.

2. An object is accelerating when it speeds up, slows down, or turns.

3. When an object moves in a straight line, its acceleration can be calculated by
$$a = \frac{(s_f - s_i)}{t}$$

**Section 3** **Momentum**

1. Momentum equals the mass of an object times its velocity:
$$p = mv$$

2. Momentum is transferred from one object to another in a collision.

3. According to the law of conservation of momentum, the total amount of momentum of a group of objects doesn't change unless outside forces act on the objects.

### Reviewing Main Ideas

Summary statements can be used by students to review the major concepts of the chapter.

### Visualizing Main Ideas

See student page.

**Science** Online

**Visit** in7.msscience.com
/self_check_quiz
/interactive_tutor
/vocabulary_puzzlemaker
/chapter_review
/standards_review

## Visualizing Main Ideas

*Copy and complete the following table on motion.*

### Describing Motion

| Quantity | Definition | Direction |
|---|---|---|
| Distance | length of path traveled | no |
| Displacement | direction and change in position | yes |
| Speed | rate of change in position | no |
| Velocity | rate of change in position and direction | yes |
| Acceleration | rate of change in velocity | yes |
| Momentum | mass times velocity | yes |

---

## ◇ Identifying Misconceptions

**Assess**

Use the assessment as follow-up to page F at the beginning of the chapter after students have completed the chapter.

**Materials** protractor, paper, ruler, string

**Procedure** Have each student use the protractor to draw a large circle and label four

points 90 degrees apart A, B, C and D. Have them place an object at point A, and tell them the object will travel around the circle. Their mission is to find the object's distance trav-

eled and displacement at points B, C, and D. Tell them the top of the paper is north.

**Expected Outcome** Ways to find the distance traveled include using a string to measure the circle or using the formula for the perimeter of a circle.

## Using Vocabulary

1. Both measure rate of change in position, but velocity includes a direction.

2. Both are rates of change in motion. Velocity is the rate of change in position, and acceleration is the rate of change in velocity.

3. Momentum is mass multiplied by velocity. The higher the velocity, the higher the momentum.

4. The law of conservation of momentum states that the total momentum of a group of objects is the same before and after they collide unless some outside force acts on the objects.

5. Momentum is mass multiplied by velocity. The higher the mass, the higher the momentum.

6. Mass is a measure of inertia.

7. An object always has inertia. It only has momentum when it is in motion. Both indicate how hard it is to change the object's motion.

8. Both measure rate of change in position. Instantaneous speed gives the speed at a moment in time; average speed gives the average of instantaneous speeds over a given time or distance interval.

## Checking Concepts

9. D
10. A
11. C
12. C
13. D
14. B
15. C
16. D
17. C
18. C

## Using Vocabulary

| | |
|---|---|
| acceleration p. 328 | mass p. 333 |
| average speed p. 325 | momentum p. 334 |
| inertia p. 333 | speed p. 324 |
| instantaneous speed p. 325 | velocity p. 327 |
| law of conservation of momentum p. 335 | |

*Explain the relationship between each pair of terms.*

1. speed—velocity

2. velocity—acceleration

3. velocity—momentum

4. momentum—law of conservation of momentum

5. mass—momentum

6. mass—inertia

7. momentum—inertia

8. average speed—instantaneous speed

## Checking Concepts

*Choose the word or phrase that best answers the question.*

9. What measures the quantity of matter?
   A) speed          C) acceleration
   B) weight          D) mass

10. Which of the following objects is NOT accelerating?
    A) a jogger moving at a constant speed
    B) a car that is slowing down
    C) Earth orbiting the Sun
    D) a car that is speeding up

11. Which of the following equals speed?
    A) acceleration/time
    B) (change in velocity)/time
    C) distance/time
    D) displacement/time

12. A parked car is hit by a moving car, and the two cars stick together. How does the speed of the combined cars compare to the speed of the car before the collision?
    A) The combined speed is the same.
    B) The combined speed is greater.
    C) The combined speed is smaller.
    D) Any of these could be true.

13. What is a measure of inertia?
    A) weight          C) momentum
    B) gravity          D) mass

14. What is 18 cm/h north an example of?
    A) speed
    B) velocity
    C) acceleration
    D) momentum

15. Ball A bumps into ball B. Which is the same before and after the collision?
    A) the momentum of ball A
    B) the momentum of ball B
    C) the sum of the momentums
    D) the difference in the momentums

16. Which of the following equals the change in velocity divided by the time?
    A) speed
    B) displacement
    C) momentum
    D) acceleration

17. You travel to a city 200 km away in 2.5 hours. What is your average speed in km/h?
    A) 180 km/h          C) 80 km/h
    B) 12.5 km/h          D) 500 km/h

18. Two objects collide and stick together. How does the total momentum change?
    A) Total momentum increases.
    B) Total momentum decreases.
    C) The total momentum doesn't change.
    D) The total momentum is zero.

 Science Online in7.msscience.com/vocabulary_puzzlemaker

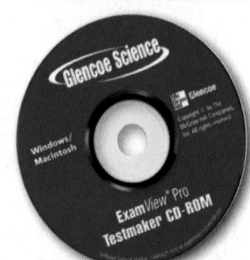

**Use the Exam*View*® Pro Testmaker CD-ROM to:**
- create multiple versions of tests
- create modified tests with one mouse click for inclusion students
- edit existing questions and add your own questions
- build tests aligned with state standards using built-in State Curriculum Tags
- change English tests to Spanish with one mouse click and vice versa

## Thinking Critically

19. **Explain** You run 100 m in 25 s. If you later run the same distance in less time, explain if your average speed increase or decrease.

**Use the graph below to answer questions 20 and 21.**

Speed Versus Time

20. **Compare** For the motion of the object plotted on the speed-time graph above, how does the acceleration between 0 s and 3 s compare to the acceleration between 3 s and 5 s?

21. **Calculate** the acceleration of the object over the time interval from 0 s to 3 s.

22. **Infer** The molecules in a gas are often modeled as small balls. If the molecules all have the same mass, infer what happens if two molecules traveling at the same speed collide head on.

23. **Calculate** What is your displacement if you walk 100 m north, 20 m east, 30 m south, 50 m west, and then 70 m south?

24. **Infer** You are standing on ice skates and throw a basketball forward. Infer how your motion after you throw the basketball compares with the motion of the basketball.

25. **Determine** You throw a ball upward and then it falls back down. How does the velocity of the ball change as it rises and falls?

**Use the graph below to answer question 26.**

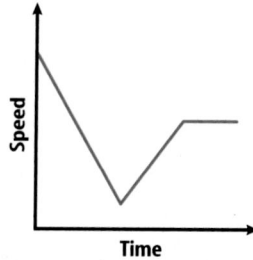

26. **Make and Use Graphs** The motion of a car is plotted on the speed-time graph above. Over which section of the graph is the acceleration of the car zero?

## Performance Activities

27. **Demonstrate** Design a racetrack and make rules that specify the types of motion allowed. Demonstrate how to measure distance, measure time, and calculate speed accurately.

## Applying Math

28. **Speed of a Ball** Calculate the speed of a 2-kg ball that has a momentum of 10 kg · m/s.

29. **Distance Traveled** A car travels for a half hour at a speed of 40 km/h. How far does the car travel?

**Use the graph below to answer question 30.**

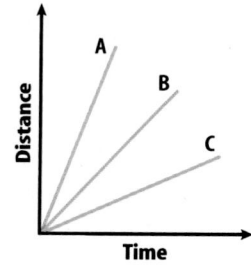

30. **Speed** From the graph determine which object is moving the fastest and which is moving the slowest.

## Thinking Critically

19. It increases; when you divide the same distance by a smaller time, the speed increases.

20. The acceleration between 0 s and 3 s is greater because the slope of this part of the line is steeper.

21. $1 \text{ m/s}^2$

22. The molecules reverse direction and travel at the same speed away from each other.

23. 30 m west

24. The basketball and I experience the same force in opposite directions, so we are accelerated in opposite directions. The basketball's acceleration is greater than my acceleration because its mass is lower.

25. The ball slows down as it moves upward, comes to a stop at the top of the throw, and speeds up as it falls back down

26. the horizontal section

## Performance Activities

27. Check students' work. Use **Performance Assessment in the Science Classroom**, p. 145.

## Applying Math

**Indiana Math Standards**
7.2.1, 7.3.1, 7.6.1

28. 10 kg·m/s ÷ 2 kg = 5 m/s

29. 40 km/h × 0.5 h = 20 km

30. Object A is moving fastest; object C is moving slowest.

---

## ✓ Assessment  Resources

📁 **Reproducible Masters**
**Chapter** *Fast File* **Resources**
   Chapter Review, pp. 37–38
   Chapter Tests, pp. 39–42
   Assessment Transparency Activity, p. 49
**Glencoe Science Web site**
   Chapter Review Test
   IN Standards Review

**Glencoe Technology**
   👆 Assessment Transparency
   ⓘ Exam*View*® Pro Testmaker
   ▭ MindJogger Videoquiz
   ⓘ Interactive Chalkboard

**Answer Sheet** A practice answer sheet can be found at in7.msscience.com/answer_sheet.

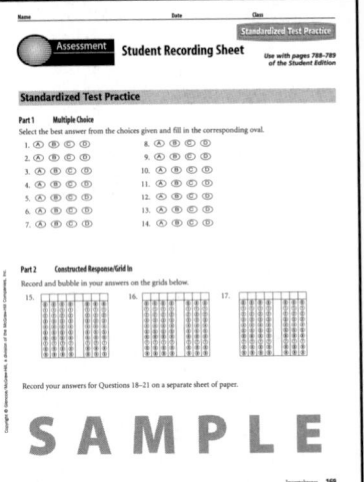

**SAMPLE**

---

### Part 1 | Multiple Choice

**1.** A
**2.** A
**3.** A
**4.** A
**5.** C
**6.** D
**7.** D
**8.** C

### Part 2 | Critical Response

**9.** Its speed is decreasing as it rises and increasing as it falls. Its velocity is changing the whole time because its speed and direction are changing. The acceleration of the ball is downward, so the ball's path turns in that direction.

**10.** The ball has positive acceleration when it is falling because it is speeding up. It has negative acceleration when it is rising because it is slowing down.

---

The assessed Indiana standard appears above the question.

*Record your answers on the answer sheet provided by your teacher or on a sheet of paper.*

### Part 1 | Multiple Choice

The illustration below show the position of a ball at one-second time intervals.

**7.7.4**

**1.** Over which time period is the ball's average speed largest?

  **A** 0 s to 1 s

  **B** 1 s to 2 s

  **C** 2 s to 3 s

  **D** 3 s to 4 s

**7.7.4**

**2.** What is the average speed of the ball over the 3-m distance in the illustration above?

  **A** 0.75 m/s

  **B** 1.0 m/s

  **C** 1.25 m/s

  **D** 1.5 m/s

---

**7.7.4**

**3.** A car's speed changes from 15 m/s to 30 m/s in 3.0 s. What is the car's acceleration?

  **A** 5 m/s$^2$

  **B** 10 m/s$^2$

  **C** 15 m/s$^2$

  **D** 45 m/s$^2$

The graph below shows a speed-time graph.

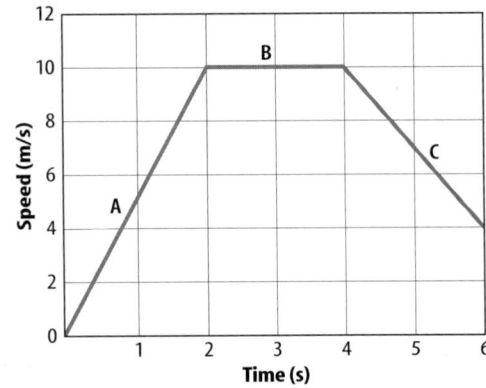

**7.7.4**

**4.** What is the acceleration over the time interval 4 s to 6 s?

  **A** $-3$ m/s$^2$

  **B** $-1.5$ m/s$^2$

  **C** 1.5 m/s$^2$

  **D** 3 m/s$^2$

**7.7.4**

**5.** Over what time interval is the speed of the object constant in the graph above?

  **A** 0 s to 1 s

  **B** 1 s to 2 s

  **C** 2 s to 3 s

  **D** 4 s to 5 s

---

**11.** Her average speed was 2 km/0.5 h = 4 km/h. It is impossible to know her instantaneous speed at 3:15 because she may not have been walking at a constant speed. Only her average speed can be found.

**12.** No; because even if the speed is constant, the car could be changing direction, which is also a form of acceleration.

**7.7.4**

**6.** A car travels for 5.5 h at an average speed of 75 km/h. How far did the car travel?

**A** 13.6 km

**B** 53.9 km

**C** 75 km

**D** 412.5 km

**7.** What is the momentum of a 21-kg bicycle traveling west at 3.0 m/s?

**A** 7 kg · m/s west

**B** 18 kg · m/s west

**C** 24 kg · m/s west

**D** 63 kg · m/s west

**7.7.4**

**8.** The graph below shows the motion of two students.

**Distance v. Time**

How does the speed of student A compare to the speed of student B?

**A** It is half as large.

**B** It is the same.

**C** It is twice as large.

**D** It is three times as large.

---

**Part 2** **Critical Response**

The illustration below shows the path of a ball.

**9.** Describe the motion of the ball in terms of its speed, velocity, and acceleration.

**10.** During which part of its path does the ball have positive acceleration? During which part of its path does it have negative acceleration? Explain.

**11.** A girl leaves school at 3:00 and starts walking home. Her house is 2 km from school. She gets home at 3:30. What was her average speed? Do you know her instantaneous speed at 3:15? Why or why not?

**12.** If a car is moving with a constant speed, can you be certain the car is not accelerating? Explain.

**Test-Taking Tip**

**Look for Missing Information** Questions sometimes will ask about missing information. Notice what is missing as well as what is given.

---

## Rubrics

The following rubric is a sample scoring device for critical response questions.

**Critical Response**

| Points | Description |
|---|---|
| 4 | The student demonstrates a thorough understanding of the science of the task. The response may contain minor flaws that do not detract from the demonstration of a thorough understanding. |
| 3 | The student demonstrates an understanding of the science of the task. The response is essentially correct and demonstrates an essential but less than thorough understanding of the science. |
| 2 | The student demonstrates only a partial understanding of the science of the task. Although the student may have used the correct approach to a solution or may have provided a correct solution, the work lacks an essential understanding of the underlying science concepts. |
| 1 | The student demonstrates a very limited understanding of the science of the task. The response is incomplete and exhibits many flaws. |
| 0 | The student provides a completely incorrect solution or no response at all. |

| Section/Objectives | Standards | | Labs/Features |
|---|---|---|---|
| **Chapter Opener** | National | State/Local | **Launch Lab:** How do forces affect a ball? p. 349 <br> **Foldables,** p. 349 |
| | See pp. 16T–17T for a Key to Standards. | Detailed standards begin on page IN8. | |
| **Section 1  Newton's First Law** <br> 🕐 2 sessions <br> 📦 1 block <br><br> 1. **Distinguish** between balanced and net forces. <br> 2. **Describe** Newton's first law of motion. <br> 3. **Explain** how friction affects motion. | National Content Standards: UCP.1–UCP.3, UCP.5, A.1, A.2, B.1, G.2, G.3 | Indiana Standards: 7.1.5, 7.3.17, 7.7.4 | **Integrate Life Science,** p. 351 <br> **Science Online,** p. 353 <br> **MiniLAB:** Observing Friction, p. 354 |
| **Section 2  Newton's Second Law** <br> 🕐 3 sessions <br> 📦 1.5 blocks <br><br> 4. **Explain** Newton's second law of motion. <br> 5. **Explain** why the direction of force is important. | National Content Standards: UCP.1–UCP.3, UCP.5, A.1, A.2, B.1–B.3 | Indiana Standards: 7.1.5, 7.3.17 | **Integrate History,** p. 357 <br> **Applying Math:** Acceleration of a Car, p. 359 |
| **Section 3  Newton's Third Law** <br> 🕐 4 sessions <br> 📦 2 blocks <br><br> 6. **Identify** the relationship between the forces that objects exert on each other. | National Content Standards: UCP.1–UCP.3, UCP.5, A.1, B.1–B.3, F.5 | Indiana Standards: 7.2.6, 7.3.17 | **Science Online,** p. 364 <br> **Visualizing Newton's Laws in Sports,** p. 365 <br> **MiniLAB:** Measuring Force Pairs, p. 367 <br> **Lab:** Balloon Races, p. 369 <br> **Lab:** Modeling Motion in Two Directions, pp. 370–371 <br> **Science and Society:** Air Bag Safety, p. 372 |

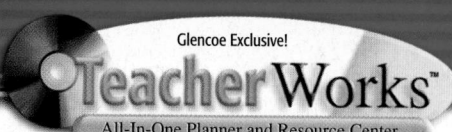
| Lab Materials | Reproducible Resources | Section Assessment | Technology |
|---|---|---|---|
| **Launch Lab:** metersticks (2), books (3), marble | **Chapter *FAST FILE* Resources**<br>Foldables Worksheet, p. 17<br>Directed Reading Overview, p. 19<br>Note-taking Worksheets, pp. 33–35 | GLENCOE'S<br>**ASSESSMENT**<br>ADVANTAGE | **Teacher Works** includes:<br>• Interactive Teacher Edition<br>• Lesson Planner with calendar<br>• Access to all program blacklines<br>• Correlations to standards<br>• Web links |
| **MiniLAB:** flat bar of soap, flat eraser, key, hard-sided notebook | **Chapter *FAST FILE* Resources**<br>Transparency Activity, p. 44<br>MiniLAB, p. 3<br>Lab Activity, pp. 9–12<br>Enrichment, p. 30<br>Reinforcement, p. 27<br>Directed Reading, p. 20<br>Transparency Activity, pp. 47–48<br>**Home and Community Involvement,** p. 23 | **Portfolio**<br>Assessment, p. 355<br>**Performance**<br>MiniLAB, p. 354<br>Applying Skills, p. 355<br>**Content**<br>Section Review, p. 355 | Section Focus Transparency<br>Teaching Transparency<br>Guided Reading Audio Program<br>Interactive Chalkboard CD-ROM |
| *Need materials?* Contact Science Kit at 1-800-828-7777 or www.sciencekit.com on the Internet. | **Chapter *FAST FILE* Resources**<br>Transparency Activity, p. 45<br>Lab Activity, pp. 13–16<br>Enrichment, p. 31<br>Reinforcement, p. 28<br>Directed Reading, p. 21<br>Transparency Activity, pp. 47–48<br>**Mathematics Skill Activities,** p. 9 | **Performance**<br>Applying Math, p. 359<br>Applying Math, p. 362<br>**Content**<br>Section Review, p. 362 | Section Focus Transparency<br>Virtual Labs CD-ROM<br>Guided Reading Audio Program<br>Interactive Chalkboard CD-ROM |
| **MiniLAB:** spring scales (2),<br>**Lab:** balloons of different sizes and shapes, drinking straws, string, tape, meterstick, stopwatch<br>**Lab:** masking tape, stop-watch, meterstick, spring scales (2), plastic lid, golf ball | **Chapter *FAST FILE* Resources**<br>Transparency Activity, p. 46<br>MiniLAB, p. 4<br>Enrichment, p. 32<br>Reinforcement, p. 29<br>Directed Reading, pp. 20, 22<br>Lab Worksheets, pp. 5–6, 7–8<br>Transparency Activity, pp. 47–48<br>**Lab Management and Safety,** p. 65 | **Portfolio**<br>MiniLAB Assessment, p. 367<br>**Performance**<br>MiniLAB, p. 367<br>Applying Math, p. 368<br>**Content**<br>Section Review, p. 368 | Section Focus Transparency<br>Guided Reading Audio Program<br>Interactive Chalkboard CD-ROM<br>Video Lab |

## End of Chapter Assessment

GLENCOE'S **ASSESSMENT** ADVANTAGE

| Blackline Masters | Technology | Professional Series |
|---|---|---|
| **Chapter *FAST FILE* Resources**<br>Chapter Review, pp. 37–38<br>Chapter Tests, pp. 39–42<br>**Mastering the Grade 7 Indiana Science Standards** | MindJogger Videoquiz<br>IN Test Prep and Practice Exam*View*®<br>Exam*View*® Pro Testmaker<br>TeacherWorks CD-ROM<br>Interactive Chalkboard CD-ROM | **Performance Assessment in the Science Classroom (PASC)** |

## Transparencies

### Section Focus

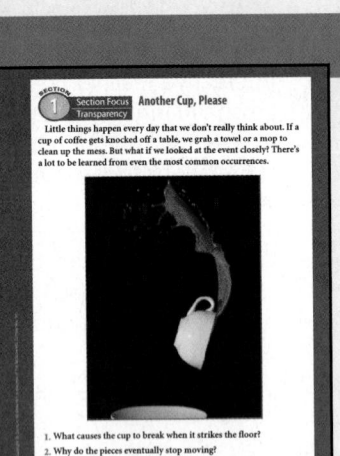

**Section Focus Transparency 1** — Another Cup, Please

Little things happen every day that we don't really think about. If a cup of coffee gets knocked off a table, we grab a towel or a mop to clean up the mess. But what if we looked at the event closely? There's a lot to be learned from even the most common occurrences.

1. What causes the cup to break when it strikes the floor?
2. Why do the pieces eventually stop moving?
3. What determines how far and in what direction the coffee cup (and coffee) will travel?

L2

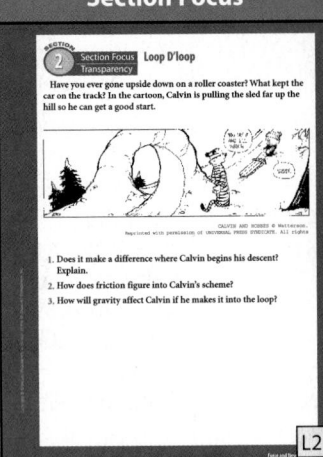

**Section Focus Transparency 2** — Loop D'loop

Have you ever gone upside down on a roller coaster? What kept the car on the track? In the cartoon, Calvin is pulling the sled far up the hill so he can get a good start.

1. Does it make a difference where Calvin begins his descent? Explain.
2. How does friction figure into Calvin's scheme?
3. How will gravity affect Calvin if he makes it into the loop?

L2

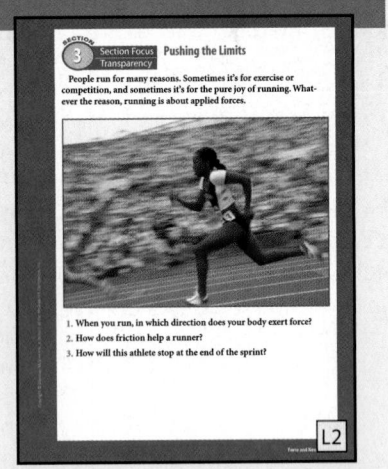

**Section Focus Transparency 3** — Pushing the Limits

People run for many reasons. Sometimes it's for exercise or competition, and sometimes it's for the pure joy of running. Whatever the reason, running is about applied forces.

1. When you run, in which direction does your body exert force?
2. How does friction help a runner?
3. How will this athlete stop at the end of the sprint?

L2

This is a representation of key blackline masters available in the Teacher Classroom Resources. See Resource Manager boxes within the chapter for additional information.

### Assessment

**Assessment Transparency** — Force and Newton's Laws

Directions: Carefully review the diagram and answer the following questions.

1. All of these objects have unbalanced forces acting upon them EXCEPT ___.
   A  A
   B  B
   C  C
   D  D
2. Rolling friction pushes on an object that is rolling. According to this definition, which of these examples shows rolling friction?
   F  A and D
   G  B and A
   H  C and B
   J  D and C
3. A force is a push or pull. Which force is acting on all of the objects in the diagram?
   A  Static friction
   B  Magnetism
   C  Gravity
   D  Acceleration

L2

### Teaching

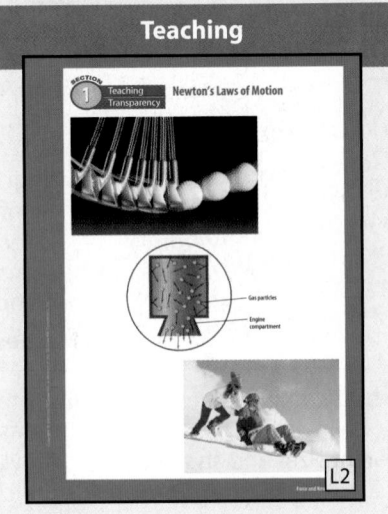

**Teaching Transparency** — Newton's Laws of Motion

L2

## Key to Teaching Strategies

The following designations will help you decide which activities are appropriate for your students.

L1 Level 1 activities should be appropriate for students with learning difficulties.

L2 Level 2 activities should be within the ability range of all students.

L3 Level 3 activities are designed for above-average students.

ELL ELL activities should be within the ability range of English Language Learners.

COOP LEARN Cooperative Learning activities are designed for small group work.

LS Multiple Learning Styles logos, as described on page 12T, are used throughout to indicate strategies that address different learning styles.

P These strategies represent student products that can be placed into a best-work portfolio.

PBL Problem-Based Learning activities apply real-world situations to learning.

## Hands-on Activities

### Student Text Lab Worksheet

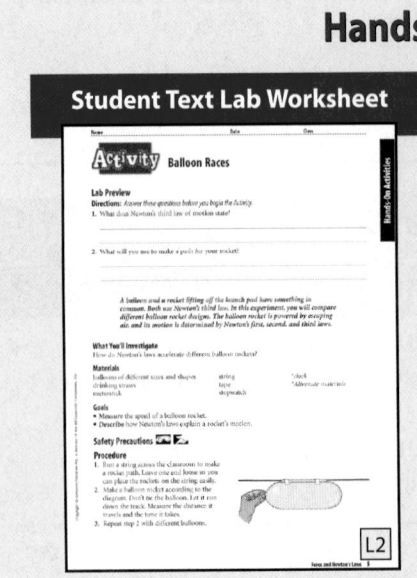

**Activity** — Balloon Races

**Lab Preview**
Directions: Answer these questions before you begin the Activity.
1. What does Newton's third law of motion state?

2. What will you use to make a path for your rocket?

A balloon and a rocket lifting off the launch pad have something in common. Both use Newton's third law. In this experiment, you will compare different balloon rocket designs. The balloon rocket is powered by escaping air, and its motion is determined by Newton's first, second, and third laws.

**What You'll Investigate**
How do Newton's laws accelerate different balloon rockets?

**Materials**
balloons of different sizes and shapes    string    *clock
drinking straws    tape    *Alternate materials
meterstick    stopwatch

**Goals**
• Measure the speed of a balloon rocket.
• Describe how Newton's laws explain a rocket's motion.

**Safety Precautions**

**Procedure**
1. Run a string across the classroom to make a rocket path. Leave one end loose so you can place the rockets on the string easily.
2. Make a balloon rocket according to the diagram. Don't tie the balloon. Let it run down the track. Measure the distance it travels and the time it takes.
3. Repeat step 2 with different balloons.

L2

### Laboratory Activities

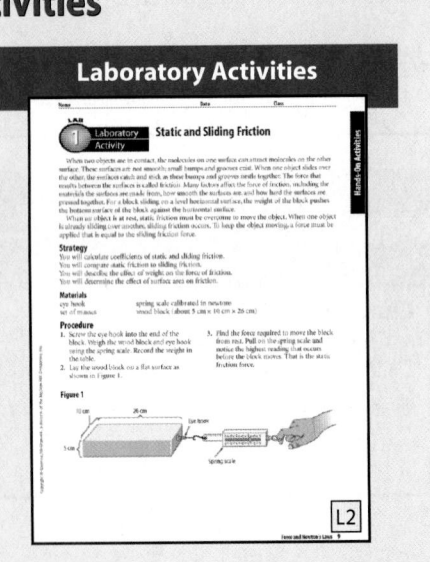

**Laboratory Activity 1** — Static and Sliding Friction

**Strategy**
You will calculate coefficients of static and sliding friction.
You will compare static friction to sliding friction.
You will describe the effect of weight on the force of friction.
You will determine the effect of surface area on friction.

**Materials**
eye hook    spring scale calibrated in newtons
set of masses    wood block (about 5 cm × 10 cm × 26 cm)

**Procedure**
1. Screw the eye hook into the end of the block. Weigh the wood block and eye hook using the spring scale. Record the weight in the table.
2. Lay the wood block on a flat surface as shown in Figure 1.

3. Find the force required to move the block from rest. Pull on the spring scale and notice the highest reading that occurs before the block moves. That is the static friction force.

**Figure 1**

L2

# Meeting Different Ability Levels

## Content Outline

L2

## Reinforcement

L2

## Enrichment

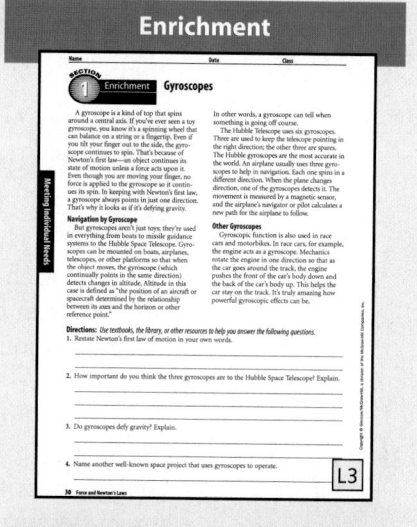

L3

## Directed Reading (English/Spanish)

L1

## Study Guide

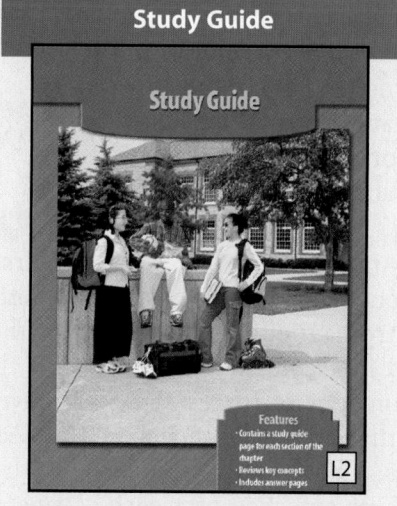

Study Guide

**Features**
- Contains a study guide page for each section of the chapter
- Reviews key concepts
- Includes answer pages

L2

## Reading Essentials

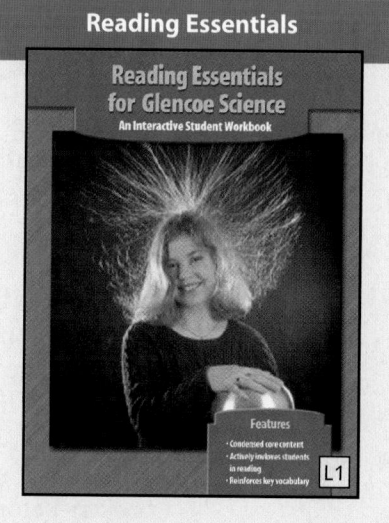

**Reading Essentials for Glencoe Science**
An Interactive Student Workbook

**Features**
- Condensed core content
- Actively involves students in reading
- Reinforces key vocabulary

L1

# Assessment

## Test Practice Workbook

L2

## Chapter Review

L2

## Chapter Tests

L2

# Science Content Background

## Force

A force is a push or a pull. If two objects must be in contact to exert forces on each other, it is a contact force, like friction between two surfaces. Other forces, such as the gravitational force, are long-ranged forces.

## Newton's First Law of Motion

According to Newton's first law of motion, a change in motion, or acceleration, is caused by a force. Because forces cause a change in motion, an object can be moving even if there are no forces acting on it. Then the object's velocity will be constant, and the object will move in a straight line with constant speed. When more than one force is acting on an object, the combination of the forces, is called the net force.

## Friction

Friction is a force that acts between any two surfaces in contact. Electromagnetic forces act between the atoms and molecules on the two surfaces. These electromagnetic forces cause bonds to be formed that weld the surfaces together in some places. These welds must be broken before the surfaces can slide past each other. This is the source of static friction.

## Gravity

Gravity acts between all objects and causes them to be attracted to each other. According to Newton's law of universal gravitation, the gravitational force between two objects is $F = G\, m_1 m_2/d_2$, where $G$ is the universal gravitational constant, $m_1$ and $m_2$ are the masses of the objects, and $d$ is the distance between them. Near Earth's surface, this equation gives the force between Earth and any other object as $F = m(9.8 \text{ m/s}^2)$.

## Action and Reaction

According to Newton's third law, forces always act in action-reaction pairs. When one object exerts a force on another, the second object always exerts a force of the same size, but in the opposite direction, on the first object. For example, the force of gravity between two objects is exerted on both objects. The size of the force is the same on both objects, and the direction of the force on one object is opposite to the direction of the force on the other.

---

## chapter content resources

**Internet Resources**
For additional content background, visit
**in7.msscience.com** to:
- access your book onlineonline
- find references to related articles in popular science magazines
- access Web links with related content background
- access current events with science journal topics

**Print Resources**
*The Spinning Blackboard,* by Paul Doherty, Don Rothjen, The Exploratorium Teacher Institute, John Wiley and Sons, 1996
*Hands-on Physics Activities with Real-Life Applications,* by James Cunningham, Norman Herr, Jossey-Bass, 2002
*Turning the World Inside Out and 174 Other Simple Physics Demonstrations,* by Robert Ehrlich, Jearl Walker, Princeton University Press, 1990

## IDENTIFYING Misconceptions

### Find Out What Students Think

**Students may think that . . .**

**An object at rest resists acceleration only because of friction.**
Students have probably learned about friction in the past and view it as the thing that works against motion.

### Demonstration
Place a small cart or car on your desk. Give it a push and give a humorous grunt to show that it is hard work to get it going. Once it is moving make the pushing seem effortless. Ask students whether they have ever had to help push a stalled car. Did they notice that it takes a lot of effort to get the car going and less effort to keep it going?

Ask students why it takes a larger force to move a stopped car than it does to push a moving car. Give students a few minutes to think about the question. Then have them share their thoughts with a partner. Ask some of the pairs to share their answers with the whole class. Finally, see if the class can come to consensus about the correct answer to this question.

### Promote Understanding

### Activity
Give each group a cart, a hanging spring scale that reads force in Newtons, five objects with different masses, and string. Show them how to find the amount of force needed to pull the cart as shown in the diagram below.

5N

- Have students practice slowly pulling the cart and measuring the maximum force needed to get the cart moving. Then have them practice measuring the force needed to move the cart with constant velocity.

  Once students are proficient in these techniques, ask them to investigate how increasing the cart's mass affects these two forces.

- They will need to know or measure the mass of the cart and the masses of each of the added objects.

- Suggest students graph their data with mass on the $x$-axis and force on the $y$-axis.

After students complete the activity, discuss with them the following questions:

- What is the relationship between the mass of the cart and the maximum force needed to get the cart moving? The greater the mass, the greater the force needed.

- Why is a force needed to have the cart move with constant velocity? to overcome friction

- Why is the force needed to start the cart moving always greater than the force to keep it moving? The friction between the cart and the table is greater when the cart is at rest.

### Assess
After completing the chapter, see *Identifying Misconceptions* in the Study Guide at the end of the chapter.

## Chapter Vocabulary

force, p. 350
net force, p. 351
balanced forces, p. 351
unbalanced forces, p. 351
Newton's first law of motion,
   p. 352
friction, p. 352
Newton's second law of motion,
   p. 356
weight, p. 357
center of mass, p. 362
Newton's third law of motion,
   p. 363

**Science Journal** Possible
answers: pulling a sled—a person supplied the force to overcome the sled's inertia; pulling
an anchored boat closer to the
dock—a person supplied the
force to overcome the boat's
inertia

**PowerPoint® Presentations**

This CD-ROM is an editable
Microsoft® PowerPoint®
presentation that includes:

• a pre-made presentation for
  every chapter
• interactive graphics
• animations
• audio clips
• image bank
• all new section and chapter
  questions
• Standardized Test Practice
• transparencies
• pre-lab questions for all labs
• Foldables directions
• links to in7.msscience.com

**Academic Standard—3:** Students collect and organize data to identify relationships between physical objects, events, and processes. They use logical reasoning to question their own ideas as new information challenges their conceptions of the natural world.

**Also covers:** Academic Standards 1, 2,7 (Detailed standards begin on page IN8.)

# Force and Newton's Laws

## chapter preview

**sections**

**1** Newton's First Law

**2** Newton's Second Law

**3** Newton's Third Law
   *Lab* Balloon Races
   *Lab* Modeling Motion in
   Two Directions

**Virtual Labs** *What is Newton's
second law of motion?*

348

### Moving at a Crawl

This enormous vehicle is a crawler that
moves a space shuttle to the launch pad. The
crawler and space shuttle together have a
mass of about 7,700,000 kg. To move the
crawler at a speed of about 1.5 km/h requires
a force of about 10,000,000 N. This force is
exerted by 16 electric motors in the crawler.

**Science Journal** Describe three examples of
pushing or pulling an object. How did the object move?

## Theme Connection

**Systems and Interactions** Newton's laws of motion
form a system that can be used to determine an
object's future motions. Objects interacting with
each other also follow these laws. If you know the
forces acting between objects, you can determine
the changes in the objects' future motion.

### About the Photo

**Crawlers** When these crawlers were built, they
were the largest tracked vehicles ever made. One
crawler requires eleven drivers. The electric
motors are powered by huge diesel engines that
use 350 liters of diesel per kilometer.

# Start-Up Activities

## Forces and Motion

Imagine being on a bobsled team speeding down an icy run. Forces are exerted on the sled by the ice, the sled's brakes and steering mechanism, and gravity. Newton's laws predict how these forces cause the bobsled to turn, speed up, or slow down. Newton's Laws tell how forces cause the motion of any object to change.

1. Lean two meter-sticks parallel, less than a marble width apart on three books as shown on the left. This is your ramp.

2. Tap a marble so it rolls up the ramp. Measure how far up the ramp it travels before rolling back.

3. Repeat step 2 using two books, one book, and zero books. The same person should tap with the same force each time.

4. **Think Critically** Make a table to record the motion of the marble for each ramp height. What would happen if the ramp were perfectly smooth and level?

**FOLDABLES**
**Study Organizer**

**Newton's Laws** Make the following Foldable to help you organize your thoughts about Newton's laws.

**STEP 1** Fold a sheet of paper in half lengthwise. Make the back edge about 5 cm longer than the front edge.

**STEP 2** Turn the paper so the fold is on the bottom. Then fold it into thirds.

**STEP 3** Unfold and cut only the top layer along both folds to make three tabs.

**STEP 4** Label the foldable as shown.

Newton's Law

| 1st Law | 2nd Law | 3rd Law |

**Make a Concept Map** As you read the chapter, record what you learn about each of Newton's laws in your concept map.

**Science Online**
Preview this chapter's content and activities at
in7.msscience.com

---

**Purpose** Use the Launch Lab to help students see the effect the steepness of a ramp has on the motion of a marble. L2 ELL LS **Kinesthetic**

**Preparation** Make sure that the books used are of similar thickness.

**Materials** 3 books, 2 metersticks, 1 marble

**Teaching Strategies** To make sure the initial speed of the marble is constant, use a flexible strip to make a launch ramp. Always release the marble from the same point on the ramp, and be sure there isn't a significant bump where the ramps join.

## Thinking Critically

Students' data should show that the flatter the incline, the longer the distance traveled by the marble. If the ramp were perfectly smooth and flat, the marble would roll forever.

## Assessment

**Oral** Show students a picture of a bobsled track, ski run, or slide. Ask them to identify the points at which a rider would have maximum speed. Ask students to write a sentence or two defending their choices. Use **Performance Assessment in the Science Classroom,** p. 159.

**FOLDABLES**
**Study Organizer**
Dinah Zike
**Study Fold**

Student preparation materials for this Foldable are available in the Chapter *FAST FILE* Resources.

# section 1

Also covers: 7.1.5, 7.7.4 (Detailed standards begin on page IN8.)

# Newton's First Law

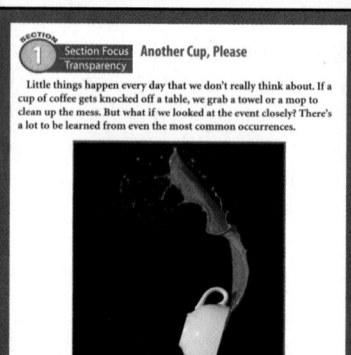
## as you read

### *What* You'll Learn
- **Distinguish** between balanced and net forces.
- **Describe** Newton's first law of motion.
- **Explain** how friction affects motion.

### *Why* It's Important
Newton's first law explains why objects change direction.

### 🔊 Review Vocabulary
**velocity:** the speed and direction of a moving object

### New Vocabulary
- force
- net force
- balanced forces
- unbalanced forces
- Newton's first law of motion
- friction

## Force

A soccer ball sits on the ground, motionless, until you kick it. Your science book sits on the table until you pick it up. If you hold your book above the ground, then let it go, gravity pulls it to the floor. In every one of these cases, the motion of the ball or book was changed by something pushing or pulling on it. An object will speed up, slow down, or turn only if something is pushing or pulling on it.

A **force** is a push or a pull. Examples of forces are shown in **Figure 1.** Think about throwing a ball. Your hand exerts a force on the ball, and the ball accelerates forward until it leaves your hand. After the ball leaves your hand, the force of gravity causes its path to curve downward. When the ball hits the ground, the ground exerts a force, stopping the ball.

A force can be exerted in different ways. For instance, a paper clip can be moved by the force a magnet exerts, the pull of Earth's gravity, or the force you exert when you pick it up. These are all examples of forces acting on the paper clip.

**Figure 1** A force is a push or a pull.

This golf club exerts a force by pushing on the golf ball.

The magnet on the crane pulls the pieces of scrap metal upward.

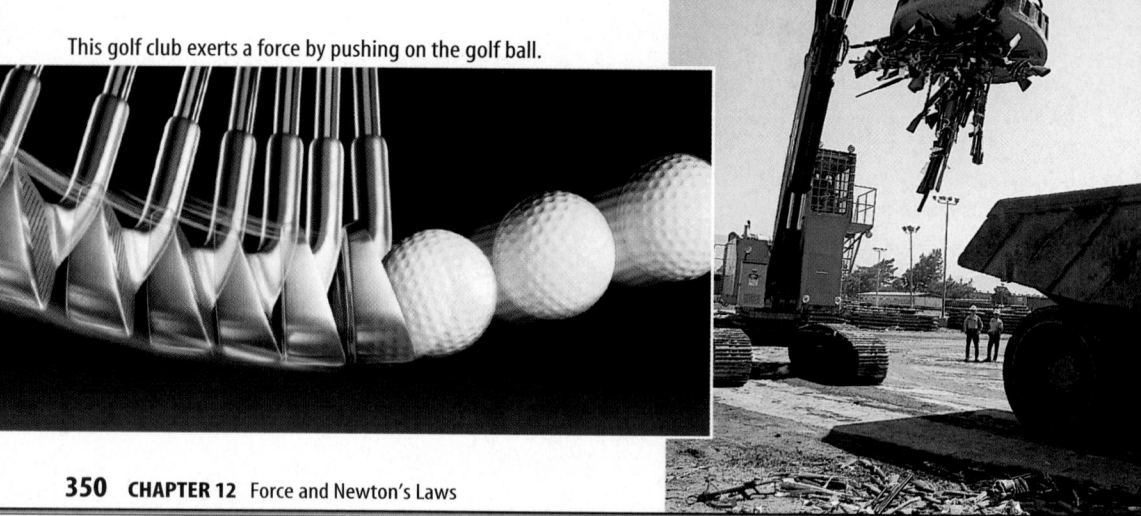

---

## Section 1 Resource Manager

### Chapter *FAST FILE* Resources
Transparency Activity, pp. 44, 47–48
Directed Reading for Content Mastery, pp. 19, 20
Note-taking Worksheets, pp. 33–35
Enrichment, p. 30

Lab Activity, pp. 9–12
MiniLAB, p. 3
Reinforcement, p. 27
**Home and Community Involvement,** p. 23

This door is not moving because the forces exerted on it are equal and in opposite directions.

The door is closing because the force pushing the door closed is greater than the force pushing it open.

**Combining Forces** More than one force can act on an object at the same time. If you hold a paper clip near a magnet, you, the magnet, and gravity all exert forces on the paper clip. The combination of all the forces acting on an object is the **net force**. When more than one force is acting on an object, the net force determines the motion of the object. In this example, the paper clip is not moving, so the net force is zero.

How do forces combine to form the net force? If the forces are in the same direction, they add together to form the net force. If two forces are in opposite directions, then the net force is the difference between the two forces, and it is in the direction of the larger force.

**Balanced and Unbalanced Forces** A force can act on an object without causing it to accelerate if other forces cancel the push or pull of the force. Look at **Figure 2.** If you and your friend push on a door with the same force in opposite directions, the door does not move. Because you both exert forces of the same size in opposite directions on the door, the two forces cancel each other. Two or more forces exerted on an object are **balanced forces** if their effects cancel each other and they do not cause a change in the object's motion. If the forces on an object are balanced, the net force is zero. If the forces are **unbalanced forces,** their effects don't cancel each other. Any time the forces acting on an object are unbalanced, the net force is not zero and the motion of the object changes.

**Figure 2** When the forces on an object are balanced, no change in motion occurs. A change in motion occurs only when the forces acting on an object are unbalanced.

**Biomechanics** Whether you run, jump, or sit, forces are being exerted on different parts of your body. Biomechanics is the study of how the body exerts forces and how it is affected by forces acting on it. Research how biomechanics has been used to reduce job-related injuries. Write a paragraph on what you've learned in your Science Journal.

## Visual Learning

**Figure 2** Point out to students the force arrows in **Figure 2.** Ask volunteers to identify the force represented by each arrow. [L1] **ELL** [L2] **Visual-Spatial**

## Use Science Words

**Word Meaning** The sum of the forces acting on an object is called the *net force*. Ask students to use a dictionary to find the meaning of the word *net*. Net is what remains after all deductions have been made. What are other familiar uses of *net* in this sense? Possible response: The net profit is the money earned after all expenses have been subtracted.

**Biomechanics** Researchers have used biomechanics to study such problems as repetitive strain injuries causing carpal tunnel syndrome and lower back pain.

**Resisting Acceleration** Some students may think that an object at rest resists acceleration only because of friction. See the beginning of this chapter for teaching strategies related to this misconception.

## Curriculum Connection

**Art** Mobiles are based on the principle of balanced forces. Have each student make a mobile with at least three arms. The only criterion students must follow is that each arm must be balanced. Hang students' mobiles in the classroom. [L2] **IS Kinesthetic**

# Newton's First Law of Motion

If you stand on a skateboard and someone gives you a push, then you and your skateboard will start moving. You will begin to move when the force was applied. An object at rest—like you on your skateboard—remains at rest unless an unbalanced force acts on it and causes it to move.

Because a force had to be applied to make you move when you and your skateboard were at rest, you might think that a force has to be applied continually to keep an object moving. Surprisingly, this is not the case. An object can be moving even if the net force acting on it is zero.

The Italian scientist Galileo Galilei, who lived from 1564 to 1642, was one of the first to understand that a force doesn't need to be constantly applied to an object to keep it moving. Galileo's ideas helped Isaac Newton to better understand the nature of motion. Newton, who lived from 1642 to 1727, explained the motion of objects in three rules called Newton's laws of motion.

Newton's first law of motion describes how an object moves when the net force acting on it is zero. According to **Newton's first law of motion,** if the net force acting on an object is zero, the object remains at rest, or if the object is already moving, continues to move in a straight line with constant speed.

## Friction

Galileo realized the motion of an object doesn't change until an unbalanced force acts on it. Every day you see moving objects come to a stop. The force that brings nearly everything to a stop is **friction,** which is the force that acts to resist sliding between two touching surfaces, as shown in **Figure 3.** Friction is why you never see objects moving with constant velocity unless a net force is applied. Friction is the force that eventually brings your skateboard to a stop unless you keep pushing on it. Friction also acts on objects that are sliding or moving through substances such as air or water.

**Figure 3** When two objects in contact try to slide past each other, friction keeps them from moving or slows them down.

Without friction, the rock climber would slide down the rock.

Force due to friction

Force due to friction

Force due to friction

Force due to gravity

Friction slows down this sliding baseball player.

Force due to friction

**Friction Opposes Sliding** Although several different forms of friction exist, they all have one thing in common. If two objects are in contact, frictional forces always try to prevent one object from sliding on the other object. If you rub your hand against a tabletop, you can feel the friction push against the motion of your hand. If you rub the other way, you can feel the direction of friction change so it is again acting against your hand's motion. Friction always will slow a moving object.

**Reading Check** *What do the different forms of friction have in common?*

**Older Ideas About Motion** It took a long time to understand motion. One reason was that people did not understand the behavior of friction and that friction was a force. Because moving objects eventually come to a stop, people thought the natural state of an object was to be at rest. For an object to be in motion, something always had to be pushing or pulling it to keep the object moving. As soon as the force stopped, the object would stop moving.

Galileo understood that an object in constant motion is as natural as an object at rest. It was usually friction that made moving objects slow down and eventually come to a stop. To keep an object moving, a force had to be applied to overcome the effects of friction. If friction could be removed, an object in motion would continue to move in a straight line with constant speed. **Figure 4** shows motion where there is almost no friction.

**Science Online**

**Topic: Galileo and Newton**
Visit in7.msscience.com for Web links to information about the lives of Galileo and Newton.

**Activity** Make a time line showing important events in the lives of either Galileo or Newton.

**Figure 4** In an air hockey game, the puck floats on a layer of air, so that friction is almost eliminated. As a result, the puck moves in a straight line with nearly constant speed after it's been hit. **Infer** *how the puck would move if there was no layer of air.*

---

**Reading Check**

**Answer** different forms of friction always slow an object down

**Activity**

**Curling** Have students investigate the sport of curling and the role friction plays in it. Curling is played on ice. Each player hurls a stone at fixed goals, and uses a broom to try to clear the path in front of the stone, thereby reducing the friction. L2 IS **Linguistic**

**Discussion**

**Fundamental Forces** Physicists hypothesize there are only four fundamental forces of nature. What do you think these forces are, and which kind is friction? The forces are gravitational force, electromagnetic force, the weak nuclear force, and the strong nuclear force. Friction is an example of electromagnetic force.

**Caption Answer**

**Figure 4** It would move in a straight line, but it would slow down and stop because of friction.

---

# Differentiated Instruction

**Physically Challenged** If you have a student in your class who uses a wheelchair, ask the student to explain its braking system and the role friction plays in making it work. Have students compare pushing the chair with the brake off and with it on. L2 IS **Kinesthetic**

## Mini LAB

**Purpose** Students observe the static and sliding friction between various objects. L2 ELL
IS **Kinesthetic**

**Materials** flat bar of soap, flat eraser, key, notebook

**Teaching Strategies** Students should conduct the experiment several times. On occasion, one of the objects may abnormally stick, which could give misleading results if not rechecked.

### Analysis

1. The eraser had the greatest static friction since it was the last to slide. The soap had the least since it was the first to slide.

2. The key slid the fastest, it had the least sliding friction. The eraser slid the slowest, it had the most sliding friction.

3. Increase the friction by pushing the surfaces together. Decrease the friction by placing a lubricant between the surfaces.

### Assessment

**Process** Ask students to explain why keeping a bicycle chain properly lubricated helps make the bicycle easier to ride. The lubricant decreases the friction between the links of the chain. Use **Performance Assessment in the Science Classroom,** p. 89.

✔ **Reading Check**

**Answer** Static friction prevents two objects at rest from moving past one another; sliding friction slows down two objects moving against each other.

## Mini LAB

### Observing Friction

**Procedure**

1. Lay a **bar of soap,** a **flat eraser,** and a **key** side by side on one end of a **hard-sided notebook.**

2. At a constant rate, slowly lift the end of notebook with objects on it. Note the order in which the objects start sliding.

**Analysis**

1. For which object was static friction the greatest? For which object was it the smallest? Explain, based on your observations.

2. Which object slid the fastest? Which slid the slowest? Explain why there is a difference in speed.

3. How could you increase and decrease the amount of friction between two materials?

**Try at Home**

---

**Static Friction** If you've ever tried pushing something heavy, like a refrigerator, you might have discovered that nothing happened at first. Then as you push harder and harder, the object suddenly will start to move. When you first start to push, friction between the heavy refrigerator and the floor opposes the force you are exerting and the net force is zero. The type of friction that prevents an object from moving when a force is applied is called static friction.

Static friction is caused by the attraction between the atoms on the two surfaces that are in contact. This causes the surfaces to stick or weld together where they are in contact. Usually, as the surface gets rougher and the object gets heavier, the force of static friction will be larger. To move the object, you have to exert a force large enough to break the bonds holding two surfaces together.

**Sliding Friction** While static friction keeps an object at rest, sliding friction slows down an object that slides. If you push an object across a room, you notice the sliding friction between the bottom of the object and the floor. You have to keep pushing to overcome the force of sliding friction. Sliding friction is due to the microscopic roughness of two surfaces, as shown in **Figure 5.** A force must be applied to move the rough areas of one surface past the rough areas of the other. A sliding friction force is produced when the brake pads in a car's brakes rub against the wheels. This force slows the car. Bicycle brakes, shown in **Figure 6,** work the same way.

✔ **Reading Check** *What is the difference between static friction and sliding friction?*

**Figure 5** Microscopic roughness, even on surfaces that seem smooth, such as the tray and metal shelf, causes sliding friction.

## Differentiated Instruction

**Challenge** Have each student choose a part of an automobile that is affected by some form of friction. Have students state the type of friction, whether the friction decreases or increases the efficiency of the car, and how the friction can be increased or decreased to improve the performance of the car. L3 IS **Logical-Mathematical**

**Visually Impaired** When these students do the MiniLAB, have them place the objects at the edge of the notebook by feel. Have a sighted student lift the end of the notebook while the first student puts his or her hand at the bottom of the notebook to catch the objects as they slide. Have students repeat the process several times, until they have had a chance to discover by feel the order in which the objects slide.

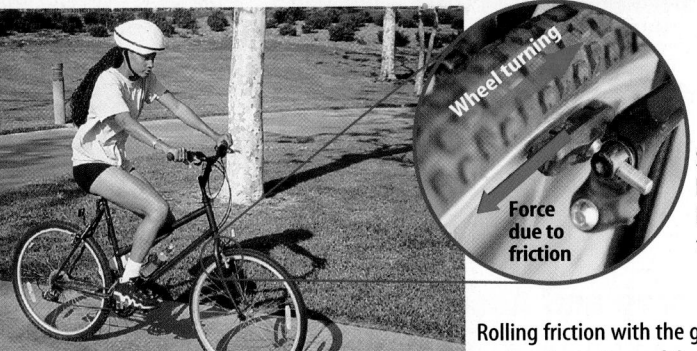

**Figure 6** A bicycle uses sliding friction and rolling friction.

Wheel turning

Force due to friction

Sliding friction is used to stop this bicycle tire. Friction between the brake pads and the wheel brings the wheel to a stop.

Rolling friction with the ground pushes the bottom of the bicycle tire, so it rolls forward.

Force due to friction

**Rolling Friction** Another type of friction, rolling friction, is needed to make a wheel or tire turn. Rolling friction occurs between the ground and the part of the tire touching the ground, as shown in **Figure 6.** Rolling friction keeps the tire from slipping on the ground. If the bicycle tires are rolling forward, rolling friction exerts the force on the tires that pushes the bicycle forward.

It's usually easier to pull a load on a wagon or cart that has wheels rather than to drag the load along the ground. This is because rolling friction between the wheels and the ground is less than the sliding friction between the load and the ground.

## section 1 review

### Summary

**Force**
- A force is a push or a pull.
- The net force on an object is the combination of all the forces acting on the object.
- The forces acting on an object can be balanced or unbalanced. If the forces are balanced, the net force is zero.

**Newton's First Law of Motion**
- If the net force on an object at rest is zero, the object remains at rest, or if the object is moving, it continues moving in a straight line with constant speed.

**Friction**
- Friction is the force that acts to resist sliding between two surfaces that are touching.
- Three types of friction are static friction, sliding friction, and rolling friction.

### Self Check

1. **Explain** whether a force is acting on a car that is moving at 20 km/h and turns to the left.
2. **Describe** the factors that cause static friction between two surfaces to increase.
3. **Discuss** why friction made it difficult to discover Newton's first law of motion.
4. **Discuss** whether an object can be moving if the net force acting on the object is zero.
5. **Think Critically** For the following actions, explain whether the forces involved are balanced or unbalanced.
   a. You push a box until it moves.
   b. You push a box but it doesn't move.
   c. You stop pushing a box and it slows down.

#### Applying Skills

6. **Compare and contrast** static, sliding, and rolling friction.

## section 1 review

1. Yes; a force is needed to keep the car moving and to change direction.
2. Static friction increases if the surface is rougher or the object is heavier.
3. Because friction usually causes objects in motion to eventually stop, it seemed that rest was the natural state of matter.
4. Yes; if an object is already in motion, it will continue at a constant velocity until acted upon by an outside force.
5. a. unbalanced, box starts moving;
   b. balanced, box doesn't move;
   c. unbalanced, box slows down
6. All three types of friction act against

the direction an object moves. Static friction keeps an object from moving; sliding friction is the friction between two objects moving against each other; rolling friction is the static friction between the rolling object and the surface on which it is rolling.

## 1 Motivate

INTERACTIVE CHALKBOARD
PowerPoint® Presentations

### Bellringer

**Section Focus Transparencies** also are available on the Interactive Chalkboard CD-ROM.

L2 ELL

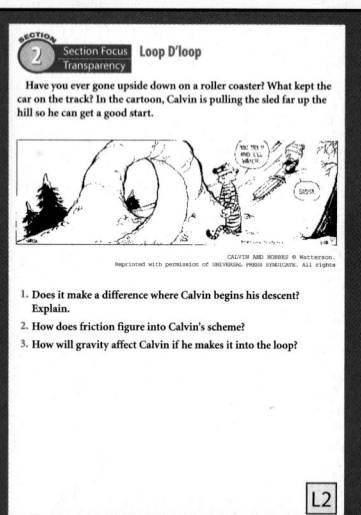

### Tie to Prior Knowledge

**Mass and Acceleration** Have students recall the definitions of mass and acceleration. In this section they will learn how the mass, acceleration and net force acting on an object are related.

### ✔ Reading Check

**Answer** An object acted upon by an unbalanced force will accelerate in the direction of the force according to $a = F_{net}/m$.

### Caption Answer

**Figure 7** The cart with less food; it has less mass.

---

Also covers: 7.1.5 (Detailed standards begin on page IN8.)

# Newton's Second Law

## as you read

### *What* You'll Learn
- **Explain** Newton's second law of motion.
- **Explain** why the direction of force is important.

### *Why* It's Important
Newton's second law of motion explains how any object, from a swimmer to a satellite, moves when acted on by forces.

### 🔎 Review Vocabulary
**acceleration:** the change in velocity divided by the time over which the change occurred

### New Vocabulary
- Newton's second law of motion
- weight
- center of mass

**Figure 7** The force needed to change the motion of an object depends on its mass.
**Predict** *which grocery cart would be easier to stop.*

## Force and Acceleration

When you go shopping in a grocery store and push a cart, you exert a force to make the cart move. If you want to slow down or change the direction of the cart, a force is required to do this, as well. Would it be easier for you to stop a full or empty grocery cart suddenly, as in **Figure 7?** When the motion of an object changes, the object is accelerating. Acceleration occurs any time an object speeds up, slows down, or changes its direction of motion. Newton's second law describes how forces cause an object's motion to change.

**Newton's second law of motion** connects force, acceleration, and mass. According to the second law of motion, an object acted upon by a force will accelerate in the direction of the force. The acceleration is given by the following equation

**Acceleration Equation**

$$\text{acceleration (in meters/second}^2) = \frac{\text{net force (in newtons)}}{\text{mass (in kilograms)}}$$

$$a = \frac{F_{net}}{m}$$

In this equation, $a$ is the acceleration, $m$ is the mass, and $F_{net}$ is the net force. If both sides of the above equation are multiplied by the mass, the equation can be written this way:

$$F_{net} = ma$$

### ✔ Reading Check    *What is Newton's second law?*

---

## Section 2 Resource Manager

### Chapter *FAST FILE* Resources
Transparency Activity, pp. 45, 47–48
Directed Reading for Content Mastery, p. 21
Lab Activity, pp. 13–16
Enrichment, p. 31

Reinforcement, p. 28
**Mathematics Skill Activities,** p. 9
**Physical Science Critical Thinking/ Problem Solving,** p. 4

---

**Units of Force** Force is measured in newtons, abbreviated N. Because the SI unit for mass is the kilogram (kg) and acceleration has units of meters per second squared (m/s²), 1 N also is equal to 1 kg•m/s². In other words, to calculate a force in newtons from the equation shown on the prior page, the mass must be given in kg and the acceleration in m/s².

## Gravity

One force that you are familiar with is gravity. Whether you're coasting down a hill on a bike or a skateboard or jumping into a pool, gravity is at work pulling you downward. Gravity also is the force that causes Earth to orbit the Sun and the Moon to orbit Earth.

**What is gravity?** The force of gravity exists between any two objects that have mass. Gravity always is attractive and pulls objects toward each other. A gravitational attraction exists between you and every object in the universe that has mass. However, the force of gravity depends on the mass of the objects and the distance between them. The gravitational force becomes weaker the farther apart the objects are and also decreases as the masses of the objects involved decrease.

For example, there is a gravitational force between you and the Sun and between you and Earth. The Sun is much more massive than Earth, but is so far away that the gravitational force between you and the Sun is too weak to notice. Only Earth is close enough and massive enough to exert a noticeable gravitational force on you. The force of gravity between you and Earth is about 1,650 times greater than between you and the Sun.

**Weight** The force of gravity causes all objects near Earth's surface to fall with an acceleration of 9.8 m/s². By Newton's second law, the gravitational force on any object near Earth's surface is:

$$F = ma = m \times (9.8 \text{ m/s}^2)$$

This gravitational force also is called the weight of the object. Your **weight** on Earth is the gravitational force between you and Earth. Your weight would change if you were standing on a planet other than Earth, as shown in **Table 1.** Your weight on a different planet would be the gravitational force between you and the planet.

**INTEGRATE History**

**Newton and Gravity** Isaac Newton was the first to realize that gravity—the force that made objects fall to Earth—was also the force that caused the Moon to orbit Earth and the planets to orbit the Sun. In 1687, Newton published a book that included the law of universal gravitation. This law showed how to calculate the gravitational force between any two objects. Using the law of universal gravitation, astronomers were able to explain the motions of the planets in the solar system, as well as the motions of distant stars and galaxies.

**Table 1  Weight of 60-kg Person on Different Planets**

| Place | Weight in Newtons If Your Mass Were 60 kg | Percent of Your Weight on Earth |
|-------|-------------------------------------------|----------------------------------|
| Mars | 221 | 38 |
| Earth | 587 | 100 |
| Jupiter | 1,387 | 236 |
| Pluto | 39 | 0.7 |

## 2 Teach

### Discussion

**Weight** In the United States, people usually measure their weight in pounds. In European countries, people speak of their weight in kilograms. When converting your weight to the metric system, should you convert it to kilograms or newtons? Why? Convert it to newtons. Weight is a measure of the force of gravity, and newtons is the unit of force. L2 IS **Logical-Mathematical**

**INTEGRATE History**

**Newton and Gravity** Isaac Newton made many contributions to science during his lifetime.

**Research** Have students research to find out about the works of Newton. Have students prepare oral reports to share their information with the class.

### Virtual Labs

**Second Law** *What is Newton's second law of motion?*

## Curriculum Connection

**History** Galileo was the first person to understand gravity's effect on objects. Have students learn more about Galileo and his understanding of gravity. Galileo discovered that the rate at which a body falls is independent of its weight or density, as long as air resistance can be neglected. He was also the first person to use mathematics to analyze his results. L2 IS **Linguistic**

## Differentiated Instruction

**English-Language Learners** Explain to students, especially those who are more familiar with seeing their "weight" in kilograms, that weight is a force, not a mass. A pound and a Newton are both forces—these are measurements of weight. A kilogram is a measure of mass. When you step on a scale, it assumes that the acceleration is always 9.8 m/s², but it varies with altitude.

**Net Force** Students might think that every force produces an acceleration in the direction in which it is applied. However, all of the forces acting on an object are added together to determine the net force on the object. The object accelerates in the direction of this net force. So, for example, if one student pushes an object west while another student pushes it north, the net force on the object will be northwest, and will cause the object to move in that direction.

## Discussion

**Relationships** $F = ma$ describes the relationship between force and acceleration. What is the relationship between force and velocity? A force causes a change in velocity. The magnitude of the change can be calculated if you know the velocity before the force acted, the velocity after the force acted, and how long the change took. L2 **IS** **Logical-Mathematical**

## Visual Learning

**Figure 9** Point out that the net force acting on the sled is a combination of gravity pulling the sled down the hill, friction between the sled and the snow, and the force exerted by the boy's feet. Ask students which forces would cause the sled to slow down and which forces would cause the sled to speed up. Gravity would cause the sled to speed up and the other two forces would cause the sled to slow down. L2 **IS** **Logical-Mathematical**

**Figure 8** The girl on the sled is speeding up because she is being pushed in the same direction that she is moving.

Applied force

Direction of motion

**Figure 9** The boy is slowing down because the force exerted by his feet is in the opposite direction of his motion.

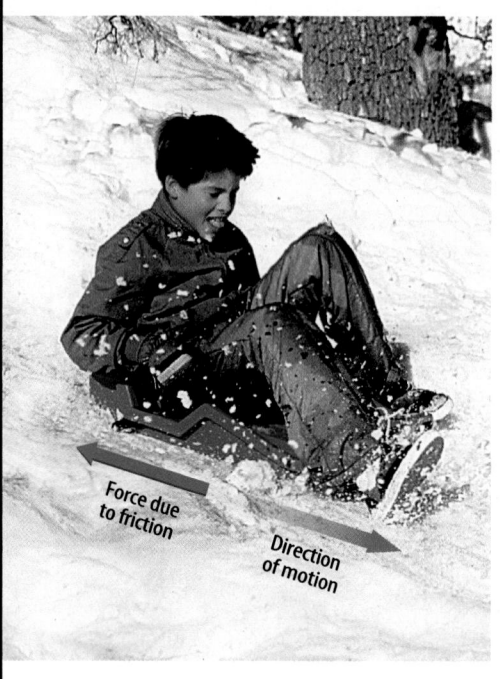

Force due to friction

Direction of motion

**Weight and Mass** Weight and mass are different. Weight is a force, just like the push of your hand is a force, and is measured in newtons. When you stand on a bathroom scale, you are measuring the pull of Earth's gravity—a force. However, mass is the amount of matter in an object, and doesn't depend on location. Weight will vary with location, but mass will remain constant. A book with a mass of 1 kg has a mass of 1 kg on Earth or on Mars. However, the weight of the book would be different on Earth and Mars. The two planets would exert a different gravitational force on the book.

## Using Newton's Second Law

How does Newton's second law determine how an object moves when acted upon by forces? The second law tells how to calculate the acceleration of an object if its mass and the forces acting on it are known. You may remember that the motion of an object can be described by its velocity. The velocity tells how fast an object is moving and in what direction. Acceleration tells how velocity changes. If the acceleration of an object is known, then the change in velocity can be determined.

**Speeding Up** Think about a soccer ball sitting on the ground. If you kick the ball, it starts moving. You exert a force on the ball, and the ball accelerates only while your foot is in contact with the ball. If you look back at all of the examples of objects speeding up, you'll notice that something is pushing or pulling the object in the direction it is moving, as in **Figure 8.** The direction of the push or pull is the direction of the force. It also is the direction of the acceleration.

**Slowing Down** If you wanted to slow down an object, you would have to push or pull it against the direction it is moving. An example is given in **Figure 9.**

Suppose you push a book across a tabletop. When you start pushing, the book speeds up. Sliding friction also acts on the book. After you stop pushing, sliding friction causes the book to slow down and stop.

**Calculating Acceleration** Newton's second law of motion can be used to calculate acceleration. For example, suppose you pull a 10-kg sled so that the net force on the sled is 5 N. The acceleration can be found as follows:

$$a = \frac{F_{net}}{m} = \frac{5 \text{ N}}{10 \text{ kg}} = 0.5 \text{ m/s}^2$$

The sled keeps accelerating as long as you keep pulling on it. The acceleration does not depend on how fast the sled is moving. It depends only on the net force and the mass of the sled.

## Applying Math — Solving a Simple Equation

**ACCELERATION OF A CAR** A net force of 4,500 N acts on a car with a mass of 1,500 kg. What is the acceleration of the car?

**Solution**

**1** *This is what you know:*
- net force: $F_{net}$ = 4,500 N²
- mass: $m$ = 1,500 kg

**2** *This is what you need to find:*
acceleration: $a$ = ? m/s²

**3** *This is the procedure you need to use:*

Substitute the known values for net force and mass into the equation for Newton's second law of motion to calculate the acceleration:

$$a = \frac{F_{net}}{m} = \frac{4,500 \text{ N}}{1,500 \text{ kg}} = 3.0 \frac{\text{N}}{\text{kg}} = 3.0 \text{ m/s}^2$$

**4** *Check your answer:*

Multiply your answer by the mass, 1,500 kg. The result should be the given net force, 4,500 N.

### Practice Problems

1. A book with a mass of 2.0 kg is pushed along a table. If the net force on the book is 1.0 N, what is the book's acceleration?

2. A baseball has a mass of 0.15 kg. What is the net force on the ball if its acceleration is 40 m/s²?

 Science Online

For more practice visit
in7.msscience.com/
math_practice

---

# Science Journal

**Forces on You** Ask students to calculate their mass in kilograms and write the results in their Science Journals. Then, ask them to calculate the amount of force it would take to accelerate them from standing still to a velocity of 10 km/h in 10 seconds. $a = (v_2 - v_1)/t$; $v_2$ = 10 km/h = 10,000 m/3,600 s = 2.8 m/s; $v_1$ = 0; therefore, $a$ = 2.8 m/s ÷ 10 s = 0.28 m/s²; $F = ma$, so the force needed will be the student's mass in kilograms times 0.28 m/s². L2  **Logical-Mathematical**

---

## Activity

**Toy Car** Have students measure the mass of a toy car, then roll it down a ramp. Have one student measure the distance the car rolled down the ramp, and have another student time how long it takes the car to get to the bottom of the ramp. Add some mass to the car and repeat. Change the mass 5 times. Have students calculate the average speed for each trial by dividing the distance traveled down the ramp by the time. Ask students whether the acceleration depended on the mass of the car. No, because the average speed was the same. Ask students whether the force on each car was different. Yes, because according to $F = ma$ the force will depend on the mass if $a$ is constant. L2  COOP LEARN
**IS Kinesthetic**

## Teacher FYI

**Translational and Angular Acceleration** This section explains how to calculate the acceleration of an object moving in a straight line. This is called the object's translational acceleration. Acceleration that causes an object to change direction is called angular acceleration. If the object is changing both speed and direction, its total acceleration is the sum of both its translational acceleration and its angular acceleration.

## Applying Math

**Indiana Math Standards**
**Correlation to Mathematics Objectives**
7.2.1, 7.3.1, 7.3.5

### Answers to Practice Problems

1. $a = \frac{F}{m} = \frac{1.0 \text{ N}}{2.0 \text{ kg}} = .5 \text{m/s}^2$
2. $F = ma = 0.15 \text{ kg} \times 40 \text{ m/s}^2 = 6 \text{ N}$

**Figure 10** The ball would fall towards Earth in a curved path.

## Visual Learning

**Figure 10** Ask students to identify the forces acting on the ball as it is being thrown and while it is in the air. Ask them to describe the motion of the ball in both of these situations. The force of the hand accelerates the ball forward and up until it loses contact with the hand. Ignoring air resistance, then only gravity acts on the ball, accelerating it downward. L2 IS **Visual-Spatial**

### Discussion

**Ball on the Moon** Tell students to imagine throwing a baseball on Earth, and then throwing the ball with the same force on the Moon. How would the paths of the ball differ? Why? The ball would travel farther in the horizontal direction before falling to the ground on the Moon. The ball would have the same horizontal force acting on it, but the force pulling it down would be less on the Moon because of the Moon's lower gravity. L2 IS **Logical-Mathematical**

### Discussion

**Gravity** What is the centripetal force that keeps the Moon in orbit around Earth? gravity L2 IS **Logical-Mathematical**

---

**Figure 10** When the ball is thrown, it doesn't keep moving in a straight line. Gravity exerts a force downward that makes it move in a curved path.
**Infer** *how the ball would move if it were thrown horizontally.*

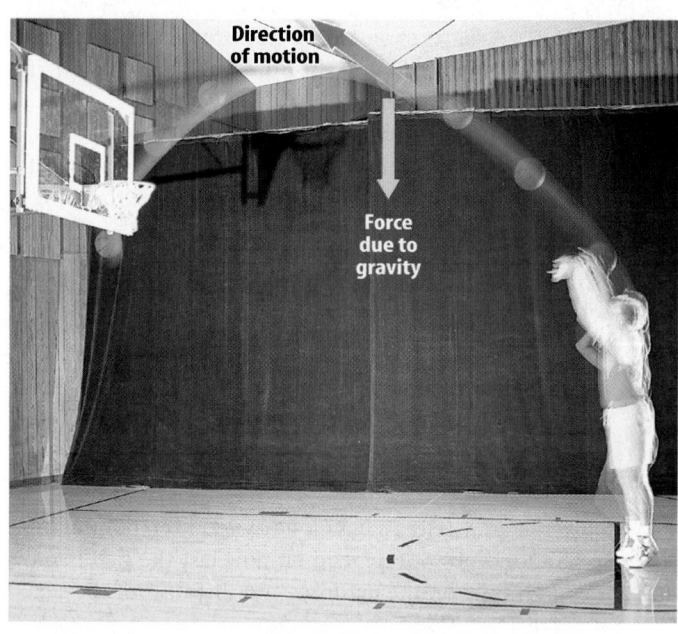

Direction of motion

Force due to gravity

---

> **Indiana Academic Standard Check**
>
> **7.3.17:** Investigate that an unbalanced force . . . may curve into an orbit around the center.
>
> ✔ In circular motion, how does the direction of the centripetal force compare to the direction of an object's motion?
>
> ✔ It is perpendicular to the object's motion.

**Turning** Sometimes forces and motion are not in a straight line. If a net force acts at an angle to the direction an object is moving, the object will follow a curved path. The object might be going slower, faster, or at the same speed after it turns.

For example, when you shoot a basketball, the ball doesn't continue to move in a straight line after it leaves your hand. Instead it starts to curve downward, as shown in **Figure 10.** The force of gravity pulls the ball downward. The ball's motion is a combination of its original motion and the downward motion due to gravity. This causes the ball to move in a curved path.

## Circular Motion

A rider on a merry-go-round ride moves in a circle. This type of motion is called circular motion. If you are in circular motion, your direction of motion is constantly changing. This means you are constantly accelerating. According to Newton's second law of motion, if you are constantly accelerating, there must be a force acting on you the entire time.

Think about an object on the end of a string whirling in a circle. The force that keeps the object moving in a circle is exerted by the string. The string pulls on the object to keep it moving in a circle. The force exerted by the string is the centripetal force and always points toward the center of the circle. In circular motion the centripetal force is always perpendicular to the motion.

**360 CHAPTER 12** Force and Newton's Laws

---

### Active Reading

**Jigsaw** In this collaborative learning technique, individuals become experts on a portion of a text and share their expertise with a small group, called their home group. Everyone shares responsibility for learning the assigned reading. Assign each person in each home group an expert number (1 through 5, for example). Have students gather into the expert groups that cor-respond to the number they were assigned. Have them read, discuss, and master chapter concepts and determine how best to teach them to their home groups. Have students return to their home groups and share the content they learned in their expert groups. Have students use the Jigsaw strategy with the material on Newton's laws of motion covered in this chapter.

**Satellite Motion** Objects that orbit Earth are satellites of Earth. Satellites go around Earth in nearly circular orbits, with the centripetal force being gravity. Why doesn't a satellite fall to Earth like a baseball does? Actually, a satellite is falling to Earth just like a baseball.

Suppose Earth were perfectly smooth and you throw a baseball horizontally. Gravity pulls the baseball downward so it travels in a curved path. If the baseball is thrown faster, its path is less curved, and it travels farther before it hits the ground. If the baseball were traveling fast enough, as it fell, its curved path would follow the curve of Earth's surface as shown in **Figure 11**. Then the baseball would never hit the ground. Instead, it would continue to fall around Earth.

Satellites in orbit are being pulled toward Earth just as baseballs are. The difference is that satellites are moving so fast horizontally that Earth's surface curves downward at the same rate that the satellites are falling downward. The speed at which a object must move to go into orbit near Earth's surface is about 8 km/s, or about 29,000 km/h.

To place a satellite into orbit, a rocket carries the satellite to the desired height. Then the rocket fires again to give the satellite the horizontal speed it needs to stay in orbit.

## Air Resistance

Whether you are walking, running, or biking, air is pushing against you. This push is air resistance. Air resistance is a form of friction that acts to slow down any object moving in the air. Air resistance is a force that gets larger as an object moves faster. Air resistance also depends on the shape of an object. A piece of paper crumpled into a ball falls faster than a flat piece of paper falls.

When an object falls it speeds up as gravity pulls it downward. At the same time, the force of air resistance pushing up on the object is increasing as the object moves faster. Finally, the upward air resistance force becomes large enough to equal the downward force of gravity.

When the air resistance force equals the weight, the net force on the object is zero. By Newton's second law, the object's acceleration then is zero, and its speed no longer increases. When air resistance balances the force of gravity, the object falls at a constant speed called the terminal velocity.

**Figure 11** The faster a ball is thrown, the farther it travels before gravity pulls it to Earth. If the ball is traveling fast enough, Earth's surface curves away from it as fast as it falls downward. Then the ball never hits the ground.

**Drop the Ball**

**Materials** sheet of paper, dense ball

**Estimated Time** five minutes

**Procedure** Display the sheet of paper and dense ball. Ask which will hit the ground first if both are dropped at the same time, and why. Have students observe as both are dropped. Then, crumple up the paper and drop it and the ball. Explain that the paper fell faster this time because its shape caused it to encounter less air resistance. L2

**LS Visual-Spatial**

## 3 Assess

### DAILY INTERVENTION

**Check for Understanding**

**Logical-Mathematical** A weight lifter lifts a 150-kg weight at a maximum acceleration of 0.25 m/s² as he lifts the weight. What was the maximum force the weight lifter exerted to lift the weight? $F = (150 \text{ kg})(0.25 \text{ m/s}^2) = 37.5 \text{ N}$

**Reteach**

**Many Forces** Have students identify the forces acting on them as they sit in a car that is speeding up. Gravity pulls down, the seat pushes up; the back of the seat pushes you forward, static friction between the students' bodies and the seat keeps you from sliding off the seat. L2 LS

**Logical-Mathematical**

### ✔ Assessment

**Process** Have students calculate the force of Earth's gravity acting on a person with a mass of 50 kg. $F = ma = 50 \text{ kg} \times 9.8 \text{ m/s}^2 = 490 \text{ N}$ Use **Performance Assessment in the Science Classroom,** p. 101.

---

**Figure 12** The wrench is spinning as it slides across the table. The center of mass of the wrench, shown by the dots, moves as if the force of friction is acting at that point.

## Center of Mass

When you throw a stick, the motion of the stick might seem to be complicated. However, there is one point on the stick, called the center of mass, that moves in a smooth path. The **center of mass** is the point in an object that moves as if all the object's mass were concentrated at that point. For a symmetrical object, such as a ball, the center of mass is at the object's center. However, for any object the center of mass moves as if the net force is being applied there.

**Figure 12** shows how the center of mass of a wrench moves as it slides across a table. The net force on the wrench is the force of friction between on the wrench and the table. This causes the center of mass to move in a straight line with decreasing speed.

### section 2 review

**Summary**

**Force and Acceleration**
- According to Newton's second law, the net force on an object, its mass, and its acceleration are related by

$$F_{net} = ma$$

**Gravity**
- The force of gravity between any two objects is always attractive and depends on the masses of the objects and the distance between them.

**Using Newton's Second Law**
- A moving object speeds up if the net force is in the direction of the motion.
- A moving object slows down if the net force is in the direction opposite to the motion.
- A moving object turns if the net force is at an angle to the direction of motion.

**Circular Motion**
- A centripetal force exerted toward the center of the circle keeps an object moving in circular motion.

**Self Check**

1. **Make a diagram** showing the forces acting on a coasting bike rider traveling at 25 km/h on a flat roadway.
2. **Analyze** how your weight would change with time if you were on a space ship traveling away from Earth toward the Moon.
3. **Explain** how the force of air resistance depends on an object's speed.
4. **Infer** the direction of the net force acting on a car as it slows down and turns right.
5. **Think Critically** Three students are pushing on a box. Under what conditions will the motion of the box change?

**Applying Math**

6. **Calculate Net Force** A car has a mass of 1,500 kg. If the car has an acceleration of 2.0 m/s², what is the net force acting on the car?
7. **Calculate Mass** During a softball game, a softball is struck by a bat and has an acceleration of 1,500 m/s². If the net force exerted on the softball by the bat is 300 N, what is the softball's mass?

 Science Online in7.msscience.com/self_check_quiz

---

### section 2 review

1. Check students' diagrams. The downward force of gravity is balanced by the upward force exerted by the ground. Rolling friction will cause the bike to slow down and stop.
2. The force of Earth's gravity will decrease so your weight will decrease.
3. The greater the speed, the greater the air resistance, but air resistance remains constant at terminal velocity.
4. The net force is pushing diagonally (at some angle) on the car and to the right.
5. When their forces are unbalanced.
6. $F = ma; F = 1,500 \text{ kg} \times 2.0 \text{ m/s}^2 = 3,000 \text{ N}$
7. $F = ma; m = F/a = 300 \text{ N}/1,500 \text{ m/s}^2 = 0.2 \text{ kg}$

# section 3

Also covers: 7.2.6 (Detailed standards begin on page IN8.)

# Newton's Third Law

## Action and Reaction

Newton's first two laws of motion explain how the motion of a single object changes. If the forces acting on the object are balanced, the object will remain at rest or stay in motion with constant velocity. If the forces are unbalanced, the object will accelerate in the direction of the net force. Newton's second law tells how to calculate the acceleration, or change in motion, of an object if the net force acting on it is known.

Newton's third law describes something else that happens when one object exerts a force on another object. Suppose you push on a wall. It may surprise you to learn that if you push on a wall, the wall also pushes on you. According to **Newton's third law of motion**, forces always act in equal but opposite pairs. Another way of saying this is for every action, there is an equal but opposite reaction. This means that when you push on a wall, the wall pushes back on you with a force equal in strength to the force you exerted. When one object exerts a force on another object, the second object exerts the same size force on the first object, as shown in **Figure 13.**

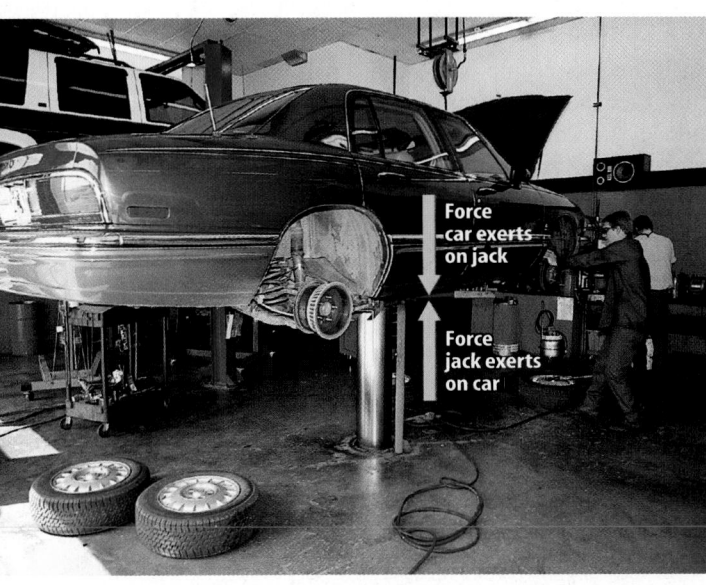

Force car exerts on jack

Force jack exerts on car

**Figure 13** The car jack is pushing up on the car with the same amount of force with which the car is pushing down on the jack. **Identify** *the other force acting on the car.*

---

### as you read

**What You'll Learn**
■ **Identify** the relationship between the forces that objects exert on each other.

**Why It's Important**
Newton's third law can explain how birds fly and rockets move.

**Review Vocabulary**
**force:** a push or a pull

**New Vocabulary**
● Newton's third law of motion

---

## Section 3 Resource Manager

**Chapter *Fast File* Resources**
Transparency Activity, pp. 46, 47–48
Directed Reading for Content Mastery,
  pp. 20, 22
MiniLAB, p. 4
Enrichment, p. 32
Reinforcement, p. 29

Lab Worksheets, pp. 5–6, 7–8
**Cultural Diversity,** p. 63
**Performance Assessment in the Science Classroom,**
  p. 36
**Lab Management and Safety,** p. 65

---

## 1 Motivate

**Bellringer**

**Section Focus Transparencies** also are available on the Interactive Chalkboard CD-ROM.
[L2] **ELL**

### Tie to Prior Knowledge

**Force Pairs** Ask students to describe the force exerted on them by their chairs. The force of the chairs pushes up on them, countering the force of gravity pulling them down. Ask students if they exert a force on their chairs. Explain that according to Newton's third law of motion, all forces act in pairs. They will learn more about these pairs of forces in this section.

### Caption Answer
**Figure 13** gravity

**Caption Answer**

**Figure 14** The car with the smaller mass accelerates more.

## Inquiry Lab

### Describing the Motion of Balls

**Purpose** to explore how mass, velocity, and size affect balls' interactions

**Possible Materials** at least ten balls having different mass and size; such as marbles, bowling, table-tennis, golf, tennis, and wiffle balls, volleyballs, raquetballs, softballs, and basketballs

**Estimated Time** 20 minutes

**Teaching Strategies**

• Students can experiment with the ways different balls interact.
• Students can plan how they want the balls to collide (one at rest, both in motion, three at a time, etc.), and then draw a diagram of the planned motion (have students indicate with arrow thickness or length the velocity of the balls).
• Student can test their plans and draw a diagram of how their balls interacted.
• Students can compare and contrast their plans with their tests.

**For additional inquiry activities, see Science Inquiry Labs.**

**Figure 14** In this collision, the first car exerts a force on the second. The second exerts the same force in the opposite direction on the first car.
**Explain** whether both cars will have the same acceleration.

**Science Online**

**Topic: How Birds Fly**
Visit in7.msscience.com for Web links to information about how birds and other animals fly.

**Activity** Make a diagram showing the forces acting on a bird as it flies.

**Figure 15** When the child pushes against the wall, the wall pushes against the child.

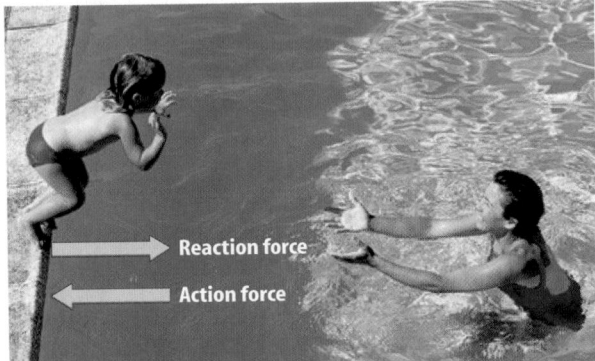

Reaction force

Action force

**Action and Reaction Forces Don't Cancel** The forces exerted by two objects on each other are often called an action-reaction force pair. Either force can be considered the action force or the reaction force. You might think that because action-reaction forces are equal and opposite that they cancel. However, action and reaction force pairs don't cancel because they act on different objects. Forces can cancel only if they act on the same object.

For example, imagine you're driving a bumper car and are about to bump a friend in another car, as shown in **Figure 14.** When the two cars collide, your car pushes on the other car. By Newton's third law, that car pushes on your car with the same force, but in the opposite direction. This force causes you to slow down. One force of the action-reaction force pair is exerted on your friend's car, and the other force of the force pair is exerted on your car. Another example of an action-reaction pair is shown in **Figure 15.**

You constantly use action-reaction force pairs as you move about. When you jump, you push down on the ground. The ground then pushes up on you. It is this upward force that pushes you into the air. **Figure 16** shows some examples of how Newton's laws of motion are demonstrated in sporting events.

**INTEGRATE Life Science** Birds and other flying creatures also use Newton's third law. When a bird flies, its wings push in a downward and a backward direction. This pushes air downward and backward. By Newton's third law, the air pushes back on the bird in the opposite directions—upward and forward. This force keeps a bird in the air and propels it forward.

## Differentiated Instruction

**Physically Challenged** Have a student in a wheelchair with the brakes off push against a student in rollerskates (or in another wheelchair or on a skate board) to demonstrate Newton's third law. Have them repeat with one student in motion, if desired.

**Figure 16**

**A**lthough it is not obvious, Newton's laws of motion are demonstrated in sports activities all the time. According to the first law, if an object is in motion, it moves in a straight line with constant speed unless a net force acts on it. If an object is at rest, it stays at rest unless a net force acts on it. The second law states that a net force acting on an object causes the object to accelerate in the direction of the force. The third law can be understood this way—for every action force, there is an equal and opposite reaction force.

◀ **NEWTON'S SECOND LAW** As Tiger Woods hits a golf ball, he applies a force that will drive the ball in the direction of that force—an example of Newton's second law.

▲ **NEWTON'S FIRST LAW** According to Newton's first law, the diver does not move in a straight line with constant speed because of the force of gravity.

▶ **NEWTON'S THIRD LAW** Newton's third law applies even when objects do not move. Here a gymnast pushes downward on the bars. The bars push back on the gymnast with an equal force.

SECTION 3 Newton's Third Law **365**

## Visualizing Newton's Laws in Sports

Have students examine the pictures and read the captions. Then ask the following questions.

A shot put has a much greater mass than a discus. How does Newton's second law explain why a discus can be thrown about twice as far as a shot put? Because of its greater mass, the shot put must be thrown with much more force than the discus to reach the same acceleration.

How does Newton's third law explain the direction a boat crew must move the oars in order to move the boat forward? The crew applies a backward force to the water through the oars. The water applies an equal and opposite force on the oars. This force propels the oars and thus the boat through the water.

### Activity

**Motion in Sports** Have groups of students cut out magazine pictures showing examples of Newton's laws of motion in sports. Have them mount each picture on poster board. Ask each group to present their pictures to the class, explaining the forces at work in each example. **LS Visual-Spatial**

## Cultural Diversity

**Lacrosse** The game of lacrosse is derived from an Iroquois game known as Galahs. This game involves catching and tossing a ball using a thin basket on a stick. Have students learn more about this game and describe it in relation to Newton's laws.

## Discussion

**Space Shuttle** Two minutes after the space shuttle's launch, all fuel in the solid rocket boosters is used up, and these boosters drop off and fall back to Earth. This makes the shuttle lighter and easier to accelerate. Predict what happens to keep the shuttle accelerating smoothly. The rate of combustion in the engine is decreased.

L3 IS **Logical-Mathematical**

## Visual Learning

**Figure 18** Review with students the action-reaction force pairs between the gas molecules and the rocket. Tell students that the force on the rocket, called the thrust, is equal to the mass ejected per second times the velocity of the expelled gases. How is this equivalent to $F = ma$? Thrust $= (m/t)v = m(v/t) = ma = f$

L2 IS **Logical-Mathematical**

## Quick Demo

**Thrust in Action-Reaction**

**Materials** $CO_2$ cartridge, nail to puncture cartridge, apparatus that rotates like a helicopter wing

**Estimated Time** five minutes

**Procedure** Attach the $CO_2$ cartridge to the end of the 'wing'. Puncture the $CO_2$ cartridge and release it to allow the apparatus to spin. Have the students explain what caused the spinning. Action-reaction similar to a rocket caused the motion.

**Figure 17** The force of the ground on your foot is equal and opposite to the force of your foot on the ground. If you push back harder, the ground pushes forward harder.
**Determine** *In what direction does the ground push on you if you are standing still?*

**Large and Small Objects** Sometimes it's easy not to notice an action-reaction pair is because one of the objects is often much more massive and appears to remain motionless when a force acts on it. It has so much inertia, or tendency to remain at rest, that it hardly accelerates. Walking is a good example. When you walk forward, you push backward on the ground. Your shoe pushes Earth backward, and Earth pushes your shoe forward, as shown in **Figure 16.** Earth has so much mass compared to you that it does not move noticeably when you push it. If you step on something that has less mass than you do, like a skateboard, you can see it being pushed back.

**A Rocket Launch** The launching of a space shuttle is a spectacular example of Newton's third law. Three rocket engines supply the force, called thrust, that lifts the rocket. When the rocket fuel is ignited, a hot gas is produced. As the gas molecules collide with the inside engine walls, the walls exert a force that pushes them out of the bottom of the engine, as shown in **Figure 18.** This downward push is the action force. The reaction force is the upward push on the rocket engine by the gas molecules. This is the thrust that propels the rocket upward.

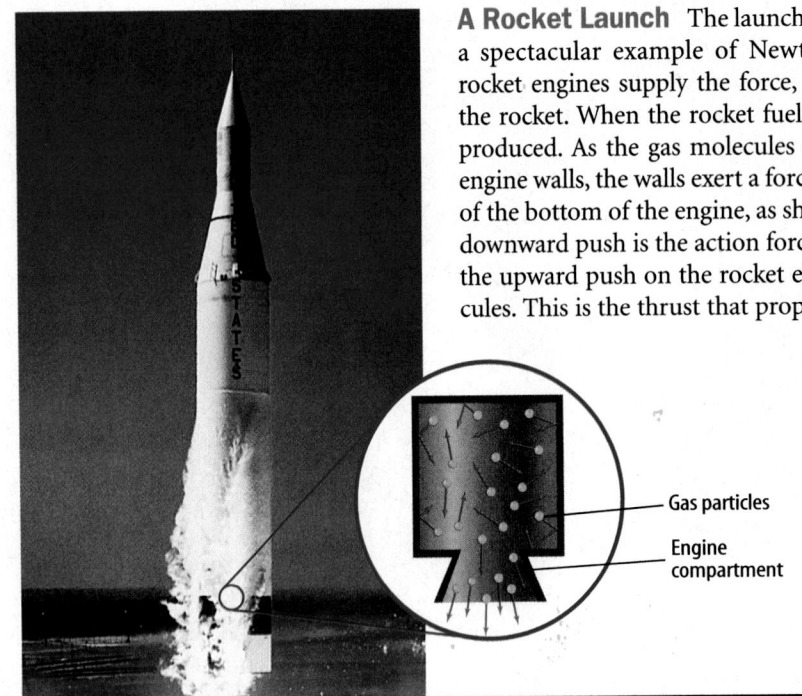

Gas particles

Engine compartment

**Figure 18** Newton's third law enables a rocket to fly. The rocket pushes the gas molecules downward, and the gas molecules push the rocket upward.

Force exerted by scale
Weight of student
Weight of student

**Figure 19** Whether you are standing on Earth or falling, the force of Earth's gravity on you doesn't change. However, your weight measured by a scale would change.

## Weightlessness

You might have seen pictures of astronauts floating inside a space shuttle as it orbits Earth. The astronauts are said to be weightless, as if Earth's gravity were no longer pulling on them. Yet the force of gravity on the shuttle is almost 90 percent as large as at Earth's surface. Newton's laws of motion can explain why the astronauts float as if there were no forces acting on them.

**Measuring Weight** Think about how you measure your weight. When you stand on a scale, your weight pushes down on the scale. This causes the scale pointer to point to your weight. At the same time, by Newton's third law the scale pushes up on you with a force equal to your weight, as shown in **Figure 19.** This force balances the downward pull of gravity on you.

**Free Fall and Weightlessness** Now suppose you were standing on a scale in an elevator that is falling, as shown in **Figure 19.** A falling object is in free fall when the only force acting on the object is gravity. Inside the free-falling elevator, you and the scale are both in free fall. Because the only force acting on you is gravity, the scale no longer is pushing up on you. According to Newton's third law, you no longer push down on the scale. So the scale pointer stays at zero and you seem to be weightless. Weightlessness is the condition that occurs in free fall when the weight of an object seems to be zero.

However, you are not really weightless in free fall because Earth is still pulling down on you. With nothing to push up on you, such as your chair, you would have no sensation of weight.

---

### Mini LAB

**Measuring Force Pairs**

**Procedure**
1. Work in pairs. Each person needs a **spring scale.**
2. Hook the two scales together. Each person should pull back on a scale. Record the two readings. Pull harder and record the two readings.
3. Continue to pull on both scales, but let the scales move toward one person. Do the readings change?
4. Try to pull in such a way that the two scales have different readings.

**Analysis**
1. What can you conclude about the pair of forces in each situation?
2. Explain how this experiment demonstrates Newton's third law.

---

### Mini LAB

**Purpose** Students study the force pairs between two spring scales that are hooked together and pulled by two students. [L2]

**ELL** **COOP LEARN** [LS]

**Kinesthetic**

**Materials** spring scales (2)

**Teaching Strategies** Be sure the scales are zeroed, and make sure students pull with the hooks facing each other directly.

**Analysis**
1. They were always equal to each other.
2. In every case, the forces of the scales pulling on each other were equal and opposite, which follows Newton's third law.

**Assessment**

**Portfolio** Have students make drawings of the spring scales and indicate the forces acting on them in each trial. Use **PASC,** p. 127. [P]

---

### Fun Fact

The space shuttle soars into space at about 4 g's. This is four times the acceleration of a falling object, and is about what you feel at the bottom of a loop on a fast roller-coaster.

---

## LAB DEMONSTRATION

**Purpose** to demonstrate Newton's third law of motion

**Materials** two identical chairs with wheels, rope, tape, meterstick

**Preparation** Set the chairs about 3 m apart, and mark their positions with tape.

**Procedure** Have two students that are about the same size sit in the chairs. Have each student pull on one end of the rope until the chairs meet. Mark and measure the distance each chair traveled.

**Expected Outcome** The chairs will both move about the same distance.

**Assessment**

How does this show Newton's third law? $F_1 = F_2$. Therefore, $m_1a_1 = m_2a_2$. If the masses of the students plus the chairs are about equal, $a_1 = a_2$; $a = v/t$, so $v_1/t_1 = v_2/t_2$. Time is the same for both, so $v_1 = v_2$; $v = d/t$, so $d_1/t_1 = d_2/t_2$, time is the same, so $d_1 = d_2$.

**Figure 20** These oranges seem to be floating because they are falling around Earth at the same speed as the space shuttle and the astronauts. As a result, they aren't moving relative to the astronauts in the cabin.

**Weightlessness in Orbit** To understand how objects move in the orbiting space shuttle, imagine you were holding a ball in the free-falling elevator. If you let the ball go, the position of the ball relative to you and the elevator wouldn't change, because you, the ball, and the elevator are moving at the same speed.

However, suppose you give the ball a gentle push downward. While you are pushing the ball, this downward force adds to the downward force of gravity. According to Newton's second law, the acceleration of the ball increases. So while you are pushing, the acceleration of the ball is greater than the acceleration of both you and the elevator. This causes the ball to speed up relative to you and the elevator. After it speeds up, it continues moving faster than you and the elevator, and it drifts downward until it hits the elevator floor.

When the space shuttle orbits Earth, the shuttle and all the objects in it are in free fall. They are falling in a curved path around Earth, instead of falling straight downward. As a result, objects in the shuttle appear to be weightless, as shown in **Figure 20.** A small push causes an object to drift away, just as a small downward push on the ball in the free-falling elevator caused it to drift to the floor.

---

## section 3 review

### Summary

**Action and Reaction**

- According to Newton's third law, when one object exerts a force on another object, the second object exerts the same size force on the first object.
- Either force in an action-reaction force pair can be the action force or the reaction force.
- Action and reaction force pairs don't cancel because they are exerted on different objects.
- When action and reaction forces are exerted by two objects, the accelerations of the objects depend on the masses of the objects.

**Weightlessness**

- A falling object is in free fall if the only force acting on it is gravity.
- Weightlessness occurs in free fall when the weight of an object seems to be zero.
- Objects orbiting Earth appear to be weightless because they are in free fall in a curved path around Earth.

### Self Check

1. **Evaluate** the force a skateboard exerts on you if your mass is 60 kg and you push on the skateboard with a force of 60 N.

2. **Explain** why you move forward and a boat moves backward when you jump from a boat to a pier.

3. **Describe** the action and reaction forces when a hammer hits a nail.

4. **Infer** You and a child are on skates and you give each other a push. If the mass of the child is half your mass, who has the greater acceleration? By what factor?

5. **Think Critically** Suppose you are walking in an airliner in flight. Use Newton's third law to describe the effect of your walk on the motion on the airliner.

#### Applying Math

6. **Calculate Acceleration** A person standing in a canoe exerts a force of 700 N to throw an anchor over the side. Find the acceleration of the canoe if the total mass of the canoe and the person is 100 kg.

Science Online in7.msscience.com/self_check_quiz

---

# BALLOON *RACES*

## ● Real-World Question

The motion of a rocket lifting off a launch pad is determined by Newton's laws of motion. Here you will make a balloon rocket that is powered by escaping air. How do Newton's laws of motion explain the motion of balloon rockets?

### Goals

- **Measure** the speed of a balloon rocket.
- **Describe** how Newton's laws explain a rocket's motion.

### Materials

| | |
|---|---|
| balloons | meterstick |
| drinking straws | stopwatch |
| string | *clock |
| tape | *Alternate materials |

### Safety Precautions

## ● Procedure

1. Make a rocket path by threading a string through a drinking straw. Run the string across the classroom and fasten at both ends.
2. Blow up a balloon and hold it tightly at the end to prevent air from escaping. Tape the balloon to the straw on the string.
3. Release the balloon so it moves along the string. Measure the distance the balloon travels and the time it takes.
4. Repeat steps 2 and 3 with different balloons.

## ● Analyze Your Data

1. **Compare and contrast** the distances traveled. Which rocket went the greatest distance?

2. **Calculate** the average speed for each rocket. Compare and contrast them. Which rocket has the greatest average speed?

## ● Conclude and Apply

1. **Infer** which aspects of these rockets made them travel far or fast.
2. **Draw** a diagram showing all the forces acting on a balloon rocket.
3. Use Newton's laws of motion to explain the motion of a balloon rocket from launch until it comes to a stop.

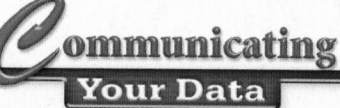

### ommunicating Your Data

Discuss with classmates which balloon rocket traveled the farthest. Why? **For more help, refer to the** Science Skill Handbook.

---

## ● Real-World Question

**Purpose** Students observe Newton's third law of motion acting on rocket balloons. **L2**

**ELL** **COOP LEARN** **IS** **Kinesthetic**

**Process Skills** observe, infer, compare and contrast, recognize cause and effect, control variables, measure, interpret data

**Time Required** 45 minutes

## ● Procedure

**Teaching Strategies** Suggest that one student handle the balloon while another measures time.

## ● Conclude and Apply

1. Answers will vary.
2. To calculate a balloon's average speed, students will need to note the time and the distance the balloon travels.
3. Answers might include the balloon's size, shape, and air capacity; the thickness of the rubber from which the balloon is made; and the size of the opening.
4. Drawings should include gravity, upward force of the straw, force of the escaping air, and friction.
5. Escaping air pushes the balloon forward (third law). When it runs out of air, it continues a short way (first law) as friction slows it to a stop (second law).

---

### ✓ Assessment

**Performance** Ask students to design nozzles that control the flow of air out the back of the balloon. Test the designs, and award a prize for the best one. Use **Performance Assessment in the Science Classroom,** p. 117.

### ommunicating Your Data

Students should discuss the process of troubleshooting their designs to get them to fly smoothly. The more successful techniques should be highlighted.

## Real-World Question

**Purpose** Students observe how to move an object from any point to another point using only two forces at right angles to each other. L2 IN **Kinesthetic**

**Process Skills** observe and infer, communicate, interpret data, diagram, hypothesize, compare and contrast, form a hypothesis, design an experiment, predict, separate and control variables, recognize cause and effect

**Time Required** 45 minutes

**Possible Materials** Any small ball can be used for the activity, but heavier balls, such as a golf ball, work best.

## Form a Hypothesis

**Possible Hypothesis** Students might hypothesize that one person can move the skid in one direction and two people can move the sled diagonally by pulling at right angles to each other.

## Design Your Own

# MODELING MOTION IN TWO DIRECTIONS

### Goals
■ **Move** the skid across the ground using two forces.
■ **Measure** how fast the skid can be moved.
■ **Determine** how smoothly the direction can be changed.

### Possible Materials
masking tape
stopwatch
* *watch or clock with a second hand*
meterstick
*metric tape measure
spring scales marked in newtons (2)
plastic lid
golf ball
*tennis ball
*Alternate materials

### Safety Precautions

## Real-World Question

When you move a computer mouse across a mouse pad, how does the rolling ball tell the computer cursor to move in the direction that you push the mouse? Inside the housing for the mouse's ball are two or more rollers that the ball rubs against as you move the mouse. They measure up-and-down and back-and-forth motions. The motion of the cursor on the screen is based on the movement of the up-and-down rollers and the back-and-forth rollers. Can any object be moved along a path by a series of motions in only two directions?

## Form a Hypothesis

How can you combine forces to move in a straight line, along a diagonal, or around corners? Place a golf ball on something that will slide, such as a plastic lid. The plastic lid is called a skid. Lay out a course to follow on the floor. Write a plan for moving your golf ball along the path without having the golf ball roll away.

## Test Your Hypothesis

**Make a Plan**

1. Lay out a course that involves two directions, such as always moving forward or left.

2. Attach two spring scales to the skid. One always will pull straight forward. One always will pull to one side. You cannot turn the skid. If one scale is pulling toward the door of your classroom, it always must pull in that direction. (It can pull with zero force if needed, but it can't push.)

3. How will you handle movements along diagonals and turns?

4. How will you measure speed?

**370 CHAPTER 12** Force and Newton's Laws

## Alternative Inquiry Lab

**Motion in All Directions** Make this Lab an Inquiry Lab by building on their experience. Have students make groups of four. Give each group masking tape to make their own course that moves through all four directions. Connect the courses and time each group in an "obstacle course" race. Make sure each group stays within the taped off area, has all four members of the group at right angles, and that the students stay in the same direction.

5. **Experiment** with your skid. How hard do you have to pull to counteract sliding friction at a given speed? How fast can you accelerate? Can you stop suddenly without spilling the golf ball, or do you need to slow down?

6. **Write** a plan for moving your golf ball along the course by pulling only forward or to one side. Be sure you understand your plan and have considered all the details.

**Follow Your Plan**

1. Make sure your teacher approves your plan before you start.

2. Move your golf ball along the path.

3. Modify your plan, if needed.

4. **Organize** your data so they can be used to run your course and write them in your Science Journal.

5. **Test** your results with a new route.

## ▶ Analyze Your Data

1. What was the difference between the two routes? How did this affect the forces you needed to use on the golf ball?

2. How did you separate and control variables in this experiment?

3. Was your hypothesis supported? Explain.

## ▶ Conclude and Apply

1. What happens when you combine two forces at right angles?

2. If you could pull on all four sides (front, back, left, right) of your skid, could you move anywhere along the floor? Make a hypothesis to explain your answer.

### Communicating
**Your Data**

**Compare** your conclusions with those of other students in your class. **For more help, refer to the** Science Skill Handbook.

**LAB 371**

---

## ▶ Test Your Hypothesis

**Teaching Strategies** Suggest that students try moving the skid by applying forces in one direction followed by the other, and then by applying forces in the two directions at the same time.

**Expected Outcome** Students will find it much easier to move the skid by moving one direction at a time. Moving the skid in both directions simultaneously requires them to be more responsive to what they see happening as they pull.

## ▶ Analyze Your Data

**Answers to Questions**

1. Students should find the new route easier than the first if they have learned from their experience.

2. The variables were the forces in each direction. The two spring scales enabled each force to be measured separately.

3. Check students' explanations.

**Error Analysis** Have students discuss problems they may have had moving the skid through their courses.

## ▶ Conclude and Apply

1. The object moves on a diagonal between the two forces.

2. Yes; forces in these four directions can be combined to move an object along any line.

---

### ☑ Assessment

**Performance** Ask students to examine a computer mouse and determine how it tells the screen how to move the cursor. Most have one roller for horizontal motion, one for vertical motion, and a third roller for stability. The information from the rollers is combined to move the cursor on the screen in any direction. Use **Performance Assessment in the Science Classroom,** p. 89.

### Communicating
**Your Data**

Encourage students to discuss how Newton's three laws affected the results of the activity. Ask them to describe how the activity would have differed if it had been done on an almost frictionless surface such as ice.

## Content Background

Air bags were originally designed as an inflatable device for use in crash landings of airplanes in World War II. Air bags inflate after a chemical reaction, triggered by an impact, releases hot nitrogen gas that expands into the bag. The inflation lasts only a fraction of a second. Between 1986 and 2000, the National Highway Traffic Safety Association estimated that air bags prevented over 5,300 fatalities. Air bags are designed to supplement, not replace, the use of seat belts. Improper use can result in injuries caused by the safety devices themselves. The NHTSA recorded 195 confirmed fatalities caused by air bags between 1990 and 2000.

## Discussion

**Collision Injuries** In addition to air bags and seat restraints, how else can injuries be avoided in collisions? Students may suggest improvements in designs of car frames such as crumpling structural frames. Also, proper use of children's seats and appropriate placement of children in the passenger compartments.

## Activity

**Egg Drop** Have students drop eggs one inch above a hard floor. Have them increase the height of the drop by half-inch increments until the eggshells break. Then have them repeat the activity several times with increasingly thick layers of fabric placed on the floor. Direct students to graph their data. Students should see that a yielding material that absorbs energy allows the eggs to withstand falls from greater heights. For further experimentation, allow the class to try different materials like balloons and pillows on the floor. [L2] [LS] **Kinesthetic**

---

TIME SCIENCE AND Society — SCIENCE ISSUES THAT AFFECT YOU!

# Air Bag Safety

## After complaints and injuries, air bags in cars are helping all passengers

The car in front of yours stops suddenly. You hear the crunch of car against car and feel your seat belt grab you. Your mom is covered with, not blood, thank goodness, but with a big white cloth. Your seat belts and air bags worked perfectly.

### Popcorn in the Dash

Air bags have saved more than a thousand lives since 1992. They are like having a giant popcorn kernel in the dashboard that pops and becomes many times its original size. But unlike popcorn, an air bag is triggered by impact, not heat. In a crash, a chemical reaction produces a gas that expands in a split second, inflating a balloonlike bag to cushion the driver and possibly the front-seat passenger. The bag deflates quickly so it doesn't trap people in the car.

### Newton and the Air Bag

When you're traveling in a car, you move with it at whatever speed it is going. According to Newton's first law, you are the object in motion, and you will continue in motion unless acted upon by a force, such as a car crash.

Unfortunately, a crash stops the car, but it doesn't stop you, at least, not right away. You continue moving forward if your car doesn't have air bags or if you haven't buckled your seat belt. You stop when you strike the inside of the car. You hit the dashboard or steering wheel while traveling at the speed of the car. When an air bag inflates, you come to a stop move slowly, which reduces the force that is exerted on you.

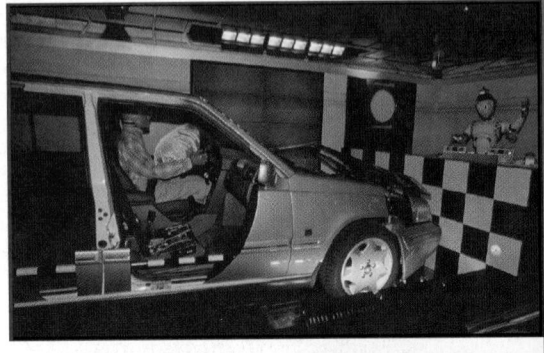

**A test measures the speed at which an air bag deploys.**

**Measure** Hold a paper plate 26 cm in front of you. Use a ruler to measure the distance. That's the distance drivers should have between the chest and the steering wheel to make air bags safe. Inform adult drivers in your family about this safety distance.

Science Online
For more information, visit
in7.msscience.com/time

---

**Measure** Ask students to investigate the proper use of seat belts and shoulder restraints. Improper placement of seat belts can result in neck injuries caused as a passenger's momentum carries them forward and under a belt. Improper positioning of shoulder restraints can result in chest and upper limb injuries.

## Resources for Teachers and Students

Air Bag and Seat Belt Safety Campaign National Safety Council
1025 Connecticut Ave., NW, Suite 1200 Washington, DC 20036

National Highway Traffic Safety Administration
Auto Safety Hotline 1-800-424-9393

## Reviewing Main Ideas

**Section 1** **Newton's First Law**

1. A force is a push or a pull.

2. Newton's first law states that objects in motion tend to stay in motion and objects at rest tend to stay at rest unless acted upon by a nonzero net force.

3. Friction is a force that resists motion between surfaces that are touching each other.

**Section 2** **Newton's Second Law**

1. Newton's second law states that an object acted upon by a net force will accelerate in the direction of this force.

2. The acceleration due to a net force is given by the equation $a = F_{net}/m$.

3. The force of gravity between two objects depends on their masses and the distance between them.

4. In circular motion, a force pointing toward the center of the circle acts on an object.

**Section 3** **Newton's Third Law**

1. According to Newton's third law, the forces two objects exert on each other are always equal but in opposite directions.

2. Action and reaction forces don't cancel because they act on different objects.

3. Objects in orbit appear to be weightless because they are in free fall around Earth.

## Reviewing Main Ideas

Summary statements can be used by students to review the major concepts of the chapter.

## Visualizing Main Ideas

See student page.

**Visit** in7.msscience.com
/self_check_quiz
/interactive_tutor
/vocabulary_puzzlemaker
/chapter_review
/standards_review

## Assessment Transparency

For additional assessment questions, use the *Assessment Transparency* located in the transparency book.

## Visualizing Main Ideas

*Copy and complete the following concept map on Newton's laws of motion.*

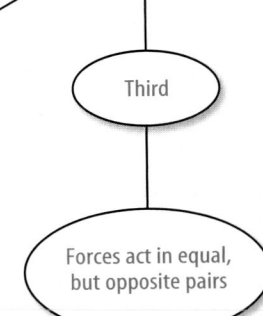

Newton's Laws of Motion
— First
— Third
— Second

First → An object at rest will remain at rest until a force is applied

Third → Forces act in equal, but opposite pairs

Second → Force = (mass) × (acceleration)

Science Online in7.msscience.com/interactive_tutor

**CHAPTER STUDY GUIDE** **373**

## Assessment

Force and Newton's Laws

**Directions:** Carefully review the diagram and answer the following questions.

1. All of these objects have unbalanced forces acting upon them **EXCEPT** ___.
   A A
   B B
   C C
   D D

2. Rolling friction pushes on an object that is rolling. According to this definition, which of these examples shows rolling friction?
   F A and D
   G B and A
   H C and B
   J D and C

3. A force is a push or pull. Which force is acting on all of the objects in the diagram?
   A Static friction
   B Magnetism
   C Gravity
   D Acceleration

L2

## Identifying Misconceptions

**Assess**

Use the assessment as a follow up to page F at the beginning of the chapter.

**Procedure** Ask students to imagine a bowling ball and a table-tennis ball in outer space so far from other objects that they experience almost no gravity. Will the force required to move the bowling ball be greater than the force required to move the ping pong ball? Why? yes, because it

has more mass How do we know friction does not play a part? In outer space there is no air and thus no friction.

**Expected Outcome** Students should begin to realize that a larger mass has more inertia, and thus a greater tendency to remain at rest.

## Using Vocabulary

1. force—a push or pull; inertia—resistance to change in motion; weight—a force due to gravity

2. Newton's first law—a body has inertia; Newton's third law—for every force there is an equal and opposite force

3. Friction is a type of force.

4. net force—total of all forces on an object; balanced forces—net force equals zero

5. weight

6. balanced forces—object does not accelerate; unbalanced forces—object accelerates

7. friction—opposing force; weight—force due to gravity

8. Newton's first law of motion—a body has inertia; Newton's second law—$a = F/m$

9. friction—opposing force; unbalanced force—accelerates an object

10. net force—sum of forces; Newton's third law—for every force there is an equal and opposite force

### Checking Concepts

| | | |
|---|---|---|
| 11. B | 14. C | 17. D |
| 12. C | 15. A | 18. D |
| 13. B | 16. B | |

### Thinking Critically

19. acceleration due to gravity increases the speed

20. Yes; the ball changed direction

21. Because Earth is so massive, the forces people exert on it cause very little acceleration.

22. The car is held on the hill by static friction. When the car moves at a constant speed, rolling friction and air resistance balance the force exerted on the wheels by the motor. When the brakes are applied, sliding friction between the brake pads and the wheels slows down the car.

**374 CHAPTER REVIEW**

## Using Vocabulary

| | |
|---|---|
| balanced forces p.351 | Newton's second law of |
| center of mass p.362 | motion p.356 |
| force p.350 | Newton's third law of |
| friction p.352 | motion p.363 |
| net force p.351 | unbalanced forces p.351 |
| Newton's first law of | weight p.357 |
| motion p.352 | |

*Explain the differences between the terms in the following sets.*

1. force—inertia—weight

2. Newton's first law of motion—Newton's third law of motion

3. friction—force

4. net force—balanced forces

5. weight—weightlessness

6. balanced forces—unbalanced forces

7. friction—weight

8. Newton's first law of motion—Newton's second law of motion

9. friction—unbalanced force

10. net force—Newton's third law of motion

## Checking Concepts

*Choose the word or phrase that best answers the question.*

11. Which of the following changes when an unbalanced force acts on an object?
    **A)** mass  **C)** inertia
    **B)** motion  **D)** weight

12. Which of the following is the force that slows a book sliding on a table?
    **A)** gravity
    **B)** static friction
    **C)** sliding friction
    **D)** inertia

**Use the illustration below to answer question 13.**

20N

5N

10N

13. Two students are pushing on the left side of a box and one student is pushing on the right. The diagram above shows the forces they exert. Which way will the box move?
    **A)** up  **C)** down
    **B)** left  **D)** right

14. What combination of units is equivalent to the newton?
    **A)** $m/s^2$  **C)** $kg \cdot m/s^2$
    **B)** $kg \cdot m/s$  **D)** $kg/m$

15. Which of the following is a push or a pull?
    **A)** force  **C)** acceleration
    **B)** momentum  **D)** inertia

16. An object is accelerated by a net force in which direction?
    **A)** at an angle to the force
    **B)** in the direction of the force
    **C)** in the direction opposite to the force
    **D)** Any of these is possible.

17. You are riding on a bike. In which of the following situations are the forces acting on the bike balanced?
    **A)** You pedal to speed up.
    **B)** You turn at constant speed.
    **C)** You coast to slow down.
    **D)** You pedal at constant speed.

18. Which of the following has no direction?
    **A)** force  **C)** weight
    **B)** acceleration  **D)** mass

## Thinking Critically

**19. Explain** why the speed of a sled increases as it moves down a snow-covered hill, even though no one is pushing on the sled.

**20. Explain** A baseball is pitched east at a speed of 40 km/h. The batter hits it west at a speed of 40 km/h. Did the ball accelerate?

**21. Form a Hypothesis** Frequently, the pair of forces acting between two objects are not noticed because one of the objects is Earth. Explain why the force acting on Earth isn't noticed.

**22. Identify** A car is parked on a hill. The driver starts the car, accelerates until the car is driving at constant speed, drives at constant speed, and then brakes to put the brake pads in contact with the spinning wheels. Explain how static friction, sliding friction, rolling friction, and air resistance are acting on the car.

**23. Draw Conclusions** You hit a hockey puck and it slides across the ice at nearly a constant speed. Is a force keeping it in motion? Explain.

**24. Infer** Newton's third law describes the forces between two colliding objects. Use this connection to explain the forces acting when you kick a soccer ball.

**25. Recognize Cause and Effect** Use Newton's third law to explain how a rocket accelerates upon takeoff.

**26. Predict** Two balls of the same size and shape are dropped from a helicopter. One ball has twice the mass of the other ball. On which ball will the force of air resistance be greater when terminal velocity is reached?

 in7.msscience.com/chapter_review

**Use the figure below to answer question 27.**

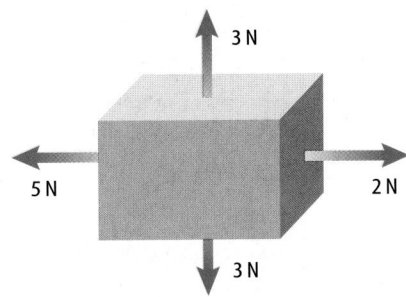

3 N

5 N                    2 N

3 N

**27. Interpreting Scientific Illustrations** Is the force on the box balanced? Explain.

## Performance Activities

**28. Oral Presentation** Research one of Newton's laws of motion and compose an oral presentation. Provide examples of the law. You might want to use a visual aid.

**29. Writing in Science** Create an experiment that deals with Newton's laws of motion. Document it using the following subject heads: *Title of Experiment, Partners' Names, Hypothesis, Materials, Procedures, Data, Results,* and *Conclusion.*

## Applying Math

**30. Acceleration** If you exert a net force of 8 N on a 2-kg object, what will its acceleration be?

**31. Force** You push against a wall with a force of 5 N. What is the force the wall exerts on your hands?

**32. Net Force** A 0.4-kg object accelerates at 2 m/s². Find the net force.

**33. Friction** A 2-kg book is pushed along a table with a force of 4 N. Find the frictional force on the book if the book's acceleration is 1.5 m/s².

**CHAPTER REVIEW 375**

**23.** When the puck is sliding on the ice, there is no force being exerted on the puck to keep it moving forward. Instead, inertia keeps the puck moving forward. Friction between the puck and the ice gradually slows the puck down.

**24.** When the foot connects with the ball, the foot accelerates the ball forward (ball has low mass) and the ball accelerates the foot backward, slowing its forward motion somewhat (foot attached to body has high mass).

**25.** The fuel inside the rocket explodes. The gas particles that are formed push against the rocket, and the rocket pushes against them. This pushes the rocket up and the gases out the bottom.

**26.** the ball with the greater mass

**27.** No; the net force is pushing to the left with a strength of 3 N

## Performance Activities

**28.** Check students' work. Use **PASC,** p. 143.

**29.** Check students' work. Use **PASC,** p. 159.

## Applying Math

### Indiana Math Standards

7.2.1, 7.3.1, 7.3.5

**30.** $a = F/m = 8\,N/2\,kg = 4\,m/s^2$

**31.** 5 N

**32.** $F = ma = 0.4\,kg \times 2\,m/s^2 = 0.8\,N$

**33.** $F = ma = (2\,kg)(1.5\,m/s^2) = 3\,N$; $4\,N - 3\,N = 1\,N$

---

## ☑ Assessment    Resources

📁 **Reproducible Masters**

**Chapter *Fast File* Resources**
 Chapter Review, pp. 39–40
 Chapter Tests, pp. 41–44
 Assessment Transparency Activity, p. 51

**Glencoe Science Web site**
 Chapter Review Test
 IN Standards Review

**Glencoe Technology**
 🖐 Assessment Transparency
 🌐 Exam*View*® Pro Testmaker
 📼 MindJogger Videoquiz
 💿 Interactive Chalkboard

**Answer Sheet** A practice answer sheet can be found at in7.msscience.com/answer_sheet.

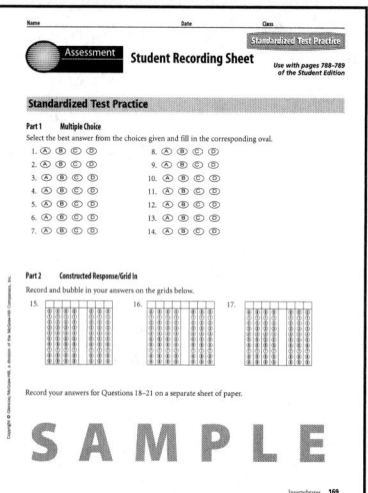

**Part 2    Critical Response**

9. Newton's first law of motion

10. A satellite's forward motion tends to keep it traveling in a straight line, but gravity continually pulls it in toward Earth. Satellites move so fast horizontally that Earth's surface curves downward at the same rate that the satellites fall downward.

11. The initial force on the ball causes it to move outward and upward. The force of gravity on the ball pulls it downward. These forces combined cause the ball to travel along a curved path.

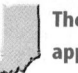 The assessed Indiana standard appears above the question.

*Record your answers on the answer sheet provided by your teacher or on a sheet of paper.*

**Part 1  Multiple Choice**

1. Which description of the gravitational force is **FALSE**?

    A It depends on the distance between objects.

    B It depends on the masses of objects.

    C It exists between all objects.

    D It is a repulsive force.

**7.3.17**

2. The table below shows the mass of some objects.

| Mass of Common Objects | |
|---|---|
| **Object** | **Mass (g)** |
| Cup | 380 |
| Book | 1,100 |
| Can | 240 |
| Ruler | 25 |
| Stapler | 620 |

Which object has an acceleration of 0.50 m/s² if you push it with a force of 0.31 N?

    A book

    B can

    C ruler

    D stapler

**Test-Taking Tip**

**Check Symbols** Be sure you understand all symbols on a table or graph before answering any questions about the table or graph.

The illustration below shows the forces acting on a box.

**7.3.17**

3. What is the acceleration of the box?

    A 0.48 m/s²

    B 4.3 m/s²

    C 4.8 m/s²

    D 27 m/s²

**7.3.17**

4. If you are pushing the box in the illustration above along the floor with a force of 12 N, what is the force of friction acting on the box?

    A 1.2 N

    B 10.8 N

    C 12 N

    D 13.2 N

**7.3.17**

5. Which best describes why astronauts in orbit seem to float in the space shuttle?

    A The gravitational force on the astronauts in orbit is nearly zero.

    B The astronauts are in free fall.

    C The astronauts are not accelerating.

    D The space shuttle exerts a reaction force that balances the force of gravity.

12. Newton's second law describes how to calculate the acceleration of an object if you know the object's mass and the force acting on the object. The book has no vertical motion because the gravitational force acting down on it equals the upward force on the book by the desktop. The horizontal acceleration of the book equals the mass of the book divided by the force you exert upon the book.

13. Newton's second law states that an object's acceleration equals the force on the object divided by the object's mass. However, this refers to the *net* force on the object. The rock experiences an upward force from the ground and an equal downward force due to gravity. The net force on the rock is zero. According to Newton's second law, the acceleration of the rock is therefore zero.

**6.** What is the weight of a book that has a mass of 0.35 kg?

**A** 0.036 N

**B** 3.4 N

**C** 28 N

**D** 34 N

7.3.17

**7.** Which best describes the force that pushes a rocket forward?

**A** The exhaust gases pushing on the air.

**B** The exhaust gases pushing on the rocket.

**C** The rocket pushing on the exhaust gases.

**D** The rocket pushing on the air.

**8.** The table below shows the acceleration of gravity at the surface of various planets.

| Acceleration of Gravity on Different Planets | |
| --- | --- |
| Planet | Gravitational acceleration $(m/s^2)$ |
| Mars | 3.69 |
| Saturn | 8.96 |
| Neptune | 11.00 |
| Pluto | 0.65 |

On which planet would your weight be greatest?

**A** Mars

**B** Neptune

**C** Pluto

**D** Saturn

## Part 2 Critical Response

7.3.17

**9.** A skater is coasting along the ice. Which law of motion explains the skater's ability to continue moving?

7.3.17

**10.** Describe how satellites are able to remain in orbit around Earth.

7.3.17

**11.** The illustration below shows the path of a ball thrown into the air.

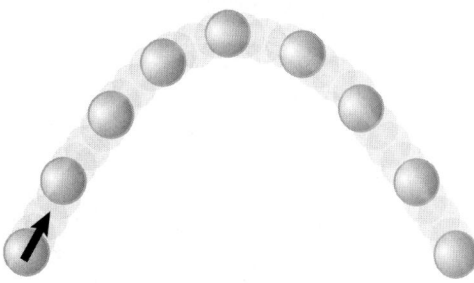

What causes the ball to move along a curved path?

7.3.17

**12.** How does Newton's second law determine the motion of a book as you push it across a desktop?

7.3.17

**13.** According to Newton's third law of motion, a rock sitting on the ground pushes against the ground, and the ground pushes back against the rock with an equal force. Explain why this force doesn't cause the rock to accelerate upward from the ground according to Newton's second law.

## Rubrics

The following rubric is a sample scoring device for critical response questions.

### Critical Response

| Points | Description |
| --- | --- |
| 4 | The student demonstrates a thorough understanding of the science of the task. The response may contain minor flaws that do not detract from the demonstration of a thorough understanding. |
| 3 | The student demonstrates an understanding of the science of the task. The response is essentially correct and demonstrates an essential but less than thorough understanding of the science. |
| 2 | The student demonstrates only a partial understanding of the science of the task. Although the student may have used the correct approach to a solution or may have provided a correct solution, the work lacks an essential understanding of the underlying science concepts. |
| 1 | The student demonstrates a very limited understanding of the science of the task. The response is incomplete and exhibits many flaws. |
| 0 | The student provides a completely incorrect solution or no response at all. |

| Section/Objectives | Standards | | Labs/Features |
|---|---|---|---|
| **Chapter Opener** | **National** | **State/Local** | **Launch Lab:** Analyze a Marble Launch, p. 379 **Foldables,** p. 379 |
| | See pp. 16T–17T for a Key to Standards. | Detailed standards begin on page IN8. | |
| **Section 1 What is energy?** 🕐 3 sessions 📦 1.5 blocks 1. **Explain** what energy is. 2. **Distinguish** between kinetic energy and potential energy. 3. **Identify** the various forms of energy. | National Content Standards: UCP.1, UCP.2, UCP.3, UCP.5, A.1, A.2, B.1, B.2, B.3, G.2, G.3 | Indiana Standards: 7.3.14 | |
| **Section 2 Energy Transformations** 🕐 3 sessions 📦 1.5 blocks 4. **Apply** the law of conservation of energy to energy transformations. 5. **Identify** how energy changes form. 6. **Describe** how electric power plants produce energy. | National Content Standards: UCP.1, UCP.2, UCP.3, UCP.5, A.1, A.2, B.1, B.2, B.3 | Indiana Standards: 7.1.10, 7.2.7, 7.3.14, 7.3.15 | **Science Online,** p. 386 **MiniLAB:** Analyzing Energy Transformations, p. 387 **Visualizing Energy Transformations,** p. 388 **Integrate History,** p. 389 **Lab:** Hearing with Your Jaw, p. 392 |
| **Section 3 Sources of Energy** 🕐 4 sessions 📦 2 blocks 7. **Explain** what renewable, nonrenewable, and alternative resources are. 8. **Describe** the advantages and disadvantages of using various energy sources. | National Content Standards: UCP.1, UCP.2, UCP.3, UCP.5, A.1, A.2, B.3, F.2, F.4 | Indiana Standards: 7.1.8, 7.2.6, 7.2.7, 7.3.15, 7.3.16 | **Integrate Earth Science,** p. 394 **Science Online,** p. 396 **Applying Science:** Is energy consumption outpacing production?, p. 396 **MiniLAB:** Building a Solar Collector, p. 397 **Lab:** Energy to Power Your Life, p. 402 **Science Stats:** Energy to Burn, p. 404 |

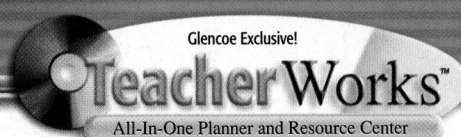
| Lab Materials | Reproducible Resources | Section Assessment | Technology |
|---|---|---|---|
| **Launch Lab:** book, glass marble, steel marbles, 3 metersticks | **Chapter *FAST FILE* Resources** <br> Foldables Worksheet, p. 15 <br> Directed Reading Overview, p. 17 <br> Note-taking Worksheets, pp. 31–32 | GLENCOE'S ASSESSMENT ADVANTAGE | **Teacher**Works includes: <br> • Interactive Teacher Edition <br> • Lesson Planner with calendar <br> • Access to all program blacklines <br> • Correlations to standards <br> • Web links <br> ▣ Video Lab |
| *Need materials?* Contact Science Kit at 1-800-828-7777 or www.sciencekit.com on the Internet. | **Chapter *FAST FILE* Resources** <br> Transparency Activity, p. 42 <br> Enrichment, p. 28 <br> Reinforcement, p. 25 <br> Directed Reading, p. 18 <br> **Reading and Writing Skill Activities,** p. 35 | **Portfolio** <br> Curriculum Connection, p. 381 <br> **Performance** <br> Applying Skills, p. 384 <br> **Content** <br> Section Review, p. 384 | Section Focus Transparency <br> Virtual Labs CD-ROM <br> Guided Reading Audio Program <br> Interactive Chalkboard CD-ROM |
| **MiniLAB:** soft clay, golf ball, steel ball, rubber ball, table-tennis ball, metric ruler <br> **Lab:** radio or CD player, small electrical motor, headphone jack | **Chapter *FAST FILE* Resources** <br> Transparency Activity, p. 43 <br> MiniLAB, p. 3 <br> Enrichment, p. 29 <br> Reinforcement, p. 26 <br> Directed Reading, p. 19 <br> Lab Activity, pp. 9–10 <br> Lab Worksheet, pp. 5–6 | **Portfolio** <br> Curriculum Connection, p. 390 <br> **Performance** <br> MiniLAB, p. 387 <br> Applying Math, p. 391 <br> **Content** <br> Section Review, p. 391 | Section Focus Transparency <br> Guided Reading Audio Program <br> Interactive Chalkboard CD-ROM |
| **MiniLAB:** black plastic garbage bag, scissors, large pot, water, clear plastic wrap, tape, computer temperature probe or thermometer, watch <br> **Lab:** Internet and other resources on energy | **Chapter *FAST FILE* Resources** <br> Transparency Activity, p. 44 <br> MiniLAB, p. 4 <br> Enrichment, p. 30 <br> Reinforcement, p. 27 <br> Directed Reading, pp. 19, 20 <br> Lab Activity, pp. 11–13 <br> Lab Worksheet, pp. 7–8 <br> Transparency Activity, pp. 45–46 <br> **Lab Management and Safety,** p. 37 | **Portfolio** <br> Activity, p. 399 <br> **Performance** <br> Applying Science, p. 396 <br> MiniLAB, p. 397 <br> Applying Math, p. 401 <br> **Content** <br> Section Review, p. 401 | Section Focus Transparency <br> Teaching Transparency <br> Guided Reading Audio Program <br> Interactive Chalkboard CD-ROM |

## End of Chapter Assessment

GLENCOE'S ASSESSMENT ADVANTAGE

| Blackline Masters | Technology | Professional Series |
|---|---|---|
| **Chapter *FAST FILE* Resources** <br> Chapter Review, pp. 35–36 <br> Chapter Tests, pp. 37–40 <br> **Mastering the Grade 7 Indiana Science Standards** | ▣ MindJogger Videoquiz <br> ◉ IN Test Prep and Practice Exam*View*® <br> ◉ Exam*View*® Pro Testmaker <br> ◉ TeacherWorks CD-ROM <br> ◉ Interactive Chalkboard CD-ROM | **Performance Assessment in the Science Classroom (PASC)** |

# Transparencies

## Section Focus

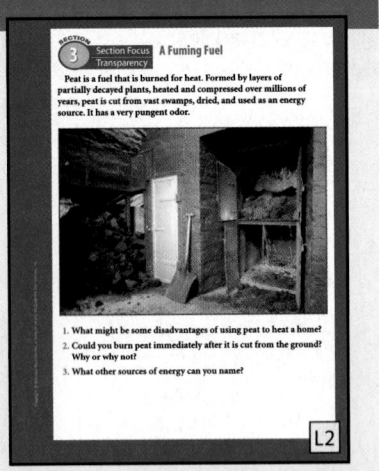

This is a representation of key blackline masters available in the Teacher Classroom Resources. See Resource Manager boxes within the chapter for additional information.

## Key to Teaching Strategies

The following designations will help you decide which activities are appropriate for your students.

L1   **Level 1** activities should be appropriate for students with learning difficulties.

L2   **Level 2** activities should be within the ability range of all students.

L3   **Level 3** activities are designed for above-average students.

ELL   **ELL** activities should be within the ability range of English-Language Learners.

COOP LEARN   **Cooperative Learning** activities are designed for small group work.

LS   **Multiple Learning Styles** logos, as described on page 12T, are used throughout to indicate strategies that address different learning styles.

P   These strategies represent student products that can be placed into a best-work portfolio.

PBL   **Problem-Based Learning** activities apply real-world situations to learning.

## Assessment

## Teaching

# Hands-on Activities

## Student Text Lab Worksheet

## Laboratory Activities

# Resource Manager

## Meeting Different Ability Levels

### Content Outline

**L2**

### Reinforcement

**L2**

### Enrichment

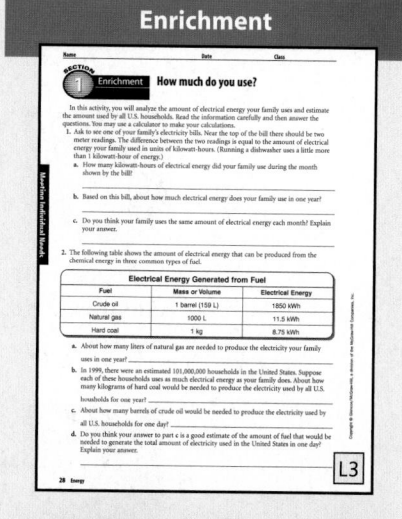

**L3**

### Directed Reading (English/Spanish)

**L1**

### Study Guide

**L2**

### Reading Essentials

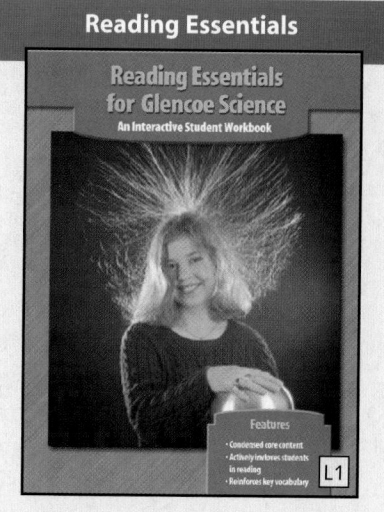

**L1**

## Assessment

### Test Practice Workbook

**L2**

### Chapter Review

**L2**

### Chapter Tests

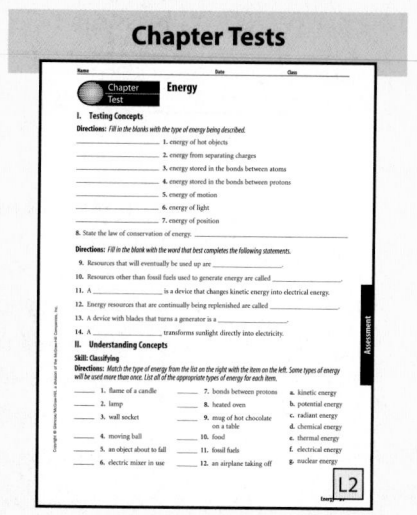

**L2**

# Science Content Background

## section 1 — What is energy?
### The Nature of Energy

Energy is not matter. Some forms of energy, such as light, can exist independent of matter. Other forms, such as chemical and kinetic energy, only can exist with matter.

## section 2 — Energy Transformations
### Changing Forms of Energy

In our common experience on Earth, energy is neither created nor destroyed, just transformed from one form into another. Heat often is produced from energy transformations.

### The Law of Conservation of Energy

The law of conservation of energy states that energy is neither created nor destroyed, only converted from one form into another. Sometimes energy may appear to be lost. For example, when a moving object slows down kinetic energy appears to be lost. However, friction converts kinetic energy into thermal energy so that the sum of the kinetic energy and thermal energy stays constant.

In processes involving nuclear fission or nuclear fusion matter can be changed to energy. Energy also can be changed to matter. According to Einstein's equation $E = mc^2$, a small amount of mass can be converted into an enormous amount of energy. However, even when nuclear reactions are involved the law of conservation of energy still is true.

## section 3 — Sources of Energy
### Fossil Fuels

Fossil fuels were once living organisms that obtained energy from the Sun, and could thus be considered a type of solar energy. Unlike more direct forms of solar energy, burning fossil fuels produces carbon dioxide gas and other pollutants.

### Geothermal Energy

You don't need to live near a volcano to use geothermal energy. Geothermal heat pumps, in use in 400,000 homes in the United States alone, take advantage of fairly constant below-ground temperatures. The temperature range in the first ten feet of soil is 10°C to 15.5°C (50°F to 60°F). This usually means the soil is warmer than the winter air and cooler than the summer air. In a heat pump, air gains or loses heat to the ground before entering a heating or cooling unit.

Iceland leads the world in its use of geothermal energy for heating. Almost 50% of its buildings are warmed using water heated by hot magma below Earth's surface. The Philippines is a leader in the use of geothermal energy to produce electricity. Approximately 22% of its electricity is produced with geothermal energy.

---

## chapter content resources

**Internet Resources**
For additional content background, visit **in7.msscience.com** to:
- access your book online
- find references to related articles in popular science magazines
- access Web links with related content background
- access current events with science journal topics

**Print Resources**
*Renewable Energy*, Sorensen, Brent, Academic Press, 2000
*The Feynman Lectures on Physics: Feynman on Fundamentals*, Feynman, Richard P., Perseus Publishing, 1999
*The Energy of Nature*, Pielou, E.C., University of Chicago Press, 2001

# Misconceptions

## Find Out What Students Think

**Students may think that . . .**

**Energy is something that is used and then disappears.**

Students may have this misconception because people commonly talk about energy as though we use it and then it's gone. An athlete may say, "I ran out of energy." A parent may say, "Turn off the lights. You're wasting energy." An environmentalist may caution that the world is running out of energy. Another problem is that energy can seem abstract. Perhaps it is easy to understand that food contains energy. But energy contained by a book sitting on a desk is more difficult to comprehend.

### Demonstration and Discussion

Hold up a windup toy. As you wind it, explain that your actions take energy. Release the toy and allow it to move until it winds down. Ask students to explain what has happened to the energy that you put into the toy. If students say that the toy used it up, ask them to explain what they mean. Did it disappear or become something else? Have students share their ideas.

## Promote Understanding

### Activity

Use books and tag board to make a U-shaped ramp. Students may have observed similar ramps used in skateboarding and bicycle stunt competitions.

- Hold a marble on top of one side of the ramp. Explain that the marble has potential energy due to its position. Gravity is pulling down on it.

- Release the marble. Explain that as the marble falls, its potential energy is converted to kinetic energy. Then, as the marble rises up the other side of the ramp, the kinetic energy is converted into potential energy.

- Now have students release the marble. Direct them to observe how high the marble rises up on each side of the ramp. Have them mark the heights achieved on each side of the ramp. Have students repeat this process at least five times.

- How does the maximum height reached by the marble change throughout each trial? Why does the marble go a little less high each time? How do we know the marble will eventually stop rolling? Help students realize that in this energy transformation between potential energy and kinetic energy, some energy is lost due to friction. This converts some kinetic energy of the marble into heat energy. Have the students rub their hands together to experience friction producing heat energy.

### Assess

After completing the chapter, see *Identifying Misconceptions* in the Study Guide at the end of the chapter.

**Academic Standard—3:** Students collect and organize data to identify relationships between physical objects, events, and processes. They use logical reasoning to question their own ideas as new information challenges their conceptions of the natural world.

**Also covers:** Academic Standards 1, 2 (Detailed standards begin on page IN8.)

# Energy and Energy Resources

## Chapter Vocabulary

**Science Journal**  Possible answers: hair dryer produces heat and blows air, toaster produces heat, TV produces sound and images, CD player produces sound

## INTERACTIVE CHALKBOARD with Image Bank

### PowerPoint® Presentations

This CD-ROM is an editable Microsoft® PowerPoint® presentation that includes:
* a pre-made presentation for every chapter
* interactive graphics
* animations
* audio clips
* image bank
* all new section and chapter questions
* Standardized Test Practice
* transparencies
* pre-lab questions for all labs
* Foldables directions
* links to in7.msscience.com

### chapter preview

**sections**

1  **What is energy?**

2  **Energy Transformations**
   *Lab  Hearing with Your Jaw*

3  **Sources of Energy**
   *Lab  Energy to Power Your Life*

◉  *Virtual Lab  What are the relationships between kinetic energy and potential energy?*

### Blowing Off Steam

The electrical energy you used today might have been produced by a coal-burning power plant like this one. Energy contained in coal is transformed into heat, and then into electrical energy. As boiling water heated by the burning coal is cooled, steam rises from these cone-shaped cooling towers.

**Science Journal**  Choose three devices that use electricity, and identify the function of each device.

378

## Theme Connection

**Systems and Interactions**  This chapter explores the various forms of energy, the interactions among them, and how they are harnessed for use in various systems.

### About the Photo

**Running on Steam**  In fossil-fuel-burning power plants and nuclear power plants, water is heated to produce steam. The steam drives turbines that are connected to electric generators. After the steam passes through the turbine, it is condensed by passing the steam over pipes containing cold water. This water then is cooled in the cooling towers.

# Start-Up Activities

## Analyze a Marble Launch

What's the difference between a moving marble and one at rest? A moving marble can hit something and cause a change to occur. How can a marble acquire energy— the ability to cause change?

1. Make a track on a table by slightly separating two metersticks placed side by side.

2. Using a book, raise one end of the track slightly and measure the height.

3. Roll a marble down the track. Measure the distance from its starting point to where it hits the floor. Repeat. Calculate the average of the two measurements.

4. Repeat steps 2 and 3 for three different heights. Predict what will happen if you use a heavier marble. Test your prediction and record your observations.

5. **Think Critically** In your Science Journal, describe how the distance traveled by the marble is related to the height of the ramp. How is the motion of the marble related to the ramp height?

 **FOLDABLES**
**Study Organizer**

**Energy** Make the following Foldable to help identify what you already know, what you want to know, and what you learned about energy.

**STEP 1** Fold a vertical sheet of paper from side to side. Make the front edge about 1 cm shorter than the back edge.

**STEP 2** Turn lengthwise and **fold** into thirds

**STEP 3** Unfold, cut, and label each tab for only the top layer along both folds to make three tabs.

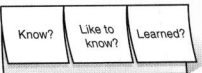

Know? | Like to know? | Learned?

**Identify Questions** Before you read the chapter, write what you know and what you want to know about the types, sources, and transformation of energy under the appropriate tabs. As you read the chapter, correct what you have written and add more questions under the *Learned* tab.

 **Science Online** | Preview this chapter's content and activities at in7.msscience.com

**Purpose** Use the Launch Lab to help students see how the height from which an object is released on a ramp affects the distance it will roll. L2 ELL COOP LEARN IS Kinesthetic

**Materials** book, glass marble, steel marble, 3 metersticks

**Teaching Strategy** Make sure students always release the marble at the same point on the ramp, and be sure there isn't a significant bump where the ramp contacts the table. An index card can be used to smooth out the bump.

## Think Critically

The higher the ramp, the farther from the table the marble hits the floor. The more massive marble lands the same distance from the table because it has the same horizontal velocity when it leaves the table as the less massive marble has.

## Assessment

**Performance** Have students redesign the experiment to explore how changes in the mass of the marble affect an object it strikes. Use **Performance Assessment in the Science Classroom,** p. 105.

 **Dinah Zike Study Fold**

Student preparation materials for this Foldable are available in the **Chapter *FAST FILE* Resources.**

Standard—7.3.14: Explain that energy in the form of heat is almost always one of the products of an energy transformation, such as in the examples of exploding stars, biological growth, the operation of machines, and the motion of people.

# What is energy?

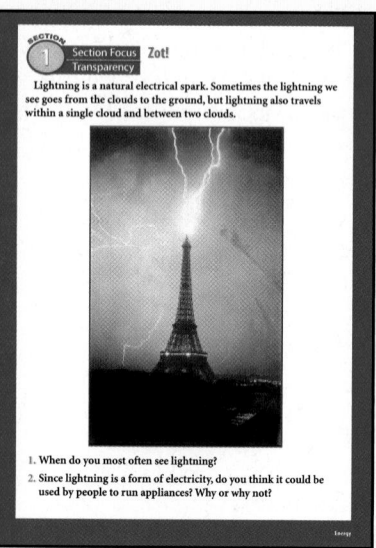
## as you read

*What* You'll Learn

- **Explain** what energy is.
- **Distinguish** between kinetic energy and potential energy.
- **Identify** the various forms of energy.

*Why* It's Important

Energy is involved whenever a change occurs.

**Review Vocabulary**

**mass:** a measure of the amount of matter in an object

**New Vocabulary**

- energy
- kinetic energy
- potential energy
- thermal energy
- chemical energy
- radiant energy
- electrical energy
- nuclear energy

## The Nature of Energy

What comes to mind when you hear the word *energy?* Do you picture running, leaping, and spinning like a dancer or a gymnast? How would you define energy? When an object has energy, it can make things happen. In other words, **energy** is the ability to cause change. What do the items shown in **Figure 1** have in common?

Look around and notice the changes that are occurring—someone walking by or a ray of sunshine that is streaming through the window and warming your desk. Maybe you can see the wind moving the leaves on a tree. What changes are occurring?

**Transferring Energy** You might not realize it, but you have a large amount of energy. In fact, everything around you has energy, but you notice it only when a change takes place. Anytime a change occurs, energy is transferred from one object to another. You hear a footstep because energy is transferred from a foot hitting the ground to your ears. Leaves are put into motion when energy in the moving wind is transferred to them. The spot on the desktop becomes warmer when energy is transferred to it from the sunlight. In fact, all objects, including leaves and desktops, have energy.

**Figure 1** Energy is the ability to cause change.
**Explain** *how these objects cause change.*

## Section 1 Resource Manager

**Chapter *FAST FILE* Resources**

Transparency Activity, p. 42

Directed Reading for Content Mastery, pp. 17, 18

Note-taking Worksheets, pp. 31–32

Enrichment, p. 28

Reinforcement, p. 25

**Reading and Writing Skill Activities,** p. 35

## Energy of Motion

Things that move can cause change. A bowling ball rolls down the alley and knocks down some pins, as in **Figure 2A.** Is energy involved? A change occurs when the pins fall over. The bowling ball causes this change, so the bowling ball has energy. The energy in the motion of the bowling ball causes the pins to fall. As the ball moves, it has a form of energy called kinetic energy. **Kinetic energy** is the energy an object has due to its motion. If an object isn't moving, it doesn't have kinetic energy.

**Kinetic Energy and Speed** If you roll the bowling ball so it moves faster, what happens when it hits the pins? It might knock down more pins, or it might cause the pins to go flying farther. A faster ball causes more change to occur than a ball that is moving slowly. Look at **Figure 2B.** The professional bowler rolls a fast-moving bowling ball. When her ball hits the pins, pins go flying faster and farther than for a slower-moving ball. All that action signals that her ball has more energy. The faster the ball goes, the more kinetic energy it has. This is true for all moving objects. Kinetic energy increases as an object moves faster.

✓ **Reading Check** *How does kinetic energy depend on speed?*

**Kinetic Energy and Mass** Suppose, as shown in **Figure 2C,** you roll a volleyball down the alley instead of a bowling ball. If the volleyball travels at the same speed as a bowling ball, do you think it will send pins flying as far? The answer is no. The volleyball might not knock down any pins. Does the volleyball have less energy than the bowling ball even though they are traveling at the same speed?

An important difference between the volleyball and the bowling ball is that the volleyball has less mass. Even though the volleyball is moving at the same speed as the bowling ball, the volleyball has less kinetic energy because it has less mass. Kinetic energy also depends on the mass of a moving object. Kinetic energy increases as the mass of the object increases.

**Figure 2** The kinetic energy of an object depends on the mass and speed of the object.

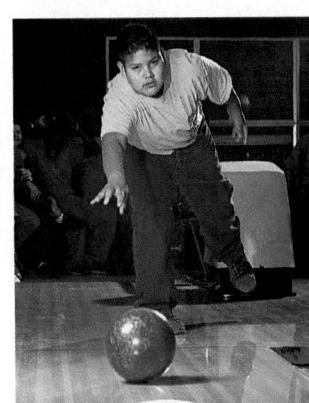

**A** This ball has kinetic energy because it is rolling down the alley.

**B** This ball has more kinetic energy because it has more speed.

**C** This ball has less kinetic energy because it has less mass.

SECTION 1 What is energy? **381**

## Inquiry Lab

**Observing Kinetic Energy**

**Purpose** To explore and observe kinetic energy, have the students shoot rubber bands of various length and width and measure the distance of their flight.

**Materials** rubber bands of varying lengths and widths, tape measure

**Estimated Time** ½ class session

**Teaching Strategies**

• Students can predict the distance based on the length and width of the rubber bands. Have them write their hypothesis down and then test it by charting their data.

• Allow students to explore how stretching the rubber bands various lengths will affect the distance.

• Allow students to explore how shooting multiple rubber bands at once affects the flight distance of each rubber band.

**For additional inquiry activities, see** *Science Inquiry Labs.*

✓ **Reading Check**

**Answer** Kinetic energy increases as speed increases.

## Curriculum Connection

**Art** Kinetic sculptures move using motors, pendulum action, or slight breezes that act upon sails. Among the most famous are the mobiles of artist Alexander Calder, who invented the art form in the 1920s. Have students research kinetic sculpture and build a sculpture of their own that models this art form. L2  ḺṠ **Kinesthetic**  P

**Figure 3** The potential energy of an object depends on its mass and height above the ground.
**Determine** *which vase has more potential energy, the red one or the blue one.*

**Figure 4** The hotter an object is, the more thermal energy it has. A cup of hot chocolate has more thermal energy than a cup of cold water, which has more thermal energy than a block of ice with the same mass.

# Energy of Position

An object can have energy even though it is not moving. For example, a glass of water sitting on the kitchen table doesn't have any kinetic energy because it isn't moving. If you accidentally nudge the glass and it falls on the floor, changes occur. Gravity pulls the glass downward, and the glass has energy of motion as it falls. Where did this energy come from?

When the glass was sitting on the table, it had potential (puh TEN chul) energy. **Potential energy** is the energy stored in an object because of its position. In this case, the position is the height of the glass above the floor. The potential energy of the glass changes to kinetic energy as the glass falls. The potential energy of the glass is greater if it is higher above the floor. Potential energy also depends on mass. The more mass an object has, the more potential energy it has. Which object in **Figure 3** has the most potential energy?

# Forms of Energy

Food, sunlight, and wind have energy, yet they seem different because they contain different forms of energy. Food and sunlight contain forms of energy different from the kinetic energy in the motion of the wind. The warmth you feel from sunlight is another type of energy that is different from the energy of motion or position.

**Thermal Energy** The feeling of warmth from sunlight signals that your body is acquiring more thermal energy. All objects have **thermal energy** that increases as its temperature increases. A cup of hot chocolate has more thermal energy than a cup of cold water, as shown in **Figure 4.** Similarly, the cup of water has more thermal energy than a block of ice of the same mass. Your body continually produces thermal energy. Many chemical reactions that take place inside your cells produce thermal energy. Where does this energy come from? Thermal energy released by chemical reactions comes from another form of energy called chemical energy.

**382   CHAPTER 13**   Energy and Energy Resources

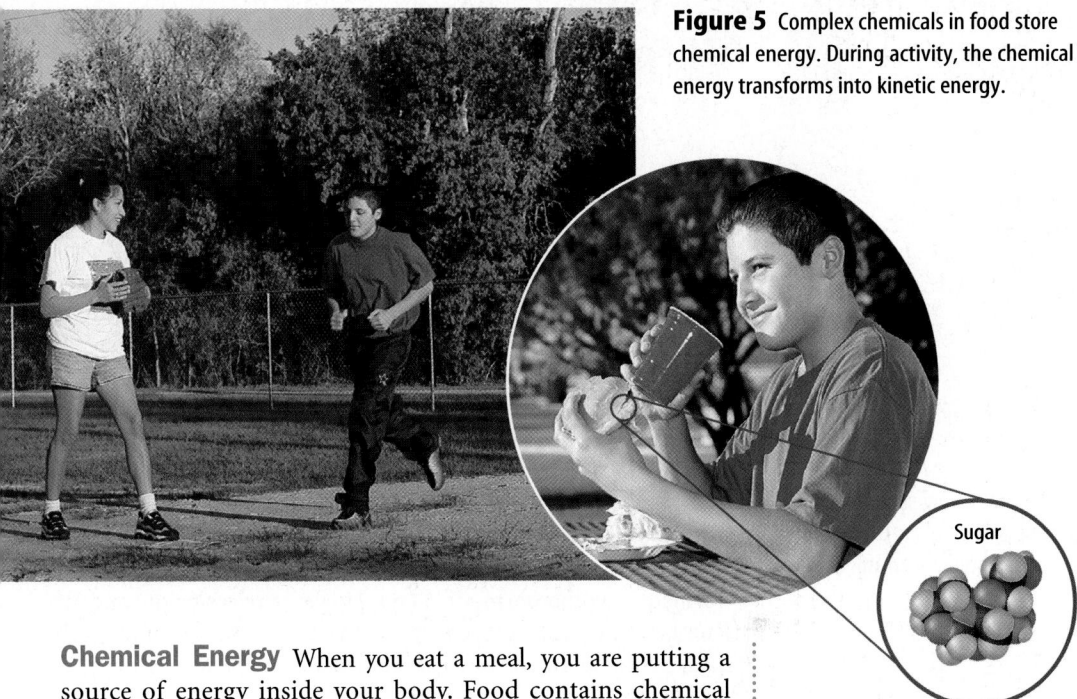

**Figure 5** Complex chemicals in food store chemical energy. During activity, the chemical energy transforms into kinetic energy.

Sugar

## Chemical Energy

When you eat a meal, you are putting a source of energy inside your body. Food contains chemical energy that your body uses to provide energy for your brain, to power your movements, and to fuel your growth. As in **Figure 5,** food contains chemicals, such as sugar, which can be broken down in your body. These chemicals are made of atoms that are bonded together, and energy is stored in the bonds between atoms. **Chemical energy** is the energy stored in chemical bonds. When chemicals are broken apart and new chemicals are formed, some of this energy is released. The flame of a candle is the result of chemical energy stored in the wax. When the wax burns, chemical energy is transformed into thermal energy and light energy.

☑ **Reading Check** *When is chemical energy released?*

## Light Energy

Light from the candle flame travels through the air at an incredibly fast speed of 300,000 km/s. This is fast enough to circle Earth almost eight times in 1 s. When light strikes something, it can be absorbed, transmitted, or reflected. When the light is absorbed by an object, the object can become warmer. The object absorbs energy from the light and this energy is transformed into thermal energy. Then energy carried by light is called **radiant energy. Figure 6** shows a coil of wire that produces radiant energy when it is heated. To heat the metal, another type of energy can be used—electrical energy.

**Figure 6** Electrical energy is transformed into thermal energy in the metal heating coil. As the metal becomes hotter, it emits more radiant energy.

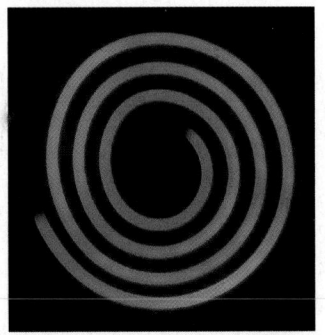

## Check For Understanding

**Interpersonal** Have students discuss why bat speed is the key factor in hitting homeruns in baseball. When a bat hits a ball, some of the kinetic energy of the bat is transferred to the ball. The more kinetic energy that is transferred to the ball, the farther it will travel. More kinetic energy can be transferred to the ball by increasing the bat's kinetic energy. The kinetic energy of an object is given by the equation $KE = \frac{1}{2}mv^2$. Because the velocity is squared in this equation, a fractional increase in the speed of the bat will have a greater effect on the bat's kinetic energy than the same fractional increase in the mass of the bat.

## Reteach

**Energy Types** Have students identify the different types of energy that they rely upon. Discuss the specific tasks each type of energy is used to perform. L1 IS
**Logical-Mathematical**

## ✔ Assessment

**Oral** During the Explore Activity, the more massive marble had the same speed as the less massive marble. What conclusion can you draw about the energy of the two marbles? Explain. *The more massive marble had more kinetic energy than the less massive marble.* Use **Performance Assessment in the Science Classroom,** p. 89.

**Electrical Energy** Electrical lighting is one of the many ways electrical energy is used. Look around at all the devices that use electricity. Electric current flows in these devices when they are connected to batteries or plugged into an electric outlet. **Electrical energy** is the energy that is carried by an electric current. An electric device uses the electrical energy provided by the current flowing in the device. Large electric power plants generate the enormous amounts of electrical energy used each day. In the United States, about 20 percent of the electrical energy used is generated by nuclear power plants.

**Figure 7** Complex power plants are required to obtain useful energy from the nucleus of an atom.

**Nuclear Energy** Nuclear power plants use the energy stored in the nucleus of an atom to generate electricity. Every atomic nucleus contains energy—**nuclear energy**—that can be transformed into other forms of energy. However, releasing the nuclear energy is a difficult process. It involves the construction of complex power plants, shown in **Figure 7.** In contrast, all that is needed to release chemical energy from wood is a lighted match.

## section 1 review

### Summary

**The Nature of Energy**
- Energy is the ability to cause change.
- Kinetic energy is the energy an object has due to its motion. Kinetic energy depends on an object's speed and mass.
- Potential energy is the energy an object has due to its position. Potential energy depends on an object's height and mass.

**Forces of Energy**
- Thermal energy increases as temperature increases.
- Chemical energy is the energy stored in chemical bonds in molecules.
- Light energy, also called radiant energy, is the energy contained in light.
- Electrical energy is the energy carried by electric current.
- Nuclear energy is the energy contained in the nucleus of an atom.

### Self Check

1. **Explain** why a high-speed collision between two cars would cause more damage than a low-speed collision between the same two cars.
2. **Describe** the energy transformations that occur when a piece of wood is burned.
3. **Identify** the form of energy that is converted into thermal energy by your body.
4. **Explain** how, if two vases are side by side on a shelf, one could have more potential energy.
5. **Think Critically** A golf ball and a bowling ball are moving and both have the same kinetic energy. Which one is moving faster? If they move at the same speed, which one has more kinetic energy?

#### Applying Skills

6. **Communicate** In your Science Journal, record different ways the word *energy* is used. Which ways of using the word *energy* are closest to the definition of energy given in this section?

**384 CHAPTER 13** Energy and Energy Resources

Science Online in7.msscience.com/self_check_quiz

## section 1 review

1. At high speed, both cars have more kinetic energy. This greater kinetic energy will result in more damage occurring when the cars collide.
2. Chemical energy in the wood is transformed into thermal energy and radiant energy.
3. chemical energy
4. The vase with the larger mass would have more potential energy.
5. The golf ball has less mass so it must be moving faster. If they move at the same speed, the bowling ball has more kinetic energy.
6. Answers will vary.

Standards—**7.3.14:** Explain that energy in the form of heat is almost always one of the products of an energy transformation, such as in the examples of exploding stars, biological growth, the operation of machines, and the motion of people. **7.3.15:** Describe how electrical energy can be produced from a variety of energy sources and can be transformed into almost any other form of energy, such as light or heat.

Also covers: 7.1.10, 7.2.7 (Detailed standards begin on page IN8.)

# section 2
# Energy Transformations

## Changing Forms of Energy

Chemical, thermal, radiant, and electrical are some of the forms that energy can have. In the world around you, energy is transforming continually between one form and another. You observe some of these transformations by noticing a change in your environment. Forest fires are a dramatic example of an environmental change that can occur naturally as a result of lightning strikes. A number of changes occur that involve energy as the mountain biker in **Figure 8** pedals up a hill. What energy transformations cause these changes to occur?

**Tracking Energy Transformations** As the mountain biker pedals, his leg muscles transform chemical energy into kinetic energy. The kinetic energy of his leg muscles transforms into kinetic energy of the bicycle as he pedals. Some of this energy transforms into potential energy as he moves up the hill. Also, some energy is transformed into thermal energy. His body is warmer because chemical energy is being released. Because of friction, the mechanical parts of the bicycle are warmer, too. Energy in the form of heat is almost always one of the products of an energy transformation. The energy transformations that occur when people exercise, when cars run, when living things grow and even when stars explode, all produce heat.

### as you read

***What* You'll Learn**
- **Apply** the law of conservation of energy to energy transformations.
- **Identify** how energy changes form.
- **Describe** how electric power plants produce energy.

***Why* It's Important**
Changing energy from one form to another is what makes cars run, furnaces heat, telephones work, and plants grow.

**⊙ Review Vocabulary**
**transformation:** a change in composition or structure

**New Vocabulary**
- law of conservation of energy
- generator
- turbine

**Figure 8** The ability to transform energy allows the biker to climb the hill.
**Identify** *all the forms of energy that are represented in the photograph.*

SECTION 2 Energy Transformations **385**

---

# 1 Motivate

**Bellringer**

**Section Focus Transparencies** also are available on the Interactive Chalkboard CD-ROM.
[L2] [ELL]

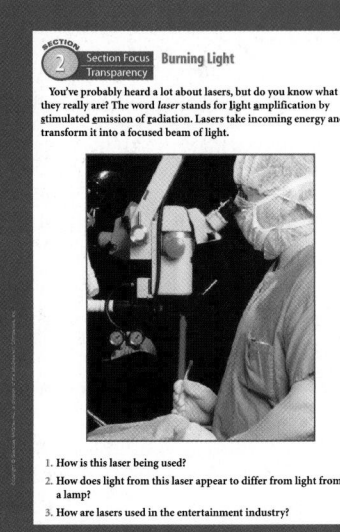

## Tie to Prior Knowledge

**Changing Energy** Ask students to give examples of energy they used to get ready for school. Possible answers: thermal energy to dry hair, electricity to run appliances. Point out that energy changes from one form to another. For example, electrical energy was transformed to thermal energy by a hairdryer.

## Caption Answer

**Figure 8** kinetic energy of the bike and rider, potential energy of the bike and rider due to the height of the hill, and chemical energy in the rider's muscles

---

### Section 2 Resource Manager

**Chapter *FAST FILE* Resources**
  Transparency Activity, p. 43
  Directed Reading for Content Mastery, p. 19
  MiniLAB, p. 3
  Lab Activity, pp. 9–10
  Enrichment, p. 29

Reinforcement, p. 26
Lab Worksheet, pp. 5–6
**Physical Science Critical Thinking/Problem Solving,** p. 17

✓ **Reading Check**

**Answer** Energy is never lost. It may be changed into a different form of energy.

**Caption Answer**

**Figure 9** The ball has the most kinetic energy as it leaves and returns to the hand. The ball's total energy is constant.

## IDENTIFYING Misconceptions

**Where Energy Goes** Students may think that energy is something that is used and then disappears. See page F at the beginning of this chapter for teacher strategies that address this misconception.

---

**Science Online**

**Topic: Energy Transformations**

Visit in7.msscience.com for Web links to information about energy transformations that occur during different activities and processes.

**Activity** Choose an activity or process and make a graph showing how the kinetic and potential energy change during it.

---

**Indiana Academic Standard Check**

**7.3.14:** Explain that energy in the form of heat is almost always one of the products of an energy transformation . . .

✓ What type of force converts mechanical energy into heat?

✓ friction

---

**Figure 9** During the flight of the baseball, energy is transforming between kinetic and potential energy.
**Determine** *where the ball has the most kinetic energy. Where does the ball have the most total energy?*

## The Law of Conservation of Energy

It can be a challenge to track energy as it moves from object to object. However, one extremely important principle can serve as a guide as you trace the flow of energy. According to the **law of conservation of energy,** energy is never created or destroyed. The only thing that changes is the form in which energy appears. When the biker is resting at the summit, all his original energy is still around. Some of the energy is in the form of potential energy, which he will use as he coasts down the hill. Some of this energy was changed to thermal energy by friction in the bike. Chemical energy was also changed to thermal energy in the biker's muscles, making him feel hot. As he rests, this thermal energy moves from his body to the air around him. No energy is missing—it can all be accounted for.

✓ **Reading Check** *Can energy ever be lost? Why or why not?*

## Changing Kinetic and Potential Energy

The law of conservation of energy can be used to identify the energy changes in a system. For example, tossing a ball into the air and catching it is a simple system. As shown in **Figure 9,** as the ball leaves your hand, most of its energy is kinetic. As the ball rises, it slows and its kinetic energy decreases. But, the total energy of the ball hasn't changed. The decrease in kinetic energy equals the increase in potential energy as the ball flies higher in the air. The total amount of energy always remains constant. Energy moves from place to place and changes form, but it never is created or destroyed.

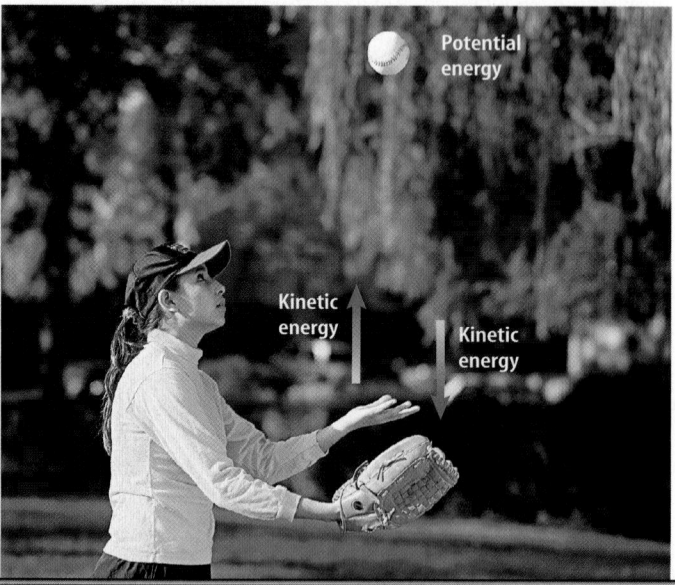

Potential energy

Kinetic energy

Kinetic energy

---

## LAB DEMONSTRATION

**Purpose** to observe the exchange of potential and kinetic energy
**Materials** 1.0-kg mass attached to a 2-m string
**Procedure** Hang the pendulum so the bob just misses the floor at its lowest point. Release the bob at different heights, and measure the height to which it rises at the other end of its swing.
**Expected Outcome** The pendulum will swing up to nearly the original height from which it was released. The final height will be slightly lower due to the effects of air resistance and friction.

**Assessment**
Where does the bob have the greatest potential energy? *just before it is released* The greatest kinetic energy? *at the bottom of its swing* How does the height at which the bob is released affect the energy? *Greater height means more total energy.*

**Figure 10** Hybrid cars that use an electric motor and a gasoline engine for power are now available. Hybrid cars make energy transformations more efficient.

Battery
Gasoline engine
Generator
Electric motor

## Energy Changes Form

## Energy Changes Form

Energy transformations occur constantly all around you. Many machines are devices that transform energy from one form to another. For example, an automobile engine transforms the chemical energy in gasoline into energy of motion. However, not all of the chemical energy is converted into kinetic energy. Instead, some of the chemical energy is converted into thermal energy, and the engine becomes hot. An engine that converts chemical energy into more kinetic energy is a more efficient engine. New types of cars, like the one shown in **Figure 10,** use an electric motor along with a gasoline engine. These engines are more efficient so the car can travel farther on a gallon of gas.

**INTEGRATE Life Science**

**Transforming Chemical Energy** Inside your body, chemical energy also is transformed into kinetic energy. Look at **Figure 11.** The transformation of chemical to kinetic energy occurs in muscle cells. There, chemical reactions take place that cause certain molecules to change shape. Your muscle contracts when many of these changes occur, and a part of your body moves.

The matter contained in living organisms, also called biomass, contains chemical energy. When organisms die, chemical compounds in their biomass break down. Bacteria, fungi, and other organisms help convert these chemical compounds to simpler chemicals that can be used by other living things.

Thermal energy also is released as these changes occur. For example, a compost pile can contain plant matter, such as grass clippings and leaves. As the compost pile decomposes, chemical energy is converted into thermal energy. This can cause the temperature of a compost pile to reach 60°C.

### Mini LAB

**Analyzing Energy Transformations**

**Procedure**
1. Place soft **clay** on the floor and smooth out its surface.
2. Hold a **marble** 1.5 m above the clay and drop it. Measure the depth of the crater made by the marble.
3. Repeat this procedure using a **golf ball** and a **plastic golf ball.**

**Analysis**
1. Compare the depths of the craters to determine which ball had the most kinetic energy as it hit the clay.
2. Explain how potential energy was transformed into kinetic energy during your activity.

Try at Home

### Quick Demo
**Radiant Energy**

**Materials** bright light source (such as a flashlight), radiometer

**Estimated Time** 1–3 minutes

**Procedure** Shine a bright light on a radiometer so that the vanes rotate. Show how the radiometer vanes stop rotating when the light is turned off. Explain that the radiant energy carried by the light is transferred to the radiometer and converted into the kinetic energy of the moving radiometer vanes.

### Mini LAB

**Purpose** Students observe the difference in kinetic energy of balls of different masses. L2

ELL IS Kinesthetic

**Materials** soft clay, marble, steel ball, rubber ball, table-tennis ball, metric ruler

**Teaching Strategies** Suggest that students hold a pencil in the crater and mark the depth of the crater on the pencil. Then they can measure the distance marked on the pencil with the metric ruler.

**Analysis**
1. The ball with the most mass had the greatest kinetic energy. This was probably the steel ball.
2. The balls had potential energy because of the height to which they were raised above the clay. This energy was transformed into kinetic energy as they fell.

### Assessment

**Oral** Ask students to explain what happened to the kinetic energy of the balls as they landed in the clay. It changed to kinetic energy in the clay and then to thermal energy. Use **Performance Assessment in the Science Classroom,** p. 89.

Try at Home

## Visual Learning

**Figure 10** Hybrid cars use an internal combustion engine as the primary power source of the car, but use a battery-powered electrical motor to assist with acceleration. The electric motor can be used alone for low speed driving. A generator converts some of the car's kinetic energy into electrical energy that keeps the batteries charged. The batteries convert chemical energy to electrical energy, which runs the electric motor.

## Fun Fact

Chemical energy is used to put on fireworks shows. Potassium nitrate, ammonium nitrate, saltpeter, sulfur, silicon, aluminum powder, and other materials give off different colors and luminescence when they burn to give off the colorful fireworks shows seen at festive times of the year.

## Visualizing Energy Transformations

Have students examine the pictures and read the captions. Then ask the following questions.

Why is it necessary for skeletal muscles in the arm to be arranged in pairs? This is necessary so that the arm can move in more than one direction. For instance, when the arm is raised by the biceps, as shown in the art drawing, the triceps are needed to lower it.

What is the source of chemical energy for the muscles? Chemical energy is provided by breaking the chemical bonds in the foods we eat.

### Activity

**Leg Muscles** Have your students research the major muscles in the human leg. Have students make drawings in their Science Journals of their leg muscles. Encourage them to make their drawings similar to those shown for the arm in **Figure 11.** L2
LS **Visual-Spatial**

---

### NATIONAL GEOGRAPHIC VISUALIZING ENERGY TRANSFORMATIONS

**Figure 11**

**P**addling a raft, throwing a baseball, playing the violin — your skeletal muscles make these and countless other body movements possible. Muscles work by pulling, or contracting. At the cellular level, muscle contractions are powered by reactions that transform chemical energy into kinetic energy.

▶ Energy transformations taking place in your muscles provide the power to move.

▲ Many skeletal muscles are arranged in pairs that work in opposition to each other. When you bend your arm, the biceps muscle contracts, while the triceps relaxes. When you extend your arm the triceps contracts, and the biceps relaxes.

Biceps

Triceps

Skeletal muscle

Muscle fiber

Bundle of muscle fibers

Filament bundle

Nerve fiber

Muscle fibers

Muscle filaments

▲ Skeletal muscles are made up of bundles of muscle cells, or fibers. Each fiber is composed of many bundles of muscle filaments.

▲ A signal from a nerve fiber starts a chemical reaction in the muscle filament. This causes molecules in the muscle filament to gain energy and move. Many filaments moving together cause the muscle to contract.

**388 CHAPTER 13**

## Differentiated Instruction

**Challenge** Have students research how electrical stimulation is being used to help paraplegics walk again. Encourage students to report their findings to the class. L3

**Figure 12** The simple act of listening to a radio involves many energy transformations. A few are diagrammed here.

Electrical energy of radio signal → Kinetic energy of speaker → Sound energy of air → Kinetic energy of eardrum and fluid → Electrical energy of brain and nerve cells

## Transforming Electrical Energy

Every day you use electrical energy. When you flip a light switch, or turn on a radio or television, or use a hair drier, you are transforming electrical energy to other forms of energy. Every time you plug something into a wall outlet, or use a battery, you are using electrical energy. **Figure 12** shows how electrical energy is transformed into other forms of energy when you listen to a radio. A loudspeaker in the radio converts electrical energy into sound waves that travel to your ear—energy in motion. The energy that is carried by the sound waves causes parts of the ear to move also. This energy of motion is transformed again into chemical and electrical energy in nerve cells, which send the energy to your brain. After your brain interprets this energy as a voice or music, where does the energy go? The energy finally is transformed into thermal energy.

## Transforming Thermal Energy

Different forms of energy can be transformed into thermal energy. For example, chemical energy changes into thermal energy when something burns. Electrical energy changes into thermal energy when a wire that is carrying an electric current gets hot. Thermal energy can be used to heat buildings and keep you warm. Thermal energy also can be used to heat water. If water is heated to its boiling point, it changes to steam. This steam can be used to produce kinetic energy by steam engines, like the steam locomotives that used to pull trains. Thermal energy also can be transformed into radiant energy. For example, when a bar of metal is heated to a high temperature, it glows and gives off light.

**INTEGRATE History**

**The Industrial Revolution** Beginning in the 18th century, machines began to be used widely to replace manual labor. This change is called the industrial revolution. The steam engine provided the source of energy for factories to manufacture various goods, such as cloth, that used to be made by hand. As the number of factory jobs increased, workers moved from rural areas to cities. This caused many cities to grow much larger, not only in Great Britain, but also in other countries such as the United States. Research the history of the steam engine. What other changes to society did the steam engine help bring about?

**Caption Answer**

**Figure 13** Its temperature decreases.

**Caption Answer**

**Figure 14** oil, natural gas, uranium, the energy from falling water, and geothermal energy

**Discussion**

**Using Electrical Energy** Discuss with students the activities in their lives that depend on electrical energy. Possible answers: operating blow-dryers, listening to radios, watching television Where does the electrical energy for these appliances come from? Possible answers: from batteries or from power plants that generate electrical energy. L2

📖 **Logical-Mathematical**

**Activity**

**Using a Generator** Have students turn a hand-held generator when it is not hooked up to a light bulb and then again when it is. Try different wattage light bulbs. Why was no electrical energy generated when the light bulb was not connected? There was no circuit in which the current could flow. L2 📖 **Kinesthetic**

✔ **Reading Check**

**Answer** A generator converts the kinetic energy of a spinning turbine into electrical energy.

Thermal energy

**Figure 13** Thermal energy moves from the hot chocolate to the cooler surroundings. **Explain** what happens to the hot chocolate as it loses thermal energy.

**Figure 14** A coal-burning power plant transforms the chemical energy in coal into electrical energy. **List** some of the other energy sources that power plants use.

**How Thermal Energy Moves** Thermal energy can move from one place to another. Look at **Figure 13.** The hot chocolate has thermal energy that moves from the cup to the cooler air around it, and to the cooler spoon. Thermal energy only moves from something at a higher temperature to something at a lower temperature.

## Generating Electrical Energy

The enormous amount of electrical energy that is used every day is too large to be stored in batteries. The electrical energy that is available for use at any wall socket must be generated continually by power plants. Every power plant works on the same principle—energy is used to turn a large generator. A **generator** is a device that transforms kinetic energy into electrical energy. In fossil fuel power plants, coal, oil, or natural gas is burned to boil water. As the hot water boils, the steam rushes through a **turbine,** which contains a set of narrowly spaced fan blades. The steam pushes on the blades and turns the turbine, which in turn rotates a shaft in the generator to produce the electrical energy, as shown in **Figure 14.**

✔ **Reading Check** What does a generator do?

Chemical energy in coal ➡ Thermal energy in water

Kinetic energy of steam ➡ Kinetic energy of turbine ➡ Electrical energy out of generator

Stack

Steam line  Turbine  Generator

Transformer that increases voltage

Coal supply

Conveyor belt

Boiler

River or reservoir

Cooling water

## Curriculum Connection

**History** The invention of the AC electric generator by Nikola Tesla in 1882 sometimes is described as the beginning of the second Industrial Revolution. Have students research and write reports about Tesla's life or his research on electricity. Tesla immigrated to the United States from Croatia. Thomas Edison advocated the use of DC electricity, and fought hard to prevent the adoption of Tesla's AC generator. L2 📖 **Linguistic** P

**Power Plants** Almost 90 percent of the electrical energy generated in the United States is produced by nuclear and fossil fuel power plants, as shown in **Figure 15.** Other types of power plants include hydroelectric (hi droh ih LEK trihk) and wind. Hydroelectric power plants transform the kinetic energy of moving water into electrical energy. Wind power plants transform the kinetic energy of moving air into electrical energy. In these power plants, a generator converts the kinetic energy of moving water or wind to electrical energy.

To analyze the energy transformations in a power plant, you can diagram the energy changes using arrows. A coal-burning power plant generates electrical energy through the following series of energy transformations.

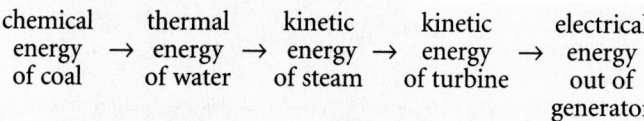

chemical energy of coal → thermal energy of water → kinetic energy of steam → kinetic energy of turbine → electrical energy out of generator

Nuclear power plants use a similar series of transformations. Hydroelectric plants, however, skip the steps that change water into steam because the water strikes the turbine directly.

**Figure 15** The graph shows sources of electrical energy in the United States.
**Name** *the energy source that you think is being used to provide the electricity for the lights overhead.*

**Caption Answer**
**Figure 15** Possible answers: fossil fuels, uranium, falling water.

## 3 Assess

### DAILY INTERVENTION

**Check For Understanding**
**Linguistic** Have students write in their Science Journals, using **Figure 12,** how the electrical energy of a radio signal is transformed into electrical energy in the brain and nerve cells. The energy in radio waves is transformed by the radio into kinetic energy in the form of sound waves. The sound waves strike the eardrum and are transformed from kinetic energy to electrical energy in the cochlea, which is then transmitted through nerve tissue to the brain.

### Reteach

**Energy Type** Have volunteers explain each type of energy discussed in this section. As each energy type is discussed, challenge students to explain how this form of energy is used in their daily lives. ⌊2⌋ 📖 **Linguistic**

---

## section 2 review

### Summary

**Changing Forms of Energy**
- Heat usually is one of the forms of energy produced in energy transformations.
- The law of conversation of energy states that energy cannot be created or destroyed; it can only change form.
- The total energy doesn't change when an energy transformation occurs.
- As an object rises and falls, kinetic and potential energy are transformed into each other, but the total energy doesn't change.

**Generating Electrical Energy**
- A generator converts kinetic energy into electrical energy.
- Burning fossil fuels produce thermal energy that is used to boil water and produce steam.
- In a power plant, steam is used to spin a turbine which then spins an electric generator.

### Self Check

1. **Describe** the conversions between potential and kinetic energy that occur when you shoot a basketball at a basket.
2. **Explain** whether your body gains or loses thermal energy if your body temperature is 37°C and the temperature around you is 25°C.
3. **Describe** a process that converts chemical energy to thermal energy.
4. **Think Critically** A lightbulb converts 10 percent of the electrical energy it uses into radiant energy. Make a hypothesis about the other form of energy produced.

### Applying Math

5. **Use a Ratio** How many times greater is the amount of electrical energy produced in the United States by coal-burning power plants than the amount produced by nuclear power plants?

Science⌐nline in7.msscience.com/self_check_quiz

SECTION 2 Energy Transformations **391**

### ✓ Assessment

**Performance** Have students make posters illustrating the energy transformations that occur when oil is used to generate electricity. Chemical energy of oil → thermal energy of water → kinetic energy of steam → kinetic energy of turbine → electrical energy out of generator Use **Performance Assessment in the Science Classroom,** p. 145.

---

## section 2 review

1. Ball has kinetic energy when it leaves your hand; kinetic energy is converted to potential energy as ball rises; potential energy is converted to kinetic energy as ball falls

2. Your temperature is higher than your surroundings, so thermal energy is transferred from you to your surroundings.

3. Possible answer: burning of wood
4. The other 90 percent is converted into thermal energy.
5. (51%)/(20%) = 2.5 times greater

## Real-World Question

**Purpose** Students track energy conversions from electrical energy to vibrations to sound.

L2 **IS** **Auditory-Musical**

**Process Skills** observing, inferring, predicting

**Time Required** 20 minutes

## Procedure

**Teaching Strategy** Have reference books about sound and electricity available.

**Troubleshooting** Make sure the wiring is securely connected. The motor will not turn even though students will be able to "hear" the music when they press the axle against their jaws.

## Conclude and Apply

1. Students should hear the sound of the radio or disc.
2. sound energy
3. Transformation should start with electrical energy (from a wall outlet or from a battery), change to mechanical energy, and end with sound energy. If a CD player is used, students also might include light energy.
4. The motor will probably get warmer as it runs. Some of the energy changes to heat because of friction.
5. All of the energy put into the system can be accounted for as motion, heat, light, or sound.

✔ **Assessment**

**Content** Have students work in groups to write a song or poem or make a picture about transfers of energy. Use **Performance Assessment in the Science Classroom**, p. 151.

# Hearing with Your Jaw

You probably have listened to music using speakers or headphones. Have you ever considered how energy is transferred to get the energy from the radio or CD player to your brain? What type of energy is needed to power the radio or CD player? Where does this energy come from? How does that energy become sound? How does the sound get to you? In this activity, the sound from a radio or CD player is going to travel through a motor before entering your body through your jaw instead of your ears.

## Real-World Question

How can energy be transferred from a radio or CD player to your brain?

### Goals
■ **Identify** energy transfers and transformations.
■ **Explain** your observations using the law of conservation of energy.

### Materials
radio or CD player
small electrical motor
headphone jack

## Procedure

1. Go to one of the places in the room with a motor/radio assembly.
2. Turn on the radio or CD player so that you hear the music.
3. Push the headphone jack into the headphone plug on the radio or CD player.
4. Press the axle of the motor against the side of your jaw.

## Conclude and Apply

1. **Describe** what you heard in your Science Journal.
2. **Identify** the form of energy produced by the radio or CD player.
3. **Draw** a diagram to show all of the energy transformations taking place.
4. **Evaluate** Did anything get hotter as a result of this activity? Explain.
5. **Explain** your observations using the law of conservation of energy.

Compare your conclusions with those of other students in your class. **For more help, refer to the** Science Skill Handbook.

Students could use an electronic presentation program to present their picture and/or events chain to the rest of the class.

**Standards—7.3.15:** Describe how electrical energy can be produced from a variety of energy sources and can be transformed into almost any other form of energy, such as light or heat. **7.3.16:** Recognize and explain that different ways of obtaining, transforming, and distributing energy have different environmental consequences.

Also covers: 7.1.8, 7.2.6, 7.2.7 (Detailed standards begin on page IN8.)

# section 3

# Sources of Energy

## Using Energy

Every day, energy is used to provide light and to heat and cool homes, schools, and workplaces. According to the law of conservation of energy, energy can't be created or destroyed. Energy only can change form. If a car or refrigerator can't create the energy they use, then where does this energy come from?

## Energy Resources

Energy cannot be made, but must come from the natural world. As you can see in **Figure 16,** the surface of Earth receives energy from two sources—the Sun and radioactive atoms in Earth's interior. The amount of energy Earth receives from the Sun is far greater than the amount generated in Earth's interior. Nearly all the energy you used today can be traced to the Sun, even the gasoline used to power the car or school bus you came to school in.

### as you read

**What You'll Learn**

- **Explain** what renewable, non-renewable, and alternative resources are.
- **Describe** the advantages and disadvantages of using various energy sources.

**Why It's Important**

Energy is vital for survival and making life comfortable. Developing new energy sources will improve modern standards of living.

**Review Vocabulary**
**resource:** a source of something that is needed

**New Vocabulary**
- nonrenewable resource
- renewable resource
- alternative resource
- inexhaustible resource
- photovoltaic

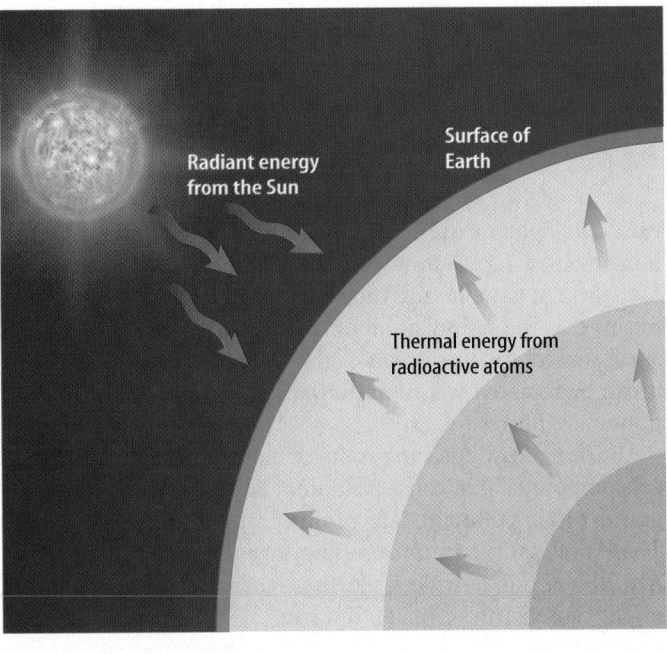

**Figure 16** All the energy you use can be traced to one of two sources—the Sun or radioactive atoms in Earth's interior.

Radiant energy from the Sun

Surface of Earth

Thermal energy from radioactive atoms

---

## 1 Motivate

**Bellringer**

**Section Focus Transparencies** also are available on the Interactive Chalkboard CD-ROM.

L2   ELL

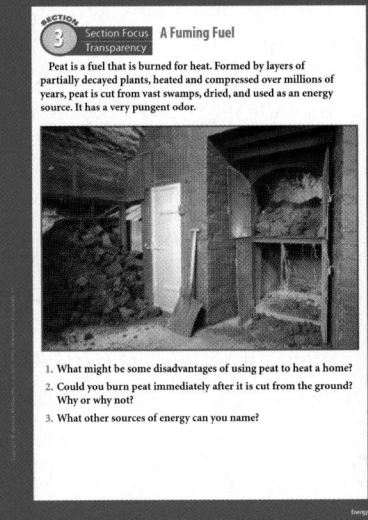

### Tie to Prior Knowledge

**Energy Sources** Ask students how their homes are heated. Possible answers: by burning oil or natural gas, or using electricity. Have them recall the sources of energy, such as fossil fuels, used to produce electricity in some power plants, and the energy transformations involved. Explain that they learn about other energy sources in this section.

---

### Section 3 Resource Manager

**Chapter FAST FILE Resources**
Transparency Activity, pp. 44, 45–46
Directed Reading for Content Mastery, pp. 19, 20
MiniLAB, p. 4
Lab Activity, pp. 11–13
Enrichment, p. 30

Reinforcement, p. 27
Lab Worksheet, pp. 7–8
**Cultural Diversity,** p. 45
**Home and Community Involvement,** p. 26
**Lab Management and Safety,** p. 73

### Use an Analogy

**Building Energy** In fossil fuels, the chemical energy between the carbon atoms and the other atoms of the original organic matter has been concentrated. Burning fossil fuel yields a high amount of energy for a period of time that is fleeting compared with the time it took to transform the organic material into fossil fuel. In the same way, professional musicians and players of professional sports spend years learning to concentrate their energy and perfecting techniques that may take mere seconds to perform.

**INTEGRATE Earth Science**

**Energy Source Origins** Coal was formed from the remains of partially decomposed plants that had accumulated hundreds of millions of years ago. Coal formation gradually occurred after the plant debris had been covered and compressed by rocks, soil, and water and then subjected to great pressure and heat over long periods of time. Oil and natural gas formed from the remains of marine life and plants that had been rapidly buried in fine-grained sediment. This rapid burial prevented these organic debris from completely decomposing; and, along with increases in temperature and pressure, oil and natural gas deposits gradually formed.

Radiant energy

Radiant energy from the Sun is stored as chemical energy in molecules.

Time
Heat
Pressure

Coal mine

**Figure 17** Coal is formed after the molecules in ancient plants are heated under pressure for millions of years. The energy stored by the molecules in coal originally came from the Sun.

**INTEGRATE Earth Science**

**Energy Source Origins** The kinds of fossil fuels found in the ground depend on the kinds of organisms (animal or plant) that died and were buried in that spot. Research coal, oil, and natural gas to find out what types of organisms were primarily responsible for producing each.

## Fossil Fuels

Fossil fuels are coal, oil, and natural gas. Oil and natural gas were made from the remains of microscopic organisms that lived in Earth's oceans millions of years ago. Heat and pressure gradually turned these ancient organisms into oil and natural gas. Coal was formed by a similar process from the remains of ancient plants that once lived on land, as shown in **Figure 17.**

Through the process of photosynthesis, ancient plants converted the radiant energy in sunlight to chemical energy stored in various types of molecules. Heat and pressure changed these molecules into other types of molecules as fossil fuels formed. Chemical energy stored in these molecules is released when fossil fuels are burned.

**Using Fossil Fuels** The energy used when you ride in a car, turn on a light, or use an electric appliance usually comes from burning fossil fuels. However, it takes millions of years to replace each drop of gasoline and each lump of coal that is burned. This means that the supply of oil on Earth will continue to decrease as oil is used. An energy source that is used up much faster than it can be replaced is a **nonrenewable resource.** Fossil fuels are nonrenewable resources.

Burning fossil fuels to produce energy also generates chemical compounds that cause pollution. Each year billions of kilograms of air pollutants are produced by burning fossil fuels. These pollutants can cause respiratory illnesses and acid rain. Also, the carbon dioxide gas formed when fossil fuels are burned might cause Earth's climate to warm.

**394 CHAPTER 13** Energy and Energy Resources

## Science Journal

**Energy Matters** Some people believe the demand for energy in the world will quadruple in the next fifty years. Have students write paragraphs in their Science Journals speculating how people will meet the demands for more energy. L2 LS
**Intrapersonal** P

## Nuclear Energy

Can you imagine running an automobile on 1 kg of fuel that releases almost 3 million times more energy than 1 L of gas? What could supply so much energy from so little mass? The answer is the nuclei of uranium atoms. Some of these nuclei are unstable and break apart, releasing enormous amounts of energy in the process. This energy can be used to generate electricity by heating water to produce steam that spins an electric generator, as shown in **Figure 18**. Because no fossil fuels are burned, generating electricity using nuclear energy helps make the supply of fossil fuels last longer. Also, unlike fossil fuel power plants, nuclear power plants produce almost no air pollution. In one year, a typical nuclear power plant generates enough energy to supply 600,000 homes with power and produces only 1 m³ of waste.

**Nuclear Wastes** Like all energy sources, nuclear energy has its advantages and disadvantages. One disadvantage is the amount of uranium in Earth's crust is nonrenewable. Another is that the waste produced by nuclear power plants is radioactive and can be dangerous to living things. Some of the materials in the nuclear waste will remain radioactive for many thousands of years. As a result the waste must be stored so no radioactivity is released into the environment for a long time. One method is to seal the waste in a ceramic material, place the ceramic in protective containers, and then bury the containers far underground. However, the burial site would have to be chosen carefully so underground water supplies aren't contaminated. Also, the site would have to be safe from earthquakes and other natural disasters that might cause radioactive material to be released.

**Indiana Academic Standard Check**

**7.3.16:** Recognize and explain that different ways of . . . transforming . . . energy have different . . . consequences.

✔ What is an environmental consequence of using fossil fuels to produce energy?

✔ Burning fossil fuels produces air pollutants.

**Figure 18** To obtain electrical energy from nuclear energy, a series of energy transformations must occur.

1. Nuclear energy of atoms
2. Thermal energy of water
3. Kinetic energy of steam
4. Kinetic energy of turbine
5. Electrical energy out of generator
Generator

The nuclear reaction used in nuclear power plants is nuclear fission. In this reaction, a neutron hits the nucleus of a uranium-235 atom and breaks it into two smaller nuclei and several neutrons. If enough reactions occur, the neutrons produced by the reaction are enough to keep the reaction going, and it becomes a chain reaction.

### Quick Demo

**Chain Reaction**

**Materials** many mousetraps, large box with short walls

**Estimated Time** 2–5 minutes

**Procedure** To model the chain reaction that can occur in nuclear fission, place many set mousetraps into a large box with fairly short walls. **Warning:** *Keep fingers clear of trap area.* The traps should be fairly close together for a good response. Drop a table-tennis ball into the box and have students observe what happens. Explain that the ball represents a loose neutron that initiates the fission process while the mousetraps model uranium-235 nuclei.

## Differentiated Instruction

**Challenge** The first human use of nuclear fission was in atomic weapons. Have students research the development of these weapons and give speeches describing their findings. During World War II, Albert Einstein twice wrote to President Franklin Delano Roosevelt to warn him that the technology needed to build nuclear weapons existed and that such weapons might be developed by Germany, which could lead to a global disaster. Einstein's warnings led to the formation of the Manhattan Project, which led to development of the world's first atomic weapons. L2 **IS Linguistic**

## Active Reading

**Four-Corner Discussion** This strategy encourages the class to debate a complex issue. Make four signs: Strongly Agree, Agree, Disagree, and Strongly Disagree. Place one sign in each corner of the room. Write on the chalkboard a statement that will elicit reactions from students. Have the students respond on paper to the statement. After several minutes, direct them to move to the corner with the sign that most closely reflects their opinions. In the corners, students share responses. Each group then selects a spokesperson to report the opinions of the group. After all groups have reported, open the floor for debate. Allow students who have changed their opinions to change corners. Have students conduct a Four-Corner Discussion about the use of nuclear energy.

**Pinwheel** Have students make a pinwheel by folding each corner of a large index card into the center and attaching it to a pencil eraser with a pin. Have students place their pinwheels under a stream of water running from a faucet to observe that the kinetic energy of moving water can be transferred to the blades of a turbine. L1 IS **Kinesthetic**

## Applying Science

**Answers to Practice Problems**

1. 1949 = ~30 quadrillion Btu; 1999 = ~70 quadrillion Btu; Production has more than doubled.

2. 1949 = ~30 quadrillion Btu; 1999 = ~95 quadrillion Btu; Consumption has more than tripled.

3. Additional energy comes from imports.

**Science Online**

**Topic: Hydroelectricity**
Visit in7.msscience.com for Web links to information about the use of hydroelectricity in various parts of the world.

**Activity** On a map of the world, show where the use of hydroelectricity is the greatest.

# Hydroelectricity

Currently, transforming the potential energy of water that is trapped behind dams supplies the world with almost 20 percent of its electrical energy. Hydroelectricity is the largest renewable source of energy. A **renewable resource** is an energy source that is replenished continually. As long as enough rain and snow fall to keep rivers flowing, hydroelectric power plants can generate electrical energy, as shown in **Figure 19.**

Although production of hydroelectricity is largely pollution free, it has one major problem. It disrupts the life cycle of aquatic animals, especially fish. This is particularly true in the Northwest where salmon spawn and run. Because salmon return to the spot where they were hatched to lay their eggs, the development of dams has hindered a large fraction of salmon from reproducing. This has greatly reduced the salmon population. Efforts to correct the problem have resulted in plans to remove a number of dams. In an attempt to help fish bypass some dams, fish ladders are being installed. Like most energy sources, hydroelectricity has advantages and disadvantages.

## Applying Science

### Is energy consumption outpacing production?

**Y**ou use energy every day—to get to school, to watch TV, and to heat or cool your home. The amount of energy consumed by an average person has increased over time. Consequently, more energy must be produced.

**U.S. Energy Overview, 1949–1999**

Energy (quadrillion Btu): 0, 30, 60, 90, 120
Year: 1949 1954 1959 1964 1969 1974 1979 1984 1989 1994 1999
Consumed in the United States; Energy imports; Produced in the United States

**Identifying the Problem**

The graph above shows the energy produced and consumed in the United States from 1949 to 1999. How does energy that is consumed by Americans compare with energy that is produced in the United States?

**Solving the Problem**

1. Determine the approximate amount of energy produced in 1949 and in 1999

and how much it has increased in 50 years. Has it doubled or tripled?

2. Do the same for consumption. Has it doubled or tripled?

3. Using your answers for steps 1 and 2 and the graph, where does the additional energy that is needed come from? Give some examples.

**396** CHAPTER 13 Energy and Energy Resources

# Differentiated Instruction

**Challenge** Have groups of students build solar-powered toy cars. The cars should be built from scratch with parts from other toys. Upon completion, students should make diagrams describing how the cars work. L3 ELL COOP LEARN IS **Kinesthetic**

# Cultural Diversity

**Three Gorges Dam** The largest hydroelectric dam in the world, Three Gorges Dam, is under construction in China. Have students find out more about this dam and present their findings to the class. The dam will produce 18,200 megawatts of electricity and is to be completed in 2009. It will submerge 13 cities, 140 towns, and 1,352 villages. L2 IS **Linguistic**

1. Potential energy of water → 2. Kinetic energy of water

3. Kinetic energy of turbine

4. Electrical energy out of generator

Long-distance power lines

**Figure 19** The potential energy of water behind a dam supplies the energy to turn the turbine. **Explain** *why hydroelectric power is a renewable energy source.*

## Alternative Sources of Energy

Electrical energy can be generated in several ways. However, each has disadvantages that can affect the environment and the quality of life for humans. Research is being done to develop new sources of energy that are safer and cause less harm to the environment. These sources often are called **alternative resources.** These alternative resources include solar energy, wind, and geothermal energy.

## Solar Energy

The Sun is the origin of almost all the energy that is used on Earth. Because the Sun will go on producing an enormous amount of energy for billions of years, the Sun is an inexhaustible source of energy. An **inexhaustible resource** is an energy source that can't be used up by humans.

Each day, on average, the amount of solar energy that strikes the United States is more than the total amount of energy used by the entire country in a year. However, less than 0.1 percent of the energy used in the United States comes directly from the Sun. One reason is that solar energy is more expensive to use than fossil fuels. However, as the supply of fossil fuels decreases, the cost of finding and mining these fuels might increase. Then, it may be cheaper to use solar energy or other energy sources to generate electricity and heat buildings than to use fossil fuels.

**Reading Check** *What is an inexhaustible energy source?*

---

### Mini LAB

**Building a Solar Collector**

**Procedure**
1. Line a **large pot** with **black plastic** and fill with **water.**
2. Stretch **clear-plastic wrap** over the pot and tape it taut.
3. Make a slit in the top and slide a **thermometer** or a **computer probe** into the water.
4. Place your solar collector in direct sunlight and monitor the temperature change every 3 min for 15 min.
5. Repeat your experiment without using any black plastic.

**Analysis**
1. Graph the temperature changes in both setups.
2. Explain how your solar collector works.

---

**Caption Answer**

**Figure 19** Precipitation falling at higher elevations will flow to lower elevations, producing rivers that can be dammed to form reservoirs.

**Discussion**

**Resource Use** How do renewable and inexhaustible energy sources differ from nonrenewable energy resources? Renewable and inexhaustible energy resources are not likely to be used up by people.

### Mini LAB

**Purpose** to construct a simple solar collector [L2] [IS] **Kinesthetic**

**Materials** black plastic garbage bag, scissors, large pot, water, clear plastic wrap, tape, thermometer, watch

**Teaching Strategies** Explain that black materials absorb more radiant energy from the Sun than shiny materials do.

**Analysis**
1. The temperature increases faster in the setup with the plastic.
2. The black plastic absorbs heat from the Sun, and the clear plastic traps the heat. This heat is transferred to the water.

**Assessment**

**Process** Have students make time/temperature graphs of their data for both collectors. Use **Performance Assessment in the Science Classroom,** p. 111.

**Reading Check**

**Answer** an energy source that can't be used up by humans

---

## Visual Learning

**Figure 19** Ask students to study the diagram of a hydroelectric plant and then explain why hydroelectric power is more efficient than fossil fuel or nuclear power. Hydroelectric power does not use heat, which is easily transferred to the surroundings, to generate electrical energy. In hydroelectric power, the energy of falling water is directly transferred to the turbine blades. [L2] [IS] **Visual-Spatial**

## Teacher **FYI**

**Geothermal Energy** Geothermal energy can be used for heating in the winter and cooling in the summer. A loop of pipe with water running through it is inserted below the frost line where the ground stays at a constant temperature of about 10°C to 20°C, as in a cave. In summer, when the house air is warmer than this underground temperature, water in the pipe carries underground heat out of the house and underground, where the water is cooled. The water then returns above ground to collect more heat. In the winter, the reverse takes place. This method of heating and cooling is more efficient than many other methods and has recently become cost effective. Also, this method does not depend on thermal vents, which occur in only a few isolated regions of the world, and it can be used nearly everywhere.

## Discussion

**Advantages of Geothermal Energy** What advantages does geothermal energy have over burning fossil fuels or using nuclear energy? Possible answers: Geothermal energy is a renewable resource. Using it instead of a nonrenewable resource such as coal or petroleum reserves fossil fuels for other uses, produces less air pollution, and eliminates waste disposal problems associated with nuclear power.

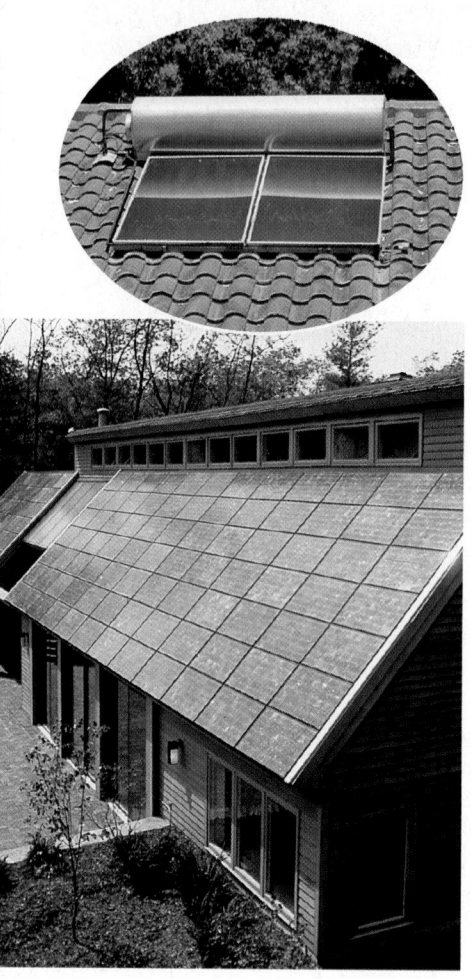

**Figure 20** Solar energy can be collected and utilized by individuals using thermal collectors or photovoltaic collectors.

**Collecting the Sun's Energy** Two types of collectors capture the Sun's rays. If you look around your neighborhood, you might see large, rectangular panels attached to the roofs of buildings or houses. If, as in **Figure 20,** pipes come out of the panel, it is a thermal collector. Using a black surface, a thermal collector heats water by directly absorbing the Sun's radiant energy. Water circulating in this system can be heated to about 70°C. The hot water can be pumped through the house to provide heat. Also, the hot water can be used for washing and bathing. If the panel has no pipes, it is a photovoltaic (foh toh vol TAY ihk) collector, like the one pictured in **Figure 20.** A **photovoltaic** is a device that transforms radiant energy directly into electrical energy. Photovoltaics are used to power calculators and satellites, including the *International Space Station.*

**Reading Check** *What does a photovoltaic do?*

## Geothermal Energy

Imagine you could take a journey to the center of Earth—down to about 6,400 km below the surface. As you went deeper and deeper, you would find the temperature increasing. In fact, after going only about 3 km, the temperature could have increased enough to boil water. At a depth of 100 km, the temperature could be over 900°C. The heat generated inside Earth is called geothermal energy. Some of this heat is produced when unstable radioactive atoms inside Earth decay, converting nuclear energy to thermal energy.

At some places deep within Earth the temperature is hot enough to melt rock. This molten rock, or magma, can rise up close to the surface through cracks in the crust. During a volcanic eruption, magma reaches the surface. In other places, magma gets close to the surface and heats the rock around it.

**Geothermal Reservoirs** In some regions where magma is close to the surface, rainwater and water from melted snow can seep down to the hot rock through cracks and other openings in Earth's surface. The water then becomes hot and sometimes can form steam. The hot water and steam can be trapped under high pressure in cracks and pockets called geothermal reservoirs. In some places, the hot water and steam are close enough to the surface to form hot springs and geysers.

**398** **CHAPTER 13** Energy and Energy Resources

## Differentiated Instruction

**Learning Disabled** Light from different sources, most notably the sun, can be transformed directly into electricity. Have a light-powered calculator available to demonstrate this. When the photovoltaic cell is in the light the light energy turns into electricity which runs the calculator. Cover the cell and the source of electricity is gone. The calculator runs out of energy and goes off.

## Cultural Diversity

**Geothermal Iceland** Iceland gets 50% of its energy from geothermal sources. Fossil fuels are only used to power automobiles, ships, and airplanes. About 86% of all space heating in Iceland is provided by geothermal energy and about 16% of Iceland's electricity is generated using geothermal energy. Geothermal energy is also used to heat outdoor pools, where people swim year round.

**Geothermal Power Plants** In places where the geothermal reservoirs are less than several kilometers deep, wells can be drilled to reach them. The hot water and steam produced by geothermal energy then can be used by geothermal power plants, like the one in **Figure 21,** to generate electricity.

Most geothermal reservoirs contain hot water under high pressure. **Figure 22** shows how these reservoirs can be used to generate electricity. While geothermal power is an inexhaustible source of energy, geothermal power plants can be built only in regions where geothermal reservoirs are close to the surface, such as in the western United States.

**Heat Pumps** Geothermal heat helps keep the temperature of the ground at a depth of several meters at a nearly constant temperature of about 10° to 20°C. This constant temperature can be used to cool and heat buildings by using a heat pump.

A heat pump contains a water-filled loop of pipe that is buried to a depth where the temperature is nearly constant. In summer the air is warmer than this underground temperature. Warm water from the building is pumped through the pipe down into the ground. The water cools and then is pumped back to the house where it absorbs more heat, and the cycle is repeated. During the winter, the air is cooler than the ground below. Then, cool water absorbs heat from the ground and releases it into the house.

**Figure 21** This geothermal power plant in Nevada produces enough electricity to power about 50,000 homes.

**Figure 22** The hot water in a geothermal reservoir is used to generate electricity in a geothermal power plant.

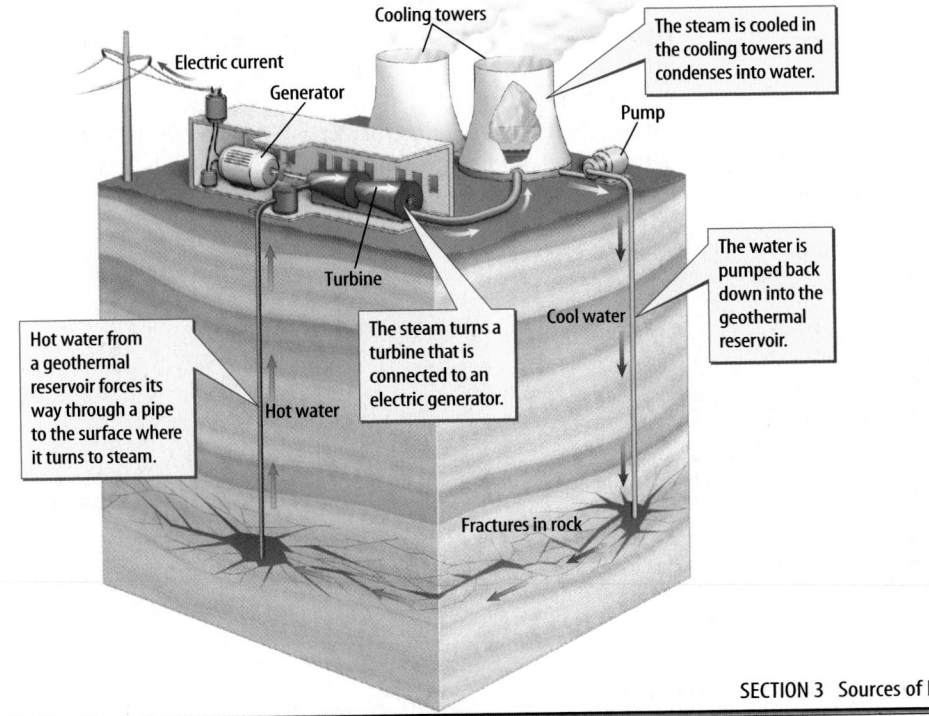

Cooling towers

The steam is cooled in the cooling towers and condenses into water.

Electric current

Generator

Pump

Turbine

The steam turns a turbine that is connected to an electric generator.

Cool water

The water is pumped back down into the geothermal reservoir.

Hot water from a geothermal reservoir forces its way through a pipe to the surface where it turns to steam.

Hot water

Fractures in rock

**Use Science Words**
**Word Origin** Have students find the origin of the word *geothermal*. The prefix *geo-* has Greek origins and means "earth." *Thermal* also has Greek origins and means "of or relating to heat."

**Activity**
**Heat Pumps** Have students research how heat pumps are used to heat and cool homes. Students should make a detailed poster showing the process. Have students present their posters to their class or a group of younger students.
[NS] **Visual-Spatial** [P]

**Discussion**
**Use of Heat Pumps** Why aren't geothermal heat pumps the primary source of heating and cooling in the United States? Possible answers: The cost of initial installation of geothermal heat pump systems is more than conventional equipment. The systems require additional land for the heat-exchanging wells. They work best in moderate climates and are not as effective in colder climates.

# Differentiated Instruction

**Learning Disabled** Have another student use a poster that was made in the activity above to explain each step in the heat pump process. Have learning disabled students define any unfamiliar words in their science journals for future reference. [NS] **Interpersonal**

# Science Journal

**Geothermal Heat Pumps** Have students make a chart in their Science Journals listing advantages and disadvantages of installing a geothermal heat pump in their home. [NS] **Logical-Mathematical**

**Figure 23** This tidal power plant in Annapolis Royal, Nova Scotia, is the only operating tidal power plant in North America.

**Figure 24** A tidal power plant can generate electricity when the tide is coming in and going out.

## Energy from the Oceans

The ocean is in constant motion. If you've been to the seashore you've seen waves roll in. You may have seen the level of the ocean rise and fall over a period of about a half day. This rise and fall in the ocean level is called a tide. The constant movement of the ocean is an inexhaustible source of mechanical energy that can be converted into electric energy. While methods are still being developed to convert the motion in ocean waves to electric energy, several electric power plants using tidal motion have been built.

**Using Tidal Energy** A high tide and a low tide each occur about twice a day. In most places the level of the ocean changes by less than a few meters. However, in some places the change is much greater. In the Bay of Fundy in Eastern Canada, the ocean level changes by 16 m between high tide and low tide. Almost 14 trillion kg of water move into or out of the bay between high and low tide.

**Figure 23** shows an electric power plant that has been built along the Bay of Fundy. This power plant generates enough electric energy to power about 12,000 homes. The power plant is constructed so that as the tide rises, water flows through a turbine that causes a electric generator to spin, as shown in **Figure 24A.** The water is then trapped behind a dam. When the tide goes out, the trapped water behind the dam is released through the turbine to generate more electricity, as shown in **Figure 24B.** Each day electric power is generated for about ten hours when the tide is rising and falling.

While tidal energy is a nonpolluting, inexhaustible energy source, its use is limited. Only in a few places is the difference between high and low tide large enough to enable a large electric power plant to be built.

**A** As the tide comes in, it turns a turbine connected to a generator. When high tide occurs, gates are closed that trap water behind a dam.

**B** As the tide goes out and the ocean level drops, the gates are opened and water from behind the dam flows through the turbine, causing it to spin and turn a generator.

# Wind

Wind is another inexhaustible supply of energy. Modern windmills, like the ones in **Figure 25,** convert the kinetic energy of the wind to electrical energy. The propeller is connected to a generator so that electrical energy is generated when wind spins the propeller. These windmills produce almost no pollution. Some disadvantages are that windmills produce noise and that large areas of land are needed. Also, studies have shown that birds sometimes are killed by windmills.

# Conserving Energy

Fossil fuels are a valuable resource. Not only are they burned to provide energy, but oil and coal also are used to make plastics and other materials. One way to make the supply of fossil fuels last longer is to use less energy. Reducing the use of energy is called conserving energy.

You can conserve energy and also save money by turning off lights and appliances such as televisions when you are not using them. Also keep doors and windows closed tightly when it's cold or hot to keep heat from leaking out of or into your house. Energy could also be conserved if buildings are properly insulated, especially around windows. The use of oil could be reduced if cars were used less and made more efficient, so they went farther on a liter of gas. Recycling materials such as aluminum cans and glass also helps conserve energy.

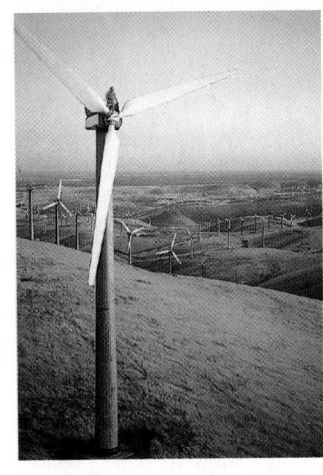

**Figure 25** Windmills work on the same basic principles as a power plant. Instead of steam turning a turbine, wind turns the rotors. **Describe** *some of the advantages and disadvantages of using windmills.*

Science⦾nline in7.msscience.com/self_check_quiz

---

## section 3 review

### Summary

**Nonrenewable Resources**

- All energy resources have advantages and disadvantages.
- Nonrenewable energy resources are used faster than they are replaced.
- Fossil fuels include oil, coal, and natural gas and are nonrenewable resources. Nuclear energy is a nonrenewable resource.

**Renewable and Alternative Resources**

- Renewable energy resources, such as hydroelectricity, are resources that are replenished continually.
- Alternative energy sources include solar energy, wind energy, and geothermal energy.

### Self Check

1. **Diagram** the energy conversions that occur when coal is formed, and then burned to produce thermal energy.
2. **Explain** why solar energy is considered an inexhaustible source of energy.
3. **Explain** how a heat pump is used to both heat and cool a building.
4. **Think Critically** Identify advantages and disadvantages of using fossil fuels, hydroelectricity, and solar energy as energy sources.

#### Applying Math

5. **Use a Ratio** Earth's temperature increases with depth. Suppose the temperature increase inside Earth is 500°C at a depth of 50 km. What is the temperature increase at a depth of 10 km?

---

## section 3 review

1. Radiant energy from the Sun is converted into chemical energy when coal is formed; chemical energy in coal is converted into thermal energy and radiant energy when coal is burned.
2. The Sun's energy cannot be used up by humans because the Sun will produce an enormous amount of energy for billions of years and humans can use only a small amount of the energy the Sun produces.
3. The ground at several meters' depth is cooler than the outside air in summer and warmer than the outside air in winter. Heat can be transferred from the building to the ground in summer, and from the ground to the building in winter.
4. fossil fuels: cheap, plentiful, but nonrenewable and produces pollution; hydroelectricity: nonpolluting, renewable, but can alter local ecosystems and available only in certain areas; solar energy: inexhaustible, but expensive
5. 100°C

---

## Caption Answer

**Figure 25** Advantages include lack of pollution and the availability of wind. Disadvantages are the potential for killing birds, variability of the wind, towers are unsightly, and a large amount of land is required.

## 3 Assess

### DAILY INTERVENTION

### Check for Understanding

**Linguistic** Have students answer the following questions in their Science Journals: "What kind of energy source is ethanol derived from corn, and why does adding it to gasoline prolong the supply of oil?" Ethanol derived from corn is a renewable source of energy. As long as corn keeps being planted and grown, there will be a source for ethanol to burn in cars. Adding ethanol to gasoline allows us to reduce our usage of gasoline, slowing down the rate at which we are using that non-renewable source of energy.

### Reteach

**Sources of Energy** Have each student make a list of all of the sources of energy discussed in this section. Ask students to explain how each energy source releases its energy and classify each source as renewable or nonrenewable. L2 IN **Linguistic**

### ☑ Assessment

**Oral** Where does all the electrical energy produced in power plants end up? It is converted into energy forms such as thermal, radiant, or sound energy.

## Use the Internet

402 CHAPTER 13 Energy and Energy Resources

### ◉ Real-World Question

**Purpose** Students will investigate the types of energy they use in everyday activities.

**Process Skills** Locate and evaluate sources of information on the Internet, in books, and in periodicals.

**Time Required** about two days

**Internet** Students use Internet sites that can be accessed through in7.msscience.com/internet_lab.

They will investigate the types of energy they use in everyday activities. L2

**IS** **Logical-Mathematical**

**Non-Internet Sources** Identify different science books to research energy sources.

### ◉ Make a Plan

**Preparation**

**Internet** To run through the steps that the students will follow, visit in7.msscience.com/internet_lab.

**Non-Internet Sources** Collect books and materials that contain information about energy sources such as gasoline, coal, and solar energy.

### ◉ Follow Your Plan

**Teaching Strategy** Ahead of time, do some Internet searches to locate and evaluate several Web sites noting their strengths and weaknesses. This will help you guide your students as they research Internet sites. Also, ask your librarian to give a short presentation on using library materials as part of their research.

# Energy to Power Your Life

**Goals**

■ **Identify** how energy you use is produced and delivered.

■ **Investigate** alternative sources for the energy you use.

■ **Outline** a plan for how these alternative sources of energy could be used.

**Data Source**

**Science**Online

Visit in7.msscience.com/internet_lab for more information about sources of energy and for data collected by other students.

### ◉ Real-World Question

Over the past 100 years, the amount of energy used in the United States and elsewhere has greatly increased. Today, a number of energy sources are available, such as coal, oil, natural gas, nuclear energy, hydroelectric power, wind, and solar energy. Some of these energy sources are being used up and are nonrenewable, but others are replaced as fast as they are used and, therefore, are renewable. Some energy sources are so vast that human usage has almost no effect on the amount available. These energy sources are inexhaustible.

Think about the types of energy you use at home and school every day. In this lab, you will investigate how and where energy is produced, and how it gets to you. You will also investigate alternative ways energy can be produced, and whether these sources are renewable, nonrenewable, or inexhaustible. What are the sources of the energy you use every day?

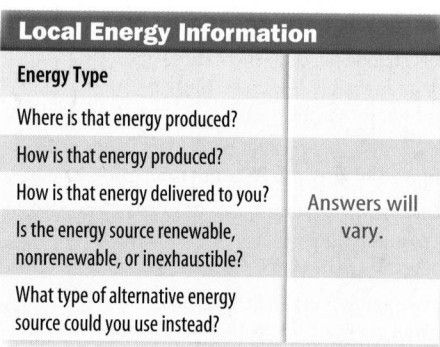

| Local Energy Information | |
|---|---|
| **Energy Type** | |
| Where is that energy produced? | |
| How is that energy produced? | |
| How is that energy delivered to you? | Answers will |
| Is the energy source renewable, nonrenewable, or inexhaustible? | vary. |
| What type of alternative energy source could you use instead? | |

**402 CHAPTER 13** Energy and Energy Resources

## Alternative Inquiry Lab

**Energy Types and Sources** Every energy source has its pros and cons. Have the students choose from a list of sources including, but not limited to, coal, gasoline, natural gas, heating oil, nuclear power, ethanol, hydrogen power, solar power, and wind power. They should summarize what the pros and cons are for that particular energy source, and take a position on the advisability of staying with or changing to that source of energy. This lab will challenge students to use critical thinking and higher order thinking skills.

## ▶ Make a Plan

1. Think about the activities you do every day and the things you use. When you watch television, listen to the radio, ride in a car, use a hair drier, or turn on the air conditioning, you use energy. Select one activity or appliance that uses energy.

2. **Identify** the type of energy that is used.

3. **Investigate** how that energy is produced and delivered to you.

4. **Determine** if the energy source is renewable, nonrenewable, or inexhaustible.

5. If your energy source is nonrenewable, describe how the energy you use could be produced by renewable sources.

## ▶ Follow Your Plan

1. Make sure your teacher approves your plan before you start.

2. Organize your findings in a data table, similar to the one that is shown.

## ▶ Analyze Your Data

1. **Describe** the process for producing and delivering the energy source you researched. How is it created, and how does it get to you?

2. How much energy is produced by the energy source you investigated?

3. Is the energy source you researched renewable, nonrenewable, or inexhaustible? Why?

## ▶ Conclude and Apply

1. **Describe** If the energy source you investigated is nonrenewable, how the use of this energy source be reduced?

2. **Organize** What alternative sources of energy could you use for everyday energy needs? On the computer, create a plan for using renewable or inexhaustible sources.

**Communicating**
**Your Data**

Find this lab using the link below. Post your data in the table that is provided. **Compare** your data to those of other students. **Combine** your data with those of other students and make inferences using the combined data.

**Science** Online
in7.msscience.com/internet_lab

**LAB** 403

## ▶ Analyze Your Data

1. Answers may vary. One example would be the process for producing gasoline, which involves drilling crude oil from wells, and the process involved in refining the crude oil into the product that we pump at the gas station.

2. If students investigated gasoline, they may discover that it is a small part of their daily energy use.

3. Gasoline is an example of a non-renewable energy source, because it is a fossil fuel.

## ▶ Conclude and Apply

1. Answers will vary.

2. One strategy may be to replace a calculator that runs on nonrechargeable batteries with one that is powered by solar cells.

---

**☑ Assessment**

**Process** Have students make displays that show their research about an activity or appliance and its energy source. They should include pictures and descriptions of how the energy source used is produced and delivered so it can be used. Use **Performance Assessment in the Science Classroom,** p.135.

**Communicating**
**Your Data**

Have students make a chart that compares the energy source they investigated with other energy sources that could be used, including alternative or renewable energy sources. Students should also compare costs and environmental impacts.

## Content Background

Solar, wind, and geothermal are inexhaustible energy sources, and biomass and hydroelectric powered systems are considered renewable energy sources. Not all sources can be used to produce a continuous supply of energy in all areas. Also, the technology needed to store and supply this energy on demand is insufficient and often far too costly to use. As technology improves, these alternative sources will supplement and possibly even replace fossil fuels.

## Discussion

**Energy Sources** What are some possible explanations for why only 18 percent of the energy used worldwide is from renewable and inexhaustible resources? Answers will vary. Currently the technology does not exist to supply energy from these sources on demand and at an affordable price.

## Activity

**Alternatives** Have students research alternative energy sources available in their area. Students should make posters showing how energy is obtained from these sources. L2 IN **Visual-Spatial**

### Applying Math

**Answer** 320 calories

## Find Out About It

Solar collectors would do well in the southwestern United States because it is sunny there for most of the year.

---

# SCIENCE Stats

# Energy to Burn

## Did you know...

**... The energy released by the average hurricane** is equal to about 200 times the total energy produced by all of the world's power plants. Almost all of this energy is released as heat when raindrops form.

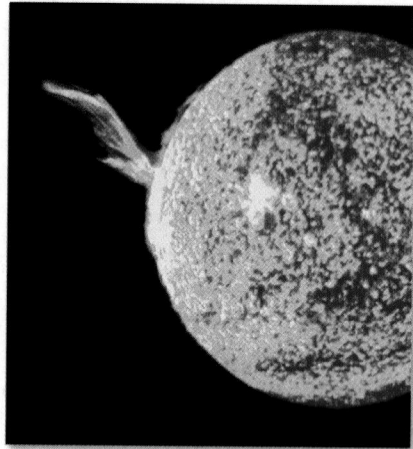

**... The energy Earth gets each half hour from the Sun** is enough to meet the world's demands for a year. Renewable and inexhaustible resources, including the Sun, account for only 18 percent of the energy that is used worldwide.

**... The Calories in one medium apple** will give you enough energy to walk for about 15 min, swim for about 10 min, or jog for about 9 min.

### Applying Math
If walking for 15 min requires 80 Calories of fuel (from food), how many Calories would someone need to consume to walk for 1 h?

## Write About It
Where would you place solar collectors in the United States? Why? For more information on solar energy, go to in7.msscience.com/science_stats.

**404 CHAPTER 13** Energy and Energy Resources

## Reviewing Main Ideas

**Section 1** What is energy?

1. Energy is the ability to cause change.

2. A moving object has kinetic energy that depends on the object's mass and speed.

3. Potential energy is energy due to position and depends on an object's mass and height.

4. Light carries radiant energy, electric current carries electrical energy, and atomic nuclei contain nuclear energy.

**Section 2** Energy Transformations

1. Energy can be transformed from one form to another. Thermal energy is usually produced when energy transformations occur.

2. The law of conservation of energy states that energy cannot be created or destroyed.

3. Electric power plants convert a source of energy into electrical energy. Steam spins a turbine which spins an electric generator.

**Section 3** Sources of Energy

1. The use of an energy source has advantages and disadvantages.

2. Fossil fuels and nuclear energy are nonrenewable energy sources that are consumed faster than they can be replaced.

3. Hydroelectricity is a renewable energy source that is continually being replaced.

4. Alternative energy sources include solar, wind, and geothermal energy. Solar energy is an inexhaustible energy source.

## Visualizing Main Ideas

*Copy and complete the concept map using the following terms:* fossil fuels, hydroelectric, solar, wind, oil, coal, photovoltaic, *and* nonrenewable resources.

Science Online in7.msscience.com/interactive_tutor

**CHAPTER STUDY GUIDE** 405

---

## Reviewing Main Ideas

Summary statements can be used by students to review the major concepts of the chapter.

## Visualizing Main Ideas

See student page.

**Visit** in7.msscience.com
/self_check_quiz
/interactive_tutor
/vocabulary_puzzlemaker
/chapter_review
/standards_review
/field_guide

### Assessment Transparency

For additional assessment questions, use the *Assessment Transparency* located in the transparency book.

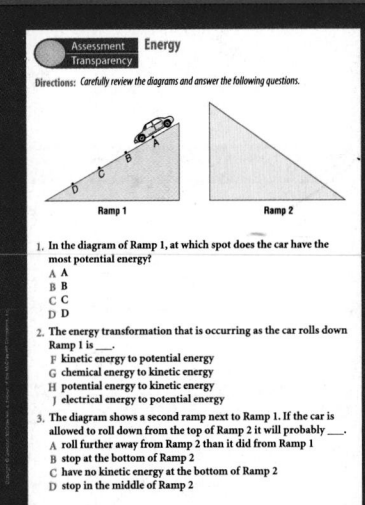

---

## Identifying Misconceptions

**Assess**

Use the assessment as follow-up to page F at the beginning of the chapter.

**Activity** Display examples of the work of the famous cartoonist Rube Goldberg. Have students draw their own Rube Goldberg style invention that includes four energy transformations. Direct students to draw red arrows to indicate areas where heat loss would occur.

**Expected Outcome** Students recognize that energy is transferred from one form into another.

**Reinforcement** Have students exchange drawings and describe the energy transformations depicted.

## Using Vocabulary

1. Nuclear energy is sometimes used to generate electrical energy.

2. A rotating turbine helps produce electrical energy by causing a generator to spin.

3. A photovoltaic collector changes radiant energy from the Sun directly into electrical energy.

4. Inexhaustible resources are resources that can't be used up by humans. Renewable resources are replenished by nature. Neither source gets used up.

5. Potential energy due to gravity changes to kinetic energy as an object falls.

6. In an electrical generator, kinetic energy is changed into electrical energy.

7. Thermal energy and radiant energy are two forms of energy that can be converted into each other or other forms of energy.

8. The law of conservation of energy states that in energy transformations, energy can be neither created nor destroyed. It only can change from one form to another.

9. Some sources of chemical energy, such as fossil fuels, are nonrenewable. Some, such as biomass, are renewable.

### Checking Concepts

| | | |
|---|---|---|
| 10. C | 14. A | 18. D |
| 11. D | 15. A | 19. B |
| 12. D | 16. B | |
| 13. C | 17. A | |

### Thinking Critically

20. When the swing is pulled back, its potential energy increases. When the swing is released, potential energy is converted into kinetic energy as it moves downward. As it moves upward, kinetic energy is converted into potential energy.

## Using Vocabulary

| | |
|---|---|
| alternative resource p. 397 | nonrenewable resource p. 394 |
| chemical energy p. 383 | nuclear energy p. 384 |
| electrical energy p. 384 | photovoltaic p. 398 |
| energy p. 380 | potential energy p. 382 |
| generator p. 390 | radiant energy p. 383 |
| inexhaustible resource p. 397 | renewable resource p. 396 |
| kinetic energy p. 381 | thermal energy p. 382 |
| law of conservation of energy p. 386 | turbine p. 390 |

*For each of the terms below, explain the relationship that exists.*

1. electrical energy—nuclear energy

2. turbine—generator

3. photovoltaic—radiant energy—electrical energy

4. renewable resource—inexhaustible resource

5. potential energy—kinetic energy

6. kinetic energy—electrical energy—generator

7. thermal energy—radiant energy

8. law of conservation of energy—energy transformations

9. nonrenewable resource—chemical energy

## Checking Concepts

*Choose the word or phrase that best answers the question.*

10. Objects that are able to fall have what type of energy?
    A) kinetic          C) potential
    B) radiant          D) electrical

11. Which form of energy does light have?
    A) electrical       C) kinetic
    B) nuclear          D) radiant

Science Online   in7.msscience.com/vocabulary_puzzlemaker

12. Muscles perform what type of energy transformation?
    A) kinetic to potential
    B) kinetic to electrical
    C) thermal to radiant
    D) chemical to kinetic

13. Photovoltaics perform what type of energy transformation?
    A) thermal to radiant
    B) kinetic to electrical
    C) radiant to electrical
    D) electrical to thermal

14. The form of energy that food contains is which of the following?
    A) chemical         C) radiant
    B) potential        D) electrical

15. Solar energy, wind, and geothermal are what type of energy resource?
    A) inexhaustible    C) nonrenewable
    B) inexpensive      D) chemical

16. Which of the following is a nonrenewable source of energy?
    A) hydroelectricity
    B) nuclear
    C) wind
    D) solar

17. A generator is NOT required to generate electrical energy when which of the following energy sources is used?
    A) solar            C) hydroelectric
    B) wind             D) nuclear

18. Which of the following are fossil fuels?
    A) gas              C) oil
    B) coal             D) all of these

19. Almost all of the energy that is used on Earth's surface comes from which of the following energy sources?
    A) radioactivity    C) chemicals
    B) the Sun          D) wind

**Use the ExamView® Pro Testmaker CD-ROM to:**
- create multiple versions of tests
- create modified tests with one mouse click for inclusion students
- edit existing questions and add your own questions
- build tests aligned with state standards using built-in State Curriculum Tags
- change English tests to Spanish with one mouse click and vice versa

## Thinking Critically

**20. Explain** how the motion of a swing illustrates the transformation between potential and kinetic energy.

**21. Explain** what happens to the kinetic energy of a skateboard that is coasting along a flat surface, slows down, and comes to a stop.

**22. Describe** the energy transformations that occur in the process of toasting a bagel in an electric toaster.

**23. Compare and contrast** the formation of coal and the formation of oil and natural gas.

**24. Explain** the difference between the law of conservation of energy and conserving energy. How can conserving energy help prevent energy shortages?

**25. Make a Hypothesis** about how spacecraft that travel through the solar system obtain the energy they need to operate. Do research to verify your hypothesis.

**26. Concept Map** Copy and complete this concept map about energy.

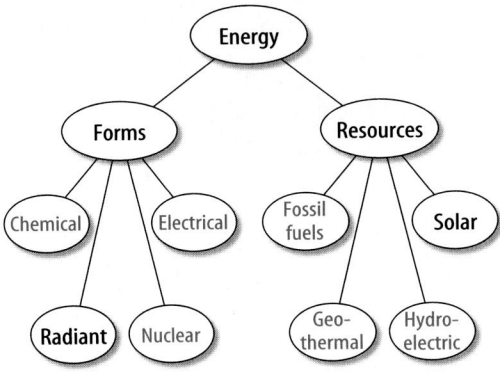

**27. Diagram** the energy transformations that occur when you rub sandpaper on a piece of wood and the wood becomes warm.

 Science Online in7.msscience.com/chapter_review

## Performance Activities

**28. Multimedia Presentation** Alternative sources of energy that weren't discussed include biomass energy, wave energy, and hydrogen fuel cells. Research an alternative energy source and then prepare a digital slide show about the information you found. Use the concepts you learned from this chapter to inform your classmates about the future prospects of using such an energy source on a large scale.

## Applying Math

**29. Calculate Number of Power Plants** A certain type of power plant is designed to provide energy for 10,000 homes. How many of these power plants would be needed to provide energy for 300,000 homes?

**Use the table below to answer questions 30 and 31.**

| Energy Sources Used in the United States | |
|---|---|
| **Energy Source** | **Percent of Energy Used** |
| Coal | 23% |
| Oil | 39% |
| Natural gas | 23% |
| Nuclear | 8% |
| Hydroelectric | 4% |
| Other | 3% |

**30. Use Percentages** According to the data in the table above, what percentage of the energy used in the United States comes from fossil fuels?

**31. Calculate a Ratio** How many times greater is the amount of energy that comes from fossil fuels than the amount of energy from all other energy sources?

## Thinking Critically

**21.** The kinetic energy of the skate is converted into thermal energy by friction.

**22.** In the toaster, electrical energy is converted into thermal energy. Thermal energy is converted into chemical energy in the bagel, causing it to become toasted.

**23.** Both formed over millions of years. Coal formed from the effects of heat and pressure on buried vegetation. Oil and natural gas formed from the effects of heat and pressure on the buried remains of microscopic organisms on the ocean floor.

**24.** Law of conservation of energy states that energy cannot be created or destroyed. Conserving energy means reducing energy usage, which can prevent energy shortages by reducing the consumption of nonrenewable energy sources.

**25.** Possible answers: spacecrafts use solar cells, spacecrafts use batteries

**26.** See student page.

**27.** chemical energy in muscles → kinetic energy of sandpaper → thermal energy of wood

## Performance Activities

**28.** Check students' work. Use **Performance Assessment in the Science Classroom,** p. 149.

## Applying Math

**Indiana Math Standards**
7.2.3, 7.7.1

**29.** 30

**30.** 85%

**31.** 5.7 times greater

---

## ☑ Assessment    Resources

📂 **Reproducible Masters**

**Chapter *Fast File* Resources**
Chapter Review, pp. 35–36
Chapter Tests, pp. 37–40
Assessment Transparency Activity, p. 47

**Glencoe Science Web site**
Chapter Review Test
IN Standards Review

**Glencoe Technology**
✋ Assessment Transparency
🌐 Exam*View*® Pro Testmaker
💻 MindJogger Videoquiz
🌐 Interactive Chalkboard

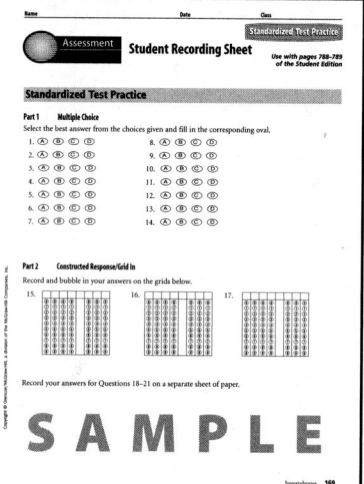

**Answer Sheet** A practice answer sheet can be found at in7.msscience.com/answer_sheet.

**Part 1** **Multiple Choice**

1. B
2. D
3. B
4. B
5. C
6. B
7. D

The assessed Indiana standard appears above the question.

*Record your answers on the answer sheet provided by your teacher or on a sheet of paper.*

**Part 1** **Multiple Choice**

**7.3.16**

1. The graph below shows global energy use from 1970 to 2000.

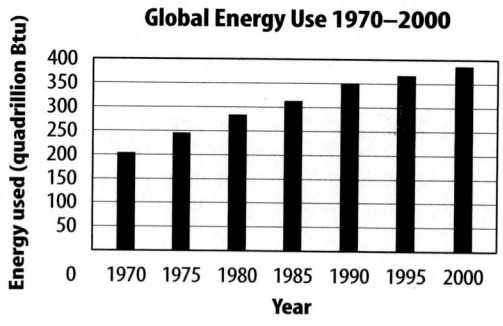

By about how many times did the global use of energy increase from 1970 to 2000?

A 1.5

B 2.0

C 2.5

D 3.0

**7.3.15**

2. Which is **TRUE** when chemical energy is transformed into thermal energy?

A Only the amount of chemical energy changes.

B Only the amount of thermal energy changes.

C The total amount of energy changes.

D The total amount of energy doesn't change.

**7.3.16**

3. Which energy source is being used faster than it can be replaced?

A hydroelectric

B oil

C tidal

D wind

4. Which energy conversion occurs as a ball falls?

A kinetic to potential

B potential to kinetic

C thermal to potential

D thermal to kinetic

5. The circle graph below shows the sources of electrical energy in the United States.

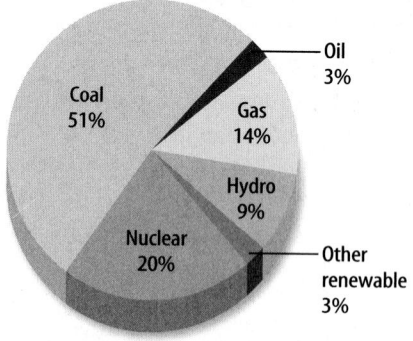

How many times greater is the amount of electrical energy produced by fossil fuels than the amount produced by nuclear energy?

A 2.4

B 3.0

C 3.4

D 4.0

**Part 2** **Critical Response**

8. During each bounce, some of the kinetic energy of the ball is converted into thermal energy. As a result, energy is not created or destroyed, but only changes form, so that the law of conservation of energy is obeyed.

9. The kinetic energy of the ball is greatest at the distances where the potential energy is smallest. This is at distances of 0 m and 40 m.

10. fossil fuels: currently cheap and plentiful, but nonrenewable and produces pollution; nuclear energy:

does not produce pollution, cheap, but produces nuclear waste and is nonrenewable; geothermal energy: inexhaustible, but only available in a few places

**6.** The kinetic energy of an object increases if which increases?

A  its height

B  its speed

C  its temperature

D  its volume

**7.** The graph below shows actual global oil production from 1930 to 2000 and estimated global oil production from 2000 to 2050.

**Global Oil Production**

In approximately what year will estimated global oil production equal the actual oil production in 1970?

A  2005

B  2010

C  2020

D  2030

---

**Part 2** | **Critical Response**

**7.3.14**

**8.** When you drop a tennis ball, it hits the floor and bounces back up. It does not reach the same height as released, and each successive upward bounce is smaller than the one previous. However, you notice the tennis ball is slightly warmer after it finishes bouncing. Explain how the law of conservation of energy is obeyed.

**9.** The graph below shows how the potential energy of a batted ball changes as the distance from the batter increases.

**Potential Energy of Batted Ball**

At what distances is the kinetic energy of the ball greatest?

**7.3.16**

**10.** List advantages and disadvantages of the following energy sources: fossil fuels, nuclear energy, and geothermal energy.

---

## Rubrics

The following rubric is a sample scoring device for critical response questions.

### Critical Response

| Points | Description |
|--------|-------------|
| 4 | The student demonstrates a thorough understanding of the science of the task. The response may contain minor flaws that do not detract from the demonstration of a thorough understanding. |
| 3 | The student demonstrates an understanding of the science of the task. The response is essentially correct and demonstrates an essential but less than thorough understanding of the science. |
| 2 | The student demonstrates only a partial understanding of the science of the task. Although the student may have used the correct approach to a solution or may have provided a correct solution, the work lacks an essential understanding of the underlying science concepts. |
| 1 | The student demonstrates a very limited understanding of the science of the task. The response is incomplete and exhibits many flaws. |
| 0 | The student provides a completely incorrect solution or no response at all. |

---

| Section/Objectives | Standards | | Labs/Features |
|---|---|---|---|
| **Chapter Opener** | **National** | **State/Local** | **Launch Lab:** Wave Properties, p. 411 **Foldables,** p. 411 |
| | See pp. 16T–17T for a Key to Standards. | Detailed standards begin on page IN8. | A data-collection lab using Probeware technology can be found in the **Probeware Lab Manual,** pp. 37–39 |
| **Section 1  Waves** ⏱ 3 sessions ▱ 1.5 blocks 1. **Explain** how waves transport energy. 2. **Distinguish** among transverse, compressional, and electromagnetic waves. 3. **Describe** the properties of waves. 4. **Describe** reflection, refraction, and diffraction of waves. | National Content Standards: UCP.1–UCP.3, UCP.5, A.1, A.2, B.1, B.2, B.3 | Indiana Standards: 7.3.18, 7.7.4 | **Applying Math:** Speed of Sound, p. 416 **MiniLAB:** Refraction of Light, p. 417 |
| **Section 2  Sound Waves** ⏱ 3 sessions ▱ 1.5 blocks 5. **Describe** how sound waves are produced. 6. **Explain** how sound waves travel through matter. 7. **Describe** the relationship between loudness and sound intensity. 8. **Explain** how humans hear sound. | National Content Standards: UCP.1–UCP.3, UCP.5, A.1, A.2, B.1, B.2, B.3 | Indiana Standards: 7.3.18, 7.3.20 | **Integrate Health,** p. 421 **Lab:** Sound Waves in Matter, p. 424 |
| **Section 3  Light** ⏱ 4 sessions ▱ 2 blocks 9. **Identify** the properties of light waves. 10. **Describe** the electromagnetic spectrum. 11. **Describe** the types of electromagnetic waves that travel from the Sun to Earth. 12. **Explain** human vision and color perception. | National Content Standards: UCP.1–UCP.3, UCP.5, A.1, A.2, B.2, B.3 | Indiana Standards: 7.1.5, 7.3.2, 7.3.11, 7.3.18, 7.3.19, 7.3.20 | **Science Online,** p. 426 **MiniLAB:** Separating Wavelengths, p. 428 **Visualizing Common Vision Problems,** p. 430 **Lab:** Bending Light, p. 432 **Oops! Accidents in Science:** Jansky's Merry-Go-Round, p. 434 |

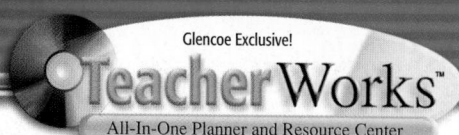
| Lab Materials | Reproducible Resources | Section Assessment | Technology |
|---|---|---|---|
| **Launch Lab:** 50-cm piece of string | **Chapter FAST FILE Resources**<br>Foldables Worksheet, p. 17<br>Directed Reading Overview, p. 19<br>Note-taking Worksheets, pp. 33–35 | GLENCOE'S **ASSESSMENT** ADVANTAGE | TeacherWorks includes:<br>• Interactive Teacher Edition<br>• Lesson Planner with calendar<br>• Access to all program blacklines<br>• Correlations to standards<br>• Web links<br>▣ Video Lab |
| **MiniLAB:** drinking glass, pencil<br><br>*Need materials?*<br>Contact Science Kit at 1-800-828-7777 or www.sciencekit.com on the Internet. | **Chapter FAST FILE Resources**<br>Transparency Activity, p. 44<br>MiniLAB, p. 3<br>Enrichment, p. 30<br>Reinforcement, p. 27<br>Directed Reading, p. 20<br>**Science Inquiry Labs,** pp. 19–20 | **Portfolio**<br>Curriculum Connection, p. 414<br>**Performance**<br>Applying Math, p. 416<br>MiniLAB, p. 417<br>Applying Math, p. 418<br>**Content**<br>Section Review, p. 418 | Section Focus Transparency<br>Virtual Labs CD-ROM<br>Guided Reading Audio Program<br>Interactive Chalkboard CD-ROM |
| **Lab:** 100-mL beakers (4), corn syrup, water, vegetable oil, pencil | **Chapter FAST FILE Resources**<br>Transparency Activity, p. 45<br>Enrichment, p. 31<br>Reinforcement, p. 28<br>Directed Reading, p. 20<br>Lab Worksheet, pp. 5–6<br>Lab Activity, pp. 9–12 | **Portfolio**<br>Differentiated Instruction, p. 420<br>**Performance**<br>Applying Math, p. 423<br>**Content**<br>Section Review, p. 423 | Section Focus Transparency<br>Guided Reading Audio Program<br>Interactive Chalkboard CD-ROM |
| **MiniLAB:** prism, flashlight, laser pointer<br>**Lab:** small piece of cardboard, scissors, tape, flashlight, flat mirror, clear plastic CD case, 250-mL beaker, prism | **Chapter FAST FILE Resources**<br>Transparency Activity, p. 46<br>MiniLAB, p. 4<br>Enrichment, p. 32<br>Reinforcement, p. 29<br>Directed Reading, p. 21<br>Lab Worksheet, pp. 7–8<br>Lab Activity, pp. 13–16<br>Transparency Activity, pp. 47–48 | **Portfolio**<br>Curriculum Connection, p. 426<br>**Performance**<br>MiniLAB, p. 428<br>Applying Skills, p. 431<br>**Content**<br>Section Review, p. 431 | Section Focus Transparency<br>Teaching Transparency<br>Guided Reading Audio Program<br>Interactive Chalkboard CD-ROM<br>▣ Probeware Lab |

## End of Chapter Assessment

GLENCOE'S **ASSESSMENT** ADVANTAGE

| Blackline Masters | Technology | Professional Series |
|---|---|---|
| **Chapter FAST FILE Resources**<br>Chapter Review, pp. 37–38<br>Chapter Tests, pp. 39–42<br>**Mastering the Grade 7 Indiana Science Standards** | ▣ MindJogger Videoquiz<br>⊙ IN Test Prep and Practice ExamView®<br>⊙ ExamView® Pro Testmaker<br>⊙ TeacherWorks CD-ROM<br>⊙ Interactive Chalkboard CD-ROM | **Performance Assessment in the Science Classroom (PASC)** |

# Transparencies

## Section Focus

## Assessment

## Teaching

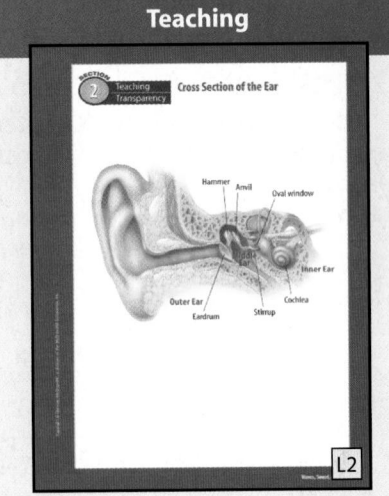

This is a representation of key blackline masters available in the Teacher Classroom Resources. See Resource Manager boxes within the chapter for additional information.

## Key to Teaching Strategies

The following designations will help you decide which activities are appropriate for your students.

L1 Level 1 activities should be appropriate for students with learning difficulties.

L2 Level 2 activities should be within the ability range of all students.

L3 Level 3 activities are designed for above-average students.

ELL ELL activities should be within the ability range of English-Language Learners.

COOP LEARN Cooperative Learning activities are designed for small group work.

LS Multiple Learning Styles logos, as described on page 12T, are used throughout to indicate strategies that address different learning styles.

P These strategies represent student products that can be placed into a best-work portfolio.

PBL Problem-Based Learning activities apply real-world situations to learning.

# Hands-on Activities

## Student Text Lab Worksheet

## Laboratory Activities

## Meeting Different Ability Levels

### Content Outline

L2

### Reinforcement

L2

### Enrichment

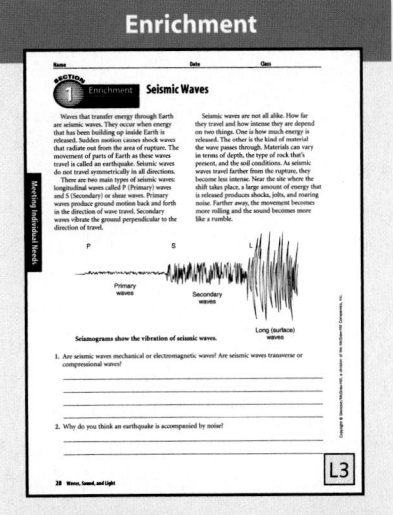

L3

### Directed Reading (English/Spanish)

L1

### Study Guide

L2

### Reading Essentials

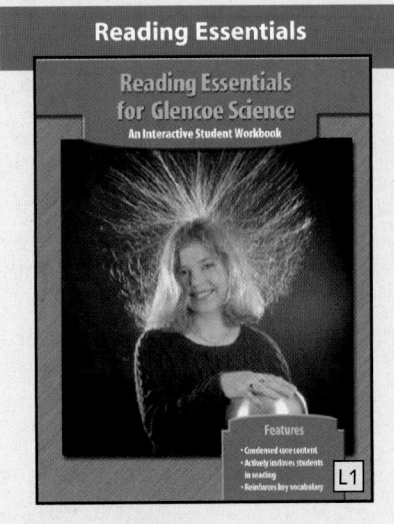

L1

## Assessment

### Test Practice Workbook

L2

### Chapter Review

L2

### Chapter Tests

L2

# Science Content Background

## section 1 Waves

### Refraction

The change in direction of a wave as it travels from one material into another is refraction. It occurs if the wave travels at different speeds in the two materials. A line perpendicular to the boundary between two materials is the normal. If a wave approaches the boundary at an angle other than perpendicular to the boundary, the wave will be bent toward the normal if it slows down as it enters the second medium. If the wave speeds up, it will be bent away from the normal.

The reason for this is apparent if you pretend a 12-inch ruler is a wave front moving toward a pan of water. The ruler approaches at an angle so that the one-inch mark hits the water before the other parts of the ruler. The ruler in the water moves slower but the rest of the ruler travels at the same speed. This causes the ruler to turn so that the ruler is more nearly parallel to the air-water boundary. This is analogous to the wave bending toward the normal when it slows down.

## section 2 Sound Waves

### Doppler Effect

You have probably noticed the change in pitch of the sound of objects as they move towards and then away from you. For example, a train's horn sounds higher in pitch as it approaches you and lower in pitch as it moves away. This phenomenon is known as the Doppler effect. As the object moves towards you, its sound waves crowd closer together making wavelengths shorter and the frequency and pitch higher. As the object moves past you, waves are spread making longer wavelengths and lower frequencies and pitch.

## section 3 Light

An electric charge that is moving back and forth or oscillating produces an electromagnetic wave. The oscillating charges create vibrating electric and magnetic fields that travel outward from the charge. These fields move outward because they mutually create each other—a changing electric field produces a changing magnetic field and vice versa.

The refraction of light, occurs because light changes its speed as it moves through different materials. The index of refraction of a material is sometimes used to describe how light is slowed when traveling in the material. The index of refraction equals the speed of light in a vacuum divided by the speed of light in the material. The slower light moves in a material, the larger the index of refraction for the material.

The index of refraction of a vacuum is 1.000. Water has an index of refraction of 1.333 and for diamond, the index of refraction is 2.417.

## chapter content resources

**Internet Resources**
For additional content background, visit
**in7.msscience.com** to:
- access your book online
- find references to related articles in popular science magazines
- access Web links with related content background
- access current events with science journal topics

**Print Resources**
*Waves: Principles of Light, Electricity, and Magnetism,* by Paul Fleisher, Lerner Publications, 2001
*Science Experiments with Sound & Music,* by Shar Levine and Leslie Johnstone, Sterling Publishing, 2002
*Great Experiments with Light,* by Phyllis Fiarotta and Noel Fiarotta, Sterling Publishing, 2000

# IDENTIFYING Misconceptions

## Find Out What Students Think

Students may think that when a wave moves through a medium that the particles of the medium travel along with the wave. Most children learn the word wave in connection with water. They might have felt an ocean or lake wave pushing them towards the shore. It is reasonable for them to think that a ripple in water or a sound moving through air is transporting the medium as it moves. In reality, however, the molecules of the medium are displaced and then return to their original position.

### Thought Experiment
Draw a picture of a cork floating in water with five letters (A, B, C, D, and E) surrounding the cork. Tell students to imagine you are going to dip your finger into the water and create waves. They should predict where the cork would be after five waves pass by the cork.

Many students will predict that the cork will move away from where you put your finger into the water. Perhaps some will suggest it will go towards your finger. Most students will not, however, say that the cork will remain in its original position after the waves pass by.

## Promote Understanding

Two demonstrations can help students develop the concept that the energy of the wave passes through the medium with no net displacement of the particles of the medium.

For a transverse wave, tie a rope to a doorknob. Stand away from the knob and pull the rope nearly taut, leaving some slack. Move your arm up quickly and back to its starting point to make a pulse in the rope. The pulse travels through the rope to the knob and back again. Help the students realize that the rope moves as the pulse goes through it and then the rope returns to its original position. Explain that this also happens in water waves.

For a compressional wave, have a student hold one end of a coiled spring and you hold the other as you stretch it across the top of a desk. Create a pulse by squeezing some coils together and then letting them go. Help students to again realize the coils of the spring moved as the pulse traveled but then it returned to its original position. Explain that this happens to the molecules as sound waves travel through air.

### Assess
After completing the chapter, see *Identifying Misconceptions* in the Study Guide at the end of the chapter.

## Chapter Vocabulary

wave, p. 412
transverse wave, p. 413
compressional wave, p. 413
wavelength, p. 414
frequency, p. 414
law of reflection, p. 417
refraction, p. 417
diffraction, p. 418
intensity, p. 420
pitch, p. 421
reverberation, p. 423
electromagnetic waves, p. 425
electromagnetic spectrum,
   p. 426
infrared waves, p. 427
ultraviolet waves, p. 428

**Science Journal** Students will likely describe the up-and-down movement of waves. The waves may move in a regular pattern, or they may move irregularly due to the movement of people or boats. Waves near a shore become larger as they approach land.

**INTERACTIVE CHALKBOARD** with Image Bank

**PowerPoint® Presentations**

This CD-ROM is an editable Microsoft® PowerPoint® presentation that includes:

- a pre-made presentation for every chapter
- interactive graphics
- animations
- audio clips
- image bank
- all new section and chapter questions
- Standardized Test Practice
- transparencies
- pre-lab questions for all labs
- Foldables directions
- links to in7.msscience.com

# Waves, Sound, and Light

### chapter preview

**sections**

1 **Waves**

2 **Sound Waves**
   *Lab  Sound Waves in Matter*

3 **Light**
   *Lab  Bending Light*

   *Virtual Lab  What are some characteristics of waves?*

410

### Ups and Downs

This wind surfer is riding high for now, but that will change soon. The energy carried by ocean waves makes this a thrilling ride, but other waves carry energy, too. Sound waves and light waves carry energy that enable you to hear and see the world around you.

**Science Journal**  Write a short paragraph describing water waves you have seen.

## Theme Connection

**Energy** Studying waves is an effective way of helping students understand the nature of energy. All waves transport energy from one place to another. Sound waves transport energy through matter from particle to particle. Light waves can transport energy through matter or through empty space.

### About the Photo

**Waves in Water** The water waves in the photograph are mechanical waves. They travel through matter, transporting energy from one place to another. The location of the water molecules changes only slightly as a result of the waves. Thus the waves only move the windsurfer up and down. It is the horizontal flow of the water, not the waves, that causes the windsurfer to move from one spot to another.

# Start-Up Activities

## Wave Properties

If you drop a pebble into a pool of water, you notice how the water rises and falls as waves spread out in all directions. How could you describe the waves? In this lab you'll make a model of one type of wave. By describing the model, you'll learn about some properties of all waves.

1. Make a model of a wave by forming a piece of thick string about 50-cm long into a series of S shapes with an up and down pattern.

2. Compare the wave you made with those of other students. Notice how many peaks you have in your wave.

3. Reform your wave so that you have a different number of peaks.

4. **Think Critically** Write a description of your wave model. How did the distance between the peaks change as the number of peaks increased?

**Preview this chapter's content and activities at**
in7.msscience.com

**FOLDABLES** Study Organizer

**Waves** Make the following Foldable to compare and contrast the characteristics of transverse and compressional waves.

**STEP 1** Fold one sheet of lengthwise paper in half.

**STEP 2** Fold into thirds.

**STEP 3** Unfold and draw overlapping ovals. Cut the top sheet along the folds.

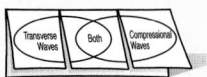
**STEP 4** Label the ovals as shown.

**Construct a Venn Diagram** As you read the chapter, list the characteristics unique to transverse waves under the left tab, those unique to compressional waves under the right tab, and those characteristics common to both under the middle tab.

411

**FOLDABLES** Study Organizer
**Dinah Zike Study Fold**

Student preparation materials for this Foldable are available in the **Chapter FAST FILE Resources.**

---

## Launch LAB

**Purpose** Students learn about properties of all waves by forming a model from clay.

**Preparation** Draw various waves on the board to show that they can vary in height (amplitude), frequency, and wavelength.

**Materials** modeling clay

**Alternative Materials** string or thin rope

**Teaching Strategy** Be sure students recognize the inverse relationship between the frequencies and wavelengths of their waves. If they make the wavelength short, the frequency increases. If they make the wavelength long, the frequency decreases.

**Troubleshooting** When students first make the waves, encourage them to make the wavelengths and amplitudes uniform. This will help them better understand the relationship of wave properties.

## Thinking Critically

Possible answer: The waves have alternating high and low points. For a fixed length of string, increasing the number of high and low points decreases the distance from one high point to the next.

## Assessment

**Portfolio** Have each student draw three different waves in his or her Science Journal. The waves should vary in height and the distance between peaks. Use **PASC,** p. 127.

**Probeware Labs**

This chapter's data-collection lab using Probeware technology is included on the *Video Labs CD-ROM.* See the *Probeware Lab Manual* pages 37–39 for student worksheets.

# section 1

# Waves

## What are waves?

When you float in the pool on a warm summer day, the up-and-down movement of the water tells you waves are moving past. Sometimes the waves are so strong they almost push you over. Other times, the waves just gently rock you. You know about water waves because you can see and feel their movement, but there are other types of waves, also. Different types of waves carry signals to televisions and radios. Sound and light waves move all around you and enable you to hear and see. Waves are even responsible for the damage caused by earthquakes.

**Waves Carry Energy, not Matter** A **wave** is a disturbance that moves through matter or space. Waves carry energy from one place to another. You can see that the waves in **Figure 1** carry energy by the way they crash against the rocks. In water waves, the energy is transferred by water molecules. When a wave moves, it may seem that the wave carries matter from place to place as the wave moves.

But that's not what really happens. When waves travel through solids, liquids, and gases, matter is not carried along with the waves. The movement of the fishing bob in **Figure 1** transfers energy to nearby water molecules. The energy is then passed from molecule to molecule as the wave spreads out. The wave disturbance moves outward, but the locations of the water molecules hardly change at all.

The energy carried by ocean waves can break rocks.

The movement of the fishing bob produces water waves that carry energy through the water.

**Figure 1** Waves carry energy from place to place without carrying matter.

**412** **CHAPTER 14** Waves, Sound, and Light

## Types of Waves

Waves usually are produced by something moving back and forth, or vibrating. It is the energy of the vibrating object that waves carry outward. This energy can spread out from the vibrating object in different types of waves. Some waves, known as mechanical waves, can travel only through matter. Other waves called electromagnetic waves can travel either through matter or through empty space.

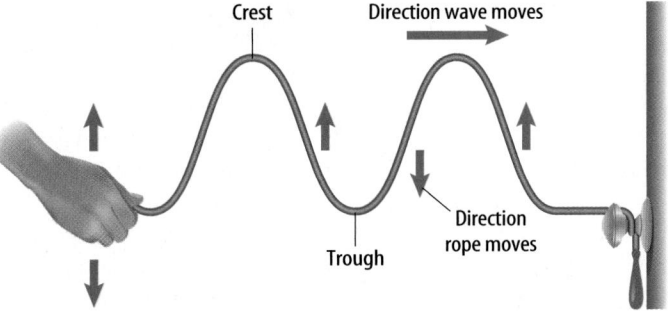

**Figure 2** You make a transverse wave when you shake the end of a rope up and down.

**Transverse Waves** One type of mechanical wave is a transverse wave, shown in **Figure 2.** A **transverse wave** causes particles in matter to move back and forth at right angles to the direction in which the wave travels. If you tie a rope to a door handle and shake the end of the rope up and down, transverse waves travel through the rope.

High points in the wave are called crests. Low points are called troughs. The series of crests and troughs forms a transverse wave. The crests and troughs travel along the rope, but the particles in the rope move only up and down.

**Compressional Waves** Another type of mechanical wave is a compressional wave. **Figure 3** shows a compressional wave traveling along a spring coil. A **compressional wave** causes particles in matter to move back and forth along the same direction in which the wave travels.

In **Figure 3** the places where the coils are squeezed together are called compressions. The places where the coils are spread apart are called rarefactions. The series of compressions and rarefactions forms a compressional wave. The compressions and rarefactions travel along the spring, but the coils move only back and forth.

**Reading Check** *How does matter move in a compressional wave?*

**Figure 3** A wave on a spring coil is an example of a compressional wave.

---

## Visual Learning

**Figure 2** Point out to students that the force exerted by the person on the rope in this figure is directed up and down. The transverse wave, however, moves horizontally away from this disturbance. After students read this page, ask them to describe the direction of compressional waves compared to the direction of the disturbance that causes the waves. Compressional waves move in the same direction as the force that causes the waves.

### Activity

**Wave Motion** Tie several brightly-colored ribbons at 30-cm intervals on a rope. Have two students hold the ends of the rope and shake it slowly up and down to create transverse waves. Other students will be able to see how the ribbons change direction vertically, but they are not displaced horizontally. Repeat the activity by having students create compressional waves using a coiled spring toy.

### Use Science Words

**Word Usage** Ask students to give an example of how they might use the word *compression* in everyday life. Have them relate this to the meaning of a *compressional wave.*

**Reading Check**

**Answer** back and forth along the same direction in which the wave travels

---

## Differentiated Instruction

**Challenge** Wave motion in water is a combination of compressional waves and transverse waves. Have students work in small groups to research these waves and learn about their properties. They should prepare a poster that describes the waves and how they move. L3

Seismic waves move through the ground during an earthquake. Some of these waves are compressional, and others are transverse. The seismic waves that cause most damage to buildings are a kind of rolling waves. These rolling waves are a combination of compressional and transverse waves.

**Electromagnetic Waves** Light, radio waves, and X rays are examples of electromagnetic waves. Just like waves on a rope, electromagnetic waves are transverse waves. However, electromagnetic waves contain electric and magnetic parts that vibrate up and down perpendicular to the direction the wave travels.

## Properties of Waves

The properties that waves have depend on the vibrations that produce the waves. For example, if you move a pencil slowly up and down in a bowl of water, the waves produced by the pencil's motion will be small and spread apart. If you move the pencil rapidly, the waves will be larger and close together.

**Wavelength** The distance between one point on a wave and the nearest point moving with the same speed and direction is the **wavelength. Figure 4** shows how the wavelengths of transverse and compressional waves are measured. The wavelength of a transverse wave is the distance between two adjacent crests or two adjacent troughs. The wavelength of a compressional wave is the distance between two adjacent compressions or rarefactions.

**Frequency** The **frequency** of a wave is the number of wavelengths that pass by a point each second. If you were watching a transverse wave on a rope, the frequency of the wave would be the number of crests or troughs that pass you each second. In the same way, the frequency of a compressional wave is the number of compressions or rarefactions would pass by each second.

**Figure 4** The wavelength of a transverse wave is the distance from crest to crest or from trough to trough. The wavelength of a compressional wave is the distance from compression to compression or rarefaction to rarefaction.

**414 CHAPTER 14** Waves, Sound, and Light

## Amplitude of a Transverse Wave

Waves have another property called amplitude. Suppose you shake the end of a rope by moving your hand up and down a large distance. Then you make a transverse wave with high crests and deep troughs. The wave you've made has a large amplitude. The amplitude of a transverse wave is half the distance between a crest and trough as shown in **Figure 5**. As the distance between crests and troughs increases, the amplitude of a transverse wave increases.

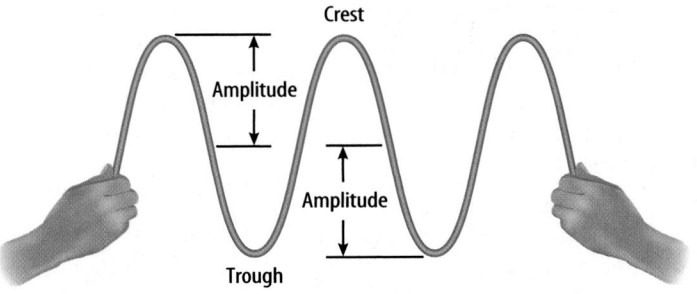

Crest

Amplitude

Amplitude

Trough

**Figure 5** The amplitude of a transverse wave depends on the height of the crests or the depth of the troughs.

## Amplitude of a Compressional Wave

The amplitude of a compressional wave depends on the density of material in compressions and rarefactions as shown in **Figure 6.** Compressional waves with greater amplitude have compressions that are more squeezed together and rarefactions that are more spread apart. For example, in a spring, squeezing some coils together more tightly causes the nearby coils to be more spread apart.

**✓ Reading Check** *What is the amplitude of a compressional wave?*

## Amplitude and Energy

The vibrations that produce a wave transfer energy to the wave. The more energy a wave carries, the larger its amplitude. By moving your hand up and down a larger distance in making a wave on a rope, you transfer more energy to the wave. Seismic waves are produced by vibrations in Earth's crust that cause earthquakes. The more energy these waves have, the larger their amplitudes and the more damage they cause as they travel along Earth's surface.

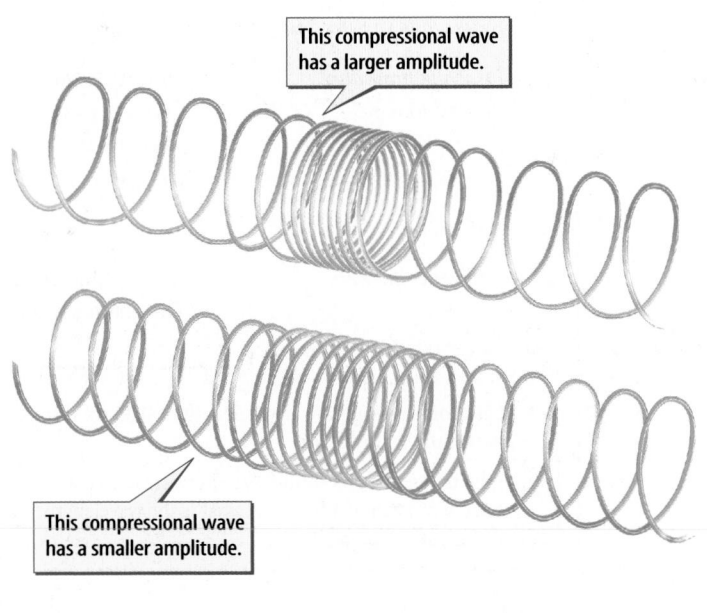

This compressional wave has a larger amplitude.

This compressional wave has a smaller amplitude.

**Figure 6** The amplitude of a compressional wave depends on the density of the material in the compressions and rarefactions.

**Wave Speed Equation** A wave moves from one material to another and slows down. If the frequency of the wave remains the same, what effect, if any, will there be on the wavelength of the wave? The wavelength will decrease.

## Misconceptions

**Wave Energy** Students may believe that the frequency and wavelength of a wave are determined by the wave's energy. Point out that a strong wave can be either slow or fast. The wave speed equation relates the wavelength and the frequency, but it does not include the wave energy.

## Fun Fact

**Tsunamis** An ocean earthquake can generate a series of powerful water waves called tsunamis. At sea, these waves may only have an amplitude of less than a meter, and the crests may be hundreds of kilometers apart. By the time a tsunami reaches land, however, it may have a height of over 10 meters and have a speed of hundreds of meters per second.

### Applying Math

**Indiana Math Standards**
7.2.1, 7.3.1

**Teaching Strategy**
Explain to students that the unit Hz is another name for the unit $\frac{1}{s}$.

**Answers to Practice Problems**
1. 3.3 m/s
2. 0.10 m

---

**Wave Speed** The speed of a wave depends on the medium in which the wave travels. The faster waves travel, the more crests or compressions pass by you each second. You can calculate the speed of a wave if you know its wavelength and frequency using the equation below.

### Wave Speed Equation

**wave speed** (in m/s) = **wavelength** (in m) × **frequency** (in Hz)

$$v = \lambda f$$

In this equation, $v$ is the symbol for wave speed and $f$ is the symbol for frequency. The SI unit for frequency is the hertz, abbreviated Hz. One hertz equals one vibration per second, or one wavelength passing a point in one second. One hertz is equal to the unit 1/s. The wavelength is represented by the Greek letter lambda, $\lambda$, and is measured in meters.

### Applying Math — Solve a Simple Equation

**SPEED OF SOUND** A sound wave produced by a lightning bolt has a frequency of 34 Hz and a wavelength of 10.0 m. What is the speed of the sound wave?

**Solution**

**1** *This is what you know:*
- wavelength: $\lambda = 10$ m
- frequency: $f = 34$ Hz

**2** *This is what you need to find:* wave speed: $v = ?$ m/s

**3** *This is the procedure you need to use:* Substitute the known values for wavelength and frequency into the wave speed equation and calculate the wave speed:

$$v = \lambda f = (10.0 \text{ m})(34 \text{ Hz})$$
$$= 340 \text{ m} \times \text{Hz} = 340 \text{ m} \times (1/s) = 340 \text{ m/s}$$

**4** *Check your answer:* Divide your answer by the wavelength 10.0 m. The result should be the given frequency 34 Hz.

### Practice Problems

1. Waves on a string have a wavelength of 0.55 m. If the frequency of the waves is 6.0 Hz, what is the wave speed?

2. If the frequency of a sound wave in water is 15,000 Hz, and the sound wave travels through water at a speed of 1,500 m/s, what is the wavelength?

 For more practice, visit in7.msscience.com/math_practice

## Cultural Diversity

**Gravitational Waves** Professor Jorge Pullin of Louisiana State University studies the movement of gravitational waves through space as part of the Laser Interferometer Gravitational Wave Observatory (LIGO). In 2001, Dr. Pullin was awarded the Edward A. Bouchet Award for his outstanding work with gravitational waves as well as his contributions to diversity in physics as a founding member of the National Society of Hispanic Physicists. Have interested students learn more about LIGO and prepare a presentation for the class.

## Waves Can Change Direction

Waves don't always travel in a straight line. When you look into a mirror, you use the mirror to make light waves change direction. Waves can change direction when they travel from one material to another. The waves can reflect (bounce off a surface), refract (change direction), or diffract (bend around an obstacle).

**The Law of Reflection** When waves reflect off a surface, they always obey the law of reflection, as shown in **Figure 7.** A line that makes an angle of 90 degrees with a surface is called the normal to the surface. According to **law of reflection,** the angle that the incoming wave makes with the normal equals the angle that the outgoing wave makes with the normal.

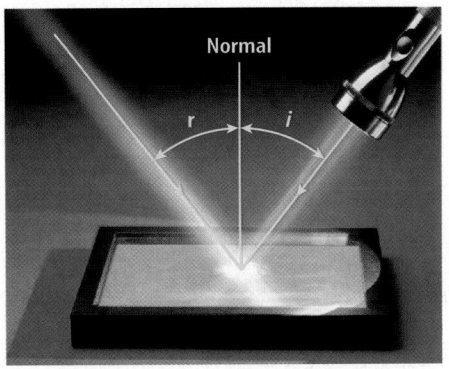

**Figure 7** All waves obey the law of reflection. The angle of reflection, $r$, always equals the angle of incidence, $i$.

**Refraction** The speed of the wave depends on properties of the material through which it travels. A light wave, for example, travels faster through air than it does through water. **Figure 8** shows that a change in a wave's speed changes the direction in which the wave travels. When the light wave moves from air to water, it slows down. This change in speed causes the light wave to bend. **Refraction** is the change in direction of a wave when it changes speed it travels from one material to another.

**Figure 8** Refraction occurs when a wave changes speed. Light waves change direction when they slow down as they pass from air to water.

### Refraction of Light

**Procedure**
1. Fill a **drinking glass** about half full with water.
2. Place a **pencil** in the glass. Describe the appearance of the pencil.
3. Slowly add water to the glass. Describe how the appearance of the pencil changes.

**Analysis**
1. How does the appearance of the pencil depend on the level of water in the glass?
2. Where do the light waves coming from the pencil change speed?
3. **Infer** how the appearance of the pencil and the change in speed of the light waves are related.

**Purpose** Students will observe the refraction of light.

**Materials** clear, drinking glass, pencil

**Troubleshooting** Be sure to use a clear drinking glass. Students should view the glass from the side to see the break in the pencil.

**Analysis**
1. The pencil appears to be broken at the water level, with the bottom shifted to the side.
2. Light waves from the pencil change speed when they pass from water into air.
3. The break in the pencil occurs where light waves change speed.

### Assessment

**Oral** Ask students whether the pencil would still look broken if it were completely covered with water.

## Differentiated Instruction

**Visually Impaired** As an alternative to the At Home MiniLab, have students glue uncooked spaghetti to construction paper to demonstrate the law of reflection. One strand of spaghetti can represent the mirror. A second strand can represent the incoming wave. A third strand can represent the outgoing wave. Students should be careful that the angle the incoming wave makes with the normal is equal to the angle the outgoing wave makes with the normal.

## Check for Understanding

**Visual-Spatial** Have students make a drawing that explains the three ways waves can change direction when they travel from one material to another.

## Reteach

**Wave Speed Equation** Help students understand the wavespeed equation by showing them how the wave speed, wavelength, and frequency depend on each other. Write the equation on the board, and ask students what would happen to the wavelength and frequency if the wave speed doubled. Replace *v* with 2*v* in the equation. Students should see that the wavelength, frequency, or both must change to maintain the equality. You can reinforce this concept with sketches of transverse waves. Repeat the exercise by varying the wavelength or frequency in the equation.

### Assessment

**Oral** Have students compare and contrast transverse waves and compressional waves.

### Virtual Labs

**Wave Traits** *What are some characteristics of waves?*

---

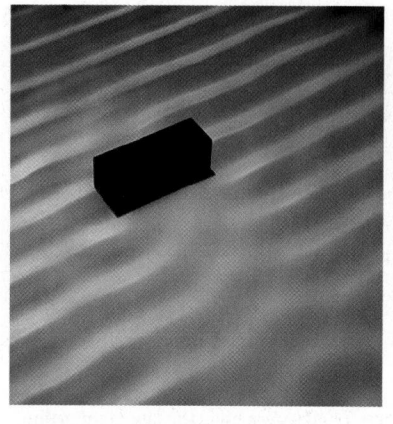

**Figure 9** The amount of diffraction or bending around an obstacle depends on the size of the obstacle and the wavelength of the wave.

**Diffraction** Waves can change direction by **diffraction**, which is the bending of waves around an object. In **Figure 9**, the water waves are not completely blocked by the obstacle, but instead bend around the obstacle.

The amount diffraction or bending of the wave depends on the size of the obstacle the wave encounters. If the size of the obstacle is much larger than the wavelength, very little diffraction occurs. Then there is a shadow behind the object where there are no waves.

As the wavelength increases compared with the size of the obstacle, the amount of diffraction increases. The amount of diffraction is greatest if the wavelength is much larger than the obstacle.

**Diffraction of Sound and Light** The wavelengths of sound waves are similar to the size of objects around you, but the wavelength of light waves are much shorter. As a result, you can hear people talking in a room with an open door even though you can't see them.

---

### section 1 review

#### Summary

**Wave Energy**

- Waves transport energy without transporting matter.

**Types of Waves**

- Transverse waves cause particles in a material to move back and forth at right angles to the direction the waves travel.
- Compressional waves cause particles in a material to move back and forth along the same direction the waves travel.
- Electromagnetic waves are transverse waves that can travel through empty space.

**Wave Properties**

- A wave can be described by its wavelength, frequency, and amplitude.
- The energy carried by a wave increases as the amplitude of the wave increases.
- The speed of a wave, *v*, equals it wavelength, $\lambda$, multiplied by its frequency, *f*:

$$v = \lambda f$$

- Reflection, refraction, or diffraction can cause waves to change direction.

#### Self Check

1. **Analyze** How can waves transport energy without transporting matter from place to another?
2. **Explain** how the spacing between coils of a spring changes if the amplitude of compressional waves traveling along the spring increases.
3. **Predict** how the wavelength of waves traveling with the same speed would change if the frequency of the waves increases.
4. **Apply** Two similar-sized stones, one heavy and one light, are dropped from the same height into a pond. Explain why the impact of the heavy stone would produce waves with higher amplitude than the impact of the light stone would.
5. **Think Critically** Water waves produced by a speed boat strike a floating inner tube. Describe the motion of the inner tube as the waves pass by.

#### Applying Math

6. **Calculate Wave Speed** Find the speed of a wave with a wavelength of 0.2 m and a frequency of 1.5 Hz.
7. **Calculate Wavelength** Find the wavelength of a wave with a speed of 3.0 m/s and a frequency of 0.5 Hz.

  Science Online in7.msscience.com/self_check_quiz

---

### section 1 review

1. The waves pass energy from particle to particle.
2. Compressional waves with greater amplitude have rarefactions that are more spread apart and compressions that are more squeezed together.
3. The wavelength would decrease.
4. The heavier stone would have a greater kinetic energy when it hit the water. A greater energy would cause the waves to have a higher amplitude.
5. The water waves cause the inner tube to move up and down as they pass by.
6. 0.3 m/s
7. 6.0 m

# section 2

# Sound Waves

## Making Sound Waves

How does the motion of a drummer's drumsticks produce sound waves? The impact of the sticks on the head of a drum causes the drum head to vibrate. These vibrations transfer energy to nearby air particles, producing sound waves in air. You can hear the sound because energy from the drums travels as sound waves to your ears. Every sound you hear is caused by something vibrating. For example, when you talk, tissues in your throat vibrate in different ways to form sounds.

**Sound Waves are Compressional Waves** Sound waves produced by a vibrating object are compressional waves. **Figure 10** shows how the vibrating drum produces compressional waves. When the drummer hits the drum, the head of the drum vibrates. Nearby air particles vibrate with the same frequency as the frequency of vibrations. The drum head moving outward compresses nearby air particles. The drum head moving inward causes rarefactions in nearby air particles. The inward and outward movement of the drum head produces the same pattern of compressions and rarefactions in the air particles.

Sound waves can only travel through matter. The energy carried by a sound wave is transferred by the collisions between the particles in the material the wave is traveling in. A spaceship traveling outside Earth's atmosphere, for example, does not make any sound outside the ship.

Compression

Compression

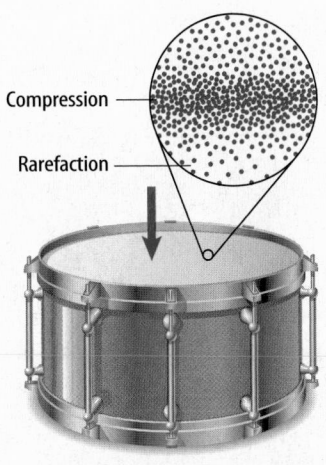

Compression

Rarefaction

### as you read

**What You'll Learn**
- **Describe** how sound waves are produced.
- **Explain** how sound waves travel through matter.
- **Describe** the relationship between loudness and sound intensity.
- **Explain** how humans hear sound.

**Why It's Important**
A knowledge of sound helps you understand how to protect your hearing.

**Review Vocabulary**
**perception:** a recognition, sense, or understanding of something

**New Vocabulary**
- intensity
- pitch
- reverberation

**Figure 10** A vibrating drumhead produces a sound wave. The drum head produces a compression each time it moves upward and a rarefaction each time it moves downward.

SECTION 2  Sound Waves  **419**

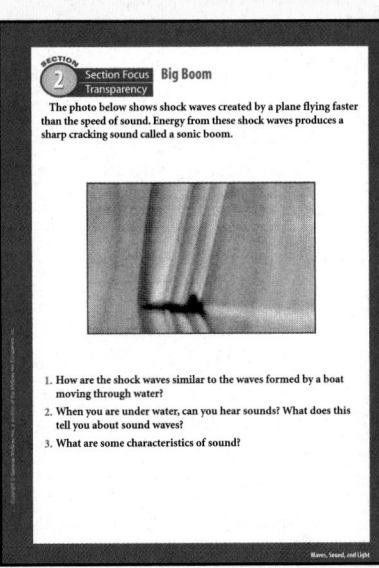
---

## Inquiry Lab

**Transmission of Sound**

**Purpose** to investigate the transmission of sound through various materials

**Possible Materials** rubber ball, polystyrene, wooden block, metal spoon, glass beaker, plastic beaker

**Estimated Time** 45 minutes

**Teaching Strategies**

• Tell students to imagine that they are part of a research team that is designing ear protectors. Some protectors should transmit sound well, and others should block most sound. What are good materials to use for the protectors?

• Remind students to follow good scientific procedures for their investigations. They should form a hypothesis, design an experiment to test their hypothesis, carry out the experiment, and write a conclusion.

• Students may wish to measure the ability of materials to transmit sound using an electronic sound detector, or they can rank the materials using a subjective comparison scale.

• Have students make a poster or graphic presentation to explain their investigation and present their conclusions to the class.

**For additional inquiry activities, see** *Science Inquiry Labs.*

 **Reading Check**

**Answer** The speed of sound increases as the temperature increases.

| Table 1 Speed of Sound in Different Materials | |
|---|---|
| **Material** | **Speed (m/s)** |
| Air (20°C) | 343 |
| Glass | 5,640 |
| Steel | 5,940 |
| Water (25°C) | 1,493 |
| Seawater (25°C) | 1,533 |
| Rubber | 1,600 |
| Diamond | 12,000 |
| Iron | 5,130 |

**Figure 11** The loudness of a sound depends on the amount of energy the sound waves carry.

**Figure 12** The intensity of a sound wave decreases as the wave spreads out from the source of the sound. The energy the wave carries is spread over a larger area.

## The Speed of Sound

Like all waves, the speed of sound depends on the matter through which it travels. Sound waves travel faster through solids and liquids. **Table 1** shows the speed of sound in different materials.

The speed of sound through a material increases as the temperature of the material increases. The effect of temperature is greatest in gases. For example, the speed of sound in air increases from about 330 m/s to about 350 m/s as the air temperature increases from 0° to 30°C.

**Reading Check** *How does temperature affect the speed of sound through a material?*

## The Loudness of Sound

What makes a sound loud or soft? The girl in **Figure 11** can make a loud sound by clapping the cymbals together sharply. She can make a soft sound by clapping the cymbals together gently. The difference is the amount of energy the girl gives to the cymbals. Loud sounds have more energy than soft sounds.

**Intensity** The amount of energy that a wave carries past a certain area each second is the **intensity** of the sound. **Figure 12** shows how the intensity of sound from the cymbals decreases with distance. A person standing close when the girl claps the cymbals would hear an intense sound. The sound would be less intense for someone standing farther away. The intensity of sound waves is related to the amplitude. Sound with a greater amplitude also has a greater intensity.

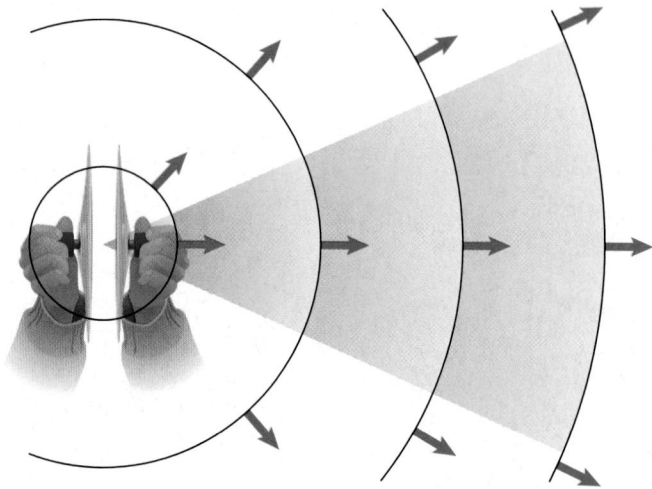

## Differentiated Instruction

**Challenge** When a jet moves faster than the speed of sound, its sound waves come together to create a cone-shaped shock wave. When this cone passes a person on the ground, the person hears a sharp bang called a sonic boom. Have students research sonic booms and create a poster describing them.

L3 P

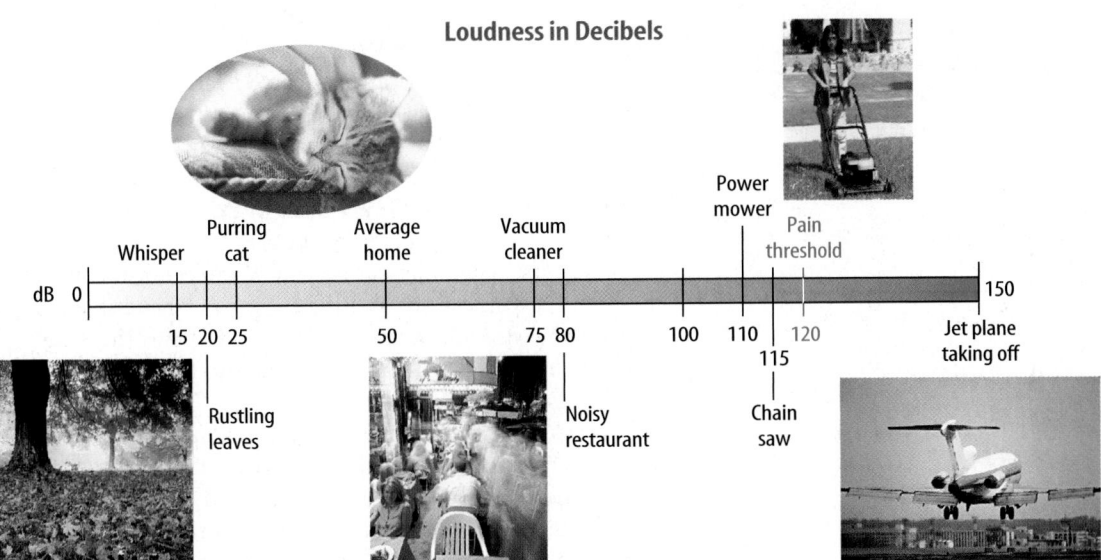

**Loudness in Decibels**

Whisper — 15
Purring cat — 20 25
Rustling leaves
Average home — 50
Vacuum cleaner — 75 80
Noisy restaurant
Power mower
Pain threshold — 110 115 120
Chain saw
dB 0 ——————————————— 150
100
Jet plane taking off

### The Decibel Scale and Loudness

The intensity of sound waves is measured in units of decibels (dB), as shown in **Figure 13.** The softest sound a person can hear has an intensity of 0 dB. Normal conversation has an intensity of about 50 dB. Sound with intensities of about 120 dB or higher are painful to people.

Loudness is the human perception of the intensity of sound waves. Each increase of 10 dB in intensity multiplies the energy of the sound waves ten times. Most people perceive this as a doubling of the loudness of the sound. An intensity increase of 20 dB corresponds to a hundred times the energy and an increase in loudness of about four times.

**Reading Check** *How much has the energy of a sound wave changed if its intensity has increased by 30 dB?*

## Frequency and Pitch

The frequency of sound waves is determined by the frequency of the vibrations that produce the sound. Recall that wave frequency is measured in units of hertz (Hz), which is the number of vibrations each second. On the musical scale, the note C has a frequency of 262 Hz. The note E has a frequency of 330 Hz. People are usually able to hear sounds with frequencies between about 20 Hz and 20,000 Hz.

**Pitch** is the human perception of the frequency of sound. The sounds from a tuba have a low pitch and the sounds from a flute have a high pitch. Sounds with low frequencies have low pitch and sounds with high frequencies have high pitch.

**Figure 13** The intensity of sound is measured on the decibel scale.
**Infer** *how many times louder a power mower is compared to a noisy restaurant.*

**Hearing Damage**
Prolonged exposure to sounds above 85 dB can damage your hearing. Research to find out the danger of noise levels you might experience at activities such as loud music concerts or basketball games.

SECTION 2 Sound Waves **421**

## Make a Model

**Catching Sound Waves** Students can model the way the outer ear catches and focuses sound waves by making a cone out of paper. Have them fold a sheet of notebook paper in half lengthwise and roll it into a cone shape. Next, have them hold the narrow end of the cone to one ear as a friend talks quietly near the other end. Students should compare the sounds they hear with and without the cone to catch and focus the waves.

## Discussion

**Hearing Under Water** Sound waves travel faster through water than through air. Why, then, can't you hear well under water? The sound waves are distorted by the water and its movement.

**Indiana Academic Standard Check**

**7.3.20:** Describe that something . . . can be "heard" when sound waves from it enter the ear.

✓ What is the function of the inner ear?

✓ to convert sound waves to signals that travel to the brain

**Figure 14** The human ear can be divided into three parts. The outer ear is the sound collector, the middle ear is the sound amplifier, and the inner ear is the sound interpreter.

## Hearing and the Ear

The ear is a complex organ that can detect a wide range of sounds. You may think that the ear is just the structure that you see on the side of your head. However, the ear can be divided into three parts—the outer ear, the middle ear, and the inner ear. **Figure 14** shows the different parts of the human ear.

**The Outer Ear** The outer ear is a sound collector. It consists of the part that you can see and the ear canal. The visible part is shaped somewhat like a funnel. This shape helps the visible part collect sound waves and direct them into the ear canal.

**The Middle Ear** The middle air is a sound amplifier. It consists of the ear drum and three tiny bones called the hammer, the anvil, and the stirrup. Sound waves that pass through the ear canal cause the eardrum to vibrate. Theses vibrations are transmitted to the three small bones, which amplify the vibrations.

**The Inner Ear** The inner ear contains the cochlea. The cochlea is filled with fluid and is lined with tiny hair-like cells. Vibrations of the stirrup bone are transmitted to the hair cells. The movement of the hair cells produce signals that travel to your brain, where they are interpreted as sound.

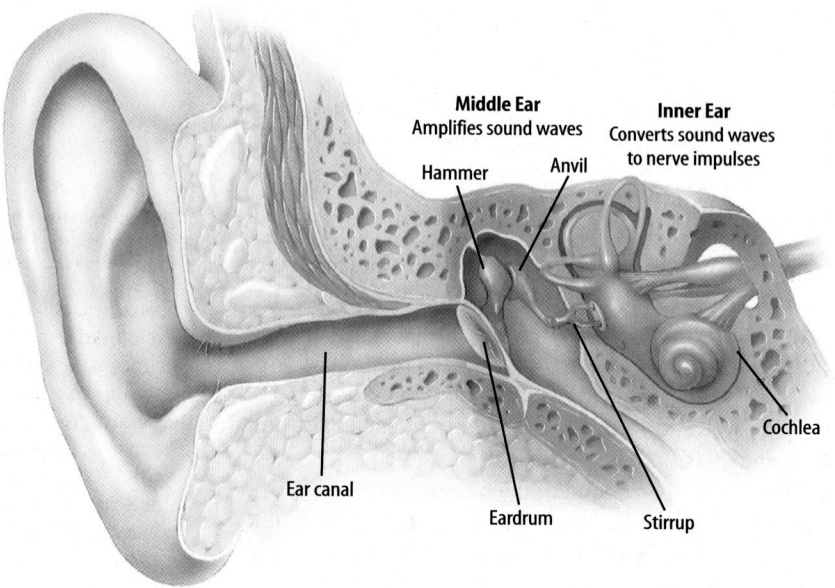

**Outer Ear** Gathers sound waves

**Middle Ear** Amplifies sound waves

Hammer    Anvil

**Inner Ear** Converts sound waves to nerve impulses

Ear canal

Eardrum    Stirrup

Cochlea

**422    CHAPTER 14** Waves, Sound, and Light

## Visual Learning

**Figure 14** Point out to students that the outer part of the cochlea is wider than the inner part. This variation enables the cochlea to distinguish different frequencies of sound. The outer part is more rigid, and the inner part is less rigid. This makes the outer part of the cochlea more responsive to high-frequency sound waves, and the inner part is more sensitive to low-frequency sound waves. Ask students how this difference in the cochlea's responsiveness enables a person to distinguish different sound pitches? The vibration of hairs at different locations on the cochlea pass information about the frequencies, and thus the pitches, of sounds to the brain.

## The Reflection of Sound

Have you ever stood in an empty room and heard echoes when you talked very loudly? Echoes are sounds that reflect off surfaces. Repeated echoes are called **reverberation.** Concert halls and auditoriums are designed with soft materials on the ceilings and walls to avoid too much reverberation. Theaters like the one in **Figure 15** often have curtains on the walls because sounds won't reflect off soft surfaces. The curtains absorb the energy of the sound waves.

The reflection of sound can be used to locate or identify objects. Echolocation is the process of locating objects by bouncing sounds off them. Bats, dolphins, and other animals emit short, high-frequency sound waves toward a certain area. By interpreting the reflected waves, the animals can locate and determine properties of other animals. Doctors use reflection of sound waves in medicine. Computers can analyze ultrasonic waves that reflect off body parts to produce an internal picture of the body. These pictures help doctors monitor pregnancies, heart problems, and other medical conditions.

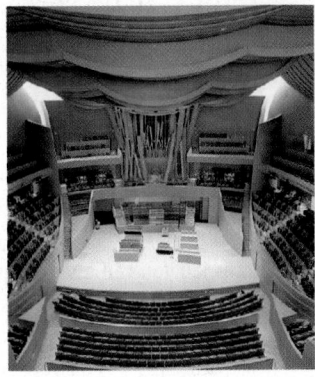

**Figure 15** A modern concert hall contains materials that absorb sound waves to control reverberation and other sound reflections.

---

### section 2 review

#### Summary

**Making Sound Waves**
- Sound waves are compressional waves produced by something vibrating.
- The speed of sound waves depends on the material in which the waves travel and its temperature.

**Loudness and Pitch**
- The intensity of a wave is the amount of energy the wave transports each second across a unit surface.
- The intensity of sound waves is measured in units of decibels.
- Loudness is the human perception of sound intensity.
- Pitch is the human perception of the frequency of a sound.

**Hearing Sound**
- You hear a sound when a sound wave reaches your ear and causes structures in your ear to vibrate.

#### Self Check

1. **Explain** why you hear a sound when you clap your hands together.
2. **Predict** whether sound will would travel faster in air in the summer or in the winter.
3. **Compare and contrast** the sound waves produced by someone whispering and someone shouting.
4. **Describe** how vibrations produced in your ear by a sound wave enable you to hear the sound.
5. **Think Critically** Vibrations cause sounds, yet if you move your hand back and forth through the air, you don't hear a sound. Explain.

##### Applying Math

6. **Calculate a Ratio** How many times louder is a sound wave with an intensity of 50 dB than a sound wave with an intensity of 20 dB?
7. **Calculate Increase in Intensity** If the energy carried by a sound wave is multiplied by a thousand times, by what factor does the intensity of the sound wave increase?

 Science Online in7.msscience.com/self_check_quiz

SECTION 2 Sound Waves **423**

---

### section 2 review

1. Your hands produce vibrations in nearby air molecules. These vibrations move through the air to your ear. Your brain interprets these vibrations as sound.
2. Sound would travel in air in the summer.
3. Both are compressional waves that can travel through air. Their frequency may be the same. Sound waves made by shouting have greater amplitude and carry more energy.
4. Sound waves enter your ear and cause the eardrum to vibrate. This, in turn, vibrates small bones in the middle ear. The bones vibrate the oval window, and this vibrates fluid in the cochlea. Vibrations in the fluid cause tiny hairs to move. Nerve cells sense this movement and send messages to the brain about the sound.
5. Your hand moves the air particles too slowly. The sound that is produced has a frequency that is too low for your ears to hear.
6. eight times
7. 30 dB increase

SECTION 2 Sound Waves **423**

## ⊙ Real-World Question

**Purpose** Students listen to variations in sounds that travel through different materials. They relate these variations to properties of the materials.

**Process Skills** make a table, observe, infer, compare and contrast, recognize cause and effect, communicate

**Time Required** 30 minutes

**Safety Precautions** Remind students that they should never eat or drink anything during a lab.

## ⊙ Procedure

**Teaching Strategy** Tell students to listen to the sounds made by tapping on the beakers several times. Have them use descriptive words that compare the sounds, such as "louder" or "higher pitch."

**Troubleshooting** Different sounds produced by tapping the beakers will be noticeable only if the liquids have different densities. Test the materials ahead of time. You may need to decrease a liquid's density by adding water.

## ⊙ Conclude and Apply

1. air, water, vegetable oil, corn syrup
2. Higher-density liquids produce lower-pitch sounds than lower-density liquids. The pitch decreased as the density increased.
3. The less dense the material, the longer the sound continued to be heard.

# Sound Waves in Matter

In this lab you can hear differences in sound when the sound waves travel through various materials.

## ⊙ Real-World Question

How does the movement of sound waves through different materials affect the sounds we hear?

### Goals
■ **Notice** the variations in sound when sound waves travel through different materials.
■ **Infer** what property of the materials cause the sound waves to produce a different sound.

### Materials
150-mL beakers (4)    corn syrup
water                 pencil
vegetable oil

### Safety Precautions

## ⊙ Procedure

1. Fill a beaker to the 140-mL line with water. Fill another beaker with 140 mL of vegetable oil. Fill a third beaker with 140 mL of corn syrup. Leave the fourth beaker empty.

2. Hold the pencil securely and tap the side of the beaker about halfway down from its rim. Use the metal band near the end of the pencil to make a clear sound.

3. Pay careful attention to the pitch of the sound. Notice whether the sound continues for a moment after the tap or if it stops suddenly. Write a description of the sound you hear in your data table.

**424** CHAPTER 14 Waves, Sound, and Light

4. Repeat steps 3 and 4 for the remaining beakers. You may wish to tap each beaker several times to be sure you hear the sound well.

5. **Compare** the sounds made by the beaker filled with air and the beaker filled with the different liquids.

## ⊙ Conclude and Apply

1. **List** the materials in the beakers in order of increasing density.

2. **Infer** how the pitch of the sound changes as the density of the material in the beaker increases.

3. How does the density of the material in the beaker affect how long the sound continued to be heard after the beaker was tapped?

### ℭommunicating Your Data

Compare your results with other students in your class.

### ℭommunicating Your Data

Encourage students to produce their data tables with an electronic spreadsheet program. They can include these with a brief written report of their conclusions.

### ☑ Assessment

**Process** Have students work in small groups to design and carry out a similar experiment testing sound transmission in solid materials. Encourage them to make predictions about the results before they begin their tests. Use **Performance Assessment in the Science Classroom,** p. 95.

Standards—**7.3.19:** Explain that human eyes respond to a narrow range of wavelengths of the electromagnetic spectrum. **7.3.20:** Describe that something can be "seen" when light waves emitted or reflected by it enter the eye ... .

Also covers: 7.1.5, 7.3.2, 7.3.11, 7.3.18 (Detailed standards begin on page IN8.)

# section

## 3

# Light

## Waves in Empty Space

On a clear night you might see the Moon shining brightly, as in **Figure 16.** Like other waves, light waves can travel through matter, but light waves are different from water waves and sound waves. Light from the Moon has traveled through space that contains almost no matter. You can see light from the moon, distant stars, and galaxies because light is an electromagnetic wave. **Electromagnetic waves** are waves that can travel through matter or through empty space.

**The Speed of Light** Have you ever seen a movie where a spaceship travels faster than the speed of light? In reality, nothing travels faster than the speed of light. In empty space, light travels at a speed of about 300,000 km/s. Light travels so fast that light emitted from the Sun travels 150 million km to Earth in only about eight and a half minutes.

However, when light travels in matter, it interacts with the atoms and molecules in the material and slows down. As a result, light travels fastest in empty space, and travels slowest in solids. In glass, for example, light travels about 197,000 km/s.

**Wavelength and Frequency of Light** Can you guess how long a wavelength of light is? Wavelengths of light are usually expressed in units of nanometers (nm). One nanometer is equal to one billionth of a meter. For example, green light has a wavelength of about 500 nm, or 500 billionths of a meter. A light wave with this wavelength has a frequency of 600 trillion Hz.

**Figure 16** The Moon reflects light from the Sun. These light waves travel through space to reach your eyes.
**Infer** *whether a sound wave could travel from the Moon to Earth.*

---

## as you read

### *What* You'll Learn
- **Identify** the properties of light waves.
- **Describe** the electromagnetic spectrum.
- **Describe** the types of electromagnetic waves that travel from the Sun to Earth.
- **Explain** human vision and color perception.

### *Why* It's Important
Light is necessary for vision. Other electromagnetic waves are used in devices such as cell phones and microwave ovens.

### Review Vocabulary
**spectrum:** a range of values or properties

### New Vocabulary
- electromagnetic waves
- electromagnetic spectrum
- infrared waves
- ultraviolet waves

---

## 1 Motivate

**Bellringer**

**Section Focus Transparencies** also are available on the Interactive Chalkboard CD-ROM.
L2 ELL

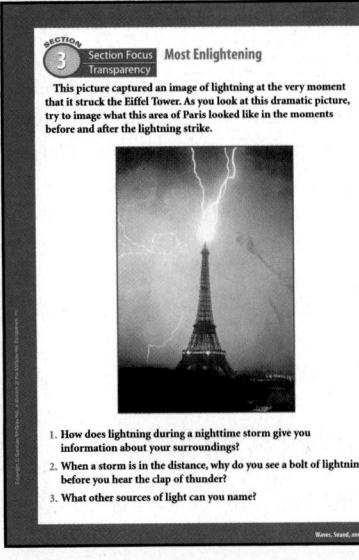

### SECTION 3 Section Focus Transparency — Most Enlightening

This picture captured an image of lightning at the very moment that it struck the Eiffel Tower. As you look at this dramatic picture, try to imagine what this area of Paris looked like in the moments before and after the lightning strike.

1. How does lightning during a nighttime storm give you information about your surroundings?
2. When a storm is in the distance, why do you see a bolt of lightning before you hear the clap of thunder?
3. What other sources of light can you name?

Waves, Sound, and Light

### Tie to Prior Knowledge

**Electromagnetic Waves** Ask students how a rainbow, a satellite signal, and an X ray are similar. Explain that these are all the same type of waves—electromagnetic waves—which they will study in this section.

### Caption Answer

**Figure 16** No. There is almost no matter between Earth and the Moon.

---

## Section 3 Resource Manager

**Chapter *FAST FILE* Resources**
- Transparency Activity, p. 46
- MiniLAB, p. 4
- Enrichment, p. 32
- Reinforcement, p. 29
- Directed Reading for Content Mastery, p. 21

- Lab Worksheet, pp. 7–8
- Lab Activity, pp. 13–16
- Life Science Critical Thinking/Problem Solving, p. 8
- Performance Assessment in the Science Classroom, p. 52

## Visual Learning

**Figure 17** The two parts of the electromagnetic wave shown in the figure are an electric field and a magnetic field. The fields are constantly changing from positive to negative. As the wave travels through space or matter, the changing electric field produces the changing magnetic field, and the changing magnetic field produces the changing electric field. A vibrating charged particle is one way that electromagnetic waves are produced. Ask students how the charged particle's frequency of vibration is related to the frequency of the wave shown in the figure. The frequency with which the particle vibrates is the same as the frequency with which the electric and magnetic fields change from positive to negative.

### ✔ Reading Check

**Answer** the amount of energy that the waves carry and the distance from the light source

## Teacher FYI

**Field Strength** The electric field of an electromagnetic wave is much stronger than the magnetic field. Because of this, wireless technology is sensitive to the electric component rather than the magnetic component of electromagnetic waves.

---

**Figure 17** A light wave is a transverse wave that contains vibrating electric and magnetic fields. The fields vibrate at right angles to the direction the wave travels.

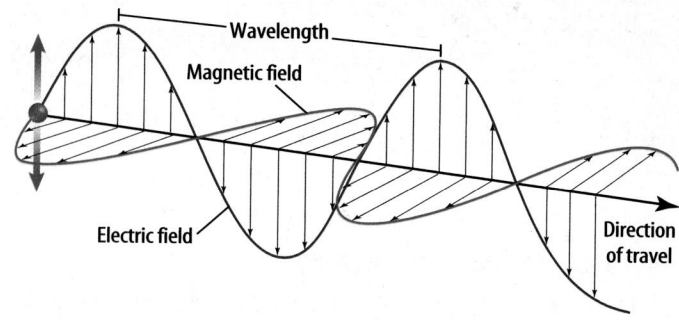

Wavelength
Magnetic field
Electric field
Direction of travel

**Science Online**

**Topic: Lasers**
Visit in7.msscience.com for Web links to information about why the intensity of light emitted by lasers makes them useful.

**Activity** Write a short paragraph describing three uses for lasers.

---

**Indiana Academic Standard Check**

**7.3.19:** Explain that human eyes respond to a narrow range of wavelengths of the electromagnetic spectrum.

✔ What range of wavelengths in the electromagnetic spectrum does the human eye detect?

✔ about 700 to 400 billionths of a meter

---

## Properties of Light Waves

Light waves, and all electromagnetic waves, are transverse waves. Recall that a wave on a rope is a transverse wave that causes the rope to move at right angles to the direction the wave is traveling. An electromagnetic wave traveling through matter also can cause matter to move at right angles to the direction the wave is moving.

An electromagnetic wave contains an electric part and a magnetic part, as shown in **Figure 17.** Both parts are called fields and vibrate at right angles to the wave motion. The number of times the electric and magnetic parts vibrate each second is the frequency of the wave. The wavelength is the distance between the crests or troughs of the vibrating electric or magnetic parts.

**Intensity of Light Waves** The intensity of waves is a measure of the amount of energy that the waves carry. For light waves, the intensity determines the brightness of the light. A dim light has lower intensity because the waves carry less energy. However, as you move away from a light source, the energy spreads out and the intensity decreases.

### ✔ Reading Check   *What determines the intensity of light waves?*

## The Electromagnetic Spectrum

Light waves aren't the only kind of electromagnetic waves. In fact, there is an entire spectrum of electromagnetic waves, as shown in **Figure 18.** The **electromagnetic spectrum** is the complete range of electromagnetic wave frequencies and wavelengths. At one end of the spectrum the waves have low frequency, long wavelength, and low energy. At the other end of the spectrum the waves have high frequency, short wavelength, and high energy. All of the waves—from radio waves to visible light to gamma rays—are the same kind of waves. They differ from each other only by their frequencies, wavelengths, and energy.

---

## Curriculum Connection

**Art** The wave property of light is not something we see, and yet it is sometimes used by artists to represent movement in nature. Have students paint a picture that shows light in this way. Interested students may also research and prepare a presentation for the class about a famous painting that represents light with waves. Some examples are Renoir's *The Seine at Chatou* and Monet's *Haystack at Giverny.*

P

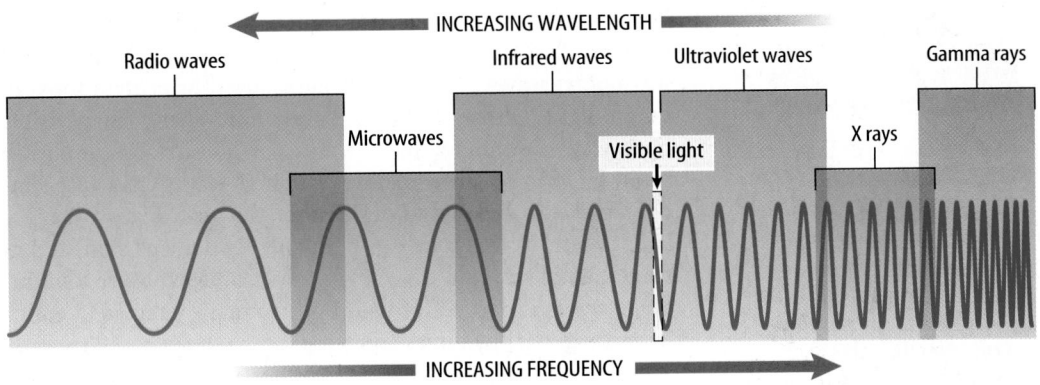

INCREASING WAVELENGTH

Radio waves | Infrared waves | Ultraviolet waves | Gamma rays

Microwaves | Visible light | X rays

INCREASING FREQUENCY

## Radio Waves and Microwaves

The waves that carry radio and television signals to your home are radio waves. The wavelengths of radio waves are greater than about 0.3 meters. Some are even thousands of meters long. The shortest radio waves are called microwaves. These waves have a wavelength between about 0.3 meters and 0.001 meters. You use these waves when you cook food in a microwave oven. Microwaves are also used to transmit information to and from cell phones.

## Infrared Waves

When you use a remote control, infrared waves travel from the remote to a receiver on your television. **Infrared waves** have wavelengths between 0.001 meters and 700 billionths of a meter. All warm bodies emit infrared waves. Because of this, law enforcement officials and military personnel sometimes use special night goggles that are sensitive to infrared waves. These goggles can be used to help locate people in the dark.

## Visible Light and Color

The range of electromagnetic waves between 700 and 400 billionths of a meter is special, because that is the range of wavelengths people can see. Electromagnetic waves in this range are called visible light. **Figure 19** shows how different wavelengths correspond to different colors of light. White light, like the light from the Sun or a flashlight, is really a combination of different colors. You can see this by using a prism to separate white light into different colors. When the light passes through the prism, the different wavelengths of light are bent different amounts. Violet light is bent the most because it has the shortest wavelength. Red light is bent the least.

**Reading Check** What range of wavelengths of electromagnetic waves can people see?

**Figure 18** Electromagnetic waves have a range of frequencies and wavelengths called the electromagnetic spectrum.
**Infer** *how the frequency of electromagnetic waves change as their wavelength decreases.*

**Figure 19** Visible light waves are electromagnetic waves with a narrow range of wavelengths from about 700 to 400 billionths of a meter. The color of visible light waves depends on their wavelength.
**Determine** *the color of the visible light waves with the highest frequency.*

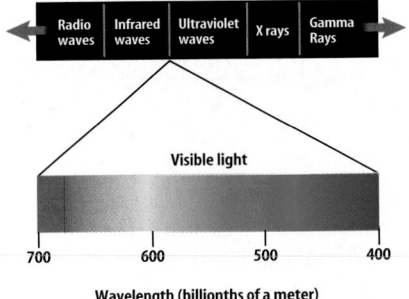

| Radio waves | Infrared waves | Ultraviolet waves | X rays | Gamma Rays |

Visible light

700      600      500      400

Wavelength (billionths of a meter)

## Discussion

**Radio Waves** Standard broadcast frequencies for AM radio stations range from 535,000 to 1,705,000 Hz. Standard frequencies for FM stations range from 88,000,000 to 108,000,000 Hz. Are the wavelengths of AM or FM radio waves longer? Explain.
All radio waves have the same speed. Because of the wave speed equation, FM waves must have shorter wavelengths because their frequencies are higher.

## Caption Answers

**Figure 18** The frequency increases.
**Figure 19** Violet light has the highest frequency.

## IDENTIFYING Misconceptions

**Wave Direction** Students should understand that electromagnetic waves spread out in many directions, not just along a line. For example, radio waves produced by electrons moving up and down a vertical radio antenna spread out in all directions except along the line of the antenna. Help students understand this by pointing out that the signal from a radio station can be received in all directions from the antenna.

## ✔ Reading Check

**Answer** between 700 and 400 billionths of a meter

## Teacher FYI

**Microwave Ovens** The frequency of microwaves used in microwave ovens is about 2,450,000,000 Hz. Because the speed of all electromagnetic waves is 300,000,000 m/s, the wavelength of these microwaves is about 12 cm.

## Fun Fact

All bodies with a temperature above absolute zero emit electromagnetic waves. As the temperature of an object increases, the wavelengths emitted decrease. At room temperature, objects emit mostly infrared waves.

**Purpose** Students will observe the dispersion of light into a spectrum of colors.

**Materials** prism, flashlight, laser pointer

**Teaching Strategy** Be sure to perform this activity on a sunny day when there is sufficient sunlight to form a rainbow of colors from the prism.

**Safety Precautions** Remind students that looking directly at the beam of light from a laser pointer could damage their eyes.

**Analysis**

1. Light changes direction when it passes into the prism. You see a spectrum of colors because different wavelengths of light bend by different amounts.

2. Laser light is made of only one wavelength of light.

## Assessment

**Oral** Based on their observations, ask students to infer whether red light waves or violet light waves are bent most by the prism. violet light waves Use **Performance Assessment in the Science Classroom**, p. 89.

---

### Separating Wavelengths

**Procedure**

1. Place a **prism** in sunlight. Adjust its position until a color spectrum is produced.
2. Place the prism on a **desktop.** Dim the lights and shine a **flashlight** on the prism.
3. Shine a **laser pointer** on the prism.

**WARNING:** *Do not shine the laser pointer into anyone's eyes.*

**Analysis**

1. Determine whether sunlight and the light emitted from the flashlight contain more than one wavelength.
2. Determine whether the light emitted from the laser pointer contains more than one wavelength.

---

**Indiana Academic Standard Check**

**7.3.11:** Explain that . . . only a tiny fraction of . . . the Sun's energy arrives as light . . . consisting of . . . untraviolet radiation.

✔ Which waves from the Sun are blocked by Earth's atmosphere?

✔ ultraviolet waves

**Figure 20** Almost all of the electromagnetic waves emitted by the Sun are infrared waves, visible light, and ultraviolet waves.

**428 CHAPTER 14** Waves, Sound, and Light

---

**Ultraviolet Waves** Electromagnetic waves with wavelengths between about 400 billionths and 10 billionths of a meter are **ultraviolet waves.** These wavelengths are shorter than those of visible light. Ultraviolet waves carry more energy than visible light waves. Sunlight that reaches Earth's surface contains a small fraction of ultraviolet waves. These waves can cause sunburn if skin is exposed to sunlight for too long. Excessive exposure to ultraviolet waves can permanently damage skin, and in some cases cause skin cancer. However, some exposure to ultraviolet waves is needed for your body to make vitamin D, which helps form healthy bones and teeth.

**X Rays and Gamma Rays** The electromagnetic waves with the highest energy, highest frequency, and shortest wavelengths are X rays and gamma rays. If you've ever broken a bone, the doctor probably took an X ray to examine the injured area. X rays are energetic enough to pass through the body. X rays pass through soft tissues, but are blocked by denser body parts, such as bones. This enables images to be made of internal body parts. Gamma rays are even more energetic than X rays. One use of gamma rays is in the food industry to kill bacteria that might increase the rate of spoilage of food.

**Electromagnetic Waves from the Sun** Most of the energy emitted by the Sun is in the form of ultraviolet, visible, and infrared waves, as shown in **Figure 20.** These waves carry energy away from the Sun and spread out in all directions. Only a tiny fraction of this energy reaches Earth. Most of the ultraviolet waves from the Sun are blocked by Earth's atmosphere. As a result, almost all energy from the Sun that reaches Earth's surface is carried by infrared and visible electromagnetic waves.

**Electromagnetic Waves from the Sun**

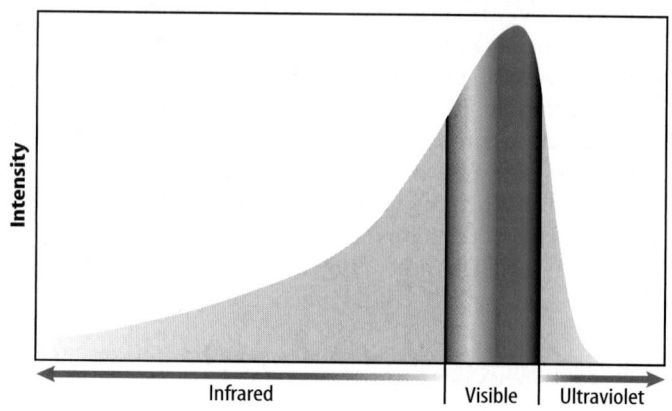

Infrared          Visible    Ultraviolet

---

## Differentiated Instruction

**Learning Disabled** Before students perform the MiniLab, be sure they understand that sunlight and light from a flashlight contain all wavelengths of light. Light from a laser pointer is just one wavelength. Reinforce this concept by having students use different colored pencils to draw light composed of many wavelengths of light. Then, have them draw laser light with just a red pencil.

Retina

Focal point

Optic nerve

Lens

Pupil

Cornea

**Figure 21** The cornea and the lens focus light waves that enter your eye so that a sharp image is formed on the retina. Special cells in the retina cause signals to be sent to the brain when they are struck by light.

## The Eye and Seeing Light

You see an object when light emitted or reflected from the object enters your eye, as shown in **Figure 21.** Light waves first pass through a transparent layer called the cornea (KOR nee uh), and then the transparent lens. The lens is flexible and changes shape to enable you to focus on objects that are nearby and far away, as shown in **Figure 22.** However, sometimes the eye is unable to form sharp images of both nearby and distant objects, as shown in **Figure 23** on the next page.

**Why do objects have color?** When light waves strike an object, some of the light waves are reflected. The wavelengths of the light waves that are reflected determine the object's color. For example, a red rose reflects light waves that have wavelengths in the red part of the visible spectrum. The color of objects that emit light is determined by the wavelengths of light that they emit. A neon sign appears to be red because it emits red light waves.

---

**Indiana Academic Standard Check**

**7.3.20:** Describe something that can be "seen" when light waves emitted or reflected by it enter the eye . . . .

✔ Which parts of the eye focus the light waves that enter the eye?

✔ the cornea and the lens

---

**Figure 22** The shape of the lens changes when you focus on nearby and distant objects.

The lens becomes flatter when you focus on a distant object.

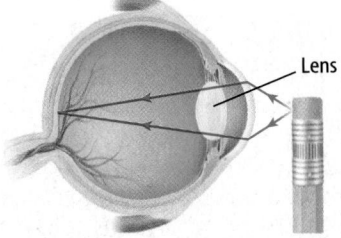

The lens becomes more curved when you focus on an object nearby.

SECTION 3 Light **429**

---

# Visualizing Common Vision Problems

Have students examine the illustrations and read the captions. Then ask the following questions.

**What are the two most common vision problems and describe each.** Farsightedness and nearsightedness; People that are farsighted see distant objects clearly, but cannot focus clearly on nearby objects. People that are nearsighted see nearby objects clearly, but distant objects seem blurry.

**Describe where the light waves are focused for people without vision problems, farsighted people, and nearsighted people.** Light waves are focused on the retina for people without vision problems; not in focus when they reach the retina of farsighted people; light waves are focused before they reach the retina of nearsighted people.

**Using the illustrations of the eyes on this page have students hypothesize how glasses or contact lenses correct vision problems.** Lenses change the way the light waves are bent, therefore changing where the light waves are focused.

## Disscussion

**Focus** Ask students if they know of anyone that wears bifocal or trifocal glasses. Ask students to describe what these terms mean.

L1 | LS | **Logical-Mathematical**

---

## Figure 23

In a human eye, light waves pass through the transparent cornea and the lens of the eye. The cornea and the lens cause light waves from an object to be focused on the retina, forming a sharp image. However, vision problems result when a sharp image is not formed on the retina. The two most common vision problems are farsightedness and nearsightedness.

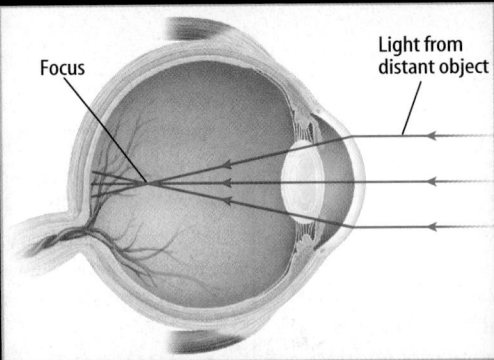

Focus | Light from distant object

◀ **Nearsightedness** A person that is nearsighted can see nearby objects clearly, but distant objects seem blurry. Nearsightedness results if the eyeball is too long, so that light waves from far away objects are brought to a focus before they reach the retina. This vision problem usually is corrected by wearing glasses or contact lenses. Laser surgery also is used to correct nearsightedness by reshaping the cornea.

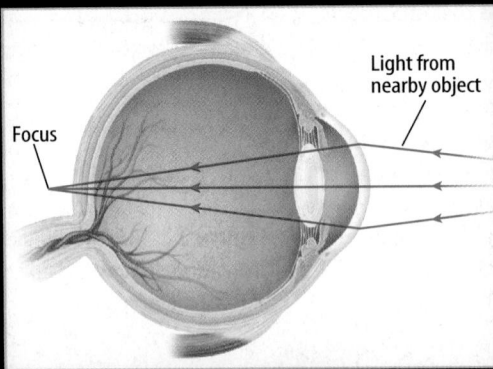

Focus | Light from nearby object

◀ **Farsightedness** A farsighted person can see distant objects clearly, but cannot focus clearly on nearby objects. Farsightedness results if the eyeball is too short, so light waves from nearby objects have not been brought to a focus when they strike the retina.

▶ Farsightedness also can be corrected by wearing glasses. People commonly become farsighted as they get older because of changes in the lens of the eye. Laser surgery sometimes is used to correct farsightedness.

**430** **CHAPTER 14** Waves, Sound, and Light

Rod

Lens

Cone

Retina

**Figure 24** Rod and cone cells in the retina of the eye detect light and send signals to the brain.

**Rod and Cone Cells** The retina contains over a hundred million light-sensitive cells called rods and cones, shown in **Figure 24.** Rod cells are sensitive to dim light, and cone cells enable you to see colors. There are three types of cone cells. One type is sensitive to red and yellow light, another type is sensitive to green and yellow light, and the third type is sensitive to blue and violet light. The combination of the signals sent to the brain by all three types of cone cells forms the color image that you see.

## section 3 review

### Summary

**Light and Electromagnetic Waves**

- Light waves are electromagnetic waves. These waves travel through empty space at a speed of 300,000 km/s.
- Electromagnetic waves are transverse waves made of vibrating electric and magnetic fields.
- Radio waves, infrared waves, visible light, ultraviolet waves, X rays, and gamma rays form the electromagnetic spectrum.
- Most of the electromagnetic waves emitted by the Sun are infrared waves, visible light, and ultraviolet waves.

**Color and Vision**

- The color of an object is the color of the light the object emits or reflects.
- You see an object when light waves emitted or reflected by the object enter your eye and strike the retina.
- Rod cells and cone cells in the retina of the eye are light-sensitive cells that send signals to the brain when light strikes them.

### Self Check

1. **Identify** the electromagnetic waves with the longest wavelengths and the electromagnetic waves with the shortest wavelengths.
2. **Describe** the difference between radio waves, visible light and gamma rays.
3. **Compare and contrast** the rod cells and the cone cells in the retina of the human eye.
4. **Explain** why most of the electromagnetic waves emitted by the Sun that strike Earth's surface are infrared and visible light waves.
5. **Think Critically** Explain why the brightness of the light emitted by a flashlight decreases as the flashlight moves farther away from you.

#### Applying Skills

6. **Make a Concept Map** Design a concept map to show the sequence of events that occurs when you see a blue object.
7. **Recognize Cause and Effect** Why does light travel faster through empty space than it does through matter?

**DAILY INTERVENTION**

### Check for Understanding

**Interpersonal** Have students work in pairs to list the types of electromagnetic waves, from longest to shortest wavelength. Have them list one or more uses or examples of each type.

### Reteach

**Intensity of Light** In a darkened room, shine a flashlight against a wall while standing about one meter away. As you slowly walk toward the wall, point out to students how the beam of light becomes brighter but the illuminated area decreases. Students should see that the intensity of light decreases with distance from the light source.

## ✓ Assessment

**Oral** Ask students to explain the following statement: White light is a combination of different colors. White light is a combination of electromagnetic waves having a range of wavelengths in the visible spectrum, from 700 to 400 nanometers. Use **Performance Assessment in the Science Classroom,** p. 89.

## section 3 review

1. Radio waves have the longest wavelengths and gamma rays have the shortest wavelengths.
2. They all are electromagnetic waves. Radio waves have the longest wavelengths and lowest frequencies. Gamma rays have the shortest wavelengths and highest frequencies. Visible light has wavelengths and frequencies between radio waves and gamma rays.
3. Both rod cells and cone cells are nerve cells in the retina of the human eye that help you see light. Rod cells are sensitive to dim light and help you see in the dark. Cone cells are sensitive to different colors.
4. The Sun emits mostly infrared waves, visible light, and ultraviolet waves. Most of the ultraviolet waves are blocked by Earth's atmosphere.
5. The energy carried by the light waves is spread out over a larger area.
6. light strikes object, object reflects blue light, light reflected from object enters eye and strikes retina, cone cells cause a signal to be sent to the brain
7. Light waves travel slower through matter because they interact with the atoms and other particles in matter.

# Bending Light

## ▶ Real-World Question

**Purpose** Students investigate the reflection and refraction of light. They infer how reflection and refraction explain rainbows.

**Process Skills** make and use a table, observe, infer, compare and contrast, predict, communicate

**Time Required** 40 minutes

**Materials** small piece of cardboard, scissors, tape, modeling clay, flashlight, flat mirror, clear plastic CD case, 250-mL beaker, prism

**Safety Precautions** Remind students that the mirror is breakable, and they should be careful when handling it.

## ▶ Procedure

**Teaching Strategies** Students may think that they are supposed to see refraction of light through the CD case, and they may not understand why they don't. Explain that the CD case is too thin for significant refraction to occur. Draw a sketch on the board showing how refraction through a material occurs. Explain that although the CD case refracts the light, the displacement of the beam is too small to see.

**Tie to Prior Knowledge** Review the meanings of *refraction* and *reflection* before students begin the lab.

### Goals
■ **Compare and contrast** the reflection, refraction, and transmission of light.
■ **Observe** how the refraction of white light can produce different colors of light.

### Materials
small piece of cardboard
scissors
tape
flashlight
flat mirror
clear plastic CD case
250-mL beaker
prism

### Safety Precautions

432

## ▶ Real-World Question

What happens to light waves when they strike the boundary between two materials? Some of the light waves might be reflected from the boundary and some of the waves might travel into the second material. These light waves can change direction and be refracted in the second material. Transmission occurs when the light waves finally pass through the second material. What happens to light waves when they strike a boundary between air and other materials?

## ▶ Procedure

1. Make a data table similar to the one shown below.

| Bending of Light by Different Surfaces | | |
|---|---|---|
| **Surface** | **How Beam is Affected** | **Colors Formed** |
| Mirror | | |
| CD case | Do not write in this book. | |
| Water | | |
| Prism | | |

2. Cut a slit about 3 cm long and 2 mm wide in a circular piece of cardboard. Tape the cardboard to the face of the flashlight.

3. In a darkened room, shine the flashlight at an angle toward the mirror. Determine whether the flashlight beam is reflected, refracted, or transmitted. Look at the color of the light beam after it strikes the mirror. Has the white light been changed into different colors of light? Record your observations on the chart.

| Bending of Light by Different Surfaces | | |
|---|---|---|
| **Surface** | **How Light Bent** | **Colors Formed** |
| Mirror | reflected | no |
| CD Case | slightly reflected and refraction | no |
| Water | refracted and slightly reflected | no |
| Prism | refracted and reflected | yes |

## Alternative Inquiry Lab

**Rainbows** Encourage critical thinking in students by using an inquiry version of this lab. Ask students to investigate how reflection and refraction of light are related to the formation of a rainbow.

4. Remove the clear plastic front from an empty CD case. Shine the flashlight at an angle toward the plastic. Does transmission occur? Record your observations about how the direction of the beam changes and colors of the light.

5. Fill the beaker with water. Shine the flashlight toward the side of the beaker so that the light shines through the water. Move the light beam from side to side. Record your observations.

6. Shine the flashlight toward a side of the prism. Move the light beam around until you see the outgoing beam spread into different colors. Record your observations.

## Analyze Your Data

1. For which objects did reflection occur? For which objects did refraction occur? For which objects did transmission occur?

2. For which objects did refraction cause the flashlight beam to be separated into different colors?

## Conclude and Apply

1. **Compare and contrast** the behavior of light waves when they strike the mirror and the CD case.

2. **Explain** why the beam that passes through the CD case does or does not change direction.

3. **Describe** how the light beam changes after it passes through the prism.

### Communicating Your Data

Create a sketch showing how light refracts in a prism and divides into different colors.

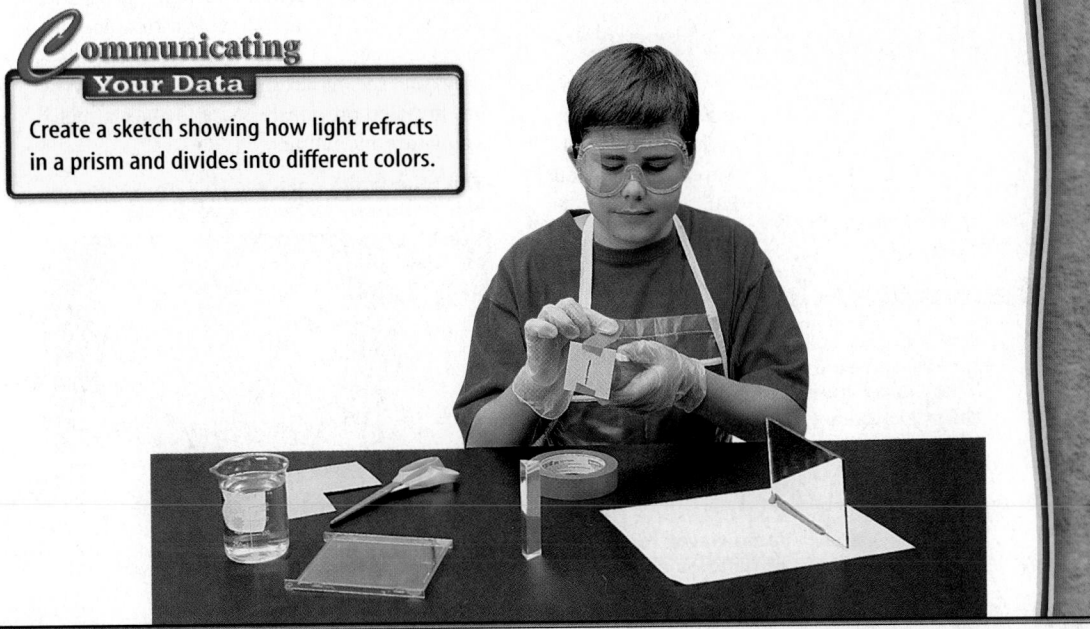

### Assessment

**Oral** Have students explain why the angled surfaces of the prism are necessary for separating light into different colors. The first angled surface separates the light as it enters the prism. The second angled surface maintains the separation as the light exits the prism.

**Expected Outcome** The mirror reflects the light but doesn't separate it into different colors. The CD case less the light through with negligible refraction, and it doesn't form colors. The water refracts light and doesn't form colors. The prism refracts light and forms colors.

### Analyze Your Data

**Answers to Questions**

1. Reflection occurred for the mirror. Refraction occurred for the water and the prism. Transmission occurs for the CD case, water, and the prism.

2. prism

**Error Analysis** At what angle did you shine the light toward the different surfaces?

### Conclude and Apply

1. Light reflects off the mirror. A small amount of reflection and refraction occur with the CD case.

2. The light refracts a small amount, but the CD case is too thin for the refraction to be significant.

3. All colors of light refract when they pass through the prism. Longer wavelengths of light, such as red light, refract less than shorter wavelengths of light, such as violet light.

### Communicating Your Data

Remind students that they must consider the refraction of light as it enters the prism and again as it exits the prism.

## Content Background

When students hear the word "radio," they may think of sound. Help them understand the difference between sound and radio waves. Sound consists of pressure variations in matter and will not travel through a vacuum. Radio waves, like visible light, infrared, and X rays, are electromagnetic waves that travel through a vacuum. The transmitter at a radio station changes the amplitude or frequency of radio waves to make them carry information about the sound of voices and music. A radio receives the radio waves, decodes this information, and changes it back into audible sound.

## Discussion

**Different Antennae** Why do you think Jansky's antenna looks so different from modern radio telescopes? *Jansky's antenna was designed to pick up radio waves on Earth rather than focus them from distant stars.*

## Analyze the Event

**Not Our Job** When Jansky discovered radio waves from outer space, his employers weren't interested. Their business was improving communication on Earth. Discuss with students why some discoveries might be lost or delayed because they were made by people in the "wrong" field. Candace Pert's discovery of endorphins is one example.

# Jansky's Merry-Go-Round

**B**efore the first radio signals were sent across the Atlantic Ocean in 1902, ships could only communicate if they could see one another. Being able to communicate using radio waves was a real breakthrough. But it wasn't without its problems—namely lots of static. Around 1930, Bell Labs was trying to improve radio communication by using radio waves with shorter wavelengths—between 10 and 20 m. They put Karl Jansky to work finding out what might be causing the static.

**Karl Jansky built the first radiotelescope.**

## An Unexpected Discovery

**This antenna built by Jansky detected radio waves from the Milky Way galaxy.**

Jansky built an antenna to receive radio waves with a wavelength of about 14.5 m. He mounted it on a turntable so that he could rotate it in any direction. His coworkers called it "Jansky's merry-go-round."

After recording signals for several months, Jansky found that there were three types of static. Two were caused by nearby and distant thunderstorms.

But the third was totally unexpected. It seemed to come from the center of our Milky Way galaxy! Jansky wanted to follow up on this unexpected discovery, but Bell Labs had the information it wanted. They were in the telephone business, not astronomy!

## A New Branch of Astronomy

Fortunately, other scientists were fascinated with Jansky's find. Grote Reber built a "radiotelescope" in his Illinois backyard. He confirmed Jansky's discovery and did the first systematic survey of radio waves from space. The field of radioastronomy was born.

Previously, astronomers could observe distant galaxies only by gathering the light arriving from their stars. But they couldn't see past the clouds of gas and small particles surrounding the galaxies. Radio waves emitted by a galaxy can penetrate much of the gas and dust in space. This allows radio astronomers to make images of galaxies and other objects they can't see. As a result, Radio astronomy has revealed previously invisible objects such as quasars and pulsars.

**The blue-white colors in this image are all you could see without radio waves.**

**Experiment** Research how astronomers convert the radio waves received by radio telescopes into images of galaxies and stars.

**Science Online**

For more information, visit in7.msscience.com/oops

**Experiment** Visit the site and read the information on the page prior to making the assignment so that you can help students understand how radio signals are converted into images. Print out and make copies of the data sheets for students. Actually filling in the data sheets will give students a better understanding of how signal strengths (numbers) can be made visible.

## Resources for Teachers and Students

*Radio Astronomy*, by Adele D. Richardson, Smart Apple Media, 2002

*Invisible Universe: The Electromagnetic Spectrum from Radio Waves to Gamma Rays*, by Alan Gould. GEMS, 2002

## Reviewing Main Ideas

### Section 1  Waves

1. Waves carry energy from place to place without transporting matter.

2. Transverse waves move particles in matter at right angles to the direction in which the waves travel.

3. Compressional waves move particles back and forth along the same direction in which the waves travel.

4. The speed of a wave equals its wavelength multiplied by its frequency.

### Section 2  Sound Waves

1. Sound waves are compressional waves produced by something vibrating.

2. The intensity of sound waves is measured in units of decibels.

3. You hear sound when sound waves reach your ear and cause parts of the ear to vibrate.

### Section 3  Light

1. Electromagnetic waves are transverse waves that can travel in matter or empty space.

2. Light waves are electromagnetic waves.

3. The range of frequencies and wavelengths of electromagnetic waves forms the electromagnetic spectrum.

4. You see an object when light waves emitted or reflected by the object enter your eye and strike light-sensitive cells inside the eye.

## Visualizing Main Ideas

*Copy and complete the following concept map on waves.*

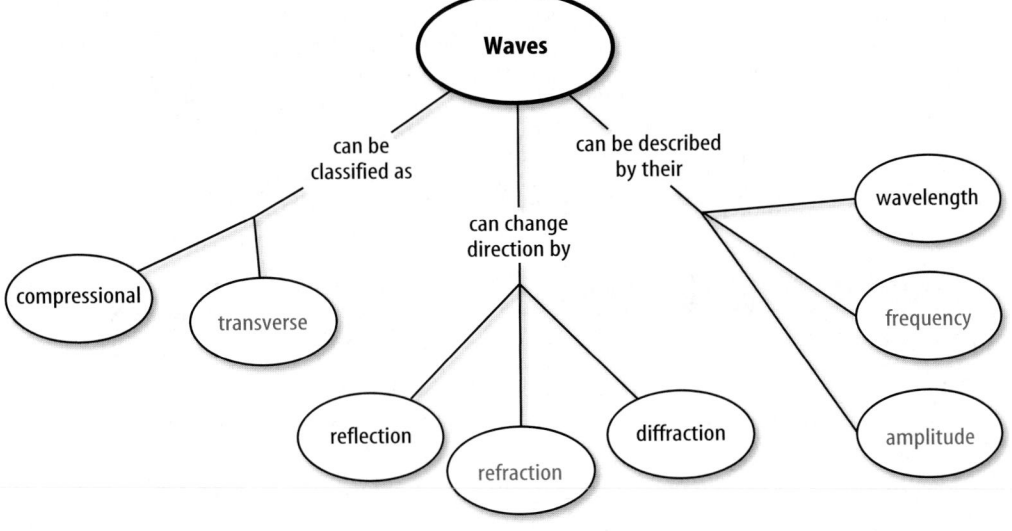

Science Online in7.msscience.com/interactive_tutor

CHAPTER STUDY GUIDE  **435**

## Reviewing Main Ideas

Summary statements can be used by students to review the major concepts of the chapter.

## Visualizing Main Ideas

See student page.

**Visit** in7.msscience.com
/self_check_quiz
/interactive_tutor
/vocabulary_puzzlemaker
/chapter_review
/standards_review

## Assessment Transparency

For additional assessment questions, use the *Assessment Transparency* located in the transparency book.

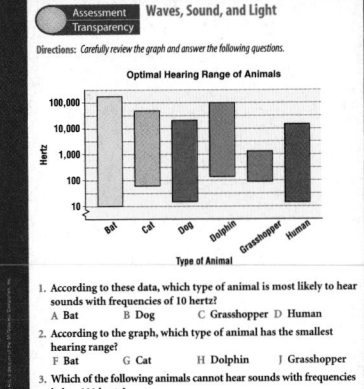

## Identifying Misconceptions

**Assess**

Use the assessment as follow-up to page F at the beginning of this chapter after students have completed the chapter.

**Activity** Give students the following scenario. There is an enormous loudspeaker on the left side of the room. In the middle of the room is a helium balloon on the ceiling. The loudspeaker produces a very loud sound. Have students predict what will happen to the balloon after the loudspeaker has been on for two minutes.

## Using Vocabulary

1. refraction
2. diffraction
3. electromagnetic spectrum
4. intensity
5. transverse wave
6. frequency
7. compressional wave

## Checking Concepts

| | | |
|---|---|---|
| **8.** A | **12.** D | **16.** D |
| **9.** B | **13.** C | **17.** C |
| **10.** C | **14.** A | |
| **11.** B | **15.** B | |

## Using Vocabulary

| | |
|---|---|
| compressional wave p. 413 | law of reflection p. 417 |
| diffraction p. 418 | pitch p. 421 |
| electromagnetic | refraction p. 417 |
| spectrum p. 426 | reverberation p. 423 |
| electromagnetic | transverse wave p. 413 |
| waves p. 425 | ultraviolet waves p. 428 |
| frequency p. 414 | wave p. 412 |
| infrared waves p. 427 | wavelength p. 414 |
| intensity p. 420 | |

*Complete each statement using a word(s) from the vocabulary list above.*

1. The bending of a wave when it moves from one material into another is _____.

2. The bending of waves around an object is due to _____.

3. The _____ is the complete range of electromagnetic wave frequencies and wavelengths.

4. The amount of energy that a wave carries past a certain area each second is the _____.

5. In a(n) _____, the particles in the material move at right angles to the direction the wave moves.

6. The _____ of a wave is the number of wavelengths that pass a point each second.

7. In a _____, particles in the material move back and forth along the direction of wave motion.

## Checking Concepts

*Choose the word or phrase that best answers the question.*

8. If the distance between the crest and trough of a wave is 0.6 m, what is the wave's amplitude?
   **A)** 0.3 m   **C)** 0.6 m
   **B)** 1.2 m   **D)** 2.4

9. Which of the following are units for measuring frequency?
   **A)** decibels   **C)** meters
   **B)** hertz   **D)** meters/second

10. Through which of these materials does sound travel fastest?
    **A)** empty space   **C)** steel
    **B)** water   **D)** air

11. An increase in a sound's pitch corresponds to an increase in what other property?
    **A)** intensity   **C)** wavelength
    **B)** frequency   **D)** loudness

12. Soft materials are sometimes used in concert halls to prevent what effect?
    **A)** refraction   **C)** compression
    **B)** diffraction   **D)** reverberation

13. Which of the following are not transverse waves?
    **A)** radio waves   **C)** sound waves
    **B)** infrared waves   **D)** visible light

14. Which of the following wave properties determines the energy carried by a wave?
    **A)** amplitude   **C)** wavelength
    **B)** frequency   **D)** wave speed

15. Which of the following best describes why refraction of a wave occurs when the wave travels from one material into another?
    **A)** The wavelength increases.
    **B)** The speed of the wave changes.
    **C)** The amplitude increases.
    **D)** The frequency decreases.

16. What produces waves?
    **A)** sound   **C)** transfer of energy
    **B)** heat   **D)** vibrations

17. Which of the following has wavelengths longer than the wavelengths of visible light?
    **A)** X rays   **C)** radio waves
    **B)** gamma rays   **D)** ultraviolet waves

 Science Online   in7.msscience.com/vocabulary_puzzlemaker

**Use the Exam*View*® Pro Testmaker CD-ROM to:**
- create multiple versions of tests
- create modified tests with one mouse click for inclusion students
- edit existing questions and add your own questions
- build tests aligned with state standards using built-in State Curriculum Tags
- change English tests to Spanish with one mouse click and vice versa

## Thinking Critically

**18. Infer** Radio waves broadcast by a radio station strike your radio and your ear. Infer whether the human ear can hear radio waves. What evidence supports your conclusion?

**19. Solve an Equation** Robotic spacecraft on Mars have sent radio signals back to Earth. The distance from Mars to Earth, at its greatest, is about 401,300,000 km. About how many minutes would it take a signal to reach Earth from that distance?

**20. Recognize Cause and Effect** When a musician plucks a string on a guitar it produces sound with a certain pitch. If the musician then presses down on the string and plucks it, the sound produced has a shorter wavelength. How does the pitch of the sound change?

**21. Interpret Scientific Illustrations** One way that radio waves can carry signals to radios is by varying the amplitude of the wave. This is known as amplitude modulation (AM). Another way is by varying the frequency. This is called frequency modulation (FM). Which of the waves below shows AM, and which shows FM? Explain.

**22. Infer** When light passes through a prism, infer how the amount of bending of a light wave depends on the frequency of the light wave. How does the amount of bending depend on the wavelength of the light wave?

**23. Describe** how the lenses in your eyes change shape when you first look at your wristwatch to read the time, and then look at a mountain in the distance.

## Performance Activities

**24. Poster** Investigate a musical instrument to find out how it produces sound. Make a poster showing the instrument and describing how it works.

**25. Model** Make an instrument out of common materials. Present the instrument to the class, and explain how it can produce different pitches.

## Applying Math

**26. Noise Levels** A noisy restaurant has an intensity of about 80 dB, and a lawn mower has an intensity of about 110 dB. How many times louder does the lawn mower noise seem?

**27. Wavelength of Sound** Sound waves with a frequency of 150 Hz travel at a speed of 340 m/s. What is the wavelength of the sound waves?

**28. Ultrasound** Physicians sometimes use high-frequency sound waves to diagnose and monitor medical conditions. A typical frequency for the sound waves is about 5,000,000.0 Hz. Sound travels through soft body tissue at about 1500.0 m/s. What is the wavelength of the sound waves?

**29. Frequency of Radio Waves** Find the frequency of radio waves that have a wavelength of 15 m if they are traveling at a speed of 300,000,000 m/s.

**CHAPTER REVIEW** 437

## Thinking Critically

**18.** The human ear can't hear radio waves. You only hear the sounds if the radio is on. The radio waves must be changed into sound waves by your radio in order for you to hear the sound.

**19.** about 22 min

**20.** increases

**21.** The spacing of the peaks in the upper figure doesn't change, but the height of the peaks, corresponding to the amplitude, does change. The upper figure is amplitude modulation. In the lower figure the amplitude of the waves doesn't change, but the spacing of the peaks does; this is frequency modulation.

**22.** Blue light is bent the most, and red light is bent the least, so the amount of bending increases with increasing frequency, and increases with decreasing wavelength.

**23.** The lens has to be more curved to focus nearby objects, and flatter to focus distant objects. So the lens changes from being more curved to less curved.

## Performance Activities

**24.** Posters should show a description of the instrument and explain how the instrument produces different frequencies of sound.

**25.** Students may construct instruments out of common materials such as cardboard tubes, boxes, rubberbands, or combs. They should demonstrate an understanding of how their instrument vibrates air molecules to produce different sounds.

## ✔ Assessment Resources

**Reproducible Masters**
**Chapter *Fast File* Resources**
Chapter Review, pp. 37–38
Chapter Tests, pp. 39–42
Assessment Transparency Activity, p. 49
**Glencoe Science Web site**
Chapter Review Test
IN Standards Review

**Glencoe Technology**
- Assessment Transparency
- Exam*View*® Pro Testmaker
- MindJogger Videoquiz
- Interactive Chalkboard

## Applying Math

### Indiana Math Standards
7.2.1, 7.3.1

**26.** eight times louder

**27.** 2.3 m

**28.** about 0.0003 m

**29.** 20,000,000 Hz

**Answer Sheet** A practice answer sheet can be found at in7.msscience.com/answer_sheet.

SAMPLE

## Part 1 Multiple Choice

1. C
2. A
3. A
4. C
5. C
6. C
7. B

## Part 2 Critical Response

8. Light waves are transverse electromagnetic waves that can travel through matter or space. Sound waves are compressional waves that can travel only through matter.

9. Light waves are focused by the lens in your eye on the retina. The light strikes rod and cone cells in the retina, which send signals to the brain, causing an image to be seen.

10. radio waves, infrared waves, visible light, ultraviolet waves, X rays, gamma rays

11. Both types of waves are produced by something vibrating. Compressional waves move by causing matter to move back and forth along the same direction the wave is moving. Transverse waves

The assessed Indiana standard appears above the question.

*Record your answers on the answer sheet provided by your teacher or on a sheet of paper.*

### Part 1 Multiple Choice

**7.3.18**

1. The table below shows the speed of sound in different materials.

| Speed of Sound in Different Materials | |
|---|---|
| **Material** | **Speed (m/s)** |
| Air (20°C) | 343 |
| Glass | 5,640 |
| Steel | 5,940 |
| Water (25°C) | 1,493 |
| Seawater (25°C) | 1,533 |

If sound travels 2,146 m through a material in 1.4 s, what is the material?

A air

B glass

C seawater

D water

2. Which term refers to the bending of waves around obstacles?

A diffraction

B reflection

C refraction

D transmission

3. Which is a **TRUE** statement?

A Waves do not transport the matter in which they travel.

B Waves can transport matter through solids, liquids, and gases, but not through empty space.

C Waves can transport matter through liquids and solids, but not through gases or empty space.

D Sound and water waves can transport matter, but light waves can't.

**7.3.20**

4. The table below shows various sound intensity levels on the decibel scale.

| Decibel Scale | |
|---|---|
| **Sound Source** | **Loudness (dB)** |
| Jet plane taking off | 150 |
| Running lawn mower | 100 |
| Average home | 50 |
| Whisper | 15 |

What would be the approximate sound intensity level of a noisy restaurant?

A 20 dB

B 40 dB

C 80 dB

D 120 dB

### Test-Taking Tip

**Be Well-Rested** Get plenty of sleep—at least eight hours every night—during test week and the week before the test.

move by causing matter to move at right angles to the direction the wave is moving.

12. Sound travels faster through materials in which the atoms tend to be closer together. The speed of sound in a material increases as the temperature of the material increases.

**5.** Which do not travel through empty space?

**A** infrared waves

**B** light waves

**C** sound waves

**D** ultraviolet waves

**6.** What is the maximum range of sound frequencies that humans can hear?

**A** 0 Hz to 3,300 Hz

**B** 0 Hz to 20,000 Hz

**C** 20 Hz to 20,000 Hz

**D** 50 Hz to 50,000 Hz

7.3.11

**7.** The graph below shows the intensity of electromagnetic waves emitted by the Sun.

**Electromagnetic Waves from the Sun**

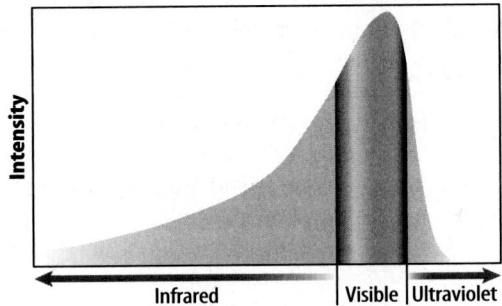

What waves emitted by the Sun have the greatest intensity?

**A** infrared

**B** visible

**C** visible and infrared

**D** visible and ultraviolet

---

**Part 2  Critical Response**

7.3.18

**8.** Compare and contrast light waves and sound waves.

7.3.20

**9.** The illustration below shows a cross section of the human eye.

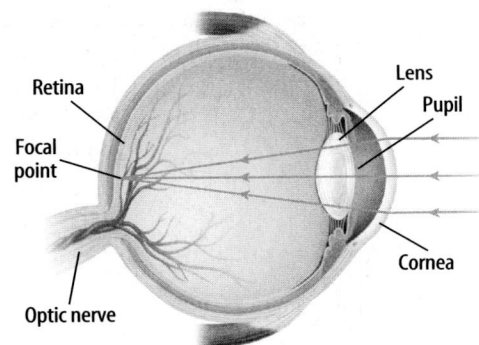

Describe the process that occurs when light waves enter your eye and produce a signal in the optic nerve.

**10.** Name the different types of electromagnetic waves from longest to shortest wavelength. Give an example of each type.

**11.** Describe compressional and transverse waves. Explain the difference between them.

7.3.18

**12.** Explain why sound travels faster through some types of matter than through others. How does temperature affect the speed of sound through a material?

---

## Rubrics

The following rubric is a sample scoring device for critical response questions.

### Critical Response

| Points | Description |
|--------|-------------|
| 4 | The student demonstrates a thorough understanding of the science of the task. The response may contain minor flaws that do not detract from the demonstration of a thorough understanding. |
| 3 | The student demonstrates an understanding of the science of the task. The response is essentially correct and demonstrates an essential but less than thorough understanding of the science. |
| 2 | The student demonstrates only a partial understanding of the science of the task. Although the student may have used the correct approach to a solution or may have provided a correct solution, the work lacks an essential understanding of the underlying science concepts. |
| 1 | The student demonstrates a very limited understanding of the science of the task. The response is incomplete and exhibits many flaws. |
| 0 | The student provides a completely incorrect solution or no response at all. |

---

| Section/Objectives | Standards | | Labs/Features |
|---|---|---|---|
| **Chapter Opener** | National | State/Local | **Launch Lab:** Electronic and Human Calculators, p. 441<br>**Foldables,** p. 441 |
| | See pp. 16T–17T for a Key to Standards. | Detailed standards begin on page IN8. | |
| **Section 1 Electronics**<br>🕐 3 sessions<br>📦 1.5 blocks<br><br>1. **Compare and contrast** analog and digital signals.<br>2. **Explain** how semiconductors are used in electronic devices. | National Content Standards: UCP.1, UCP.2, UCP.3, UCP.5, A.1, A.2, E.2, F.5 | Indiana Standards: This section builds a foundation for Standard 7.1.11. | **Science Online,** p. 445<br>**Lab:** Investigating Diodes, p. 448 |
| **Section 2 Computers**<br>🕐 5 sessions<br>📦 2.5 blocks<br><br>3. **Describe** the different parts of a computer.<br>4. **Compare** computer hardware with computer software.<br>5. **Discuss** the different types of memory and storage in a computer. | National Content Standards: UCP.1, UCP.2, UCP.3, UCP.5, A.1, A.2, E.2, F.5, G.3 | Indiana Standards: 7.1.8, 7.1.11, 7.2.7 | **MiniLAB:** Using Binary Numbers, p. 450<br>**Applying Science:** How much information can be stored?, p. 451<br>**Science Online,** p. 452<br>**MiniLAB:** Observing Memory, p. 453<br>**Integrate Career,** p. 454<br>**Integrate Environment,** p. 456<br>**Science Online,** p. 456<br>**Visualizing a Hard Disk,** p. 457<br>**Science Online,** p. 458<br>**Lab:** Does your computer have a virus?, pp. 460–461<br>**Science and Society:** E-Lectrifying E-Books, p. 462 |

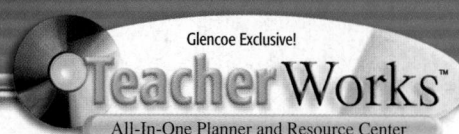
| Lab Materials | Reproducible Resources | Section Assessment | Technology |
|---|---|---|---|
| **Launch Lab:** stopwatch, calculator, pencil and paper | **Chapter FAST FILE Resources**<br>Foldables Worksheet, p. 17<br>Directed Reading Overview, p. 19<br>Note-taking Worksheets, pp. 31–32 | GLENCOE'S ASSESSMENT ADVANTAGE | Teacher**Works** includes:<br>• Interactive Teacher Edition<br>• Lesson Planner with calendar<br>• Access to all program blacklines<br>• Correlations to standards<br>• Web links |
| **Lab:** light-emitting diode, lightbulb and holder, D-cell battery and holder, wire<br><br>*Need materials?* Contact Science Kit at 1-800-828-7777 or www.sciencekit.com on the Internet. | **Chapter FAST FILE Resources**<br>Transparency Activity, p. 42<br>Lab Activity, pp. 9–11<br>Enrichment, p. 29<br>Reinforcement, p. 27<br>Directed Reading, p. 20<br>Lab Worksheet, pp. 5–6<br>**Lab Management and Safety,** p. 76 | **Portfolio**<br>Reteach, p. 447<br>**Performance**<br>Applying Math, p. 447<br>**Content**<br>Section Review, p. 447 | ♪ Section Focus Transparency<br>♫ Guided Reading Audio Program<br>◉ Interactive Chalkboard CD-ROM |
| **MiniLAB:** 8 small paper squares<br>**MiniLAB:** 3-in × 5-in cards (6)<br>**Lab:** paper and pencil | **Chapter FAST FILE Resources**<br>Transparency Activity, p. 43<br>MiniLAB, pp. 3, 4<br>Transparency Activity, pp. 45–46<br>Lab Activity, pp. 13–16<br>Enrichment, p. 30<br>Reinforcement, p. 28<br>Directed Reading, pp. 21, 22<br>Lab Worksheet, pp. 7–8<br>**Cultural Diversity,** p. 27 | **Portfolio**<br>Differentiated Instruction, p. 455<br>**Performance**<br>MiniLAB, p. 450<br>Applying Science, p. 451<br>MiniLAB, p. 453<br>Applying Skills, p. 459<br>**Content**<br>Section Review, p. 459 | ♪ Section Focus Transparency<br>♪ Teaching Transparency<br>◉ Virtual Labs CD-ROM<br>♫ Guided Reading Audio Program<br>◉ Interactive Chalkboard CD-ROM<br>▦ Video Lab |

## End of Chapter Assessment

GLENCOE'S ASSESSMENT ADVANTAGE

| Blackline Masters | Technology | Professional Series |
|---|---|---|
| **Chapter FAST FILE Resources**<br>Chapter Review, pp. 35–36<br>Chapter Tests, pp. 37–40<br>**Mastering the Grade 7 Indiana Science Standards** | ▦ MindJogger Videoquiz<br>◉ IN Test Prep and Practice ExamView®<br>◉ ExamView® Pro Testmaker<br>◉ TeacherWorks CD-ROM<br>◉ Interactive Chalkboard CD-ROM | **Performance Assessment in the Science Classroom (PASC)** |

## Transparencies

### Section Focus

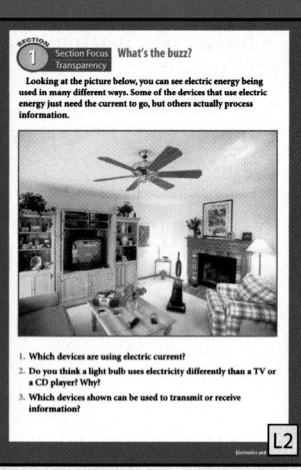

This is a representation of key blackline masters available in the Teacher Classroom Resources. See Resource Manager boxes within the chapter for additional information.

## Key to Teaching Strategies

The following designations will help you decide which activities are appropriate for your students.

L1 Level 1 activities should be appropriate for students with learning difficulties.

L2 Level 2 activities should be within the ability range of all students.

L3 Level 3 activities are designed for above-average students.

ELL ELL activities should be within the ability range of English Language Learners.

COOP LEARN Cooperative Learning activities are designed for small group work.

LS Multiple Learning Styles logos, as described on page 12T, are used throughout to indicate strategies that address different learning styles.

P These strategies represent student products that can be placed into a best-work portfolio.

PBL Problem-Based Learning activities apply real-world situations to learning.

### Assessment

### Teaching

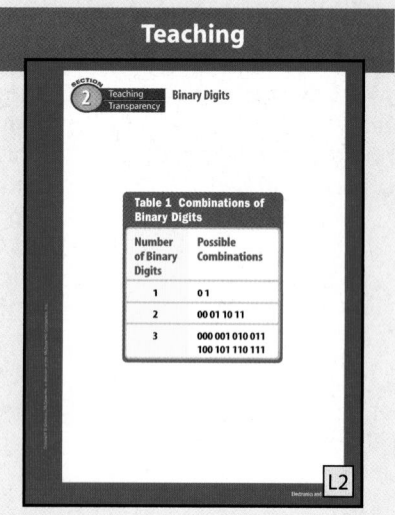

## Hands-on Activities

### Student Text Lab Worksheet

### Laboratory Activities

# Resource Manager

## Meeting Different Ability Levels

### Content Outline

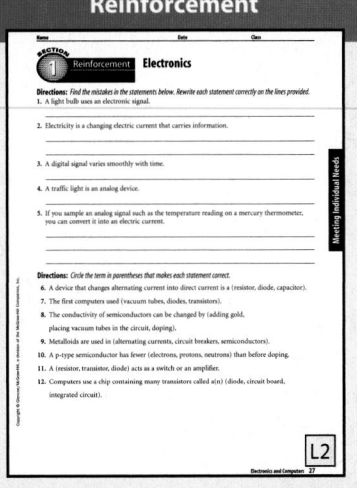

Note-taking Worksheet — **Electronics and Computers**

L2

### Reinforcement

Reinforcement — **Electronics**

L2

### Enrichment

Enrichment — **Digital TV**

L3

### Directed Reading (English/Spanish)

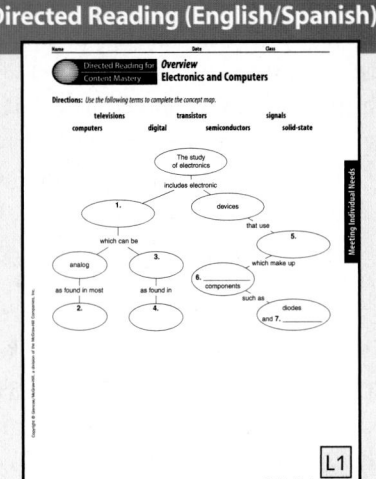

Directed Reading for Content Mastery — Overview **Electronics and Computers**

L1

### Study Guide

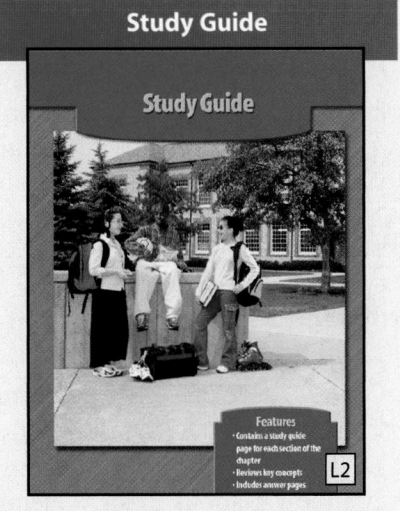

**Study Guide**

Features
- Contains a study guide page for each section of the chapter
- Reviews key concepts
- Includes answer pages

L2

### Reading Essentials

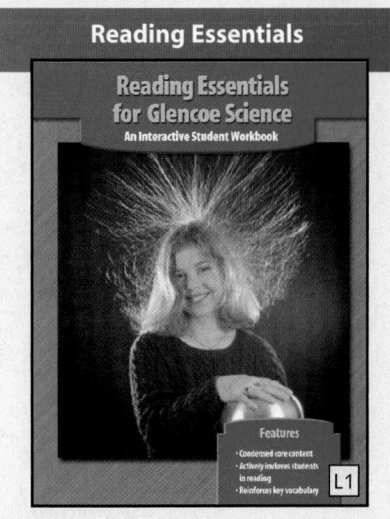

**Reading Essentials for Glencoe Science**
An Interactive Student Workbook

Features
- Condensed core content
- Actively involves students in reading
- Reinforces key vocabulary

L1

## Assessment

### Test Practice Workbook

Chapter 3 Electronics and Computers — Chapter Test

L2

### Chapter Review

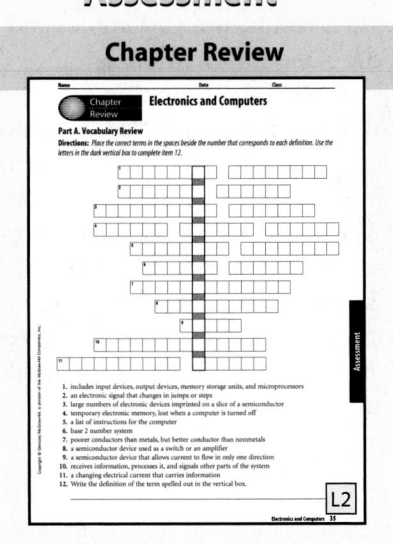

Chapter Review — **Electronics and Computers**

L2

### Chapter Tests

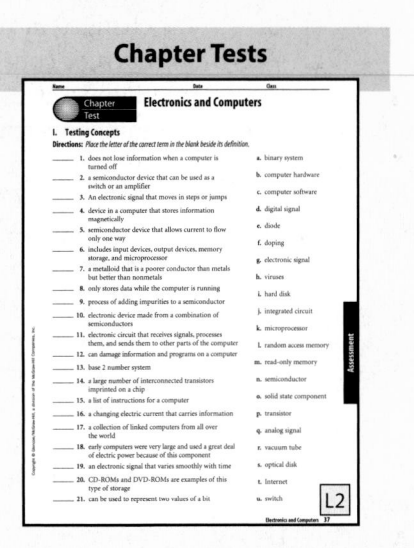

Chapter Test — **Electronics and Computers**

L2

**CHAPTER 15** Resource Manager  **440D**

# Science Content Background

## Electronics

### Electronic Signals

Information can be transmitted by an electric current. However, the electric current doesn't carry the information directly. Rather, it is the changes in the current that contain the information. For example, a song is the result of variations in air pressure. These air pressure variations are information that your ears and brain use to produce the sensation of hearing the song.

---

**Teacher to Teacher**

Deborah Peters Huffine
Noblesville Intermediate School
Noblesville, IN

"I have groups of six to eight students create a human circuit by holding hands. The class identifies the circuit as a series or parallel and predicts whether it will work. Using a set of electrical equipment, have another group create the demonstrated circuit."

*Deborah Peters Huffine*

---

A microphone converts the variations in air pressure into a varying electric current. It does this in such a way that there is a relationship between the variations in air pressure and changes in the current. As a result, the varying current contains nearly the same information as the air pressure variations. A loudspeaker then can convert the information in the varying electric current, or electronic signal, into air pressure variations that you interpret as the song.

The electronic signal produced by a microphone is an example of an analog signal. Here the word *analog* means the electric current varies smoothly. In contrast, a *digital* signal varies in jumps, with each jump giving the value of the signal over some time interval. As a result, a digital signal can be represented as a collection of numbers.

Music is stored as a digital signal on a CD. The analog signal originally produced by the musicians is converted into a digital signal by *sampling*. In the sampling process, the analog signal is measured at a fixed time interval, such as every 0.001 s. The number of samples measured per second is the *sampling rate*. The measured value is converted into a number that can vary only in steps or have only certain values. The number of possible measured values or steps is the *sampling precision*.

As the sampling rate and the sampling precision increase, the digital signal more closely resembles the analog signal being sampled. However, more numbers must be stored. A stereo digital signal on a CD is recorded at a sampling rate of 44,100 samples per second for each channel, and a sampling precision of 65,536, or $2^{16}$. Each sample requires 16 bits, or 2 bytes of storage. So one minute of stereo music on a CD requires 44,100 samples $\times$ 60 s $\times$ 2 bytes/sample $\times$ 2 channels = 10,584,000 bytes.

### Semiconductors

Most electronic devices contain integrated circuits that usually consist of a number of layers of semiconductor material, and can contain thousands or millions of electronic components, such as transistors. These electronic components are formed by etching away regions of certain layers, and can be made microscopic in size.

The electrical conductivity of metals usually is only slightly affected if the metal contains small amounts of impurities, However, the electrical behavior of semiconductor elements, such as silicon, can be altered greatly by the addition of small amounts of impurities, a process called *doping*.

For example, a silicon atom has four outer electrons, and an arsenic atom has five outer electrons. When a small amount of arsenic is added to a silicon crystal, the arsenic atoms supply extra electrons that are free to move through the crystal. A doped semiconductor with extra electrons is an n-type semiconductor. An aluminum atom has only three outer electrons, so a silicon crystal doped with aluminum has an electron deficit. A doped semiconductor with an electron deficiency is a p-type semiconductor.

Electronic components can be made simply by joining an n-type and a p-type semiconductor to form a p-n junction. A diode contains a single p-n junction, and transistors are made from several p-n junctions.

Unlike metals, the electrical resistance of semiconductors decreases with increasing temperature. By measuring the resistance of a semiconductor device called a thermistor, temperatures can be determined. The electrical properties of some semiconductors vary, depending on the amount of light that shines on them. These semiconductors are used in light meters, in photo cells that are used as switches, and in photovoltaic cells.

## section 2 — Computers
### What are computers?

Some people consider the 5,000-year-old abacus to be the first computer. Others consider Pascal's wheel calculator, created in 1642, to be the first. The impetus for the development of the first modern computer came from the U.S. census in 1880, when it took seven years to tally the information. It was realized that as the U.S. population grew, it would be impossible to tally all the census information in the ten-year period prior to the next census. Herman Hollerith invented a machine to store the information on punched cards. He got the idea from watching a train conductor punch train tickets. The 1890 census was done using this machine, and the data was processed in only six weeks. Hollerith formed a business to market his machines, which eventually became known as International Business Machines, or IBM.

In the 1950s and 1960s the development of transistors and integrated circuits allowed computers to shrink in size and energy usage. An early computer had 18,000 vacuum tubes, which took up a lot of space, produced a great deal of heat, and consumed a large amount of energy. Later, vacuum tubes were replaced with transistors and other solid-state components packed tightly together on an integrated circuit.

## chapter content resources

**Internet Resources**
For additional content background, visit
**in7.msscience.com** to:
- access your book online
- find references to related articles in popular science magazines
- access Web links with related content background
- access current events with science journal topics

**Print Resources**
*Teach Yourself Electricity and Electronics,* by Stan Bigilisco, McGraw-Hill Companies, 2001
*Techno-Matter: The Materials Behind the Marvels,* by Alfred B. Bortz, Millbrook Press, 2001
*Computers,* by Brian K. Williams and Brian Williams, Heinemann Library, 2001
*How Computers Work,* by Ron White, Timothy Downs, Timothy Edward Downs, Pearson Education, 2001

## Chapter Vocabulary

electronic signal, p. 442
analog signal, p. 442
digital signal, p. 443
semiconductor, p. 445
diode, p. 446
transistor, p. 447
integrated circuit, p. 447
binary system, p. 450
random-access memory, p. 452
read-only memory, p. 452
computer software, p. 453
microprocessor, p. 455

**Science Journal** Student responses will vary, but could include playing games, word processing, surfing the web.

**with Image Bank**

**PowerPoint® Presentations**

This CD-ROM is an editable Microsoft® PowerPoint® presentation that includes:
- a pre-made presentation for every chapter
- interactive graphics
- animations
- audio clips
- image bank
- all new section and chapter questions
- Standardized Test Practice
- transparencies
- pre-lab questions for all labs
- Foldables directions
- links to in7.msscience.com

**Academic Standard—1:** Students further their scientific understanding of the natural world through investigations, experiences, and readings. They design solutions to practical problems by using a variety of scientific methodologies.

**Also covers:** Academic Standard 2 (Detailed standards begin on page IN8.)

# Electronics and Computers

### chapter preview

**sections**

**1** Electronics
*Lab Investigating Diodes*

**2** Computers
*Lab Does your computer have a virus?*

*Virtual Lab How can a decision tree be used to generate binary numbers?*

### Deep in Thought?

You are looking at a brain—the brain of a computer. This is a microprocessor—a device that controls a computer. Even though this microprocessor is only a few cm on a side, it contains over a million microscopic circuits that enable it to store and process information very quickly.

**Science Journal** Describe three activities that you do using a computer.

440

## Theme Connection

**Systems and Interactions** A study of electronics provides the basis for understanding computers. Computers are complex systems of interacting components.

### About the Photo

**Microprocessor** This is a scanning electron microscope photo of a CX486 microprocessor at a magnification of 50× for the original image size of 6 × 7 cm. The gold microwires at the edge of the microprocessor connect it to pins that plug into a socket on the computer motherboard. In this way the microprocessor is connected to the rest of the computer.

# Start-Up Activities

## Electronic and Human Calculators

Imagine how your life would be different if you had been born before the invention of electronic devices. You could not watch television or use a computer. Besides providing entertainment, electronic devices and computers can make many tasks easier. For example, how much quicker is an electronic calculator than a human calculator?

1. Use a stopwatch to time how long it takes a volunteer to add the numbers 423, 21, 84, and 1,098.

2. Time how long it takes another volunteer to add these numbers using a calculator.

3. Repeat steps 1 and 2 this time asking the competitors to multiply 149 and 876.

4. Divide the time needed by the student calculator by the time needed by the calculator to solve each problem. How many times faster is the calculator?

5. **Think Critically** Write a paragraph describing which step in each calculation takes the most time.

Preview this chapter's content and activities at in7.msscience.com

---

**FOLDABLES** Study Organizer

### Electronics and Computers
Make the following Foldable to help you identify what you already know and what you want to learn about electronics and computers.

**STEP 1** Fold a vertical sheet of paper from side to side. Make the front edge about 1 cm shorter than the back edge.

**STEP 2** Turn lengthwise and fold into thirds.

**STEP 3** Unfold and cut only the top layer along both folds to make three tabs.

**STEP 4** Label the tabs as shown.

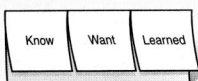

Know | Want | Learned

**Identify Questions** Before you read the chapter, write what you know under the left tab and what you want to know under the middle tab. As you read the chapter, add to and correct what you have written. After you read the chapter, write what you have learned under the right tab of your Foldable.

**441**

---

## Bellringer

**Section Focus Transparencies** also are available on the Interactive Chalkboard CD-ROM.

## Tie to Prior Knowledge

**Electrical v. Electronic** Many students can probably distinguish between electrical devices and electronic devices, but they may not be able to describe in words what distinguishes one from the other. Have each student make a list of electrical devices and a list of electronic devices. After students have worked through this section, have them read over their lists to see if their ideas were correct.

# section 1 Electronics

## as you read

### *What* You'll Learn
- **Compare and contrast** analog and digital signals.
- **Explain** how semiconductors are used in electronic devices.

### *Why* It's Important
You use electronic devices every day to make your life easier and more enjoyable.

### Review Vocabulary
**crystal:** a solid substance which has a regularly repeating internal arrangement of atoms

### New Vocabulary
- electronic signal
- analog signal
- digital signal
- semiconductor
- diode
- transistor
- integrated circuit

## Electronic Signals

You've popped some popcorn, put a video in the VCR, and turned off the lights. Now you're ready to watch a movie. The VCR, television, and lamp shown in **Figure 1** use electricity to operate. However, unlike the lamp, the VCR and the TV are electronic devices. An electronic device uses electricity to store, process, and transfer information.

The VCR and the TV use information recorded on the videotape to produce the images and sounds you see as a movie. As the videotape moves inside the VCR, it produces a changing electric current. This changing electric current is the information the VCR uses to send signals to the TV. The TV then uses these signals to produce the images you see and the sounds you hear.

A changing electric current that carries information is an **electronic signal.** The information can be used to produce sounds, images, printed words, numbers, or other data. For example, a changing electric current causes a loudspeaker to produce sound. If the electric current didn't change, no sound would be produced by the loudspeaker. There are two types of electronic signals—analog and digital.

**Analog Signals** Most TVs, VCRs, radios, and telephones process and transmit information that is in the form of analog electronic signals. An **analog signal** is a signal that varies smoothly in time. In an analog electronic signal the electric current increases or decreases smoothly in time, just as your hand can move smoothly up and down.

Electronic signals are not the only types of analog signals. An analog signal can be produced by something that varies in a smooth, continuous way and contains information. For example, a person's temperature changes smoothly and contains information about a person's health.

**Figure 1** A VCR sends electronic signals to the TV, which uses the information in these signals to produce images and sound.

442

---

### Section 1 Resource Manager

**Chapter *FAST FILE* Resources**
Transparency Activity, p. 42
Directed Reading for Content Mastery, pp. 19, 20
Note-taking Worksheets, pp. 31–32
Enrichment, p. 29
Reinforcement, p. 27

Lab Worksheet, p. 56
Lab Activity, pp. 9–12
**Home and Community Involvement,** p. 23
**Lab Management and Safety,** p. 76

**Figure 2** Clocks can be analog or digital devices.

The information displayed on an analog device such as this clock changes continuously.

On this digital clock, the displayed time jumps from one number to another.

**Analog Devices** The clock with hands shown in **Figure 2** is an example of an analog device. The hands move smoothly from one number to the next to represent the time of day. Fluid-filled and dial thermometers also are analog devices. In a fluid-filled thermometer, the height of the fluid column smoothly rises or falls as the temperature changes. In a dial thermometer, a spring smoothly expands or contracts as the temperature changes.

You have used another analog device if you ever have made a recording on a magnetic tape recorder. When voices or music are recorded on magnetic tape, the tape stores an analog signal of the sounds. When you play the tape, the tape recorder converts the analog signal to an electric current. This current changes smoothly with time and causes a loudspeaker to vibrate, recreating the sounds for you to hear.

**Digital Signals** Some devices, such as CD players, use a different kind of electronic signal called a digital signal. Unlike an analog signal, a **digital signal** does not vary smoothly, but changes in jumps or steps. If each jump is represented by a number, a digital signal can be represented by a series of numbers.

**✔ Reading Check** *How is a digital signal different from an analog signal?*

You might have a digital clock or watch similar to the one shown on the right in **Figure 2** that displays the time as numbers. The display changes from 6:29 to 6:30 in a single jump, rather than sweeping smoothly from second to second. You might have seen digital thermometers that display temperature as a number. Some digital thermometers display temperature to the nearest whole degree, such as 23°C. The displayed temperature changes by jumps of 1°C. As a result, temperatures between two whole degrees, such as 22.7°C, are not displayed.

SECTION 1 Electronics **443**

## Differentiated Instruction

**Learning Disabled** Students may benefit from a review of atoms, electrons, and electrical circuits. Remind them that electrons will only flow in a closed circuit.

**IDENTIFYING Misconceptions**

**Direction of Current Flow** Students may not understand the correct way to refer to the direction of current flow in a circuit. On the board, draw a picture of a circuit containing a battery and a lamp. Label the battery terminals negative and positive. Remind students that negative means the terminal is a source of electrons, and positive means the terminal accepts electrons. Explain that although electrons flow from the negative to the positive terminal, the direction of current is conventionally taken to be the direction in which positive charge would flow. So in a circuit containing a battery, conventional current would flow from the positive terminal to the negative terminal.

**✔ Reading Check**

**Answer** An analog signal varies smoothly. A digital signal can have only certain values.

### Discussion

**Watches** Bring to class a digital watch and an analog watch (a watch with hands that mark the time). Display both watches. What are some advantages of each type of watch? Possible answer: It is easier to tell the time to the minute on a digital watch, but an analog watch shows not only the present time, but also how far past one hour it is and how long until the next hour. L2 LS
**Visual-Spatial**

**Figure 3** Point out that in the graph the temperature seems to change in steps, although in reality the temperature changes smoothly. The height of the bars on the graph would be different if the temperature were recorded more often or less often. Ask students how the graph would differ if the temperature had been recorded every thirty minutes instead of every hour. The bars would be narrower and the change in height from one bar to the next would be less, making the graph smoother. **L2** **IS**
**Visual-Spatial**

## Quick Demo

### Analog v. Digital

**Materials** digital thermometer, analog thermometer, container of ice water, container of warm water

**Estimated Time** ten minutes

**Procedure** Place digital and analog thermometers in ice water. Have students note readings. Place digital and analog thermometers in warm water. Have students note readings. Have students discuss which thermometer is more accurate, and which thermometer is easier to use. **L2**
**ELL** **IS** **Visual-Spatial**

## IDENTIFYING
# Misconceptions

**Electronic and Electric** Students may confuse an electronic device with an electrical device. Explain that an electronic device produces or uses a varying electric current that represents information. An electrical device uses the current only to provide energy to the device.

**Digitized Analog Signal**

**Figure 3** A temperature record made by recording the temperature every hour changes in steps and is a digital signal.

**Figure 4** An analog signal can be converted to a digital signal. At a fixed time interval, the strength of the analog signal is measured and recorded. The resulting digital signal changes in steps.

**Analog Signal**

**Digital Signal**

**444** CHAPTER 15 Electronics and Computers

**Making Digital Signals** A smoothly varying analog signal can be converted to a digital signal. For example, suppose you wish to create a record of how the temperature outside changed over a day. One way to do this would be read an outdoor thermometer every hour and record the temperature and time. At the end of the day your temperature record would be a series of numbers. If you used these numbers to make a graph of the temperature record, it might look like the one shown in **Figure 3.** The temperature information shown by the graph changes in steps and is a digital signal.

**Sampling an Analog Signal** By recording the temperature every hour, you have sampled the smoothly varying outdoor temperature. When an analog signal is sampled, a value of the signal is read and recorded at some time interval, such as every hour or every second. An example is shown in **Figure 4.** As a result, a smoothly changing analog signal is converted to a series of numbers. This series of numbers is a digital signal.

The process of converting an analog signal to a digital signal is called digitization. The analog signal on a magnetic tape can be converted to a digital signal by sampling. In this way, a song can be represented by a series of numbers.

**Using Digital Signals** It might seem that analog signals would be more useful than digital signals. After all, when an analog signal is converted to a digital signal, some information is lost. However, think about how analog and digital signals might be stored. Suppose a song that is stored as an analog signal on a small cassette tape were digitized and converted into a series of numbers. It might take millions of numbers to digitize a song, so how could these numbers be stored? As you will see later in this chapter, there is one electronic device that can store these numbers easily—a computer.

Once a digital signal is stored on a computer as a series of numbers, the computer can change these numbers using mathematical formulas. This process changes the signal and is called signal processing. For example, background noise can be removed from a digitized song using signal processing.

# Curriculum Connection

**Music** Using signal processing, even musicians with minimal experience can produce professional quality music. Have students discuss the differences between hearing music produced by nonmusicians using advanced technology and music performed by a professional musician. Students might debate quality of sound or the emotional impact of the sound. **L2** **IS** **Auditory-Musical**

## Active Reading

**Write-Draw-Discuss** This strategy encourages students to actively participate in reading and lectures, assimilating content creatively. Have students write about an idea, clarify it, then make an illustration or drawing. Ask students to share responses with the class and display several examples. Have students Write-Draw-Discuss about analog and digital electronic signals.

**Early Television**

**Vacuum Tube**

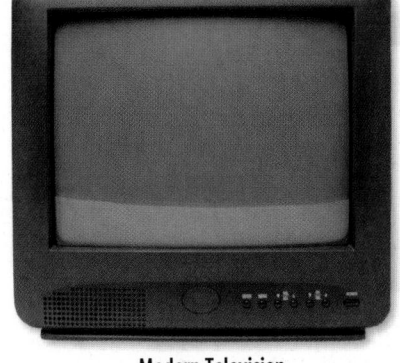

**Modern Television**

## Electronic Devices

An electronic device, such as a calculator or a CD player, uses the information contained in electronic signals to do a job. For example, the job can be adding two numbers together or making sounds and images. The electronic signals are electric currents that flow through circuits in the electronic device. An electronic device, such as a calculator or a VCR, may contain hundreds or thousands of complex electric circuits.

**Electronic Components** The electric circuits in an electronic device usually contain electronic components. These electronic components are small devices that use the information in the electronic signals to control the flow of current in the circuits.

Early electronic devices, such as the early television shown in **Figure 5,** used electronic components called vacuum tubes, such as the one shown in the middle of **Figure 5,** to help create sounds and images. Vacuum tubes were bulky and generated a great deal of heat. As a result, early electronic devices used more electric power and were less dependable than those used today, such as the modern television shown in **Figure 5.** Today, televisions and radios no longer use vacuum tubes. Instead, they contain electronic components made from semiconductors.

## Semiconductors

On the periodic table, the small number of elements found between the metals and nonmetals are called metalloids. Some metalloids, such as silicon and germanium, are semiconductors. A **semiconductor** is an element that is a poorer conductor of electricity than metals but a better conductor than nonmetals. However, semiconductors have a special property that ordinary conductors and insulators lack—their electrical conductivity can be controlled by adding impurities.

**Figure 5** Because early televisions used vacuum tubes, they used more electrical power and were less reliable than their modern versions.

**Science Online**

**Topic: Semiconductor Devices**

Visit in7.msscience.com for Web links to information about semiconductor devices.

**Activity** Choose one semiconductor device and write a paragraph explaining one way that it is used.

## Teacher FYI

**Digital Sound** Sound, such as music, is naturally analog. To convert a sound to a digital signal, the intensity of the sound is measured thousands of times per second. Each of these measurements is assigned a number value that depends on the amplitude of the sound waves. This process is known as digital sound recording.

## Make a Model

**Doped Semiconductors** Have students work in pairs using modeling clay, colored beads, construction paper, or other materials to create two models of doped semiconductors. One model should be an n-type semiconductor and the other should be a p-type semiconductor. Students should use the models to demonstrate how adding impurities to the semiconductor alters its conductivity so that it either donates or accepts electrons. L2 COOP LEARN [IS] **Kinesthetic**

## Use an Analogy

**One-Way Doors** Ask students if they have ever gone into a building that had an in door that could only be pushed inward and an out door that could only be pushed outward. Explain that a diode is similar to these one-way doors. Electrons can only travel one way through the diode.

## Quick Demo

**Electronic Components**

**Materials** diodes, LEDs, transistors, integrated circuits

**Estimated Time** five minutes

**Procedure** Remind students that an integrated circuit can contain thousands of miniature transistors and diodes. L2 [ELL] [IS] **Visual-Spatial**

### ✓ Reading Check

The n-type semiconductor gives electrons and the p-type superconductor takes electrons.

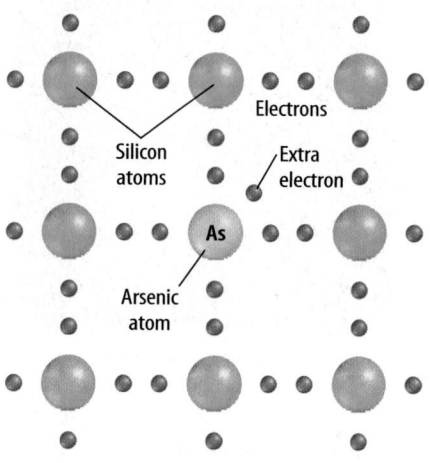

**Figure 6** When arsenic atoms are added to a silicon crystal, they add extra electrons that are free to move about. This causes the electrical conductivity of the silicon crystal to increase.

**Figure 7** Diodes like these allow current to flow in only one direction.

**Adding Impurities** Adding even a single atom of an element such as gallium or arsenic to a million silicon atoms significantly changes the conductivity. This process of adding impurities is called doping.

Doping can produce two different kinds of semiconductors. One type of semiconductor can be created by adding atoms like arsenic to a silicon crystal, as shown in **Figure 6.** Then the silicon crystal contains extra electrons. A semiconductor with extra electrons is an n-type semiconductor.

A p-type semiconductor is produced when atoms like gallium are added to a silicon crystal. Then the silicon crystal has fewer electrons than it had before. An n-type semiconductor can give, or donate, electrons and a p-type semiconductor can take, or accept, electrons.

### ✓ Reading Check
*How are n-type and p-type semiconductors different?*

## Solid-State Components

The two types of semiconductors can be put together to form electronic components that can control the flow of electric current in a circuit. Combinations of n-type and p-type semiconductors can form components that behave like switches that can be turned off and on. Other combinations can form components that can increase, or amplify, the change in an electric current or voltage. Electronic components that are made from combinations of semiconductors are called solid-state components. Diodes and transistors are examples of solid-state components that often are used in electric circuits.

**Diodes** A **diode** is a solid-state component that, like a one-way street, allows current to flow only in one direction. In a diode, a p-type semiconductor is connected to an n-type semiconductor. Because an n-type semiconductor gives electrons and a p-type semiconductor accepts electrons, current can flow from the n-type to the p-type semiconductor, but not in the opposite direction. **Figure 7** shows common types of diodes. Diodes are useful for converting alternating current (AC) to direct current (DC). Recall that an alternating current constantly changes direction. When an alternating current reaches a diode, the diode allows the current to flow in only one direction. The result is direct current.

## Visual Learning

**Figure 6** Point out that silicon atoms have four electrons available for sharing (outer electrons), and arsenic atoms have five. The extra electron moves freely. Gallium has three electrons for sharing. Doping with it creates a "hole" that seems to move as nearby electrons fill the hole. Have students draw the figure using gallium instead of arsenic. L3 [IS] **Visual-Spatial**

## Differentiated Instruction

**Challenge** An integrated circuit is often referred to simply as a chip. Ask students to find out why this is an appropriate name. A chip is a thin, flat piece of something. An integrated circuit is made of a thin slice of semiconductor material. L3 [IS] **Linguistic**

**Transistors** A **transistor** is a solid-state component that can be used to amplify signals in an electric circuit. A transistor also is used as an electronic switch. Electronic signals can cause a transistor to allow current to pass through it or to block the flow of current. **Figure 8** shows examples of transistors that are used in many electronic devices. Unlike a diode, a transistor is made from three layers of n-type and p-type semiconductor material sandwiched together.

**Figure 8** Transistors such as these are used in electric circuits to amplify signals or to act as switches.

**Integrated Circuits** Personal computers usually contain millions of transistors, and would be many times larger if they used transistors the size of those shown in **Figure 8.** Instead, computers and other electronic devices use integrated circuits. An **integrated circuit** contains large numbers of interconnected solid-state components and is made from a single chip of semiconductor material such as silicon. An integrated circuit, like the one shown in **Figure 9,** may be smaller than 1 mm on each side and still can contain millions of transistors, diodes, and other components.

**Figure 9** This tiny integrated circuit contains thousands of diodes and transistors.

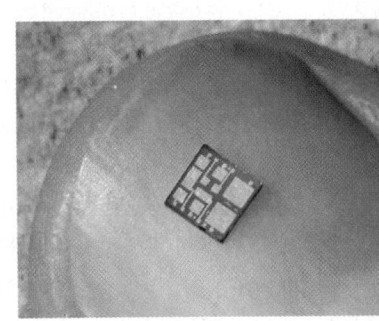

---

## section 1 review

### Summary

**Electronic Signals**

- An electronic signal is a changing electric current that carries information.
- Analog electronic signals change continuously and digital electronic signals change in steps.
- An analog signal can be converted to a digital signal that is a series of numbers.

**Solid-State Components**

- Adding impurities to silicon can produce n-type semiconductors that donate electrons and p-type semiconductors that accept electrons.
- Solid-state components are electronic devices, such as diodes and transistors, made from n-type and p-type semiconductors.
- An integrated circuit contains a large number of solid-state components on a single semiconductor chip.

### Self Check

1. **Explain** why the electric current that flows in a lamp is not an electronic signal.
2. **Describe** two advantages of using integrated circuits instead of vacuum tubes in electronic devices.
3. **Explain** why a digital signal can be stored on a computer.
4. **Compare and contrast** diodes and transistors.
5. **Think Critically** When an analog signal is sampled, what are the advantages and disadvantages of decreasing the time interval?

#### Applying Math

6. **Digital Signal** A song on a cassette tape is sampled and converted to a digital signal that is stored on a computer. The strength of the analog signal produced by the tape is sampled every 0.1 s. If the song is 3 min and 20 s long, how many numbers are in the digital signal stored on the computer?

 nline  in7.msscience.com/self_check_quiz

---

### DAILY INTERVENTION

#### Check for Understanding

**Linguistic** Have students research and report on different ways integrated circuits are fabricated. Students might discuss photolithography (writing on the chips with beams of light), chemical etching (using chemicals to imprint the circuits), or diffusion (adding chemical impurities to the silicon by diffusing). L3 IS

#### Reteach

**Electronic Components** Have students use colored pencils to draw a layer of p-type semiconductor on a layer of n-type semiconductor and label the drawing "Diode." Have them make similar drawings for n-p-n and p-n-p transistors. For each of these, students should draw arrows to represent the direction of electron flow. L2 IS **Visual-Spatial** P

### ✓ Assessment

**Process** Ask students to write paragraphs comparing and contrasting diodes and transistors. Both are solid state components based on doped semiconductors. A diode has an n-type and a p-type semiconductor and allows current to flow in only one direction. A transistor is a layer of three semiconductors. It is used as a switch or to amplify signals. Use **Performance Assessment in the Science Classroom,** p. 159.

---

## section 1 review

1. The electric current in a lamp is steady and does not carry information.
2. Integrated circuits are smaller, lighter, and more reliable than vacuum tubes. Integrated circuits do not generate as much heat as vacuum tubes and do not use as much electricity. Vacuum tubes also break easily.
3. Digital signals can be stored as numbers.
4. Diodes allow current to flow in only one direction. A diode is a p-type semiconductor connected to an n-type semiconductor. A diode converts alternate current to direct current. A transistor can amplify a

signal and can be used as an electronic switch. It contains 3 semiconductors joined together (an n-p-n transistor or a p-n-p transistor).
5. Decreasing the time interval increases the number of signal samples. This enables the analog signal to be converted more accurately to a digital sig-

nal, but increases the amount of information that must be stored.
6. $3 \times 60$ s $= 180$ s; $180$ s $+ 20$ s $= 200$ s; $200/.1 = 2000$ numbers.

## ▶ Real-World Question

**Purpose** Students determine how a current flows through a diode. [L2] [IS] **Kinesthetic**

**Process Skills** observe, infer, compare and contrast, recognize cause and effect, interpret scientific illustrations, communicate

**Time Required** 30 minutes

## ▶ Procedure

**Safety Precautions** Remind students that the part of the wire that isn't insulated can become very hot.

**Teaching Strategy** Test all batteries ahead of time to be sure all are good.

**Troubleshooting** If students' bulbs do not light, have them check their connections.

## ▶ Conclude and Apply

1. The bulb lit up only when an electric current flowed in the bulb.
2. The LED lit up when the wires were connected to the battery terminals in one way, but not the other because current can only flow in one direction through a diode.
3. The bulb lights up when current flows in the bulb, regardless of the current direction. The LED lights up only when current flows in a certain direction.
4. When the LED lights up, the lead from the positive terminal of the battery is attached to the p-type semiconductor and the lead from the negative terminal of the battery is connected to the n-type semiconductor.

# Investigating Diodes

Diodes are found in most electronic devices. They are used to control the flow of electrons through a circuit. Electrons will flow through a diode in only one direction, from the n-type semiconductor to the p-type semiconductor. In this lab you will use a type of diode called an LED (light-emitting diode) to observe how a diode works.

## ▶ Real-World Question

How does electric current flow through a diode?

**Goals**
■ **Create** an electronic circuit.
■ **Observe** how an LED works.

**Materials**
light-emitting diode    D-cell battery and holder
lightbulb and holder    wire

**Safety Precautions**

## ▶ Procedure

1. Set up the circuit shown below. Record your observations. Then reverse the connections so each wire is connected to the other battery terminals. Record your observations.
2. Disconnect the wires from the lightbulb and attach one wire to each end of an LED. Observe whether the LED lights up when you connect the battery.

1.5V Battery    Lightbulb

**448    CHAPTER 15** Electronics and Computers

3. Reverse the connections on the LED so the current goes into the opposite end. Observe whether the LED lights up this time. Record your observation.

## ▶ Conclude and Apply

1. **Explain** why the bulb did or did not light up each time.
2. **Explain** why the LED did or did not light up each time.
3. **Describe** how the behavior of the lightbulb is different from that of the LED.
4. **Infer** which wire on the LED is connected to the n-type semiconductor and which is connected to the p-type semiconductor based on your observations.

### 𝒞ommunicating
**Your Data**

Discuss your results with other students in your class. Did their LEDs behave in the same way? **For more help, refer to the Science Skill Handbook.**

### 𝒞ommunicating
**Your Data**

Have each student prepare a chart explaining the results they obtained in the lab. When comparing their results with those of other students, students should refer to the charts and discuss any differences.

### ✓ Assessment

**Process** Ask students to hypothesize what would happen if they had two LEDs connected in series in the circuit. Have students test their hypotheses. In order for the LEDs to light up, both must be positioned so that the electrons can flow from the n-type to the p-type semiconductor. Use **Performance Assessment in the Science Classroom,** p. 93.

# section 2

Also covers: 7.1.8, 7.2.7 (Detailed standards begin on page IN8.)

# Computers

## What are computers?

When was the last time you used a computer? Computers are found in libraries, grocery stores, banks, and gas stations. Computers seem to be everywhere. A computer is an electronic device that can carry out a set of instructions, or a program. By changing the program, the same computer can be made to do a different job.

Compared to today's desktop and laptop computers, the first electronic computers, like the one shown in **Figure 10,** were much bigger and slower. Several of the first electronic computers were built in the United States between 1946 and 1951. Solid-state components and the integrated circuit had not been developed yet. So these early computers contained thousands of vacuum tubes that used a great deal of electric power and produced large amounts of heat.

Computers became much smaller, faster, and more efficient after integrated circuits became available in the 1960s. Today, even a game system, like the one in **Figure 10,** can carry out many more operations each second than the early computers.

### as you read

**What You'll Learn**
- **Describe** the different parts of a computer.
- **Compare** computer hardware with computer software.
- **Discuss** the different types of memory and storage in a computer.

**Why It's Important**
You can do more with computers if you understand how they work.

**Review Vocabulary**
**laser:** a device that produces a concentrated beam of light

**New Vocabulary**
- binary system
- random-access memory
- read-only memory
- computer software
- microprocessor

**Figure 10** One of the first electronic computers was ENIAC, which was built in 1946 and weighed more than 30 tons. ENIAC could do 5,000 additions per second.

This handheld game system can do millions of operations per second.

SECTION 2 Computers **449**

## 1 Motivate

INTERACTIVE CHALKBOARD
PowerPoint® Presentations

**Bellringer**

**Section Focus Transparencies** also are available on the Interactive Chalkboard CD-ROM.
L2 ELL

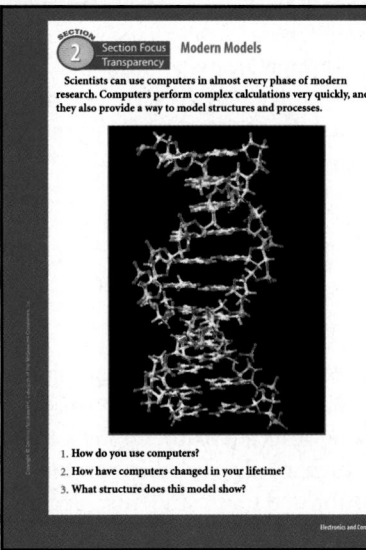

**Section Focus Transparency** Modern Models

Scientists can use computers in almost every phase of modern research. Computers perform complex calculations very quickly, and they also provide a way to model structures and processes.

1. How do you use computers?
2. How have computers changed in your lifetime?
3. What structure does this model show?

Electronics and Computers

### Tie to Prior Knowledge

**Using Computers** Have students discuss the many ways they use computers. They might mention word processing, video games, accessing the Internet, and graphics.

---

## Section 2 Resource Manager

**Chapter *FAST FILE* Resources**
   Transparency Activity, pp. 43, 45–46
   Directed Reading for Content Mastery,
     pp. 21, 22
   MiniLAB, pp. 3, 4

Enrichment, p. 30
Reinforcement, p. 28
Lab Worksheet, pp. 7–8
Lab Activity, pp. 13–16

**Mini LAB**

**Purpose** Students investigate binary numbers. L1 ELL LS

**Kinesthetic**

**Materials** paper, scissors

**Teaching Strategy** Students are most likely to discover all combinations if they make changes in an orderly way.

**Analysis**

1. It doubles.
2. 32

## Assessment

**Process** Have the class produce their own binary code by assigning a letter of the alphabet to each of the five-bit combinations. Have students decide what other characters, such as blank space or a period, could be assigned to the remaining six combinations, and then use their code to send and decipher short messages. Use **Performance Assessment in the Science Classroom,** p 169.

*Try at Home*

## Text Question Answer

no

---

**Mini LAB**

### Using Binary Numbers

**Procedure**

1. Cut out **8 small paper squares.**
2. On four of the squares, draw the number zero, and on the other four, draw the number one.
3. Use the numbered squares to help determine the number of different combinations possible from four binary digits. List the combinations.

**Analysis**

1. From **Table 1** and your results from this MiniLAB, what happens to the number of combinations each time the number of binary digits is increased by one?
2. Infer how many combinations would be possible using five binary digits.

*Try at Home*

### Table 1 Combinations of Binary Digits

| Number of of Binary Digits | Possible Combinations |
|---|---|
| 1 | 0 1 |
| 2 | 00 01 10 11 |
| 3 | 000 001 010 011 100 101 110 111 |

---

# Computer Information

How does a computer display images, generate sounds, and manipulate numbers and words? Every piece of information that is stored in or used by a computer must be converted to a series of numbers. The words you write with a word processor, or the numbers in a spreadsheet are stored in the computer's memory as numbers. An image or a sound file also is stored as a series of numbers. Information stored in this way is sometimes called digital information.

**Binary Numbers** Imagine what it would be like if you had to communicate with just two words—on and off. Could you use these words to describe your favorite music or to read a book out loud? Communication with just two words seems impossible, but that's exactly what a computer does.

All the digital information in a computer is converted to a type of number that is expressed using only two digits—0 and 1. This type of number is called a binary (BI nuh ree) number. Each 0 or 1 is called a binary digit, or bit. Because this number system uses only two digits, it is called the **binary system,** or base-2 number system.

### ✔ Reading Check *Which digits are used in the binary system?*

**Combining Binary Digits** You might think that using only two digits would limit the amount of information you can represent. However, a small number of binary digits can be used to generate a large number of combinations, as shown in **Table 1.**

While one binary digit has only two possible combinations—0 or 1—there are four possible combinations for a group of two binary digits, as shown in **Table 1.** By using just one more binary digit the possible number of combinations is increased to eight. The number of combinations increases quickly as more binary digits are added to the group. For example, there are 65,536 combinations possible for a group of 16 binary digits.

### Representing Information with Binary Digits

Combinations of binary digits can be used to represent information. For example, the English alphabet has 26 letters. Suppose each letter was represented by one combination of binary digits. To represent both lowercase and uppercase letters would require a total of 52 different combinations of binary digits. Would a group of five binary digits have enough possible combinations?

**450** CHAPTER 15 Electronics and Computers

---

**LAB DEMONSTRATION**

**Purpose** demonstrate how electronic switches can represent binary code

**Materials** four D-cell batteries in holders, four 1.5-V light bulbs with sockets, four switches, insulated wire

**Preparation** Connect a battery, a light bulb, and a switch four times.

**Procedure** Start with all switches in the circuits open. This represents the binary code 0000. Close only the second switch. This represents the binary code 0010. Demonstrate other combinations.

**Expected Outcome** Students will be able to determine the possible number of combi-

nations that four bits can make.

## Assessment

**Oral** Ask students how many bits are represented by these four lightbulbs. 4 Ask students how many possible unique combinations can be made with four bits. 16

**Representing Letters and Numbers** A common system that is used by computers represents each letter, number, or other text character by eight binary digits, or one byte. There are 256 combinations possible for a group of eight binary digits. In this system, the letter "A" is represented by the byte 01000001, while the letter "a" is represented by the byte 01100001, and a question mark is represented by 00111111.

## Computer Memory

Why are digital signals stored in a computer as binary numbers? A binary number is a series of bits that can have only one of two values—0 and 1. A switch, such as a light switch on a wall, can have two positions: on or off. A switch could be used to represent the two values of a bit. A switch in the "off" position could represent a 0, and a switch in the "on" position could represent a 1. **Table 2** shows how switches could be used to represent combinations of binary digits.

**Table 2 Representing Binary Digits**

| Binary Number | Switches |
|---|---|
| 0000 | |
| 0001 | |
| 0010 | |
| 0011 | |
| 0100 | |
| 1010 | |

### Applying Science

### How much information can be stored?

Information can be stored in a computer's memory or in storage devices such as hard disks or CDs. The amount of information that can be stored is so large that special units, shown in the table on the right, are used. Desktop computers often have hard disks that can store many gigabytes of information. How much information can be stored in one gigabyte of storage?

**Size of Information Storage Units**

| Information Storage Unit | Number of Bytes |
|---|---|
| kilobyte | 1,024 |
| megabyte | 1,048,576 |
| gigabyte | 1,073,741,824 |

#### Identifying the Problem

When words are stored on a computer, every letter, punctuation mark, and space between words is represented by one byte. A page of text, such as this page, might contain as many as 2,900 characters. So to store a page of text on a computer might require 2,900 bytes.

If you write a page of text using a word-processing program, more bytes might be needed to store the page. This is because when the page is stored, some word-processing programs include other information along with the text.

#### Solving the Problem

1. If it takes 2,900 bytes to store one page of text on a computer, how many pages can be stored in 1 gigabyte of storage?
2. Suppose a book contains 400 pages of text. How many books could be stored on a 1-gigabyte hard disk?
3. A CD can hold 650 megabytes of information. How many 400-page books could be stored on a CD?

### Activity

**ASCII** ASCII (American Standard Code for Information Interchange) is a code used in computers to represent digits, letters, and symbols. For example, the letters *d o g* are assigned the ASCII numbers 100, 111, and 103. These can be represented by the binary numbers 01100100, 01101111, and 01100111. Display a copy of the ASCII table on an overhead projector. Have students use the table to write the letters of their first name in binary numbers. L2 ELL IS **Logical-Mathematical** P

### IDENTIFYING Misconceptions

**Microscopic Switches** Students may think of switches in a computer as mechanical objects that can be flipped one way or the other like a wall switch. Point out that the smallest imaginable mechanical switch would be far too large to use in a computer. Remind students that switches in computer memory are microscopic in size and are made by combining microscopic layers of semiconductor materials. The switch is turned on or off by the movement of electrons.

### Applying Science

**Answers**
1. 1,073,741,824/2,900 = about 370,255 pages
2. 370,255/400 = about 926 books
3. 650 × 1,048,576 = 681,574,400; 681,574,400/2,900/400 = about 588 books

## Curriculum Connection

**Language Arts** Have students find ways the word *binary* is used in other branches of science. Possible answers: In chemistry, a binary compound is composed of two elements. In astronomy, a binary star is two stars revolving about a common center of mass. L2 IS **Linguistic**

## Use an Analogy

**Pencil v. Pen** Compare RAM and ROM to writing with a pencil and writing with an ink pen. Storing information in RAM is like writing with a pencil. You can erase and rewrite the information repeatedly. ROM is like information written in ink. Once it is written, it can't be erased.

**Reading Check**

**Answer** It is lost.

## Teacher **FYI**

**Computer Booting** Turning on a computer is typically called booting the computer. The name for this procedure comes from the term bootstrap, meaning able to function independently of outside direction. When the computer is turned on, the bootstrap program, contained in ROM, transfers the computer's operating system to RAM.

### IDENTIFYING
## Misconceptions

**Computer Chips** Students may not realize that many devices they use every day, such as calculators, televisions, and microwaves, are controlled by tiny computer chips. Explain that computers used this way are known as embedded or hidden computers.

**Figure 11** Computer memory is made of integrated circuits like this one. This integrated circuit can contain millions of microscopic circuits, shown here under high magnification.

---

**Indiana Academic Standard Check**

**7.1.11:** Illustrate how numbers can be represented using sequences of only two symbols . . .

 How many microscopic circuits in a computer's memory are needed to store 1 byte?

 eight

---

**Science Online**

**Topic: Computer Software**
Visit in7.msscience.com for Web links to information about types of computer software.

**Activity** Choose one type of software application and write a paragraph explaining why it is useful. Create a chart that summarizes what the software does.

---

**Storing Information** The memory in a computer is an integrated circuit that contains millions of tiny electronic circuits, as shown in **Figure 11.** In the most commonly used type of computer memory, each circuit is able to store electric charge and can be either charged or uncharged. If the circuit is charged, it represents the bit 1 and if it is uncharged it represents the bit 0. Because computer memory contains millions of these circuits, it can store tremendous amounts of information using only the numbers 1 and 0.

What is your earliest memory? When you remember something from long ago, you use your long-term memory. On the other hand, when you work on a math problem, you may keep the numbers in your head long enough to find the answer. Like you, a computer has a long-term memory and a short-term memory that are used for different purposes.

**Random-Access Memory** A computer's **random-access memory,** or RAM, is short-term memory that stores documents, programs, and data while they are being used. Program instructions and data are temporarily stored in RAM while you are using a program or changing the data.

For example, a computer game is kept in RAM while you are playing it. If you are using a word-processing program to write a report, the report is temporarily held in RAM while you are working on it. Because information stored in RAM is lost when the computer is turned off, this type of memory cannot store anything that you want to use later.

The amount of RAM depends on the number of binary digits it can store. Recall that eight bits is called a byte. A megabyte is more than one million bytes. A computer that has 128 megabytes of memory can store more than 128 million bytes of information in its RAM, or nearly one billion bits.

**Reading Check** *What happens to information in RAM when the computer is turned off?*

**Read-Only Memory** Some information that is needed to enable the computer to operate is stored in its permanent memory. The computer can read this memory, but it cannot be changed. Memory that can't be changed and is permanently stored inside the computer is called **read-only memory,** or ROM. ROM is not lost when the computer is turned off.

**452 CHAPTER 15** Electronics and Computers

---

## Visual Learning

**Figure 11** Point out to students that integrated circuits, such as the one shown here, are much too small to contain large transistors like those shown in **Figure 8.** This figure shows thin strips of metal imprinted onto a small silicon chip. The metal connects microscopic layers of doped silicon that form the transistors and other electronic components. L2 **IS Visual-Spatial**

## Computer Programs

It's your mother's birthday and you decide to surprise her by baking a chocolate cake. You find a recipe for chocolate cake in a cookbook and follow the directions in the order the recipe tells you to. However, if the person who wrote the recipe left out any steps or put them in the wrong order, the cake probably will not turn out the way you expected. A computer program is like a recipe. A program is a series of instructions that tell the computer how to do a job. Unlike the recipe for a cake, some computer programs contain millions of instructions that tell the computer how to do many different jobs.

All the functions of a computer, such as displaying an image on the computer monitor or doing a math calculation, are controlled by programs. These instructions tell the computer how to add two numbers, how to display a word, or how to change an image on the monitor when you move a joystick. Many different programs can be stored in a computer's memory.

**Computer Software** When you type a report, play a video game, draw a picture, or look through an encyclopedia on a computer, you are using computer software. **Computer software** is any list of instructions for the computer. The instructions that are part of the software tell the computer what to display on the monitor. If you respond to what you see, for example by moving the mouse, the software instructions tell the computer how to respond to your action.

## Computer Programming

The process of writing computer software is called computer programming. To write a computer program, you must decide what you want the computer to do, plan the best way to organize the instructions, write the instructions, and test the program to be sure it works. A person who writes computer programs is called a computer programmer. Computer programmers write software in computer languages such as Basic, C++, and Java.

**Figure 12** shows part of a computer program. After the program is written, it is converted into binary digits to enable it to be stored in the computer's memory. Then the computer can carry out the program's instructions.

### Mini LAB

**Observing Memory**

**Procedure**
1. Write a different five-digit number on six 3 × 5 cards.
2. Show a card to a partner for 3 s. Turn the card over and ask your partner to repeat the number. Repeat with two other cards.
3. Repeat this procedure with the last three cards, but wait 20 s before asking your partner to repeat each number.

**Analysis**
Is your partner's memory of the five-digit numbers more like computer RAM or ROM? Explain.

*Try at Home*

**Figure 12** The text below is part of a computer program that directs the operation of a computer.

```
int request_dma(unsigned int dmanr, const char * device_id)
{
    if (dmanr > = MAX_DMA_CHANNELS)
        return -EINVAL;

    if (xchg(&dma_chan_busy[dmanr].lock, 1) != 0)
        return -EBUSY;

    dma_chan_busy[dmanr].device_id = device_id;

    /* old flag was 0, now contains 1 to indicate busy */
    return 0;
} /* request_dma */

void free_dma(unsigned int dmanr)
{
    if (dmanr > = MAX_DMA_CHANNELS) {
        printk("Trying to free DMA%d\n", dmanr);
        return;
    }
```

# Computer Hardware

When you press a key on a computer's keyboard, a letter appears on the screen. This seems to occur all at once, but actually three steps are involved. In the first step, the computer receives information from an input device, such as a keyboard or mouse. For example, when you press a key on the keyboard, the computer receives and stores an electronic signal from the keyboard.

The next step is to process the input signal from the keyboard. This means to change the input signal into an electronic signal that can be understood by the computer monitor. The computer does this by following instructions contained in the programs stored in the computer's memory. The third step is to send the processed signal to the monitor.

All three steps can be carried out with a combination of hardware and software components. Computer hardware consists of input devices, output devices, storage devices, and integrated circuits for storing information. A keyboard and a mouse are examples of input devices, while a monitor, a printer, and loudspeakers are examples of output devices. Storage devices, such as floppy disks, hard disks, and CDs, are used to store information outside of the computer memory. A computer also contains a microprocessor that controls the computer hardware. Examples of computer hardware are shown in **Figure 13.**

**Figure 13** Computer hardware includes input devices, output devices, and storage devices.

**The Microprocessor** Modern computers contain a microprocessor, like the one shown in **Figure 14,** that serves as the brain of the computer. A **microprocessor,** which is also called the central processing unit, or CPU, is an integrated circuit that controls the flow of information between different parts of the computer. A microprocessor can contain millions of interconnected transistors and other components. The microprocessor receives electronic signals from various parts of the computer, processes these signals, and sends electronic signals to other parts of the computer. For example, the microprocessor might tell the hard-disk drive to write data to the hard disk or the monitor to change the image on the screen. The microprocessor does this by carrying out instructions that are contained in computer programs stored in the computer's memory.

The microprocessor was developed in the late 1970s as the result of a process that made it possible to fit thousands of electronic components on a silicon chip. In the 1980s, the number of components on a silicon chip increased to hundreds of thousands. In the 1990s, microprocessors were developed that contained several million components on a single chip.

**Figure 14** The pencil points to the microprocessor in the photo above. This microprocessor has dimensions of about one centimeter on a side, but contains millions of transistors and other solid-state components.

Monitor

Speakers

Printer

Compact disc

SECTION 2 Computers **455**

## Visual Learning

**Figure 14** The small square on the inside of the photo is the microprocessor. The circles arranged outside are electrical connections between the microprocessor and the rest of the computer. Why do you think microprocessors must be produced in a dust-free environment? The microprocessor circuits are so small that even the slightest amount of dust would cause them to malfunction. L2 IS **Logical-Mathematical**

### Quick Demo
**Microprocessors**

**Materials** a microprocessor from a discarded computer

**Estimated Time** five minutes

**Procedure** Show students how small the microprocessor is. Explain that it is encapsulated to prevent dust from damaging the circuits. L2 ELL IS **Visual-Spatial**

## Teacher FYI

**Microprocessors** Some large computers have several microprocessors that work together to perform tasks.

### Virtual Labs

 **Computer Instructions**
*How can a decision tree be used to generate binary numbers?*

## Differentiated Instruction

**Challenge** A microprocessor has three primary tasks: fetch, decode, and execute. Have students research microprocessors and learn about these tasks. They should prepare posters describing what they learn. L3 IS **Visual-Spatial** P

**Recycling Computers** The glass in computer monitors contains lead to shield the user from electromagnetic radiation emitted by the cathode ray tube. The amount of lead and other toxic substances in computers is so high that some states ban them from landfills. Donating old computers to charity or schools is a possibility, but the need for up-to-date technology often makes this difficult. Some states send computers to computer recycling companies where the metal, plastic, and lead glass parts are recycled.

**Research** Have students research where they can bring computer parts for recycling in their communities.

## Activity

**Hard Drives** To show students how information is organized on a hard disk, have them draw about ten concentric circles on a piece of paper. Next, have them draw lines through the center of the circles so that they are divided into eight equal parts. Explain that the concentric circles represent the platter's tracks where information is stored. The slices formed by the diameters split the tracks into sectors. The hard disk is able to retrieve information by labeling these tracks and sectors and remembering the location where information is stored. L2 ELL LS **Visual-Spatial**

## Discussion

**Pocket of Air** Explain to students that the heads of the hard disk don't actually touch the platters. The heads and platters are kept apart by a pocket of air formed as the platters spin. Why is this necessary? The platter would have to be extremely smooth to allow the head to slide over it smoothly. Also, if they touched, the head and the platter would wear out easily. L2 LS **Logical-Mathematical**

**Recycling Computers** Changes in computer technology occur so rapidly that computers are often replaced after being used for only a few years. What happens to old computers? Some computer parts contain lead, mercury, and other toxic substances. Research how toxic materials can be recovered from old computers, and disposed of safely. Summarize your findings in your Science Journal.

**Science Online**

**Topic: Magnetic Disks**
Visit in7.msscience.com for Web links to information about storing data on magnetic disks.

**Activity** Write a paragraph explaining why hard disks can store more information than floppy disks.

## Storing Information

You have decided to type your homework assignment on a computer. The resulting paper is quite long and you make many changes to it each time you read it. How does the computer make it possible for you to store your information and make changes to it?

Both RAM and ROM are integrated circuits inside the computer. You might wonder, then, why other types of information storage are needed. Information stored in RAM is lost when the computer is turned off, and information stored in ROM can only be read—it can't be changed. If you want to store information that can be changed but isn't lost when the computer is off, you must store that information on a storage device, such as a disk. Several different types of disks are available.

**Hard Disks** A hard disk is a device that stores computer information magnetically. A hard disk is usually located inside a computer. **Figure 15** shows the inside of a hard disk, and **Figure 16** shows how a hard disk stores data. The hard disk contains one or more metal disks that have magnetic particles on one surface. When you save information on a hard disk, a device called a read/write head inside the disk drive changes the orientation of the magnetic particles on the disk's surface. Orientation in one direction represents 0 and orientation in the opposite direction represents 1. When a magnetized disk is read, the read/write head converts the digital information on the disk to pulses of electric current.

Information stored magnetically cannot be read by the computer as quickly as information stored on RAM and ROM. However, because the information on a hard disk is stored magnetically rather than with electronic switches like RAM, the information isn't lost when the computer is turned off.

**Figure 15** A hard disk contains a disk or platter that is coated with magnetic particles. A read/write head moves over the surface of the disk.

## Science Journal

**The Information Age** The age we live in is sometimes referred to as the Information Age because so much information is available to everyone. Have each student write a paragraph in his or her Science Journal discussing the relationship between the development of digital computers and the increase in the amount of information available to people. L2 LS **Linguistic**

## Fun Fact

Modern hard drives may have platters with more than 60,000 tracks per inch. Some platters spin more than 10,000 times per second.

**NATIONAL GEOGRAPHIC**

**Figure 16**

**C**omputers are useful because they can process large amounts of information quickly. Almost all desktop computers use a hard disk to store information. A hard disk is an electronic filing cabinet that can store enormous amounts of information and retrieve them quickly.

Read/Write head

Platters

**A** A hard-disk drive is made of a stack of aluminum disks, called platters, that are coated with a thin layer that contains magnetic particles. Like tiny compasses, these particles will line up along magnetic field lines. The hard disk also contains read/write heads that contain electromagnets. When the hard disk is turned on, the platters spin under the heads.

Read/Write head

Magnetic particles

N

S

S

N

**B** To write information on the disk, a magnetic field is created around the head by an electric current. As the platter rotates past the head, this magnetic field causes the magnetic particles on the platter to line up in bands. One direction of the bands corresponds to the digital bit 0, the other to the digital bit 1.

**C** To read information on the disk, no current is sent to the heads. Instead, the magnetized bands create a changing current in the head as it passes over the platter. This current is the electronic signal that represents the needed information.

SECTION 2 Computers **457**

## Visualizing a Hard Disk

Have students examine the pictures and read the captions. Then ask the following questions.

Why is it important for hard drives to be enclosed in a metal casing? The metal casing keeps out dust that could get in the space between a head and a platter, preventing it from working properly.

Why is more than one platter used in most hard drives? to increase the amount of information that can be stored on the hard drive

### Activity

**Investigate Hard Drives** Obtain an old hard drive from a computer repair store. Open it and allow students to identify the platters, read/write heads, and actuator arms. Point out that each platter has a head on either side of it. Explain that when the hard drive is off, the heads rest on the platters. When the platters spin, the air flow forces the heads slightly away from the surface.

## Teacher **FYI**

**Capacitors** Each bit of information is stored on RAM in a capacitor. A charged capacitor has a value of 1, and a capacitor without charge has a value of 0. Capacitors must be read and recharged hundreds of times every second. This is why information stored on RAM is lost when the computer is turned off.

**Floppy Disks** Storing information on a hard disk is convenient, but sometimes you might want to store information that you can carry with you. The original storage device of this type was the floppy disk. A floppy disk is a thin, flexible, plastic disk. You might be confused by the term *floppy* if you have heard it used to describe disks that seem quite rigid. That is because you don't actually hold the floppy disk. Instead, you hold the harder plastic case in which the floppy disk is encased. Just as for a hard disk, the floppy disk is coated with a magnetic material that is magnetized and read by a read/write head. Floppy disks have lower storage capacity than hard disks. Also, compared to hard disks, information is read from and written to floppy disks much more slowly.

**Optical Disks** An optical storage disk, such as a CD, is a thin, plastic disk that has information digitally stored on it. The disk contains a series of microscopic pits and flat spots as shown on the left in **Figure 17.** A tiny laser beam shines on the surface of the disk. The information on the disk is read by measuring the intensity of the laser light reflected from the surface of the disk. This intensity will depend on whether the laser beam strikes a pit or a flat spot. The original optical storage disks, laser discs, CD-ROMs, and DVD-ROMs, were read-only. Several of these are shown on the right in **Figure 17.** However, CD-RW disks can be erased and rewritten many times. Information is written by a CD burner that causes a metal alloy in the disk to change form when heated by a laser. When the disk is read, the intensity of reflected laser light depends on which form of the alloy the beam strikes.

**Figure 17** An optical storage disk stores information that is read by a laser.

**Explain** the difference between a read-only disk and a reusable disk.

Information is stored on an optical disk by a series of pits and flat spots, representing a binary 1 or 0.

CDs, laser disks, and DVDs are all examples of optical storage disks.

## Computer Networks

People can communicate using a computer if it is part of a computer network. A computer network is two or more computers that are connected to share files or other information. The computers might be linked by cables, telephone lines, or radio signals.

The Internet is a collection of computer networks from all over the world. The Internet is linked together by cable or satellite. The Internet itself has no information. No documents or files exist on the Internet, but you can use the Internet to access a tremendous amount of information by linking to other computers.

The World Wide Web is part of the Internet. The World Wide Web is the ever-changing collection of information (text, graphics, audio, and video) on computers all over the world. The computers that store these documents are called servers. When you connect with a server through the Internet, you can view any of the Web documents that are stored there, like the Web page shown in **Figure 18.** A particular collection of information that is stored in one place is known as a Web site.

**Figure 18** When you connect to the Internet, you can be linked with other computers that are part of the World Wide Web. Then you can have access to the information stored at millions of Web sites.

---

### section 2 review

#### Summary

**Computer Information**
- A binary digit can be a 0 or a 1.
- Computers store information as groups of binary digits.
- Computers use tiny electronic circuits to represent binary digits and store information.

**Computer Software and Hardware**
- Computer software and computer programs are lists of instructions for a computer.
- Computer programs are written in special computer languages.
- Computer hardware, such as keyboards and hard disks, is controlled by a microprocessor.

**Storing Information**
- Hard disks and floppy disks store information on disks coated with magnetic particles.
- Optical disks store information as a series of pits and flat spots that is read by a laser.

#### Self Check

1. **Explain** why the binary number system is used for storing information in computers.

2. **Compare and contrast** the Internet and the World Wide Web.

3. **Describe** what a microprocessor does with the signals it receives from various parts of a computer.

4. **Compare and contrast** three different computer information storage devices.

5. **Think Critically** Why can't computer information be stored only in RAM and ROM, making storage devices such as hard disks and optical disks unnecessary?

#### Applying Skills

6. **Make a Concept Map** Develop a spider map about computers. Include the following terms in your spider map: *keyboard, monitor, microprocessor, software, printer, RAM, ROM, floppy disk, hard disk, CD, Internet,* and *World Wide Web*.

**Science** Online in7.msscience.com/self_check_quiz

---

### 3 Assess

#### DAILY INTERVENTION

**Check for Understanding**

**Logical-Mathematical** Ask students to explain why optical disks are a better choice than floppy disks for storing information for a long time. The magnetization on a floppy disk is likely to degrade with time, and the information will be lost. L2 LS

**Reteach**

**Computer-Related Terms** Write the headings *hardware, software,* and *other* on the board. Have students recall new vocabulary words. Have them place the new word under a heading and state their reason for doing so. Words under *hardware* might include microprocessor, floppy disk, and Internet. Words under *software* might include programs and the World Wide Web. Words under *other* might include byte and random-access memory. L2 LS
**Logical-Mathematical**

### ☑ Assessment

**Oral** If a computer has 256 megabytes of memory, does this refer to RAM, ROM, or memory on the hard disk? RAM

---

### section 2 review

1. Binary numbers use only two digits. Information represented by binary numbers can be stored by on/off switches.

2. The World Wide Web contains information from all over the world. The Internet contains no information. One can use the Internet to access the World Wide Web.

3. It processes the signals and sends other signals to the various parts of the computer.

4. Floppy and hard disks use magnetic memory. Hard disks are internal, but floppy disks are external. Optical disks are external but they store information as pits and flat spots on the disk.

5. Information stored in RAM is erased when the computer is turned off. Information in ROM cannot be changed easily.

6. Check students' work.

## Use the Internet

### ▶ Real-World Question

#### Purpose

**Internet** Students use Internet sites that can be accessed through in7.msscience.com/internet_lab.

Students can post their findings on the site and get information from other schools around the country.

**Non-Internet Sources** Students can obtain library books that describe computer viruses and discuss the problem with network administrators at schools, libraries, or businesses.

**Time Required** one week

### ▶ Make a Plan

#### Preparation

**Internet** Use the Internet site on the student text to run through the steps that the students will follow.

**Non-Internet** Bring books to class about computers that contain information on computer viruses.

**Virus Protection** Computer viruses can be avoided by being aware of the problem and taking proper precautions.

### ▶ Follow Your Plan

**Teaching Strategy** You might also want to have students research other harmful computer programs that are similar to viruses (*i.e.*, Trojan horses, logic bombs, and worms). Have students find out how each of these affects a computer.

### Goals

- **Understand** what a computer virus is.
- **Identify** different types of computer viruses.
- **Describe** how a computer virus is spread.
- **Create** a plan for protecting electronic files and computers from computer viruses.

### Data Source

**Science Online**

Visit in7.msscience.com/internet_lab to get more information about computer viruses and for data collected by other students.

# Does your computer have a virus?

### ▶ Real-World Question

The Internet has provided many ways to share information and become connected with people near and far. People can communicate ideas and information quickly and easily. Unfortunately, some people use computers and the Internet as an opportunity to create and spread computer viruses. Many new viruses are created each year that can damage information and programs on a computer. Viruses create problems for computers in homes and schools. Computer problems caused by viruses can be costly for business and government computers as well. How can acquiring and transmitting computer viruses be prevented?

### ▶ Make a Plan

People share information and ideas by exchanging electronic files with one another. Perhaps you send email to your friends and family. Many people send word processing or spreadsheet files to friends and associates. What happens if a computer file is infected with a virus? How is that virus spread among different users? How can you protect your computer and your information from being attacked by a virus?

## Differentiated Instruction

**Learning Disabled** Students who are not as capable or experienced with using a computer for Internet searches can be paired with students who can provide guidance.

## Alternative Inquiry Lab

**Other Viruses** To extend this Lab into an Inquiry Lab, have students make a biology connection by researching how biological viruses work, and drawing an analogy to computer viruses. Exploring the exponential growth patterns of biological viruses in cells will help them understand how they propagate so quickly through computer systems. Students may write a paragraph to explain their analogy.

### Follow Your Plan

1. Do research to find out what a computer virus is and the difference between various types of viruses. Also research the ways that a computer virus can damage computer files and programs.

2. After you know what a computer virus is, make a list of different types of viruses and how they are passed from computer to computer. For example, some viruses can be passed through attachments to email. Others can be passed by sharing spreadsheet files. Be specific about how a virus is passed.

3. Discover how you can protect yourself from viruses that attack your computer. Make a list of steps to follow to avoid infection.

4. Make sure your teacher approves your plan before you start.

5. Visit the link below to post your data.

### Analyze Your Data

1. **Explain** how computer viruses are transferred from one computer to another.

2. **Explain** how you can prevent your computer from becoming infected by a virus.

3. **Explain** how you can prevent other people from getting computer viruses.

4. **Describe** what steps you should take to make sure you do not spread viruses to the computers of people you share information with.

5. **Describe** the different ways computer viruses can damage computer files and programs.

### Conclude and Apply

1. **List** five to eight steps a computer user should follow to prevent getting a computer virus or passing a computer virus to another computer.

2. **Discuss** how antivirus software can keep viruses from spreading. Could antivirus software always prevent you from getting a computer virus? Why or why not?

### Communicating Your Data

Find this lab using the link below. Post your data in the table that is provided. **Compare** your data on types of viruses and how they infect computers with that of other students.

in7.msscience.com/internet_lab

### Analyze Your Data

1. Possible answer: by opening infected e-mail attachments, copying or downloading infected files

2. Possible answers: Install virus protection. Don't open unknown e-mail attachments or copy programs unless you know they are not infected. Obtain software only from legitimate sources; use scanning or monitoring software on your computer; use only write-protected disks.

3. Possible answers: Don't share suspicious files without checking them. Be sure that files sent with e-mail don't contain viruses.

4. Possible answers: They can make your hard disk unusable, make files unreadable, alter programs so they cannot be run, and mail themselves to addresses on your e-mail address list.

5. Viruses can damage files and programs so that they are no longer useable. They also can alter programs so that the programs transmit the virus to other files and programs on different computers. Some viruses can erase the programs and files on a hard disk.

### Conclude and Apply

1. Possible answers: Don't open unknown e-mail attachments. Use up-to-date anti-virus software. Don't copy unknown files. Don't download Internet files unless they are checked by anti-virus software. See if your software provider has software security patches. Use write-protected disks. Obtain software only from legitimate sources.

2. It identifies a virus and deletes it. It compares files with known viruses. It checks to see if an unknown program is trying to alter the operating system on your computer. A virus could still infect your operating system if anti-virus software is not up-to-date or if the type of virus is unknown.

### Assessment

**Pamphlets** Have groups of students design and produce pamphlets about computer viruses and security measures. Some of the best pamphlets can be copied and distributed to other students in the school. Use **Performance Assessment in the Science Classroom,** p. 129.

### Communicating Your Data

Have students use their data and the data they find at the link in the lab to prepare posters about the types of viruses and ways to protect against them. The posters can be displayed at various places throughout the school for other students to see. L2 LS **Visual-Spatial**

# TIME ) SCIENCE AND
## Society

**SCIENCE ISSUES THAT AFFECT YOU!**

## Content Background

There are many different types of books being converted into electronic books. Books being converted range in subject from education and government, to medicine, to name a few.

There are a number of different formats that can be adapted depending on the publisher's specifications. E-books can simply be book text that appears on the screen or clients can order a reformatted edition of a text with links to web pages and slick graphics. It can take anywhere from a few weeks to four months to complete such a conversion.

## Discussion

**E-books** What are some of the benefits e-books provide that traditional books cannot? Answers should include that e-books save space in that many books can be stored in one unit. Also more information can be accessed such as photos and videos of a subject, as well as provide links to other sources. Also, the reading experience can be more interactive. L2 IS **Logical-Mathematical**

## Activity

**Making an E-book** Have each student choose a favorite book to convert into an e-book. Remind students that they can include illustrations or photos that are not printed in the book. They can also include more information about the author or addresses of related web sites. Allow students to collaborate and share ideas for this project. Have them report on the plot of the book as well as how the student designed the e-book and how the changes affect the experience of reading the book.

# E-Lectrifying E-Books

**Here's a look at how computers and the Internet are changing what—and how—you read**

**All of these stacked books can fit into one e-book.**

In recent years, people have been using their computers to order books from online bookstores. That's no big deal. What might become a big deal is the ordering of electronic books—books that you download to your own computer and read on the screen or print out to read later. Some famous authors are writing books just for that purpose. Some of the books are published only online—you can't find them anywhere else.

Many other Web sites, however, are selling any book anybody wishes to write—including students like you. In fact, you could start your own online bookstore with your own stories and reports. It will be up to readers to pick and choose what's good from the huge number of e-books that will be on the Web.

## Curling Up with a Good Disk

Downloading books to your home computer is just one way to get an e-book. You can also buy versions of books to read on hand-held devices that are about the size of a paperback book. With one device, the books come on CD-ROM disks. With another, the books download to the device over a modem.

Current e-book devices are expensive, heavy, and awkward, and the number of books you can get for them is small. But if improvements come quickly, it might not be long before you check out of the library with a pocketful of disks instead of a heavy armload of books!

## Will Traditional Books Disappear?

Most people think that the traditional printed book will never disappear. Publishers will still be printing books on paper with soft and hard covers. But publishers also predict there will be more and more kinds of formats for books. E-books, for example, might be best for interactive works that blend video, sound, and words the way many Web sites already do. For example, an e-book biography might allow the reader to click on photos and videos of the subject, and even provide links to other sources of information.

**Interview** Talk to a bookstore employee to find out how book publishing and selling has changed in the last five years. Can he or she predict how people will read books in the future? Report to the class.

**Science online**

**For more information, visit in7.msscience.com/time**

**Interview** Provide students with a list of bookstores in your area. If possible, include in the list booksellers who deal specifically with used books. Require each student to speak to both sellers of new books and sellers of used books, as there should be some differences as well as similarities in the information they provide.

## Resources for Teachers and Students

*Instant American History of the 20th Century*, by Richard Rubin, Format: Microsoft Reader. ibooks, inc.

*Careers in Computers*, by Lile B. Stair, Leslie Stair, Format: Adobe Reader, McGraw-Hill

## Reviewing Main Ideas

### Section 1  Electronics

1. A changing electric current used to carry information is an electronic signal. Electronic signals can be either analog or digital.

2. Semiconductor elements, such as silicon and germanium, conduct electricity better than nonmetals but not as well as metals. If a small amount of some impurities is added to a semiconductor, its conductivity can be controlled.

3. Diodes and transistors are solid-state components. Diodes allow current to flow in one direction only. Transistors are used as switches or amplifiers.

### Section 2  Computers

1. The binary system consists of two digits, 0 and 1. Switches within electronic devices such as computers can store information by turning on (1) and off (0).

2. Electronic memory within a computer can be random-access (RAM) or read-only (ROM).

3. Computer hardware consists of the physical parts of a computer. Computer software is a list of instructions for a computer.

4. A microprocessor is a complex integrated circuit that receives signals from various parts of the computer, processes these signals, and then sends instructions to various parts of the computer.

5. Floppy disks, hard disks, and optical disks are types of computer information storage devices.

6. The Internet is a collection of linked computer networks from all over the world. The World Wide Web is part of the Internet.

## Reviewing Main Ideas

Summary statements can be used by students to review the major concepts of the chapter.

## Visualizing Main Ideas

See student page.

**Science** Online

**Visit** in7.msscience.com
/self_check_quiz
/interactive_tutor
/vocabulary_puzzlemaker
/chapter_review
/standards_review

### Assessment Transparency

For additional assessment questions, use the *Assessment Transparency* located in the transparency book.

## Visualizing Main Ideas

*Copy and complete the following concept map on computers.*

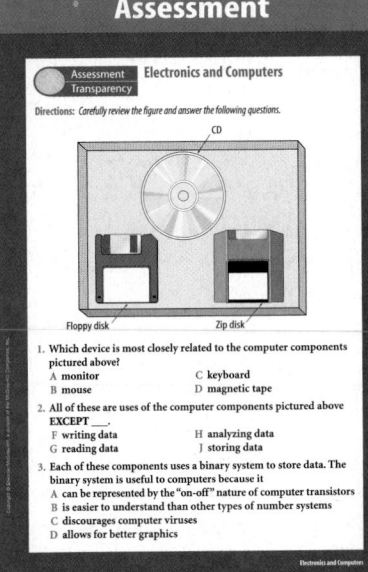

## Using Vocabulary

1. binary system
2. diode
3. integrated circuit
4. RAM
5. transistor
6. microprocessor
7. analog signal

## Checking Concepts

| | |
|---|---|
| 8. D | 12. D |
| 9. C | 13. A |
| 10. C | 14. B |
| 11. B | 15. C |

## Thinking Critically

16. Possible answer: A liquid thermometer is analog and displays temperature variations smoothly as liquid expands and contracts. A digital camera has sensors that convert light into an electrical signal that is stored in digital form.

17. A diode has two semiconductors, one n-type and one p-type. It can be used to change AC to DC. A transistor has three semiconductor layers. It is used as a switch or to amplify signals. An integrated circuit has many interconnected solid-state components on a semiconductor chip. Integrated circuits can be used as microprocessors and to electronically control devices such as video cameras.

18. Binary has two digits rather than ten. On/off switches in a computer can be used to represent information using the binary system.

19. See student page.

20. Before integrated circuits were developed, computers were larger, used more power, and were less reliable.

## Using Vocabulary

| | |
|---|---|
| analog signal p. 442 | microprocessor p. 455 |
| binary system p. 450 | random access |
| computer software p. 453 | memory p. 452 |
| digital signal p. 443 | read-only memory p. 452 |
| diode p. 446 | semiconductor p. 445 |
| electronic signal p. 442 | transistor p. 447 |
| integrated circuit p. 447 | |

*Fill in the blanks with the correct vocabulary word or words.*

1. _____ is a base-2 number system.

2. A(n) _____ can change AC current to DC current.

3. A(n) _____ is made from a single piece of semiconductor material and can contain thousands of solid-state components.

4. The information in a computer's _____ changes each time the computer is used.

5. An electronic device that can be used as a switch or to amplify electronic signals is a(n) _____.

6. A(n) _____ is also called a CPU.

7. An electronic signal that varies smoothly with time is a(n) _____.

## Checking Concepts

*Choose the word or phrase that best answers the question.*

8. Which of the following best describes integrated circuits?
   A) They can be read with a laser.
   B) They use vacuum tubes as transistors and diodes.
   C) They contain pits and flat areas.
   D) They can be small and contain a large number of solid-state components.

9. Which type of elements are semiconductors?
   A) metals          C) metalloids
   B) nonmetals       D) gases

10. How is a digital signal different from an analog signal?
    A) It uses electric current.
    B) It varies continuously.
    C) It changes in steps.
    D) It is used as a switch.

11. Which of the following uses magnetic materials to store digital information.
    A) DVD             C) RAM
    B) hard disk       D) compact disk

12. Which part of a computer carries out the instructions contained in computer programs and software?
    A) RAM             C) hard disk
    B) ROM             D) microprocessor

13. Which type of computer memory is used when a computer is first turned on?
    A) ROM             C) DVD
    B) RAM             D) floppy disk

14. The instructions contained in a computer program are stored in which type of computer memory while the program is being used?
    A) ROM             C) CD
    B) RAM             D) floppy disk

**Use the figure below to answer question 15.**

15. What binary number is represented by the positions of the switches?
    A) 1110            C) 0101
    B) 0010            D) 0001

Science Online in7.msscience.com/vocabulary_puzzlemaker

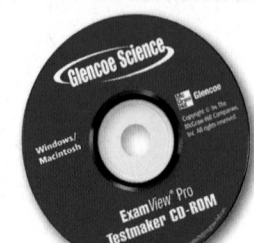

**Use the ExamView® Pro Testmaker CD-ROM to:**
- create multiple versions of tests
- create modified tests with one mouse click for inclusion students
- edit existing questions and add your own questions
- build tests aligned with state standards using built-in State Curriculum Tags
- change English tests to Spanish with one mouse click and vice versa

## Thinking Critically

**16. Compare and contrast** an analog device and a digital device.

**17. Make and Use Tables** Copy and complete the following table that describes solid-state components.

### Solid-State Components

| Component | Description | Use |
|---|---|---|
| Diode | | |
| Transistor | | |
| Integrated circuit | | |

**18. Explain** why the binary number system is used to store digital information in computers, instead of the decimal number system you use every day.

**19. Concept Map** Copy and complete the following events-chain map showing the sequence of events that occurs when a computer mouse is moved.

Mouse is moved by computer user

↓

Signal is sent to microprocessor

↓

Microprocessor processes signal

↓

Microprocessor sends signal to monitor

↓

Mouse pointer moves on screen

**20. Discuss** how the development of solid-state components and integrated circuits affected devices such as TVs and computers.

**21. Make a table** to classify the different types of internal and external computer memory and storage.

## Performance Activities

**22. Make a Poster** Microprocessors continue to be developed that are more complex and contain an ever-increasing number of solid state components. Visit **in7.msscience.com** for links to information about different microprocessors and how they have changed. Make a poster that summarizes what you have learned.

## Applying Math

Students at a middle school researched the storage capacity of different computer storage devices. The information is summarized in the table below. The storage capacity is listed in units of gigabytes. A gigabyte is 1,074,000,000 bytes.

**Use the table below to answer questions 23–25.**

### Computer Storage Devices

| Device | Capacity (Gb) |
|---|---|
| Floppy disk | 0.00144 |
| Compact disc | 0.650 |
| DVD | 4.7 |
| Hard Disk A | 8.60 |
| Hard Disk B | 120.2 |

**23. Music Files Storage** In a certain format, to store 1 min of music as a digital signal requires 10,584,000 bytes. How many minutes of music in this format can be stored on the compact disc?

**24. Digital Pictures Storage** A certain digital camera produces digital images that require 921,600 bytes to store. How many of these images could be stored on hard disk A?

**25. Documents Storage** Seven documents produced by word processing software are stored on a floppy disk. If there are 40,000 bytes of storage still available on the disk, what is the average amount of storage used by each of the documents?

 **Science** nline  in7.msscience.com/chapter_review

**21.** ROM (read-only) and RAM (random access) are internal electronic memory. Floppy disks are external magnetic memory. Optical disks are external and store information as pits and flat spots on disks. Hard disks are magnetic and usually internal.

## Performance Activities

**22.** Students could investigate how the newest microprocessors are used as well as their speed and performance abilities. They could also research state-of-the-art techniques for producing microprocessors. Use **PASC,** p. 91.

## Applying Math

### Indiana Math Standards
7.2.1, 7.3.1
**23.** 65.95 minutes
**24.** 10,022
**25.** 215,222 bytes

**CHAPTER REVIEW** 465

---

### ✓ Assessment  Resources

📁 **Reproducible Masters**
**Chapter Fast File Resources**
   Chapter Review, pp. 35–36
   Chapter Tests, pp. 37–40
   Assessment Transparency Activity, p. 47
**Glencoe Science Web site**
   Chapter Review Test
   IN Standards Review

**Glencoe Technology**
🔦 Assessment Transparency
💿 ExamView® Pro Testmaker
📼 MindJogger Videoquiz
🔵 Interactive Chalkboard

**Answer Sheet** A practice answer sheet can be found at in7.msscience.com/answer_sheet.

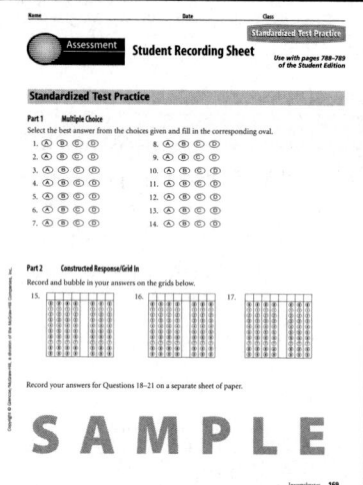

**Part 1 | Multiple Choice**

| 1. | B | 5. | C |
|----|---|----|---|
| 2. | C | 6. | C |
| 3. | C | 7. | B |
| 4. | B | | |

**Part 2 | Critical Response**

8. A monitor is an output device that lets the computer communicate with the operator. It lets you see what you have typed into the computer. A keyboard is an input device. It lets you type in the report. The hard drive is a storage device. It stores the word-processing program you are using, and file that the word-processing program produces.

9. A floppy disk is a thin, flexible, plastic disk. It is coated with a magnetic material that is magnetized and read by a read/write head. An optical disk is a thin, plastic disk. It has a series of microscopic pits and flat spots. The information on the disk is read by measuring the intensity of laser light reflected from the disk's surface. Optical disks also can be written to by a CD burner that uses a laser.

---

The assessed Indiana standard appears above the question.

*Record your answers on the answer sheet provided by your teacher or on a sheet of paper.*

**Part 1 | Multiple Choice**

The table below shows the number of combinations for different numbers of binary digits.

**Number of Binary Digit Combinations**

| Number of Binary Digits | Total Number of Combinations |
|---|---|
| 1 | 2 |
| 2 | 4 |
| 3 | 8 |
| 4 | ? |
| 5 | 32 |

**7.1.11**

1. What is the total number of combinations of four binary digits?

A  8

B  16

C  32

D  64

**7.1.11**

2. Based on the trend in the table above, what is the total number of combinations of six binary digits?

A  40

B  44

C  64

D  96

---

3. What materials are used to make solid-state components?

A  conductors

B  insulators

C  semiconductors

D  superconductors

4. Which best describes computer software?

A  It is the central processing unit.

B  It is a list of instructions.

C  It is a type of magnetic disk.

D  It is a type of optical disk.

5. The graph below shows a digitized signal.

What is the process that produces this digital signal from an analog signal?

A  doping

B  programming

C  sampling

D  switching

---

10. The memory in a computer is an integrated circuit that consists of millions of tiny electrical circuits. Each circuit can be either charged, which corresponds to a binary one, or uncharged, which corresponds to a binary zero. In this way, binary numbers can be stored in memory as groups of microcircuits that are charged and uncharged.

11. To write information, an electric current in a read/write head produces a magnetic field around the head. This magnetic field causes magnetic particles on the platter to line up in bands. The direction of the bands corresponds to a binary zero or one.

12. To read information, the magnetic bands on the platter produce an electric current in the head as the platter rotates past the head. This electric current changes as different bands move past the head. The changing current is the electronic signal corresponding to the information stored on the disk.

**6.** Which is **NOT** an electronic device?

  **A** calculator

  **B** CD player

  **C** lightbulb

  **D** television

**7.** The illustration below shows arsenic atoms in a silicon crystal.

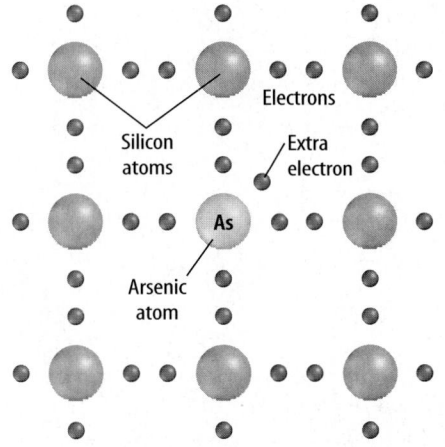

Adding atoms of other elements to a semiconductor material mainly affects which physical property?

  **A** density

  **B** electrical conductivity

  **C** heat generated

  **D** weight

---

**Test-Taking Tip**

**Some Questions Have Qualifiers** Look for qualifiers in a question. Such questions are not looking for absolute answers. Qualifiers could be words such as *best describes, most common,* or *least common.*

---

## Part 2   Critical Response

**7.1.11**

**8.** Classify each of the following as an input, output, or storage device: monitor, keyboard, printer, hard disk. Explain the function of each device if you are using a word processing program to write a report.

**7.1.11**

**9.** Compare and contrast a floppy disk with an optical disk, such as a CD.

**7.1.11**

**10.** Explain why electric circuits that can be charged or uncharged are used as the components of computer memory.

The photo below shows a hard disk drive.

**7.1.11**

**11.** Describe how the read/write heads write information on a platter in the hard disk drive.

**7.1.11**

**12.** Describe how the read/write heads read information that is stored on the platters in the hard disk drive shown in the photo above.

## Rubrics

The following rubric is a sample scoring device for critical response questions.

**Critical Response**

| Points | Description |
|--------|-------------|
| 4 | The student demonstrates a thorough understanding of the science of the task. The response may contain minor flaws that do not detract from the demonstration of a thorough understanding. |
| 3 | The student demonstrates an understanding of the science of the task. The response is essentially correct and demonstrates an essential but less than thorough understanding of the science. |
| 2 | The student demonstrates only a partial understanding of the science of the task. Although the student may have used the correct approach to a solution or may have provided a correct solution, the work lacks an essential understanding of the underlying science concepts. |
| 1 | The student demonstrates a very limited understanding of the science of the task. The response is incomplete and exhibits many flaws. |
| 0 | The student provides a completely incorrect solution or no response at all. |

## Unit Contents

 **WebQuest** *Created Gemstones: The Real Thing?* is a real-world scenario. Students research how natural gems form, what their chemical, physical, and optical properties are, how their flaws are corrected, and their colors enhanced. Students will compare the laboratory processes used to create gems, their prices and properties, and decide if they are the same as their natural counterparts. They must be able to give their reasons and justify their decision.

# How Are Canals & the Paleozoic Era Connected?

**B**efore the invention of the locomotive, canals, such as the one at upper right, were an important means of transportation. In the 1790s, an engineer traveled around England to study new canals. The engineer noticed something odd: All across the country, certain types of rocks seemed to lie in predictable layers, or strata. And the same strata always had the same kinds of fossils in them. Since each layer of sedimentary rock typically forms on top of the previous one, scientists realized that the strata recorded the history of life on Earth. By the mid-1800s, the known rock strata had been organized into a system that we now know as the geologic time scale. In this system, Earth's history is divided into units called eras, which in turn are divided into periods. Many of the rock layers in the Grand Canyon (background) date from the Paleozoic, or "ancient life," Era.

468

**PROJECT**
**CRISS** SM

**Study Skills**

**Organize Information** Frame-use is an effective strategy when comparing various concepts. Have students break into cooperative teams. Each member of the team researches a time period in Earth's history. After researching the period, including the characteristics of Earth and the flora and fauna present during the period, they can compile their findings on a content frame.

| | Triassic | Jurassic | Cretaceous |
|---|---|---|---|
| Flora | | | |
| Fauna | | | |
| Earth's characteristics | | | |

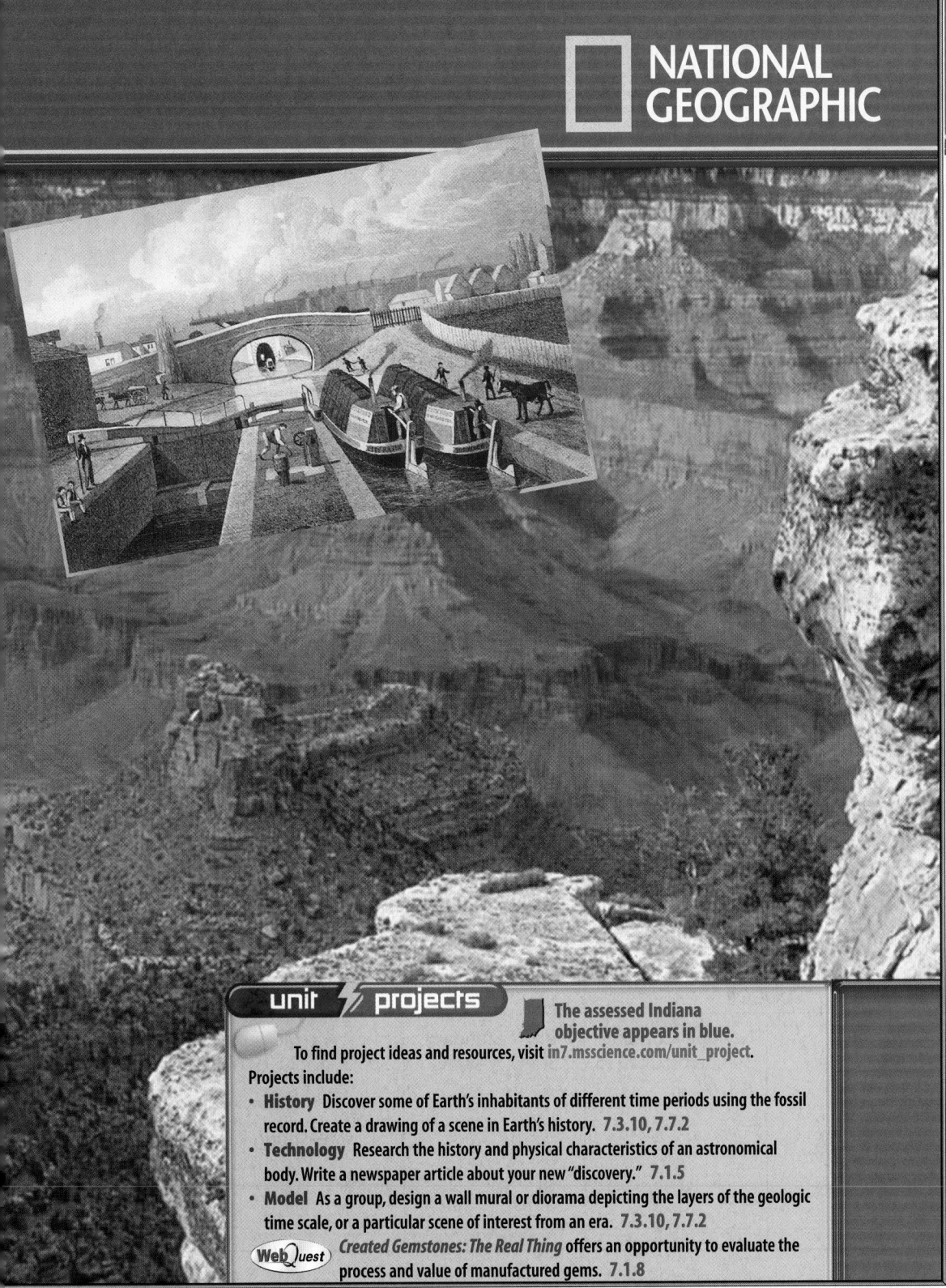

# NATIONAL GEOGRAPHIC

**unit ⚡ projects**

**History** Have students research a period in the geologic time scale and then chart the possible Earth inhabitants of that period. Categories may include: plants, fish, reptiles, mammals, and birds. Students can create a drawing that shows what they think might have been a typical scene during that period in Earth's history.

**Technology** Have students choose a planet, moon, star, asteroid, galaxy, or other astronomical body to research. Using word processing or other technology, have students write a newspaper article about their "new discovery." This factual information might include size, distance, composition, physical characteristics, who discovered it and when, and what exploration is planned for the future.

**Model** Students may cooperatively design a large diorama or class mural to demonstrate the knowledge they have acquired about past eras in Earth's history. A written key to the plants and animals present in their model should accompany their final presentation. Projects may include a geologic time scale with layers, or a scene of one particular era of interest.

**Additional Resources** For more information, resources, and assessment rubrics, visit in7.msscience.com/unit_project.

---

**unit ⚡ projects**

🏛 The assessed Indiana objective appears in blue.

To find project ideas and resources, visit in7.msscience.com/unit_project.
Projects include:
- **History** Discover some of Earth's inhabitants of different time periods using the fossil record. Create a drawing of a scene in Earth's history. 7.3.10, 7.7.2
- **Technology** Research the history and physical characteristics of an astronomical body. Write a newspaper article about your new "discovery." 7.1.5
- **Model** As a group, design a wall mural or diorama depicting the layers of the geologic time scale, or a particular scene of interest from an era. 7.3.10, 7.7.2
- **WebQuest** *Created Gemstones: The Real Thing* offers an opportunity to evaluate the process and value of manufactured gems. 7.1.8

---

## NATIONAL GEOGRAPHIC    How are Canals & the Paleozoic Era Connected?

The excavation of land to build canals exposed previously unseen layers of rock and sediment. In other areas of the world, rivers have eroded rock and sediment, creating deep canyons. The walls of the canyon contain exposed layers of rocks containing fossils. Some of these layers date back to the Paleozoic Era. By studying the age of the rock and the fossils contained in them, scientists have been able to construct a history of life on Earth. Fossils provide clues to the types of species inhabiting Earth during a particular era. Scientists also study the changing traits in fossils to determine how organisms may have adapted to changing environments.

| Section/Objectives | Standards | | Labs/Features |
|---|---|---|---|
| **Chapter Opener** | **National** | **State/Local** | **Launch Lab:** Why do clusters of galaxies move apart?, p. 471 **Foldables,** p. 471 |
| | See pp. 16T–17T for a Key to Standards. | Detailed standards begin on page IN8. | |
| Section 1 **Stars** ⏱ 1 session  📦 5 block 1. **Explain** why some constellations are visible only during certain seasons. 2. **Distinguish** between absolute magnitude and apparent magnitude. | National Content Standards: UCP.1–3, UCP.5, A.1, A.2 | Indiana Standards: 7.1.5 | **MiniLAB:** Observing Star Patterns, p. 473 **Applying Science:** Are distance and brightness related?, p. 474 |
| Section 2 **The Sun** ⏱ 2 sessions  📦 1 block 3. **Explain** that the Sun is the closest star to Earth. 4. **Describe** the structure of the Sun. 5. **Describe** sunspots, prominences, and solar flares. | National Content Standards: UCP.1–3, UCP.5, A.1, A.2, D.3 | Indiana Standards: 7.3.2, 7.3.11 | **Science Online,** p. 479 **Lab:** Sunspots, p. 481 |
| Section 3 **Evolution of Stars** ⏱ 2 sessions  📦 1 block 6. **Describe** how stars are classified. 7. **Compare** the Sun to other types of stars on the H-R diagram. 8. **Describe** how stars evolve. | National Content Standards: UCP.1–5, A.1, A.2, B.1–3, G.3 | Indiana Standards: 7.1.5, 7.3.11 | **Science Online,** p. 484 **Integrate Chemistry,** p. 485 **Integrate History,** p. 486 |
| Section 4 **Galaxies and the Universe** ⏱ 4 sessions  📦 2 blocks 9. **Describe** the Sun's position in the Milky Way Galaxy. 10. **Explain** that the same natural laws that apply to our solar system also apply in other galaxies. | National Content Standards: UCP.1–5, A.1, A.2 | Indiana Standards: 7.3.1 | **MiniLAB:** Measuring Distance in Space, p. 490 **Visualizing the Big Bang Theory,** p. 492 **Lab:** Measuring Parallax, p. 494 **Science Stats:** Stars and Galaxies, p. 496 |

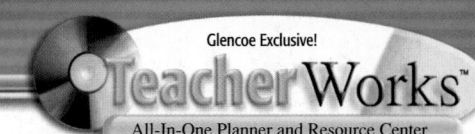

| Lab Materials | Reproducible Resources | Section Assessment | Technology |
|---|---|---|---|
| **Launch Lab:** balloon, felt-tip marker, string, metric ruler | **Chapter FAST FILE Resources**<br>Foldables Worksheet, p. 17<br>Directed Reading Overview, p. 19<br>Note-taking Worksheets, pp. 35–38 | GLENCOE'S ASSESSMENT ADVANTAGE | **TeacherWorks includes:**<br>• Interactive Teacher Edition<br>• Lesson Planner with calendar<br>• Access to all program blacklines<br>• Correlations to standards<br>• Web links |
| **MiniLAB:** paper, drawing materials | **Chapter FAST FILE Resources**<br>Transparency Activity, p. 48<br>MiniLAB, p. 3<br>Enrichment, p. 31<br>Reinforcement, p. 27<br>Directed Reading, p. 20<br>Lab Activity, pp. 9–12, 13–15<br>Transparency Activity, pp. 53–54 | Portfolio<br>Science Journal, p. 473<br>Performance<br>MiniLAB, p. 473<br>Applying Science, p. 474<br>Applying Skills, p. 476<br>Content<br>Section Review, p. 476 | Section Focus Transparency<br>Teaching Transparency<br>Guided Reading Audio Program<br>Interactive Chalkboard CD-ROM |
| **Lab:** several books, piece of cardboard, drawing paper, refracting telescope, clipboard, small tripod, scissors | **Chapter FAST FILE Resources**<br>Transparency Activity, p. 49<br>Lab Worksheets, pp. 5–6<br>Enrichment, p. 32<br>Reinforcement, p. 28<br>Directed Reading, p. 20<br>**Cultural Diversity,** p. 29 | Portfolio<br>Differentiated Instruction, p. 478<br>Performance<br>Applying Skills, p. 480<br>Content<br>Section Review, p. 480 | Section Focus Transparency<br>Guided Reading Audio Program<br>Interactive Chalkboard CD-ROM |
| *Need materials?* Contact Science Kit at 1-800-828-7777 or www.sciencekit.com on the Internet. | **Chapter FAST FILE Resources**<br>Transparency Activity, p. 50<br>Enrichment, p. 33<br>Reinforcement, p. 29<br>Directed Reading, p. 21 | Portfolio<br>Differentiated Instruction, p. 483<br>Performance<br>Applying Math, p. 487<br>Content<br>Section Review, p. 487 | Section Focus Transparency<br>Virtual Labs CD-ROM<br>Guided Reading Audio Program<br>Interactive Chalkboard CD-ROM |
| **MiniLAB:** large sheet of paper, metric ruler or meterstick, markers<br>**Lab:** meterstick, metric ruler, masking tape, pencil | **Chapter FAST FILE Resources**<br>Transparency Activity, p. 51<br>Lab Worksheets, pp. 7–8<br>MiniLAB, p. 4<br>Enrichment, p. 34<br>Reinforcement, p. 30<br>Directed Reading, pp. 21, 22<br>**Cultural Diversity,** p. 31 | Portfolio<br>Assessment, p. 493<br>Performance<br>MiniLAB, p. 490<br>Applying Skills, p. 493<br>Content<br>Section Review, p. 493 | Guided Reading Audio Program<br>Interactive Chalkboard CD-ROM<br>Video Lab |

## End of Chapter Assessment

GLENCOE'S ASSESSMENT ADVANTAGE

| Blackline Masters | Technology | Professional Series |
|---|---|---|
| **Chapter FAST FILE Resources**<br>Chapter Review, pp. 41–42<br>Chapter Tests, pp. 43–46<br>**Mastering the Grade 7 Indiana Science Standards** | MindJogger Videoquiz<br>IN Test Prep and Practice ExamView®<br>ExamView® Pro Testmaker<br>TeacherWorks CD-ROM<br>Interactive Chalkboard CD-ROM | **Performance Assessment in the Science Classroom (PASC)** |

## Transparencies

### Section Focus

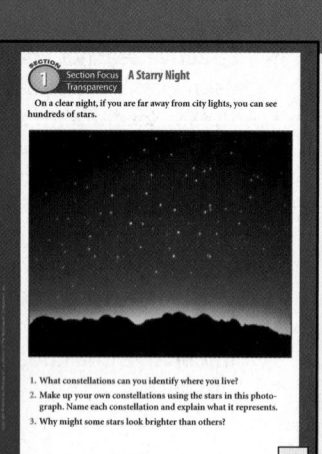

**SECTION 1** Section Focus Transparency — **A Starry Night**

On a clear night, if you are far away from city lights, you can see hundreds of stars.

1. What constellations can you identify where you live?
2. Make up your own constellations using the stars in this photograph. Name each constellation and explain what it represents.
3. Why might some stars look brighter than others?

L2

**SECTION 2** Section Focus Transparency — **A Hot Topic**

Light isn't the only thing that comes from the Sun; the solar wind, which consists mainly of charged particles, also flows from the Sun. These particles are the reason that the tails of comets point away from the Sun, and they are thought to play a role in the auroral light displays.

1. How does the Sun make life on Earth possible?
2. Describe the features of the Sun that you can see in the image above.

L2

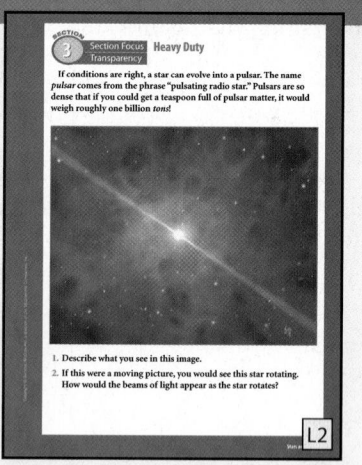

**SECTION 3** Section Focus Transparency — **Heavy Duty**

If conditions are right, a star can evolve into a pulsar. The name *pulsar* comes from the phrase "pulsating radio star." Pulsars are so dense that if you could get a teaspoon full of pulsar matter, it would weigh roughly one billion *tons!*

1. Describe what you see in this image.
2. If this were a moving picture, you would see this star rotating. How would the beams of light appear as the star rotates?

L2

This is a representation of key blackline masters available in the Teacher Classroom Resources. See Resource Manager boxes within the chapter for additional information.

### Key to Teaching Strategies

The following designations will help you decide which activities are appropriate for your students.

**L1** Level 1 activities should be appropriate for students with learning difficulties.

**L2** Level 2 activities should be within the ability range of all students.

**L3** Level 3 activities are designed for above-average students.

**ELL** ELL activities should be within the ability range of English Language Learners.

**COOP LEARN** Cooperative Learning activities are designed for small group work.

**LS** Multiple Learning Styles logos, as described on page 12T, are used throughout to indicate strategies that address different learning styles.

**P** These strategies represent student products that can be placed into a best-work portfolio.

**PBL** Problem-Based Learning activities apply real-world situations to learning.

### Assessment

Assessment Transparency — **Stars and Galaxies**

**Directions:** *Carefully review the table and answer the following questions.*

| Light Waves | |
| --- | --- |
| Color | Wavelength (nanometers) |
| Violet | 380-450 |
| Blue | 450-490 |
| Green | 490-560 |
| Yellow | 560-590 |
| Orange | 590-630 |
| Red | 630-760 |

1. According to the table, what will be the color of a light wave with a wavelength of 500 nanometers?
   A Violet     C Green
   B Blue       D Yellow
2. In a clear sky, the Sun is bright yellow. What is the approximate wavelength of the light coming from the Sun?
   F 380–340 nanometers
   G 450–490 nanometers
   H 560–590 nanometers
   J 630–760 nanometers
3. The shorter the wavelength of a light wave, the greater its energy. A light wave of which of the colors listed below has the greatest energy?
   A Red
   B Orange
   C Green
   D Violet

L2

### Teaching

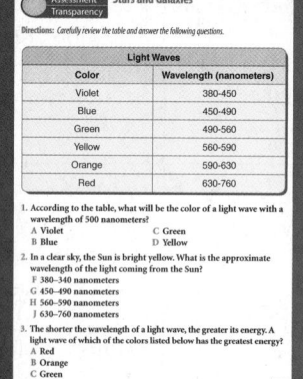

**SECTION 1** Teaching Transparency — **Circumpolar Constellations**

L2

## Hands-on Activities

### Activity Worksheets

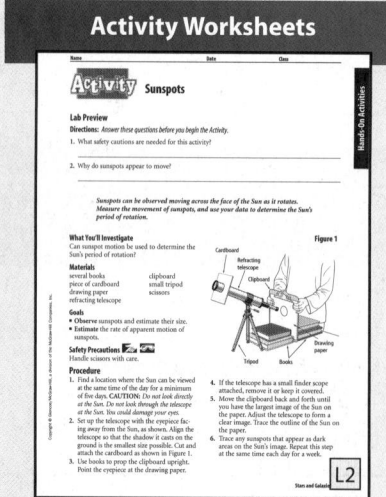

**Activity** — **Sunspots**

L2

### Laboratory Activities

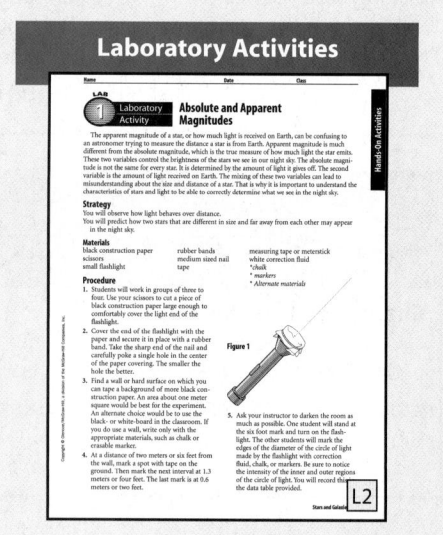

**LAB 1** Laboratory Activity — **Absolute and Apparent Magnitudes**

L2

## Meeting Different Ability Levels

### Content Outline

### Reinforcement

### Enrichment

### Directed Reading (English/Spanish)

### Study Guide

### Reading Essentials

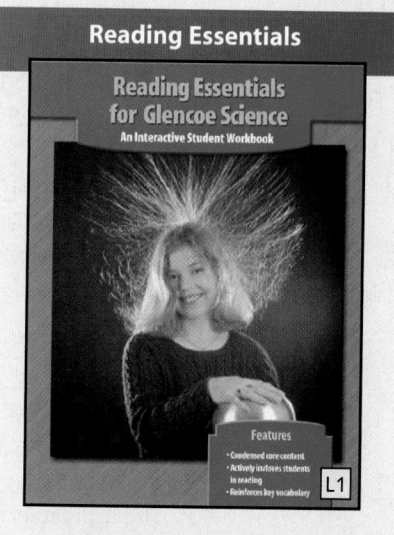

## Assessment

### Test Practice Workbook

### Chapter Review

### Chapter Tests

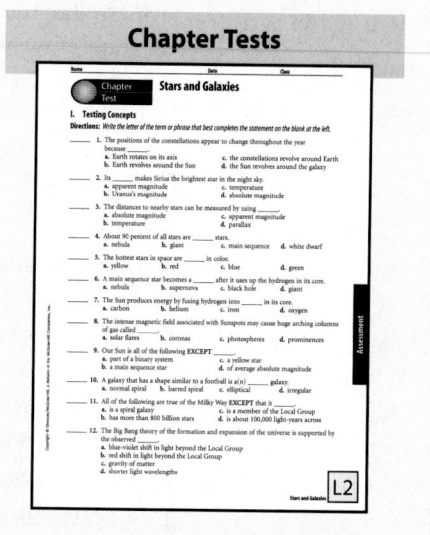

# Science Content Background

## Stars
### Absolute and Apparent Magnitudes

The size and temperature of a star affect its absolute magnitude. The size and temperature of a star, along with its distance from Earth, affect its apparent magnitude. If the absolute and apparent magnitudes of a star are known, the distance from the star to Earth can be determined.

---

**Teacher to Teacher**

Dennis L. Stockdale
Asheville High School
Asheville, N.C.

"While studying the stars, my students build a planetarium from a 50-foot square of plastic film. The final product will be 30 feet in diameter and 16 feet tall. Plans are available in *The Science Teacher*, vol. 64, no. 7, October 1997."

*Dennis L. Stockdale*

---

Clouds of gas and dust in space, called nebulae, can obscure starlight, thus reducing a star's apparent magnitude. Interstellar nebulae reduce the apparent magnitude of stars in many parts of our galaxy to the point where they cannot be seen. The gas and dust from these interstellar nebulae can also make a star appear red in color. Interstellar material tends to be opaque to light of shorter wavelengths, allowing longer wavelengths of red light to pass through.

## The Sun
### Surface Features

The phenomenon called granulation seen on the surface of the Sun was first observed by Galileo. He thought the patterns he observed resembled grains of wheat and thus called the features granules. Granules on the Sun's surface are the tops of large convection cells that extend deep into the Sun. Their presence is evidence that convection currents do exist inside the Sun, just under the photosphere. These granules form when hot gases are forced upward by surrounding denser gases. The hot gases flow toward the surface, emit energy, cool, and sink back toward the Sun's interior. Each granule measures about 1,000 km across.

### Sunspots

Sunspots occur in a periodic pattern. Magnetic reversals occur every 11 years; therefore, a sunspot cycle is complete after 22 years. Solar activity affects circulation within Earth's atmosphere. Some scientists see a correlation between the Sun's 22-year activity cycle and droughts on Earth. Solar activity might affect Earth's climate over longer periods of time. The Little Ice Age that gripped northern Europe for over 300 years has been associated with the Maunder minimum, a time during the late 1600s when sunspot occurrences were very low.

## chapter content resources

**Internet Resources**

For additional content background, visit **in7.msscience.com** to:

- access your book onlineonline
- find references to related articles in popular science magazines
- access Web links with related content background
- access current events with science journal topics

**Print Resources**

*Discovering the Universe,* by Neil F. Comins, and William J. Kaufmann, W.H. Freeman, 2003

*A Dictionary of Astronomy,* Ian Ridpath (ed.), Oxford University Press, 1998

*Star Chart Map,* American Map Corporation, 1995

## section 3 Evolution of Stars

### Classifying Stars

Not all stars shine with a steady light. Stars that change brightness in a cyclic manner are called variable stars. Stars may vary because the outer layers of the star expand and contract, causing a change in the temperature and the absolute magnitude of the star.

One class of variable stars, the Cepheid variable, provides important information related to the study of the universe. These stars vary regularly, and their period of variation is an indication of their absolute magnitudes. Because of this, they can be used to determine distances to faraway clusters and galaxies. If two Cepheid variables have the same period of pulsation, they are the same average size and have the same average absolute magnitude. Any difference noted in the apparent magnitudes of the two stars is caused by a difference in the distance to each of the stars. Polaris is an example of a Cepheid variable.

### Black Holes

New infrared studies of the center of the Milky Way provide more evidence for a supermassive black hole at the core of our galaxy. The total output of energy from this object at the Milky Way's core is more than 1 million times that of the Sun, and it appears to contain more than 2 million solar masses (1 solar mass = mass of the Sun = $2 \times 10^{30}$ kg). Most other galaxies also contain supermassive black holes.

Quasars are supermassive black holes that existed billions of years ago but still can be seen today at great distances. These objects emitted much more energy than modern supermassive black holes emit. Some quasars are thousands of times brighter than entire galaxies. Some have suggested that today's supermassive black holes might be "fossil" quasars.

## section 4 Galaxies and the Universe

### Galaxies

The Milky Way and Andromeda Galaxies both have a number of companion dwarf spheroidal galaxies. A dwarf spheroidal galaxy called the Sagittarius Dwarf Galaxy is about 50,000 light-years from the nucleus of the Milky Way. It lies in the direction of the constellation Sagittarius on the opposite side of the Milky Way from Earth. Researchers hypothesize that the Sagittarius Dwarf Galaxy has orbited the Milky Way many times. The stars from this small galaxy eventually will be incorporated into the Milky Way. This supports a theory that large galaxies, such as the Milky Way, are formed, in part, by the incorporation of smaller galaxies. Larger galaxies, therefore, are thought to have been built up over time from smaller galaxies.

Luke Dodd/Science Library/Photo Researchers, Inc.

## Chapter Vocabulary

constellation, p. 472
absolute magnitude, p. 474
apparent magnitude, p. 474
light-year, p. 475
photosphere, p. 477
chromosphere, p. 477
corona, p. 477
sunspot, p. 478
nebula, p. 484
giant, p. 485
white dwarf, p. 485
supergiant, p. 486
neutron star, p. 486
black hole, p. 486
galaxy, p. 488
big bang theory, p. 493

**Science Journal** Students'
descriptions should include spiral
arms and a bright galactic core.

**PowerPoint® Presentations**

This CD-ROM is an editable
Microsoft® PowerPoint®
presentation that includes:
- a pre-made presentation for
  every chapter
- interactive graphics
- animations
- audio clips
- image bank
- all new section and chapter
  questions
- Standardized Test Practice
- transparencies
- pre-lab questions for all labs
- Foldables directions
- links to in7.msscience.com

**Academic Standard—3:** Students collect and organize data to identify relationships between physical objects, events, and processes. They use logical reasoning to question their own ideas as new information challenges their conceptions of the natural world.

**Also covers:** Academic Standard 1 (Detailed standards begin on page IN8.)

# Stars and Galaxies

## chapter preview

### sections
1 Stars
2 The Sun
   *Lab* Sunspots
3 Evolution of Stars
4 Galaxies and the Universe
   *Lab* Measuring Parallax
   *Virtual Lab* How does the chemical composition of stars determine their classification?

### What's your address?

You know your address at home. You also know your address at school. But do you know your address in space? You live on a planet called Earth that revolves around a star called the Sun. Earth and the Sun are part of a galaxy called the Milky Way. It looks similar to galaxy M83, shown in the photo.

**Science Journal** Write a description in your Science Journal of the galaxy shown on this page.

470

## Theme Connection

**Scale and Structure** and **Stability and Change** The major themes of this chapter deal with the vast scale and structure of the universe and how the universe, and the matter that it contains, changes.

### About the Photo

**Galaxy M83** The photo shows galaxy M83 in the constellation Hydra. M83 is a barred spiral galaxy that probably is similar to the Milky Way.

# Start-Up Activities

## Why do clusters of galaxies move apart?

Astronomers know that most galaxies occur in groups of galaxies called clusters. These clusters are moving away from each other in space. The fabric of space is stretching like an inflating balloon.

1. Partially inflate a balloon. Use a piece of string to seal the neck.

2. Draw six evenly spaced dots on the balloon with a felt-tipped marker. Label the dots A through F.

3. Use string and a ruler to measure the distance, in millimeters, from dot A to each of the other dots.

4. Inflate the balloon more.

5. Measure the distances from dot A again.

6. Inflate the balloon again and make new measurements.

7. **Think Critically** Imagine that each dot represents a cluster of galaxies and that the balloon represents the universe. Describe the motion of the clusters in your Science Journal.

**Science Online** Preview this chapter's content and activities at in7.msscience.com

---

**FOLDABLES** Study Organizer

**Stars, Galaxies, and the Universe** Make the following Foldable to show what you know about stars, galaxies, and the universe.

**STEP 1** Fold a sheet of paper from side to side. Make the front edge about 1.25 cm shorter than the back edge.

**STEP 2** Turn lengthwise and **fold** into thirds.

**STEP 3** Unfold and cut only the top layer along both folds to make three tabs.

**STEP 4** Label the tabs *Stars, Galaxies,* and *Universe.*

**Read and Write** Before you read the chapter, write what you already know about stars, galaxies, and the universe. As you read the chapter, add to or correct what you have written under the tabs.

471

---

**Launch LAB**

**Purpose** Students are introduced to the concept of an expanding universe. L1 ELL COOP LEARN

**LS Kinesthetic**

**Materials** balloon, felt-tipped marker, string, metric ruler

**Teaching Strategies**

• Divide the class into groups of four students. Assign roles to students. One student should blow up the balloon and tie it shut. Another should draw the dots on the balloon. The remaining students should measure the distance between the dots.

• Have students compare their results with those of classmates. Discuss differences and similarities.

**Safety Precautions** Caution students not to blow up the balloons to the breaking point.

## Think Critically

The galaxy clusters are moving away from each other. This type of motion implies that the universe is expanding.

## Assessment

**Process** Have students make illustrations that depict the motion of galaxy clusters. Drawings should indicate that clusters are moving away from each other. Use **Performance Assessment in the Science Classroom,** p. 127.

**FOLDABLES** Study Organizer **Dinah Zike Study Fold**

Student preparation materials for this Foldable are available in the Chapter *FAST FILE* Resources.

## 1 Motivate

### Bellringer

INTERACTIVE CHALKBOARD
PowerPoint® Presentations

**Section Focus Transparencies** also are available on the Interactive Chalkboard CD-ROM.

L2 ELL

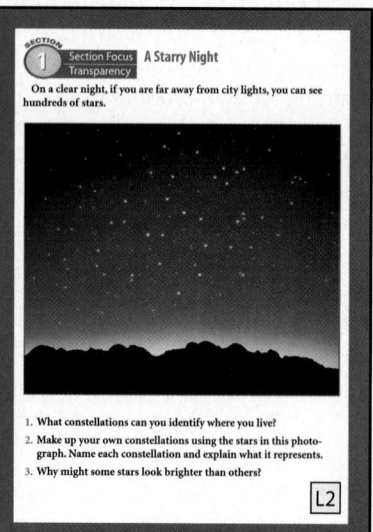

SECTION 1 Section Focus Transparency A Starry Night

On a clear night, if you are far away from city lights, you can see hundreds of stars.

1. What constellations can you identify where you live?
2. Make up your own constellations using the stars in this photograph. Name each constellation and explain what it represents.
3. Why might some stars look brighter than others?

L2

Stars and Galaxies

### Tie to Prior Knowledge

**Big Dipper** Ask students if they have observed the Big Dipper, part of the constellation known as Ursa Major. Invite a volunteer to draw the stars of the Big Dipper on the chalkboard to illustrate why it's called a dipper.

---

# section 1

# Stars

## as you read

### *What* You'll Learn

■ **Explain** why some constellations are visible only during certain seasons.
■ **Distinguish** between absolute magnitude and apparent magnitude.

### *Why* It's Important

The Sun is a typical star.

### Review Vocabulary

**star:** a large, spherical mass of gas that gives off light and other types of radiation

### New Vocabulary

● constellation
● absolute magnitude
● apparent magnitude
● light-year

## Constellations

It's fun to look at clouds and find ones that remind you of animals, people, or objects that you recognize. It takes more imagination to play this game with stars. Ancient Greeks, Romans, and other early cultures observed patterns of stars in the night sky called **constellations.** They imagined that the constellations represented mythological characters, animals, or familiar objects.

From Earth, a constellation looks like spots of light arranged in a particular shape against the dark night sky. **Figure 1** shows how the constellation of the mythological Greek hunter Orion appears from Earth. It also shows that the stars in a constellation often have no relationship to each other in space.

Stars in the sky can be found at specific locations within a constellation. For example, you can find the star Betelgeuse (BEE tul jooz) in the shoulder of the mighty hunter Orion. Orion's faithful companion is his dog, Canis Major. Sirius, the brightest star that is visible from the northern hemisphere, is in Canis Major.

**Figure 1** The stars in Orion appear close together, but they really are many light-years apart.

Meissa
Betelgeuse
Bellatrix
Mintaka
Alnilam
Alnitak
Orion nebula
Na'ir al Saif
Rigel
Salph

500    1,000    2,000

Distances from Earth in light-years

**472    CHAPTER 16** Stars and Galaxies

---

## Section 1 Resource Manager

Looking north

**Figure 2** The Big Dipper, in red, is part of the constellation Ursa Major. It is visible year-round in the northern hemisphere. Constellations close to Polaris rotate around Polaris, which is almost directly over the north pole.

**Modern Constellations** Modern astronomy divides the sky into 88 constellations, many of which were named by early astronomers. You probably know some of them. Can you recognize the Big Dipper? It's part of the constellation Ursa Major, shown in **Figure 2.** Notice how the front two stars of the Big Dipper point almost directly at Polaris, which often is called the North Star. Polaris is located at the end of the Little Dipper in the constellation Ursa Minor. It is positioned almost directly over Earth's north pole.

**Circumpolar Constellations** As Earth rotates, Ursa Major, Ursa Minor, and other constellations in the northern sky circle around Polaris. Because of this, they are called circumpolar constellations. The constellations appear to move, as shown in **Figure 2,** because Earth is in motion. The stars appear to complete one full circle in the sky in about 24 h as Earth rotates on its axis. One circumpolar constellation that's easy to find is Cassiopeia (ka see uh PEE uh). You can look for five bright stars that form a big W or a big M in the northern sky, depending on the season.

As Earth orbits the Sun, different constellations come into view while others disappear. Because of their unique position, circumpolar constellations are visible all year long. Other constellations are not. Orion, which is visible in the winter in the northern hemisphere, can't be seen there in the summer because the daytime side of Earth is facing it.

**Mini LAB**

## Observing Star Patterns

**Procedure**

1. On a clear night, go outside after dark and study the stars. Take an adult with you.
2. Let your imagination flow to find patterns of stars that look like something familiar.
3. Draw the stars you see, note their positions, and include a drawing of what you think each star pattern resembles.

**Analysis**

1. Which of your constellations match those observed by your classmates?
2. How can recognizing star patterns be useful?

Try at Home

**Mini LAB**

**Purpose** Students identify constellations. [L2] ELL [IS] Visual-Spatial

**Materials** paper, pencil

**Teaching Strategy** Provide star charts for students to refer to.

**Analysis**

1. Many students will likely include familiar constellations; other constellations will be unique.
2. Possible answer: Constellations can be used to identify directions.

**Assessment**

**Performance** Have students write a myth about one of the drawings they made. Use **Performance Assessment in the Science Classroom,** p. 155.

Try at Home

**IDENTIFYING Misconceptions**

**Constellations** Students might think that stars within a constellation are close to one another in space. Explain that two stars that appear to be side by side can be separated by hundreds of light-years.

## Teacher FYI

**Asterisms** A recognizable pattern of stars within a constellation or among stars in different constellations is called an asterism. The Big Dipper and Little Dipper are asterisms in the constellations of Ursa Major and Ursa Minor.

## Science Journal

**Constellations from Mythology** Have students research a constellation of their choice and write a report in their Science Journals that identifies the stars in the constellation and describes the mythological character or story for which the constellation is named. [L2] [IS] **Linguistic** [P]

**Procedure** Move students into a hallway. Give two volunteers identical flashlights, have them walk to different locations, and have them shine the flashlights toward the class. Which has a brighter apparent magnitude? the closer flashlight Which has the brighter absolute magnitude? Neither; they have equal absolute magnitudes. L2 LS **Visual-Spatial**

## Text Question Answer

The brighter star may be bigger or hotter.

### Reading Check

**Answer** absolute—a measure of the amount of light given off by a star; apparent—a measure of the amount of light received on Earth from a star

## Fun Fact

Luminosity, $L$, is a measure of how many times brighter or dimmer a star is compared with the Sun.

### Applying Science

## Answers

1. As distance is doubled (20 cm to 40 cm), light intensity decreases to 1/4 the original. As distance is tripled (20 cm to 60 cm), light intensity decreases to 1/9 the original.

2. The relationship can be expressed as 1 divided by the square of how many times distance is increased. At 100 cm, the distance will have increased five fold (to five times the original), and the light intensity will be decreased to 1/25 of its original intensity, or 166 luxes.

# Absolute and Apparent Magnitudes

When you look at constellations, you'll notice that some stars are brighter than others. For example, Sirius looks much brighter than Rigel. Is Sirius a brighter star, or is it just closer to Earth, making it appear to be brighter? As it turns out, Sirius is 100 times closer to Earth than Rigel is. If Sirius and Rigel were the same distance from Earth, Rigel would appear much brighter in the night sky than Sirius would.

When you refer to the brightness of a star, you can refer to its absolute magnitude or its apparent magnitude. The **absolute magnitude** of a star is a measure of the amount of light it gives off. A measure of the amount of light received on Earth is the **apparent magnitude.** A star that's dim can appear bright in the sky if it's close to Earth, and a star that's bright can appear dim if it's far away. If two stars are the same distance away, what might cause one of them to be brighter than the other?

### Reading Check

*What is the difference between absolute and apparent magnitude?*

### Applying Science

## Are distance and brightness related?

The apparent magnitude of a star is affected by its distance from Earth. This activity will help you determine the relationship between distance and brightness.

### Identifying the Problem

Luisa conducted an experiment to determine the relationship between distance and the brightness of stars. She used a meterstick, a light meter, and a lightbulb. She placed the bulb at the zero end of the meterstick, then placed the light meter at the 20-cm mark and recorded the distance and the light-meter reading in her data table. Readings are in luxes, which are units for measuring light intensity. Luisa then increased the distance from the bulb to the light meter and took more readings. By examining the data in the table, can you see a relationship between the two variables?

| Effect of Distance on Light | |
| --- | --- |
| Distance (cm) | Meter Reading (luxes) |
| 20 | 4150.0 |
| 40 | 1037.5 |
| 60 | 461.1 |
| 80 | 259.4 |

### Solving the Problem

1. What happened to the amount of light recorded when the distance was increased from 20 cm to 40 cm? When the distance was increased from 20 cm to 60 cm?

2. What does this indicate about the relationship between light intensity and distance? What would the light intensity be at 100 cm? Would making a graph help you visualize the relationship?

# Differentiated Instruction

**Challenge** Have students measure the distance between their eyes in centimeters. Then have them do calculations using the following equation to determine the parallax angle they observe at various distances from an object: $P° = (360°)(B)/2\pi r$, where $P°$ is the parallax angle, $B$ is the student's baseline (distance between eyes), and $r$ is the distance to the object. Students should plug in different values for $r$ in centimeters. L3

**Learning Disabled** Pair each learning disabled student with another student. Have pairs cut a 4-cm square from black construction paper and punch pinholes in the square to show a constellation's outline. Then have students put the square at one end of a cardboard tube and point the tube toward a light source to view the constellation. L2 ELL LS **Visual-Spatial**

# Measurement in Space

How do scientists determine the distance from Earth to nearby stars? One way is to measure parallax—the apparent shift in the position of an object when viewed from two different positions. Extend your arm and look at your thumb first with your left eye closed and then with your right eye closed, as the girl in **Figure 3A** is doing. Your thumb appears to change position with respect to the background. Now do the same experiment with your thumb closer to your face, as shown in **Figure 3B.** What do you observe? The nearer an object is to the observer, the greater its parallax is.

Astronomers can measure the parallax of relatively close stars to determine their distances from Earth. **Figure 4** shows how a close star's position appears to change. Knowing the angle that the star's position changes and the size of Earth's orbit, astronomers can calculate the distance of the star from Earth.

Because space is so vast, a special unit of measure is needed to record distances. Distances between stars and galaxies are measured in light-years. A **light-year** is the distance that light travels in one year. Light travels at 300,000 km/s, or about 9.5 trillion km in one year. The nearest star to Earth, other than the Sun, is Proxima Centauri. Proxima Centauri is a mere 4.2 light-years away, or about 40 trillion km.

**Figure 3** **A** Your thumb appears to move less against the background when it is farther away from your eyes. **B** It appears to move more when it is closer to your eyes.

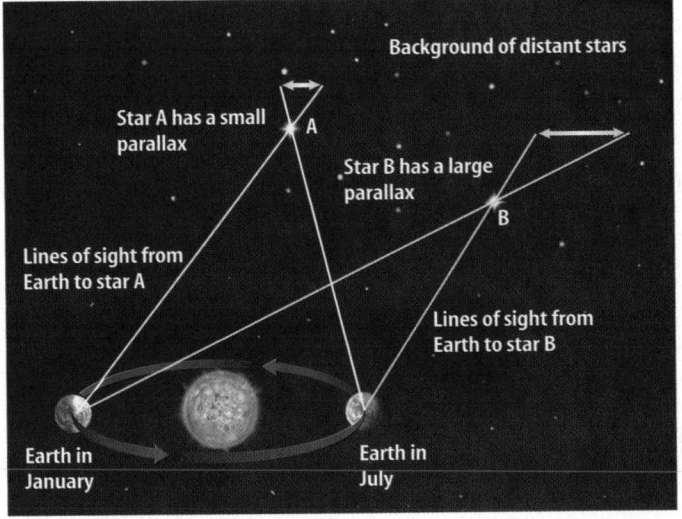

Background of distant stars

Star A has a small parallax

Star B has a large parallax

Lines of sight from Earth to star A

Lines of sight from Earth to star B

Earth in January

Earth in July

**Figure 4** Parallax is determined by observing the same star when Earth is at two different points in its orbit around the Sun. The star's position relative to more distant background stars will appear to change.
**Infer** *whether star* **A** *or* **B** *is farther from Earth.*

## Activity

**Parallax Angle** Arrange a numbered scale in the front of the room. Place two objects at different distances from the scale. Have students observe the objects relative to the scale from three different classroom locations. Ask them to explain differences in their observations. Students should note that as the distance to the viewed object decreases, the shift in the position of the object in relation to the scale increases. This occurs because the parallax angle of the closer object is greater than that of the farther object.
**LS** **Visual-Spatial**

## Visual Learning

**Figure 3** Have students repeat the activity shown in the figure. They should notice that the closer their thumb is to their face, the more the position of the thumb appears to shift and the greater the parallax.

### Caption Answer
**Figure 4** Star A is more distant.

### Discussion
**Parallax** Why can the parallax of close stars be measured against the background of distant stars? The distant stars have no measurable parallax. Why are the two positions in Earth's orbit that are chosen for parallax measurements usually far apart? A longer baseline produces higher parallax angles, which are easier to measure.

## Curriculum Connection

**Math** Use the following equation to calculate the distance in light-years to two stars:
$$d = 3.26/p$$
In this equation, *d* represents light-years and *p* represents parallax angle. Star 1 has a parallax angle of 0.77″, and Star 2 has a parallax angle of 0.04″. Star 1 = 4.23 light-years; Star 2 = 81.5 light-years

## 3 Assess

### DAILY INTERVENTION

#### Check for Understanding

**Visual-Spatial** Provide students with unlabeled star charts and have them make and explain their own constellations. [L2] **ELL** **LS**

#### Reteach

**Compass Headings** Take students to an open area to demonstrate parallax. Have two volunteers stand approximately 50 m apart. Give one student a compass with a sighting mirror. Have the student determine the exact compass heading to the other student. Now have the student holding the compass move sideways 20 m, and determine the new compass heading to the other student. Repeat this activity, varying the distances between students. [L2] **ELL**

**COOP LEARN** **LS** **Kinesthetic**

### Assessment

**Performance** Have students write paragraphs explaining why Deneb appears so bright and yet is more than 1,400 light-years away. Deneb is either very large, very hot, or both. Use **Performance Assessment in the Science Classroom,** p. 159.

---

**Figure 5** This star spectrum was made by placing a diffraction grating over a telescope's objective lens. A diffraction grating produces a spectrum by causing interference of light waves. **Explain** *what causes the lines in spectra.*

## Properties of Stars

The color of a star indicates its temperature. For example, hot stars are a blue-white color. A relatively cool star looks orange or red. Stars that have the same temperature as the Sun have a yellow color.

Astronomers study the composition of stars by observing their spectra. When fitted into a telescope, a spectroscope acts like a prism. It spreads light out in the rainbow band called a spectrum. When light from a star passes through a spectroscope, it breaks into its component colors. Look at the spectrum of a star in **Figure 5.** Notice the dark lines caused by elements in the star's atmosphere. Light radiated from a star passes through the star's atmosphere. As it does, elements in the atmosphere absorb some of this light. The wavelengths of visible light that are absorbed appear as dark lines in the spectrum. Each element absorbs certain wavelengths, producing a unique pattern of dark lines. Like a fingerprint, the patterns of lines can be used to identify the elements in a star's atmosphere.

---

## section 1 review

### Summary

**Constellations**
- Constellations are patterns of stars in the night sky.
- The stars in a constellation often have no relationship to each other in space.

**Absolute and Apparent Magnitudes**
- Absolute magnitude is a measure of how much light is given off by a star.
- Apparent magnitude is a measure of how much light from a star is received on Earth.

**Measurement in Space**
- Distances between stars are measured in light-years.

**Properties of Stars**
- Astronomers study the composition of stars by observing their spectra.

### Self Check

1. **Describe** circumpolar constellations.
2. **Explain** why some constellations are visible only during certain seasons.
3. **Infer** how two stars could have the same apparent magnitude but different absolute magnitudes.
4. **Explain** how a star is similar to the Sun if it has the same absorption lines in its spectrum that occur in the Sun's spectrum.
5. **Think Critically** If a star's parallax angle is too small to measure, what can you conclude about the star's distance from Earth?

#### Applying Skills

6. **Recognize Cause and Effect** Suppose you viewed Proxima Centauri, which is 4.2 light-years from Earth, through a telescope. How old were you when the light that you see left this star?

Science Online in7.msscience.com/self_check_quiz

---

## section 1 review

1. Circumpolar constellations are constellations that occur high above or below Earth's celestial equator. In the northern hemisphere, these constellations appear to rotate around Polaris.

2. As Earth revolves around the Sun, its nighttime side faces different directions. As a result, different constellations are visible during the year.

3. The star with the greater absolute magnitude is farther away.

4. The star's composition is similar to the Sun's composition.

5. The star is not close to Earth.

6. student's current age minus 4.3 years

**Also covers:** 7.3.11 (Detailed standards begin on page IN8.)

# The Sun

## The Sun's Layers

The Sun is an ordinary star, but it's important to you. The Sun is the center of the solar system, and the closest star to Earth. Almost all of the life on Earth depends on energy from the Sun.

Notice the different layers of the Sun, shown in **Figure 6,** as you read about them. Like other stars, the Sun is an enormous ball of gas that produces energy by fusing hydrogen into helium in its core. This energy travels outward through the radiation zone and the convection zone. In the convection zone, gases circulate in giant swirls. Finally, energy passes into the Sun's atmosphere.

## The Sun's Atmosphere

The lowest layer of the Sun's atmosphere and the layer from which light is given off is the **photosphere.** The photosphere often is called the surface of the Sun, although the surface is not a smooth feature. Temperatures there are about 6,000 K. Above the photosphere is the **chromosphere.** This layer extends upward about 2,000 km above the photosphere. A transition zone occurs between 2,000 km and 10,000 km above the photosphere. Above the transition zone is the **corona.** This is the largest layer of the Sun's atmosphere and extends millions of kilometers into space. Temperatures in the corona are as high as 2 million K. Charged particles continually escape from the corona and move through space as solar wind.

**Figure 6** Energy produced in the Sun's core by fusion travels outward by radiation and convection. The Sun's atmosphere shines by the energy produced in the core.

### as you read

*What* **You'll Learn**

- **Explain** that the Sun is the closest star to Earth.
- **Describe** the structure of the Sun.
- **Describe** sunspots, prominences, and solar flares.

*Why* **It's Important**

The Sun is the source of most energy on Earth.

**Review Vocabulary**

**cycle:** a repeating sequence of events, such as the sunspot cycle

**New Vocabulary**

- photosphere
- corona
- chromosphere
- sunspot

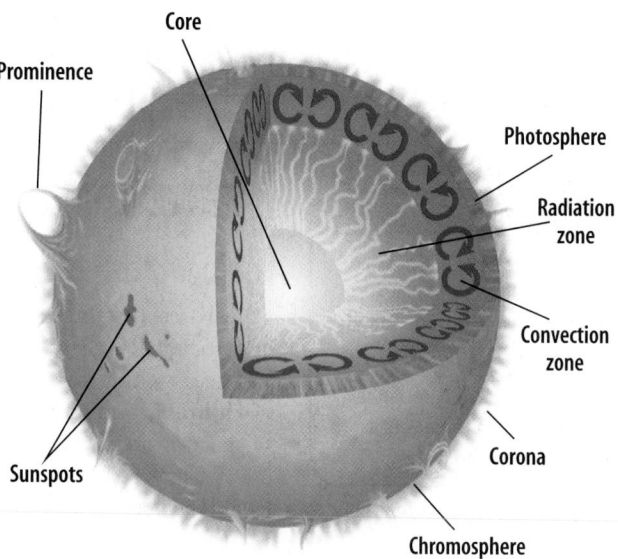

Core

Prominence

Photosphere

Radiation zone

Convection zone

Corona

Sunspots

Chromosphere

**Bellringer**

**Section Focus Transparencies** also are available on the Interactive Chalkboard CD-ROM.

 L2 ELL

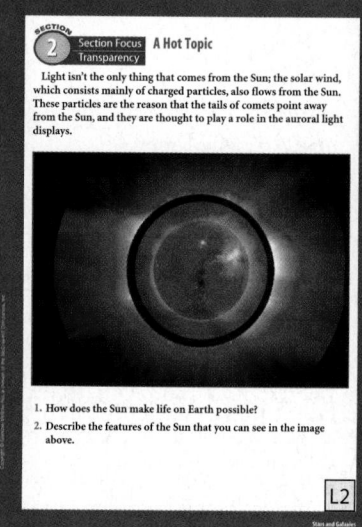

## Tie to Prior Knowledge

**The Sun's Warmth** Have students recall the warmth of a sunny summer day. Remind them that the Sun's energy keeps Earth's temperatures appropriate for life.

---

### Section 2 Resource Manager

**Chapter *FAST FILE* Resources**

Transparency Activity, p. 49

Directed Reading for Content Mastery, p. 20

Enrichment, p. 32

Lab Worksheets, pp. 5–6

Reinforcement, p. 28

**Cultural Diversity,** p. 29

**Caption Answer**

**Figure 7** counterclockwise

## Fun Fact

Temperatures rise from 6,000 K to more than 1,000,000 K in a transition zone between the chromosphere and corona.

### Quick Demo

**Sunspots**

**Materials** overhead projector, blank transparency

**Estimated Time** 10 minutes

**Procedure** Use this demo to help students understand why sunspots look dark even though they are quite bright. Turn on an overhead projector, and have students observe the light that falls on the screen. Then partially cover the surface of the projector with a blank transparency. Have students compare both sides of the screen. They should note a difference in brightness. This is analogous to what occurs on the Sun's surface. Next to the brighter surrounding areas of the Sun's surface, the sunspots look dark.

### ✔ Reading Check

**Answer** the regular pattern of increasing and decreasing sunspot activity on the Sun

**Figure 7** Sunspots are bright, but when viewed against the rest of the photosphere, they appear dark. Notice how these sunspots move as the Sun rotates.
**Describe** the Sun's direction of rotation.

This is a close-up photo of a large sunspot.

---

**Indiana Academic Standard Check**

**7.3.2:** Recognize and describe that the Sun is many thousands of times closer to Earth than any other star, . . . .

✔ How many times farther from Earth is the nearest star compared to the Sun?

✔ about 270,000 times farther

---

## Surface Features

From the viewpoint that you observe the Sun, its surface appears to be a smooth layer. But the Sun's surface has many features, including sunspots, prominences, flares, and CMEs.

**Sunspots** Areas of the Sun's surface that appear dark because they are cooler than surrounding areas are called **sunspots.** Ever since Galileo Galilei made drawings of sunspots, scientists have been studying them. Because scientists could observe the movement of individual sunspots, shown in **Figure 7,** they concluded that the Sun rotates. However, the Sun doesn't rotate as a solid body, as Earth does. It rotates faster at its equator than at its poles. Sunspots at the equator take about 25 days to complete one rotation. Near the poles, they take about 35 days.

Sunspots aren't permanent features on the Sun. They appear and disappear over a period of several days, weeks, or months. The number of sunspots increases and decreases in a fairly regular pattern called the sunspot, or solar activity, cycle. Times when many large sunspots occur are called sunspot maximums. Sunspot maximums occur about every 10 to 11 years. Periods of sunspot minimum occur in between.

### ✔ Reading Check   *What is a sunspot cycle?*

**Prominences and Flares** Sunspots are related to several features on the Sun's surface. The intense magnetic fields associated with sunspots might cause prominences, which are huge, arching columns of gas. Notice the huge prominence in **Figure 8.** Some prominences blast material from the Sun into space at speeds ranging from 600 km/s to more than 1,000 km/s.

Gases near a sunspot sometimes brighten suddenly, shooting outward at high speed. These violent eruptions are called solar flares. You can see a solar flare in **Figure 8.**

## Differentiated Instruction

**Challenge** Have students research the relationship between sunspot activity and Earth's climate. Have students research and write a report about the Maunder Minimum, a period from 1645 through 1715 when few sunspots were observed. Possible answer: During this time, Europe experienced record low temperatures, and severe droughts occurred in the western United States. L3 P

## Teacher FYI

**Sunspots** Sunspots are caused by intense magnetic storms on the Sun. As the Sun rotates, lines of magnetic force wrap around it. These lines dip into the Sun's interior and then back out, forming sunspots. This explains why many sunspots occur in pairs and why the members of the pair have opposite magnetic polarity.

**CMEs** Coronal mass ejections (CMEs) occur when large amounts of electrically charged gas are ejected suddenly from the Sun's corona. CMEs can occur as often as two or three times each day during a sunspot maximum.

CMEs present little danger to life on Earth, but they do have some effects. CMEs can damage satellites in orbit around Earth. They also can interfere with radio and power distribution equipment. CMEs often cause auroras. High-energy particles contained in CMEs and the solar wind are carried past Earth's magnetic field. This generates electric currents that flow toward Earth's poles. These electric currents ionize gases in Earth's atmosphere. When these ions recombine with electrons, they produce the light of an aurora, shown in **Figure 8.**

**Science Online**

**Topic: Space Weather**
Visit in7.msscience.com for Web links to information about space weather and its effects.

**Activity** Record space weather conditions for several weeks. How does space weather affect Earth?

**Figure 8** Features such as solar prominences and solar flares can reach hundreds of thousands of kilometers into space. CMEs are generated as magnetic fields above sunspot groups rearrange. CMEs can trigger events that produce auroras.

Solar prominence

Solar flare

Aurora borealis, or northern lights

## Discussion

**Coronagraph** Ask the class to suggest ways to view a CME around the bright disk of the Sun. Encourage students to be inventive and brainstorm the topic for several minutes. After the discussion, tell students that CMEs are viewed through telescopes called coronagraphs. These telescopes use a disk to block light from the Sun's surface. **WARNING:** *Students should not attempt to view the Sun with the unaided eye.*

## Visual Learning

**Figure 8** Explain that CMEs can send as much as ten billion tons of plasma away from the Sun at speeds up to 2,000 km/s. It takes from 2 to 4 days for the shock wave caused by a CME to reach Earth. If a CME is observed, additional sightings of auroras can be expected within a few days as the shock wave passes Earth. Additional geomagnetic activity lasts for 1 to 2 days after the shock wave passes. Have students make an events-chain concept map using the information from Figure 8 and the text detailing the events from the production of a CME to the sighting of auroras on Earth.

### Use Science Words

**Word Meaning** Have students find out why a study of sunspots, solar flares, CMEs, and magnetic disturbances such as auroras on Earth are part of a study called *space weather.* Space weather deals with any factors affecting the environment of space in the vicinity of Earth and the Sun.

## Curriculum Connection

**Math** Using the data provided, have student groups graph sunspot activity. Have each group describe any observed trends. Sunspot activity seems to increase and decrease in a cycle. [L2] COOP LEARN

| Year | Sunspots | Year | Sunspots | Year | Sunspots | Year | Sunspots |
|------|----------|------|----------|------|----------|------|----------|
| 1985 | 18 | 1989 | 159 | 1993 | 54 | 1997 | 22 |
| 1986 | 14 | 1990 | 147 | 1994 | 31 | 1998 | 65 |
| 1987 | 29 | 1991 | 145 | 1995 | 18 | 1999 | 94 |
| 1988 | 100 | 1992 | 94 | 1996 | 9 | 2000 | 127 |

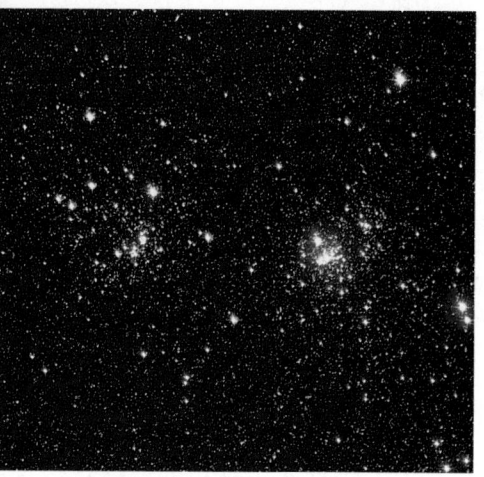

**Figure 9** Most stars originally formed in large clusters containing hundreds, or even thousands, of stars.
**Draw and label** *a sketch of the double cluster.*

## The Age of the Sun

The nuclear fusion reactions in the Sun that convert hydrogen to helium have been going on for about five billion years. As these reactions occur, the Sun emits energy. As a result, the Sun continually loses energy as nuclear energy in the Sun's interior is converted to other forms of energy that are radiated into space. However, it is estimated that the Sun still has enough hydrogen to keep these nuclear reactions going for another five billion years.

## The Sun in Space

In some ways the Sun is an average star. Compared to other stars, its mass, absolute magnitude, and age are about average. However, the Sun is unusual in one way— it is relatively far from any other stars. As a result, the Sun is much closer to Earth than any other star. The next closest star, Proxima Centauri, is about 270,000 times farther from Earth than the Sun. Light from this star takes over four years to reach Earth while light from the Sun reaches Earth in only about 8 min.

Unlike the Sun, most stars are part of a system in which two or more stars orbit each other. For example, the stars closest to the Sun form a star system in which three stars orbit each other. Larger groups of stars sometimes form star clusters that are held together by the gravitational attraction between the stars. **Figure 9** shows the double star cluster in the constellation Perseus.

### section 2 review

**Summary**

**The Sun's Layers**
- The Sun's interior has layers that include the core, radiation zone, and convection zone.

**The Sun's Atmosphere**
- The Sun's atmosphere includes the photosphere, chromosphere, and corona.

**Surface Features**
- The number of sunspots on the Sun varies in a 10- to 11-year cycle.
- Auroras occur when charged particles from the Sun interact with Earth's magnetic field.

**The Sun—An Average Star**
- The Sun is an average star, but it is much closer to Earth than any other star.

**Self Check**

1. **Explain** why the Sun is important for life on Earth.
2. **Describe** the sunspot cycle.
3. **Explain** why sunspots appear dark.
4. **Explain** why the Sun, which is an average star, appears so much brighter from Earth than other stars do.
5. **Think Critically** When a CME occurs on the Sun, it takes a couple of days for effects to be noticed on Earth. Explain.

**Applying Skills**

6. **Communicate** Make a sketch that shows the Sun's layers in your Science Journal. Write a short description of each layer.

 Science Online in7.msscience.com/self_check_quiz

### section 2 review

# LAB

# sunsp☉ts

Sunspots can be observed moving across the face of the Sun as it rotates. Measure the movement of sunspots, and use your data to determine the Sun's period of rotation.

## ◉ Real-World Question

Can sunspot motion be used to determine the Sun's period of rotation?

### Goals
- **Observe** sunspots and estimate their size.
- **Estimate** the rate at which sunspots move across the face of the Sun.

### Materials
several books                clipboard
piece of cardboard           small tripod
drawing paper                scissors
refracting telescope

### Safety Precautions

**WARNING:** *Handle scissors with care.*

## ◉ Procedure

1. Find a location where the Sun can be viewed at the same time of day for a minimum of five days. **WARNING:** *Do not look directly at the Sun. Do not look through the telescope at the Sun. You could damage your eyes.*

2. If the telescope has a small finder scope attached, remove it or keep it covered.

3. Set up the telescope with the eyepiece facing away from the Sun, as shown. Align the telescope so that the shadow it casts on the ground is the smallest size possible. Cut and attach the cardboard as shown in the photo.

4. Use books to prop the clipboard upright. Point the eyepiece at the drawing paper.

5. Move the clipboard back and forth until you have the largest image of the Sun on the paper. Adjust the telescope to form a clear image. Trace the outline of the Sun on the paper.

6. Trace any sunspots that appear as dark areas on the Sun's image. Repeat this step at the same time each day for a week.

7. Using the Sun's diameter (approximately 1,390,000 km), estimate the size of the largest sunspots that you observed.

8. **Calculate** how many kilometers the sunspots move each day.

9. **Predict** how many days it will take for the same group of sunspots to return to the same position in which they appeared on day 1.

## ◉ Conclude and Apply

1. What was the estimated size and rate of motion of the largest sunspots?

2. **Infer** how sunspots can be used to determine that the Sun's surface is not solid like Earth's surface.

### 𝒞ommunicating
### Your Data

**Compare** your conclusions with those of other students in your class. **For more help, refer to the** Science Skill Handbook.

LAB  **481**

---

### 𝒞ommunicating
### Your Data

Use a computer to produce a table to record calculations and predictions. Explain possible causes of differences. Possible answer: Students' estimates of sunspot movement might vary.

---

### Bellringer

**Section Focus Transparencies** also are available on the Interactive Chalkboard CD-ROM.

 L2 ELL

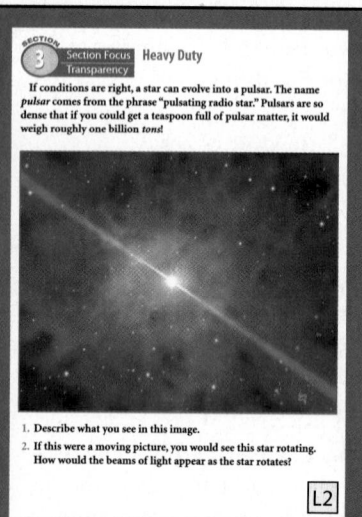

SECTION 3 Section Focus Transparency **Heavy Duty**

If conditions are right, a star can evolve into a pulsar. The name *pulsar* comes from the phrase "pulsating radio star." Pulsars are so dense that if you could get a teaspoon full of pulsar matter, it would weigh roughly one billion *tons!*

1. Describe what you see in this image.
2. If this were a moving picture, you would see this star rotating. How would the beams of light appear as the star rotates?

L2

Stars and Galaxies

### Tie to Prior Knowledge

**Plasma** Have students recall the four states of matter: solid, liquid, gas, and plasma. Explain that stars are composed of matter in the plasma state. Ask students to describe traits of matter in this state. Plasma is the state of matter in which there are roughly equal numbers of positively and negatively charged particles. It is produced when the atoms in a gas become ionized.

### Caption Answer

**Figure 10** white dwarf

---

**Standard—7.3.11:** Explain that the Sun loses energy by emitting light. Note that only a tiny fraction of that light reaches Earth. Understand that the Sun's energy arrives as light with a wide range of wavelengths, consisting of visible light, infrared, and ultraviolet radiation.

# Evolution of Stars

**as you read**

## *What* You'll Learn

- **Describe** how stars are classified.
- **Compare** the Sun to other types of stars on the H-R diagram.
- **Describe** how stars evolve.

## *Why* It's Important

Earth and your body contain elements that were made in stars.

### 🔍 Review Vocabulary

**gravity:** an attractive force between objects that have mass

### New Vocabulary

- nebula
- giant
- white dwarf
- supergiant
- neutron star
- black hole

**Figure 10** The relationships among a star's color, temperature, and brightness are shown in this H-R diagram. Stars in the upper left are hot, bright stars, and stars in the lower right are cool, dim stars.
**Classify** *Which type of star shown in the diagram is the hottest, dimmest star?*

## Classifying Stars

When you look at the night sky, all stars might appear to be similar, but they are quite different. Like people, they vary in age and size, but stars also vary in temperature and brightness.

In the early 1900s, Ejnar Hertzsprung and Henry Russell made some important observations. They noticed that, in general, stars with higher temperatures also have brighter absolute magnitudes.

Hertzsprung and Russell developed a graph, shown in **Figure 10,** to show this relationship. They placed temperatures across the bottom and absolute magnitudes up one side. A graph that shows the relationship of a star's temperature to its absolute magnitude is called a Hertzsprung-Russell (H-R) diagram.

**The Main Sequence** As you can see, stars seem to fit into specific areas of the graph. Most stars fit into a diagonal band that runs from the upper left to the lower right of the graph. This band, called the main sequence, contains hot, blue, bright stars in the upper left and cool, red, dim stars in the lower right. Yellow main sequence stars, like the Sun, fall in between.

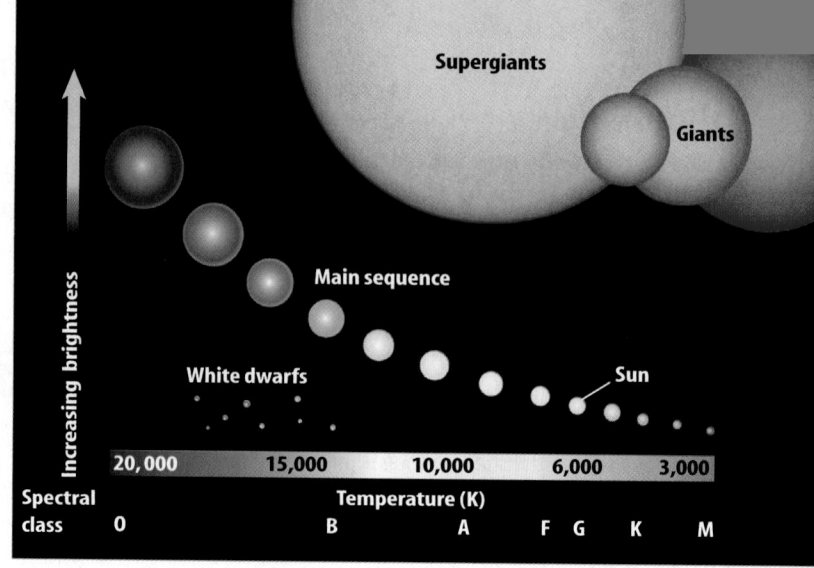

Supergiants

Giants

Main sequence

White dwarfs

Sun

Increasing brightness

| | | | | |
|---|---|---|---|---|
| 20,000 | 15,000 | 10,000 | 6,000 | 3,000 |

Temperature (K)

Spectral class

| O | B | A | F G | K | M |

**482 CHAPTER 16** Stars and Galaxies

---

## Section 3 Resource Manager

**Chapter FAST FILE Resources**

Transparency Activity, p. 50

Directed Reading for Content Mastery, p. 21

Enrichment, p. 33

Reinforcement, p. 29

**Dwarfs and Giants** About 90 percent of all stars are main sequence stars. Most of these are small, red stars found in the lower right of the H-R diagram. Among main sequence stars, the hottest stars generate the most light and the coolest ones generate the least. What about the ten percent of stars that are not part of the main sequence? Some of these stars are hot but not bright. These small stars are located on the lower left of the H-R diagram and are called white dwarfs. Other stars are extremely bright but not hot. These large stars on the upper right of the H-R diagram are called giants, or red giants, because they are usually red in color. The largest giants are called super-giants. **Figure 11** shows the supergiant, Antares—a star 300 times the Sun's diameter—in the constellation Scorpius. It is more than 11,000 times as bright as the Sun.

**Reading Check** *What kinds of stars are on the main sequence?*

## How do stars shine?

For centuries, people were puzzled by the questions of what stars were made of and how they produced light. Many people had estimated that Earth was only a few thousand years old. The Sun could have been made of coal and shined for that long. However, when people realized that Earth was much older, they wondered what material possibly could burn for so many years. Early in the twentieth century, scientists began to understand the process that keeps stars shining for billions of years.

**Generating Energy** In the 1930s, scientists discovered reactions between the nuclei of atoms. They hypothesized that temperatures in the center of the Sun must be high enough to cause hydrogen to fuse to make helium. This nuclear fusion reaction releases tremendous amounts of energy. Much of this energy is emitted as different wavelengths of light, including visible, infrared, and ultraviolet light. Only a tiny fraction of this light comes to Earth. During the nuclear fusion reaction, four hydrogen nuclei combine to create one helium nucleus. The mass of one helium nucleus is less than the mass of four hydrogen nuclei, so some mass is lost in the reaction.

Years earlier, in 1905, Albert Einstein had proposed a theory stating that mass can be converted into energy. This was stated as the famous equation $E = mc^2$. In this equation, $E$ is the energy produced, $m$ is the mass, and $c$ is the speed of light. A small amount of mass is converted to a large amount of energy when hydrogen atoms fuse to form a helium atom.

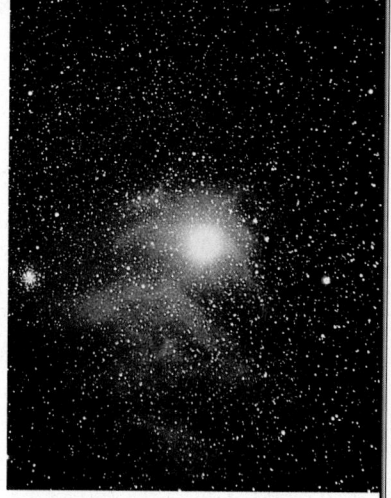

**Figure 11** Antares is a bright supergiant located 400 light-years from Earth. Although its temperature is only about 3,500 K, it is the 16th brightest star in the sky.

**Indiana Academic Standard Check**

**7.3.11:** Explain that the Sun loses energy by emitting light . . . consisting of visible light, infrared, and ultraviolet radiation.

✓ What type of reaction in the Sun converts a small amount of mass into a large amount of energy?

✓ a nuclear fusion reaction

---

---

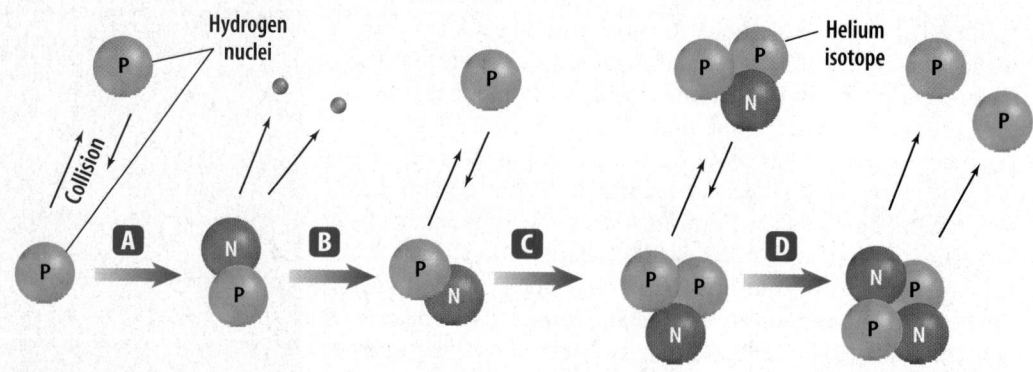

Hydrogen nuclei

Helium isotope

**A** Two protons (hydrogen nuclei) collide. One proton decays to a neutron, releasing subatomic particles and some energy.

**B** Another proton fuses with a proton and neutron to form an isotope of helium. Energy is given off again.

**C** Two helium isotopes collide with enough energy to fuse.

**D** A helium nucleus (two protons and two neutrons) forms as two protons break away. During the process, still more energy is released.

**Figure 12** Fusion of hydrogen into helium occurs in a star's core. **Infer** *why nuclear reactions occur only in the core of a star.*

**Fusion** Shown in **Figure 12,** fusion occurs in the cores of stars. Only in the core are temperatures high enough to cause atoms to fuse. Normally, they would repel each other, but in the core of a star where temperatures can exceed 15,000,000 K, atoms can move so fast that some of them fuse upon colliding.

## Evolution of Stars

INTEGRATE Physics

The H-R diagram explained a lot about stars. However, it also led to more questions. Many wondered why some stars didn't fit in the main sequence group and what happened when a star depleted its supply of hydrogen fuel. Today, scientists have theories about how stars evolve, what makes them different from one another, and what happens when they die. **Figure 13** illustrates the lives of different types of stars.

When hydrogen fuel is depleted, a star loses its main sequence status. This can take less than 1 million years for the brightest stars to many billions of years for the dimmest stars. The Sun has a main sequence life span of about 10 billion years. Half of its life span is still in the future.

**Nebula** Stars begin as a large cloud of gas and dust called a **nebula.** As the particles of gas and dust exert a gravitational force on each other, the nebula begins to contract. Gravitational forces cause instability within the nebula. The nebula can break apart into smaller and smaller pieces. Each piece eventually might collapse to form a star.

---

## LAB DEMONSTRATION

**Purpose** to demonstrate how color changes as a material is heated
**Materials** Bunsen burner, wire, tongs, insulated pad
**Preparation** Set up the Bunsen burner and obtain safety goggles and gloves.
**Procedure** Using tongs, hold a wire over a burner flame until it begins to glow. Have students record the color of the glowing wire. Continue heating the wire as students record changes and summarize their observations.
**Expected Outcome** The wire changed from red to reddish-orange as it became hotter.

**Assessment**
How do the color changes you observed relate to star colors? Hotter stars shine at different colors than cooler stars.

**A Star Is Born** As the particles in the smaller pieces of nebula move closer together, the temperatures in each nebula piece increase. When the temperature inside the core of a nebula piece reaches 10 million K, fusion begins. The energy released radiates outward through the condensing ball of gas. As the energy radiates into space, stars are born.

**✓ Reading Check** *How are stars born?*

**Main Sequence to Giant Stars** In the newly formed star, the heat from fusion causes pressure to increase. This pressure balances the attraction due to gravity. The star becomes a main sequence star. It continues to use its hydrogen fuel.

When hydrogen in the core of the star is depleted, a balance no longer exists between pressure and gravity. The core contracts, and temperatures inside the star increase. This causes the outer layers of the star to expand and cool. In this late stage of its life cycle, a star is called a **giant.**

After the core temperature reaches 100 million K, helium nuclei fuse to form carbon in the giant's core. By this time, the star has expanded to an enormous size, and its outer layers are much cooler than they were when it was a main sequence star. In about 5 billion years, the Sun will become a giant.

**White Dwarfs** After the star's core uses much of its helium, it contracts even more and its outer layers escape into space. This leaves behind the hot, dense core. At this stage in a star's evolution, it becomes a **white dwarf.** A white dwarf is about the size of Earth. Eventually, the white dwarf will cool and stop giving off light.

**INTEGRATE Chemistry**

**White Dwarf Matter** The matter in white dwarf stars is more than 500,000 times as dense as the matter in Earth. In white dwarf matter, there are free electrons and atomic nuclei. The resistance of the electrons to pack together more provides pressure that keeps the star from collapsing. This state of matter is called electron degeneracy.

**Figure 13** The life of a star depends on its mass. Massive stars eventually become neutron stars or black holes.
**Explain** *what happens to stars that are the size of the Sun.*

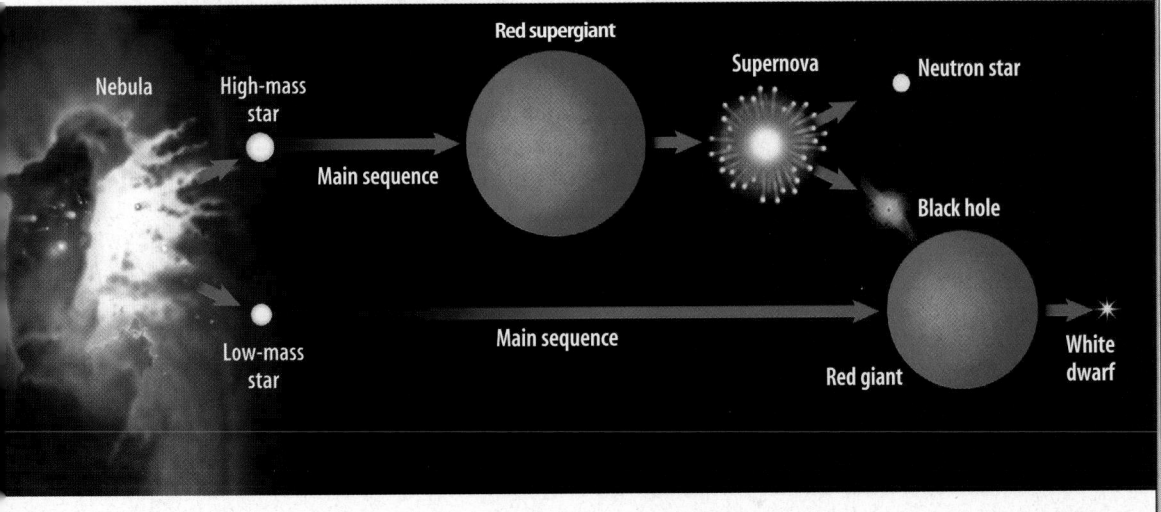

Nebula · High-mass star · Main sequence · Red supergiant · Supernova · Neutron star · Black hole

Low-mass star · Main sequence · Red giant · White dwarf

SECTION 3 Evolution of Stars **485**

**INTEGRATE Chemistry**

**White Dwarf Matter** White dwarf matter is electron degenerate. Electron degeneracy is effective to 1.4 solar masses, a value called the Chandrasekhar Limit. If a white dwarf acquires more than 1.4 solar masses, it will collapse and explode as a type IA supernova.

**✓ Reading Check**

**Answer** temperatures in nebulae increase, fusion begins; energy radiates

**Activity**

**Nebulae** Have students research the Horsehead and Orion nebulae, located in the constellation of Orion. Ask them to describe each nebula. The Horsehead Nebula is composed of a dust cloud that blocks light from behind it, whereas the Orion Nebula is composed of young stars and hot, glowing gases. [L3] **ILS Linguistic**

**Caption Answer**

**Figure 13** Stars the size of the Sun will become giants, white dwarfs, and finally black dwarfs.

**Visual Learning**

**Figure 13** Have students construct sequence diagrams showing the evolution of a massive star. After students read about black holes, ask the following questions: After a supernova, what type of object forms if the remaining dense core collapses? a black hole If no light is given off, how are black holes located? X-rays are emitted by matter as it is pulled into the black hole.

## Teacher FYI

**Orion Nebula** A nebula may produce a steady stream of stars over a given period. In the Orion Nebula (M42), a star nursery 1,500 light-years away, hundreds of stars have already formed and more will follow. The brightest star seen in the Orion Nebula by the *Hubble Space Telescope* is the Becklin-Neugebauer object.

**Research** Historic accounts like the description of the 386 supernova are very important to astronomers. Knowing the exact age of this pulsar provides an opportunity to test and calibrate models of how pulsars evolve.

**386 Supernova** In 386 A.D., Chinese observers described a new star—a supernova—in the night sky. More recently, astronomers using the *Chandra X-ray Observatory* found evidence of a spinning neutron star, called a pulsar, in exactly the same location. Because of the Chinese account, astronomers better understand how neutron stars form and evolve.

**Supergiants and Supernovas** In stars that are more than about eight times more massive than the Sun, the stages of evolution occur more quickly and more violently. Look back at **Figure 13.** In massive stars, the core heats up to much higher temperatures. Heavier and heavier elements form by fusion, and the star expands into a **supergiant.** Eventually, iron forms in the core. Because of iron's atomic structure, it cannot release energy through fusion. The core collapses violently, and a shock wave travels outward through the star. The outer portion of the star explodes, producing a supernova. A supernova can be millions of times brighter than the original star was.

**Neutron Stars** If the collapsed core of a supernova is between about 1.4 and 3 times as massive as the Sun, it will shrink to approximately 20 km in diameter. Only neutrons can exist in the dense core, and it becomes a **neutron star.** Neutron stars are so dense that a teaspoonful would weigh more than 600 million metric tons in Earth's gravity. As dense as neutron stars are, they can contract only so far because the neutrons resist the inward pull of gravity.

**Black Holes** If the remaining dense core from a supernova is more than about three times more massive than the Sun, probably nothing can stop the core's collapse. Under these conditions, all of the core's mass collapses to a point. The gravity near this mass is so strong that nothing can escape from it, not even light. Because light cannot escape, the region is called a **black hole.** If you could shine a flashlight on a black hole, the light simply would disappear into it.

### ✔ Reading Check

**Answer** the remaining dense core from a massive supernova, collapsed down into a point, where gravity is so strong nothing can escape, not even light

### ✔ Reading Check  *What is a black hole?*

Black holes, however, are not like giant vacuum cleaners, sucking in distant objects. A black hole has an event horizon, which is a region inside of which nothing can escape. If something—including light—crosses the event horizon, it will be pulled into the black hole. Beyond the event horizon, the black hole's gravity pulls on objects just as it would if the mass had not collapsed. Stars and planets can orbit around a black hole.

The photograph in **Figure 14** was taken by the *Hubble Space Telescope.* It shows a jet of gas streaming out of the center of galaxy M87. This jet of gas formed as matter flowed toward a black hole, and some of the gas was ejected along the polar axis.

## Fun Fact

In a star with a mass similar to that of the Sun, outer layers become unstable and begin escaping into space when the core runs out of hydrogen fuel. The escaping gases form a shell around the star, producing a nebula. The Ring Nebula in the constellation Lyra is a result of this process.

**Figure 14** The black hole at the center of galaxy M87 pulls matter into it at extremely high velocities. Some matter is ejected to produce a jet of gas that streams away from the center of the galaxy at nearly light speed.

## Teacher FYI

**Brown Dwarfs** Brown dwarfs are stars that never generated fusion in their cores. These dim stars are found by observing the movement of a companion star. A single star's path through space is a nearly straight line. The path of a star orbited by a brown dwarf has a distinct wobble. This wobble is used to locate brown dwarfs as well as planets beyond the solar system.

### ✔ Active Reading

**Learning Journal** Students should draw a vertical line down each page of their Learning Journals. The left-column entries can be research notes, lecture notes, or vocabulary terms. The right-column entries are the student's response to, interpretation of, questions about, or analysis of the left-column entries. Have students write a Learning Journal related to stars and galaxies.

**Recycling Matter** A star begins its life as a nebula, such as the one shown in **Figure 15**. Where does the matter in a nebula come from? Nebulas form partly from the matter that was once in other stars. A star ejects enormous amounts of matter during its lifetime. Some of this matter is incorporated into nebulas, which can evolve to form new stars. The matter in stars is recycled many times.

What about the matter created in the cores of stars and during supernova explosions? Are elements such as carbon and iron also recycled? These elements can become parts of new stars. In fact, spectrographs have shown that the Sun contains some carbon, iron, and other heavier elements. Because the Sun is an average, main sequence star, it is too young and its mass is too small to have formed these elements itself. The Sun condensed from material that was created in stars that died many billions of years ago.

Some elements condense to form planets and other bodies rather than stars. In fact, your body contains many atoms that were fused in the cores of ancient stars. Evidence suggests that the first stars formed from hydrogen and helium and that all the other elements have formed in the cores of stars or as stars explode.

**Figure 15** Stars are forming in the Orion Nebula and other similar nebulae.
**Describe** *a star-forming nebula.*

## section 3 review

### Summary

**Classifying Stars**
- Most stars plot on the main sequence of an H-R diagram.
- As stars near the end of their lives, they move off of the main sequence.

**How do stars shine?**
- Stars shine because of a process called fusion.
- During fusion, nuclei of a lighter element merge to form a heavier element.

**Evolution of Stars**
- Stars form in regions of gas and dust called nebulae.
- Stars evolve differently depending on how massive they are.

### Self Check

1. **Explain** how the Sun is different from other stars on the main sequence. How is it different from a giant star? How is it different from a white dwarf?
2. **Describe** how stars release energy.
3. **Outline** the past and probable future of the Sun.
4. **Define** a black hole.
5. **Think Critically** How can white dwarf stars be both hot and dim?

#### Applying Math

6. **Convert Units** A neutron star has a diameter of 20 km. One kilometer equals 0.62 miles. What is the neutron star's diameter in miles?

Science Online in7.msscience.com/self_check_quiz

SECTION 3 Evolution of Stars **487**

## section 3 review

1. The Sun is smaller and its surface is hotter than a giant star. The Sun is larger and cooler than a white dwarf.
2. Stars release energy by fusing a lighter element, such as hydrogen, into a heavier element, such as helium.
3. The Sun formed when a solar nebula contracted. It has been a main sequence star for about 4.6 billion years. In another 5 billion years, the Sun will become a giant star. Eventually, its core will shrink to a white dwarf, and it will cool gradually.
4. A black hole is the completely collapsed core of a massive star.
5. White dwarfs are very small, so they can be both hot and dim.
6. 12.4 miles

## section 4

# Galaxies and the Universe

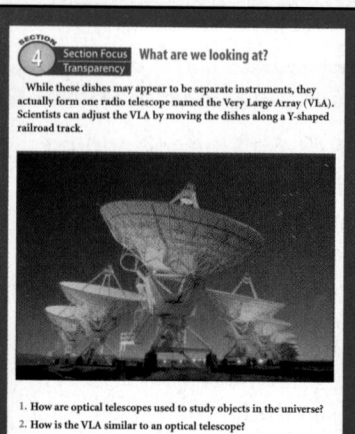
### as you read

**What You'll Learn**

- **Describe** the Sun's position in the Milky Way Galaxy.
- **Explain** that the same natural laws that apply to our solar system also apply in other galaxies.

**Why It's Important**

Studying the universe could determine whether life exists elsewhere.

**Review Vocabulary**
**universe:** the space that contains all known matter and energy

**New Vocabulary**
- galaxy
- big bang theory

## Galaxies

If you enjoy science fiction, you might have read about explorers traveling through the galaxy. On their way, they visit planets around other stars and encounter strange alien beings. Although this type of space exploration is futuristic, it is possible to explore galaxies today. Using a variety of telescopes, much is being learned about the Milky Way and other galaxies.

A **galaxy** is a large group of stars, gas, and dust held together by gravity. Earth and the solar system are in a galaxy called the Milky Way. It might contain as many as one trillion stars. The universe contains many billions of galaxies. Most of these galaxies contain billions of stars. Some, like the Milky Way, might contain a trillion stars or more. Galaxies are separated by huge distances—often millions of light-years.

In the same way that stars are grouped together within galaxies, galaxies are grouped into clusters. The cluster that the Milky Way belongs to is called the Local Group. It contains about 45 galaxies of various sizes and types. The three major types of galaxies are spiral, elliptical, and irregular.

**Spiral Galaxies** Spiral galaxies are galaxies that have spiral arms that wind outward from the center. The arms consist of bright stars, dust, and gas. The Milky Way Galaxy, shown in **Figure 16,** is a spiral galaxy. The Sun and the rest of the solar system are located near the outer edge of the Milky Way Galaxy.

Spiral galaxies can be normal or barred. Arms in a normal spiral start close to the center of the galaxy. Barred spirals have spiral arms extending from a large bar of stars and gas that passes through the center of the galaxy.

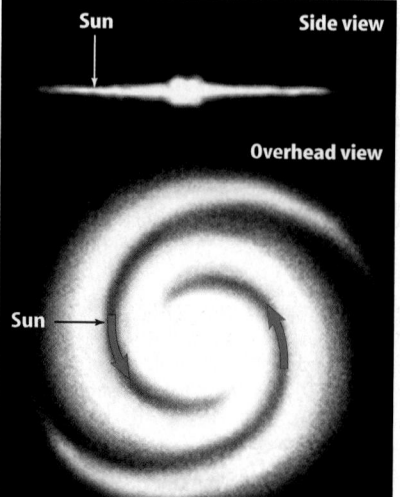

**Figure 16** This illustration shows a side view and an overhead view of the Milky Way.
**Describe** where the Sun is in the Milky Way.

**Elliptical Galaxies** A common type of galaxy is the elliptical galaxy. **Figure 17** shows an elliptical galaxy in the constellation Andromeda. These galaxies are shaped like large, three-dimensional ellipses. Many are football shaped, but others are round. Some elliptical galaxies are small, while others are so large that several galaxies the size of the Milky Way would fit inside one of them.

**Irregular Galaxies** The third type—an irregular galaxy—includes most of those galaxies that don't fit into the other categories. Irregular galaxies have many different shapes. They are smaller than the other types of galaxies. Two irregular galaxies called the Clouds of Magellan orbit the Milky Way. The Large Magellanic Cloud is shown in **Figure 18.**

> ☑ **Reading Check** *How do the three different types of galaxies differ?*

## The Milky Way Galaxy

The Milky Way might contain one trillion stars. The visible disk of stars shown in **Figure 16** is about 100,000 light-years across. Find the location of the Sun. Notice that it is located about 26,000 light-years from the galaxy's center in one of the spiral arms. In the galaxy, all stars orbit around a central region, or core. It takes about 225 million years for the Sun to orbit the center of the Milky Way.

The Milky Way often is classified as a normal spiral galaxy. However, recent evidence suggests that it might be a barred spiral. It is difficult to know for sure because astronomers have limited data about how the galaxy looks from the outside.

You can't see the shape of the Milky Way because you are located within one of its spiral arms. You can, however, see the Milky Way stretching across the sky as a misty band of faint light. You can see the brightest part of the Milky Way if you look low in the southern sky on a moonless summer night. All the stars you can see in the night sky belong to the Milky Way.

Like many other galaxies, the Milky Way has a supermassive black hole at its center. This black hole might be more than 2.5 million times as massive as the Sun. Evidence for the existence of the black hole comes from observing the orbit of a star near the galaxy's center. Additional evidence includes X-ray emissions detected by the *Chandra X-ray Observatory.* X rays are produced when matter spirals into a black hole.

**Figure 17** This photo shows an example of an elliptical galaxy. **Identify** *the two other types of galaxies.*

**Figure 18** The Large Magellanic Cloud is an irregular galaxy. It's a member of the Local Group, and it orbits the Milky Way.

## Cultural Diversity

**The Milky Way** The names various cultures have assigned to the Milky Way show that most observers are struck by its fluid form. Akkadians called it the River of the Snake. In Judea, Armenia, and Syria, it was a long bandage. In China and Japan it was called the Celestial River. Polynesians called it the Long, Blue, Cloud-Eating Shark. In India, it was known as the Bed of the Ganges.

**Purpose** Students develop a scale illustrating the vastness of space. L2 ELL LS **Logical-Mathematical**

**Materials** large sheet of paper, metric ruler or meterstick

**Teaching Strategies** Help students conceptualize the vast scale of their model. If our Sun were represented by a dot, the circle representing the distance to Proxima Centauri would be nearly within that same dot.

**Analysis**

1. Answers will vary depending on the scale chosen.
2. The distance to the Andromeda Galaxy should be 29 times the diameter of the student's Milky Way model. This can be determined by dividing the distance to the Andromeda Galaxy (2.9 million light-years) by the diameter of the Milky Way (100,000 light-years).

## Assessment

**Content** Have students determine the scale distance to the Large Magellanic Cloud. Its true distance is about 169,000 light-years. The distance to the Large Magellanic Cloud should be about 1.69 times the diameter of the student's Milky Way model. Use **Performance Assessment in the Science Classroom,** p. 123.

**Measuring Distance in Space**

**Procedure**

1. On a large sheet of **paper,** draw an overhead view of the Milky Way. If necessary, refer to **Figure 16.** Choose a scale to show distance in light-years.
2. Mark the approximate location of the solar system, which is about two-thirds of the way out on one of the spiral arms.
3. Now, draw a side view of the Milky Way Galaxy. Mark the position of the solar system.

**Analysis**

1. What scale did you use to represent distance on your model of the Milky Way?
2. The Andromeda Galaxy is about 2.9 million light-years from Earth. What scale distance would this represent?

## Origin of the Universe

People long have wondered how the universe formed. Several models of its origin have been proposed. One model is the steady state theory. It suggests that the universe always has been the same as it is now. The universe always existed and always will. As the universe expands, new matter is created to keep the overall density of the universe the same or in a steady state. However, evidence indicates that the universe was much different in the past.

A second idea is called the oscillating model. In this model, the universe began with expansion. Over time, the expansion slowed and the universe contracted. Then the process began again, oscillating back and forth. Some scientists still hypothesize that the universe expands and contracts in a cycle.

A third model of how the universe formed is called the big bang theory. The universe started with a big bang and has been expanding ever since. This theory will be described later.

## Expansion of the Universe

What does it sound like when a train is blowing its whistle while it travels past you? The whistle has a higher pitch as the train approaches you. Then the whistle seems to drop in pitch as the train moves away. This effect is called the Doppler shift. The Doppler shift occurs with light as well as with sound. **Figure 19** shows how the Doppler shift causes changes in the light coming from distant stars and galaxies. If a star is moving toward Earth, its wavelengths of light are compressed. If a star is moving away from Earth, its wavelengths of light are stretched.

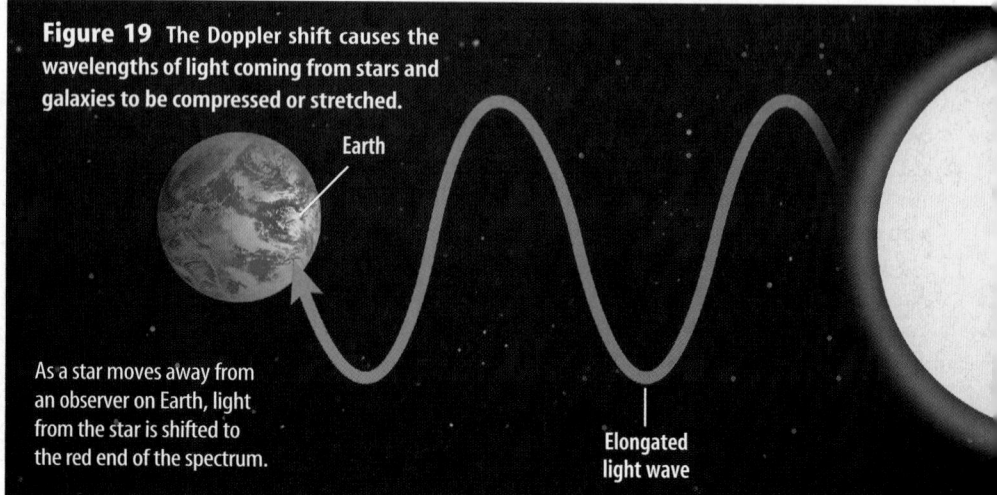

**Figure 19** The Doppler shift causes the wavelengths of light coming from stars and galaxies to be compressed or stretched.

Earth

As a star moves away from an observer on Earth, light from the star is shifted to the red end of the spectrum.

Elongated light wave

## Curriculum Connection

**Art** Suggest that a group of students research and draw a diagram of the *Hubble Space Telescope,* which is used to gather data about the origin of the universe. When they present their diagram, have students explain the advantage of having a telescope in space. Images are clearer because there is no interference from the atmosphere. L2 COOP LEARN LS **Visual-Spatial**

## Differentiated Instruction

**Learning Disabled** Use a balloon to demonstrate the oscillating model of the origin of the universe. Blow up the balloon, and explain that this is like the expansion phase of this model. Then slowly let the air out of the balloon, and explain that this is like the contraction phase of this model. Have students describe what would happen next. The balloon (universe) would again begin to expand. L1 ELL LS **Visual-Spatial**

**The Doppler Shift** Look at the spectrum of a star in **Figure 20A.** Note the position of the dark lines. How do they compare with the lines in **Figures 20B** and **20C?** They have shifted in position. What caused this shift? As you just read, when a star is moving toward Earth, its wavelengths of light are compressed, just as the sound waves from the train's whistle are. This causes the dark lines in the spectrum to shift toward the blue-violet end of the spectrum. A red shift in the spectrum occurs when a star is moving away from Earth. In a red shift, the dark lines shift toward the red end of the spectrum.

**Red Shift** In 1929, Edwin Hubble published an interesting fact about the light coming from most galaxies. When a spectrograph is used to study light from galaxies beyond the Local Group, a red shift occurs in the light. What does this red shift tell you about the universe?

Because all galaxies beyond the Local Group show a red shift in their spectra, they must be moving away from Earth. If all galaxies outside the Local Group are moving away from Earth, then the entire universe must be expanding. Remember the Launch Lab at the beginning of the chapter? The dots on the balloon moved apart as the model universe expanded. Regardless of which dot you picked, all the other dots moved away from it. In a similar way, galaxies beyond the Local Group are moving away from Earth.

**Figure 20** **A** This spectrum shows dark absorption lines. **B** The dark lines shift toward the blue-violet end for a star moving toward Earth. **C** The lines shift toward the red end for a star moving away from Earth.

> **Indiana Academic Standard Check**
>
> **7.3.1:** Recognize and describe that . . . each galaxy contains many billions of stars.
>
> ✔ In which galaxy is the Sun located?
>
> ✔ the Milky Way Galaxy

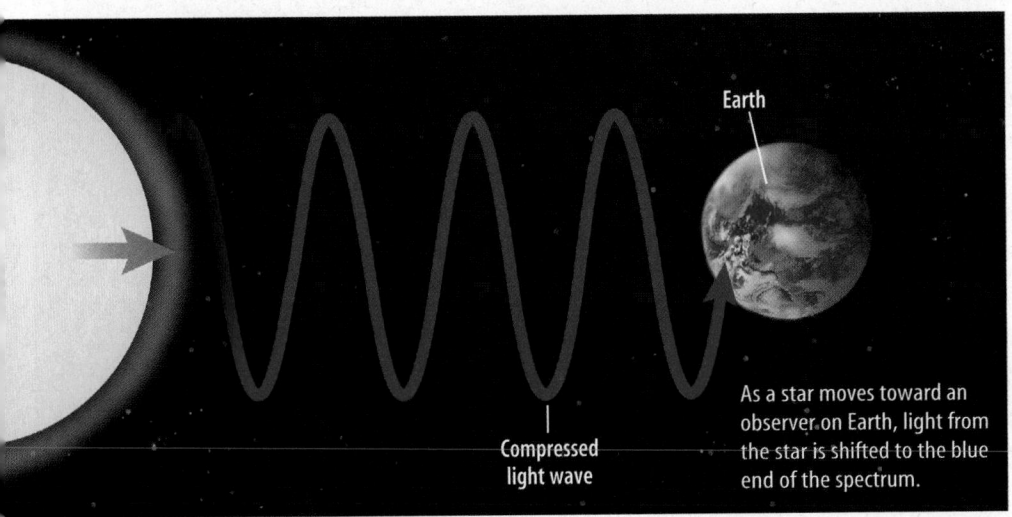

As a star moves toward an observer on Earth, light from the star is shifted to the blue end of the spectrum.

Earth

Compressed light wave

## Differentiated Instruction

## Visualizing the Big Bang Theory

Have students examine the pictures and read the captions. Then ask the following questions.

If a galaxy were discovered at a distance of 24 billion light years from Earth, how would this change the estimated age of the universe? According to the big bang theory, it would mean that the universe had been expanding for at least 24 billion years, making it much older that its present estimated age.

When you look at distant galaxies, why can you say that you are looking back in time? Because light that is now reaching Earth left those galaxies millions or even billions of years ago.

### Activity

**Penzias and Wilson** Have small groups of students research the work of Arno A. Penzias and Robert W. Wilson that resulted in their winning a Nobel Prize. Ask each group to make a comic book that illustrates the story of their work and explains how it relates to the big bang theory. L2 COOP LEARN Ⓚ **Visual-Spatial and Linguistic**

**Figure 21**

The big bang theory states that the universe probably began about 13.7 billion years ago with an enormous explosion. Even today, galaxies are rushing apart from this explosion.

Ⓐ Within fractions of a second of the initial explosion, the universe grew from the size of a pinhead to 2,000 times the size of the Sun.

Ⓑ By the time the universe was one second old, it was a dense, opaque, swirling mass of elementary particles.

Ⓒ Matter began collecting in clumps. As matter cooled, hydrogen and helium gases formed.

Ⓓ More than a billion years after the initial explosion, the first stars were born.

**492 CHAPTER 16** Stars and Galaxies

## Science Journal

**The Big Bang Theory** Ask students to write a short newspaper article about the big bang theory in their Science Journals. Students should copy the style of articles in the local paper. They also should assume that they are writing for an audience that is not familiar with the theory.

## The Big Bang Theory

When scientists determined that the universe was expanding, they developed a theory to explain their observations. The leading theory about the formation of the universe is called the **big bang theory**. **Figure 21** illustrates the big bang theory. According to this theory, approximately 13.7 billion years ago, the universe began with an enormous explosion. The entire universe began to expand everywhere at the same time.

**Looking Back in Time** The time-exposure photograph shown in **Figure 22** was taken by the *Hubble Space Telescope*. It shows more than 1,500 galaxies at distances of more than 10 billion light-years. These galaxies could date back to when the universe was no more than 1 billion years old. The galaxies are in various stages of development. One astronomer says that humans might be looking back to a time when the Milky Way was forming.

Whether the universe will expand forever or stop expanding is still unknown. If enough matter exists, gravity might halt the expansion, and the universe will contract until everything comes to a single point. However, studies of distant supernovae indicate that an energy, called dark energy, is causing the universe to expand faster. Scientists are trying to understand how dark energy might affect the fate of the universe.

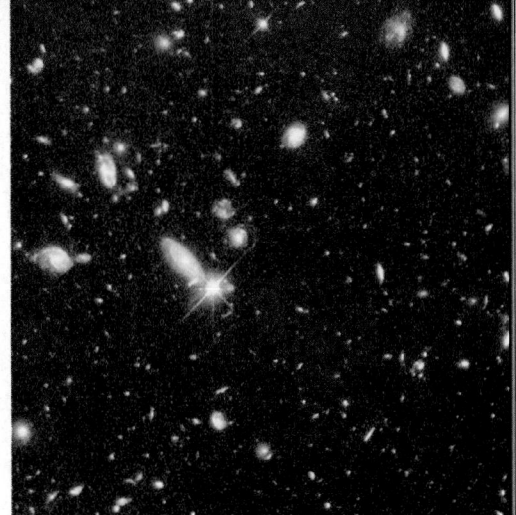

**Figure 22** The light from the galaxies in this photo mosaic took billions of years to reach Earth.

---

## section ④ review

### Summary

**Galaxies**
- The three main types of galaxies are spiral, elliptical, and irregular.

**The Milky Way Galaxy**
- The Milky Way is a spiral galaxy and the Sun is about 26,000 light-years from its center.

**Origin of the Universe**
- Theories about how the universe formed include the steady state theory, the oscillating universe theory, and the big bang theory.

**The Big Bang Theory**
- This theory states that the universe began with an explosion about 13.7 billion years ago.

### Self Check

1. **Describe** elliptical galaxies. How are they different from spiral galaxies?
2. **Identify** the galaxy that you live in.
3. **Explain** the Doppler shift.
4. **Explain** how all galaxies are similar.
5. **Think Critically** All galaxies outside the Local Group show a red shift. Within the Local Group, some show a red shift and some show a blue shift. What does this tell you about the galaxies in the Local Group?

#### Applying Skills

6. **Compare and contrast** the theories about the origin of the universe.

Science Online in7.msscience.com/self_check_quiz   SECTION 4   Galaxies and the Universe   **493**

---

## section ④ review

1. Elliptical galaxies have ellipsoidal shapes. Spiral galaxies have flattened, pinwheel shapes.
2. the Milky Way
3. The Doppler shift occurs when waves of light or sound are stretched or compressed because of relative motion between the source and the receiver.
4. Answers will vary. Possible answer: All galaxies are made of similar chemical elements and have the same forms of energy.
5. Some galaxies are moving toward the Milky Way, and some are moving away from the Milky Way.
6. Student answers will vary.

---

---

### Use an Analogy

**Raisin Bread** Ask students to think of a loaf of raisin bread. When the bread is unbaked, the raisins are relatively close together. As the bread bakes, all the raisins move apart from one another. Have students compare this to the way scientists hypothesize galaxies are moving in the universe.

## 3 Assess

### DAILY INTERVENTION

#### Check for Understanding

**Logical-Mathematical** Have students write brief paragraphs in their Science Journals explaining why the spiral shape of the Milky Way Galaxy is not visible from Earth. To see the spiral shape, an observer would have to be above or below the plane of the galaxy. Earth is located in one of the spiral arms. **LS**

#### Reteach

**Light Waves** Have a student use a spring toy to demonstrate the compression and expansion of light waves described by the Doppler shift. **L1** **LS** **Visual-Spatial**

## ✔ Assessment

**Content** Have students write a paragraph about galaxies. Encourage them to illustrate their summaries. Use **Performance Assessment in the Science Classroom**, p. 159. **P**

## ⊙ Real-World Question

**Purpose** Students conduct an experiment that shows how distance from an object affects the object's parallax shift. L2 **ELL** **COOP LEARN** IS **Logical-Mathematical**

**Process Skills** measure in SI, use numbers, compare and contrast, recognize cause and effect, formulate models, communicate

**Time Required** one class period

**Materials** meterstick, metric ruler, masking tape, pencil

**Safety Precautions** Caution students to wear goggles during the experiment.

## ⊙ Form a Hypothesis

**Possible Hypothesis** Students may hypothesize that the amount of observed parallax increases as an object is moved closer and that a simple demonstration can illustrate this effect.

## ⊙ Test Your Hypothesis

**Possible Procedures** Choose and mark three different positions on the meterstick (20 cm, 40 cm, and 60 cm). Attach a metric ruler to one end, forming a T shape, and place it on a table. Hold a pencil upright at one of the marked positions. Observe the pencil's apparent movement against the meterstick with one eye closed and then the other. Repeat for all positions.

---

# LAB Design Your Own

# Measuring Parallax

## ⊙ Real-World Question

Parallax is the apparent shift in the position of an object when viewed from two locations. How can you build a model to show the relationship between distance and parallax?

## ⊙ Form a Hypothesis

State a hypothesis about how parallax varies with distance.

## ⊙ Test Your Hypothesis

**Make a Plan**

1. As a group, agree upon and write your hypothesis statement.
2. **List** the steps you need to take to build your model. Be specific, describing exactly what you will do at each step.
3. **Devise** a method to test how distance from an observer to an object, such as a pencil, affects the parallax of the object.
4. **List** the steps you will take to test your hypothesis. Be specific, describing exactly what you will do at each step.
5. Read over your plan for the model to be used in this experiment.

### Goals
- **Design** a model to show how the distance from an observer to an object affects the object's parallax shift.
- **Describe** how parallax can be used to determine the distance to a star.

### Possible Materials
meterstick
masking tape
metric ruler
pencil

### Safety Precautions
👓

**WARNING:** *Be sure to wear goggles to protect your eyes.*

**494 CHAPTER 16** Stars and Galaxies

---

## Alternative Inquiry Lab

**Extend the Activity** Ask students to develop demonstrations that show how people observe parallax as part of their everyday experience. For example, students might demonstrate that a moving person loses sight of nearby objects very quickly but can see a distant object for a long time. One notices this effect when driving—trees along the roadside pass quickly, but one can observe the Moon during the entire drive.

6. How will you determine changes in observed parallax? Remember, these changes should occur when the distance from the observer to the object is changed.

7. You should measure shifts in parallax from several different positions. How will these positions differ?

8. How will you measure distances accurately and compare relative position shift?

**Follow Your Plan**

1. Make sure your teacher approves your plan before you start.

2. **Construct** the model your team has planned.

3. Carry out the experiment as planned.

4. While conducting the experiment, record any observations that you or other members of your group make in your Science Journal.

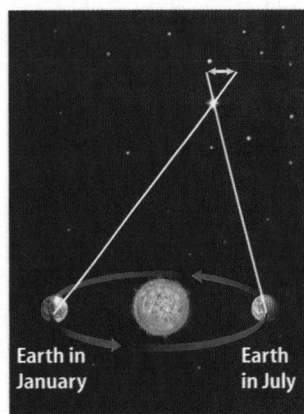

Earth in January

Earth in July

## Analyze Your Data

1. **Compare** what happened to the object when it was viewed with one eye closed, then the other.

2. At what distance from the observer did the object appear to shift the most?

3. At what distance did it appear to shift the least?

## Conclude and Apply

1. **Infer** what happened to the apparent shift of the object's location as the distance from the observer was increased or decreased.

2. **Describe** how astronomers might use parallax to study stars.

### Communicating Your Data

Prepare a chart showing the results of your experiment. Share the chart with members of your class. **For more help, refer to the Science Skill Handbook.**

**LAB** 495

---

**Teaching Strategy** Pair students and have one act as holder while the other student views the pencil. Students should then switch roles.

## Analyze Your Data

**Expected Outcome** If students position themselves so that the meterstick is lined up with their noses and distances of 20 cm, 40 cm, and 60 cm are used, the following results can be expected: Observed parallax is about 20 cm at the 20-cm mark, 8.5 cm at the 40-cm mark, and 4.9 cm at the 60-cm mark.

**Answers to Questions**

1. The position of the pencil seemed to shift, but this motion was only apparent.
2. the closest distance used
3. the farthest distance

**Error Analysis** It important that students not move while viewing the pencil. Movement could cause erroneous results.

## Conclude and Apply

1. As distance from the observer increased, the pencil's apparent shift decreased. As the distance from the observer decreased, the pencil's apparent shift increased.
2. Astronomers use parallax angles or shifts in the apparent position of astronomical objects to determine distances to the objects.

---

### Assessment

**Oral** How can astronomers use parallax to determine distances to stars relatively close to Earth? Parallax angle decreases with distance from observer. Very distant stars will show no parallax.

### Communicating Your Data

Have students use a computer to prepare a table on which they can enter the data from their experiment.

## Content Background

Supernova explosions often are hypothesized to initiate the contraction of a gaseous nebula and hence star formation. The shock wave of a supernova can compress gas in a nebula. The increased density can be enough to initiate contraction under the influence of gravity.

## Discussion

**Betelgeuse** Tell students that Betelgeuse is 520 light-years from Earth. If Betelgeuse is so much larger than the Sun, why isn't it brighter than the Sun? It is much farther away from Earth, so it looks much smaller and dimmer than the Sun.

## Activity

**Scale Models** Have students select a scale to use and make scale models that compare the diameters of the Sun and Betelgeuse. Then have students research the sizes of other stars and make additional scale models showing how their diameters compare to those of the Sun and Betelgeuse.

### Applying Math

**Answer** four hundred fifty million five hundred twenty thousand

## Write About It

Student reports will vary.

---

# SCIENCE Stats

## Stars and Galaxies

### Did you know...

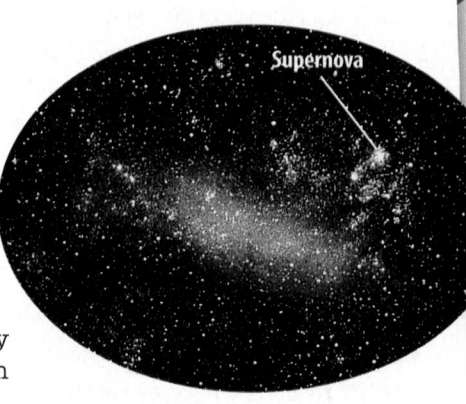
Supernova

**... A star in Earth's galaxy explodes** as a supernova about once a century. The most famous supernova of this galaxy occurred in 1054 and was recorded by the ancient Chinese and Koreans. The explosion was so powerful that it could be seen during the day, and its brightness lasted for weeks. Other major supernovas in the Milky Way that were observed from Earth occurred in 185, 386, 1006, 1181, 1572, and 1604.

**... The large loops of material** called solar prominences can extend more than 320,000 km above the Sun's surface. This is so high that two Jupiters and three Earths could fit under the arch.

**... The red giant star** Betelgeuse has a diameter larger than that of Earth's Sun. This gigantic star measures 450,520,000 km in diameter, while the Sun's diameter is a mere 1,390,176 km.

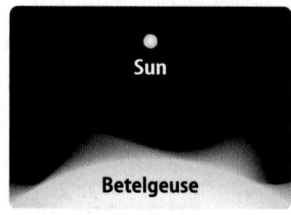
Sun
Betelgeuse

### Applying Math
Use words to express the number 450,520,000.

### Write About It

Visit in7.msscience.com/science_stats to learn whether it might be possible for Earth astronauts to travel to the nearest stars. How long would such a trip take? What problems would have to be overcome? Write a brief report about what you find.

---

## Visual Learning

**Solar Prominence Art** Make certain that students notice the relative sizes of Earth and Jupiter. Have them estimate how many Earths would need to be stacked to equal the diameter of Jupiter. about 11

## Reviewing Main Ideas

### Section 1 Stars

1. Constellations are patterns of stars in the night sky. Some constellations can be seen all year. Other constellations are visible only during certain seasons.

2. Parallax is the apparent shift in the position of an object when viewed from two different positions. Parallax is used to find the distance to nearby stars.

### Section 2 The Sun

1. The Sun is the closest star to Earth.

2. Sunspots are areas on the Sun's surface that are cooler and less bright than surrounding areas.

### Section 3 Evolution of Stars

1. Stars are classified according to their position on the H-R diagram.

2. Low-mass stars end their lives as white dwarfs. High-mass stars become neutron stars or black holes.

### Section 4 Galaxies and the Universe

1. A galaxy consists of stars, gas, and dust held together by gravity.

2. Earth's solar system is in the Milky Way, a spiral galaxy.

3. The universe is expanding. Scientists don't know whether the universe will expand forever or contract to a single point.

## Visualizing Main Ideas

*Copy and complete the following concept map that shows the evolution of a main sequence star with a mass similar to that of the Sun.*

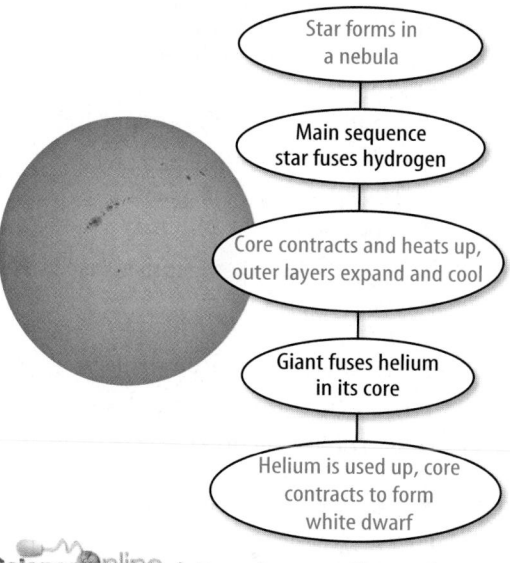

- Star forms in a nebula
- Main sequence star fuses hydrogen
- Core contracts and heats up, outer layers expand and cool
- Giant fuses helium in its core
- Helium is used up, core contracts to form white dwarf

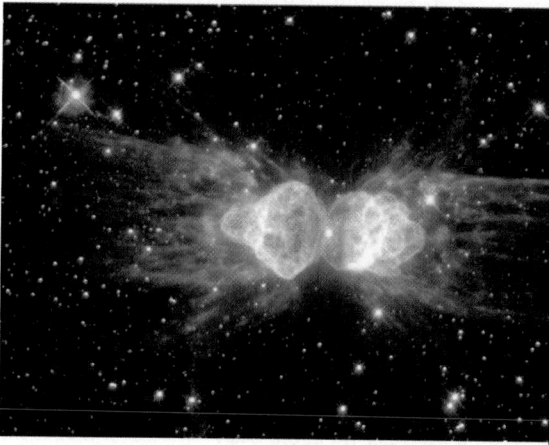

**Science Online** in7.msscience.com/interactive_tutor

**CHAPTER STUDY GUIDE 497**

## Reviewing Main Ideas

Summary statements can be used by students to review the major concepts of the chapter.

## Visualizing Main Ideas

See student page.

**Visit in7.msscience.com**
/self_check_quiz
/interactive_tutor
/vocabulary_puzzlemaker
/chapter_review
/standards_review

## Assessment Transparency

For additional assessment questions, use the *Assessment Transparency* located in the transparency book.

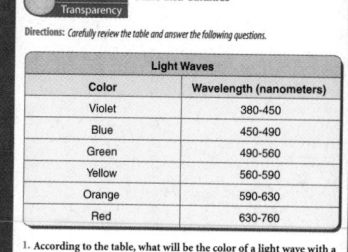

**Assessment**

Assessment Transparency — Stars and Galaxies

Directions: Carefully review the table and answer the following questions.

| Light Waves | |
|---|---|
| Color | Wavelength (nanometers) |
| Violet | 380-450 |
| Blue | 450-490 |
| Green | 490-560 |
| Yellow | 560-590 |
| Orange | 590-630 |
| Red | 630-760 |

1. According to the table, what will be the color of a light wave with a wavelength of 500 nanometers?
   A Violet       C Green
   B Blue         D Yellow

2. In a clear sky, the Sun is bright yellow. What is the approximate wavelength of the light coming from the Sun?
   F 380-340 nanometers
   G 450-490 nanometers
   H 560-590 nanometers
   J 630-760 nanometers

3. The shorter the wavelength of a light wave, the greater its energy. A light wave of which of the colors listed below has the greatest energy?
   A Red
   B Orange
   C Green
   D Violet

L2

Stars and Galaxies

## Using Vocabulary

1. Absolute magnitude is a measure of the light given off by a star. Apparent magnitude is a measure of the light received on Earth.

2. A constellation is a pattern of stars in the night sky. A galaxy is a group of stars held together by gravity.

3. A giant is the late stage of a relatively low mass star. A supergiant is the late stage of a very massive star.

4. The photosphere is the lowest layer of the Sun's atmosphere. The chromosphere is directly above it.

5. Black holes form when the cores of very massive stars collapse to a point. Neutron stars form when slightly less massive stars collapse to a small core consisting of neutrons.

## Checking Concepts

| | |
|---|---|
| 6. B | 11. D |
| 7. C | 12. D |
| 8. C | 13. A |
| 9. C | 14. B |
| 10. D | 15. A |

## Using Vocabulary

| | |
|---|---|
| absolute magnitude p.474 | giant p.485 |
| apparent magnitude p.474 | light-year p.475 |
| big bang theory p.493 | nebula p.484 |
| black hole p.486 | neutron star p.486 |
| chromosphere p.477 | photosphere p.477 |
| constellation p.472 | sunspot p.478 |
| corona p.477 | supergiant p.486 |
| galaxy p.488 | white dwarf p.485 |

*Explain the difference between the terms in each of the following sets.*

1. absolute magnitude—apparent magnitude

2. galaxy—constellation

3. giant—supergiant

4. chromosphere—photosphere

5. black hole—neutron star

## Checking Concepts

*Choose the word or phrase that best answers the question.*

6. What is a measure of the amount of a star's light that is received on Earth?
   A) absolute magnitude
   B) apparent magnitude
   C) fusion
   D) parallax

7. What is higher for closer stars?
   A) absolute magnitude
   B) red shift
   C) parallax
   D) blue shift

8. What happens after a nebula contracts and its temperature increases to 10 million K?
   A) a black hole forms
   B) a supernova occurs
   C) fusion begins
   D) a white dwarf forms

9. Which of these has an event horizon?
   A) giant
   B) white dwarf
   C) black hole
   D) neutron star

10. What forms when the Sun fuses hydrogen?
    A) carbon
    B) oxygen
    C) iron
    D) helium

**Use the illustration below to answer question 11.**

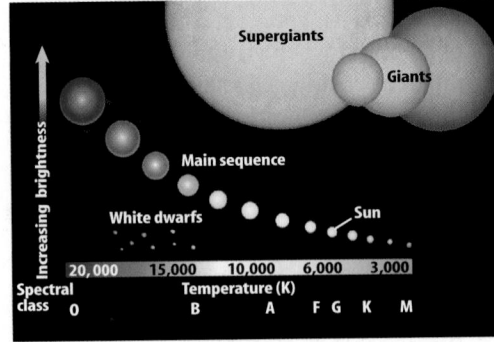

11. Which of the following best describes giant stars?
    A) hot, dim stars
    B) cool, dim stars
    C) hot, bright stars
    D) cool, bright stars

12. Which of the following are loops of matter flowing from the Sun?
    A) sunspots
    B) auroras
    C) coronas
    D) prominences

13. What are groups of galaxies called?
    A) clusters
    B) supergiants
    C) giants
    D) binary systems

14. Which galaxies are sometimes shaped like footballs?
    A) spiral
    B) elliptical
    C) barred
    D) irregular

15. What do scientists study to determine shifts in wavelengths of light?
    A) spectrum
    B) parallax
    C) corona
    D) nebula

 Science Online in7.msscience.com/vocabulary_puzzlemaker

**Use the Exam*View*® Pro Testmaker CD-ROM to:**
- create multiple versions of tests
- create modified tests with one mouse click for inclusion students
- edit existing questions and add your own questions
- build tests aligned with state standards using built-in State Curriculum Tags
- change English tests to Spanish with one mouse click and vice versa

## Thinking Critically

**Use the table below to answer question 16.**

### Magnitude and Distance of Stars

| Star | Apparent Magnitude | Absolute Magnitude | Distance in Light-Years |
|---|---|---|---|
| A | −26 | 4.8 | 0.00002 |
| B | −1.5 | 1.4 | 8.7 |
| C | 0.1 | 4.4 | 4.3 |
| D | 0.1 | −7.0 | 815 |
| E | 0.4 | −5.9 | 520 |
| F | 1.0 | −0.6 | 45 |

16. **Interpret Data** Use the table above to answer the following questions. *Hint: lower magnitude values are brighter than higher magnitude values.*
   a. Which star appears brightest from Earth?
   b. Which star would appear brightest from a distance of 10 light-years?
   c. Infer which star in the table above is the Sun.

17. **Infer** How do scientists know that black holes exist if these objects don't emit visible light?

18. **Recognize Cause and Effect** Why can parallax only be used to measure distances to stars that are relatively close to Earth?

19. **Compare and contrast** the Sun with other stars on the H-R diagram.

20. **Concept Map** Make a concept map showing the life history of a very large star.

21. **Make Models** Make a model of the Sun. Include all of the Sun's layers in your model.

Science Online in7.msscience.com/chapter_review

## Performance Activities

22. **Story** Write a short science-fiction story about an astronaut traveling through the universe. In your story, describe what the astronaut observes. Use as many vocabulary words as you can.

23. **Photomontage** Gather photographs of the aurora borealis from magazines and other sources. Use the photographs to create a photomontage. Write a caption for each photo.

## Applying Math

24. **Travel to Vega** Vega is a star that is 26 light-years away. If a spaceship could travel at one-tenth the speed of light, how long would it take to reach this star?

**Use the illustration below to answer question 25.**

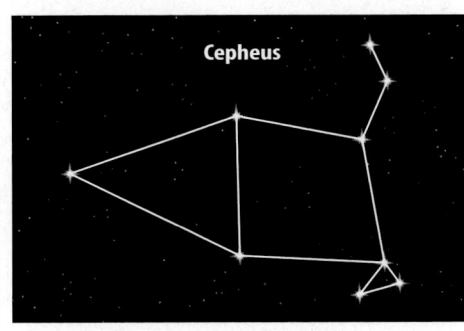
Cepheus

25. **Constellation Cepheus** The illustration above shows the constellation Cepheus. Answer the following questions about this contellation.
   a. Which of the labeled line segments are nearly parallel?
   b. Which line segments are nearly perpendicular?
   c. Which line segments are oblique?
   d. What geometric shape do the three stars at the left side of the drawing form?

## Thinking Critically

16. a. A
   b. D
   c. A
17. Matter emits radiation as it is drawn into black holes. A black hole's gravity can affect nearby objects.
18. Stars that are far from Earth have parallax angles that are too small to measure accurately.
19. The Sun is smaller and hotter than giants and supergiants. It is larger and cooler than white dwarf stars.
20. Student maps should parallel the upper branch of **Figure 13**.
21. Make certain that student models are accurate and complete.

## Performance Activities

22. Stories will be futuristic. However, they should be based on sound science. Use **PASC**, p. 155
23. Students also might create a photomontage for the aurora australis. Use **PASC**, p. 149

## Applying Math

### Indiana Math Standards
7.2.1
24. 260 years
25. a. $\overline{AE}$ and $\overline{CD}$; $\overline{BC}$ and $\overline{DE}$
   b. $\overline{BE}$ and $\overline{ED}$
   c. $\angle AED$; $\angle ABC$; $\angle BCD$
   d. triangle

---

## ✓ Assessment Resources

📂 **Reproducible Masters**
**Chapter *Fast File* Resources**
   Chapter Review, pp. 41–42
   Chapter Tests, pp. 43–46
   Assessment Transparency Activity, p. 55
**Glencoe Science Web site**
   Chapter Review Test
   IN Standards Review

**Glencoe Technology**
   🗲 Assessment Transparency
   💿 Exam*View*® Pro Testmaker
   📼 MindJogger Videoquiz
   💿 Interactive Chalkboard

**Answer Sheet** A practice answer sheet can be found at in7.msscience.com/answer_sheet.

## Part 1 | Multiple Choice

1. A
2. C
3. C
4. A
5. B
6. A
7. D
8. B

## Part 2 | Critical Response

9. The hydrogen is converted into helium by nuclear fusion reactions.

10. The supernova was brightest about 7.5 days after discovery when it had an apparent magnitude of about 12.9. After this, the brightness decreased to an apparent magnitude of about 14.3 about 13 days after discovery, and then decreased more slowly 25 days after discovery to an apparent magnitude of about 15.5.

11. Constellations appear to move because Earth rotates. Their visibility depends on their location. The circumpolar constellations are visible all year, but others are not. Other constellations can be seen only in summer or winter when Earth's dark side faces them.

---

The assessed Indiana standard appears above the question.

*Record your answers on the answer sheet provided by your teacher or on a sheet of paper.*

### Part 1 | Multiple Choice

The illustration below shows parts of the Sun.

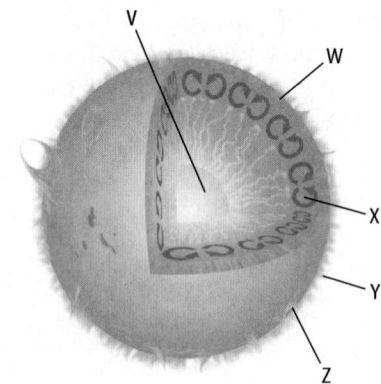

**7.3.11**

1. In which layer of the Sun is energy produced?

   A  V

   B  X

   C  Y

   D  Z

2. In the illustration above, which layer of the Sun is the source of solar wind?

   A  V

   B  W

   C  Y

   D  Z

---

3. Which is the most abundant element in the Sun?

   A  carbon

   B  helium

   C  hydrogen

   D  oxygen

**7.3.1**

4. The illustration below shows a side view of the Milky Way Galaxy.

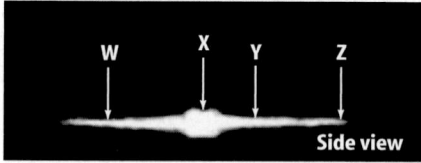

Side view

Where is the Sun located?

   A  W

   B  X

   C  Y

   D  Z

**7.3.2**

5. About how long does it take light from the Sun to reach Earth?

   A  8 seconds

   B  8 minutes

   C  8 hours

   D  8 days

**Test-Taking Tip**

**Process of Elimination** If you don't know the answer to a multiple-choice question, eliminate as many incorrect choices as possible. Mark your best guess from the remaining answers before moving on to the next question.

12. The position of a star is measured when Earth is on opposite sides of its orbit around the Sun. The distance to the star can then be calculated from the shift in the star's position and the size of Earth's orbit.

13. The dark lines in a star's spectrum are due to the presence of various elements in the star. The pattern of these lines enables the elements in the star to be identified.

**6.** What type of object do the most massive stars become at the end of their lives?

  **A** black hole

  **B** neutron star

  **C** red giant

  **D** white dwarf

**7.** The illustration below shows the distance between Earth and the nearest star besides the Sun, Proxima Centauri.

Scale:
1 cm = 1 light-year

How far away from Earth is Proxima Centauri?

  **A** 8.4 AU's

  **B** 8.4 light-years

  **C** 4.2 AU's

  **D** 4.2 light-years

**7.3.1**

**8.** Which series is ordered from smallest to largest?

  **A** universe, galaxy clusters, galaxies, stars

  **B** stars, galaxies, galaxy clusters, universe

  **C** galaxies, stars, star clusters, universe

  **D** galaxy clusters, galaxies, stars, universe

**Part 2   Critical Response**

**7.3.11**

**9.** Why do nuclear fusion reactions cause the amount of hydrogen in the Sun to decrease?

**10.** The graph below shows how the brightness of a supernova changed over time.

**Visual Light Curve of Supernova**

On what day after discovery was the supernova brightest? Describe how the brightness changed after that day.

**11.** Explain why the constellations appear to move. Why are some visible all year and others only visible during certain seasons?

**7.3.2**

**12.** Explain how parallax is used to measure the distance to nearby stars.

**13.** What can be learned by studying the dark lines in a star's spectrum?

## Rubrics

The following rubric is a sample scoring device for critical response questions.

**Critical Response**

| Points | Description |
|---|---|
| 4 | The student demonstrates a thorough understanding of the science of the task. The response may contain minor flaws that do not detract from the demonstration of a thorough understanding. |
| 3 | The student demonstrates an understanding of the science of the task. The response is essentially correct and demonstrates an essential but less than thorough understanding of the science. |
| 2 | The student demonstrates only a partial understanding of the science of the task. Although the student may have used the correct approach to a solution or may have provided a correct solution, the work lacks an essential understanding of the underlying science concepts. |
| 1 | The student demonstrates a very limited understanding of the science of the task. The response is incomplete and exhibits many flaws. |
| 0 | The student provides a completely incorrect solution or no response at all. |

| Section/Objectives | Standards | | Labs/Features |
|---|---|---|---|
| | National | State/Local | |
| **Chapter Opener** | See p. 16T–17T for a Key to Standards. | Detailed standards begin on page IN8. | **Launch Lab:** Distinguish Rocks from Minerals; p. 503<br>**Foldables,** p. 503 |
| **Section 1  Minerals**<br>⏱ 2 sessions<br>📦 1 block<br><br>1. **Describe** characteristics that all minerals share.<br>2. **Explain** how minerals form. | National Content Standards: UCP.1, UCP.2, UCP.3, UCP.5, A.1, A.2, D.1, D.2 | Indiana standards: 7.5.3 | **MiniLAB:** Inferring Salt's Crystal System, p. 505<br>**Visualizing Crystal Systems,** p. 506<br>**Integrate Physics,** p. 507<br>**Lab:** Crystal Formation, p. 509 |
| **Section 2  Mineral Identification**<br>⏱ 2 sessions<br>📦 1 block<br><br>3. **Describe** physical properties used to identify minerals.<br>4. **Identify** minerals using physical properties such as hardness and streak. | National Content Standards: UCP.1, UCP.2, UCP.3, UCP.5, A.1, A.2, B.2, D.1, G.2, G.3 | Indiana standards: This section builds a foundation for standards 7.3.8 and 7.3.9. | **Applying Science:** How can you identify minerals?, p. 512<br>**MiniLab:** Observing Mineral Properties, p. 514 |
| **Section 3  Uses of Minerals**<br>⏱ 2 sessions<br>📦 1 block<br><br>5. **Describe** characteristics of gems that make them more valuable than other minerals.<br>6. **Identify** useful elements that are contained in minerals. | National Content Standards: UCP.1, UCP.2, UCP.5, A.1, A.2, D.2, G.1, G.2, G.3 | Indiana standards: 7.1.5, 7.1.6 | **Science Online,** p. 518<br>**Integrate Social Studies,** p. 519<br>**Lab:** Mineral Identification, p. 522<br>**Science and History:** Dr. Dorothy Crowfoot Hodgkin, p. 524 |

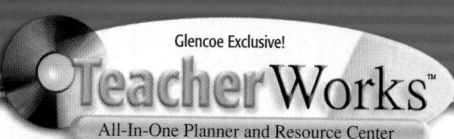
| Lab Materials | Reproducible Resources | Section Assessment | Technology |
|---|---|---|---|
| **Launch Lab:** magnifying lens, quartz crystal, table salt, samples of sandstone, granite, gypsum, mica, schist | **Chapter FAST FILE Resources**<br>Foldables Worksheet, p. 13<br>Directed Reading Overview, p. 15<br>Note-taking Worksheets, p. 29, 30 | GLENCOE'S **ASSESSMENT** ADVANTAGE | Teacher**Works** includes:<br>• Interactive Teacher Edition<br>• Lesson Planner with calendar<br>• Access to all program blacklines<br>• Correlations to standards<br>• Web links |
| **MiniLAB:** magnifying lens, table salt, construction paper<br>**Lab:** 250-mL beakers (2), cardboard, large paper clip, table salt, flat wooden stick, granulated sugar, cotton string, hot plate, magnifying lens, thermal mitt, shallow pan, spoon | **Chapter FAST FILE Resources**<br>Transparency Activity, p. 40<br>MiniLAB, p. 3<br>Enrichment, p. 26<br>Reinforcement, p. 23<br>Directed Reading, p. 16<br>Lab Worksheets, pp. 5–6<br>Lab Activity, pp. 9–10<br>**Cultural Diversity,** p. 37<br>**Mathematics Skill Activities,** p. 47 | **Portfolio**<br>Activity, p. 507<br>**Performance**<br>MiniLAB, p. 505<br>Applying Skills, p. 508<br>**Content**<br>Section Review, p. 508 | • Section Focus Transparency<br>• Guided Reading Audio Program<br>• Interactive Chalkboard CD-ROM |
| **MiniLAB:** samples of clear minerals such as gypsum, muscovite mica, halite, and calcite<br><br>*Need materials?* Contact Science Kit at 1-800-828-7777 or www.sciencekit.com on the Internet. | **Chapter FAST FILE Resources**<br>Transparency Activity, p. 41<br>MiniLAB, p. 4<br>Enrichment, p. 27<br>Reinforcement, p. 24<br>Directed Reading, p. 17<br>Transparency Activity, pp. 43–44<br>**Science Inquiry Lab,** pp. 31–32 | **Portfolio**<br>Activity, p. 511<br>**Performance**<br>Applying Science, p. 512<br>MiniLAB, p. 514<br>Applying Skills, p. 514<br>**Content**<br>Section Review, p. 514 | • Section Focus Transparency<br>• Teaching Transparency<br>• Virtual Labs CD-ROM<br>• Guided Reading Audio Program<br>• Interactive Chalkboard CD-ROM<br>• Video Lab |
| **Lab:** mineral samples, magnifying lens, pan balance, graduated cylinder, water, penny, glass plate, small iron nail, steel file, streak plate, 5% HCl with dropper, Mohs scale of hardness, Minerals Appendix, safety goggles | **Chapter FAST FILE Resources**<br>Transparency Activity, p. 42<br>Enrichment, p. 28<br>Reinforcement, p. 25<br>Directed Reading, pp. 17, 18<br>Lab Worksheets, pp. 7–8<br>Lab Activity, pp. 11–12<br>**Lab Management and Safety,** pp. 54–57<br>**Home and Community Involvement,** p. 34 | **Portfolio**<br>Use Science Words, p. 516<br>Differentiated Instruction, p. 518<br>**Performance**<br>Applying Math, p. 521<br>**Content**<br>Section Review, p. 521 | • Section Focus Transparency<br>• Guided Reading Audio Program<br>• Interactive Chalkboard CD-ROM<br>• Video Lab |

## GLENCOE'S ASSESSMENT ADVANTAGE — End of Chapter Assessment

| Blackline Masters | Technology | Professional Series |
|---|---|---|
| **Chapter FAST FILE Resources**<br>Chapter Review, pp. 33–34<br>Chapter Tests, pp. 35–38<br>**Mastering the Grade 7 Indiana Science Standards** | • MindJogger Videoquiz<br>• IN Test Prep and Practice Exam*View*®<br>• Exam*View*® Pro Testmaker<br>• TeacherWorks CD-ROM<br>• Interactive Chalkboard CD-ROM | **Performance Assessment in the Science Classroom (PASC)** |

## Transparencies

### Section Focus

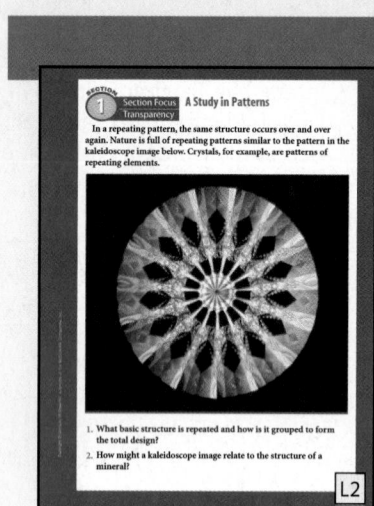

**SECTION 1 Section Focus Transparency — A Study in Patterns**

In a repeating pattern, the same structure occurs over and over again. Nature is full of repeating patterns similar to the pattern in the kaleidoscope image below. Crystals, for example, are patterns of repeating elements.

1. What basic structure is repeated and how is it grouped to form the total design?
2. How might a kaleidoscope image relate to the structure of a mineral?

L2

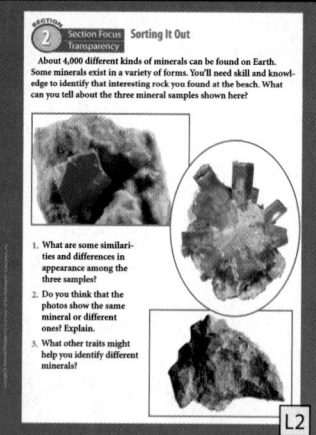

**SECTION 2 Section Focus Transparency — Sorting It Out**

About 4,000 different kinds of minerals can be found on Earth. Some minerals exist in a variety of forms. You'll need skill and knowledge to identify that interesting rock you found at the beach. What can you tell about the three mineral samples shown here?

1. What are some similarities and differences in appearance among the three samples?
2. Do you think that the photos show the same mineral or different ones? Explain.
3. What other traits might help you identify different minerals?

L2

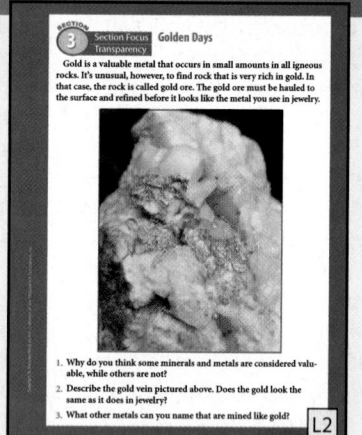

**SECTION 3 Section Focus Transparency — Golden Days**

Gold is a valuable metal that occurs in small amounts in all igneous rocks. It's unusual, however, to find rock that is very rich in gold. In that case, the rock is called gold ore. The gold ore must be hauled to the surface and refined before it looks like the metal you see in jewelry.

1. Why do you think some minerals and metals are considered valuable, while others are not?
2. Describe the gold vein pictured above. Does the gold look the same as it does in jewelry?
3. What other metals can you name that are mined like gold?

L2

This is a representation of key blackline masters available in the Teacher Classroom Resources. See Resource Manager boxes within the chapter for additional information.

### Assessment

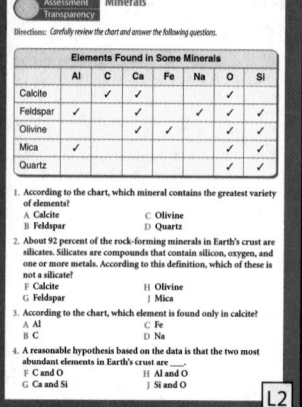

**Assessment Transparency — Minerals**

Directions: *Carefully review the chart and answer the following questions.*

**Elements Found in Some Minerals**

| | Al | C | Ca | Fe | Na | O | Si |
|---|---|---|---|---|---|---|---|
| Calcite | | ✓ | ✓ | | | ✓ | |
| Feldspar | ✓ | | ✓ | | ✓ | ✓ | ✓ |
| Olivine | | | ✓ | ✓ | | ✓ | ✓ |
| Mica | ✓ | | | | ✓ | ✓ | ✓ |
| Quartz | | | | | | ✓ | ✓ |

1. According to the chart, which mineral contains the greatest variety of elements?
   A Calcite   C Olivine
   B Feldspar   D Quartz
2. About 92 percent of the rock-forming minerals in Earth's crust are silicates. Silicates are compounds that contain silicon, oxygen, and one or more metals. According to this definition, which of these is not a silicate?
   F Calcite   H Olivine
   G Feldspar   J Mica
3. According to the chart, which element is found only in calcite?
   A Al   C Fe
   B C   D Na
4. A reasonable hypothesis based on the data is that the two most abundant elements in Earth's crust are ____.
   F C and O   H Al and O
   G Ca and Si   J Si and O

L2

### Teaching

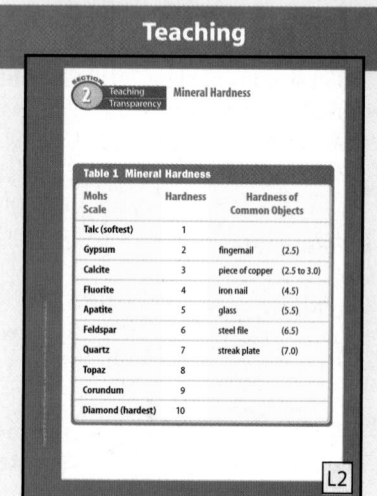

**SECTION 2 Teaching Transparency — Mineral Hardness**

**Table 1 Mineral Hardness**

| Mohs Scale | Hardness | Hardness of Common Objects |
|---|---|---|
| Talc (softest) | 1 | |
| Gypsum | 2 | fingernail (2.5) |
| Calcite | 3 | piece of copper (2.5 to 3.0) |
| Fluorite | 4 | iron nail (4.5) |
| Apatite | 5 | glass (5.5) |
| Feldspar | 6 | steel file (6.5) |
| Quartz | 7 | streak plate (7.0) |
| Topaz | 8 | |
| Corundum | 9 | |
| Diamond (hardest) | 10 | |

L2

## Hands-on Activities

### Student Text Lab Worksheet

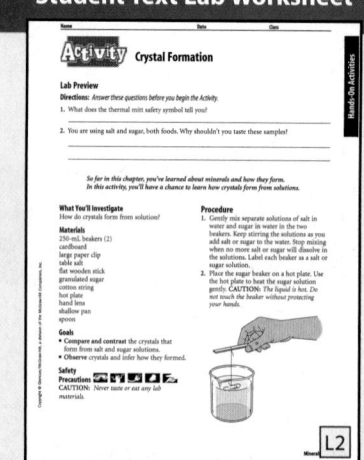

**Activity — Crystal Formation**

**Lab Preview**

Directions: *Answer these questions before you begin the Activity.*

1. What does the thermal mitt safety symbol tell you?

2. You are using salt and sugar, both foods. Why shouldn't you taste these samples?

*So far in this chapter, you've learned about minerals and how they form. In this activity, you'll have a chance to learn how crystals form from solutions.*

**What You'll Investigate**
How do crystals form from solution?

**Materials**
250-mL beakers (2)
cardboard
large paper clip
table salt
flat wooden stick
granulated sugar
cotton string
hot plate
hand lens
shallow pan
spoon

**Procedure**

1. Gently mix separate solutions of salt in water and sugar in water in the two beakers. Keep stirring the solutions as you add salt or sugar to the water. Stop mixing when no more salt or sugar will dissolve in the solutions. Label each beaker as a salt or sugar solution.
2. Place the sugar beaker on a hot plate. Use the hot plate to heat the sugar solution gently. **CAUTION:** *The liquid is hot. Do not touch the beaker without protecting your hands.*

**Goals**
• Compare and contrast the crystals that form from salt and sugar solutions.
• Observe crystals and infer how they formed.

**Safety Precautions**
**CAUTION:** *Never taste or eat any lab materials.*

L2

### Laboratory Activities

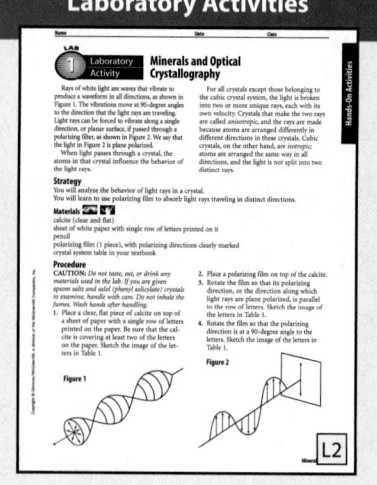

**LAB 1 Laboratory Activity — Minerals and Optical Crystallography**

Rays of white light are waves that vibrate to produce a waveform in all directions, as shown in Figure 1. The vibrations move at 90-degree angles to the direction that the light rays are traveling. Light rays can be forced to vibrate along a single direction, or planar surface, if passed through a polarizing filter, as shown in Figure 2. We say that the light in Figure 2 is plane polarized. When light passes through a crystal, the atoms in that crystal influence the behavior of the light rays.

For all crystals except those belonging to the cubic crystal system, the light is broken into two or more unique rays, each with its own velocity. Crystals that make the two rays are called anisotropic, and the rays are made because atoms are arranged differently in different directions in these crystals. Cubic crystals, on the other hand, are isotropic; atoms are arranged the same way in all directions, and the light is not split into two distinct rays.

**Strategy**
You will analyze the behavior of light rays in a crystal.
You will learn to use polarizing film to absorb light rays traveling in distinct directions.

**Materials**
calcite (clear and flat)
sheet of white paper with single row of letters printed on it
pencil
polarizing film (1 piece), with polarizing directions clearly marked
crystal system table in your textbook

**Procedure**
**CAUTION:** *Do not taste, eat, or drink any materials used in the lab. If you are given epsom salts and salol (phenyl salicylate) crystals to examine, handle with care. Do not inhale the fumes. Wash hands after handling.*

1. Place a clear, flat piece of calcite on top of a sheet of paper with a single row of letters printed on the paper. Be sure that the calcite is covering at least two of the letters on the paper. Sketch the image of the letters in Table 1.
2. Place a polarizing film on top of the calcite. Rotate the film so that its polarizing direction, or the direction along which light rays are plane polarized, is parallel to the row of letters. Sketch the image of the letters in Table 1.
3. Rotate the film so that the polarizing direction is at a 90-degree angle to the letters. Sketch the image of the letters in Table 1.

**Figure 1**

**Figure 2**

L2

## Meeting Different Ability Levels

### Content Outline

**L2**

### Reinforcement

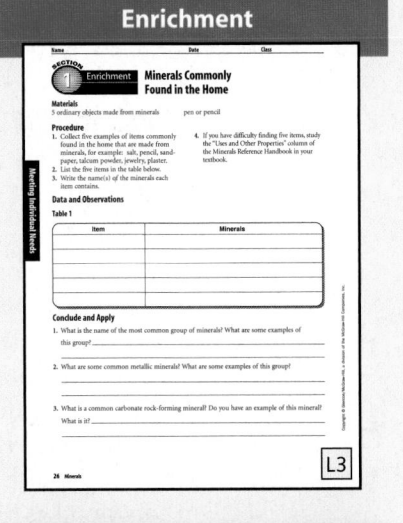

**L2**

### Enrichment

**L3**

### Directed Reading (English/Spanish)

**L1**

### Study Guide

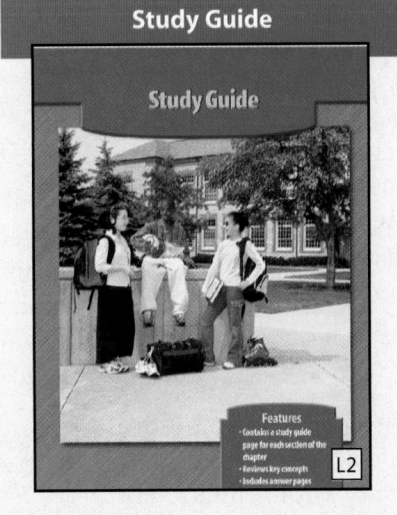

**Features**
- Contains a study guide page for each section of the chapter
- Reviews key concepts
- Includes answer pages

**L2**

### Reading Essentials

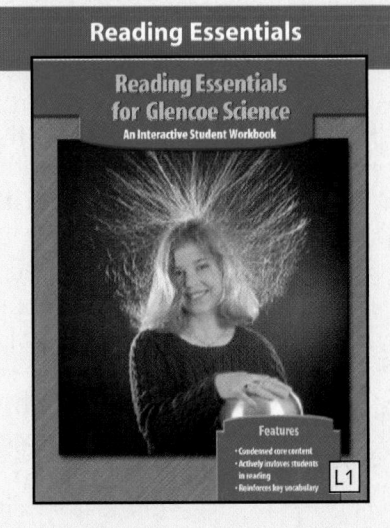

**Reading Essentials for Glencoe Science**
An Interactive Student Workbook

**Features**
- Condensed core content
- Actively involves students in reading
- Reinforces key vocabulary

**L1**

## Assessment

### Test Practice Workbook

**L2**

### Chapter Review

**L2**

### Chapter Tests

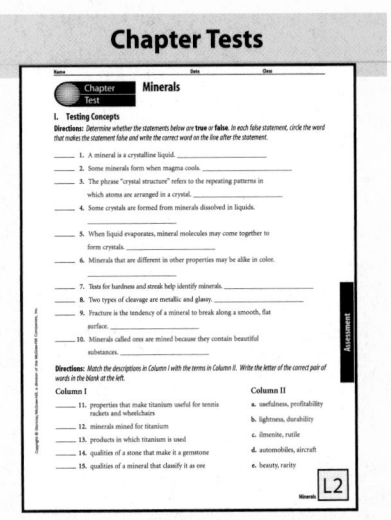

**L2**

# Science Content Background

## section 1 Minerals
### General Characteristics

Between 40 and 50 new minerals are identified each year. Only eight elements comprise the majority of minerals. The 24 or so minerals that make up most rocks are called the rock-forming minerals. Coal, which fits many of the characteristics of minerals, is not a mineral because it comes from once-living material.

Graphite is among the softest minerals, and diamond is the hardest mineral. Both of these minerals are composed of carbon. The type of bond between the atoms of carbon and different atomic arrangements cause the differences in the properties of these minerals. Because of these differences, the two minerals have widely different uses. Diamonds are used in jewelry, as abrasives, and in cutting tools. Graphite is used as a lubricant and in pencil lead. Minerals that have identical composition but different properties are called polymorphs.

### Mineral Composition

Although each type of mineral has a unique composition, the composition of individual mineral specimens can vary within limits. For example, the chemical composition of olivine ranges from $Fe_2SiO_4$ to $Mg_2SiO_4$. For this reason, the composition of olivine is often written $(Fe,Mg)_2SiO_4$. A more precise chemical formula can be written when the amounts of iron and magnesium are known, for example $(Fe_{.77}Mg_{.23})_2SiO_4$.

## section 2 Mineral Identification
### Hardness

Most silicate minerals do not leave a streak because they have a hardness greater than 6 on the Mohs scale. The hardness of a mineral is related to its crystal structure and to the type of atomic bonds in the mineral. The difference between the hardness of diamond (Mohs 10) and corundum (Mohs 9) is far greater than the difference in hardness between corundum and the softest mineral, talc. This means that the Mohs scale is nonlinear.

## section 3 Uses of Minerals
### Valuing Diamonds

The value of diamonds varies depending on whether they are tinted. The most common diamonds of gem quality have yellow or brown tints. These diamonds are less valuable than those with no tint. Diamonds with blue or pink tints are the most valuable.

### chapter content resources

**Internet Resources**
For additional content background, visit **in7.msscience.com** to:
- access your book online
- find references to related articles in popular science magazines
- access Web links with related content background
- access current events with science journal topics

**Print Resources**
*A Field Guide to Rocks and Minerals* (The Peterson Field Guide series), by Frederick H. Pough, Houghton Mifflin Company, 1998

*Minerals of the World,* by Charles A. Sorrell, Golden Press, 1973

*The Mineral Kingdom,* by Paul E. Desautels, The Ridge Press, Inc., 1968

*Barry L. Runk/Grant Heilman Photography, Inc.*

# Misconceptions

## Find Out What Students Think

**Students may think that . . .**

**Minerals are rare objects that are seldom used in everyday materials.**

Students are often asked to observe and classify minerals. However, some students fail to understand that these materials are part of their everyday lives.

### Discussion

Ask students to raise their hands if they used minerals before coming to school this morning.

Then ask how many brushed their teeth using toothpaste. Explain that when they use toothpaste, they are using a product made from minerals. Phosphate materials, aluminum oxide, and silica are used as abrasives in toothpaste. Fluoride comes from the mineral fluorite. Stannous fluoride (or tin fluoride) is also found in toothpaste. The sparkle in toothpaste comes from the mineral mica.

Have students handle and observe the minerals that furnish the ingredients for toothpaste.

## Promote Understanding

### Discussion

Reproduce the information shown below, which lists the amount of elements, minerals, and other earth materials the average person uses in a lifetime. Have students discuss the different ways in which minerals impact their lives.

**Every American Born Will Need...**

1,841 lbs. Copper

21,476 lbs. Clays

32,061 lbs. Salt

997 lbs. Zinc

1.64 million lbs. Stone, Sand, & Gravel

2.196 Troy oz. Gold

81,585 gallons Petroleum

586,218 lbs. Coal

68,110 lbs. Cement

23,700 lbs. Phospate

5,599 lbs. Aluminum

1,074 lbs. Lead

45,176 lbs. Iron Ore

+57,448 lbs. Other Minerals & Metals

5.9 million cu. ft. Natural Gas

**3.7 million pounds of minerals, metals, and fuels in his/her lifetime**

© 2001 Mineral Information Institute, Golden, Colorado

## Assess

After completing the chapter, see *Identifying Misconceptions* in the Study Guide at the end of the chapter.

## Chapter Vocabulary

**Science Journal** Student responses will vary, but may include questions about the properties of gem-quality minerals, where they are found, and how valuable they are.

**INTERACTIVE CHALKBOARD with Image Bank**

**PowerPoint® Presentations**

This CD-ROM is an editable Microsoft® PowerPoint® presentation that includes:
- a pre-made presentation for every chapter
- interactive graphics
- animations
- audio clips
- image bank
- all new section and chapter questions
- Standardized Test Practice
- transparencies
- pre-lab questions for all labs
- Foldables directions
- links to in7.msscience.com

chapter

17

**Academic Standard—1:** Students further their scientific understanding of the natural world through investigations, experiences, and readings. They design solutions to practical problems by using a variety of scientific methodologies.

# Minerals

## chapter preview

**sections**

1. **Minerals**
   *Lab  Crystal Formation*

2. **Mineral Identification**

3. **Uses of Minerals**
   *Lab  Mineral Identification*

   *Virtual Lab  How can minerals be defined by their properties?*

### Nature's Beautiful Creation

Some physical properties of minerals arise from the way in which light is reflected and transmitted by them. These natural diamonds are beautiful in the rough, yet gemologists will cut the stones to produce new, flat surfaces. New surfaces and edges enhance the way light rays interact with gems, adding to their brilliance and fire.

**Science Journal** Write two questions you would ask a gemologist about the minerals that he or she works with.

## Theme Connection

**Scale and Structure** The structure of minerals is discussed. On the atomic scale, minerals have orderly crystal structures, that is, regularly repeating patterns of atoms. Emphasizing the relationship between the internal structure of a mineral and its properties and uses will help clarify its uniqueness among these solids that make up Earth's rocks.

## About the Photo

**Earth's Jewels** The extreme physical processes required to produce diamonds contribute to their rarity. Gem-quality diamonds are found in rocks that once were subjected to great pressures. One example is a kimberlite pipe, which forms after magma moves from great depths in Earth at high speeds, bringing diamonds closer to the surface.

# Start-Up Activities

## Distinguish Rocks from Minerals

When examining rocks, you'll notice that many of them are made of more than one material. Some rocks are made of many different crystals of mostly the same mineral. A mineral, however, will appear more like a pure substance and will tend to look the same throughout. Can you tell a rock from a mineral?

1. Use a magnifying lens to observe a quartz crystal, salt grains, and samples of sandstone, granite, calcite, mica, and schist (SHIHST).

2. Draw a sketch of each sample.

3. Infer which samples are made of one type of material and should be classified as minerals.

4. Infer which samples should be classified as rocks.

5. **Think Critically** In your Science Journal, compile a list of descriptions for the minerals you examined and a second list of descriptions for the rocks. Compare and contrast your observations of minerals and rocks.

**Minerals** Make the following Foldable to help you better understand minerals.

**STEP 1** Fold a vertical sheet of notebook paper from side to side.

**STEP 2** Cut along every third line of only the top layer to form tabs.

**STEP 3** Label each tab with a question.

**Ask Questions** Before you read the chapter, write questions you have about minerals on the front of the tabs. As you read the chapter, add more questions and write answers under the appropriate tabs.

**Science Online** Preview this chapter's content and activities at in7.msscience.com

---

503

Standards—This section builds a foundation for standards 7.3.8 and 7.3.9.

# Minerals

### Bellringer

INTERACTIVE CHALKBOARD
PowerPoint® Presentations

**Section Focus Transparencies** also are available on the Interactive Chalkboard CD-ROM.

L2  ELL

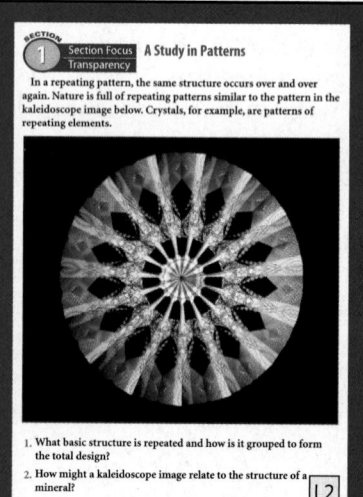

**Section Focus Transparency**  A Study in Patterns

In a repeating pattern, the same structure occurs over and over again. Nature is full of repeating patterns similar to the pattern in the kaleidoscope image below. Crystals, for example, are patterns of repeating elements.

1. What basic structure is repeated and how is it grouped to form the total design?
2. How might a kaleidoscope image relate to the structure of a mineral?

L2

### Tie to Prior Knowledge

**Atom Patterns** Help students recall that atoms are the building blocks of matter and that atoms can combine to form compounds. The structure of a mineral is determined by the repeating pattern of atoms in the mineral.

### Caption Answer

**Figure 1** Students might list parts of the building, such as cement and glass. They should not list living items, such as trees.

---

### as you read

**What You'll Learn**
- **Describe** characteristics that all minerals share.
- **Explain** how minerals form.

**Why It's Important**
You use minerals and products made from them every day.

**Review Vocabulary**
**atoms:** tiny particles that make up matter; composed of protons, electrons, and neutrons

**New Vocabulary**
- mineral
- crystal
- magma
- silicate

**Figure 1** You probably use minerals or materials made from minerals every day without thinking about it.
**Infer** *How many objects in this picture might be made from minerals?*

---

## What is a mineral?

How important are minerals to you? Very important? You actually own or encounter many things made from minerals every day. Ceramic, metallic, and even some paper items are examples of products that are derived from or include minerals. **Figure 1** shows just a few of these things. Metal bicycle racks, bricks, and the glass in windows would not exist if it weren't for minerals. A **mineral** is a naturally occurring, inorganic solid with a definite chemical composition and an orderly arrangement of atoms. About 4,000 different minerals are found on Earth, but they all share these four characteristics.

**Mineral Characteristics** First, all minerals are formed by natural processes. These are processes that occur on or inside Earth with no input from humans. For example, salt formed by the natural evaporation of seawater is the mineral halite, but salt formed by evaporation of saltwater solutions in laboratories is not a mineral. Second, minerals are inorganic. This means that they aren't made by life processes. Third, every mineral is an element or compound with a definite chemical composition. For example, halite's composition, NaCl, gives it a distinctive taste that adds flavor to many foods. Fourth, minerals are crystalline solids. All solids have a definite volume and shape. Gases and liquids like air and water have no definite shape, and they aren't crystalline. Only a solid can be a mineral, but not all solids are minerals.

**Atom Patterns** The word *crystalline* means that atoms are arranged in a pattern that is repeated over and over again. For example, graphite's atoms are arranged in layers. Opal, on the other hand, is not a mineral in the strictest sense because its atoms are not all arranged in a definite, repeating pattern, even though it is a naturally occurring, inorganic solid.

---

### Section 1 Resource Manager

**Chapter FAST FILE Resources**
Transparency Activity, p. 40
Directed Reading for Content Mastery, pp. 15, 16
MiniLAB, p. 3
Enrichment, p. 26

Lab Activity, pp. 9–10
Lab Worksheets, pp. 5–6
**Mathematics Skill Activities,** p. 47
**Cultural Diversity,** p. 37

**Figure 2** More than 200 years ago, the smooth, flat surfaces on crystals led scientists to infer that minerals had an orderly structure inside.

Even though this rose quartz looks uneven on the outside, its atoms have an orderly arrangement on the inside.

The well-formed crystal shapes exhibited by these clear quartz crystals suggest an orderly structure.

## The Structure of Minerals

Do you have a favorite mineral sample or gemstone? If so, perhaps it contains well-formed crystals. A **crystal** is a solid in which the atoms are arranged in orderly, repeating patterns. You can see evidence for this orderly arrangement of atoms when you observe the smooth, flat outside surfaces of crystals. A crystal system is a group of crystals that have similar atomic arrangements and therefore similar external crystal shapes.

✓ **Reading Check** *What is a crystal?*

**Crystals** Not all mineral crystals have smooth surfaces and regular shapes like the clear quartz crystals in **Figure 2.** The rose quartz in the smaller photo of **Figure 2** has atoms arranged in repeating patterns, but you can't see the crystal shape on the outside of the mineral. This is because the rose quartz crystals developed in a tight space, while the clear quartz crystals developed freely in an open space. The six-sided, or hexagonal crystal shape of the clear quartz crystals in **Figure 2,** and other forms of quartz can be seen in some samples of the mineral. **Figure 3** illustrates the six major crystal systems, which classify minerals according to their crystal structures. The hexagonal system to which quartz belongs is one example of a crystal system.

Crystals form by many processes. Next, you'll learn about two of these processes—crystals that form from magma and crystals that form from solutions of salts.

### Inferring Salt's Crystal System

**Procedure** 🔬 ⚗️
1. Use a **magnifying lens** to observe grains of common **table salt** on a dark sheet of **construction paper.** Sketch the shape of a salt grain. WARNING: *Do not taste or eat mineral samples. Keep hands away from your face.*
2. Compare the shapes of the salt crystals with the shapes of crystals shown in **Figure 3.**

**Analysis**
1. Which characteristics do all the grains have in common?
2. Research another mineral with the same crystal system as salt. What is this crystal system called?

SECTION 1 Minerals **505**

SECTION 1 Minerals **505**

## Visualizing Crystal Systems

Have students examine the pictures and read the captions. Then ask the following question.

Which of the crystal systems includes the fewest right angles? Triclinic crystals have no right angles; all angles where the crystal surfaces meet are oblique.

### Inquiry Lab

**Modeling Mineral Coordinate Systems**

**Purpose** students practice working with coordinate systems and thinking in 3-D

**Possible Materials,** toothpicks, tongue depressors, pipe cleaners, protractor, connecting toys, glue, tape, string, ruler, **Figure 3**

**Estimated Time** 1 class session

**Teaching Strategies**

• Students can build 3-D models of the coordinate systems that describe each crystal system. L3
• Students could sketch the model coordinate systems of their choice in different orientations. L2
• Students who are having difficulties can focus on the cubic, tetragonal, and orthorhombic crystal systems. L2
• Allow students to explore other questions that arise.

**For additional inquiry activities, see** *Science Inquiry Labs.*

---

## NATIONAL GEOGRAPHIC VISUALIZING CRYSTAL SYSTEMS

### Figure 3

A crystal's shape depends on how its atoms are arranged. Crystal shapes can be organized into groups known as crystal systems—shown here in 3-D with geometric models (in blue). Knowing a mineral's crystal system helps researchers understand its atomic structure and physical properties.

▲ **CUBIC** Fluorite is an example of a mineral that forms cubic crystals. Minerals in the cubic crystal system are equal in size along all three principal dimensions.

▲ **HEXAGONAL** (hek SA guh nul) In hexagonal crystals, horizontal distances between opposite crystal surfaces are equal. These crystal surfaces intersect to form 60° or 120° angles. The vertical length is longer or shorter than the horizontal lengths.

◀ **TETRAGONAL** (te TRA guh nul) Zircon crystals are tetragonal. Tetragonal crystals are much like cubic crystals, except that one of the principal dimensions is longer or shorter than the other two dimensions.

▲ **ORTHORHOMBIC** (awr thuh RAHM bihk) Minerals with orthorhombic structure, such as barite, have dimensions that are unequal in length, resulting in crystals with a brick-like shape.

▲ **MONOCLINIC** (mah nuh KLIH nihk) Minerals in the monoclinic system, such as orthoclase, also exhibit unequal dimensions in their crystal structure. Only one right angle forms where crystal surfaces meet. The other angles are oblique, which means they don't form 90° angles where they intersect.

▲ **TRICLINIC** (tri KLIH nihk) The triclinic crystal system includes minerals exhibiting the least symmetry. Triclinic crystals, such as rhodonite (ROH dun ite), are unequal in all dimensions, and all angles where crystal surfaces meet are oblique.

---

## Teacher FYI

**Hexagonal Crystal System** The hexagonal crystal system possesses one axis of six-fold or three-fold symmetry perpendicular to, and not equal in length to, three equal axes intersecting at 120°. Crystals with six-fold symmetry are classified as hexagonal—apatite and graphite are examples. Crystals with three-fold symmetry are classified as trigonal—calcite and some varieties of quartz are examples.

**Figure 4** Minerals form by many natural processes.

**A** This rock formed as magma cooled slowly, allowing large mineral grains to form.

Labradorite

**B** Some minerals form when salt water evaporates, such as these white crystals of halite in Death Valley, California.

## Crystals from Magma

Natural processes form minerals in many ways. For example, hot melted rock material, called **magma,** cools when it reaches Earth's surface, or even if it's trapped below the surface. As magma cools, its atoms lose heat energy, move closer together, and begin to combine into compounds. During this process, atoms of the different compounds arrange themselves into orderly, repeating patterns. The type and amount of elements present in a magma partly determine which minerals will form. Also, the size of the crystals that form depends partly on how rapidly the magma cools.

When magma cools slowly, the crystals that form are generally large enough to see with the unaided eye, as shown in **Figure 4A.** This is because the atoms have enough time to move together and form into larger crystals. When magma cools rapidly, the crystals that form will be small. In such cases, you can't easily see individual mineral crystals.

## Crystals from Solution

Crystals also can form from minerals dissolved in water. When water evaporates, as in a dry climate, ions that are left behind can come together to form crystals like the halite crystals in **Figure 4B.** Or, if too much of a substance is dissolved in water, ions can come together and crystals of that substance can begin to form in the solution. Minerals can form from a solution in this way without the need for evaporation.

**INTEGRATE Physics**

**Crystal Formation**
Evaporites commonly form in dry climates. Research the changes that take place when a saline lake or shallow sea evaporates and halite or gypsum forms.

SECTION 1 Minerals **507**

**DAILY INTERVENTION**

### Check for Understanding

**Visual-Spatial** Have groups of students compete to brainstorm the greatest number of ordinary, non-mineral objects that conform to the described crystal systems. Examples might include a skyscraper, tissue box, and unsharpened colored pencil. Offer a special bonus to any group that can describe an object conforming to the triclinic system. [L2]

### Reteach

**Illustrating Elements** Hold up an unlabeled circle graph showing the weight percentages of elements in Earth's crust. Ask students to identify the portions of the graph that represent aluminum, oxygen, and silicon. [L2]

### ☑ Assessment

**Process** Have students make a Venn diagram that compares and contrasts crystals formed from magma with crystals formed from solutions. Use **Performance Assessment in the Science Classroom,** p. 167. [L2]

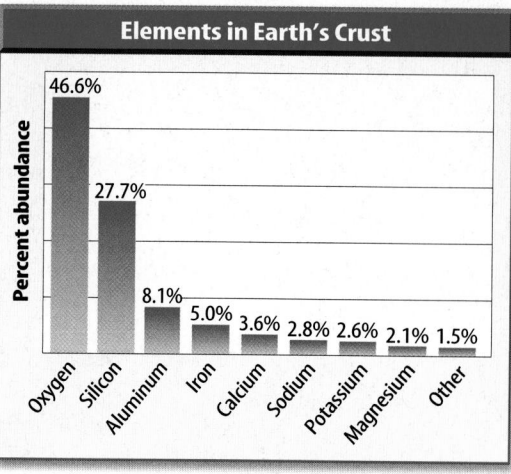

**Figure 5** Most of Earth's crust is composed of eight elements.

## Mineral Compositions and Groups

Ninety elements occur naturally in Earth's crust. Approximately 98 percent (by weight) of the crust is made of only eight of these elements, as shown in **Figure 5.** Of the thousands of known minerals, only a few dozen are common, and these are mostly composed of the eight most common elements in Earth's crust.

Most of the common rock-forming minerals belong to a group called the silicates. **Silicates** (SIH luh kayts) are minerals that contain silicon (Si) and oxygen (O) and usually one or more other elements. Silicon and oxygen are the two most abundant elements in Earth's crust. These two elements alone combine to form the basic building blocks of most of the minerals in Earth's crust and mantle. Feldspar and quartz, which are silicates, and calcite, which is a carbonate, are examples of common, rock-forming minerals. Other mineral groups also are defined according to their compositions.

### section ① review

**Summary**

**What is a mineral?**
- Many products used by humans are made from minerals.
- Minerals are defined by four main characteristics.

**The Structure of Minerals**
- The crystal shape of a mineral reflects the way in which its atoms are arranged.
- Minerals are classified according to the types of atoms in their structures and the way that the atoms are arranged.

**Mineral Compositions and Groups**
- Only eight elements form approximately 98 percent (by weight) of Earth's crust.
- The majority of Earth's crust is composed of silicate minerals.

**Self Check**

1. **List** four characteristics that all minerals share.
2. **Describe** two ways that minerals can form from solution.
3. **Explain** whether diamonds made in the laboratory are considered to be minerals.
4. **Describe** how crystals of minerals are classified.
5. **Think Critically** The mineral dolomite, a rock-forming mineral, contains oxygen, carbon, magnesium, and calcium. Is dolomite a silicate? Explain.

**Applying Skills**

6. **Graph** Make a graph of your own design that shows the relative percentages of the eight most common elements in Earth's crust. Then determine the approximate percentage of the crust that is made up of iron and aluminum. If one is available, you may use an electronic spreadsheet program to make your graph and perform the calculation.

  Science Online in7.msscience.com/self_check_quiz

### section ① review

1. A mineral must be a naturally occurring, inorganic, crystalline solid with a definite chemical composition.
2. Minerals can precipitate out of a solution where too much of a substance is dissolved, or form as a solution evaporates.
3. No; because the diamonds are made in the lab, they are not naturally occurring.
4. Crystals are classified by the shapes produced by the internal arrangement of their atoms.
5. No; this rock-forming mineral is a carbonate. Silicate rock-forming minerals contain silicon and oxygen, both of which are very common. Silicates are one type of rock-forming mineral.
6. Student's graphs should include the information from **Figure 5.** They can be bar graphs, shaded-block graphs, or circle graphs; 13.1 percent.

# Crystal Formation

In this lab, you'll have a chance to learn how crystals form from solutions.

## ● Real-World Question

How do crystals form from solution?

### Goals
- **Compare and contrast** the crystals that form from salt and sugar solutions.
- **Observe** crystals and infer how they formed.

### Materials
| | |
|---|---|
| 250-mL beakers (2) | cotton string |
| cardboard | hot plate |
| large paper clip | magnifying lens |
| table salt | thermal mitt |
| flat wooden stick | shallow pan |
| granulated sugar | spoon |

### Safety Precautions

**WARNING:** *Never taste or eat any lab materials.*

## ● Procedure

1. Gently mix separate solutions of salt in water and sugar in water in the two beakers. Keep stirring the solutions as you add salt or sugar to the water. Stop mixing when no more salt or sugar will dissolve in the solutions. Label each beaker.

2. Place the sugar solution beaker on a hot plate. Use the hot plate to heat the sugar solution gently. **WARNING:** *Do not touch the hot beaker without protecting your hands.*

3. Tie one end of the thread to the middle of the wooden stick. Tie a large paper clip to the free end of the string for weight. Place the stick across the opening of the sugar beaker so the thread dangles in the sugar solution.

4. Remove the beaker from the hot plate and cover it with cardboard. Place it in a location where it won't be disturbed.

5. Pour a thin layer of the salt solution into the shallow pan.

6. Leave the beaker and the shallow pan undisturbed for at least one week.

7. After one week, examine each solution with a magnifying lens to see whether crystals have formed.

## ● Conclude and Apply

1. **Compare and contrast** the crystals that formed from the salt and the sugar solutions. How do they compare with samples of table salt and sugar?

2. **Describe** what happened to the saltwater solution in the shallow pan.

3. Did this same process occur in the sugar solution? Explain.

### *Communicating* Your Data

Make a poster that describes your methods of growing salt and sugar crystals. Present your results to your class.

**LAB 509**

---

---

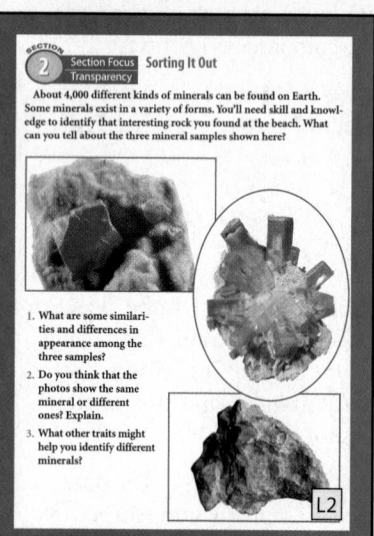
## section 2

# Mineral Identification

### as you read

**What You'll Learn**

- **Describe** physical properties used to identify minerals.
- **Identify** minerals using physical properties such as hardness and streak.

**Why It's Important**

Identifying minerals helps you recognize valuable mineral resources.

**Review Vocabulary**

**physical property:** any characteristic of a material that you can observe without changing the identity of the material

**New Vocabulary**

- hardness
- streak
- luster
- cleavage
- specific gravity
- fracture

## Physical Properties

Why can you recognize a classmate when you see him or her in a crowd away from school? A person's height or the shape of his or her face helps you tell that person from the rest of your class. Height and facial shape are two properties unique to individuals. Individual minerals also have unique properties that distinguish them.

**Mineral Appearance** Just like height and facial characteristics help you recognize someone, mineral properties can help you recognize and distinguish minerals. Color and appearance are two obvious clues that can be used to identify minerals.

However, these clues alone aren't enough to recognize most minerals. The minerals pyrite and gold are gold in color and can appear similar, as shown in **Figure 6.** As a matter of fact, pyrite often is called fool's gold. Gold is worth a lot of money, whereas pyrite has little value. You need to look at other properties of minerals to tell them apart. Some other properties to study include how hard a mineral is, how it breaks, and its color when crushed into a powder. Every property you observe in a mineral is a clue to its identity.

**Figure 6** The general appearance of a mineral often is not enough to identify it.

Gold

Azurite

Pyrite

Using only color, observers can be fooled when trying to distinguish between pyrite and gold.

The mineral azurite is identified readily by its striking blue color.

**510 CHAPTER 17** Minerals

**Hardness** A measure of how easily a mineral can be scratched is its **hardness**. The mineral talc is so soft you can scratch it loose with your fingernail. Talcum powder is made from this soft mineral. Diamonds, on the other hand, are the hardest mineral. Some diamonds are used as cutting tools, as shown in **Figure 7**. A diamond can be scratched only by another diamond. Diamonds can be broken, however.

**Reading Check** *Why is hardness sometimes referred to as scratchability?*

Sometimes the concept of hardness is confused with whether or not a mineral will break. It is important to understand that even though a diamond is extremely hard, it can shatter if given a hard enough blow in the right direction along the crystal.

**Mohs Scale** In 1824, the Austrian scientist Friedrich Mohs developed a list of common minerals to compare their hardnesses. This list is called Mohs scale of hardness, as seen in **Table 1.** The scale lists the hardness of ten minerals. Talc, the softest mineral, has a hardness value of one, and diamond, the hardest mineral, has a value of ten.

Here's how the scale works. Imagine that you have a clear or whitish-colored mineral that you know is either fluorite or quartz. You try to scratch it with your fingernail and then with an iron nail. You can't scratch it with your fingernail but you can scratch it with the iron nail. Because the hardness of your fingernail is 2.5 and that of the iron nail is 4.5, you can determine the unknown mineral's hardness to be somewhere around 3 or 4. Because it is known that quartz has a hardness of 7 and fluorite has a hardness of 4, the mystery mineral must be fluorite.

Some minerals have a hardness range rather than a single hardness value. This is because atoms are arranged differently in different directions in their crystal structures.

**Figure 7** Some saw blades have diamonds embedded in them to help slice through materials, such as this limestone. Blades are kept cool by running water over them.

**Table 1  Mineral Hardness**

| Mohs Scale | Hardness | Hardness of Common Objects | |
|---|---|---|---|
| Talc (softest) | 1 | | |
| Gypsum | 2 | fingernail | (2.5) |
| Calcite | 3 | piece of copper | (2.5 to 3.0) |
| Fluorite | 4 | iron nail | (4.5) |
| Apatite | 5 | glass | (5.5) |
| Feldspar | 6 | steel file | (6.5) |
| Quartz | 7 | streak plate | (7.0) |
| Topaz | 8 | | |
| Corundum | 9 | | |
| Diamond (hardest) | 10 | | |

SECTION 2 Mineral Identification **511**

## 2 Teach

**Activity**

**Synthetic Diamonds** Diamonds that are used in cutting tools can be made synthetically. Have students research how synthetic diamonds are produced. Have them write a one-page report on their findings. Synthetic diamonds can be made by heating graphite at high pressure. [L2] [IS] **Linguistic** [P]

**Reading Check**

**Answer** Hardness is a measure of how easily a mineral can be scratched. It is tested by attempting to scratch one mineral with a common object or another mineral of known hardness.

**Discussion**

**Fake Diamonds** Tell students that someone has placed an ad in the newspaper that reads, "Real gems for sale! We'll prove these are genuine diamonds by cutting glass with them before your very eyes!" Have students describe why cutting glass wouldn't prove the stones were diamonds. Possible answer: Many minerals other than diamonds cut glass. [IS] **Linguistic**

## Curriculum Connection

**Auto Mechanics** Some motor oil is dark gray in color. This is caused by the presence of graphite in the oil. Have students find out why graphite is added to motor oil. Because of its softness and atomic arrangement, graphite can be used to lubricate the moving parts of a motor. Graphite can also be used to lubricate moving parts in door hinges and locks. [L2]

**Figure 8** The two minerals shown have metallic and glassy lusters. Have students relate the way that light reflects off different minerals to the way it reflects off a piece of chrome, a stainless-steel butter knife, brushed aluminum framing, a chalkboard, and a piece of plastic. The lusters of the pieces of metal are all metallic. However, some are shiny and others are not. The luster of the plastic is shiny, but not metallic.

 **Visual-Spatial**

## Applying Science

### Answers

1. Hardness test: Hematite would scratch an iron nail; copper would not scratch an iron nail.
2. streak test; unglazed porcelain tile
3. Apply other tests; observe luster, specific gravity, etc.

Graphite

Fluorite

**Figure 8** Luster is an important physical property that is used to distinguish minerals. Graphite has a metallic luster. Fluorite has a nonmetallic, glassy luster.

**Luster** The way a mineral reflects light is known as **luster.** Luster can be metallic or nonmetallic. Minerals with a metallic luster, like the graphite shown in **Figure 8,** shine like metal. Metallic luster can be compared to the shine of a metal belt buckle, the shiny chrome trim on some cars, or the shine of metallic cooking utensils. When a mineral does not shine like metal, its luster is nonmetallic. Examples of terms for nonmetallic luster include dull, pearly, silky, and glassy. Common examples of minerals with glassy luster are quartz, calcite, halite, and fluorite.

**Specific Gravity** Minerals also can be distinguished by comparing the weights of equal-sized samples. The **specific gravity** of a mineral is the ratio of its weight compared with the weight of an equal volume of water. Like hardness, specific gravity is expressed as a number. If you were to research the specific gravities of gold and pyrite, you'd find that gold's specific gravity is about 19, and pyrite's is 5. This means that gold is about 19 times heavier than water and pyrite is 5 times heavier than water. You could experience this by comparing equal-sized samples of gold and pyrite in your hands—the pyrite would feel much lighter. The term *heft* is sometimes used to describe how heavy a mineral sample feels.

## Applying Science

### How can you identify minerals?

| Properties of Minerals | | |
| --- | --- | --- |
| Mineral | Hardness | Streak |
| Copper | 2.5–3 | copper-red |
| Galena | 2.5 | dark gray |
| Gold | 2.5–3 | yellow |
| Hematite | 5.5–6.5 | red to brown |
| Magnetite | 6–6.5 | black |
| Silver | 2.5–3 | silver-white |

You have learned that minerals are identified by their physical properties, such as streak, hardness, cleavage, and color. Use your knowledge of mineral properties and your ability to read a table to solve the following problems.

**Identifying the Problem**

The table includes hardnesses and streak colors for several minerals. How can you use these data to distinguish minerals?

**Solving the Problem**

1. What test would you perform to distinguish hematite from copper? How would you carry out this test?
2. How could you distinguish copper from galena? What tool would you use?
3. What would you do if two minerals had the same hardness and the same streak color?

**512** CHAPTER 17 Minerals

 ## LAB DEMONSTRATION

**Purpose** to show that minerals can be identified by unique physical properties

**Materials** sulfur, calcite, magnetite

**Preparation** Wear safety goggles and an apron.

**Procedure** Show students the bright yellow color of sulfur. Drop dilute HCl on calcite to show its fizzing reaction. Show the magnetic property of magnetite by using it to attract a magnet.

**Expected Outcome** Students will see that color can help identify certain minerals, and that unique properties might be the only clue needed to identify certain minerals.

### Assessment

What would happen if HCl were dropped on other minerals in the same group as calcite? The minerals would probably fizz (although not all carbonates will readily react to acid).

**Streak** When a mineral is rubbed across a piece of unglazed porcelain tile, as in **Figure 9,** a streak of powdered mineral is left behind. **Streak** is the color of a mineral when it is in a powdered form. The streak test works only for minerals that are softer than the streak plate. Gold and pyrite can be distinguished by a streak test. Gold has a yellow streak and pyrite has a greenish-black or brownish-black streak.

Some soft minerals will leave a streak even on paper. The last time you used a pencil to write on paper, you left a streak of the mineral graphite. One reason that graphite is used in pencil lead is because it is soft enough to leave a streak on paper.

 **Reading Check** *Why do gold and pyrite leave a streak, but quartz does not?*

**Cleavage and Fracture** The way a mineral breaks is another clue to its identity. Minerals that break along smooth, flat surfaces have **cleavage** (KLEE vihj). Cleavage, like hardness, is determined partly by the arrangement of the mineral's atoms. Mica is a mineral that has one perfect cleavage. **Figure 10** shows how mica breaks along smooth, flat planes. If you were to take a layer cake and separate its layers, you would show that the cake has cleavage. Not all minerals have cleavage. Minerals that break with uneven, rough, or jagged surfaces have **fracture.** Quartz is a mineral with fracture. If you were to grab a chunk out of the side of that cake, it would be like breaking a mineral that has fracture.

**Figure 9** Streak is more useful for mineral identification than is mineral color. Hematite, for example, can be dark red, gray, or silver in color. However, its streak is always dark reddish-brown.

Mica

Halite

**Figure 10** Weak or fewer bonds within the structures of mica and halite allow them to be broken along smooth, flat cleavage planes. **Infer** *If you broke quartz, would it look the same?*

SECTION 2 Mineral Identification **513**

**Reading Check**

**Answer** Both gold and pyrite are softer than the streak plate; quartz is harder than the streak plate.

## Use an Analogy

**Cleavage** Explain that some minerals show perfect cleavage, breaking into thin sheets that can be compared to sheets of paper. Relatively large samples of muscovite or biotite are called "books," because thin sheets can be separated along one cleavage plane, similar to separating the pages of a book.

## Quick Demo

**Pyrite Properties**

**Materials** pyrite, glass plate, streak plate

**Estimated Time** 5 minutes

**Procedure** Demonstrate how pyrite can be distinguished from gold with two simple tests. Rub the sample on a streak plate and show students the greenish streak. Place the glass plate flat on a tabletop and firmly scrape the pyrite against the glass. Have students feel for the scratch left in the glass.

## Caption Answer

**Figure 10** No; quartz breaks with uneven, often conchoidal, fracture surfaces.

**Virtual Labs**

 **Mineral Properties** *How can minerals be defined by their properties?*

## Differentiated Instruction

**Challenge** Have students research the atomic structure of a mica, such as muscovite. Have them write about the chemical bonds that exist between structural layers, and relate this to cleavage in micas. L3

## Teacher FYI

**Mica Uses** Sheets of white mica once were used to make the "isinglass" heatproof windows of stoves and ranges. It was also used in Russia for windowpanes and became known as "Muscovy glass." This later became "muscovite," the current name for white mica.

## Mini LAB

**Purpose** to observe how properties can be used to identify minerals **IS** Visual-Spatial

**Teaching Strategy** Place a clear calcite cleavage fragment over a dot on an overhead projector transparency. Rotate the calcite so that one dot revolves around the other.

**Analysis**

1. calcite
2. reaction with HCl

### Assessment

**Oral** Have students describe the double image of a dot through different thicknesses of calcite. The greater the distance between cleavage planes, the farther apart the dots appear. Use **PASC**, p. 89. L2

---

## 3 Assess

### DAILY INTERVENTION

**Check for Understanding**

**Kinesthetic** Have students hypothesize whether mineral samples contain iron. Iron content will make a mineral feel heavy, give it a dark color, and possibly make it magnetic.

**Reteach**

**Observing Properties** Obtain samples of magnetite. Have students determine its properties. magnetic, has a metallic luster, hardness greater than glass, black in color and streak, exhibits uneven fracture

---

### ☑ Assessment

**Performance** Have students make a table classifying familiar minerals according to types of cleavage. Use **PASC**, p. 109. L2

---

## Mini LAB

**Observing Mineral Properties**

**Procedure** 🐾 🥽 👋 🏚️

1. Obtain samples of some of the following clear minerals: **gypsum, muscovite mica, halite,** and **calcite.**
2. Place each sample over the print on this page and observe the letters.

**Analysis**

1. Which mineral can be identified by observing the print's double image?
2. What other special property is used to identify this mineral?

---

**Figure 11** Some minerals are natural magnets, such as this lodestone, which is a variety of magnetite.

**Other Properties** Some minerals have unique properties. Magnetite, as you can guess by its name, is attracted to magnets. Lodestone, a form of magnetite, will pick up iron filings like a magnet, as shown in **Figure 11.** Light forms two separate rays when it passes through calcite, causing you to see a double image when viewed through transparent specimens. Calcite also can be identified because it fizzes when hydrochloric acid is put on it.

Now you know that you sometimes need more information than color and appearance to identify a mineral. You also might need to test its streak, hardness, luster, and cleavage or fracture. Although the overall appearance of a mineral can be different from sample to sample, its physical properties remain the same.

---

## section 2 review

### Summary

**Physical Properties**

- Minerals are identified by observing their physical properties.
- Hardness is a measure of how easily a mineral can be scratched.
- Luster describes how a mineral reflects light.
- Specific gravity is the ratio of the weight of a mineral sample compared to the weight of an equal volume of water.
- Streak is the color of a powdered mineral.
- Minerals with cleavage break along smooth, flat surfaces in one or more directions.
- Fracture describes any uneven manner in which a mineral breaks.
- Some minerals react readily with acid, form a double image, or are magnetic.

### Self Check

1. **Compare and contrast** a mineral fragment that has one cleavage direction with one that has only fracture.
2. **Explain** how an unglazed porcelain tile can be used to identify a mineral.
3. **Explain** why streak often is more useful for mineral identification than color.
4. **Determine** What hardness does a mineral have if it does not scratch glass but it scratches an iron nail?
5. **Think Critically** What does the presence of cleavage planes within a mineral tell you about the chemical bonds that hold the mineral together?

#### Applying Skills

6. **Draw Conclusions** A large piece of the mineral halite is broken repeatedly into several perfect cubes. How can this be explained?

Science Online in7.msscience.com/self_check_quiz

---

## section 2 review

1. A mineral with cleavage breaks along smooth, flat planes. One that fractures breaks with uneven or jagged surfaces.
2. A mineral softer than an unglazed porcelain tile will leave a powdered streak on the tile. The streak color can help identify the mineral.
3. Several different samples of one mineral may have different colors, but they usually will have the same streak.
4. between 4.5 and 5.5
5. Cleavage planes occur where relatively weak bonds exist within the mineral's structure.
6. Halite has three directions of cleavage oriented at 90° to each other.

**Standards—7.1.5:** Identify some important contributions to the advancement of science ... and technology that have been made by different kinds of people, in different cultures, at different times. **7.1.6:** Provide examples of people who overcame bias and/or limited opportunities in education and employment to excel in the fields of science.

# Uses of Minerals

## Gems

Walking past the window of a jewelry store, you notice a large selection of beautiful jewelry—a watch sparkling with diamonds, a necklace holding a brilliant red ruby, and a gold ring. For thousands of years, people have worn and prized minerals in their jewelry. What makes some minerals special? What unusual properties do they have that make them so valuable?

**Properties of Gems** As you can see in **Figure 12, gems** or gemstones are highly prized minerals because they are rare and beautiful. Most gems are special varieties of a particular mineral. They are clearer, brighter, or more colorful than common samples of that mineral. The difference between a gem and the common form of the same mineral can be slight. Amethyst is a gem form of quartz that contains just traces of iron in its structure. This small amount of iron gives amethyst a desirable purple color. Sometimes a gem has a crystal structure that allows it to be cut and polished to a higher quality than that of a non-gem mineral. **Table 2** lists popular gems and some locations where they have been collected.

### as you read

*What* **You'll Learn**
- **Describe** characteristics of gems that make them more valuable than other minerals.
- **Identify** useful elements that are contained in minerals.

*Why* **It's Important**

Minerals are necessary materials for decorative items and many manufactured products.

**Review Vocabulary**
**metal:** element that typically is a shiny, malleable solid that conducts heat and electricity well

**New Vocabulary**
- gem
- ore

**Bellringer**

**Section Focus Transparencies** also are available on the Interactive Chalkboard CD-ROM.

L2 ELL

**Figure 12** It is easy to see why gems are prized for their beauty and rarity. Shown here is The Imperial State Crown, made for Queen Victoria of England in 1838. It contains thousands of jewels, including diamonds, rubies, sapphires, and emeralds.

### Tie to Prior Knowledge

**Jewelry** Have students recall the last time they saw jewelry in a jewelry store or department store. Have students describe the jewelry. Most will say it was shiny, colorful, or looked brilliant under the lights in the store. Explain that jewelry is one common use of minerals. L1 LS
**Visual-Spatial**

SECTION 3 Uses of Minerals **515**

---

## Use Science Words

**Word Usage** Have students read advertisements and use **Table 2** to discover what gems are commonly used in jewelry. Ask them also to find out what minerals the gems are set in. They also could discover where the minerals were found. Have them write their findings in their Science Journals. Possible answer: gems used in jewelry—emeralds, rubies, tanzanite, topaz, peridot, almandine, pyrope, amethyst, sapphires, diamonds; gem settings—gold, silver, platinum; where minerals found—quartz veins and placer deposits, among others L2
ELL IS **Visual-Spatial and Linguistic** P

## Make a Model

**Crystal Systems** Have students research the crystal systems of the gemstones listed in **Table 2.** Once the crystal system has been identified, have students construct models of each crystal system. Students should use **Figure 3** and a book on mineralogy to assist in planning their models. Student models should include the following crystal systems: cubic—spinel and garnet; hexagonal—beryl, quartz, and corundum; orthorhombic—zoisite, topaz, and olivine. L3 ELL IS **Kinesthetic**

### Table 2 Minerals and Their Gems

| Fun Facts | Mineral | Gem Example | Some Important Locations |
|---|---|---|---|
| Beryl is named for the element beryllium, which it contains. Some crystals reach several meters in length. | Beryl | Emerald | Colombia, Brazil, South Africa, North Carolina |
| A red spinel in the British crown jewels has a mass of 352 carats. A carat is 0.2 g. | Spinel | Ruby spinel | Sri Lanka, Thailand, Myanmar (Burma) |
| Purplish-blue examples of zoisite were discovered in 1967 near Arusha, Tanzania. | Zoisite | Tanzanite | Tanzania |
| The most valuable examples are yellow, pink, and blue varieties. | Topaz (uncut) | Topaz (gem) | Siberia, Germany, Japan, Mexico, Brazil, Colorado, Utah, Texas, California, Maine, Virginia, South Carolina |

**516 CHAPTER 17** Minerals

## Cultural Diversity

**Quartz** The mineral quartz has been recognized for its hardness and utility since prehistoric times. Quartz tools that are more than 350,000 years old have been found at sites such as Zhoukoudianzhen, China. Quartz has also been esteemed by many cultures for its beauty. The Japanese and Chinese carved clear rock quartz into art objects and spheres, as did the Greeks. Large transparent crystals are found in Madagascar, Japan, Burma, and Brazil. Quartz occurs in many colors and has been used for ornamentation. Purple amethyst comes from Mexico and Brazil. Cairngorm, a brown quartz, was named after the Cairngorm Mountains of Scotland. It also can be found in Switzerland, Japan, and Colorado. Have students research modern uses of quartz. Possible answer: timepieces and jewelry L2

| Fun Facts | Mineral | Gem Example | Some Important Locations |
|---|---|---|---|
| Olivine composes a large part of Earth's upper mantle. It is also present in moon rocks. | Olivine | Peridot | Myanmar (Burma), Zebirget (Saint John's Island, located in the Red Sea), Arizona, New Mexico |
| Garnet is a common mineral found in a wide variety of rock types. The red color of the variety almandine is caused by iron in its crystal structure. | Garnet | Almandine | Ural Mountains, Italy, Madagascar, Czech Republic, India, Sri Lanka, Brazil, North Carolina, Arizona, New Mexico |
| Quartz makes up about 30 percent of Earth's continental crust. | Quartz | Amethyst | Colorless varieties in Hot Springs, Arkansas; Amethyst in Brazil, Uruguay, Madagascar, Montana, North Carolina, California, Maine |
| The blue color of sapphire is caused by iron or titanium in corundum. Chromium in corundum produces the red color of ruby. | Corundum | Blue sapphire | Thailand, Cambodia, Sri Lanka, Kashmir |

## Activity

**Separating Crystals** Have students suppose that they have a liquid that has a density of 4.0 g/cm³. Ask students to design an experiment that would enable them to separate several gems into two piles; one of diamonds and the other of cubic zirconium crystals. Possible answer: The density of diamond is 3.52 g/cm³ and the density of cubic zirconium is 4.7 g/cm³. Place the gems in the liquid. The diamonds will float and the cubic zirconium crystals will sink. L3 **LS** **Logical-Mathematical**

## Discussion

**Gem Color** Ruby and sapphire are varieties of the mineral corundum. Why are rubies red and some sapphires blue? Blue sapphire is colored by iron and titanium impurities, while the red color of ruby is caused by the presence of minor chromium.

## Differentiated Instruction

**Challenge** Have students research a method used to make diamond-edged surgical scalpels, razor blades, dental drills, and diamond-coated computer parts. Possible answer: Microwaves are used to strip the hydrogen atoms away from the methane molecule. The carbon atoms then link together on the surface of the instrument being coated, forming tiny rows of diamonds. L3

**Figure 13** Two famous and very valuable diamonds are shown here. What makes a diamond valuable? The value of diamonds depends partly on whether or not they are tinted. The most common diamonds of gem quality have yellow or brown tints and are less valuable than diamonds with no tints. Diamonds with blue or pink tints are more valuable than those with no tints. Why might these stones be exceptionally valuable? Possible answer: They are rare and have large carat weights. The Hope diamond is tinted blue.

**Science Online**

**Topic: Gemstone Data**

Visit in7.msscience.com for Web links to information about gems at the Smithsonian Museum of Natural History.

**Activity** List three important examples of gems other than those described on this page. Prepare a data table with the heads *Gem Name/Type, Weight (carats/grams), Mineral,* and *Location.* Fill in the table entries for the gemstones you selected.

**Figure 13** These gems are among the most famous examples of precious stones.

**Important Gems** All gems are prized, but some are truly spectacular and have played an important role in history. For example, the Cullinan diamond, found in South Africa in 1905, was the largest uncut diamond ever discovered. Its mass was 3,106.75 carats (about 621 g). The Cullinan diamond was cut into 9 main stones and 96 smaller ones. The largest of these is called the Cullinan 1 or Great Star of Africa. Its mass is 530.20 carats (about 106 g), and it is now part of the British monarchy's crown jewels, shown in **Figure 13A.**

Another well-known diamond is the blue Hope diamond, shown in **Figure 13B.** This is perhaps the most notorious of all diamonds. It was purchased by Henry Philip Hope around 1830, after whom it is named. Because his entire family as well as a later owner suffered misfortune, the Hope diamond has gained a reputation for bringing its owner bad luck. The Hope diamond's mass is 45.52 carats (about 9 g). Currently it is displayed in the Smithsonian Institution in Washington, D.C.

**Useful Gems** In addition to their beauty, some gems serve useful purposes. You learned earlier that diamonds have a hardness of 10 on Mohs scale. They can scratch almost any material—a property that makes them useful as industrial abrasives and cutting tools. Other useful gems include rubies, which are used to produce specific types of laser light. Quartz crystals are used in electronics and as timepieces. When subjected to an electric field, quartz vibrates steadily, which helps control frequencies in electronic devices and allows for accurate timekeeping.

Most industrial diamonds and other gems are synthetic, which means that humans make them. However, the study of natural gems led to their synthesis, allowing the synthetic varieties to be used by humans readily.

**A** The Great Star of Africa is part of a sceptre in the collection of British crown jewels.

**B** Beginning in 1668, the Hope diamond was part of the French crown jewels. Then known as the French Blue, it was stolen in 1792 and later surfaced in London, England in 1812.

## Curriculum Connection

**Art** Ask an art teacher to bring jewelry-making supplies to class. Materials might include copper, brass, and silver, as well as precut and polished stones. Students could even make jewelry from stones they find near their homes. Have samples of the mineral ores that copper and other materials come from available for students to observe. L2 ELL IS **Visual-Spatial**

## Differentiated Instruction

**Challenge** Students can investigate the areas of the world that produce most of the world's gems. Have them make a collage of what they discover. Their collages could include images of the gems and the places where they are found. L3 IS **Visual-Spatial** P

**Figure 14** Bauxite, an ore of aluminum, is processed to make pure aluminum metal for useful products.

**Bauxite**

## Useful Elements in Minerals

Gemstones are perhaps the best-known use of minerals, but they are not the most important. Look around your home. How many things made from minerals can you name? Can you find anything made from iron?

**Ores** Iron, used in everything from frying pans to ships, is obtained from its ore, hematite. A mineral or rock is an **ore** if it contains a useful substance that can be mined at a profit. Magnetite is another mineral that contains iron.

**☑ Reading Check** *When is a mineral also an ore?*

**INTEGRATE Chemistry** Aluminum sometimes is refined, or purified, from the ore bauxite, shown in **Figure 14.** In the process of refining aluminum, aluminum oxide powder is separated from unwanted materials that are present in the original bauxite. After this, the aluminum oxide powder is converted to molten aluminum by a process called smelting.

During smelting, a substance is melted to separate it from any unwanted materials that may remain. Aluminum can be made into useful products like bicycles, soft-drink cans, foil, and lightweight parts for airplanes and cars. The plane flown by the Wright brothers during the first flight at Kitty Hawk had an engine made partly of aluminum.

**INTEGRATE Social Studies**

**Historical Mineralogy** An early scientific description of minerals was published by Georgius Agricola in 1556. Use print and online resources to research the mining techniques discussed by Agricola in his work *De Re Metallica*.

**Figure 15** The mineral sphalerite (greenish when nearly pure) is an important source of zinc. Iron often is coated with zinc to prevent rust in a process called galvanization.

**Vein Minerals** Under certain conditions, metallic elements can dissolve in fluids. These fluids then travel through weaknesses in rocks and form mineral deposits. Weaknesses in rocks include natural fractures or cracks, faults, and surfaces between layered rock formations. Mineral deposits left behind that fill in the open spaces created by the weaknesses are called vein mineral deposits.

### ✔ Reading Check *How do fluids move through rocks?*

Sometimes vein mineral deposits fill in the empty spaces after rocks collapse. An example of a mineral that can form in this way is shown in **Figure 15.** This is the shiny mineral sphalerite, a source of the element zinc, which is used in batteries. Sphalerite sometimes fills spaces in collapsed limestone.

**Minerals Containing Titanium** You might own golf clubs with titanium shafts or a racing bicycle containing titanium. Perhaps you know someone who has a titanium hip or knee replacement. Titanium is a durable, lightweight, metallic element derived from minerals that contain this metal in their crystal structures. Two minerals that are sources of the element titanium are ilmenite (IHL muh nite) and rutile (rew TEEL), shown in **Figure 16.** Ilmenite and rutile are common in rocks that form when magma cools and solidifies. They also occur as vein mineral deposits and in beach sands.

**Figure 16** Rutile and ilmenite are common ore minerals of the element titanium.

**Rutile**

**Ilmenite**

## Science Journal

**Copper Wire** Have students research the property of copper that makes it useful in electrical wire. Ask them to determine what types of chemical elements have this property. Possible answer: The electrical conductivity of copper makes it useful in electrical wire. Usually, metals are the types of chemical elements that conduct electricity well. L2

**Uses for Titanium** Titanium is used in automobile body parts, such as connecting rods, valves, and suspension springs. Low density and durability make it useful in the manufacture of aircraft, eyeglass frames, and sports equipment such as tennis rackets and bicycles. Wheelchairs used by people who want to race or play basketball often are made from titanium, as shown in **Figure 17.** Titanium is one of many examples of useful materials that come from minerals and that enrich humans' lives.

**Figure 17** Wheelchairs used for racing and playing basketball often have parts made from titanium.

## section 3 review

### Summary

**Gems**

- Gems are highly prized mineral specimens often used as decorative pieces in jewelry or other items.
- Some gems, especially synthetic ones, have industrial uses.

**Useful Elements in Minerals**

- Economically important quantities of useful elements or compounds are present in ores.
- Ores generally must be processed to extract the desired material.
- Iron, aluminum, zinc, and titanium are common metals that are extracted from minerals.

### Self Check

1. **Explain** why the Cullinan diamond is an important gem.
2. **Identify** Examine **Table 2.** What do rubies and sapphires have in common?
3. **Describe** how vein minerals form.
4. **Explain** why bauxite is considered to be a useful rock.
5. **Think Critically** Titanium is nontoxic. Why is this important in the manufacture of artificial body parts?

**Applying Skills**

6. **Use Percentages** Earth's average continental crust contains 5 percent iron and 0.007 percent zinc. How many times more iron than zinc is present in average continental crust?

 **Science Online** in7.msscience.com/self_check_quiz

SECTION 3 Uses of Minerals **521**

## section 3 review

1. It was the largest uncut diamond ever found. Part of it is now among the British Monarchy's crown jewels.
2. Both are forms of corundum.
3. Vein minerals form when minerals precipitate from fluids moving along faults or fractures.
4. Bauxite is an ore of aluminum.
5. Body parts manufactured from titanium are less likely to damage body tissues.
6. 0.05/0.00007 = 714; average continental crust contains about 714 times more iron than zinc.

### 3 Assess

**DAILY INTERVENTION**

**Check for Understanding**

**Visual-Spatial** Show students a photograph of a rock that contains a vein mineral deposit that formed within it. Ask them to infer how the vein mineral formed. Possible answer: As a fluid solution flowed through cracks in the host rock, conditions changed to favor the precipitation of the vein mineral in the cracks. L2

**Reteach**

**Mineral Resources** Ask students to describe how a mineral deposit containing a useful element might not be classified as an ore. Possible answers: The mineral deposit cannot be mined at a profit because the need for the mineral has decreased.

### ☑ Assessment

**Content** What must be true for a mineral or rock to be classified as an ore? It must contain a useful substance that can be mined at a profit. L2

## Real-World Question

**Purpose** Students investigate how physical properties are used to identify unknown mineral samples. L2 IS **Interpersonal**

**Process Skills** compare and contrast, hypothesize, interpret data, observe and infer

**Time Required** 60–80 minutes

**Materials** Mineral testing kits can be purchased from scientific supply houses.

## Procedure

**Safety Precaution** Students should never hold a glass plate in their hands while testing hardness because the plate could break.

### Teaching Strategies

- Spread out all minerals on a lab bench so students can study their appearance and specific gravity.
- Begin by having students determine the hardness of each mineral and use this property to attempt mineral identification.
- Narrow possibilities or confirm ID by subjecting the sample to further tests.

**Troubleshooting** Encourage students to test the same physical properties of each specimen several times.

### Goals
- **Hypothesize** which properties of each mineral are most useful for identification purposes.
- **Test** your hypothesis as you attempt to identify unknown mineral samples.

### Materials
mineral samples
magnifying lens
pan balance
graduated cylinder
water
piece of copper
*copper penny
glass plate
small iron nail
steel file
streak plate
5% HCl with dropper
Mohs scale of hardness
Minerals Appendix
*minerals field guide
safety goggles
*Alternate materials

### Safety Precautions

**WARNING:** *If an HCl spill occurs, notify your teacher and rinse with cool water until you are told to stop. Do not taste, eat, or drink any lab materials.*

# Mineral Identification

## Real-World Question

Although certain minerals can be identified by observing only one property, others require testing several properties to identify them. How can you identify unknown minerals?

## Procedure

1. Copy the data table into your Science Journal. Obtain a set of unknown minerals.
2. Observe a numbered mineral specimen carefully. Write a star in the table entry that represents what you hypothesize is an important physical property. Choose one or two properties that you think will help most in identifying the sample.
3. Perform tests to observe your chosen properties first.
   **a.** To estimate hardness:
   - Rub the sample firmly against objects of known hardness and observe whether it leaves a scratch on the objects.
   - Estimate a hardness range based on which items the mineral scratches.
   **b.** To estimate specific gravity: Perform a density measurement.
   - Use the pan balance to determine the sample's mass, in grams.

## Alternative Inquiry Lab

**Sorting Minerals** To make this Lab an Inquiry Lab, ask students to divide minerals into groups according to a property of their choice before they attempt serious identification. For example, they could sort the minerals first by luster (metallic or nonmetallic) or heft (heavy, medium, light-weight). L2

## Differentiated Instruction

**English-Language Learners** After students have completed the lab, have them play a game based on 20 Questions. One student can think of a mineral while others try to narrow the choices by asking five *yes* or *no* questions related to luster, hardness, cleavage or fracture, and so on. This will encourage students to use good questioning strategies and classification and memory skills. L1 ELL IS **Interpersonal**

## Using Scientific Methods

■ Measure its volume using a graduated cylinder partially filled with water. The amount of water displaced by the immersed sample, in mL, is an estimate of its volume in cm³.

■ Divide mass by volume to determine density. This number, without units, is comparable to specific gravity.

4. With the help of the Mineral Appendix or a field guide, attempt to identify the sample using the properties from step 2. Perform more physical property observations until you can identify the sample. Repeat steps 2 through 4 for each unknown.

### Physical Properties of Minerals

| Sample Number | Hardness | Cleavage or Fracture | Color | Specific Gravity | Luster and Streak | Crystal Shape | Other Properties | Mineral Name |
|---|---|---|---|---|---|---|---|---|
| 1 | | | | | | | | |
| 2 | | | Answers will vary. | | | | | |
| etc. | | | | | | | | |

### ◗ Analyze Your Data

1. Which properties were most useful in identifying your samples? Which properties were least useful?

2. **Compare** the properties that worked best for you with those that worked best for other students.

### ◗ Conclude and Apply

1. **Determine** two properties that distinguish clear, transparent quartz from clear, transparent calcite. Explain your choice of properties.

2. Which physical properties would be easiest to determine if you found a mineral specimen in the field?

### 𝒞ommunicating Your Data

For three minerals, list physical properties that were important for their identification. **For more help, refer to the** Science Skill Handbook.

### ◗ Analyze Your Data

**Expected Outcome** Students will discover that using a combination of properties is best when identifying unknown mineral samples.

**Answers to Questions**

1. Although answers will vary, hardness and streak will generally be the properties commonly cited as most useful. Color usually is the least helpful property.

2. Comparisons among groups will vary but should lead to discussions about different ways to test minerals.

**Error Analysis** Have students compare their results and explain why any differences occurred. Students who did not get the correct outcome should repeat tests or examine other physical properties of the same specimens.

### ◗ Conclude and Apply

1. Students could choose hardness, cleavage/fracture, reaction to acid, or double refraction.

2. Properties easily field tested include color, luster, crystal shape, and the presence of cleavage and/or fracture.

---

### ☑ Assessment

**Performance** Ask students to bring mineral samples from home or supply students with additional mineral samples. Have them repeat this lab to identify the additional samples. Use **Performance Assessment in the Science Classroom**, p. 121. L2

### 𝒞ommunicating Your Data

Have students compare conclusions by asking each group to prepare and deliver a five-minute presentation. Have each group use their data table as a visual aid for the presentation. L2

## Content Background

In 1895 Wilhelm Conrad Roentgen discovered a type of non-visible radiation, which he termed X rays because their nature was unknown.

In 1912 Max von Laue showed that X rays were part of the electromagnetic spectrum and, like visible light, could be diffracted, absorbed, and polarized. Two years later William and Lawrence Bragg developed the means to analyze the patterns created by the diffraction of X rays in crystalline substances.

Applying this knowledge to biochemistry, Dorothy Hodgkin was able to describe the atomic structure of insulin and vitamin B12. Her work led to a better understanding of how organic chemicals function and the development of synthetic versions of the same compounds.

## Discussion

**Atom Positions** Why is the knowledge of atomic structure important? Possible answers: Knowing the atomic structure of substances helps chemists make those substances artificially and manufacture new products and medicines based on their structures.

What problems might Dr. Hodgkin have faced as a result of being excluded from her colleagues' meetings because she was a woman? Possible answers: She would not have been in a position to easily communicate the results of her work or gain the necessary support from her colleagues to acquire funding.

# Dr. Dorothy Crowfoot Hodgkin

Like X rays, electrons are diffracted by crystalline substances, revealing information about their internal structures and symmetry. This electron diffraction pattern of titanium was obtained with an electron beam focused along a specific direction in the crystal.

## Trailblazing scientist and humanitarian

### What contributions did Dorothy Crowfoot Hodgkin make to science?

Dr. Hodgkin used a method called X-ray crystallography (kris tuh LAH gruh fee) to figure out the structures of crystalline substances, including vitamin $B^{12}$, vitamin D, penicillin, and insulin.

### What's X-ray crystallography?

Scientists expose a crystalline sample to X rays. As X rays travel through a crystal, the crystal diffracts, or scatters, the X rays into a regular pattern. Like an individual's fingerprints, each crystalline substance has a unique diffraction pattern.

Crystallography has applications in the life, Earth, and physical

1910–1994

sciences. For example, geologists use X-ray crystallography to identify and study minerals found in rocks.

### What were some obstacles Hodgkin overcame?

During the 1930s, there were few women scientists. Hodgkin was not even allowed to attend meetings of the chemistry faculty where she taught because she was a woman. Eventually, she won over her colleagues with her intelligence and tenacity.

### How does Hodgkin's research help people today?

Dr. Hodgkin's discovery of the structure of insulin helped scientists learn how to control diabetes, a disease that affects more than 15 million Americans. Diabetics' bodies are unable to process sugar efficiently. Diabetes can be fatal. Fortunately, Dr. Hodgkin's research with insulin has saved many lives.

**Research** Look in reference books or go to the Glencoe Science Web site for information on how X-ray crystallography is used to study minerals. Write your findings and share them with your class.

**For more information, visit in7.msscience.com/time**

## Resources for Teachers and Students

*X ray: The First Hundred Years*, edited by Alan Michette and Slawka Pfauntsch Chichester; New York, John Wiley & Sons, 1996

*Women in Chemistry and Physics, a Bibliographic Sourcebook*, edited by L.S. Grinstein, R.K. Rose, M.H. Rafailovich; Westport, CT; Greenwood Press, 1993

**Research** X-ray crystallography is routinely used to identify minerals of interest in many geological studies. It also is applied to research new minerals or structural and chemical variations in known minerals.

## Reviewing Main Ides

### Section 1 Minerals

1. Much of what you use each day is made at least in some part from minerals.

2. All minerals are formed by natural processes and are inorganic solids with definite chemical compositions and orderly arrangements of atoms.

3. Minerals have crystal structures in one of six major crystal systems.

### Section 2 Mineral Identification

1. Hardness is a measure of how easily a mineral can be scratched.

2. Luster describes how light reflects from a mineral's surface.

3. Streak is the color of the powder left by a mineral on an unglazed porcelain tile.

4. Minerals that break along smooth, flat surfaces have cleavage. When minerals break with rough or jagged surfaces, they are displaying fracture.

5. Some minerals have special properties that aid in identifying them. For example, magnetite is identified by its attraction to a magnet.

### Section 3 Uses of Minerals

1. Gems are minerals that are more rare and beautiful than common minerals.

2. Minerals are useful for their physical properties and for the elements they contain.

## Visualizing Main Ideas

*Copy and complete the following concept map about minerals. Use the following words and phrases:* the way a mineral breaks, the way a mineral reflects light, ore, a rare and beautiful mineral, how easily a mineral is scratched, streak, *and* a useful substance mined for profit.

Science Online in7.msscience.com/interactive_tutor

**CHAPTER STUDY GUIDE 525**

---

chapter **Study Guide** **17**

### Reviewing Main Ideas

Summary statements can be used by students to review the major concepts of the chapter.

### Visualizing Main Ideas

See student page.

**Visit** in7.msscience.com
/self_check_quiz
/interactive_tutor
/vocabulary_puzzlemaker
/chapter_review
/standards_review

### Assessment Transparency

For additional assessment questions, use the *Assessment Transparency* located in the transparency book.

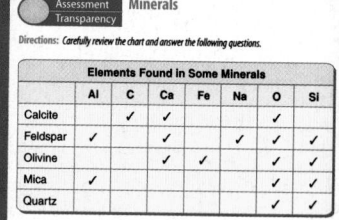

## Identifying Misconceptions

**Assess**

Use the assessment as follow-up to page F at the beginning of the chapter after students have completed the chapter.

**Materials** mineral samples that correspond to substances found in vitamin tablets, such as compounds of calcium, iron, and zinc

**Procedure** Provide each small group of students with a mineral sample and the matching vitamin supplement. Samples could include the mineral halite from salt or the mineral calcite and the supplement calcium.

**Expected Outcome** Students will realize that they use minerals every day, even as essential parts of the foods they eat. L2

## Using Vocabulary

1. Cleavage—mineral breaks along flat surfaces; Fracture—mineral breaks along uneven surfaces

2. crystal—regular, repeating pattern of atoms in a solid; mineral—a naturally occurring, inorganic crystalline solid

3. luster—how light reflects from a mineral; streak—color of the powdered mineral

4. Magma is molten rock material. Crystals form from magma as it cools and hardens.

5. hardness—how easily a mineral can be scratched; specific gravity—weight of a mineral relative to weight of an equal volume of water

6. ore—mineral or rock with useful substance that can be mined for profit; mineral—naturally occurring inorganic crystalline solid with a definite chemical composition

7. crystal—solid with an orderly internal arrangement of atoms; luster—the way a mineral reflects light

8. Minerals make up rocks. Silicate is a rock-forming mineral that contains silicon and oxygen.

9. A gem is a rare and beautiful mineral. A crystal is a solid with an orderly arrangement of atoms.

10. streak—color of the powdered form of a mineral; specific gravity—weight of a mineral relative to weight of an equal volume of water

## Checking Concepts

11. D
12. B
13. B
14. B
15. C
16. D
17. C

## Using Vocabulary

cleavage  p. 513
crystal  p. 505
fracture  p. 513
gem  p. 515
hardness  p. 511
luster  p. 512

magma  p. 507
mineral  p. 504
ore  p. 519
silicate  p. 508
specific gravity  p. 512
streak  p. 513

*Explain the difference between the vocabulary words in each of the following sets.*

1. cleavage—fracture

2. crystal—mineral

3. luster—streak

4. magma—crystal

5. hardness—specific gravity

6. ore—mineral

7. crystal—luster

8. mineral—silicate

9. gem—crystal

10. streak—specific gravity

## Checking Concepts

*Choose the word or phrase that best answers the question.*

11. Which is a characteristic of a mineral?
    A) It can be a liquid.
    B) It is organic.
    C) It has no crystal structure.
    D) It is inorganic.

12. What must all silicates contain?
    A) magnesium
    B) silicon and oxygen
    C) silicon and aluminum
    D) oxygen and carbon

13. What is the measure of how easily a mineral can be scratched?
    A) luster
    B) hardness
    C) cleavage
    D) fracture

**Use the photo below to answer question 14.**

14. Examine the photo of quartz above. In what way does quartz break?
    A) cleavage        C) luster
    B) fracture        D) flat planes

15. Which of the following must crystalline solids have?
    A) carbonates
    B) cubic structures
    C) orderly arrangement of atoms
    D) cleavage

16. What is the color of a powdered mineral formed when rubbing it against an unglazed porcelain tile?
    A) luster
    B) density
    C) hardness
    D) streak

17. Which is hardest on Mohs scale?
    A) talc
    B) quartz
    C) diamond
    D) feldspar

Science Online  in7.msscience.com/vocabulary_puzzlemaker

**Use the Exam*View*® Pro Testmaker CD-ROM to:**
- create multiple versions of tests
- create modified tests with one mouse click for inclusion students
- edit existing questions and add your own questions
- build tests aligned with state standards using built-in State Curriculum Tags
- change English tests to Spanish with one mouse click and vice versa

## Thinking Critically

**18. Classify** Water is an inorganic substance that is formed by natural processes on Earth. It has a unique composition. Sometimes water is a mineral and other times it is not. Explain.

**19. Determine** how many sides a perfect salt crystal has.

**20. Apply** Suppose you let a sugar solution evaporate, leaving sugar crystals behind. Are these crystals minerals? Explain.

**21. Predict** Will a diamond leave a streak on a streak plate? Explain.

**22. Collect Data** Make an outline of how at least seven physical properties can be used to identify unknown minerals.

**23. Explain** how you would use **Table 1** to determine the hardness of any mineral.

**24. Concept Map** Copy and complete the concept map below, which includes two crystal systems and two examples from each system. Use the following words and phrases: *hexagonal, corundum, halite, fluorite,* and *quartz.*

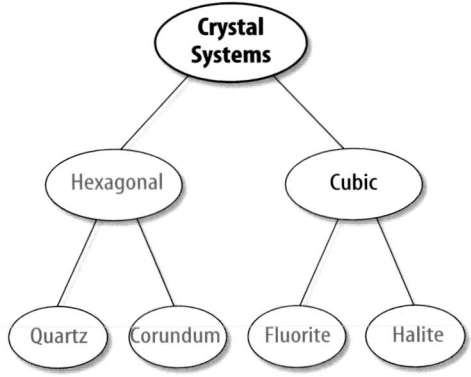

## Performance Activities

**25. Display** Make a display that shows the six crystal systems of minerals. Research the crystal systems of minerals and give three examples for each crystal system. Indicate whether any of the minerals are found in your state. Describe any important uses of these minerals. Present your display to the class.

## Applying Math

**26. Mineral Volume** Recall that $1 \text{ mL} = 1 \text{ cm}^3$. Suppose that the volume of water in a graduated cylinder is 107.5 mL. A specimen of quartz, tied to a piece of string, is immersed in the water. The new water level reads 186 mL. What is the volume, in $\text{cm}^3$, of the piece of quartz?

**Use the graph below to answer questions 27 and 28.**

**27. Zinc Use** According to the graph above, what was the main use of zinc consumed in the United States between 1978 and 1998?

**28. Metal Products** According to the graph, approximately how many thousand metric tons of zinc were used to make brass and bronze products in 1998?

## Thinking Critically

**18.** On Earth, water can exist as a solid, a liquid, or a gas. Water is a mineral only when it is a solid that has formed naturally such as glacial ice.

**19.** Each perfect cubic salt crystal has six sides.

**20.** No; sugar, although it is a solid formed in nature with a definite composition and internal structure, is not a mineral because it is an organic compound.

**21.** No; a diamond is harder than a streak plate and will scratch the plate.

**22.** Accept all reasonable outlines.

**23.** Using common objects and the minerals on the Mohs hardness scale allows you to determine the relative hardness of any mineral. Minerals are harder than other minerals or objects they scratch and softer than minerals or objects that scratch them.

**24.** See student page.

## Performance Activities

**25.** Displays should correctly show the six crystal systems with three examples listed for each one. Be sure students answer the directives concerning their minerals. Use **Performance Assessment in the Science Classroom,** p. 145.

## Applying Math

### Indiana Math Standards
7.5.4, 7.6.1

**26.** $186 \text{ mL} - 107.5 \text{ mL} = 78.5 \text{ mL} = 78.5 \text{ cm}^3$

**27.** galvanizing

**28.** about 175 thousand metric tons

## ✔ Assessment    Resources

**📁 Reproducible Masters**
**Chapter *Fast File* Resources**
Chapter Review, pp. 33–34
Chapter Tests, pp. 35–38
Assessment Transparency Activity, p. 45
**Glencoe Science Web site**
Chapter Review Test
IN Standards Review

**Glencoe Technology**
🔊 Assessment Transparency
💿 Exam*View*® Pro Testmaker
📺 MindJogger Videoquiz
💿 Interactive Chalkboard

## Answer Sheet

**Answer Sheet** A practice answer sheet can be found at in7.msscience.com/answer_sheet.

S A M P L E

1. A
2. D
3. B
4. C
5. D
6. C
7. D

The assessed Indiana standard appears above the question.

*Record your answers on the answer sheet provided by your teacher or on a sheet of paper.*

### Part 1 Multiple Choice

1. The photo below shows a crystal of pyrite.

To which crystal system does the crystal shown above belong?

A cubic

B hexagonal

C monoclinic

D triclinic

2. Which is a common rock-forming mineral?

A azurite

B diamond

C gold

D quartz

**Test-Taking Tip**

**Pace Yourself** If you are taking a timed test, keep track of time during the test. If you find that you're spending too much time on a multiple-choice question, mark your best guess and move on.

3. Which term refers to the resistance of a mineral to scratching?

A fracture

B hardness

C luster

D streak

4. Which is the most abundant element in Earth's crust?

A iron

B manganese

C oxygen

D silicon

5. The table below is the Mohs hardness scale.

| Mineral | Hardness |
|---------|----------|
| Talc | 1 |
| Gypsum | 2 |
| Calcite | 3 |
| Fluorite | 4 |
| Apatite | 5 |
| Feldspar | 6 |
| Quartz | 7 |
| Topaz | 8 |
| Corundum | 9 |
| Diamond | 10 |

Use the table above to determine which mineral scratches feldspar but not topaz.

A apatite

B calcite

C diamond

D quartz

### Part 2 Critical Response

8. Sample hypothesis: The magma cooled slowly beneath Earth's surface, giving crystals enough time to grow to substantial sizes.

9. Most industrial diamonds are synthesized by humans.

10. Minerals are useful because most products could not be made without them. Society depends on minerals for metals, chemicals, building materials, and more.

11. They are not minerals. Minerals cannot be gases or liquids.

12. silicates; Silicates always contain oxygen and silicon.

13. This illustrates mineral cleavage. Muscovite mica has one direction of perfect cleavage.

The table below contains facts about selected diamonds and diamond production.

**1.0 carat = 0.2 grams**

| Diamond | Carats | Grams |
|---|---|---|
| *Uncle Sam:* largest diamond found in United States | 40.4 | ? |
| *Punch Jones:* second largest U.S. diamond; named after boy who discovered it | ? | 6.89 |
| *Theresa:* discovered in Wisconsin in 1888 | 21.5 | 4.3 |
| 2001 diamond production from western Australia | 21,679,930 | ? |

**6.** How many grams is the *Uncle Sam* diamond?

**A** 4.30 g

**B** 6.89 g

**C** 8.08 g

**D** 202 g

**7.** Using the table above, how many grams, to the nearest million, were produced in western Australia in 2001?

**A** 7,000,000 g

**B** 6,000,000 g

**C** 5,000,000 g

**D** 4,000,000 g

**Part 2** **Critical Response**

**8.** The photo below shows a sample of granite.

The mineral crystals in the granite formed when magma cooled and are visible with the unaided eye. Hypothesize about how fast the magma cooled.

**9.** What is the source of most of the diamonds that are used for industrial purposes?

**10.** Explain how minerals are useful to society. Describe some of their uses.

**11.** Are gases that are given off by volcanoes minerals? Why or why not?

**12.** What is the most abundant mineral group in Earth's crust? What elements always are found in the minerals included in this group?

**13.** Several layers are peeled from a piece of muscovite mica. What property of minerals does this illustrate? Describe this property in mica.

## Rubrics

The following rubric is a sample scoring device for critical response questions.

**Critical Response**

| Points | Description |
|---|---|
| 4 | The student demonstrates a thorough understanding of the science of the task. The response may contain minor flaws that do not detract from the demonstration of a thorough understanding. |
| 3 | The student demonstrates an understanding of the science of the task. The response is essentially correct and demonstrates an essential but less than thorough understanding of the science. |
| 2 | The student demonstrates only a partial understanding of the science of the task. Although the student may have used the correct approach to a solution or may have provided a correct solution, the work lacks an essential understanding of the underlying science concepts. |
| 1 | The student demonstrates a very limited understanding of the science of the task. The response is incomplete and exhibits many flaws. |
| 0 | The student provides a completely incorrect solution or no response at all. |

| Section/Objectives | Standards | | Labs/Features |
|---|---|---|---|
| | National | State/Local | |
| **Chapter Opener** | See pp. 16T–17T for a Key to Standards. | Detailed standards begin on page IN8. | **Launch Lab:** Observe and Describe Rocks, p. 531 **Foldables**, p. 531 |
| **Section 1  The Rock Cycle** ⏱ 2 sessions  📦 1 block  1. **Distinguish** between a rock and a mineral. 2. **Describe** the rock cycle and some changes that a rock could undergo. | National Content Standards: UCP.1–3, UCP.5, A.1, A.2, D.1, D.2 | Indiana Standards: 7.1.5 | **MiniLAB:** Modeling Rock, p. 533 **Visualizing the Rock Cycle,** p. 534 |
| **Section 2  Igneous Rocks** ⏱ 2 sessions  📦 1 block  3. **Recognize** magma and lava as the materials that cool to form igneous rocks. 4. **Contrast** the formation of intrusive and extrusive igneous rocks. 5. **Contrast** granitic and basaltic igneous rocks. | National Content Standards: UCP.1–3, UCP.5, A.1, A.2, D.1, D.2 | Indiana Standards: This section builds a foundation for Standards 7.38 and 7.39. | **Science Online**, p. 538 **Integrate Chemistry**, p. 539 **Lab:** Igneous Rock Clues, p. 540 |
| **Section 3  Metamorphic Rocks** ⏱ 2 sessions  📦 1 block  6. **Describe** the conditions in Earth that cause metamorphic rocks to form. 7. **Classify** metamorphic rocks as foliated or nonfoliated. | National Content Standards: UCP.1–3, UCP.5, A.1, A.2, D.1, D.2 | Indiana Standards: 7.3.9 | **Science Online**, p. 542 |
| **Section 4  Sedimentary Rocks** ⏱ 3 sessions  📦 1.5 blocks  8. **Explain** how sedimentary rocks form from sediments. 9. **Classify** sedimentary rocks as detrital, chemical, or organic in origin. 10. **Summarize** the rock cycle. | National Content Standards: UCP.1–3, UCP.5, A.1, A.2, D.1, D.2 | Indiana Standards: 7.3.8, 7.3.9 | **MiniLAB:** Classifying Sediments, p. 546 **Integrate Career**, p. 548 **Applying Math:** Coal Formation, p. 550 **Lab:** Sedimentary Rocks pp. 552–553 **Science and Society:** Australia's Controversial Rock Star, p. 554 |

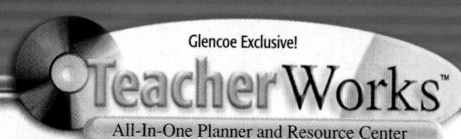
| Lab Materials | Reproducible Resources | Section Assessment | Technology |
|---|---|---|---|
| **Launch Lab:** 3 rock samples, magnifying lens | **Chapter** *FAST FILE* **Resources**<br>Foldables Worksheet, p. 13<br>Directed Reading Overview, p. 15<br>Note-taking Worksheets, pp. 31–33 | GLENCOE'S ASSESSMENT ADVANTAGE | **Teacher**Works includes:<br>• Interactive Teacher Edition<br>• Lesson Planner with calendar<br>• Access to all program blacklines<br>• Correlations to standards<br>• Web links |
| **MiniLAB:** white glue (about 10 mL), dirt or sand (about 7 g), small paper cup | **Chapter** *FAST FILE* **Resources**<br>Transparency Activity, p. 42<br>MiniLAB, p. 3<br>Enrichment, p. 27<br>Reinforcement, p. 23<br>Directed Reading, p. 16<br>Lab Activity, pp. 9–10<br>Transparency Activity, pp. 47–48 | **Portfolio**<br>Curriculum Connection, p. 534<br>**Performance**<br>MiniLAB, p. 533<br>Applying Skills, p. 535<br>**Content**<br>Section Review, p. 535 | Section Focus Transparency<br>Teaching Transparency<br>Guided Reading Audio Program<br>Interactive Chalkboard CD-ROM |
| **Lab:** rhyolite, basalt, vesicular basalt, pumice, granite, obsidian, gabbro, magnifying lens<br><br>*Need materials?* Contact Science Kit at 1-800-828-7777 or www.sciencekit.com on the Internet. | **Chapter** *FAST FILE* **Resources**<br>Transparency Activity, p. 43<br>Lab Worksheets, pp. 5–6<br>Enrichment, p. 28<br>Reinforcement, p. 24<br>Directed Reading, p. 16<br>**Reading and Writing Skill Activities,** p. 27 | **Portfolio**<br>Reteach, p. 539<br>**Performance**<br>Applying Skills, p. 539<br>**Content**<br>Section Review, p. 539 | Section Focus Transparency<br>Virtual Labs CD-ROM<br>Guided Reading Audio Program<br>Interactive Chalkboard CD-ROM |
| | **Chapter** *FAST FILE* **Resources**<br>Transparency Activity, p. 44<br>Enrichment, p. 29<br>Reinforcement, p. 25<br>Directed Reading, p. 17<br>Lab Activity, pp. 11–12<br>**Science Inquiry Labs,** p. 31–32 | **Portfolio**<br>Differentiated Instruction, p. 543<br>**Performance**<br>Applying Skills, p. 544<br>**Content**<br>Section Review, p. 544 | Section Focus Transparency<br>Guided Reading Audio Program<br>Interactive Chalkboard CD-ROM |
| **MiniLAB:** paper, samples of sediment, tweezers, magnifying lens<br>**Lab:** sedimentary rocks, marking pen, 5% hydrochloric acid or vinegar, dropper, paper towels, magnifying lens, metric ruler | **Chapter** *FAST FILE* **Resources**<br>Transparency Activity, p. 45<br>MiniLAB, p. 4<br>Enrichment, p. 30<br>Reinforcement, p. 26<br>Directed Reading, pp. 17, 18<br>Lab Worksheets, pp. 7–8 | **Portfolio**<br>Science Journal, p. 547<br>**Performance**<br>MiniLAB, p. 546<br>Applying Math, p. 550<br>Applying Math, p. 551<br>**Content**<br>Section Review, p. 551 | Section Focus Transparency<br>Guided Reading Audio Program<br>Interactive Chalkboard CD-ROM<br>Video Lab |

## End of Chapter Assessment

GLENCOE'S ASSESSMENT ADVANTAGE

| Blackline Masters | Technology | Professional Series |
|---|---|---|
| **Chapter** *FAST FILE* **Resources**<br>Chapter Review, pp. 35–36<br>Chapter Tests, pp. 37–40<br>**Mastering the Grade 7 Indiana Science Standards** | MindJogger Videoquiz<br>IN Test Prep and Practice Exam*View*®<br>Exam*View*® Pro Testmaker<br>TeacherWorks CD-ROM<br>Interactive Chalkboard CD-ROM | **Performance Assessment in the Science Classroom (PASC)** |

## Transparencies

### Section Focus

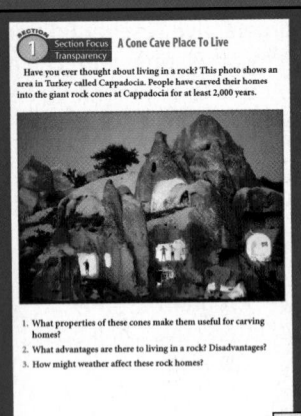

**Section Focus Transparency 1** — A Cone Cave Place To Live

Have you ever thought about living in a rock? This photo shows an area in Turkey called Cappadocia. People have carved their homes into the giant rock cones at Cappadocia for at least 2,000 years.

1. What properties of these cones make them useful for carving homes?
2. What advantages are there to living in a rock? Disadvantages?
3. How might weather affect these rock homes?

L2

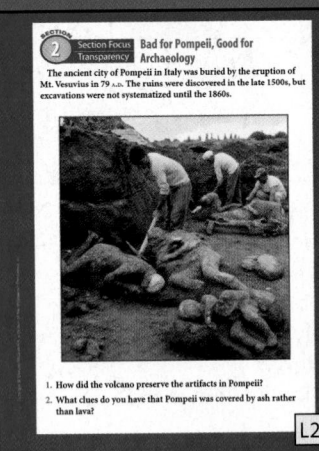

**Section Focus Transparency 2** — Bad for Pompeii, Good for Archaeology

The ancient city of Pompeii in Italy was buried by the eruption of Mt. Vesuvius in 79 A.D. The ruins were discovered in the late 1500s, but excavations were not systematized until the 1860s.

1. How did the volcano preserve the artifacts in Pompeii?
2. What clues do you have that Pompeii was covered by ash rather than lava?

L2

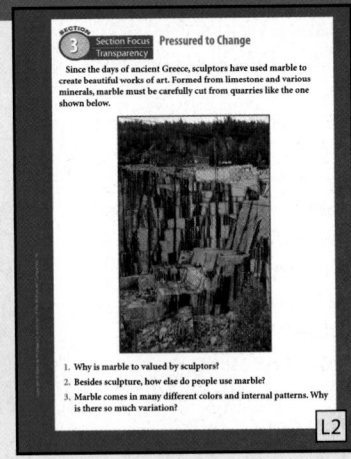

**Section Focus Transparency 3** — Pressured to Change

Since the days of ancient Greece, sculptors have used marble to create beautiful works of art. Formed from limestone and various minerals, marble must be carefully cut from quarries like the one shown below.

1. Why is marble to valued by sculptors?
2. Besides sculpture, how else do people use marble?
3. Marble comes in many different colors and internal patterns. Why is there so much variation?

L2

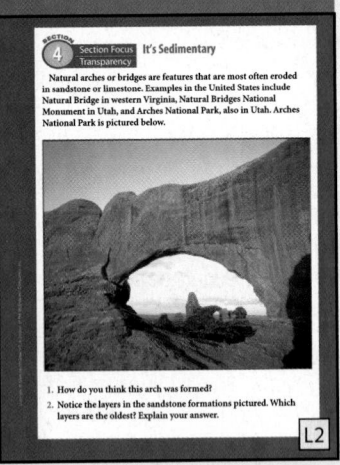

**Section Focus Transparency 4** — It's Sedimentary

Natural arches or bridges are features that are most often eroded in sandstone or limestone. Examples in the United States include Natural Bridge in western Virginia, Natural Bridges National Monument in Utah, and Arches National Park, also in Utah. Arches National Park is pictured below.

1. How do you think this arch was formed?
2. Notice the layers in the sandstone formations pictured. Which layers are the oldest? Explain your answer.

L2

This is a representation of key blackline masters available in the Teacher Classroom Resources. See Resource Manager boxes within the chapter for additional information.

### Assessment

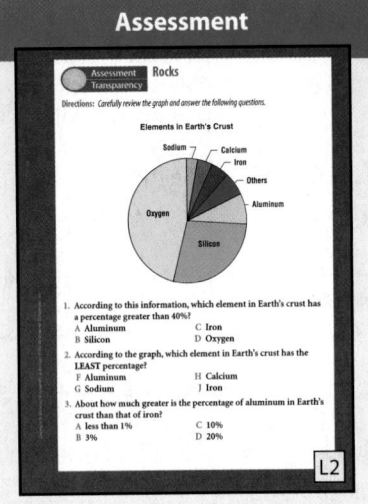

**Assessment Transparency** — Rocks

**Directions:** Carefully review the graph and answer the following questions.

**Elements in Earth's Crust**

1. According to this information, which element in Earth's crust has a percentage greater than 40%?
   A Aluminum    C Iron
   B Silicon    D Oxygen
2. According to the graph, which element in Earth's crust has the LEAST percentage?
   F Aluminum    H Calcium
   G Sodium    J Iron
3. About how much greater is the percentage of aluminum in Earth's crust than that of iron?
   A less than 1%    C 10%
   B 3%    D 20%

L2

### Teaching

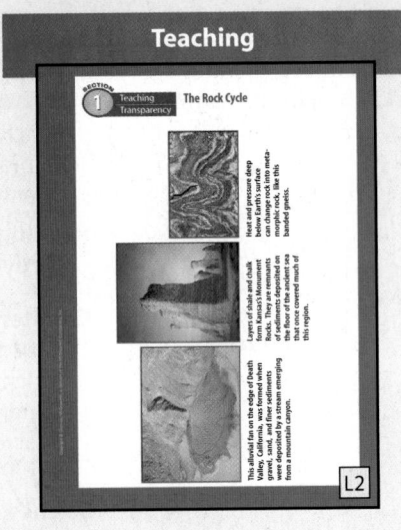

**Teaching Transparency 1** — The Rock Cycle

L2

## Key to Teaching Strategies

The following designations will help you decide which activities are appropriate for your students.

**L1** Level 1 activities should be appropriate for students with learning difficulties.

**L2** Level 2 activities should be within the ability range of all students.

**L3** Level 3 activities are designed for above-average students.

**ELL** ELL activities should be within the ability range of English Language Learners.

**COOP LEARN** Cooperative Learning activities are designed for small group work.

**LS** Multiple Learning Styles logos, as described on page 12T, are used throughout to indicate strategies that address different learning styles.

**P** These strategies represent student products that can be placed into a best-work portfolio.

**PBL** Problem-Based Learning activities apply real-world situations to learning.

## Hands-on Activities

### Student Text Lab Worksheet

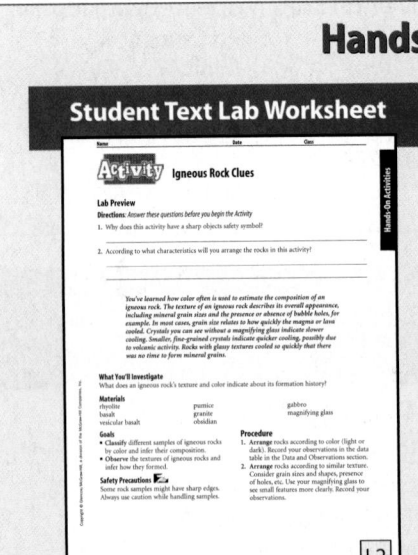

**Activity** — Igneous Rock Clues

**Lab Preview**
**Directions:** Answer these questions before you begin the Activity.

1. Why does this activity have a sharp objects safety symbol?

2. According to what characteristics will you arrange the rocks in this activity?

You've learned how color often is used to estimate the composition of an igneous rock. The texture of an igneous rock describes its overall appearance, including mineral grain sizes and the presence or absence of bubble holes, for example. In most cases, grain size relates to how quickly the magma or lava cooled. Crystals you can see without a magnifying glass indicate slower cooling. Smaller, fine-grained crystals indicate quicker cooling, possibly due to volcanic activity. Rocks with glassy textures cooled so quickly that there was no time to form mineral grains.

**What You'll Investigate**
What does an igneous rock's texture and color indicate about its formation history?

**Materials**
rhyolite   pumice   gabbro
basalt   granite   magnifying glass
vesicular basalt   obsidian

**Goals**
- **Classify** different samples of igneous rocks by color and infer their composition.
- **Observe** the textures of igneous rocks and infer how they formed.

**Safety Precautions**
Some rock samples might have sharp edges. Always use caution while handling samples.

**Procedure**
1. **Arrange** rocks according to color (light or dark). Record your observations in the data table in the Data and Observations section.
2. **Arrange** rocks according to similar texture. Consider grain sizes and shapes, presence of holes, etc. Use your magnifying glass to see small features more clearly. Record your observations.

L2

### Laboratory Activities

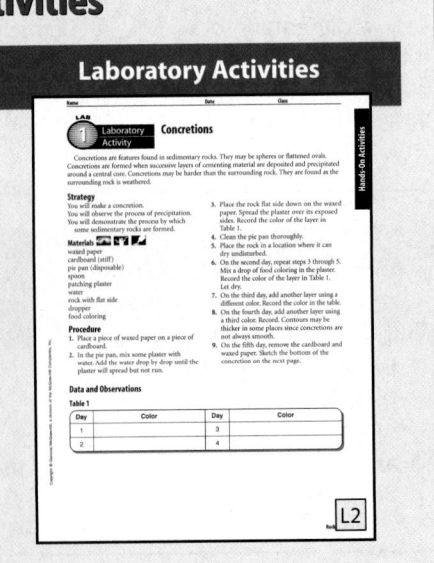

**Laboratory Activity 1** — Concretions

Concretions are features found in sedimentary rocks. They may be spheres or flattened ovals. Concretions are formed when successive layers of cementing material are deposited and precipitated around a central core. Concretions may be harder than the surrounding rock. They are found as the surrounding rock is weathered.

**Strategy**
You will make a concretion.
You will observe the process of precipitation.
You will demonstrate the process by which some sedimentary rocks are formed.

**Materials**
waxed paper
cardboard (stiff)
pie pan (disposable)
spoon
patching plaster
water
rock with flat side
dropper
food coloring

**Procedure**
1. Place a piece of waxed paper on a piece of cardboard.
2. In the pie pan, mix some plaster with water. Add the water drop by drop until the plaster will spread but not run.
3. Place the rock flat side down on the waxed paper. Spread the plaster over its exposed surface. Record the color of the layer in Table 1.
4. Clean the pie pan thoroughly.
5. Place the rock in a location where it can dry undisturbed.
6. On the second day, repeat steps 3 through 5. Mix a drop of food coloring in the plaster. Record the color of the layer in Table 1. Let dry.
7. On the third day, add another layer using a different color. Record the color in the table.
8. On the fourth day, add another layer using a third color. Record. Contours may be thicker in some places since concretions are not always smooth.
9. On the fifth day, remove the cardboard and waxed paper. Sketch the bottom of the concretion on the next page.

**Data and Observations**
Table 1

| Day | Color | Day | Color |
|-----|-------|-----|-------|
| 1 | | 3 | |
| 2 | | 4 | |

L2

# Resource Manager

## Meeting Different Ability Levels

### Content Outline

L2

### Reinforcement

L2

### Enrichment

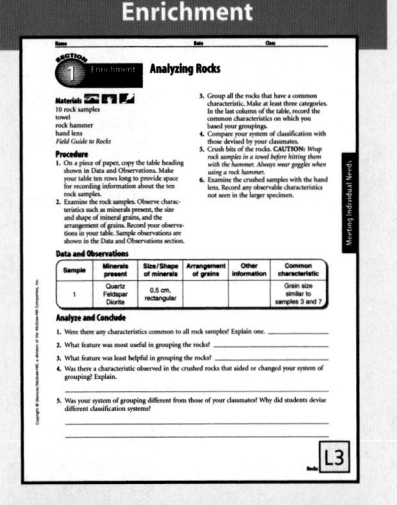

L3

### Directed Reading (English/Spanish)

L1

### Study Guide

**Features**
- Contains a study guide page for each section of the chapter
- Reviews key concepts
- Includes answer pages

L2

### Reading Essentials

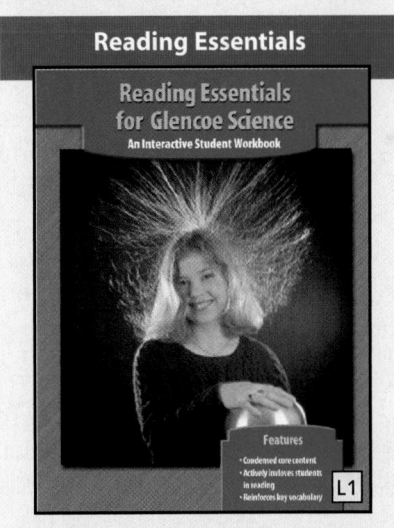

**Reading Essentials for Glencoe Science**
An Interactive Student Workbook

**Features**
- Condensed core content
- Actively involves students in reading
- Reinforces key vocabulary

L1

## Assessment

### Test Practice Workbook

L2

### Chapter Review

L2

### Chapter Tests

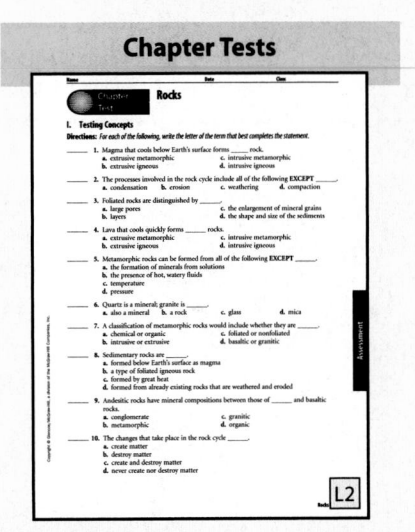

L2

# Science Content Background

### section 1 The Rock Cycle
### Many Paths

There is no set path through the rock cycle. A rock from any of the three groups of rocks can be changed into a rock belonging to another group, or it can be changed into a rock belonging to its original group. A study of the rock cycle reveals the relationships among the three groups of rocks.

### section 2 Igneous Rocks
### Texture and Grain Size

The size and arrangement of mineral grains determine igneous rock textures. Some rocks are coarse grained, and individual grains can be seen with the unaided eye. Other rocks are fine grained, and individual minerals are not visible with the unaided eye. In rocks with glassy textures, few or no mineral crystals are present. The sizes of mineral grains in most igneous rocks are determined by cooling rates. The faster the magma or lava cooled during an igneous rock's formation, the smaller the grain size is.

### Magma

As magma cools, different minerals will crystallize at different temperatures. This relationship is known as Bowen's reaction series. The first silicate minerals to crystallize from magma are lower in silica and higher in iron and magnesium. As crystallization progresses, minerals higher in silica and lower in iron and magnesium form.

Olivine is one of the first minerals to crystallize. Next, pyroxenes such as augite form, which have a different composition and structure. This reaction continues through amphiboles such as hornblende, and biotite mica. One of the last minerals to crystallize is potassium feldspar. Quartz ($SiO_2$) crystallizes when most of the remaining melt consists of silicon and oxygen.

*D. Cavagnaro/DRK Photo*

---

**Teacher to Teacher**
Steve Federman
Loveland Middle School
Loveland, Ohio

"I have students review characteristics of sedimentary, igneous, and metamorphic rocks by working with a partner to create a dichotomous key. Students consider characteristics such as grain size, texture, cement type, sediment type, foliated or nonfoliated, and so on, then write *if, then* type statements that apply."

*Steve Federman*

As minerals continue to crystallize from a melt, igneous rocks of different composition form, from ultramafic through mafic (basaltic) and intermediate (andesitic) to felsic (granitic).

## section 3 Metamorphic Rocks

### How Rocks Change

The overall chemical compositions of metamorphic rocks can be similar to the compositions of the rocks from which they form. However, new minerals may form in response to changes in temperature and pressure.

### Heat, Pressure, and Fluids

Changes in temperature, pressure, and fluids can have several causes. One common cause is mountain building. Processes of mountain building cause metamorphism of rock over a large area. This type of metamorphism, called regional metamorphism, produces large amounts of metamorphic rock. Another type of metamorphism, called contact metamorphism, occurs when magma comes in contact with surrounding rocks. A zone of metamorphic rock called an aureole forms around the magma. No melting occurs to form this metamorphic aureole, but hot fluids from the magma do pass into and react with the surrounding rock.

## section 4 Sedimentary Rocks

### Formation

Understanding the processes by which sedimentary rocks form allows one to discern the history of the rock: the source of the sediment, the means by which the sediment was transported, and the environment that existed where the sediment was deposited.

Sedimentary rocks form under two main sets of conditions. These are referred to as environments of deposition and are either marine (in the sea) or terrestrial (on continents). Rocks that form in a shore zone are considered to form under conditions that are transitional between the marine and terrestrial environments.

### Sedimentary Rock Layers

Three of the most important principles used by geologists to interpret sedimentary rock layers were formulated by Nicholas Steno in 1669 and are referred to as Steno's principles. The principle of superposition states that the oldest rock layers lie at the bottom of an undisturbed sequence of sedimentary rock. The principle of original horizontality states that tilted sedimentary rock layers must have been disturbed after they were deposited. The principle of original lateral continuity states that sedimentary rock layers originally extended until they thinned to zero thickness or butted into the edge of the area in which they were deposited. This last principle allows geologists to conclude that a rock layer now cut by a canyon was once continuous across it.

## chapter content resources

**Internet Resources**

For additional content background, visit **in7.msscience.com** to:
- access your book online
- find references to related articles in popular science magazines
- access Web links with related content background
- access current events with science journal topics

**Print Resources**

*Peterson First Guide to Rocks and Minerals,* by Frederick H. Pough, Houghton Mifflin Company, 1998

*Encyclopedia of Rocks, Minerals and Gemstones,* by Chris Pellant and Henry Russell, Thunder Bay Press, 2001

*How the Earth Works,* by John Farndon, Dorling Kindersley Limited, 1992

## Chapter Vocabulary

rock, p. 532
rock cycle, p. 533
igneous rock, p. 536
lava, p. 536
intrusive, p. 537
extrusive, p. 537
basaltic, p. 539
granitic, p. 539
metamorphic rock, p. 541
foliated, p. 543
nonfoliated, p. 544
sediment, p. 545
sedimentary rock, p. 545
compaction, p. 546
cementation, p. 547

**Science Journal** Students might discuss the rock's color or shape, or where it was found; descriptions of rocks in the photo should be detailed and vivid.

## INTERACTIVE CHALKBOARD
### with Image Bank

**PowerPoint® Presentations**

This CD-ROM is an editable Microsoft® PowerPoint® presentation that includes:

- a pre-made presentation for every chapter
- interactive graphics
- animations
- audio clips
- image bank
- all new section and chapter questions
- Standardized Test Practice
- transparencies
- pre-lab questions for all labs
- Foldables directions
- links to in7.msscience.com

---

**Academic Standard—3:** Students collect and organize data to identify relationships between physical objects, events, and processes. They use logical reasoning to question their own ideas as new information challenges their conceptions of the natural world.

**Also covers:** Academic Standard 1 (Detailed standards begin on page IN8.)

# Rocks

## chapter preview
### sections

**1** The Rock Cycle

**2** Igneous Rocks
   *Lab* Igneous Rock Clues

**3** Metamorphic Rocks

**4** Sedimentary Rocks
   *Lab* Sedimentary Rocks

*Virtual Lab* How are rocks classified?

### How did it get there?

The giant rocky peak of El Capitan towers majestically in Yosemite National Park. Surrounded by flat landscape, it seems out of place. How did this expanse of granite rock come to be?

**Science Journal** Are you a rock collector? If so, write two sentences about your favorite rock. If not, describe the rocks you see in the photo in enough detail that a nonsighted person could visualize them.

530

## Theme Connection

**Systems and Interactions** Physical conditions, such as heat and pressure inside Earth and weathering and erosion on Earth's surface, interact with Earth materials, constantly changing rock through processes of the rock cycle.

### About the Photo

**Exposed Rock** El Capitan is a huge granite batholith that rises straight up from the valley floor in Yosemite National Park, California. It is igneous rock that formed at high temperatures and pressures. Exposed to Earth's surface today, it is unstable, gradually weathering and shedding material as wind and water come in contact with it.

# Start-Up Activities

## Observe and Describe Rocks

Some rocks are made of small mineral grains that lock together, like pieces of a puzzle. Others are grains of sand tightly held together or solidified lava that once flowed from a volcano. If you examine rocks closely, you sometimes can tell what they are made of.

1. Collect three different rock samples near your home or school.

2. Draw a picture of the details you see in each rock.

3. Use a magnifying lens to look for different types of materials within the same rock.

4. Describe the characteristics of each rock. Compare your drawings and descriptions with photos, drawings, and descriptions in a rocks and minerals field guide.

5. Use the field guide to try to identify each rock.

6. **Think Critically** Decide whether you think your rocks are mixtures. If so, infer or suggest what these mixtures might contain. Write your explanations in your Science Journal.

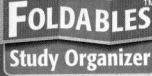

**Major Rock Types** Make the following Foldable to help you organize facts about types of rocks.

**STEP 1** Fold a sheet of paper in half lengthwise. Make the back edge about 5 cm longer than the front edge.

**STEP 2** Turn the paper so the fold is on the bottom. Then fold it into thirds.

**STEP 3** Unfold and cut only the top layer along both folds to make three tabs.

**STEP 4** Label the Foldable as shown.

**Make an Organizational Study Fold** As you read the chapter, write and illustrate what you learn about the three main types of rocks in your study fold.

Preview this chapter's content and activities at in7.msscience.com

531

# section 1

# The Rock Cycle

## 1 Motivate

### Bellringer

**Section Focus Transparencies**
also are available on the
Interactive Chalkboard CD-ROM.

L2 ELL

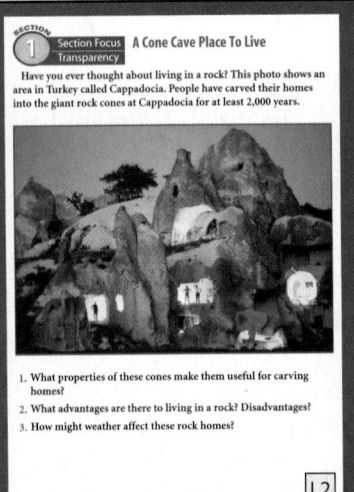

**A Cone Cave Place To Live**

## as you read

### *What* You'll Learn
- **Distinguish** between a rock and a mineral.
- **Describe** the rock cycle and some changes that a rock could undergo.

### *Why* It's Important
Rocks exist everywhere, from under deep oceans and in high mountain ranges, to the landscape beneath your feet.

### Review Vocabulary
**mineral:** a naturally occurring, inorganic solid with a definite chemical composition and an orderly arrangement of atoms

### New Vocabulary
- rock
- rock cycle

## What is a rock?

Imagine you and some friends are exploring a creek. Your eye catches a glint from a piece of rock at the edge of the water. As you wander over to pick up the rock, you notice that it is made of different-colored materials. Some of the colors reflect light, while others are dull. You put the rock in your pocket for closer inspection in science lab.

**Common Rocks** The next time you walk past a large building or monument, stop and take a close look at it. Chances are that it is made out of common rock. In fact, most rock used for building stone contains one or more common minerals, called rock-forming minerals, such as quartz, feldspar, mica, or calcite. When you look closely, the sparkles you see are individual crystals of minerals. A **rock** is a mixture of such minerals, rock fragments, volcanic glass, organic matter, or other natural materials. **Figure 1** shows minerals mixed together to form the rock granite. You might even find granite near your home.

### Tie to Prior Knowledge

**Rock Formation** Ask students to recall rocks they have seen. Do all rocks look the same? no What differences can you recall? Possible answers: color, texture, density, luster (shininess). Tell students that the composition of rocks, and the way they look, are clues to how they formed. Let students know that they will learn how rocks form and change in this section.

**Figure 1** Mount Rushmore, in South Dakota, is made of granite. Granite is a mixture of feldspar, quartz, mica, hornblende, and other minerals.

Feldspar
Quartz
Mica
Hornblende

**532 CHAPTER 18** Rocks

## Section 1 Resource Manager

**Chapter *FAST FILE* Resources**
Transparency Activity, pp. 42, 47–48
Directed Reading for Content Mastery, pp. 15, 16
MiniLAB, p. 3
Lab Activity, pp. 9–10

Enrichment, p. 27
Reinforcement, p. 23
Note-taking Worksheets, pp. 31–33

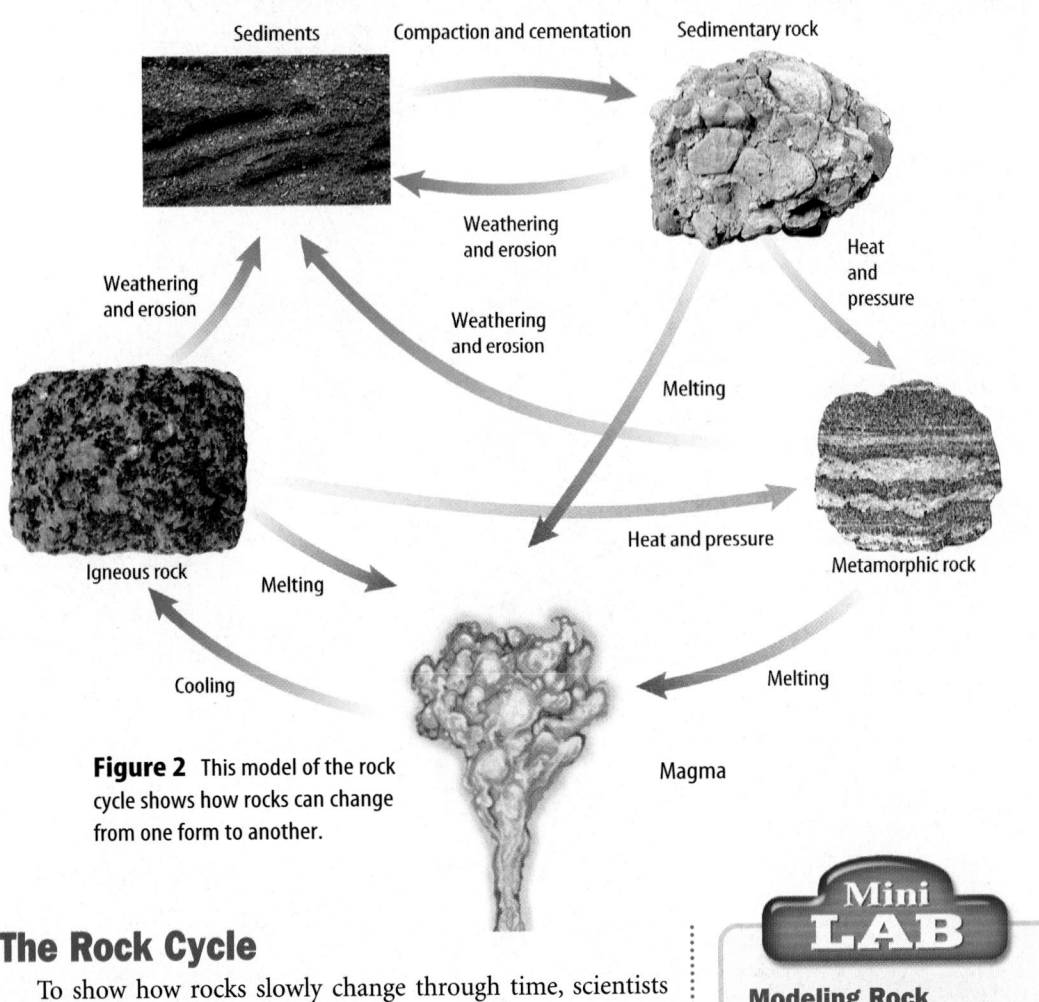

Figure 2 labels: Sediments — Compaction and cementation — Sedimentary rock — Weathering and erosion — Weathering and erosion — Weathering and erosion — Heat and pressure — Melting — Heat and pressure — Metamorphic rock — Igneous rock — Melting — Cooling — Melting — Magma

**Figure 2** This model of the rock cycle shows how rocks can change from one form to another.

## The Rock Cycle

To show how rocks slowly change through time, scientists have created a model called the **rock cycle**, shown in **Figure 2**. It illustrates the processes that create and change rocks. The rock cycle shows the three types of rock—igneous, metamorphic, and sedimentary—and the processes that form them.

Look at the rock cycle and notice that rocks change by many processes. For example, a sedimentary rock can change by heat and pressure to form a metamorphic rock. The metamorphic rock then can melt and later cool to form an igneous rock. The igneous rock then could be broken into fragments by weathering and erode away. The fragments might later compact and cement together to form another sedimentary rock. Any given rock can change into any of the three major rock types. A rock even can transform into another rock of the same type.

> ✔ **Reading Check** *What is illustrated by the rock cycle?*

### Mini LAB

**Modeling Rock**

**Procedure** 🖐️ 🧤 📋

1. Mix about 10 mL of **white glue** with about 7 g of **dirt** or **sand** in a **small paper cup.**
2. Stir the mixture and then allow it to harden overnight.
3. Tear away the paper cup carefully from your mixture.

**Analysis**

1. Which rock type is similar to your hardened mixture?
2. Which part of the rock cycle did you model?

 Try at Home

## Visual Learning

**Figure 2** What are some of the processes that can change rock from one form to another? melting, cooling, weathering and erosion, compaction and cementation, and heat and pressure

### Mini LAB

**Purpose** Students will model sedimentary rock. L2 ELL LS **Kinesthetic**

**Materials** glue, sand or dirt, paper cups

**Teaching Strategy** Explain to students that sedimentary rocks forming under natural conditions may require thousands to millions of years.

**Analysis**

1. sedimentary rock
2. the cementation of mineral and rock fragments into sedimentary rock.

### Assessment

**Process** Ask students to model sedimentary rock using a variety of different materials such as gravel, ground-up shells, and different-colored sand. Make a display of student rock models in the classroom. Use **Performance Assessment in the Science Classroom,** p. 123.

Try at Home

## Differentiated Instruction

**Learning Disabled** Place large, labeled samples of basalt, granite, gneiss, slate, shale, sandstone, and limestone in a science center. Ask students in groups of three to study the samples and to take turns selecting a rock and telling its type and the processes that formed it. L1 COOP LEARN LS **Logical-Mathematical and Naturalist**

> ✔ **Reading Check**

**Answer** the three types of rocks, how they form, and the processes that change one type into another

## Visualizing the Rock Cycle

Have students examine the pictures and read the captions. Then ask the following questions.

What are some possible ways the black beach sand could become rock? It could be compacted and cemented to become sedimentary rock; it could be melted and cooled to once again form igneous rock.

What processes formed Kansas's Monument Rocks? Layers of sediments that formed on the ancient seafloor were compacted and/or cemented to form the sedimentary rocks.

### Activity

**Travel Brochure** Assign small groups a rock structure, such as Garden of the Gods in Colorado, the Palisades in New York, the White Cliffs of Dover in England, the Cathedral Spires of South Dakota's Black Hills, or Devil's Postpile in California. Ask each group to prepare a travel brochure that shows a map of the feature's location and a description of how it was formed. L2 ELL LS **Visual-Spatial and Linguistic**

### Discussion

**Metamorphic Rock** What could happen to rock to cause the pressure and temperature conditions necessary to metamorphose it? It could become deeply buried by many younger rock formations situated above it.

---

**NATIONAL GEOGRAPHIC VISUALIZING THE ROCK CYCLE**

### Figure 3

Rocks continuously form and transform in a process that geologists call the rock cycle. For example, molten rock—from volcanoes such as Washington's Mount Rainier, background—cools and solidifies to form igneous rock. It slowly breaks down when exposed to air and water to form sediments. These sediments are compacted or cemented into sedimentary rock. Heat and pressure might transform sedimentary rock into metamorphic rock. When metamorphic rock melts and hardens, igneous rock forms again. There is no distinct beginning, nor is there an end, to the rock cycle.

▲ The black sand beach of this Polynesian island is sediment weathered and eroded from the igneous rock of a volcano nearby.

▲ This alluvial fan on the edge of Death Valley, California, was formed when gravel, sand, and finer sediments were deposited by a stream emerging from a mountain canyon.

▲ Layers of shale and chalk form Kansas's Monument Rocks. They are remnants of sediments deposited on the floor of the ancient sea that once covered much of this region.

▲ Heat and pressure deep below Earth's surface can change rock into metamorphic rock, like this banded gneiss.

**534 CHAPTER 18** Rocks

---

## Curriculum Connection

**Language Arts** The word igneous comes from the Latin word *ignis*, which means "fire." Ask students to write a paragraph describing where the words *metamorphic* and *sedimentary* come from. *Metamorphic*, which means "change of form," comes from the Greek roots *meta*, meaning "after" and *morphe*, meaning "form." *Sedimentary* comes from the word "sediment." L2

P

**Matter and the Rock Cycle**
The rock cycle, illustrated in **Figure 3,** shows how rock can be weathered to small rock and mineral grains. This material then can be eroded and carried away by wind, water, or ice. When you think of erosion, it might seem that the material is somehow destroyed and lost from the cycle. This is not the case. The chemical elements that make up minerals and rocks are not destroyed. This fact illustrates the principle of conservation of matter. The changes that take place in the rock cycle never destroy or create matter. The elements are just redistributed in other forms.

**✔ Reading Check** *What is the principle of conservation of matter?*

**Discovering the Rock Cycle** James Hutton, a Scottish physician and naturalist, first recognized in 1788 that rocks undergo profound changes. Hutton noticed, among other things, that some layers of solid rock in Siccar Point, shown in **Figure 4,** had been altered since they formed. Instead of showing a continuous pattern of horizontal layering, some of the rock layers at Siccar Point are tilted and partly eroded. However, the younger rocks above them are nearly horizontal.

Hutton published these and other observations, which proved that rocks are subject to constant change. Hutton's early recognition of the rock cycle continues to influence geologists.

**Figure 4** The rock formations at Siccar Point, Scotland, show that rocks undergo constant change.

## section 1 review

**Summary**

**What is a rock?**
- Rocks are mixtures of minerals, rock fragments, organic matter, volcanic glass, and other materials found in nature.

**The Rock Cycle**
- The three major types of rock are igneous, metamorphic, and sedimentary.
- Rock cycle processes do not create or destroy matter.
- Processes that are part of the rock cycle change rocks slowly over time.
- In the late eighteenth century, James Hutton recognized some rock cycle processes by observing rocks in the field.
- Some of Hutton's ideas continue to influence geologic thinking today.

**Self Check**

1. **Explain** how rocks differ from minerals.
2. **Compare and contrast** igneous and metamorphic rock formation.
3. **Describe** the major processes of the rock cycle.
4. **Explain** one way that the rock cycle can illustrate the principle of conservation of matter.
5. **Think Critically** How would you define magma based on the illustration in **Figure 2?** How would you define sediment and sedimentary rock?

**Applying Skills**

6. **Communicate** Review the model of the rock cycle in **Figure 2.** In your Science Journal, write a story or poem that explains what can happen to a sedimentary rock as it changes throughout the rock cycle.

 in7.msscience.com/self_check_quiz

## section 1 review

1. Minerals are naturally occurring crystalline solids with definite chemical compositions. Rocks most often are mixtures of more than one mineral or other natural materials.
2. Both form at relatively high temperatures. Igneous rocks solidify from melted rock material; metamorphic

rocks begin and remain in the solid state as they form.
3. Weathering breaks down rock; erosion and deposition transport and deposit the sediment, which is compacted and cemented into new rock; pressure and heat inside Earth change rock from one form to

another. Magma from melting of preexisting rock solidifies to form igneous rock.
4. The changes never destroy or create matter. For example, weathering of existing rock produces sediment that is eroded and deposited to form new rock. Accept any reasonable answers.

5. Magma is melted rock material. Sediments are loose mineral and rock fragments. Sedimentary rock is formed from compacted and cemented sediment.
6. Stories or poems can include any logical pathways through the rock cycle.

# 1 Motivate

INTERACTIVE CHALKBOARD
PowerPoint® Presentations

## Bellringer

**Section Focus Transparencies** also are available on the Interactive Chalkboard CD-ROM.

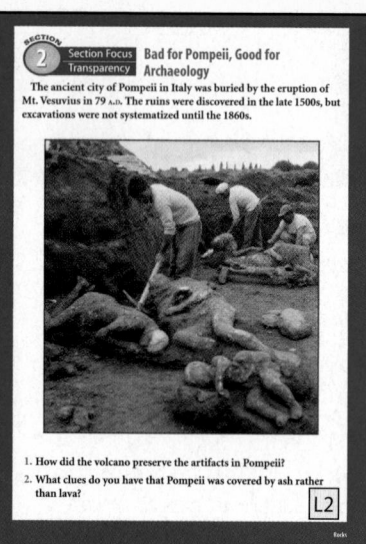

SECTION
**2** Section Focus Transparency — **Bad for Pompeii, Good for Archaeology**

The ancient city of Pompeii in Italy was buried by the eruption of Mt. Vesuvius in 79 A.D. The ruins were discovered in the late 1500s, but excavations were not systematized until the 1860s.

1. How did the volcano preserve the artifacts in Pompeii?
2. What clues do you have that Pompeii was covered by ash rather than lava?

L2

## Tie to Prior Knowledge

**Lava** Have students recall a volcanic eruption they've seen in person or on television. What comes out of erupting volcanoes? lava, ash, rock, steam Describe lava. They might describe it as hot material that flows out of a volcano. Inform students that lava is a basic ingredient for a certain type of igneous rock and that in this section they will learn how lava becomes rock.

---

## section 2

# Igneous Rocks

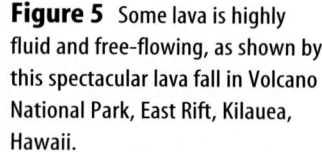
### as you read

**What You'll Learn**

■ **Recognize** magma and lava as the materials that cool to form igneous rocks.
■ **Contrast** the formation of intrusive and extrusive igneous rocks.
■ **Contrast** granitic and basaltic igneous rocks.

**Why It's Important**

Igneous rocks are the most abundant kind of rock in Earth's crust. They contain many valuable resources.

**Review Vocabulary**
**element:** substance made of one type of atom that cannot be broken down by ordinary chemical or physical means

**New Vocabulary**
• igneous rock   • extrusive
• lava           • basaltic
• intrusive      • granitic

## Formation of Igneous Rocks

Perhaps you've heard of recent volcanic eruptions in the news. When some volcanoes erupt, they eject a flow of molten rock material, as shown in **Figure 5.** Molten rock material, called magma, flows when it is hot and becomes solid when it cools. When hot magma cools and hardens, it forms **igneous** (IHG nee us) **rock.** Why do volcanoes erupt, and where does the molten material come from?

**Magma** In certain places within Earth, the temperature and pressure are just right for rocks to melt and form magma. Most magmas come from deep below Earth's surface. Magma is located at depths ranging from near the surface to about 150 km below the surface. Temperatures of magmas range from about 650°C to 1,200°C, depending on their chemical compositions and pressures exerted on them.

The heat that melts rocks comes from sources within Earth's interior. One source is the decay of radioactive elements within Earth. Some heat is left over from the formation of the planet, which originally was molten. Radioactive decay of elements contained in rocks balances some heat loss as Earth continues to cool.

Because magma is less dense than surrounding solid rock, it is forced upward toward the surface, as shown in **Figure 6.** When magma reaches Earth's surface and flows from volcanoes, it is called **lava.**

**Figure 5** Some lava is highly fluid and free-flowing, as shown by this spectacular lava fall in Volcano National Park, East Rift, Kilauea, Hawaii.

**536   CHAPTER 18** Rocks

---

## Section 2 Resource Manager

**Chapter FAST FILE Resources**
  Transparency Activity, p. 43
  Directed Reading for Content Mastery, p. 16
  Enrichment, p. 28

  Reinforcement, p. 24
  Lab Worksheets, pp. 5–6
  **Reading and Writing Skill Activities,** p. 27

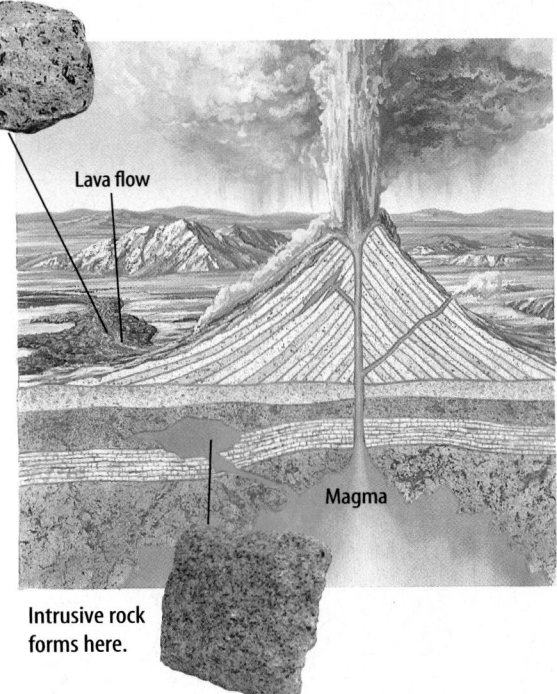

Extrusive rock forms here.

Lava flow

Magma

Intrusive rock forms here.

**Figure 6** Intrusive rocks form from magma trapped below Earth's surface. Extrusive rocks form from lava flowing at the surface.

**Intrusive Rocks** Magma is melted rock material composed of common elements and fluids. As magma cools, atoms and compounds in the liquid rearrange themselves into new crystals called mineral grains. Rocks form as these mineral grains grow together. Rocks that form from magma below the surface, as illustrated in **Figure 6,** are called **intrusive** igneous rocks. Intrusive rocks are found at the surface only after the layers of rock and soil that once covered them have been removed by erosion. Erosion occurs when the rocks are pushed up by forces within Earth. Because intrusive rocks form at depth and they are surrounded by other rocks, it takes a long time for them to cool. Slowly cooled magma produces individual mineral grains that are large enough to be observed with the unaided eye.

**Extrusive Rocks** **Extrusive** igneous rocks are formed as lava cools on the surface of Earth. When lava flows on the surface, as illustrated in **Figure 6,** it is exposed to air and water. Lava, such as the basaltic lava shown in **Figure 5,** cools quickly under these conditions. The quick cooling rate keeps mineral grains from growing large, because the atoms in the liquid don't have the time to arrange into large crystals. Therefore, extrusive igneous rocks are fine grained.

✔ **Reading Check** *What controls the grain size of an igneous rock?*

## Differentiated Instruction

**English-Language Learners** Provide students with one extrusive and one intrusive igneous rock sample. Have them make sketches of the rocks and then compare and contrast the textures of each in their own words. L2

## Visual Learning

**Figure 6** Ask students to contrast magma and lava. Magma is molten rock material that is beneath Earth's surface. Magma becomes lava upon reaching the surface.

## Use Science Words

**Word Origin** Have students use dictionaries to compare the origins of the words *intrusive* and *extrusive* with the origins of *interior* and *exterior.* L2 IN **Linguistic**

## Quick Demo

**Porous Rocks**

**Materials** pumice, scoria, plastic container of water

**Estimated Time** 5 to 10 minutes

**Procedure** Place pumice and scoria in the container of water. Students should observe that pumice floats in the water, but scoria does not. Ask them to make inferences based on their observations. Both samples contain holes from trapped gases, but scoria is darker in color and denser. Scoria contains a higher proportion of heavier elements, such as iron, than pumice does.

✔ **Reading Check**

**Answer** the rate at which magma or lava cools

## Discussion

**Obsidian Properties** Obsidian is a solid, dense volcanic glass. Examine the photo of obsidian in **Table 2.** Why do you think it has been used as a cutting tool? It can be sculpted into an object with sharp, thin edges.

# Differentiated Instruction

**Challenge** Invite interested students to collect rocks from various parts of your community and then use a rock and mineral guide to identify any igneous rocks they find among them. Have students label the rocks and display them in class. Invite other students to do the same with sedimentary and metamorphic rocks in upcoming sections. L2 ELL COOP LEARN LS **Visual-Spatial and Naturalist**

### Reading Check

**Answer** whether they form above or below the ground, and the type of magma from which they form

| Table 1 Common Igneous Rocks | | | |
|---|---|---|---|
| Magma Type | Basaltic | Andesitic | Granitic |
| Intrusive | Gabbro | Diorite | Granite |
| Extrusive | Basalt / Scoria | Andesite | Rhyolite / Pumice / Obsidian |

**Topic: Rock Formation**
Visit in7.msscience.com for Web links to information about intrusive and extrusive rocks.

**Activity** List several geographic settings where intrusive or extrusive rocks are found. Select one setting for intrusive rocks, and one for extrusive rocks. Describe how igneous rocks form in the two settings, and locate an example of each on a map.

**Volcanic Glass** Pumice, obsidian, and scoria are examples of volcanic glass. These rocks cooled so quickly that few or no mineral grains formed. Most of the atoms in these rocks are not arranged in orderly patterns, and few crystals are present.

In the case of pumice and scoria, gases become trapped in the gooey molten material as it cools. Some of these gases eventually escape, but holes are left behind where the rock formed around the pockets of gas.

## Classifying Igneous Rocks

Igneous rocks are intrusive or extrusive depending on how they are formed. A way to further classify these rocks is by the magma from which they form. As shown in **Table 1,** an igneous rock can form from basaltic, andesitic, or granitic magma. The type of magma that cools to form an igneous rock determines important chemical and physical properties of that rock. These include mineral composition, density, color, and melting temperature.

### Reading Check *Name two ways igneous rocks are classified.*

### Active Reading

**Buddy Interviews** Have students interview one another to find out what helps them understand what they are reading, how they find answers, and how they assimilate new vocabulary terms. Have students use Buddy Interviews to help them master the differences among igneous rocks.

### Teacher FYI

**Rock Textures** Some intrusive igneous rocks have textures similar to extrusive rocks. These rocks may form as dikes and sills, and are intruded into relatively shallow levels of Earth's crust.

**Basaltic Rocks** **Basaltic** (buh SAWL tihk) igneous rocks are dense, dark-colored rocks. They form from magma that is rich in iron and magnesium and poor in silica, which is the compound SiO$_2$. The presence of iron and magnesium in minerals in basalt gives basalt its dark color. Basaltic lava is fluid and flows freely from volcanoes in Hawaii, such as Kilauea. How does this explain the black beach sand common in Hawaii?

**Granitic Rocks** **Granitic** igneous rocks are light-colored rocks of a lower density than basaltic rocks. Granitic magma is thick and stiff and contains lots of silica but lesser amounts of iron and magnesium. Because granitic magma is stiff, it can build up a great deal of gas pressure, which is released explosively during violent volcanic eruptions.

**Andesitic Rocks** Andesitic igneous rocks have mineral compositions between those of basaltic and granitic rocks. Many volcanoes around the rim of the Pacific Ocean formed from andesitic magmas. Like volcanoes that erupt granitic magma, these volcanoes also can erupt violently.

Take another look at **Table 1.** Basalt forms at the surface of Earth because it is an extrusive rock. Granite forms below Earth's surface from magma with a high concentration of silica. When you identify an igneous rock, you can infer how it formed and the type of magma that it formed from.

**Melting Rock** Inside Earth, materials contained in rocks can melt. In your Science Journal, describe what is happening to the atoms and molecules to cause this change of state.

**Melting Rock** As thermal energy increases, atoms move faster, and the material changes from solid to liquid.

**Text Question Answer**

The black beach sand is sediment derived from erosion of black basalt.

## 3 Assess

**DAILY INTERVENTION**

### Check for Understanding

**Kinesthetic** Have students compare granitic and basaltic rocks of similar size. Have one student close his or her eyes while another student places the rocks in the first student's hands. Have students hypothesize which rocks are basaltic and which are granitic based on the heft of the rock. L2 LS

### Reteach

**Magma Composition** Ask students to make a concept map that shows basaltic, andesitic, and granitic magmas and the rocks that form from them. L2 LS
**Visual-Spatial** P

## section 2 review

### Summary

**Formation of Igneous Rocks**

- When molten rock material, called magma, cools and hardens, igneous rock forms.
- Intrusive igneous rocks form as magma cools and hardens slowly, beneath Earth's surface.
- Extrusive igneous rocks form as lava cools and hardens rapidly, at or above Earth's surface.

**Classifying Igneous Rocks**

- Igneous rocks are further classified according to their mineral compositions.
- The violent nature of some volcanic eruptions is partly explained by the composition of the magma that feeds them.

### Self Check

1. **Explain** why some types of magma form igneous rocks that are dark colored and dense.
2. **Identify** the property of magma that causes it to be forced upward toward Earth's surface.
3. **Explain** The texture of obsidian is best described as glassy. Why does obsidian contain few or no mineral grains?
4. **Think Critically** Study the photos in **Table 1.** How are granite and rhyolite similar? How are they different?

**Applying Skills**

5. **Make and Use Graphs** Four elements make up most of the rocks in Earth's crust. They are: *oxygen—46.6 percent, aluminum—8.1 percent, silicon—27.7 percent,* and *iron—5.0 percent.* Make a bar graph of these data. What might you infer from the low amount of iron?

### Assessment

**Oral** Have students write questions on the material in the section and then take turns quizzing each other aloud. Use **Performance Assessment in the Science Classroom,** p. 91.

## section 2 review

1. The magma or lava is rich in iron and magnesium, which are contained in relatively dark and dense minerals.
2. Magma is less dense than surrounding rocks and is forced upward.
3. Obsidian solidifies so quickly that there is no time for mineral grains to form.
4. Granite and rhyolite both are granitic igneous rocks composed of the same minerals. Granite is intrusive—cooled slowly beneath Earth's surface; rhyolite is extrusive—cooled rapidly at the surface.
5. Students' bar graphs should be drawn to scale and properly labeled. On average, crustal rocks contain a fairly low concentration of iron as compared to oxygen, silicon, and aluminum.

## Real-World Question

**Purpose** Students observe the texture and color of igneous rocks to determine how they formed. **L2** **ELL** **IS** **Kinesthetic**

**Process Skills** observe, classify, record data, make and use tables, analyze, infer

**Time Required** 45–50 minutes

**Materials** Supply magnifying lenses that students can use to observe the rocks.

## Procedure

**Teaching Strategy** Have students work in pairs. If rock samples are in short supply, allow students to take turns using the same samples.

## Conclude and Apply

1. rocks that are light in color
2. Rocks with smaller grains; quick cooling does not allow large grains (crystals) to form.
3. Pumice and vesicular basalt; holes in rock suggest that gas was escaping as it cooled.
4. Obsidian and pumice; they cool so quickly that individual grains (crystals) do not have the chance to form.
5. Answers will vary depending on samples observed. The presence of grains that all are visible to the unaided eye indicates rocks are not volcanic.

# Igneous Rock Clues

You've learned how color often is used to estimate the composition of an igneous rock. The texture of an igneous rock describes its overall appearance, including mineral grain sizes and the presence or absence of bubble holes, for example. In most cases, grain size relates to

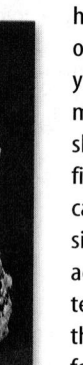

how quickly the magma or lava cooled. Crystals you can see without a magnifying lens indicate slower cooling. Smaller, fine-grained crystals indicate quicker cooling, possibly due to volcanic activity. Rocks with glassy textures cooled so quickly that there was no time to form mineral grains.

## Real-World Question

What does an igneous rock's texture and color indicate about its formation history?

### Goals

- **Classify** different samples of igneous rocks by color and infer their composition.
- **Observe** the textures of igneous rocks and infer how they formed.

### Materials

| | |
|---|---|
| rhyolite | granite |
| basalt | obsidian |
| vesicular basalt | gabbro |
| pumice | magnifying lens |

### Safety Precautions 🔥 🥽 ✋

**WARNING:** *Some rock samples might have sharp edges. Always use caution while handling samples.*

## Procedure

1. **Arrange** rocks according to color (light or dark). Record your observations in your Science Journal.
2. **Arrange** rocks according to similar texture. Consider grain sizes and shapes, presence of holes, etc. Use your magnifying lens to see small features more clearly. Record your observations.

## Conclude and Apply

1. **Infer** which rocks are granitic based on color.
2. **Infer** which rocks cooled quickly. What observations led you to this inference?
3. **Identify** any samples that suggest gases were escaping from them as they cooled.
4. **Describe** Which samples have a glassy appearance? How did these rocks form?
5. **Infer** which samples are not volcanic. Explain.

### Communicating Your Data

Research the compositions of each of your samples. Did the colors of any samples lead you to infer the wrong compositions? Communicate to your class what you learned.

---

### ✔ Assessment

**Process** Encourage students to use a word processing program to make a table that lists and classifies the rocks used in the activity. Use **Performance Assessment in the Science Classroom,** p. 109.

### Communicating Your Data

Some granitic rocks are dark in color, and might lead to incorrect inferences. Students should show pictures they have located in print or Internet resources to support their conclusions.

**Standard—7.3.9:** Explain that sedimentary rock, when buried deep enough, may be reformed by pressure and heat, perhaps melting and recrystallizing into different kinds of rock. Describe that these reformed rock layers may be forced up again to become land surface and even mountains, and subsequently erode.

# section 3

# Metamorphic Rocks

## Formation of Metamorphic Rocks

Have you ever packed your lunch in the morning and not been able to recognize it at lunchtime? You might have packed a sandwich, banana, and a large bottle of water. You know you didn't smash your lunch on the way to school. However, you didn't think about how the heavy water bottle would damage your food if the bottle was allowed to rest on the food all day. The heat in your locker and the pressure from the heavy water bottle changed your sandwich. Like your lunch, rocks can be affected by changes in temperature and pressure.

**Metamorphic Rocks** Rocks that have changed because of changes in temperature and pressure or the presence of hot, watery fluids are called **metamorphic rocks.** Changes that occur can be in the form of the rock, shown in **Figure 7,** the composition of the rock, or both. Metamorphic rocks can form from igneous, sedimentary, or other metamorphic rocks. What Earth processes can change these rocks?

### as you read

**What You'll Learn**
- **Describe** the conditions in Earth that cause metamorphic rocks to form.
- **Classify** metamorphic rocks as foliated or nonfoliated.

**Why It's Important**
Metamorphic rocks are useful because of their unique properties.

**Review Vocabulary**
**pressure:** the amount of force exerted per unit of area

**New Vocabulary**
- metamorphic rock
- foliated
- nonfoliated

+ pressure

Granite

Gneiss

**Figure 7** The mineral grains in granite are flattened and aligned when heat and pressure are applied to them. As a result, gneiss is formed. **Describe** *other conditions that can cause metamorphic rocks to form.*

SECTION 3  Metamorphic Rocks  **541**

### Section 3 Resource Manager

**Chapter FAST FILE Resources**
Transparency Activity, p. 44
Directed Reading for Content Mastery, p. 17
Enrichment, p. 29

Lab Activity, pp. 11–12
Reinforcement, p. 25
MiniLAB, p. 4
**Cultural Diversity,** p. 27
**Science Inquiry Labs,** pp. 31–32

# 1 Motivate

**Bellringer**

**Section Focus Transparencies** also are available on the Interactive Chalkboard CD-ROM.

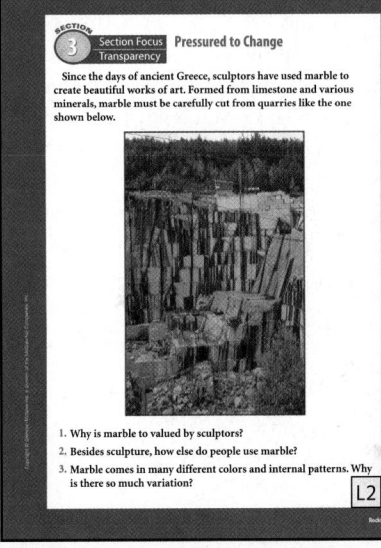

**Tie to Prior Knowledge**

**Metamorphic** Help students recall the meaning of the word *metamorphosis.* Have them use this knowledge to speculate about the nature of metamorphic rocks.

**Text Question Answer**

high temperatures and pressures deep inside Earth

**Caption Answer**

**Figure 7** a change in temperature or pressure and the presence of hot fluids

### Use an Analogy

**Contact Metamorphism** Use this analogy to explain how heat generated from hot magma can cause an adjacent area of rock to change. Remind students what happens to beef as it is seared in a pan. The outside of the meat is cooked as it comes in contact with the pan. If removed from the heat soon enough, the inside of the meat remains unchanged. If the cooking continues, the center of the meat will eventually change. Hot magma changes rock in contact with its surface. The longer it continues, the more the rock body in contact with the magma will be changed. **LS** **Visual-Spatial**

### ✔ Reading Check

**Answer** Different types of metamorphic rock form depending on the temperature, pressure, and fluid conditions.

## Visual Learning

**Figure 8** What is the source of the heat in the fluids? The heat source is the melted rock material, or magma.

### Discussion

**Reactive Fluids** Why might fluids at high temperatures be more effective at changing rock than low-temperature fluids? High temperature fluids would transport more thermal energy to initiate chemical reactions within rock.

---

**Science Online**

**Topic: Shale Metamorphism**
Visit in7.msscience.com for Web links to information about the metamorphism of shale. Communicate to your class what you learn.

**Activity** Make a table with headings that are major rock types that form from shale metamorphism. Under each rock heading, make a list of minerals that can occur in the rock.

---

### Indiana Academic Standard Check

**7.3.9:** Explain that sedimentary rock, when buried deep enough, may be reformed by pressure and heat, perhaps ... recrystallizing into different kinds of rock. ...

✔ Beginning with shale, name the sequence of rock types as increasing temperature and pressure are applied.

✔ shale, slate, phyllite, schist, gneiss

---

**Heat and Pressure** Rocks beneath Earth's surface are under great pressure from rock layers above them. Temperature also increases with depth in Earth. In some places, the heat and pressure are just right to cause rocks to melt and magma to form. In other areas where melting doesn't occur, some mineral grains can change by dissolving and recrystallizing—especially in the presence of fluids. Sometimes, under these conditions, minerals exchange atoms with surrounding minerals and new, bigger minerals form.

Depending upon the amount of pressure and temperature applied, one type of rock can change into several different metamorphic rocks, and each type of metamorphic rock can come from several kinds of parent rocks. For example, the sedimentary rock shale will change into slate. As increasing pressure and temperature are applied, the slate can change into phyllite, then schist, and eventually gneiss. Schist also can form when basalt is metamorphosed, or changed, and gneiss can come from granite.

### ✔ Reading Check

*How can one type of rock change into several different metamorphic rocks?*

**Hot Fluids** Did you know that fluids can move through rock? These fluids, which are mostly water with dissolved elements and compounds, can react chemically with a rock and change its composition, especially when the fluids are hot. That's what happens when rock surrounding a hot magma body reacts with hot fluids from the magma, as shown in **Figure 8.** Most fluids that transform rocks during metamorphic processes are hot and mainly are comprised of water and carbon dioxide.

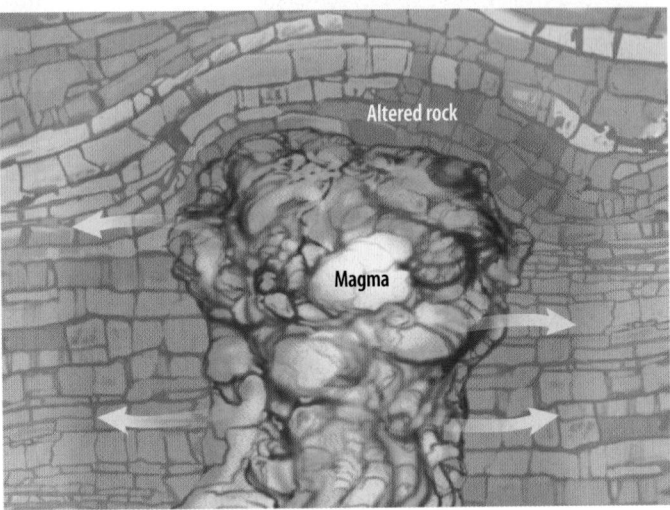

**Figure 8** In the presence of hot, water-rich fluids, solid rock can change in mineral composition without having to melt.

---

### Active Reading ✔

**Jigsaw** In this collaborative learning strategy, individuals become experts on a portion of a text and share their expertise with their "home" group. Everyone shares responsibility for learning the assigned reading. Assign each person in each home group an "expert" number (1 through 5, for example). Have students gather into the expert groups that correspond to the number they were assigned. There, have them read, discuss, and master chapter concepts and determine how best to teach them to their home groups. Have students return to home groups and share the content they learned in their expert groups. Have students use the Jigsaw strategy to learn about conditions in Earth that cause metamorphic rocks to form.

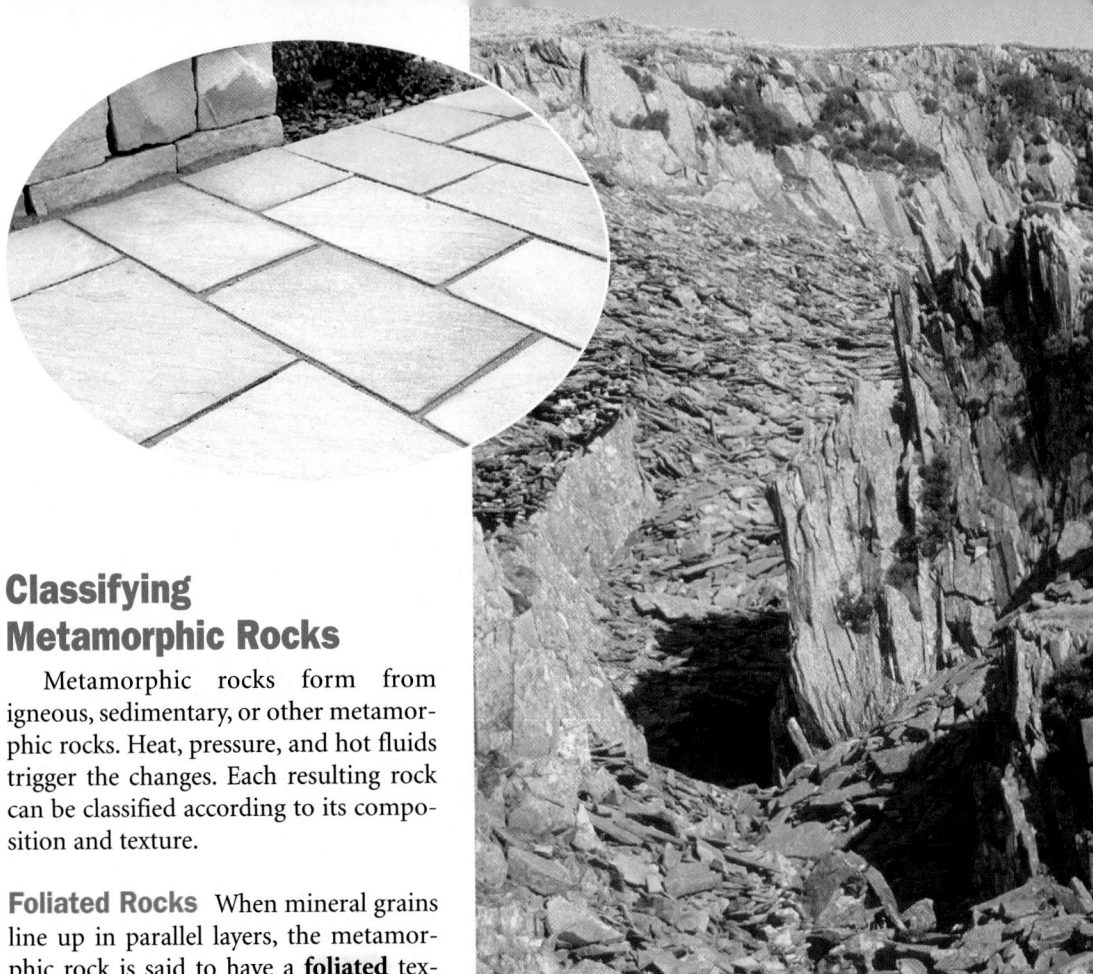

## Classifying Metamorphic Rocks

Metamorphic rocks form from igneous, sedimentary, or other metamorphic rocks. Heat, pressure, and hot fluids trigger the changes. Each resulting rock can be classified according to its composition and texture.

**Foliated Rocks** When mineral grains line up in parallel layers, the metamorphic rock is said to have a **foliated** texture. Two examples of foliated rocks are slate and gneiss. Slate forms from the sedimentary rock shale. The minerals in shale arrange into layers when they are exposed to heat and pressure. As **Figure 9** shows, slate separates easily along these foliation layers.

The minerals in slate are pressed together so tightly that water can't pass between them easily. Because it's watertight, slate is ideal for paving around pools and patios. The naturally flat nature of slate and the fact that it splits easily make it useful for roofing and tiling many surfaces.

Gneiss (NISE), another foliated rock, forms when granite and other rocks are changed. Foliation in gneiss shows up as alternating light and dark bands. Movement of atoms has separated the dark minerals, such as biotite mica, from the light minerals, which are mainly quartz and feldspar.

**Figure 9** Slate often is used as a building or landscaping material.
**Identify** *the properties that make slate so useful for these purposes.*

✓ **Reading Check** *What type of metamorphic rock is composed of mineral grains arranged in parallel layers?*

SECTION 3 Metamorphic Rocks **543**

### Check for Understanding

**Visual-Spatial** Have students sketch foliated and nonfoliated metamorphic rocks. Call on individual students to describe what their sketches show. Encourage students to obtain samples of the rocks they have sketched. L2 LS

### Reteach

**Rock Facts** Have students take turns brainstorming facts they now know about metamorphic rocks. Write their contributions on the board. Use this information to stimulate discussion about the origins and classification of metamorphic rocks. L1
LS **Interpersonal**

### ✓ Assessment

**Performance** Provide students with a variety of metamorphic rocks. Have them infer a possible parent rock for each sample. Use **Performance Assessment in the Science Classroom,** p. 121.

**Figure 10** This exhibit in Vermont shows the beauty of carved marble.

**Nonfoliated Rocks** In some metamorphic rocks, layering does not occur. The mineral grains grow and rearrange, but they don't form layers. This process produces a **nonfoliated** texture.

Sandstone is a sedimentary rock that's often composed mostly of quartz grains. When sandstone is heated under a lot of pressure, the grains of quartz grow in size and become interlocking, like the pieces of a jigsaw puzzle. The resulting rock is called quartzite.

Marble is another nonfoliated metamorphic rock. Marble forms from the sedimentary rock limestone, which is composed of the mineral calcite. Usually, marble contains several other minerals besides calcite. For example, hornblende and serpentine give marble a black or greenish tone, whereas hematite makes it red. As **Figure 10** shows, marble is a popular material for artists to sculpt because it is not as hard as other rocks.

So far, you've investigated only a portion of the rock cycle. You still haven't observed how sedimentary rocks are formed and how igneous and metamorphic rocks evolve from them. The next section will complete your investigation of the rock cycle.

## section 3 review

### Summary

**Formation of Metamorphic Rocks**

- Changes in pressure, temperature, or the presence of fluids can cause metamorphic rocks to form.
- Rock, altered by metamorphic processes at high temperatures and pressures, changes in the solid state without melting.
- Hot fluids that move through and react with preexisting rock are composed mainly of water and carbon dioxide.
- One source of hot, watery fluids is magma bodies close to the changing rock.
- Any parent rock type—igneous, metamorphic, or sedimentary—can become a metamorphic rock.

**Classifying Metamorphic Rocks**

- Texture and mineral composition determine how a metamorphic rock is classified.
- Physical properties of metamorphic rocks, such as the watertight nature of slate, make them useful for many purposes.

### Self Check

1. **Explain** what role fluids play in rock metamorphism.
2. **Describe** how metamorphic rocks are classified. What are the characteristics of rocks in each of these classifications?
3. **Identify** Give an example of a foliated and a nonfoliated metamorphic rock. Name one of their possible parent rocks.
4. **Think Critically** Marble is a common material used to make sculptures, but not just because it's a beautiful stone. What properties of marble make it useful for this purpose?

#### Applying Skills

5. **Concept Map** Put the following events in an events-chain concept map that explains how a metamorphic rock might form from an igneous rock. *Hint: Start with "Igneous Rock Forms."* Use each event just once.

    Events: *sedimentary rock forms, weathering occurs, heat and pressure are applied, igneous rock forms, metamorphic rock forms, erosion occurs, sediments are formed, deposition occurs*

 in7.msscience.com/self_check_quiz

## section 3 review

1. Hot fluids chemically react with rocks with which they are in contact, changing their compositions.
2. Foliated or nonfoliated; foliated rocks have layers of mineral grains; nonfoliated rocks have little or no layering.
3. foliated: slate; parent rock: shale; nonfoliated: marble; parent rock: limestone
4. It also is relatively homogeneous and easy to shape. It is composed mainly of the mineral calcite, which has a hardness of only 3 on the Mohs scale.
5. Igneous rock forms. Weathering occurs. Sediments are formed. Erosion occurs. Deposition occurs. Sedimentary rock forms. Heat and pressure are applied. Metamorphic rock forms.

section

4

Standard—7.3.8: Describe how sediments of sand and smaller particles, sometimes containing the remains of organisms, are gradually buried and are cemented together by dissolved minerals to form solid rock again.

Also covers: 7.3.9, 7.3.10 (Detailed standards begin on page IN8.)

# Sedimentary Rocks

## Formation of Sedimentary Rocks

Igneous rocks are the most common rocks on Earth, but because most of them exist below the surface, you might not have seen too many of them. That's because 75 percent of the rocks exposed at the surface are sedimentary rocks.

**Sediments** are loose materials such as rock fragments, mineral grains, and bits of shell that have been moved by wind, water, ice, or gravity. If you look at the model of the rock cycle, you will see that sediments come from already-existing rocks that are weathered and eroded. **Sedimentary rock** forms when sediments are pressed and cemented together, or when minerals form from solutions.

**Stacked Rocks** Sedimentary rocks often form as layers. The older layers are on the bottom because they were deposited first. Sedimentary rock layers are a lot like the books and papers in your locker. Last week's homework is on the bottom, and today's notes will be deposited on top of the stack. However, if you disturb the stack, the order in which the books and papers are stacked will change, as shown in **Figure 11.** Sometimes, forces within Earth such as folding and faulting overturn or displace layers of rock, so that oldest are no longer on the bottom.

### as you read

**What You'll Learn**

- **Explain** how sedimentary rocks form from sediments.
- **Classify** sedimentary rocks as detrital, chemical, or organic in origin.
- **Summarize** the rock cycle.

**Why It's Important**

Some sedimentary rocks, like coal, are important sources of energy.

**Review Vocabulary**
**weathering:** surface processes that work to break down rock mechanically or chemically

**New Vocabulary**
- sediment
- sedimentary rock
- compaction
- cementation

**Figure 11** Like sedimentary rock layers, the oldest paper is at the bottom of the stack. If the stack is disturbed, then it is no longer in order.

## 1 Motivate

INTERACTIVE CHALKBOARD
PowerPoint® Presentations

**Bellringer**

**Section Focus Transparencies** also are available on the Interactive Chalkboard CD-ROM.
L2 ELL

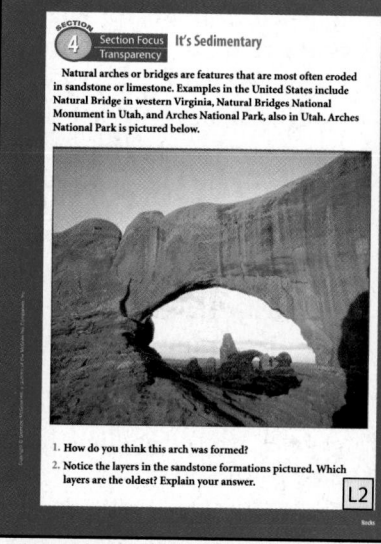

SECTION 4 Section Focus Transparency It's Sedimentary

Natural arches or bridges are features that are most often eroded in sandstone or limestone. Examples in the United States include Natural Bridge in western Virginia, Natural Bridges National Monument in Utah, and Arches National Park, also in Utah. Arches National Park is pictured below.

1. How do you think this arch was formed?
2. Notice the layers in the sandstone formations pictured. Which layers are the oldest? Explain your answer.
L2

**Tie to Prior Knowledge**

**Sedimentary Rock Formation** Have students describe what happens when sugar is stirred into a glass of cold water. What happens? Some grains dissolve, others drop to the bottom of the glass. Explain that some rocks form from sediment that drops to the bottom of water bodies. Others form from chemicals dissolved in water. Tell students they will learn in this section how this happens.

## Section 4 Resource Manager

**Chapter FAST FILE Resources**
Transparency Activity, p. 45
Directed Reading for Content Mastery, pp. 17, 18
MiniLAB, p. 4
Enrichment, p. 30

Reinforcement, p. 26
Lab Worksheets, pp. 7–8
**Reading and Writing Skill Activities,** p. 21
**Mathematics Skill Activities,** p. 29
**Lab Management and Safety,** p. 70

**Purpose** Students classify sediments according to grain size.

L2 ELL COOP LEARN LS

**Kinesthetic**

**Materials** paper, samples of silt, sand, and gravel-sized sediment grains (with both rounded and sharp edges), tweezers or dissecting probe, magnifying lens

**Teaching Strategy** Review with students the appearance of rounded grains as opposed to grains with sharp edges. For example, grains need not be spherical in shape to be considered well-rounded.

**Safety Precautions** Caution students to handle sharp instruments with care and to wear goggles while handling samples.

**Analysis**

1. Students should describe grains by size and the smoothness or angularity of their edges.
2. Conglomerate from rounded gravel, breccia from angular gravel; If other sediments are used: shale from clay, siltstone from silt, sandstone from sand.

**Assessment**

**Performance** Have students paste silt, sand, and gravel-sized sediment onto a note card. Then use the cards to determine the grain sizes of several sedimentary rock samples. Use **Performance Assessment in the Science Classroom,** p. 121.

**☑ Reading Check**

**Answer** As layers of sediment build up, pressure from upper layers on lower layers compacts lower layers into rock.

---

**Classifying Sediments**

**Procedure**

**WARNING:** *Use care when handling sharp objects.*

1. Collect different samples of **sediment.**
2. Spread them on a sheet of **paper.**
3. Use **Table 2** to determine the size range of gravel-sized sediment.
4. Use **tweezers or a dissecting probe** and a **magnifying lens** to separate the gravel-sized sediments.
5. Separate the gravel into piles—rounded or angular.

**Analysis**

1. Describe the grains in both piles.
2. Determine what rock could form from each type of sediment you have.

**Figure 12**  During compaction, pore space between sediments decreases, causing them to become packed together more tightly.

---

# Classifying Sedimentary Rocks

Sedimentary rocks can be made of just about any material found in nature. Sediments come from weathered and eroded igneous, metamorphic, and sedimentary rocks. Sediments also come from the remains of some organisms. The composition of a sedimentary rock depends upon the composition of the sediments from which it formed.

Like igneous and metamorphic rocks, sedimentary rocks are classified by their composition and by the manner in which they formed. Sedimentary rocks usually are classified as detrital, chemical, or organic.

## Detrital Sedimentary Rocks

The word *detrital* (dih TRI tul) comes from the Latin word *detritus,* which means "to wear away." Detrital sedimentary rocks, such as those shown in **Table 2,** are made from the broken fragments of other rocks. These loose sediments are compacted and cemented together to form solid rock.

**Weathering and Erosion**  When rock is exposed to air, water, or ice, it is unstable and breaks down chemically and mechanically. This process, which breaks rocks into smaller pieces, is called weathering. **Table 2** shows how these pieces are classified by size. The movement of weathered material is called erosion.

**Compaction**  Erosion moves sediments to a new location, where they then are deposited. Here, layer upon layer of sediment builds up. Pressure from the upper layers pushes down on the lower layers. If the sediments are small, they can stick together and form solid rock. This process, shown in **Figure 12,** is called **compaction.**

**☑ Reading Check**   *How do rocks form through compaction?*

---

# Differentiated Instruction

**Visually Impaired**  Provide students with samples of rounded and angular gravel that they can feel to determine the size and shape of grains. Also provide samples of conglomerate and breccia in which the students can feel the embedded grains.
L2

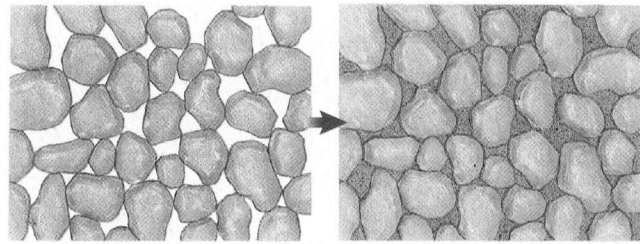

**Figure 13** Sediments are cemented together as minerals crystallize between grains.

**Cementation** If sediments are large, like sand and pebbles, pressure alone can't make them stick together. Large sediments have to be cemented together. As water moves through soil and rock, it picks up materials released from minerals during weathering. The resulting solution of water and dissolved materials moves through open spaces between sediments. **Cementation,** which is shown in **Figure 13,** occurs when minerals such as quartz, calcite, and hematite are deposited between the pieces of sediment. These minerals, acting as natural cements, hold the sediment together like glue, making a detrital sedimentary rock.

**Shape and Size of Sediments** Detrital rocks have granular textures, much like granulated sugar. They are named according to the shapes and sizes of the sediments that form them. For example, conglomerate and breccia both form from large sediments, as shown in **Table 2.** If the sediments are rounded, the rock is called conglomerate. If the sediments have sharp angles, the rock is called breccia. The roundness of sediment particles depends on how far they have been moved by wind or water.

| Table 2 Sediment Sizes and Detrital Rocks | | | | |
|---|---|---|---|---|
| **Sediment** | Clay | Silt | Sand | Gravel |
| **Size Range** | <0.004 mm | 0.004–0.063 mm | 0.063–2 mm | >2 mm |
| **Example** | Shale | Siltstone | Sandstone | Conglomerate (shown) or Breccia |

## Visual Learning

**Figure 13** Why is a cementing material needed to hold coarse-grained sedimentary rocks together? Pressure alone can't make large grains stick together. A cementing material acts to hold them together.

### Discussion

**Sediment Sizes** Have students imagine a swiftly-flowing river that empties into a quiet bay.

- Where in the bay would you expect to find the coarsest sediments being deposited? Explain. The coarsest sediments would be deposited nearest the mouth of the river. This is where the water loses velocity and drops the largest sediments in its load.

- Where would you expect to find the finest sediments being deposited? Explain. The finest sediments would be deposited farther from the mouth of the river. Because these sediments are lighter in weight than the coarser sediments, they stay suspended longer, even when the velocity of the water slows.

- Have students use **Table 2** to answer this question. If these sediments became cemented together, what type of rock would form in each location? Sandstone or conglomerate would form near the mouth of the river. Shale or siltstone would form farther out in the bay.

## Science Journal

**Observing Rock** Exhibit a piece of sandstone. Have students examine the rock and write a brief geologic history that explains how the sandstone could have formed. Then have students hypothesize what might happen to the rock if it were exposed to weathering and erosion, or to heat and pressure. L2 LS **Logical-Mathematical** P

## Activity

**Detrital Rocks** Form groups of three students. Supply each group with containers of clay, silt, fine sand, coarse sand, and rounded and angular gravel. Make samples of shale, siltstone, sandstone, conglomerate, and breccia available to each group. Have students use a hand lens to match sediment type with the appropriate rock sample. One student in each group should present a report containing the conclusions drawn by the group. L2 COOP LEARN **N** **Interpersonal**

**INTEGRATE**
**Career**

**Sedimentary Petrology** People who study to become sedimentary petrologists focus on the formation of sedimentary rocks. They could pursue careers in industrial minerals, or in petroleum exploration, research, and development, among others. Other careers include continuing advanced research and becoming professors at colleges and universities. Graduate degrees are strongly recommended for industrial fields, and essential for academic fields.

✅ **Reading Check**

**Answer** They form when dissolved minerals come out of solution or when liquid evaporates.

**Figure 14** Although concrete strongly resembles conglomerate, concrete is not a rock because it does not occur in nature.

**INTEGRATE**
**Career**

**Sedimentary Petrology** Research the work done by sedimentary petrologists. Include examples of careers in academia and in industry.

**Materials Found in Sedimentary Rocks** The gravel-sized sediments in conglomerate and breccia can consist of any type of rock or mineral. Often, they are composed of chunks of the minerals quartz and feldspar. They also can be pieces of rocks such as gneiss, granite, or limestone. The cement that holds the sediments together usually is made of quartz or calcite.

Have you ever looked at the concrete in sidewalks, driveways, and stepping stones? The concrete in **Figure 14** is made of gravel and sand grains that have been cemented together. Although the structure is similar to that of naturally occurring conglomerate, it cannot be considered a rock.

Sandstone is formed from smaller particles than conglomerates and breccias. Its sand-sized sediments can be just about any mineral, but they are usually grains of minerals such as quartz and feldspar that are resistant to weathering. Siltstone is similar to sandstone except it is made of smaller, silt-sized particles. Shale is a detrital sedimentary rock that is made mainly of clay-sized particles. Clay-sized sediments are compacted together by pressure from overlying layers.

## Chemical Sedimentary Rocks

Chemical sedimentary rocks form when dissolved minerals come out of solution. You can show that salt is deposited in the bottom of a glass or pan when saltwater solution evaporates. In a similar way, minerals collect when seas or lakes evaporate. The deposits of minerals that come out of solution form sediments and rocks. For example, the sediment making up New Mexico's White Sands desert consists of pieces of a chemical sedimentary rock called rock gypsum. Chemical sedimentary rocks are different. They are not made from pieces of preexisting rocks.

✅ **Reading Check** *How do chemical sedimentary rocks form?*

## Cultural Diversity

**Rock Art** Native Americans used flint to make arrowheads, axes, and other tools that need a sharp edge. Flint is an extremely fine-grained, dense, glossy sedimentary rock made of quartz. It often is found embedded in deposits of chalk or limestone. Flint is an even-grained rock that breaks easily into smooth, curved flakes with sharp edges. This makes it ideal for the manufacture of cutting tools.

Today people learn the art of flint napping as a craft. *Napping* is the method of striking a flint rock in such a way that a sharp-edged flake results. Have students find out what archaeologists have learned about the flint tools used by ancient Americans. Then have them make a classroom bulletin board showing the locations, types, and appearances of the flint artifacts. L2

**Limestone** Calcium carbonate is carried in solution in ocean water. When calcium carbonate ($CaCO_3$) comes out of solution as calcite and its many crystals grow together, limestone forms. Limestone also can contain other minerals and sediments, but it must be at least 50 percent calcite. Limestone usually is deposited on the bottom of lakes or shallow seas. Large areas of the central United States have limestone bedrock because seas covered much of the country for millions of years. It is hard to imagine Kansas being covered by ocean water, but it has happened several times throughout geological history.

**Rock Salt** When water that is rich in dissolved salt evaporates, it often deposits the mineral halite. Halite forms rock salt, shown in **Figure 15**. Rock salt deposits can range in thickness from a few meters to more than 400 m. Companies mine these deposits because rock salt is an important resource. It's used in the manufacturing of glass, paper, soap, and dairy products. The halite in rock salt is processed and used as table salt.

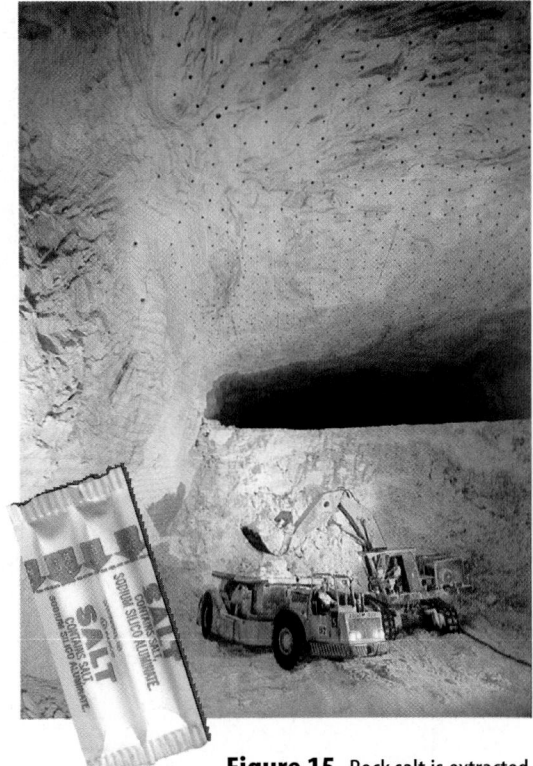

**Figure 15** Rock salt is extracted from this mine in Germany.

## Organic Sedimentary Rocks

Rocks made of the remains of once-living things are called organic sedimentary rocks. One of the most common organic sedimentary rocks is fossil-rich limestone. Like chemical limestone, fossil-rich limestone is made of the mineral calcite. However, fossil-rich limestone mostly contains remains of once-living ocean organisms instead of only calcite that formed directly from ocean water.

Animals such as mussels, clams, corals, and snails make their shells from $CaCO_3$ that eventually becomes calcite. When they die, their shells accumulate on the ocean floor. When these shells are cemented together, fossil-rich limestone forms. If a rock is made completely of shell fragments that you can see, the rock is called coquina (koh KEE nuh).

**Chalk** Chalk is another organic sedimentary rock that is made of microscopic shells. When you write with naturally occurring chalk, you're crushing and smearing the calcite-shell remains of once-living ocean organisms.

**Indiana Academic Standard Check**

**7.3.8:** Describe how sediments . . . sometimes containing the remains of organisms, are . . . buried and cemented together . . . to form solid rock.

✔ Name the three classifications of sedimentary rocks and describe how they are formed.

✔ detrital: formed from compacted and cemented rock fragments; chemical: deposits of dissolved minerals; organic: formed from the remains of living things

SECTION 4 Sedimentary Rocks **549**

**Teacher FYI**

**Chalk Formation** Many deposits of chalk formed during the Cretaceous Period, between 145 and 65 million years ago. The word *cretaceous* comes from the Latin word for chalk, which is *creta*.

## Discussion

**Coal Types** Display samples of peat, lignite, and bituminous and anthracite coal. Have students observe the peat to see that it is made of plant material. Demonstrate the relative ease with which you can break the lignite and the bituminous coal as opposed to the harder anthracite. Infer what happens to the hardness of coal as it changes from peat to lignite, bituminous, and anthracite. The coal becomes harder.

**Coal** Another useful organic sedimentary rock is coal, shown in **Figure 16.** Coal forms when pieces of dead plants are buried under other sediments in swamps. These plant materials are chemically changed by microorganisms. The resulting sediments are compacted over millions of years to form coal, an important source of energy. Much of the coal in North America and Europe formed during a period of geologic time that is so named because of this important reason. The Carboniferous Period, which spans from approximately 360 to 286 million years ago, was named in Europe. So much coal formed during this interval of time that coal's composition—primarily carbon—was the basis for naming a geologic period.

### Applying Math    Calculate Thickness

**COAL FORMATION** It took 300 million years for a layer of plant matter about 0.9 m thick to produce a bed of bituminous coal 0.3 m thick. Estimate the thickness of plant matter that produced a bed of coal 0.15 m thick.

#### Solution

**1** *This is what you know:*
- original thickness of plant matter = 0.9 m
- original coal thickness = 0.3 m
- new coal thickness = 0.15 m

**2** *This is what you need to know:* thickness of plant matter needed to form 0.15 m of coal

**3** *This is the equation you need to use:* (thickness of plant matter)/(new coal thickness) = (original thickness of plant matter)/(original coal thickness)

**4** *Substitute the known values:* (? m plant matter)/(0.15 m coal) = (0.9 m plant matter)/(0.3 m coal)

**5** *Solve the equation:* (? m plant matter) = (0.9 m plant matter) (0.15 m coal)/(0.3 m coal) = 0.45 m plant matter

**6** *Check your answer:* Multiply your answer by the original coal thickness. Divide by the original plant matter thickness to get the new coal thickness.

#### Practice Problems

**1.** Estimate the thickness of plant matter that produced a bed of coal 0.6 m thick.

**2.** About how much coal would have been produced from a layer of plant matter 0.50 m thick?

 Science Online | For more practice, visit in7.msscience.com/ math_practice

**550    CHAPTER 18** Rocks

---

 **LAB DEMONSTRATION**

**Purpose** to observe that some sedimentary rocks react with hydrochloric acid (HCl)

**Materials** samples of quartz sandstone, limestone, and shale; dilute HCl

**Procedure** Place a few drops of dilute HCl on each sample. **WARNING:** *Wear goggles and protect clothing and work surfaces.*

**Expected Outcome** Students will observe that the limestone sample fizzes readily.

**Assessment**

Which of the samples react to acid? Students should infer that the limestone sample contains a substance that reacts with HCl. Limestone reacts because it contains calcite.

## Another Look at the Rock Cycle

You have seen that the rock cycle has no beginning and no end. Rocks change continually from one form to another. Sediments can become so deeply buried that heat and pressure can reform them to become metamorphic or igneous rocks. These reformed rocks later can be uplifted and exposed to the surface—possibly as mountains to be worn away again by erosion.

All of the rocks that you've learned about in this chapter formed through some process within the rock cycle. All of the rocks around you, including those used to build houses and monuments, are part of the rock cycle. Slowly, they are all changing, because the rock cycle is a continuous, dynamic process.

**Figure 16** This coal layer in Alaska is easily identified by its jet-black color, as compared with other sedimentary layers.

 **Indiana Academic Standard Check**

**7.3.9:** ...Describe that these reformed rock layers may be forced up again to become land surface and even mountains, and subsequently erode.

✔ Does the rock cycle end when the rocks erode into sediment?

✔ No. The sediment can eventually become sedimentary rock, metamorphic rock, or even igneous rock.

**Make a Model**

**Rock Cycle** Have students make a model of the rock cycle. Encourage them to be creative and to present their models in class. L2

## ③ Assess

### DAILY INTERVENTION

**Check for Understanding**

**Logical-Mathematical** Have students explain which is older: detrital sedimentary rock or the sediments it contains. The sediments are older; they had to be present first in order for the sedimentary rock to form from them. L2

**Reteach**

**Rock Properties** Have students construct a table that summarizes the characteristics of detrital, chemical, and organic sedimentary rocks. L2

### ☑ Assessment

**Process** Assess students' abilities to sequence events by having them make an events chain for the process of changing a metamorphic rock to a sedimentary rock. Use **Performance Assessment in the Science Classroom,** p. 163.

## section ④ review

### Summary

**Formation of Sedimentary Rocks**
- Sedimentary rocks form as layers, with older layers near the bottom of an undisturbed stack.

**Classifying Sedimentary Rocks**
- To classify a sedimentary rock, determine its composition and texture.

**Detrital Sedimentary Rocks**
- Rock and mineral fragments make up detrital rocks.

**Chemical Sedimentary Rocks**
- Chemical sedimentary rocks form from solutions of dissolved minerals.

**Organic Sedimentary Rocks**
- The remains of once-living organisms make up organic sedimentary rocks.

### Self Check

1. **Identify** where sediments come from.
2. **Explain** how compaction is important in the formation of coal.
3. **Compare and contrast** detrital and chemical sedimentary rock.
4. **List** chemical sedimentary rocks that are essential to your health or that are used to make life more convenient. How is each used?
5. **Think Critically** Explain how pieces of granite and slate could both be found in the same conglomerate. How would the granite and slate pieces be held together?

### Applying Math

6. **Calculate Ratios** Use information in **Table 2** to estimate how many times larger the largest grains of silt and sand are compared to the largest clay grains.

 Science online in7.msscience.com/self_check_quiz

## section ④ review

1. weathered rock and mineral material
2. Compaction concentrates transformed plant matter to form an important energy resource.
3. Detrital rocks are made from the pieces of weathered rocks; chemical rocks form as dissolved minerals

come out of solution or as liquid evaporates.
4. Possible answers: salt: preservation, seasoning, manufacture of glass, paper and soap; limestone: material for buildings, roads, and statues
5. Granite and slate could be weathered in separate locations, then

transported and deposited in the same location. Mineral cements would hold grains together.
6. The largest grains of silt are about 16 times larger than clay, and the largest grains of sand about 500 times larger than clay.

**BENCH TESTED**

# Sedimentary Rocks

Sedimentary rocks are formed by compaction and cementation of sediment. Because sediment is found in all shapes and sizes, do you think these characteristics could be used to classify detrital sedimentary rocks? Sedimentary rocks also can be classified as chemical or organic.

## ▶ Real-World Question

**Purpose** Students use various characteristics to classify sedimentary rocks. [L2] [ELL]

[COOP LEARN] [IS] **Interpersonal**

**Process Skills** observe and infer, communicate, classify, form operational definitions, interpret qualitative data, compare and contrast

**Time Required** 45 minutes

## ▶ Procedure

**Safety Precautions** Have students wear goggles, aprons, and rubber gloves when handling acid in the lab. **WARNING:** *When mixing concentrated acid and water, always add the acid to the water (never add water to acid). Mix in a well-ventilated area.*

**Teaching Strategies**

- Suitable rocks include: fossil-rich limestone, rock salt, shale, siltstone, sandstone, and conglomerate.

- Dilute (5%) HCl can be made by mixing 1 part concentrated HCl with 19 parts tap water.

- Make several rock and mineral identification books available in class. The books should identify the characteristics of rocks that students encounter in class.

### Goals

- **Observe** sedimentary rock characteristics.
- **Compare and contrast** sedimentary rock textures.
- **Classify** sedimentary rocks as detrital, chemical, or organic.

### Materials

unknown sedimentary rock samples
marking pen
5% hydrochloric acid (HCl) solution
dropper
paper towels
water
magnifying lens
metric ruler

### Safety Precautions

**WARNING:** *HCl is an acid and can cause burns. Wear goggles and a lab apron. Rinse spills with water and wash hands afterward.*

## ▶ Real-World Question

How are rock characteristics used to classify sedimentary rocks as detrital, chemical, or organic?

## ▶ Procedure

1. **Make** a Sedimentary Rock Samples chart in your Science Journal similar to the one shown on the next page.

2. **Determine** the sizes of sediments in each sample, using a magnifying lens and a metric ruler. Using **Table 2,** classify any grains of sediment in the rocks as gravel, sand, silt, or clay. In general, the sediment is silt if it is gritty and just barely visible, and clay if it is smooth and if individual grains are not visible.

3. **Place** a few drops of 5% HCl solution on each rock sample. Bubbling on a rock indicates the presence of calcite.

4. **Examine** each sample for fossils and describe any that are present.

5. **Determine** whether each sample has a granular or nongranular texture.

## Alternative Inquiry Lab

**Classification System** To make this Lab an Inquiry Lab, ask students to devise a classification system of their own to categorize a second set of unknown sedimentary rocks. Then they should use their own systems to help them identify the rocks. Have them critique their classification methods according to how helpful they were in arriving at correct identifications. [L3]

## Science Journal

**Emphasizing Safety** In preparation for this lab exercise, demonstrate how to check samples for reaction with HCl. Be sure to wear goggles and an apron. Ask students to write a description of the reaction in their Science Journals. Also, have students explain the need for wearing goggles and an apron while performing this activity. [L2] [ELL] [IS] **Linguistic**

### Sedimentary Rock Samples

| Sample | Observations | Minerals or Fossils Present | Sediment Size | Detrital, Chemical, or Organic | Rock Name |
|--------|-------------|----------------------------|---------------|-------------------------------|-----------|
| A | fizzes in acid | calcite, fossils | varies | organic | fossil-rich limestone |
| B | feels gritty | quartz, feldspar | sand | detrital | sandstone |
| C | breaks in layers | kaolinite, quartz | clay | detrital | shale |
| D | sediment easily seen | pebbles of any rock or mineral | pebble and sand | detrital | shale |
| E | soft | halite | not grainy | chemical | rock salt |

## Analyze Your Data

1. **Classify** your samples as detrital, chemical, or organic.
2. **Identify** each rock sample.

## Conclude and Apply

1. **Explain** why you tested the rocks with acid. What minerals react with acid?
2. **Compare and contrast** sedimentary rocks that have a granular texture with sedimentary rocks that have a nongranular texture.

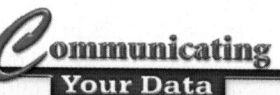

**Communicating Your Data**

**Compare** your conclusions with those of other students in your class. **For more help, refer to the** Science Skill Handbook.

LAB **553**

---

## Analyze Your Data

**Expected Outcome** Students will identify the rock samples based on characteristics such as hardness, texture, layering, size and feel of grains, and reaction to acid. They also will classify them as detrital, chemical, or organic.

**Error Analysis** Rocks could be misclassified if students were not able to correctly identify grain size or the relative hardness of samples, or if they had trouble getting the samples to react in the presence of acid. Some carbonates must be powdered before they readily react with acid.

### Answers to Questions

1. Classifications will vary according to available samples. As a general rule, detrital specimens have a granular, or grainy texture, organic specimens contain fossils or other remains of organisms, and chemical specimens often are not grainy and contain primarily one mineral such as limestone (calcite), rock salt (halite) and rock gypsum (gypsum).
2. Check students' identifications by comparing their observations to text and photos in a rock and mineral field guide.

## Conclude and Apply

1. to determine whether calcite was present; carbonates
2. Rocks of both textures form from sedimentary processes. Rocks with a granular, or clastic texture are made of pieces of other rocks, minerals, and/or shells. Rocks with a nongranular texture are formed by chemical or organic means.

---

### ☑ Assessment

**Performance** Provide students with large samples of unidentified rocks. Ask them to determine whether the rocks are sedimentary, and if so, whether they are detrital, chemical, or organic. Use **Performance Assessment in the Science Classroom,** p. 89.

**Communicating Your Data**

Encourage students to use a spreadsheet program to display the characteristics of sedimentary rock samples used in this activity.

# TIME › SCIENCE AND Society

## Content Background

According to Anangu, Earth's surface once was featureless. Places like Uluru did not exist until ancestral beings—in the form of people, plants, and animals—started to travel across the land. As they traveled from one area to another, these ancestral beings formed the features of the landscape. The travels and activities of the ancestral beings linked places throughout the country by iwara (paths or tracks). Iwara often link places separated by hundreds of kilometers. Uluru represents one meeting point in a network of such ancestral tracks.

Anangu knowledge of their land is based on Tjukurpa, or Dream Time. This knowledge is passed on through ceremony, song, dance, and art. The four major elements of the Tjukurpa for Uluru are Kuniya (woma python), Liru (poisonous snake), Kurpany (monster dog-like creature), and Mala (hare-wallaby). These beings and the stories associated with them connect Anangu with the land around them. To the Anangu, the huge grooves in rocks of Uluru were made by Kuniya as she came and went on her search for food.

## Discussion

**Tourism** What are the advantages and disadvantages to the Anangu of having tourists visit Uluru? Possible answer: advantages—financial rewards, opportunity to explain their beliefs to tourists; disadvantages—tourists climbing their sacred rock; tourists not respecting their beliefs and traditions.

# Australia's controversial rock star

## One of the most famous rocks in the world is causing serious problems for Australians

Uluru (yew LEW rew), also known as Ayers Rock, is one of the most popular tourist destinations in Australia. This sandstone skyscraper is more than 8 km around, over 300 m high, and extends as much as 4.8 km below the surface. One writer describes it as an iceberg in the desert. Geologists hypothesize that the mighty Uluru rock began forming 550 million years ago during Precambrian time. That's when large mountain ranges started to form in Central Australia.

For more than 25,000 years, this geological wonder has played an important role in the lives of the Aboriginal peoples, the Anangu (a NA noo). These native Australians are the original owners of the rock and have spiritual explanations for its many caves, holes, and scars.

### Tourists Take Over

In the 1980s, some 100,000 tourists visited—and many climbed—Uluru. In 2000, the rock attracted about 400,000 tourists. The Anangu take offense at anyone climbing their sacred rock. However, if climbing the rock were outlawed, tourism would be seriously hurt. That would mean less income for Australians.

To respect the Anangu's wishes, the Australian government returned Ayers Rock to the Anangu

Athlete Nova Benis-Kneebone had the honor of receiving the Olympic torch near the sacred Uluru and carried it partway to the Olympic stadium.

in 1985 and agreed to call it by its traditional name. The Anangu leased back the rock to the Australian government until the year 2084, when its management will return to the Anangu. Until then, the Anangu will collect 25 percent of the money people pay to visit the rock.

The Aboriginal people encourage tourists to respect their beliefs. They offer a walking tour around the rock, and they show videos about Aboriginal traditions. The Anangu sell T-shirts that say "I *didn't* climb Uluru." They hope visitors to Uluru will wear the T-shirt with pride and respect.

**Write** Research a natural landmark or large natural land or water formation in your area. What is the geology behind it? When was it formed? How was it formed? Write a folktale that explains its formation. Share your folktale with the class.

Science Online

For more information, visit in7.msscience.com/time

**Write** Have students examine physical maps of your state to locate natural landforms and water formations. After a site is selected, have students research the geology of the formation to answer the questions in the student text before writing their folktales. Before sharing their folktales, have students explain the formation's geologic history to the class. L2

## Resources for Teachers and Students

*A Natural History of Australia*, by Tim M. Berra, Academic Press, 1998

*Australian Dreaming: 40,000 Years of Aboriginal History*, edited by Jennifer Isaacs, Lansdowne Press, 1980

## Reviewing Main Ideas

### Section 1 The Rock Cycle

1. A rock is a mixture of one or more minerals, rock fragments, organic matter, or volcanic glass.

2. The rock cycle includes all processes by which rocks form.

### Section 2 Igneous Rocks

1. Magma and lava are molten materials that harden to form igneous rocks.

2. Intrusive igneous rocks form when magma cools slowly below Earth's surface. Extrusive igneous rocks form when lava cools rapidly at the surface.

3. The compositions of most igneous rocks range from granitic to andesitic to basaltic.

### Section 3 Metamorphic Rocks

1. Heat, pressure, and fluids can cause metamorphic rocks to form.

2. Slate and gneiss are examples of foliated metamorphic rocks. Quartzite and marble are examples of nonfoliated metamorphic rocks.

### Section 4 Sedimentary Rocks

1. Detrital sedimentary rocks form when fragments of rocks and minerals are compacted and cemented together.

2. Chemical sedimentary rocks come out of solution or are left behind by evaporation.

3. Organic sedimentary rocks contain the remains of once-living organisms.

## Reviewing Main Ideas

Summary statements can be used by students to review the major concepts of the chapter.

## Visualizing Main Ideas

See student page.

**Science** nline

**Visit** in7.msscience.com
/self_check_quiz
/interactive_tutor
/vocabulary_puzzlemaker
/chapter_review
/standards_review

### Assessment Transparency

For additional assessment questions, use the *Assessment Transparency* located in the transparency book.

## Visualizing Main Ideas

*Copy and complete the following concept map on rocks. Use the following terms:* organic, metamorphic, foliated, extrusive, igneous, *and* chemical.

## Using Vocabulary

1. Foliated metamorphic rocks are layered; nonfoliated metamorphic rocks are not layered.

2. Compaction is the pressing of mineral grains together during the formation of sedimentary rock; cementation is the gluing of grains together by dissolved mineral matter coming out of solution.

3. Sediment is weathered pieces of solid Earth materials; lava is molten rock material that reaches Earth's surface through volcanic activity.

4. Extrusive rock forms above Earth's surface; intrusive rock forms below Earth's surface.

5. A rock is a mixture of minerals, volcanic glass, organic matter, or other materials; the rock cycle describes how one type of rock can change into another.

6. Igneous rock forms when magma or lava solidifies; sedimentary rock forms from compaction and cementation of sediment or when minerals form from solution; metamorphic rock forms when any type of rock is changed by heat, pressure, or fluids inside Earth.

7. Sediment consists of grains of weathered and eroded rock; sedimentary rock is formed by the compaction and cementation of sediment or when minerals form from solution.

8. Lava is molten rock that has reached Earth's surface; igneous rock forms from magma or lava that has cooled and solidified.

9. Rock is a mixture of minerals, volcanic glass, organic matter, or other materials; sediment is composed of weathered pieces of rock and other Earth materials.

10. Basaltic magma is low in silica and high in magnesium and iron compared to granitic magma.

## Checking Concepts

| 11. D | 14. C | 17. C |
|-------|-------|-------|
| 12. D | 15. D | 18. B |
| 13. A | 16. B | 19. A |

**556  CHAPTER REVIEW**

## Using Vocabulary

*Explain the difference between the vocabulary words in each of the following sets.*

1. foliated—nonfoliated

2. cementation—compaction

3. sediment—lava

4. extrusive—intrusive

5. rock—rock cycle

6. metamorphic rock—igneous rock—sedimentary rock

7. sediment—sedimentary rock

8. lava—igneous rock

9. rock—sediment

10. basaltic—granitic

## Checking Concepts

*Choose the word or phrase that best answers the question.*

11. Why does magma tend to rise toward Earth's surface?
    A) It is more dense than surrounding rocks.
    B) It is more massive than surrounding rocks.
    C) It is cooler than surrounding rocks.
    D) It is less dense than surrounding rocks.

12. During metamorphism of granite into gneiss, what happens to minerals?
    A) They partly melt.
    B) They become new sediments.
    C) They grow smaller.
    D) They align into layers.

13. Which rock has large mineral grains?
    A) granite        C) obsidian
    B) basalt         D) pumice

14. Which type of rock is shown in this photo?
    A) foliated
    B) nonfoliated
    C) intrusive
    D) extrusive

15. What do igneous rocks form from?
    A) sediments      C) gravel
    B) mud            D) magma

16. What sedimentary rock is made of large, angular pieces of sediments?
    A) conglomerate   C) limestone
    B) breccia        D) chalk

17. Which of the following is an example of a detrital sedimentary rock?
    A) limestone      C) breccia
    B) evaporite      D) chalk

18. What is molten material at Earth's surface called?
    A) limestone      C) breccia
    B) lava           D) granite

19. Which of these is an organic sedimentary rock?
    A) coquina        C) rock salt
    B) sandstone      D) conglomerate

Science online in7.msscience.com/vocabulary_puzzlemaker

**Use the ExamView® Pro Testmaker CD-ROM to:**
- create multiple versions of tests
- create modified tests with one mouse click for inclusion students
- edit existing questions and add your own questions
- build tests aligned with state standards using built-in State Curriculum Tags
- change English tests to Spanish with one mouse click and vice versa

## Thinking Critically

**20. Infer** Granite, pumice, and scoria are igneous rocks. Why doesn't granite have airholes like the other two?

**21. Infer** why marble rarely contains fossils.

**22. Predict** Would you expect quartzite or sandstone to break more easily? Explain your answer.

**23. Compare and contrast** basaltic and granitic magmas.

**24. Form Hypotheses** A geologist was studying rocks in a mountain range. She found a layer of sedimentary rock that had formed in the ocean. Hypothesize how this could happen.

**25. Concept Map** Copy and complete the concept map shown below. Use the following terms and phrases: *magma, sediments, igneous rock, sedimentary rock, metamorphic rock*. Add and label any missing arrows.

## Performance Activities

**26. Poster** Collect a group of rocks. Make a poster that shows the classifications of rocks, and glue your rocks to the poster under the proper headings. Describe your rocks and explain where you found them.

## Applying Math

**27. Grain Size** Assume that the conglomerate shown on the second page of the "Sedimentary Rocks" lab is one-half of its actual size. Determine the average length of the gravel in the rock.

**28. Plant Matter** Suppose that a 4-m layer of plant matter was compacted to form a coal layer 1 m thick. By what percent has the thickness of organic material been reduced?

**Use the graph below to answer questions 29 and 30.**

**29. Melting Granite** Determine the melting temperature of a water-rich granite at a pressure of 0.2 GPa.

**Pressure conversions:**
1 GPa, or gigapascal, = 10,000 bars
1 bar = 0.9869 atmospheres

**30. Melting Pressure** At about what pressure will a water-rich granite melt at 680°C?

## Thinking Critically

**20.** Because granite is an intrusive rock. Pumice and scoria form above ground where escaping gases can form bubbles in lava.

**21.** Marble is metamorphic. The processes that form it often destroy organic remains.

**22.** Sandstone; quartz grains in sandstone are held together by cement, whereas quartz grains in quartzite have grown in size and have become interlocking.

**23.** Both are molten materials that form deep within Earth. Basaltic magma is fluid and is rich in iron and magnesium. Granitic magma is more viscous and is rich in silica compared with basaltic magma.

**24.** Sample hypothesis: sedimentary layer forms in ocean basin; more sediments accumulate; mountain building processes uplift sedimentary layers originally formed in ocean.

**25.** See student page.

## Performance Activities

**26.** Posters should classify rocks as igneous, sedimentary, or metamorphic, and list their names. Use **Performance Assessment in the Science Classroom**, p. 145.

## Applying Math

### Indiana Math Standards
7.2.1, 7.2.2, 7.6.1

**27.** approximately 9 mm. Accept reasonable answers.

**28.** 75 percent

**29.** approximately 720 °C

**30.** approximately 0.3 GPa

## ☑ Assessment ▶ Resources

**📁 Reproducible Masters**

**Chapter *Fast File* Resources**
Chapter Review, pp. 35–36
Chapter Tests, pp. 37–40
Assessment Transparency Activity, p. 49

**Glencoe Science Web site**
Chapter Review Test
IN Standards Review

**Glencoe Technology**
- Assessment Transparency
- Exam*View*® Pro Testmaker
- MindJogger Videoquiz
- Interactive Chalkboard

chapter **18** Indiana

**Answer Sheet** A practice answer sheet can be found at in7.msscience.com/answer_sheet.

**S A M P L E**

## Part 1 Multiple Choice

1. D
2. A
3. A
4. C
5. B
6. B

## Part 2 Critical Response

7. Chemical sedimentary rocks, like the cements of detrital sedimentary rocks, form when minerals precipitate from solution.

8. The loose sediment can be buried, compacted, and/or cemented to become sediimentary rock. During compaction, pressure from the upper layers causes small sediments to become tightly packed and stick together, forming solid rock. If sediments are large, dissolved minerals can precipitate in the pore spaces, acting as natural cements, and hold the sediments together to become sedimentary rock.

 The assessed Indiana standard appears above the question.

*Record your answers on the answer sheet provided by your teacher or on a sheet of paper.*

### Part 1 Multiple Choice

**7.3.10**

1. The illustration below shows layers of sedimentary rock.

These layers of rock were not disturbed after they were deposited. Which layer was deposited first?

A layer L

B layer Z

C layer A

D layer M

**7.3.8**

2. During which process do minerals precipitate in the spaces between sediment grains?

A cementation

B compaction

C conglomerate

D weathering

**7.3.8**

3. Which rock consists mostly of pieces of seashell?

A coquina

B granite

C pumice

D sandstone

The illustration below shows processes of the rock cycle.

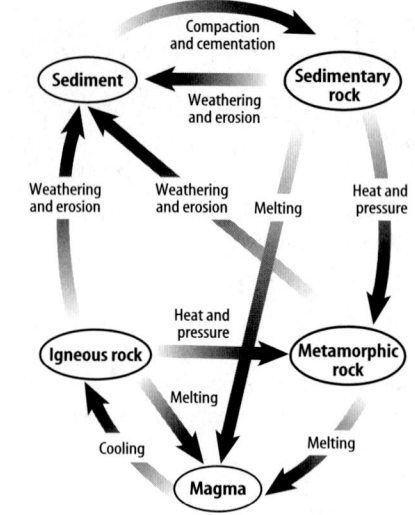

4. Which process in the rock cycle causes magma to form?

A cooling

B erosion

C melting

D weathering

### Test-Taking Tip

**Careful Reading** Read each question carefully for full understanding.

9. Pressure increases with depth because rocks deeper in Earth have more overburden above them. Higher pressure can cause metamorphism of rocks to occur. High pressures also can inhibit melting, which is why much of Earth's mantle is solid despite the high temperatures.

10. Igneous rocks are classified accordiing to composition and crystal size.

11. Sample hypothesis: Tectonic forces caused the older layer to be thrust over the younger layer.

The graph below shows how temperature changes with depth beneath the continents.

### Temperature Beneath the Continents

**5.** About how deep below a continent does the temperature reach 1000°C?

**A** 100 km

**B** 120 km

**C** 140 km

**D** 160 km

**6.** Using the graph above, what is the approximate temperature at a depth of about 60 km beneath a continent?

**A** 500°C

**B** 750°C

**C** 1000°C

**D** 1250°C

---

**Part 2   Critical Response**

`7.3.8`

**7.** How is the formation of chemical sedimentary rocks similar to the formation of cement in detrital sedimentary rocks?

`7.3.8`

**8.** Explain how loose sediment can become sedimentary rock. Describe two processes that hold sediments together when forming sedimentary rock.

**9.** Why does pressure increase with depth in Earth? How does higher pressure affect rocks?

**10.** The table below shows an igneous rock classification.

| Magma Type | Basaltic | Andesitic | Granitic |
|---|---|---|---|
| **Intrusive** | Gabbro | Diorite | Granite |
| **Extrusive** | Basalt or scoria | Andesite | Rhyolite, pumice, or obsidian |

Explain how igneous rocks are classified.

`7.3.10`

**11.** A geologist found a sequence of rocks in which 200-million-year-old shales were on top of 100-million-year-old sandstones. Hypothesize how this could happen.

---

## Rubrics

The following rubric is a sample scoring device for critical response questions.

### Critical Response

| Points | Description |
|---|---|
| 4 | The student demonstrates a thorough understanding of the science of the task. The response may contain minor flaws that do not detract from the demonstration of a thorough understanding. |
| 3 | The student demonstrates an understanding of the science of the task. The response is essentially correct and demonstrates an essential but less than thorough understanding of the science. |
| 2 | The student demonstrates only a partial understanding of the science of the task. Although the student may have used the correct approach to a solution or may have provided a correct solution, the work lacks an essential understanding of the underlying science concepts. |
| 1 | The student demonstrates a very limited understanding of the science of the task. The response is incomplete and exhibits many flaws. |
| 0 | The student provides a completely incorrect solution or no response at all. |

---

unit 6

# Processes that Shape Earth

## Unit Contents

**WebQuest** *Fossils of Antarctica* provides a list of questions to guide students as they research literature on fossils found in Antarctica. The young researchers will learn what kinds of fossils are present and what those fossils indicate about the climate and location of Antarctica millions of years ago. Students will form their own opinions to support or disprove Alfred Wegener's theory of plate tectonics and complete the 10-question summary.

# How Are Rivers & Writing Connected?

560

## PROJECT CRISS℠

### Study Skills

**Summarize** Using one-sentence summary frames is an effective method for helping students to learn how to summarize. Students can use the frame, "_____ happens because…," including factors—such as erosion—that change the Earth's surface as the sentence's subject. The causes of erosion are described in the second half of the sentence.

R ivers change the surface of Earth by moving material from place to place. In the process, rivers help build up fertile soil. Thousands of years ago, the Egyptian civilization took root in the extremely fertile soil along the Nile River (seen here as it looks today). Agriculture flourished, society grew more complex, and people needed a way to keep track of everything from harvests to history. Around 3100 B.C., the Egyptians developed one of the first systems of writing—a type of picture writing called hieroglyphics (left). Later peoples probably borrowed from the Egyptian system to create their own writing systems. By about 1000 B.C., the Phoenicians had developed an alphabet, with symbols that stood for individual sounds. The Phoenician alphabet was adopted and modified by other peoples, eventually giving rise to the alphabet we use today.

## unit projects

The assessed Indiana objective appears in blue.

To find project ideas and resources, visit **in7.msscience.com/unit_project**.

Projects include:
- **History** Discover the characteristics of a variety of landforms and then design a tourist brochure about your specific feature. **7.3.7**
- **Career** Explore a geology-related career, learn the tools of the trade, and present your career at a class job fair. **7.1.2, 7.1.7, 7.1.9**
- **Model** Create a picture book with adventurous characters to demonstrate your new knowledge of Earth's changing surface. **7.7.2**
- **WebQuest** Investigate the *Fossils of Antarctica* and what they could tell us about its ancient climate and location on Earth. **7.1.2, 7.1.4, 7.1.5, 7.1.6, 7.1.7, 7.1.10**

## unit projects

**History** Have students research a particular type of land form: cave, canyon, cliffs, islands, mountains, plains, or plateaus. Ask the students to focus on the location of their land form, how it developed, the forces of nature that act on it, why they feel their landform is unique, and what is being done to preserve it. Students may design a tourist brochure about their landform and some of the more famous examples around the world.

**Career** Have students explore a career related to geology. Students should brainstorm a set of questions that include training/schooling required, location, expected income, availability of jobs, or even clothing to wear on the job. Encourage students to investigate creative job opportunities, such as soil analyst, meteorologist, climatologist, hydrologist, or bioengineer designing new crops that can grow in desert conditions. Students can present their knowledge at a mock job fair.

**Model** Ask students to review new vocabulary and concepts from this unit and prepare an adventurous picture/story book that will demonstrate their understanding of the information presented in this unit. Story books should contain a given number of new vocabulary (25–40 words suggested), correctly used, effective illustrations, and characters in a simple plot line.

**Additional Resources** For more information, resources, and assessment rubrics, visit in7.msscience.com/unit_project.

---

## NATIONAL GEOGRAPHIC  How Are Rivers & Writing Connected?

An important factor in the history of civilization was the development of agriculture. The ability to cultivate and harvest crops allowed the development of sedentary, and much larger, populations capable of almost unlimited growth. Certain agricultural practices have led to an increased rate of topsoil erosion, which can in turn result in decreased harvests and food shortages. The water requirements of large urban centers have necessitated the damming of rivers and streams to produce large reservoirs. The long-term effects of this practice on local climate conditions are still unclear.

| Section/Objectives | Standards | | Labs/Features |
|---|---|---|---|
| | **National** | **State/Local** | |
| **Chapter Opener** | See pp. 16T–17T for a Key to Standards. | Detailed standards begin on page IN8. | **Launch Lab:** Model Earth's Interior, p. 563 **Foldables,** p. 563 |
| **Section 1 Earth's Moving Plates** ⏱ 4 sessions 📦 2 blocks 1. **Describe** how Earth's interior is divided into layers. 2. **Explain** how plates of Earth's lithosphere move. 3. **Discuss** why Earth's plates move. | National Content Standards: UCP.1, UCP.2, UCP.3, UCP.5, A.1, A.2, B.2, B.3, D.1, D.2 | Indiana Standards: 7.1.1, 7.1.4, 7.3.4, 7.3.7, 7.3.18 | **Integrate Chemistry,** p. 566 **Science Online,** p. 569 **Visualizing Rift Valleys,** p. 570 **MiniLAB:** Modeling Tension and Compression, p. 571 **Lab:** Earth's Moving Plates, p. 574 |
| **Section 2 Uplift of Earth's Crust** ⏱ 4 sessions 📦 2 blocks 4. **Describe** how Earth's mountains form and erode. 5. **Compare** types of mountains. 6. **Identify** the forces that shape Earth's mountains. | National Content Standards: UCP.1, UCP.2, UCP.3, UCP.5, A.1, A.2, B.2, B.3, D.1, D.2 | Indiana Standards: 7.2.7, 7.3.4, 7.3.7 | **MiniLAB:** Modeling Mountains, p. 577 **Science Online,** p. 578 **Integrate Language Arts,** p. 580 **Applying Science:** How can glaciers cause land to rise?, p. 580 **Lab:** Isostasy, p. 582 **Science Stats:** Mountains, p. 584 |

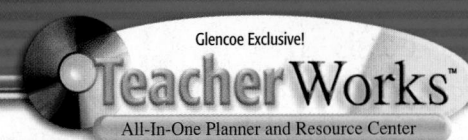

Glencoe Exclusive!
**TeacherWorks™**
All-In-One Planner and Resource Center

| Lab Materials | Reproducible Resources | Section Assessment | Technology |
|---|---|---|---|
| **Launch Lab:** 4 pieces of different-colored clay, plastic knife | **Chapter** *FAST FILE* **Resources**<br>Foldables Worksheet, p. 19<br>Note-taking Worksheets, pp. 33–34 | GLENCOE'S<br>**ASSESSMENT**<br>ADVANTAGE | **Teacher Works** includes:<br>• Interactive Teacher Edition<br>• Lesson Planner with calendar<br>• Access to all program blacklines<br>• Correlations to standards<br>• Web links |
| **MiniLAB:** 2 bars of taffy<br>**Lab:** 1-L beakers (2), food coloring, aluminum foil, pencil, rubber band, water, 2-cm paper squares (3), small clear-plastic cup<br><br>*Need materials?*<br>Contact Science Kit at 1-800-828-7777 or www.sciencekit.com on the Internet. | **Chapter** *FAST FILE* **Resources**<br>Transparency Activity, p. 44<br>MiniLAB, p. 3<br>Enrichment, p. 31<br>Reinforcement, p. 29<br>Directed Reading, p. 22<br>Lab Worksheet, pp. 5–6<br>Lab Activity, pp. 9–13<br>Transparency Activity, pp. 47–48<br>**Cultural Diversity,** p. 47<br>**Earth Science Critical Thinking/ Problem Solving,** pp. 8, 9, 10<br>**Reading and Writing Skill Activities,** p. 21 | **Portfolio**<br>Differentiated Instruction, p. 565<br>**Performance**<br>MiniLAB, p. 571<br>Applying Skills, p. 573<br>**Content**<br>Section Review, p. 573 | Section Focus Transparency<br>Teaching Transparency<br>Guided Reading Audio Program<br>Interactive Chalkboard CD-ROM |
| **MiniLAB:** clay, plastic knife, ball<br>**Lab:** 5-cm × 5-cm × 2-cm wooden blocks (3), 10-cm × 35-cm × 15-cm clear-plastic storage box or other bin, water, permanent marker, ruler | **Chapter** *FAST FILE* **Resources**<br>Transparency Activity, p. 45<br>MiniLAB, p. 4<br>Enrichment, p. 32<br>Reinforcement, p. 30<br>Directed Reading, pp. 23, 24<br>Lab Worksheet, pp. 7–8<br>Lab Activity, pp. 15–18<br>**Lab Management and Safety,** p. 50<br>**Home and Community Involvement,** p. 23<br>**Performance Assessment in the Science Classroom,** p. 39<br>**Cultural Diversity,** p. 27<br>**Earth Science Critical Thinking/ Problem Solving,** p. 1 | **Portfolio**<br>Science Journal, p. 576<br>**Performance**<br>MiniLAB, p. 577<br>Applying Science, p. 580<br>Applying Skills, p. 581<br>**Content**<br>Section Review, p. 581 | Section Focus Transparency<br>Virtual Labs CD-ROM<br>Guided Reading Audio Program<br>Interactive Chalkboard CD-ROM<br>Video Lab |

GLENCOE'S
**ASSESSMENT**
ADVANTAGE

## End of Chapter Assessment

| Blackline Masters | Technology | Professional Series |
|---|---|---|
| **Chapter** *FAST FILE* **Resources**<br>Chapter Review, pp. 37–38<br>Chapter Tests, pp. 39–42<br>**Mastering the Grade 7 Indiana Science Standards** | MindJogger Videoquiz<br>IN Test Prep and Practice Exam*View*®<br>Exam*View*® Pro Testmaker<br>TeacherWorks CD-ROM<br>Interactive Chalkboard CD-ROM | **Performance Assessment in the Science Classroom (PASC)** |

# Transparencies

## Section Focus

**Section 1 Focus Transparency** Not a Place to Drop Your Keys

Have you ever thought about the deepest place on Earth? It's the Mariana Trench in the western Pacific Ocean. The trench is so deep, you'd have to stack a medium-sized mountain *on top of* Mount Everest just to reach the surface. Try to locate the Mariana Trench on this map of the Pacific Ocean floor.

1. Describe some features of the ocean floor shown on this map.
2. What continental features are similar to the features of the ocean floor?

L2

**Section 2 Focus Transparency** Mythological Heights

Mount Olympus, the highest mountain in Greece, was once thought to be the home of Zeus, Hera, Hermes, Aphrodite and all the other gods and goddesses of Greek mythology. Formed when sections of Earth's crust pressed together, Olympus is often shrouded in clouds. The ancient Greeks believed that these clouds hid the doorway to the home of the gods.

1. Do you think all mountains are formed in the same way? Explain.
2. What does it mean for an area to be geologically active?
3. There's a major fault line near Greece. Would you predict that the area might experience earthquakes? Why or why not?

L2

This is a representation of key blackline masters available in the Teacher Classroom Resources. See Resource Manager boxes within the chapter for additional information.

## Key to Teaching Strategies

The following designations will help you decide which activities are appropriate for your students.

**L1** Level 1 activities should be appropriate for students with learning difficulties.

**L2** Level 2 activities should be within the ability range of all students.

**L3** Level 3 activities are designed for above-average students.

**ELL** ELL activities should be within the ability range of English Language Learners.

**COOP LEARN** Cooperative Learning activities are designed for small group work.

**LS** Multiple Learning Styles logos, as described on page 12T, are used throughout to indicate strategies that address different learning styles.

**P** These strategies represent student products that can be placed into a best-work portfolio.

**PBL** Problem-Based Learning activities apply real-world situations to learning.

## Assessment

**Assessment Transparency** Forces Shaping Earth

Directions: Carefully review the table and answer the following questions.

| Layers of Earth | Thickness in Earth | Thickness in scale model |
|---|---|---|
| Crust | 40 km | 0.8 mm |
| Mantle | 2660 km | 53 mm |
| Outer core | 2260 km | 45 mm |
| Inner core | 1300 km | ? |

1. According to the table, which layer has the greatest thickness?
   A crust
   B mantle
   C outer core
   D inner core

2. About how much thicker is the outer core than the inner core?
   F 960 km
   G 1600 km
   H 1950 km
   J 2250 km

3. A student wants to draw a scale model of the layers of Earth. She has already calculated the thickness in the scale model for the crust, mantle, and outer core. If everything remains the same, what will be the thickness of the inner core in the scale model?
   A 2.6 mm
   B 20 mm
   C 26 mm
   D 50 mm

L2

## Teaching

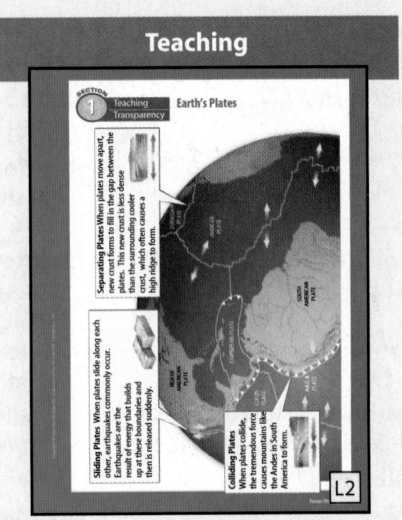

**Section 1 Teaching Transparency** Earth's Plates

**Separating Plates** When plates move apart, new crust forms to fill in the gap between the plates. This new crust is less dense than the surrounding cooler crust, which often causes a high ridge to form.

**Sliding Plates** When plates slide along each other, earthquakes commonly occur. Earthquakes are the result of energy that builds up at these boundaries and then is released suddenly.

**Colliding Plates** When plates collide, the tremendous force causes mountain ranges such as the Andes in South America to form.

L2

# Hands-on Activities

## Student Text Lab Worksheet

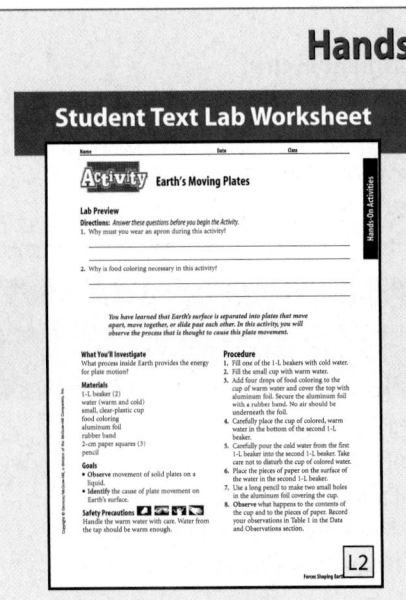

**Activity** Earth's Moving Plates

**Lab Preview**
Directions: Answer these questions before you begin the Activity.
1. Why must you wear an apron during this activity?

2. Why is food coloring necessary in this activity?

You have learned that Earth's surface is separated into plates that move apart, move together, or slide past each other. In this activity, you will observe the process that is thought to cause this plate movement.

**What You'll Investigate**
What process inside Earth provides the energy for plate motion?

**Materials**
1-L beaker (2)
water (warm and cold)
small, clear-plastic cup
food coloring
aluminum foil
rubber band
2-cm paper squares (3)
pencil

**Goals**
- Observe movement of solid plates on a liquid.
- Identify the cause of plate movement on Earth's surface.

**Safety Precautions**
Handle the warm water with care. Water from the tap should be warm enough.

**Procedure**
1. Fill one of the 1-L beakers with cold water.
2. Fill the small cup with warm water.
3. Add four drops of food coloring to the cup of warm water and cover the top with aluminum foil. Secure the aluminum foil with a rubber band. No air should be underneath the foil.
4. Carefully place the cup of colored, warm water in the bottom of the second 1-L beaker.
5. Carefully pour the cold water from the first 1-L beaker into the second 1-L beaker. Take care not to disturb the cup of colored water.
6. Place the pieces of paper on the surface of the water in the second 1-L beaker.
7. Use a long pencil to make two small holes in the aluminum foil covering the cup.
8. Observe what happens to the contents of the cup and to the pieces of paper. Record your observations in Table 1 in the Data and Observations section.

L2

## Laboratory Activities

**Laboratory Activity** Earth's Plates

Earth's lithosphere is divided into about 30 sections, or plates, that fit together like a puzzle. The plates extend below Earth's surface to a depth of about 100 km; each plate includes crust that is above sea level and crust that is below sea level. With a few exceptions, each continent is contained within one plate, but the plates do not necessarily resemble the continents in shape or size.

**Strategy**
You will construct a puzzle to show how Earth's lithosphere is broken into plates that fit together.

**Materials**
scissors
map showing Earth's plates (Figure 1)
1/2-in foam board
sharp knife or tool for cutting foam board
glue
map showing Earth's continents (Figure 2)
black marker
red marker

**Procedure**

**Part A**
1. Use the scissors to cut out each of the plates in Figure 1.
2. Trace the shape of each plate onto the foam board.
3. Cut out each piece of foam board and glue to the back of each paper plate piece. Allow the pieces to dry.
4. Try to fit the plates together as they were on the worksheet.

**Part B**
5. Cut out each of the continents in Figure 2.
6. Place them over the plate puzzle where you think they would go.
7. Use Figure 5 in the text to check the position of the plates and continents.
8. Use the black marker and Figure 5 in your text to label each of the plates.

**Part C**
9. Research earthquakes and volcanic eruptions in the last 10 years. On your plate puzzle, mark the location of each earthquake/eruption with a red dot.

L2

# Resource Manager

## Meeting Different Ability Levels

### Content Outline

L2

### Reinforcement

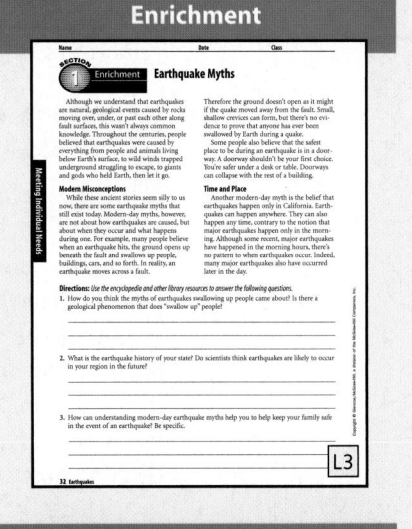

L2

### Enrichment

L3

### Directed Reading (English/Spanish)

L1

### Study Guide

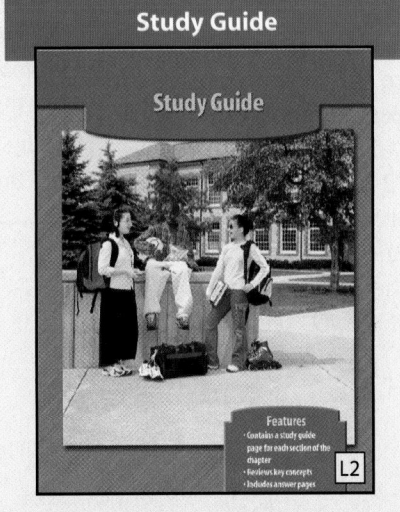

Study Guide

Features
• Contains a study guide page for each section of the chapter
• Reviews key concepts
• Includes answer pages

L2

### Reading Essentials

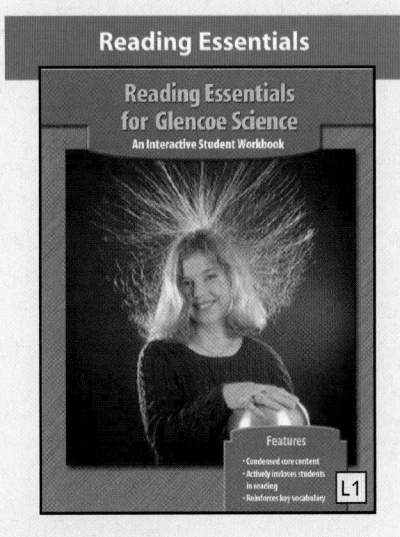

Reading Essentials for Glencoe Science
An Interactive Student Workbook

Features
• Condensed core content
• Actively involves students in reading
• Reinforces key vocabulary

L1

## Assessment

### Test Practice Workbook

L2

### Chapter Review

L2

### Chapter Tests

L2

# Science Content Background

### section 1 · Earth's Moving Plates

### Earth's Layers

An important study defining the boundary between two of Earth's layers was conducted by Yugoslavian seismologist Andrija Mohorovicic in 1909. He discovered that the velocity of seismic waves increased abruptly at about 50 km below the continents. This is the boundary that separates the crust from the mantle. It is called the Mohorovicic discontinuity.

### Divergent (Separating) Plate Boundaries

Although the mountain chains formed at divergent plate boundaries are the most extensive on Earth, they remain unseen, submerged beneath the water in the form of mid-oceanic ridges. Mid-oceanic ridges are 2 km to 3 km in elevation and form an interconnecting system of mountains 65,000 km long.

In some places the mid-oceanic ridge is elevated higher than sea level. Iceland, on the

## chapter content resources

**Internet Resources**
For additional content background, visit **in7.msscience.com** to:

- access your book online
- find references to related articles in popular science magazines
- access Web links with related content background
- access current events with science journal topics

**Print Resources**
*The New View of the Earth* by Seiya Uyeda, W.H. Freeman and Co, 1978
*Global Tectonics* by Philip Kearey & Frederick J. Vine, Blackwell Sciences LTD, 1996
*Physical Geology* by Carla W. Montgomery, Wm. C. Brown Publishers, 1987

*Y. Arthus-B./Peter Arnold, Inc.*

Mid-Atlantic Ridge, and Easter Island, on the East Pacific Rise, were formed as a result of hot spots located beneath the spreading ridges. The plume of magma has caused the ridges in these areas to rise above sea level.

Divergent boundaries can begin on continents. The East African rift valley is being created as eastern Africa separates from the rest of the continent. In the Red Sea the formation of new oceanic crust, a prelude to an oceanic ridge, has already begun.

## Convergent Plate Boundaries— Collision

Mountains formed from the collision of two continental plates are not usually volcanic. Because subduction is not complete and the continental crust becomes over-thickened as a result of the collision, the production and ascent of magma to the surface is arrested. Most major mountain ranges were formed as a result of continental plate collision. These include the older chains of the Appalachians in the U.S. and the Ural Mountains in Russia, and the more recently formed European Alps and the Himalayas. As India is still moving northward into the Eurasian Plate, the Himalayas are still a work in progress.

## section 2 Uplift of Earth's Crust
### Underwater Volcanic Mountains

While mapping seamounts in the Pacific, geologists discovered a chain of volcanic underwater mountains stretching from the Hawaiian Islands to Midway Island and on north to the Aleutian trench. Studies indicate that the structures farthest from Hawaii are the oldest. Their conclusion is that the chain was formed by a hot spot, which is in process of building the island of Hawaii.

E.R. Degginger/Photo Researcher, Inc. AFP/Corbis

## Isostasy

Icebergs have a ratio that relates the volume of the exposed portion of the iceberg to the volume of the submerged portion. The submerged portion of the iceberg is always nine times greater than the exposed portion. A similar ratio exists for continental mountains. The thickness of the crust beneath the mountain must be at least four and one half times the mountain's elevation. For example, Mount Everest's elevation is 8 km; therefore, the thickness of the crust beneath it must be at least 36 km. The thickness of the crust beneath Mount Everest is actually 80 km.

Mid-oceanic ridges are not in isostatic equilibrium; rather, they are uplifted by the buoyancy of the heated magma beneath them. The hotter and more extensive the magma, the higher the ridge. As seafloor spreading continues, however, basaltic crust moves away from its area of formation and its heat source, and it will lose height as it cools.

## Chapter Vocabulary

inner core, p. 565
outer core, p. 566
mantle, p. 566
crust, p. 566
lithosphere, p. 568
plate, p. 568
fault, p. 569
subduction, p. 571
fault-block mountain, p. 576
folded mountain, p. 577
upwarped mountain, p. 577
volcanic mountain, p. 578
isostasy, p. 580

**Science Journal** Accept all reasonable answers.

**with Image Bank**

### PowerPoint® Presentations

This CD-ROM is an editable Microsoft® PowerPoint® presentation that includes:

• a pre-made presentation for every chapter
• interactive graphics
• animations
• audio clips
• image bank
• all new section and chapter questions
• Standardized Test Practice
• transparencies
• pre-lab questions for all labs
• Foldables directions
• links to in7.msscience.com

---

**Academic Standard—3:** Students collect and organize data to identify relationships between physical objects, events, and processes. They use logical reasoning to question their own ideas as new information challenges their conceptions of the natural world.

**Also covers:** Academic Standards 1, 2 (Detailed standards begin on page IN8.)

# Forces Shaping Earth

### chapter preview

**sections**

**1** Earth's Moving Plates
 *Lab  Earth's Moving Plates*

**2** Uplift of Earth's Crust
 *Lab  Isostasy*

 *Virtual Lab  How do glaciers shape the land?*

### Young or Old Mountains?

These majestic, snow-capped mountains are in their infancy. It would take a few hundred million years of erosion for their sharp, jagged peaks to become smooth. In this chapter, you'll learn how the movement of plates formed these mountains and about other Earth forces that shape mountains.

**Science Journal** Use descriptive adjectives to describe these mountains in a short paragraph.

562

## Theme Connection

**Scale, Structure, and Energy** The structure of Earth's interior and the relative thicknesses of each layer involve the theme of scale and structure. Energy is involved in the movement of Earth's plates and in the production of forces necessary for mountain building.

### About the Photo

**Baby Mountains** These majestic, snow-capped mountains are in their infancy. It would take a few hundred million years of erosion for their sharp, jagged peaks to become smooth.

# Start-Up Activities

## Model Earth's Interior

Geologists know many things about the interior of Earth even though its center is over 6,000 km deep. Use modeling clay to make a model of Earth's interior.

1. Obtain four pieces of different-colored clay.

2. Roll one piece of clay into a ball. This clay represents the inner core.

3. Wrap another piece of clay around the first ball of clay, making an even bigger ball. This clay represents the outer core.

4. Repeat step 3 with the third piece of clay, which represents Earth's mantle. Wrap your model with a thin layer of the fourth piece of clay to represent the crust.

5. Use a plastic knife to cut the ball of clay in half.

6. **Think Critically** Make a sketch of your model and label each of Earth's layers.

**Earth's Interior and Surface**
Make the following cause and effect Foldable to help you understand the relationship between Earth's interior and surface.

**STEP 1** Collect 2 sheets of paper and layer them about 2.5 cm apart vertically. Keep the edges level.

**STEP 2** Fold up the bottom edges of the paper to form 4 equal tabs.

**STEP 3** Fold the papers and crease well to hold the tabs in place. Staple along the fold. Label each tab as shown.

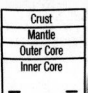

**Cause and Effect** As you read the chapter, record information about each layer and how it is related to the layer above it under the tabs.

Preview this chapter's content and activities at in7.msscience.com

563

## section 1

Also covers: 7.1.1, 7.1.4, 7.3.7, 7.3.18 (Detailed standards begin on page IN8.)

# Earth's Moving Plates

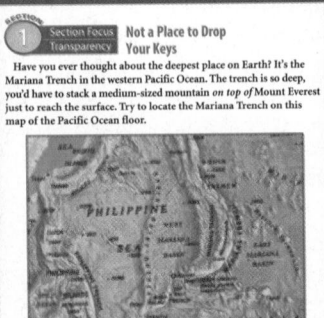
## as you read

**What You'll Learn**

■ **Describe** how Earth's interior is divided into layers.
■ **Explain** how plates of Earth's lithosphere move.
■ **Discuss** why Earth's plates move.

**Why It's Important**

Forces that cause Earth's plates to move apart, together, or past each other cause events that shape Earth's surface, such as mountain building, volcanoes, and earthquakes.

**Review Vocabulary**
**magma:** melted rock material found beneath Earth's surface

**New Vocabulary**
● inner core     ● lithosphere
● outer core     ● plate
● mantle          ● fault
● crust           ● subduction

**Figure 1** Waves carry energy across water just like seismic waves carry energy through Earth.

## Clues to Earth's Interior

If someone gives you a wrapped present, how could you figure out what was in it? You might hold it, shake it gently, or weigh it. You'd look for clues that could help you identify the contents of the box. Even though you can't see what's inside the package, these types of clues can help you figure out what it might be. Because you can't see what's inside, the observations you make are known as indirect observations.

Geologists do the same thing when they try to learn about Earth's interior. Although the best way to find out what's inside Earth might be to dig a tunnel to its center, that isn't possible. The deepest mines in the world only scratch Earth's surface. A tunnel would need to be more than 6,000 km deep to reach the center, so geologists must use indirect observations to gather clues about what Earth's interior is made of and how it is structured. This indirect evidence includes information learned by studying earthquakes and rocks that are exposed at Earth's surface.

 **INTEGRATE Physics**

**Waves** When you throw a rock into a calm puddle or pond, you observe waves like those shown in **Figure 1.** Waves are disturbances that carry energy through matter or space. When a rock hits water, waves carry some of the rock's kinetic energy, or energy of motion, away from where it hit the water. When an earthquake occurs, as shown in **Figure 2,** energy is carried through objects by waves. The speed of these waves depends on the density and nature of the material they are traveling through. For example, a wave travels faster in solid rock than it does in a liquid. By studying the speed of these waves and the paths they take, geologists uncover clues as to how the planet is put together. In fact, these waves, called seismic waves, speed up in some areas, slow down in other areas, and can be bent or stopped.

564

**Figure 2** As seismic waves travel across Earth's surface, the ground shakes and damage occurs.

**Rock Clues** Another clue to what's inside Earth comes in the form of certain rocks found in different places on Earth's surface. These rocks are made of material similar to what is thought to exist deep inside Earth. The rocks formed far below the surface. Forces inside Earth pushed them closer to the surface, where they eventually were exposed by erosion. The seismic clues and the rock clues suggest that Earth is made up of layers of different kinds of materials.

## Earth's Layers

Based on evidence from earthquake waves and exposed rocks, scientists have produced a model of Earth's interior. The model shows that Earth's interior has at least four distinct layers—the inner core, the outer core, the mantle, and the crust. Earth's structure is similar in some ways to the structure of a peach, shown in **Figure 3.** A peach has a thin skin covering the thick, juicy part that you eat. Under that is a large pit that surrounds a seed.

**Inner Core** The pit and seed are similar to Earth's core. Earth's core is divided into two distinct parts—one that is liquid and one that is solid. The innermost layer of Earth's interior is the solid **inner core.** This part of the core is dense and composed mostly of solid iron. When seismic waves produced by earthquakes reach this layer they speed up, indicating that the inner core is solid.

Conditions in the inner core are extreme compared to those at the surface. At about 5,000°C, the inner core is the hottest part of Earth. Also, because of the weight of the surrounding rock, the core is under tremendous pressure. Pressure, or the force pushing on an area, increases the deeper you go beneath Earth's surface. Pressure increases because more material is pushing toward Earth's center as a result of gravity. The inner core, at the center of Earth, experiences the greatest amount of pressure.

**Figure 3** The structure of Earth can be compared to a peach.
**Explain** *If the part of Earth that you live on is like the skin of the peach, what does that tell you about this layer of Earth?*

## Inquiry Lab

**A World Puzzle**

**Purpose** To see how the continents may have fit together at one point in Earth's history.

**Possible Materials** line map of the world—2 per student, scissors, construction paper

**Estimated Time** 1 class period

**Teaching Strategies**

- Students should study the world map and make initial guesses as to which continents may have fit together in the past.
- Instruct them to carefully cut out the continents and large masses from one of the maps.
- Students should assemble the pieces as if they were pieces. There are several possible ways to assemble them so encourage students to use the other map in the same fashion.
- Have students research Pangaea, Gondwanaland, and Laurasia to see how their puzzle matches that of early scientists.

**For additional inquiry activities, see** *Science Inquiry Labs.*

## Fun Fact

Originally, Earth's entire core was most likely liquid. As Earth cooled, the solid, inner core formed. Eventually the entire core will be solid.

**Caption Answer**

**Figure 3** It is the thinnest layer, just as the skin is the thinnest layer of a peach.

## Differentiated Instruction

**Challenge** Have students research how the P- and S- waves generated by earthquakes are affected by the different layers of Earth's interior. Have them create a model of the interior showing the behavior of each wave. L3 P

## Curriculum Connection

**Language Arts** Have students use a dictionary to look up *crust, mantle,* and *core.* Ask students to write a brief description in their Science Journals that explains why these terms are used to name parts of Earth's structure. *Crust* refers to any hard surface layer, *mantle* refers to anything that envelops or conceals, and *core* refers to the central part of anything. L2 LS

**Linguistic**

## Iron Core

**Iron Core** Support for this theory comes from the study of meteorites, which are considered to be representative samples of solar system material. Like Earth, they are composed of iron and other minerals; however, they contain a much higher percentage of iron than Earth's crust does. Earth's density increases with depth toward its center, so geologists assume denser substances such as iron must exist there.

**Research** Have students research how scientists determined the density of Earth's core. Does this density support or disprove the theory that Earth's core is made mostly of iron? Explain.

**Answer** The outer woody layer of the pit.

## Caption Answer

**Figure 4** earthquakes and exposure by erosion of rocks formed far below the surface

**Iron Core** Earth's crust is composed of about five percent iron. However, geologists theorize that Earth's core is composed mostly of iron. Research the theory that Earth's core is composed mostly of iron. Analyze, review, and critique the strengths and weaknesses of this theory using scientific evidence and information.

**Figure 4** Earth is made up of many layers.
**Identify** *geologic events that have allowed scientists to study Earth's interior.*

The lithosphere is composed of crust and uppermost mantle. The asthenosphere is a plasticlike layer upon which the plates of the lithosphere float and move.

**Outer Core** The **outer core** lies above the inner core and is thought to be composed mostly of molten metal. The outer core stops one type of seismic wave and slows down another. Because of this, scientists have concluded that the outer core is a liquid. The location of the outer core is similar to the location of the pit in the peach model. Even the wrinkled surface of the pit resembles the uneven nature of the boundary between Earth's outer core and its mantle as indicated by seismic studies.

**Reading Check** *What peach layer is similar to the outer core?*

**Mantle** The layer in Earth's interior above the outer core is the mantle. In the peach model, the mantle would be the juicy part of the peach that you would eat. The **mantle** is the largest layer of Earth's interior. Even though it's solid, the mantle flows slowly, similar to putty.

**Crust** Earth's outermost layer is the **crust.** In the model of the peach, this layer would be the fuzzy skin of the peach. Earth's crust is thin when compared to the other layers, though its thickness does vary. It is thinnest under the oceans and thickest through the continents. All features on Earth's surface are part of the crust.

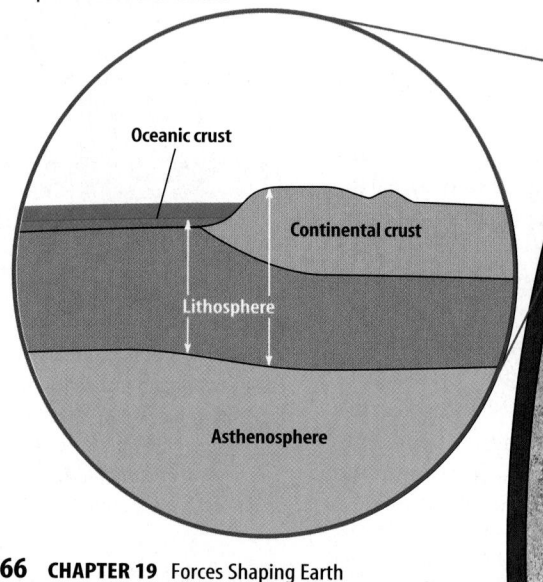

Oceanic crust
Continental crust
Lithosphere
Asthenosphere

**566** **CHAPTER 19** Forces Shaping Earth

---

## LAB DEMONSTRATION

**Purpose** to show how properties of an unknown substance can be discovered
**Materials** empty boxes with lids, tape, and several common items
**Preparation** While you are not looking, have a student select an item, place it in a box, and tape the box shut.

**Procedure** Shake the box, heft it, and slide the object around to show how an object's properties (mass, approximate size, probable shape, density) can be indirectly determined.
**Expected Outcome** Students can determine the properties of an unknown object without seeing the object.

**Assessment**

Have students make mystery boxes for each other. Discuss which properties are easy to determine, which are more difficult, and which are not able to be determined. Compare this to how scientists study Earth's interior.

## Earth's Structure

Although Earth's structure can be divided into four basic layers, it also can be divided into other layers based on physical properties that change with depth beneath the surface. **Figure 4** shows the structure of Earth and describes some of the properties of its layers. Density, temperature, and pressure are properties that are lowest in the crust and greatest in the inner core.

## Visual Learning

**Figure 4** Have students compare the Pressure versus Depth graph and the Temperature versus Depth graph. What statement can they make about these two factors as one goes deeper beneath Earth's surface? Both temperature and pressure increase with depth.

Crust

Mantle

**Distribution of Earth's Mass**

Inner core
2.5%

Outer core
30%

Crust
0.5%

Mantle
67%

Outer core

Inner core

**Temperature v. Depth**

Increasing temperature

Increasing depth

**Pressure v. Depth**

Increasing pressure

Increasing depth

567

## Differentiated Instruction

**Visually Impaired** Use modeling clay to construct a three-dimensional scale model of Earth's structure that separates into layers. Use balled-up aluminum foil for the core. Cover the model with paper to represent the crust. Help visually-impaired students remove each layer of the model and explain what each layer represents. Point out the relative thickness of each layer. L1
**ELL** **IS** **Kinesthetic**

**Earth's Crust** Students may think that plate tectonics results in motion of only Earth's continents. In fact, Earth's crust covers the entire planet, underlying even the oceans. Therefore, ocean plates are also in motion.

### ✔ Reading Check

**Answer** crust and upper part of mantle

### Quick Demo
**Plate Interactions**
**Materials** large clear bowl, water, thin sponge, scissors
**Estimated Time** 15 minutes
**Procedure** Half-fill a large bowl with tap water. Cut irregular shapes from a thin cleaning sponge. Randomly place four sections of the sponge on top of the water. Gently move the bowl back and forth in order to set the sponge sections in motion. Ask volunteers to describe their observations. The sponge sections move around on the water. Some move together, others move apart, and still others move past each other. L2 LS
**Visual-Spatial**

### Caption Answer
**Figure 5** Plates move apart, move together, or move past each other at plate boundaries.

**Figure 5** Earth's plates fit together like the pieces of a jigsaw puzzle.
**Draw Conclusions** *If the plates are moving, what do you suppose happens at the plate boundaries?*

## Earth's Plates

Although the crust is separated from the mantle, the uppermost, rigid layer of the mantle moves as if it were part of Earth's crust. The rigid, upper part of Earth's mantle and the crust is called the **lithosphere.** It is broken into about 30 sections or **plates** that move around on the plasticlike asthenosphere, which also is part of the mantle. Earth's major plates vary greatly in size and shape, as shown in **Figure 5.**

### ✔ Reading Check    *What parts of Earth make up the lithosphere?*

The movements of the plates are fairly slow, often taking more than a year to creep a few centimeters. This means that they have not always looked the way they do in **Figure 5.** The plates have not always been their current size and shape, and continents have moved great distances. Antarctica, which now covers the south pole, was once near the equator, and North America was once connected to Africa and Europe.

Lasers and satellites are used to measure the small plate movements, which can add up to great distances over time. If a plate is found to move at 2 centimeters per year on average, how far will it move in 1,000 years? What about in 10 million years?

## Cultural Diversity

**Pieces of the Puzzle** Have students work in cooperative groups to discover the contributions made by Alfred Wegener, Harry Hess, and J. Tuzo Wilson that helped lead to plate tectonics theory. Wegener proposed continental drift. Hess discovered sea floor spreading. Wilson called broken sections of crust *plates* and discovered the nature of transform faults.
COOP LEARN LS **Interpersonal**

### ✔ Active Reading

**Metacognition Journal** Have students divide sheets of paper in half. On the left, have them record what they have learned about Earth's plates. On the right, have them record the reason they learned it.

## Plate Boundaries

The places where the edges of different plates meet are called plate boundaries. The constant movement of plates creates forces that affect Earth's surface at the boundaries of the plates. At some boundaries, these forces are large enough to cause mountains to form. Other boundaries form huge rift valleys with active volcanoes. At a third type of boundary, huge faults form. **Faults** are large fractures in rocks along which movement occurs. The movement can cause earthquakes. **Figure 6** shows the different plate motions.

**Plates That Move Apart** Plates move apart as a result of pulling forces that act in opposite directions on each plate. This pulling force is called tension. **Figure 7** shows what happens as tension continues to pull two plates apart.

One important result of plates separating is the formation of new crust. New crust forms in gaps where the plates pull apart. As tension continues along these boundaries, new gaps form and are filled in by magma that is pushed up from the mantle. Over time, the magma in the gaps cools to become new crust. This process of plate separation and crust formation takes place under the oceans at places called mid-ocean ridges. As new crust moves away from the mid-ocean ridges, it cools and becomes denser.

**Science Online**

**Topic: Plate Boundaries**
Visit in7.msscience.com for Web links to information about Earth's plates and the different boundaries that they form.

**Activity** Create a table of the information on plates and plate boundaries. Try to include specific plates and boundary locations. Share your findings with your classmates.

**Figure 6** Earth's plates can collide, move away from each other, or slide past each other.

**Sliding Plates** When plates slide along each other, earthquakes commonly occur. Earthquakes are the result of energy that builds up at these boundaries and then is released suddenly.

**Separating Plates** When plates move apart, new crust forms to fill in the gap between the plates. This new crust is less dense than the surrounding cooler crust, which often causes a high ridge to form.

**Colliding Plates** When plates collide, the tremendous force causes mountains like the Andes in South America to form.

NORTH AMERICAN PLATE

EURASIAN PLATE

AFRICAN PLATE

CARIBBEAN PLATE

COCOS PLATE

PACIFIC PLATE

NAZCA

SOUTH AMERICAN

569

## Visualizing Rift Valleys

Have students examine the pictures and read the captions. Then ask the following questions.

The Red Sea represents which stage in the rifting process? The Red Sea is a narrow sea generated by spreading as depicted by the red arrows. It represents the third stage in the rifting process.

Why do slabs of rocks sink when the crust is pulled apart? After cracking separates them from the crust, they are unsupported by surrounding rock layers. They are pulled by gravity down toward the mantle.

How is seawater allowed to enter rift valleys? Eventually slabs of rock in the rift zone fall below sea level, allowing for the inflow of seawater if the rift is near a coastline.

## Activity

**Rifting Process** Have students work in groups to model each stage of the rifting process in brightly colored modeling clay. Have them label their models, showing the directions in which the crust is moving, slabs of sinking rock, magma, crustal fractures, valley walls, and seawater.

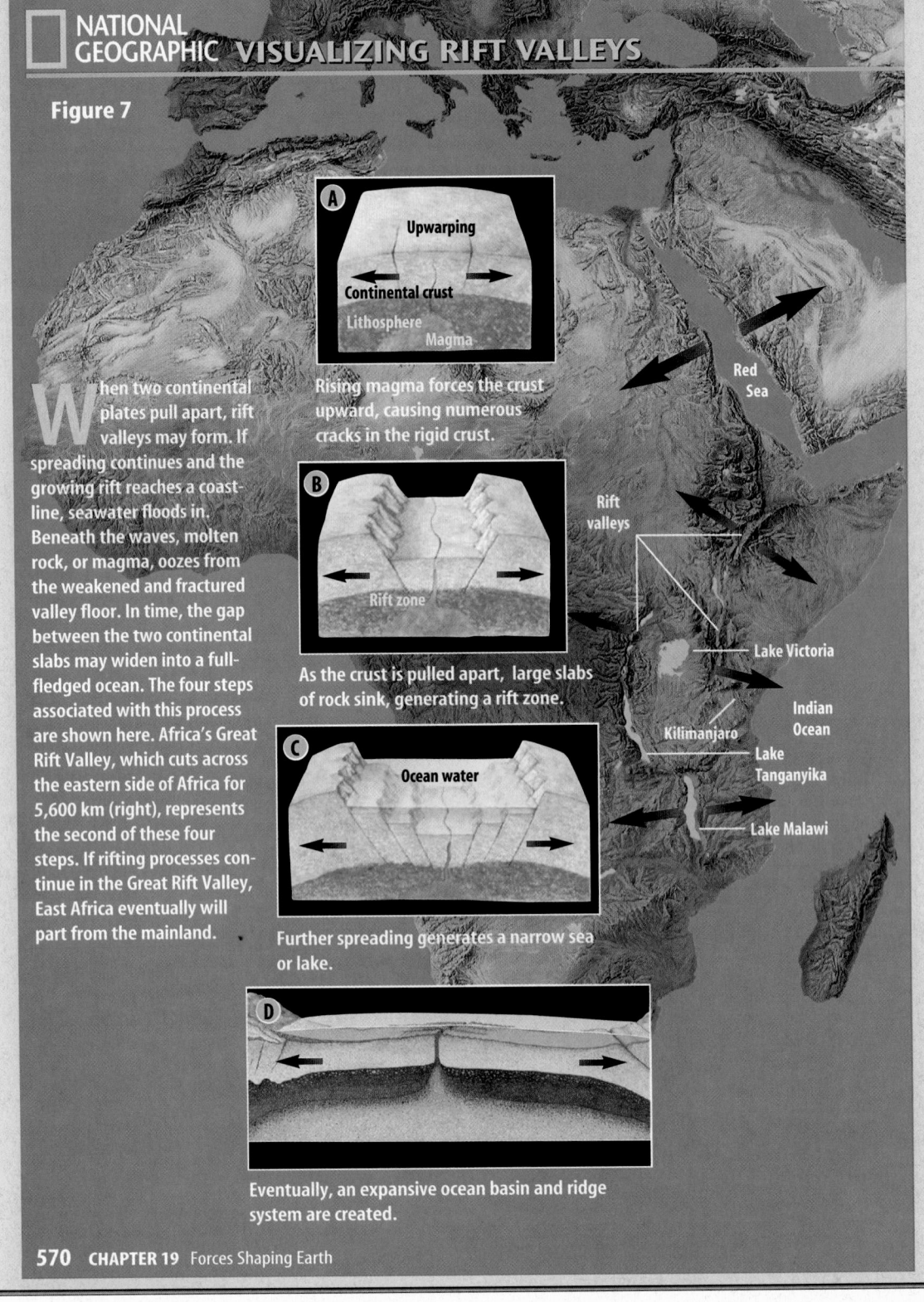

**NATIONAL GEOGRAPHIC** VISUALIZING RIFT VALLEYS

Figure 7

When two continental plates pull apart, rift valleys may form. If spreading continues and the growing rift reaches a coastline, seawater floods in. Beneath the waves, molten rock, or magma, oozes from the weakened and fractured valley floor. In time, the gap between the two continental slabs may widen into a full-fledged ocean. The four steps associated with this process are shown here. Africa's Great Rift Valley, which cuts across the eastern side of Africa for 5,600 km (right), represents the second of these four steps. If rifting processes continue in the Great Rift Valley, East Africa eventually will part from the mainland.

**A** Rising magma forces the crust upward, causing numerous cracks in the rigid crust.

Upwarping
Continental crust
Lithosphere
Magma

**B** As the crust is pulled apart, large slabs of rock sink, generating a rift zone.

Rift zone

**C** Further spreading generates a narrow sea or lake.

Ocean water

**D** Eventually, an expansive ocean basin and ridge system are created.

Red Sea
Rift valleys
Lake Victoria
Indian Ocean
Kilimanjaro
Lake Tanganyika
Lake Malawi

**Plates That Collide** When plates move toward each other, they collide, causing several different things to occur. As you can see in **Figure 8,** the outcome depends on the density of the two plates involved. The crust that forms the ocean floors, called oceanic crust, is more dense than the continental crust, which forms continents.

If two continental plates collide, they have a similar density which is less than the mantle underneath. Therefore, the collision causes the crust to pile up. When rock converges like this, the force is called compression. Compression causes the rock layers on both plates to crumple and fold. Imagine laying a piece of fabric flat on your desk. If you push the edges of the cloth toward each other, the fabric will crumple and fold over on itself. A similar process occurs when plates crash into each other, causing mountains to form.

Flat rock layers are pushed up into folds. Sometimes the folding is so severe that rock layers bend completely over on themselves, turning upside down. As rock layers are folded and faulted, they pile up and form mountains. The tallest mountains in the world, the Himalaya in Asia, are still rising as two continental plates collide.

**Plate Subduction** When an oceanic plate collides with another oceanic plate or a continental plate, the more dense one plunges underneath the other, forming a deep trench. When one plate sinks underneath another plate, it's called **subduction.** When a plate subducts, it sinks into the mantle. In this way, Earth's crust does not continue to grow larger. As new crust material is generated at a rift, older crustal material subducts into the mantle.

**Figure 8** There are three types of convergent plate boundaries.

**Continental-continental collisions** Two continental plates have similar densities, which are less than underlying mantle rock. As a result, they buckle and fold when they collide, piling up into high mountain ranges, such as the Himalaya.

**Oceanic-oceanic collisions** The collision of two oceanic plates causes subduction of the denser plate, which forms a deep ocean trench where the plates meet. Erupting lava forms islands near the trench.

**Continental-oceanic collisions** When a continental plate collides with an oceanic plate, the more dense oceanic plate slides underneath the continental plate, forming volcanoes.

## Visual Learning

**Figure 8** Have students compare and contrast the convergent boundaries shown. At all of these boundaries, plates are moving together and colliding. At continental-continental collisions, mountains form. At oceanic-oceanic and continental-oceanic collisions, one plate slides under the other.

## Differentiated Instruction

**Learning Disabled** Have students use their hands to demonstrate the types of plate movements that occur at plate boundaries: Colliding plates—bring hands together and fold fingers to make mountains; diverging plates—move hands apart; plates sliding past each other—press hands together and then move hands in opposite directions. L1 ELL IS **Kinesthetic**

**San Andeas Fault** Earthquakes often occur along plates that are sliding past each other along a transform fault, such as the San Andreas. Why is there so much earthquake activity along the San Andreas Fault? As the North American and Pacific plates slide past each other along the fault, the two plates stick and build stress. When the stress builds to a high enough level, a sudden movement along the fault releases energy. This causes an earthquake.

## Teacher FYI

**Mantle Convection** Convection in Earth's interior is thought to be responsible for the movement of Earth's plates. This movement produces mountain-building processes, including volcanism and earthquakes. Scientists have different ideas as to how convection in the mantle works. One model shows large convection cells throughout the mantle. Another shows convection in the upper mantle only. Still another shows convection through rising plumes and subduction zones.

## Use Science Words

**Word Meaning** Help students learn why the movement of molten material inside Earth is referred to as *convection*. Convection deals with movement caused by differences in density. Hot, partially molten rock is less dense than the cooler surrounding rock, causing the hot rock to be forced upward. When it rises, the hot rock cools, becomes more dense, and sinks again. This process forms a convection current.

**Figure 9** As two plates slide past each other, their edges grind and scrape. The jerky movement that results causes earthqakes like those frequently felt in California along the San Andreas Fault.

---

**Indiana Academic Standard Check**

**7.3.4:** Explain how heat flow ... within Earth causes earthqakes and volcanic eruptions and creates mountains and ocean basins.

✔ What causes convection currents in Earth's mantle?

✔ density differences due to uneven heating

---

**Plates That Slide Past** In addition to moving toward and away from one another, plates also can slide past one another. For example, one plate might be moving north while the plate next to it is moving south. The boundary where these plates meet is called a transform boundary. When a force pushes something in two different directions, it's called shearing. Shearing causes the area between the plates to form faults and experience many earthquakes. **Figure 9** shows part of the San Andreas Fault near Taft, California, which is an example of the features that form along a transform boundary.

## Why do plates move?

As you can see, Earth's plates are large. To move something so massive requires a tremendous amount of energy. Where does the energy that drives plate movement come from? The reason plates move is complex, and geologists still are trying to understand it fully. So far, scientists have come up with several possible explanations about what is happening inside Earth to cause plate movement. Most of these theories suggest that gravity is the driving force behind it. However, gravity pulls things toward the center of Earth, and plates move sideways across the globe. How does gravity make something move across the surface of Earth?

One theory that could explain plate movement is convection of the mantle. Convection in any material is driven by differences in density. In the mantle, density differences are caused by uneven heating, which results in a cycling of material, as shown in **Figure 10.** The theory suggests that the plates move as part of this circulation of mantle material.

**572 CHAPTER 19** Forces Shaping Earth

## Science Journal

**Features of Transform Fault Boundaries** Have students study **Figure 9,** and then describe in their Science Journals some of the features caused by the shearing forces along the fault. Surface features are offset as the plates move slowly past one another. L2

**IS** **Linguistic**

**Figure 10** Convection, ridge-push, and slab-pull might all contribute to the motions of Earth's plates.

Uneven heating of the upper mantle could cause convection.

Mid-ocean ridge

Ridge-push could occur at mid-ocean ridges.

**Ridge-push and Slab-pull** Other factors, as shown in **Figure 10,** that could play a role in plate movement are ridge-push and slab-pull. Ridge-push occurs at mid-ocean ridges, which are higher than surrounding ocean floor. The plates respond to gravity by sliding down the slope. Slab-pull occurs as the plates move away from the mid-ocean ridges and become cooler, which makes them more dense. A plate can get so dense that it sinks when it collides with another plate. When the more dense plate begins to sink, it becomes easier for it to move across Earth's surface because resistance to movement is reduced.

Slab-pull could occur where oceanic plates meet other oceanic or continental plates.

---

## section 1 review

### Summary

**Clues to Earth's Interior**
- Earth's interior has been explored using information from seismic waves and rocks.

**Earth's Layers**
- The interior of Earth is made of the inner core, outer core, mantle, and crust.

**Plate Boundaries**
- Plates can move apart, collide, subduct, or slide past each other.
- Plates probably move by convection and factors such as ridge-push and slab-pull.

### Self Check

1. **Explain** How are earthquake waves used to provide information about Earth's interior?
2. **Identify** Give examples of where the three types of plate movements occur.
3. **Describe** the layer of Earth's interior that is the largest.
4. **List** the layers of Earth's interior in order of density.
5. **Think Critically** How can slab-pull and ridge-push contribute to the movement of a plate at the same time?

> **Applying Skills**
>
> 6. **Compare and contrast** the following pairs of terms: *inner core, outer core; ridge-push, slab-pull.*

 Science Online in7.msscience.com/self_check_quiz

SECTION 1 Earth's Moving Plates **573**

## section 1 review

1. If the path or speed of earthquake waves is changed, it indicates a difference in the material through which they are traveling.
2. move together (converge), move apart (diverge), and move past each other; possible examples: converge–Himalaya, diverge–Rift Valley, slide past–San Andreas Fault
3. mantle—solid but flows slowly
4. crust, mantle, outer core, and inner core
5. Ridge-push occurs as plates slide down the slope of a mid-ocean ridge. As the plate moves away from the ridge, it becomes denser, eventually beginning to sink into the mantle. Once the plate starts to sink, resistance to movement is reduced, causing slab-pull.
6. Inner/outer core: both are parts of Earth's innermost layer; the outer core is liquid; the inner core is solid. Ridge-push/slab-pull: both are mechanisms that contribute to the movement of plates; ridge-push occurs at divergent boundaries; slab-pull occurs at convergent boundaries.

---

**3 Assess**

**DAILY INTERVENTION**

**Check for Understanding**

**Visual-Spatial** Have students work together in small groups to label a world map with the different types of plate boundaries.

**Reteach**

**Plate Boundaries** Request three groups of students pantomime the types of interactions that occur at plate boundaries. Have each group perform for the class so that all three boundaries are modeled. L2 COOP LEARN IS Interpersonal

**☑ Assessment**

**Oral** Pair students and have them work together to write one question and answer covering the content in this section. Collect the questions, and divide the class into teams to play Moving Plate Jeopardy. Provide each team an answer, and have them come up with the appropriate question. Use **Performance Assessment in the Science Classroom,** p. 91.

**BENCH TESTED**

## ● Real-World Question

**Purpose** Students observe the process of convection and infer its relationship to plate movement. L1 ELL LS **Visual-Spatial**

**Process Skills** interpret data, recognize cause and effect, communicate, measure in SI, recognize and use spatial relationships, formulate models

**Time Required** 35 minutes

## ● Procedure

### Teaching Strategies

• Be sure students use a sharpened pencil in Step 7. Caution students to poke the holes with care.

• Pair students who are physically challenged with students who can help with Steps 4-7.

**Troubleshooting** Caution students not to bump the beaker or the table. Explain that all currents within the beaker must be caused by changes within the beaker. Paper squares must be nearly at rest prior to performing Step 7.

## ● Conclude and Apply

1. The warm water begins to flow out of the cup and toward the top of the beaker.
2. Movement of the warm water upward causes the positions of the paper to change. The paper moves around as it floats.
3. The warm water rises through the colder water. In a similiar way, hot plasticlike rock and magma rise through cooler surrounding rock in Earth. One reason that the processes are different is because convection in

# EARTH'S MOVING PLATES

You have learned that Earth's surface is separated into plates that move apart, move together, or slide past each other. In this lab, you will observe a process that is thought to cause this plate movement.

## ● Real-World Question

What process inside Earth provides the energy for plate motion?

### Goals
■ **Observe** movement of solid plates on a liquid.
■ **Identify** the cause of plate movement on Earth's surface.

### Materials
| | |
|---|---|
| 1-L beakers (2) | rubber band |
| food coloring | water (warm and cold) |
| aluminum foil | 2-cm paper squares (3) |
| pencil | small, clear-plastic cup |

### Safety Precautions

**WARNING:** *Handle the warm water with care. Water from the tap should be warm enough.*

## ● Procedure

1. Fill one of the 1-L beakers with cold water.
2. Fill the small cup with warm water.
3. Add four drops of food coloring to the cup of warm water and cover the top with aluminum foil. Secure the aluminum foil with a rubber band. No air should be underneath the foil.
4. Carefully place the cup of colored, warm water in the bottom of the second 1-L beaker.

**574 CHAPTER 19** Forces Shaping Earth

5. Carefully pour the cold water from the first 1-L beaker into the second 1-L beaker. Take care not to disturb the cup of colored water.

6. Place the pieces of paper on the surface of the water in the second 1-L beaker.

7. Use a long pencil to make two small holes in the aluminum foil covering the cup.

8. **Observe** what happens to the contents of the cup and to the pieces of paper. Record your observations in your Science Journal.

## ● Conclude and Apply

1. **Describe** What happened to the colored, warm water originally located in the cup?

2. **Infer** What effect, if any, does the warm water have on the positions of the floating paper?

3. **Compare and Contrast** How is what happens to the warm water similar to processes that occur inside Earth? How is it different?

4. **Explain** After observing the pieces of paper floating on the cold water, explain what features on Earth's surface they are similar to.

### Communicating Your Data

Compare your conclusions with those of other students in your class. **For more help, refer to the** Science Skill Handbook.

---

Earth occurs much more slowly than convection in water.

4. The pieces of paper are similar to Earth's tectonic plates.

### Communicating Your Data

Ask students to make a series of drawings illustrating what they observed happening in the beaker. Then have students compare their drawings and discuss any differences they note.

**Standards—7.3.4:** Explain how heat flow and movement of material within Earth causes earthquakes and volcanic eruptions and creates mountains and ocean basins. **7.3.7:** Give examples of some changes in Earth's surface that are abrupt, such as earthquakes and volcanic eruptions, and some changes that happen very slowly, such as uplift and wearing down of mountains and the action of glaciers.

**Also covers:** 7.2.7 (Detailed standards begin on page IN8.)

# section 2

# Uplift of Earth's Crust

## Building Mountains

One popular vacation that people enjoy is a trip to the mountains. Mountains tower over the surrounding land, often providing spectacular views from their summits or from surrounding areas. The highest mountain peak in the world is Mount Everest in the Himalaya in Tibet. Its elevation is more than 8,800 m above sea level. In the United States, the highest mountains reach an elevation of more than 6,000 m. There are four main types of mountains—fault-block, folded, upwarped, and volcanic. Each type forms in a different way and can produce mountains that vary greatly in size.

**Age of a Mountain** As you can see in **Figure 11,** mountains can be rugged with high, snowcapped peaks, or they can be rounded and forested with gentle valleys and babbling streams. The ruggedness of a mountain chain depends largely on whether or not it is still forming. Mountains like the Himalaya are currently forming at a rate of several centimeters per year, while much older mountains like the Ouachita Mountains in Arkansas stopped forming millions of years ago and are now being eroded by geological processes.

**Figure 11** Mountains can be high and rugged like the mountains of the Himalaya shown on the left, or they can be large, gently rolling hills like the Ouachita Mountains in Arkansas, shown above.
**Infer** *What determines how rugged and high a mountain chain is?*

### as you read

**What You'll Learn**
- **Describe** how Earth's mountains form and erode.
- **Compare** types of mountains.
- **Identify** the forces that shape Earth's mountains.

**Why It's Important**
The forces inside Earth that cause Earth's plates to move around also are responsible for forming Earth's mountains.

**Review Vocabulary**
**erosion:** process by which products of weathering are moved

**New Vocabulary**
- fault-block mountain
- folded mountain
- upwarped mountain
- volcanic mountain
- isostasy

SECTION 2 Uplift of Earth's Crust **575**

## Caption Answer

**Figure 11** Whether the mountain is still growing; older mountain chains that contain gently rolling hills have undergone extensive erosion.

## Quick Demo

**Mountain Building**

**Materials** three text books, all the same size

**Estimated Time** 10 minutes

**Procedure** Explain that the books represent blocks of crust. Have students describe the landforms that would result from each movement. (1) Hold the books with the spines all upward. Have students observe as you push up on the middle book so that it slides upward. Compression on the inner block, combined with upward pressure, causes a block of crust to upwarp. (2) Firmly hold the books out away from your body. Release some of the pressure so that the middle book slips slightly. Tension causes the inner block to slip below the other crustal blocks.

## Use an Analogy

**Folding Paper** Have students observe as they apply opposite sliding forces to both ends of a sheet of paper lying flat on their desk. Now ask them to determine how this act is analogous to the formation of folded mountains. Compression was applied to the sheet of paper, which caused it to fold. The same force causes rock layers to fold.

**Figure 12** Before tension is applied, the layers of rock are even and fairly level. After tension is applied, huge blocks of rock separate and slip downward. This leaves large, tilted blocks that become mountains.

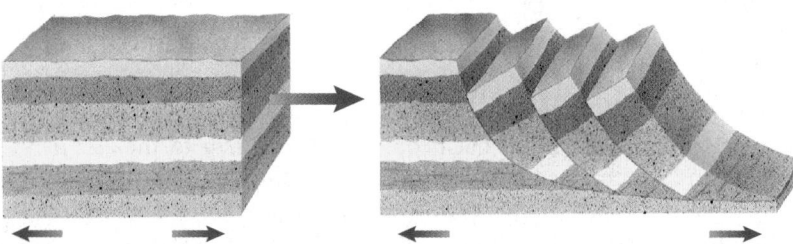

**Figure 13** The Teton Range in the Grand Teton National Park has sharp, jagged peaks that are characteristic of fault-block mountains.

**Fault-Block Mountains** The first mountains you'll study are fault-block mountains. Some examples are the Sierra Nevada in California and the Teton Range in Wyoming. Recall that pulling, or tension, forces that occur at the boundaries of plates moving apart, work to create surface features such as rift valleys and faults. Fault-block mountains also form from pulling forces. **Fault-block mountains** are made of huge, tilted blocks of rock that are separated from surrounding rock by faults. When rock layers are pulled from opposite directions, large blocks slide downward, creating peaks and valleys, as shown in **Figure 12.**

**Models of Mountain Building** If you hold a candy bar between your hands and then begin to pull it apart, cracks might form within the chocolate. Similarly, when rocks are pulled apart, faults form. Unlike rocks deep in Earth, rocks at Earth's surface are hard and brittle. When they are pulled apart, large blocks of rock can move along the faults. The Teton Range of Wyoming formed when a block of crust was tilted as one side of the range was uplifted above the neighboring valley. As shown in **Figure 13,** if you travel to the Grand Teton National Park, you will see sharp, jagged peaks that are characteristic of fault-block mountains.

Now, hold a flat piece of clay between your hands and then push your hands together gently. What happens? As you push your hands together, the clay begins to bend and fold over on itself. A similar process causes rocks to fold and bend, causing folded mountains to form on Earth's surface.

**576** **CHAPTER 19** Forces Shaping Earth

## Curriculum Connection

**Math** The Sierra Nevada formed over a period of at least 10 million years. Mount Whitney is one of many peaks in this mountain range. Its elevation is 4,400 m above sea level. If the total uplift is 4,400 m in 10 million years, have students compute the average annual rate of uplift. 4,400 m ÷ 10 million years = 0.44 mm/year [L2] [IS] **Logical-Mathematical**

## Science Journal

**Mountain Characteristics** Have students write in their Science Journals brief descriptions of one basic characteristic of each type of mountain. Fault-block mountains have sharp, jagged peaks. Folded mountains have folds in the rock layers. Upwarped mountains form in broad domes. Volcanic mountains are cone-shaped. [L2] [IS] **Linguistic** [P]

**Folded Mountains** Traveling along a road that is cut into the side of the Appalachian Mountains, you can see that rock layers were folded just as the clay was when it was squeezed, or compressed. Tremendous pushing forces exerted by two of Earth's plates moving together squeezed rock layers from opposite sides. This caused the rock layers to buckle and fold, forming folded mountains. **Folded mountains** are mountains formed by the folding of rock layers caused by compression forces.

**Reading Check** *What type of force causes folded mountains to form?*

The Appalachian Mountains are folded mountains that formed about 250 million to 300 million years ago. A small part of the folded Appalachians is shown in **Figure 14.** The compression occurred as the North American Plate and the African Plate moved together. The Appalachians are the oldest mountain range in North America, and also one of the longest. They extend from Alabama northward to Quebec, Canada. Erosion has been acting on these mountains since they were formed. As a result, the Appalachians are small compared to other mountain ranges. At one time, the Appalachian Mountains were higher than the Rocky Mountains are today.

**Upwarped Mountains** The Adirondack Mountains in New York, the southern Rocky Mountains in Colorado and New Mexico, and the Black Hills in South Dakota are examples of upwarped mountains. **Upwarped mountains** form when forces inside Earth push up the crust. With time, sedimentary rock layers on top will erode, exposing the igneous or metamorphic rocks underneath. The igneous and metamorphic rocks can erode further to form sharp peaks and ridges.

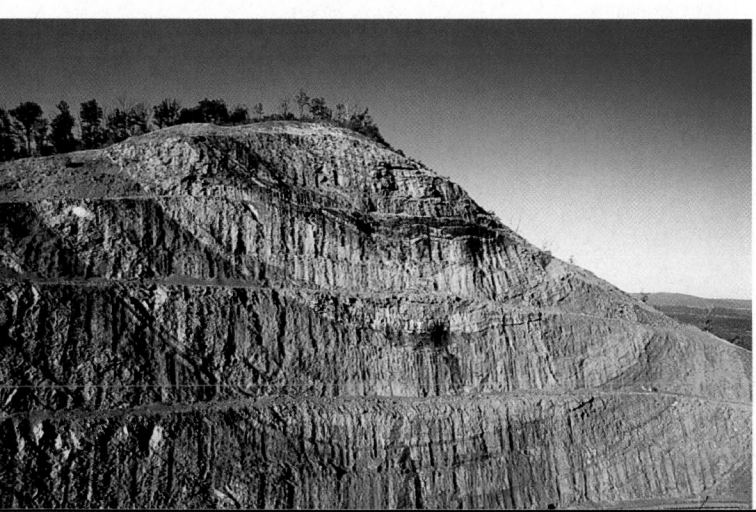

**Figure 14** This roadcut in Maryland exposes folded rock layers that formed when the North American Plate and the African Plate collided.

577

## Modeling Mountains
**Procedure**
1. Use layers of **clay** to build a model of each major type of mountain.
2. For fault-block mountains, cut the layers of clay with a **plastic knife** to show how one block moves upward and another moves downward.
3. For folded mountains, push on the layers of clay from directly opposite directions.
4. For upwarped mountains, push a large, round object, such as a **ball**, upward from below, forcing the layers of clay to warp.
5. For volcanic mountains, place layer upon layer of clay to form a cone-shaped feature.

**Analysis**
1. Do any of the mountains you have modeled look similar? Explain.
2. How could you recognize the different types of mountains?

**Purpose** Students model the four different types of mountains L2 IS **Kinesthetic**

**Materials** modeling clay, plastic knife, ball

**Teaching Strategy** Have students work with a partner to model upwarped mountains. One student can hold the clay layers while the other pushes the ball upward.

**Safety Precautions** Caution students to handle the plastic knife with care.

**Analysis**
1. Yes, upwarped mountains and folded mountains can look similar. In both cases rock layers are bent upward.
2. Each type of mountain can be distinguished by its form and structure.

## Assessment

**Oral** Have students develop questions about the four types of mountains and then quiz each other aloud. Use **Performance Assessment in the Science Classroom,** p. 91.

## Teacher FYI

**Continental Accretion** Plate collisions and subduction are considered the causes of most mountain belts. In a proposed mechanism, called continental accretion, small crustal fragments collide and attach to larger continental masses. It is thought that many of the mountains around the Pacific Ocean were formed in this way.

## Activity

**Topographic Maps** Provide students with topographic maps of areas that have fault-block, folded, upwarped, and volcanic mountains. Ask students to describe the pattern on the map formed by each type of mountain. Fault-block mountains have jagged peaks indicated by closely-spaced contour lines. Folded mountains appear as long ridges of closely-spaced lines (mountains) separated by wider-spaced lines (valleys). Streams on upwarped mountains might form parallel lines. Volcanic mountains are steeply cone-shaped and streams run down their sides in a radial pattern. L2

**LS** Visual-Spatial and Linguistic

## Visual Learning

**Figure 15** Movements of magma in the magma chamber and into the pipe can generate earthquakes. Earthquakes around volcanoes are an indication of magma movement near the volcano. Have students make an events-chain concept map summarizing the sequence of events that lead up to a volcanic eruption. Magma rises from the magma chamber, up the pipe, to the vent in the crater. Magma, now called lava, then flows across the surface and down the sides of the volcano.

## Use Science Words

**Word Origins** Geologists refer to mountain-building as *orogenesis*. Have students research the Greek roots of this word, and use the word in a sentence. Orogenesis is derived from the Greek word *oros*, meaning "mountain" and *genesis*, meaning "coming into being." Orogenesis explains how mountains are formed.

**Science Online**

**Topic: Volcanic Mountains**
Visit in7.msscience.com for Web links to information about volcanic mountains.

**Activity** Collect as many photographs of volcanic mountains as possible. Create a large map of the world with the photographs in their proper locations. Include some information about the volcanic mountains and the impact they have had on the environment around there.

**Figure 15** Volcanic mountains form when lava and ash build up in one area over time.

**Volcanic Mountains** Occasionally, magma from inside Earth reaches the surface. When this happens, the magma is called lava. When hot, molten lava flows onto Earth's surface, volcanic mountains can form. Over time, layer upon layer of lava piles up until a cone-shaped feature called a **volcanic mountain** forms. Washington's Mount St. Helens and Mexico's Mount Popocateptl, shown in **Figure 15,** are examples. Next, you will take a closer look at how volcanic mountains form.

Some volcanic mountains form when large plates of Earth's lithosphere sink into Earth's mantle at subduction zones. As the plates sink deeper into the mantle, they cause melting to occur. The magma produced is less dense than the surrounding rock, so it is forced slowly upward to Earth's surface. If the magma reaches the surface, it can erupt as lava and ash. Layers of these materials can pile up over time to form volcanic mountains.

**Crater** This bowl-shaped part of the volcano surrounds the vent. Lava often collects here before it flows down the slope.

**Vent** As magma flows up the pipe, it reaches the surface at an opening called the vent. Side vents often branch off of the main pipe.

**Pipe** Magma flows through this nearly vertical crack in the rock called the pipe.

**Magma Chamber** Magma that has been forced upward forms and fills a large pocket underneath the volcano. This pocket is called the magma chamber. In some cases, one magma chamber feeds several volcanoes.

**Magma** The hot, molten mixture of rock material and gases is called magma.

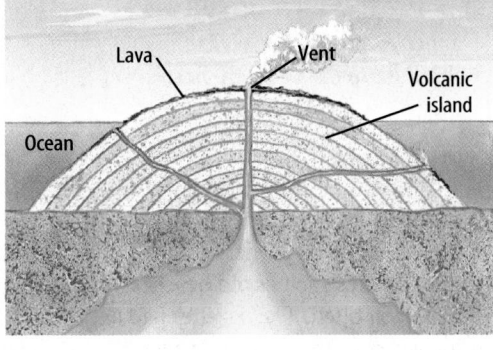

**Underwater Volcanic Mountains** You know that volcanic mountains form on land, but did you know that these mountains also form on the ocean floor? Underwater eruptions can produce mountains beneath the sea. Eventually, if enough lava is erupted, these mountains grow above sea level. For example, Hawaii, shown above in **Figure 16,** is the peak of a huge volcanic mountain that extends above the surface of the water of the Pacific Ocean. **Figure 16** also illustrates how the Hawaiian Islands formed.

Volcanic mountains like the Hawaiian Islands are different from the volcanic mountains that form where one plate subducts beneath another. The Hawaiian Islands formed from material that came from near the boundary between Earth's core and mantle. Hot rock is forced upward through the mantle as a plume and melts to form a hot spot in Earth's crust. As plates travel over the hot spot, a series of volcanoes, as seen in Hawaii, forms. Magma from subduction volcanoes forms much closer to Earth's surface. Hot spot volcanoes also are much larger and have more gently sloping sides than subduction volcanoes.

**Reading Check** *What type of mountains make up the Hawaiian Islands?*

## Discussion

**New Island** Loihi is a submerged volcanic mountain off the southern coast of the Big Island of Hawaii. It is being formed as the Pacific plate moves over a stationary hot spot in the mantle. Have students discuss what the formation of this island means about the future of the Hawaiian Islands. When it breaks the surface, which at its present rate of growth will take tens of thousands of years Loihi will be the next island in the chain that forms the Hawaiian Islands. At that time, the volcanoes on the big island of Hawaii will likely be inactive. L2 **IS** **Linguistic**

**Reading Check**

**Answer** volcanic mountains

## Fun Fact

Pillow lava forms when lava is extruded under oceans. The cooling nature of the water forms pillow-like formations of hardened lava.

SECTION 2 Uplift of Earth's Crust **579**

---

# Differentiated Instruction

**Behaviorally Disordered** To help students keep focused on the lesson about volcanic mountains, provide them with a model of a volcano with parts labeled. After students study the model and **Figure 15,** encourage them to make their own model volcano. Challenge them to find a way to make their volcano erupt. For example, students might mix baking soda and vinegar to simulate lava pouring down the slope of a volcano. A more accurate model would include rubber tubing built into the bottom of the volcano. When the model is complete, have students fill the pipe of their volcanoes with puffed cereal to represent magma. They can make their volcano erupt by blowing into the end of the rubber tubing. The harder they blow, the more violent the eruption will be. L2 **ELL** **IS** **Visual-Spatial and Kinesthetic**

## Use Science Words

**Word Meaning** Folded mountains have areas that are folded upward and other areas that are folded downward. Have students research and determine which of the following terms, *anticline* or *syncline*, refers to each area. Syncline refers to downfolded areas; anticline refers to upfolded areas.

**The Isostasy Story** The prefix *iso* means "equal". The suffix *stasis* means "remain constant." Isostasy is the condition of equilibrium that occurs when the downward force of gravity on a portion of Earth's crust is equal to the upward force of buoyancy on the crust.

### Applying Science

**Answers**
1. The land rebounds, or pushes back up, after a glacier melts.
2. Accept reasonable answers. Rising crust would likely cause beaches to be tilted. It is unlikely that the crust would rise the same amount everywhere. The glacier may have been thicker in some areas, causing a greater depression. Also, some areas of crust may be less elastic than others, and thus move less than other areas.

### Virtual Labs

**Glaciers** *How do glaciers shape the land?*

**The Isostasy Story**
Using the principle of isostasy, explain in your Science Journal why large features on Earth's surface, such as mountains, float on the layers of Earth beneath them.

## Other Types of Uplift

You have learned about the origin of the pushing forces that bend crustal rocks during mountain-building processes. However, another force also works to keep mountains elevated above the surrounding land. If you place wooden blocks of various thicknesses in a container of water, you will notice that different blocks of wood float in the water at different heights. Also, the thicker blocks of wood float higher in the water than the thinner blocks do. The buoyant force of the water is balancing the force of gravity. A similar process called isostasy occurs in Earth. According to the principle of **isostasy,** Earth's lithosphere floats on a plasticlike upper part of the mantle, the asthenosphere.

The effects of isostasy were first noticed near large mountain ranges. Earth's crust is thicker under mountains than it is elsewhere. Also, if mountains continue to get uplifted, the crust under the mountains will become thicker and will extend farther down into the mantle. This is similar to the floating wooden blocks. If you pile another wooden block on a block that is already floating in the water, you will see that the new, larger block will sink down into the water farther than before. You also will see that the new block floats higher than it did before.

### Applying Science

#### How can glaciers cause land to rise?

About 20,000 years ago, much of North America was covered by a large glacial ice sheet. How do you think an ice sheet can affect Earth's crust? What do you think happens when the ice melts?

**Identifying the Problem**
More than 100 years ago, people living in areas that once had been covered by glaciers noticed that features such as old beaches had been tilted. The beaches had a higher elevation in some places and a lower elevation in others. How do you think old beaches could be tilted?

**Solving the Problem**
1. The weight of glaciers pushes down Earth's crust. What do you think happens after the glacier melts?
2. How could rising crust cause beaches to be tilted? Do you think the crust would rise the same amount everywhere? Explain.

## Differentiated Instruction

**Challenge** Mount St. Helens, Mount Hood, Crater Lake, and Mount Rainer are part of the Cascade Mountain Range. Have students research the Cascade Mountain Range and learn more specifically about the formation of these mountains. Then have them chose one of the mountains mentioned above and create a model of the mountain and the surrounding areas. L3

**English-Language Learners** Students who are just learning English may find it difficult to understand the concept of isostasy. Demonstrate isostasy as described in the text using a water-filled aquarium and wooden blocks. Have students describe what is happening both above and below the water surface as you add blocks to the water.

**Text Question Answer**
As a mountain erodes, its mass is reduced and the buoyant force of isostasy pushes the root of the mountain upward.

**3 | Assess**

**Adjusting to Gravity** Similar to the wooden blocks, if mountains continue to grow larger, they will sink even farther into the mantle. Once mountains stop forming, erosion lowers the mountains and the crust rises again because weight has been removed. If the process continues, the once-thick crust under the mountains will be reduced to the thickness of the crust where no mountains exist.

Icebergs behave in much the same way, as shown in **Figure 17.** The iceberg is largest when it first breaks off of a glacier. As the iceberg floats, it melts and starts to lose mass. This causes the iceberg to rise in the water. Eventually, the iceberg will be much smaller and will not extend as deeply into the water. How is this similar to what happens to mountains?

**Figure 17** Isostasy makes Earth's crust behave in a similar way to these icebergs. As an iceberg melts and becomes smaller, ice from below the water's surface is forced up.

**DAILY INTERVENTION**

**Check for Understanding**
**Logical-Mathematical** Have students locate several mountain systems on a world map. Then have them draw conclusions as to which of these mountains are associated with active tectonic boundaries and are therefore still growing.

**Reteach**
**Mountains** Have students identify each mountain type as you read its description: (1) can form from the movement of magma volcanoes and upwarped mountains; (2) most likely formed from tension fault-block mountains; (3) most likely formed from compression folded mountains. L1

## section 2 review

### Summary

**Building Mountains**
- A rugged, tall mountain is geologically young. An old mountain is rounded and lower in elevation.
- There are four main types of mountains: fault block, folded, upwarped, and volcanic.
- Volcanic mountains can form on the surface of the continents or under the ocean at ridges.

**Other Types of Uplift**
- The principle of isostasy explains how the lithosphere floats on the asthenosphere.
- The crust will also adjust to gravity as erosion and weathering wear away older mountains.

### Self Check

1. **Predict** If compression were exerted on rock layers, what type of mountains would form?
2. **Describe** how fault-block mountains form.
3. **Explain** how a volcano forms.
4. **Think Critically** Put the Appalachian, Himalaya, and Rocky Mountains in order from youngest to oldest knowing that the Himalaya are most rugged and the Appalachians are the least rugged.

**Applying Skills**

5. **Concept Map** Make a chain-of-events concept map that describes how folded mountains form.

**Performance** Have students make a model of the mountain-building process of their choosing and explain how the mountains form. Use **Performance Assessment in the Science Classroom,** p. 123.

**Science Online** in7.msscience.com/self_check_quiz    SECTION 2 Uplift of Earth's Crust **581**

## section 2 review

1. folded mountains
2. Fault-block mountains are huge tilted blocks of rock that are separated from surrounding rock by faults.
3. Magma inside Earth is forced upward until it flows out onto the surface. A volcano forms when layer after layer of lava piles up, forming a cone-shaped mountain.
4. Himalaya, Rocky, Appalachian
5. Answers should include the following in order: compression pushes from opposite directions, rock layers crumple and fold, folded mountains form.

## Model and Invent

# Isostasy

## Real-World Question

**Purpose** Students will determine how adding or removing mass affects the way an object floats in a fluid.

**Process Skills** model, compare, observe, predict, recognize cause and effect, interpret data

**Time Required** 45 minutes

## Procedure

**Possible Materials** You may want to test your wooden blocks ahead of time to make sure they are stable as they float in water.

**Alternate Materials** You might want to provide students with large metal washers or nuts that can be added to or removed from the wooden blocks to increase or decrease the mass of the floating object.

### Goals
- **Observe** the results of isostasy.
- **Predict** what will happen to floating objects when mass is removed or added.

### Possible Materials
5-cm × 5-cm × 2-cm wooden blocks (3)
10-cm × 35-cm × 15-cm clear-plastic storage box or other bin
water
permanent marker
ruler

### Safety Precautions

## Real-World Question

The principle of isostasy states that Earth's crust floats on the more dense mantle beneath. This is similar to the way objects float in water. What do you think will happen when you add mass to a floating object? What if you take away mass? How does adding or removing mass affect the way an object floats in a fluid?

## Make the Model

1. **Decide** what object(s) you will float in the water initially. How will you remove mass from that object? How will you add mass?
2. What will you observe as the mass changes? How will you record the effects of adding or removing mass?
3. How much water will you use? What problems might you encounter if you have too much or too little water?

## Alternative Inquiry Lab

**Make a Model** Make this Lab an Inquiry Lab by extending the exercise. Instruct students that icebergs operate on the same principle as isostasy. Ask students to create a plan for a model iceberg where they will calculate the amount of ice below the water compared to the amount of ice visible above the surface. Once the plan has been approved, provide students with the necessary materials to create their model.

4. Will you make any additional measurements or record any other data?

5. **List** all the steps that you plan to do in this activity. Are the steps in a logical order?

6. **Compare** your model plans to those of other students.

7. Make sure your teacher approves your plans before you start.

## Test the Model

1. Fill the storage box or bin with an appropriate amount of water.

2. Start by floating the initial object you planned to use in the water. Observe and record relevant data.

3. Follow the list of steps you planned in order to obtain data for removing and adding mass. Observe your model and record all relevant data in your Science Journal.

## Conclude and Apply

1. **Describe** What did your initial object look like? What level did the water rise to when your initial object was placed in the bin? How did you add and remove mass?

2. **Summarize** What happened to the amount of the object that was submerged and the amount sticking out of the water when mass was removed from the object?

3. **Summarize** What happened to the amount of the object that was submerged and the amount sticking out of the water when mass was added?

4. **Explain** How can you explain your observations about how much of the object was submerged and how much was sticking out of the water? How is this similar to processes that occur in Earth?

### 𝒞ommunicating Your Data

Make a poster that illustrates what you have learned about isostasy. **For more help, refer to the** Science Skill Handbook.

**LAB 583**

### 𝒞ommunicating Your Data

Students may choose to include information obtained from the Glencoe science web site in their posters.

## Analyze Your Data

**Teaching Strategy** Do not leave the wood in water too long because it will become water-logged and heavy.

## Make a Model

**Expected Outcome** The model should include blocks that float at different levels in the water, depending on the amount of mass added to or removed from the block. The greater the mass, the lower the block will float.

## Conclude and Apply

1. The height at which the object floated will vary according to the density of the material used. Methods used to add and remove mass will vary according to the model.

2. The object floated higher in the water—less of it was submerged.

3. More of the object was submerged and less was above the water level.

4. Removing mass from the object causes it to float higher. This is similar to a mountain eroding away, having less mass, and its root floating higher in Earth's mantle.

### ✔ Assessment

**Oral** Ask students to describe how this activity relates to the advance and retreat of continental glaciers. Use **Performance Assessment in the Science Classroom,** p. 91.

## SCIENCE Stats

### Content Background

The tallest mountain—Mauna Kea, Hawaii—is taller than Mount Everest. Mauna Kea rises 10,205 m from the ocean floor, but rises only 4,205 m above sea level. Mount Everest is 8,850 m tall, as measured from sea level.

### Discussion

**Old Mountains** Since the Rockies are much taller than the Appalachians, what does this tell you about the age of the Rockies? Explain. The Rockies must be younger than the Appalachians and not as worn down by erosion.

How is it possible that some mountains are still becoming taller? Volcanic mountains can be taller as they continue to erupt. Also plate movement can continue to push mountains up.

### Find Out About It

Have students compare their drawings with those made by other members of the class. Discuss why the view from the top of different mountains can vary so much.

**Applying Math**

**Answer** 3.3 m

---

## SCIENCE Stats

## Mountains

### Did you know...

**... The world's longest mountain range** is underwater. The mid-ocean ridge that winds around Earth beneath the Arctic, Atlantic, and Pacific Oceans is 65,000 km long. That's four times longer than the combined lengths of the Andes Mountains, the Rocky Mountains, and the Himalaya.

**... The beautiful Appalachian Mountains** are among the oldest in the world. By 250 million years ago, their formation was complete. Today, the mountains aren't among the tallest because they have been worn down by many millions of years of erosion.

**... In 1963, Surtsey,** a small island, formed when an underwater volcano erupted off the coast of Iceland. The 1.6-km-long island rose to the height of 183 m—about as tall as a 55-story building.

**Applying Math** Using this relationship, how many meters would there be in a one-story building?

### Find Out About It

Research a mountain on **in7.msscience.com/science_stats.** Pinpoint its location on a map, and then accurately draw the mountain and the view from its top.

**584 CHAPTER 19** Forces Shaping Earth

---

## Visual Learning

**Highest Mountain Peaks on Each of the Seven Continents** Ask students which continent has the highest mountain peak. Asia Then ask them to rank the peaks from tallest to smallest. Have them locate each continent on a globe or world map and then locate the position of each mountain. Suggest that they research which of the mountains in the graph are volcanic mountains and which are not. Of those that are volcanic, have students find out which are still active volcanoes.

## Reviewing Main Ideas

### Section 1 — Earth's Moving Plates

1. Earth's interior is divided into four layers, the inner core, the outer core, the mantle, and the crust.

2. Earth's inner and outer cores are thought to be composed mostly of iron. The outer core is thought to be liquid and the inner core is solid.

3. Plates composed of sections of Earth's crust and rigid upper mantle move around on the plasticlike asthenosphere.

4. Earth's plates move together, move apart, and slide past each other.

5. Convection in Earth's mantle, ridge-push, and slab-pull might all contribute to plate movement.

### Section 2 — Uplift of Earth's Crust

1. Uplift causes mountains to form. Faulting, folding, upwarping, and volcanic eruptions are all processes that build mountains.

2. Four main types of mountains are fault-block, folded, upwarped, and volcanic.

3. As erosion removes material, the mass of the mountains is reduced. Isostasy, then forces the crust upward.

## Visualizing Main Ideas

*Copy and complete the following table comparing examples and causes of the four types of mountains.*

### The Four Types of Mountains

| Mountain Type | Example | Cause |
|---|---|---|
| Fault-block mountain | Teton Range | tension |
| Folded mountain | Appalachian Mountains | compression |
| Upwarped mountain | Adirondack Mountains | upward pressure |
| Volcanic mountain | Mount St. Helens | lava flows |

 in7.msscience.com/interactive_tutor

**CHAPTER STUDY GUIDE** 585

---

chapter Study Guide **19**

### Reviewing Main Ideas

Summary statements can be used by students to review the major concepts of the chapter.

### Visualizing Main Ideas

See student page.

**Visit** in7.msscience.com
/self_check_quiz
/interactive_tutor
/vocabulary_puzzlemaker
/chapter_review
/standards_review

### Assessment Transparency

For additional assessment questions, use the *Assessment Transparency* located in the transparency book.

### Assessment

Assessment Transparency — Forces Shaping Earth

**Directions:** *Carefully review the table and answer the following questions.*

| Layers of Earth | Thickness in Earth | Thickness in scale model |
|---|---|---|
| Crust | 40 km | 0.8 mm |
| Mantle | 2660 km | 53 mm |
| Outer core | 2260 km | 45 mm |
| Inner core | 1300 km | ? |

1. According to the table, which layer has the greatest thickness?
   A crust
   B mantle
   C outer core
   D inner core

2. About how much thicker is the outer core than the inner core?
   F 960 km
   G 1600 km
   H 1950 km
   J 2250 km

3. A student wants to draw a scale model of the layers of Earth. She has already calculated the thickness in the scale model for the crust, mantle, and outer core. If everything remains the same, what will be the thickness of the inner core in the scale model?
   A 2.6 mm
   B 20 mm
   C 26 mm
   D 50 mm

Forces Shaping Earth

## Using Vocabulary

1. Earth's <u>outer core</u> is thought to be liquid.
2. The Sierra Nevada are <u>fault-block mountains</u>.
3. <u>Folded mountains</u> commonly form in areas where plates are being pushed together.
4. <u>Subduction</u> occurs when a more dense plate sinks beneath a less dense plate
5. A <u>volcanic mountain</u> forms when magma is forced upward and flows onto Earth's surface.

## Checking Concepts

| | |
|---|---|
| 6. B | 11. D |
| 7. A | 12. B |
| 8. B | 13. C |
| 9. A | 14. D |
| 10. D | 15. B |

## Using Vocabulary

| | |
|---|---|
| crust p. 566 | lithosphere p. 568 |
| fault p. 569 | mantle p. 566 |
| fault-block mountain p. 576 | outer core p. 566 |
| | plate p. 568 |
| folded mountain p. 577 | subduction p. 571 |
| inner core p. 565 | upwarped mountain p. 577 |
| isostasy p. 580 | volcanic mountain p. 578 |

*Answer the following questions with complete sentences.*

1. Which part of Earth's core do scientists think is liquid?
2. The Sierra Nevada mountains in California are which type of mountain?
3. What type of mountains form in areas where rocks are being pushed together?
4. What process occurs when a more dense plate sinks beneath a less dense plate?
5. Which type of mountain forms when magma is forced upward and flows onto Earth's surface?

## Checking Concepts

*Choose the word or phrase that best answers the question.*

6. Which part of Earth is largest?
   **A)** crust   **C)** outer core
   **B)** mantle   **D)** inner core

7. Earth's plates are pieces of which layer of Earth?
   **A)** lithosphere
   **B)** asthenosphere
   **C)** inner core
   **D)** mantle

8. Which force pushes plates together?
   **A)** tension   **C)** shearing
   **B)** compression   **D)** isostasy

9. Which force occurs where Earth's plates are moving apart?
   **A)** tension   **C)** shear
   **B)** compression   **D)** isostasy

10. Which layer of Earth is thought to be solid and composed mostly of the metal iron?
   **A)** crust   **C)** outer core
   **B)** mantle   **D)** inner core

11. Which suggests that Earth's lithosphere floats on the asthenosphere?
   **A)** tension
   **B)** compression
   **C)** shear
   **D)** isostasy

12. Which type of mountain forms because of compression forces?
   **A)** fault-block mountains
   **B)** folded mountains
   **C)** upwarped mountains
   **D)** volcanic mountains

13. Which type of mountain forms because forces inside Earth push up overlying rock layers?
   **A)** fault-block mountains
   **B)** folded mountains
   **C)** upwarped mountains
   **D)** volcanic mountains

14. Which type of plate movement occurs at transform boundaries?
   **A)** plates moving together
   **B)** plates moving apart
   **C)** plates sinking
   **D)** plates sliding past each other

15. Which type of plate movement produces deep rifts such as the mid-ocean rift?
   **A)** plates moving together
   **B)** plates moving apart
   **C)** plates sliding past each other
   **D)** plates sinking

 Science Online in7.msscience.com/vocabulary_puzzlemaker

**Use the Exam*View*® Pro Testmaker CD-ROM to:**
- create multiple versions of tests
- create modified tests with one mouse click for inclusion students
- edit existing questions and add your own questions
- build tests aligned with state standards using built-in State Curriculum Tags
- change English tests to Spanish with one mouse click and vice versa

## Thinking Critically

**16. Explain** Which is older, the Great Rift Valley in East Africa, or the Mid-Atlantic Ridge in the Atlantic Ocean?

**17. Explain** how you can determine whether or not a mountain is still forming.

**18. Infer** Seismic waves slow down when entering the asthenosphere. What does this tell you about the nature of the asthenosphere?

**19. Predict** what would happen to the elevation of the island of Greenland if the ice sheet were to melt away.

**20. Describe** If you wanted to know whether a certain mountain was formed by compression, what would you look for?

**21. Compare and contrast** volcanic and folded mountains. Draw a diagram of each type of mountain. Label important features.

**22. Make Models** Use layers of clay to make a model of fault-block mountains. Draw a diagram of your model.

**23. Draw Conclusions** The speed of seismic waves suddenly increases when they go from the upper mantle into the lower mantle. What does this indicate about the comparative densities of the rock in both layers?

**24. Use graphics software** to generate a scale illustration of Earth's interior. Include the thickness of each layer in kilometers.

**25. Recognize Cause and Effect** What is the effect of subduction at the boundary of two plates?

 Science Online in7.msscience.com/chapter_review

## Performance Activities

**26. Poem** Write a poem in a style of your choosing about the spectacular view often associated with mountains. You may wish to write about the scene from the top of a mountain or the one you see from the bottom of the mountain looking up to its peak.

## Applying Math

**27. Mountain Climbing** The most standard climb for climbers of Mount Everest is up to Base Camp, an elevation of 5400 m. If the summit is 8850 m high, what percentage of Mount Everest's elevation is the Base Camp?

**Use the map below to answer question 28.**

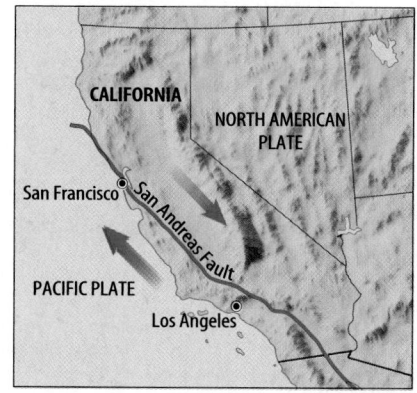

**28. Moving Cities** The distance between San Francisco and Los Angeles is 616 km. If the San Andreas fault is moving at an average rate of 2.0 cm per year, how long will it be before Los Angeles is next to San Francisco?

**CHAPTER REVIEW** **587**

## Thinking Critically

**16.** The Mid-Atlantic Ridge is older, because the continents along its edges are farther apart.

**17.** Mountains that are still forming have sharp, jagged peaks.

**18.** It may be less dense than surrounding rock. It also may be somewhat molten.

**19.** Because of isostasy, the elevation of Greenland would increase as the ice sheet melted away.

**20.** folded rock layers

**21.** Both are formed by forces pushing upward. Volcanic mountains are cone-shaped, whereas folded mountains show folded rock layers. Drawings should show these features.

**22.** Models should show blocks of rock tilted upward along a fault.

**23.** The density of the rock in the lower mantle is greater than the rock in the upper mantle.

**24.** Student illustrations should resemble **Figure 4.**

**25.** Rock layers are folded by compression as two plates move together. The denser plate sinks under the other plate. As it sinks deep into Earth it melts, and the magma rises to the surface to form volcanoes.

## Performance Activities

**26.** Poems may be of any style as long as they describe the beauty of a mountain view. Use **Performance Assessment in the Science Classroom,** p. 151.

## Applying Math

**Indiana Math Standards**
7.2.3, 7.7.1

**27.** 61 percent

**28.** 616 km $\times$ 100,000 cm/km = 61,600,000 cm

61,600,000 cm $\div$ 2.0 cm/yr = 30,800,000 years

## ☑ Assessment   Resources

📁 **Reproducible Masters**
**Chapter *Fast File* Resources**
Chapter Review, pp. 37–38
Chapter Tests, pp. 39–42
Assessment Transparency Activity, p. 49
**Glencoe Science Web site**
Chapter Review Test
IN Standards Review

**Glencoe Technology**
🖌 Assessment Transparency
⊕ Exam*View*® Pro Testmaker
▭ MindJogger Videoquiz
◉ Interactive Chalkboard

**Answer Sheet** A practice answer sheet can be found at in7.msscience.com/answer_sheet.

S A M P L E

*Record your answers on the answer sheet provided by your teacher or on a sheet of paper.*

### Part 1 Multiple Choice

**7.3.4**

**1.** The graph below shows how temperature varies with depth.

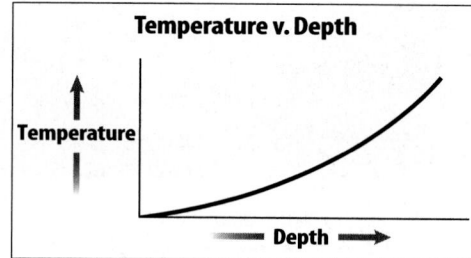

**Temperature v. Depth**

What happens to temperature as you go deeper into Earth?

- **A** decreases
- **B** decreases then increases
- **C** increases
- **D** increases then decreases

**7.3.4**

**2.** Which is believed to cause tectonic plate movement?

- **A** compression
- **B** convection
- **C** isostasy
- **D** tension

**7.3.4**

**3.** Which mountains form when forces pull from opposite directions?

- **A** fault-block
- **B** folded
- **C** upwarped
- **D** volcanic

**7.3.7**

**4.** The illustration below shows relative tectonic plate movement.

Which force is involved when Earth's plates slide past each other?

- **A** compression
- **B** isostasy
- **C** shear
- **D** tension

**7.3.7**

**5.** Which mountains form when forces inside Earth push up the crust?

- **A** fault-block
- **B** folded
- **C** upwarped
- **D** volcanic

### Part 1 Multiple Choice

1. C
2. B
3. A
4. C
5. C
6. B
7. D
8. C

### Part 2 Critical Response

9. Compression pushes rock layers together from opposite directions causing rock layers to bend, buckle, and fold. Compression is applied very slowly, perhaps over millions of years, to form folded mountains.

10. Ridge-push occurs at mid-ocean ridges, which are higher than the surrounding ocean floor. Portions of the ridges respond to gravity by sliding down the slope and pushing the plates.

11. Both types of mountains may produce peaks that tower over the surrounding land. Upwarped mountains form when forces inside Earth push up the crust. Sedimentary rock layers on top will erode, exposing igneous or metamorphic rocks underneath, that can eventually form sharp peaks and ridges. In contrast to mountains formed by other processes, a volcanic mountain is cone-shaped and has a bowl-shaped opening at the top. This bowl-shaped opening is a crater, the part of the volcano that surrounds the vent. The vent is the opening for the magma to flow through and reach the surface as lava. Lava flows outward from the volcano's vent and builds up layer upon layer. The buildup of layers gives the mountain its cone shape. None of the other types of mountains form entirely from layers of lava.

**7.3.4**

**6.** Which is produced by differences in density in Earth's mantle?

**A** compression

**B** convection

**C** shear

**D** tension

**7.3.4**

**7.** The illustration below shows a type of mountain.

Which type of mountain is shown above?

**A** fault-block

**B** folded

**C** upwarped

**D** volcanic

**8.** Which lists the layers of Earth's interior from the inside out?

**A** crust, mantle, outer core, inner core

**B** inner core, outer core, crust, mantle

**C** inner core, outer core, mantle, crust

**D** mantle, crust, outer core, inner core

---

### Part 2 Critical Response

**7.3.4**

**9.** The photo below shows folded mountains.

Explain how compression causes folded mountains to form. How must this force be applied for folded mountains to form?

**7.3.4**

**10.** Where does ridge-push occur? How is it involved in the movement of Earth's tectonic plates?

**7.3.4**

**11.** Compare and contrast mountains formed by volcanic activity and those formed by upwarping. Describe how characteristics of a volcanic mountain differ from the characteristics of mountains formed in other ways.

---

### Test-Taking Tip

**Check** Never leave any critical-response answer blank. Answer each question as best as you can. You can receive partial credit for partially correct answers.

---

## Rubrics

The following rubric is a sample scoring device for critical response questions.

### Critical Response

| Points | Description |
|---|---|
| 4 | The student demonstrates a thorough understanding of the science of the task. The response may contain minor flaws that do not detract from the demonstration of a thorough understanding. |
| 3 | The student demonstrates an understanding of the science of the task. The response is essentially correct and demonstrates an essential but less than thorough understanding of the science. |
| 2 | The student demonstrates only a partial understanding of the science of the task. Although the student may have used the correct approach to a solution or may have provided a correct solution, the work lacks an essential understanding of the underlying science concepts. |
| 1 | The student demonstrates a very limited understanding of the science of the task. The response is incomplete and exhibits many flaws. |
| 0 | The student provides a completely incorrect solution or no response at all. |

| Section/Objectives | Standards | | Labs/Features |
|---|---|---|---|
| | **National** | **State/Local** | |
| **Chapter Opener** | See pp. 16T–17T for a Key to Standards. | Detailed standards begin on page IN8. | **Launch Lab:** Construct with Strength, p. 591<br>**Foldables,** p. 591<br><br>A data-collection lab using Probeware technology can be found in the **Probeware Lab Manual,** pp. 29–31 |
| **Section 1 Earthquakes**<br>🕐 2 sessions<br>📦 1 block<br><br>1. **Explain** how earthquakes are caused by a buildup of strain in Earth's crust.<br>2. **Compare and contrast** primary, secondary, and surface waves.<br>3. **Recognize** earthquake hazards and how to prepare for them. | National Content Standards UCP.1, UCP.2, UCP.3, UCP.5, A.1, A.2, B.2, B.3, D.1, F.3 | Indiana Standards: 7.3.7, 7.3.18 | **MiniLAB:** Observing Deformation, p. 593<br>**Science Online,** p. 597<br>**Visualizing Tsunamis,** p. 598 |
| **Section 2 Volcanoes**<br>🕐 2 sessions<br>📦 1 block<br><br>4. **Explain** how volcanoes can affect people.<br>5. **Describe** how types of materials are produced by volcanoes.<br>6. **Compare** how three different volcano forms develop. | National Content Standards UCP.1, UCP.2, UCP.3, UCP.5, A.1, A.2, B.2, B.3, D.1, D.2 | Indiana Standards: 7.3.7 | **MiniLAB:** Modeling an Eruption, p. 602<br>**Science Online,** p. 603<br>**Lab:** Disruptive Eruptions, p. 607 |
| **Section 3 Earthquakes, Volcanoes, and Plate Tectonics**<br>🕐 4 sessions<br>📦 2 blocks<br><br>7. **Explain** how the locations of volcanoes and earthquake epicenters are related to tectonic plate boundaries.<br>8. **Explain** how heat within Earth causes Earth's plates to move. | National Content Standards UCP.1, UCP.2, UCP.3, UCP.5, A.1, A.2, B.2, B.3, D.1, D.2, G.3 | Indiana Standards: 7.3.4, 7.3.7, 7.3.18 | **Integrate Chemistry,** p. 610<br>**Integrate Language Arts,** p. 611<br>**Applying Math:** P-wave Travel Time, p. 612<br>**Lab:** Seismic Waves, pp. 614–615<br>**Science and History:** Quake, p. 616 |

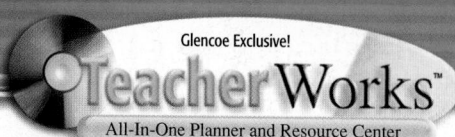
| Lab Materials | Reproducible Resources | Section Assessment | Technology |
|---|---|---|---|
| **Launch Lab:** 4 wooden blocks, sheet of cardboard, large rubber bands | **Chapter FAST FILE Resources** <br> Foldables Worksheet, p. 15 <br> Directed Reading Overview, pp. 17–18 <br> Note-taking Worksheets, pp. 31–33 | GLENCOE'S **ASSESSMENT** ADVANTAGE | Teacher**Works** includes: <br> • Interactive Teacher Edition <br> • Lesson Planner with calendar <br> • Access to all program blacklines <br> • Correlations to standards <br> • Web links |
| **MiniLAB:** 3 bars of taffy <br><br> *Need materials?* Contact Science Kit at 1-800-828-7777 or www.sciencekit.com on the Internet. | **Chapter FAST FILE Resources** <br> Transparency Activity, p. 42 <br> MiniLAB, p. 3 <br> Enrichment, p. 28 <br> Reinforcement, p. 25 <br> Directed Reading, p. 18 <br> Transparency Activity, pp. 45–46 <br> Lab Activity, pp. 9–10 <br> **Cultural Diversity,** p. 47 | **Portfolio** <br> Science Journal, p. 595 <br> **Performance** <br> MiniLAB, p. 593 <br> Applying Skills, p. 600 <br> **Content** <br> Section Review, p. 600 | Section Focus Transparency <br> Teaching Transparency <br> Guided Reading Audio Program <br> Interactive Chalkboard CD-ROM |
| **MiniLAB:** red-colored gelatin, self-sealing plastic bag, pin <br> **Lab:** plastic film canisters, baking soda, vinegar, 50-ml graduated cylinder, teaspoon | **Chapter FAST FILE Resources** <br> Transparency Activity, p. 43 <br> MiniLAB, p. 4 <br> Enrichment, p. 29 <br> Reinforcement, p. 26 <br> Directed Reading, p. 19 <br> Lab Worksheet, pp. 5–6 <br> Lab Activity, pp. 11–14 | **Portfolio** <br> Differentiated Instruction, p. 603 <br> **Performance** <br> MiniLAB, p. 602 <br> Applying Math, p. 606 <br> **Content** <br> Section Review, p. 606 | Section Focus Transparency <br> Virtual Labs CD-ROM <br> Guided Reading Audio Program <br> Interactive Chalkboard CD-ROM <br> Video Lab |
| **Lab:** coiled spring toy, yarn or string, metric ruler | **Chapter FAST FILE Resources** <br> Transparency Activity, p. 44 <br> Enrichment, p. 30 <br> Reinforcement, p. 27 <br> Directed Reading, pp. 19–20 <br> Lab Worksheet, pp. 7–8 <br> **Lab Management and Safety,** p. 38 <br> **Mathematics Skill Activities,** p. 11 | **Portfolio** <br> Science Journal, p. 611 <br> **Performance** <br> Applying Math, p. 612 <br> Applying Skills, p. 613 <br> **Content** <br> Section Review, p. 613 | Section Focus Transparency <br> Guided Reading Audio Program <br> Interactive Chalkboard CD-ROM <br> Probeware Lab |

## End of Chapter Assessment

GLENCOE'S **ASSESSMENT** ADVANTAGE

| Blackline Masters | Technology | Professional Series |
|---|---|---|
| **Chapter FAST FILE Resources** <br> Chapter Review, pp. 35–36 <br> Chapter Tests, pp. 37–40 <br> **Mastering the Grade 7 Indiana Science Standards** | MindJogger Videoquiz <br> IN Test Prep and Practice Exam*View*® <br> Exam*View*® Pro Testmaker <br> TeacherWorks CD-ROM <br> Interactive Chalkboard CD-ROM | **Performance Assessment in the Science Classroom (PASC)** |

## Transparencies

### Section Focus

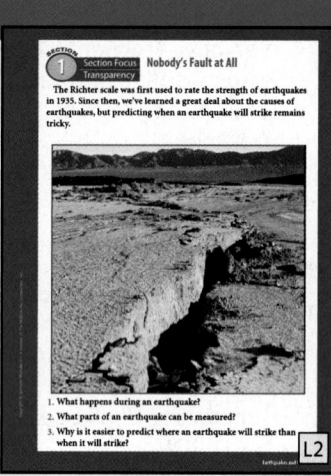

**Section Focus Transparency 1** — Nobody's Fault at All

The Richter scale was first used to rate the strength of earthquakes in 1935. Since then, we've learned a great deal about the causes of earthquakes, but predicting when an earthquake will strike remains tricky.

1. What happens during an earthquake?
2. What parts of an earthquake can be measured?
3. Why is it easier to predict where an earthquake will strike than when it will strike?

L2

**Section Focus Transparency 2** — Does the stork bring baby islands?

In November of 1963, the Atlantic Ocean got a new island. The island was named Surtsey after Sutur, a mythological fire god. The new island was the result of a volcanic eruption very near Iceland.

1. Looking at the photo, how did the island of Surtsey form?
2. What do volcanoes and earthquakes have in common?
3. What unique learning opportunities might scientists have on Surtsey?

L2

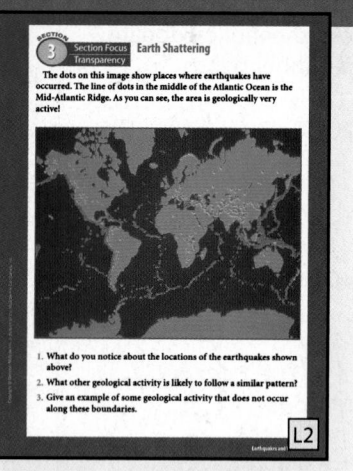

**Section Focus Transparency 3** — Earth Shattering

The dots on this image show places where earthquakes have occurred. The line of dots in the middle of the Atlantic Ocean is the Mid-Atlantic Ridge. As you can see, the area is geologically very active!

1. What do you notice about the locations of the earthquakes shown above?
2. What other geological activity is likely to follow a similar pattern?
3. Give an example of some geological activity that does not occur along these boundaries.

L2

This is a representation of key blackline masters available in the Teacher Classroom Resources. See Resource Manager boxes within the chapter for additional information.

### Key to Teaching Strategies

The following designations will help you decide which activities are appropriate for your students.

**L1** Level 1 activities should be appropriate for students with learning difficulties.

**L2** Level 2 activities should be within the ability range of all students.

**L3** Level 3 activities are designed for above-average students.

**ELL** ELL activities should be within the ability range of English-Language Learners.

**COOP LEARN** Cooperative Learning activities are designed for small group work.

**LS** Multiple Learning Styles logos, as described on page 12T, are used throughout to indicate strategies that address different learning styles.

**P** These strategies represent student products that can be placed into a best-work portfolio.

**PBL** Problem-Based Learning activities apply real-world situations to learning.

### Assessment

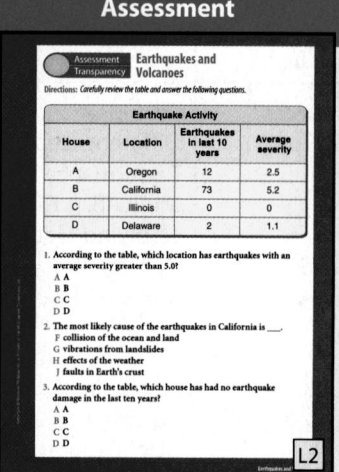

**Assessment Transparency** — Earthquakes and Volcanoes

Directions: Carefully review the table and answer the following questions.

**Earthquake Activity**

| House | Location | Earthquakes in last 10 years | Average severity |
|-------|----------|------------------------------|------------------|
| A | Oregon | 12 | 2.5 |
| B | California | 73 | 5.2 |
| C | Illinois | 0 | 0 |
| D | Delaware | 2 | 1.1 |

1. According to the table, which location has earthquakes with an average severity greater than 5.0?
   A A
   B B
   C C
   D D
2. The most likely cause of the earthquakes in California is ___.
   F collision of the ocean and land
   G vibrations from landslides
   H effects of the weather
   J faults in Earth's crust
3. According to the table, which house has had no earthquake damage in the last ten years?
   A A
   B B
   C C
   D D

L2

### Teaching

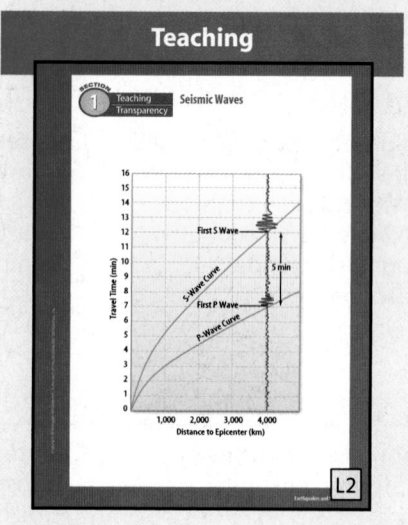

**Teaching Transparency 1** — Seismic Waves

L2

## Hands-on Activities

### Student Text Lab Worksheet

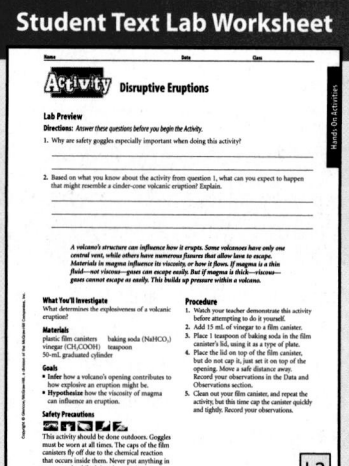

**Activity** — Disruptive Eruptions

**Lab Preview**

Directions: Answer these questions before you begin the Activity.

1. Why are safety goggles especially important when doing this activity?

2. Based on what you know about the activity from question 1, what can you expect to happen that might resemble a cinder-cone volcanic eruption? Explain.

A volcano's structure can influence how it erupts. Some volcanoes have only one central vent, while others have numerous fissures that allow lava to escape. Materials in magma influence its viscosity, or how it flows. If magma is a thin fluid—not viscous—gases can escape easily. But if magma is thick—viscous—gases cannot escape as easily. This builds up pressure within a volcano.

**What You'll Investigate**
What determines the explosiveness of a volcanic eruption?

**Materials**
plastic film canisters   baking soda (NaHCO₃)
vinegar (CH₃COOH)   teaspoon
50-mL graduated cylinder

**Goals**
- Infer how a volcano's opening contributes to how explosive an eruption might be.
- Hypothesize how the viscosity of magma can influence an eruption.

**Safety Precautions**
This activity should be done outdoors. Goggles must be worn at all times. The caps of the film canisters fly off due to the chemical reaction that occurs inside them. Never put anything in your mouth while doing the experiment.

**Procedure**
1. Watch your teacher demonstrate this activity before attempting to do it yourself.
2. Add 15 mL of vinegar to a film canister.
3. Place 1 teaspoon of baking soda in the film canister's lid, using it as a type of plate.
4. Place the lid on top of the film canister, but do not cap it, just set it on top of the opening. Move a safe distance away. Record your observations in the Data and Observations section.
5. Clean out your film canister, then repeat the activity, but this time cap the canister quickly and tightly. Record your observations.

L2

### Laboratory Activities

**Laboratory Activity 1** — Wave Detecting

Today, scientists use seismographs to observe and record seismic waves. Before the nineteenth century, however, scientists used other types of instruments to study earthquakes. These instruments did not record seismic waves. Instead, they indicated the magnitude or direction of an earthquake in a general way. In the 1600s in Italy, for example, scientists used a device that contained water to detect seismic waves. The amount of water spilling out during an earthquake indicated the amount of shaking. In this lab, you will make a simple earthquake-detecting device and determine how it is affected by seismic waves.

**Strategy**
You will model and observe the effects of seismic waves.
You will infer how the energy released by an earthquake affects the amplitude, or height, of seismic waves.

**Materials**
baking pan
large ceramic or stainless steel bowl
pitcher of tap water
dropper
meterstick
textbook
paper towels

**Procedure**
1. Work with a partner. Place the baking pan on a flat surface such as a desk or counter. Set the bowl inside the pan.
2. Pour water into the bowl from the pitcher. Fill the bowl to within 1 or 2 mm of the rim.
3. Using the dropper add water to the bowl until the surface of the water arches above the rim (Figure 1). This is your earthquake detector.
4. Model an earthquake by having a partner drop a book near the detector from a height of 2 cm. Observe what happens to the water in the bowl. Does water spill over? Record your observation in the Data and Observations section. Add more water to the bowl with the dropper if any spills out. Then repeat this step, switching roles with your partner.
5. Repeat step 4 several more times. Each time, you should increase the height at which you drop the book by several centimeters.
6. If any water spills outside the baking pan, be sure to wipe it up with the paper towels.

Figure 1

L2

## Meeting Different Ability Levels

### Content Outline

**L2**

### Reinforcement

**L2**

### Enrichment

**L3**

### Directed Reading (English/Spanish)

**L1**

### Study Guide

**L2**

### Reading Essentials

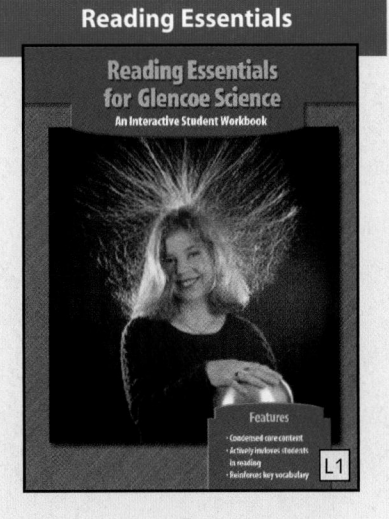

**L1**

## Assessment

### Test Practice Workbook

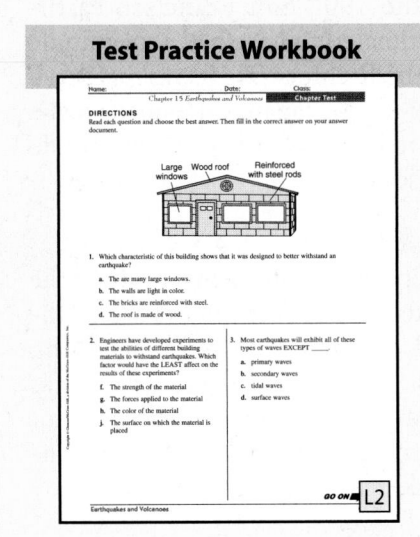

**L2**

### Chapter Review

**L2**

### Chapter Tests

**L2**

# Science Content Background

## section 1  Earthquakes
### Types of Faults

Normal faults, created by tension forces pulling rocks apart, are associated with areas of extension such as mid-ocean ridges. Compression forces, from which reverse faults result, also are the forces that are usually responsible for building mountains. Faults can be very evident in the structure of Earth's surface, even to the untrained eye. The San Andreas Fault, a 1,300-km long, 16-km deep strike-slip fault network that separates the North American and Pacific Plates, is so large it can be seen from the air.

---

**Teacher to Teacher**

Steve Federman
6th Grade Teacher
Loveland Middle School
Loveland, Ohio

"To demonstrate the three basic deformational forces that change Earth's surface, I supply students with candy bars, large pieces of soft bubble gum, and a data sheet to record observations. Unwrap the gum and using fingers, apply a **compressional** force on the gum. Record observations. Reshape the gum and apply a **tensional** force. Have them use the second piece of gum followed by the candy bar to apply a **transversal** force with their fingers. Compare the results among students."

*Steve Federman*

---

## Measuring Earthquake Strength

Seismologists today also measure the moment magnitude of an earthquake. This measurement is based on the total amount of energy released by the earthquake, rather than just the amplitudes of seismic waves. Measuring the moment magnitude is particularly important for larger earthquakes, which cannot always be measured with accuracy by the traditional Richter scale. For example, the 1906 San Francisco earthquake is now estimated to have had a magnitude of 7.7–7.9. On the Richter scale it was measured at 8.3. The 1995 Kobe, Japan, earthquake had a moment magnitude of 6.9 and a 7.2 magnitude on the Richter scale.

## Earthquake Safety

Earthquake safety also means being aware of the potential for aftershocks. Aftershocks are earthquakes created by further movements along a fault after a main earthquake event has occurred. Although aftershocks usually are not as strong as the main earthquake, they can continue to cause destruction to structures already

*Corbis*

weakened or damaged by the earthquake. Aftershocks can occur for several days to several months following a quake.

Aside from more obvious dangers, such as those posed by tsunamis, earthquakes can set off other events, the effects of which can be as disastrous as the earthquake itself. Fire can result from broken gas and power lines. In a severe earthquake, water mains can also be broken, which leaves people virtually powerless to fight the fires. In some cases, out of control fires have caused as much, if not more damage than the earthquake itself.

## Predicting Earthquakes

Seismologists have shown that detectable changes, both on Earth's surface and below, can occur before an earthquake takes place. Some of these changes may result from a change in the porosity of the rock. Small cracks in rock are created as forces act on it, and water subsequently flows into the cracks. Differences in the elevation and tilt of land that occur on either side of a fault also have been observed just before an earthquake.

The influx of water to the rock is thought to account for local changes of water level in wells and groundwater, changes that have also been noted to occur before some earthquakes. The presence of water in the rock also changes the electrical properties of the rock and the ground.

Other changes that have been recorded before an earthquake include an increase in the emission of radon gas from water wells and a change in the speed of seismic waves.

### section 2 Volcanoes
#### Predicting Volcanic Eruptions

Subtle changes can be detected before a volcano erupts. These changes have been successfully used to forecast a volcanic event. Magma rising into the chamber directly beneath a volcano can be associated with low to moderate seismic activity. This phenomenon also can cause the chamber to become

inflated, a change that can be measured relative to sea level on Earth's surface. The new magma mixing with existing magma in the chamber can cause changes in hydrochloric acid and in the gases, including carbon dioxide and sulfur dioxide, released by the volcano. Monitoring these changes led to the successful prediction of the 1991 eruption of Mount Pinatubo in the Philippines, which saved thousands of lives.

### section 3 Earthquakes, Volcanoes, and Plate Tectonics
#### Where Volcanoes Form

Much of Earth's volcanic activity occurs unobserved at divergent plate boundaries in the ocean. The only above-sea volcanoes formed along divergent plate boundaries are in Iceland and East Africa. Most of Earth's active above-sea volcanoes occur along convergent plate boundaries including Mount St. Helens in the state of Washington. Islands formed by hot spots include Easter Island and the Galápagos Islands in the Pacific Ocean, and the Azores and the Canary Islands in the Atlantic.

## chapter content resources

**Internet Resources**
For additional content background, visit
in7.msscience.com to:
- access your book online
- find references to related articles in popular science magazines
- access Web links with related content background
- access current events with science journal topics

**Print Resources**
*Geology Rocks!* by Cindy Blobaum, Williamson Publishing, 1999
*Volcanoes,* by Janice VanCleave, John Wiley & Sons, Inc., 1994
*Earthquakes,* by Janice VanCleave, John Wiley & Sons, 1993

## Chapter Vocabulary

### Science Journal

Earthquakes and volcanic eruptions do not have to occur at the same time or place. However, if students examine a world map showing the history and locations of earthquakes and volcanoes, they may discover patterns that will help draw a connection to a common cause.

**with Image Bank**

### PowerPoint® Presentations

This CD-ROM is an editable Microsoft® PowerPoint® presentation that includes:
- a pre-made presentation for every chapter
- interactive graphics
- animations
- audio clips
- image bank
- all new section and chapter questions
- Standardized Test Practice
- transparencies
- pre-lab questions for all labs
- Foldables directions
- links to in7.msscience.com

**Academic Standard—3:** Students collect and organize data to identify relationships between physical objects, events, and processes. They use logical reasoning to question their own ideas as new information challenges their conceptions of the natural world.

# Earthquakes and Volcanoes

### chapter preview

#### sections

**1** Earthquakes

**2** Volcanoes
   *Lab* Disruptive Eruptions

**3** Earthquakes, Volcanoes, and Plate Tectonics
   *Lab* Seismic Waves

⊙ *Virtual Lab* How does magma's composition affect a volcano's eruption?

### Earth's upset stomach?

Rivers of boiling lava poured down the mountain, engulfing small buildings and threatening a lodge after a series of earthquakes awakened this volcano. What causes Earth to behave this way? Are earthquakes and volcanoes related?

**Science Journal** Are earthquakes and volcanoes completely unrelated, or could there be a possible connection? Propose several ideas that might explain what causes these events.

590

## Theme Connection

**Energy** Energy generated by forces inside Earth is released as seismic waves during an earthquake. Energy is involved in the formation of magma and the eruption of volcanoes.

### About the Photo

**Mount Etna, Sicily** In October of 2002, Mount Etna erupted. With hot lava flowing, fire, and smoke, this volcanic activity engulfed everything in its path. What caused this volcano to erupt this time? A series of earthquakes triggered Mount Etna's eruption.

# Start-Up Activities

## Construct with Strength

One of the greatest dangers associated with an earthquake occurs when people are inside buildings during the event. In the following lab, you will see how construction materials can be used to help strengthen a building.

1. Using wooden blocks, construct a building with four walls. Place a piece of cardboard over the four walls as a ceiling.

2. Gently shake the table under your building. Describe what happens.

3. Reconstruct the building. Wrap large rubber bands around each section, or wall, of blocks. Then wrap large rubber bands around the entire building.

4. Gently shake the table again.

5. **Think Critically** In your Science Journal, note any differences you observed as the two buildings were shaken. Hypothesize how the construction methods you used in this activity might be applied to the construction of real buildings.

 **Preview this chapter's content and activities at** in7.msscience.com

---

**FOLDABLES** Study Organizer

**Earthquakes and Volcanoes** Make the following Foldable to help you compare and contrast the characteristics of earthquakes and volcanoes.

**STEP 1** Draw a mark at the midpoint of a vertical sheet of paper.

**STEP 2** Turn the paper horizontally and **fold** the outside edges in to touch at the midpoint mark.

**STEP 3** Draw a volcano on one flap and label the flap *Volcanoes*. Draw an earthquake on the other flap and label it *Earthquakes*. The inside portion should be labeled *Both* and include characteristics that both events share.

**Analyze and Critique** Before you read the chapter, write what you know about earthquakes and volcanoes on the back of each flap. As you read the chapter, add more information about earthquakes and volcanoes.

591

---

**Purpose** Use the Launch Lab to introduce students to the power of earthquakes. Explain that reinforcing structures provides support that helps buildings withstand the enormous power of an earthquake. L1 ELL COOP LEARN IS **Kinesthetic**

**Materials** wooden blocks, large rubber bands, cardboard

**Teaching Strategy** Have students compare their structures with those of others. Discuss similarities and differences in how vibrations affected their structures.

## Think Critically

Students will likely note that motion had a greater effect on the first building than the second. The rubber bands acted as reinforcements that supported the blocks. This demonstrates the need to provide buildings with additional support to withstand earthquakes.

## Assessment

**Performance** Show students pictures of highway supports and building reinforcements. Ask whether these structures will increase or decrease an earthquake's effects. decrease Use **Performance Assessment in the Science Classroom**, p. 89.

**FOLDABLES** Study Organizer **Dinah Zike Study Fold**

Student preparation materials for this Foldable are available in the **Chapter** *FAST FILE* Resources.

**Probeware Labs**

This chapter's data-collection lab using Probeware technology is included on the *Video Labs CD-ROM*. See the *Probeware Lab Manual* pages 29–31 for student worksheets.

# section 1

Also covers: 7.3.7 (Detailed standards begin on page IN8.)

# Earthquakes

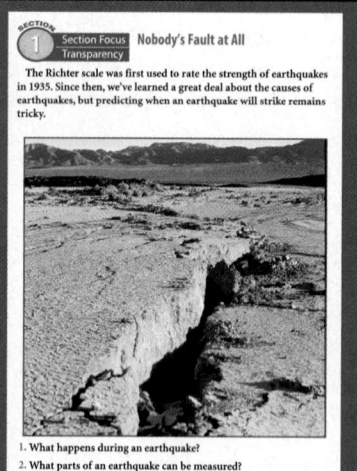
## as you read

### *What* You'll Learn

- **Explain** how earthquakes are caused by a buildup of strain in Earth's crust.
- **Compare and contrast** primary, secondary, and surface waves.
- **Recognize** earthquake hazards and how to prepare for them.

### *Why* It's Important

Studying earthquakes will help you learn where they might occur and how you can prepare for their hazards.

### ❓ Review Vocabulary

**energy:** the ability to cause change

### New Vocabulary

- earthquake
- fault
- seismic wave
- focus
- epicenter
- seismograph
- magnitude
- tsunami
- seismic safe

## What causes earthquakes?

If you've gone for a walk in the woods lately, maybe you picked up a stick along the way. If so, did you try to bend or break it? If you've ever bent a stick slowly, you might have noticed that it changes shape but usually springs back to normal form when you stop bending it. If you continue to bend the stick, you can do it for only so long before it changes permanently. When this elastic limit is passed, the stick may break, as shown in **Figure 1.** When the stick snaps, you can feel vibrations in the stick.

**Elastic Rebound** As hard as they seem, rocks act in much the same way when forces push or pull on them. If enough force is applied, rocks become strained, which means they change shape. They may even break, and the ends of the broken pieces may snap back. This snapping back is called elastic rebound.

Rocks usually change shape, or deform, slowly over long periods of time. As they are strained, potential energy builds up in them. This energy is released suddenly by the action of rocks breaking and moving. Such breaking, and the movement that follows, causes vibrations that move through rock or other earth materials. If they are large enough, these vibrations are felt as **earthquakes.**

✓ **Reading Check** *What is an earthquake?*

**Figure 1** A stick can bend only so far before it breaks.

When a stick is bent, potential energy is stored in the stick.

The energy is released as vibrations when the stick breaks.

**592 CHAPTER 20** Earthquakes and Volcanoes

## Section 1 Resource Manager

**Chapter *FAST FILE* Resources**

Transparency Activity, pp. 42, 45–46

Directed Reading for Content Mastery, pp. 17, 18

MiniLAB, p. 3

Note-taking Worksheets, pp. 31–33

Enrichment, p. 28

Reinforcement, p. 25

Lab Activity, pp. 9–10

**Earth Science Critical Thinking/Problem Solving,** p. 9

**Cultural Diversity,** p. 47

**Performance Assessment in the Science Classroom,** p. 42

**Figure 2** When rocks change shape by breaking, faults form. The type of fault formed depends on the type of stress exerted on the rock.

**A** When rocks are pulled apart, a normal fault may form.

**B** When rocks are compressed, a reverse fault may form.

**C** When rocks are sheared, a strike-slip fault may form.

**Types of Faults** When a section of rock breaks, rocks on either side of the break along which rocks move might move as a result of elastic rebound. The surface of such a break along which rocks move is called a **fault.** Several types of faults exist. The type that forms depends on how forces were applied to the rocks.

When rocks are pulled apart under tension forces, normal faults form, as shown in **Figure 2A.** Along a normal fault, rock above the fault moves down compared to rock below the fault. Compression forces squeeze rocks together, like an accordion. Compression might cause rock above a fault to move up compared to rock below the fault. This movement forms reverse faults, as shown in **Figure 2B.** As illustrated in **Figure 2C,** rock experiencing shear forces can break to form a strike-slip fault. Shear forces cause rock on either side of a strike-slip fault to move past one another in opposite directions along Earth's surface. You could infer the motion of a strike-slip fault while walking along and observing an offset feature, such as a displaced fence line, on Earth's surface.

Where do the forces come from that cause rocks to deform by bending or breaking? Why do faults form and why do earthquakes occur in certain areas? As you'll learn later in this chapter, forces inside Earth are caused by the constant motion of plates, or sections, of Earth's crust and upper mantle.

## Mini LAB

### Observing Deformation

**WARNING:** *Do not taste or eat any lab materials. Wash hands when finished.*

**Procedure**
1. Remove the wrapper from three bars of **taffy.**
2. Hold a bar of taffy lengthwise between your hands and gently push on it from opposite directions.
3. Hold another bar of taffy and pull it in opposite directions.

**Analysis**
1. Which of the procedures that you performed on the taffy involved applying tension? Which involved applying compression?
2. Infer how to apply a shear stress to the third bar of taffy.

---

## Visual Learning

**Figure 1** What would it feel like if you were holding the stick when it broke? Vibrations would be felt in the hands and arms. How is this like an earthquake? When rocks break, they also cause vibrations that move through the surrounding rock. [L2]

### Reading Check

**Answer** vibrations caused by breaking and moving rock

## Mini LAB

**Purpose** Students model the effect of forces on rock. [L1] **ELL** **IS** **Kinesthetic**

**Materials** three bars of taffy

**Teaching Strategy** Remind students not to eat the taffy.

**Troubleshooting** If students have difficulty with the directions, use a rubber band to demonstrate compression and tension.

**Analysis**
1. tension: when the taffy was pulled in opposite directions; compression: when the taffy was pushed together
2. To apply shear, push the two ends of the taffy together, but not from directly opposite directions.

### Assessment

**Oral** Explain why the taffy bent but did not break when force was applied. The force was applied gradually. The taffy would have broken if the force was applied suddenly. Use **Performance Assessment in the Science Classroom,** p. 89.

## Fun Fact

Almost 2000 years ago in China, the first earthquake detector was created. An elaborately decorated vase had dragon heads, each with a ball in its mouth, that extended out near the top of the vase. If the vase moved, presumably as a result of seismic activity, the balls would drop from the dragons' mouths.

## Making Waves

Do you recall the last time you shouted for a friend to save you a seat on the bus? When you called out, energy was transmitted through the air to your friend, who interpreted the familiar sound of your voice as belonging to you. These sound waves were released by your vocal cords and were affected by your tongue and mouth. They traveled outward through the air. Earthquakes also release waves. Earthquake waves are transmitted through materials in Earth and along Earth's surface. Earthquake waves are called **seismic waves.** In the two-page activity, you'll make waves similar to seismic waves by moving a coiled spring toy.

**Earthquake Focus and Epicenter** Movement along a fault releases strain energy. Strain energy is potential energy that builds up in rock when it is bent. When this potential energy is released, it moves outward from the fault in the form of seismic waves. The point inside Earth where this movement first occurs and energy is released is called the **focus** of an earthquake, as shown in **Figure 3.** The point on Earth's surface located directly above the earthquake focus is called the **epicenter** of the earthquake.

✔ **Reading Check** *Where is the focus of an earthquake located?*

**Figure 3** During an earthquake, several types of seismic waves form. Primary and secondary waves travel in all directions from the focus and can travel through Earth's interior. Surface waves travel at shallow depths and along Earth's surface.
**Infer** *Which seismic waves are the most destructive?*

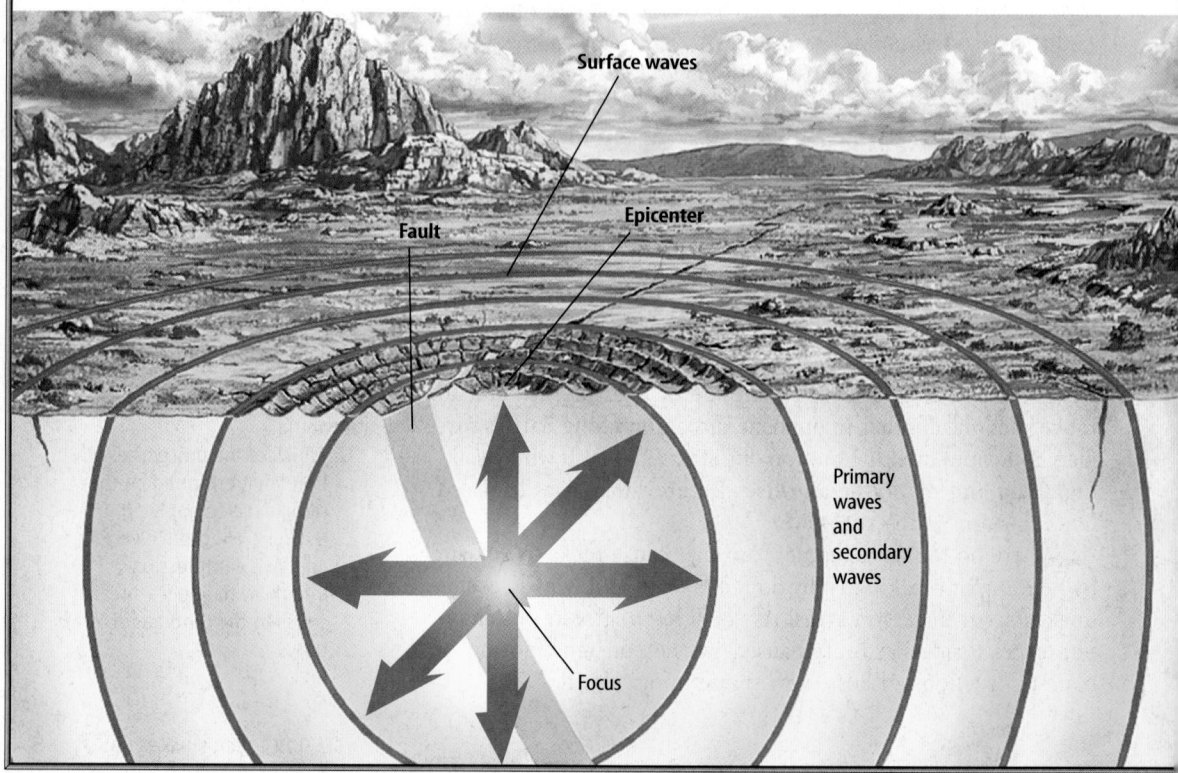

Surface waves

Fault

Epicenter

Primary waves and secondary waves

Focus

## Differentiated Instruction

**Learning Disabled** Use this activity to help students understand the different motions of surface waves. First, have several students place their chairs side-by-side in a line. Have them do "the wave" as seen at sporting events, by lifting and lowering their arms, one after another. Now have them try another human "wave." Have them turn their chairs so that they are lined up one behind the other. Have students sway side to side, swaying in the same direction as, but slightly after, the person in front of them. Allow students to switch off observing and "waving," until all students have had a chance to observe both phenomena. L1 **ELL** COOP LEARN **IS Visual-Spatial and Kinesthetic**

**Seismic Waves** After they are produced at the focus, seismic waves travel away from the focus in all directions, as illustrated in **Figure 3.** Some seismic waves travel throughout Earth's interior, and others travel along Earth's surface. The surface waves cause the most damage during an earthquake event.

Primary waves, also known as P-waves, travel the fastest through rock material by causing particles in the rock to move back and forth, or vibrate, in the same direction as the waves are moving. Secondary waves, known as S-waves, move through rock material by causing particles in the rock to vibrate at right angles to the direction in which the waves are moving. P- and S-waves travel through Earth's interior. Studying them has revealed much information about Earth's interior.

Surface waves are the slowest and largest of the seismic waves, and they cause most of the destruction during an earthquake. The movements of surface waves are complex. Some surface waves move along Earth's surface in a manner that moves rock and soil in a backward rolling motion. They have been observed moving across the land like waves of water. Some surface waves vibrate in a side-to-side, or swaying, motion parallel to Earth's surface. This motion can be particularly devastating to human-built structures.

## Learning from Earthquakes

On your way to lunch tomorrow, suppose you were to walk twice as fast as your friend does. What would happen to the distance between the two of you as you walked to the lunchroom? The distance between you and your friend would become greater the farther you walked, and you would arrive first. Using this same line of reasoning, scientists use the different speeds of seismic waves and their differing arrival times to calculate the distance to an earthquake epicenter.

**Earthquake Measurements** Seismologists are scientists who study earthquakes and seismic waves. The instrument they use to obtain a record of seismic waves from all over the world is called a **seismograph,** shown in the top photo of **Figure 4.**

One type of seismograph has a drum holding a roll of paper on a fixed frame. A pendulum with an attached pen is suspended from the frame. When seismic waves are received at the station, the drum vibrates but the pendulum remains at rest. The pen on the pendulum traces a record of the vibrations on the paper. The height of the lines traced on the paper is a measure of the energy released by the earthquake, also known as its **magnitude.**

**Figure 4** Scientists study seismic waves using seismographs located around the world.

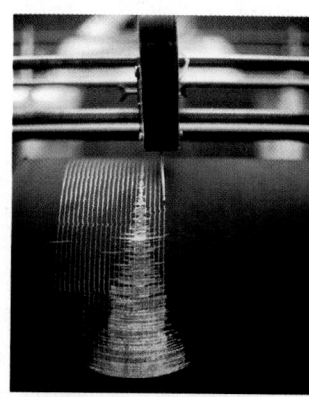

This seismograph records incoming seismic waves using a fixed mass.

Some seismographs collect and store data on a computer.

**Indiana Academic Standard Check**

7.3.18: Describe that light waves, sound waves, and other waves move at different speeds in different materials.

✔ Which seismic waves travel fastest through Earth's interior?

✔ primary waves, or P-waves

**Quick Demo**

**Visualize Sound Waves**

**Materials** plastic ruler

**Estimated Time** 10 minutes

**Procedure** Use a plastic ruler to demonstrate sound waves. Hold the ruler flat on a desktop with one end sticking out over the edge. Firmly pull down on the ruler and then release it. Pressure waves generated by the ruler's movement will move through the air and produce a sound. Varying the length of ruler protruding from the desk produces different wavelengths that result in sounds with different pitches. L1 ELL

IS Auditory-Musical

**Use an Analogy**

**Student Waves** Place two students side-by-side on one side of the room. Tell one student to walk slowly and the other to walk quickly when you say, "start." By telling the students to start and stop several times, demonstrate that one person travels farther than the other in an equal amount of time. Explain that this movement is analogous to the manner in which P- and S-waves travel through Earth. P-waves travel faster and farther over a specific period of time than S-waves. L1

IS Visual-Spatial

## Science Journal

**Surface Waves** Show photographs of buildings damaged by an earthquake's surface waves. Ask students to write brief paragraphs in their Science Journals explaining how they would design a building that could resist the surface waves. Possible answer: Structures that absorb the up-and-down motion of surface waves, such as shock absorbers, might be used in the foundation. L2 P

**Word Usage** The word *epicenter* is derived from the Greek term *epi-*, which means "at" and the Latin term *centrum*, which means "center." Ask students to use the word in a sentence that illustrates its Greek and Latin derivations. Possible answer: An earthquake's epicenter is located directly above the focus or center from which surface waves originate. L2

## Seismographs

**Purpose** To observe the energy released in a model earthquake by building a model seismograph. L2

**Possible Materials** shoebox, sand, pen, masking tape, 1 kg weight, 2 kg weight, balance, paper, ruler

**Estimated Time** one class period

**Teaching Strategies**

• Students should set up the box with the sand inside and the pen taped to the top, sticking off of one end.
• One person should move the paper past the pen, at a slow constant rate.
• At the same time, the other partner should drop the 1 kg weight from a height of 30 cm directly on the center of the top.
• Label the resulting line.
• Repeat with the next weight and label the line.
• Students should be able to conclude the relationship between seismograph records and the energy an earthquake releases.

**For additional inquiry activities, see *Science Inquiry Labs*.**

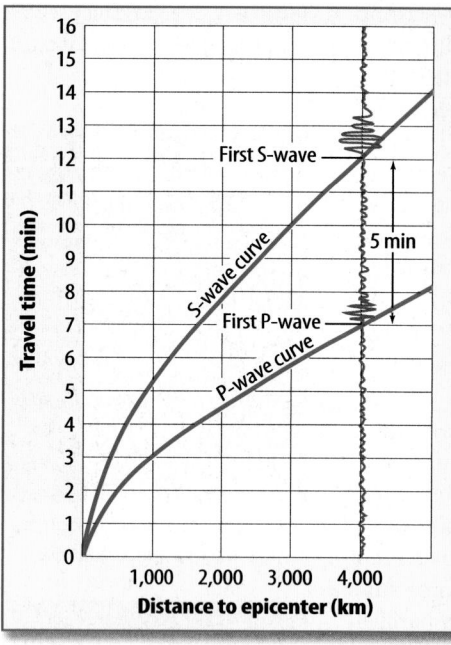

**Figure 5** P-waves and S-waves travel at different speeds. These speeds are used to determine how close a seismograph station is to an earthquake.

**Figure 6** After distances from at least three seismograph stations are determined, they are plotted as circles with radii equal to these distances on a map. The epicenter is the point at which the circles intersect.

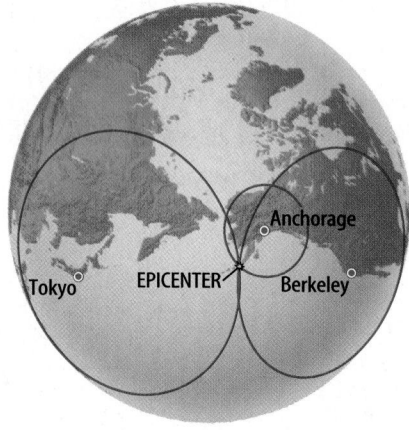

**Epicenter Location** When seismic-wave arrival times are recorded at a seismograph station, the distance from that station to the epicenter can be determined. The farther apart the arrival times for the different waves are, the farther away the earthquake epicenter is. This difference is shown by the graph in **Figure 5.** Using this information, scientists draw a circle with a radius equal to the distance from the earthquake for each of at least three seismograph stations, as illustrated in **Figure 6.** The point where the three circles meet is the location of the earthquake epicenter. Data from many stations normally are used to determine an epicenter location.

## How strong are earthquakes?

As shown in **Table 1,** major earthquakes cause much loss of life. For example, on September 20, 1999, a major earthquake struck Taiwan, leaving more than 2,400 people dead, more than 8,700 injured, and at least 100,000 homeless. Sometimes earthquakes are felt and can cause destruction in areas hundreds of kilometers away from their epicenters. The Mexico City earthquake in 1985 is an example of this. The movement of the soft sediment underneath Mexico City caused extensive damage to this city, even though the epicenter was nearly 400 km away.

**The Richter Scale** Richter (RIHK tur) magnitude is based on measurements of amplitudes, or heights, of seismic waves as recorded on seismographs. Richter magnitude describes how much energy an earthquake releases. For each increase of 1.0 on the Richter scale, the amplitude of the highest recorded seismic wave increases by 10. However, about 32 times more energy is released for every increase of 1.0 on the scale. For example, an earthquake with a magnitude of 7.5 releases about 32 times more energy than one with a magnitude of 6.5, and the wave height for a 7.5-magnitude quake is ten times higher than for a quake with a magnitude of 6.5.

---

## Visual Learning

**Figure 5** What could you infer if P- and S-waves were to arrive at a seismograph station almost at the same time? The seismic station is close to the epicenter. The farther away from the epicenter, the farther apart the arrival times of the two waves. L2

## Differentiated Instruction

**Challenge** Have students estimate how many magnitude-3.0 earthquakes would be needed to release the same energy as one magnitude-8.0 earthquake. Since the difference in magnitude is 5, the difference in released energy is $32^5$ or about 33,554,432 times. Therefore, it would take over 33.5 million magnitude-3.0 earthquakes to release the energy of one magnitude-8.0 earthquake. L3

## Curriculum Connection

**Math** Primary waves travel about 6.0 km/s through granite. Secondary waves travel about 3.5 km/s through granite. Have students calculate how much farther ahead the primary waves would be after two minutes. In 2 min (120 s) the primary waves would have traveled 720 km, and the secondary waves would have traveled 420 km. Thus, the primary waves would be 300 km ahead of the secondary waves. L3

**Earthquake Damage** Another way to measure earthquakes is available. The modified Mercalli intensity scale measures the intensity of an earthquake. Intensity is a measure of the amount of structural and geologic damage done by an earthquake in a specific location. The range of intensities spans Roman numerals I through XII. The amount of damage done depends on several factors—the strength of the earthquake, the nature of the surface material, the design of structures, and the distance from the epicenter. An intensity-I earthquake would be felt only by a few people under ideal conditions. An intensity-VI earthquake would be felt by everyone. An intensity-XII earthquake would cause major destruction to human-built structures and Earth's surface. The 1994 earthquake in Northridge, California was a Richter magnitude 6.7, and its intensity was listed at IX. An intensity-IX earthquake causes considerable damage to buildings and could cause cracks in the ground.

| Table 1 Strong Earthquakes | | | |
|------|------------------|-----------|--------|
| Year | Location | Magnitude | Deaths |
| 1989 | Loma Prieta, CA | 7.1 | 62 |
| 1990 | Iran | 7.7 | 50,000 |
| 1993 | Guam | 8.1 | none |
| 1993 | Maharashtra, India | 6.4 | 30,000 |
| 1994 | Northridge, CA | 6.7 | 61 |
| 1995 | Kobe, Japan | 6.8 | 5,378 |
| 1999 | Taiwan | 7.7 | 2,400 |
| 2000 | Indonesia | 7.9 | 103 |
| 2001 | India | 7.7 | 20,000 |
| 2003 | Iran | 6.6 | 30,000 |

**Tsunamis** Most damage from an earthquake is caused by surface waves. Buildings can crack or fall down. Elevated bridges and highways can collapse. However, people living near the seashore must protect themselves against another hazard from earthquakes. When an earthquake occurs on the ocean floor, the sudden movement pushes against the water and powerful water waves are produced. These waves can travel outward from the earthquake thousands of kilometers in all directions.

When these seismic sea waves, or **tsunamis,** are far from shore, their energy is spread out over large distances and great water depths. The wave heights of tsunamis are less than a meter in deep water, and large ships can ride over them and not even know it. In the open ocean, the speed of tsunamis can reach 950 km/h. However, when tsunamis approach land, the waves slow down and their wave heights increase as they encounter the bottom of the seafloor. This creates huge tsunami waves that can be as much as 30 m in height. Just before a tsunami crashes to shore, the water near a shoreline may move rapidly out toward the sea. If this should happen, there is immediate danger that a tsunami is about to strike. **Figure 7** illustrates the behavior of a tsunami as it approaches the shore.

**Science Online**

**Topic: Earthquake Magnitude**

Visit in7.msscience.com for Web links to information about determining earthquake magnitudes.

**Activity** Create a table that compares the damage in dollars, the magnitude, and the general location of six recent earthquakes.

## Visualizing Tsunamis

Have students examine the pictures and read the captions. Then ask the following questions.

Why would it be more important to have a tsunami warning system for the Pacific Ocean than for the Atlantic Ocean? Earthquakes are much more common in and around the Pacific Ocean than they are in the Atlantic Ocean.

How long would it take for a tsunami generated by an earthquake off the coast of California to reach Hawaii? approximately 6 hours

### Activity

**TV Broadcast** Have small groups of students prepare a script for a TV broadcast designed to make the public more aware of what tsunamis are, the dangers of tsunamis, and what people should do if a tsunami warning is issued. Allow students to perform their broadcasts for the class. L2

---

# NATIONAL GEOGRAPHIC VISUALIZING TSUNAMIS

### Figure 7

The diagram below shows stages in the development of a tsunami. A tsunami is an ocean wave that is usually generated by an earthquake and is capable of inflicting great destruction.

▶ TSUNAMI ALERT  The red dots on this map show the tide monitoring stations that make up part of the Tsunami Warning System for the Pacific Ocean. The map shows approximately how long it would take for tsunamis that originate at different places in the Pacific to reach Hawaii. Each ring represents two hours of travel time.

**TSUNAMI WARNING SYSTEM**

6  4  2 hr.  6  8  8  10  6  10  8  14

**Displacement**

**C** When a tsunami wave reaches shallow water, friction slows it down and causes it to roll up into a wall of water—sometimes 30 m high—before it breaks against the shore.

**B** The waves travel across the ocean at speeds ranging from about 500 to 950 km/h

**A** The vibrations set off by a sudden movement along a fault in Earth's crust are transferred to the water's surface and spread across the ocean in a series of long waves.

**Tsunami Warning System buoy**

# Earthquake Safety

You've just read about the destruction that earthquakes cause. Fortunately, there are ways to reduce the damage and the loss of life associated with earthquakes.

Learning the earthquake history of an area is one of the first things to do to protect yourself. If the area you are in has had earthquakes before, chances are it will again and you can prepare for that.

**Is your home seismic safe?** What could you do to make your home earthquake safe? As shown in **Figure 8,** it's a good idea to move all heavy objects to lower shelves so they can't fall on you. Make sure your gas hot-water heater and appliances are well secured. A new method of protecting against fire is to place sensors on your gas line that would shut off the gas when the vibrations of an earthquake are felt.

In the event of an earthquake, keep away from all windows and avoid anything that might fall on you. Watch for fallen power lines and possible fire hazards. Collapsed buildings and piles of rubble can contain many sharp edges, so keep clear of these areas.

**Seismic-Safe Structures** If a building is considered **seismic safe,** it will be able to stand up against the vibrations caused by most earthquakes. Residents in earthquake-prone areas are constantly improving the way structures are built. Since 1971, stricter building codes have been enforced in California. Older buildings have been reinforced. Many high-rise office buildings now stand on huge steel-and-rubber supports that could enable them to ride out the vibrations of an earthquake. Underground water and gas pipes are replaced with pipes that will bend during an earthquake. This can help prevent broken gas lines and therefore reduce damage from fires.

Seismic-safe highways have cement pillars with spiral reinforcing rods placed within them. One structure that was severely damaged in the 1989 Loma Prieta, California earthquake was Interstate Highway 880. The collapsed highway was due to be renovated to make it seismic safe. It was built in the 1950s and did not have spiral reinforcing rods in its concrete columns. When the upper highway went in one direction, the lower one went in the opposite direction. The columns collapsed and the upper highway came down onto the lower one.

**Figure 8** You can minimize your risk of getting hurt by preparing for an earthquake in advance.

Placing heavy or breakable objects on lower shelves means they won't fall too far during an earthquake.

Vibration sensors on gas lines shut off the supply of gas automatically during an earthquake. **Draw Conclusions** *What hazard can be prevented if the gas is turned off?*

## Discussion

**Earthquake Resistance** Explain that the two main strategies for building earthquake-resistant structures are shock absorption and reinforcement. How could reinforcing the walls in a structure increase earthquake safety? It would reduce the amount of debris that might fall on victims. How might placing shock absorbers in the foundation of a building help increase safety during an earthquake? Shock absorbers could absorb some of the up-and-down movement within a structure, thus reducing the amount of structural failure within walls and supports. L2

## Caption Answer

**Figure 8** fire hazard

## Science Journal

**Safety Checklist** Have students make an earthquake safety checklist in their Science Journals. Checklists should note actions people should take when an earthquake occurs. Students should include staying away from power lines, keeping clear of heavy objects that might fall on them, and using the "DUCK (get down), COVER (head), and HOLD (stay put under a sturdy piece of furniture)" safety routine. L2

## Check for Understanding

**Kinesthetic** Give pairs of students a rope and coiled spring toy. Have them model the three types of seismic waves using the rope and coiled spring toy. L2

## Reteach

**Earthquake Damage** Show students pictures illustrating damage caused by the 1995 earthquake in Kobe, Japan, the 1989 earthquake in Loma Prieta, California, and the 1906 earthquake in San Francisco, California. Ask them to hypothesize what caused the greatest amount of damage. falling structures and fires caused by breaking gas lines L2 IS **Logical-Mathematical**

## ✓ Assessment

**Oral** How might warning the public of an impending earthquake help save lives? People could remain outside of buildings and avoid being trapped by falling debris. Would a warning help reduce structural damage? No, structural damage would still occur. Use **Performance Assessment in the Science Classroom**, p. 89. L2

**Figure 9** One way to monitor changes along a fault is to detect any movement that occurs.

**Predicting Earthquakes** Imagine how many lives could be saved if only the time and location of a major earthquake could be predicted. Because most injuries from earthquakes occur when structures fall on top of people, it would help if people could be warned to move outside of buildings.

Researchers try to predict earthquakes by noting changes that precede them. That way, if such changes are observed again, an earthquake warning may be issued.

For example, movement along faults is monitored using laser-equipped, distance-measuring devices, such as the one shown in **Figure 9**. Changes in groundwater level or in electrical properties of rocks under stress have been measured by some scientists. Some people even study rock layers that have been affected by ancient earthquakes. Whether any of these studies will lead to the accurate and reliable prediction of earthquakes, no one knows. A major problem is that no single change in Earth occurs for all earthquakes. Each earthquake is unique.

Long-range forecasts predict whether an earthquake of a certain magnitude is likely to occur in a given area within 30 to 100 years. Forecasts of this nature are used to update building codes to make a given area more seismic safe.

## section 1 review

### Summary

**What causes earthquakes?**

- The sudden release of energy in rock and the resulting movement causes an earthquake.
- Faults are breaks in rocks along which movement occurs.

**Making Waves**

- The focus is where an earthquake occurs. The epicenter is directly above it.
- Earthquakes generate seismic waves.

**How strong are earthquakes?**

- The Richter Scale measures magnitude.
- The modified Mercalli scale measures intensity.

**Earthquake Safety**

- Structures can be made seismic safe.

### Self Check

1. **Explain** what happens to rocks after their elastic limit is passed.
2. **Identify** Which seismic waves cause most of the damage during an earthquake?
3. **Apply** What has been done to make structures more seismic safe?
4. **Summarize** How can seismic waves be used to determine an earthquake's epicenter?
5. **Think Critically** Explain how a magnitude-8.0 earthquake could be classified as a low-intensity earthquake.

#### Applying Skills

6. **Make and Use Tables** Use **Table 1** to research the earthquakes that struck Indonesia in 2000, Loma Prieta, California in 1989, and Iran in 1990. Why was there such a great difference in the number of deaths?

**600 CHAPTER 20** Earthquakes and Volcanoes

Science Online in7.msscience.com/self_check_quiz

## section 1 review

1. Rocks bend or break.
2. Surface waves cause the most damage.
3. Reinforcements and shock absorbers have been added to structures to make them safer.
4. The different speeds at which P- and S-waves travel can be used
to determine distance.
5. Intensity is a measure of damage. If the earthquake occurred far from populated areas or if structures in the area had been built to withstand a large earthquake, damage, and thus intensity, might be low.
6. The structures in California were built to withstand earthquakes. Buildings in Indonesia and Iran lacked support structures and were more likely to crumble, killing people inside the buildings.

# section

# 2 Volcanoes

## How do volcanoes form?

Much like air bubbles that are forced upward toward the bottom of an overturned bottle of denser syrup, molten rock material, or magma, is forced upward toward Earth's surface by denser surrounding rock. Rising magma eventually can lead to an eruption, where magma, solids, and gas are spewed out to form cone-shaped mountains called **volcanoes.** As magma flows onto Earth's surface through a vent, or opening, it is called **lava.** Volcanoes have circular holes near their summits called craters. Lava and other volcanic materials can be expelled through a volcano's crater.

Some explosive eruptions throw lava and rock thousands of meters into the air. Bits of rock or solidified lava dropped from the air are called tephra. Tephra varies in size from volcanic ash to cinders to larger rocks called bombs or blocks.

**Where Plates Collide** Some volcanoes form because of collision of large plates of Earth's crust and upper mantle. This process has produced a string of volcanic islands, much like those illustrated in **Figure 10,** which includes Montserrat. These islands are forming as plates made up of oceanic crust and mantle collide. The older and denser oceanic plate subducts, or sinks beneath, the less dense plate, as shown in **Figure 10.** When one plate sinks under another plate, rock in and above the sinking plate melts, forming chambers of magma. This magma is the source for volcanic eruptions that have formed the Caribbean Islands.

Montserrat

### as you read

**What You'll Learn**

- **Explain** how volcanoes can affect people.
- **Describe** how types of materials are produced by volcanoes.
- **Compare** how three different volcano forms develop.

**Why It's Important**

Volcanic eruptions can cause serious consequences for humans and other organisms.

**Review Vocabulary**

**plate:** a large section of Earth's crust and rigid upper mantle that moves around on the asthenosphere

**New Vocabulary**

- volcano
- lava
- shield volcano
- cinder cone volcano
- composite volcano

**Figure 10** A string of Caribbean Islands known as the Lesser Antilles formed because of subduction. The island of Montserrat is among these.

SECTION 2 Volcanoes **601**

## 1 Motivate

**Bellringer**

**Section Focus Transparencies** also are available on the Interactive Chalkboard CD-ROM.

L2 ELL

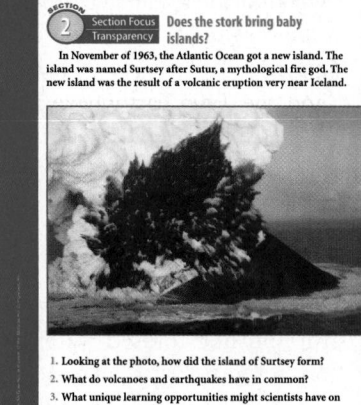

SECTION 2 Section Focus Transparency — Does the stork bring baby islands?

In November of 1963, the Atlantic Ocean got a new island. The island was named Surtsey after Sutur, a mythological fire god. The new island was the result of a volcanic eruption very near Iceland.

1. Looking at the photo, how did the island of Surtsey form?
2. What do volcanoes and earthquakes have in common?
3. What unique learning opportunities might scientists have on Surtsey?

Earthquakes and Volcanoes

**Tie to Prior Knowledge**

**Recent Eruptions** Help students identify the locations of recent volcano eruptions described in the media. Ask them to name materials that are extruded from an erupting volcano. lava, tephra, gases L2

---

## Section 2 Resource Manager

**Chapter FAST FILE Resources**

Transparency Activity, p. 43

Directed Reading for Content Mastery, p. 19

MiniLAB, p. 4

Enrichment, p. 29

Reinforcement, p. 26

Lab Activity, pp. 11–14

Lab Worksheet, pp. 5–6

**Earth Science Critical Thinking/Problem Solving,** p. 1

**Reading and Writing Skill Activities,** p. 2

**Purpose** Students model the forces involved in a volcanic eruption. L1 ELL

**LS Kinesthetic**

**Materials** red-colored gelatin, self-sealing bag, pin

**Teaching Strategy** Remind students not to eat the gelatin and to be careful with the pin.

**Analysis**

1. gelatin: magma; plastic bag: Earth's crust; pinhole: vent
2. pressure building within the crust
3. super-heated steam and gases

### Assessment

**Process** Infer why you used gelatin and not colored water in this activity. Gelatin more closely resembles thick, sticky silica-rich magma than does colored water. Use **Performance Assessment in the Science Classroom,** p. 89.

*Try at Home*

## Teacher FYI

**Early Earth Water** During eruptions, volcanoes extrude lava, gases, and tephra. Most gases released from volcanoes consist of water vapor. Scientists think that water vapor from magma was the source of Earth's early oceans and that gases released by volcanoes may have contributed to the composition of Earth's early atmosphere.

**Figure 11** Several volcanic hazards are associated with explosive activity.

Volcanic ash blanketing an area can cause collapse of structures or—when mixed with precipitation—mudflows.

Objects in the path of a pyroclastic flow are subject to complete destruction.

### Modeling an Eruption

**Procedure**

1. Place **red-colored gelatin** into a **self-sealing plastic bag** until the bag is half full.
2. Seal the bag and press the gelatin to the bottom of the bag.
3. Put a hole in the bottom of the bag with a **pin**.

**Analysis**

1. What parts of a volcano do the gelatin, the plastic bag, and the hole represent?
2. What force in nature did you mimic as you moved the gelatin to the bottom of the bag?
3. What factors in nature cause this force to increase and lead to an eruption?

*Try at Home*

**Eruptions on a Caribbean Island** Soufrière (soo free UR) Hills volcano on the island of Montserrat was considered dormant until recently. However, in 1995, Soufrière Hills volcano surprised its inhabitants with explosive activity. In July 1995, plumes of ash soared to heights of more than 10,000 m. This ash covered the capital city of Plymouth and many other villages, as shown at left in **Figure 11.**

Every aspect of a once-calm tropical life changed when the volcano erupted. Glowing avalanches and hot, boiling mudflows destroyed villages and shut down the main harbor of the island and its airport. During activity on July 3, 1998, volcanic ash reached heights of more than 14,000 m. This ash settled over the entire island and was followed by mudflows brought on by heavy rains.

Pyroclastic flows are another hazard for inhabitants of Montserrat. They can occur anytime on any side of the volcano. Pyroclastic flows are massive avalanches of hot, glowing rock flowing on a cushion of intensely hot gases, as shown at right in **Figure 11.** Speeds at which these flows travel can reach 200 km/h.

More than one half of Montserrat has been converted to a barren wasteland by the volcano. Virtually all of the farmland is now unusable, and most of the island's business and leisure centers are gone. Many of the inhabitants of the island have been evacuated to England, surrounding islands, or northern Montserrat, which is considered safe from volcanic activity.

**602 CHAPTER 20** Earthquakes and Volcanoes

## Curriculum Connection

**Geography** Place a world map on a bulletin board. Ask each student to use the Internet or library sources to determine the location of a volcano. Have students place a pin on the map to show the location of the volcano researched. Use a piece of string to connect each pin to a card labeled with the volcano's name, latitude, and longitude. L2

## Differentiated Instruction

**English-Language Learners** Students who are beginning to learn English may find the different types of volcanoes difficult to remember. Display pictures of a shield volcano and a cinder cone volcano. Also have a picture of a medieval shield and an ice cream cone handy. Ask students to compare the shield and the ice cream cone to the volcano pictures and match up the ones that look similar.

**Volcanic Risks** According to the volcanic-risk map shown in **Figure 12,** inactive volcanic centers exist at Silver Hill, Centre Hill, and South Soufrière Hills. The active volcano, Soufrière Hills volcano, is located just north of South Soufrière Hills. The risk map shows different zones of the island where inhabitants still are able to stay and locations from which they have been evacuated. Twenty people who had ignored evacuation orders were killed by pyroclastic flows from the June 25, 1997, event. These are the first and only deaths that have occurred since July 1995.

## Forms of Volcanoes

As you have learned, volcanoes can cause great destruction. However, volcanoes also add new rock to Earth's crust with each eruption. The way volcanoes add this new material to Earth's surface varies greatly. Different types of eruptions produce different types of volcanoes.

**What determines how a volcano erupts?** Some volcanic eruptions are violent, while during others lava flows out quietly around a vent. The composition of the magma plays a big part in determining the manner in which energy is released during a volcanic eruption. Lava that contains more silica, which is a compound consisting of silicon and oxygen, tends to be thicker and is more resistant to flow. Lava containing more iron and magnesium and less silica tends to flow easily. The amount of water vapor and other gases trapped in the lava also influences how lava erupts.

When you shake a bottle of carbonated soft drink before opening it, the pressure from the gas in the drink builds up and is released suddenly when the container is opened. Similarly, steam builds pressure in magma. This pressure is released as magma rises toward Earth's surface and eventually erupts. Sticky, silica-rich lava tends to trap water vapor and other gases.

Water is carried down from the surface of Earth into the mantle when one plate subducts beneath another, as in the case of the Lesser Antilles volcanoes. In hotter regions of Earth's interior, part of a descending plate and nearby rock will melt to form magma. The magma produced is more silica rich than the rock that melts to form the magma. Superheated steam produces tremendous pressure in such thick, silica-rich magmas. After enough pressure builds up, an eruption occurs. The type of lava and the gases contained in that lava determine the type of eruption that occurs.

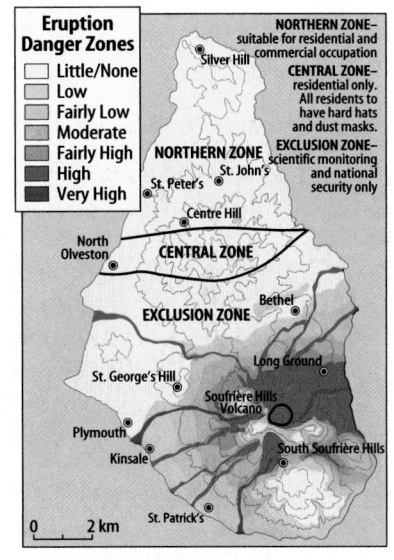

**Figure 12** A volcanic risk map for Montserrat was prepared to warn inhabitants and visitors about unsafe areas on the island.

**Eruption Danger Zones**
- Little/None
- Low
- Fairly Low
- Moderate
- Fairly High
- High
- Very High

NORTHERN ZONE– suitable for residential and commercial occupation

CENTRAL ZONE– residential only. All residents to have hard hats and dust masks.

EXCLUSION ZONE– scientific monitoring and national security only

---

**Indiana Academic Standard Check**

**7.3.7:** Give examples of... changes in Earth's surface that are abrupt, such as... volcanic eruptions...

✔ How fast can pyroclastic flows move?

✔ Speeds can reach 200 km/h.

---

**Science Online**

**Topic: Montserrat Volcano**
Visit in7.msscience.com for Web links to an update of data on Soufrière Hills volcano.

**Activity** Compare the recent activity of the Soufrière Hills volcano on Montserrat to another recently active volcano. Gather your findings into a table and include dates as well as amount of area destroyed in your report.

SECTION 2 Volcanoes **603**

---

## Discussion

**Lava Composition** Would the lava flowing from Kilauea Iki be hotter or cooler than lava from Mount Saint Helens? *Hotter; freely flowing lava is usually rich in iron and magnesium.* How would the composition of slow moving, viscous (thick) lava compare to fast moving, runny lava? *Viscous lava is usually silica-rich and cooler, whereas fast moving lava is usually iron- and magnesium-rich and hotter.* L2

## Activity

**Illustrate Volcanoes** Have students work in pairs to illustrate the three forms of volcanoes. Encourage students to use proper size ratios in their illustrations. For example, Mauna Loa (shield) is 3 times higher and 10 times wider than Mount Rainier (composite). In turn, Mount Rainier is 10 times higher and 11 times wider than Sunset Crater (cinder cone). L2
**IS** Visual-Spatial

### ✔ Reading Check

**Answer** basaltic lava

---

**Figure 13** Volcanic landforms vary greatly in size and shape.

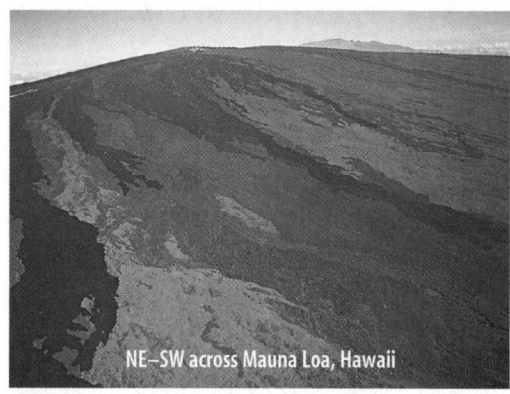

NE–SW across Mauna Loa, Hawaii

**A** The fluid nature of basaltic lava has produced extensive flows at Mauna Loa, Hawaii—the largest active volcano on Earth.

Cinder cone volcano          Crater

0.3 km

0.5 km

N–S View across Sunset Crater, Arizona

**B** Sunset Crater is small and steep along its flanks—typical of a cinder cone. Compare the scale given for Sunset Crater with that shown in Figure 13A.

---

Shield volcano
Caldera
Sea level
9 km
50 km

**Shield Volcanoes** Basaltic lava, which is high in iron and magnesium and low in silica, flows in broad, flat layers. The buildup of basaltic layers forms a broad volcano with gently sloping sides called a **shield volcano.** Shield volcanoes, shown in **Figure 13A,** are the largest type of volcano. They form where magma is being forced up from extreme depths within Earth, or in areas where Earth's plates are moving apart. The separation of plates enables magma to be forced upward to Earth's surface.

### ✔ Reading Check
*What materials are shield volcanoes composed of?*

**Cinder Cone Volcanoes** Rising magma accumulates gases on its way to the surface. When the gas builds up enough pressure, it erupts. Moderate to violent eruptions throw volcanic ash, cinders, and lava high into the air. The lava cools quickly in midair and the particles of solidified lava, ash, and cinders fall back to Earth. This tephra forms a relatively small cone of volcanic material called a **cinder cone volcano.** Cinder cones are usually less than 300 m in height and often form in groups near other larger volcanoes. Because the eruption is powered by the high gas content, it usually doesn't last long. After the gas is released, the force behind the eruption is gone. Sunset Crater, an example of a cinder cone near Flagstaff, Arizona, is shown in **Figure 13B.**

---

## Teacher **FYI**

**Ring of Fire** The Pacific Ring of Fire contains Mount Rainier, Mount Hood, Mount Jefferson, Crater Lake, Mount Shasta, and Mount Saint Helens. These and other volcanoes all have formed around the Pacific and Juan de Fuca plates where they converge with other plates.

## Cultural Diversity

**Effects of Volcanic Eruptions** Have students make a classroom collage about volcanoes around the world. Ask them to research and discuss cultural effects each volcano might have had on people living nearby. Have the class discuss why people continue to live near large, dangerous volcanoes. *Possible answer: Volcanic eruptions provide fertile soil. People might be able to evacuate when volcanoes erupt. People might be reluctant to leave their homes.* L2

**Composite Volcanoes** Steep-sided mountains composed of alternating layers of lava and tephra are **composite volcanoes**. They sometimes erupt violently, releasing large quantities of ash and gas. This forms a tephra layer of solid materials. Then a quieter eruption forms a lava layer.

Composite volcanoes form where one plate sinks beneath another. Soufrière Hills volcano is an example of a composite volcano. Another volcanic eruption from a composite volcano was the May 1980 eruption of Mount St. Helens in the state of Washington. It erupted explosively, spewing ash that fell on regions hundreds of kilometers away from the volcano. A composite volcano is shown in **Figure 13C**.

**Fissure Eruptions** Magma that is highly fluid can ooze from cracks or fissures in Earth's surface. This is the type of magma that usually is associated with fissure eruptions. The lava that erupts has a low viscosity, which means it can flow freely across the land to form flood basalts. Flood basalts that have been exposed to erosion for millions of years can become large, relatively flat landforms known as lava plateaus, as shown in **Figure 13D**. The Columbia River Plateau in the northwestern United States was formed about 15 million years ago when several fissures erupted and the flows built up layer upon layer.

**C** Composite cones are intermediate in size and shape compared to shield volcanoes and cinder cone volcanoes.

Mount Rainier, Washington

Crater
Composite volcano
3 km
6 km

**D** No modern example compares with the extensive flood basalts making up the Columbia River Plateau.

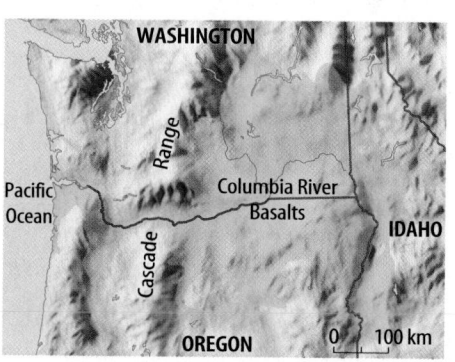
WASHINGTON
Pacific Ocean
Range
Columbia River Basalts
IDAHO
Cascade
OREGON
0    100 km

**DAILY INTERVENTION**

## Check for Understanding

**Intrapersonal** Ask students to work in small groups to brainstorm the following problem. How did the eruption of Mount Saint Helens generate a massive mudflow that caused great destruction? Have them support their hypothesis with facts about Mount Saint Helens and the surrounding area.
**L3**

## Reteach

**Subduction Zones** Draw a cross section of a subduction zone on the board. Have a student volunteer use the diagram to explain how the denser plate carries water with it as it sinks. Have a second volunteer explain that the partial melting of the sinking block and the water content of the material produce a silica-rich magma that contains water vapor and other gases **L3** **IS** **Visual-Spatial**

### ✔ Assessment

**Content** Have students work in groups of three or four to write a song or poem about how volcanoes like those in Hawaii erupt. Poems or songs should include reference to the runny, quickly moving, basaltic lava that flows from Hawaiian volcanoes. Use **Performance Assessment in the Science Classroom,** p. 151. **L2**

**Table 2 Seven Selected Eruptions in History**

| Volcano (Year) | Type | Eruptive Force | Silica Content | Gas Content | Eruption Products |
|---|---|---|---|---|---|
| Krakatau, Indonesia (1883) | composite | high | high | high | gas, cinders, ash |
| Katmai, Alaska (1912) | composite | high | high | high | lava, ash, gas |
| Paricutín, Mexico (1943) | cinder cone | moderate | high | low | gas, cinders, ash |
| Helgafell, Iceland (1973) | cinder cone | moderate | low | high | gas, ash |
| Mount St. Helens, Washington (1980) | composite | high | high | high | gas, ash |
| Kilauea Iki, Hawaii (1989) | shield | low | low | low | gas, lava |
| Soufrière Hills, Montserrat (1995–) | composite | high | high | high | gas, ash, rocks |

You have read about some variables that control the type of volcanic eruption that will occur. Examine **Table 2** for a summary of these important factors. In the next section, you'll learn that the type of magma produced is associated with properties of Earth's plates and how these plates interact.

## section 2 review

### Summary

**How do volcanoes form?**

- Some volcanoes form as two or more large plates collide.
- The Caribbean Islands formed from volcanic eruptions as one plate sinks under another plate.

**Forms of volcanoes**

- Lava high in silica produces explosive eruptions, lava low in silica but high in iron and magnesium produces more fluid eruptions.
- The amount of water vapor and gases impacts how volcanoes erupt.
- The types of volcanoes include shield, cinder cone and composite volcanoes, and fissure eruptions.

### Self Check

1. **Identify** Which types of lava eruptions cover the largest area on Earth's surface?
2. **Describe** the processes that have led to the formation of the Soufrière Hills volcano.
3. **Explain** why a cinder cone has steep sides?
4. **List** What types of materials are volcanoes like Mount St. Helens made of?
5. **Think Critically** Why is silica-rich magma explosive?

#### Applying Math

6. **Solve One-Step Equations** Mauna Loa in Hawaii rises 9 km above the seafloor. Sunset Crater in Arizona rises to an elevation of 300 m. How many times higher is Mauna Loa than Sunset Crater?

**606** **CHAPTER 20** Earthquakes and Volcanoes

Science Online in7.msscience.com/self_check_quiz

## section 2 review

1. fissure eruptions
2. As one plate sinks under another, rock material is melted and forced upward toward Earth's surface, where it erupts to form a volcano.
3. The solids extruded by a cinder cone form a steep-sided pile.
4. alternating layers of lava and tephra
5. Silica-rich magma is sticky and thick. It tends to hold in gases that cause pressure to build until finally the volcano erupts explosively.
6. Mauna Loa is 30 times higher than Sunset Crater (9,000 m ÷ 300 m = 30).

# Disruptive Eruptions

A volcano's structure can influence how it erupts. Some volcanoes have only one central vent, while others have numerous fissures that allow lava to escape. Materials in magma influence its viscosity, or how it flows. If magma is a thin fluid—not viscous—gases can escape easily. But if magma is thick—viscous—gases cannot escape as easily. This builds up pressure within a volcano.

## Real-World Question

What determines the explosiveness of a volcanic eruption?

### Goals
- **Infer** how a volcano's opening contributes to how explosive an eruption might be.
- **Hypothesize** how the viscosity of magma can influence an eruption.

### Materials
plastic film canisters    50-mL graduated
baking soda ($NaHCO_3$)    cylinder
vinegar ($CH_3COOH$)    teaspoon

### Safety Precautions

This lab should be done outdoors. Goggles must be worn at all times. The caps of the film canisters fly off due to the chemical reaction that occurs inside them. Never put anything in your mouth while doing the experiment.

## Procedure

1. Watch your teacher demonstrate this lab before attempting to do it yourself.
2. Add 15 mL of vinegar to a film canister.
3. Place 1 teaspoon of baking soda in the film

canister's lid, using it as a type of plate.

4. Place the lid on top of the film canister, but do not cap it. The baking soda will fall into the vinegar. Move a safe distance away. Record your observations in your Science Journal.
5. Clean out your film canister and repeat the lab, but this time cap the canister quickly and tightly. Record your observations.

## Conclude and Apply

1. **Identify** Which of the two labs models a more explosive eruption?
2. **Explain** Was the pressure greater inside the canister during the first or second lab? Why?
3. **Explain** What do the bubbles have to do with the explosion? How do they influence the pressure in the container?
4. **Infer** If the vinegar were a more viscous substance, how would the eruption be affected?

### Communicating Your Data

**Research** three volcanic eruptions that have occurred in the past five years. Compare each eruption to one of the eruption styles you modeled in this lab. Communicate to your class what you learn.

**LAB 607**

### Communicating Your Data

Students should provide descriptive evidence of each eruption to support their comparisons.

## Real-World Question

**Purpose** Students will investigate what determines the explosiveness of a volcanic eruption.

**Process Skills** observe, infer, hypothesize

**Time Required** 30 minutes

## Procedure

**Safety Precautions** Be sure students move a safe distance away from the canisters.

**Teaching Strategy** Review with students that the reaction between vinegar and baking soda produces carbon dioxide gas.

**Troubleshooting** Some film canisters will not seal tightly enough to pop the top off in step 5. You may want to test the canisters ahead of time.

## Conclude and Apply

1. the second one
2. during the second one because the gas produced could not easily escape
3. The bubbles are carbon dioxide gas produced by the reaction. The more gas that is trapped in the canister, the greater the pressure is.
4. The gas bubbles would have a harder time escaping from a more viscous liquid so the pressure would build up more before it erupted.

### ☑ Assessment

**Oral** Have students describe how they think a reaction between baking soda and vinegar mixed with ketchup would appear. Use **Performance Assessment in the Science Classroom**, p. 89

## section

## 3

Also covers: 7.3.4, 7.3.18 (Detailed standards begin on page IN8.)

# Earthquakes, Volcanoes, and Plate Tectonics

## as you read

### *What* You'll Learn

- **Explain** how the locations of volcanoes and earthquake epicenters are related to tectonic plate boundaries.
- **Explain** how heat within Earth causes Earth's plates to move.

### *Why* It's Important

Most volcanoes and earthquakes are caused by the motion and interaction of Earth's plates.

### Review Vocabulary

**asthenosphere:** plasticlike layer of mantle under the lithosphere

### New Vocabulary

- rift
- hot spot

## Earth's Moving Plates

At the beginning of class, your teacher asks for volunteers to help set up the cafeteria for a special assembly. You and your classmates begin to move the tables carefully, like the students shown in **Figure 14.** As you move the tables, two or three of them crash into each other. Think about what could happen if the students moving those tables kept pushing on them. For a while one or two of the tables might keep another from moving. However, if enough force were used, the tables would slide past one another. One table might even slide up on top of another. It is because of this possibility that your teacher has asked that you move the tables carefully.

The movement of the tables and the possible collisions among them is like the movement of Earth's crust and uppermost mantle, called the lithosphere. Earth's lithosphere is broken into separate sections, or plates. When these plates move around, they collide, move apart, or slide past each other. The movement of these plates can cause vibrations known as earthquakes and can create conditions that cause volcanoes to form.

**Figure 14** Like the tables pictured here, Earth's plates are in contact with one another and can slide beneath each other. The way Earth's plates interact at boundaries is an important factor in the locations of earthquakes and volcanoes.

**608**  **CHAPTER 20**  Earthquakes and Volcanoes

Figure 15 Earth's lithosphere is divided into about 13 major plates. Where plates collide, separate, and slip past one another at plate boundaries, interesting geological activity results.

**Map legend:**
- ↞↠ Convergent plate boundaries
- ⊢⊣ Divergent plate boundaries
- ⇌ Transform plate boundaries
- • Volcano locations

## Where Volcanoes Form

A plot of the location of plate boundaries and volcanoes on Earth shows that most volcanoes form along plate boundaries. Examine the map in **Figure 15.** Can you see how this indicates that plate tectonics and volcanic activity are related? Perhaps the energy involved in plate tectonics is causing magma to form deep under Earth's surface. You'll recall that the Soufrière Hills volcano formed where plates converge. Plate movement often explains why volcanoes form in certain areas.

**Divergent Plate Boundaries** Tectonic plates move apart at divergent plate boundaries. As the plates separate, long cracks called **rifts** form between them. Rifts contain fractures that serve as passageways for magma originating in the mantle. Rift zones account for most of the places where lava flows onto Earth's surface. Fissure eruptions often occur along rift zones. These eruptions form lava that cools and solidifies into basalt, the most abundant type of rock in Earth's crust.

> ✓ **Reading Check** *Where does magma along divergent boundaries originate?*

## Visual Learning

**Figure 15** Explain that volcanoes occur where plates pull apart or are pushed together. Which type of eruption is likely to occur where plates pull apart? Explain. A fracture forms in Earth's crust where plates pull apart. Thus, fissure eruptions are likely to occur there. L2

### Quick Demo

**Materials** chocolate-covered nougat or caramel candy bar

**Estimated Time** 10 minutes

**Procedure** Ask students to observe the behavior of the chocolate layer at the top and bottom of the candy bar as you slowly pull it apart. Explain to them that this is similar to the behavior of the crust at a divergent plate boundary.

### Make a Model

**Model Volcanoes** Organize the class into four groups and assign each group one of the following topics: volcanoes caused by convergence, volcanoes caused by divergence, volcanoes caused by hot spots, and different forms of volcanoes. Ask each group to make a model of their assigned topic using everyday materials. Allow groups to present their models to the class. L2 ELL COOP LEARN IS **Kinesthetic**

> ✓ **Reading Check**

**Answer** the mantle

---

### Teacher FYI

**Magma in the Cascades** Sinking of the remaining portion of the Farallon Plate, called the Juan de Fuca Plate, has caused melting that is the source of magma for the Cascade range of volcanic mountains. These volcanoes are located in the western United States and include Mount Rainier, Mount Shasta, and Mount Saint Helens.

## Differentiated Instruction

**Challenge** Have students locate Iceland on a physical map of the ocean floors. Encourage them to predict what the climate may be like on Iceland, what physical features, and power sources the island may possess. Then have them research Iceland and compare their hypothesis with the correct information. The students should then create a travel brochure enticing people to visit Iceland. L3

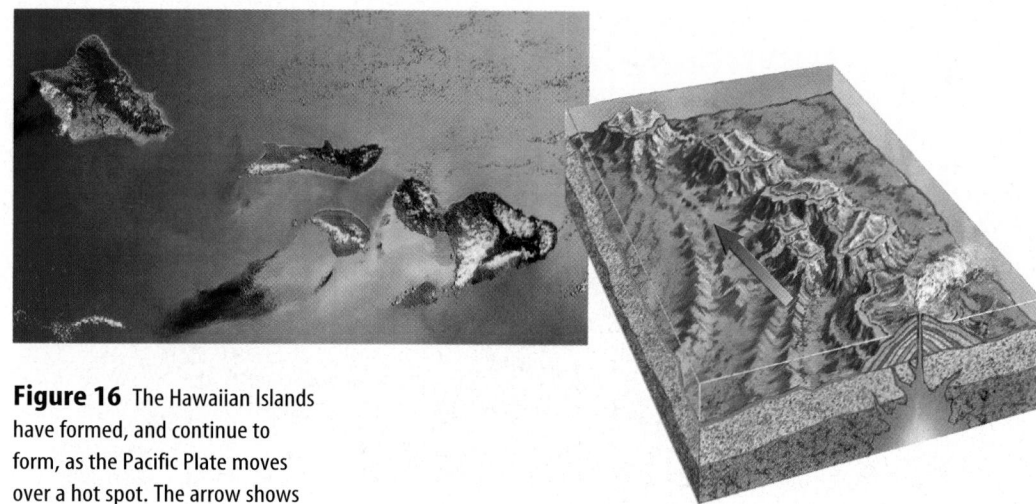

**Figure 16** The Hawaiian Islands have formed, and continue to form, as the Pacific Plate moves over a hot spot. The arrow shows that the Pacific Plate is moving north-northwest.

**Convergent Plate Boundaries** A common location for volcanoes to form is along convergent plate boundaries. More dense oceanic plates sink beneath less dense plates that they collide with. This sets up conditions that form volcanoes.

When one plate sinks beneath another, basalt and sediment on an oceanic plate move down into the mantle. Water from the sediment and altered basalt lowers the melting point of the surrounding rock. Heat in the mantle causes part of the sinking plate and overlying mantle to melt. This melted material then is forced upward. Volcanoes have formed in this way all around the Pacific Ocean, where the Pacific Plate, among others, collides with several other plates. This belt of volcanoes surrounding the Pacific Ocean is called the Pacific Ring of Fire.

**Hot Spots** The Hawaiian Islands are volcanic islands that have not formed along a plate boundary. In fact, they are located well within the Pacific Plate. What process causes them to form? Large bodies of magma, called **hot spots,** are forced upward through Earth's mantle and crust, as shown in **Figure 16.** Scientists suggest that this is what is occurring at a hot spot that exists under the present location of Hawaii.

☑ **Reading Check** *What is a hot spot?*

Volcanoes on Earth usually form along rift zones, subduction zones (where one plate sinks beneath another), or over hot spots. At each of these locations, magma from deep within Earth is forced upward toward the surface. Lava breaks through and flows out, where it piles up into layers or forms a volcanic cone.

**610** CHAPTER 20 Earthquakes and Volcanoes

## Moving Plates Cause Earthquakes

Place two notebooks on your desk with the page edges facing each other. Then push them together slowly. The individual sheets of paper gradually will bend upward from the stress. If you continue to push on the notebooks, one will slip past the other suddenly. This sudden movement is like an earthquake.

Now imagine what would happen if tectonic plates were moving like the notebooks. What would happen if the plates collided and stopped moving? Forces generated by the locked-up plates would cause strain to build up. Both plates would begin to deform until the elastic limit was passed. The breaking and elastic rebound of the deformed material would produce vibrations felt as earthquakes.

Earthquakes often occur where tectonic plates come together at a convergent boundary, where tectonic plates move apart at a divergent boundary, and where tectonic plates grind past each other, called a transform boundary.

**Earthquake Locations** If you look at a map of earthquakes, you'll see that most occur in well-known belts. About 80 percent of them occur in the Pacific Ring of Fire—the same belt in which many of Earth's volcanoes occur. If you compare **Figure 17** with **Figure 15,** you will notice a definite relationship between earthquake epicenters and tectonic plate boundaries. Movement of the plates produces forces that generate the energy to cause earthquakes.

**Friction** Friction is a force that opposes the motion of two objects in contact. Do research to find out different types of friction in a literary and figurative sense.

**Figure 17** Locations of earthquakes that have occurred between 1990 and 2000 are plotted below.

• Earthquake epicenter

**Discussion**

**Plate Relationships** Why does a strong relationship exist between earthquakes and plate boundaries? As plates move away from, toward, or past each other, tension, compression, and shear forces are generated and build up in rocks. When energy from these forces is released, vibrations are caused, which are felt as earthquakes. L2

**Activity**

**Block Movement** Provide blocks of wood to small groups of students. Have them use the blocks to demonstrate how the movement of plates at convergent, divergent, and transform boundaries causes earthquakes. L1 **ELL** COOP LEARN **IS** **Kinesthetic**

## Visual Learning

**Figure 17** Have students compare **Figures 17 and 15** and describe ways in which the two figures are similar. Students should note that the locations of earthquake epicenters shown in **Figure 17** align well with plate boundaries shown in **Figure 15.**

**Friction** When two of Earth's plates meet, friction keeps them from moving freely past each other. In literature, friction may occur between two characters who do not get along.

## Science Journal

**New Madrid Earthquake** In 1811–1812, three of the strongest earthquakes to ever strike the United States occurred in New Madrid, Missouri. Have students research these earthquakes and write a paragraph hypothesizing how the earthquakes might be related to plate tectonics. It is thought that a failed divergent plate boundary lies under New Madrid. L2
**IS** **Linguistic** P

## Make a Model

**Earth's Interior** Use different colors of modeling clay to make a model of Earth's interior. Form a clay ball with a radius of 24 mm. Cut the ball in half and mold a 55-mm thick layer around the half ball. Continue by molding a 47-mm thick layer around the other two. Mold a final, thin layer around the other three. Display the model of Earth's inner core, outer core, mantle, and crust.

### Applying Math

**Indiana Math Standards**
**Correlation to Mathematics Objectives**
7.2.1, 7.3.1

### Teaching Strategy

Explain that as the density of a material increases, the velocity of a P-wave traveling through it increases. The velocity of the S-waves through the outer core is zero because the core is liquid and S-waves do not travel through liquids.

### Answers to Practice Problems

1. $t = 300$ km $\div$ 8 km/s $= 37.5$ s
2. $t = 500$ km $\div$ 6 km/s $= 83.3$ s

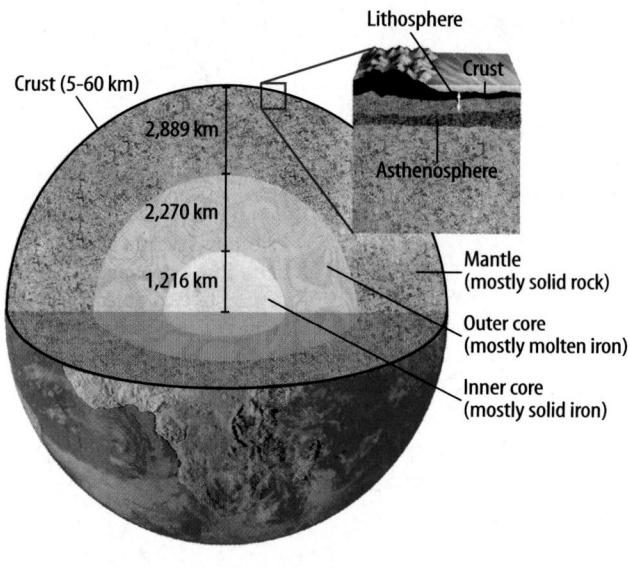

**Figure 18** Seismic waves generated by earthquakes allow researchers to figure out the structure and composition of Earth's layers.

## Earth's Plates and Interior

Researchers have learned much about Earth's interior and plate tectonics by studying seismic waves. The way in which seismic waves pass through a material depends on the properties of that material. Seismic wave speeds, and how they travel through different levels in the interior, have allowed scientists to map out the major layers of Earth, as shown in **Figure 18.**

For example, the asthenosphere was discovered when seismologists noted that seismic waves slowed when they reached the base of the lithosphere of the Earth. This partially molten layer forms a warmer, softer layer over which the colder, brittle, rocky plates move.

### Applying Math    Calculate

**P-WAVE TRAVEL TIME** There is a relationship between the density of a region in Earth and the velocity of P-waves. How can you calculate the time it would take P-waves to travel 100 km in the crust of Earth?

| Density and Wave Velocity | | |
|---|---|---|
| **Region** | **Density** | **P-Wave Velocity** |
| Crust | 2.8 g/cm³ | 6 km/s |
| Upper mantle | 3.3 g/cm³ | 8 km/s |

**Solution**

**1** *This is what you know:*
- velocity: $v = 6$ km/s
- distance: $d = 100$ km

**2** *This is what you need to find:*

How long would it take a P wave to travel?

**3** *This is the procedure you need to use:*
- $t = d/v$
- $t = (100$ km$)/(6$ km/s$) = 16.7$ s

**4** *Check your answer:*

Solve $v = d/t = (100$ km$)/(16.7$ s$) = 6$ km/s

### Practice Problems

1. Calculate the time it takes P-waves to travel 300 km in the upper mantle.

2. How long will it take a P-wave to travel 500 km in the crust?

 For more practice, visit in7.msscience.com/math_practice

## Teacher FYI

**Wave Pace** P-waves are slowed and bent by the asthenosphere. They speed up in denser parts of the mantle and then slow and bend at the outer core. At the inner core, P-waves again speed up. S-waves are formed in the inner core when P-waves strike its surface.

**What is driving Earth's plates?** There are several hypotheses about where all the energy comes from to power the movement of Earth's plates.

In one case, mantle material deep inside Earth is heated by Earth's core. This hot, less dense rock material is forced toward the surface. The hotter, rising mantle material eventually cools. The cooler material then sinks into the mantle toward Earth's core, completing the convection current. Convection currents inside Earth, shown in **Figure 19,** provide the mechanism for plate motion, which then produces the conditions that cause volcanoes and earthquakes. Sometimes magma is forced up directly within a plate. Volcanic activity in Yellowstone National Park is caused by a hot spot beneath the North American Plate. Such hot spots might be related to larger-scale convection in Earth's mantle.

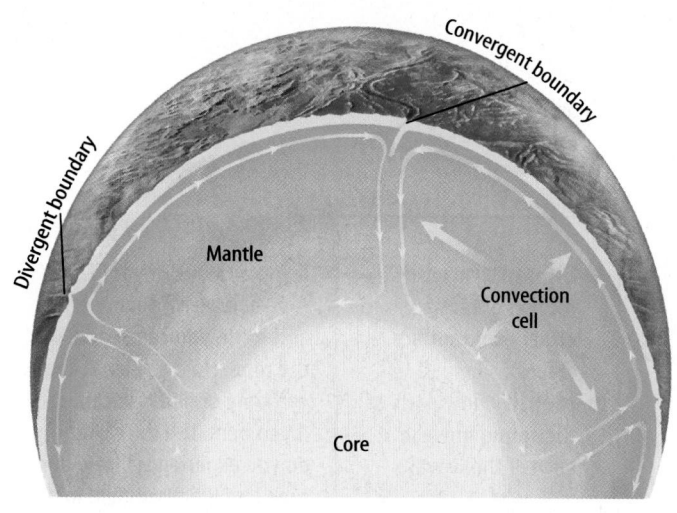

**Figure 19** Convection of material in Earth's interior drives the motion of tectonic plates.

---

## section 3 review

### Summary

**Earth's Moving Plates**
- Earth's lithosphere is broken into plates that move around the planet.

**Where Volcanoes Form**
- Plates move apart at divergent plate boundaries, creating fissure eruptions.
- Plates collide at convergent plate boundaries.
- Many volcanoes form at convergent plate boundaries.
- Volcanoes may also form along rift zones, subduction zones, or over hot spots.

**Moving Plates Cause Earthquakes**
- Earthquakes often form at plate boundaries.
- Seismic waves have been used to determine the characteristics of Earth's interior.
- Convection currently may drive tectonic plate movement.

### Self Check

1. **Identify** Along which type of plate boundary has the Soufrière Hills volcano formed?
2. **Predict** At which type of plate boundary does rift-volcanism occur?
3. **Explain** how volcanoes in Hawaii form.
4. **Recognize Cause and Effect** Why do most deep earthquakes occur at convergent boundaries?
5. **Think Critically** Subduction occurs where plates converge. This causes water-rich sediment and altered rock to be forced down to great depths. Explain how water can help form a volcano.

### Applying Skills

6. **Form Hypotheses** Write a hypothesis concerning the type of lava that will form a hot spot volcano. Consider that magma in a hot spot comes from deep inside Earth's mantle.

Science Online in7.msscience.com/self_check_quiz

**613**

## Use an Analogy

**Warming Soup** Explain that convection currents in a warming pan of soup are similar to the convection currents located inside Earth's interior. L2

## 3 Assess

### DAILY INTERVENTION

### Check for Understanding

**Visual-Spatial** Give students a map of the Pacific Ocean. Ask them to use what they know about hot spots and plate tectonics to explain why Hawaii is made of a chain of volcanic islands, not just one large island. L2

### Reteach

**Earth's Plates** Have students describe what is occurring in Earth's crust as you move your hands together to demonstrate converging plates, apart to demonstrate diverging plates, and past each other to demonstrate plates moving along a transform boundary. L1 **ELL** **LS** Visual-Spatial

## Assessment

**Oral** Explain why magma coming from deep inside Earth's mantle is likely to be basaltic. Earth's interior is denser than the crust and it contains more iron and magnesium. Thus, magma from that area should be richer in iron and magnesium also. Use **Performance Assessment in the Science Classroom,** p. 89. L2

---

## section 3 review

1. convergent boundary with one oceanic plate sinking beneath the other
2. divergent boundary
3. Hot magma is forced upward through Earth's mantle and crust, forming a hot spot.
4. Deep earthquakes occur where one tectonic plate sinks beneath another. This occurs at convergent boundaries.
5. As ocean sediment sinks into Earth's mantle, water travels along with it. The pressure of water vapor in mantle rock lowers the melting point of the rock. The lowered melting point helps to form some magma. Magma is forced upward, reaches Earth's surface, and flows out as lava.
6. Possible answer: Lava from a hot spot will be basaltic in composition and flow easily.

## Real-World Question

**Purpose** Students use a coiled spring toy to demonstrate seismic waves and to show how material is affected by the waves. L2 ELL COOP LEARN IS **Visual-Spatial**

**Process Skills** observe, infer, communicate, make and use tables, interpret data, make models

**Time Required** one class period

**Safety Precautions** Caution students to wear safety goggles when manipulating the spring.

## Procedure

**Teaching Strategies**

- Caution students not to over-stretch the coiled spring.
- Keep individual coiled spring toys in separate boxes or bags to avoid tangled coils.

**Troubleshooting** If students wish to measure the amount of movement in the coiled spring toy, advise them to tape the metric ruler to the desktop or floor.

**Expected Outcome** The yarn or string moves perpendicular to the wave for transverse waves (S-waves). It moves parallel to the wave for compression waves (P-waves).

### Goals
- **Demonstrate** the motion of primary, secondary, and surface waves.
- **Identify** how parts of the spring move in each of the waves.

### Materials
coiled spring toy
yarn or string
metric ruler

### Safety Precautions

# Seismic Waves

## Real-World Question

If you and one of your friends hold a long piece of rope between you and move one end of the rope back and forth, you can send a wave through the length of the rope. Hold a ruler at the edge of a table securely with one end of it sticking out from the table's edge. If you bend the ruler slightly and then release it, what do you experience? How does what you see in the rope and what you feel in the ruler relate to seismic waves? How do seismic waves differ?

## Procedure

1. Copy the following data table in your Science Journal.
2. Tie a small piece of yarn or string to every tenth coil of the spring.
3. Place the spring on a smooth, flat surface. Stretch it so it is about 2 m long (1 m for shorter springs).
4. Hold your end of the spring firmly. Make a wave by having your partner snap the spring from side to side quickly.
5. **Record** your observations in your Science Journal and draw the wave you and your partner made in the data table.
6. Have your lab partner hold his or her end of the spring firmly. Make a wave by quickly pushing your end of the spring toward your partner and bringing it back to its original position.

| Comparing Seismic Waves | | | |
|---|---|---|---|
| **Observation of Wave** | **Observation of Yarn or String** | **Drawing** | **Wave Type** |
| | | | |
| Answers will vary. | | | |
| | | | |

# Differentiated Instruction

**Learning Disabled** Be sure each student has a specific job to do during the activity. In this way, your learning disabled students will be assured of having a role in the activity and serving as an important part of the team. Also, check with each group and see that learning disabled students observe the movements of the toy when each different type of wave is transmitted.

# Alternative Inquiry Lab

**Wave Hypothesis** Make this lab an Inquiry Lab by building on the experience. Encourage students to use what they have learned about the behavior of the different seismic waves to predict what materials each one can travel through. Ask them to create a hypothesis as to why certain waves will travel through solids, liquids, and gases. Then ask them to create a model which will demonstrate this.

7. **Record** your observations of the wave and of the yarn or string and draw the wave in the data table.

8. Have your lab partner hold his or her end of the spring firmly. Move the spring off of the table. Gently move your end of the spring side to side while at the same time moving it in a rolling motion, first up and away and then down and toward your partner.

9. **Record** your observations and draw the wave in the data table.

## ⬤ Conclude and Apply

1. Based on your observations, detrmine which of the waves that you and your partner have generated demonstrates a primary, or pressure, wave. Record in your data table and explain why you chose the wave you did.

2. Do the same for the secondary, or shear wave, and for the surface wave. Explain why you chose the wave you did.

3. **Explain** Based on your observations of wave motion, which of the waves that you and your partner generated probably would cause the most damage during an earthquake?

4. **Observe** What was the purpose of the yarn or string?

5. **Compare and contrast** the motion of the yarn or string when primary and secondary waves travel through the spring. Which of these waves is a compression wave? Explain your answer.

6. **Compare and Contrast** Which wave most closely resembled wave motion in a body of water? How was it different? Explain.

ommunicating
**Your Data**

**Compare** your conclusions with those of other students in your class. **For more help, refer to the** Science Skill Handbook.

**LAB 615**

ommunicating
**Your Data**

Fill out your data table and compare your results with those of others in the class. Comment on similarities and differences that you notice.

## Content Background

A method for measuring earthquakes, the Richter scale, was developed by Charles Richter. This system assigns a number to an earthquake according to the amount of energy released at the focus. On the logarithmic scale, each increasing number indicates an earthquake that produces a deflection on a seismogram that is ten times larger than the next lower number. In actuality, the energy released is 32 times greater.

## Discussion

**Emergency Preparedness** What should be included in an emergency preparedness plan for your family? Remind students that natural disasters like earthquakes, hurricanes, floods, and tornadoes may cause homes to collapse, broken gas and water lines, injury, and loss of power. Possible answers: Learn how to protect yourself against the most common natural disasters that occur in your area. Hold regular drills with family members. Take a first aid class. Learn how to use a fire extinguisher. Store first aid supplies, food, water, battery-powered radio, fresh batteries, flashlight, and protective clothing. L2

## Historical Significance

Explain to students that most of the buildings in San Francisco at the time of the 1906 earthquake were made of wood and brick. While the shaking itself devastated many of the poorly built structures, most of the damage was caused by fires that swept through the city. Broken water lines forced firefighters to haul water into the city from the ocean and reservoirs.

# Quake

### The 1906 San Francisco earthquake taught people valuable lessons

It struck without warning. "We found ourselves staggering and reeling. It was as if the earth was slipping gently from under our feet. Then came the sickening swaying of the earth that threw us flat upon our faces. We struggled in the street. We could not get on our feet. Then it seemed as though my head were split with the roar that crashed into my ears. Big buildings were crumbling as one might crush a biscuit in one's hand."

That's how survivor P. Barrett described the San Francisco earthquake of 1906. Duration of the quake on the morning of April 18—one minute. Yet, in that short time, Earth opened a gaping hole stretching more than 430 km. The tragic result was one of the worst natural disasters in U.S. history.

Fires caused by falling chimneys and fed by broken gas mains raged for three days. Despite the estimated 3,000 deaths and enormous devastation to San Francisco, the earthquake did have a positive effect. It led to major building changes that would help protect people and property from future quakes.

Computers analyze information from seismographs that have helped to map the San Andreas Fault—the area along which many California earthquakes take place. This information is helping scientists better understand how and when earthquakes might strike.

The 1906 quake also has led to building codes that require stronger construction materials for homes, offices, and bridges. Laws have been passed saying where hospitals, homes, and nuclear power plants can be built—away from soft ground and away from the San Andreas Fault.

Even today, scientists can't predict an earthquake. But thanks to what they learned from the 1906 quake—and others—people are safer today than ever before.

**Write** Prepare a diary entry pretending to be a person who experienced the 1906 San Francisco earthquake. Possible events to include in your entry: What were you doing at 5:15 A.M.? What began to happen around you? What did you see and hear?

Science Online

For more information, visit in7.msscience.com/time

**Write** Ask students to brainstorm possible responses for their diary entries. List the answers to each question in separate columns as students suggest them. Direct the class to choose several of the ideas from each list to incorporate into their own diary entry. Encourage students to use other original ideas while composing their diaries. L2

## Resources for Teachers and Students

*Earthquake: The World Reacts* by Paul Bennett. Smart Apple Media, Mankato, MN. 1999

*Magnitude 8: Earthquakes and Life Along the San Andreas Fault* by Philip L. Fradkin. Henry Holt and Company, New York 1998

## Reviewing Main Ideas

### Section 1    Earthquakes

1. Earthquakes occur whenever rocks inside Earth pass their elastic limit, break, and experience elastic rebound.

2. Seismic waves are vibrations inside Earth. P- and S-waves travel in all directions away from the earthquake focus. Surface waves travel along the surface.

3. Earthquakes are measured by their magnitudes—the amount of energy they release—and by their intensity—the amount of damage they produce.

### Section 2    Volcanoes

1. The Soufrière Hills volcano is a composite volcano formed by converging plates.

2. The way a volcano erupts is determined by the composition of the lava and the amount of water vapor and other gases in the lava.

3. Three different forms of volcanoes are shield volcanoes, cinder cone volcanoes, and composite volcanoes.

### Section 3    Earthquakes, Volcanoes, and Plate Tectonics

1. The locations of volcanoes and earthquake epicenters are related to the locations of plate boundaries.

2. Volcanoes occur along rift zones, subduction zones, and at hot spots.

3. Most earthquakes occur at convergent, divergent, and transform plate boundaries.

## Visualizing Main Ideas

*Copy and complete the following table comparing characteristics of shield, composite, and cinder cone volcanoes.*

| Volcanoes | | | |
|---|---|---|---|
| **Characteristic** | **Shield Volcano** | **Cinder Cone Volcano** | **Composite Volcano** |
| Relative size | large | small | moderate |
| Nature of eruption | low eruptive force | high eruptive force | moderate to high eruptive force |
| Materials extruded | lava, gas | cinders, gas | lava, ash, gas |
| Composition of lava | low silica | variable | high silica |
| Ability of lava to flow | high | low | variable |

**Science Online** in7.msscience.com/interactive_tutor

**CHAPTER STUDY GUIDE** 617

---

chapter **Study Guide** **20**

### Reviewing Main Ideas

Summary statements can be used by students to review the major concepts of the chapter.

### Visualizing Main Ideas

See student page.

**Science Online**

**Visit** in7.msscience.com
/self_check_quiz
/interactive_tutor
/vocabulary_puzzlemaker
/chapter_review
/standards_review

### Assessment Transparency

For additional assessment questions, use the *Assessment Transparency* located in the transparency book.

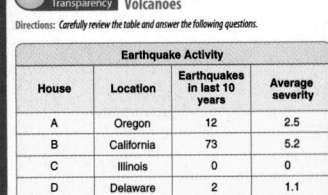

**Assessment**

Assessment Transparency — Earthquakes and Volcanoes

Directions: Carefully review the table and answer the following questions.

| Earthquake Activity | | | |
|---|---|---|---|
| **House** | **Location** | **Earthquakes in last 10 years** | **Average severity** |
| A | Oregon | 12 | 2.5 |
| B | California | 73 | 5.2 |
| C | Illinois | 0 | 0 |
| D | Delaware | 2 | 1.1 |

1. According to the table, which location has earthquakes with an average severity greater than 5.0?
   A A
   B B
   C C
   D D

2. The most likely cause of the earthquakes in California is ___.
   F collision of the ocean and land
   G vibrations from landslides
   H effects of the weather
   J faults in Earth's crust

3. According to the table, which house has had no earthquake damage in the last ten years?
   A A
   B B
   C C
   D D

*Earthquakes and Volcanoes*

## Using Vocabulary

1. fault—a break along which there is motion; earthquake—vibrations generated by the movement along a fault

2. shield—largest type of volcano, made from basaltic lava; composite—medium-sized volcano, made from alternating lava and tephra layers

3. focus—where earthquake originates; epicenter—point on surface directly above focus

4. seismic wave—wave produced by an earthquake; seismograph—instrument used to record earthquake waves

5. tsunami—seismic sea wave; seismic wave—waves caused by earthquakes

6. epicenter—point on surface directly above focus; earthquake—vibrations caused by fault movement

7. cinder cone—smallest volcano, made of tephra; shield—largest volcano, made from basaltic lava

### Checking Concepts

| | | |
|---|---|---|
| 8. D | 11. C | 14. A |
| 9. A | 12. D | 15. D |
| 10. B | 13. B | 16. B |

## Using Vocabulary

| | |
|---|---|
| cinder cone volcano p. 604 | magnitude p. 595 |
| composite volcano p. 605 | rift p. 609 |
| earthquake p. 592 | seismic safe p. 599 |
| epicenter p. 594 | seismic wave p. 594 |
| fault p. 593 | seismograph p. 595 |
| focus p. 594 | shield volcano p. 604 |
| hot spot p. 610 | tsunami p. 597 |
| lava p. 601 | volcano p. 601 |

*Explain the differences between the vocabulary words in each of the following sets.*

1. fault—earthquake

2. shield volcano—composite volcano

3. focus—epicenter

4. seismic wave—seismograph

5. tsunami—seismic wave

6. epicenter—earthquake

7. cinder cone volcano—shield volcano

## Checking Concepts

*Choose the word or phrase that best answers the question.*

8. Which type of plate boundary caused the formation of the Soufrière Hills volcano?
   **A)** divergent        **C)** rift
   **B)** transform        **D)** convergent

9. What is a cone-shaped mountain that is built from layers of lava?
   **A)** volcano        **C)** vent
   **B)** lava flow        **D)** crater

10. What is the cause of the volcanoes on Hawaii?
    **A)** rift zone
    **B)** hot spot
    **C)** divergent plate boundary
    **D)** convergent plate boundary

11. Which type of lava flows easily?
    **A)** silica-rich        **C)** basaltic
    **B)** composite        **D)** smooth

12. Which type of volcano is built from alternating layers of lava and tephra?
    **A)** shield        **C)** lava dome
    **B)** cinder cone        **D)** composite

13. Which type of volcano is relatively small with steep sides?
    **A)** shield        **C)** lava dome
    **B)** cinder cone        **D)** composite

14. Which seismic wave moves through Earth at the fastest speed?
    **A)** primary wave
    **B)** secondary wave
    **C)** surface wave
    **D)** tsunami

15. Which of the following is a wave of water caused by an earthquake under the ocean?
    **A)** primary wave
    **B)** secondary wave
    **C)** surface wave
    **D)** tsunami

**Use the illustration below to answer question 16.**

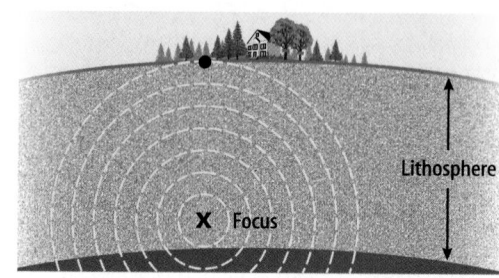

16. What is the point on Earth's surface directly above an earthquake's focus?
    **A)** earthquake center
    **B)** epicenter
    **C)** fault
    **D)** focus

 **Science** Online in7.msscience.com/vocabulary_puzzlemaker

**Use the Exam*View*® Pro Testmaker CD-ROM to:**
- create multiple versions of tests
- create modified tests with one mouse click for inclusion students
- edit existing questions and add your own questions
- build tests aligned with state standards using built-in State Curriculum Tags
- change English tests to Spanish with one mouse click and vice versa

## Thinking Critically

**17. Infer** Why does the Soufrière Hills volcano erupt so explosively?

**18. Compare and contrast** composite and cinder cone volcanoes.

**19. Explain** how the composition of magma can affect the way a volcano erupts.

**20. Evaluate** What factors determine an earthquake's intensity on the modified Mercalli scale?

**21. Compare and contrast** magnitude and intensity.

**22. Make Models** Select one of the three forms of volcanoes and make a model, using appropriate materials.

**23. Draw Conclusions** You are flying over an area that has just experienced an earthquake. You see that most of the buildings are damaged or destroyed and much of the surrounding countryside is disrupted. What level of intensity would you conclude for this earthquake?

**24. Concept Map** Copy and complete this concept map on examples of features produced along plate boundaries. Use the following terms: *Mid-Atlantic Ridge, Soufrière Hills volcano, divergent, San Andreas Fault, convergent,* and *transform.*

## Performance Activities

**25. Oral Presentation** Research the earthquake or volcano history of your state or community. Find out how long ago your area experienced earthquake- or volcano-related problems. Present your findings in a speech to your class.

## Applying Math

**Use the graph below to answer questions 26 and 27.**

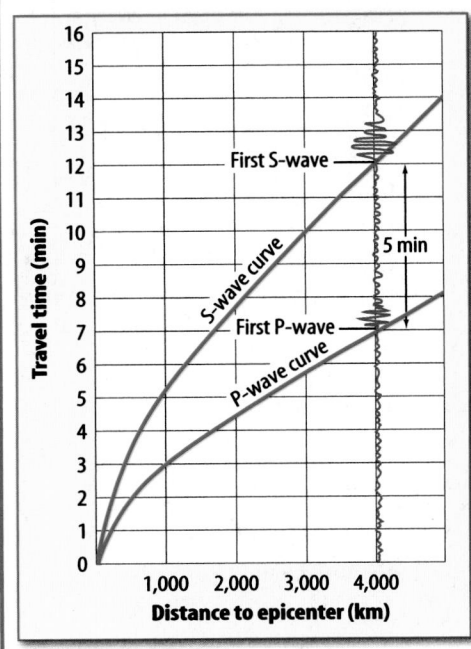

**26. Earthquake Epicenter** If a P-wave arrives at a seismograph station at 9:07 AM and the S-wave arrives at the same seismograph station at 9:09 AM, about how far is that station from the epicenter of the earthquake?

**27. Arrival Time** A seismograph station is 2,500 km from the epicenter of an earthquake. What is the difference in time between the P-wave arrival time and the S-wave arrival time?

## Thinking Critically

**17.** The silica-rich magma contains water vapor and other gases under intense pressure in the magma, causing it to erupt explosively.

**18.** Tephra can erupt from both, however eruptions of composite volcanoes alternate between tephra and lava.

**19.** Silica-rich magma is viscous and can trap gases and build up pressure. Iron- and magnesium-rich magma is hotter and flows more easily, and allows gases to escape more readily.

**20.** the amount of structural and geologic damage done

**21.** Both magnitude and intensity are used to measure earthquakes. Magnitude measures energy released, and intensity measures damage done.

**22.** Models will vary, but should follow data presented in the text for each form.

**23.** Accept any answer between IX and XII.

**24.** See student page.

## Performance Activities

**25.** Answers will vary depending on your location. Use **Performance Assessment in the Science Classroom,** p. 143.

## Applying Math

### Indiana Math Standards

**7.6.1**

**26.** 1,000 km

**27.** 3.5 seconds

---

## ✔ Assessment    Resources

**📁 Reproducible Masters**

**Chapter *Fast File* Resources**
  Chapter Review, pp. 35–36
  Chapter Tests, pp. 37–40
  Assessment Transparency Activity, p. 47

**Glencoe Science Web site**
  Chapter Review Test
  IN Standards Review

**Glencoe Technology**

  🖌 Assessment Transparency
  ⦿ Exam*View*® Pro Testmaker
  💿 MindJogger Videoquiz
  ⦿ Interactive Chalkboard

**Answer Sheet** A practice answer sheet can be found at **in7.msscience.com/answer_sheet**.

**SAMPLE**

---

### Part 1 | Multiple Choice

1. A
2. D
3. C
4. B
5. B
6. B
7. C
8. D

### Part 2 | Critical Response

9. An earthquake is the vibrations felt as a result of rock breaking. The vibrations move through rock and other earth materials. Faults form when rocks change shape by breaking. Movement along a fault releases strain energy. When this potential energy is released, it moves outward from the fault in the form of seismic waves.

10. explosive

---

The assessed Indiana standard appears above the question.

*Record your answers on the answer sheet provided by your teacher or on a sheet of paper.*

### Part 1 | Multiple Choice

The table below shows the number of convergent and divergent boundaries for different plates in Earth's crust.

| Plate Boundaries | | |
|---|---|---|
| **Plate** | **Number of convergent boundaries** | **Number of divergent boundaries** |
| African | 1 | 4 |
| Antarctic | 1 | 2 |
| Indo-Australian | 4 | 2 |
| Eurasian | 4 | 1 |
| North American | 2 | 1 |
| Pacific | 6 | 2 |
| South American | 2 | 1 |

1. Determine which plate has the most spreading boundaries.

   A African

   B Antarctic

   C Indo-Australian

   D Pacific

**7.3.4**

2. Use the table above to predict which plate will be surrounded by the most volcanoes.

   A Antarctic

   B Eurasian

   C Indo-Australian

   D Pacific

**7.3.8**

3. Which are created by earthquakes, and travel through Earth's interior at various speeds?

   A energy waves

   B light waves

   C seismic waves

   D sound waves

The illustration below shows the Hawaiian Islands and its active volcanoes.

4. In which direction is the Pacific Plate moving?

   A north-northeast

   B north-northwest

   C south-southeast

   D south-southwest

5. Which island is the oldest?

   A Hawaii

   B Kauai

   C Maui

   D Molokai

---

11. Mantle material deep inside Earth is heated by Earth's core. The hot, less dense material is forced upward toward Earth's surface. As the material reaches the surface, it cools and becomes more dense. The cooler material then sinks back into the mantle towards Earth's core, setting up a convection current. Convection currents provide the mechanism for plate motion. Earthquakes and volcanoes result from Earth's plates moving. When plates collide, diverge, or slide past each other, earthquakes can occur. Volcanoes can be formed as plates collide or diverge.

12. shield volcanoes, cinder cone volcanoes, and composite volcanoes; Volcanoes form as molten lava is forced upward toward Earth's surface by denser surrounding rock. Rising magma can lead to an eruption, where magma, solids, and gas are spewed out to form cone-shaped mountains called volcanoes. Shield volcanoes form from fluid, basaltic lava which flows in broad, flat layers and

**6.** Which instrument is used to study the waves produced by earthquakes?

**A** lithograph

**B** seismograph

**C** creepmeter

**D** tiltmeter

The illustration below shows a fault in Earth's crust.

**7.** Identify the type of fault shown.

**A** normal fault

**B** reverse fault

**C** strike-slip fault

**D** thrust fault

**8.** Which force creates this type of fault?

**A** compression

**B** deformation

**C** extension

**D** shear

**Test-Taking Tip**

**Watch the Time** If you are taking a timed test, keep track of time during the test. If you find you're spending too much time on a multiple-choice question, mark your best guess and move on.

---

**Part 2 Critical Response**

7.3.7

**9.** What is an earthquake? Explain the relationship between faults and earthquakes.

7.3.7

**10.** The lava of a particular volcano is high in silica and water vapor and other gases. What kind of eruptive force will likely result from this volcano?

7.3.7

**11.** The illustration below shows Earth's interior.

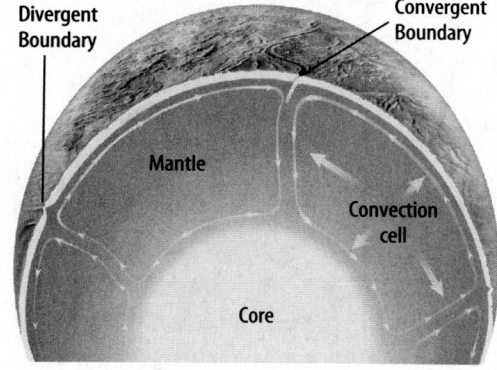

Divergent Boundary

Convergent Boundary

Mantle

Convection cell

Core

Explain how convection currents may be related to plate tectonics. How is plate tectonics related to earthquakes and volcanoes?

7.3.4

**12.** Name three types of volcanoes. Describe how each volcano forms.

7.3.4

**13.** Some surface waves vibrate in a side-to-side, or swaying, motion parallel to Earth's surface. Why is this type of motion so devastating to human-built structures?

---

## Rubrics

The following rubric is a sample scoring device for critical response questions.

### Critical Response

| Points | Description |
|---|---|
| 4 | The student demonstrates a thorough understanding of the science of the task. The response may contain minor flaws that do not detract from the demonstration of a thorough understanding. |
| 3 | The student demonstrates an understanding of the science of the task. The response is essentially correct and demonstrates an essential but less than thorough understanding of the science. |
| 2 | The student demonstrates only a partial understanding of the science of the task. Although the student may have used the correct approach to a solution or may have provided a correct solution, the work lacks an essential understanding of the underlying science concepts. |
| 1 | The student demonstrates a very limited understanding of the science of the task. The response is incomplete and exhibits many flaws. |
| 0 | The student provides a completely incorrect solution or no response at all. |

---

forms broad volcanoes with gently sloping sides. Cinder cone volcanoes form from ash, cinders, and lava that are thrown high into the air, cool quickly, and fall back to Earth as tephra, forming small, steep-sided cinder cones. Composite volcanoes form from alternating layers of lava and tephra that form large, steep-sided mountains.

**13.** Surface waves combine the effects of primary and secondary waves, resulting in a backward, rolling motion and a side-to-side, swaying motion. The resulting amplitude of surface waves is greater than those of primary and secondary waves. The materials that make up the structures cannot withstand the motion.

| Section/Objectives | Standards | | Labs/Features |
|---|---|---|---|
| **Chapter Opener** | National | State/Local | **Launch Lab:** Tracking World Climates, p. 623 **Foldables,** p. 623 |
| | See pp. 16T–17T for a Key to Standards. | Detailed standards begin on page IN8. | |
| **Section 1  What is climate?** ⏱ 2 sessions 📦 1 block 1. **Describe** what determines climate. 2. **Explain** how latitude, oceans, and other factors affect the climate of a region. | National Content Standards: UCP.1–3, UCP.5, A.1–2, D.1 | Indiana Standards: 7.3.5, 7.5.1 | **MiniLAB:** Observing Solar Radiation, p. 625 **Integrate Physics,** p. 626 **Applying Science:** How do cities influence temperature?, p. 626 |
| **Section 2  Climate Types** ⏱ 1 session 📦 0.5 block 3. **Describe** a climate classification system. 4. **Explain** how organisms adapt to particular climates. | National Content Standards: UCP.1–3, UCP.5, A.1–2, D.1 | Indiana Standards: 7.1.5 | |
| **Section 3  Climatic Changes** ⏱ 3 sessions 📦 1.5 blocks 5. **Explain** what causes seasons. 6. **Describe** how El Niño affects climate. 7. **Explore** possible causes of climatic change. | National Content Standards: UCP.1–3, UCP.5, A.1–2, B.2–3, D.1–2, F.3 | Indiana Standards: 7.1.4, 7.2.6, 7.2.7, 7.3.3, 7.3.5, 7.3.6, 7.4.14 | **MiniLAB:** Modeling El Niño, p. 633 **Visualizing El Niño and La Niña,** p. 634 **Science Online,** p. 639 **Integrate Career,** p. 641 **Science Online,** p. 641 **Lab:** The Greenhouse Effect, p. 643 **Lab:** Microclimates, p. 644 **Science and History:** The Year There Was No Summer, p. 646 |

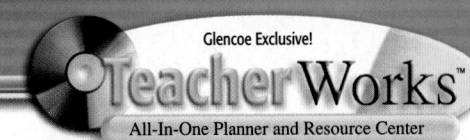
| Lab Materials | Reproducible Resources | Section Assessment | Technology |
|---|---|---|---|
| **Launch Lab:** world atlas, globe, or classroom map; sources for researching world temperatures | **Chapter *FAST FILE* Resources** Foldables Worksheet, p. 17 Note-taking Worksheets, pp. 33–35 **Science Inquiry Labs,** pp. 17–18 | GLENCOE'S ASSESSMENT ADVANTAGE | Teacher**Works** includes: • Interactive Teacher Edition • Lesson Planner with calendar • Access to all program blacklines • Correlations to standards • Web links |
| **MiniLAB:** flashlight, globe | **Chapter *FAST FILE* Resources** Transparency Activity, p. 44 MiniLAB, p. 3 Enrichment, p. 30 Reinforcement, p. 27 Directed Reading, p. 20 Lab Activity, pp. 9–11 **Mathematics Skill Activities,** p. 11 | Portfolio Reteach, p. 627 Performance MiniLAB, p. 625 Applying Science, p. 626 Applying Math, p. 627 Content Section Review, p. 627 | Section Focus Transparency Virtual Labs CD-ROM Guided Reading Audio Program Interactive Chalkboard CD-ROM |
| *Need materials?* Contact Science Kit at 1-800-828-7777 or www.sciencekit.com on the Internet. | **Chapter *FAST FILE* Resources** Transparency Activity, p. 45 Enrichment, p. 31 Reinforcement, p. 28 Directed Reading, p. 20 Transparency Activity, pp. 47–48 **Reading and Writing Skill Activities,** p. 3 | Portfolio Make a Model, p. 630 Performance Applying Skills, p. 631 Content Section Review, p. 631 | Section Focus Transparency Teaching Transparency Guided Reading Audio Program Interactive Chalkboard CD-ROM |
| **MiniLAB:** baking pan (9 in x 13 in), warm water **Lab:** 2 identical large, glass jars, lid for one jar, 3 alcohol thermometers **Lab:** thermometers, psychrometer, paper strip or wind sock, 4–5 large cans, unlined paper | **Chapter *FAST FILE* Resources** Transparency Activity, p. 46 MiniLAB, p. 4 Enrichment, p. 32 Reinforcement, p. 29 Lab Worksheets, pp. 5–6, 7–8 Directed Reading, pp. 21, 22 Lab Activity, pp. 13–16 **Lab Management and Safety,** p. 37 | Portfolio Curriculum Connection, p. 634 Science Journal, p. 636 Performance MiniLAB, p. 633 Applying Skills, p. 642 Content Section Review, p. 642 | Section Focus Transparency Virtual Labs CD-ROM Guided Reading Audio Program Interactive Chalkboard CD-ROM Video Lab |

## End of Chapter Assessment

GLENCOE'S ASSESSMENT ADVANTAGE

| Blackline Masters | Technology | Professional Series |
|---|---|---|
| **Chapter *FAST FILE* Resources** Chapter Review, pp. 37–38 Chapter Tests, pp. 39–42 **Mastering the Grade 7 Indiana Science Standards** | MindJogger Videoquiz IN Test Prep and Practice Exam*View*® Exam*View*® Pro Testmaker TeacherWorks CD-ROM Interactive Chalkboard CD-ROM | **Performance Assessment in the Science Classroom (PASC)** |

## Transparencies

### Section Focus

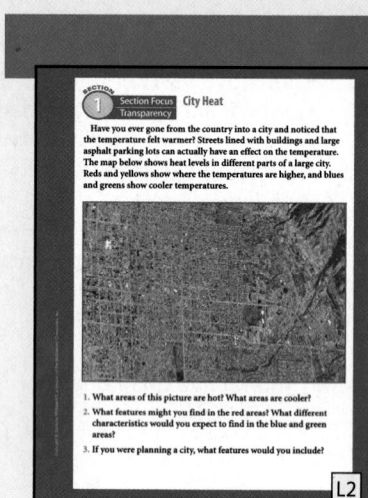

Section Focus Transparency 1 — City Heat

Have you ever gone from the country into a city and noticed that the temperature felt warmer? Streets lined with buildings and large asphalt parking lots can actually have an effect on the temperature. The map below shows heat levels in different parts of a large city. Reds and yellows show where the temperatures are higher, and blues and greens show cooler temperatures.

1. What areas of this picture are hot? What areas are cooler?
2. What features might you find in the red areas? What different characteristics would you expect to find in the blue and green areas?
3. If you were planning a city, what features would you include?

L2

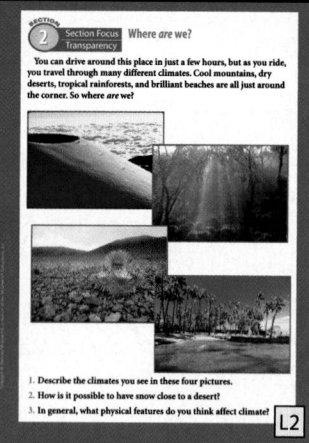

Section Focus Transparency 2 — Where are we?

You can drive around this place in just a few hours, but as you ride, you travel through many different climates. Cool mountains, dry deserts, tropical rainforests, and brilliant beaches are all just around the corner. So where are we?

1. Describe the climates you see in these four pictures.
2. How is it possible to have snow close to a desert?
3. In general, what physical features do you think affect climate?

L2

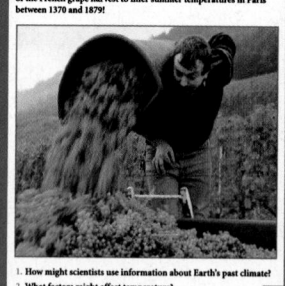

Section Focus Transparency 3 — Informative Fruit

Up-to-the-minute weather and climate information is used to plan a day's events or to know when to take cover from a storm. However, information about Earth's past climate is also very useful to scientists. Ice cores, fossils, and sediments provide a lot of data about the climate long ago, but what about grapes? One study used the recorded dates of the French grape harvest to infer summer temperatures in Paris between 1370 and 1879!

1. How might scientists use information about Earth's past climate?
2. What factors might affect temperature?

L2

This is a representation of key blackline masters available in the Teacher Classroom Resources. See Resource Manager boxes within the chapter for additional information.

### Key to Teaching Strategies

The following designations will help you decide which activities are appropriate for your students.

**L1** Level 1 activities should be appropriate for students with learning difficulties.

**L2** Level 2 activities should be within the ability range of all students.

**L3** Level 3 activities are designed for above-average students.

**ELL** ELL activities should be within the ability range of English Language Learners.

**COOP LEARN** Cooperative Learning activities are designed for small group work.

**LS** Multiple Learning Styles logos, as described on page 12T, are used throughout to indicate strategies that address different learning styles.

**P** These strategies represent student products that can be placed into a best-work portfolio.

**PBL** Problem-Based Learning activities apply real-world situations to learning.

### Assessment

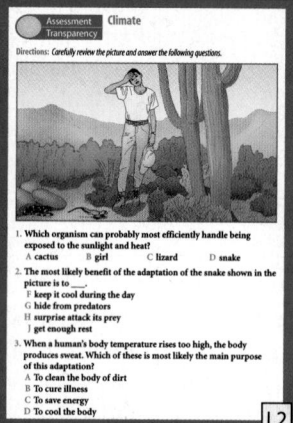

Assessment Transparency — Climate

Directions: Carefully review the picture and answer the following questions.

1. Which organism can probably most efficiently handle being exposed to the sunlight and heat?
   A cactus    B girl    C lizard    D snake
2. The most likely benefit of the adaptation of the snake shown in the picture is to ____.
   F keep it cool during the day
   G hide from predators
   H surprise attack its prey
   J get enough rest
3. When a human's body temperature rises too high, the body produces sweat. Which of these is most likely the main purpose of this adaptation?
   A To clean the body of dirt
   B To cure illness
   C To save energy
   D To cool the body

L2

### Teaching

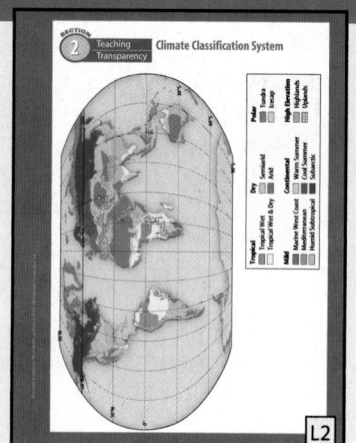

Teaching Transparency 2 — Climate Classification System

L2

## Hands-on Activities

### Student Text Lab Worksheet

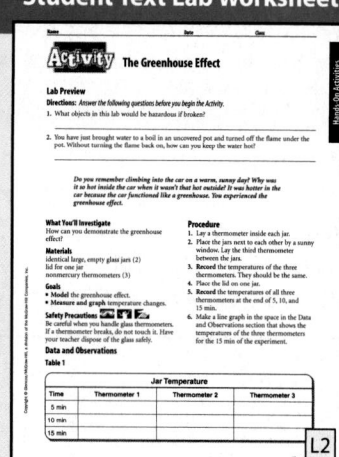

Activity — The Greenhouse Effect

**Lab Preview**

Directions: Answer the following questions before you begin the Activity.

1. What objects in this lab would be hazardous if broken?

2. You have just brought water to a boil in an uncovered pot and turned off the flame under the pot. Without turning the flame back on, how can you keep the water hot?

*Do you remember climbing into the car on a warm, sunny day? Why was it so hot inside the car when it wasn't that hot outside? It was hotter in the car because the car functioned like a greenhouse. You experienced the greenhouse effect.*

**What You'll Investigate**
How can you demonstrate the greenhouse effect?

**Materials**
identical large, empty glass jars (2)
lid for one jar
nonmercury thermometers (3)

**Goals**
- Model the greenhouse effect.
- Measure and graph temperature changes.

**Safety Precautions**
Be careful when you handle glass thermometers. If a thermometer breaks, do not touch it. Have your teacher dispose of the glass safely.

**Data and Observations**
Table 1

| Jar Temperature | | | |
|---|---|---|---|
| Time | Thermometer 1 | Thermometer 2 | Thermometer 3 |
| 5 min | | | |
| 10 min | | | |
| 15 min | | | |

**Procedure**
1. Lay a thermometer inside each jar.
2. Place the jars next to each other by a sunny window. Lay the third thermometer between the jars.
3. Record the temperatures of the three thermometers. They should be the same.
4. Place the lid on one jar.
5. Record the temperatures of all three thermometers at the end of 5, 10, and 15 min.
6. Make a line graph in the space in the Data and Observations section that shows the temperatures of the three thermometers for the 15 min of the experiment.

L2

### Laboratory Activities

Laboratory Activity 1 — How do the oceans affect climate?

Meteorologists, people who study weather and climate, are always looking at what happens in the oceans. Most of the climate we experience on land is a result of winds and evaporated water at sea. One of the effects of the oceans is to keep the climate near their shores fairly constant. This happens because the water maintains a relatively even temperature. As a result of the weak attractions that form between the hydrogen atoms of one molecule of water and the oxygen atoms of nearby water molecules, a large amount of heat energy can be absorbed by water before its temperature rises. Air molecules do not have this type of attraction between them; therefore the temperature rises more quickly with heat input from the Sun. Volume is also an important consideration in looking at the effects of the Sun's energy on water molecules. It is much easier for the Sun to heat or cool a small pond than it is for the Sun to heat or cool the ocean. In this laboratory exercise, you will compare the effect of the Sun's energy on water with its effect on the atmosphere. From your data, you will make conclusions about climate in different regions.

**Strategy**
You will model and observe the effect of energy from the Sun on water and on air. You will infer how oceans and energy from the Sun affect climate.

**Materials**
2 plastic soda bottles (labels removed)
2 cork or rubber stoppers with center holes
2 long, chemistry-type thermometers
water
paper towels
*100-watt light source (if no sunlight is available)
*apparatus for holding light source stationary
*Alternate materials

Figure 1

**Procedure**
1. Work with a partner. Obtain two bottles, stoppers, and thermometers from your instructor. (The thermometers might be fitted into the stopper holes already.)
2. Place the thermometer GENTLY through the stopper hole. The fit should be snug so the stopper will hold the thermometer, but not so tight that it breaks. If your thermometer breaks, DO NOT pick up the pieces of glass yourself. Tell your instructor what happened. If you are uncomfortable doing this step, ask for help from your instructor.
3. Pour water that has reached room temperature into one of your bottles. You do not need to fill the bottle all the way to the top. You need just enough water to insert the thermometer about 8–10 cm into the water. Use paper towels to wipe up any water spills.
4. Check the temperatures on your thermometers and record them on the table provided. They should both be at room temperature.
5. If you have a sunny window in your classroom, place your bottles side by side in the window. If possible, it is even better to place the thermometer out in the Sun. If no sunshine is available, place your bottles under a light bulb, as shown in Figure 1.

L2

# Resource Manager

## Meeting Different Ability Levels

### Content Outline

### Reinforcement

### Enrichment

### Directed Reading (English/Spanish)

### Study Guide

### Reading Essentials

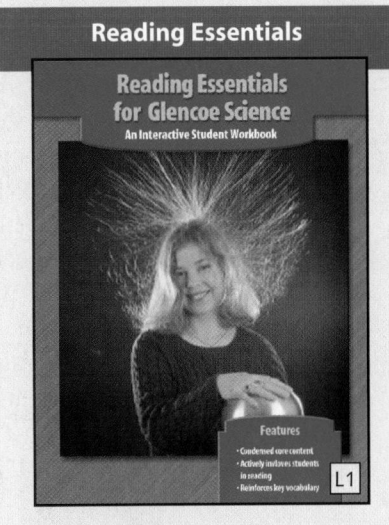

## Assessment

### Test Practice Workbook

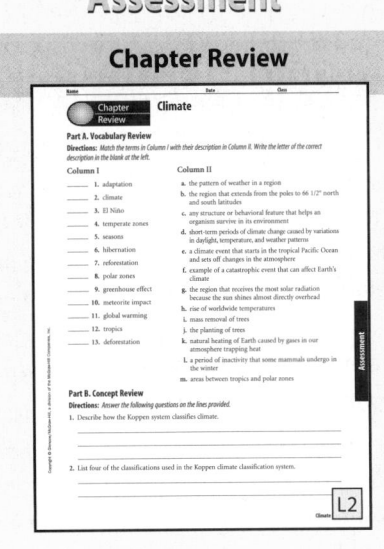

### Chapter Review

### Chapter Tests

# Science Content Background

## What is climate?

### Latitude and Climate

On a sunny day at 0° latitude, the average amount of solar energy received is 300 W/m². At 60° latitude, it is 110 W/m², and at 90° only 60 W/m² of solar energy is received. At any latitude, the amount of energy received is lower when skies are cloudy.

### Mountains

Mountains typically have higher precipitation and lower temperatures than surrounding lower elevations. Mountain slopes also affect climate. Orographic lifting occurs when an air mass encounters a mountain range and is forced upward. As the air rises, it cools and condensation occurs, forming precipitation on the side of the mountain. When the air mass descends down the other side, it sinks and dries. As a result, little precipitation occurs on the other side of the mountain. This phenomenon is known as a rain shadow. The eastern half of Washington State falls in the rain shadow of the Cascades, resulting in the near-arid climate of the Columbia basin.

## Climate Types

### Classifying Climates

The early Greeks devised the first climate classification system. It was based on differences in temperature. Köppen's classification system is more biological in nature, based on the different types of flora found in a specific climate.

## Climatic Changes

### Earth's Seasons

As a result of changes in temperature and pressure in different regions throughout the year, winds often shift direction, causing predictable changes in the climate of an area. The word *monsoon* comes from the Arabic word *mausim*, meaning "season." Monsoon season occurs in both India and Arizona when the winds shift, pulling in air from a very moist region. During this season the affected area experiences a significant increase in precipitation.

### Climatic Change

The first great ice age occurred between 2.5 billion and 2 billion years ago. Evidence suggests that a warm period followed that lasted until about 950 million years ago. Between 950 million and 200 million years ago, at least five major ice ages occurred. Since that time, there have been several periods when glaciers have formed and then melted. The last ice age reached its peak about 18,000 years ago.

## chapter content resources

**Internet Resources**

For additional content background, visit **in7.msscience.com** to:

- access your book online
- find references to related articles in popular science magazines
- access Web links with related content background
- access current events with science journal topics

**Print Resources**

*What If The Polar Ice Caps Melted?,* by Katherine Friedman, Children's Press, 2002

*Global Warming,* by Alvin Silverstein, Virginia Silverstein, and Laura Silverstein, Twenty-First Century Books, 2003

*Restless Earth,* by National Geographic Society, National Geographic Society, 1997

*What's The Weather Today?,* by Allan Fowler, Children's Press, 1991

# IDENTIFYING ⟩ **Misconceptions**

## Find Out What Students Think

### Students may think that . . .

**Seasons are affected by the distance between Earth and the Sun.**

Because Earth's orbit around the Sun is an ellipse and not a circle, Earth is not the same distance from the Sun throughout the year. However, summer and winter are not caused by Earth's changing distance from the Sun during its orbit. In fact, during winter in the Northern Hemisphere, Earth is actually closer to the Sun than it is during summer. The changing of the seasons is caused by Earth's tilt.

If Earth's axis were not tilted relative to its orbit around the Sun, each of Earth's hemispheres would receive the same amount of sunlight at all times throughout the year. The days would not grow longer during the summer and shorter in winter. Every day of the year would have about 12 hours of daylight and about 12 hours of night, and there would be no seasons.

Because of Earth's axial tilt, during most of its orbit around the Sun one or the other of Earth's hemispheres is tilted toward the Sun. The part of Earth that is tilted toward the Sun experiences summer, and the part tilted away from the Sun experiences winter. As Earth orbits the Sun, this orientation constantly changes throughout the year. At two points in Earth's orbit, the first day of spring and the first day of autumn, neither hemisphere is tilted toward the sun. On those days, the Sun appears to us to be directly over the equator, and all points on Earth experience nearly equal lengths of day and night.

### Demonstration

Using a lightbulb to represent the Sun and a globe to represent Earth, have two students demonstrate the position of Earth and the Sun during the various seasons. Refer to **Figure 8.** Ask students to record which season they think will occur at various locations, first for the northern hemisphere and then for the southern hemisphere. Ask them what months these seasons would represent in each hemisphere, for example, winter-northern-December, or winter-southern-June. Be sure to reinforce the concept that seasons are not occurring because of the changing distance between Earth and the Sun but rather because part of Earth is tilted toward the Sun.

## Promote Understanding

### Activity

Reinforce that the greatest contributor to the change of seasons is the inclination of Earth's axis with respect to its orbital plane.

- Give each group a flashlight and a sheet of construction paper.

- Have students shine the flashlight straight onto the paper. Instruct them to draw a circle around the light beam on the paper.

- Next, direct them to slowly tilt the paper so that the circle elongates into an ellipse. Again

have students draw an outline around the ellipse, this time using a different color of pencil.

Students should infer that the same amount of light energy is spread over a greater area when the paper is tilted relative to the flashlight. Therefore, each point on the paper receives less energy from the light when the paper is tilted.

### Assess

After completing the chapter, see *Identifying Misconceptions* in the Study Guide at the end of the chapter.

## Chapter Vocabulary

climate, p. 624
tropics, p. 624
polar zone, p. 624
temperate zone, p. 624
adaptation, p. 628
hibernation, p. 630
season, p. 632
El Niño, p. 633
greenhouse effect, p. 639
global warming, p. 640
deforestation, p. 641

**Science Journal** Answers will vary but should say that seasons occur due to Earth being at different positions and angles relative to the Sun at different times of the year causing the northern hemisphere to have more sunlight on occasion, and the southern hemisphere to have more sunlight on other occasions.

### INTERACTIVE CHALKBOARD
#### with Image Bank

**PowerPoint® Presentations**

This CD-ROM is an editable Microsoft® PowerPoint® presentation that includes:
- a pre-made presentation for every chapter
- interactive graphics
- animations
- audio clips
- image bank
- all new section and chapter questions
- Standardized Test Practice
- transparencies
- pre-lab questions for all labs
- Foldables directions
- links to in7.msscience.com

**Academic Standard—3:** Students collect and organize data to identify relationships between physical objects, events, and processes. They use logical reasoning to question their own ideas as new information challenges their conceptions of the natural world.

**Also covers:** Academic Standards 1, 2, 4, 5 (Detailed standards begin on page IN8.)

# Climate

## chapter preview

### sections

**1** What is climate?

**2** Climate Types

**3** Climatic Changes

*Lab* The Greenhouse Effect
*Lab* Microclimates
*Virtual Lab* How can locations be identified by their climate and topography?

## Why do seasons change?

Why do some places have four distinct seasons, while others have only a wet and dry season? In this chapter, you will learn what climate is and how climates are classified. You will also learn what causes climate changes and how humans and animals adapt to different climates.

**Science Journal** Write a paragraph explaining what you already know about the causes of seasons.

## Theme Connection

**Stability and Change** Although climate may appear to be constant, this chapter illustrates that Earth's climates undergo both short-term seasonal changes as well as long-term shifts, such as ice ages.

### About the Photo

**Change of Seasons** Why do some places have four distinct seasons, while others have only a wet and dry season? A family of snowmen shows a most wintry season!

# Start-Up Activities

## Tracking World Climates

You wouldn't go to Alaska to swim or to Jamaica to snow ski. You know the climates in these places aren't suited for these sports. In this lab, you'll explore the climates in different parts of the world.

1. Obtain a world atlas, globe, or large classroom map. Select several cities from different parts of the world.

2. Record the longitude and latitude of your cities. Note if they are near mountains or an ocean.

3. Research the average temperature of your cities. In what months are they hottest? Coldest? What is the average yearly rainfall? What kinds of plants and animals live in the region? Record your findings.

4. Compare your findings with those of the rest of your class. Can you see any relationship between latitude and climate? Do cities near an ocean or a mountain range have different climatic characteristics?

5. **Think Critically** Keep track of the daily weather conditions in your cities. Are these representative of the kind of climates your cities are supposed to have? Suggest reasons why day-to-day weather conditions may vary.

---

**FOLDABLES™**
**Study Organizer**

**Classifying Climates** Make the following Foldable to help you compare climatic types.

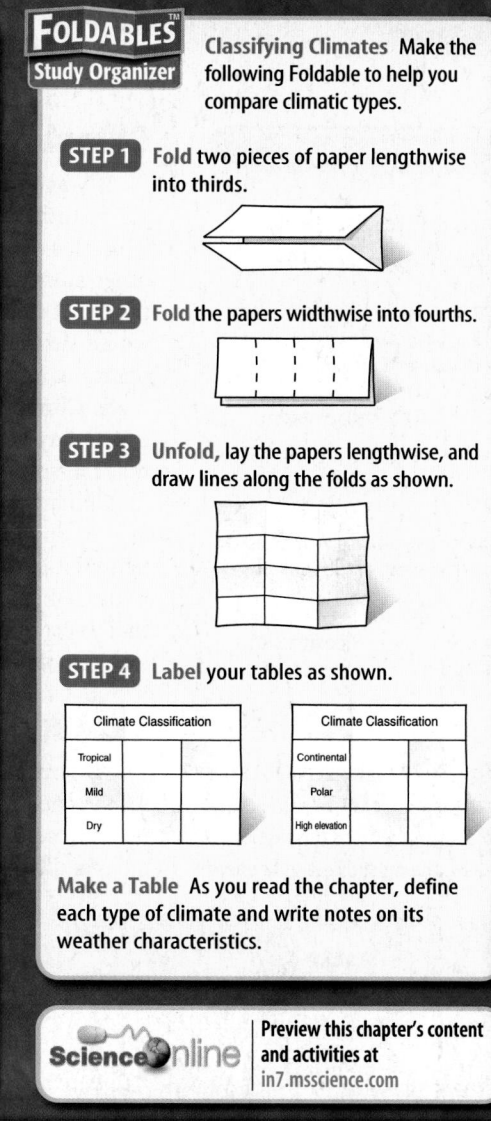

**STEP 1** Fold two pieces of paper lengthwise into thirds.

**STEP 2** Fold the papers widthwise into fourths.

**STEP 3** Unfold, lay the papers lengthwise, and draw lines along the folds as shown.

**STEP 4** Label your tables as shown.

| Climate Classification | | |
|---|---|---|
| Tropical | | |
| Mild | | |
| Dry | | |

| Climate Classification | | |
|---|---|---|
| Continental | | |
| Polar | | |
| High elevation | | |

**Make a Table** As you read the chapter, define each type of climate and write notes on its weather characteristics.

 **Science Online** Preview this chapter's content and activities at in7.msscience.com

---

**623**

## section 1

Also covers: 7.5.1 (Detailed standards begin on page IN8.)

# What is climate?

## 1 Motivate

### Bellringer

**Section Focus Transparencies** also are available on the Interactive Chalkboard CD-ROM.

L2 ELL

1. What areas of this picture are hot? What areas are cooler?
2. What features might you find in the red areas? What different characteristics would you expect to find in the blue and green areas?
3. If you were planning a city, what features would you include?

L2

### Tie to Prior Knowledge

**Community Climate** Ask students to list the temperature and precipitation characteristics where they live, for both summer and winter. Write these characteristics on the board. Tell students they will later use these characteristics to determine their community's climate.

### Quick Demo

**Heat Distribution**

**Materials** globe, lamp without the lamp shade

**Estimated Time** 10 minutes

**Procedure** Place your globe to one side of the lamp, then to the other side so the students can visually observe how Earth's tilt and location affect which hemisphere receives the most energy from the Sun.

### as you read

**What You'll Learn**

■ **Describe** what determines climate.
■ **Explain** how latitude, oceans, and other factors affect the climate of a region.

**Why It's Important**

Climate affects the way you live.

**Review Vocabulary**
**latitudes:** distance in degrees north or south of the equator

**New Vocabulary**
● climate   ● polar zone
● tropics   ● temperate zone

**Figure 1** The tropics are warmer than the temperate zones and the polar zones because the tropics receive the most direct solar energy.

66.5°  Polar zone
Temperate zone
23.5°
Tropic of Cancer
Equator  0°  Tropics
Tropic of Capricorn  23.5°
Temperate zone
66.5°
Polar zone

## Climate

If you wandered through a tropical rain forest, you would see beautiful plants flowering in shades of pink and purple beneath a canopy of towering trees. A variety of exotic birds and other animals would dart among the tree branches and across the forest floor. The sounds of singing birds and croaking frogs would surround you. All of these organisms thrive in hot temperatures and abundant rainfall. Rain forests have a hot, wet climate. **Climate** is the pattern of weather that occurs in an area over many years. It determines the types of plants or animals that can survive, and it influences how people live.

Climate is determined by averaging the weather of a region over a long period of time, such as 30 years. Scientists average temperature, precipitation, air pressure, humidity, and number of days of sunshine to determine an area's climate. Some factors that affect the climate of a region include latitude, landforms, location of lakes and oceans, and ocean currents.

## Latitude and Climate

As you can see in **Figure 1,** regions close to the equator receive the most solar radiation. Latitude, a measure of distance north or south of the equator, affects climate. **Figure 2** compares cities at different latitudes. The **tropics**—the region between latitudes 23.5°N and 23.5°S—receive the most solar radiation because the Sun shines almost directly over these areas. The tropics have temperatures that are always hot, except at high elevations. The **polar zones** extend from 66.5°N and 66.5°S latitude to the poles. Solar radiation hits these zones at a low angle, spreading energy over a large area. During winter, polar regions receive little or no solar radiation. Polar regions are never warm.

**Reading Check** *How does latitude affect climate?*

Between the tropics and the polar zones are the **temperate zones.** Temperatures here are moderate. Most of the United States is in a temperate zone.

## Section 1 Resource Manager

**Chapter FAST FILE Resources**
Transparency Activity, p. 44
Directed Reading for Content Mastery, p. 20
MiniLAB, p. 3
Note-taking Worksheets, pp. 33–35

Enrichment, p. 30
Reinforcement, p. 27
Lab Activity, pp. 9–11
**Mathematics Skill Activities,** p. 11
**Science Inquiry Labs,** pp. 17–18

## Other Factors

In addition to the general climate divisions of polar, temperate, and tropical, natural features such as large bodies of water, ocean currents, and mountains affect climate within each zone. Large cities also change weather patterns and influence the local climate.

**Large Bodies of Water** If you live or have vacationed near an ocean, you may have noticed that water heats up and cools down more slowly than land does. This is because it takes a lot more heat to increase the temperature of water than it takes to increase the temperature of land. In addition, water must give up more heat than land does for it to cool. Large bodies of water can affect the climate of coastal areas by absorbing or giving off heat. This causes many coastal regions to be warmer in the winter and cooler in the summer than inland areas at similar latitude. Look at **Figure 2** again. You can see the effect of an ocean on climate by comparing the average temperatures in a coastal city and an inland city, both located at 37°N latitude.

**Figure 2** This map shows average daily low temperatures in four cities during January and July. It also shows average yearly precipitation.

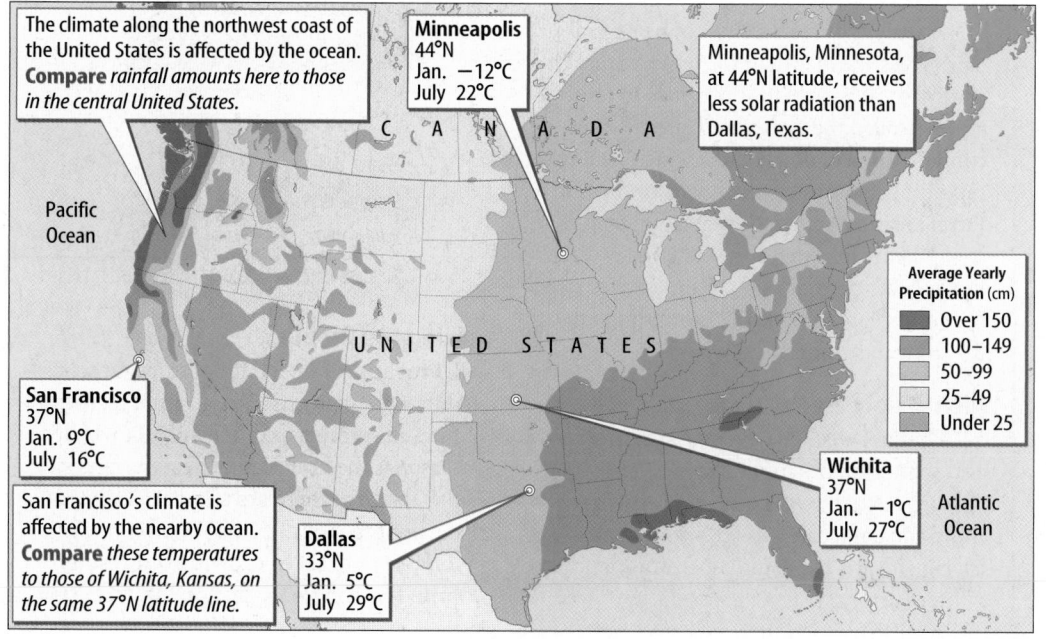

The climate along the northwest coast of the United States is affected by the ocean. **Compare** rainfall amounts here to those in the central United States.

**Minneapolis**
44°N
Jan. −12°C
July 22°C

Minneapolis, Minnesota, at 44°N latitude, receives less solar radiation than Dallas, Texas.

Pacific Ocean

CANADA

UNITED STATES

Average Yearly Precipitation (cm)
- Over 150
- 100–149
- 50–99
- 25–49
- Under 25

**San Francisco**
37°N
Jan. 9°C
July 16°C

San Francisco's climate is affected by the nearby ocean. **Compare** these temperatures to those of Wichita, Kansas, on the same 37°N latitude line.

**Dallas**
33°N
Jan. 5°C
July 29°C

**Wichita**
37°N
Jan. −1°C
July 27°C

Atlantic Ocean

## Observing Solar Radiation

### Procedure
1. Darken the room.
2. Hold a **flashlight** about 30 cm from a **globe**. Shine the light directly on the equator. With your finger, trace around the light.
3. Now, tilt the flashlight to shine on 30°N latitude. The size of the lighted area should increase. Repeat at 60°N latitude.

### Analysis
1. How did the size and shape of the light beam change as you directed the light toward higher latitudes?
2. How does Earth's tilt affect the solar radiation received by different latitudes?

### Reading Check

**Answer** In general, the closer one is to the equator, the warmer the climate.

## Mini LAB

**Purpose** Students observe how Earth's tilt affects the amount of solar radiation received at different latitudes. L2 **Kinesthetic**

**Materials** globe, flashlight

**Teaching Strategy** Have students use string and a ruler to measure the diameter of each lighted area.

**Troubleshooting** Instruct students to keep the light steady as they change its angle.

### Analysis
1. The size of the area lit by the beam increases. The shape changes from fairly circular to more oval.
2. As latitude increases, sunlight strikes Earth at a lower angle and solar radiation is spread over a larger area. Thus, higher latitudes receive less concentrated solar radiation than lower latitudes.

### Assessment
**Process** Have students illustrate the different angles at which sunlight hits Earth's surface at the equator, 30°, and 60° latitude. Use **Performance Assessment in the Science Classroom,** p. 127.

---

# Differentiated Instruction

**Visually Impaired** For visually impaired children, have them take their hand and tilt it. Shine the flashlight right into the middle of their hand on one side, than on the other side and ask them to feel the difference in heat on each half of their hand so that they may understand this concept a little better.

# Curriculum Connection

**Geography** Oceans and large lakes modify the nearby climate. Sandusky, Ohio, a town on Lake Erie, has more frost-free days and a smaller monthly temperature range than Bucyrus, Ohio, a city farther south and farther from the lake. As a result, the growing season is longer in Sandusky than in Bucyrus for crops such as peaches and grapes. Have students locate Lake Erie, Sandusky, and Bucyrus on a map. L1

**Ocean Currents** Ocean currents affect coastal climates. Warm currents begin near the equator and flow toward higher latitudes, warming the land regions they pass. When the currents cool off and flow back toward the equator, they cool the air and climates of nearby land.

**Reading Check** *How do ocean currents affect climate?*

Winds blowing from the sea are often moister than those blowing from land. Therefore, some coastal areas have wetter climates than places farther inland. Look at the northwest coast of the United States shown in **Figure 2.** The large amounts of precipitation in Washington, Oregon, and northern California can be explained by this moist ocean air.

**Mountains** At the same latitude, the climate is colder in the mountains than at sea level. When radiation from the Sun is absorbed by Earth's surface, it heats the land. Heat from Earth then warms the atmosphere. Because Earth's atmosphere gets thinner at higher altitudes, the air in the mountains has fewer molecules to absorb heat.

## Applying Science

### How do cities influence temperature?

The temperature in a city can be several degrees warmer than the temperature of nearby rural areas. This difference in temperature is called the heat island effect. Cities contain asphalt and concrete which heat up rapidly as they absorb energy from the Sun. Rural areas covered with vegetation stay cooler because plants and soil contain water. Water heats up more slowly and carries away heat as it evaporates. Is the heat island effect the same in summer and winter?

#### Identifying the Problem

The table lists the average summer and winter high temperatures in and around a city in 1996 and 1997. By examining the data, can you tell if the heat island effect is the same in summer and winter?

| Average Seasonal Temperatures | | |
|---|---|---|
| **Season** | **Temperature (°C)** | |
| | **City** | **Rural** |
| Winter 1996 | −3.0 | −4.4 |
| Summer 1996 | 23.5 | 20.9 |
| Winter 1997 | −0.1 | −1.8 |
| Summer 1997 | 23.6 | 21.2 |

#### Solving the Problem

1. Use a number line to find the average difference between city and rural temperatures in summer and in winter. In which season is the heat island effect the largest?
2. For this area there are about 15 hours of daylight in summer and 9 hours in winter. Use this fact to explain your results from the previous question.

**Rain Shadows** Mountains also affect regional climates, as shown in **Figure 3**. On the windward side of a mountain range, air rises, cools, and drops its moisture. On the leeward side of a mountain range air descends, heats up, and dries the land. Deserts are common on the leeward sides of mountains.

**Cities** Large cities affect local climates. Streets, parking lots, and buildings heat up, in turn heating the air. Air pollution traps this heat, creating what is known as the heat-island effect. Temperatures in a city can be 5°C higher than in surrounding rural areas.

**Figure 3** Large mountain ranges can affect climate by forcing air to rise over the windward side, cooling and bringing precipitation. The air descends with little or no moisture, creating desertlike conditions on the leeward side.

## section 1 review

### Summary

**Latitude and Climate**
- Climate is the pattern of weather that occurs in an area over many years.
- The tropics receive the most solar radiation because the Sun shines most directly there.
- The polar zones receive the least solar energy due to the low-angled rays.
- Temperate zones, located between the tropics and the polar zones, have moderate temperatures.

**Other Factors**
- Natural features such as large bodies of water, ocean currents, and mountains can affect local and regional climates.
- Large cities can change weather patterns and influence local climates.

### Self Check

1. **Explain** how two cities located at the same latitude can have different climates.
2. **Describe** how mountains affect climate.
3. **Define** the heat island effect.
4. **Compare and contrast** tropical and polar climates.
5. **Think Critically** Explain why plants found at different elevations on a mountain might differ. How can latitude affect the elevation at which some plants are found?

#### Applying Math

6. **Solve One-Step Equations** The coolest average summer temperature in the United States is 2°C at Barrow, Alaska, and the warmest is 37°C at Death Valley, California. Calculate the range of average summer temperatures in the United States.

Science Online in7.msscience.com/self_check_quiz

SECTION 1 What is climate? **627**

---

## section 1 review

1. If they are located at different altitudes, on different sides of mountains, or if only one is near a large water body, they will likely have different climates.
2. On the side facing the wind, air rises, cools, and precipitation occurs.

On the other side, air descends, warms, and produces a dry climate.
3. Paved surfaces heat up and air pollution traps heat, producing higher temperatures in cities than in the surrounding countryside.

4. Both are affected by the angle of the Sun's rays. The tropics receive the most direct rays and are always hot. Polar zones get little solar energy, and are never warm.
5. The climate would differ at different elevations and plants adapt to their

climates. Plants found at high elevation near the equator might be found only at low elevation at higher latitudes.
6. $37° − 2° = 35°C$

---

## Visual Learning

**Figure 3** How would farming be different on each side of this mountain range? windward: wide range of crops that need plentiful rainfall; leeward: smaller range of crops, especially those that grow in dry areas

### Discussion

**City Heat** Why are temperatures noticeably cooler in the suburbs of big cities? In big cities, heat from the Sun is absorbed by large buildings which conserve heat. The suburbs have few such buildings.

## 3 Assess

### DAILY INTERVENTION

#### Check For Understanding

**Visual-Kinesthetic** Make photocopies of **Figure 3** to give to your students. Ask them questions relating to the climate differences on both sides of the mountain, and how even at the same latitude, the climate can be different in these conditions

### Reteach

**Climate Concept Map** Have students make a concept map that shows how latitude and topographic features affect climate.
L2 IS Visual-Spatial P

## Assessment

**Process** Ask students to infer what has the greatest effect on the climate where you live. Use **PASC**, p. 89.

# section 2

# Climate Types

## 1 Motivate

### Bellringer

**Section Focus Transparencies** also are available on the Interactive Chalkboard CD-ROM.

L2 ELL

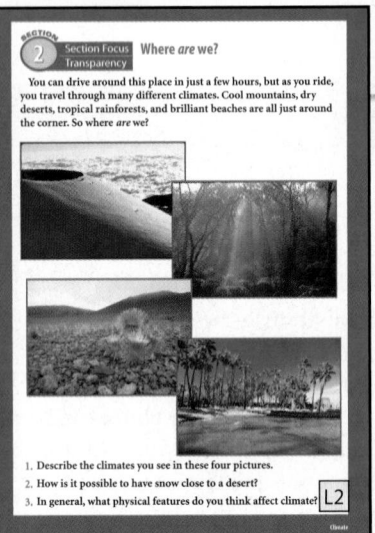

### Tie to Prior Knowledge

**Climate Characteristics** Recall the climate characteristics that students listed at the start of Section 1. Have students use this list to determine the climate in which their community is located as they read this Section.

### Caption Answer

**Figure 4** that it's a desert

### Activity

**Water Vapor** Have students do research to learn about the effects of water vapor as a greenhouse gas. Students should report the results of their research to the class. Water vapor is the most abundant greenhouse gas in the atmosphere, and some scientists have suggested that changes in its abundance could have large impacts on Earth's climates.

---

### as you read

#### *What* You'll Learn
- **Describe** a climate classification system.
- **Explain** how organisms adapt to particular climates.

#### *Why* It's Important
Many organisms can survive only in climates to which they are adapted.

#### Review Vocabulary
**regions:** places united by specific characteristics

#### New Vocabulary
- adaptation
- hibernation

**Figure 4** The type of vegetation in a region depends on the climate. **Describe** *what these plants tell you about the climate shown here.*

628

---

## Classifying Climates

What is the climate like where you live? Would you call it generally warm? Usually wet and cold? Or different depending on the time of year? How would you classify the climate in your region? Life is full of familiar classification systems—from musical categories to food groups. Classifications help to organize your thoughts and to make your life more efficient. That's why Earth's climates also are classified and are organized into the various types that exist. Climatologists—people who study climates—usually use a system developed in 1918 by Wladimir Köppen to classify climates. Köppen observed that the types of plants found in a region depended on the climate of the area. **Figure 4** shows one type of region Köppen might have observed. He classified world climates by using the annual and monthly averages of temperature and precipitation of different regions. He then related the types and distribution of native vegetation to the various climates.

The climate classification system shown in **Figure 5** separates climates into six groups—tropical, mild, dry, continental, polar, and high elevation. These groups are further separated into types. For example, the dry climate classification is separated into semiarid and arid.

## Adaptations

Climates vary around the world, and as Köppen observed, the type of climate that exists in an area determines the vegetation found there. Fir trees aren't found in deserts, nor are cacti found in rain forests. In fact, all organisms are best suited for certain climates. Organisms are adapted to their environment. An **adaptation** is any structure or behavior that helps an organism survive in its environment. Structural adaptations are inherited. They develop in a population over a long period of time. Once adapted to a particular climate, organisms may not be able to survive in other climates.

---

### Section 2 Resource Manager

**Chapter** *FAST FILE* **Resources**
Transparency Activity, pp. 45, 47–48
Directed Reading for Content Mastery, p. 20

Enrichment, p. 31
Reinforcement, p. 28
**Reading and Writing Skill Activities**, p. 3

| Tropical | Dry | Polar |
|---|---|---|
| ■ Tropical wet | ■ Semiarid | ■ Tundra |
| □ Tropical wet & dry | ■ Arid | ■ Icecap |
| **Mild** | **Continental** | **High Elevation** |
| ■ Marine west coast | □ Warm summer | ■ Highlands |
| ■ Mediterranean | ■ Cool summer | ▨ Uplands |
| ■ Humid subtropical | ■ Subarctic | |

**Structural Adaptations** Some organisms have body structures that help them survive in certain climates. The fur of mammals is really hair that insulates them from cold temperatures. A cactus has a thick, fleshy stem. This structural adaptation helps a cactus hold water. The waxy stem covering prevents water inside the cactus from evaporating. Instead of broad leaves, these plants have spiny leaves, called needles, that further reduce water loss.

**✔ Reading Check** *How do cacti conserve water?*

**Figure 5** This map shows a climate classification system similar to the one developed by Köppen. **Describe** *the patterns you can see in the locations of certain climate types.*

**Behavioral Adaptations** Some organisms display behavioral adaptations that help them survive in a particular climate. For example, rodents and certain other mammals undergo a period of greatly reduced activity in winter called **hibernation.** During hibernation, body temperature drops and body processes are reduced to a minimum. Some of the factors thought to trigger hibernation include cooler temperatures, shorter days, and lack of adequate food. The length of time that an animal hibernates varies depending on the particular species of animal and the environmental conditions.

### Reading Check *What is hibernation?*

Other animals have adapted differently. During cold weather, bees cluster together in a tight ball to conserve heat. On hot, sunny days, desert snakes hide under rocks. At night when it's cooler, they slither out in search of food. Instead of drinking water as turtles and lizards do in wet climates, desert turtles and lizards obtain the moisture they need from their food. Some behavioral and structural adaptations are shown in **Figure 6.**

**Figure 6** Organisms have structural and behavioral adaptations that help them survive in particular climates.

The needles and the waxy skin of a cactus are structural adaptations to a desert climate. **Infer** *how these adaptations help cacti conserve water.*

These hibernating bats have adapted their behavior to survive winter.

Polar bears have structural adaptations to keep them warm. The hairs of their fur trap air and heat.

630

## Differentiated Instruction

**English-Language Learners** A good way to involve an English-language learner student in your class might be to have that student wrap the thermometer in gauze, dip the thermometer in water, and reveal to the students the new temperature of the thermometer dipped in water.

## Visual Learning

**Figure 6** How can you tell that the bat is not adapted to live in a polar climate? Students should infer the bat would need thick fur or long hair to keep it warm in frigid polar temperatures. This bat has neither of these structural adaptations.

**Estivation** Lungfish, shown in **Figure 7,** survive periods of intense heat by entering an inactive state called estivation (es tuh VAY shun). As the weather gets hot and water evaporates, the fish burrows into mud and covers itself in a leathery mixture of mud and mucus. It lives this way until the warm, dry months pass.

Like other organisms, you have adaptations that help you adjust to climate. In hot weather, your sweat glands release water onto your skin. The water evaporates, taking some heat with it. As a result, you become cooler. In cold weather, you may shiver to help your body stay warm. When you shiver, the rapid muscle movements produce some heat. What other adaptations to climate do people have?

**Figure 7** Lungfish survive periods of intense heat and drought by going into an inactive state called estivation. During the dry season when water evaporates, lungfish dig into the mud and curl up in a small chamber they make at the lake's bottom. During the wet season, lungfish reemerge to live in small lakes and pools.

---

## section 2 review

### Summary

**Classifying Climates**

- Climatologists classify climates into six main groups: tropical, mild, dry, continental, polar, and high elevation.

**Adaptations**

- Adaptations are any structures or behaviors that help an organism to survive.
- Structural adaptations such as fur, hair, and spiny needles help an organism to survive in certain climates.
- Behavioral adaptations include hibernation, a period of greatly reduced activity in winter; estivation, an inactive state during intense heat; clustering together in the cold; and obtaining water from food when water is not found elsewhere.

### Self Check

1. **List** Use **Figure 5** and a world map to identify the climate type for each of the following locations: Cuba, North Korea, Egypt, and Uruguay.
2. **Compare and contrast** hibernation and estivation.
3. **Think Critically** What adaptations help dogs keep cool during hot weather?

#### Applying Skills

4. **Form Hypotheses** Some scientists have suggested that Earth's climate is getting warmer. What effects might this have on vegetation and animal life in various parts of the United States?
5. **Communicate** Research the types of vegetation found in the six climate regions shown in **Figure 5.** Write a paragraph in your Science Journal describing why vegetation can be used to help define climate boundaries.

 **Science**Online  in7.msscience.com/self_check_quiz

SECTION 2 Climate Types **631**

---

## section 2 review

1. Cuba: tropical wet and dry; North Korea: warm summer; Egypt: arid; Uruguay: humid subtropical
2. Estivation is an inactive state; hibernation is a period in which body temperature drops and life

processes slow. Both help animals survive extreme climate conditions.
3. They pant to reduce body heat, sit in shade, and drink water.
4. Those species adapted to live in warm climates will survive, others

may not. Accept any reasonable answers.
5. Sample answer: Vegetation varies with temperature and precipitation. Thus, it can define climatic regions.

---

**Text Question Answer**
Students might suggest that skin color, body stature, and possibly the presence of hair are adaptations to climate.

**Discussion**
**Sweat** How does sweat help your body adapt to the heat of the summer months? The water produced from sweat glands on skin evaporates, taking some of the heat with it. As a result, you become cooler as more sweat is produced and evaporated.

### 3 Assess

**DAILY INTERVENTION**

### Check for Understanding

**Logical-Mathematical** Challenge students to consider the direction-finding advice that moss grows on the north side of tree trunks. Ask them what this has to do with moss adaptation. Moss is adapted for growing in the shade. In the northern hemisphere, the north side of a tree trunk is never in direct sunlight and usually sees no sunshine at all. L3 IS

### Reteach

**Climates** Have students look in books and magazines for photos that show different types of climates. Have students share the pictures in class, and then discuss the characteristics of temperature and precipitation evident or suggested by vegetation, animals, or clothing worn by people in each picture. L1 IS **Visual-Spatial**

### ✓ Assessment

**Process** If Earth gets hotter, ice caps will melt, sea level will rise, and coasts will flood. Have students predict which adaptations might allow some of today's coastal organisms to survive these changes. Adaptations to shallow, warm water. Use **Performance Assessment in the Science Classroom,** p. 89.

SECTION 2 Climate Types **631**

632 **CHAPTER 21** Climate

**Bellringer**

**Section Focus Transparencies** also are available on the Interactive Chalkboard CD-ROM.

 **ELL**

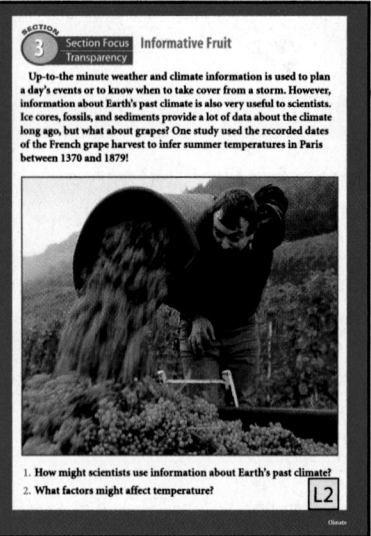

**Tie to Prior Knowledge**

**Season's Reasons** Tell students that seasons are short-term climate changes. Ask them to write a brief paragraph contrasting any two seasons where you live. Then have students share their ideas.

**Caption Answer**

**Figure 8** winter

**Answer** The tropics have both dry and rainy seasons.

---

**Standards—7.3.6:** Describe how gas and dust from large volcanoes can change the atmosphere. **7.3.3:** Describe how climates have changed abruptly in the past as a result of changes in Earth's crust, such as volcanic eruptions or impacts of huge rocks from space.

## section 3

**Also covers:** 7.1.4, 7.2.6, 7.2.7, 7.3.5, 7.4.14 (Detailed standards begin on page IN8.)

# Climatic Changes

**as you read**

*What* **You'll Learn**

- **Explain** what causes seasons.
- **Describe** how El Niño affects climate.
- **Explore** possible causes of climatic change.

*Why* **It's Important**

Changing climates could affect sea level and life on Earth.

**Review Vocabulary**

**solar radiation:** energy from the Sun transferred by waves or rays

**New Vocabulary**

- season
- El Niño
- greenhouse effect
- global warming
- deforestation

## Earth's Seasons

In temperate zones, you can play softball under the summer Sun and in the winter go sledding with friends. Weather changes with the season. **Seasons** are short periods of climatic change caused by changes in the amount of solar radiation an area receives. **Figure 8** shows Earth revolving around the Sun. Because Earth is tilted, different areas of Earth receive changing amounts of solar radiation throughout the year.

**Seasonal Changes** Because of fairly constant solar radiation near the equator, the tropics do not have much seasonal temperature change. However, they do experience dry and rainy seasons. The middle latitudes, or temperate zones, have warm summers and cool winters. Spring and fall are usually mild.

**Reading Check** *What are seasons like in the tropics?*

**Figure 8** As Earth revolves around the Sun, different areas of Earth are tilted toward the Sun, which causes different seasons.
**Identify** *During which northern hemisphere season is Earth closer to the Sun?*

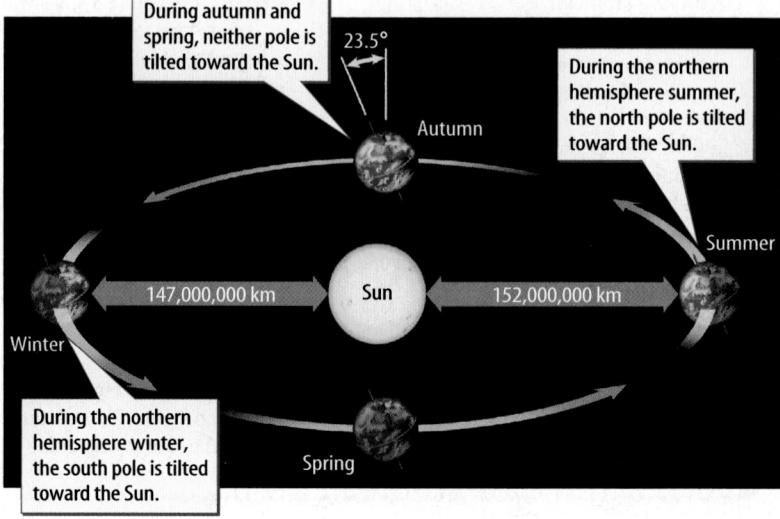

During autumn and spring, neither pole is tilted toward the Sun.

23.5°

During the northern hemisphere summer, the north pole is tilted toward the Sun.

Autumn

Summer

147,000,000 km   Sun   152,000,000 km

Winter

During the northern hemisphere winter, the south pole is tilted toward the Sun.

Spring

---

## Section 3 Resource Manager

**Chapter FAST FILE Resources**

Transparency Activity, p. 46

Directed Reading for Content Mastery, pp. 21, 22

MiniLAB, p. 4

Enrichment, p. 32

Lab Activity, pp. 13–16

Lab Worksheets, pp. 5–6, 7–8

Reinforcement, p. 29

**Earth Science Critical Thinking/Problem Solving,** pp. 13, 14, 18

**Reading and Writing Skill Activities,** p. 19

**Figure 9** A strong El Niño, like the one that occurred in 1998, can affect weather patterns around the world.

California was plagued by large storms that produced pounding surf and shoreline erosion.

A severe drought struck Indonesia, contributing to forest fires.

**High Latitudes** During the year, the high latitudes near the poles have great differences in temperature and number of daylight hours. As shown in **Figure 8,** during summer in the northern hemisphere, the north pole is tilted toward the Sun. During summer at the north pole, the Sun doesn't set for nearly six months. During that same time, the Sun never rises at the south pole. At the equator days are about the same length all year long.

## El Niño and La Niña

**El Niño** (el NEEN yoh) is a climatic event that involves the tropical Pacific Ocean and the atmosphere. During normal years, strong trade winds that blow east to west along the equator push warm surface water toward the western Pacific Ocean. Cold, deep water then is forced up from below along the coast of South America. During El Niño years, these winds weaken and sometimes reverse. The change in the winds allows warm, tropical water in the upper layers of the Pacific to flow back eastward to South America. Cold, deep water is no longer forced up from below. Ocean temperatures increase by 1°C to 7°C off the coast of Peru.

El Niño can affect weather patterns. It can alter the position and strength of one of the jet streams. This changes the atmospheric pressure off California and wind and precipitation patterns around the world. This can cause drought in Australia and Africa. This also affects monsoon rains in Indonesia and causes storms in California, as shown in **Figure 9.**

The opposite of El Niño is La Niña, shown in **Figure 10.** During La Niña, the winds blowing across the Pacific are stronger than normal, causing warm water to accumulate in the western Pacific. The water in the eastern Pacific near Peru is cooler than normal. La Niña may cause droughts in the southern United States and excess rainfall in the northwestern United States.

### Mini LAB

**Modeling El Niño**

**Procedure**
1. During El Niño, trade winds blowing across the Pacific Ocean from east to west slacken or even reverse. Surface waters move back toward the coast of Peru.
2. Add **warm water** to a **9-in × 13-in baking pan** until it is two-thirds full. Place the pan on a smooth countertop.
3. Blow as hard as you can across the surface of the water along the length of the pan. Next, blow with less force. Then, blow in the opposite direction.

**Analysis**
1. What happened to the water as you blew across its surface? What was different when you blew with less force and when you blew from the opposite direction?
2. Explain how this is similar to what happens during an El Niño event.

Try at Home

SECTION 3 Climatic Changes **633**

---

## 2 Teach

### IDENTIFYING Misconceptions

**Summer's Cause** Many students think summer occurs when Earth is closest to the Sun. Refer to page F at the beginning of the chapter for teaching strategies that address this misconception.

### Mini LAB

**Purpose** Students model winds that blow during El Niño. L1
**Kinesthetic**
**Materials** baking pan (9 in × 9 in), warm water
**Teaching Strategy** Have students concentrate their breath by blowing through a straw.
**Analysis**
1. Water moved in ripples toward the opposite end of the pan; the water moved in the same direction with less force; water moved in the opposite direction.
2. Winds weaken and can reverse, causing warm surface water to move to the eastern Pacific.

### Assessment

**Oral** Ask students to explain what blowing across the water and ripples on the water modeled. wind; surface currents Use **Performance Assessment in the Science Classroom,** p. 143.

Try at Home

---

## Differentiated Instruction

**Visually Impaired** For visually impaired students, suggest that they place their hand into the pan of water (fingers together) while a parent or sibling blows on the water. Have the student report what they feel so that they may understand the concept of this experiment.

## Cultural Diversity

**Peru** El Niño is Spanish for "the Christ child," so named because it usually appears near Christmas. Because fish become less abundant during El Niño, fishers use this time to repair equipment and spend time with their families. Have students infer why there are fewer fish during El Niño. During El Niño, upwelling of nutrients stops or is greatly reduced. Less upwelling means less food for fish.

## Visualizing El Niño and La Niña

Have students examine the pictures and read the captions. Then ask the following questions.

**How does El Niño affect the weather in your area?** Students should use the map on page 501 to determine their answer.

**What effect can La Niña have on farming?** Possible answer: In areas that are affected by La Niña, the drought conditions can ruin an entire season or year's worth of crops.

### Activity

**Recent El Niño** The two most extreme El Niño events in recent history were in 1982–83 and 1997–98. Have students research how these events affected different areas worldwide. Students can make a simple world map and symbolically represent the effects of the events in the appropriate area. Possible answer: In February 1998 the southeastern U.S. experienced a rash of tornadoes, while in Peru heavy rains caused flooding and mud slides.

---

**NATIONAL GEOGRAPHIC VISUALIZING EL NIÑO AND LA NIÑA**

**Figure 10**

**W**eather in the United States can be affected by changes that occur thousands of kilometers away. Out in the middle of the Pacific Ocean, periodic warming and cooling of a huge mass of seawater—phenomena known as El Niño and La Niña, respectively—can impact weather across North America. During normal years (right), when neither El Niño nor La Niña is in effect, strong winds tend to keep warm surface waters contained in the western Pacific while cooler water wells up to the surface in the eastern Pacific.

EL NIÑO During El Niño years, winds blowing west weaken and may even reverse. When this happens, warm waters in the western Pacific move eastward, preventing cold water from upwelling. These changes can alter global weather patterns and trigger heavier-than-normal precipitation across much of the United States.

LA NIÑA During La Niña years, stronger-than-normal winds push warm Pacific waters farther west, toward Asia. Cold, deep-sea waters then well up strongly in the eastern Pacific, bringing cooler and often drier weather to many parts of the United States.

**634 CHAPTER 21** Climate

---

## Curriculum Connection

**Social Studies** In 1982–1983 and 1998, two powerful El Niños caused billions of dollars worth of damage and thousands of deaths. Have students research and write a report about the reasons for El Niño's destructiveness. Floods destroyed crops and drowned people; drought resulted in fires and crop destruction; crop loss led to starvation. L2  P  LS **Linguistic**

## Differentiated Instruction

**Challenge** Have students investigate how El Niño events may be responsible for coral bleaching. Have students make a poster showing their results. Possible answer: Under the stress of a change in water temperature, the corals expel the algae that live symbiotically in their tissues. It is these algae that give corals their brilliant colors. When the algae are no longer present, the corals' own transparent tissues allow the white calcium carbonate skeleton to show through. L3

**El Niño**

| Warmer than normal | decreased rain |
|---|---|
| Cooler than normal | increased rain |

Sun-warmed surface water spans the Pacific Ocean during El Niño years. Clouds form above the warm ocean, carrying moisture aloft. The jet stream, shown by the white arrow above, helps bring some of this warm, moist air to the United States.

▲ LANDSLIDE Heavy rains in California resulting from El Niño can lead to landslides. This upended house in Laguna Niguel, California, took a ride downhill during the El Niño storms of 1998.

**La Niña**

| Warmer than normal | decreased rain |
|---|---|
| Cooler than normal | increased rain |

During a typical La Niña year, warm ocean waters, clouds, and moisture are pushed away from North America. A weaker jet stream often brings cooler weather to the northern parts of the continent and hot, dry weather to southern areas.

▲ PARCHED LAND The Southeast may experience drought conditions, like those that struck the cornfields of Montgomery County, Maryland, during the La Niña summer of 1988.

SECTION 3 Climatic Changes **635**

## Content Background

Scientists are still not sure what causes an El Niño Southern Oscillation (ENSO) event to occur. Careful study of data from recent ENSO events has provided scientists with information about the change in conditions that occurs at the onset of an ENSO. However, the trigger for these changes remains a mystery. Under normal conditions, a high-pressure system sits over the eastern Pacific and a low-pressure system over the western Pacific. The position of these pressure systems drives the trade winds, which blow from east to west across the Pacific.

The onset of an ENSO is marked by a reversal in the position of these pressure systems. This reversal causes the trade winds to weaken and sometimes even to reverse in direction. The change in atmospheric pressure across the Pacific is referred to as the Southern Oscillation. Aside from the extreme weather conditions, often created worldwide as a result of an ENSO, these events can also cause problems for organisms living in the waters of the eastern Pacific. The cold water that is normally upwelled brings large amounts of nutrients to the surface. Primary producers that live on these nutrients thrive in this area, providing a large base for the food web. Thus, fish, birds, and marine mammals such as sea lions depend on these primary producers. When the upwelling stops and the warm water at the surface during an ENSO event does not provide the necessary nutrients, the number of producers decreases and greater numbers of consumers face starvation.

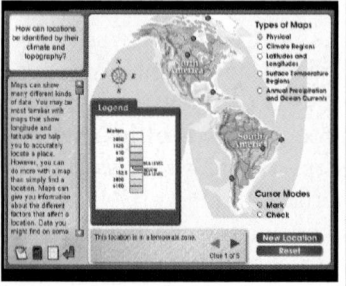
# Climatic Change

If you were exploring in Antarctica near Earth's south pole and found a 3-million-year-old fossil of a warm-weather plant or animal, what would it tell you? You might conclude that the climate of that region changed because Antarctica is much too cold for similar plants and animals to survive today. Some warm-weather fossils found in polar regions indicate that at times in Earth's past, worldwide climate was much warmer than at present. At other times Earth's climate has been much colder than it is today.

Sediments in many parts of the world show that at several different times in the past 2 million years, glaciers covered large parts of Earth's surface. These times are called ice ages. During the past 2 million years, ice ages have alternated with warm periods called interglacial intervals. Ice ages seem to last 60,000 to 100,000 years. Most interglacial periods are shorter, lasting 10,000 to 15,000 years. We are now in an interglacial interval that began about 11,500 years ago. Additional evidence suggests that climate can change even more quickly. Ice cores record climate in a way similar to tree rings. Cores drilled in Greenland show that during the last ice age, colder times lasting 1,000 to 2,000 years changed quickly to warmer spells that lasted about as long. **Figure 11** shows a scientist working with ice cores.

## What causes climatic change?

Climatic change has many varied causes. These causes of climatic change can operate over short periods of time or very long periods of time. Catastrophic events, including meteorite collisions and large volcanic eruptions, can affect climate over short periods of time, such as a year or several years. These events add solid particles and liquid droplets to the upper atmosphere, which can change climate. Another factor that can alter Earth's climate is short- or long-term changes in solar output, which is the amount of energy given off by the Sun. Changes in Earth's movements in space affect climate over many thousands of years, and movement of Earth's crustal plates can change climate over millions of years. All of these things can work separately or together to alter Earth's climate.

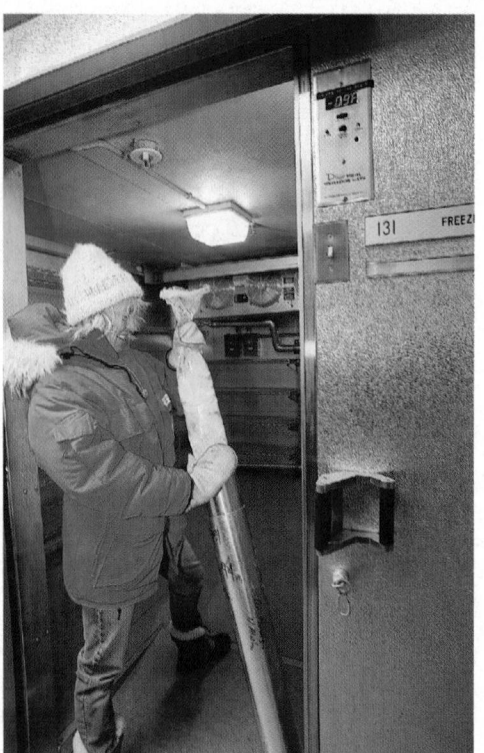

**Figure 11** Some ice cores consist of layers of ice that record detailed climate information for individual years. These ice cores can cover more than 300,000 years. **Describe** *how this is helpful.*

## Science Journal

**Glacial Living** Have students imagine that they are living near the edge of a thick sheet of glacial ice during an ice age. Have them write a story describing the difficulties of daily survival, including where they would live, how they would keep warm, and how they would get food. Have students share their stories. L2 LS **Linguistic** P

### Fun Fact

Major ice ages occurred 2 billion, 650 million, 250 million, and 3.0 million to 10,000 years ago. In the most recent ice age, the ice sheet in some places was 3,000 meters thick.

**Atmospheric Solids and Liquids** Small solid and liquid particles always are present in Earth's atmosphere. These particles can enter the atmosphere naturally or be added to the atmosphere by humans as pollution. Some ways that particles enter the atmosphere naturally include volcanic eruptions, soot from fires, and wind erosion of soil particles. Humans add particles to the atmosphere through automobile exhaust and smokestack emissions. These small particles can affect climate.

Catastrophic events such as meteorite collisions and volcanic eruptions put enormous volumes of dust, ash, and other particles into the atmosphere. These particles block so much solar radiation that they can cool the planet. **Figure 12** shows how a major volcanic eruption affected Earth's atmosphere.

In cities, particles put into the atmosphere as pollution can change the local climate. These particles can increase the amount of cloud cover downwind from the city. Some studies have even suggested that rainfall amounts can be reduced in these areas. This may happen because many small cloud droplets form rather than larger droplets that could produce rain.

**Energy from the Sun** Solar radiation provides Earth's energy. If the output of radiation from the Sun varies, Earth's climate could change. Some changes in the amount of energy given off by the Sun seem to be related to the presence of sunspots. Sunspots are dark spots on the surface of the Sun. **WARNING:** *Never look directly at the Sun.* Evidence supporting the link between sunspots and climate includes an extremely cold period in Europe between 1645 and 1715. During this time, very few sunspots appeared on the Sun.

**Figure 12** Mount Pinatubo in the Philippines erupted in 1991. During the eruption, particles were spread high into the atmosphere and circled the globe. Over time, particles spread around the world, blocking some of the Sun's energy from reaching Earth. The gray areas show how particles from the eruption moved around the world.

> **Indiana Academic Standard Check**
>
> **7.3.3:** Describe how climates . . . have changed abruptly in the past as a result of changes in Earth's crust, such as volcanic eruptions or impacts of huge rocks from space.
>
> ✔ How can volcanic eruptions or meteorite collisions affect climate?
>
> ✔ They affect climate for short periods of time by rapidly injecting particles into the atmosphere that block solar radiation and cause the planet to cool.

SECTION 3 Climatic Changes **637**

## Active Reading

**Cause-and-Effect Chart** This strategy is used to focus on cause-and-effect reasoning. In the center, have students write the topic that they are trying to understand. To the left of center, write the apparent causes of the topic. On the right side, write the apparent effects of the topic. Have students design a Cause-and-Effect Chart for a concept about climate. A sample is shown here.

**Caption Answer**

**Figure 13** Low; during the middle of the last ice age—the solar energy reaching the northern hemisphere was lower than normal.

**Quick Demo**

**Spinning Like a Top**

**Materials** a top

**Estimated Time** 5 minutes

**Procedure** Use a top to demonstrate the wobble of a spinning object on its axis. Remind students that Earth's wobbling is so slow that one complete wobble takes thousands of years.

## Teacher FYI

**Cooler Summers** If the northern hemisphere summer occurs when Earth is farthest from the Sun and Earth's axis is tilted the least, it is cooler than normal. This situation encourages the growth of ice sheets in the middle latitudes, possibly triggering ice ages.

## Use Science Words

**Word Origin** Paleoclimatology is the study of ancient climates. Have students find the meaning of the word part *paleo*. Have them list other words that include this word part and explain their meanings. Paleo means dealing with or involved with ancient forms or conditions. Possible examples: Paleobotany is the study of fossil plants. Paleontology is the study of ancient life forms. L3 IN **Linguistic**

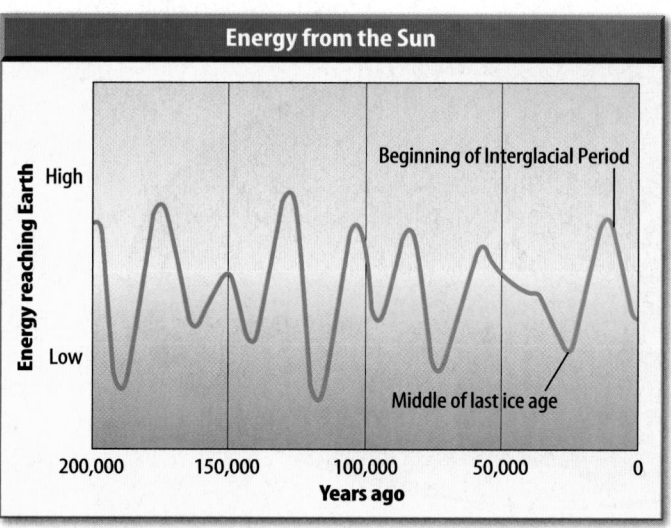

**Energy from the Sun**

Beginning of Interglacial Period

Middle of last ice age

Energy reaching Earth — High / Low

200,000  150,000  100,000  50,000  0

**Years ago**

**Figure 13** The curving line shows how the amount of the Sun's energy that strikes the northern hemisphere changed over the last 200,000 years.
**Describe** *the amount of energy that reached the northern hemisphere during the last ice age.*

**Indiana Academic Standard Check**

**7.3.6:** Describe how gas and dust from large volcanoes can change the atmosphere.

✔ Why can gas and dust from large volcanic eruptions cause Earth to cool?

✔ They can reduce the amount of solar radiation reaching Earth's surface.

**Earth Movements** Another explanation for some climatic changes involves Earth's movements in space. Earth's axis currently is tilted 23.5° from perpendicular to the plane of its orbit around the Sun. In the past, this tilt has increased to 24.5° and has decreased to 21.5°. When this tilt is at its maximum, the change between summer and winter is probably greater. Earth's tilt changes about every 41,000 years. Some scientists hypothesize that the change in tilt affects climate.

Two additional Earth movements also cause climatic change. Earth's axis wobbles in space just like the axis of a top wobbles when it begins to spin more slowly. This can affect the amount of solar energy received by different parts of Earth. Also, the shape of Earth's orbit changes. Sometimes it is more circular than at present and sometimes it is more flattened. The shape of Earth's orbit changes over a 100,000-year cycle.

**Amount of Solar Energy** These movements of Earth cause the amount of solar energy reaching different parts of Earth to vary over time, as shown in **Figure 13.** These changes might have caused glaciers to grow and shrink over the last few million years. However, they do not explain why glaciers have occurred so rarely over long spans of geologic time.

**Crustal Plate Movement** Another explanation for major climatic change over tens or hundreds of millions of years concerns the movement of Earth's crustal plates. The movement of continents and oceans affects the transfer of heat on Earth, which in turn affects wind and precipitation patterns. Through time, these altered patterns can change climate. One example of this is when movement of Earth's plates created the Himalaya about 40 million years ago. The growth of these mountains changed climate over much of Earth.

As you've learned, many theories attempt to answer questions about why Earth's climate has changed through the ages. Probably all of these things play some role in changing climates. More study needs to be done before all the factors that affect climate will be understood.

## Curriculum Connection

**Geography** A new ocean might form where Earth's crust is pulling apart in Africa's Great Rift Valley. If this ocean grows, it will affect the transfer of heat on Earth's surface and change wind and precipitation patterns. Have students locate the Great Rift Valley on a map. Have them also locate photographs that show evidence of the growing rift.

## Differentiated Instruction

**Visually Impaired** For visually impaired students, suggest that they place their hand into the pan of water (fingers together) while a parent or sibling blows on the water. Have the student report what they feel so that they may understand the concept of this experiment.

## Climatic Changes Today

Beginning in 1992, representatives from many countries have met to discuss the greenhouse effect and global climate change. These subjects also have appeared frequently in the headlines of newspapers and magazines. Some people are concerned that the greenhouse effect could be responsible for some present-day warming of Earth's atmosphere and oceans.

The **greenhouse effect** is a natural heating process that occurs when certain gases in Earth's atmosphere trap heat. Radiation from the Sun strikes Earth's surface and causes it to warm. Some of this heat then is radiated back toward space. Some gases in the atmosphere, known as greenhouse gases, absorb a portion of this heat and then radiate heat back toward Earth, as shown in **Figure 14.** This keeps Earth warmer than it would be otherwise.

There are many natural greenhouse gases in Earth's atmosphere. Water vapor, carbon dioxide, and methane are some of the most important ones. Without these greenhouse gases, life would not be possible on Earth. Like Mars, Earth would be too cold. However, if the greenhouse effect is too strong, Earth could get too warm. High levels of carbon dioxide in its atmosphere indicate that this has happened on the planet Venus.

**Science Online**

**Topic: Greenhouse Effect**
Visit in7.msscience.com for Web links to information about the greenhouse effect.

**Activity** Research changes in the greenhouse effect over the last 200 years. Infer what might be causing the changes.

## Discussion

**Reducing CO$_2$** Tell students that scientists recently pumped iron into a patch of seawater. The number of phytoplankton in their test patch increased significantly as the iron fertilized the water. Infer what happened to the concentration of CO$_2$ in the water. How might this process reduce the concentration of CO$_2$ in the atmosphere? CO$_2$ decreased because it was used by the phytoplankton during photosynthesis. Since CO$_2$ is a greenhouse gas, removing it from the air might slow global warming. Inform students that testing must be done to find out if this process has negative effects.

## Caption Answer

**Figure 14** In a greenhouse the Sun's energy heats the air inside. Heat is trapped because convection is limited and the air cannot escape. On Earth, heat is trapped because the energy "bounces" back/reradiates at a different frequency that can be absorbed by the atmospheric gases. The glass of a greenhouse does not absorb the air.

**Figure 14** The Sun's radiation travels through Earth's atmosphere and heats the surface. Gases in our atmosphere trap the heat. **Compare and contrast** *this to the way a greenhouse works.*

SECTION 3 Climatic Changes **639**

## Teacher FYI

**Venus Greenhouse** An extreme example of the greenhouse effect at work has been observed on Venus. Boiling-hot temperatures are common on the planet's surface both at night and during the day. Venus's atmosphere is dense with carbon dioxide, a greenhouse gas that traps heat around the planet.

## Visual Learning

## Check For Understanding

## Global Warming

Over the past 100 years, the average global surface temperature on Earth has increased by about 0.6°C. This increase in temperature is known as **global warming.** Over the same time period, atmospheric carbon dioxide has increased by about 20 percent. As a result, researchers hypothesize that the increase in global temperatures may be related to the increase in atmospheric carbon dioxide. Other hypotheses include the possibility that global warming might be caused by changes in the energy emitted by the Sun.

If Earth's average temperature continues to rise, many glaciers could melt. When glaciers melt, the extra water causes sea levels to rise. Low-lying coastal areas could experience increased flooding. Already some ice caps and small glaciers are beginning to melt and recede, as shown in **Figure 15.** Sea level is rising in some places. Some scientific studies show that these events are related to Earth's increased temperature.

You learned in the previous section that organisms are adapted to their environments. When environments change, can organisms cope? In some tropical waters around the world, corals are dying. Many people think these deaths are caused by warmer water to which the corals are not adapted.

Some climate models show that in the future, Earth's temperatures will increase faster than they have in the last 100 years. However, these predictions might change because of uncertainties in the climate models and in estimating future increases in atmospheric carbon dioxide.

**Figure 15** This glacier in Greenland might have receded from its previous position because of global warming. The pile of sediment in front shows how far the glacier once reached.

 **LAB DEMONSTRATION**

**Purpose** to show that burning hydrocarbons produces $CO_2$

**Materials** phenol red; candle; match; two petri dishes; tall, narrow jar; clay

**Preparation** Explain that coal, oil, natural gas, trees, and candles contain hydrocarbons; phenol red is an indicator for $CO_2$.

**Procedure** Secure the candle to the bottom of one petri dish with clay. Cover the bottoms of each dish with phenol red. Light the candle. Invert the jar over the candle.

**Expected Outcome** The phenol red turns yellow in the dish with the candle; it stays red in the other petri dish.

**Assessment**

What caused the color change? presence of carbon dioxide What was the source of the carbon dioxide? Carbon from the burning candle combined with oxygen to produce CO2. Why was the second petri dish used? It was a control.

## Human Activities

Human activities affect the air in Earth's atmosphere. Burning fossil fuels and removing vegetation increase the amount of carbon dioxide in the atmosphere. Because carbon dioxide is a greenhouse gas, it might contribute to global warming. Each year, the amount of carbon dioxide in the atmosphere continues to increase.

**Burning Fossil Fuels** When natural gas, oil, and coal are burned for energy, the carbon in these fossil fuels combines with atmospheric oxygen to form carbon dioxide. This increases the amount of carbon dioxide in Earth's atmosphere. Studies indicate that humans have increased carbon dioxide levels in the atmosphere by about 25 percent over the last 150 years.

**Deforestation** Destroying and cutting down trees, called **deforestation**, also affects the amount of carbon dioxide in the atmosphere. Forests, such as the one shown in **Figure 16,** are cleared for mining, roads, buildings, and grazing cattle. Large tracts of forest have been cleared in every country on Earth. Tropical forests have been decreasing at a rate of about one percent each year for the past two decades.

As trees grow, they take in carbon dioxide from the atmosphere. Trees use this carbon dioxide to produce wood and leaves. When trees are cut down, the carbon dioxide they could have removed from the atmosphere remains in the atmosphere. Cut-down trees often are burned for fuel or to clear the land. Burning trees produces even more carbon dioxide.

**✓ Reading Check** *What can humans do to slow carbon dioxide increases in the atmosphere?*

---

**Figure 16** When forests are cleared or burned, carbon dioxide levels increase in the atmosphere.

**Air Quality Control/Monitor**
Atmospheric particles from pollution can affect human health as well as climate. These small particles, often called particulates, can enter the lungs and cause tissue damage. The Department of Environmental Protection employs people to monitor air pollution and its causes. Research what types of laws air quality control monitors must enforce.

**Topic: Deforestation**
Visit in7.msscience.com for Web links to information about deforestation.

**Activity** Collect data on the world's decline in forests. Infer what the world's forests will be like in 100 years.

---

## Check For Understanding

**Linguistic** Challenge students to access the Glencoe Science Web site to find out about the role of the ocean in absorbing atmospheric $CO_2$. Instruct students to report on their findings. L3 LS

## Reteach

**Forecasting Climate** Have students explain why scientists don't all agree on their forecasts for Earth's climate. Students should discuss the many variables that must be considered in making such predictions. L2 LS
**Logical-Mathematical**

### ✔ Assessment

**Oral** Have students contrast the effects of volcanic aerosols and $CO_2$ on atmospheric temperature. Volcanic aerosols reflect solar energy, making Earth cooler. $CO_2$ traps heat, making Earth warmer. Use **Performance Assessment in the Science Classroom, p. 99.**

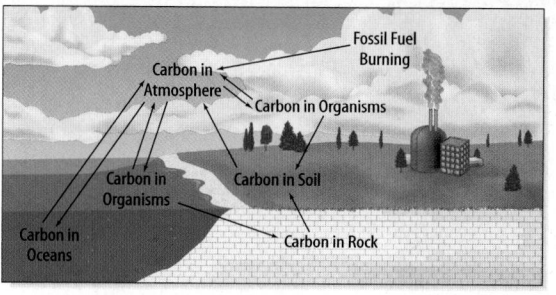

**Figure 17** Carbon constantly is cycled among the atmosphere, oceans, solid earth, and biosphere.

## The Carbon Cycle

Carbon, primarily as carbon dioxide, is constantly recycled in nature among the atmosphere, Earth's oceans, and organisms that inhabit the land. Organisms that undergo photosynthesis on land and in the water take in carbon dioxide and produce and store carbon-based food. This food is consumed by non-photosynthetic organisms. Carbon dioxide is released as food is broken down to release energy. When organisms die and decay, some carbon is stored as humus in soil and some carbon is released as carbon dioxide. This carbon cycle is illustrated in **Figure 17.**

Some carbon dioxide in the atmosphere dissolves in the oceans, and is used by algae and other photosynthetic, aquatic organisms. Just as on land, aquatic organisms give off carbon dioxide. However, Earth's oceans currently absorb more carbon dioxide from the atmosphere than they give off.

When Earth's climate changes, the amount of carbon dioxide that cycles among atmosphere, ocean, and land also can change. Some people hypothesize that if Earth's climate continues to warm, more carbon dioxide may be absorbed by oceans and land. Scientists continue to collect data to study any changes in the global carbon cycle.

### section 3 review

#### Summary

**Earth's Seasons**

- Seasons are short periods of climatic changes due to Earth's tilt on its axis while revolving around the Sun, causing differing amounts of solar energy to reach areas of Earth.

**El Niño and La Niña**

- El Niño begins in the tropical Pacific Ocean when trade winds weaken or reverse directions, disrupting the normal temperature and precipitation patterns around the globe.

**Climatic Changes Today**

- The greenhouse effect is a natural heating process that occurs when certain gases in Earth's atmosphere trap heat.
- Burning fossil fuels increases the amount of carbon dioxide in the air.
- Deforestation increases the amount of carbon dioxide in the atmosphere.

#### Self Check

1. **Explain** how Earth's tilted axis is responsible for seasons.
2. **Compare and contrast** El Niño and La Niña. What climate changes do they demonstrate?
3. **List** factors that can cause Earth's climate to change.
4. **Explain** how people are adding carbon dioxide to the atmosphere.
5. **Think Critically** If Earth's climate continues to warm, how might your community be affected?

#### Applying Skills

6. **Use Models** Using a globe, model the three movements of Earth in space that can cause climatic change.
7. **Use a word processor** to make a table that lists the different processes that might cause Earth's climate to change. Include in your table a description of the process and how it causes climate to change.

Science Online in7.msscience.com/self_check_quiz

### section 3 review

1. It causes areas to receive changing amounts of solar radiation throughout the year.
2. El Niño: drought in Australia and Africa, less dependable monsoons in Indonesia, storms in California; La Niña: droughts in southern U.S., excess rainfall in northwestern U.S.
3. Factors include: seasons, El Niño/La Niña, Earth's tilt, Earth's wobble, changes in the shape of Earth's orbit, volcanic eruptions, meteorite impacts, excess $CO_2$.
4. by burning fossil fuels, deforestation
5. Answers could include a need for more energy for air conditioning and possibility of flooding as sea level rises.
6. Students should model Earth's changing orbit, tilt, and wobble.
7. Students should include several of the processes discussed in this section, such as changes in solar output, changes in Earth's orbital parameters, crustal plate movement, and variations in greenhouse gases.

# The Greenhouse Effect

Do you remember climbing into the car on a warm, sunny day? Why was it so hot inside the car when it wasn't that hot outside? It was hotter in the car because the car functioned like a greenhouse. You experienced the greenhouse effect.

## Real-World Question

How can you demonstrate the greenhouse effect?

### Goals
- **Model** the greenhouse effect.
- **Measure and graph** temperature changes.

### Materials
identical large, empty glass jars (2)
lid for one jar
nonmercury thermometers (3)

### Safety Precautions

**WARNING:** *Be careful when you handle glass thermometers. If a thermometer breaks, do not touch it. Have your teacher dispose of the glass safely.*

## Procedure

1. Lay a thermometer inside each jar.
2. Place the jars next to each other by a sunny window. Lay the third thermometer between the jars.
3. **Record** the temperatures of the three thermometers. They should be the same.
4. Place the lid on one jar.
5. **Record** the temperatures of all three thermometers at the end of 5, 10, and 15 min.
6. Make a line graph that shows the temperatures of the three thermometers for the 15 min of the experiment.

## Conclude and Apply

1. **Explain** why you placed a thermometer between the two jars.
2. **List** the constants in this experiment. What was the variable?
3. **Identify** which thermometer showed the greatest temperature change during your experiment.
4. **Analyze** what occurred in this experiment. How was the lid in this experiment like the greenhouse gases in the atmosphere?
5. **Infer** from this experiment why you should never leave a pet inside a closed car in warm weather.

## Communicating
### Your Data

Give a brief speech describing your conclusions to your class.

LAB **643**

---

---

**BENCH TESTED**

# MICROCLIMATES

## Real-World Question

**Purpose** Students observe characteristics of microclimates near school. L2 COOP LEARN P

**Naturalist**

**Process Skills** measure in SI, use numbers, observe and infer, record, interpret data, relate cause and effect, analyze, communicate, compare and contrast

**Time Required** 40 minutes to set up testing sites, 20 minutes twice each day for a week to observe and record measurements, 40 minutes to do Procedure #5 and the Conclude and Apply questions

## Procedure

**Materials** Make a thermometer and rain gauge available for each test site. Have a psychrometer and windsock available for each group.

**Alternate Materials** If psychrometers need to be assembled, have students do this prior to the activity. To make a wet bulb thermometer, have students wrap the tip of a thermometer with gauze, as was done in the Quick Demo earlier in this chapter.

**Safety Precautions** Students should handle thermometers with care.

### Goals
■ **Observe** temperature, wind speed, relative humidity, and precipitation in areas outside your school.
■ **Identify** local microclimates.

### Materials
thermometers
psychrometer
paper strip or wind sock
large cans (4 or 5)
* *beakers or rain gauges (4 or 5)*
unlined paper
*Alternate materials*

### Safety Precautions

**WARNING:** *If a thermometer breaks, do not touch it. Have your teacher dispose of the glass safely.*

## Real-World Question

A microclimate is a localized climate that differs from the main climate of a region. Buildings in a city, for instance, can affect the climate of the surrounding area. Large buildings, such as the Bank of America Plaza in Dallas, Texas, can create microclimates by blocking the Sun or changing wind patterns. Does your school create microclimates?

## Procedure

1. Select four or five sites around your school building. Also, select a control site well away from the school.

2. Attach a thermometer to an object near each of the locations you selected. Set up a rain gauge, beaker, or can to collect precipitation.

3. Visit each site at two predetermined times, one in the morning and one in the afternoon, each day for a week. Record the temperature and measure any precipitation that might have fallen. Use a wind sock or paper strip to determine wind direction.

### Relative Humidity

| Dry Bulb Temperature (°C) | Dry Bulb Temperature Minus Wet Bulb Temperature (°C) | | | | | | | | | |
|---|---|---|---|---|---|---|---|---|---|---|
| | 1 | 2 | 3 | 4 | 5 | 6 | 7 | 8 | 9 | 10 |
| 14 | 90 | 79 | 70 | 60 | 51 | 42 | 34 | 26 | 18 | 10 |
| 15 | 90 | 80 | 71 | 61 | 53 | 44 | 36 | 27 | 20 | 13 |
| 16 | 90 | 81 | 71 | 63 | 54 | 46 | 38 | 30 | 23 | 15 |
| 17 | 90 | 81 | 72 | 64 | 55 | 47 | 40 | 32 | 25 | 18 |
| 18 | 91 | 82 | 73 | 65 | 57 | 49 | 41 | 34 | 27 | 20 |
| 19 | 91 | 82 | 74 | 65 | 58 | 50 | 43 | 36 | 29 | 22 |
| 20 | 91 | 83 | 74 | 66 | 59 | 51 | 44 | 37 | 31 | 24 |
| 21 | 91 | 83 | 75 | 67 | 60 | 53 | 46 | 39 | 32 | 26 |
| 22 | 92 | 83 | 76 | 68 | 61 | 54 | 47 | 40 | 34 | 28 |
| 23 | 92 | 84 | 76 | 69 | 62 | 55 | 48 | 42 | 36 | 30 |
| 24 | 92 | 84 | 77 | 69 | 62 | 56 | 49 | 43 | 37 | 31 |
| 25 | 92 | 84 | 77 | 70 | 63 | 57 | 50 | 44 | 39 | 33 |

**644 CHAPTER 21** Climate

### Sample Student Data Table: Test Site 1

| Day | Time | Temp. | Precip. | Wind |
|---|---|---|---|---|
| 1 | AM | | | |
| | PM | | | |
| 2 | AM | | | |
| | PM | | | |
| 3 | AM | | | |
| | PM | | | |
| 4 | AM | | | |
| | PM | | | |
| 5 | AM | | | |
| | PM | | | |

### Alternative Inquiry Lab

**Exploring Questions** Have students share questions they have about climate. For example, students may wish to know how scientists use ice cores to study the environment. They can design an experiment to study their own ice cores.

4. To find relative humidity, you'll need to use a psychrometer. A psychrometer is an instrument with two thermometers—one wet and one dry. As moisture from the wet thermometer evaporates, it takes heat energy from its environment, and the environment immediately around the wet thermometer cools. The thermometer records a lower temperature. Relative humidity can be found by finding the difference between the wet thermometer and the dry thermometer and by using the chart on the previous page. Record all of your weather data.

5. **Analyze** your data to find patterns. Make separate line graphs for temperature, relative humidity, and precipitation for your morning and afternoon data. Make a table showing wind direction data.

### ▶ Conclude and Apply

1. **Explain** Why did you take weather data at a control site away from the school building? How did the control help you analyze and interpret your data?

2. **Compare and contrast** weather data for each of your sites. What microclimates did you identify around your school building? How did these climates differ from the control site? How did they differ from each other?

3. **Infer** what conditions could have caused the microclimates that you identified. Are your microclimates similar to those that might exist in a large city? Explain.

### Communicating
#### Your Data

Use your graphs to make a large poster explaining your conclusions. Display your poster in the school building. **For more help, refer to the** Science Skill Handbook.

### Teaching Strategies

- Students should dip the wet bulb thermometer in water at each site and wait several minutes before reading both thermometers.
- Students can find relative humidity at the intersection of the "dry bulb" temperature and the "dry bulb minus wet bulb" temperature on the Relative Humidity table.

**Expected Outcome** Students should find that microclimate varies with location.

### ▶ Conclude and Apply

1. To see what the climate was like when not influenced by the building; when test sites were compared to the control, climatic effects caused by the building could be determined.
2. Answers will be subjective and based on the student's individual research.
3. Possible answers: shaded areas, walls blocking wind or rainfall. Students may infer that a large city would have similar microclimates because of the effects of the buildings.

**Error Analysis** If students did not find differences, they may not have read the thermometers correctly.

### ✔ Assessment

**Performance** Have students hypothesize how microclimates change throughout a 24-hour period around the school building. Use **Performance Assessment in the Science Classroom,** p. 93.

### Communicating
#### Your Data

Students may wish to use electronic spreadsheets to make their graphs.

## Content Background

Volcanoes are found throughout the world. However, not all volcanoes erupt in the same way. Kilauea, on the island of Hawaii, erupts quietly, pouring lava out slowly. Others, such as Mount St. Helens, spew out hot ash and debris in violent explosions. The type of eruption that occurs largely depends on the location of the volcano with respect to the boundaries of tectonic plates.

Volcanoes similar to Mount St. Helens occur where an oceanic plate converges with a continental plate. A large trench is formed as the oceanic plate sinks below the continental plate. Water included in the structure of some minerals subducts along with the plate. Part of the plate and overlying mantle rock melt, and some water is incorporated into the melt. As the magma rises toward the surface and pressure is reduced, the water vapor and other gases escape from the magma. These escaping gases can build pressure, causing the volcano to erupt explosively. During the eruption, escaping gas fragments the magma. Small pieces of magma and rock fragments are thrown into the air. The small pieces of magma cool in the air to form volcanic ash and pumice.

## Discussion

**Volcanic Debris** What are some of the other unfavorable effects that may result from debris blown into the atmosphere during a volcanic eruption? Possible answers: As the ash settles to the ground, breathing problems and long-term lung damage may result from inhaling ash; engines in aircraft and motor vehicles could clog up; and rivers could become rivers of mud jeopardizing aquatic life and human populations downstream.

## The Year there was No Summer

You've seen pictures of erupting volcanoes. One kind of volcano sends smoke, rock, and ash high into the air above the crater. Another kind of volcano erupts with fiery, red-hot rivers of lava snaking down its sides. Erupting volcanoes are nature's forces at their mightiest, causing destruction and death. But not everyone realizes how far-reaching the destruction can be. Large volcanic eruptions can affect people thousands of kilometers away. In fact, major volcanic eruptions can have effects that reach around the globe.

An erupting volcano can temporarily change Earth's climate. The ash a volcano ejects into the atmosphere can create day after day without sunshine. Other particles move high into the atmosphere and are carried all the way around Earth, sometimes causing global temperatures to drop for several months.

### The Summer That Never Came

An example of a volcanic eruption with wide-ranging effects occurred in 1783 in Iceland, an island nation in the North Atlantic Ocean. Winds carried a black cloud of ash from an erupting volcano in Iceland westward across northern Canada, Alaska, and across the Pacific Ocean to Japan. The summer turned bitterly cold in these places. Water froze, and heavy snowstorms pelted the land. Sulfurous gases from the erupting volcano combined with water to form particles of acid that reflected solar energy back into space. This "blanket" in the atmosphere kept the Sun's rays from heating up part of Earth.

The most tragic result of this eruption was the death of many Kauwerak people, who lived in western Alaska. Only a handful of Kauwerak survived the summer that never came. They had no opportunity to catch needed foods to keep them alive through the following winter.

**Locate** Using an atlas, locate Indonesia and Iceland. Using reference materials, find five facts about each place. Make a map of each nation and illustrate the map with your five facts.

Science Online

For more information, visit in7.msscience.com/time

**Locate** Collect books from your school library and local public library for students to use while researching facts on Iceland and Indonesia. Encourage the students to look for unique details. Have students share their maps in small groups. Let each group select five facts from their collection to share with the class.

## Resources for Teachers and Students

*How the Weather Works*, by Nicholas Turpin, ed. Dorling Kindersley Limited, London. 1995

*Volcano Cowboys: the Rocky Evolution of a Dangerous Science*, by Dick Thompson. St. Martin's Press, New York. 2000

## Reviewing Main Ideas

### Section 1 What is climate?

1. An area's climate is the average weather over a long period of time, such as 30 years.

2. The three main climate zones are tropical, polar, and temperate.

3. Features such as oceans, mountains, and even large cities affect climate.

### Section 2 Climate Types

1. Climates can be classified by various characteristics, such as temperature, precipitation, and vegetation. World climates commonly are separated into six major groups.

2. Organisms have structural and behavioral adaptations that help them survive in particular climates. Many organisms can survive only in the climate they are adapted to.

3. Adaptations develop in a population over a long period of time.

### Section 3 Climatic Changes

1. Seasons are caused by the tilt of Earth's axis as Earth revolves around the Sun.

2. El Niño disrupts normal temperature and precipitation patterns around the world.

3. Geological records show that over the past few million years, Earth's climate has alternated between ice ages and warmer periods.

4. The greenhouse effect occurs when certain gases trap heat in Earth's atmosphere.

5. Carbon dioxide enters the atmosphere when fossil fuels such as oil and coal are burned.

## Visualizing Main Ideas

*Copy and complete the following concept map on climate.*

 in7.msscience.com/interactive_tutor

**CHAPTER STUDY GUIDE 647**

---

## Reviewing Main Ideas

Summary statements can be used by students to review the major concepts of the chapter.

## Visualizing Main Ideas

See student page.

**Visit** in7.msscience.com
/self_check_quiz
/interactive_tutor
/vocabulary_puzzlemaker
/chapter_review
/standards_review

## Assessment Transparency

For additional assessment questions, use the *Assessment Transparency* located in the transparency book.

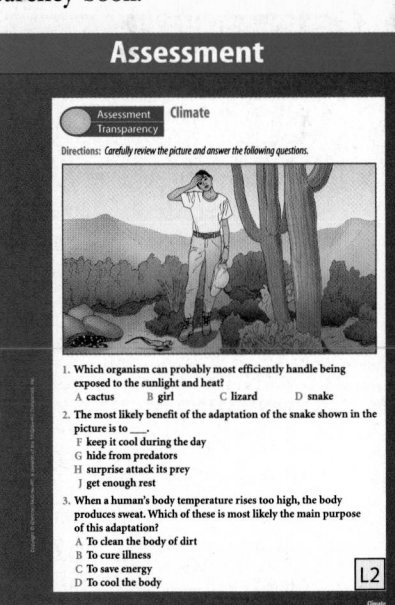

---

## ◇ Identifying Misconceptions

**Assess**

Use this assessment as follow-up to page F at the beginning of the chapter after students have completed the chapter.
**Materials** (for each group) globe, light source
**Procedure** Using **Figure 8**, have each group determine the location of Earth and the axis tilts that illustrate the four seasons in the northern hemisphere. Repeat the activity to illustrate the four seasons in the southern hemisphere.
**Expected Outcome** Students will recognize that the major contributor to the cause of seasons is the tilt of Earth on its axis at about 23.5° and that the distance between Earth and the Sun is not a major factor in causing seasons.

### Using Vocabulary

1. Earth's north pole is in the <u>polar zone.</u>
2. <u>El Niño</u> causes the Pacific Ocean to become warmer off the coast of Peru.
3. During <u>hibernation</u>, an animal's body temperature drops.
4. <u>Climate</u> is the pattern of weather that occurs over many years.
5. <u>Global warming</u> means global temperatures are rising.

### Checking Concepts

6. B
7. A
8. D
9. A
10. D
11. B
12. A
13. C
14. C
15. C

### Thinking Critically

16. Some organisms may not be adapted to the new climate conditions. Some of these organisms may migrate to more suitable environments. Organisms that cannot migrate to more suitable areas might die. Other organisms that are adapted to the new conditions might appear.
17. The region was wetter and possibly warmer in the past.
18. During the day, air near water is often cooler than air inland.
19. Earth's temperature would increase.
20. Temperature decreases with altitude.
21. When air pressure is high, air molecules move toward low pressure and produce wind. If air pressure is high in the eastern Pacific, winds blow west; if air pressure is high in the western Pacific, winds blow east.

### Using Vocabulary

| | |
|---|---|
| adaptation p.628 | hibernation p.630 |
| climate p.624 | polar zone p.624 |
| deforestation p.641 | season p.632 |
| El Niño p.633 | temperate zone p.624 |
| global warming p.640 | tropics p.624 |
| greenhouse effect p.639 | |

*Fill in the blanks with the correct vocabulary word or words.*

1. Earth's north pole is in the _____.

2. _____ causes the Pacific Ocean to become warmer off the coast of Peru.

3. During _____, an animal's body temperature drops.

4. _____ is the pattern of weather that occurs over many years.

5. _____ means global temperatures are rising.

### Checking Concepts

*Choose the word or phrase that best answers the question.*

6. Which of the following is a greenhouse gas in Earth's atmosphere?
   A) helium     C) hydrogen
   B) carbon dioxide     D) oxygen

7. During which of the following is the eastern Pacific warmer than normal?
   A) El Niño     C) summer
   B) La Niña     D) spring

8. Which latitude receives the most direct rays of the Sun year-round?
   A) 60°N     C) 30°S
   B) 90°N     D) 0°

9. What happens as you climb a mountain?
   A) temperature decreases
   B) temperature increases
   C) air pressure increases
   D) air pressure remains constant

10. Which of the following is true of El Niño?
    A) It cools the Pacific Ocean near Peru.
    B) It causes flooding in Australia.
    C) It cools the waters off Alaska.
    D) It may occur when the trade winds slacken or reverse.

11. What do changes in Earth's orbit affect?
    A) Earth's shape     C) Earth's rotation
    B) Earth's climate     D) Earth's tilt

12. The Köppen climate classification system includes categories based on precipitation and what other factor?
    A) temperature     C) winds
    B) air pressure     D) latitude

13. Which of the following is an example of structural adaptation?
    A) hibernation     C) fur
    B) migration     D) estivation

14. Which of these can people do in order to help reduce global warming?
    A) burn coal     C) conserve energy
    B) remove trees     D) produce methane

**Use the illustration below to answer question 15.**

N ↑

15. What would you most likely find on the leeward side of this mountain range?
    A) lakes     C) deserts
    B) rain forests     D) glaciers

Science**online** in7.msscience.com/vocabulary_puzzlemaker

**Use the ExamView® Pro Testmaker CD-ROM to:**
- create multiple versions of tests
- create modified tests with one mouse click for inclusion students
- edit existing questions and add your own questions
- build tests aligned with state standards using built-in State Curriculum Tags
- change English tests to Spanish with one mouse click and vice versa

## Thinking Critically

**16. Draw a Conclusion** How could climate change cause the types of organisms in an area to change?

**17. Infer** What might you infer if you find fossils of tropical plants in a desert?

**18. Describe** On a summer day, why would a Florida beach be cooler than an orange grove that is 2 km inland?

**19. Infer** what would happen to global climates if the Sun emitted more energy.

**20. Explain** why it will be cooler if you climb to a higher elevation in a desert.

**21. Communicate** Explain how atmospheric pressure over the Pacific Ocean might affect how the trade winds blow.

**22. Predict** Make a chain-of-events chart to explain the effect of a major volcanic eruption on climate.

**23. Form Hypotheses** A mountain glacier in South America has been getting smaller over several decades. What hypotheses should a scientist consider to explain why this is occurring?

**24. Concept Map** Copy and complete the concept map using the following: *tropics, 0°–23.5° latitude, polar, temperate, 23.5°–66.5° latitude,* and *66.5° latitude to poles.*

**25. Explain** how global warming might lead to the extinction of some organisms.

**26. Describe** how dust and ash from large volcanoes can change the atmosphere.

**27. Explain** how heat energy carried by ocean currents influences climate.

**28. Describe** how sediments, fossils, and ice cores record Earth's geologic history.

**29. Describe** how volcanic eruptions or meteorite collisions have changed past climates.

## Performance Activities

**30. Science Display** Make a display illustrating different factors that can affect climate. Be sure to include detailed diagrams and descriptions for each factor in your display. Present your display to the class.

## Applying Math

**Use the table below to answer questions 31 and 32.**

| Precipitation in Phoenix, Arizona | |
|---|---|
| Season | Precipitation (cm) |
| Winter | 5.7 |
| Spring | 1.2 |
| Summer | 6.7 |
| Autumn | 5.9 |
| Total | 19.5 |

**31. Precipitation Amounts** The following table gives average precipitation amounts for Phoenix, Arizona. Make a bar graph of these data. Which climate type do you think Phoenix represents?

**32. Local Precipitation** Use the table above to help estimate seasonal precipitation for your city or one that you choose. Create a bar graph for that data.

**CHAPTER REVIEW 649**

---

**22.** Charts may include the following steps: volcano erupts, ash rises into air, ash spreads around world, ash blocks solar radiation, world climate cools.

**23.** Climate is getting warmer; perhaps precipitation is less. Accept reasonable responses.

**24.** See student page.

**25.** Habitats might be altered or destroyed.

**26.** Large amounts of dust and ash can increase the atmosphere's particulate composition, and thus, block solar radiation and cool the planet.

**27.** Warm currents that begin near the equator and flow toward higher latitudes warm the land regions they pass. When they cool and flow back toward the equator, they cool the air and climates of nearby land.

**28.** Sediments, fossils, and ice cores can provide clues to Earth's past climates. For example, sediments from glacial deposits might be found in tropical regions, marine fossils might be found in deserts. All would indicate changes in Earth's climate.

**29.** Particulates ejected by volcanic eruptions and meteorite collisions have blocked solar radiation and cooled the planet.

### Performance Activities

**30.** Displays should include data about seasons; El Niño; volcanic eruptions; meteorite impacts; changes in Earth's tilt, wobble, and orbit shape; and the effect of greenhouse gases. Use the Performance Task Assessment List for Science Displays in **Performance Assessment in the Science Classroom,** p. 135.

### Applying Math

**Indiana Math Standards**

7.6.1

**31.** Check students' graphs against data in table; desert

**32.** Answers will vary.

---

## ✔ Assessment    Resources

📁 **Reproducible Masters**
**Chapter *Fast File* Resources**
  Chapter Review, pp. 37–38
  Chapter Tests, pp. 39–42
  Assessment Transparency Activity, p. 49
**Glencoe Science Web site**
  Chapter Review Test
  IN Standards Review

**Glencoe Technology**
  🖌 Assessment Transparency
  💿 Exam*View*® Pro Testmaker
  📼 MindJogger Videoquiz
  💿 Interactive Chalkboard

**Answer Sheet** A practice answer sheet can be found at in7.msscience.com/answer_sheet.

SAMPLE

The assessed Indiana standard appears above the question.

*Record your answers on the answer sheet provided by your teacher or on a sheet of paper.*

**Part 1** **Multiple Choice**

1. The graph below shows the levels of carbon dioxide in the atmosphere along with changes in temperature for the last 160,000 years.

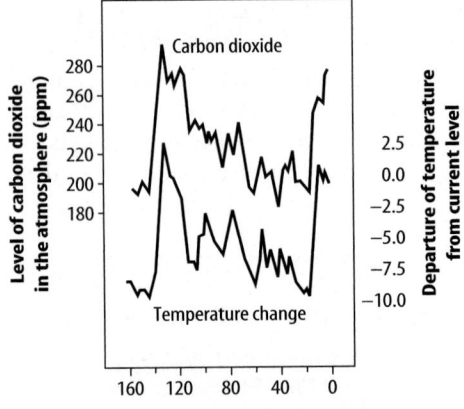

Which statement best describes the data in the graph above?

**A** As $CO_2$ levels have increased, global temperature has decreased.

**B** As $CO_2$ levels have increased, global temperature increased.

**C** As global temperature has decreased, $CO_2$ levels have increased.

**D** As global temperature has increased, $CO_2$ levels have decreased.

2. The table below shows the apparent temperature for a given air temperature and relative humidity.

| Apparent Temperature Index | | | | |
|---|---|---|---|---|
| | Relative Humidity (%) | | | |
| Air Temperature (°F) | 80 | 85 | 90 | 95 |
| 85 | 97 | 99 | 102 | 105 |
| 80 | 86 | 87 | 88 | 89 |
| 75 | 78 | 78 | 79 | 79 |
| 70 | 71 | 71 | 71 | 71 |

If the relative humidity is 85% and the temperature is 75°F, what is the apparent temperature?

**A** 78°F

**B** 79°F

**C** 88°F

**D** 89°F

3. The temperature of a city can be up to 5°C warmer than in surrounding rural areas. What is this phenomenon called?

**A** the Coriolis effect

**B** the greenhouse effect

**C** the heat island effect

**D** the rain shadow effect

**Test-Taking Tip**

**Fill In The Blanks** Never leave any answer blank.

dioxide which is released into the atmosphere. This leads to an increase in carbon dioxide in the atmosphere. The oceans absorb more carbon dioxide than they give off, which could mean the extra carbon dioxide may be absorbed by oceans and land.

Trees, which are photosynthetic, absorb carbon dioxide from the atmosphere. When large areas of forest are removed through deforestation, the carbon dioxide they could have removed remains in the atmosphere. Cut-down trees are often burned for fuel or to clear the

land. This also allows more carbon dioxide to enter the atmosphere.

7. When particles from volcanic eruptions enter the atmosphere, they block solar radiation. This can lead to decreased temperatures across the globe.

**4.** What is global warming?

**A** the average difference in temperature between tropical regions and polar regions

**B** the daily change in temperature as the Sun heats Earth's surface

**C** the increase in average surface temperature on Earth over the past 100 years

**D** the natural heating process that occurs when certain gases in the atmosphere trap heat

**5.** The illustration below shows what happens as the Sun's radiation passes through Earth's atmosphere.

What specific process does this illustration depict?

**A** El Niño

**B** global warming

**C** greenhouse effect

**D** La Niña

---

**Part 2 Critical Response**

**6.** The illustration below shows the carbon cycle.

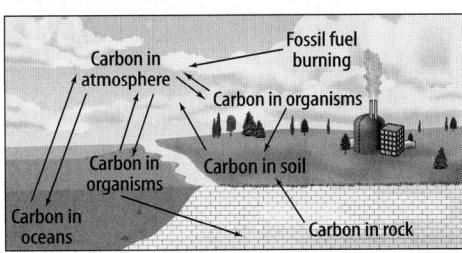

Describe the carbon cycle. How does the burning of fossil fuels affect the amount of carbon dioxide entering the carbon cycle? How does deforestation affect the amount of carbon dioxide entering the carbon cycle?

**7.3.3** **7.3.6**

**7.** In 1991, Mt. Pinatubo erupted, releasing volcanic particulates into the atmosphere. Temperatures around the world fell by as much as 0.7°C below average during 1992. How was this global temperature change related to the volcanic eruption?

**7.3.5**

**8.** Explain how a large body of water can affect the climate of a nearby area.

**7.3.5**

**9.** Describe the relationship between ocean currents and precipitation in a coastal region.

---

## Rubrics

The following rubric is a sample scoring device for critical response questions.

### Critical Response

| Points | Description |
| --- | --- |
| 4 | The student demonstrates a thorough understanding of the science of the task. The response may contain minor flaws that do not detract from the demonstration of a thorough understanding. |
| 3 | The student demonstrates an understanding of the science of the task. The response is essentially correct and demonstrates an essential but less than thorough understanding of the science. |
| 2 | The student demonstrates only a partial understanding of the science of the task. Although the student may have used the correct approach to a solution or may have provided a correct solution, the work lacks an essential understanding of the underlying science concepts. |
| 1 | The student demonstrates a very limited understanding of the science of the task. The response is incomplete and exhibits many flaws. |
| 0 | The student provides a completely incorrect solution or no response at all. |

---

 **Science** Online in7.msscience.com/standards_review

**8.** Large bodies of water can affect the climate of coastal ares by absorbing or giving off heat. This causes many coastal regions to be warmer in winter and cooler in summer than inland areas at similar latitude.

**9.** Winds blowing from the sea are often moister than those blowing from land. Some coastal areas have wetter climates than places farther inland.

| Section/Objectives | Standards | | Labs/Features |
|---|---|---|---|
| **Chapter Opener** | **National** | **State/Local** | **Launch Lab:** Clues to Life's Past, p. 653 |
| | See pp. 16T–17T for a Key to Standards. | Detailed standards begin on page IN8. | **Foldables,** p. 653 |
| **Section 1 Fossils** ⏱ 2 sessions 📦 1 block <br><br> 1. **List** the conditions necessary for fossils to form. <br> 2. **Describe** several processes of fossil formation. <br> 3. **Explain** how fossil correlation is used to determine rock ages. <br> 4. **Determine** how fossils can be used to explain changes in Earth's surface, life forms, and environment. | National Content Standards: UCP.1, UCP.2, UCP.3, UCP.5, A.1, A.2, F.5 | Indiana Standards: 7.3.8, 7.3.10 | **MiniLAB:** Predicting Fossil Preservation, p. 655 <br> **Integrate Social Studies,** p. 657 <br> **Integrate Life Science,** p. 660 |
| **Section 2 Relative Ages of Rocks** ⏱ 2 sessions 📦 1 block <br><br> 5. **Describe** methods used to assign relative ages to rock layers. <br> 6. **Interpret** gaps in the rock record. <br> 7. **Give** an example of how rock layers can be correlated with other rock layers. | National Content Standards: UCP.1, UCP.2, UCP.3, UCP.5, A.1, A.2 | Indiana Standards: 7.3.10 | **Science Online,** p. 663 <br> **Visualizing Unconformities,** p. 665 <br> **Science Online,** p. 666 <br> **Lab:** Relative Ages, p. 668 |
| **Section 3 Absolute Ages of Rocks** ⏱ 3 sessions 📦 1.5 blocks <br><br> 8. **Identify** how absolute age differs from relative age. <br> 9. **Describe** how the half-lives of isotopes are used to determine a rock's age. | National Content Standards: UCP.1, UCP.2, UCP.3, UCP.5, A.1, A.2, B.1, F.5, G.3 | Indiana Standards: 7.1.5 | **MiniLAB:** Modeling Carbon-14 Dating, p. 670 <br> **Science Online,** p. 672 <br> **Applying Science:** When did the Iceman die?, p. 672 <br> **Lab:** Trace Fossils, p. 674 <br> **Oops! Accidents in Science:** The World's Oldest Fish Story, p. 676 |

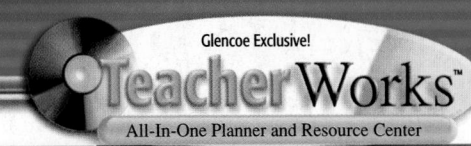
| Lab Materials | Reproducible Resources | Section Assessment | Technology |
|---|---|---|---|
| **Launch Lab:** 500-mL jar with lid, plaster of paris, water, several small shells, paper or plastic bowl | **Chapter FAST FILE Resources** <br> Foldables Worksheet, p. 17 <br> Directed Reading Overview, p. 19 <br> Note-taking Worksheets, pp. 33–34 | GLENCOE'S ASSESSMENT ADVANTAGE | **TeacherWorks includes:** <br> • Interactive Teacher Edition <br> • Lesson Planner with calendar <br> • Access to all program blacklines <br> • Correlations to standards <br> • Web links |
| | **Chapter FAST FILE Resources** <br> Transparency Activity, p. 44 <br> MiniLAB, p. 3 <br> Enrichment, p. 30 <br> Reinforcement, p. 27 <br> Directed Reading, p. 20 <br> Transparency Activity, pp. 47–48 <br> Lab Activities, pp. 9–12 <br> **Science Inquiry Labs,** p. 30 | **Portfolio** <br> Integrate Social Studies, p. 657 <br> **Performance** <br> MiniLAB, p. 655 <br> Applying Skills, p. 661 <br> **Content** <br> Section Review, p. 661 | Section Focus Transparency <br> Teaching Transparency <br> Guided Reading Audio Program <br> Interactive Chalkboard CD-ROM |
| **Lab:** no materials needed <br><br> *Need materials?* Contact Science Kit at 1-800-828-7777 or www.sciencekit.com on the Internet. | **Chapter FAST FILE Resources** <br> Transparency Activity, p. 45 <br> Enrichment, p. 31 <br> Reinforcement, p. 28 <br> Directed Reading, p. 21 <br> Lab Worksheets, pp. 5–6 <br> Lab Activities, pp. 13–15 <br> **Reading and Writing Skill Activities,** p. 21 | **Performance** <br> Applying Skills, p. 667 <br> **Content** <br> Section Review, p. 667 | Section Focus Transparency <br> Virtual Labs CD-ROM <br> Guided Reading Audio Program <br> Interactive Chalkboard CD-ROM |
| **MiniLAB:** 80 red jelly beans, 80 green jelly beans <br> **Lab:** construction paper, rigid plastic, plaster of paris, sturdy cardboard, pipe cleaners, wire, scissors, toothpicks, clay, glue | **Chapter FAST FILE Resources** <br> Transparency Activity, p. 46 <br> MiniLAB, p. 4 <br> Enrichment, p. 32 <br> Reinforcement, p. 29 <br> Directed Reading, p. 21, 22 <br> Lab Worksheets, pp. 7–8 <br> **Lab Management and Safety,** p. 39 | **Portfolio** <br> Science Journal, p. 672 <br> **Performance** <br> MiniLAB, p. 670 <br> Applying Science, p. 672 <br> Applying Math, p. 673 <br> **Content** <br> Section Review, p. 673 | Section Focus Transparency <br> Guided Reading Audio Program <br> Interactive Chalkboard CD-ROM <br> Video Lab |

## End of Chapter Assessment

GLENCOE'S ASSESSMENT ADVANTAGE

| Blackline Masters | Technology | Professional Series |
|---|---|---|
| **Chapter FAST FILE Resources** <br> Chapter Review, pp. 37–38 <br> Chapter Tests, pp. 39–42 <br> **Mastering the Grade 7 Indiana Science Standards** | MindJogger Videoquiz <br> IN Test Prep and Practice ExamView® <br> ExamView® Pro Testmaker <br> TeacherWorks CD-ROM <br> Interactive Chalkboard CD-ROM | **Performance Assessment in the Science Classroom (PASC)** |

# Transparencies

## Section Focus

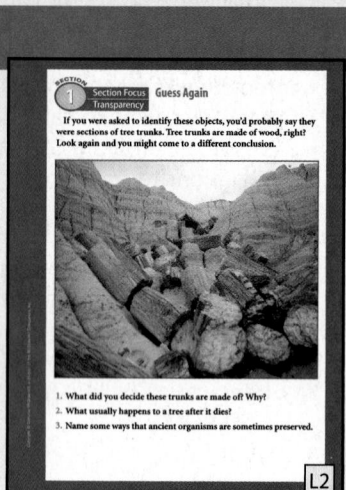

SECTION 1 — Section Focus Transparency — **Guess Again**

If you were asked to identify these objects, you'd probably say they were sections of tree trunks. Tree trunks are made of wood, right? Look again and you might come to a different conclusion.

1. What did you decide these trunks are made of? Why?
2. What usually happens to a tree after it dies?
3. Name some ways that ancient organisms are sometimes preserved.

L2

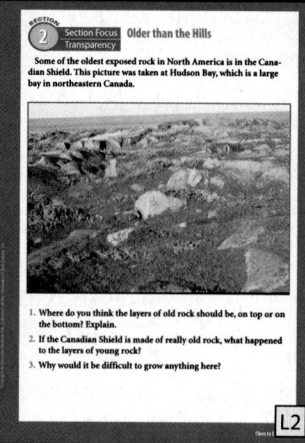

SECTION 2 — Section Focus Transparency — **Older than the Hills**

Some of the oldest exposed rock in North America is in the Canadian Shield. This picture was taken at Hudson Bay, which is a large bay in northeastern Canada.

1. Where do you think the layers of old rock should be, on top or on the bottom? Explain.
2. If the Canadian Shield is made of really old rock, what happened to the layers of young rock?
3. Why would it be difficult to grow anything here?

L2

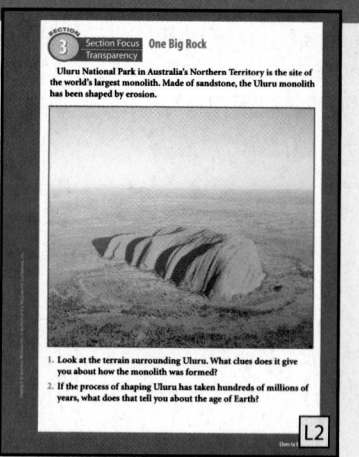

SECTION 3 — Section Focus Transparency — **One Big Rock**

Uluru National Park in Australia's Northern Territory is the site of the world's largest monolith. Made of sandstone, the Uluru monolith has been shaped by erosion.

1. Look at the terrain surrounding Uluru. What clues does it give you about how the monolith was formed?
2. If the process of shaping Uluru has taken hundreds of millions of years, what does that tell you about the age of Earth?

L2

---

This is a representation of key blackline masters available in the Teacher Classroom Resources. See Resource Manager boxes within the chapter for additional information.

## Key to Teaching Strategies

The following designations will help you decide which activities are appropriate for your students.

**L1** Level 1 activities should be appropriate for students with learning difficulties.

**L2** Level 2 activities should be within the ability range of all students.

**L3** Level 3 activities are designed for above-average students.

**ELL** ELL activities should be within the ability range of English Language Learners.

**COOP LEARN** Cooperative Learning activities are designed for small group work.

**LS** Multiple Learning Styles logos, as described on page 12T, are used throughout to indicate strategies that address different learning styles.

**P** These strategies represent student products that can be placed into a best-work portfolio.

**PBL** Problem-Based Learning activities apply real-world situations to learning.

## Assessment

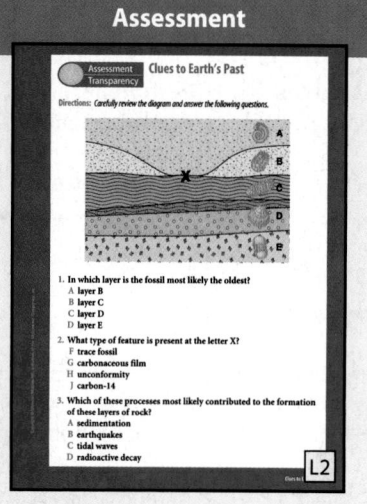

Assessment Transparency — **Clues to Earth's Past**

Directions: Carefully review the diagram and answer the following questions.

1. In which layer is the fossil most likely the oldest?
   A layer B
   B layer C
   C layer D
   D layer E
2. What type of feature is present at the letter X?
   F trace fossil
   G carbonaceous film
   H unconformity
   J carbon-14
3. Which of these processes most likely contributed to the formation of these layers of rock?
   A sedimentation
   B earthquakes
   C tidal waves
   D radioactive decay

L2

## Teaching

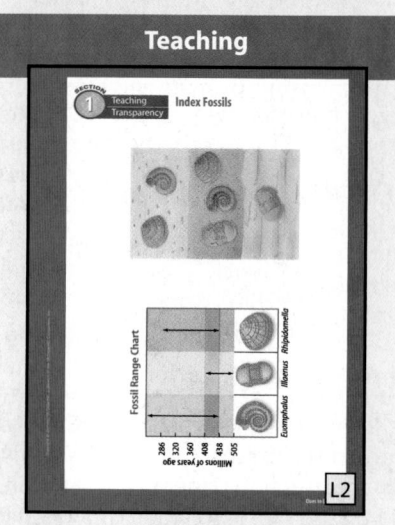

SECTION 1 — Teaching Transparency — **Index Fossils**

L2

# Hands-on Activities

## Student Text Lab Worksheet

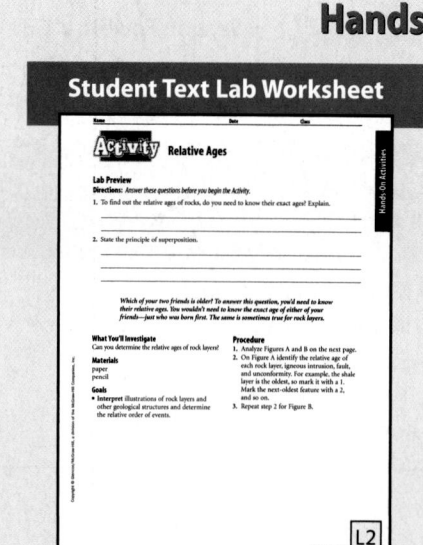

**Activity** — Relative Ages

**Lab Preview**
Directions: Answer these questions before you begin the Activity.

1. To find out the relative ages of rocks, do you need to know their exact ages? Explain.

2. State the principle of superposition.

*Which of your two friends is older? To answer this question, you'd need to know their relative ages. You wouldn't need to know the exact age of either of your friends—just who was born first. The same is sometimes true for rock layers.*

**What You'll Investigate**
Can you determine the relative ages of rock layers?

**Materials**
paper
pencil

**Goals**
• Interpret illustrations of rock layers and other geological structures and determine the relative order of events.

**Procedure**
1. Analyze Figures A and B on the next page.
2. On Figure A identify the relative age of each rock layer, igneous intrusion, fault, and unconformity. For example, the oldest layer is the oldest, so mark it with a 1. Mark the next-oldest feature with a 2, and so on.
3. Repeat step 2 for Figure B.

L2

## Laboratory Activities

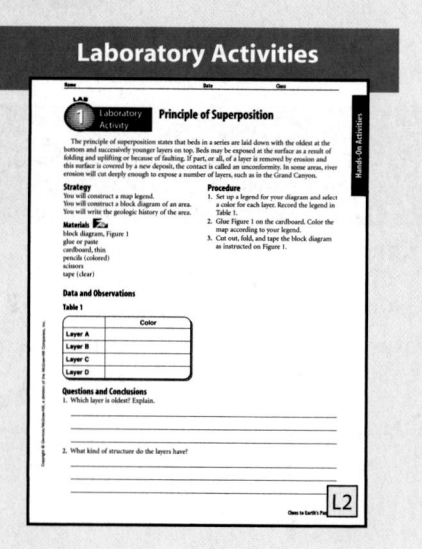

LAB 1 — Laboratory Activity — **Principle of Superposition**

The principle of superposition states that beds in a series are laid down with the oldest at the bottom and successively younger layers on top. Beds may be exposed at the surface as a result of folding and uplifting or because of faulting. If part, or all, of a layer is removed by erosion and this surface is covered by a new deposit, the contact is called an unconformity. In some areas, river erosion will cut deeply enough to expose a number of layers, such as in the Grand Canyon.

**Strategy**
You will construct a map legend.
You will construct a block diagram of an area.
You will write the geologic history of the area.

**Materials**
block diagram, Figure 1
glue or paste
cardboard, thin
pencils (colored)
scissors
tape (clear)

**Procedure**
1. Set up a legend for your diagram and select a color for each layer. Record the legend in Table 1.
2. Glue Figure 1 on the cardboard. Color the map according to your legend.
3. Cut out, fold, and tape the block diagram as instructed on Figure 1.

**Data and Observations**
Table 1

| | Color |
|---|---|
| Layer A | |
| Layer B | |
| Layer C | |
| Layer D | |

**Questions and Conclusions**
1. Which layer is oldest? Explain.

2. What kind of structure do the layers have?

L2

# Resource Manager

## Meeting Different Ability Levels

### Content Outline

L2

### Reinforcement

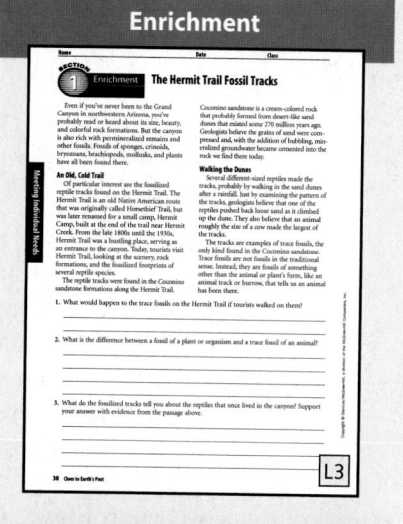

L2

### Enrichment

L3

### Directed Reading (English/Spanish)

L1

### Study Guide

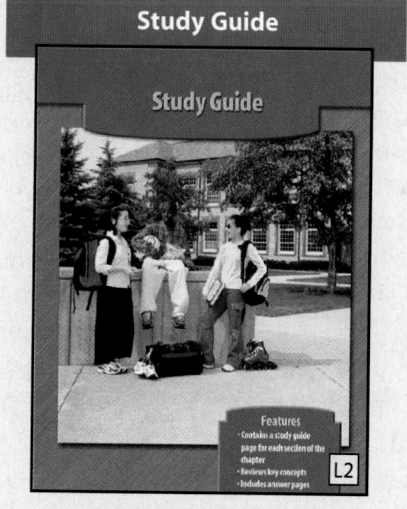

**Study Guide**

**Features**
- Contains a study guide page for each section of the chapter
- Reviews key concepts
- Includes answer pages

L2

### Reading Essentials

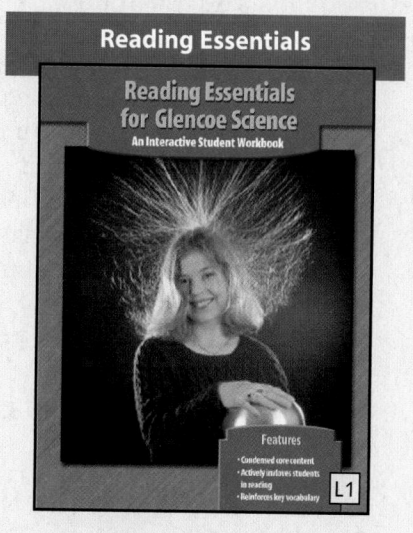

**Reading Essentials for Glencoe Science**
**An Interactive Student Workbook**

**Features**
- Condensed core content
- Actively involves students in reading
- Reinforces key vocabulary

L1

## Assessment

### Test Practice Workbook

L2

### Chapter Review

L2

### Chapter Tests

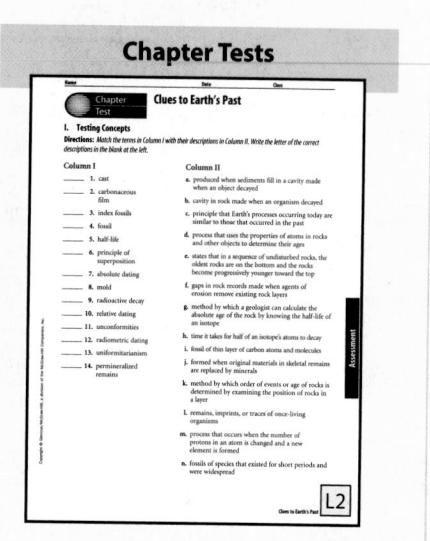

L2

# Science Content Background

## section 1 Fossils

### Trace Fossils

Scientists hypothesize that certain reptiles swallowed stones to aid in digestion. When the organism died and decayed, the polished stones, called gastroliths, were left behind. Because gastroliths are traces of the original organism and not the organism itself, they are called trace fossils. Another trace fossil is a coprolite, or fossilized fecal material. Jewelry has been made from cut and polished coprolites.

### Fossil Formation

Some fossils consist of the original parts of the organism. An insect trapped in amber and the skin and hair of some woolly mammoths have been found intact because they were protected from bacteria which would cause decay. Most fossils are formed as dead organisms are buried by layers of sediment that harden to form sedimentary rocks.

## section 2 Relative Ages of Rocks

### Relative Dating

The principle of faunal succession states that fossil organisms occur in rocks in a definite and determinable order. Thus, rocks formed during a particular interval of geological time can be recognized by their fossils. A geological column is a composite diagram that shows the rocks of an area in the sequence in which they occur. Correlation of geological columns from many locations enables geologists to construct geologic maps. Geologic maps show the relative age, distribution, and structural features of surface rocks.

## section 3 Absolute Ages of Rocks

### Isotopes

When daughter isotopes are part of the original makeup of a rock, the calculated age of that rock can be wrong. However, for some isotopes, geologists are able to distinguish between original daughter isotopes and those that formed during radioactive decay. In order to cross-check their work in radiometric dating, geologists use several parent isotopes for the same age measurement. Because the different parent isotopes decay at different rates, using them for the same age measurement can ensure accuracy or expose errors.

## chapter content resources

**Internet Resources**
For additional content background, visit
in7.msscience.com to:
- access your book online
- find references to related articles in popular science magazines
- access Web links with related content background
- access current events with science journal topics

**Print Resources**
*Roadside Geology* Series, by various authors, Mountain Press Publishing Company, various dates
*Fossils*, Frank H. Rhodes, Raymond Perlman, and Herbert Spencer Zim, St. Martin's Press, 2001
*Janice VanCleave's Earth Science for Every Kid*, Janice Pratt VanCleave, Barbara Clark, John Wiley & Sons, 1991

## IDENTIFYING ▷ Misconceptions

### Find Out What Students Think

**Students may think that . . .**

**The present is not the key to the past.**
Students are often confused about uniformitarianism, which is one of the fundamental principles of geology. The principle of uniformitarianism states that Earth processes occurring today are similar to those that occurred in the past. Thus, our understanding of past Earth processes is based on those that are presently taking place.

**Discussion**
Have students imagine that they are geologists. During a field study, they observe that deposits of sediment in a mudflat contain cracks and ripple marks. Back in the lab, you observe several sedimentary rocks that also contain these features. Have students discuss what they can infer from these observations, and how observations such as these help scientists explain past events. Students should infer that the same processes that cause the ripple marks to form today also caused them to form in the past.

### Promote Understanding

**Activity**

• Organize the class into small groups. Have groups examine samples of a layered sedimentary rock, such as shale. Ask each student to record his or her observations of the shale and then share these observations with their group members.

• Provide each group with a jar of water into which you have put sediment containing fine particles of clay. After students make sure that the lids are tightly sealed, have them gently shake the jar and observe the contents as they settle. Have students compare the rock sample and the layered sediments and determine how many of their original observations "fit" the sediments in the jar. Students should recognize that many of their observations are the same for both samples.

• Have each student group present their list of common characteristics to illustrate the principle of uniformitarianism.

### Assess

After completing the chapter, see *Identifying Misconceptions* in the Study Guide at the end of the chapter.

## Chapter Vocabulary

fossil, p. 655
permineralized remains, p. 656
carbon film, p. 656
mold, p. 657
cast, p. 657
index fossil, p. 659
principle of superposition, p. 662
relative age, p. 663
unconformity, p. 664
absolute age, p. 669
radioactive decay, p. 669
half-life, p. 670
radiometric dating, p. 671
uniformitarianism, p. 673

**Science Journal** Answers
will vary, but should make sense
for the local environment. If
near water, include mollusks.
Insects in amber also are likely.
Point out that animal bones are
unlikely to survive for fossilization. Leaf impressions or pollen
grains may be possible.

### PowerPoint® Presentations

This CD-ROM is an editable
Microsoft® PowerPoint®
presentation that includes:
* a pre-made presentation for
  every chapter
* interactive graphics
* animations
* audio clips
* image bank
* all new section and chapter
  questions
* Standardized Test Practice
* transparencies
* pre-lab questions for all labs
* Foldables directions
* links to in7.msscience.com

**Academic Standard—3:** Students collect and organize data to identify relationships between physical objects, events, and processes. They use logical reasoning to question their own ideas as new information challenges their conceptions of the natural world.

**Also covers:** Academic Standard 4 (Detailed standards begin on page IN8.)

# Clues to Earth's Past

## chapter preview

### sections

**1** Fossils

**2** Relative Ages of Rocks
*Lab* Relative Ages

**3** Absolute Ages of Rocks
*Lab* Trace Fossils

*Virtual Lab* How can fossil
and rock data determine when
an organism lived?

## Reading the Past

The pages of Earth's history, much like the
pages of human history, can be read if you look
in the right place. Unlike the pages of a book,
the pages of Earth's past are written in stone. In
this chapter you will learn how to read the
pages of Earth's history to understand what the
planet was like in the distant past.

**Science Journal** List three fossils that you would expect
to find a million years from now in the place you live today.

652

## Theme Connection

**Stability and Change** The evolution of organisms
throughout geologic time as shown by the fossil
record is a major focus of the chapter. The
changes in organisms on Earth can be used
to obtain relative ages of rocks and to date
geologic events.

## About the Photo

**Grand Canyon** Aside from being a famous tourist
attraction, the Grand Canyon is studied exten-
sively by geologists. Since it cuts deeply into
Earth's crust, it exposes rocks that are millions of
years old. This allows scientists access to rocks
that formed in Earth's distant past.

# Start-Up Activities

## Clues to Life's Past

Fossil formation begins when dead plants or animals are buried in sediment. In time, if conditions are right, the sediment hardens into sedimentary rock. Parts of the organism are preserved along with the impressions of parts that don't survive. Any evidence of once-living things contained in the rock record is a fossil.

1. Fill a small jar (about 500 mL) one-third full of plaster of paris. Add water until the jar is half full.
2. Drop in a few small shells.
3. Cover the jar and shake it to model a swift, muddy stream.
4. Now model the stream flowing into a lake by uncovering the jar and pouring the contents into a paper or plastic bowl. Let the mixture sit for an hour.
5. Crack open the hardened plaster to locate the model fossils.
6. **Think Critically** Remove the shells from the plaster and study the impressions they made. In your Science Journal, list what the impressions would tell you if found in a rock.

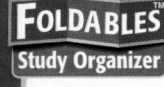 **Study Organizer**

**Age of Rocks** Make the following Foldable to help you understand how scientists determine the age of a rock.

**STEP 1** Fold a sheet of paper in half lengthwise.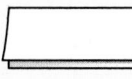

**STEP 2** Fold paper down 2.5 cm from the top. (Hint: From the tip of your index finger to your middle knuckle is about 2.5 cm.)

**STEP 3** Open and draw lines along the 2.5-cm fold. Label as shown.

**Summarize in a Table** As you read the chapter, in the left column, list four different ways in which one could determine the age of a rock. In the right column, note whether each method gives an absolute or a relative age.

 **Science Online**

**Preview this chapter's content and activities at in7.msscience.com**

653

## section

## 1

# Fossils

## 1 Motivate

**Bellringer**

INTERACTIVE CHALKBOARD
PowerPoint® Presentations

**Section Focus Transparencies** also are available on the Interactive Chalkboard CD-ROM.

L2 ELL

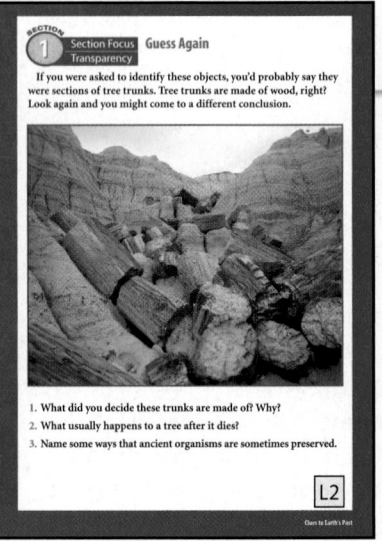

SECTION 1 Section Focus Transparency — **Guess Again**

If you were asked to identify these objects, you'd probably say they were sections of tree trunks. Tree trunks are made of wood, right? Look again and you might come to a different conclusion.

1. What did you decide these trunks are made of? Why?
2. What usually happens to a tree after it dies?
3. Name some ways that ancient organisms are sometimes preserved.

L2

**Tie to Prior Knowledge**

**Fossilization** Ask students to list things that can become fossils. In this section, they will learn that, under certain conditions, the remains of almost any organism or evidence of its activities can become a fossil.

### as you read

***What* You'll Learn**

■ **List** the conditions necessary for fossils to form.
■ **Describe** several processes of fossil formation.
■ **Explain** how fossil correlation is used to determine rock ages.
■ **Determine** how fossils can be used to explain changes in Earth's surface, life forms, and environments.

***Why* It's Important**

Fossils help scientists find oil and other sources of energy necessary for society.

🔍 **Review Vocabulary**
**paleontologist:** a scientist who studies fossils

**New Vocabulary**
● fossil          ● mold
● permineralized  ● cast
  remains         ● index fossil
● carbon film

## Traces of the Distant Past

A giant crocodile lurks in the shallow water of a river. A herd of *Triceratops* emerges from the edge of the forest and cautiously moves toward the river. The dinosaurs are thirsty, but danger waits for them in the water. A large bull *Triceratops* moves into the river. The others follow.

Does this scene sound familiar to you? It's likely that you've read about dinosaurs and other past inhabitants of Earth. But how do you know that they really existed or what they were like? What evidence do humans have of past life on Earth? The answer is fossils. Paleontologists, scientists who study fossils, can learn about extinct animals from their fossil remains, as shown in **Figure 1.**

**Figure 1** Scientists can learn how dinosaurs looked and moved using fossil remains. A skeleton can then be reassembled and displayed in a museum.

654

---

## Section 1 Resource Manager

**Chapter *FAST FILE* Resources**
Transparency Activity, pp. 44, 47–48
Directed Reading for Content Mastery, pp. 19, 20
Note-taking Worksheets, pp. 33–35
MiniLAB, p. 3

Enrichment, p. 30
Lab Activities, pp. 9–12
Reinforcement, p. 27
**Earth Science Critical Thinking/Problem Solving,** p. 12
**Science Inquiry Labs,** p. 30

## Formation of Fossils

**Fossils** are the remains, imprints, or traces of prehistoric organisms. Fossils have helped scientists determine approximately when life first appeared, when plants and animals first lived on land, and when organisms became extinct. Fossils are evidence of not only when and where organisms once lived, but also how they lived.

For the most part, the remains of dead plants and animals disappear quickly. Scavengers eat and scatter the remains of dead organisms. Fungi and bacteria invade, causing the remains to rot and disappear. If you've ever left a banana on the counter too long, you've seen this process begin. In time, compounds within the banana cause it to break down chemically and soften. Microorganisms, such as bacteria, cause it to decay. What keeps some plants and animals from disappearing before they become fossils? Which organisms are more likely to become fossils?

**Conditions Needed for Fossil Formation** Whether or not a dead organism becomes a fossil depends upon how well it is protected from scavengers and agents of physical destruction, such as waves and currents. One way a dead organism can be protected is for sediment to bury the body quickly. If a fish dies and sinks to the bottom of a lake, sediment carried into the lake by a stream can cover the fish rapidly. As a result, no waves or scavengers can get to it and tear it apart. The body parts then might be fossilized and included in a sedimentary rock like shale. However, quick burial alone isn't always enough to make a fossil.

Organisms have a better chance of becoming fossils if they have hard parts such as bones, shells, or teeth. One reason is that scavengers are less likely to eat these hard parts. Hard parts also decay more slowly than soft parts do. Most fossils are the hard parts of organisms, such as the fossil teeth in **Figure 2.**

## Types of Preservation

Perhaps you've seen skeletal remains of *Tyrannosaurus rex* towering above you in a museum. You also have some idea of what this dinosaur looked like because you've seen illustrations. Artists who draw *Tyrannosaurus rex* and other dinosaurs base their illustrations on fossil bones. What preserves fossil bones?

**Figure 2** These fossil shark teeth are hard parts. Soft parts of animals do not become fossilized as easily.

### Predicting Fossil Preservation

**Procedure**
1. Take a brief walk outside and observe your neighborhood.
2. Look around and notice what kinds of plants and animals live nearby.

**Analysis**
1. Predict what remains from your time might be preserved far into the future.
2. Explain what conditions would need to exist for these remains to be fossilized.

SECTION 1 Fossils **655**

---

### 2 Teach

**Purpose** Students consider what conditions are necessary for living things to become fossils. [L2]

**[IS] Logical-Mathematical**

**Teaching Strategy** Introduce this activity by asking students how we know about conditions that existed long ago on Earth's surface. Scientists study evidence of past life preserved in Earth's crust.

**Analysis**

1. The objects named must be the remains of living things or evidence of their activities, such as footprints or burrows. Possible answers: leaves, sticks, bones, shells
2. To best be preserved, the remains should have hard parts and be buried quickly.

### Assessment

**Oral** Have students explain why shark teeth are often found as fossils but impressions of jellyfish are rarely found. Shark teeth are hard, and thus likely to be preserved. Jellyfish have no hard parts and thus are unlikely to be preserved. Use **Performance Assessment in the Science Classroom,** p. 89.

---

## Differentiated Instruction

**Challenge** Have students investigate the process of fossilization. Scientists often study the decay of today's organisms to understand which animals from the past could become fossils and to help interpret the marks seen on those fossils. Have the students prepare a poster that discusses how current organisms can provide information on ancient fossils. [L3]

**Figure 3** Opal and various minerals have replaced original materials and filled the hollow spaces in this permineralized dinosaur bone. **Explain** *why this fossil retained the shape of the original bone.*

**Mineral Replacement** Most hard parts of organisms such as bones, teeth, and shells have tiny spaces within them. In life, these spaces can be filled with cells, blood vessels, nerves, or air. When the organism dies and the soft materials inside the hard parts decay, the tiny spaces become empty. If the hard part is buried, groundwater can seep in and deposit minerals in the spaces. **Permineralized remains** are fossils in which the spaces inside are filled with minerals from groundwater. In permineralized remains, some original material from the fossil organism's body might be preserved—encased within the minerals from groundwater. It is from these original materials that DNA, the chemical that contains an organism's genetic code, can sometimes be recovered.

Sometimes minerals replace the hard parts of fossil organisms. For example, a solution of water and dissolved silica (the compound $SiO_2$) might flow into and through the shell of a dead organism. If the water dissolves the shell and leaves silica in its place, the original shell is replaced.

Often people learn about past forms of life from bones, wood, and other remains that became permineralized or replaced with minerals from groundwater, as shown in **Figure 3,** but many other types of fossils can be found.

**Figure 4** Graptolites lived hundreds of millions of years ago and drifted on currents in the oceans. These organisms often are preserved as carbon films.

**Carbon Films** The tissues of organisms are made of compounds that contain carbon. Sometimes fossils contain only carbon. Fossils usually form when sediments bury a dead organism. As sediment piles up, the organism's remains are subjected to pressure and heat. These conditions force gases and liquids from the body. A thin film of carbon residue is left, forming a silhouette of the original organism called a **carbon film. Figure 4** shows the carbonized remains of graptolites, which were small marine animals. Graptolites have been found in rocks as old as 500 million years.

**656** **CHAPTER 22** Clues to Earth's Past

**Coal** In swampy regions, large volumes of plant matter accumulate. Over millions of years, these deposits become completely carbonized, forming coal. Coal is an important fuel source, but since the structure of the original plant is usually lost, it cannot reveal as much about the past as other kinds of fossils.

☑ **Reading Check** *In what sort of environment does coal form?*

**Molds and Casts** In nature, impressions form when seashells or other hard parts of organisms fall into a soft sediment such as mud. The object and sediment are then buried by more sediment. Compaction, together with cementation, which is the deposition of minerals from water into the pore spaces between sediment particles, turns the sediment into rock. Other open pores in the rock then let water and air reach the shell or hard part. The hard part might decay or dissolve, leaving behind a cavity in the rock called a **mold**. Later, mineral-rich water or other sediment might enter the cavity, form new rock, and produce a copy or **cast** of the original object, as shown in **Figure 5.**

**INTEGRATE Social Studies**

**Coal Mining** Many of the first coal mines in the United States were located in eastern states like Pennsylvania and West Virginia. In your Science Journal, discuss how the environments of the past relate to people's lives today.

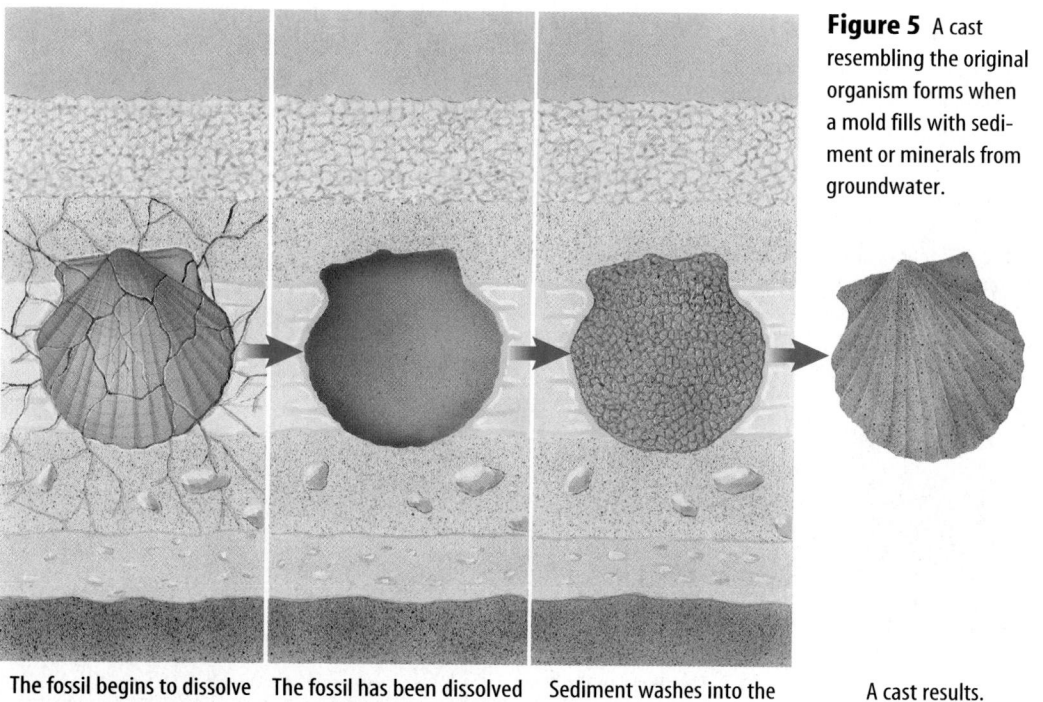

**Figure 5** A cast resembling the original organism forms when a mold fills with sediment or minerals from groundwater.

The fossil begins to dissolve as water moves through spaces in the rock layers.

The fossil has been dissolved away. The harder rock once surrounding it forms a mold.

Sediment washes into the mold and is deposited, or mineral crystals form.

A cast results.

---

☑ **Reading Check**

**Answer** Coal forms in swampy regions.

**Coal Mining** Answers will vary; accept anything reasonable

**Career** Have students investigate how geologists find coal deposits. They also should learn what training is required. Have students prepare a recruitment poster to attract students to the field. P

## Visual Learning

**Figure 5** After students have studied the figure, provide them with a mold and cast of the same organism. Which of your fossils is a mold and which is a cast? The mold is the hollow or depression in the original rock, and the cast will be the bump that fits into the hollow.

## Use an Analogy

**Molds in Nature** Have students discuss an analogy between molds used in making ceramic statues and those formed in nature. Use modeling clay and a small statue to demonstrate why the internal structure of an organism is not preserved when casts are formed. L2

---

## Fun Fact

Scientists have extracted DNA from frozen mammoths and compared it with modern elephants to determine their relationships.

## Curriculum Connection

**Geography** Have students research and find on a map where replacement fossils have been found in the United States. As part of the task, have students explain what the name "Petrified Forest" refers to. This name refers to the Petrified Forest National Monument in Arizona, where there is wood in which much of the original matter has been replaced by minerals. L2 LS
**Visual-Spatial**

**Figure 6** The original soft parts of this mosquito have been preserved in amber for millions of years.

**Figure 7** Tracks made in soft mud, and now preserved in solid rock, can provide information about animal size, speed, and behavior.

The dinosaur track below is from the Glen Rose Formation in north-central Texas.

The tracks to the right are located on a Navajo reservation in Arizona.

**Original Remains** Sometimes conditions allow original soft parts of organisms to be preserved for thousands or millions of years. For example, insects can be trapped in amber, a hardened form of sticky tree resin. The amber surrounds and protects the original material of the insect's exoskeleton from destruction, as shown in **Figure 6.** Some organisms, such as the mammoth, have been found preserved in frozen ground in Siberia. Original remains also have been found in natural tar deposits, such as the La Brea tar pits in California.

**Trace Fossils** Do you have a handprint in plaster that you made when you were in kindergarten? If so, it's a record that tells something about you. From it, others can guess your size and maybe your weight at that age. Animals walking on Earth long ago left similar tracks, such as those in **Figure 7.** Trace fossils are fossilized tracks and other evidence of the activity of organisms. In some cases, tracks can tell you more about how an organism lived than any other type of fossil. For example, from a set of tracks at Davenport Ranch, Texas, you might be able to learn something about the social life of sauropods, which were large, plant-eating dinosaurs. The largest tracks of the herd are on the outer edges and the smallest are on the inside. These tracks led some scientists to hypothesize that adult sauropods surrounded their young as they traveled—perhaps to protect them from predators. A nearby set of tracks might mean that another type of dinosaur, an allosaur, was stalking the herd.

## Cultural Diversity

**The Copper Man of the Alps** On September 19, 1991, a German couple hiking in the Alps came across a 5,000-year-old traveler, naturally mummified in a small depression covered by glacial ice. The Iceman is now known to be one of the oldest and best-preserved mummified humans. Plant remains on his clothing suggest that he came from lowland South Tyrol. He wore finely stitched skin clothing, a woven grass cape, and boots. His deerskin quiver held two arrows tipped with flint and 12 unfinished arrows. He carried two antibiotic fungi, a backpack, a half-finished longbow, high-quality flint, and a flint dagger. One of his most intriguing possessions was an axe, originally thought to be bronze but now known to be copper. It is flanged in a style not found anywhere nearby until nearly 800 years later.

**Trails and Burrows** Other trace fossils include trails and burrows made by worms and other animals. These, too, tell something about how these animals lived. For example, by examining fossil burrows you can sometimes tell how firm the sediment the animals lived in was. As you can see, fossils can tell a great deal about the organisms that have inhabited Earth.

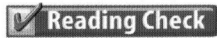 **Reading Check** *How are trace fossils different from fossils that are the remains of an organism's body?*

## Index Fossils

One thing you can learn by studying fossils is that species of organisms have changed over time. Some species of organisms inhabited Earth for long periods of time without changing. Other species changed a lot in comparatively short amounts of time. It is these organisms that scientists use as index fossils.

**Index fossils** are the remains of species that existed on Earth for relatively short periods of time, were abundant, and were widespread geographically. Because the organisms that became index fossils lived only during specific intervals of geologic time, geologists can estimate the ages of rock layers based on the particular index fossils they contain. However, not all rocks contain index fossils. Another way to approximate the age of a rock layer is to compare the spans of time, or ranges, over which more than one fossil appears. The estimated age is the time interval where fossil ranges overlap, as shown in **Figure 8.**

**Figure 8** The fossils in a sequence of sedimentary rock can be used to estimate the ages of each layer. The chart shows when each organism inhabited Earth.
**Explain** why it is possible to say that the middle layer of rock was deposited between 440 million and 410 million years ago.

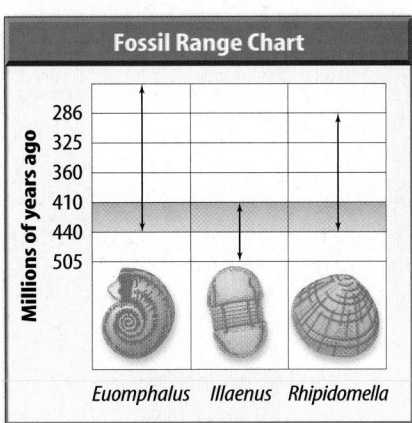

**Fossil Range Chart**

Millions of years ago: 286, 325, 360, 410, 440, 505

Euomphalus   Illaenus   Rhipidomella

**Indiana Academic Standard Check**

**7.3.10:** Explain how thousands of layers of sedimentary rock can confirm . . . the changing life forms whose remains are found in successive layers.

✔ What is the importance of index fossils?

✔ Index fossils make it possible to estimate the age of the rock layers in which they are found.

 **Reading Check**

**Answer** Trace fossils are fossilized tracks and other evidence of an organism's activity. They are not parts of the original organism.

## Make a Model

**Fossil Models** Encourage pairs of students to produce a model of a fossil that depicts one of the five methods of formation. Display student models and actual samples in the classroom. [L2] ELL COOP LEARN IS **Kinesthetic**

## Caption Answer

**Figure 8** The three fossils have ranges that overlap between 440 and 410 million years. The age of the layer cannot be dated more accurately than that.

## Activity

**Index Fossils** Have students prepare a list of index fossils for North America, including the periods in which they are found. Give them maps of various geologic formations in the United States. Have students show the class which index fossils might be found in their formations.

## Science Journal

**Traces of the Past** Have students research and write a summary of what can be learned about extinct animals from studying gastroliths and coprolites. Possible answer: Gastroliths are stones swallowed to aid in digestion; coprolites are petrified feces. Both might provide clues about an organism's diet. [L2] IS
**Linguistic**

**Ancient Ecology** Possible answers: Study of fossils might indicate predator-prey relationships, migratory patterns, and climatic changes. Accept reasonable answers.

**Research** Have students investigate the Burgess Shale, dinosaur footprints, or dinosaur nests. Let them put together a presentation that discusses the ecological insights available from these discoveries. If possible, have them connect these past organisms to current animals with similar behaviors.

**Text Question Answer**

Because different organisms live at different depths, fossils can be general indicators of water depth in a region.

## Visual Learning

**Figure 9** How does the position of North America explain the presence of fern fossils in shale beds of the Pennsylvanian Period? North America was closer to the equator during the Pennsylvanian Period. Much of the region was covered by swamps, in which ferns thrived. As ferns died, they fell into the swamp and were covered by sediments.

**Ancient Ecology**
Ecology is the study of how organisms interact with each other and with their environment. Some paleontologists study the ecology of ancient organisms. Discuss the kinds of information you could use to determine how ancient organisms interacted with their environment.

**Figure 9** The equator passed through North America 310 million years ago. At this time, warm, shallow seas and coal swamps covered much of the continent, and ferns like the *Neuropteris,* below, were common.

## Fossils and Ancient Environments

Scientists can use fossils to determine what the environment of an area was like long ago. Using fossils, you might be able to find out whether an area was land or whether it was covered by an ocean at a particular time. If the region was covered by ocean, it might even be possible to learn the depth of the water. What clues about the depth of water do you think fossils could provide?

Fossils also are used to determine the past climate of a region. For example, rocks in parts of the eastern United States contain fossils of tropical plants. The environment of this part of the United States today isn't tropical. However, because of the fossils, scientists know that it was tropical when these plants were living. **Figure 9** shows that North America was located near the equator when these fossils formed.

**660** CHAPTER 22 Clues to Earth's Past

## Differentiated Instruction

**Learning Disabled** To help students better understand how fossils can indicate ancient environments, show them samples of rocks that contain fossils of organisms that once lived in a shallow sea. Ask students to explain the environment that existed when the organisms were alive.
L1 IS **Visual-Spatial**

**Shallow Seas** How would you explain the presence of fossilized crinoids—animals that lived in shallow seas—in rocks found in what is today a desert? **Figure 10** shows a fossil crinoid and a living crinoid. When the fossil crinoids were alive, a shallow sea covered much of western and central North America. The crinoid hard parts were included in rocks that formed from the sediments at the bottom of this sea. Fossils provide information about past life on Earth and also about the history of the rock layers that contain them. Fossils can provide information about the ages of rocks and the climate and type of environment that existed when the rocks formed.

**Figure 10** The crinoid on the left lived in warm, shallow seas that once covered part of North America. Crinoids like the one on the right typically live in warm, shallow waters in the Pacific Ocean.

## section 1 review

### Summary

**Formation of Fossils**

- Fossils are the remains, imprints, or traces of past organisms.
- Fossilization is most likely if the organism had hard parts and was buried quickly.

**Fossil Preservation**

- Permineralized remains have open spaces filled with minerals from groundwater.
- Thin carbon films remain in the shapes of dead organisms.
- Hard parts dissolve to leave molds.
- Trace fossils are evidence of past activity.

**Index Fossils**

- Index fossils are from species that were abundant briefly, but over wide areas.
- Scientists can estimate the ages of rocks containing index fossils.

**Fossils and Ancient Environments**

- Fossils tell us about the environment in which the organisms lived.

### Self Check

1. **Describe** the typical conditions necessary for fossil formation.
2. **Explain** how a fossil mold is different from a fossil cast.
3. **Discuss** how the characteristics of an index fossil are useful to geologists.
4. **Describe** how carbon films form.
5. **Think Critically** What can you say about the ages of two widely separated layers of rock that contain the same type of fossil?

#### Applying Skills

6. **Communicate** what you learn about fossils. Visit a museum that has fossils on display. Make an illustration of each fossil in your Science Journal. Write a brief description, noting key facts about each fossil and how each fossil might have formed.
7. **Compare and contrast** original remains with other kinds of fossils. What kinds of information would only be available from original remains? Are there any limitations to the use of original remains?

**Science** nline    in7.msscience.com/self_check_quiz

SECTION 1 Fossils **661**

## section 1 review

1. hard parts that are quickly buried
2. A buried object decays, leaving a cavity, or mold. Later, sediments fill the cavity, harden, and produce a cast.
3. They lived for a relatively short period of time, were abundant, and were geographically widespread. Geologists can define the ages of rock layers based on the particular index fossils they contain.
4. Pressure and heat force out gases and liquids; only a film of carbon residue is left.
5. Both rock layers formed when the fossil-producing organism lived; they may be similar in age if the organism existed for a short time.
6. Encourage students to set up their observations as a field notebook.
7. Original remains include structures like hair and organs that are usually absent in fossils. Original remains only exist in a few places, like glaciers or tar pits.

SECTION 1 Fossils **661**

---

## 3 Assess

### DAILY INTERVENTION

### Check for Understanding

**Visual-Spatial** Give groups of students stacks of magazines in chronological order. Insert an undated item in the middle of the stack. Have each group determine the relative age of the item based on the magazine dates.

### Reteach

**Fossils** Have students form groups of four. Have them press shells or bones into mixtures of sand and water, soft clay and water, and gravel and water. The recorder should report which sediment allowed the best imprint to be formed. soft clay and water L2 COOP LEARN

**IS Kinesthetic and Interpersonal**

### ✓ Assessment

**Performance** Have students devise concept maps summarizing the major concepts of this section. Have pairs exchange maps and make suggestions as to how to improve the maps. Use **Performance Assessment in the Science Classroom,** p. 161.

## section 2

# Relative Ages of Rocks

## 1 Motivate

### Bellringer

**Section Focus Transparencies** also are available on the Interactive Chalkboard CD-ROM.

**Section Focus Transparency** — Older than the Hills

Some of the oldest exposed rock in North America is in the Canadian Shield. This picture was taken at Hudson Bay, which is a large bay in northeastern Canada.

1. Where do you think the layers of old rock should be, on top or on the bottom? Explain.
2. If the Canadian Shield is made of really old rock, what happened to the layers of young rock?
3. Why would it be difficult to grow anything here?

### Tie to Prior Knowledge

**Daily Superposition** Students may be surprised to find that they observe superposition every day. Discuss how they know which layers of bricks were laid first as they observe a wall, or where they would look for last week's paper in a stack of newspapers set aside to be recycled. Explain that scientists use these same principles when they determine the age of rock layers.

### Text Question Answer

Sediments accumulate to form rocks; the oldest layer is on the bottom.

---

### as you read

#### *What* You'll Learn

- **Describe** methods used to assign relative ages to rock layers.
- **Interpret** gaps in the rock record.
- **Give** an example of how rock layers can be correlated with other rock layers.

#### *Why* It's Important

Being able to determine the age of rock layers is important in trying to understand a history of Earth.

#### Review Vocabulary
**sedimentary rock:** rock formed when sediments are cemented and compacted or when minerals are precipitated from solution

#### New Vocabulary
- principle of superposition
- relative age
- unconformity

---

## Superposition

Imagine that you are walking to your favorite store and you happen to notice an interesting car go by. You're not sure what kind it is, but you remember that you read an article about it. You decide to look it up. At home you have a stack of magazines from the past year, as seen in **Figure 11.**

You know that the article you're thinking of came out in the January edition, so it must be near the bottom of the pile. As you dig downward, you find magazines from March, then February. January must be next. How did you know that the January issue of the magazine would be on the bottom? To find the older edition under newer ones, you applied the principle of superposition.

**Oldest Rocks on the Bottom** According to the **principle of superposition,** in undisturbed layers of rock, the oldest rocks are on the bottom and the rocks become progressively younger toward the top. Why is this the case?

**Figure 11** The pile of magazines illustrates the principle of superposition. According to this principle, the oldest rock layer (or magazine) is on the bottom.

662

---

### Section 2 Resource Manager

**Chapter *FAST FILE* Resources**
- Transparency Activity, p. 45
- Directed Reading for Content Mastery, p. 21
- Lab Activities, pp. 13–15
- Lab Worksheets, pp. 5–6

**Reading and Writing Skill Activities,** p. 21
**Earth Science Critical Thinking/Problem Solving,** pp. 11 and 14
**Cultural Diversity,** p. 13

---

**Rock Layers** Sediment accumulates in horizontal beds, forming layers of sedimentary rock. The first layer to form is on the bottom. The next layer forms on top of the previous one. Because of this, the oldest rocks are at the bottom. However, forces generated by mountain formation sometimes can turn layers over. When layers have been turned upside down, it's necessary to use other clues in the rock layers to determine their original positions and relative ages.

## Relative Ages

Now you want to look for another magazine. You're not sure how old it is, but you know it arrived after the January issue. You can find it in the stack by using the principle of relative age.

The **relative age** of something is its age in comparison to the ages of other things. Geologists determine the relative ages of rocks and other structures by examining their places in a sequence. For example, if layers of sedimentary rock are offset by a fault, which is a break in Earth's surface, you know that the layers had to be there before a fault could cut through them. The relative age of the rocks is older than the relative age of the fault. Relative age determination doesn't tell you anything about the age of rock layers in actual years. You don't know if a layer is 100 million or 10,000 years old. You only know that it's younger than the layers below it and older than the fault cutting through it.

**Other Clues Help** Determination of relative age is easy if the rocks haven't been faulted or turned upside down. For example, look at **Figure 12.** Which layer is the oldest? In cases where rock layers have been disturbed you might have to look for fossils and other clues to date the rocks. If you find a fossil in the top layer that's older than a fossil in a lower layer, you can hypothesize that layers have been turned upside down by folding during mountain building.

### Science Online

**Topic: Relative Dating**

Visit in7.msscience.com for Web links to information about relative dating of rocks and other materials.

**Activity** You have found a rare artifact. Make a list of clues you might look for to provide a relative date and explain how each would allow you to approximate the artifact's age.

### Indiana Academic Standard Check

**7.3.10:** . . . although the youngest layers are not always found on top, because of folding, breaking, and uplift of layers.

✔ What are clues that a geologist might use to determine the relative age of a rock?

✔ fossil evidence and faults

**Figure 12** In a stack of undisturbed sedimentary rocks, the oldest rocks are at the bottom. This stack of rocks can be folded by forces within Earth.

Limestone

Coal

Sandstone

**Undisturbed Layers**

Limestone

Coal

Sandstone

**Folded Layers**

## 2 Teach

**Quick Demo**

**Relative Ages**

**Materials** 6 different colors of clay, knife

**Estimated Time** 10 minutes

**Procedure** Place layers of five different colored clays on top of a desk. Use a knife to carefully cut a fault through all of the layers. Place a sixth layer on top of the faulted ones. Ask students to determine the relative ages of each layer and the fault. L2

LS **Visual-Spatial**

### Fun Fact

An inclusion forms when one type of rock is included in another. The rock with inclusions is younger than the rock from which the inclusions came. For example, if granite inclusions are found within a layer of sedimentary rock, the sedimentary rock formed after the granite.

### Virtual Labs

**How old is it?** *How can fossil and rock data determine when an organism lived?*

## Differentiated Instruction

**Challenge** Have students research how index fossils can be used in relative dating. What index fossils are found in your state? Students can prepare a chart showing the rock layers in your area and the index fossils that might be in those layers. L3

**Answer** Unconformities form when rock is eroded, and new sediment is deposited on top of the erosion surface.

# Visual Learning

**Figure 13** Use several books from a set of encyclopedias to reinforce the appearance of an angular unconformity shown in Figure D. Place volumes 1, 2, 3, and 4 in numerical order, with volume 1 on the bottom. Tilt the books at an angle and then horizontally place volumes 5 and 6 on top of the tilted books.
[LS] **Visual-Spatial**

## Discussion

**Unconformities** What does an unconformity indicate about past geological processes of an area? At some point, erosion removed some rock, or time passed without any sediment deposition and rock formation, or both. Explain that angular unconformities form when rock layers are uplifted, tilted, and eroded. Ask students to explain what causes the forces that produce angular unconformities. Plate tectonics generates compression, tension, and shear forces, which in turn cause rock layers to be folded, tilted, or faulted. The agents of erosion produce forces that wear away exposed rock. [L2]
[LS] **Logical-Mathematical**

**Figure 13** An angular unconformity results when horizontal layers cover tilted, eroded layers.

**A** Sedimentary rocks are deposited originally as horizontal layers.

**B** The horizontal rock layers are tilted as forces within Earth deform them.

**C** The tilted layers erode.

Angular unconformity

**D** An angular unconformity results when new layers form on the tilted layers as deposition resumes.

# Unconformities

A sequence of rock is a record of past events. But most rock sequences are incomplete—layers are missing. These gaps in rock sequences are called **unconformities** (un kun FOR muh teez). Unconformities develop when agents of erosion such as running water or glaciers remove rock layers by washing or scraping them away.

**Reading Check** *How do unconformities form?*

**Angular Unconformities** Horizontal layers of sedimentary rock often are tilted and uplifted. Erosion and weathering then wear down these tilted rock layers. Eventually, younger sediment layers are deposited horizontally on top of the tilted and eroded layers. Geologists call such an unconformity an angular unconformity. **Figure 13** shows how angular unconformities develop.

**Disconformity** Suppose you're looking at a stack of sedimentary rock layers. They look complete, but layers are missing. If you look closely, you might find an old surface of erosion. This records a time when the rocks were exposed and eroded. Later, younger rocks formed above the erosion surface when deposition of sediment began again. Even though all the layers are parallel, the rock record still has a gap. This type of unconformity is called a disconformity. A disconformity also forms when a period of time passes without any new deposition occurring to form new layers of rock.

**Nonconformity** Another type of unconformity, called a nonconformity, occurs when metamorphic or igneous rocks are uplifted and eroded. Sedimentary rocks are then deposited on top of this erosion surface. The surface between the two rock types is a nonconformity. Sometimes rock fragments from below are incorporated into sediments deposited above the nonconformity. All types of unconformities are shown in **Figure 14.**

# Differentiated Instruction

**Visually Impaired** To help students participate in the discussion of unconformities, mold models of each type of unconformity from clay. Allow students to handle the models and to remove each of the layers. [L1] [ELL] [LS] **Kinesthetic**

# NATIONAL GEOGRAPHIC VISUALIZING UNCONFORMITIES

## Figure 14

**A**n unconformity is a gap in the rock record caused by erosion or a pause in deposition. There are three major kinds of unconformities—nonconformity, angular unconformity, and disconformity.

**Nonconformity**

▲ In a nonconformity, horizontal layers of sedimentary rock overlie older igneous or metamorphic rocks. A nonconformity in Big Bend National Park, Texas, is shown above.

**Angular unconformity**

▲ An angular unconformity develops when new horizontal layers of sedimentary rock form on top of older sedimentary rock layers that have been folded by compression. An example of an angular unconformity at Siccar Point in southeastern Scotland is shown above.

▼ A disconformity develops when horizontal rock layers are exposed and eroded, and new horizontal layers of rock are deposited on the eroded surface. The disconformity shown below is in the Grand Canyon.

**Disconformity**

## Visualizing Unconformities

Have students examine the pictures and read the captions. Then ask the following questions.

How do geologists know there is a gap in the rock record in the disconformity shown at the Grand Canyon? The sequence of rock layers does not match the complete sequence found in surrounding areas. Some layers are missing and somewhere younger layers abut older layers. Fossils are often used to date the layers.

Could an unconformity occur that has metamorphic rock on top of sedimentary rock? Not likely. The forces of heat and pressure responsible for the metamorphism would likely occur throughout the rock layers.

## Activity

**Modeling Unconformities** Have students work in groups of three, with each student modeling one of the three types of unconformities shown in the feature. Have them use several colors of modeling clay so the models are vivid and obvious. Have students explain their models to each other.

# Inquiry Lab

## Modeling Relative Dating

**Purpose** To understand how various geologic features allow us to determine the ages of rocks.

**Possible Materials** modeling clay

**Estimated Time** one class period

**Teaching Strategies**

• Have students make models involving multiple rock layers with unconformities and faults.

• Students can then present their models to the class, including the relative ages of all features.

• Allow students to investigate other features that contribute to relative dating, such as index fossils.

**For additional inquiry activities, see Science Inquiry Labs.**

**Answer** If the fossils are the same type or can be shown to be the same age, it is likely that the rocks are part of the same layer.

---

**Science Online**

**Topic: Correlating with Index Fossils**

Visit in7.msscience.com for Web links to information about using index fossils to match up layers of rock.

**Activity** Make a chart that shows the rock layers of both the Grand Canyon and Capitol Reef National Park in Utah. For each layer that appears in both parks, list an index fossil you could find to correlate the layers.

**Figure 15** These rock layers, exposed at Hopi Point in Grand Canyon National Park, Arizona, can be correlated, or matched up, with rocks from across large areas of the western United States.

---

## Matching Up Rock Layers

Suppose you're studying a layer of sandstone in Bryce Canyon in Utah. Later, when you visit Canyonlands National Park, Utah, you notice that a layer of sandstone there looks just like the sandstone in Bryce Canyon, 250 km away. Above the sandstone in the Canyonlands is a layer of limestone and then another sandstone layer. You return to Bryce Canyon and find the same sequence—sandstone, limestone, and sandstone. What do you infer? It's likely that you're looking at the same layers of rocks in two different locations. **Figure 15** shows that these rocks are parts of huge deposits that covered this whole area of the western United States. Geologists often can match up, or correlate, layers of rocks over great distances.

**Evidence Used for Correlation** It's not always easy to say that a rock layer exposed in one area is the same as a rock layer exposed in another area. Sometimes it's possible to walk along the layer for kilometers and prove that it's continuous. In other cases, such as at the Canyonlands area and Bryce Canyon as seen in **Figure 16,** the rock layers are exposed only where rivers have cut through overlying layers of rock and sediment. How can you show that the limestone sandwiched between the two layers of sandstone in Canyonlands is likely the same limestone as at Bryce Canyon? One way is to use fossil evidence. If the same types of fossils were found in the limestone layer in both places, it's a good indication that the limestone at each location is the same age, and, therefore, one continuous deposit.

**Reading Check** *How do fossils help show that rocks at different locations belong to the same rock layer?*

**666**

---

Canyonlands National Park

Bryce Canyon National Park

Date deposited (millions of years ago)

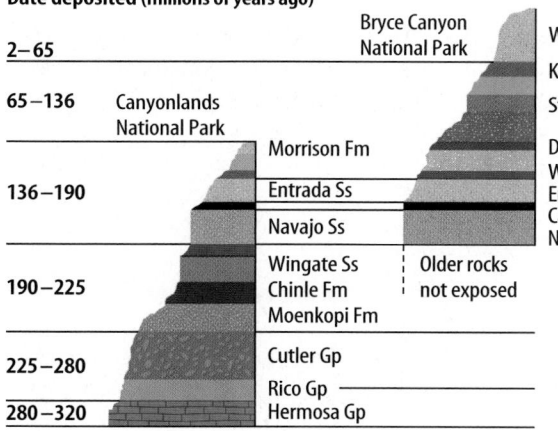

Bryce Canyon National Park — Wasatch Fm, Kaiparowits Fm, Straight Cliffs Ss, Dakota Ss, Winsor Fm, Entrada Ss, Carmel Fm, Navajo Ss

Canyonlands National Park — Morrison Fm, Entrada Ss, Navajo Ss, Wingate Ss, Chinle Fm, Moenkopi Fm, Older rocks not exposed, Cutler Gp, Rico Gp, Hermosa Gp

2–65
65–136
136–190
190–225
225–280
280–320

**Figure 16** Geologists have named the many rock layers, or formations, in Canyonlands and in Bryce Canyon, Utah. They also have correlated some formations between the two canyons.
**List** *the labeled layers present at both canyons.*

Can layers of rock be correlated in other ways? Sometimes determining relative ages isn't enough and other dating methods must be used. In Section 3, you'll see how the numerical ages of rocks can be determined and how geologists have used this information to estimate the age of Earth.

## section 2 review

### Summary

**Superposition**
- Superposition states that in undisturbed rock, the oldest layers are on the bottom.

**Relative Ages**
- Rock layers can be ranked by relative age.

**Unconformities**
- Angular unconformities are new layers deposited over tilted and eroded rock layers.
- Disconformities are gaps in the rock record.
- Nonconformities divide uplifted igneous or metamorphic rock from new sedimentary rock.

**Matching Up Rock Layers**
- Rocks from different areas may be correlated if they are part of the same layer.

### Self Check

1. **Discuss** how to find the oldest paper in a stack of papers.
2. **Explain** the concept of relative age.
3. **Illustrate** a disconformity.
4. **Describe** one way to correlate similar rock layers.
5. **Think Critically** Explain the relationship between the concept of relative age and the principle of superposition.

#### Applying Skills

6. **Interpret data** to determine the oldest rock bed. A sandstone contains a 400-million-year-old fossil. A shale has fossils that are over 500 million years old. A limestone, below the sandstone, contains fossils between 400 million and 500 million years old. Which rock bed is oldest? Explain.

Science Online in7.msscience.com/self_check_quiz

SECTION 2 Relative Ages of Rocks **667**

## 3 Assess

### DAILY INTERVENTION

#### Check for Understanding
**Visual-Spatial** Obtain a geologic map and correlation chart for the area that includes your state. Invite students to illustrate the correlation between any two points in the state.

#### Reteach
**Geologic History** Draw a geologic column on transparency acetate. Include layers of limestone, sandstone, shale, and metamorphic rock, a fault, a disconformity (indicated by a jagged line), and an igneous intrusion. Project the illustration, and have students explain the history of the area. L2 ELL IS **Visual-Spatial**

### ☑ Assessment

**Performance** Illustrate Question 6 of the Section Review on the board. Then have students interpret the relative ages of the rock layers. Assume that the rocks are undisturbed and that shale underlies the limestone. Use **Performance Assessment in the Science Classroom,** p. 89.

## section 2 review

1. Applying the principle of superposition would help in finding the papers.
2. Relative age describes the age of one rock layer in relation to another; it does not describe age in actual years.
3. a stack of sedimentary rock layers in which one or more layers is missing
4. Possible answers: match rock types, look for presence of matching fossils, compare relative positions in the geologic column
5. The principle of superposition states that older rock is on the bottom; therefore, the relative age of the bottom layer is older.
6. The shale; its fossils are older than those found in the other layers.

SECTION 2 Relative Ages of Rocks **667**

**BENCH TESTED**

## ⊙ Real-World Question

**Purpose** Students determine the relative order of events by interpreting geologic cross sections. **L2** **ELL** **LS** **Logical-Mathematical**

**Process Skills** infer, interpret data, formulate models, recognize and use spatial relationships, sequence, interpret scientific illustrations

**Time Required** 40–45 minutes

## ⊙ Procedure

**Teaching Strategy** If students are having trouble, reproduce the cross sections on an overhead. Then work as a class to identify the relative ages of the different layers.

## ⊙ Conclude and Apply

1. Disconformity; yes, other rock layers could have been eroded.
2. The rocks moved upward.
3. as a result of a fault
4. A fault cuts through the intrusion but stops at the unconformity. Thus the fault occurred after the intrusion but while erosion was occurring. Therefore, the intrusion is older.
5. The one on the left is older than the one on the right. The one on the right intrudes the sandstone and is therefore younger. The one offset by the fault is older than the sandstone.
6. The sandstone and the upper shale may have been thicker. They exhibit erosional disconformities at their upper surfaces.

# Relative Ages

Which of your two friends is older? To answer this question, you'd need to know their relative ages. You wouldn't need to know the exact age of either of your friends—just who was born first. The same is sometimes true for rock layers.

## ⊙ Real-World Question

Can you determine the relative ages of rock layers?

### Goals
■ **Interpret** illustrations of rock layers and other geological structures and determine the relative order of events.

### Materials
paper          pencil

## ⊙ Procedure

1. **Analyze** Figures **A** and **B**.
2. Make a sketch of **Figure A**. On it, identify the relative age of each rock layer, igneous intrusion, fault, and unconformity. For example, the shale layer is the oldest, so mark it with a 1. Mark the next-oldest feature with a 2, and so on.
3. Repeat step 2 for **Figure B**.

## ⊙ Conclude and Apply

### Figure A
1. **Identify** the type of unconformity shown. Is it possible that there were originally more layers of rock than are shown?
2. **Describe** how the rocks above the fault moved in relation to rocks below the fault.
3. **Hypothesize** how the hill on the left side of the figure formed.

**A**

**B**

| | |
|---|---|
| Granite | Limestone |
| Sandstone | Shale |

**Figure B**

4. Is it possible to conclude if the igneous intrusion on the left is older or younger than the unconformity nearest the surface?
5. **Describe** the relative ages of the two igneous intrusions. How did you know?
6. **Hypothesize** which two layers of rock might have been much thicker in the past.

### **Communicating** Your Data

**Compare** your results with other students' results. **For more help, refer to the** Science Skill Handbook.

---

### ✓ Assessment

**Performance** Based on what was learned about relative ages of rock layers, have students draw a block diagram similar to those in the Lab. Tell them to include all three rock types. Have students exchange and interpret their diagrams. Use **Performance Assessment in the Science Classroom,** p. 127.

### **Communicating** Your Data

Oldest to youngest: A: shale, sandstone, limestone, disconformity, sandstone, limestone, intrusion, fault; B: sandstone, shale, limestone, sandstone, disconformity, limestone, shale, intrusion (left), fault, disconformity, sandstone, intrusion (right)

# section

# 3

# Absolute Ages of Rocks

## Absolute Ages

As you sort through your stack of magazines looking for that article about the car you saw, you decide that you need to restack them into a neat pile. By now, they're in a jumble and no longer in order of their relative age, as shown in **Figure 17.** How can you stack them so the oldest are on the bottom and the newest are on top? Fortunately, magazine dates are printed on the cover. Thus, stacking magazines in order is a simple process. Unfortunately, rocks don't have their ages stamped on them. Or do they? **Absolute age** is the age, in years, of a rock or other object. Geologists determine absolute ages by using properties of the atoms that make up materials.

## Radioactive Decay

**INTEGRATE Physics** Atoms consist of a dense central region called the nucleus, which is surrounded by a cloud of negatively charged particles called electrons. The nucleus is made up of protons, which have a positive charge, and neutrons, which have no electric charge. The number of protons determines the identity of the element, and the number of neutrons determines the form of the element, or isotope. For example, every atom with a single proton is a hydrogen atom. Hydrogen atoms can have no neutrons, a single neutron, or two neutrons. This means that there are three isotopes of hydrogen.

**Reading Check** *What particles make up an atom's nucleus?*

Some isotopes are unstable and break down into other isotopes and particles. Sometimes a lot of energy is given off during this process. The process of breaking down is called **radioactive decay.** In the case of hydrogen, atoms with one proton and two neutrons are unstable and tend to break down. Many other elements have stable and unstable isotopes.

*What* **You'll Learn**
- **Identify** how absolute age differs from relative age.
- **Describe** how the half-lives of isotopes are used to determine a rock's age.

*Why* **It's Important**

Events in Earth's history can be better understood if their absolute ages are known.

**Review Vocabulary**
**isotopes:** atoms of the same element that have different numbers of neutrons

**New Vocabulary**
- absolute age
- radioactive decay
- half-life
- radiometric dating
- uniformitarianism

**Figure 17** The magazines that have been shuffled through no longer illustrate the principle of superposition.

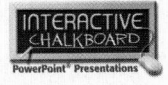
INTERACTIVE CHALKBOARD
PowerPoint® Presentations

**Bellringer**

**Section Focus Transparencies** also are available on the Interactive Chalkboard CD-ROM.

L2 ELL

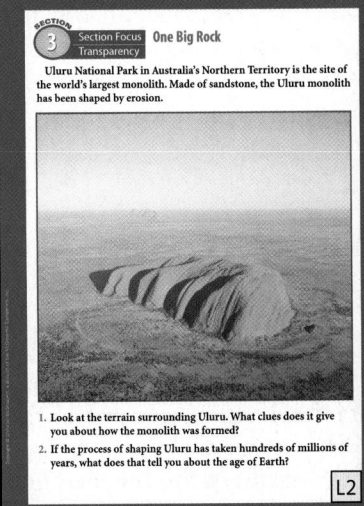

## Tie to Prior Knowledge

**Atom Parts and Positions** Have students recall the main parts of the atom and their positions within an atom. Protons and neutrons—in nucleus; electrons—around nucleus

**Reading Check**

**Answer** protons and neutrons

SECTION 3 Absolute Ages of Rocks **669**

## Section 3 Resource Manager

**Chapter *FAST FILE* Resources**
Transparency Activity, p. 46
Directed Reading for Content Mastery, pp. 21, 22
MiniLAB, p. 4
Enrichment, p. 32

Reinforcement, p. 29
Lab Worksheets, pp. 7–8
**Mathematics Skill Activities,** p. 3
**Cultural Diversity,** p. 69
**Lab Management and Safety,** p. 39

## Mini LAB

**Purpose** Students will model the principle of carbon-14 dating.

**Materials** red and green jelly beans

**Teaching Strategy** Advise students not to eat the jelly beans and to wash hands thoroughly after the activity.

**Analysis**

1. As in carbon-14, each half-life resulted in half of the remaining jelly beans being removed.
2. 4
3. 22, 920 years old

## Assessment

**Performance** Have students determine the relative and absolute ages of students in the classroom. Use **Performance Assessment in the Science Classroom**, p. 99.

## Discussion

**Dating Errors** What would happen to your estimate of age if some of the daughter isotope escaped? Since this would make it appear that less daughter has formed, the rock will seem younger.

## Mini LAB

**Modeling Carbon-14 Dating**

**Procedure**

1. Count out 80 **red jelly beans.**
2. Remove half the red jelly beans and replace them with **green jelly beans.**
3. Continue replacing half the red jelly beans with green jelly beans until only 5 red jelly beans remain. Count the number of times you replace half the red jelly beans.

**Analysis**

1. How did this activity model the decay of carbon-14 atoms?
2. How many half lives of carbon-14 did you model during this activity?
3. If the atoms in a bone experienced the same number of half lives as your jelly beans, how old would the bone be?

**Figure 18** In beta decay, a neutron changes into a proton by giving off an electron. This electron has a lot of energy and is called a beta particle.

In the process of alpha decay, an unstable parent isotope nucleus gives off an alpha particle and changes into a new daughter product. Alpha particles contain two neutrons and two protons.

**Alpha and Beta Decay** In some isotopes, a neutron breaks down into a proton and an electron. This type of radioactive decay is called beta decay because the electron leaves the atom as a beta particle. The nucleus loses a neutron but gains a proton. When the number of protons in an atom is changed, a new element forms. Other isotopes give off two protons and two neutrons in the form of an alpha particle. Alpha and beta decay are shown in **Figure 18.**

**Half-Life** In radioactive decay reactions, the parent isotope undergoes radioactive decay. The daughter product is produced by radioactive decay. Each radioactive parent isotope decays to its daughter product at a certain rate. Based on this decay rate, it takes a certain period of time for one half of the parent isotope to decay to its daughter product. The **half-life** of an isotope is the time it takes for half of the atoms in the isotope to decay. For example, the half-life of carbon-14 is 5,730 years. So it will take 5,730 years for half of the carbon-14 atoms in an object to change into nitrogen-14 atoms. You might guess that in another 5,730 years, all of the remaining carbon-14 atoms will decay to nitrogen-14. However, this is not the case. Only half of the atoms of carbon-14 remaining after the first 5,730 years will decay during the second 5,730 years. So, after two half-lives, one fourth of the original carbon-14 atoms still remain. Half of them will decay during another 5,730 years. After three half-lives, one eighth of the original carbon-14 atoms still remain. After many half-lives, such a small amount of the parent isotope remains that it might not be measurable.

## LAB DEMONSTRATION

**Purpose** to demonstrate how half-life works

**Materials** 100 pennies, 100 paper clips, box with lid

**Preparation** Place the pennies in the box, heads up.

**Procedure** Close the lid and shake the box twice (half-life). Open the lid and count and record the flipped (decayed) pennies. Remove the flipped pennies and replace them with paper clips. Repeat until all pennies have been replaced.

**Expected Outcome** About half of the remaining pennies decay during each half-life.

## Assessment

What do the pennies represent? atoms of the parent isotope What do the paper clips represent? daughter products What is each two shakes? a half-life Why do fewer isotopes decay in each successive half-life? There are fewer atoms left to decay.

## Radiometric Ages

Decay of radioactive isotopes is like a clock keeping track of time that has passed since rocks have formed. As time passes, the amount of parent isotope in a rock decreases as the amount of daughter product increases, as in **Figure 19.** By measuring the ratio of parent isotope to daughter product in a mineral and by knowing the half-life of the parent, in many cases you can calculate the absolute age of a rock. This process is called **radiometric dating.**

A scientist must decide which parent isotope to use when measuring the age of a rock. If the object to be dated seems old, then the geologist will use an isotope with a long half-life. The half-life for the decay of potassium-40 to argon-40 is 1.25 billion years. As a result, this isotope can be used to date rocks that are many millions of years old. To avoid error, conditions must be met for the ratios to give a correct indication of age. For example, the rock being studied must still retain all of the argon-40 that was produced by the decay of potassium-40. Also, it cannot contain any contamination of daughter product from other sources. Potassium-argon dating is good for rocks containing potassium, but what about other things?

**Radiocarbon Dating** Carbon-14 is useful for dating bones, wood, and charcoal up to 75,000 years old. Living things take in carbon from the environment to build their bodies. Most of that carbon is carbon-12, but some is carbon-14, and the ratio of these two isotopes in the environment is always the same. After the organism dies, the carbon-14 slowly decays. By determining the amounts of the isotopes in a sample, scientists can evaluate how much the isotope ratio in the sample differs from that in the environment. For example, during much of human history, people built campfires. The wood from these fires often is preserved as charcoal. Scientists can determine the amount of carbon-14 remaining in a sample of charcoal by measuring the amount of radiation emitted by the carbon-14 isotope in labs like the one in **Figure 20.** Once they know the amount of carbon-14 in a charcoal sample, scientists can determine the age of the wood used to make the fire.

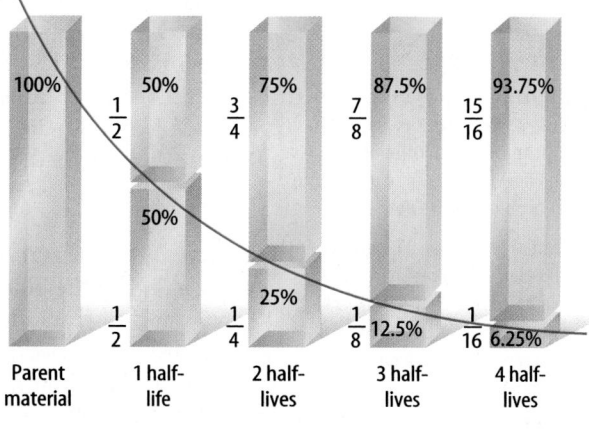

**Figure 19** During each half-life, one half of the parent material decays to the daughter product. **Explain** *how one uses both parent and daughter material to estimate age.*

**Figure 20** Radiometric ages are determined in labs like this one.

## Teacher FYI

**Half-Lives** The half-life of carbon-14 is about 5,730 years. The half-life of uranium-238 in its decay to lead-206 is 4.5 billion years (nearly the age of Earth). By contrast, the half-life of uranium-235 in its decay to lead-207 is 713 million years.

## Activity

**Calculate Absolute Age** The half-life of potassium-40 is 1.3 billion years. An igneous rock is found with 25% potassium-40 and 75% daughter product. Calculate the absolute age of this rock. 2.6 billion years (two half-lives)

L2 IS **Logical-Mathematical**

## Quick Demo

**Paper Half-Lives**

**Materials** piece of paper

**Estimated time** 3 minutes

**Procedure** Have students imagine that a sheet of paper is analogous to parent isotope in a rock. The half-life of this isotope is 10 seconds. After 10 seconds, tear the paper in half and set one of the halves aside as the daughter isotope. Repeat the process every 10 seconds with the remaining paper.

## Visual Learning

**Figure 19** After students have studied the graph, discuss whether the overall amount of material changes after each half-life. Reinforce that the overall amount of material stays nearly the same; it is the makeup of the material that changes.

## Caption Answer

**Figure 19** The ratio of parent to daughter materials allows scientists to estimate how many half-lives have passed.

**Answer** Sedimentary rocks are made of particles eroded from older rocks. Dating these particles gives the age of the preexisting rock, not the newer sedimentary rock.

## Teaching Strategy

Explain that the age given by this method is an estimate. Radiometric dating does not give exact answers.

## Answers to Questions

1. Since the Iceman is about 5,300 years old, students should estimate that about 55% of the original carbon-14 was still present.

2. Using the chart, you can see that after 17, 190 years, 12.5 percent of the carbon-14 would remain; $10 \times 0.125 = 1.25$ grams

## IDENTIFYING
# Misconceptions

**Uniformitarianism** Students may think that the present is not the key to the past. Refer to page F at the beginning of this chapter for teaching strategies that address this misconception.

## Science Online

**Topic: Isotopes in Ice Cores**
Visit in7.msscience.com for Web links to information about ice cores and how isotopes in ice are used to learn about Earth's past.

**Activity** Prepare a report that shows how isotopes in ice cores can tell us about past Earth environments. Include how these findings can help us understand today's climate.

**Age Determinations** Aside from carbon-14 dating, rocks that can be radiometrically dated are mostly igneous and metamorphic rocks. Most sedimentary rocks cannot be dated by this method. This is because many sedimentary rocks are made up of particles eroded from older rocks. Dating these pieces only gives the age of the preexisting rock from which it came.

**The Oldest Known Rocks** Radiometric dating has been used to date the oldest rocks on Earth. These rocks are about 3.96 billion years old. By determining the age of meteorites, and using other evidence, scientists have estimated the age of Earth to be about 4.5 billion years. Earth rocks greater than 3.96 billion years old probably were eroded or changed by heat and pressure.

✓ **Reading Check** *Why can't most sedimentary rocks be dated radiometrically?*

### When did the Iceman die?

Carbon-14 dating has been used to date charcoal, wood, bones, mummies from Egypt and Peru, the Dead Sea Scrolls, and the Italian Iceman. The Iceman was found in 1991 in the Italian Alps, near the Austrian border. Based on carbon-14 analysis, scientists determined that the Iceman is 5,300 years old. Determine approximately in what year the Iceman died.

**Half-Life of Carbon-14**

| Percent Carbon-14 | Years Passed |
| --- | --- |
| 100 | 0 |
| 50 | 5,730 |
| 25 | 11,460 |
| 12.5 | 17,190 |
| 6.25 | 22,920 |
| 3.125 | |

Reconstruction of Iceman

### Identifying the Problem

The half-life chart shows the decay of carbon-14 over time. Half-life is the time it takes for half of a sample to decay. Fill in the years passed when only 3.125 percent of carbon-14 remain. Is there a point at which no carbon-14 would be present? Explain.

### Solving the Problem

1. Estimate, using the data table, how much carbon-14 still was present in the Iceman's body that allowed scientists to determine his age.
2. If you had an artifact that originally contained 10.0 g of carbon-14, how many grams would remain after 17,190 years?

**672** CHAPTER 22 Clues to Earth's Past

---

# Science Journal

**Uniformitarianism** Have students research and write a brief report in their Science Journals about uniformitarianism and the contributions of James Hutton, John Playfair, and Sir Charles Lyell. James Hutton thought Earth processes of today were similar to those of the past. John Playfair wrote about Hutton's ideas, but Sir Charles Lyell's written works were easier to read. L2 ⓝ **Linguistic** P

# Differentiated Instruction

**English-Language Learners** Have students prepare 100 squares of paper, one side red and the other side blue. Start with all of one color facing up and have a student keep time. Every 30 seconds, have someone turn over half of the squares. Explain half-lives and show that the total number of atoms remains constant.

## Uniformitarianism

Can you imagine trying to determine the age of Earth without some of the information you know today? Before the discovery of radiometric dating, many people estimated that Earth is only a few thousand years old. But in the 1700s, Scottish scientist James Hutton estimated that Earth is much older. He used the principle of **uniformitarianism**. This principle states that Earth processes occurring today are similar to those that occurred in the past. Hutton's principle is often paraphrased as "the present is the key to the past."

Hutton observed that the processes that changed the landscape around him were slow, and he inferred that they were just as slow throughout Earth's history. Hutton hypothesized that it took much longer than a few thousand years to form the layers of rock around him and to erode mountains that once stood kilometers high. **Figure 21** shows Hutton's native Scotland, a region shaped by millions of years of geologic processes.

Today, scientists recognize that Earth has been shaped by two types of change: slow, everyday processes that take place over millions of years, and violent, unusual events such as the collision of a comet or asteroid about 65 million years ago that might have caused the extinction of the dinosaurs.

**Figure 21** The rugged highlands of Scotland were shaped by erosion and uplift.

Science Online  in7.msscience.com/self_check_quiz

---

## Visual Learning

**Figure 21** Have students list some of the processes that helped shape this landscape.

### 3 Assess

#### DAILY INTERVENTION

**Check for Understanding**

**Visual-Spatial** Give students red and blue marbles, and have them illustrate the decay of blue marbles to red marbles, one half-life at a time.

**Reteach**

**Radiometric Dates** Have students determine the age of a rock containing 1/32 of the radium-226 originally in the rock. The half-life of radium-226 is 1,600 years. After five half-lives, or 8,000 years, 1/32 of the original isotope remains. **L2** **IS**

**Logical-Mathematical**

#### ✓ Assessment

**Performance** Have students plot the data from the tables they make in Question 6. Half-lives should appear on the horizontal axis, and the percentage of parent material should appear on the vertical axis. Use **Performance Assessment in the Science Classroom,** p. 111.

---

## section 3 review

### Summary

**Absolute Ages**
- The absolute age is the actual age of an object.

**Radioactive Decay**
- Some isotopes are unstable and decay into other isotopes and particles.
- Decay is measured in half-lives, the time it takes for half of a given isotope to decay.

**Radiometric Ages**
- By measuring the ratio of parent isotope to daughter product, one can determine the absolute age of a rock.
- Living organisms less than 75,000 years old can be dated using carbon-14.

**Uniformitarianism**
- Processes observable today are the same as the processes that took place in the past.

### Self Check

1. **Evaluate** the age of rocks. You find three undisturbed rock layers. The middle layer is 120 million years old. What can you say about the ages of the layers above and below it?
2. **Determine** the age of a fossil if it had only one eighth of its original carbon-14 content remaining.
3. **Explain** the concept of uniformitarianism.
4. **Describe** how radioactive isotopes decay.
5. **Think Critically** Why can't scientists use carbon-14 to determine the age of an igneous rock?

#### Applying Math

6. **Make and use a table** that shows the amount of parent material of a radioactive element that is left after four half-lives if the original parent material had a mass of 100 g.

---

## section 3 review

1. The top layer is less than 120 million years old; the bottom layer is more than 120 million years old.
2. 17,190 years old
3. Earth processes occurring today are like those that have occurred in the past.

4. In some isotopes, a neutron breaks down into a proton and an electron (beta decay). In others, an isotope gives off two protons and two neutrons (alpha decay).

5. Carbon-14 dating works only for materials that were once alive and contain carbon. Igneous rocks are nonliving materials.
6. See chart in side column.

| Half-Life | Parent |
|-----------|--------|
| 0 | 100 g |
| 1 | 50 g |
| 2 | 25 g |
| 3 | 12.5 g |
| 4 | 6.25 g |

## Real-World Question

**Purpose** Students will research information and create a model of trace fossils that shows some behaviors of animals.

**Process Skills** make a model, use reference materials, observe and infer

**Time Required** one or two class periods, depending on the amount of research required

## Make a Model

**Teaching Strategies** Have references available for students in the classroom where they can look up information.

**Troubleshooting** Tell students to limit the number of specific behaviors that they show so that the model does not get too confusing.

## Model and Invent

### Goals
- **Construct** a model of trace fossils.
- **Describe** the information that you can learn from looking at your model.

### Possible Materials
construction paper
wire
plastic (a fairly rigid type)
scissors
plaster of paris
toothpicks
sturdy cardboard
clay
pipe cleaners
glue

### Safety Precautions

# Trace Fossils

## Real-World Question

Trace fossils can tell you a lot about the activities of organisms that left them. They can tell you how an organism fed or what kind of home it had. How can you model trace fossils that can provide information about the behavior of organisms? What materials can you use to model trace fossils? What types of behavior could you show with your trace fossil model?

## Make a Model

1. **Decide** how you are going to make your model. What materials will you need?

2. **Decide** what types of activities you will demonstrate with your model. Were the organisms feeding? Resting? Traveling? Were they predators? Prey? How will your model indicate the activities you chose?

3. What is the setting of your model? Are you modeling the organism's home? Feeding areas? Is your model on land or water? How can the setting affect the way you build your model?

4. Will you only show trace fossils from a single species or multiple species? If you include more than one species, how will you provide evidence of any interaction between the species?

### Check the Model Plans

1. Compare your plans with those of others in your class. Did other groups mention details that you had forgotten to think about? Are there any changes you would like to make to your plan before you continue?

2. Make sure your teacher approves your plan before you continue.

## Test Your Model

1. Following your plan, construct your model of trace fossils.
2. Have you included evidence of all the behaviors you intended to model?

## Analyze Your Data

1. **Evaluate** Now that your model is complete, do you think that it adequately shows the behaviors you planned to demonstrate? Is there anything that you think you might want to do differently if you were going to make the model again?
2. **Describe** how using different kinds of materials might have affected your model. Can you think of other materials that would have allowed you to show more detail than you did?

## Conclude and Apply

1. **Compare and contrast** your model of trace fossils with trace fossils left by real organisms. Is one more easily interpreted than the other? Explain.
2. **List** behaviors that might not leave any trace fossils. Explain.

### Communicating Your Data

Ask other students in your class or another class to look at your model and describe what information they can learn from the trace fossils. Did their interpretations agree with what you intended to show?

**LAB 675**

## Test Your Model

**Expected Outcome** Students will create a model that includes trace fossils that indicate certain behaviors of one or more species.

## Analyze Your Data

1. Answers will be individualized and based on the students' opinion of their research. Look for depth and quality of research performed.
2. Answers will vary depending on the materials students used. Clay would show three-dimensional fossils whereas paper or fabric would only be two-dimensional.

## Conclude and Apply

1. The models may be easier to interpret because they will not have any extraneous features and were not subject to weather or other factors that could damage them.
2. Answers will vary. Look for behaviors like mating rituals or communication that wouldn't necessarily leave any marks on sediments for later fossilization.

### ✔ Assessment

**Process** Have students use reference materials, such as textbooks or magazines, to find photographs of trace fossils. Students should write a brief description of the type of animals and the behavior indicated. Then, groups of students can trade photographs and try to interpret those found by others. Use **Performance Assessment in the Science Classroom,** p. 159.

### Communicating Your Data

Students should discuss why their interpretations did or did not agree. They can cite their references to support their arguments.

## Content Background

The coelacanths are an ancient group, appearing in the fossil record about 395 million years ago. They are characterized by lobelike, fleshy fins, and live at great depths, where they are difficult to find. The limblike skeletal structure of the fleshy fins of coelacanths is thought to be an ancestral condition of all animals with four limbs.

## Discussion

**Survival** Hypothesize how a fish could survive when many of the animals that evolved from it on land no longer exist. Conditions in the sea, such as temperature, salinity, and food sources are slow to change and are relatively constant, allowing marine species long periods to adjust to environmental changes.

## Analyze the Event

**Serendipity** Ask students to brainstorm the characteristics or circumstances that helped Courtenay-Latimer to recognize the significance of her find. Possible answers: She was observant; she had friends who fished; she was curious; she knew to whom to send her sketch. Point out that she was not a scientist but had characteristics that are important for scientists, such as curiosity.

# The World's Oldest Fish Story

*A catch-of-the-day set science on its ears*

Camouflage marks

First dorsal fin

Second dorsal fin

Pectoral fin

Anal fin

Pelvic fin

*Some scientists call the coelacanth "Old Four Legs." It got its nickname because the fish has paired fins that look something like legs.*

On a December day in 1938, just before Christmas, Marjorie Courtenay-Latimer went to say hello to her friends on board a fishing boat that had just returned to port in South Africa. Courtenay-Latimer, who worked at a museum, often went aboard her friends' ship to check out the catch. On this visit, she received a surprise Christmas present—an odd-looking fish. As soon as the woman spotted its strange blue fins among the piles of sharks and rays, she knew it was special.

Courtenay-Latimer took the fish back to her museum to study it. "It was the most beautiful fish I had ever seen, five feet long, and a pale mauve blue with iridescent silver markings," she later wrote. Courtenay-Latimer sketched it and sent the drawing to a friend of hers, J. L. B. Smith.

Smith was a chemistry teacher who was passionate about fish. After a time, he realized it was a coelacanth (SEE luh kanth). Fish experts knew that coelacanths had first appeared on Earth 400 million years ago. But the experts thought the fish were extinct. People had found fossils of coelacanths, but no one had seen one alive. It was assumed that the last coelacanth species had died out 65 million years ago. They were wrong. The ship's crew had caught one by accident.

Smith figured there might be more living coelacanths. So he decided to offer a reward for anyone who could find a living specimen. After 14 years of silence, a report came in that a coelacanth had been caught off the east coast of Africa.

Today, scientists know that there are at least several hundred coelacanths living in the Indian Ocean, just east of central Africa. Many of these fish live near the Comoros Islands. The coelacanths live in underwater caves during the day but move out at night to feed. The rare fish are now a protected species. With any luck, they will survive for another hundred million years.

**Write** a short essay describing the discovery of the coelacanths and describe the reaction of scientists to this discovery.

Science online

For more information, visit in7.msscience.com/oops

**Write** People around the world read about the discovery in newspapers and were fascinated by it. Courtenay-Latimer became famous. Thousands of people gathered to view the mounted fish. A prehistoric animal, the fish appealed to people the way dinosaurs appeal to many people today.

## Resources for Teachers and Students

"Dispute Over a Legendary Fish," by Constance Holden, *Science*, April 2, 1999

*A Fish Caught in Time*, by Samantha Weinberg, HarperCollins Publishers, 2000

## Reviewing Main Ideas

### Section 1  Fossils

1. Fossils are more likely to form if hard parts of the dead organisms are buried quickly.

2. Some fossils form when original materials that made up the organisms are replaced with minerals. Other fossils form when remains are subjected to heat and pressure, leaving only a carbon film behind. Some fossils are the tracks or traces left by ancient organisms.

### Section 2  Relative Ages of Rocks

1. The principle of superposition states that, in undisturbed layers, older rocks lie underneath younger rocks.

2. Unconformities, or gaps in the rock record, are due to erosion or periods of time during which no deposition occurred.

3. Rock layers can be correlated using rock types and fossils.

### Section 3  Absolute Ages of Rocks

1. Absolute dating provides an age in years for the rocks.

2. The half-life of a radioactive isotope is the time it takes for half of the atoms of the isotope to decay into another isotope.

## Visualizing Main Ideas

*Copy and complete the following concept map on fossils.*

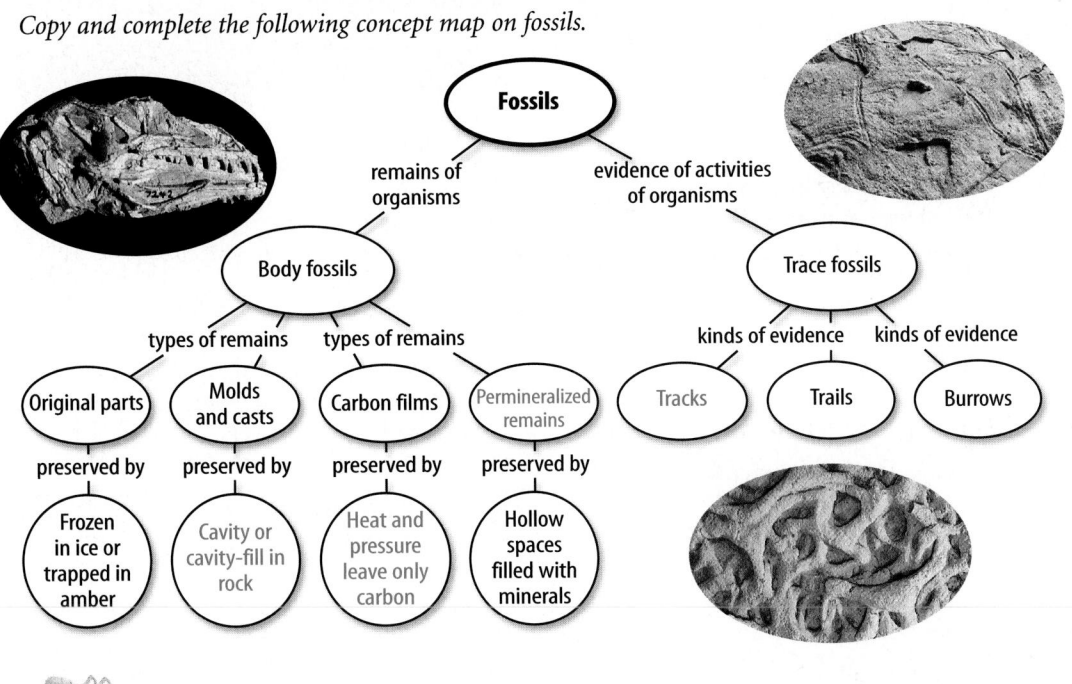

## Reviewing Main Ideas

Summary statements can be used by students to review the major concepts of the chapter.

## Visualizing Main Ideas

See student page.

**Science** Online

**Visit** in7.msscience.com
/self_check_quiz
/interactive_tutor
/vocabulary_puzzlemaker
/chapter_review
/standards_review

### Assessment Transparency

For additional assessment questions, use the *Assessment Transparency* located in the transparency book.

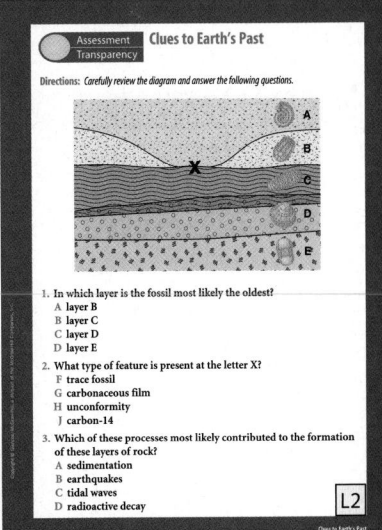

## Identifying Misconceptions

**Assess**

Use the assessment as follow-up to page 652F after students have completed the chapter.

**Procedure** Set up a stream table with a meandering stream in it that flows into a lake. Have students observe the water flowing through the stream into the lake. After several minutes, ask the students to make a drawing of the feature created where the river flows into the lake.

Show the students a photo of the Mississippi River delta. Ask them how they think the Mississippi River delta was formed.

**Expected Outcome** Students will recognize that the process of delta formation is a natural Earth process and that the process has been the same throughout Earth's history.

## Using Vocabulary

1. A <u>carbon film</u> is a thin film of carbon preserved as a fossil.

2. The <u>principle of superposition</u> states that older rocks lie under younger rocks in an undisturbed area.

3. According to <u>uniformitarianism</u>, processes occur today as they did in the past.

4. An <u>unconformity</u> is a gap in the rock record.

5. The time needed for half of the atoms to decay is called <u>half-life</u>.

6. An <u>index fossil</u> is the fossil of a group that lived for a short time but was widespread.

7. <u>Absolute ages</u> give the ages of rocks in years.

8. In <u>permineralized remains</u>, tiny spaces inside a fossil are filled with minerals.

9. A <u>cast</u> is a copy of a fossil produced inside a mold.

## Checking Concepts

| | |
|---|---|
| 10. B | 14. D |
| 11. C | 15. C |
| 12. B | 16. D |
| 13. D | 17. D |

## Thinking Critically

18. Possible answers: Decay can destroy organic remains if they are not buried quickly; erosion destroys layers of rock; deeply buried materials are frequently destroyed by metamorphism.

19. Since the lava contains radioactive elements, an absolute age for the flow can be determined. This age can then be used to determine relative ages for the rocks above and below the flow.

## Using Vocabulary

| | |
|---|---|
| absolute age p. 669 | principle of superposition |
| carbon film p. 656 | p. 662 |
| cast p. 657 | radioactive decay p. 669 |
| fossil p. 655 | radiometric dating p. 671 |
| half-life p. 670 | relative age p. 663 |
| index fossil p. 659 | unconformity p. 664 |
| mold p. 657 | uniformitarianism p. 673 |
| permineralized remains | |
| p. 656 | |

*Write an original sentence using the vocabulary word to which each phrase refers.*

1. thin film of carbon preserved as a fossil

2. older rocks lie under younger rocks

3. processes occur today as they did in the past

4. gap in the rock record

5. time needed for half the atoms to decay

6. fossil organism that lived for a short time

7. gives the age of rocks in years

8. minerals fill spaces inside fossil

9. a copy of a fossil produced by filling a mold with sediment or crystals

## Checking Concepts

*Choose the word or phrase that best answers the question.*

10. What is any evidence of ancient life called?
    A) half-life       C) unconformity
    B) fossil          D) disconformity

11. Which of the following conditions makes fossil formation more likely?
    A) buried slowly
    B) attacked by scavengers
    C) made of hard parts
    D) composed of soft parts

12. What are cavities left in rocks when a shell or bone dissolves called?
    A) casts           C) original remains
    B) molds           D) carbon films

13. To say "the present is the key to the past" is a way to describe which of the following principles?
    A) superposition   C) radioactivity
    B) succession      D) uniformitarianism

14. A fault can be useful in determining which of the following for a group of rocks?
    A) absolute age    C) radiometric age
    B) index age       D) relative age

15. Which of the following is an unconformity between parallel rock layers?
    A) angular unconformity
    B) fault
    C) disconformity
    D) nonconformity

**Use the illustration below to answer question 16.**

16. Which of the following puts the layers in order from oldest to youngest?
    A) 5-4-3-2-1       C) 2-3-4-5-1
    B) 1-2-3-4-5       D) 4-3-2-5-1

17. Which process forms new elements?
    A) superposition
    B) uniformitarianism
    C) permineralization
    D) radioactive decay

 Science Online in7.msscience.com/vocabulary_puzzlemaker

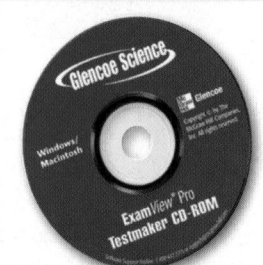

**Use the Exam*View*® Pro Testmaker CD-ROM to:**
- create multiple versions of tests
- create modified tests with one mouse click for inclusion students
- edit existing questions and add your own questions
- build tests aligned with state standards using built-in State Curriculum Tags
- change English tests to Spanish with one mouse click and vice versa

## Thinking Critically

**18. Explain** why the fossil record of life on Earth is incomplete. Give some reasons why.

**19. Infer** Suppose a lava flow was found between two sedimentary rock layers. How could you use the lava flow to learn about the ages of the sedimentary rock layers? *(Hint: Most lava contains radioactive isotopes.)*

**20. Infer** Suppose you're correlating rock layers in the western United States. You find a layer of volcanic ash deposits. How can this layer help you in your correlation over a large area?

**21. Recognize Cause and Effect** Explain how some woolly mammoths could have been preserved intact in frozen ground. What conditions must have persisted since the deaths of these animals?

**22. Classify** each of the following fossils in the correct category in the table below: *dinosaur footprint, worm burrow, dinosaur skull, insect in amber, fossil woodpecker hole,* and *fish tooth.*

### Types of Fossils

| Trace Fossils | Body Fossils |
|---|---|
| dinosaur footprint | dinosaur skull |
| worm burrow | insect in amber |
| fossil woodpecker hole | fish tooth |

**23. Compare and contrast** the three different kinds of unconformities. Draw sketches of each that illustrate the features that identify them.

**24. Describe** how relative and absolute ages differ. How might both be used to establish ages in a series of rock layers?

**25. Discuss** uniformitarianism in the following scenario. You find a shell on the beach, and a friend remembers seeing a similar fossil while hiking in the mountains. What does this suggest about the past environment of the mountain?

## Performance Activities

**26. Illustrate** Create a model that allows you to explain how to establish the relative ages of rock layers.

**27. Use a Classification System** Start your own fossil collection. Label each find as to type, approximate age, and the place where it was found. Most state geological surveys can provide you with reference materials on local fossils.

## Applying Math

**28. Calculate** how many half-lives have passed in a rock containing one-eighth the original radioactive material and seven-eighths of the daughter product.

**Use the graphs below to answer question 29.**

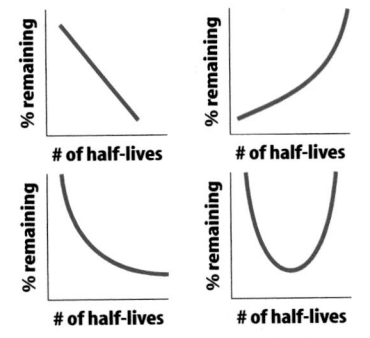

**29. Interpret Data** Which of the above curves best illustrates radioactive decay?

Science**Online** in7.msscience.com/chapter_review

---

## ✔ Assessment    Resources

📁 **Reproducible Masters**

**Chapter *Fast File* Resources**
Chapter Review, pp. 37–38
Chapter Tests, pp. 39–42
Assessment Transparency Activity, p. 49

**Glencoe Science Web site**
Chapter Review Test
IN Standards Review

**Glencoe Technology**
🔹 Assessment Transparency
💿 ExamView® Pro Testmaker
📼 MindJogger Videoquiz
💿 Interactive Chalkboard

---

**20.** The layer of volcanic ash would have been deposited quickly during a volcanic eruption. Therefore, you have a marker rock layer that you know is the same age everywhere and can be dated by using radioactive isotopes.

**21.** The cold temperatures preserved the entire animal, much like freezing helps preserve foods.

**22.** See student page.

**23.** Sketches should show angular unconformities with parallel layers over tilted layers, disconformities with parallel layers over an eroded surface, and nonconformities with sedimentary over igneous or metamorphic rock.

**24.** Relative age is in relation to other rocks while absolute age gives an actual estimate. Any rocks aged absolutely can be used to determine relative ages of adjacent layers.

**25.** Answers will vary; students should recognize that the material that formed the mountain was once under water.

### Performance Activities

**26.** Model should show layers, preferably disturbed by fault or unconformity. Student should then tell oldest to youngest and explain how it is possible to do so.

**27.** Fossil collections should indicate type of fossil formation, how old each is, and where each was found. Use **Performance Assessment in the Science Classroom**, p. 121.

### Applying Math

**Indiana Math Standards**
7.2.1, 7.6.1, 7.6.2

**28.** three

**29.** the lower left graph

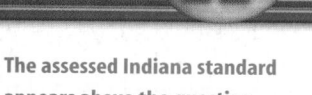

**Answer Sheet** A practice answer sheet can be found at in7.msscience.com/answer_sheet.

**Part 1  Multiple Choice**

1. D    5. B
2. C    6. B
3. A    7. B
4. B    8. D

**Part 2  Critical Response**

9. Fossils are important because they provide information about past life on Earth. Fossils also provide information about the evolution of organisms, past environments, and past climates, among others.

10. In the geologic past, shallow oceans covered much of North America.

11. The preservation potential increases as the burial rate increases. Burial by sediment slows decay and protects remains from scavengers, wave action, and other destructive processes.

12. Students should answer that the presence of hard parts increases the likelihood of fossilization. Low-oxygen, marine environments also favor fossilization because aerobic decay cannot occur.

---

The assessed Indiana standard appears above the question.

*Record your answers on the answer sheet provided by your teacher or on a sheet of paper.*

**Part 1  Multiple Choice**

1. The photo below shows a kind of fossil.

Which type of fossil preservation is this?

A carbon film

B original remain

C permineralized remain

D trace fossil

**7.3.10**

2. Which are the remains of species that existed on Earth for relatively short periods, and were abundant and widespread geographically?

A body fossils

B carbon fossils

C index fossils

D trace fossils

**Test-Taking Tip**

**Check It Again** Double check your answers before turning in the test.

---

3. Which separates tilted rocks below from horizontal rocks above?

A angular unconformity

B conformity

C disconformity

D nonconformity

The illustration below shows the strata at a certain locale.

4. Which sequence of letters describes the rock layers from oldest to youngest?

A D, Q, A, Z, L

B L, Z, A, Q, D

C Q, D, L, Z, A

D Z, L, A, D, Q

5. What does the wavy line between layers A and Q in the illustration above represent?

A an angular unconformity

B a disconformity

C an erosion

D a fault

**7.3.10**

**6.** Which means matching up rock layers in different places?

**A** absolute dating

**B** correlation

**C** relative dating

**D** uniformitarianism

The table below shows the percent remaining parent isotope per half-life of a radioisotope.

| Number of Half-lives | Parent Isotope Remaining (%) |
|:---:|:---:|
| 1 | 100 |
| 2 | X |
| 3 | 25 |
| 4 | 12.5 |
| 5 | Y |

**7.** Which replaces the letter X?

**A** 40

**B** 50

**C** 62.5

**D** 75

**8.** Which letter replaces the letter Y in the table above?

**A** 0

**B** 2.5

**C** 3.13

**D** 6.25

**Part 2   Critical Response**

**7.3.8**

**9.** Why are fossils important? What information do they provide?

**10.** How could a fossil of an organism that lived in ocean water millions of years ago be found in the middle of North America?

**11.** Below is a graph showing the relationship between preservation potential and burial rate.

**Relationship Between Sediment Burial Rate and Potential for Remains to Become Fossils**

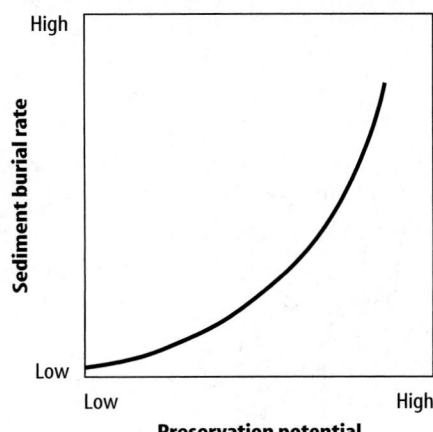

How does the potential for remains to be preserved change as the rate of burial by sediment increases? Why do you think this relationship exists?

**7.3.8**

**12.** What other factors affect the potential for the remains of organisms to become fossils?

## Rubrics

The following rubric is a sample scoring device for critical response questions.

### Critical Response

| Points | Description |
|:---:|:---|
| 4 | The student demonstrates a thorough understanding of the science of the task. The response may contain minor flaws that do not detract from the demonstration of a thorough understanding. |
| 3 | The student demonstrates an understanding of the science of the task. The response is essentially correct and demonstrates an essential but less than thorough understanding of the science. |
| 2 | The student demonstrates only a partial understanding of the science of the task. Although the student may have used the correct approach to a solution or may have provided a correct solution, the work lacks an essential understanding of the underlying science concepts. |
| 1 | The student demonstrates a very limited understanding of the science of the task. The response is incomplete and exhibits many flaws. |
| 0 | The student provides a completely incorrect solution or no response at all. |

# Student Resources

## CONTENTS

Science Skill Handbook

# Scientific Methods

Scientists use an orderly approach called the scientific method to solve problems. This includes organizing and recording data so others can understand them. Scientists use many variations in this method when they solve problems.

## Identify a Question

The first step in a scientific investigation or experiment is to identify a question to be answered or a problem to be solved. For example, you might ask which gasoline is the most efficient.

## Gather and Organize Information

After you have identified your question, begin gathering and organizing information. There are many ways to gather information, such as researching in a library, interviewing those knowledgeable about the subject, testing and working in the laboratory and field. Fieldwork is investigations and observations done outside of a laboratory.

**Researching Information** Before moving in a new direction, it is important to gather the information that already is known about the subject. Start by asking yourself questions to determine exactly what you need to know. Then you will look for the information in various reference sources, like the student is doing in **Figure 1.** Some sources may include textbooks, encyclopedias, government documents, professional journals, science magazines, and the Internet. Always list the sources of your information.

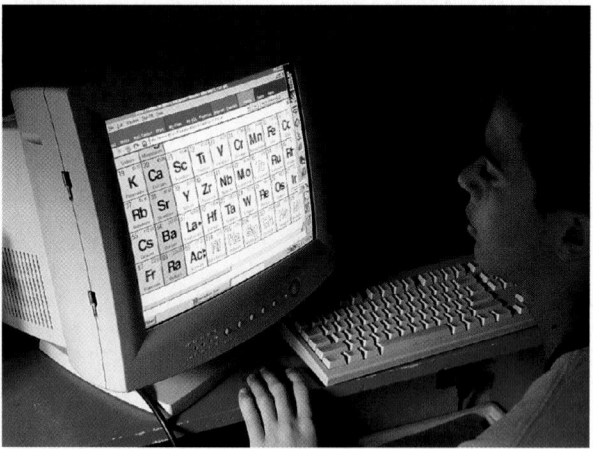

**Figure 1** The Internet can be a valuable research tool.

**Evaluate Sources of Information** Not all sources of information are reliable. You should evaluate all of your sources of information, and use only those you know to be dependable. For example, if you are researching ways to make homes more energy efficient, a site written by the U.S. Department of Energy would be more reliable than a site written by a company that is trying to sell a new type of weatherproofing material. Also, remember that research always is changing. Consult the most current resources available to you. For example, a 1985 resource about saving energy would not reflect the most recent findings.

Sometimes scientists use data that they did not collect themselves, or conclusions drawn by other researchers. This data must be evaluated carefully. Ask questions about how the data were obtained, if the investigation was carried out properly, and if it has been duplicated exactly with the same results. Would you reach the same conclusion from the data? Only when you have confidence in the data can you believe it is true and feel comfortable using it.

**Interpret Scientific Illustrations** As you research a topic in science, you will see drawings, diagrams, and photographs to help you understand what you read. Some illustrations are included to help you understand an idea that you can't see easily by yourself, like the tiny particles in an atom in **Figure 2.** A drawing helps many people to remember details more easily and provides examples that clarify difficult concepts or give additional information about the topic you are studying. Most illustrations have labels or a caption to identify or to provide more information.

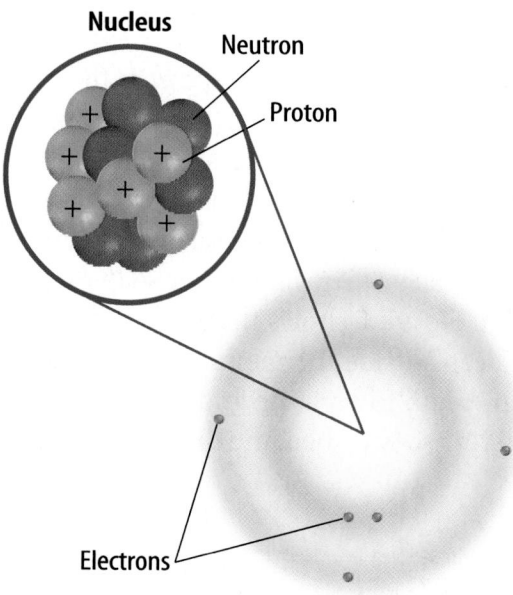

**Figure 2** This drawing shows an atom of carbon with its six protons, six neutrons, and six electrons.

**Concept Maps** One way to organize data is to draw a diagram that shows relationships among ideas (or concepts). A concept map can help make the meanings of ideas and terms more clear, and help you understand and remember what you are studying. Concept maps are useful for breaking large concepts down into smaller parts, making learning easier.

**Network Tree** A type of concept map that not only shows a relationship, but how the concepts are related is a network tree, shown in **Figure 3.** In a network tree, the words are written in the ovals, while the description of the type of relationship is written across the connecting lines.

When constructing a network tree, write down the topic and all major topics on separate pieces of paper or notecards. Then arrange them in order from general to specific. Branch the related concepts from the major concept and describe the relationship on the connecting line. Continue to more specific concepts until finished.

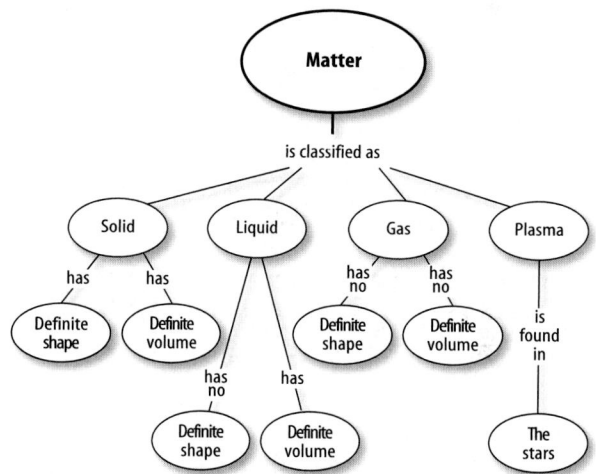

**Figure 3** A network tree shows how concepts or objects are related.

**Events Chain** Another type of concept map is an events chain. Sometimes called a flow chart, it models the order or sequence of items. An events chain can be used to describe a sequence of events, the steps in a procedure, or the stages of a process.

When making an events chain, first find the one event that starts the chain. This event is called the initiating event. Then, find the next event and continue until the outcome is reached, as shown in **Figure 4.**

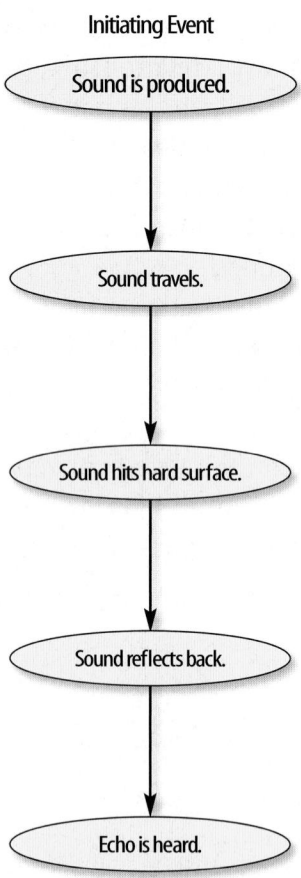

**Figure 4** Events-chain concept maps show the order of steps in a process or event. This concept map shows how a sound makes an echo.

**Cycle Map** A specific type of events chain is a cycle map. It is used when the series of events do not produce a final outcome, but instead relate back to the beginning event, such as in **Figure 5.** Therefore, the cycle repeats itself.

To make a cycle map, first decide what event is the beginning event. This is also called the initiating event. Then list the next events in the order that they occur, with the last event relating back to the initiating event. Words can be written between the events that describe what happens from one event to the next. The number of events in a cycle map can vary, but usually contain three or more events.

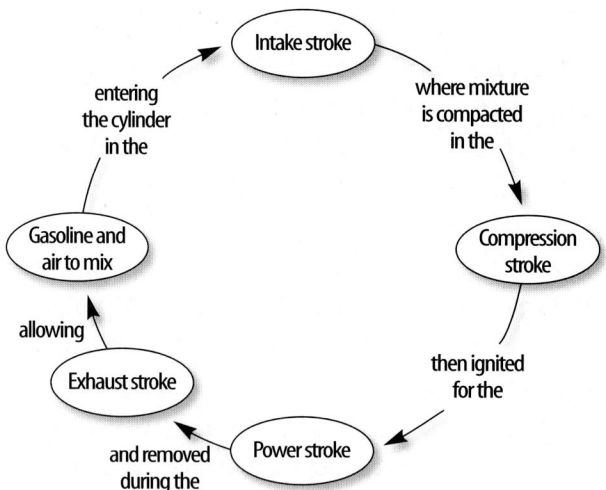

**Figure 5** A cycle map shows events that occur in a cycle.

**Spider Map** A type of concept map that you can use for brainstorming is the spider map. When you have a central idea, you might find that you have a jumble of ideas that relate to it but are not necessarily clearly related to each other. The spider map on sound in **Figure 6** shows that if you write these ideas outside the main concept, then you can begin to separate and group unrelated terms so they become more useful.

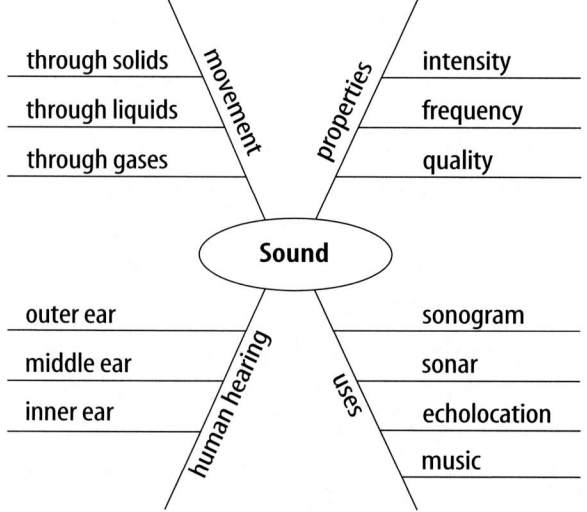

**Figure 6** A spider map allows you to list ideas that relate to a central topic but not necessarily to one another.

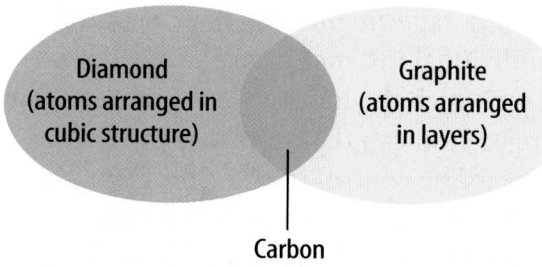

**Figure 7** This Venn diagram compares and contrasts two substances made from carbon.

**Venn Diagram** To illustrate how two subjects compare and contrast you can use a Venn diagram. You can see the characteristics that the subjects have in common and those that they do not, shown in **Figure 7.**

To create a Venn diagram, draw two overlapping ovals that that are big enough to write in. List the characteristics unique to one subject in one oval, and the characteristics of the other subject in the other oval. The characteristics in common are listed in the overlapping section.

**Make and Use Tables** One way to organize information so it is easier to understand is to use a table. Tables can contain numbers, words, or both.

To make a table, list the items to be compared in the first column and the characteristics to be compared in the first row. The title should clearly indicate the content of the table, and the column or row heads should be clear. Notice that in **Table 1** the units are included.

| Table 1 Recyclables Collected During Week | | | |
|---|---|---|---|
| **Day of Week** | **Paper (kg)** | **Aluminum (kg)** | **Glass (kg)** |
| Monday | 5.0 | 4.0 | 12.0 |
| Wednesday | 4.0 | 1.0 | 10.0 |
| Friday | 2.5 | 2.0 | 10.0 |

**Make a Model** One way to help you better understand the parts of a structure, the way a process works, or to show things too large or small for viewing is to make a model. For example, an atomic model made of a plastic-ball nucleus and pipe-cleaner electron shells can help you visualize how the parts of an atom relate to each other. Other types of models can by devised on a computer or represented by equations.

## Form a Hypothesis

A possible explanation based on previous knowledge and observations is called a hypothesis. After researching gasoline types and recalling previous experiences in your family's car you form a hypothesis—our car runs more efficiently because we use premium gasoline. To be valid, a hypothesis has to be something you can test by using an investigation.

**Predict** When you apply a hypothesis to a specific situation, you predict something about that situation. A prediction makes a statement in advance, based on prior observation, experience, or scientific reasoning. People use predictions to make everyday decisions. Scientists test predictions by performing investigations. Based on previous observations and experiences, you might form a prediction that cars are more efficient with premium gasoline. The prediction can be tested in an investigation.

**Design an Experiment** A scientist needs to make many decisions before beginning an investigation. Some of these include: how to carry out the investigation, what steps to follow, how to record the data, and how the investigation will answer the question. It also is important to address any safety concerns.

## Test the Hypothesis

Now that you have formed your hypothesis, you need to test it. Using an investigation, you will make observations and collect data, or information. This data might either support or not support your hypothesis. Scientists collect and organize data as numbers and descriptions.

**Follow a Procedure** In order to know what materials to use, as well as how and in what order to use them, you must follow a procedure. **Figure 8** shows a procedure you might follow to test your hypothesis.

### Procedure
1. Use regular gasoline for two weeks.
2. Record the number of kilometers between fill-ups and the amount of gasoline used.
3. Switch to premium gasoline for two weeks.
4. Record the number of kilometers between fill-ups and the amount of gasoline used.

**Figure 8** A procedure tells you what to do step by step.

**Identify and Manipulate Variables and Controls** In any experiment, it is important to keep everything the same except for the item you are testing. The one factor you change is called the independent variable. The change that results is the dependent variable. Make sure you have only one independent variable, to assure yourself of the cause of the changes you observe in the dependent variable. For example, in your gasoline experiment the type of fuel is the independent variable. The dependent variable is the efficiency.

Many experiments also have a control—an individual instance or experimental subject for which the independent variable is not changed. You can then compare the test results to the control results. To design a control you can have two cars of the same type. The control car uses regular gasoline for four weeks. After you are done with the test, you can compare the experimental results to the control results.

## Collect Data

Whether you are carrying out an investigation or a short observational experiment, you will collect data, as shown in **Figure 9.** Scientists collect data as numbers and descriptions and organize it in specific ways.

**Observe** Scientists observe items and events, then record what they see. When they use only words to describe an observation, it is called qualitative data. Scientists' observations also can describe how much there is of something. These observations use numbers, as well as words, in the description and are called quantitative data. For example, if a sample of the element gold is described as being "shiny and very dense" the data are qualitative. Quantitative data on this sample of gold might include "a mass of 30 g and a density of 19.3 g/cm$^3$."

**Figure 9** Collecting data is one way to gather information directly.

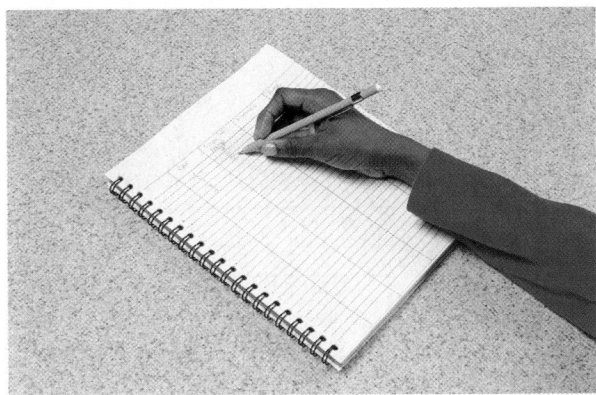

**Figure 10** Record data neatly and clearly so it is easy to understand.

When you make observations you should examine the entire object or situation first, and then look carefully for details. It is important to record observations accurately and completely. Always record your notes immediately as you make them, so you do not miss details or make a mistake when recording results from memory. Never put unidentified observations on scraps of paper. Instead they should be recorded in a notebook, like the one in **Figure 10.** Write your data neatly so you can easily read it later. At each point in the experiment, record your observations and label them. That way, you will not have to determine what the figures mean when you look at your notes later. Set up any tables that you will need to use ahead of time, so you can record any observations right away. Remember to avoid bias when collecting data by not including personal thoughts when you record observations. Record only what you observe.

**Estimate** Scientific work also involves estimating. To estimate is to make a judgment about the size or the number of something without measuring or counting. This is important when the number or size of an object or population is too large or too difficult to accurately count or measure.

**Sample** Scientists may use a sample or a portion of the total number as a type of estimation. To sample is to take a small, representative portion of the objects or organisms of a population for research. By making careful observations or manipulating variables within that portion of the group, information is discovered and conclusions are drawn that might apply to the whole population. A poorly chosen sample can be unrepresentative of the whole. If you were trying to determine the rainfall in an area, it would not be best to take a rainfall sample from under a tree.

**Measure** You use measurements everyday. Scientists also take measurements when collecting data. When taking measurements, it is important to know how to use measuring tools properly. Accuracy also is important.

**Length** To measure length, the distance between two points, scientists use meters. Smaller measurements might be measured in centimeters or millimeters.

Length is measured using a metric ruler or meter stick. When using a metric ruler, line up the 0-cm mark with the end of the object being measured and read the number of the unit where the object ends. Look at the metric ruler shown in **Figure 11.** The centimeter lines are the long, numbered lines, and the shorter lines are millimeter lines. In this instance, the length would be 4.50 cm.

**Figure 11** This metric ruler has centimeter and millimeter divisions.

**Mass** The SI unit for mass is the kilogram (kg). Scientists can measure mass using units formed by adding metric prefixes to the unit gram (g), such as milligram (mg). To measure mass, you might use a triple-beam balance similar to the one shown in **Figure 12.** The balance has a pan on one side and a set of beams on the other side. Each beam has a rider that slides on the beam.

When using a triple-beam balance, place an object on the pan. Slide the largest rider along its beam until the pointer drops below zero. Then move it back one notch. Repeat the process for each rider proceeding from the larger to smaller until the pointer swings an equal distance above and below the zero point. Sum the masses on each beam to find the mass of the object. Move all riders back to zero when finished.

Instead of putting materials directly on the balance, scientists often take a tare of a container. A tare is the mass of a container into which objects or substances are placed for measuring their masses. To mass objects or substances, find the mass of a clean container. Remove the container from the pan, and place the object or substances in the container. Find the mass of the container with the materials in it. Subtract the mass of the empty container from the mass of the filled container to find the mass of the materials you are using.

**Figure 12** A triple-beam balance is used to determine the mass of an object.

— Meniscus

**Figure 13** Graduated cylinders measure liquid volume.

**Liquid Volume** To measure liquids, the unit used is the liter. When a smaller unit is needed, scientists might use a milliliter. Because a milliliter takes up the volume of a cube measuring 1 cm on each side it also can be called a cubic centimeter ($cm^3 = cm \times cm \times cm$).

You can use beakers and graduated cylinders to measure liquid volume. A graduated cylinder, shown in **Figure 13,** is marked from bottom to top in milliliters. In lab, you might use a 10-mL graduated cylinder or a 100-mL graduated cylinder. When measuring liquids, notice that the liquid has a curved surface. Look at the surface at eye level, and measure the bottom of the curve. This is called the meniscus. The graduated cylinder in **Figure 13** contains 79.0 mL, or 79.0 $cm^3$, of a liquid.

**Temperature** Scientists often measure temperature using the Celsius scale. Pure water has a freezing point of 0°C and boiling point of 100°C. The unit of measurement is degrees Celsius. Two other scales often used are the Fahrenheit and Kelvin scales.

**Figure 14** A thermometer measures the temperature of an object.

Scientists use a thermometer to measure temperature. Most thermometers in a laboratory are glass tubes with a bulb at the bottom end containing a liquid such as colored alcohol. The liquid rises or falls with a change in temperature. To read a glass thermometer like the thermometer in **Figure 14,** rotate it slowly until a red line appears. Read the temperature where the red line ends.

**Form Operational Definitions** An operational definition defines an object by how it functions, works, or behaves. For example, when you are playing hide and seek and a tree is home base, you have created an operational definition for a tree.

Objects can have more than one operational definition. For example, a ruler can be defined as a tool that measures the length of an object (how it is used). It can also be a tool with a series of marks used as a standard when measuring (how it works).

## Analyze the Data

To determine the meaning of your observations and investigation results, you will need to look for patterns in the data. Then you must think critically to determine what the data mean. Scientists use several approaches when they analyze the data they have collected and recorded. Each approach is useful for identifying specific patterns.

**Interpret Data** The word *interpret* means "to explain the meaning of something." When analyzing data from an experiment, try to find out what the data show. Identify the control group and the test group to see whether or not changes in the independent variable have had an effect. Look for differences in the dependent variable between the control and test groups.

**Classify** Sorting objects or events into groups based on common features is called classifying. When classifying, first observe the objects or events to be classified. Then select one feature that is shared by some members in the group, but not by all. Place those members that share that feature in a subgroup. You can classify members into smaller and smaller subgroups based on characteristics. Remember that when you classify, you are grouping objects or events for a purpose. Keep your purpose in mind as you select the features to form groups and subgroups.

**Compare and Contrast** Observations can be analyzed by noting the similarities and differences between two more objects or events that you observe. When you look at objects or events to see how they are similar, you are comparing them. Contrasting is looking for differences in objects or events.

**Science Skill Handbook**

**Recognize Cause and Effect** A cause is a reason for an action or condition. The effect is that action or condition. When two events happen together, it is not necessarily true that one event caused the other. Scientists must design a controlled investigation to recognize the exact cause and effect.

## Draw Conclusions

When scientists have analyzed the data they collected, they proceed to draw conclusions about the data. These conclusions are sometimes stated in words similar to the hypothesis that you formed earlier. They may confirm a hypothesis, or lead you to a new hypothesis.

**Infer** Scientists often make inferences based on their observations. An inference is an attempt to explain observations or to indicate a cause. An inference is not a fact, but a logical conclusion that needs further investigation. For example, you may infer that a fire has caused smoke. Until you investigate, however, you do not know for sure.

**Apply** When you draw a conclusion, you must apply those conclusions to determine whether the data supports the hypothesis. If your data do not support your hypothesis, it does not mean that the hypothesis is wrong. It means only that the result of the investigation did not support the hypothesis. Maybe the experiment needs to be redesigned, or some of the initial observations on which the hypothesis was based were incomplete or biased. Perhaps more observation or research is needed to refine your hypothesis. A successful investigation does not always come out the way you originally predicted.

**Avoid Bias** Sometimes a scientific investigation involves making judgments. When you make a judgment, you form an opinion. It is important to be honest and not to allow any expectations of results to bias your judgments. This is important throughout the entire investigation, from researching to collecting data to drawing conclusions.

## Communicate

The communication of ideas is an important part of the work of scientists. A discovery that is not reported will not advance the scientific community's understanding or knowledge. Communication among scientists also is important as a way of improving their investigations.

Scientists communicate in many ways, from writing articles in journals and magazines that explain their investigations and experiments, to announcing important discoveries on television and radio. Scientists also share ideas with colleagues on the Internet or present them as lectures, like the student is doing in **Figure 15.**

**Figure 15** A student communicates to his peers about his investigation.

| SAFETY SYMBOLS | HAZARD | EXAMPLES | PRECAUTION | REMEDY |
|---|---|---|---|---|
| **DISPOSAL** | Special disposal procedures need to be followed. | certain chemicals, living organisms | Do not dispose of these materials in the sink or trash can. | Dispose of wastes as directed by your teacher. |
| **BIOLOGICAL** | Organisms or other biological materials that might be harmful to humans | bacteria, fungi, blood, unpreserved tissues, plant materials | Avoid skin contact with these materials. Wear mask or gloves. | Notify your teacher if you suspect contact with material. Wash hands thoroughly. |
| **EXTREME TEMPERATURE** | Objects that can burn skin by being too cold or too hot | boiling liquids, hot plates, dry ice, liquid nitrogen | Use proper protection when handling. | Go to your teacher for first aid. |
| **SHARP OBJECT** | Use of tools or glassware that can easily puncture or slice skin | razor blades, pins, scalpels, pointed tools, dissecting probes, broken glass | Practice common-sense behavior and follow guidelines for use of the tool. | Go to your teacher for first aid. |
| **FUME** | Possible danger to respiratory tract from fumes | ammonia, acetone, nail polish remover, heated sulfur, moth balls | Make sure there is good ventilation. Never smell fumes directly. Wear a mask. | Leave foul area and notify your teacher immediately. |
| **ELECTRICAL** | Possible danger from electrical shock or burn | improper grounding, liquid spills, short circuits, exposed wires | Double-check setup with teacher. Check condition of wires and apparatus. | Do not attempt to fix electrical problems. Notify your teacher immediately. |
| **IRRITANT** | Substances that can irritate the skin or mucous membranes of the respiratory tract | pollen, moth balls, steel wool, fiberglass, potassium permanganate | Wear dust mask and gloves. Practice extra care when handling these materials. | Go to your teacher for first aid. |
| **CHEMICAL** | Chemicals can react with and destroy tissue and other materials | bleaches such as hydrogen peroxide; acids such as sulfuric acid, hydrochloric acid; bases such as ammonia, sodium hydroxide | Wear goggles, gloves, and an apron. | Immediately flush the affected area with water and notify your teacher. |
| **TOXIC** | Substance may be poisonous if touched, inhaled, or swallowed. | mercury, many metal compounds, iodine, poinsettia plant parts | Follow your teacher's instructions. | Always wash hands thoroughly after use. Go to your teacher for first aid. |
| **FLAMMABLE** | Flammable chemicals may be ignited by open flame, spark, or exposed heat. | alcohol, kerosene, potassium permanganate | Avoid open flames and heat when using flammable chemicals. | Notify your teacher immediately. Use fire safety equipment if applicable. |
| **OPEN FLAME** | Open flame in use, may cause fire. | hair, clothing, paper, synthetic materials | Tie back hair and loose clothing. Follow teacher's instruction on lighting and extinguishing flames. | Notify your teacher immediately. Use fire safety equipment if applicable. |

 **Eye Safety** Proper eye protection should be worn at all times by anyone performing or observing science activities.

 **Clothing Protection** This symbol appears when substances could stain or burn clothing.

 **Animal Safety** This symbol appears when safety of animals and students must be ensured.

 **Handwashing** After the lab, wash hands with soap and water before removing goggles.

# Safety in the Science Laboratory

The science laboratory is a safe place to work if you follow standard safety procedures. Being responsible for your own safety helps to make the entire laboratory a safer place for everyone. When performing any lab, read and apply the caution statements and safety symbol listed at the beginning of the lab.

## General Safety Rules

1. Obtain your teacher's permission to begin all investigations and use laboratory equipment.

2. Study the procedure. Ask your teacher any questions. Be sure you understand safety symbols shown on the page.

3. Notify your teacher about allergies or other health conditions which can affect your participation in a lab.

4. Learn and follow use and safety procedures for your equipment. If unsure, ask your teacher.

5. Never eat, drink, chew gum, apply cosmetics, or do any personal grooming in the lab. Never use lab glassware as food or drink containers. Keep your hands away from your face and mouth.

6. Know the location and proper use of the safety shower, eye wash, fire blanket, and fire alarm.

## Prevent Accidents

1. Use the safety equipment provided to you. Goggles and a safety apron should be worn during investigations.

2. Do NOT use hair spray, mousse, or other flammable hair products. Tie back long hair and tie down loose clothing.

3. Do NOT wear sandals or other open-toed shoes in the lab.

4. Remove jewelry on hands and wrists. Loose jewelry, such as chains and long necklaces, should be removed to prevent them from getting caught in equipment.

5. Do not taste any substances or draw any material into a tube with your mouth.

6. Proper behavior is expected in the lab. Practical jokes and fooling around can lead to accidents and injury.

7. Keep your work area uncluttered.

## Laboratory Work

1. Collect and carry all equipment and materials to your work area before beginning a lab.

2. Remain in your own work area unless given permission by your teacher to leave it.

3. Always slant test tubes away from yourself and others when heating them, adding substances to them, or rinsing them.

4. If instructed to smell a substance in a container, hold the container a short distance away and fan vapors towards your nose.

5. Do NOT substitute other chemicals/substances for those in the materials list unless instructed to do so by your teacher.

6. Do NOT take any materials or chemicals outside of the laboratory.

7. Stay out of storage areas unless instructed to be there and supervised by your teacher.

## Laboratory Cleanup

1. Turn off all burners, water, and gas, and disconnect all electrical devices.

2. Clean all pieces of equipment and return all materials to their proper places.

3. Dispose of chemicals and other materials as directed by your teacher. Place broken glass and solid substances in the proper containers. Never discard materials in the sink.

4. Clean your work area.

5. Wash your hands with soap and water thoroughly BEFORE removing your goggles.

## Emergencies

1. Report any fire, electrical shock, glassware breakage, spill, or injury, no matter how small, to your teacher immediately. Follow his or her instructions.

2. If your clothing should catch fire, STOP, DROP, and ROLL. If possible, smother it with the fire blanket or get under a safety shower. NEVER RUN.

3. If a fire should occur, turn off all gas and leave the room according to established procedures.

4. In most instances, your teacher will clean up spills. Do NOT attempt to clean up spills unless you are given permission and instructions to do so.

5. If chemicals come into contact with your eyes or skin, notify your teacher immediately. Use the eyewash or flush your skin or eyes with large quantities of water.

6. The fire extinguisher and first-aid kit should only be used by your teacher unless it is an extreme emergency and you have been given permission.

7. If someone is injured or becomes ill, only a professional medical provider or someone certified in first aid should perform first-aid procedures.

## 1 Your Daily Drink

**Time required** one day (no class time)

### Materials
- Purchase inexpensive measuring cups at a discount department store.
- Students can make inexpensive measuring cups by using a new graduated cylinder to fill up a clear plastic cup 50 mL at a time. They can mark the 50 mL increments on the outside of the cup with a permanent marker.

### Safety Precaution
Students should make certain their measuring cups are clean and have never contained toxic substances.

### Teaching Strategy
Students can convert the number of milliliters of liquid they drank in one day to liters by dividing their total number of milliliters by 1,000.

### Conclude and Apply
1. Answers should include the units of milliliters or liters.
2. The mass in grams of individually wrapped foods is printed on the packaging, and a balance could be used to measure the mass of fresh foods or foods poured from a larger container.

---

# EXTRA Try at Home Labs

**From Your Kitchen, Junk Drawer, or Yard**

### 1 Your Daily Drink

▶ **Real-World Question**
How much liquid do you consume in a day?

**Possible Materials**
- 500-mL measuring cup
- calculator

▶ **Procedure**
1. When you drink a bottle or can of juice, soda, water, or other beverage, look on the label of the container to find the volume in milliliters.

2. Record the volumes of all the canned and bottled drinks you consume in one day in your Science Journal.
3. Use a measuring cup to measure the liquids that you pour from larger containers. Record these volumes in your Science Journal.
4. Add up the volumes of all the drinks you consumed during the day.

▶ **Conclude and Apply**
1. How much liquid did you drink during the day?
2. Infer how you would measure the mass of the foods you ate in one day.

### 2 Cell Sizes

▶ **Real-World Question**
How do different cells compare in size?

**Possible Materials**
- meterstick
- metric ruler
- white paper
- pencil
- pen
- masking tape

▶ **Procedure**
1. Make a dot on a white sheet of paper with a pencil.
2. Use a metric ruler to make a second dot 1 mm away from the first dot. This distance represents the average length of a bacteria cell.
3. Measure a distance 8 mm away from the first dot and make a third dot. This distance represents the average length of a red blood cell.

4. Mark a spot on the floor with a piece of tape and use the meterstick to measure a distance of 7 m. Mark this distance with a second piece of tape. This distance represents the average length of an amoeba cell.

▶ **Conclude and Apply**
1. The distance between the first and second dot is 1,000 times longer than the actual size of a bacterium cell. Calculate the length of an actual bacterium cell.
2. A large chicken egg is just one cell, and it is 100 times longer than an amoeba cell. Using your measurement from step 4, calculate the distance you would have to measure to represent the average length of a hen's egg.

Adult supervision required for all labs.

These labs are available at in7.msscience.com.

---

## 2 Cell Sizes

**Time required** 15 minutes

**Materials** Students can complete this lab by using only metersticks.

**Safety Precaution** Metal metersticks bend easily and can harm others if used carelessly.

### Teaching Strategies
- Clear away space on the classroom floor for this lab or have students complete it outside.
- Students can research the length of other types of cells and measure their relative distances on the white sheet of paper or on the floor.

### Conclude and Apply
1. 0.001 mm or 1 micrometer
2. 700 m

## 3 Expanding Eggs

▶ **Real-World Question**
How can you observe liquids passing through a cell membrane?

**Possible Materials**
- glass jar with lid
- white vinegar
- medium chicken egg
- tape measure or string and ruler
- tongs
- measuring cup

▶ **Procedure**
1. Obtain a glass jar with a lid and a medium egg.
2. Make certain your egg easily fits into your jar.
3. Measure the circumference of your egg.
4. Pour 250 mL of white vinegar into the jar.
5. Carefully place your egg in the jar so that it is submerged in the vinegar. Be careful not to crack or break the egg.
6. Observe your egg each day for three days. Measure the circumference of the egg after three days.

▶ **Conclude and Apply**
1. Describe the changes that happened to your egg.
2. Infer why the egg's circumference changed. *HINT: A hen's egg is a single cell.*

## 4 Putting Down Roots

▶ **Real-World Question**
Can cells from a plant's stem produce root cells for a new plant?

**Possible Materials**
- houseplant
- scissors
- metric ruler
- glasses or jars (3)
- water
- magnifying lens

▶ **Procedure**
1. Examine the stems of a houseplant, such as *Pothos,* and locate a node on three different stems. A node looks like a small bump.
2. Cut 3 stems off the plant at a 45° angle about 3–4 mm below the node.
3. Place the end of each stem into a separate glass of water and observe them for a week.

▶ **Conclude and Apply**
1. Describe what happened to the ends of the stems.
2. Infer how plant stem cells can produce root cells.

---

**Time Required** several two-to-three minute observation periods for a week

**Materials** The plant roots will grow more quickly when dipped in rooting hormone, but the hormone is not necessary to complete the lab.

**Safety Precaution** Students should wash their hands thoroughly after the lab.

**Teaching Strategies**
- Not all the cuttings will grow roots.
- Roots more visible when under a hand lens.
- Consider having students plant their cuttings in soil once roots have grown.

## 3 Expanding Eggs

**Time Required** five minutes for set-up; five-minute observation periods for three days

**Materials**
- Make certain the egg will fit into the jar both before and after the lab is completed. Avoid using large or extra large eggs.
- Spaghetti sauce or pickle jars work well for this lab.
- Students also can measure egg circumferences with lengths of string and metric rulers.

**Safety Precaution**
Students should wash their hands thoroughly after handling eggs.

**Teaching Strategy** The eggshell is made of calcium carbonate and has the same chemical composition as limestone. Vinegar dissolves the calcium carbonate, producing bubbles of carbon dioxide during the reaction.

**Conclude and Apply**
1. The egg's shell will dissolve. The outer membrane of the egg will become rubbery, and the egg will increase in circumference by about 15 percent.
2. The water in the vinegar passes through the membrane of the egg cell expanding the egg's size. The particles inside the egg are too large to move out through the membrane.

## 4 Putting Down Roots

**Conclude and Apply**
1. Tiny roots should grow on one or more stems.
2. Flowers and buds consume energy for growth. Cuttings can conserve more energy without them.
3. The DNA of each plant cell contains all the information needed to make every type of plant cell.

Extra Try at Home Labs

## 5 Vitamin Search

**Time Required** 40 minutes

### Materials
- Purchase inexpensive nutrition guidebooks at a local grocery store.
- Many cookbooks contain nutritional information about fresh foods.

**Safety Precaution** Caution students never to eat or drink anything in science class.

### Teaching Strategy
Encourage students to evaluate the percentages of vitamins and minerals in their favorite foods and in the foods they eat most frequently.

### Conclude and Apply
1. Fresh fruits and vegetables have many vitamins and minerals people need.
2. A single fruit or vegetable will have a high content of one vitamin or mineral but not others. A varied diet will ensure enough of all essential vitamins and minerals are consumed.

---

# Extra Try at Home Labs

## 5 Vitamin Search

▶ **Real-World Question**
How many vitamins and minerals are in the foods you eat?

**Possible Materials**
- labels from packaged foods and drinks
- nutrition guidebook or cookbook

▶ **Procedure**
1. Create a data table to record the "% Daily Value" of important vitamins and minerals for a variety of foods.
2. Collect packages from a variety of packaged foods and check the Nutrition Facts chart for the "% Daily Value" of all the vitamins and minerals it contains. These values are listed at the bottom of the chart.
3. Use cookbooks or nutrition guidebooks to research the "% Daily Value" of vitamins and minerals found in several fresh fruits and vegetables such as strawberries, spinach, oranges, and lentils.

▶ **Conclude and Apply**
1. Infer why a healthy diet includes fresh fruits and vegetables.
2. Infer why a healthy diet includes a wide variety of nutritious foods.

---

## 6 Acid Defense

▶ **Real-World Question**
How is stomach acid your internal first line of defense?

**Possible Materials**
- drinking glasses (2)
- milk
- cola or lemon juice
- masking tape
- marker
- measuring cup

▶ **Procedure**
1. Pour 100 mL of milk into each glass.
2. Pour 20 mL of cola into the second glass.
3. Using the masking tape and marker, label the first glass *No Acid* and the second glass *Acid*.
4. Place the glasses in direct sunlight and observe the mixture each day for several days.

▶ **Conclude and Apply**
1. Compare the odor of the mixture in both glasses after one or two days.
2. Infer how this experiment modeled one of your internal defenses against disease.

Adult supervision required for all labs.

These labs are available at in7.msscience.com.

---

## 6 Acid Defense

**Time Required** ten minutes for set-up; two-minute observation periods for several days

### Safety Precautions
- If acid splashes into the eyes, flush with water immediately and seek help.
- Caution students never to eat or drink anything in science class.

**Teaching Strategy** The pH of stomach acid is around 1, similar to the pH of concentrated hydrochloric acid. Have students research the pH of the acid they used.

### Conclude and Apply
1. After one day, the milk without the added acid will become thick with white lumps floating in it, and it will smell sour. The milk with the acid in it will not sour until two or three days later.
2. Stomach acid kills many disease-causing bacteria that enter the digestive system in foods or drinks.

*(Image: Nutrition Facts label)*

**Nutrition Facts**
Serving Size 1 Meal

**Amount Per Serving**
Calories 330    Calories from Fat 60

| | % Daily Value* |
|---|---|
| **Total Fat** 7g | 10% |
| Saturated Fat 3.5g | 17% |
| Polyunsaturated Fat 1g | |
| Monounsaturated Fat 2.5g | |
| **Cholesterol** 35mg | 12% |
| **Sodium** 460mg | 19% |
| **Total Carbohydrate** 52g | 18% |
| Dietary Fiber 6g | 24% |
| Sugars 17g | |
| **Protein** 15g | |

| | |
|---|---|
| Vitamin A 15% | Vitamin C 70% |
| Calcium 4% | Iron 10% |

* Percent Daily Values are based on a 2,000 calorie diet. Your daily values may be higher or lower depending on your calorie needs.

| | Calories | 2,000 | 2,500 |
|---|---|---|---|
| Total Fat | Less than | 65g | 80g |
| Sat Fat | Less than | 20g | 25g |
| Cholesterol | Less than | 300mg | 300mg |
| Sodium | Less than | 2,400mg | 2,400mg |
| Total Carbohydrate | | 300g | 375g |
| Dietary Fiber | | 25g | 30g |

## 7 Feeding Frenzy

### Real-World Question
How can you observe predation?

**Possible Materials** 🔲 ⚠️ 📷 🧤 🔬 🗂️
- large jar with metal lid
- hammer and nail
- plant-eating insect
- insect net
- magnifying lens
- leaves, grass, flowers
- water

### Procedure
1. Poke tiny holes in the metal lid of a jar with a nail so the insect has fresh air.
2. Observe a plant-eating insect in the wild. Collect one for indoor observation as well.
3. Put leaves, grass, and flowers in the bottom of the jar. Add a few drops of water.
4. Add the insect. Watch how it behaves.
5. When the experiment is finished, release the insect back into the wild.

### Conclude and Apply
1. Describe the predation behaviors of the insect.
2. Compare the insect's behavior in the wild and in captivity. Did its diet change?

## 8 UV Watch

### Real-World Question
How can you find out about the risks of ultraviolet radiation each day?

**Possible Materials**
- daily newspaper with weekly weather forecasts
- graph paper

### Procedure
1. Use the local newspaper or another resource to get the weather forecast for the day.
2. Check the UV (ultraviolet light) index for the day. If it provides an hourly UV index level, record the level for 1:00 P.M.
3. Find a legend or do research to discover what the numbers of the UV index mean.
4. Record the UV index everyday for ten days and graph your results on graph paper.

### Conclude and Apply
1. Explain how the UV index system works.
2. Research several ways you can protect yourself from too much ultraviolet light exposure.

---

## 7 Feeding Frenzy

**Time Required** 45 minutes

**Safety Precaution** Students should use caution when gathering insects and plants.

### Teaching Strategies
- If you have an extensive knowledge of the aquatic insects in your area, you could try setting up an aquatic insect ecosystem. It is more difficult to find aquatic predatory insects, however.
- If you have an aquarium, this experiment can be done using brine shrimp or small guppies as prey. Carnivorous tropical fish include swordtails, fancytail guppies, and large barbs.

### Conclude and Apply
1. Students should describe feeding habits and other behaviors of the insects they collect.
2. Answers will vary depending on the animals used.

---

## 8 UV Watch

**Time Required** one-to-two minute sessions for ten consecutive days

**Materials** Online resources, daily newspapers, and some local TV news channels provide daily UV index levels.

**Safety Precaution** Students should use computers only with adult supervision.

**Teaching Strategy** This lab works best during warm weather seasons.

### Conclude and Apply
1. Ultraviolet light levels range from 0–10. Levels of 0–3 are low levels of UV radiation; 4–6 are moderate, and 7–10 are high levels of exposure.
2. When in the Sun, wear a wide brim hat, sunscreen with an SPF of 15, long sleeves, and UV protection sunglasses. Time in the Sun between 10:00 A.M. and 3:00 P.M. should be limited.

## ⑨ Comparing Atom Sizes

**Time Required** 25 minutes

**Safety Precaution** Caution students to handle the meter-sticks with care.

### Teaching Strategies
- Instruct students to start measuring the relative diameters at one end of the paper.
- If necessary, remind students that these measurements are relative diameters not the actual diameters of atoms.

### Conclude and Apply
1. $1 \times 10^{-12}$ m
2. hydrogen: 7.4 cm; oxygen: 14.6 cm; iron: 24.8 cm; gold: 28.8 cm; and francium: 54.0 cm

---

**Extra Try at Home Labs**

### ⑨ Comparing Atom Sizes

🔵 *Real-World Question*
**How do the sizes of different types of atoms compare?**

**Possible Materials** 🔲 🔲
- metric ruler or meterstick
- 1-m length of white paper
- transparent or masking tape
- colored pencils

🔵 *Procedure*
1. Tape a 1-m sheet of paper on the floor.
2. Use a scale of 1 mm: 1 picometer for measuring and drawing the relative diameters of all the atoms.
3. Study the chart of atomic sizes.
4. Use your scale to measure the relative size of a hydrogen atom on the sheet of paper. Use a red pencil to draw the relative diameter of a hydrogen atom on your paper.
5. Use your scale to measure the relative sizes of an oxygen atom, iron atom, gold atom, and francium atom. Use four other colored pencils to draw the relative diameters of these atoms on the paper.
6. Compare the relative sizes of these different atoms.

🔵 *Conclude and Apply*
1. Research the length of a picometer.
2. Using your scale, list the diameters of the atoms that you drew on your paper.

| Atomic Sizes (picometers) | |
|---|---|
| **Element** | **Diameter** |
| Hydrogen | 50 |
| Oxygen | 146 |
| Iron | 248 |
| Gold | 288 |
| Francium | 540 |

---

### ⑩ A Good Mix?

🔵 *Real-World Question*
**Which liquids will dissolve in water?**

**Possible Materials** 🔲 🔲 🔲
- cooking oil
- water
- apple or grape juice
- rubbing alcohol
- spoon
- glass
- measuring cup

🔵 *Procedure*
1. Pour 100 mL of water into a large glass.
2. Pour 100 mL of apple juice into the glass and stir the water and juice together. Observe your mixture to determine whether juice is soluble in water.
3. Empty and rinse out your glass.
4. Pour 100 mL of water and 100 mL of cooking oil into the glass and stir them together. Observe your mixture to determine whether oil is soluble in water.
5. Empty and rinse out your glass.
6. Pour 100 mL of water and 100 mL of rubbing alcohol into the glass and stir them together. Observe your mixture to determine whether alcohol is soluble in water.

🔵 *Conclude and Apply*
1. List the liquid(s) that are soluble in water.
2. List the liquid(s) that are not soluble in water.
3. Infer why some liquids are soluble in water and others are not.

**Adult supervision required for all labs.**

**These labs are available at** in7.msscience.com.

---

## ⑩ A Good Mix?

**Time Required** 20 minutes

### Materials
- Orange, grapefruit, tomato, and other juices will also dissolve in water.
- Olive, peanut, and other oils are also insoluble in water.
- Students can also test various types of sodas, which are soluble in water.
- Students will need dish soap to rinse the oil from beakers.

**Safety Precaution** Warn students not to drink anything during science class.

**Teaching Strategy** Students can complete this lab at home by using equal volumes of water and each liquid.

### Conclude and Apply
1. juices and rubbing alcohol
2. cooking oil
3. Like dissolves like. Water, juices, and alcohols are all polar, but oils are nonpolar.

## 11 Measuring Momentum

▶ **Real-World Question**
How much momentum do rolling balls have?

**Possible Materials** 🔌 🔲
- meterstick
- orange cones or tape
- scale
- stopwatch
- bucket
- bowling ball
- plastic baseball
- golf ball
- tennis ball
- calculator

▶ **Procedure**
1. Use a balance to measure the masses of the tennis ball, golf ball, and plastic baseball. Convert their masses from grams to kilograms.
2. Find the weight of the bowling ball in pounds. The weight should be written on the ball. Divide the ball's weight by 2.2 to calculate its mass in kilograms.

3. Go outside and measure a 10-m distance on a blacktop or concrete surface. Mark the distance with orange cones or tape.
4. Have a partner roll each ball the 10-m distance. Measure the time it takes each ball to roll 10 m.
5. Use the formula: velocity $= \frac{distance}{time}$ to calculate each ball's velocity.

▶ **Conclude and Apply**
1. Calculate the momentum of each ball.
2. Infer why the momentums of the balls differed so greatly.

## 12 Friction in Traffic

▶ **Real-World Question**
How do the various kinds of friction affect the operation of vehicles?

**Possible Materials** 🔲 🔲 🔌
- erasers taken from the ends of pencils (4)
- needles (2)
- small match box
- toy car

▶ **Procedure**
1. Build a match box car with the materials listed, or use a toy car.
2. Invent ways to demonstrate the effects of static friction, sliding friction, and rolling friction on the car. Think of hills, ice or rain conditions, graveled roads and paved roads, etc.

3. Make drawings of how friction is acting on the car, or how the car uses friction to work.

▶ **Conclude and Apply**
1. In what ways are static, sliding, and rolling friction helpful to drivers?
2. In what ways are static, sliding, and rolling friction unfavorable to car safety and operation?
3. Explain what your experiment taught you about driving in icy conditions.

**Adult supervision required for all labs.**

## 11 Measuring Momentum

**Time Required** 40 minutes

### Materials
- Students can transport the bowling balls in heavy-duty 5-gallon construction buckets.
- You might have to help students find the weights of the bowling balls.

### Safety Precautions
- Caution students not to throw or drop the bowling balls.
- Students should use the metersticks with care.

### Teaching Strategies
- Students should roll each ball so that it does not bounce.
- Instruct students to use the formula: momentum = mass × velocity to calculate each ball's momentum.

### Conclude and Apply
1. Answers will vary, but all answers should have the units kg m/s.
2. The masses of balls varied greatly.

## 12 Friction in Traffic

**Time Required** one to one-and-a-half hours, including building the car

**Materials** For an icy hill, you could use a cookie sheet with ice, soap, or cornstarch. Use books to elevate it.

### Teaching Strategies
- Combine this lab with force drawings to help students understand the types of friction.
- Introduce the idea that heavier objects are acted upon more by forces.

### Conclude and Apply
1. Static friction helps a car park on a hill. Sliding friction helps it stop by braking. Rolling friction is necessary for the wheels to move. Other answers are possible.
2. The engine needs to overcome static friction. Without enough sliding friction, cars skid (like on wet and/or icy roads). Too much friction decreases fuel economy.
3. Answers will vary.

## 13 The Heat is On

**Time Required** ten minutes

### Materials
- Use an incandescent, not fluorescent, lightbulb.
- The lightbulbs should not be turned on before the lab.
- Black cloth can be used instead of the paper.

### Safety Precaution
Warn students never to touch a lightbulb even if it is not lit.

### Teaching Strategies
- Have students lay the sheet of paper in direct sunlight first, complete the other parts of the lab, and then return to the paper after ten minutes.
- Extend the lab by using thermometers.

### Conclude and Apply
1. solar energy to heat energy
2. kinetic energy (energy of motion) to heat energy
3. electrical energy to heat energy

---

## 13 The Heat is On

▶ **Real-World Question**
How can different types of energy be transformed into thermal energy?

**Possible Materials**
- lamp
- incandescent light bulb
- black construction paper or cloth

▶ **Procedure**
1. Feel the temperature of a black sheet of paper. Lay the paper in direct sunlight, wait 10 min, and observe how it feels.
2. Rub the palms of your hands together quickly for 10 s and observe how they feel.
3. Switch on a lamp that has a bare light bulb. *Without touching the lightbulb,* cup your hand 2 cm above the bulb for 30 s and observe what you feel.

▶ **Conclude and Apply**
1. Infer the type of energy transformation that happened on the paper.
2. Infer the type of energy transformation that happened between the palms of your hands.
3. Infer the type of energy transformation that happened to the lightbulb.

## 14 Disappearing Dots

▶ **Real-World Question**
Do your eyes have a blind spot?

**Possible Materials**
- white paper
- metric ruler
- colored pencils

▶ **Procedure**
1. Hold a sheet of white paper horizontally. Near the left edge of the paper, draw a black dot about 0.5 cm in diameter.
2. Draw a red dot 5 cm to the right of the black dot.
3. Hold the paper out in front of you, close your left eye, and look at the black dot with your right eye. Slowly move the paper toward you and observe what happens to the red dot.
4. Draw a blue dot 10 cm to the right of the black dot and a green dot 15 cm from the black dot.
5. Hold the paper out at arm's length, close your left eye, and look at the black dot with your right eye. Slowly move the paper toward you and observe what happens to the dots.

▶ **Conclude and Apply**
1. Describe what happened to the red, blue, and green dots as you moved the paper toward you.
2. The optic nerve carries visual images to the brain, and it is attached to the retina in your eye. Infer why the dots disappeared.

**702 STUDENT RESOURCES**

**Adult supervision required for all labs.**

These labs are available at in7.msscience.com.

---

## 14 Disappearing Dots

**Time Required** 20 minutes

**Materials** Students can use any type of pen or pencil for this lab, but colored pencils help them keep track of the disappearing dots.

**Safety Precaution** Students should do this lab while seated to prevent becoming dizzy and falling.

**Teaching Strategy** Show students a labeled diagram of the human eye and point out the location where the optic nerve attaches to the retina.

### Conclude and Apply
1. The green dot will disappear when the paper is about 60 cm away and then reappear as the paper moves closer. The blue dot will disappear at about 40 cm and the red dot at about 20 cm.
2. There are no nerve cells where the optic nerve attaches to the retina. Without light striking this region, no image is visible at that small spot.

**15** Pattern Counting

*Real-World Question*

What pattern is used to count in binary?

*Procedure*

1. Study the pattern used for counting in 4-bit binary.
2. Describe the pattern in your own words.
3. To test your understanding of the pattern, close the book and write the counting pattern from 0–15 by using your notes.

*Conclude and Apply*

1. Can this pattern continue past 15? Explain.
2. Develop a pattern to count to 32.

| Decimal Number | Binary Number | Decimal Number | Binary Number |
|---|---|---|---|
| 0 | 0000 | 8 | 1000 |
| 1 | 0001 | 9 | 1001 |
| 2 | 0010 | 10 | 1010 |
| 3 | 0011 | 11 | 1011 |
| 4 | 0100 | 12 | 1100 |
| 5 | 0101 | 13 | 1101 |
| 6 | 0110 | 14 | 1110 |
| 7 | 0111 | 15 | 1111 |

Extra Try at Home Labs

**16** Big Stars

*Real-World Question*

How does the size of Earth compare to the size of stars?

**Possible Materials**
- metric ruler
- meterstick
- tape measure
- masking tape
- white paper
- black marker

*Procedure*

1. Tape a sheet of white paper to the floor.
2. Draw a dot in the center to the paper. Measure a 1-mm distance from the dot and draw a second dot. This distance represents the diameter of Earth.
3. Measure a distance of 10.9 cm from the first dot and draw a third dot. This distance represents the diameter of the Sun.
4. Measure a distance of 5 m from the first dot and mark the location on the floor with a piece of masking tape. This distance represents the average diameter of a red giant star.
5. Measure a distance of 30 m from the first dot and mark the location on the floor with a piece of masking tape. This distance represents the diameter of the supergiant star Antares.

*Conclude and Apply*

1. The diameter of Earth is 12,756 km. What is the diameter of the Sun?
2. What is the diameter of an average red giant?

Adult supervision required for all labs.

**15** Pattern Counting

**Time Required** one class period

**Teaching Strategies**
- Have students study the pattern individually and write down their answers. Then have them work in groups and discuss their thoughts.
- You could make a quiz game with two teams and test the students' knowledge of binary.
- There are many online resources about binary counting. You could make a research project of having them research hexadecimal and octadecimal counting.

**Conclude and Apply**

1. No. All of the combinations of four digits have already been used.
2. Any reasonable system should be accepted.

**16** Big Stars

**Time Required** 25 minutes

**Materials** Instead of using masking tape, tennis balls or small orange cones can be used to mark the comparative diameters of the giant stars.

**Safety Precaution** Students should use the metersticks with care.

**Teaching Strategy** Plan to complete this lab outside or in a gymnasium if you want students to complete the final measurement.

**Conclude and Apply**

1. 1,390,404 km
2. 63,780,000 km

## 17 Panning Minerals

**Time Required** one period to pan the sand; an additional one-to-two periods to examine the black sand

### Materials
- The sand should be mostly free of silt, clay, and organic matter.
- Clean sand can be collected at many locations. Clean, natural sand also can be obtained from some hardware suppliers, concrete plants, and aggregate pits.

### Safety Precaution
To ensure safety, obtain the sand for the students in advance.

### Teaching Strategies
- You might want to practice the panning technique in advance.
- Inform students that the black sand appears black because it contains a high percentage of dark minerals, such as magnetite, ilmenite, pyroxene, and hornblende.

### Conclude and Apply
1. The sand grains that were left are denser than the sand grains that washed over the pan's rim.
2. Students should see many well-formed crystals with a variety of shapes, sizes, and colors. If very lucky, someone might find a fleck of gold.
3. Grains of magnetite were attracted to the magnet.

---

# Extra Try at Home Labs

## 17 Panning Minerals

▶ **Real-World Question**
How can minerals be separated from sand?

**Possible Materials**
- large, aluminum pie pan
- gallon jug filled with water
- empty gallon jug
- clean sand
- funnel
- coffee filter
- squirt bottle of water
- magnifying lens
- white paper
- hand magnet

▶ **Procedure**
1. Conduct this lab outdoors.
2. Line the funnel with a coffee filter. Insert the funnel stem into an empty gallon jug.
3. Add a small amount of sand to the pie pan. Add some water and swirl the pan.
4. Continue to shake and swirl the pan until only black sand is left in the pan.
5. Use the squirt bottle to wash the black sand into the coffee filter. Repeat steps 3–5 until you have a good sample of black sand.
6. Let the black sand dry. Then observe it with a magnifying lens. Test the sand with a magnet.

▶ **Conclude and Apply**
1. Why was black sand left in the gold pan after swirling it?
2. Describe how the sand looked under the lens. Did you see any well-shaped crystals?
3. What happened when you tested the sand with a magnet? Explain.

## 18 Changing Rocks

▶ **Real-World Question**
How can the change of metamorphic rock be modeled?

**Possible Materials**
- soil
- water
- measuring cup
- bowl
- spoon
- shale sample
- slate sample
- schist sample
- gneiss sample

▶ **Procedure**
1. Mix equal parts of soil and water in a measuring cup or bowl. Stir the mixture until you make mud.

2. Place the bowl of mud on the table near the top edge.
3. Lay a sample of shale below the mud, a sample of slate below the shale, a sample of schist below the slate, a sample of gneiss below the schist.
4. Observe the different stages of sedimentary and metamorphic rocks that are formed by heat and pressure over long periods of time.

▶ **Conclude and Apply**
1. Identify which rock sample(s) are sedimentary rock and which sample(s) are metamorphic rock.
2. Infer which type of rock is found at the greatest depth beneath the surface of Earth.

Adult supervision required for all labs.

**These labs are available at** in7.msscience.com.

---

## 18 Changing Rocks

**Time required** 30 minutes

**Materials** Save class time by preparing the mud beforehand.

**Safety Precaution** Students should wear aprons.

**Teaching Strategy** Have students hypothesize the approximate depth beneath Earth's surface where each type of rock is found. shale—5 km below; slate—10 km below; schist—15 km below; gneiss—20 km below; and hornfel—25 km below

### Conclude and Apply
1. Shale is a sedimentary rock; all other samples are metamorphic rocks.
2. hornfel

### 19 Continental Movement

**Real-World Question**

How far will the continents move in the future?

**Possible Materials**
- meterstick or metric tape measure
- masking tape or sidewalk chalk
- tennis balls

**Procedure**

1. Go outside and measure a 1-cm distance. Mark this distance with two pieces of tape. This is the distance traveled by the slowest plate in one year.
2. Measure a 2.5-cm distance and mark this distance with two pieces of tape. This is the distance traveled by the North American plate in one year.
3. Measure a 15-cm distance and mark this distance with two pieces of tape. This is the distance traveled by the fastest plate in one year.
4. Measure the distances the slowest plate, North American plate, and fastest plate will travel in the next 50 years. Use tennis balls to mark your distances.
5. Measure the distances these three plates will move in the next 300 years. Use tennis balls to mark your distances.

**Conclude and Apply**

1. How many centimeters will these three plates travel in the next 50 years?
2. How many meters will these three plates travel in the next 300 years?

### 20 Earth's Layers

**Real-World Question**

What is the relative thickness of Earth's different layers?

**Possible Materials**
- meterstick
- masking tape

**Procedure**

1. Use a piece of masking tape to mark a spot on the floor. This spot represents the center of Earth.
2. Measure a distance of 1.22 m from the first tape mark and place a second piece of tape.
3. From the second piece of tape, measure a distance of 2.27 m and place a third piece of tape.
4. From the third piece of tape, measure a distance of 2.89 m and place a fourth piece of tape.
5. From the fourth piece of tape, make two measurements. Measure a distance of 0.005 m and a distance of 0.06 m. Place two more pieces of tape to mark these two distances.

**Conclude and Apply**

1. Identify the name of each of the levels you drew.
2. Calculate the scale you used for the thickness of your earth layers.

**Extra Try at Home Labs**

Adult supervision required for all labs.

### 19 Continental Movement

**Time Required** 25 minutes

**Materials**
- Students can complete this lab outside using sidewalk chalk on an asphalt or concrete surface.
- For the longer distances, students can use tennis balls or small orange cones as markers.

**Safety Precautions**
- Caution students to use the metersticks carefully.
- Be certain measurements do not take them near streets or traffic.

**Teaching Strategy** Have students complete this lab outside in an open space where they can measure a 45-m distance.

**Conclude and Apply**

1. 50 cm, 125 cm, 750 cm
2. 3 m, 7.5 m, 45 m

### 20 Earth's Layers

**Time Required** 15 minutes

**Materials** Students can also complete this lab outside on an asphalt or cement surface using sidewalk chalk.

**Safety Precaution** Caution students to handle the metersticks with care.

**Teaching Strategies**
- Clear away floor space in your classroom to complete the lab.
- Instruct students to make their measurements in a straight line.
- Explain to students that earth's crust varies from 5–60 km thick.

**Conclude and Apply**

1. In order, the levels are inner core, outer core, mantle, crust.
2. 1 cm: 10 km

## 21 Getting Warmer

**Time Required** 30 minutes

**Materials** Students can collect moist grass clippings to use instead of leaf litter.

### Safety Precautions
- Students should wash their hands thoroughly after handling the leaf litter.
- Use only nonmercury thermometers.

### Teaching Strategy
This lab works best on a hot sunny day. Students can also compare the temperature inside a forest with the temperature of asphalt in direct sunlight.

### Conclude and Apply
1. Answers will vary, but on hot days, the temperatures of the artificial surfaces can be up to 10°C higher than the temperature of the grass and leaf litter. Typical temperature differences range between 3–5°C.
2. The heat-island effect measures the temperature increase of artificial, paved surfaces.

---

## 21 Getting Warmer

▶ **Real-World Question**
How do different surfaces affect temperature?

**Possible Materials**
- thermometer
- moist leaf litter
- large self-sealing bag
- stopwatch or watch

▶ **Procedure**
1. Collect moist leaf litter in a large self-sealing bag.
2. Pile the leaf litter on a patch of grass that is exposed to direct sunlight.
3. Set the thermometer in the center of the leaf litter, wait 3 min, and measure the temperature.
4. Place the thermometer on the grass in direct sunlight, wait 3 min, and measure the temperature.
5. Place the thermometer on a cement surface in direct sunlight, wait 3 min, and measure the temperature.
6. Place the thermometer on an asphalt surface in direct sunlight, wait 3 min, and measure the temperature.

▶ **Conclude and Apply**
1. Compare the temperatures of the different surfaces.
2. Explain how you measured the heat-island effect.

## 22 Making Burrows

▶ **Real-World Question**
How does burrowing affect sediment layers?

**Possible Materials**
- clear-glass bowl
- white flour
- colored gelatin powder (3 packages)
- paintbrush
- pencil

▶ **Procedure**
1. Add 3 cm of white flour to the bowl. Flatten the top of the flour layer.
2. Carefully sprinkle gelatin powder over the flour to form a colored layer about 0.25 cm thick.
3. The two layers represent two different layers of sediment.
4. Use a paintbrush or pencil to make "burrows" in the "sediment."
5. Make sure to make some of the burrows at the edge of the bowl so that you can see how it affects the sediment.
6. Continue to make more burrows and observe the effect on the two layers.

▶ **Conclude and Apply**
1. How did the two layers of powder change as you continued to make burrows?
2. Were the "trace fossils" easy to recognize at first? How about after a lot of burrowing?
3. How do you think burrowing animals affect layers of sediment on the ocean floor? How could this burrowing be recognized in rock?

Adult supervision required for all labs.

These labs are available at in7.msscience.com

---

## 22 Making Burrows

**Time Required** 30 minutes

**Materials** A bright color gelatin works best for the top layer.

**Safety Precaution** Caution students not to mix the powder too vigorously.

### Teaching Strategy
Remind students that many marine organisms burrow into the sediment and that these burrows are a type of trace fossil.

### Conclude and Apply
1. The two layers became more mixed as more burrows were made.
2. At first, distinct burrows are visible. After a lot of burrowing, individual burrows no longer can be discerned. The layers have a mottled appearance.
3. Burrowing animals mix thin layers of sediment on the ocean floor. This burrowing can be recognized in rock, such as limestone. The amount of mottling indicates how intensely the sediment was burrowed.

# Computer Skills

People who study science rely on computers, like the one in **Figure 16,** to record and store data and to analyze results from investigations. Whether you work in a laboratory or just need to write a lab report with tables, good computer skills are a necessity.

Using the computer comes with responsibility. Issues of ownership, security, and privacy can arise. Remember, if you did not author the information you are using, you must provide a source for your information. Also, anything on a computer can be accessed by others. Do not put anything on the computer that you would not want everyone to know. To add more security to your work, use a password.

## Use a Word Processing Program

A computer program that allows you to type your information, change it as many times as you need to, and then print it out is called a word processing program. Word processing programs also can be used to make tables.

**Figure 16** A computer will make reports neater and more professional looking.

**Learn the Skill** To start your word processing program, a blank document, sometimes called "Document 1," appears on the screen. To begin, start typing. To create a new document, click the *New* button on the standard tool bar. These tips will help you format the document.

- The program will automatically move to the next line; press *Enter* if you wish to start a new paragraph.
- Symbols, called non-printing characters, can be hidden by clicking the *Show/Hide* button on your toolbar.
- To insert text, move the cursor to the point where you want the insertion to go, click on the mouse once, and type the text.
- To move several lines of text, select the text and click the *Cut* button on your toolbar. Then position your cursor in the location that you want to move the cut text and click *Paste.* If you move to the wrong place, click *Undo.*
- The spell check feature does not catch words that are misspelled to look like other words, like "cold" instead of "gold." Always reread your document to catch all spelling mistakes.
- To learn about other word processing methods, read the user's manual or click on the *Help* button.
- You can integrate databases, graphics, and spreadsheets into documents by copying from another program and pasting it into your document, or by using desktop publishing (DTP). DTP software allows you to put text and graphics together to finish your document with a professional look. This software varies in how it is used and its capabilities.

## Use a Database

A collection of facts stored in a computer and sorted into different fields is called a database. A database can be reorganized in any way that suits your needs.

**Learn the Skill** A computer program that allows you to create your own database is a database management system (DBMS). It allows you to add, delete, or change information. Take time to get to know the features of your database software.

- Determine what facts you would like to include and research to collect your information.
- Determine how you want to organize the information.
- Follow the instructions for your particular DBMS to set up fields. Then enter each item of data in the appropriate field.
- Follow the instructions to sort the information in order of importance.
- Evaluate the information in your database, and add, delete, or change as necessary.

## Use the Internet

The Internet is a global network of computers where information is stored and shared. To use the Internet, like the students in **Figure 17,** you need a modem to connect your computer to a phone line and an Internet Service Provider account.

**Learn the Skill** To access internet sites and information, use a "Web browser," which lets you view and explore pages on the World Wide Web. Each page is its own site, and each site has its own address, called a URL. Once you have found a Web browser, follow these steps for a search (this also is how you search a database).

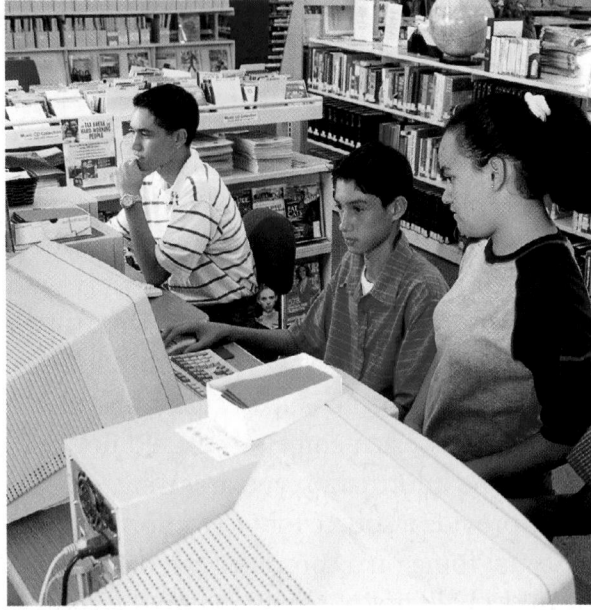

**Figure 17** The Internet allows you to search a global network for a variety of information.

- Be as specific as possible. If you know you want to research "gold," don't type in "elements." Keep narrowing your search until you find what you want.
- Web sites that end in *.com* are commercial Web sites; *.org, .edu,* and *.gov* are non-profit, educational, or government Web sites.
- Electronic encyclopedias, almanacs, indexes, and catalogs will help locate and select relevant information.
- Develop a "home page" with relative ease. When developing a Web site, NEVER post pictures or disclose personal information such as location, names, or phone numbers. Your school or community usually can host your Web site. A basic understanding of HTML (hypertext mark-up language), the language of Web sites, is necessary. Software that creates HTML code is called authoring software, and can be downloaded free from many Web sites. This software allows text and pictures to be arranged as the software is writing the HTML code.

## Use a Spreadsheet

A spreadsheet, shown in **Figure 18,** can perform mathematical functions with any data arranged in columns and rows. By entering a simple equation into a cell, the program can perform operations in specific cells, rows, or columns.

**Learn the Skill** Each column (vertical) is assigned a letter, and each row (horizontal) is assigned a number. Each point where a row and column intersect is called a cell, and is labeled according to where it is located— Column A, Row 1 (A1).

- Decide how to organize the data, and enter it in the correct row or column.
- Spreadsheets can use standard formulas or formulas can be customized to calculate cells.
- To make a change, click on a cell to make it activate, and enter the edited data or formula.
- Spreadsheets also can display your results in graphs. Choose the style of graph that best represents the data.

**Figure 18** A spreadsheet allows you to perform mathematical operations on your data.

## Use Graphics Software

Adding pictures, called graphics, to your documents is one way to make your documents more meaningful and exciting. This software adds, edits, and even constructs graphics. There is a variety of graphics software programs. The tools used for drawing can be a mouse, keyboard, or other specialized devices. Some graphics programs are simple. Others are complicated, called computer-aided design (CAD) software.

**Learn the Skill** It is important to have an understanding of the graphics software being used before starting. The better the software is understood, the better the results. The graphics can be placed in a word-processing document.

- Clip art can be found on a variety of internet sites, and on CDs. These images can be copied and pasted into your document.
- When beginning, try editing existing drawings, then work up to creating drawings.
- The images are made of tiny rectangles of color called pixels. Each pixel can be altered.
- Digital photography is another way to add images. The photographs in the memory of a digital camera can be downloaded into a computer, then edited and added to the document.
- Graphics software also can allow animation. The software allows drawings to have the appearance of movement by connecting basic drawings automatically. This is called in-betweening, or tweening.
- Remember to save often.

# Presentation Skills

## Develop Multimedia Presentations

Most presentations are more dynamic if they include diagrams, photographs, videos, or sound recordings, like the one shown in **Figure 19.** A multimedia presentation involves using stereos, overhead projectors, televisions, computers, and more.

**Learn the Skill** Decide the main points of your presentation, and what types of media would best illustrate those points.

- Make sure you know how to use the equipment you are working with.
- Practice the presentation using the equipment several times.
- Enlist the help of a classmate to push play or turn lights out for you. Be sure to practice your presentation with him or her.
- If possible, set up all of the equipment ahead of time, and make sure everything is working properly.

**Figure 19** These students are engaging the audience using a variety of tools.

## Computer Presentations

There are many different interactive computer programs that you can use to enhance your presentation. Most computers have a compact disc (CD) drive that can play both CDs and digital video discs (DVDs). Also, there is hardware to connect a regular CD, DVD, or VCR. These tools will enhance your presentation.

Another method of using the computer to aid in your presentation is to develop a slide show using a computer program. This can allow movement of visuals at the presenter's pace, and can allow for visuals to build on one another.

**Learn the Skill** In order to create multimedia presentations on a computer, you need to have certain tools. These may include traditional graphic tools and drawing programs, animation programs, and authoring systems that tie everything together. Your computer will tell you which tools it supports. The most important step is to learn about the tools that you will be using.

- Often, color and strong images will convey a point better than words alone. Use the best methods available to convey your point.
- As with other presentations, practice many times.
- Practice your presentation with the tools you and any assistants will be using.
- Maintain eye contact with the audience. The purpose of using the computer is not to prompt the presenter, but to help the audience understand the points of the presentation.

# Math Review

## Use Fractions

A fraction compares a part to a whole. In the fraction $\frac{2}{3}$, the 2 represents the part and is the numerator. The 3 represents the whole and is the denominator.

**Reduce Fractions** To reduce a fraction, you must find the largest factor that is common to both the numerator and the denominator, the greatest common factor (GCF). Divide both numbers by the GCF. The fraction has then been reduced, or it is in its simplest form.

**Example** Twelve of the 20 chemicals in the science lab are in powder form. What fraction of the chemicals used in the lab are in powder form?

**Step 1** Write the fraction.

$$\frac{\text{part}}{\text{whole}} = \frac{12}{20}$$

**Step 2** To find the GCF of the numerator and denominator, list all of the factors of each number.

Factors of 12: 1, 2, 3, 4, 6, 12 (the numbers that divide evenly into 12)
Factors of 20: 1, 2, 4, 5, 10, 20 (the numbers that divide evenly into 20)

**Step 3** List the common factors.
1, 2, 4.

**Step 4** Choose the greatest factor in the list.
The GCF of 12 and 20 is 4.

**Step 5** Divide the numerator and denominator by the GCF.

$$\frac{12 \div 4}{20 \div 4} = \frac{3}{5}$$

In the lab, $\frac{3}{5}$ of the chemicals are in powder form.

**Practice Problem** At an amusement park, 66 of 90 rides have a height restriction. What fraction of the rides, in its simplest form, has a height restriction?

**Add and Subtract Fractions** To add or subtract fractions with the same denominator, add or subtract the numerators and write the sum or difference over the denominator. After finding the sum or difference, find the simplest form for your fraction.

**Example 1** In the forest outside your house, $\frac{1}{8}$ of the animals are rabbits, $\frac{3}{8}$ are squirrels, and the remainder are birds and insects. How many are mammals?

**Step 1** Add the numerators.

$$\frac{1}{8} + \frac{3}{8} = \frac{(1+3)}{8} = \frac{4}{8}$$

**Step 2** Find the GCF.

$$\frac{4}{8} \text{ (GCF, 4)}$$

**Step 3** Divide the numerator and denominator by the GCF.

$$\frac{4}{4} = 1, \ \frac{8}{4} = 2$$

$\frac{1}{2}$ of the animals are mammals.

**Example 2** If $\frac{7}{16}$ of the Earth is covered by freshwater, and $\frac{1}{16}$ of that is in glaciers, how much freshwater is not frozen?

**Step 1** Subtract the numerators.

$$\frac{7}{16} - \frac{1}{16} = \frac{(7-1)}{16} = \frac{6}{16}$$

**Step 2** Find the GCF.

$$\frac{6}{16} \text{ (GCF, 2)}$$

**Step 3** Divide the numerator and denominator by the GCF.

$$\frac{6}{2} = 3, \ \frac{16}{2} = 8$$

$\frac{3}{8}$ of the freshwater is not frozen.

**Practice Problem** A bicycle rider is going 15 km/h for $\frac{4}{9}$ of his ride, 10 km/h for $\frac{2}{9}$ of his ride, and 8 km/h for the remainder of the ride. How much of his ride is he going over 8 km/h?

## Reduce Fractions

$$\frac{66 \div 6}{90 \div 6} = \frac{11}{15}$$

## Add and Subtract Fractions

$$\frac{4}{9} + \frac{2}{9} = \frac{6}{9}$$
$$\frac{6 \div 3}{9 \div 3} = \frac{2}{3}$$

## Unlike Denominators

**Problem 1**

$1 \times 5 = 5, 8 \times 5 = 40$

$1 \times 4 = 4, 10 \times 4 = 40$

$\dfrac{5}{40} + \dfrac{4}{40} = \dfrac{9}{40}$

**Problem 2**

If $\dfrac{7}{10}$ are involuntary, the remainder are voluntary.

$\dfrac{10}{10} - \dfrac{7}{10} = \dfrac{3}{10}$

**Unlike Denominators** To add or subtract fractions with unlike denominators, first find the least common denominator (LCD). This is the smallest number that is a common multiple of both denominators. Rename each fraction with the LCD, and then add or subtract. Find the simplest form if necessary.

**Example 1** A chemist makes a paste that is $\dfrac{1}{2}$ table salt (NaCl), $\dfrac{1}{3}$ sugar ($C_6H_{12}O_6$), and the rest water ($H_2O$). How much of the paste is a solid?

**Step 1** Find the LCD of the fractions.

$\dfrac{1}{2} + \dfrac{1}{3}$  (LCD, 6)

**Step 2** Rename each numerator and each denominator with the LCD.

$1 \times 3 = 3, \quad 2 \times 3 = 6$

$1 \times 2 = 2, \quad 3 \times 2 = 6$

**Step 3** Add the numerators.

$\dfrac{3}{6} + \dfrac{2}{6} = \dfrac{(3+2)}{6} = \dfrac{5}{6}$

$\dfrac{5}{6}$ of the paste is a solid.

**Example 2** The average precipitation in Grand Junction, CO, is $\dfrac{7}{10}$ inch in November, and $\dfrac{3}{5}$ inch in December. What is the total average precipitation?

**Step 1** Find the LCD of the fractions.

$\dfrac{7}{10} + \dfrac{3}{5}$  (LCD, 10)

**Step 2** Rename each numerator and each denominator with the LCD.

$7 \times 1 = 7, \quad 10 \times 1 = 10$

$3 \times 2 = 6, \quad 5 \times 2 = 10$

**Step 3** Add the numerators.

$\dfrac{7}{10} + \dfrac{6}{10} = \dfrac{(7+6)}{10} = \dfrac{13}{10}$

$\dfrac{13}{10}$ inches total precipitation, or $1\dfrac{3}{10}$ inches.

**Practice Problem** On an electric bill, about $\dfrac{1}{8}$ of the energy is from solar energy and about $\dfrac{1}{10}$ is from wind power. How much of the total bill is from solar energy and wind power combined?

**Example 3** In your body, $\dfrac{7}{10}$ of your muscle contractions are involuntary (cardiac and smooth muscle tissue). Smooth muscle makes $\dfrac{3}{15}$ of your muscle contractions. How many of your muscle contractions are made by cardiac muscle?

**Step 1** Find the LCD of the fractions.

$\dfrac{7}{10} - \dfrac{3}{15}$  (LCD, 30)

**Step 2** Rename each numerator and each denominator with the LCD.

$7 \times 3 = 21, \quad 10 \times 3 = 30$

$3 \times 2 = 6, \quad 15 \times 2 = 30$

**Step 3** Subtract the numerators.

$\dfrac{21}{30} - \dfrac{6}{30} = \dfrac{(21-6)}{30} = \dfrac{15}{30}$

**Step 4** Find the GCF.

$\dfrac{15}{30}$  (GCF, 15)

$\dfrac{1}{2}$

$\dfrac{1}{2}$ of all muscle contractions are cardiac muscle.

**Example 4** Tony wants to make cookies that call for $\dfrac{3}{4}$ of a cup of flour, but he only has $\dfrac{1}{3}$ of a cup. How much more flour does he need?

**Step 1** Find the LCD of the fractions.

$\dfrac{3}{4} - \dfrac{1}{3}$  (LCD, 12)

**Step 2** Rename each numerator and each denominator with the LCD.

$3 \times 3 = 9, \quad 4 \times 3 = 12$

$1 \times 4 = 4, \quad 3 \times 4 = 12$

**Step 3** Subtract the numerators.

$\dfrac{9}{12} - \dfrac{4}{12} = \dfrac{(9-4)}{12} = \dfrac{5}{12}$

$\dfrac{5}{12}$ of a cup of flour.

**Practice Problem** Using the information provided to you in Example 3 above, determine how many muscle contractions are voluntary (skeletal muscle).

**Multiply Fractions** To multiply with fractions, multiply the numerators and multiply the denominators. Find the simplest form if necessary.

**Example** Multiply $\frac{3}{5}$ by $\frac{1}{3}$.

**Step 1** Multiply the numerators and denominators.

$$\frac{3}{5} \times \frac{1}{3} = \frac{(3 \times 1)}{(5 \times 3)} = \frac{3}{15}$$

**Step 2** Find the GCF.

$$\frac{3}{15} \quad (\text{GCF, 3})$$

**Step 3** Divide the numerator and denominator by the GCF.

$$\frac{3}{3} = 1, \quad \frac{15}{3} = 5$$

$$\frac{1}{5}$$

$\frac{3}{5}$ multiplied by $\frac{1}{3}$ is $\frac{1}{5}$.

**Practice Problem** Multiply $\frac{3}{14}$ by $\frac{5}{16}$.

**Find a Reciprocal** Two numbers whose product is 1 are called multiplicative inverses, or reciprocals.

**Example** Find the reciprocal of $\frac{3}{8}$.

**Step 1** Inverse the fraction by putting the denominator on top and the numerator on the bottom.

$$\frac{8}{3}$$

The reciprocal of $\frac{3}{8}$ is $\frac{8}{3}$.

**Practice Problem** Find the reciprocal of $\frac{4}{9}$.

**Divide Fractions** To divide one fraction by another fraction, multiply the dividend by the reciprocal of the divisor. Find the simplest form if necessary.

**Example 1** Divide $\frac{1}{9}$ by $\frac{1}{3}$.

**Step 1** Find the reciprocal of the divisor.

The reciprocal of $\frac{1}{3}$ is $\frac{3}{1}$.

**Step 2** Multiply the dividend by the reciprocal of the divisor.

$$\frac{\frac{1}{9}}{\frac{1}{3}} = \frac{1}{9} \times \frac{3}{1} = \frac{(1 \times 3)}{(9 \times 1)} = \frac{3}{9}$$

**Step 3** Find the GCF.

$$\frac{3}{9} \quad (\text{GCF, 3})$$

**Step 4** Divide the numerator and denominator by the GCF.

$$\frac{3}{3} = 1, \quad \frac{9}{3} = 3$$

$$\frac{1}{3}$$

$\frac{1}{9}$ divided by $\frac{1}{3}$ is $\frac{1}{3}$.

**Example 2** Divide $\frac{3}{5}$ by $\frac{1}{4}$.

**Step 1** Find the reciprocal of the divisor.

The reciprocal of $\frac{1}{4}$ is $\frac{4}{1}$.

**Step 2** Multiply the dividend by the reciprocal of the divisor.

$$\frac{\frac{3}{5}}{\frac{1}{4}} = \frac{3}{5} \times \frac{4}{1} = \frac{(3 \times 4)}{(5 \times 1)} = \frac{12}{5}$$

$\frac{3}{5}$ divided by $\frac{1}{4}$ is $\frac{12}{5}$ or $2\frac{2}{5}$.

**Practice Problem** Divide $\frac{3}{11}$ by $\frac{7}{10}$.

**Multiply Fractions**

$$\frac{3}{14} \times \frac{5}{16} = \frac{(3 \times 5)}{(14 \times 16)} = \frac{15}{224}$$

**Find a Reciprocal**

$$\frac{9}{4}$$

**Divide Fractions**

The reciprocal of $\frac{7}{10}$ is $\frac{10}{7}$.

$$\frac{3}{11} \times \frac{10}{7} = \frac{(3 \times 10)}{(11 \times 7)} = \frac{30}{77}$$

Math Skill Handbook

Math Skill Handbook

## Use Ratios

$$\frac{100\ cm}{144\ cm} = \frac{100 \div 4}{144 \div 4} = \frac{25}{36}$$

25:36

## Add or Subtract Decimals

$$\begin{array}{r} 1 \\ 1.245 \\ + 3.842 \\ \hline 5.087 \end{array}$$

## Use Ratios

When you compare two numbers by division, you are using a ratio. Ratios can be written 3 to 5, 3:5, or $\frac{3}{5}$. Ratios, like fractions, also can be written in simplest form.

Ratios can represent probabilities, also called odds. This is a ratio that compares the number of ways a certain outcome occurs to the number of outcomes. For example, if you flip a coin 100 times, what are the odds that it will come up heads? There are two possible outcomes, heads or tails, so the odds of coming up heads are 50:100. Another way to say this is that 50 out of 100 times the coin will come up heads. In its simplest form, the ratio is 1:2.

**Example 1** A chemical solution contains 40 g of salt and 64 g of baking soda. What is the ratio of salt to baking soda as a fraction in simplest form?

**Step 1** Write the ratio as a fraction.
$$\frac{salt}{baking\ soda} = \frac{40}{64}$$

**Step 2** Express the fraction in simplest form.
The GCF of 40 and 64 is 8.
$$\frac{40}{64} = \frac{40 \div 8}{64 \div 8} = \frac{5}{8}$$

The ratio of salt to baking soda in the sample is 5:8.

**Example 2** Sean rolls a 6-sided die 6 times. What are the odds that the side with a 3 will show?

**Step 1** Write the ratio as a fraction.
$$\frac{number\ of\ sides\ with\ a\ 3}{number\ of\ sides} = \frac{1}{6}$$

**Step 2** Multiply by the number of attempts.
$$\frac{1}{6} \times 6\ attempts = \frac{6}{6}\ attempts = 1\ attempt$$

1 attempt out of 6 will show a 3.

**Practice Problem** Two metal rods measure 100 cm and 144 cm in length. What is the ratio of their lengths in simplest form?

## Use Decimals

A fraction with a denominator that is a power of ten can be written as a decimal. For example, 0.27 means $\frac{27}{100}$. The decimal point separates the ones place from the tenths place.

Any fraction can be written as a decimal using division. For example, the fraction $\frac{5}{8}$ can be written as a decimal by dividing 5 by 8. Written as a decimal, it is 0.625.

**Add or Subtract Decimals** When adding and subtracting decimals, line up the decimal points before carrying out the operation.

**Example 1** Find the sum of 47.68 and 7.80.

**Step 1** Line up the decimal places when you write the numbers.
$$\begin{array}{r} 47.68 \\ + 7.80 \\ \hline \end{array}$$

**Step 2** Add the decimals.
$$\begin{array}{r} 47.68 \\ + 7.80 \\ \hline 55.48 \end{array}$$

The sum of 47.68 and 7.80 is 55.48.

**Example 2** Find the difference of 42.17 and 15.85.

**Step 1** Line up the decimal places when you write the number.
$$\begin{array}{r} 42.17 \\ - 15.85 \\ \hline \end{array}$$

**Step 2** Subtract the decimals.
$$\begin{array}{r} 42.17 \\ - 15.85 \\ \hline 26.32 \end{array}$$

The difference of 42.17 and 15.85 is 26.32.

**Practice Problem** Find the sum of 1.245 and 3.842.

Math Skill Handbook

## Multiply Decimals

**Multiply Decimals** To multiply decimals, multiply the numbers like any other number, ignoring the decimal point. Count the decimal places in each factor. The product will have the same number of decimal places as the sum of the decimal places in the factors.

**Example** Multiply 2.4 by 5.9.

**Step 1** Multiply the factors like two whole numbers.

$$24 \times 59 = 1416$$

**Step 2** Find the sum of the number of decimal places in the factors. Each factor has one decimal place, for a sum of two decimal places.

**Step 3** The product will have two decimal places.

14.16

The product of 2.4 and 5.9 is 14.16.

**Practice Problem** Multiply 4.6 by 2.2.

**Divide Decimals** When dividing decimals, change the divisor to a whole number. To do this, multiply both the divisor and the dividend by the same power of ten. Then place the decimal point in the quotient directly above the decimal point in the dividend. Then divide as you do with whole numbers.

**Example** Divide 8.84 by 3.4.

**Step 1** Multiply both factors by 10.

$$3.4 \times 10 = 34, \ 8.84 \times 10 = 88.4$$

**Step 2** Divide 88.4 by 34.

```
        2.6
   34)88.4
     −68
      204
     −204
        0
```

8.84 divided by 3.4 is 2.6.

**Practice Problem** Divide 75.6 by 3.6.

## Use Proportions

An equation that shows that two ratios are equivalent is a proportion. The ratios $\frac{2}{4}$ and $\frac{5}{10}$ are equivalent, so they can be written as $\frac{2}{4} = \frac{5}{10}$. This equation is a proportion.

When two ratios form a proportion, the cross products are equal. To find the cross products in the proportion $\frac{2}{4} = \frac{5}{10}$, multiply the 2 and the 10, and the 4 and the 5. Therefore $2 \times 10 = 4 \times 5$, or $20 = 20$.

Because you know that both proportions are equal, you can use cross products to find a missing term in a proportion. This is known as solving the proportion.

**Example** The heights of a tree and a pole are proportional to the lengths of their shadows. The tree casts a shadow of 24 m when a 6-m pole casts a shadow of 4 m. What is the height of the tree?

**Step 1** Write a proportion.

$$\frac{\text{height of tree}}{\text{height of pole}} = \frac{\text{length of tree's shadow}}{\text{length of pole's shadow}}$$

**Step 2** Substitute the known values into the proportion. Let $h$ represent the unknown value, the height of the tree.

$$\frac{h}{6} = \frac{24}{4}$$

**Step 3** Find the cross products.

$$h \times 4 = 6 \times 24$$

**Step 4** Simplify the equation.

$$4h = 144$$

**Step 5** Divide each side by 4.

$$\frac{4h}{4} = \frac{144}{4}$$

$$h = 36$$

The height of the tree is 36 m.

**Practice Problem** The ratios of the weights of two objects on the Moon and on Earth are in proportion. A rock weighing 3 N on the Moon weighs 18 N on Earth. How much would a rock that weighs 5 N on the Moon weigh on Earth?

## Multiply Decimals

Multiply 4.6 and 2.2 by 10.

$$46 \times 22 = 1012$$

Each factor had one decimal place.

10.12

## Divide Decimals

Multiply both factors by 10.

Divide 756 by 36.

```
        21
   36)756
      72
      36
      36
       0
```

## Use Proportions

$$\frac{3}{18} = \frac{5}{w}$$

$$w \times 3 = 5 \times 18$$

$$\frac{3w}{3} = \frac{90}{3}$$

$$w = 30$$

Math Skill Handbook

## Use Percentages

The word *percent* means "out of one hundred." It is a ratio that compares a number to 100. Suppose you read that 77 percent of the Earth's surface is covered by water. That is the same as reading that the fraction of the Earth's surface covered by water is $\frac{77}{100}$. To express a fraction as a percent, first find the equivalent decimal for the fraction. Then, multiply the decimal by 100 and add the percent symbol.

**Example** Express $\frac{13}{20}$ as a percent.

**Step 1** Find the equivalent decimal for the fraction.

$$\begin{array}{r} 0.65 \\ 20\overline{)13.00} \\ \underline{12\,0} \\ 1\,00 \\ \underline{1\,00} \\ 0 \end{array}$$

**Step 2** Rewrite the fraction $\frac{13}{20}$ as 0.65.

**Step 3** Multiply 0.65 by 100 and add the % sign.

$$0.65 \times 100 = 65 = 65\%$$

So, $\frac{13}{20} = 65\%$.

This also can be solved as a proportion.

**Example** Express $\frac{13}{20}$ as a percent.

**Step 1** Write a proportion.

$$\frac{13}{20} = \frac{x}{100}$$

**Step 2** Find the cross products.

$$1300 = 20x$$

**Step 3** Divide each side by 20.

$$\frac{1300}{20} = \frac{20x}{20}$$
$$65\% = x$$

**Practice Problem** In one year, 73 of 365 days were rainy in one city. What percent of the days in that city were rainy?

## Solve One-Step Equations

A statement that two things are equal is an equation. For example, $A = B$ is an equation that states that $A$ is equal to $B$.

An equation is solved when a variable is replaced with a value that makes both sides of the equation equal. To make both sides equal the inverse operation is used. Addition and subtraction are inverses, and multiplication and division are inverses.

**Example 1** Solve the equation $x - 10 = 35$.

**Step 1** Find the solution by adding 10 to each side of the equation.

$$x - 10 = 35$$
$$x - 10 + 10 = 35 + 10$$
$$x = 45$$

**Step 2** Check the solution.

$$x - 10 = 35$$
$$45 - 10 = 35$$
$$35 = 35$$

Both sides of the equation are equal, so $x = 45$.

**Example 2** In the formula $a = bc$, find the value of $c$ if $a = 20$ and $b = 2$.

**Step 1** Rearrange the formula so the unknown value is by itself on one side of the equation by dividing both sides by $b$.

$$a = bc$$
$$\frac{a}{b} = \frac{bc}{b}$$
$$\frac{a}{b} = c$$

**Step 2** Replace the variables $a$ and $b$ with the values that are given.

$$\frac{a}{b} = c$$
$$\frac{20}{2} = c$$
$$10 = c$$

**Step 3** Check the solution.

$$a = bc$$
$$20 = 2 \times 10$$
$$20 = 20$$

Both sides of the equation are equal, so $c = 10$ is the solution when $a = 20$ and $b = 2$.

**Practice Problem** In the formula $h = gd$, find the value of $d$ if $g = 12.3$ and $h = 17.4$.

---

### Use Percentages

$$\frac{73}{365} = \frac{x}{100}$$
$$\frac{7300}{365} = \frac{365x}{365}$$
$$20\% = x$$

### Solve One-Step Equations

$$h = gd$$
$$\frac{17.4}{12.3} = \frac{12.3d}{12.3}$$
$$1.41 = d$$

## Use Statistics

The branch of mathematics that deals with collecting, analyzing, and presenting data is statistics. In statistics, there are three common ways to summarize data with a single number—the mean, the median, and the mode.

The **mean** of a set of data is the arithmetic average. It is found by adding the numbers in the data set and dividing by the number of items in the set.

The **median** is the middle number in a set of data when the data are arranged in numerical order. If there were an even number of data points, the median would be the mean of the two middle numbers.

The **mode** of a set of data is the number or item that appears most often.

Another number that often is used to describe a set of data is the range. The **range** is the difference between the largest number and the smallest number in a set of data.

A **frequency table** shows how many times each piece of data occurs, usually in a survey. **Table 2** below shows the results of a student survey on favorite color.

| Table 2 Student Color Choice | | |
|---|---|---|
| **Color** | **Tally** | **Frequency** |
| red | IIII | 4 |
| blue | HHt | 5 |
| black | II | 2 |
| green | III | 3 |
| purple | HHt II | 7 |
| yellow | HHt I | 6 |

Based on the frequency table data, which color is the favorite?

**Example** The speeds (in m/s) for a race car during five different time trials are 39, 37, 44, 36, and 44.

**To find the mean:**

**Step 1** Find the sum of the numbers.
$$39 + 37 + 44 + 36 + 44 = 200$$

**Step 2** Divide the sum by the number of items, which is 5.
$$200 \div 5 = 40$$

The mean is 40 m/s.

**To find the median:**

**Step 1** Arrange the measures from least to greatest.
36, 37, 39, 44, 44

**Step 2** Determine the middle measure.
36, 37, $\underline{39}$, 44, 44

The median is 39 m/s.

**To find the mode:**

**Step 1** Group the numbers that are the same together.
44, 44, 36, 37, 39

**Step 2** Determine the number that occurs most in the set.
$\underline{44, 44}$, 36, 37, 39

The mode is 44 m/s.

**To find the range:**

**Step 1** Arrange the measures from largest to smallest.
44, 44, 39, 37, 36

**Step 2** Determine the largest and smallest measures in the set.
$\underline{44}$, 44, 39, 37, $\underline{36}$

**Step 3** Find the difference between the largest and smallest measures.
$$44 - 36 = 8$$

The range is 8 m/s.

**Practice Problem** Find the mean, median, mode, and range for the data set 8, 4, 12, 8, 11, 14, 16.

## Use Statistics

**mean**
$$8 + 4 + 12 + 8 + 11 + 14 + 16 = 73$$
$$73 \div 7 = 10.4$$

**median**
4, 8, 8, $\underline{11}$, 12, 14, 16

**mode**
4, $\underline{8}$, $\underline{8}$, 11, 12, 14, 16

**range**
$\underline{4}$, 8, 8, 11, 12, 14, $\underline{16}$
$$16 - 4 = 12$$

## Perimeter

**Problem 1**

$P = 2(18\,m + 7\,m)$

$P = 2(25\,m)$

$P = 50\,m$

**Problem 2**

$P = 1.6\,cm + 2.4\,cm + 2.4\,cm$

$P = 6.4\,cm$

## Area of a Rectangle

$A = (4\,m \times 4\,m)$

$A = 16\,m^2$

## Area of a Triangle

$A = \frac{1}{2}(27\,cm \times 17\,cm)$

$A = \frac{1}{2}(459\,cm^2)$

$A = 229.5\,cm^2$

## Use Geometry

The branch of mathematics that deals with the measurement, properties, and relationships of points, lines, angles, surfaces, and solids is called geometry.

**Perimeter** The **perimeter** ($P$) is the distance around a geometric figure. To find the perimeter of a rectangle, add the length and width and multiply that sum by two, or $2(l + w)$. To find perimeters of irregular figures, add the length of the sides.

**Example 1** Find the perimeter of a rectangle that is 3 m long and 5 m wide.

**Step 1** You know that the perimeter is 2 times the sum of the width and length.

$P = 2(3\,m + 5\,m)$

**Step 2** Find the sum of the width and length.

$P = 2(8\,m)$

**Step 3** Multiply by 2.

$P = 16\,m$

The perimeter is 16 m.

**Example 2** Find the perimeter of a shape with sides measuring 2 cm, 5 cm, 6 cm, 3 cm.

**Step 1** You know that the perimeter is the sum of all the sides.

$P = 2 + 5 + 6 + 3$

**Step 2** Find the sum of the sides.

$P = 2 + 5 + 6 + 3$

$P = 16$

The perimeter is 16 cm.

**Practice Problem** Find the perimeter of a rectangle with a length of 18 m and a width of 7 m.

**Practice Problem** Find the perimeter of a triangle measuring 1.6 cm by 2.4 cm by 2.4 cm.

**Area of a Rectangle** The **area** ($A$) is the number of square units needed to cover a surface. To find the area of a rectangle, multiply the length times the width, or $l \times w$. When finding area, the units also are multiplied. Area is given in square units.

**Example** Find the area of a rectangle with a length of 1 cm and a width of 10 cm.

**Step 1** You know that the area is the length multiplied by the width.

$A = (1\,cm \times 10\,cm)$

**Step 2** Multiply the length by the width. Also multiply the units.

$A = 10\,cm^2$

The area is 10 cm².

**Practice Problem** Find the area of a square whose sides measure 4 m.

**Area of a Triangle** To find the area of a triangle, use the formula:

$$A = \frac{1}{2}(\text{base} \times \text{height})$$

The base of a triangle can be any of its sides. The height is the perpendicular distance from a base to the opposite endpoint, or vertex.

**Example** Find the area of a triangle with a base of 18 m and a height of 7 m.

**Step 1** You know that the area is $\frac{1}{2}$ the base times the height.

$A = \frac{1}{2}(18\,m \times 7\,m)$

**Step 2** Multiply $\frac{1}{2}$ by the product of $18 \times 7$. Multiply the units.

$A = \frac{1}{2}(126\,m^2)$

$A = 63\,m^2$

The area is 63 m².

**Practice Problem** Find the area of a triangle with a base of 27 cm and a height of 17 cm.

**Math Skill Handbook**

**Math Skill Handbook**

**Circumference of a Circle** The **diameter** (*d*) of a circle is the distance across the circle through its center, and the **radius** (*r*) is the distance from the center to any point on the circle. The radius is half of the diameter. The distance around the circle is called the **circumference** (C). The formula for finding the circumference is:

$$C = 2\pi r \ or \ C = \pi d$$

The circumference divided by the diameter is always equal to 3.1415926... This nonterminating and nonrepeating number is represented by the Greek letter $\pi$ (pi). An approximation often used for $\pi$ is 3.14.

**Example 1** Find the circumference of a circle with a radius of 3 m.

**Step 1** You know the formula for the circumference is 2 times the radius times $\pi$.
$$C = 2\pi(3)$$

**Step 2** Multiply 2 times the radius.
$$C = 6\pi$$

**Step 3** Multiply by $\pi$.
$$C = 19 \ m$$

The circumference is 19 m.

**Example 2** Find the circumference of a circle with a diameter of 24.0 cm.

**Step 1** You know the formula for the circumference is the diameter times $\pi$.
$$C = \pi(24.0)$$

**Step 2** Multiply the diameter by $\pi$.
$$C = 75.4 \ cm$$

The circumference is 75.4 cm.

**Practice Problem** Find the circumference of a circle with a radius of 19 cm.

**Area of a Circle** The formula for the area of a circle is:
$$A = \pi r^2$$

**Example 1** Find the area of a circle with a radius of 4.0 cm.

**Step 1** $A = \pi(4.0)^2$

**Step 2** Find the square of the radius.
$$A = 16\pi$$

**Step 3** Multiply the square of the radius by $\pi$.
$$A = 50 \ cm^2$$

The area of the circle is 50 cm$^2$.

**Example 2** Find the area of a circle with a radius of 225 m.

**Step 1** $A = \pi(225)^2$

**Step 2** Find the square of the radius.
$$A = 50625\pi$$

**Step 3** Multiply the square of the radius by $\pi$.
$$A = 158962.5$$

The area of the circle is 158,962 m$^2$.

**Example 3** Find the area of a circle whose diameter is 20.0 mm.

**Step 1** You know the formula for the area of a circle is the square of the radius times $\pi$, and that the radius is half of the diameter.
$$A = \pi\left(\frac{20.0}{2}\right)^2$$

**Step 2** Find the radius.
$$A = \pi(10.0)^2$$

**Step 3** Find the square of the radius.
$$A = 100\pi$$

**Step 4** Multiply the square of the radius by $\pi$.
$$A = 314 \ mm^2$$

The area is 314 mm$^2$.

**Practice Problem** Find the area of a circle with a radius of 16 m.

## Circumference of a Circle

$C = 2\pi r$
$C = 2\pi(19)$
$C = 38\pi$
$C = 119.3$

## Area of a Circle

$A = \pi r^2$
$A = \pi(16 \ m)^2$
$A = \pi \ 256 \ m^2$
$A = 803.8 \ m^2$

## Volume

**Problem 1**

$V = 8\,\text{m} \times 4\,\text{m} \times 4\,\text{m}$

$V = 128\,\text{m}^3$

**Problem 2**

$V = \pi r^2 \times \text{height}$

$V = \left[\pi\left(\frac{1}{2} \times 7\right)^2\right] \times 16$

$V = [\pi(3.5)^2] \times 16$

$V = [\pi(12.25)] \times 16$

$V = 38.46 \times 16$

$V = 615.36$

---

# Math Skill Handbook

**Volume**  The measure of space occupied by a solid is the **volume** ($V$). To find the volume of a rectangular solid multiply the length times width times height, or $V = l \times w \times h$. It is measured in cubic units, such as cubic centimeters ($\text{cm}^3$).

**Example**  Find the volume of a rectangular solid with a length of 2.0 m, a width of 4.0 m, and a height of 3.0 m.

**Step 1**  You know the formula for volume is the length times the width times the height.

$V = 2.0\,\text{m} \times 4.0\,\text{m} \times 3.0\,\text{m}$

**Step 2**  Multiply the length times the width times the height.

$V = 24\,\text{m}^3$

The volume is 24 $\text{m}^3$.

**Practice Problem**  Find the volume of a rectangular solid that is 8 m long, 4 m wide, and 4 m high.

To find the volume of other solids, multiply the area of the base times the height.

**Example 1**  Find the volume of a solid that has a triangular base with a length of 8.0 m and a height of 7.0 m. The height of the entire solid is 15.0 m.

**Step 1**  You know that the base is a triangle, and the area of a triangle is $\frac{1}{2}$ the base times the height, and the volume is the area of the base times the height.

$V = \left[\frac{1}{2}(b \times h)\right] \times 15$

**Step 2**  Find the area of the base.

$V = \left[\frac{1}{2}(8 \times 7)\right] \times 15$

$V = \left(\frac{1}{2} \times 56\right) \times 15$

**Step 3**  Multiply the area of the base by the height of the solid.

$V = 28 \times 15$

$V = 420\,\text{m}^3$

The volume is 420 $\text{m}^3$.

**Example 2**  Find the volume of a cylinder that has a base with a radius of 12.0 cm, and a height of 21.0 cm.

**Step 1**  You know that the base is a circle, and the area of a circle is the square of the radius times $\pi$, and the volume is the area of the base times the height.

$V = (\pi r^2) \times 21$

$V = (\pi 12^2) \times 21$

**Step 2**  Find the area of the base.

$V = 144\pi \times 21$

$V = 452 \times 21$

**Step 3**  Multiply the area of the base by the height of the solid.

$V = 9490\,\text{cm}^3$

The volume is 9490 $\text{cm}^3$.

**Example 3**  Find the volume of a cylinder that has a diameter of 15 mm and a height of 4.8 mm.

**Step 1**  You know that the base is a circle with an area equal to the square of the radius times $\pi$. The radius is one-half the diameter. The volume is the area of the base times the height.

$V = (\pi r^2) \times 4.8$

$V = \left[\pi\left(\frac{1}{2} \times 15\right)^2\right] \times 4.8$

$V = (\pi 7.5^2) \times 4.8$

**Step 2**  Find the area of the base.

$V = 56.25\pi \times 4.8$

$V = 176.63 \times 4.8$

**Step 3**  Multiply the area of the base by the height of the solid.

$V = 847.8$

The volume is 847.8 $\text{mm}^3$.

**Practice Problem**  Find the volume of a cylinder with a diameter of 7 cm in the base and a height of 16 cm.

# Science Applications

## Measure in SI

The metric system of measurement was developed in 1795. A modern form of the metric system, called the International System (SI), was adopted in 1960 and provides the standard measurements that all scientists around the world can understand.

The SI system is convenient because unit sizes vary by powers of 10. Prefixes are used to name units. Look at **Table 3** for some common SI prefixes and their meanings.

| Table 3 Common SI Prefixes | | | |
|---|---|---|---|
| **Prefix** | **Symbol** | **Meaning** | |
| kilo– | k | 1,000 | thousand |
| hecto– | h | 100 | hundred |
| deka– | da | 10 | ten |
| deci– | d | 0.1 | tenth |
| centi– | c | 0.01 | hundredth |
| milli– | m | 0.001 | thousandth |

**Example** How many grams equal one kilogram?

**Step 1** Find the prefix *kilo* in **Table 3.**

**Step 2** Using **Table 3,** determine the meaning of *kilo*. According to the table, it means 1,000. When the prefix *kilo* is added to a unit, it means that there are 1,000 of the units in a "*kilo*unit."

**Step 3** Apply the prefix to the units in the question. The units in the question are grams. There are 1,000 grams in a kilogram.

**Practice Problem** Is a milligram larger or smaller than a gram? How many of the smaller units equal one larger unit? What fraction of the larger unit does one smaller unit represent?

## Dimensional Analysis

**Convert SI Units** In science, quantities such as length, mass, and time sometimes are measured using different units. A process called dimensional analysis can be used to change one unit of measure to another. This process involves multiplying your starting quantity and units by one or more conversion factors. A conversion factor is a ratio equal to one and can be made from any two equal quantities with different units. If 1,000 mL equal 1 L then two ratios can be made.

$$\frac{1{,}000 \text{ mL}}{1 \text{ L}} = \frac{1 \text{ L}}{1{,}000 \text{ mL}} = 1$$

One can covert between units in the SI system by using the equivalents in **Table 3** to make conversion factors.

**Example 1** How many cm are in 4 m?

**Step 1** Write conversion factors for the units given. From **Table 3,** you know that 100 cm = 1 m. The conversion factors are

$$\frac{100 \text{ cm}}{1 \text{ m}} \quad and \quad \frac{1 \text{ m}}{100 \text{ cm}}$$

**Step 2** Decide which conversion factor to use. Select the factor that has the units you are converting from (m) in the denominator and the units you are converting to (cm) in the numerator.

$$\frac{100 \text{ cm}}{1 \text{ m}}$$

**Step 3** Multiply the starting quantity and units by the conversion factor. Cancel the starting units with the units in the denominator. There are 400 cm in 4 m.

$$4 \text{ m} \times \frac{100 \text{ cm}}{1 \text{ m}} = 400 \text{ cm}$$

**Practice Problem** How many milligrams are in one kilogram? (Hint: You will need to use two conversion factors from **Table 3.**)

## Dimensional Analysis

$$x \text{ mg} = 1 \text{ kg} \times \frac{1000 \text{ g}}{1 \text{ kg}} \times \frac{1000 \text{ mg}}{1 \text{ g}} =$$
1,000,000 mg

1,000,000 mg = 1 kg

## Convert Between Unit Systems

**Problem 1**

$5 \text{ lbs} \times \dfrac{0.45 \text{ kg}}{1 \text{ lb}} = 2.25 \text{ kg}$

**Problem 2**

$\dfrac{(1 \text{ in})^3}{(2.54 \text{ cm})^3}$

$= \dfrac{1 \text{ in} \times 1 \text{ in} \times 1 \text{ in}}{2.54 \text{ cm} \times 2.54 \text{ cm} \times 2.54 \text{ cm}}$

$= \dfrac{1 \text{ in}^3}{16.39 \text{ cm}^3}$

### Table 4  Unit System Equivalents

| Type of Measurement | Equivalent |
|---|---|
| Length | 1 in = 2.54 cm |
|  | 1 yd = 0.91 m |
|  | 1 mi = 1.61 km |
| Mass and Weight* | 1 oz = 28.35 g |
|  | 1 lb = 0.45 kg |
|  | 1 ton (short) = 0.91 tonnes (metric tons) |
|  | 1 lb = 4.45 N |
| Volume | $1 \text{ in}^3 = 16.39 \text{ cm}^3$ |
|  | 1 qt = 0.95 L |
|  | 1 gal = 3.78 L |
| Area | $1 \text{ in}^2 = 6.45 \text{ cm}^2$ |
|  | $1 \text{ yd}^2 = 0.83 \text{ m}^2$ |
|  | $1 \text{ mi}^2 = 2.59 \text{ km}^2$ |
|  | 1 acre = 0.40 hectares |
| Temperature | $^\circ C = \dfrac{(^\circ F - 32)}{1.8}$ |
|  | $K = {}^\circ C + 273$ |

*Weight is measured in standard Earth gravity.

**Convert Between Unit Systems** **Table 4** gives a list of equivalents that can be used to convert between English and SI units.

**Example** If a meterstick has a length of 100 cm, how long is the meterstick in inches?

**Step 1** Write the conversion factors for the units given. From **Table 4**, 1 in = 2.54 cm.

$\dfrac{1 \text{ in}}{2.54 \text{ cm}}$ *and* $\dfrac{2.54 \text{ cm}}{1 \text{ in}}$

**Step 2** Determine which conversion factor to use. You are converting from cm to in. Use the conversion factor with cm on the bottom.

$\dfrac{1 \text{ in}}{2.54 \text{ cm}}$

**Step 3** Multiply the starting quantity and units by the conversion factor. Cancel the starting units with the units in the denominator. Round your answer based on the number of significant figures in the conversion factor.

$100 \text{ cm} \times \dfrac{1 \text{ in}}{2.54 \text{ cm}} = 39.37 \text{ in}$

The meterstick is 39.4 in long.

**Practice Problem** A book has a mass of 5 lbs. What is the mass of the book in kg?

**Practice Problem** Use the equivalent for in and cm (1 in = 2.54 cm) to show how $1 \text{ in}^3 = 16.39 \text{ cm}^3$.

Math Skill Handbook

## Precision and Significant Digits

When you make a measurement, the value you record depends on the precision of the measuring instrument. This precision is represented by the number of significant digits recorded in the measurement. When counting the number of significant digits, all digits are counted except zeros at the end of a number with no decimal point such as 2,050, and zeros at the beginning of a decimal such as 0.03020. When adding or subtracting numbers with different precision, round the answer to the smallest number of decimal places of any number in the sum or difference. When multiplying or dividing, the answer is rounded to the smallest number of significant digits of any number being multiplied or divided. Because a calculator may give you more digits than are significant, this method also is used to round the results of calculator operations.

**Example** The lengths 5.28 and 5.2 are measured in meters. Find the sum of these lengths and record your answer using the correct number of significant digits.

**Step 1** Find the sum.

| | |
|---|---|
| 5.28 m | 2 digits after the decimal |
| + 5.2 m | 1 digit after the decimal |
| 10.48 m | |

**Step 2** Round to one digit after the decimal because the least number of digits after the decimal of the numbers being added is 1.

The sum is 10.5 m.

**Practice Problem** How many significant digits are in the measurement 7,071,301 m? How many significant digits are in the measurement 0.003010 g?

**Practice Problem** Multiply 5.28 and 5.2 using the rule for multiplying and dividing. Record the answer using the correct number of significant digits.

## Scientific Notation

Many times numbers used in science are very small or very large. Because these numbers are difficult to work with scientists use scientific notation. To write numbers in scientific notation, move the decimal point until only one non-zero digit remains on the left. Then count the number of places you moved the decimal point and use that number as a power of ten. For example, the average distance from the Sun to Mars is 227,800,000,000 m. In scientific notation, this distance is $2.278 \times 10^{11}$ m. Because you moved the decimal point to the left, the number is a positive power of ten.

The mass of an electron is about 0.000 000 000 000 000 000 000 000 000 000 911 kg. Expressed in scientific notation, this mass is $9.11 \times 10^{-31}$ kg. Because the decimal point was moved to the right, the number is a negative power of ten.

**Example** Earth is 149,600,000 km from the Sun. Express this in scientific notation.

**Step 1** Move the decimal point until one non-zero digit remains on the left.
1.496 000 00

**Step 2** Count the number of decimal places you have moved. In this case, eight.

**Step 3** Show that number as a power of ten, $10^8$.

The Earth is $1.496 \times 10^8$ km from the Sun.

**Practice Problem** How many significant digits are in 149,600,000 km? How many significant digits are in $1.496 \times 10^8$ km?

**Practice Problem** Parts used in a high performance car must be measured to $7 \times 10^{-6}$ m. Express this number as a decimal.

**Practice Problem** A CD is spinning at 539 revolutions per minute. Express this number in scientific notation.

## Precision and Significant Digits
**Problem 1**
7; 4

**Problem 2**
$5.28 \times 5.2 = 27.456$

5.28 has 3 significant digits.

5.2 has 2 significant digits.

When multiplying and dividing, the answer is rounded to the smallest number of significant digits of the numbers being multiplied or divided—in this case, 2.

27.456 is rounded to 27.

## Scientific Notation
**Problem 1**
4; 4

**Problem 2**
0.000007

**Problem 3**
$5.39 \times 10^2$

Math Skill Handbook

## Line Graph

| x | y |
|---|---|
| 3 | 52 |
| 6 | 72 |
| 9 | 83 |
| 12 | 86 |

**Puppy Growth**

## Make and Use Graphs

Data in tables can be displayed in a graph—a visual representation of data. Common graph types include line graphs, bar graphs, and circle graphs.

**Line Graph** A line graph shows a relationship between two variables that change continuously. The independent variable is changed and is plotted on the *x*-axis. The dependent variable is observed, and is plotted on the *y*-axis.

**Example** Draw a line graph of the data below from a cyclist in a long-distance race.

| Table 5  Bicycle Race Data | |
|---|---|
| **Time (h)** | **Distance (km)** |
| 0 | 0 |
| 1 | 8 |
| 2 | 16 |
| 3 | 24 |
| 4 | 32 |
| 5 | 40 |

**Step 1** Determine the *x*-axis and *y*-axis variables. Time varies independently of distance and is plotted on the *x*-axis. Distance is dependent on time and is plotted on the *y*-axis.

**Step 2** Determine the scale of each axis. The *x*-axis data ranges from 0 to 5. The *y*-axis data ranges from 0 to 40.

**Step 3** Using graph paper, draw and label the axes. Include units in the labels.

**Step 4** Draw a point at the intersection of the time value on the *x*-axis and corresponding distance value on the *y*-axis. Connect the points and label the graph with a title, as shown in **Figure 20.**

**Distance v. Time**

**Figure 20**  This line graph shows the relationship between distance and time during a bicycle ride.

**Practice Problem** A puppy's shoulder height is measured during the first year of her life. The following measurements were collected: (3 mo, 52 cm), (6 mo, 72 cm), (9 mo, 83 cm), (12 mo, 86 cm). Graph this data.

**Find a Slope** The slope of a straight line is the ratio of the vertical change, rise, to the horizontal change, run.

$$\text{Slope} = \frac{\text{vertical change (rise)}}{\text{horizontal change (run)}} = \frac{\text{change in } y}{\text{change in } x}$$

**Example** Find the slope of the graph in **Figure 20.**

**Step 1** You know that the slope is the change in *y* divided by the change in *x*.

$$\text{Slope} = \frac{\text{change in } y}{\text{change in } x}$$

**Step 2** Determine the data points you will be using. For a straight line, choose the two sets of points that are the farthest apart.

$$\text{Slope} = \frac{(40-0) \text{ km}}{(5-0) \text{ hr}}$$

**Step 3** Find the change in *y* and *x*.

$$\text{Slope} = \frac{40 \text{ km}}{5 \text{ h}}$$

**Step 4** Divide the change in *y* by the change in *x*.

$$\text{Slope} = \frac{8 \text{ km}}{\text{h}}$$

The slope of the graph is 8 km/h.

Math Skill Handbook

**Bar Graph** To compare data that does not change continuously you might choose a bar graph. A bar graph uses bars to show the relationships between variables. The *x*-axis variable is divided into parts. The parts can be numbers such as years, or a category such as a type of animal. The *y*-axis is a number and increases continuously along the axis.

**Example** A recycling center collects 4.0 kg of aluminum on Monday, 1.0 kg on Wednesday, and 2.0 kg on Friday. Create a bar graph of this data.

**Step 1** Select the *x*-axis and *y*-axis variables. The measured numbers (the masses of aluminum) should be placed on the *y*-axis. The variable divided into parts (collection days) is placed on the *x*-axis.

**Step 2** Create a graph grid like you would for a line graph. Include labels and units.

**Step 3** For each measured number, draw a vertical bar above the *x*-axis value up to the *y*-axis value. For the first data point, draw a vertical bar above Monday up to 4.0 kg.

**Aluminum Collected During Week**

**Practice Problem** Draw a bar graph of the gases in air: 78% nitrogen, 21% oxygen, 1% other gases.

**Circle Graph** To display data as parts of a whole, you might use a circle graph. A circle graph is a circle divided into sections that represent the relative size of each piece of data. The entire circle represents 100%, half represents 50%, and so on.

**Example** Air is made up of 78% nitrogen, 21% oxygen, and 1% other gases. Display the composition of air in a circle graph.

**Step 1** Multiply each percent by 360° and divide by 100 to find the angle of each section in the circle.

$$78\% \times \frac{360°}{100} = 280.8°$$

$$21\% \times \frac{360°}{100} = 75.6°$$

$$1\% \times \frac{360°}{100} = 3.6°$$

**Step 2** Use a compass to draw a circle and to mark the center of the circle. Draw a straight line from the center to the edge of the circle.

**Step 3** Use a protractor and the angles you calculated to divide the circle into parts. Place the center of the protractor over the center of the circle and line the base of the protractor over the straight line.

**Practice Problem** Draw a circle graph to represent the amount of aluminum collected during the week shown in the bar graph to the left.

**Math Skill Handbook**

**Bar Graph**

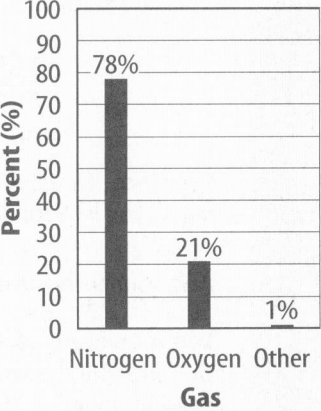

**Composition of Air**

**Circle Graph**

The total amount of aluminum collected is:

$$4.0 \text{ kg} + 1.0 \text{ kg} + 2.0 \text{ kg} = 7.0 \text{ kg}$$

$$\frac{4.0 \text{ kg}}{7.0 \text{ kg}} = \frac{x}{360°}; \ x = 206°$$

$$\frac{1.0 \text{ kg}}{7.0 \text{ kg}} = \frac{x}{360°}; \ x = 51°$$

$$\frac{2.0 \text{ kg}}{7.0 \text{ kg}} = \frac{x}{360°}; \ x = 103°$$

Math Skill Handbook

# Use and Care of a Microscope

**Eyepiece** Contains magnifying lenses you look through.

**Arm** Supports the body tube.

**Low-power objective** Contains the lens with the lowest power magnification.

**Stage clips** Hold the microscope slide in place.

**Coarse adjustment** Focuses the image under low power.

**Fine adjustment** Sharpens the image under high magnification.

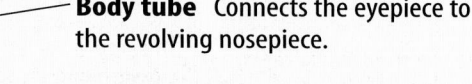

**Body tube** Connects the eyepiece to the revolving nosepiece.

**Revolving nosepiece** Holds and turns the objectives into viewing position.

**High-power objective** Contains the lens with the highest magnification.

**Stage** Supports the microscope slide.

**Light source** Provides light that passes upward through the diaphragm, the specimen, and the lenses.

**Base** Provides support for the microscope.

## Caring for a Microscope

1. Always carry the microscope holding the arm with one hand and supporting the base with the other hand.

2. Don't touch the lenses with your fingers.

3. The coarse adjustment knob is used only when looking through the lowest-power objective lens. The fine adjustment knob is used when the high-power objective is in place.

4. Cover the microscope when you store it.

## Using a Microscope

1. Place the microscope on a flat surface that is clear of objects. The arm should be toward you.

2. Look through the eyepiece. Adjust the diaphragm so light comes through the opening in the stage.

3. Place a slide on the stage so the specimen is in the field of view. Hold it firmly in place by using the stage clips.

4. Always focus with the coarse adjustment and the low-power objective lens first. After the object is in focus on low power, turn the nosepiece until the high-power objective is in place. Use ONLY the fine adjustment to focus with the high-power objective lens.

## Making a Wet-Mount Slide

1. Carefully place the item you want to look at in the center of a clean, glass slide. Make sure the sample is thin enough for light to pass through.

2. Use a dropper to place one or two drops of water on the sample.

3. Hold a clean coverslip by the edges and place it at one edge of the water. Slowly lower the coverslip onto the water until it lies flat.

4. If you have too much water or a lot of air bubbles, touch the edge of a paper towel to the edge of the coverslip to draw off extra water and draw out unwanted air.

# Rocks

| Rocks | | |
|---|---|---|
| **Rock Type** | **Rock Name** | **Characteristics** |
| **Igneous** (intrusive) | Granite | Large mineral grains of quartz, feldspar, hornblende, and mica. Usually light in color. |
| | Diorite | Large mineral grains of feldspar, hornblende, and mica. Less quartz than granite. Intermediate in color. |
| | Gabbro | Large mineral grains of feldspar, augite, and olivine. No quartz. Dark in color. |
| **Igneous** (extrusive) | Rhyolite | Small mineral grains of quartz, feldspar, hornblende, and mica, or no visible grains. Light in color. |
| | Andesite | Small mineral grains of feldspar, hornblende, and mica or no visible grains. Intermediate in color. |
| | Basalt | Small mineral grains of feldspar, augite, and possibly olivine or no visible grains. No quartz. Dark in color. |
| | Obsidian | Glassy texture. No visible grains. Volcanic glass. Fracture looks like broken glass. |
| | Pumice | Frothy texture. Floats in water. Usually light in color. |
| **Sedimentary** (detrital) | Conglomerate | Coarse grained. Gravel or pebble-size grains. |
| | Sandstone | Sand-sized grains 1/16 to 2 mm. |
| | Siltstone | Grains are smaller than sand but larger than clay. |
| | Shale | Smallest grains. Often dark in color. Usually platy. |
| **Sedimentary** (chemical or organic) | Limestone | Major mineral is calcite. Usually forms in oceans and lakes. Often contains fossils. |
| | Coal | Forms in swampy areas. Compacted layers of organic material, mainly plant remains. |
| **Sedimentary** (chemical) | Rock Salt | Commonly forms by the evaporation of seawater. |
| **Metamorphic** (foliated) | Gneiss | Banding due to alternate layers of different minerals, of different colors. Parent rock often is granite. |
| | Schist | Parallel arrangement of sheetlike minerals, mainly micas. Forms from different parent rocks. |
| | Phyllite | Shiny or silky appearance. May look wrinkled. Common parent rocks are shale and slate. |
| | Slate | Harder, denser, and shinier than shale. Common parent rock is shale. |
| **Metamorphic** (nonfoliated) | Marble | Calcite or dolomite. Common parent rock is limestone. |
| | Soapstone | Mainly of talc. Soft with greasy feel. |
| | Quartzite | Hard with interlocking quartz crystals. Common parent rock is sandstone. |

# Minerals

| Mineral (formula) | Color | Streak | Hardness | Breakage Pattern | Uses and Other Properties |
|---|---|---|---|---|---|
| **Graphite** (C) | black to gray | black to gray | 1–1.5 | basal cleavage (scales) | pencil lead, lubricants for locks, rods to control some small nuclear reactions, battery poles |
| **Galena** (PbS) | gray | gray to black | 2.5 | cubic cleavage perfect | source of lead, used for pipes, shields for X rays, fishing equipment sinkers |
| **Hematite** ($Fe_2O_3$) | black or reddish-brown | reddish-brown | 5.5–6.5 | irregular fracture | source of iron; converted to pig iron, made into steel |
| **Magnetite** ($Fe_3O_4$) | black | black | 6 | conchoidal fracture | source of iron, attracts a magnet |
| **Pyrite** ($FeS_2$) | light, brassy, yellow | greenish-black | 6–6.5 | uneven fracture | fool's gold |
| **Talc** ($Mg_3 Si_4O_{10}(OH)_2$) | white, greenish | white | 1 | cleavage in one direction | used for talcum powder, sculptures, paper, and tabletops |
| **Gypsum** ($CaSO_4 \cdot 2H_2O$) | colorless, gray, white, brown | white | 2 | basal cleavage | used in plaster of paris and dry wall for building construction |
| **Sphalerite** (ZnS) | brown, reddish-brown, greenish | light to dark brown | 3.5–4 | cleavage in six directions | main ore of zinc; used in paints, dyes, and medicine |
| **Muscovite** ($KAl_3Si_3O_{10}(OH)_2$) | white, light gray, yellow, rose, green | colorless | 2–2.5 | basal cleavage | occurs in large, flexible plates; used as an insulator in electrical equipment, lubricant |
| **Biotite** ($K(Mg,Fe)_3(AlSi_3O_{10})(OH)_2$) | black to dark brown | colorless | 2.5–3 | basal cleavage | occurs in large, flexible plates |
| **Halite** (NaCl) | colorless, red, white, blue | colorless | 2.5 | cubic cleavage | salt; soluble in water; a preservative |

# Minerals

| Mineral (formula) | Color | Streak | Hardness | Breakage Pattern | Uses and Other Properties |
|---|---|---|---|---|---|
| **Calcite** ($CaCO_3$) | colorless, white, pale blue | colorless, white | 3 | cleavage in three directions | fizzes when HCI is added; used in cements and other building materials |
| **Dolomite** ($CaMg(CO_3)_2$) | colorless, white, pink, green, gray, black | white | 3.5–4 | cleavage in three directions | concrete and cement; used as an ornamental building stone |
| **Fluorite** ($CaF_2$) | colorless, white, blue, green, red, yellow, purple | colorless | 4 | cleavage in four directions | used in the manufacture of optical equipment; glows under ultraviolet light |
| **Hornblende** $(CaNa)_{2-3}$ $(Mg,Al, Fe)_5-(Al,Si)_2$ $Si_6O_{22}$ $(OH)_2)$ | green to black | gray to white | 5–6 | cleavage in two directions | will transmit light on thin edges; 6-sided cross section |
| **Feldspar** ($KAlSi_3O_8$) ($NaAl Si_3O_8$), ($CaAl_2Si_2 O_8$) | colorless, white to gray, green | colorless | 6 | two cleavage planes meet at 90° angle | used in the manufacture of ceramics |
| **Augite** $((Ca,Na) (Mg,Fe,Al) (Al,Si)_2 O_6)$ | black | colorless | 6 | cleavage in two directions | square or 8-sided cross section |
| **Olivine** $((Mg,Fe)_2 SiO_4)$ | olive, green | none | 6.5–7 | conchoidal fracture | gemstones, refractory sand |
| **Quartz** ($SiO_2$) | colorless, various colors | none | 7 | conchoidal fracture | used in glass manufacture, electronic equipment, radios, computers, watches, gemstones |

# Physical Science Reference Tables

## Standard Units

| Symbol | Name | Quantity |
|--------|------|----------|
| m | meter | length |
| kg | kilogram | mass |
| Pa | pascal | pressure |
| K | kelvin | temperature |
| mol | mole | amount of a substance |
| J | joule | energy, work, quantity of heat |
| s | second | time |
| C | coulomb | electric charge |
| V | volt | electric potential |
| A | ampere | electric current |
| $\Omega$ | ohm | resistance |

## Wavelengths of Light in a Vacuum

| | |
|---|---|
| Violet | $4.0 - 4.2 \times 10^{-7}$ m |
| Blue | $4.2 - 4.9 \times 10^{-7}$ m |
| Green | $4.9 - 5.7 \times 10^{-7}$ m |
| Yellow | $5.7 - 5.9 \times 10^{-7}$ m |
| Orange | $5.9 - 6.5 \times 10^{-7}$ m |
| Red | $6.5 - 7.0 \times 10^{-7}$ m |

## Physical Constants and Conversion Factors

| | | |
|---|---|---|
| Acceleration due to gravity | g | 9.8 m/s/s or m/s$^2$ |
| Avogadro's Number | $N_A$ | $6.02 \times 10^{23}$ particles per mole |
| Electron charge | e | $1.6 \times 10^{-19}$ C |
| Electron rest mass | $m_e$ | $9.11 \times 10^{-31}$ kg |
| Gravitation constant | G | $6.67 \times 10^{-11}$ N $\times$ m$^2$/kg$^2$ |
| Mass-energy relationship | | 1 u (amu) = $9.3 \times 10^2$ MeV |
| Speed of light in a vacuum | c | $3.00 \times 10^8$ m/s |
| Speed of sound at STP | | 331 m/s |
| Standard Pressure | | 1 atmosphere |
| | | 101.3 kPa |
| | | 760 Torr or mmHg |
| | | 14.7 lb/in.$^2$ |

## The Index of Refraction for Common Substances

($\lambda = 5.9 \times 10^{-7}$ m)

| | |
|---|---|
| Air | 1.00 |
| Alcohol | 1.36 |
| Canada Balsam | 1.53 |
| Corn Oil | 1.47 |
| Diamond | 2.42 |
| Glass, Crown | 1.52 |
| Glass, Flint | 1.61 |
| Glycerol | 1.47 |
| Lucite | 1.50 |
| Quartz, Fused | 1.46 |
| Water | 1.33 |

## Heat Constants

| | Specific Heat (average) (kJ/kg $\times$ °C) (J/g $\times$ °C) | Melting Point (°C) | Boiling Point (°C) | Heat of Fusion (kJ/kg) (J/g) | Heat of Vaporization (kJ/kg) (J/g) |
|---|---|---|---|---|---|
| Alcohol (ethyl) | 2.43 (liq.) | −117 | 79 | 109 | 855 |
| Aluminum | 0.90 (sol.) | 660 | 2467 | 396 | 10500 |
| Ammonia | 4.71 (liq.) | −78 | −33 | 332 | 1370 |
| Copper | 0.39 (sol.) | 1083 | 2567 | 205 | 4790 |
| Iron | 0.45 (sol.) | 1535 | 2750 | 267 | 6290 |
| Lead | 0.13 (sol.) | 328 | 1740 | 25 | 866 |
| Mercury | 0.14 (liq.) | −39 | 357 | 11 | 295 |
| Platinum | 0.13 (sol.) | 1772 | 3827 | 101 | 229 |
| Silver | 0.24 (sol.) | 962 | 2212 | 105 | 2370 |
| Tungsten | 0.13 (sol.) | 3410 | 5660 | 192 | 4350 |
| Water (solid) | 2.05 (sol.) | 0 | – | 334 | – |
| Water (liquid) | 4.18 (liq.) | – | 100 | – | – |
| Water (vapor) | 2.01 (gas) | – | – | – | 2260 |
| Zinc | 0.39 (sol.) | 420 | 907 | 113 | 1770 |

## Standard Units

## Heat Constants

**Atomic number and chemical symbol**

$^{4}_{2}$He ($\alpha$ particle) Helium nucleus emission

$^{0}_{-1}$e ($\beta$ particle) electron emission

# PERIODIC TABLE OF THE ELEMENTS

Columns of elements are called groups. Elements in the same group have similar chemical properties.

Gas
Liquid
Solid
Synthetic

Element — Hydrogen
Atomic number — 1
Symbol — H
Atomic mass — 1.008
State of matter

The first three symbols tell you the state of matter of the element at room temperature. The fourth symbol identifies elements that are not present in significant amounts on Earth. Useful amounts are made synthetically.

| 1 | 2 | 3 | 4 | 5 | 6 | 7 | 8 | 9 |
|---|---|---|---|---|---|---|---|---|
| **1** Hydrogen 1 H 1.008 | | | | | | | | |
| **2** Lithium 3 Li 6.941 | Beryllium 4 Be 9.012 | | | | | | | |
| **3** Sodium 11 Na 22.990 | Magnesium 12 Mg 24.305 | | | | | | | |
| **4** Potassium 19 K 39.098 | Calcium 20 Ca 40.078 | Scandium 21 Sc 44.956 | Titanium 22 Ti 47.867 | Vanadium 23 V 50.942 | Chromium 24 Cr 51.996 | Manganese 25 Mn 54.938 | Iron 26 Fe 55.845 | Cobalt 27 Co 58.933 |
| **5** Rubidium 37 Rb 85.468 | Strontium 38 Sr 87.62 | Yttrium 39 Y 88.906 | Zirconium 40 Zr 91.224 | Niobium 41 Nb 92.906 | Molybdenum 42 Mo 95.94 | Technetium 43 Tc (98) | Ruthenium 44 Ru 101.07 | Rhodium 45 Rh 102.906 |
| **6** Cesium 55 Cs 132.905 | Barium 56 Ba 137.327 | Lanthanum 57 La 138.906 | Hafnium 72 Hf 178.49 | Tantalum 73 Ta 180.948 | Tungsten 74 W 183.84 | Rhenium 75 Re 186.207 | Osmium 76 Os 190.23 | Iridium 77 Ir 192.217 |
| **7** Francium 87 Fr (223) | Radium 88 Ra (226) | Actinium 89 Ac (227) | Rutherfordium 104 Rf (261) | Dubnium 105 Db (262) | Seaborgium 106 Sg (266) | Bohrium 107 Bh (264) | Hassium 108 Hs (277) | Meitnerium 109 Mt (268) |

The number in parentheses is the mass number of the longest-lived isotope for that element.

Rows of elements are called periods. Atomic number increases across a period.

The arrow shows where these elements would fit into the periodic table. They are moved to the bottom of the table to save space.

| Lanthanide series | Cerium 58 Ce 140.116 | Praseodymium 59 Pr 140.908 | Neodymium 60 Nd 144.24 | Promethium 61 Pm (145) | Samarium 62 Sm 150.36 |
|---|---|---|---|---|---|
| Actinide series | Thorium 90 Th 232.038 | Protactinium 91 Pa 231.036 | Uranium 92 U 238.029 | Neptunium 93 Np (237) | Plutonium 94 Pu (244) |

**Metal**

**Metalloid**

**Nonmetal**

The color of an element's block tells you if the element is a metal, nonmetal, or metalloid.

**Science Online**

Visit in7.msscience.com for updates to the periodic table.

| 13 | 14 | 15 | 16 | 17 | 18 |
|---|---|---|---|---|---|

| | | | | | | Helium 2 **He** 4.003 |

| Boron 5 **B** 10.811 | Carbon 6 **C** 12.011 | Nitrogen 7 **N** 14.007 | Oxygen 8 **O** 15.999 | Fluorine 9 **F** 18.998 | Neon 10 **Ne** 20.180 |

| 10 | 11 | 12 |

| Aluminum 13 **Al** 26.982 | Silicon 14 **Si** 28.086 | Phosphorus 15 **P** 30.974 | Sulfur 16 **S** 32.065 | Chlorine 17 **Cl** 35.453 | Argon 18 **Ar** 39.948 |

| Nickel 28 **Ni** 58.693 | Copper 29 **Cu** 63.546 | Zinc 30 **Zn** 65.409 | Gallium 31 **Ga** 69.723 | Germanium 32 **Ge** 72.64 | Arsenic 33 **As** 74.922 | Selenium 34 **Se** 78.96 | Bromine 35 **Br** 79.904 | Krypton 36 **Kr** 83.798 |

| Palladium 46 **Pd** 106.42 | Silver 47 **Ag** 107.868 | Cadmium 48 **Cd** 112.411 | Indium 49 **In** 114.818 | Tin 50 **Sn** 118.710 | Antimony 51 **Sb** 121.760 | Tellurium 52 **Te** 127.60 | Iodine 53 **I** 126.904 | Xenon 54 **Xe** 131.293 |

| Platinum 78 **Pt** 195.078 | Gold 79 **Au** 196.967 | Mercury 80 **Hg** 200.59 | Thallium 81 **Tl** 204.383 | Lead 82 **Pb** 207.2 | Bismuth 83 **Bi** 208.980 | Polonium 84 **Po** (209) | Astatine 85 **At** (210) | Radon 86 **Rn** (222) |

| Darmstadtium 110 **Ds** (281) | Unununium * 111 **Uuu** (272) | Ununbium * 112 **Uub** (285) | | Ununquadium * 114 **Uuq** (289) | | ** 116 | | ** 118 |

* The names and symbols for elements 111–114 are temporary. Final names will be selected when the elements' discoveries are verified.

** Elements 116 and 118 were thought to have been created. The claim was retracted because the experimental results could not be repeated.

| Europium 63 **Eu** 151.964 | Gadolinium 64 **Gd** 157.25 | Terbium 65 **Tb** 158.925 | Dysprosium 66 **Dy** 162.500 | Holmium 67 **Ho** 164.930 | Erbium 68 **Er** 167.259 | Thulium 69 **Tm** 168.934 | Ytterbium 70 **Yb** 173.04 | Lutetium 71 **Lu** 174.967 |

| Americium 95 **Am** (243) | Curium 96 **Cm** (247) | Berkelium 97 **Bk** (247) | Californium 98 **Cf** (251) | Einsteinium 99 **Es** (252) | Fermium 100 **Fm** (257) | Mendelevium 101 **Md** (258) | Nobelium 102 **No** (259) | Lawrencium 103 **Lr** (262) |

**Cómo usar el glosario en español:**
1. Busca el término en inglés que desees encontrar.
2. El término en español, junto con la definición, se encuentran en la columna de la derecha.

## Pronunciation Key

Use the following key to help you sound out words in the glossary.

| | | | |
|---|---|---|---|
| **a** | back (BAK) | **ew** | food (FEWD) |
| **ay** | day (DAY) | **yoo** | pure (PYOOR) |
| **ah** | father (FAH thur) | **yew** | few (FYEW) |
| **ow** | flower (FLOW ur) | **uh** | comma (CAH muh) |
| **ar** | car (CAR) | **u (+ con)** | rub (RUB) |
| **e** | less (LES) | **sh** | shelf (SHELF) |
| **ee** | leaf (LEEF) | **ch** | nature (NAY chur) |
| **ih** | trip (TRIHP) | **g** | gift (GIHFT) |
| **i (i + con + e)** | idea (i DEE uh) | **j** | gem (JEM) |
| **oh** | go (GOH) | **ing** | sing (SING) |
| **aw** | soft (SAWFT) | **zh** | vision (VIH zhun) |
| **or** | orbit (OR buht) | **k** | cake (KAYK) |
| **oy** | coin (COYN) | **s** | seed, cent (SEED, SENT) |
| **oo** | foot (FOOT) | **z** | zone, raise (ZOHN, RAYZ) |

**English** — **A** — **Español**

**abiotic (ay bi AH tihk) factor:** any nonliving part of the environment, such as water, sunlight, temperature, and air. (p. 196)

**absolute age:** age, in years, of a rock or other object; can be determined by using properties of the atoms that make up materials. (p. 669)

**absolute magnitude:** measure of the amount of light a star actually gives off. (p. 474)

**acceleration:** equals the change in velocity divided by the time for the change to take place; occurs when an object speeds up, slows down, or turns. (p. 328)

**acid:** substance that releases $H^+$ ions and produces hydronium ions when dissolved in water. (p. 302)

**acid precipitation:** precipitation with a pH below 5.6—which occurs when air pollutants from the burning of fossil fuels react with water in the atmosphere to form strong acids—that can pollute water, kill fish and plants, and damage soils. (p. 233)

**active immunity:** long-lasting immunity that results when the body makes its own antibodies in response to a specific antigen. (p. 176)

**factor abiótico:** cualquier parte no viva del medio ambiente, tal como el agua, la luz solar, la temperatura y el aire. (p. 196)

**edad absoluta:** edad, en años, de una roca u otro objeto; puede determinarse utilizando las propiedades de los átomos de los materiales. (p. 669)

**magnitud absoluta:** medida de la cantidad real de luz que genera una estrella. (p. 474)

**aceleración:** es igual al cambio de velocidad dividido por el tiempo que toma en realizarse dicho cambio; sucede cuando un objeto aumenta su velocidad, la disminuye o gira. (p. 328)

**ácido:** sustancia que libera iones $H^+$ y produce iones de hidronio al ser disuelta en agua. (p. 302)

**lluvia ácida:** precipitación con un pH menor de 5.6—lo cual ocurre cuando los contaminantes del aire provenientes de la quema de combustibles fósiles reaccionan con el agua en la atmósfera para formar ácidos fuertes—que puede contaminar el agua, matar peces y plantas, y dañar los suelos. (p. 233)

**inmunidad activa:** inmunidad duradera que se presenta cuando el cuerpo crea sus propios anticuerpos como respuesta a un antígeno específico. (p. 176)

**active transport:** energy-requiring process in which transport proteins bind with particles and move them through a cell membrane. (p. 77)

**adaptation:** any structural or behavioral change that helps an organism survive in its particular environment. (p. 628)

**allergen:** substance that causes an allergic reaction. (p. 183)

**alternative resource:** new renewable or inexhaustible energy source; includes solar energy, wind, and geothermal energy. (p. 397)

**alveoli (al VEE uh li):** tiny, thin-walled, grapelike clusters at the end of each bronchiole that are surrounded by capillaries; carbon dioxide and oxygen exchange takes place. (p. 142)

**amino acid:** building block of protein. (p. 133)

**amplitude:** for a transverse wave, one half the distance between a crest and a trough. (p. 415)

**analog signal:** a electronic signal that carries information and varies smoothly with time. (p. 442)

**antibody:** a protein made in response to a specific antigen that can attach to the antigen and cause it to be useless. (p. 175)

**antigen (AN tih jun):** complex molecule that is foreign to your body. (p. 175)

**apparent magnitude:** measure of the amount of light from a star that is received on Earth. (p. 474)

**aqueous (A kwee us):** solution in which water is the solvent. (p. 294)

**artery:** blood vessel that carries blood away from the heart. (p. 170)

**asexual reproduction:** a type of reproduction—fission, budding, and regeneration—in which a new organism is produced from one organism and has DNA identical to the parent organism. (p. 101)

**atom:** a very small particle that makes up most kinds of matter and consists of smaller parts called protons, neutrons, and electrons. (p. 259)

**atomic mass:** average mass of an atom of an element; its unit of measure is the atomic mass unit (u), which is 1/12 the mass of a carbon-12 atom. (p. 270)

**atomic number:** number of protons in the nucleus of each atom of a given element; is the top number in the periodic table. (p. 269)

**average speed:** equals the total distance traveled divided by the total time taken to travel the distance. (p. 325)

**transporte activo:** proceso que requiere energía y en el cual las proteínas de transporte se unen con partículas y las trasladan a través de la membrana celular. (p. 77)

**adaptación:** cualquier cambio de estructura o comportamiento que ayude a un organismo a sobrevivir en su medio ambiente particular. (p. 628)

**alergeno:** sustancia que produce una reacción alérgica. (p. 183)

**recurso alternativo:** nueva fuente de energía renovable o inagotable; incluye energía solar, eólica y geotérmica. (p. 397)

**alvéolos:** racimos parecidos a las uvas, pequeños y de paredes finas encontrados en el extremo de cada bronquiolo, los cuales están rodeados de capilares y en donde se realiza el intercambio de dióxido de carbono y oxígeno. (p. 142)

**aminoácido:** bloque formador de las proteínas. (p. 133)

**amplitud:** para una onda transversal, es la mitad de la distancia entre la cresta y la depresión. (p. 415)

**señal analógica:** señal electrónica que conduce información y varía de manera uniforme con el tiempo. (p. 442)

**anticuerpo:** proteína creada como respuesta a un antígeno específico y que se puede adherir al antígeno inutilizándolo. (p. 175)

**antígeno:** molécula compleja extraña al cuerpo. (p. 175)

**magnitud aparente:** medida de la cantidad de luz recibida en la Tierra desde una estrella. (p. 474)

**acuoso:** solución en la cual el agua es el solvente. (p. 294)

**arteria:** vaso sanguíneo que transporta la sangre desde el corazón. (p. 170)

**reproducción asexual:** tipo de reproducción—fisión, gemación y regeneración—en el que un organismo da origen a uno nuevo de ADN idéntico al organismo progenitor. (p. 101)

**átomo:** partícula muy pequeña que constituye la mayoría de los tipos de materia y que está formada por partes más pequeñas llamadas protones, neutrones y electrones. (p. 259)

**masa atómica:** masa promedio de un átomo de un elemento; su unidad de medida es la unidad de masa atómica (u), la cual es 1/12 de la masa de un átomo de carbono-12. (p. 270)

**número atómico:** número de protones en el núcleo de un átomo de determinado elemento; es el número superior en la tabla periódica. (p. 269)

**velocidad promedio:** es igual al total de la distancia recorrida dividida por el tiempo total necesario para recorrer dicha distancia. (p. 325)

**B**

**balanced forces:** two or more forces whose effects cancel each other out and do not change the motion of an object. (p. 351)

**basaltic:** describes dense, dark-colored igneous rock formed from magma rich in magnesium and iron and poor in silica. (p. 539)

**base:** substance that accepts $H^+$ ions and produces hydroxide ions when dissolved in water. (p. 305)

**Big Bang theory:** states that about 13.7 billion years ago, the universe began with a huge, fiery explosion. (p. 493)

**binary system:** number system consisting of two digits, 0 and 1, that can be used by devices such as computers to store or use information. (p. 450)

**binomial nomenclature (bi NOH mee ul • NOH mun klay chur):** two-word naming system that gives all organisms their scientific name. (p. 24)

**biogenesis (bi oh JEH nuh sus):** theory that living things come only from other living things. (p. 19)

**biosphere (BI uh sfihr):** part of Earth that supports life—the top part of Earth's crust, all the waters covering Earth's surface, and the surrounding atmosphere; includes all biomes, ecosystems, communities, and populations. (p. 201)

**biotic (bi AHT ihk) factor:** any living or once-living organism in the environment. (p. 196)

**black hole:** final stage in the evolution of a very massive star, where the core's mass collapses to a point that it's gravity is so strong that not even light can escape. (p. 486)

**bladder:** elastic, muscular organ that holds urine until it leaves the body through the urethra. (p. 149)

**bronchi (BRAHN ki):** two short tubes that branch off the lower end of the trachea and carry air into the lungs. (p. 142)

**fuerzas balanceadas:** dos o más fuerzas cuyos efectos se cancelan mutuamente sin cambiar el movimiento de un objeto. (p. 351)

**basáltica:** roca ígnea densa de color oscuro que se forma a partir de magma rico en magnesio y hierro pero pobre en sílice. (p. 539)

**base:** sustancia que acepta los iones $H^+$ y produce iones de hidróxido al ser disuelta en agua. (p. 305)

**teoría de la Gran Explosión:** establece que hace aproximadamente 13.7 billones de años el universo se originó con una enorme explosión. (p. 493)

**sistema binario:** sistema numérico que consiste en dos dígitos, 0 y 1, que se puede usar con dispositivos como las computadoras para almacenar o usar información. (p. 450)

**nomenclatura binomial:** sistema de denominación de dos palabras que da a todos los organismos su nombre científico. (p. 24)

**biogénesis:** teoría que sostiene que los seres vivos sólo provienen de otros seres vivos. (p. 19)

**biosfera:** parte de la Tierra que alberga la vida, es decir, la parte superior de la corteza terrestre, toda el agua que cubre la superficie terrestre y la atmósfera circundante; incluye todas las biomasas, ecosistemas, comunidades y poblaciones. (p. 201)

**factor biótico:** cualquier organismo vivo, o que estuvo vivo, del medio ambiente. (p. 196)

**agujero negro:** etapa final en la evolución de una estrella masiva, en donde la masa del núcleo se colapsa hasta el punto de que su gravedad es tan fuerte que ni siquiera la luz puede escapar. (p. 486)

**vejiga:** órgano muscular elástico que retiene la orina hasta que ésta sale del cuerpo a través de la uretra. (p. 149)

**bronquios:** dos tubos cortos que salen del extremo inferior de la tráquea y llevan el aire a los pulmones. (p. 142)

**C**

**capillary (KA puh ler ee):** blood vessel that connects arteries and veins. (p. 170)

**carbohydrate (kar boh HI drayt):** nutrient that usually is the body's main source of energy. (p. 134)

**carbon film:** thin film of carbon residue preserved as a fossil. (p. 656)

**capilar:** vaso sanguíneo que conecta las arterias y las venas. (p. 170)

**carbohidrato:** nutriente que por lo general es la principal fuente de energía del cuerpo. (p. 134)

**película de carbono:** capa delgada de residuos de carbono preservada como un fósil. (p. 656)

**cast:** a type of body fossil that forms when crystals fill a mold or sediments wash into a mold and harden into rock. (p. 657)

**cell:** smallest unit of an organism that can carry on life functions. (p. 14)

**cell membrane:** protective outer covering of all cells that regulates the interaction between the cell and the environment. (p. 38)

**cell theory:** states that all organisms are made up of one or more cells, the cell is the basic unit of life, and all cells come from other cells. (p. 51)

**cell wall:** rigid structure that encloses, supports, and protects the cells of plants, algae, fungi, and most bacteria. (p. 39)

**cementation:** sedimentary rock-forming process in which sediment grains are held together by natural cements that are produced when water moves through rock and soil. (p. 547)

**center of mass:** point in a object that moves as if all of the object's mass were concentrated at that point. (p. 362)

**chemical energy:** energy stored in chemical bonds. (p. 383)

**chloroplast:** green, chlorophyll-containing, plant-cell organelle that uses light energy to produce sugar from carbon dioxide and water. (p. 42)

**chromosome:** structure in a cell's nucleus that contains hereditary material. (p. 98)

**chromosphere:** layer of the Sun's atmosphere above the photosphere. (p. 477)

**chyme (KIME):** liquid product of digestion. (p. 131)

**cinder cone volcano:** relatively small volcano formed by moderate to explosive eruptions of tephra. (p. 604)

**cleavage:** physical property of some minerals that causes them to break along smooth, flat surfaces. (p. 513)

**climate:** average weather pattern in an area over a long period of time; can be classified by temperature, humidity, precipitation, and vegetation. (p. 624)

**community:** all of the populations of different species in a given area that interact in some way and depend on one another for food, shelter, and other needs. (p. 200)

**compaction:** process that forms sedimentary rocks when layers of sediments are compressed by the weight of the layers above them. (p. 546)

**vaciado:** tipo de cuerpo fósil que se forma cuando los cristales llenan un molde o los sedimentos son lavados hacia un molde y se endurecen convirtiéndose en roca. (p. 657)

**célula:** la unidad más pequeña de un organismo que puede continuar con sus funciones vitales. (p. 14)

**membrana celular:** capa externa protectora de todas las células y reguladora de la interacción entre la célula y su entorno. (p. 38)

**teoría celular:** establece que todos los organismos están formados por una o más células, que la célula es la unidad básica de la vida y que las células provienen de otras células. (p. 51)

**pared celular:** estructura rígida que envuelve, sostiene y protege a las células de las plantas, algas, hongos y de la mayoría de las bacterias. (p. 39)

**cementación:** proceso de formación de la roca sedimentaria en el que las partículas de sedimento están unidas por cementos naturales producidos cuando el agua se mueve a través de la roca y el suelo. (p. 547)

**centro de masa:** punto en un objeto que se mueve como si toda la masa del objeto estuviera concentrada en ese punto. (p. 362)

**energía química:** energía almacenada en enlaces químicos. (p. 383)

**cloroplasto:** organelo de las células vegetales, de color verde, que contiene clorofila y que usa la luz solar para convertir el dióxido de carbono y el agua en azúcar. (p. 42)

**cromosoma:** estructura en el núcleo celular que contiene el material hereditario. (p. 98)

**cromosfera:** capa de la atmósfera del sol que se encuentra sobre la fotosfera. (p. 477)

**quimo:** líquido producido durante la digestión. (p. 131)

**volcán de cono de cenizas:** volcán relativamente pequeño formado por erupciones moderadas o explosivas de tefra. (p. 604)

**exfoliación:** propiedad física de algunos minerales que causa que se rompan junto a superficies planas y lisas. (p. 513)

**clima:** modelo meteorológico en un área durante un periodo de tiempo largo; puede clasificarse por temperatura, humedad, precipitación y vegetación. (p. 624)

**comunidad:** todas las poblaciones de diferentes especies en una determinada área, que interactúan de alguna forma y que dependen unas de otras en cuanto a alimento, refugio y otras necesidades. (p. 200)

**compactación:** proceso que forma rocas sedimentarias cuando las capas de sedimento son comprimidas por el peso de las capas superiores. (p. 546)

**composite volcano:** steep-sided volcano formed from alternating layers of violent eruptions of tephra and quieter eruptions of lava. (p. 605)

**compound:** a substance produced when elements combine and whose properties are different from each of the elements in it. (p. 273)

**compressional wave:** mechanical wave that causes particles in matter to move back and forth along the direction the wave travels. (p. 413)

**computer software:** any list of instructions for a computer to follow that is stored in the computer's memory. (p. 453)

**concentration:** describes how much solute is present in a solution compared to the amount of solvent. (p. 299)

**constellation:** group of stars that forms a pattern in the sky that looks like a familiar object (Libra), animal (Pegasus), or character (Orion). (p. 472)

**control:** standard to which the outcome of a test is compared. (p. 9)

**corona:** outermost, largest layer of the Sun's atmosphere; extends millions of kilometers into space and has temperatures up to 2 million K. (p. 477)

**crust:** Earth's outermost layer that is thinnest under the oceans and thickest through the mountains and contains all features of Earth's surface. (p. 566)

**crystal:** solid in which the atoms are arranged in an orderly, repeating pattern. (p. 505)

**cytoplasm:** constantly moving gel-like mixture inside the cell membrane that contains heredity material and is the location of most of a cell's life processes. (p. 38)

**volcán compuesto:** volcán de costados inclinados formado por capas alternas producto de erupciones violentas de tefra y erupciones silenciosas de lava. (p. 605)

**compuesto:** sustancia resultante de la combinación de elementos cuyas propiedades son diferentes de los elementos que la componen. (p. 273)

**onda de compresión:** onda mecánica que hace que las partículas de materia se muevan hacia adelante y hacia atrás en la dirección en que viaja la onda. (p. 413)

**software para computadoras:** cualquier lista de instrucciones que debe realizar una computadora y que se almacena en la memoria de ésta. (p. 453)

**concentración:** describe la cantidad de soluto presente en una solución, comparada con la cantidad de solvente. (p. 299)

**constelación:** grupo de estrellas que forma un patrón en el cielo y que semeja un objeto (Libra), un animal (Pegaso) o un personaje familiar (Orión). (p. 472)

**control:** estándar contra el que se compara el resultado de una prueba. (p. 9)

**corona:** capa más externa y más grande de la atmósfera solar; se extiende millones de kilómetros dentro del espacio y tiene una temperatura hasta de 2 millones de grados Kelvin. (p. 477)

**corteza:** capa más externa de la Tierra, la cual es más delgada debajo de los océanos y más gruesa en las montañas y contiene todas las características de la superficie terrestre. (p. 566)

**cristal:** sólido en el que los átomos están alineados en forma ordenada y repetitiva. (p. 505)

**citoplasma:** mezcla parecida al gel y que está en constante movimiento dentro de la membrana celular, contiene material hereditario y es en donde tiene lugar la mayor parte de los procesos vitales de la célula. (p. 38)

---

**D**

---

**deforestation:** destruction and cutting down of forests—often to clear land for mining, roads, and grazing of cattle—resulting in increased atmospheric $CO_2$ levels. (p. 641)

**diffraction:** bending of waves around an object. (p. 418)

**diffusion:** a type of passive transport in cells in which molecules move from areas where there are more of them to areas where there are fewer of them. (p. 75)

**deforestación:** destrucción y tala de los bosques—a menudo el despeje de la tierra para minería, carreteras y ganadería—resultando en el aumento de los niveles atmosféricos de dióxido de carbono. (p. 641)

**difracción:** curvatura de las ondas alrededor de un objeto. (p. 418)

**difusión:** tipo de transporte pasivo en las células en el que las moléculas se mueven de áreas de mayor concentración de éstas hacia áreas de menor concentración. (p. 75)

**digital signal:** electronic signal that varies information that does not vary smoothly with time, but changes in steps between certain values, and can be represented by a series of numbers. (p. 443)

**diode:** a solid-state component made from two layers of semiconductor material that allows electric current to flow in only one direction and is commonly used to change alternating current to direct current. (p. 446)

**diploid (DIHP loyd):** cell whose similar chromosomes occur in pairs. (p. 104)

**DNA:** deoxyribonucleic acid; the genetic material of all organisms; made up of two twisted strands of sugar-phosphate molecules and nitrogen bases. (p. 110)

**señal digital:** señal electrónica que varía aquella información que no varía de manera uniforme con el tiempo, pero que cambia por grados entre ciertos valores y que puede ser representada por una serie de números. (p. 443)

**diodo:** componente de estado sólido conformado por dos capas de material semiconductor que permite el flujo de corriente eléctrica en una sola dirección y que comúnmente se utiliza para cambiar la corriente alterna a corriente directa. (p. 446)

**diploide:** célula cuyos cromosomas similares están en pares. (p. 104)

**ADN:** Ácido desoxirribonucleico; material genético de todos los organismos constituido por dos cadenas trenzadas de moléculas de azúcar-fosfato y bases de nitrógeno (p. 110)

**E**

**earthquake:** movement of the ground that occurs when rocks inside Earth pass their elastic limit, break suddenly, and experience elastic rebound. (p. 592)

**ecology:** study of all the interactions among organisms and their environment. (p. 196)

**ecosystem:** all of the communities in a given area and the abiotic factors that affect them. (p. 200)

**egg:** haploid sex cell formed in the female reproductive organs. (p. 104)

**El Niño (el NEEN yoh):** climatic event that begins in the tropical Pacific Ocean; may occur when trade winds weaken or reverse, and can disrupt normal temperature and precipitation patterns around the world. (p. 633)

**electrical energy:** energy carried by electric current. (p. 384)

**electromagnetic spectrum:** complete range of electromagnetic wave frequencies and wavelengths. (p. 426)

**electromagnetic waves:** waves that can travel through matter or empty space, include radio waves, infrared waves, visible light waves, ultraviolet waves, X rays and gamma rays. (p. 425)

**electron:** invisible, negatively charged particle located in a cloudlike formation that surrounds the nucleus of an atom. (p. 262)

**electronic signal:** a changing electric current that is used to carry information; can be analog or digital. (p. 442)

**terremoto:** movimiento del suelo que ocurre cuando las rocas del interior de la Tierra sobrepasan su límite de elasticidad, se rompen súbitamente y experimentan rebotes elásticos. (p. 592)

**ecología:** estudio de todas las interacciones entre los organismos y su medio ambiente. (p. 196)

**ecosistema:** todas las comunidades en un área determinada y los factores abióticos que las afectan. (p. 200)

**óvulo:** célula sexual haploide que se forma en los órganos reproductivos femeninos. (p. 104)

**El Niño:** evento climático que comienza en el Océano Pacífico tropical; puede ocurrir cuando los vientos alisios se debilitan o se invierten; puede desestabilizar los patrones normales de precipitación y temperatura del mundo. (p. 633)

**energía eléctrica:** energía transportada por corriente eléctrica. (p. 384)

**espectro electromagnético:** rango total de las frecuencias y longitudes de onda de las ondas electromagnéticas. (p. 426)

**ondas electromagnéticas:** ondas que pueden viajar a través de la materia o del espacio vacío; incluyen las ondas de radio, las infrarrojas, las de luz visible, las ultravioleta y los rayos X y gama. (p. 425)

**electrón:** partícula invisible con carga negativa, localizada en una formación parecida a una nube que rodea el núcleo de un átomo. (p. 262)

**señal electrónica:** corriente eléctrica dinámica que se usa para conducir información; puede ser analógica o digital. (p. 442)

**element:** natural or synthetic material that cannot be broken down into simpler materials by ordinary means; has unique properties and is generally classified as a metal, metalloid, or nonmetal. (p. 266)

**endocytosis (en duh si TOH sus):** process by which a cell takes in a substance by surrounding it with the cell membrane. (p. 78)

**endoplasmic reticulum (ER):** cytoplasmic organelle that moves materials around in a cell and is made up of a complex series of folded membranes; can be rough (with attached ribosomes) or smooth (without attached ribosomes). (p. 43)

**energy:** the ability to cause change. (p. 380)

**enzyme:** a type of protein that speeds up chemical reactions in the body without being changed or used up itself. (pp. 71, 128)

**epicenter:** point on Earth's surface directly above an earthquake's focus. (p. 594)

**equilibrium:** occurs when molecules of one substance are spread evenly throughout another substance. (p. 75)

**erosion:** movement of soil from one place to another. (p. 239)

**exocytosis (ek soh si TOH sus):** process by which vesicles release their contents outside the cell. (p. 78)

**extrusive:** describes fine-grained igneous rock that forms when magma cools quickly at or near Earth's surface. (p. 537)

**elemento:** material natural o sintético que no puede ser descompuesto fácilmente en materiales más simples por medios ordinarios; tiene propiedades únicas y generalmente es clasificado como metal, metaloide o no metal. (p. 266)

**endocitosis:** proceso mediante el cual una célula capta una sustancia rodeándola con su membrana celular. (p. 78)

**retículo endoplásmático (RE):** organelo citoplasmático que transporta materiales dentro de una célula y está formado por una serie compleja de membranas plegadas; puede ser rugoso (con ribosomas adosados) o liso (sin ribosomas adosados). (p. 43)

**energía:** capacidad de producir cambios. (p. 380)

**enzima:** tipo de proteína que acelera las reacciones químicas en el cuerpo sin que ésta sufra modificaciones o se agote. (pp. 71, 128)

**epicentro:** punto de la superficie terrestre directamente encima del foco del terremoto. (p. 594)

**equilibrio:** ocurre cuando las moléculas de una sustancia están diseminadas completa y uniformemente a lo largo de otra sustancia. (p. 75)

**erosión:** movimiento del suelo de un lugar a otro. (p. 239)

**exocitosis:** proceso mediante el cual las vesículas liberan su contenido fuera de la célula. (p. 78)

**extrusivo:** describe rocas ígneas de grano fino que se forman cuando el magma se enfría rápidamente en o cerca de la superficie terrestre. (p. 537)

**fault:** fracture that occurs when rocks break and that results in relative movement of opposing sides; can form as a result of compression (reverse fault), being pulled apart (normal fault), or shear (strike-slip fault). (pp. 569, 593)

**fault-block mountains:** sharp, jagged mountains made of huge, tilted blocks of rock that are separated from surrounding rock by faults and form because of pulling forces. (p. 576)

**fermentation:** process by which oxygen-lacking cells and some one-celled organisms release small amounts of energy from glucose molecules and produce wastes such as alcohol, carbon dioxide, and lactic acid. (p. 84)

**fertilization:** in sexual reproduction, the joining of a sperm and egg. (p. 104)

**falla:** fractura que ocurre cuando al romperse una roca se presentan relativos movimientos de los lados opuestos; se pueden formar como resultado de una compresión (falla reversa), al separarse (falla normal) o al deslizarse (falla por desplazamiento). (pp. 569, 593)

**montañas con bloques de fallas:** montañas afiladas y dentadas formadas por enormes bloques de roca inclinados, separados de las rocas adyacentes por fallas y que se forman debido a fuerzas atrayentes. (p. 576)

**fermentación:** proceso mediante el cual las células carentes de oxígeno y algunos organismos unicelulares liberan pequeñas cantidades de energía a partir de moléculas de glucosa y producen desechos como alcohol, dióxido de carbono y ácido láctico. (p. 84)

**fertilización:** en la reproducción sexual, la unión de un óvulo y un espermatozoide. (p. 104)

# Glossary/Glosario

**focus:** point deep inside Earth where energy is released, causing an earthquake. (p. 594)

**folded mountain:** mountain that forms by the folding of rock layers caused by compressive forces. (p. 577)

**foliated:** describes metamorphic rock, such as slate and gneiss, whose mineral grains line up in parallel layers. (p. 543)

**food chain:** model that describes how energy passes from one organism to another. (p. 208)

**food web:** model that describes how energy from food moves through a community; a series of overlapping food chains. (p. 210)

**force:** a push or a pull. (p. 350)

**fossil fuels:** nonrenewable energy resources—coal, oil, and natural gas—that formed in Earth's crust over hundreds of millions of years. (p. 226)

**fossils:** remains, imprints, or traces of prehistoric organisms that can tell when and where organisms once lived and how they lived. (p. 655)

**fracture:** physical property of some minerals that causes them to break with uneven, rough, or jagged surfaces. (p. 513)

**frequency:** number of wavelengths that pass a given point in one second, measured in hertz (Hz). (p. 414)

**friction:** force that acts to oppose sliding between two surfaces that are touching. (p. 352)

**foco:** punto profundo de la Tierra donde se genera energía causando un terremoto. (p. 594)

**montañas plegadas:** montañas que se forman por el plegamiento de capas de rocas causado por fuerzas de tracción. (p. 577)

**foliado:** describe rocas metamórficas, como pizarra y gneis, cuyas vetas minerales se alinean en capas paralelas. (p. 543)

**cadena alimenticia:** modelo que describe la forma como pasa la energía de un organismo a otro. (p. 208)

**red alimenticia:** modelo que describe cómo la energía proveniente de los alimentos pasa a una comunidad; es una serie de cadenas alimenticias entrelazadas. (p. 210)

**fuerza:** presión o tracción. (p. 350)

**combustibles fósiles:** recursos energéticos no renovables—carbón, petróleo y gas natural—que se formaron en la corteza terrestre durante cientos de millones de años. (p. 226)

**fósiles:** restos, huellas o trazas de organismos pre-históricos que pueden informar cuándo, dónde y cómo vivieron tales organismos. (p. 655)

**fractura:** propiedad física de algunos minerales que causa que se rompan formando superficies irregulares, ásperas o dentadas. (p. 513)

**frecuencia:** número de longitudes de onda que pasan un punto determinado en un segundo; se mide en hertz (Hz). (p. 414)

**fricción:** fuerza que actúa para oponerse al deslizamiento entre dos superficies que se tocan. (p. 352)

## G

**galaxy:** large group of stars, dust, and gas held together by gravity; can be elliptical, spiral, or irregular. (p. 488)

**gem:** beautiful, rare, highly prized mineral that can be worn in jewelry. (p. 515)

**gene:** section of DNA on a chromosome that contains instructions for making specific proteins. (p. 112)

**generator:** device that transforms kinetic energy into electrical energy. (p. 390)

**genus:** first word of the two-word scientific name used to identify a group of similar species. (p. 24)

**geothermal energy:** heat energy within Earth's crust, available only where natural geysers or volcanoes are located. (p. 229)

**galaxia:** grupo grande de estrellas, polvo y gas en donde todo está unido por gravedad; puede ser elíptica, espiral o irregular. (p. 488)

**gema:** mineral hermoso, raro y altamente valorado que puede usarse como joya. (p. 515)

**gen:** sección de ADN en un cromosoma, el cual contiene instrucciones para la formación de proteínas específicas. (p. 112)

**generador:** dispositivo que transforma la energía cinética en energía eléctrica. (p. 390)

**género:** primera palabra, de las dos palabras del nombre científico, que se usa para identificar a un grupo de especies similares. (p. 24)

**energía geotérmica:** energía calórica en el interior de la corteza terrestre disponible sólo donde existen géiseres o volcanes. (p. 229)

**Glossary/Glosario**

**giant:** late stage in the life of comparatively low-mass main sequence star in which hydrogen in the core is deleted, the core contracts and temperatures inside the star increase, causing its outer layers to expand and cool. (p. 485)

**global warming:** increase in the average global temperature of Earth. (p. 640)

**Golgi bodies:** organelles that package cellular materials and transport them within the cell or out of the cell. (p. 43)

**granitic:** describes generally light-colored, silica-rich igneous rock that is less dense than basaltic rock. (p. 539)

**greenhouse effect:** natural heating that occurs when certain gases in Earth's atmosphere, such as methane, $CO_2$, and water vapor, trap heat. (pp. 234, 639)

**gigante:** etapa tardía en la vida de una estrella de secuencia principal, de relativamente poca masa, en la que el hidrógeno en el núcleo está agotado, el núcleo se contrae y la temperatura en el interior de la estrella aumenta, causando que las capas externas se expandan y enfríen. (p. 485)

**calentamiento global:** incremento del promedio de la temperatura global. (p. 640)

**aparato de Golgi:** organelo que concentra los materiales celulares y los transporta hacia adentro o afuera de la célula. (p. 43)

**granítica:** roca ígnea rica en sílice, generalmente de color claro y menos densa que la rocas basáltica. (p. 539)

**efecto invernadero:** calentamiento natural que ocurre cuando ciertos gases en la atmósfera terrestre, como el metano, el dióxido de carbono y el vapor de agua atrapan el calor. (pp. 234, 639)

**H**

**habitat:** place where an organism lives. (p. 207)

**half-life:** time it takes for half the atoms of an isotope to decay. (p. 670)

**haploid (HAP loyd):** cell that has half the number of chromosomes as body cells. (p. 105)

**hardness:** measure of how easily a mineral can be scratched. (p. 511)

**hazardous wastes:** waste materials, such as pesticides and leftover paints, that are harmful to human health or poisonous to living organisms. (p. 240)

**hemoglobin (HEE muh gloh bun):** a molecule in red blood cells that carries oxygen and carbon dioxide. (p. 163)

**heterogeneous mixture:** type of mixture where the substances are not evenly mixed. (p. 289)

**hibernation:** behavioral adaptation for winter survival in which an animal's activity is greatly reduced, its body temperature drops, and body processes slow down. (p. 630)

**homeostasis:** regulation of an organism's internal, life-maintaining conditions. (p. 15)

**homogeneous mixture:** type of mixture where two or more substances are evenly mixed on a molecular level but are not bonded together. (p. 290)

**host cell:** living cell in which a virus can actively multiply or in which a virus can hide until activated by environmental stimuli. (p. 52)

**hábitat:** lugar donde viven los organismos. (p. 207)

**vida media:** tiempo que le toma a la mitad de los átomos de un isótopo para desintegrarse. (p. 670)

**haploide:** célula que posee la mitad del número de cromosomas que tienen las células somáticas. (p. 105)

**dureza:** medida de la facilidad con que un mineral puede ser rayado. (p. 511)

**desperdicios peligrosos:** materiales de desecho como los pesticidas y residuos de pintura nocivos para la salud humana o dañinos para los organismos vivos. (p. 240)

**hemoglobina:** molécula presente en los glóbulos rojos que transporta oxígeno y dióxido de carbono. (p. 163)

**mezcla heterogénea:** tipo de mezcla en la cual las sustancias no están mezcladas de manera uniforme. (p. 289)

**hibernación:** adaptación del comportamiento para sobrevivir durante el invierno en la cual la actividad del animal se ve fuertemente reducida, su temperatura corporal se reduce y los procesos corporales disminuyen su ritmo. (p. 630)

**homeostasis:** control de las condiciones internas que mantienen la vida de un organismo. (p. 15)

**mezcla homogénea:** tipo de mezcla en la cual dos o más sustancias están mezcladas en de manera uniforme a nivel molecular pero no están enlazadas. (p. 290)

**célula huésped:** célula viva en la que un virus puede reproducirse activamente o en la que un virus puede ocultarse hasta que es activado por estímulos del medio ambiente. (p. 52)

**hot spot:** hot, molten rock material that has been forced upward from deep inside Earth, which may cause magma to break through Earth's mantle and crust and may form volcanoes. (p. 610)

**hydroelectric power:** electricity produced when the energy of falling water turns the blades of a generator turbine. (p. 227)

**hydronium ion:** hydrogen ion combines with a water molecule to form a hydronium ion, $H_3O^+$. (p. 302)

**hypothesis:** prediction that can be tested. (p. 8)

**punto caliente:** material de roca fundida, caliente, que ha sido lanzado hacia arriba desde lo más profundo de la Tierra y que puede producir que el magma se rompa a través del manto y la corteza pudiendo formar volcanes. (p. 610)

**energía hidroeléctrica:** electricidad producida cuando la energía generada por la caída del agua hace girar las aspas de una turbina generadora. (p. 227)

**ion de hidronio:** ion de hidrógeno combinado con una molécula de agua para formar un ion de hidronio, $H_3O^+$. (p. 302)

**hipótesis:** predicción que puede probarse. (p. 8)

## I

**igneous rock:** rock formed when magma or lava cools and hardens. (p. 536)

**index fossils:** remains of species that existed on Earth for a relatively short period of time, were abundant and widespread geographically, and can be used by geologists to assign the ages of rock layers. (p. 659)

**indicator:** compound that changes color at different pH values when it reacts with acidic or basic solutions. (p. 308)

**inertia:** tendency of an object to resist a change in its motion. (p. 333)

**inexhaustible resource:** energy source that can't be used up by humans. (p. 397)

**infectious disease:** disease caused by a virus, bacterium, fungus, or protest that is spread from one person to another. (p. 179)

**infrared waves:** electromagnetic waves with wavelengths between about one thousandth of a meter and 700 billionths of a meter (p. 427)

**inner core:** solid, innermost layer of Earth's interior that is the hottest part of Earth and experiences the greatest amount of pressure. (p. 565)

**inorganic compound:** compound, such as $H_2O$, that is made from elements other than carbon and whose atoms usually can be arranged in only one structure. (p. 71)

**instantaneous speed:** the speed of an object at one instant of time. (p. 325)

**integrated circuit:** circuit that can contain millions of interconnected transistors and diodes imprinted on a single small chip of semiconductor material. (p. 447)

**roca ígnea:** roca formada cuando se enfría y endurece el magma o la lava. (p. 536)

**fósiles índice:** restos de especies que existieron sobre la Tierra durante un periodo de tiempo relativamente corto y que fueron abundantes y ampliamente diseminadas geográficamente; los geólogos pueden usarlos para inferir las edades de las capas rocosas. (p. 659)

**indicador:** compuesto que cambia de color con diferentes valores de pH al reaccionar con soluciones ácidas o básicas. (p. 308)

**inercia:** tendencia de un objeto a resistirse a un cambio de movimiento. (p. 333)

**recurso inagotable:** fuente de energía que no puede ser agotada por los seres humanos. (p. 397)

**enfermedad infecciosa:** enfermedad causada por un virus, bacteria, hongo o protista y que se propaga de una persona a otra. (p. 179)

**ondas infrarrojas:** ondas electromagnéticas con longitudes de onda entre aproximadamente una milésima y 700 billonésimas de metro. (p. 427)

**núcleo interior:** la capa sólida más interna del centro de la Tierra, la cual constituye la parte más caliente de ésta y en donde se ejerce la mayor cantidad de presión. (p. 565)

**compuesto inorgánico:** compuesto, como $H_2O$, formado por elementos distintos al carbono y cuyos átomos generalmente pueden estar organizados en sólo una estructura. (p. 71)

**velocidad instantánea:** la velocidad de un objeto en un instante de tiempo. (p. 325)

**circuito integrado:** circuito que puede contener millones de transistores y diodos interconectados y fijados en un solo chip de tamaño reducido y hecho de material semiconductor. (p. 447)

**intensity:** amount of energy a wave carries past a certain area each second. (p. 420)

**intrusive:** describes a type of igneous rock that generally contains large crystals and forms when magma cools slowly beneath Earth's surface. (p. 537)

**isostasy:** principle stating that Earth's lithosphere floats on a plasticlike upper part of the mantle called the athenosphere. (p. 580)

**isotopes (I suh tohps):** two or more atoms of the same element that have different numbers of neutrons in their nuclei. (p. 269)

**intensidad:** cantidad de energía que transporta una onda al pasar por un área determinada en un segundo. (p. 420)

**intrusivo:** describe un tipo de roca ígnea que generalmente contiene cristales grandes y se forma cuando el magma se enfría lentamente por debajo de la superficie terrestre. (p. 537)

**isostasía:** principio que establece que la litosfera de la Tierra flota en la parte superior del manto, semejante a un plástico, llamada astenosfera. (p. 580)

**isótopos:** dos o más átomos del mismo elemento que tienen diferente número de neutrones en su núcleo. (p. 269)

## K

**kinetic energy:** energy an object has due to its motion. (p. 381)

**kingdom:** first and largest category used to classify organisms. (p. 23)

**energía cinética:** energía que posee un objeto debido a su movimiento. (p. 381)

**reino:** la primera y más grande categoría utilizada para clasificar a los organismos. (p. 23)

## L

**larynx:** airway to which the vocal cords are attached. (p. 142)

**lava:** molten rock flowing onto Earth's surface. (pp. 536, 601)

**law:** statement about how things work in nature that seems to be true consistently. (p. 10)

**law of conservation of energy:** states that energy can change its form but is never created or destroyed. (p. 386)

**law of conservation of matter:** states that matter is not created or destroyed but only changes its form. (p. 260)

**law of conservation of momentum:** states that the total momentum of objects that collide with each other is the same before and after the collision. (p. 335)

**law of reflection:** states that the angle the incoming wave makes with the normal to the reflecting surface equals the angle the reflected wave makes with the surface. (p. 417)

**light-year:** unit representing the distance light travels in one year—about 9.5 trillion km—used to record distances between stars and galaxies. (p. 475)

**laringe:** pasaje aéreo al cual están adheridas las cuerdas vocales. (p. 142)

**lava:** roca fundida que fluye en la superficie terrestre. (pp. 536, 601)

**ley:** enunciado acerca de cómo funciona todo en la naturaleza y que constantemente parece ser verdadero. (p. 10)

**ley de la conservación de la energía:** establece que la energía puede cambiar de forma pero nunca puede ser creada ni destruida. (p. 386)

**ley de la conservación de la materia:** establece que la materia no se crea ni se destruye, solamente cambia de forma. (p. 260)

**ley de conservación de momento:** establece que el momento total de los objetos que chocan entre sí es el mismo antes y después de la colisión. (p. 335)

**ley de reflexión:** establece que el ángulo que forman la onda que llega y la normal hacia la superficie reflejante es igual al ángulo que la onda reflejada forma con la superficie. (p. 417)

**año luz:** unidad que representa la distancia que la luz viaja en un año—cerca de 9.5 trillones de kilómetros—usada para registrar las distancias entre las estrellas y las galaxias. (p. 475)

**limiting factor:** any biotic or abiotic factor that limits the number of individuals in a population. (p. 205)

**lithosphere (LIH thuh sfihr):** rigid layer of Earth about 100 km thick, made of the crust and a part of the upper mantle. (p. 568)

**luster:** describes the way a mineral reflects light from its surface; can be metallic or nonmetallic. (p. 512)

**lymph:** fluid that has diffused into the lymphatic capillaries. (p. 173)

**factor limitante:** cualquier factor biótico o abiótico que limite el número de individuos en una población. (p. 205)

**litosfera:** capa rígida de la Tierra de aproximadamente 100 kilómetros de grosor, formada por la corteza y una parte del manto superior. (p. 568)

**brillo:** describe la forma en que un mineral refleja la luz desde su superficie; puede ser metálicos o no metálicos. (p. 512)

**linfa:** fluido que se encuentra difundido en los capilares linfáticos. (p. 173)

**M**

**magma:** hot, melted rock material beneath Earth's surface. (p. 507)

**magnitude:** a measure of the energy released by an earthquake. (p. 595)

**mantle:** largest layer of Earth's interior that lies above the outer core and is solid yet flows slowly. (p. 566)

**mass:** amount of matter in an object. (p. 333)

**mass number:** sum of the number of protons and neutrons in the nucleus of an atom. (p. 269)

**matter:** anything that has mass and takes up space and is made up of different kinds of atoms; includes all things that can be seen, tasted, smelled, or touched but does not include heat, sound, or light. (p. 258)

**meiosis (mi OH sus):** reproductive process that produces four haploid sex cells from one diploid cell and ensures offspring will have the same number of chromosomes as the parent organisms. (p. 105)

**metabolism:** the total of all chemical reactions in an organism. (p. 81)

**metal:** element that is malleable, ductile, a good conductor of electricity, and generally has a shiny or metallic luster. (p. 270)

**metalloid:** element that has characteristics of both metals and nonmetals and is a solid at room temperature. (p. 271)

**metamorphic rock:** forms when heat, pressure, or fluids act on igneous, sedimentary, or other metamorphic rock to change its form or composition, or both. (p. 541)

**microprocessor:** integrated circuit that controls the flow of information between different parts of the computer; also called the central processing unit or CPU. (p. 455)

**magma:** material rocoso fundido y caliente que se encuentra por debajo de la superficie terrestre. (p. 507)

**magnitud:** medida de la energía generada por un terremoto. (p. 595)

**manto:** la capa más grande del interior de la Tierra que yace sobre el núcleo exterior y que es sólida aunque fluye lentamente. (p. 566)

**masa:** cantidad de materia en un objeto. (p. 333)

**número de masa:** suma del número de protones y neutrones en el núcleo de un átomo. (p. 269)

**materia:** todo lo que tenga masa, ocupe espacio y esté hecho de diferentes tipos de átomos; incluye todo lo que se puede ver, saborear, oler o tocar, pero no incluye el calor, el sonido o la luz. (p. 258)

**meiosis:** proceso reproductivo que produce cuatro células sexuales haploides a partir de una célula diploide y asegura que la descendencia tendrá el mismo número de cromosomas que los organismos progenitores. (p. 105)

**metabolismo:** el conjunto de todas las reacciones químicas en un organismo. (p. 81)

**metal:** elemento maleable, dúctil y buen conductor de electricidad que generalmente tiene un lustre brillante o metálico. (p. 270)

**metaloide:** elemento que comparte características de los metales y de los no metales y es sólido a temperatura ambiente. (p. 271)

**roca metamórfica:** se forma cuando el calor, la presión o los fluidos actúan sobre una roca ígnea, sedimentaria u otra roca metamórfica para cambiar su forma, composición o ambas. (p. 541)

**microprocesador:** circuito integrado que controla el flujo de información entre diferentes partes de una computadora; también se lo denomina la unidad central de procesamiento o CPU. (p. 455)

# Glossary/Glosario

**mineral:** naturally occurring inorganic solid that has a definite chemical composition and an orderly internal atomic structure. (pp. 136, 504)

**mitochondrion:** cell organelle that breaks down food and releases energy. (p. 42)

**mitosis (mi TOH sus):** cell process in which the nucleus divides to form two nuclei identical to each other, and identical to the original nucleus, in a series of steps (prophase, metaphase, anaphase, and telophase). (p. 98)

**mixture:** a combination of substances in which the individual substances do not change or combine chemically but instead retain their own individual properties; can be gases, solids, liquids, or any combination of them. (pp. 69, 275)

**mold:** a type of body fossil that forms in rock when an organism with hard parts is buried, decays or dissolves, and leaves a cavity in the rock. (p. 657)

**momentum:** a measure of how difficult it is to stop a moving object; equals the product of mass and velocity. (p. 334)

**mutation:** any permanent change in a gene or chromosome of a cell; may be beneficial, harmful, or have little effect on an organism. (p. 114)

**mineral:** sólido inorgánico que se encuentra en la naturaleza, tiene una composición química definida y una estructura atómica ordenada. (pp. 136, 504)

**mitocondria:** organelo celular que degrada nutrientes y libera energía. (p. 42)

**mitosis:** proceso celular en el que el núcleo se divide para formar dos núcleos idénticos entre sí e idénticos al núcleo original, a través de varias etapas (profase, metafase, anafase y telofase). (p. 98)

**mezcla:** una combinación de sustancias en la que las sustancias individuales no cambian ni se combinan químicamente pero mantienen sus propiedades individuales; pueden ser gases, sólidos, líquidos o una combinación de ellos. (pp. 69, 275)

**moldura:** tipo de cuerpo fósil que se formó en la roca cuando un organismo con partes duras fue enterrado, descompuesto o disuelto, dejando una cavidad en la roca. (p. 657)

**momento:** medida de la dificultad para detener un objeto en movimiento; es igual al producto de la masa por la velocidad. (p. 334)

**mutación:** cualquier cambio permanente en un gen o cromosoma de una célula; puede ser benéfica, perjudicial o tener un pequeño efecto sobre un organismo. (p. 114)

## N

**natural resources:** parts of Earth's environment that supply materials useful or necessary for the survival of living organisms. (p. 224)

**nebula:** large cloud of gas and dust that contracts under gravitational force and breaks apart into smaller pieces, each of which might collapse to form a star. (p. 484)

**nephron (NEF rahn):** tiny filtering unit of the kidney. (p. 149)

**net force:** combination of all forces acting on an object. (p. 351)

**neutralization (new truh luh ZAY shun):** reaction in which an acid reacts with a base and forms water and a salt. (p. 308)

**neutron:** an uncharged particle located in the nucleus of an atom. (p. 264)

**neutron star:** collapsed core of a supernova that can shrink to about 20 km in diameter and contains only neutrons in the dense core. (p. 486)

**recursos naturales:** partes del medio ambiente terrestre que proporcionan materiales útiles o necesarios para la supervivencia de los organismos vivos. (p. 224)

**nebulosa:** nube grande de polvo y gas que se contrae bajo la fuerza gravitacional y se descompone en pedazos más pequeños, cada uno de los cuales se puede colapsar para formar una estrella. (p. 484)

**nefrona:** pequeña unidad de filtración en el riñón. (p. 149)

**fuerza neta:** la combinación de todas las fuerzas que actúan sobre un objeto. (p. 351)

**neutralización:** reacción en la cual un ácido reacciona con una base para formar agua y una sal. (p. 308)

**neutrón:** partícula sin carga localizada en el núcleo de un átomo (p. 264)

**estrella de neutrones:** núcleo colapsado de una supernova que puede contraerse hasta tener un diámetro de 20 kilómetros y contiene sólo neutrones en su denso núcleo. (p. 486)

**Newton's first law of motion:** states that if the net force acting on an object is zero, the object will remain at rest or move in a straight line with a constant speed. (p. 352)

**Newton's second law of motion:** states that an object acted upon by a net force will accelerate in the direction of the force, and that the acceleration equals the net force divided by the object's mass. (p. 356)

**Newton's third law of motion:** states that forces always act in equal but opposite pairs. (p. 363)

**niche (NICH):** role of an organism in the ecosystem, including what it eats, how it interacts with other organisms, and how it gets its food. (p. 207)

**nonfoliated:** describes metamorphic rock, such as quartzite or marble, whose mineral grains grow and rearrange but generally do not form layers. (p. 544)

**noninfectious disease:** disease that is not caused by a pathogen. (p. 183)

**nonmetals:** elements that are usually gases or brittle solids and poor conductors of electricity and heat; are the basis of the chemicals of life. (p. 271)

**nonrenewable resources:** natural resources, such as petroleum, minerals, and metals, that are used more quickly than they can be replaced by natural processes. (pp. 225, 394)

**nuclear energy:** energy contained in atomic nuclei. (pp. 228, 384)

**nucleus (NEW klee us):** organelle that controls all the activities of a cell and contains hereditary material made of proteins and DNA; positively charged, central part of an atom. (pp. 40, 263)

**nutrients (NEW tree unts):** substances in foods—proteins, carbohydrates, fats, vitamins, minerals, and water—that provide energy and materials for cell development, growth, and repair. (p. 128)

**primera ley de movimiento de Newton:** establece que si la fuerza neta que actúa sobre un objeto es igual a cero, el objeto se mantendrá en reposo o se moverá en línea recta a una velocidad constante. (p. 352)

**segunda ley de movimiento de Newton:** establece que si una fuerza neta se ejerce sobre un objeto, éste se acelerará en la dirección de la fuerza y la aceleración es igual a la fuerza neta dividida por la masa del objeto. (p. 356)

**tercera ley de movimiento de Newton:** establece que las fuerzas siempre actúan en pares iguales pero opuestos. (p. 363)

**nicho:** papel que juega un organismo en un ecosistema, incluyendo lo que come, cómo interactúa con los otros organismos y cómo consigue su alimento. (p. 207)

**no foliado:** describe rocas metamórficas, como la cuarcita o el mármol, cuyas vetas minerales se acumulan y reestructuran pero rara vez forman capas. (p. 544)

**enfermedad no infecciosa:** enfermedad que no es causada por un patógeno. (p. 183)

**no metales:** elementos que por lo general son gases o sólidos frágiles y malos conductores de electricidad y calor; son la base de los compuestos químicos biológicos. (p. 271)

**recursos no renovables:** recursos naturales, como el petróleo, los minerales y los metales, que son utilizados más rápidamente de lo que pueden ser reemplazados mediante procesos naturales. (pp. 225, 394)

**energía nuclear:** energía contenida en los núcleos de los átomos. (pp. 228, 384)

**núcleo:** organelo que controla todas las actividades de una célula y que contiene el material hereditario formado por proteínas y ADN; parte central con carga positiva del átomo. (pp. 40, 263)

**nutrientes:** sustancias en los alimentos (proteínas, carbohidratos, grasas, vitaminas, minerales y agua) que suministran energía y materiales para el desarrollo, crecimiento y reparación de las células. (p. 128)

**O**

**ore:** deposit in which a mineral exists in large enough amounts to be mined at a profit. (p. 519)

**organ:** structure, such as the heart, made up of different types of tissues that all work together. (p. 45)

**mena:** depósito en el que existe un mineral en cantidades suficientes para la explotación minera. (p. 519)

**órgano:** estructura, como el corazón, que consiste en diferentes tipos de tejidos que trabajan conjuntamente. (p. 45)

**organelle:** structure in the cytoplasm of a eukaryotic cell that can act as a storage site, process energy, move materials, or manufacture substances. (p. 40)

**organic compounds:** compounds that always contain hydrogen and carbon; carbohydrates, lipids, proteins, and nucleic acids are organic compounds found in living things. (p. 70)

**organism:** any living thing. (p. 14)

**osmosis:** a type of passive transport that occurs when water diffuses through a cell membrane. (p. 76)

**outer core:** layer of Earth that lies above the inner core and is thought to be composed mostly of molten metal. (p. 566)

**ozone depletion:** thinning of Earth's ozone layer caused by chlorofluorocarbons (CFCs) leaking into the air and reacting chemically with ozone, breaking the ozone molecules apart. (p. 235)

**organelo:** estructura del citoplasma de una célula eucariota que puede actuar como sitio de almacenamiento, procesamiento de energía, movimiento de materiales o elaboración de sustancias. (p. 40)

**compuestos orgánicos:** compuestos que siempre contienen hidrógeno y carbono; los carbohidratos, lípidos, proteínas y ácidos nucleicos son compuestos orgánicos que se encuentran en los seres vivos. (p. 70)

**organismo:** cualquier ser vivo. (p. 14)

**ósmosis:** tipo de transporte pasivo que ocurre cuando el agua se difunde a través de una membrana celular. (p. 76)

**núcleo exterior:** capa de la Tierra que yace sobre el núcleo interior y que se piensa que está compuesta principalmente de metal fundido. (p. 566)

**agotamiento del ozono:** adelgazamiento de la capa de ozono de la Tierra causado por los clorofluorocarbonos (CFC) que escapan al aire y reaccionan químicamente con el ozono rompiendo sus moléculas. (p. 235)

**P**

**passive immunity:** immunity that results when antibodies produced in one animal are introduced into another's body; does not last as long as active immunity. (p. 176)

**passive transport:** movement of substances through a cell membrane without the use of cellular energy; includes diffusion, osmosis, and facilitated diffusion. (p. 74)

**pasteurization (pas chuh ruh ZAY shun):** process in which a liquid is heated to a temperature that kills most bacteria. (p. 178)

**peristalsis (per uh STAHL sus):** waves of muscular contractions that move food through the digestive tract. (p. 130)

**permineralized remains:** fossils in which the spaces inside are filled with minerals from groundwater. (p. 656)

**petroleum:** nonrenewable resource formed over hundreds of millions of years mostly from the remains of microscopic marine organisms buried in Earth's crust. (p. 225)

**pH:** measure of how acidic or basic a solution is, ranging in a scale from 0 to 14. (p. 306)

**photosphere:** lowest layer of the Sun's atmosphere; gives off light and has temperatures of about 6,000K. (p. 477)

**inmunidad pasiva:** inmunidad que se presenta cuando los anticuerpos producidos en un animal son introducidos en el cuerpo de otro animal, la cual no es tan duradera como la inmunidad activa. (p. 176)

**transporte pasivo:** movimiento de sustancias a través de la membrana celular sin usar energía celular; incluye difusión, ósmosis y difusión facilitada. (p. 74)

**pasteurización:** proceso mediante el cual un líquido es calentado a una temperatura que mata a la mayoría de las bacterias. (p. 178)

**peristalsis:** ondas de contracciones musculares que mueven al alimento a través del sistema digestivo. (p. 130)

**restos permineralizados:** fósiles en los que los espacios interiores son llenados con minerales de aguas subterráneas. (p. 656)

**petróleo:** recurso no renovable formado durante cientos de millones de años, en su mayoría a partir de los restos de organismos marinos microscópicos sepultados en la corteza terrestre. (p. 225)

**pH:** medida para saber qué tan básica o ácida es una solución, en una escala de 0 a 14. (p. 306)

**fotosfera:** capa más interna de la atmósfera del sol; emite luz y tiene temperaturas de cerca de 6,000 grados Kelvin. (p. 477)

# Glossary/Glosario

**photosynthesis:** process by which plants and many other producers use light energy to produce a simple sugar from carbon dioxide and water and give off oxygen. (p. 82)

**photovoltaic:** device that transforms radiant energy directly into electrical energy. (p. 398)

**phylogeny (fi LAH juh nee):** evolutionary history of an organism; used today to group organisms into six kingdoms. (p. 23)

**pitch:** human perception of the frequency of sound. (p. 421)

**plasma:** the liquid part of blood, which is made mostly of water. (p. 162)

**plate:** section of Earth's crust and rigid, upper mantle that moves slowly around on the asthenosphere. (p. 568)

**platelet:** irregularly shaped cell fragments that help clot blood. (p. 163)

**polar zones:** climate zones that receive solar radiation at a low angle, extend from 66°N and S latitude to the poles, and are never warm. (p. 624)

**pollutant:** substance that contaminates any part of the environment. (p. 232)

**population:** all of the individuals of one species that live in the same space at the same time. (p. 200)

**population density:** number of individuals in a population that occupies an area of limited size. (p. 204)

**potential energy:** energy stored in an object due to its position. (p. 382)

**precipitate:** solid that comes back out of its solution because of a chemical reaction or physical change. (p. 290)

**principle of superposition:** states that in undisturbed rock layers, the oldest rocks are on the bottom and the rocks become progressively younger toward the top. (p. 662)

**proton:** positively charged particle located in the nucleus of an atom and that is counted to identify the atomic number. (p. 263)

**fotosíntesis:** proceso mediante el cual las plantas y muchos otros organismos productores usan la energía solar para producir azúcares simples a partir de dióxido de carbono y agua y desprender oxígeno. (p. 82)

**fotovoltaico:** dispositivo que transforma la energía radiante directamente en energía eléctrica. (p. 398)

**filogenia:** historia evolutiva de un organismo; usada hoy para agrupar a los organismos en seis reinos. (p. 23)

**tono:** percepción humana de la frecuencia del sonido. (p. 421)

**plasma:** parte líquida de la sangre compuesto principalmente por agua. (p. 162)

**placa:** sección de la corteza terrestre y del manto superior rígido que se mueve lentamente sobre la astenosfera. (p. 568)

**plaqueta:** fragmentos de célula de forma irregular que ayudan a coagular la sangre. (p. 163)

**zonas polares:** zonas climáticas que reciben radiación solar a un ángulo reducido, se extienden desde los 66° de latitud norte y sur hasta los polos y nunca son cálidas. (p. 624)

**contaminante:** sustancia que contamina cualquier parte del medio ambiente. (p. 232)

**población:** todos los individuos de una especie que viven en el mismo espacio al mismo tiempo. (p. 200)

**densidad de población:** número de individuos en una población que ocupa un área de tamaño limitado. (p. 204)

**energía potencial:** energía almacenada en un objeto debido a su posición. (p. 382)

**precipitado:** sólido que se aísla de su solución mediante una reacción química o un cambio físico. (p. 290)

**principio de superposición:** establece que en las capas rocosas no perturbadas, las rocas más antiguas están en la parte inferior y las rocas son más jóvenes conforme están más cerca de la superficie. (p. 662)

**protón:** partícula cargada positivamente, localizada en el núcleo de un átomo y que se cuenta para identificar el número atómico. (p. 263)

**R**

**radiant energy:** energy carried by light. (p. 383)

**energía radiante:** energía transportada por la luz. (p. 383)

**radioactive decay:** process in which some isotopes break down into other isotopes and particles. (p. 669)

**radiometric dating:** process used to calculate the absolute age of rock by measuring the ratio of parent isotope to daughter product in a mineral and knowing the half-life of the parent. (p. 671)

**random-access memory (RAM):** temporary electronic memory within a computer. (p. 452)

**read-only memory (ROM):** electronic memory that is permanently stored within a computer. (p. 452)

**recycling:** conservation method that is a form of reuse and requires changing or reprocessing an item or natural resource. (p. 243)

**refraction:** change in direction of a wave when it changes speed as it travels from one material into another. (p. 417)

**relative age:** the age of something compared with other things. (p. 663)

**renewable resources:** natural resources, such as water, sunlight, and crops, that are constantly being recycled or replaced by nature. (pp. 225, 396)

**respiration:** process by which producers and consumers release stored energy from food molecules. (p. 83)

**reverberation:** repeated echoes of sound waves. (p. 423)

**ribosome:** small cytoplasmic structure on which cells make their own proteins. (p. 42)

**rift:** long crack, fissure, or trough that forms between tectonic plates moving apart at plate boundaries. (p. 609)

**RNA:** ribonucleic acid; a type of nucleic acid that carries codes for making proteins from the nucleus to the ribosomes. (p. 112)

**rock:** mixture of one or more minerals, rock fragments, volcanic glass, organic matter, or other natural materials; can be igneous, metamorphic, or sedimentary. (p. 532)

**rock cycle:** model that describes how rocks slowly change from one form to another through time. (p. 533)

**desintegración radiactiva:** proceso en el que algunos isótopos se desintegran en otros isótopos y partículas. (p. 669)

**fechado radiométrico:** proceso utilizado para calcular la edad absoluta de las rocas midiendo la relación isótopo parental a producto derivado en un mineral y conociendo la vida media del parental. (p. 671)

**memoria de acceso aleatorio (RAM):** memoria electrónica temporal dentro de una computadora. (p. 452)

**memoria de sólo lectura (ROM):** memoria electrónica almacenada permanentemente dentro de una computadora. (p. 452)

**reciclaje:** método de conservación como una forma de reutilización y que requiere del cambio o reprocesamiento del producto o recurso natural. (p. 243)

**refracción:** cambio de dirección de una onda al cambiar su velocidad cuando pasa de un material a otro. (p. 417)

**edad relativa:** la edad de algo comparado con otras cosas. (p. 663)

**recursos renovables:** recursos naturales, como el agua, la luz solar y los cultivos, que son reciclados o reemplazados constantemente por la naturaleza. (pp. 225, 396)

**respiración:** proceso mediante el cual los organismos productores y consumidores liberan la energía almacenada en las moléculas de los alimentos. (p. 83)

**reverberación:** ecos repetidos de ondas sonoras. (p. 423)

**ribosoma:** estructura citoplasmática pequeña en la que las células producen sus propias proteínas. (p. 42)

**ruptura:** grieta larga, fisura o hueco que se forma entre placas tectónicas que se separan en los límites de las placas. (p. 609)

**ARN:** Ácido ribonucleico; tipo de ácido nucleico que transporta los códigos para la formación de proteínas del núcleo a los ribosomas. (p. 112)

**roca:** mezcla de uno o más minerales, fragmentos de roca, obsidiana, materia orgánica u otros materiales naturales; puede ser ígnea, metamórfica o sedimentaria. (p. 532)

**ciclo de la roca:** modelo que describe cómo cambian lentamente las rocas de una forma a otra a través del tiempo. (p. 533)

## S

**saturated:** describes a solution that holds the total amount of solute that it can hold under given conditions. (p. 298)

**saturado:** describe a una solución que retiene toda la cantidad de soluto que puede retener bajo determinadas condiciones. (p. 298)

**scientific methods:** procedures used to solve problems and answer questions that can include stating the problem, gathering information, forming a hypothesis, testing the hypothesis with an experiment, analyzing data, and drawing conclusions. (p. 7)

**season:** short period of climate change in an area caused by the tilt of Earth's axis as Earth revolves around the Sun. (p. 632)

**sedimentary rock:** forms when sediments are compacted and cemented together or when minerals form from solutions. (p. 545)

**sediments:** loose materials, such as rock fragments, mineral grains, and the remains of once-living plants and animals, that have been moved by wind, water, ice, or gravity. (p. 545)

**seismic safe:** describes the ability of structures to stand up against the vibrations caused by an earthquake. (p. 599)

**seismic waves:** earthquake waves, including primary waves, secondary waves, and surface waves. (p. 594)

**seismograph:** instrument used to record seismic waves. (p. 595)

**semiconductor:** element, such as silicon, that is a poorer electrical conductor that a metal, but a better conductor than a nonmetal, and whose electrical conductivity can be changed by adding impurities. (p. 445)

**sexual reproduction:** a type of reproduction in which two sex cells, usually an egg and a sperm, join to form a zygote, which will develop into a new organism with a unique identity. (p. 104)

**shield volcano:** large, broad volcano with gently sloping sides that is formed by the buildup of basaltic layers. (p. 604)

**silicate:** mineral that contains silicon and oxygen and usually one or more other elements. (p. 508)

**solubility (sahl yuh BIH luh tee):** measure of how much solute can be dissolved in a certain amount of solvent. (p. 297)

**solute:** substance that dissolves and seems to disappear into another substance. (p. 290)

**solution:** homogeneous mixture whose elements and/or compounds are evenly mixed at the molecular level but are not bonded together. (p. 290)

**solvent:** substance that dissolves the solute. (p. 290)

**specific gravity:** ratio of a mineral's weight compared with the weight of an equal volume of water. (p. 512)

**métodos científicos:** procedimientos utilizados para solucionar problemas y responder a preguntas; puede incluir el establecimiento de un problema, recopilación de información, formulación de una hipótesis, comprobación de la hipótesis con un experimento, análisis de la información y presentación de conclusiones. (p. 7)

**estación:** periodo corto de cambio climático en un área, causado por la inclinación del eje de la Tierra conforme gira alrededor del sol. (p. 632)

**roca sedimentaria:** se forma cuando los sedimentos son compactados y cementados o cuando se forman minerales a partir de soluciones. (p. 545)

**sedimentos:** materiales sueltos, como fragmentos de roca, granos minerales y restos de animales y plantas, que han sido arrastrados por el viento, el agua, el hielo o la gravedad. (p. 545)

**seguridad antisísmica:** describe la capacidad de las estructuras de resistir las vibraciones producidas por los terremotos. (p. 599)

**ondas sísmicas:** ondas producidas durante los terremotos, las cuales pu ser primarias, secundarias y superficiales. (p. 594)

**sismógrafo:** instrumento usado para registrar las ondas sísmicas. (p. 595)

**semiconductor:** elemento, como el silicio, que no es tan buen conductor de electricidad como un metal, pero que es mejor conductor que un no metal y cuya conductividad eléctrica puede ser modificada al añadirle impurezas. (p. 445)

**reproducción sexual:** tipo de reproducción en la que dos células sexuales, generalmente un óvulo y un espermatozoide, se unen para formar un zigoto, el cual se desarrollará para formar un nuevo organismo con identidad única. (p. 104)

**volcán escudo:** volcán grande y ancho con lados ligeramente inclinados que se forma por la aparición de capas basálticas. (p. 604)

**silicato:** mineral que contiene sílice y oxígeno y generalmente uno o varios elementos distintos. (p. 508)

**solubilidad:** medida de la cantidad de soluto que puede disolverse en cierta cantidad de solvente. (p. 297)

**soluto:** sustancia que se disuelve y parece desaparecer en otra sustancia. (p. 290)

**solución:** mezcla homogénea cuyos elementos o compuestos están mezclados de manera uniforme a nivel molecular pero no se enlazan. (p. 290)

**solvente:** sustancia que disuelve al soluto. (p. 290)

**gravedad específica:** cociente del peso de un mineral comparado con el peso de un volumen igual de agua. (p. 512)

**Glossary/Glosario**

**speed:** equals the distance traveled divided by the time it takes to travel that distance. (p. 324)

**sperm:** haploid sex cell formed in the male reproductive organs. (p. 104)

**spontaneous generation:** idea that living things come from nonliving things. (p. 19)

**streak:** color of a mineral when it is in powdered form. (p. 513)

**subduction:** a type of plate movement that occurs when one plate sinks beneath another plate. (p. 571)

**substance:** matter that has the same composition and properties throughout. (pp. 273, 288)

**sunspots:** areas on the Sun's surface that are cooler and less bright than surrounding areas, are caused by the Sun's magnetic field, and occur in cycles. (p. 478)

**supergiant:** late stage in the life cycle of a massive star in which the core heats up, heavy elements form by fusion, and the star expands; can eventually explode to form a supernova. (p. 487)

**symbiosis (sihm bee OH sus):** any close interaction among two or more different species, including mutualism, commensalism, and parasitism. (p. 206)

**rapidez:** equivale a dividir la distancia recorrida por el tiempo que toma recorrer dicha distancia. (p. 324)

**espermatozoides:** células sexuales haploides que se forman en los órganos reproductores masculinos. (p. 104)

**generación espontánea:** idea que sostiene que los seres vivos proceden de seres inertes. (p. 19)

**veta:** color de un mineral en forma de polvo. (p. 513)

**subducción:** tipo de movimiento de placas que ocurre cuando una placa se ubica debajo de otra. (p. 571)

**sustancia:** materia que siempre tiene la misma composición y las mismas propiedades. (pp. 273, 288)

**manchas solares:** áreas en la superficie solar que son más frías y menos brillantes que las áreas circundantes, son causadas por el campo magnético solar y ocurren en ciclos. (p. 478)

**supergigante:** etapa tardía en el ciclo de vida de una estrella masiva en la que el núcleo se calienta, se forman elementos pesados por fusión y la estrella se expande; eventualmente puede explotar para formar una supernova. (p. 487)

**simbiosis:** cualquier interacción cercana entre dos o más especies diferentes, incluyendo mutualismo, asociaciones y parasitismo. (p. 206)

**temperate zones:** climate zones with moderate temperatures that are located between the tropics and the polar zones. (p. 624)

**theory:** explanation of things or events based on scientific knowledge resulting from many observations and experiments. (p. 10)

**thermal energy:** energy that all objects have that increases as the object's temperature increases. (p. 382)

**tissue:** group of similar cells that work together to do one job. (p. 45)

**trachea (TRAY kee uh):** air-conducting tube that connects the larynx with the bronchi, is lined with mucous membranes and cilia, and contains strong cartilage rings. (p. 142)

**transistor:** a solid-state component made from three layers of semiconductor material that can amplify the strength of an electric signal or act as an electronic switch. (p. 447)

**transverse wave:** mechanical wave that causes particles in matter to move at right angles to the direction the wave travels. (p. 413)

**zonas templadas:** zonas climáticas con temperaturas moderadas que están localizadas entre los trópicos y las zonas polares. (p. 624)

**teoría:** explicación de cosas o eventos basándose en el conocimiento científico resultante de muchas observaciones y experimentos. (p. 10)

**energía térmica:** energía que poseen todos los objetos y que aumenta al aumentar la temperatura de éstos. (p. 382)

**tejido:** grupo de células similares que trabajan conjuntamente para hacer una tarea. (p. 45)

**tráquea:** tubo conductor de aire que conecta a la laringe con los bronquios, está forrada con membranas mucosas y cilios y contiene fuertes anillos de cartílagos. (p. 142)

**transistor:** componente de estado sólido formado por tres capas de material semiconductor que puede amplificar la fuerza de una señal eléctrica o actuar a manera de interruptor electrónico. (p. 447)

**onda transversal:** onda mecánica que hace que las partículas de materia se muevan en ángulos rectos respecto a la dirección en que viaja la onda. (p. 413)

**tropics:** climate zone that receives the most solar radiation, is located between latitudes 23°N and 23°S, and is always hot, except at high elevations. (p. 624)

**tsunami:** powerful seismic sea wave that begins over an ocean-floor earthquake, can reach 30 m in height when approaching land, and can cause destruction in coastal areas. (p. 597)

**turbine:** set of steam-powered fan blades that spins a generator at a power plant. (p. 390)

**trópicos:** zonas climáticas que reciben la mayor parte de la radiación solar, están localizadas entre los 23° de latitud norte y 23° de latitud sur y siempre son cálidas excepto a grandes alturas. (p. 624)

**tsunami:** poderosa onda sísmica marina que comienza en un terremoto en el lecho oceánico, pudiendo alcanzar 30 metros de altura al acercarse a la tierra y causar gran destrucción en las áreas costeras. (p. 597)

**turbina:** conjunto de aspas de ventilador impulsadas por vapor que hacen girar a un generador en una planta de energía eléctrica. (p. 390)

**ultraviolet waves:** electromagnetic waves with wavelengths between about 400 billionths and 10 billionths of a meter. (p. 428)

**unbalanced forces:** two or more forces acting on an object that do not cancel, and cause the object to accelerate. (p. 351)

**unconformity (un kun FOR mih tee):** gap in the rock layer that is due to erosion or periods without any deposition. (p. 664)

**uniformitarianism:** principle stating that Earth processes occurring today are similar to those that occurred in the past. (p. 673)

**upwarped mountain:** mountain that forms when forces inside Earth push up the crust. (p. 577)

**ureter:** tube that carries urine from each kidney to the bladder. (p. 149)

**ondas ultravioleta:** ondas electromagnéticas con longitudes de onda entre aproximadamente 10 y 400 billonésimas de metro. (p. 428)

**fuerzas no balanceadas:** dos o más fuerzas que actúan sobre un objeto sin anularse y que hacen que el objeto se acelere. (p. 351)

**discordancia:** brecha en la capa rocosa que es debida a la erosión o a periodos sin deposición. (p. 664)

**uniformitarianismo:** principio que establece que los procesos de la Tierra que ocurren actualmente son similares a los que ocurrieron en el pasado. (p. 673)

**montaña encorvada:** montaña que se forma cuando las fuerzas internas de la Tierra levantan la corteza. (p. 577)

**uréter:** tubo que transporta la orina desde cada uno de los riñones hasta la vejiga. (p. 149)

**variable:** something in an experiment that can change. (p. 9)

**vein:** blood vessel that carries blood to the heart. (p. 170)

**velocity:** speed and direction of a moving object. (p. 327)

**villi (VIH li):** fingerlike projections covering the wall of the small intestine that increase the surface area for food absorption. (p. 131)

**virus:** a strand of hereditary material surrounded by a protein coating. (p. 52)

**variable:** condición que puede cambiar en un experimento. (p. 9)

**vena:** vasos sanguíneos que transportan la sangre al corazón. (p. 170)

**velocidad:** rapidez y dirección de un objeto en movimiento. (p. 327)

**vellosidades:** proyecciones en forma de dedo que cubren las paredes del intestino delgado y aumentan el área de superficie para la absorción de los alimentos. (p. 131)

**virus:** cadena de material hereditario rodeada por una membrana proteica. (p. 52)

**Glossary/Glosario**

**vitamin:** water-soluble or fat-soluble organic nutrient needed in small quantities for growth, for preventing some diseases, and for regulating body functions. (p. 135)

**volcanic mountain:** mountain that forms when magma is forced upward and flows onto Earth's surface. (p. 578)

**volcano:** cone-shaped hill or mountain formed when hot magma, solids, and gas erupt onto Earth's surface through a vent. (p. 601)

**vitamina:** nutriente orgánico soluble en agua o en grasa, necesario en pequeñas cantidades para el crecimiento, para prevenir algunas enfermedades y para regular las funciones biológicas. (p. 135)

**montaña volcánica:** montaña que se forma cuando el magma es empujado hacia arriba y fluye sobre la superficie terrestre. (p. 578)

**volcán:** colina o montaña cónica que se forma cuando el magma caliente, sólidos y gases, hacen erupción en la superficie terrestre a través de una abertura. (p. 601)

## W

**water cycle:** continuous cycle of water molecules on Earth as they rise into the atmosphere, fall back to Earth as rain or other precipitation, and flow into rivers and oceans through the processes of evaporation, condensation, and precipitation. (p. 212)

**wave:** disturbance that moves through matter and space and carries energy. (p. 412)

**wavelength:** distance between one point on a wave and the nearest point moving with the same speed and direction. (p. 414)

**weight:** gravitational force between an object and Earth. (p. 357)

**white dwarf:** late stage in the life cycle of a comparatively low-mass main sequence star; formed when its core depletes its helium and its outer layers escape into space, leaving behind a hot, dense core. (p. 486)

**ciclo del agua:** ciclo continuo de las moléculas de agua en la Tierra en su proceso de subir a la atmósfera, regresar a la Tierra en forma de lluvia u otra forma de precipitación y fluir hacia los ríos y océanos a través de la evaporación, condensación y precipitación. (p. 212)

**onda:** perturbación que se mueve a través de la materia y el espacio y que transporta energía. (p. 412)

**longitud de onda:** distancia entre un punto en una onda y el punto más cercano, moviéndose con la misma rapidez y dirección. (p. 414)

**peso:** fuerza gravitacional entre un objeto y la Tierra. (p. 357)

**enana blanca:** etapa tardía en el ciclo de vida de una estrella de secuencia principal, de relativamente poca masa, formada cuando el núcleo agota su helio y sus capas externas escapan al espacio, dejando atrás un núcleo denso y caliente. (p. 486)

## Z

**zygote:** new diploid cell formed when a sperm fertilizes an egg; will divide by mitosis and develop into a new organism. (p. 104)

**zigoto:** célula diploide nueva formada cuando un espermatozoide fertiliza a un óvulo; se dividirá por mitosis y se desarrollará para formar un nuevo organismo. (p. 104)

## A

Index

# Index

Index

# Index

Index

Index

**Magnification Key:** Magnifications listed are the magnifications at which images were originally photographed.
LM–Light Microscope
SEM–Scanning Electron Microscope
TEM–Transmission Electron Microscope

**Acknowledgments:** Glencoe would like to acknowledge the artists and agencies who participated in illustrating this program: Absolute Science Illustration; Andrew Evansen; Argosy; Articulate Graphics; Craig Attebery, represented by Frank & Jeff Lavaty; CHK America; John Edwards and Associates; Gagliano Graphics; Pedro Julio Gonzalez, represented by Melissa Turk & The Artist Network; Robert Hynes, represented by Mendola Ltd.; Morgan Cain & Associates; JTH Illustration; Laurie O'Keefe; Matthew Pippin, represented by Beranbaum Artist's Representative; Precision Graphics; Publisher's Art; Rolin Graphics, Inc.; Wendy Smith, represented by Melissa Turk & The Artist Network; Kevin Torline, represented by Berendsen and Associates, Inc.; WILDlife ART; Phil Wilson, represented by Cliff Knecht Artist Representative; Zoo Botanica.

## Photo Credits

**Cover i ii** (bkgd)Sharon Gerig/Tom Stack & Assoc., (bl)Steve Raymer/CORBIS, (r)Zephyr/Photo Researchers; **vii** Aaron Haupt; **viii** John Evans; **ix** (t)PhotoDisc, (b)John Evans; **x** (l)John Evans, (r)Geoff Butler; **xi** (l)John Evans, (r)PhotoDisc; **xii** PhotoDisc; **xiii** Michael Fogden/Earth Scenes; **xiv** (t)Roland Seitre-Bios/Peter Arnold, Inc., (b)KS Studios; **xv** AFP/CORBIS; **xvi** Ray Massey/Getty Images; **xvii** (t)Breck P. Kent/Earth Scenes, (c)Charles D. Winters/Photo Researchers, (b)Matt Meadows; **xviii** (t)PhotoTake NYC/PictureQuest, (b)David Hosking/CORBIS; **xix** Tim Courlas; **xx** (t)Dennis Johnson/Papilio/CORBIS, (b)Joe McDonald/CORBIS; **xxi** Alexis Duclos/Getty News Images; **xxiii** (l)Archivo Iconografico, S.A./CORBIS, (r)John Reader/Science Photo Library/Photo Researchers; **xxiv** Aaron Haupt; **xxvi** George Bernard/Earth Scenes; **1** David W. Hamilton/Getty Images; **2** Microworks/PhotoTake NYC; **2–3** Doug Wilson/CORBIS; **4–5** A. Witte/C. Mahaney/Getty Images; **6** Kjell B. Sandved/Visuals Unlimited; **8 9** Mark Burnett; **11** Tek Image/Science Photo Library/Photo Researchers; **12 13** Mark Burnett; **14** (t)Michael Abbey/Science Source/Photo Researchers, (bl)Aaron Haupt, (br)Michael Delannoy/Visuals Unlimited; **15** Mark Burnett; **16** (tcr)A. Glauberman/Photo Researchers, (tr)Mark Burnett, (bl bcl br)Runk/Schoenberger from Grant Heilman, (others)Dwight Kuhn; **17** (t)Bill Beaty/Animals Animals, (bl)Tom & Therisa Stack/Tom Stack & Assoc., (br)Michael Fogden/Earth Scenes; **18** Aaron Haupt; **19** Geoff Butler; **22** (t)Arthur C. Smith III From Grant Heilman, (bl)Hal Beral/Visuals Unlimited, (br)Larry L. Miller/Photo Researchers; **23** Doug Perrine/Innerspace Visions; **24** (l)Brandon D. Cole, (r)Gregory Ochocki/Photo Researchers; **25** (l)Zig Leszczynski/Animals Animals, (r)R. Andrew Odum/Peter Arnold, Inc.; **26** Alvin E. Staffan; **27** Geoff Butler; **28** (t)Jan Hinsch/Science Photo Library/Photo Researchers, (b)Mark Burnett; **29** Mark Burnett; **30** Marc Von Roosmalen/AP; **31** (l)Mark Burnett, (r)Will & Deni McIntyre/Photo Researchers; **32** KS Studios/Mullenix; **33** Jeff Greenberg/Rainbow; **34** Dwight Kuhn; **35** Dave Spier/Visuals Unlimited; **36–37** Nancy Kedersha/Science Photo Library/Photo Researchers; **39** David M.

Phillips/Visuals Unlimited; **40** (t)Don Fawcett/Photo Researchers, (b)M. Schliwa/Visuals Unlimited; **42** (t)George B. Chapman/Visuals Unlimited, (b)P. Motta & T. Naguro/Science Photo Library/Photo Researchers; **43** (t)Don Fawcett/Photo Researchers, (b)Biophoto Associates/Photo Researchers; **47** (l)Biophoto Associates/Photo Researchers, (r)Matt Meadows; **48–49** David M. Phillips/Visuals Unlimited; **48** (cw from top)Kathy Talaro/Visuals Unlimited, Michael Abbey/Visuals Unlimited, Michael Gabridge/Visuals Unlimited, David M. Phillips/Visuals Unlimited, David M. Phillips/Visuals Unlimited, courtesy Nikon Instruments Inc.; **49** (tl)Michael Abbey/Visuals Unlimited, (tr)Bob Krist/CORBIS, (cl)courtesy Olympus Corporation, (cr)James W. Evarts, (bl)Karl Aufderheide/Visuals Unlimited, (br)Lawrence Migdale/Stock Boston/PictureQuest; **52** (l)Richard J. Green/Photo Researchers, (c)Dr. J.F.J.M. van der Heuvel, (r)Gelderblom/Eye of Science/Photo Researchers; **55** Pam Wilson/Texas Dept. of Health; **56 57** Matt Meadows; **58** (t)Quest/Science Photo Library/Photo Researchers, (b)courtesy California University; **59** (l)Keith Porter/Photo Researchers, (r)NIBSC/Science Photo Library/Photo Researchers; **61** Biophoto Associates/Science Source/Photo Researchers; **62** P. Motta & T. Naguro/Science Photo Library/Photo Researchers; **64–65** Jane Grushow/Grant Heilman Photography; **67** Bob Daemmrich; **69** (t)Runk/Schoenberger from Grant Heilman, (b)Klaus Guldbrandsen/Science Photo Library/Photo Researchers; **74** (l)John Fowler, (r)Richard Hamilton Smith/CORBIS; **75** KS Studios; **76** Aaron Haupt; **77** Visuals Unlimited; **78** Biophoto Associates/Science Source/Photo Researchers; **80** Matt Meadows; **82** Craig Lovell/CORBIS; **83** John Fowler; **84** David M. Phillips/Visuals Unlimited; **85** (l)Grant Heilman Photography, (r)Bios (Klein/Hubert)/Peter Arnold; **86** (t)Runk/Schoenberger from Grant Heilman, (b)Matt Meadows; **87** Matt Meadows; **88** Lappa/Marquart; **89** CNRI/Science Photo Library/Photo Researchers; **90** Biophoto Associates/Science Source/Photo Researchers; **94–95** Zig Leszczynski/Animals Animals; **96** (l)Dave B. Fleetham/Tom Stack & Assoc., (r)Cabisco/Visuals Unlimited; **98** Cabisco/Visuals Unlimited; **99** (tl)Michael Abbey/Visuals Unlimited, (others)John D. Cunningham/Visuals Unlimited; **100** (l)Matt Meadows, (r)Nigel Cattlin/Photo Researchers; **101** (l)Barry L. Runk from Grant Heilman, (r)Runk/Schoenberger from Grant Heilman; **102** (l)Walker England/Photo Researchers, (r)Tom Stack & Assoc.; **103** Runk/Schoenberger from Grant Heilman; **104** Dr. Dennis Kunkel/PhotoTake NYC; **105** (tl)Gerald & Buff Corsi/Visuals Unlimited, (r)Fred Bruenner/Peter Arnold, Inc., (bl)Susan McCartney/Photo Researchers; **107** (l)John D. Cunningham/Visuals Unlimited, (c)Jen & Des Bartlett/Bruce Coleman, Inc., (r)Breck P. Kent; **108** (tl)Artville, (tr)Tim Fehr, (c)Bob Daemmrich/Stock Boston/PictureQuest, (bl)Troy Mary Parlee/Index Stock/PictureQuest, (br)Jeffery Myers/Southern Stock/PictureQuest; **114** Stewart Cohen/Stone/Getty Images; **116** (t)Tom McHugh/Photo Researchers, (b)file photo; **117** Monica Dalmasso/Stone/Getty Images; **118** (t)Philip Lee Harvey/Stone, (b)Lester V. Bergman/CORBIS; **120** Walker England/Photo Researchers; **122** Barry L. Runk from Grant Heilman; **123** Cabisco/Visuals Unlimited; **125** Don Mason/The Stock Market/CORBIS; **124–125** Birgid Allig/Stone/Getty Images; **126–127** Chris Trotman/NewSport/Corbis; **129** Geoff Butler; **133 134** KS Studios; **135** Visuals Unlimited; **137 138** KS Studios; **140** Dominic Oldershaw; **141** Bob Daemmrich; **144** Richard T. Nowitz; **146** Renee Lynn/Photo

Researchers; **151** Richard Hutchings/Photo Researchers; **152** KS Studios; **153** Matt Meadows; **154** (t)Lane Medical Library, (b)Custom Medical Stock Photo; **155** (l)Ed Beck/The Stock Market/CORBIS, (r)Tom & DeeAnn McCarthy/The Stock Market/CORBIS; **160–161** Julian Calder/CORBIS; **163** National Cancer Institute/Science Photo Library/Photo Researchers; **166** Meckes/Ottawa/Photo Researchers; **167** Aaron Haupt; **170** Matt Meadows, (inset)StudiOhio; **171** Aaron Haupt; **173** Runk/Schoenberger from Grant Heilman; **175** CC Studio/Science Photo Library/Photo Researchers; **178** Holt Studios International (Nigel Cattlin)/ Photo Researchers; **179** (tc br)Visuals Unlimited, (tr bl)Jack Bostrack/Visuals Unlimited, (cl)Cytographics Inc./Visuals Unlimited, (cr)Cabisco/Visuals Unlimited; **181** Oliver Meckes/E.O.S/Gelderblom/Photo Researchers; **182** Andrew Syred/Science Photo Library/Photo Researchers; **186** Matt Meadows/Peter Arnold, Inc.; **187** Matt Meadows; **188** (bkgd)Science Photo Library/Photo Researchers, TIME; **189** (tl)Manfred Kage/Peter Arnold, Inc., (tr)K.G. Murti/ Visuals Unlimited, (bl)Don W. Fawcett/Visuals Unlimited; **192** Aaron Haupt; **194–195** Clem Haagner/A.B.P.L./Photo Researchers; **196** WM. J. Jahoda/Photo Researchers; **197** (t)Stuart Westmorland/Photo Researchers, (c)Michael P. Gadomski/Earth Scenes, (b)George Bernard/Earth Scenes; **198** Francis Lepine/Earth Scenes; **200** (t)Roland Seitre-Bios/Peter Arnold, Inc., (bl)Robert C. Gildart/Peter Arnold, Inc., (br)Carr Clifton/Minden Pictures; **202** Bob Daemmrich; **204** Dan Suzio/Photo Researchers; **205** (t)Tim Davis/Photo Researchers, (b)Arthur Gloor/Animals Animals; **206** Gilbert Grant/Photo Researchers; **207** John Gerlach/Animals Animals; **208** Michael P. Gadomski/Photo Researchers; **209** (bkgd bl)Michael Boys/CORBIS, (t)Joe McDonald/ CORBIS, (c)David A. Northcott/CORBIS, (bc)Dennis Johnson/Papilio/CORBIS, (br)Kevin Jackson/Animals Animals; **211** (from top)Ray Richardson/Animals Animals, Suzanne L. Collins/Photo Researchers, William E. Grenfell Jr./Visuals Unlimited, Zig Leszczynski/Earth Scenes; **214** (t)Geoff Butler, (b)KS Studios; **215** Matt Meadows; **216** Allen Russell/Index Stock; **217** (l)Richard Reid/Earth Scenes, (r)Helga Lade/Peter Arnold, Inc.; **218** Helga Lade/ Peter Arnold, Inc.; **220** (l)George Bernard/Earth Scenes, (r)Tim Davis/Photo Researchers; **221** Arthur Gloor/Animals Animals; **222–223** Grant Heilman Photography; **224** (l)Keith Lanpher/Liaison Agency/Getty Images, (r)Richard Thatcher/ David R. Frazier Photolibrary; **225** (t)Solar Cookers International, (bl)Brian F. Peterson/The Stock Market/ CORBIS, (br)Ron Kimball Photography; **226** Larry Mayer/ Liaison Agency/Getty Images; **229** (tr)Torleif Svenson/The Stock Market/CORBIS, (bl)Rob Williamson, (br)Les Gibbon/ Cordaiy Photo Library Ltd./CORBIS; **230** Sean Justice; **231** (t)Lowell Georgia/Science Source/Photo Researchers, (cl)NASA, (c)CORBIS, (cr)Sean Sprague/Impact Visuals/ PictureQuest, (bl)Lee Foster/Bruce Coleman, Inc., (br)Robert Perron; **232** Philippe Renault/Liaison Agency/Getty Images; **233** (l)NYC Parks Photo Archive/Fundamental Photographs, (r)Kristen Brochmann/Fundamental Photographs; **237** (l)Jeremy Walker/Science Photo Library/Photo Researchers, (c)John Colwell from Grant Heilman, (r)Telegraph Colour Library/FPG/Getty Images; **238** Wilford Haven/Liaison Agency/Getty Images; **239** (tl)Larry Mayer/ Liaison Agency/Getty Images, (tr)ChromoSohm/The Stock Market/CORBIS, (cr)David R. Frazier Photolibrary, (br)Inga Spence/Visuals Unlimited; **240** (r)Andrew Holbrooke/The Stock Market/CORBIS, (Paint Cans)Amanita Pictures,

(Turpantine, Paint thinner, epoxy)Icon Images, (Batteries) Aaron Haupt; **242** Paul A. Souders/CORBIS; **243** Icon Images; **245** Larry Lefever from Grant Heilman; **246** (t)Howard Buffett from Grant Heilman, (b)Solar Cookers International; **247** John D. Cunningham/Visuals Unlimited; **248** Frank Cezus/FPG/Getty Images; **250** Robert Cameron/Stone/Getty Images; **251** (l)Steve McCutcheon/ Visuals Unlimited, (r)James N. Westwater; **252** David R. Frazier Photolibrary; **254** CORBIS/PictureQuest; **254–255** Stephen Frisch/Stock Boston/PictureQuest; **256–257** Russell Dohrman/Index Stock; **257** Morrison Photography; **258** (l)Gary C. Will/Visuals Unlimited, (c)Mark Burnett/Stock Boston, (r)CORBIS; **260** Mark Burnett; **261** (l)Mark Burnett, (r)NASA; **262** Van Bucher/Photo Researchers; **266** Fermi National Accelerator Laboratory/ Science Photo Library/Photo Researchers; **267** Tom Stewart/ The Stock Market/CORBIS; **268** (br)New York Public Library, General Research Division, Astor, Lenox, and Tilden Foundations, (others)Bettmann/CORBIS; **270** Emmanuel Scorcelletti/Liaison Agency/Getty Images; **272** Doug Martin; **273** NASA; **274** Mark Burnett; **275** Klaus Guldbrandsen/ Science Photo Library/Photo Researchers; **276–277** KS Studios; **276** (tl)Mark Thayer, (tr)CORBIS, (bl)Kenneth Mengay/Liaison Agency/Getty Images, (bc)Arthur Hill/ Visuals Unlimited, (br)RMIP/Richard Haynes; **278** (t)Mark Burnett, (b)Michael Newman/PhotoEdit, Inc.; **280** (tl)Robert Essel/The Stock Market/CORBIS,(tr)John Eastcott & Yva Momatiuk/DRK Photo, (cl)Ame Hodalic/CORBIS, (cr)Diaphor Agency/Index Stock, (br)TIME; **286–287** Joseph Sohm/ChromoSohm, Inc./CORBIS; **289** (l)Stephen W. Frisch/Stock Boston, (r)Doug Martin; **290** (t)HIRB/Index Stock, (b)Doug Martin; **291** Richard Hamilton/CORBIS; **292** John Evans; **293** (l)SuperStock, (r)Annie Griffiths/ CORBIS; **296** John Evans; **298** Richard Nowitz/Phototake/ PictureQuest; **300** Aaron Haupt; **301** KS Studios/Mullenix; **303** John Evans; **304** (l)Joe Sohm, Chromosohm/Stock Connection/PictureQuest, (c)Andrew Popper/Phototake/ PictureQuest, (r)A. Wolf/Explorer, Photo Researchers; **305** John Evans; **306** (tl tr)Elaine Shay, (tcl)Brent Turner/BLT Productions, (tcr)Matt Meadows, (bl bcl)CORBIS, (bcr)Icon Images, (br)StudiOhio; **310 311** KS Studios; **312** CORBIS; **314** Royalty-Free/CORBIS; **317** Stephen W. Frisch/Stock Boston; **318–319** Matthew Borkoski/Stock Boston/ PictureQuest; **319** L. Fritz/H. Armstrong Roberts; **320–321** Brian Snyder/Reuters Newmedia Inc./CORBIS; **322** Telegraph Colour Library/FPG/Getty Images; **323** Geoff Butler; **326** Richard Hutchings; **329** Runk/Schoenberger from Grant Heilman; **331** Mark Doolittle/Outside Images/ Picturequest; **333** (l)Ed Bock/The Stock Market/CORBIS, (r)Will Hart/PhotoEdit, Inc.; **335** (t)Tom & DeeAnn McCarthy/The Stock Market/CORBIS, (bl)Jodi Jacobson/ Peter Arnold, Inc., (br)Jules Frazier/PhotoDisc; **336** Mark Burnett; **338** Robert Brenner/PhotoEdit, Inc.; **339** Laura Sifferlin; **340 341** Icon Images; **342** Alexis Duclos/Liaison/ Getty Images; **343** (l r)Rudi Von Briel/PhotoEdit, Inc., (c)PhotoDisc; **348–349** Wendell Metzen/Index Stock; **349** Richard Hutchings; **350** (l)Globus Brothers Studios, NYC, (r)Stock Boston; **351** Bob Daemmrich; **352** (t)Beth Wald/ImageState, (b)David Madison; **353** Rhoda Sidney/ Stock Boston/PictureQuest; **355** (l)Myrleen Cate/PhotoEdit, Inc., (r)David Young-Wolff/PhotoEdit, Inc.; **356** Bob Daemmrich; **358** (t)Stone/Getty Images, (b)Myrleen Cate/ PhotoEdit, Inc.; **360** David Madison; **362** Richard Megna/ Fundamental Photographs; **363** Mary M. Steinbacher/

# PERIODIC TABLE OF THE ELEMENTS

Columns of elements are called groups. Elements in the same group have similar chemical properties.

Gas

Liquid

Solid

Synthetic

Element — Hydrogen
Atomic number — 1
Symbol — H
Atomic mass — 1.008

State of matter

The first three symbols tell you the state of matter of the element at room temperature. The fourth symbol identifies elements that are not present in significant amounts on Earth. Useful amounts are made synthetically.

| 1 | 2 | 3 | 4 | 5 | 6 | 7 | 8 | 9 |
|---|---|---|---|---|---|---|---|---|
| **1** Hydrogen 1 **H** 1.008 | | | | | | | | |
| **2** Lithium 3 **Li** 6.941 | Beryllium 4 **Be** 9.012 | | | | | | | |
| **3** Sodium 11 **Na** 22.990 | Magnesium 12 **Mg** 24.305 | | | | | | | |
| **4** Potassium 19 **K** 39.098 | Calcium 20 **Ca** 40.078 | Scandium 21 **Sc** 44.956 | Titanium 22 **Ti** 47.867 | Vanadium 23 **V** 50.942 | Chromium 24 **Cr** 51.996 | Manganese 25 **Mn** 54.938 | Iron 26 **Fe** 55.845 | Cobalt 27 **Co** 58.933 |
| **5** Rubidium 37 **Rb** 85.468 | Strontium 38 **Sr** 87.62 | Yttrium 39 **Y** 88.906 | Zirconium 40 **Zr** 91.224 | Niobium 41 **Nb** 92.906 | Molybdenum 42 **Mo** 95.94 | Technetium 43 **Tc** (98) | Ruthenium 44 **Ru** 101.07 | Rhodium 45 **Rh** 102.906 |
| **6** Cesium 55 **Cs** 132.905 | Barium 56 **Ba** 137.327 | Lanthanum 57 **La** 138.906 | Hafnium 72 **Hf** 178.49 | Tantalum 73 **Ta** 180.948 | Tungsten 74 **W** 183.84 | Rhenium 75 **Re** 186.207 | Osmium 76 **Os** 190.23 | Iridium 77 **Ir** 192.217 |
| **7** Francium 87 **Fr** (223) | Radium 88 **Ra** (226) | Actinium 89 **Ac** (227) | Rutherfordium 104 **Rf** (261) | Dubnium 105 **Db** (262) | Seaborgium 106 **Sg** (266) | Bohrium 107 **Bh** (264) | Hassium 108 **Hs** (277) | Meitnerium 109 **Mt** (268) |

The number in parentheses is the mass number of the longest-lived isotope for that element.

Rows of elements are called periods. Atomic number increases across a period.

The arrow shows where these elements would fit into the periodic table. They are moved to the bottom of the table to save space.

| | Cerium 58 **Ce** 140.116 | Praseodymium 59 **Pr** 140.908 | Neodymium 60 **Nd** 144.24 | Promethium 61 **Pm** (145) | Samarium 62 **Sm** 150.36 |
|---|---|---|---|---|---|
| **Lanthanide series** | | | | | |
| **Actinide series** | Thorium 90 **Th** 232.038 | Protactinium 91 **Pa** 231.036 | Uranium 92 **U** 238.029 | Neptunium 93 **Np** (237) | Plutonium 94 **Pu** (244) |